Office for
National Statistics

47.47
SJ 9/09

Annual Abstract
of Statistics

No 145
2009 Edition

Editor: Ian Macrory
Office for National Statistics

palgrave
macmillan

ISBN 978-0-230-57609-4

ISSN 0072–5730

A National Statistics publication

National Statistics are produced to high professional standards as set out in the Code of Practice for Official Statistics. They are produced free from political influence.

Not all of the statistics contained in this publication are National Statistics because it is a compilation from various data sources.

About us

The Office for National Statistics

The Office for National Statistics (ONS) is the executive office of the UK Statistics Authority, a non-ministerial department which reports directly to Parliament. ONS is the UK government's single largest statistical producer. It compiles information about the UK's society and economy which provides evidence for policy and decision-making and in the allocation of resources.

The Director of ONS is also the National Statistician.

Palgrave Macmillan

This publication first published 2009 by Palgrave Macmillan.

Palgrave Macmillan in the UK is an imprint of Macmillan Publishers Limited, registered in England, company number 785998, of Houndmills, Basingstoke, Hampshire RG21 6XS.

Palgrave Macmillan in the US is a division of St Martin's Press LLC, 175 Fifth Avenue, New York, NY 10010.

Palgrave Macmillan is the global academic imprint of the above companies and has companies and representatives throughout the world.

Palgrave® and Macmillan® are registered trademarks in the United States, the United Kingdom, Europe and other countries.

A catalogue record for this book is available from the British Library.

10 9 8 7 6 5 4 3 2 1

18 17 16 15 14 13 12 11 10 09

Contacts

This publication

For information about the content of this publication, contact the ONS Core Table Unit

Tel: 01633 455851

Email: ctu@ons.gsi.gov.uk

Other customer enquiries

ONS Customer Contact Centre

Tel: 0845 601 3034

International: +44 (0)845 601 3034

Minicom: 01633 812399

Email: info@statistics.gsi.gov.uk

Fax: 01633 652747

Post: Room 1015, Government Buildings, Cardiff Road, Newport, South Wales NP10 8XG

www.ons.gov.uk

Media enquiries

Tel: 0845 604 1858

Email: press.office@ons.gsi.gov.uk

Publication orders

To obtain the print version of this publication, contact Palgrave Macmillan

Tel: 01256 302611

www.palgrave.com/ons

Price: £52.00

Copyright and reproduction

© Crown copyright 2009

Published with the permission of the Office of Public Sector Information (OPSI)

You may use this publication (excluding logos) free of charge in any format for research, private study or internal circulation within an organisation providing it is used accurately and not in a misleading context. The material must be acknowledged as Crown copyright and you must give the title of the source publication. Where we have identified any third party copyright material you will need to obtain permission from the copyright holders concerned.

For re-use of this material you must apply for a Click-Use Public Sector Information (PSI) Licence from:

Office of Public Sector Information, Crown Copyright Licensing and Public Sector Information, Kew, Richmond, Surrey TW9 4DU

Tel: 020 8876 3444

www.opsi.gov.uk/click-use/index.htm

Printing

This book is printed on paper suitable for recycling and made from fully managed and sustained forest sources. Logging, pulping and manufacturing processes are expected to conform to the environmental regulations of the country of origin.

Printed and bound in Great Britain by Hobbs the Printer Ltd, Totton, Southampton

Typeset by Kerrypress Ltd, Luton

Contents Whether items are National Statistics, non National Statistics

Contents

6: Education

7: Labour market

		Page	**Type***

Contents

		Page	Type*

13: Environment

14: Housing

15: Transport and communications

Contents

		Page	Type*

17: Prices

18: Government finance

Central government

Local authorities

Contents

19: External trade and investment

20: Research and Development

21: Agriculture, fisheries and food

		Page	Type*

22: Production

Contents

* This publication contains a mixture of 'National Statistics' and 'Other Official Statistics'. Statistics accredited as 'National Statistics' (NS) are fully compliant with the Code of Practice for Official Statistics and carry the National Statistics Kitemark. Statistics labelled as 'Other Official Statistics' (Non NS) follow many of the best practice principles set out in the Code but have not been accredited as fully compliant.

Contributors and acknowledgements

The editor would like to thank the following people for their help in producing this book:

Production team: Angela Collin

Marc Evans

Tammy Powell

Dilys Rosen

Andrew White

Contributors

The Editor also wishes to thank all his colleagues in ONS, the rest of the Government Statistical Service and all contributors in other organisations for their generous support and helpful comments, without whose help this publication would not be possible.

Design: ONS Design
Typesetting: Kerrypress Typesetters Ltd
Publishing management: Mark Bristow

Units of measurement

Length

1 millimetre (mm)	= 0.03937 inch	
1 centimetre (cm)	= 10 millimetres	= 0.3937 inch
1 metre (m)	= 1,000 millimetres	= 1.094 yards
1 kilometre (km)	= 1,000 metres	= 0.6214 mile
1 inch (in.)		= 25.40 millimetres or 2.540 centimetres
1 foot (ft.)	= 12 inches	= 0.3048 metre
1 yard (yd.)	= 3 feet	= 0.9144 metre
1 mile	= 1,760 yards	= 1.609 kilometres

Area

1 square millimetre (mm2)		= 0.001550 square inch
1 square metre (m2)	= one million square millimetres	= 1.196 square yards
1 hectare (ha)	= 10,000 square metres	= 2.471 acres
1 square kilometre (km2)	= one million square metres	= 247.1 acres
1 square inch (sq. in.)		= 645.2 square millimetres or 6.452 square centimetres
1 square foot (sq. ft.)	= 144 square inches	= 0.09290 square metre or 929.0 square centimetres
1 square yard (sq. yd.)	= 9 square feet	= 0.8361 square metre
1 acre	= 4,840 square yards	= 4,046 square metres or 0.4047 hectare
1 square mile (sq. mile)	= 640 acres	= 2.590 square kilometres or 259.0 hectares

Volume

1 cubic centimetre (cm3)		= 0.06102 cubic inch
1 cubic decimetre (dm3)	= 1,000 cubic centimetres	= 0.03531 cubic foot
1 cubic metre (m3)	= one million cubic centimetres	= 1.308 cubic yards
1 cubic inch (cu.in.)		=16.39 cubic centimetres
1 cubic foot (cu. ft.)	= 1,728 cubic inches	= 0.02832 cubic metre or 28.32 cubic decimetres
1 cubic yard (cu. yd.)	= 27 cubic feet	= 0.7646 cubic metre

Capacity

1 litre (l)	= 1 cubic decimetre	= 0.2200 gallon
1 hectolitre (hl)	= 100 litres	= 22.00 gallons
1 pint		= 0.5682 litre
1 quart	= 2 pints	= 1.137 litres
1 gallon	= 8 pints	= 4.546 litres
1 bulk barrel	= 36 gallons (gal.)	= 1.637 hectolitres

Weight

1 gram (g)		= 0.03527 ounce avoirdupois
1 hectogram (hg)	= 100 grams	= 3.527 ounces or 0.2205 pound
1 kilogram (kg)	= 1,000 grams or 10 hectograms	= 2.205 pounds
1 tonne (t)	= 1,000 kilograms	= 1.102 short tons or 0.9842 long ton
1 ounce avoirdupois (oz.)	= 437.5 grains	= 28.35 grams
1 pound avoirdupois (lb.)	= 16 ounces	= 0.4536 kilogram
1 hundredweight (cwt.)	= 112 pounds	= 50.80 kilograms
1 short ton	= 2,000 pounds	= 907.2 kilograms or 0.9072 tonne
1 long ton (referred to as ton)	= 2,240 pounds	= 1,016 kilograms or 1.016 tonnes
1 ounce troy	= 480 grains	= 31.10 grams

Energy

British thermal unit (Btu)	= 0.2520 kilocalorie (kcal) = 1.055 kilojoule (kj)
Therm	= 105 British thermal units = 25,200 kcal = 105,506 kj
Megawatt hour (MWh)	= 106 watt hours (Wh)
Gigawatt hour (GWh)	= 106 kilowatt hours = 34,121 therms

Food and drink

Butter	23,310 litres milk	= 1 tonne butter (average)
Cheese	10,070 litres milk	= 1 tonne cheese
Condensed milk	2,550 litres milk	= 1 tonne full cream condensed milk
	2,953 litres skimmed milk	= 1 tonne skimmed condensed milk
Milk	1 million litres	= 1,030 tonnes
Milk powder	8,054 litres milk	= 1 tonne full cream milk powder
	10,740 litres skimmed milk	= 1 tonne skimmed milk powder
Eggs	17,126 eggs	= 1 tonne (approximate)
Sugar	100 tonnes sugar beet	= 92 tonnes refined sugar
	100 tonnes cane sugar	= 96 tonnes refined sugar

Shipping

Gross tonnage	= The total volume of all the enclosed spaces of a vessel, the unit of measurement being a 'ton' of 100 cubic feet.
Deadweight tonnage	= Deadweight tonnage is the total weight in tons of 2,240 lb. that a ship can legally carry, that is the total weight of cargo, bunkers, stores and crew.

Introduction

Introduction

Welcome to the 2009 edition of the *Annual Abstract of Statistics*. This compendium draws together statistics from a wide range of official and other authoritative sources. Their help is gratefully acknowledged.

Regional information, supplementary to the national figures in *Annual Abstract*, appear in *Regional Trends*. The latest edition of *Regional Trends* is available electronically on the Office for National Statistics Website free of charge. This can be accessed at: *www.statistics.gov.uk/regionaltrends41*. Earlier editions are available via Palgrave Macmillan.

Current data for many of the series appearing in this Annual Abstract are contained in other ONS publications, such as *Economic & Labour Market Review, Population Trends, Health Statistics Quarterly* and *Financial Statistics*. All are published by Palgrave Macmillan.

Other Office for National Statistics (ONS) publications which contain related data are the *Monthly Digest of Statistics* and *Social Trends*, these are also published by Palgrave Macmillan or can be found directly at:

www.statistics.gov.uk/statbase/Product.asp?vlnk=611

www.statistics.gov.uk/socialtrends39/

The name (and telephone number, where this is available) of the organisation providing the statistics are shown under each table. In addition, a list of Sources is given at the back of the book, which sets out the official publications or other sources to which further reference can be made.

Identification codes

The four-letter identification code at the top of each data column, or at the side of each row is the ONS reference for this series of data on our database. Please quote the relevant code if you contact us requiring any further information about the data. On some tables it is not possible to include these codes, so please quote the table number in these cases.

Definitions and classification

Time series

So far as possible annual totals are given throughout, but quarterly or monthly figures are given where these are more suitable to the type of series.

Explanatory notes

Most sections are preceded by explanatory notes which should be read in conjunction with the tables. Definitions and explanatory notes for many of the terms occurring in the *Annual Abstract* are also given in the *Annual Supplement to the Monthly Digest of Statistics*, published in the January edition. Detailed notes on items which appear in both the *Annual Abstract* and *Financial Statistics* are given in an annual supplement to the latter entitled *Financial Statistics Explanatory Handbook*. The original sources listed in the Sources may also be consulted.

Standard Industrial Classification

A Standard Industrial Classification (SIC) was first introduced into the UK in 1948 for use in classifying business establishments and other statistical units by the type of economic activity in which they are engaged. The classification provides a framework for the collection, tabulation, presentation and analysis of data about economic activities. Its use promotes uniformity of data collected by various government departments and agencies. Since 1948 the classification has been revised in 1958, 1968, 1980, 1992, 2003 and 2007. One of the principal objectives of the 1980 revision was to eliminate differences from the activity classification issued by the Statistical Office of the European Communities (Eurostat) and entitled 'Nomenclature générale des activités économiques dans les Communautés Européennes', usually abbreviated to NACE. In 1990 the European Communities introduced a new statistical classification of economic activities (NACE Rev 1) by regulation. The regulation made it obligatory for the UK to introduce a new Standard Industrial Classification SIC(92), based on NACE Rev 1. UK SIC(92) was based exactly on NACE Rev 1 but, where it was thought necessary or helpful, a fifth digit was added to form subclasses of the NACE 1 four digit system. Classification systems need to be revised periodically because, over time, new products, processes and industries emerge. In January 2003 a minor revision of NACE Rev 1, known as NACE Rev 1.1, was published in the *Official Journal of the European Communities*.

Consequently, the UK was obliged to introduce a new Standard Industrial Classification, SIC(2003) consistent with NACE Rev 1.1. The UK took the opportunity of the 2003 revision also to update the national Subclasses. Full details are available in UK Standard Industrial Classification of Economic Activities 2003 and the Indexes to the UK Standard Industrial Classification of Economic Activities 2003. These are the most recent

Introduction

that are currently used. The most up to date version is the UK Standard Industrial Classification of Economic activities 2007 (SIC2007). It will be implemented in 5 stages and came into effect on 1 January 2008.

- For reference year 2008, the Annual Business Inquiry (parts 1 & 2) will be based on SIC 2007

- PRODCOM will also be based on SIC 2007 from reference year 2008

- Other annual outputs will be based on SIC 2007 from reference year 2009, unless otherwise determined by regulation

- Quarterly and monthly surveys will be based on SIC 2007 from the first reference period in 2010, unless otherwise determined by regulation

- National Accounts will move to SIC 2007 in September 2011

ONS is currently working on a detailed implementation plan for the introduction of the new classification, covering all of our surveys and outputs.
For further information see:
www.statistics.gov.uk/statbase/Product.asp?vlnk=14012

Revisions to contents

Some of the figures, particularly for the latest year, are provisional and may be revised in a subsequent issue of the *Annual Abstract*.

Symbols and conventions used

Change of basis
Where consecutive figures have been compiled on different bases and are not strictly comparable, a footnote is added indicating the nature of the difference.

Geographic coverage
Statistics relate mainly to the UK. Where figures relate to other areas, this is indicated on the table.

Units of measurement
The various units of measurement used are listed after the Contents.

Rounding of figures
In tables where figures have been rounded to the nearest final digit, the constituent items may not add up exactly to the total.

Symbols
The following symbols have been used throughout:

.. = not available or not applicable (also information supressed to avoid disclosure)

- = nil or less than half the final digit shown

Office for National Statistics online: www.ons.gov.uk

Web-based access to time series, cross-sectional data and metadata from across the Government Statistical Service (GSS), is available using the site search function from the homepage. Download many datasets, in whole or in part, or consult directory information for all GSS statistical resources, including censuses, surveys, periodicals and enquiry services. Information is posted as PDF electronic documents or in XLS and CSV formats, compatible with most spreadsheet packages. Complete copies of this publication are available to download free of charge on the following web page:
www.statistics.gov.uk/statbase/product.asp?vlnk=94

Contact point

The ONS welcomes any feedback on the content of the *Annual Abstract*, including comments on the format of the data and the selection of topics. Comments and requests for general information should be addressed to:

Core Table Unit
Household, Labour Market and Social Wellbeing Division
Room 1.024
Office for National Statistics
Government Buildings
Cardiff Road
Newport
South Wales
NP10 8XG

or

Email: info@statistics.gov.uk

July 2009

Area

Chapter 1

Area

The UK comprises Great Britain and Northern Ireland. Great Britain comprises England, Wales and Scotland.

Physical Features

The UK constitutes the greater part of the British Isles. The largest of the islands is Great Britain. The next largest comprises Northern Ireland and the Irish Republic. Western Scotland is fringed by the large island chain known as the Hebrides, and to the north east of the Scottish mainland are the Orkney and Shetland Islands. All these, along with the Isle of Wight, Anglesey and the Isles of Scilly, form part of the UK. The Isle of Man, in the Irish Sea, and the Channel Islands, between Great Britain and France, are largely self-governing and are not part of the UK. The UK is one of the 27 member states of the European Union following the accession of Bulgaria and Romania on 1 January 2007. With an area of about 243,000 sq km (about 94,000 sq miles), the UK is just under 1,000 km (about 600 miles) from the south coast to the extreme north of Scotland and just under 500 km (around 300 miles) across at the widest point.

- Highest mountain: Ben Nevis, in the highlands of Scotland, at 1,343 m (4,406 ft)

- Longest river: the Severn, 354 km (220 miles) long, which rises in central Wales and flows through Shrewsbury, Worcester and Gloucester in England to the Bristol Channel

- Largest lake: Lough Neagh, Northern Ireland, at 396 sqkm (153 sq miles)

- Deepest lake: Loch Morar in the Highlands of Scotland, 310 m (1,017 ft) deep

- Highest waterfall: Eas a'Chual Aluinn, from Glas Bheinn, in the highlands of Scotland, with a drop of 200 m (660 ft)

- Deepest cave: Ogof Ffynnon Ddu, Wales, at 308 m (1,010 ft) deep

- Most northerly point on the British mainland: Dunnet Head, north-east Scotland

- Most southerly point on the British mainland: Lizard Point, Cornwall

- Closest point to mainland continental Europe: Dover, Kent. The Channel Tunnel, which links England and France, is a little over 50 km (31 miles) long, of which nearly 38 km (24 miles) are actually under the Channel.

1.1 Area of the United Kingdom[1,2], 2007

	sq km		sq km
		Shropshire	3 197
United Kingdom	242 495	Staffordshire	2 620
		Warwickshire	1 975
Great Britain[3]	228 919	West Midlands (Met County)	902
		Worcestershire	1 741
England and Wales	151 012		
		East of England	19 109
		Luton UA	43
England	130 279	Peterborough UA	343
		Southend-on-Sea UA	42
North East	8 573	Thurrock UA	163
Darlington UA	197	Bedfordshire	1 192
Hartlepool UA	94	Cambridgeshire	3 046
Middlesbrough UA	54	Essex	3 465
Redcar and Cleveland UA	245	Hertfordshire	1 643
Stockton-on-Tees UA	204	Norfolk	5 371
		Suffolk	3 800
Durham	2 226		
Northumberland	5 013	**London**	1 572
Tyne and Wear (Met County)	540		
		Inner London	319
North West	14 106	Outer London	1 253
Blackburn with Darwen UA	137	**South East**	19 069
Blackpool UA	35		
Halton UA	79	Bracknell Forest UA	109
Warrington UA	181	Brighton and Hove UA	83
		Isle of Wight UA	380
Cheshire	2 083	Medway UA	192
Cumbria	6 768	Milton Keynes UA	309
Greater Manchester (Met County)	1 276	Portsmouth UA	40
Lancashire	2 903	Reading UA	40
Merseyside (Met County)	645	Slough UA	33
		Southampton UA	50
Yorkshire and The Humber	15 408	West Berkshire UA	704
		Windsor and Maidenhead UA	197
East Riding of Yorkshire UA	2 408	Wokingham UA	179
Kingston upon Hull, City of UA	71		
North East Lincolnshire UA	192	Buckinghamshire	1 565
North Lincolnshire UA	846	East Sussex	1 709
York UA	272	Hampshire	3 679
		Kent	3 544
North Yorkshire	8 038	Oxfordshire	2 605
South Yorkshire (Met County)	1 552	Surrey	1 663
West Yorkshire (Met County)	2 029	West Sussex	1 991
East Midlands	15 607	**South West**	23 837
Derby UA	78	Bath and North East Somerset UA	346
Leicester UA	73	Bournemouth UA	46
Nottingham UA	75	Bristol, City of UA	110
Rutland UA	382	North Somerset UA	374
		Plymouth UA	80
Derbyshire	2 547	Poole UA	65
Leicestershire	2 083	South Gloucestershire UA	497
Lincolnshire	5 921	Swindon UA	230
Northamptonshire	2 364	Torbay UA	63
Nottinghamshire	2 085		
		Cornwall and the Isles of Scilly	3 563
West Midlands	12 998	Devon	6 564
		Dorset	2 542
Herefordshire, County of UA	2 180	Gloucestershire	2 653
Stoke-on-Trent UA	93	Somerset	3 451
Telford and Wrekin UA	290	Wiltshire	3 255

3

Area

1.1 Area of the United Kingdom[1,2], 2007
continued

	sq km		sq km
Wales	20 733	Dumfries & Galloway	6 426
		Dundee City	60
Blaenau Gwent	109	East Ayrshire	1 262
Bridgend	251	East Dunbartonshire	175
Caerphilly	277	East Lothian	679
Cardiff	140		
Carmarthenshire	2 371	East Renfrewshire	174
		Edinburgh, City of	263
Ceredigion	1 785	Eilean Siar[4]	3 055
Conwy	1 126	Falkirk	297
Denbighshire	837	Fife	1 325
Flintshire	438		
Gwynedd	2 535	Glasgow City	175
		Highland	25 659
Isle of Anglesey	711	Inverclyde	160
Merthyr Tydfil	111	Midlothian	354
Monmouthshire	849	Moray	2 238
Neath Port Talbot	441		
Newport	190	North Ayrshire	885
Pembrokeshire	1 619	North Lanarkshire	470
		Orkney Islands	990
Powys	5 181	Perth & Kinross	5 286
Rhondda, Cynon, Taff	424	Renfrewshire	261
Swansea	378	Scottish Borders	4 732
Torfaen	126		
The Vale of Glamorgan	331	Shetland Islands	1 466
Wrexham	504	South Ayrshire	1 222
		South Lanarkshire	1 772
		Stirling	2 187
Scotland	77 907	West Dunbartonshire	159
		West Lothian	427
Aberdeen City	186		
Aberdeenshire	6 313		
Angus	2 182	**Northern Ireland**	13 576
Argyll & Bute	6 908		
Clackmannanshire	159		

1 Figures relate to land area only.
2 The area measurements are a definitive set derived from boundaries maintained by Ordnance Survey and Ordnance Survey of Northern Ireland. The current measurements may differ from those published previously in tables, publications or other statistical outputs, even allowing for boundary changes or changes to the physical structure of the land because of improvements to the source of the data.
3 Excludes inland water for all countries.
4 Formerly known as the Western Isles.

Source: Office for National Statistics

Parliamentary elections

Chapter 2

Elections

2.1 Parliamentary elections[1]
United Kingdom

		15 Oct 1964	31 Mar 1966	18 June 1970[1]	28 Feb 1974		10 Oct 1974	3 May 1979	9 June 1983	11 June 1987	9 April 1992	1 May 1997	7 June 2001	5 May 2005
United Kingdom														
Electorate	DZ5P	35 894	35 957	39 615	40 256	DZ6V	40 256	41 573	42 704	43 666	43 719	43 846	44 403	44 246
Average-electors per seat	DZ5T	57.0	57.1	62.9	63.4	DZ6R	63.4	65.5	66.7	67.2	67.2	66.5	67.4	68.5
Valid votes counted	DZ5X	27 657	27 265	28 345	31 340	DZ6N	29 189	31 221	30 671	32 530	33 614	31 286	26 367	27 149
As percentage of electorate	DZ63	77.1	75.8	71.5	77.9	DZ6J	72.5	75.1	71.8	74.5	76.7	71.4	59.4	61.4
England and Wales														
Electorate	DZ5Q	31 610	31 695	34 931	35 509	DZ6W	35 509	36 695	37 708	38 568	38 648	38 719	39 228	39 266
Average-electors per seat	DZ5U	57.8	57.9	63.9	64.3	DZ6S	64.3	66.5	67.2	68.8	68.8	68.0	68.9	69.0
Valid votes counted	DZ5Y	24 384	24 116	24 877	27 735	DZ6O	25 729	27 609	27 082	28 832	29 897	27 679	23 243	24 097
As percentage of electorate	DZ64	77.1	76.1	71.2	78.1	DZ6K	72.5	75.2	71.8	74.8	77.5	71.5	59.3	61.4
Scotland														
Electorate	DZ5R	3 393	3 360	3 659	3 705	DZ6X	3 705	3 837	3 934	3 995	3 929	3 949	3 984	3 840
Average-electors per seat	DZ5V	47.8	47.3	51.5	52.2	DZ6T	52.2	54.0	54.6	55.5	54.6	54.8	55.3	65.1
Valid votes counted	DZ5Z	2 635	2 553	2 688	2 887	DZ6P	2 758	2 917	2 825	2 968	2 931	2 817	2 313	2 334
As percentage of electorate	DZ65	77.6	76.0	73.5	77.9	DZ6L	74.5	76.0	71.8	74.3	74.2	71.3	58.1	60.8
Northern Ireland														
Electorate	DZ5S	891	902	1 025	1 027	DZ6Y	1 037	1 028	1 050	1 090	1 141	1 178	1 191	1 140
Average-electors per seat	DZ5W	74.2	75.2	85.4	85.6	DZ6U	86.4	85.6	61.8	64.1	67.1	65.4	66.2	63.3
Valid votes counted	DZ62	638	596	779	718	DZ6Q	702	696	765	730	785	791	810	718
As percentage of electorate	DZ66	71.7	66.1	76.0	69.9	DZ6M	67.7	67.7	72.9	67.0	68.8	67.1	68.0	62.9
Members of Parliament elected: (numbers)	DZV7	630	630	630	635	DZV8	635	635	650	650	651	659	659	646
Conservative	DZ67	303	253	330	296	DZ6D	276	339	396	375	336	165	166	198
Labour	DZ68	317	363	287	301	DZ6E	319	268	209	229	271	418	412	355
Liberal Democrat[2]	DZ69	9	12	6	14	DZ6F	13	11	23	22	20	46	52	62
Scottish National Party	DZ6A	–	–	1	7	DZ6G	11	2	2	3	3	6	5	6
Plaid Cymru	DZ6B	–	–	–	2	DZ6H	3	2	2	3	4	4	4	3
Other[3]	DZ6C	1	2	6	15	DZ6I	13	13	18	18	17	20	20	22

1 The Representation of the People Act 1969 lowered the minimum voting age from 21 to 18 years with effect from 16 February 1970.
2 Liberal before 1992. The figures for 1983 and 1987 include six and five MPs respectively who were elected for the Social Democratic Party.
3 Including the Speaker.

Sources: British Electoral Facts 1832-2006.;
University of Plymouth for the Electoral Commission: 01752 233207

2.2 Parliamentary by-elections
United Kingdom

	May 1997 - June 2001	General[1,2] Election May 1997	June 2001 - November 2004	General[1] Election June 2001	May 2005 - November 2008	General[1] Election May 2005
Numbers of by-elections	17		6		12	
Votes recorded						
By party (percentages)						
Conservative	27.0	25.1	17.7	21.2	27.6	26.5
Labour	29.7	40.1	40.8	58.3	28.4	36.9
Liberal Democrat	22.1	14.4	31.3	13.7	21.3	22.0
Scottish National Party	6.0	4.1	-	-	10.8	6.2
Plaid Cymru	2.5	2.3	2.7	2.1	0.5	0.2
Other	12.7	14.1	7.4	4.7	11.5	8.3
Total votes recorded (percentages)	100.0	100.0	100.0	100.0	100.0	100.0
(thousands)	435	723	140	205	385	510

1 Votes recorded in the same seats in the previous General Election.
2 Proportions of 'other' votes inflated by the fact that votes were cast for the retiring Speaker as 'The Speaker seeking re-election' and not as a party candidate.

Source: University of Plymouth for the Electoral Commission: 01752 233207

2.3 Devolved assembly elections
Wales and Scotland

		6 May 1999	1 May 2003	3 May 2007
Welsh Assembly				
Electorate	E28K	2 205	2 230	2 248
Average-electors per seat[1]	E28N	55.1	55.7	56.2
Valid votes counted	E28Q	1 023	850	978
As percentage of electorate	E28T	46.4	38.1	43.5
Members elected:[2] (numbers)	E2XI	60	60	60
Conservative	E2WG	9	11	12
Labour	E2WU	28	30	26
Liberal Democrat	E2WW	6	6	6
Plaid Cymru	E2X3	17	12	15
Other	E2WY	–	1	1
Scottish Parliament				
Electorate	E28L	4 024	3 879	3 899
Average-electors per seat[1]	E28O	55.1	53.1	53.4
Valid votes counted	E28R	2 342	1 916	2 017
As percentage of electorate	E28U	58.2	49.4	51.7
Members elected:[3] (numbers)	E2XJ	129	129	129
Conservative	E2WH	18	18	17
Labour	E2WV	56	50	46
Liberal Democrat	E2WX	17	17	16
Scottish National Party	E2X4	35	27	47
Other	E2WZ	3	17	3

1 This is the average in each first-past-the-post constituency. Additional members are then elected on the basis of a regional 'list' vote.
2 Comprising 40 from constituencies and 20 from the regional 'list'.
3 Comprising 73 from constituencies and 56 from the regional 'list'.

Sources: British Electoral Facts 1832-2006;
University of Plymouth for the Electoral Commission: 01752 233207

2.4 Devolved assembly elections
Northern Ireland

		25 June 1998	26 Nov 2003	8 Mar 2007
Electorate	E28M	1 179	1 098	1 108
Average-electors per seat[1]	E28P	65.5	61.0	61.6
Valid votes counted	E28S	810	702	690
As percentage of electorate	E28V	68.7	64.0	63.0
Members elected: (numbers)	E2XK	108	108	108
Alliance Party	E2X5	6	6	7
SDLP	E2X6	24	18	16
Sinn Fein	E2X7	18	24	28
Democratic Unionist Party	E2X8	20	30	36
UK Unionist Party	E2X9	5	1	–
Ulster Unionist Party	E2XA	28	27	18
Other	E2X2	7	2	3

1 This is the average in each Westminster constituency. Six members are elected by single transferable vote (STV) in each constituency.

Sources: British Electoral Facts 1832-2006;
University of Plymouth for the Electoral Commission: 01752 233207

International development

Chapter 3

International development

Overseas development assistance

(Tables 3.1 and 3.2)

The Department for International Development (DFID) is the UK government department with lead responsibility for overseas development. DFID's aim is to eliminate poverty in poorer countries through achievement of the Millennium Development Goals (MDGs) by 2015. Statistics relating to international development are published on a financial year basis and on a calendar year basis. Statistics on a calendar year basis allow comparisons of aid expenditure with other donor countries. Aid flows can be measured before (gross) or after (net) deductions of repayments of principal on past loans. These tables show only the gross figures.

Aid is provided in two main ways: Bilateral funding is provided directly to partner countries while multilateral funding is provided through international organisations.

Funds can only be classified as multilateral if they are channelled through one of the organisations listed in the OECD Development Assistance Committee (DAC) statistical reporting directives which identifies all multilateral organisations. This list also highlights some bodies that might appear to be multilateral but are actually bilateral (in particular this latter category includes some international non-governmental organisations such as the International Committee of the Red Cross and some public–private partnerships such as the Global Alliance for Vaccines and Immunisation). The DAC list of multilaterals is updated annually based on members nominations. Organisations must be engaged in development work to be classified as multilateral aid channels.[1]

While core funding to multilateral organisations is always classified as multilateral expenditure, additional funding channelled through multilaterals is often classified as bilateral expenditure. This would be the case in circumstances where a DFID country office transfers some money to a multilateral organisation (for example, a UN agency) for a particular programme in that country (or region). That is, where DFID has control over what the money is being spent on and/or where it is being spent. Likewise, if DFID responds to an emergency appeal from an agency for a particular country

---

[1]   money may be classified as bilateral while a case is being made for a new multilateral organisation to be recognised.

or area, the funds will be allocated as bilateral spend to that country or region. As a result, some organisations, such as UN agencies have some of their DFID funding classified as bilateral and some as multilateral.

DFID is planning to introduce a new activity reporting system between 2007/08 and 2009/10. The new system will integrate all DFID's current financial and project management systems. To coincide with the introduction of the new system, DFID is reviewing how it classifies its aid delivery types. The outcome of this review may lead to the introduction of a new set of classifications which may result in changes to the format in future publications.

Table 3.1 shows the main groups of multilateral agencies; the International Development Association being the largest in the World Bank Group.

Bilateral assistance takes various forms:

Financial aid: Poverty Reduction Budget Support (PRBS) – funds provided to developing countries for them to spend in support of their expenditure programmes whose long-term objective is to reduce poverty. Funds are spent using the overseas governments' own financial management, procurement and accountability systems to increase ownership and long-term sustainability. PRBS can take the form of a general contribution to the overall budget – general budget support – or support with a more restricted focus which is earmarked for a specific sector – sector budget support.

Other financial aid – funding of projects and programmes such as sector-wide programmes not classified as PRBS. Financial aid in its broader sense covers all bilateral aid expenditure other than technical cooperation and administrative costs but in *Statistics on International Development* (SID) Humanitarian Assistance, DFID Debt Relief, and 'Other bilateral aid' are separately categorised. Aid and Trade Provision which was previously identified in SID has now been merged into 'Other financial aid' as it is a rapidly declining flow.

Technical co-operation – activities designed to enhance the knowledge, intellectual skills, technical expertise or the productive capability of people in recipient countries. It also covers funding of services which contribute to the design or implementation of development projects and programmes.

This assistance is mainly delivered through research and development, the use of consultants, training (generally overseas partners visiting the UK or elsewhere for a training programme) and employment of 'other personnel' (non-DFID experts on fixed-term contracts). This latter category is growing less significant over time as existing contracted staff reach the end of their assignments.

Other bilateral aid – this category comprises support to the development work of UK and international voluntary organisations, grants to the British Council and for other development work by UK institutions, and non-emergency special appeals through multilateral agencies. The remaining element of 'Other bilateral aid' is made up of a number of categories including, for example, DFID's contributions to two multi-donor trust funds for Sudan, the Development Awareness Fund and the provision of books, equipment and other supplies.

Humanitarian assistance – provides food, aid and other humanitarian assistance including shelter, medical care and advice in emergency situations and their aftermath. Work of the conflict pools is also included.

DFID debt relief – this includes sums for debt relief on DFID aid loans and cancellation of debt under the Commonwealth Debt Initiative (CDI). The non-CDI DFID debt relief is reported on the basis of the 'benefit to the recipient country'. This means that figures shown represent the money available to the country in the year in question that would otherwise have been spent on debt servicing. The CDI debt cancellation is reported on a 'lump sum' basis where all outstanding amounts on a loan are shown at the time the agreement to cancel is made.

CDC investments – CDC Group plc (or CDC) replaced the former Commonwealth Development Corporation in 1999. CDC was founded in 1948 and is now the UK Government's instrument for investing in the private sector in developing economies (it does so through fund management companies, of whom the largest is Actis Capital LLP). CDC has activities in more than 50 developing countries. CDC provides equities an concessional loans to companies in some aid-eligible countries, and these disbursements and repayments are included as UK flows. Although CDC no longer provides loans to governments, it did in the past and these existing loans can become eligible for debt relief.

Non-DFID debt relief – comprises CDC debt and Export Credit Guarantee Department (ECGD) debt. CDC has a portfolio of loans to governments which can become eligible for debt relief under the HIPC (Heavily Indebted Poor Countries) or other debt relief deals. In 2005/06 £90 million of debts owed to CDC were reorganised. ECGD is the UK's official Export Credit Agency which provides insurance for exporters against the main risks in selling overseas and guarantees to banks providing export finance. It also negotiates debt relief arrangements on commercial debt.

Other – This includes contributions from other government departments to civil society organisations, British Council and Global Conflict Pool, and small amounts of drug related assistance funded by the Home Office and the Foreign and Commonwealth Office.

Further details on the UK's development assistance can be found in the Department for International Developments publication *Statistics on International Development* which can be found on the website at: www.dfid.gov.uk/About-DFID/Finance-and-performance/DFID-Expenditure-Statistics/. International Comparisons are available in the OECD Development Assistance Committee's annual report.

3.1 Gross public expenditure on aid (GPEX)[1]
United Kingdom

£ Thousand

		1999 /00	2000 /01	2001 /02	2002 /03	2003 /04	2004 /05	2005 /06	2006 /07	2007 /08
Bilateral Assistance										
Department for International Development										
Poverty Reduction Budget Support (General)	LUJS	15 000	239 900	245 500	184 500	288 750	286 500	347 320	297 553	366 453
Poverty Reduction Budget Support (Sector)	I4UJ	11 000	24 098	22 718	23 685	20 724	60 492	128 232	166 064	268 631
Other Financial Aid	LUJW	327 648	206 113	264 905	319 145	389 853	411 018	469 631	454 631	460 554
Technical Co-operation Projects	LUOS	457 188	455 401	473 519	508 574	459 754	462 633	481 052	522 722	474 287
Other Bilateral Aid	LUOT	273 476	370 184	367 736	450 749	480 252	573 382	712 489	810 993	889 723
Humanitarian Assistance	LUOU	224 700	222 431	192 446	294 981	311 602	333 318	447 978	383 513	430 773
DFID Debt Relief	LUOV	23 140	20 367	17 682	20 364	59 534	71 485	68 120	147 106	71 386
CDC Investments	LUOX	268 518	201 427	159 352	237 324	350 356	238 279	172 808	278 787	360 821
Debt Relief	EQ4B	70 101	79 850	242 097	399 844	163 059	627 402	1 588 414	1 866 591	3 760
Other	LUOY	30 620	66 978	67 795	79 459	111 197	143 564	153 535	196 122	191 002
Total	LUOZ	1 742 967	1 918 441	2 081 504	2 540 613	2 635 081	3 208 072	4 569 524	5 124 083	3 517 389
Multilateral Assistance										
European Community[2]	LUPA	749 668	723 651	744 141	897 826	1 082 389	1 222 018	1 191 961	1 123 215	1 200 319
World Bank Group	LUPB	167 298	342 410	173 722	300 021	150 000	150 000	364 909	493 333	493 387
IMF Poverty Reduction and Growth Facility	LUPC	17 000	–	11 147	11 434	9 417	1 767	23 728	15	..
Global Environmental Assistance	EQ4C	17 095	21 144	25 337	27 338	61 213	52 445	53 460	50 260	..
HIPC Trust Funds	EQ4D	..	27 518	23 400	17 855	22 910	42 123	11 094	18 666	
UN Agencies	LUPD	151 572	122 423	163 645	176 487	196 406	211 638	252 745	245 019	296 940
Regional Development Banks	LUPE	67 179	54 784	75 383	90 648	80 391	82 166	77 759	123 591	
Other[3]	LUPF	73 273	134 086	111 076	151 473	155 861	164 750	105 891	360 443	256 349
Total	LUPG	974 513	1 322 571	1 192 584	1 525 807	1 584 656	1 748 406	1 915 506	2 222 010	2 246 995
Administrative costs	LUPH	104 601	138 507	132 214	154 127	248 698	227 769	256 451	245 893	262 731
Total Gross Public Expenditure on Aid	LUPI	2 822 081	3 379 519	3 406 301	4 220 547	4 468 435	5 184 247	6 741 481	7 591 986	6 027 115

1 See chapter text.
2 The institution, not the member states of the European Union.
3 IMF Poverty Reduction and Growth Facility, Global Environmental Assistance, HIPC Trust Funds and Regional Development Banks are now included in Multilateral Assistance Other.

Source: Department for International Development: 01355 843764.

3.2 Total bilateral gross public expenditure on aid (GPEX): by main recipient countries and regions[1]
United Kingdom

£ Thousand

		1999 /00	2000 /01	2001 /02	2002 /03	2003 /04	2004 /05	2005 /06	2006 /07	2007 /08
Main recipients										
Nigeria	C227	14 395	15 940	20 561	29 287	32 630	73 113	1 227 717	1 750 694	157 722
India	LUPJ	104 016	126 700	198 576	182 708	242 736	267 510	270 065	293 706	312 751
Afghanistan	C224	5 452	7 465	50 027	76 018	99 595	98 959	126 949	123 011	146 818
Pakistan	LUPY	23 472	15 890	44 838	46 852	66 299	55 277	97 688	118 150	88 145
Cameroon	I53M	7 005	5 467	3 652	28 971	7 764	16 547	3 170	115 408	2 013
Tanzania	LUPK	74 709	110 590	203 830	102 614	162 372	130 009	114 134	115 023	125 353
Sudan	EU5S	3 189	4 912	5 598	19 222	24 663	83 964	117 114	109 917	138 702
Bangladesh	LUPM	69 670	75 005	60 375	73 246	155 364	149 152	128 258	109 313	129 725
Serbia	I53N	6 393	15 670	11 531	305 036	4 795	4 001	48 971	95 713	3 491
Ethiopia	C225	7 299	16 484	12 088	44 224	43 665	73 044	62 562	90 506	140 011
Malawi	LUPP	49 058	54 648	46 651	49 206	54 437	56 429	68 653	88 686	72 619
Ghana	LUPL	51 887	74 700	54 479	86 294	73 448	145 835	96 315	93 147	93 076
Congo, Dem Rep	C223	2 132	6 752	10 262	15 574	151 657	36 585	58 832	79 283	82 910
Uganda	LUPN	89 978	98 352	68 091	54 041	59 694	62 928	72 064	79 035	77 231
Iraq	C222	6 585	9 545	7 760	18 853	214 313	391 507	426 249	71 829	40 649
Kenya	EU5W	32 665	62 620	34 227	63 404	28 647	37 824	65 486	67 054	52 135
Zambia	LUPO	46 657	93 345	59 203	45 140	32 304	163 537	101 707	63 412	41 942
Indonesia	LUPZ	58 812	28 405	18 232	42 613	17 449	34 526	58 553	62 290	32 715
China	LUPS	26 246	56 740	50 266	44 386	42 406	42 476	36 854	60 086	83 743
Mozambique	LUPV	70 643	43 876	134 133	39 101	36 713	47 941	56 540	56 273	67 799
Total	LUQD	750 261	923 108	1 094 379	1 366 848	1 550 951	1 971 164	3 237 881	3 642 536	1 889 550
Total other countries	LUQE	899 776	837 292	886 021	1 095 698	1 084 130	1 236 908	1 331 643	1 481 547	1 627 839
Regional totals										
Africa	LUQF	628 719	774 692	865 317	891 954	1 058 005	1 282 423	2 425 880	3 071 676	1 552 123
America	LUQG	237 961	180 165	166 949	221 526	103 358	126 278	85 389	119 491	68 545
Asia	LUQH	375 839	413 294	534 954	609 138	969 466	1 243 004	1 356 415	1 091 488	1 116 528
Europe	LUQI	191 697	113 859	97 609	384 240	74 871	62 295	90 086	135 699	39 496
Pacific	LUQJ	7 248	5 029	6 885	5 362	4 484	3 272	3 823	2 670	2 842
World unallocated[2]	LUQK	208 574	273 363	308 686	350 327	451 897	490 800	607 931	703 059	737 855
Total Bilateral GPEX	LUQL	1 650 037	1 760 400	1 980 400	2 462 546	2 635 081	3 208 072	4 569 524	5 124 083	3 517 389

1 See chapter text.
2 Includes grants to VSO, CSOs, Research Institutions and Commonwealth Organisations based in the UK.

Source: Department for International Development: 01355 843764.

Defence

Chapter 4

Defence

This section includes figures on defence expenditure, on the size and role of the Armed Forces and on related support activities.

Much of the material in this section can be found in UK Defence Statistics 2007 (The Stationery Office).

Defence expenditure

(Table 4.1)

UK Defence Expenditure – the move from cash to resource accounting

Up until financial year 1998/99, government expenditure was accounted for on a cash basis. In April 1999 the introduction of Resource Accounting and Budgeting (RAB) brought in an accruals-based accounting system, although government departments were still controlled on a cash basis. This transitional accounting regime remained for two financial years. Government expenditure has been accounted for on a resource basis only since 2001/02.

The main difference arising from the adoption of RAB is that costs are accounted for as they are incurred (the principle of accruals), rather than when payment is made (the principle of cash). This gives rise to timing differences in accounting between the cash and RAB systems and also to the recognition of depreciation, which expends the cost of an asset over its useful economic life, and the cost of capital charge, equivalent to an interest charge on the net assets held on the balance sheet. At the time that RAB was introduced the cost of capital charge was 6 per cent of the net value of assets; although this was reduced to 3.5 per cent in 2003/04.

The change from cash based accounting to resource (accruals) based accounting, and the two-stage introduction of RAB (outlined below) has affected the time series comparability of the data.

Please refer to UK Defence Statistics 2007 Chapter 1 – Resource Accounting & Budgeting section for a summary of the key events leading to the introduction of RAB. Back copies of this publication are available at: www.dasa.mod.uk/natstats/natstatsindex.html

Control regime

Under Resource Accounting, government departments are accountable for their spending against Resource and Capital Departmental Expenditure Limits (DELs). Spending against the Resource DEL includes current items, which are explained in the following two paragraphs. The Capital DEL, while part of the overall DEL, reflects investment spending that will appear on the department's balance sheet and be consumed over a number of years, net of the receipts from sale of assets. Departments are also responsible for Annually Managed Expenditure (AME). This spending is demand led (for example, payment of war pensions) and therefore cannot be controlled by departments in the same way.

In Stage 1 of RAB, which was introduced at the start of financial year 2001/02, the Resource DEL covered current costs such as in-year personnel costs, equipment, and maintenance of land and buildings. Non-cash costs such as depreciation and the cost of capital charge fell within Annually Managed Expenditure (AME) and were not controlled to the same degree as DELs. This allowed departments an interim period to gain experience of managing the new non-cash costs and to review their holdings of stocks and fixed assets, which impact the non-cash costs, prior to the charge impacting on the more tightly controlled DELs.

Stage 2 of RAB was introduced at the start of the financial year 2003/04. This involved the movement of the primary non-cash costs (depreciation and the cost of capital charge) from AME into the Resource DEL, and a reduction of the cost of capital charge to 3.5 per cent of the net value of assets.

The change in definition of the DELs combined with volatile non-cash costs over the Stage 1 period make time series comparisons over the period 2001/02 to 2003/04 complex.

From 2006/07, the MOD has transferred ownership of fixed assets into two top level budgets (TLBs): Defence Estates (DE) for land and buildings, and Defence Equipment & Support (DE&S) for plant and machinery, transport, IT and communications equipment, and single use military equipment (SUME).

Factors affecting Cash to RAB data consistency

- There are timing differences as to when payments are recognised

- The movement of non-cash items of expenditure from AME into the Resource DEL from 2003/04 onwards has the 'apparent' effect of inflating the Resource DEL

- In the financial year 2003/04 the rate of interest used to calculate the cost of capital charge was reduced from 6 per cent to 3.5 per cent

- The discount rate for provisions was changed from 3.5 per cent real to 2.2 per cent real with effect from 1 April 2005

- The discount rate for pension's liabilities was changed from 2.8 per cent real to 1.8 per cent real with effect from 1 April 2007

Resource DEL includes expenditure under the following headings:

- *Equipment support:* internal and contracted-out costs for equipment repair and maintenance

- *Stock consumption:* consumption of armament, medical, dental, veterinary, oil, clothing, and general stores

- *Property management:* estate and facilities management services and costs for building maintenance

- *Movements:* cost of transportation of freight and personnel

- *Accommodation and utilities:* charges include rent, rates, gas, electricity, water and sewerage costs

- *Professional fees:* fees, such as legal costs paid to professional organisations

- *Fuel:* relates to fuel consumption by military vehicles, ships and aircraft

- *Other costs:* includes stock and fixed assets written off, research and expensed development and rentals paid under operating leases

Expenditure on fixed asset categories in Capital DEL includes:

- *Intangible assets:* comprise the development costs of major equipment projects and Intellectual property rights.

- *Single use military equipment (SUME):* Prior to 2004/05, this category was called 'Fighting equipment'. The category contains assets which only have a military use, such as tanks and fighter aircrafts. Dual use items such as those that also have a civilian use are recorded under the other categories

- *Assets under construction:* largely consist of major weapons platforms under construction in the Defence Procurement Agency, and a smaller element of buildings under construction. Once construction is complete, those platforms will transfer to the relevant TLB holder as SUME on their balance sheets

- *Transport/Capital spares:* from 2004/05 'Transport' has been recorded as a separate category and 'Capital spares' has been removed as a category, with the costs previously recorded here being incorporated into Transport or SUME

- *Other costs:* include, amongst others, items of Capital DEL and capital income

Annual Managed Expenditure includes:

- *Other:* for 2001/02 and 2002/03, AME included depreciation and the cost of capital charge. Under Stage 2 of RAB, this category now contains only demand led payments, such as cash release and cost of capital credit on nuclear provisions and QinetiQ loan repayments

In order to give a single measure of spending on public services under full resource budgeting, the Defence Spending line is presented as the sum of the resource and capital budgets, net of depreciation and impairments. This reflects the resources required plus the net investment in them, but avoids double counting the writing down of the existing capital stock and the cash outlay on new assets. Control is exercised separately on gross Capital and Resource DEL.

Service personnel

(Tables 4.2, 4.4, 4.5, 4.8 and 4.10)

The Regular Forces consist entirely of volunteer members serving on a whole-time basis, figures for which include both trained and untrained personnel and exclude Gurkhas, Full Time Reserve Service personnel, the Home Service battalions of the Royal Irish Regiment, mobilised reservists and Naval Activated Reservists.

Locally Entered Personnel are recruited outside the UK for whole-time service in special formations with special conditions of service and normally restricted locations. The Brigade of Gurkhas is an example.

The Regular Forces are supported by Reserves and Auxiliary Forces. There are both regular and volunteer Reserves. Regular Reserves consist of former Service personnel with a Reserve liability. Volunteer Reserves are open to both former personnel and civilians. The call out liabilities of the various reserve forces differ in accordance with their roles.

Defence

All three Services run cadet forces for young people and the Combined Cadet Force, which is found in certain schools where education is continued to the age of 17 or above, may operate sections for any or all of the Services.

Full Time Reserve Service (FTRS) personnel represent reserves serving full-time in regular posts. This was made possible by the Reserve Forces Act 1996. None existed before 1998. FTRS figures include Full Commitment (FC), Home Commitment (HC) and Limited Commitment (LC) individuals.

Home Service battalions of the Royal Irish Regiment were, until 1 July 1992, the Ulster Defence Regiment. The figures for the Territorial Army include Officer Training Corps and non-regular permanent staff.

The figures for cadet forces for each Service include the Combined Cadet Force. Naval Service figures include officers and civilian instructors. The Army and Royal Air Force figures exclude officers and civilian instructors.

Intake of UK regular forces from civilian life: by service

(Table 4.2)

This table shows all intakes to UK Regular Forces including re-enlistments and rejoined reservists.

Formation of the armed forces

(Table 4.3)

This table shows the number of units which comprise the 'teeth' elements of the Armed Forces and excludes supporting units.

Outflow of UK regular forces: by service

(Table 4.4)

This table does not include promotions to officer from other ranks and miscellaneous outflow.

Civilian personnel

(Table 4.6)

In previous years, the Ministry of Defence civilian workforce definition has reflected the historical requirement to understand the number of civil servants being directly funded. However with changes in employment legislation and the requirement to plan the future of the civilian workforce there was a need to change the definition to a more inclusive one, better reflecting modern human resources methods and policies. In the longer term it will be used for skills planning, ensuring that the Ministry of Defence has a well-equipped workforce able to provide the best support to the UK Armed Forces.

In summary, the change over previous years is the addition of two further categories of individuals:

Casual personnel – those employed on a short-term casual contract

Those not directly funded – personnel who are employed by the Ministry of Defence, but whose salaries are paid for by another department/agency etc. This includes personnel on loan to other government departments or working for NATO, as well as those on a career break or long-term sickness absence

These additions allow two levels of definition to be established:

Definition - Level 1 This includes permanent and casual personnel, Royal Fleet Auxiliaries, but excludes Trading Funds. This is generally used for internal reporting and planning.

Definition - Level 0 This contains all those at Level 1 plus Trading Funds and Locally Engaged Civilians. This is used for external reporting, including National Statistics publications CPS1 (Civilian Personnel Statistics) and UKDS (UK Defence Statistics), and Parliamentary business.

For more information on the revised civilian workforce definition, visit: www.dasa.mod.uk/natstats/consultation/consultation.html

As from 1 April 2000 a new top level budget was formed in the Centre called Defence Logistics Organisation, replacing the top level budgets CinC Fleet Support, Quarter Master General and RAF Logistics Command.

At 1 April 2007, Chief of Defence Logistics and Defence Procurement Agency merged to form Defence Equipment and Support.

The QinetiQ portion of the Defence Evaluation and Research Agency was established as a private company in July 2001. The War Pensions Agency transferred from the Department of Work and Pensions in 2001. The Clyde Dockyards were contractorised in 2002.

Data on manually paid personnel before 1999 is not available, so estimates are used.

Totals and subtotals have been rounded separately and so may not appear to be the sums of their parts.

Family accommodation and defence land holdings

(Table 4.7)

In November 1996 most of the Ministry of Defence (MOD) housing stock in England and Wales was sold to a private company, Annington Homes. The homes retained for use by Service families were leased back with the condition that the MOD releases a certain number of houses each year for disposal by Annington. The proceeds of the sale are being used to upgrade the housing stock.

The table also presents statistics of land and foreshore in the UK owned or leased by the MOD or over which it has limited rights under grants or licences. Land declared as surplus to Defence requirements is also included.

Deployment of Service personnel

(Table 4.8)

The figures for Service personnel in England, Wales, Scotland and Northern Ireland are obtained from a different source from that used to compile the UK total. Consequently the sum of the national figures can differ from the UK total. The figures for Northern Ireland include all personnel who are serving on emergency tours of duty but exclude the former Ulster Defence Regiment, now the Home Services element of the Royal Irish Regiment. The figures for overseas countries include service personnel who are on loan to countries in the areas shown. Royal Navy and Royal Marines personnel on board ship are included in the UK figure if the ship was in home waters on the situation date or otherwise against the appropriate overseas area. All Defence Attaches and Advisers and their staffs are included under 'Other locations' and not identified within specific areas. From 2001 the grouping of overseas locations has been changed to give a more relevant overview.

The table reports personnel against their stationed location (where they are normally based). It does not show the location of troops on operational deployments.

UK regular forces – deaths

(Table 4.9)

Rates have been standardised to 2004 Tri-Service age and gender structure. In previous publications, deaths among the Brigade of Gurkhas were excluded, even though they belong to the regular Army, owing to the lack of reliable data on date of birth from which to calculate mortality rates. Gurkhas have been included in the number of deaths provided in Table 4.9. However they have been excluded from calculations for age- and gender-standardised rates.

Health

(Table 4.10)

The Services operate a number of hospitals in this country and in areas abroad where there is a significant British military presence. These hospitals take as patients, members of all three Services and their dependants. In addition, the hospitals in the UK take civilian patients under arrangements agreed with the National Health Service. Medical support is also supplied by service medical staff at individual units, ships and stations.

Defence services and the civilian community

(Table 4.11)

Search & Rescue (SAR)

This table covers incidents attended by military SAR units. The Royal Air Force and Royal Navy provide an essential service to the search and rescue effort around the UK forming part of the national UK SAR coverage throughout the year for air, land and maritime operations. Military SAR teams' primary purpose is to recover aircrew from crashed military aircraft although, each year, over 90 per cent of call-outs are to civilian incidents. The SAR force currently consists of 6 x RAF and 2 x RN SAR Sea King helicopter units and 4 RAF mountain rescue teams operating from bases around the UK plus specially equipped RAF Nimrod aircraft based in RAF Kinloss in Scotland.

The table also includes urgent medical incidents in which the military SAR facilities gave assistance (for example, inter-hospital transfers).

More than one SAR unit may be called to the same incident; consequently the number of call-outs is likely to be greater than the number of incidents.

Persons moved involves moving people from a hostile environment to a safe environment or to a medical facility to receive urgent medical attention. People assisted by RAF mountain rescue teams, but subsequently transported from the scene by helicopter, are recorded as having been rescued by the helicopter unit concerned.

Fisheries Protection

The Royal Navy Fishery Protection squadron operates within the British fishery limits under contract to the Department for Environment, Food and Rural Affairs. Boardings carried out by vessels of the Scottish Executive Environment and Rural Affairs Department and the Department of Agriculture for Northern Ireland are not included.

Defence

4.1 United Kingdom defence expenditure[1]

Inclusive of non-recoverable VAT at current prices (£ million)

		2002/03	2003/04	2004/05	2005/06	2006/07	2007/08
Defence Spending	C228	..	30 861	32 515	33 164	34 045	37 407
Departmental Expenditure Limits (DEL)	SNKJ	26 148	37 174	38 323	39 751	40 654	43 654
Resource DEL	E2XV	19 944	31 266	31 798	32 911	33 457	35 709
Expenditure on personnel	SNKK	9 969	10 435	10 996	11 255	11 204	11 485
of which: Armed forces	SNKL	7 385	7 974	8 047	8 263	8 423	8 649
of which: Civilians	SNKM	2 584	2 461	2 948	2 992	2 781	2 836
Depreciation/impairments	SNKN	..	6 313	5 808	6 587	6 609	6 247
Cost of capital	SNKO	..	2 770	3 026	3 106	3 242	3 371
Equipment support	SNKP	3 135	3 804	3 623	3 542	3 793	4 272
Stock consumption	SNKQ	1 222	1 060	1 079	1 039	1 140	1 071
Property management	SNKR	1 453	1 393	1 509	1 367	1 258	1 523
Movements	SNKS	505	491	711	729	774	858
Accommodation and utilities	SNKT	544	643	581	735	786	750
Professional fees	SNKU	468	549	565	553	482	471
Fuel	SNKV	185	161	239	369	416	537
Hospitality & Entertainment	I4SS	7	8	6	5	4	4
PFI Service Charges	I4ST	..	..	..	870	1 148	1 276
IT & Communications	I4SU	628	738	678	643	719	655
Other costs	SNKW	1 827	2 900	2 977	2 111	1 882	3 189
Capital DEL	E2YW	6 204	5 908	6 525	6 840	7 197	7 945
Expenditure on fixed asset categories							
Intangible assets	SNKX	1 756	1 665	1 580	1 550	1 744	1 756
Land and buildings	SNKY	96	54	389	31	45	126
Single Use Military Equipment	SNKZ	42	90	434	402	404	657
Plant, machinery and vehicles	SNLA	45	78	124	64	32	36
IT and communications equipment	SNLB	96	183	134	180	206	361
Assets under construction	SNLC	3 986	3 931	4 335	4 879	5 099	5 450
Transport	E2XX	..	..	73	13	33	55
Capital spares	SNLD	467	581	..	..	..	..
Capital loan repayment	E2XY	–	−28	−25	−53	−8	−10
Other Costs	E2Y3	−284	−646	−519	−225	−358	−486
Annually Managed Expenditure (AME)	SNLF	19 293	1 011	908	890	582	510
War pensions	SNLG	1 166	1 116	1 110	1 067	1 038	1 014
Other	SNLH	18 127	−105	−202	−177	−456	−504

1 See chapter text. Where rounding has been used, totals and sub-totals have been rounded separately and so may not equal the sums of their rounded parts.

Sources: Ministry of Defence/DASA (Economic Statistics); 0117 913 4529/30

4.2 Intake of United Kingdom regular forces from civilian life: by service[1]

Numbers

		1997[2]/98	1998/99	1999/00	2000/01	2001/02	2002/03	2003/04	2004/05	2005/06	2006[3]/07	2007[3]/08
All services:												
Male	KCJB	20 190	22 560	22 390	20 410	20 950	23 040	20 760	15 660	16 410	17 830	19 230
Female	KCJC	3 340	3 440	3 160	2 610	2 700	3 240	2 710	1 900	1 740	1 960	2 090
Total	KCJA	23 530	26 000	25 550	23 020	23 650	26 280	23 470	17 560	18 150	19 790	21 330
Naval service:												
Male	KCJE	3 970	4 110	4 250	3 990	4 270	4 420	3 530	3 240	3 480	3 300	3 400
Female	KCJF	630	660	700	630	740	800	580	460	460	460	470
Total	KCJD	4 600	4 770	4 950	4 620	5 010	5 220	4 120	3 690	3 940	3 770	3 860
Army:												
Male	KCJJ	13 390	15 010	14 750	13 450	13 620	15 060	13 930	10 780	11 740	13 160	13 390
Female	KCJK	2 010	1 980	1 750	1 320	1 240	1 550	1 260	910	990	1 140	1 150
Total	KCJI	15 400	16 990	16 500	14 770	14 850	16 610	15 190	11 690	12 730	14 300	14 540
Royal Air Force:												
Male	KCJM	2 830	3 450	3 380	2 980	3 070	3 550	3 290	1 640	1 190	1 370	2 450
Female	KCJN	700	800	710	660	720	890	870	530	290	360	480
Total	KCJL	3 530	4 250	4 100	3 630	3 780	4 450	4 160	2 180	1 480	1 720	2 930

1 See chapter text.
2 The definitions of intake used have been standardised from 1997/98 to give a more consistent picture across the three services.
3 Due to ongoing validation of data from the new Personnel Administration System, Naval Service statistics from 1 October 2006, Army statistics from 1 April 2007 and RAF statistics from 1 May 2007 are provisional and subject to review.

Source: Ministry of Defence/DASA (Quad-Service): 0207 8078772

4.3 Formation of the United Kingdom armed forces[1]
As at 1 April 2008

Numbers

			1998	1999	2000	2001	2002	2003	2004	2005	2006	2007	2008
		Front Line Units											
Royal Navy[2]													
Submarines	KCGA	Vessels	15	15	16	16	16	16	15	15	14[3]	13[4]	13
Carriers and assault ships	KCGB	"	5	6	6	6	4	4	5	6	5[5]	5	5
Destroyers and frigates	KCGC	"	35	35	32	32	32	31	31	28	25[6]	25	25
Mine counter-measure	KCGE	"	19	20	21	23	22	22	19	16	16	16	16
Patrol ships and craft	KCGF	"	28	24	23	23	23	22	26	26	22[7]	22	18
Fixed wing aircraft[8]	KCGG	Squadrons	3	3	1	1	1	1	1	1	1	1	1
Helicopters[9]	KCGH	"	12	12	9	9	8	8	5	6	6	7	7
Royal Marines	KCGI	Commandos	3	3	3	3	3	3	3	3	3	3	3
Regular Army													
Royal Armoured Corps[10]	KCGJ	Regiments	11	11	10	10	10	10	10	10	10	10	10
Royal Artillery	KCGK	"	15	15	15	15	15	15	14	14	14	14	14
Royal Engineers[11]	KCGL	"	10	10	11	11	11	11	11	11	11	11	11
Infantry	KCGM	Battalions	40	40	40	40	40	40	40	40	36	36	36
Special Air Service	KCGN	Regiments	1	1	..	..	..	..	..	..	..	..	..
Army Air Corps[9]	KCGO	"	5	5	..	..	..	..	..	..	..	..	..
Royal Air Force													
Strike/attack	KCGP	Squadrons	6	5	5	5	5	5	5	5)			
Offensive support[8]	KCGQ ZIZM	"	5	5	2	2	2	2	2	1)	13[12]	13	11[13]
Reconnaissance	KCGT	"	5	5	5	5	5	5	5	5)			
Air defence	KCGR	"	6	5	5	5	5	4	4	4)	..	..	..
Maritime patrol	KCGS	"	3	3	3	3	3	3	3	3	2[14]	2	2
Airborne early warning & ISTAR[15]	KCGU	"	2	2	2	2	2	2	2	2	3	3	4
Air transport and tankers and helicopters[9]	KCGV	"	14	14	8	9	9	9	9	9	8	8	8
Search and rescue	KCGY	"	2	2	2	2	2	2	2	2	2	2	2
RAF FP Wg	GHN7	HQs	..	..	..	4	4	4	4	4	6	6	7
RAF Ground based air defence[16]	GHN8	Squadrons	..	..	..	4	4	4	4	4	3	2	–
RAF Regiment Field[17]	GJ2F	"	..	..	..	6	6	6	6	6	6	6	7
RAF Regt (Jt CBRN)	I63Y	"	..	..	..	..	..	..	..	..	..	1	1
Tactical Provost Wg	GJ2G	HQs	–	–	–	–	–	–	–	–	1	1	1
Tactical Provost	GJ2H	Squadrons	–	–	–	–	–	–	–	–	2	1	1
Joint Helicopter Command													
Royal Navy Helicopter	JUAT	"	..	..	4	4	4	4	4	4	4	4	4
Army Aviation	JUAU	Regiments	..	..	5	5	5	5	5	5	5	5	5
Royal Air Force Helicopter	JUAV	Squadrons	..	..	6	6	6	6	6	6	6	5	6[18]
Joint Force Harrier													
Royal Navy	JUAW	"	..	..	3	3	3	3	2	1	1	2[19]	2
Royal Air Force	JUAX	"	..	..	3	3	3	3	3	3	2	2	2

1 See chapter text.
2 Only active vessels are shown.
3 HMS Spartan was withdrawn from service during the year.
4 HMS Sovereign was withdrawn from the service during the year.
5 HMS Invincible went into Extended Readiness in late 2005.
6 HMS Cardiff, HMS Marlborough and HMS Grafton were withdrawn from service during the year.
7 HMS Leeds Castle and the NI Squadron, consisting of HMS Brecon, HMS Cottesmore and HMS Dulverton, were withdrawn from service during the year.
8 From 2000 excludes aircraft transferred to the Joint Force Harrier squadron.
9 From 2000 excludes helicopters transferred to the Joint Helicopter command.
10 From 2000 includes one Armoured Regiment which is committed to the new Joint Nuclear Biological and Chemical Regiment.
11 Figure for 2000 includes an additional Close Support Regiment formed as a result of the Stategic Defence Review.

12 From 2006, 4 Air Defence squadrons amalgamated with Strike/Attack, Offensive support and Reconnaissance to form multi-roled squadrons. One squadron moved from reconnaissance to ISTAR, and one squadron was disbanded.
13 6 Squadron (Jag) was disbanded 30 April 2007, 25 Squadron was disbanded 1 April 2008. 43 Squadron also cover the role of the OCU since the disbandment of 56 Squadron, however this is not their only role.
14 206 Squadron was disbanded on 1 April 2005.
15 Figure for 2001 includes an embedded Operational Conversion Unit at the Sentry Operation Establishments.
16 Delivery of Ground Based Air Defence is now vested with the Army. The remaining 2 Squadrons were reroled on 1 April 2008 to increase the numbers of FP WGS and field Regts.
17 In UKDS editions 2003 and 2004, Ground Based Air Defence and Field Squadrons for years 2001 to 2004 were also included under Regular Air Force.
18 Reflects the standing up of 78 Squadron RAF to accommodate the endorsed increase in Merlin Mk3 crews and aircraft.
19 The Fleet Air Arm Strike wing, the equivalent to an RAF Squadron, comprises 800 and 801 Naval Air Squadrons.

Source: MOD/DASA: 020 7218 0390

Defence

4.4 Outflow of United Kingdom regular forces: by service[1]

Numbers

		1997[2]/98	1998/99	1999/00	2000/01	2001/02	2002/03	2003/04	2004/05	2005/06	2006[3]/07	2007[3]/08
All Services:												
Male	KDNA	21 860	24 500	23 870	22 520	22 360	21 770	21 200	21 330	21 290	23 000	22 510
Female	KDNB	2 490	2 970	2 750	2 430	2 350	2 340	2 200	2 100	1 980	2 160	2 170
Total	KDNC	24 350	27 470	26 620	24 950	24 710	24 100	23 400	23 430	23 260	25 160	24 690
Naval Service:												
Male	KDND	4 650	4 920	5 160	4 480	5 110	4 680	4 230	4 150	4 000	3 830	3 870
Female	KDNE	620	610	630	550	690	620	540	490	480	490	470
Total	KDNF	5 270	5 530	5 800	5 040	5 800	5 300	4 770	4 630	4 490	4 320	4 340
Army:												
Male	KDNI	13 190	15 320	14 620	13 900	13 290	13 420	13 500	13 990	13 240	14 660	14 230
Female	KDNJ	1 280	1 730	1 580	1 330	1 090	1 140	1 090	1 080	950	1 110	1 100
Total	KDNK	14 470	17 050	16 200	15 230	14 380	14 560	14 600	15 070	14 190	15 770	15 330
Royal Air Force:												
Male	KDNL	4 020	4 250	4 080	4 140	3 960	3 670	3 470	3 200	4 050	4 500	4 420
Female	KDNM	590	640	540	540	570	580	570	530	540	560	610
Total	KDNN	4 610	4 890	4 620	4 680	4 530	4 250	4 040	3 730	4 590	5 070	5 020

1 See chapter text. Comprises all those who left the Regular Forces and includes deaths.

2 The definitions of outflow used have been standardised from 1997/98 to give a more consistent picture across the three services.

3 Due to ongoing validation of data from the new Personnel Administration System, Naval Service statistics from 1 October 2006, Army statistics from 1 April 2007 and RAF statistics from 1 May 2007 are provisional and subject to review.

Source: Ministry of Defence/DASA (Quad-Service): 0207 8078772

4.5 United Kingdom Defence: service manpower strengths[1]
As at 1 April

Thousands

		1998	1999	2000	2001	2002	2003	2004	2005	2006	2007	2008
UK service personnel												
Full-time trained strength	ZBTR	194.0	191.1	190.3	189.1	187.1	188.5	190.2	188.1	183.2	177.8	174.0
Trained Naval Service	ZBTS	40.5	39.3	38.9	38.5	37.5	37.6	37.5	36.4	35.6	34.9	35.1
UK regulars	ZBTT	40.4	39.1	38.5	38.0	36.8	36.6	36.4	35.5	34.9	34.3	34.5
Full-time reserve service	ZBTU	0.1	0.3	0.3	0.5	0.7	1.0	1.1	0.9	0.7	0.6	0.5
Trained Army	ZBTV	100.9	99.8	100.2	100.4	100.4	102.0	103.6	102.4	100.6	99.3	98.3
UK regulars	ZBTW	97.5	96.3	96.5	96.3	96.0	97.6	99.4	98.5	96.8	95.4	93.8
Full-time reserve service[2]	ZBTX	..	0.2	0.5	0.7	0.9	1.0	0.7	0.4	0.5	0.7	0.9
Gurkhas	ZBTY	3.4	3.4	3.4	3.5	3.4	3.4	3.4	3.5	3.3	3.3	3.6
Trained Royal Air Force	ZBTZ	52.7	51.9	51.2	50.1	49.2	48.9	49.1	49.2	46.9	43.6	40.6
UK regulars	ZBUA	52.7	51.8	51.0	49.8	48.9	48.5	48.7	48.8	46.6	43.2	40.3
Full-time reserve service	ZBUB	..	0.1	0.2	0.3	0.3	0.4	0.4	0.4	0.3	0.3	0.4
Untrained UK regulars	ZBUC	19.7	21.5	21.6	21.5	23.0	24.2	22.5	18.3	17.5	17.5	18.4
Naval Service	ZBUD	4.1	4.6	4.3	4.4	4.9	5.0	4.5	4.4	4.5	4.5	4.0
Army	ZBUE	12.4	13.4	13.6	13.2	14.0	14.5	13.3	10.8	10.9	10.8	11.3
Royal Air Force	ZBUF	3.2	3.5	3.7	3.9	4.1	4.7	4.7	3.0	2.1	2.2	3.1
Locally Entered Personnel (excluding Gurkhas)	ZBUG	0.4	0.4	0.4	0.3	0.4	0.4	0.4	0.4	0.4	0.4	0.4
Royal Irish Regiment[3]												
Home Service batallions	ZBUH	4.6	4.4	4.2	3.8	3.6	3.5	3.4	3.2	3.1	2.1	–
Reserve personnel	ZBUI	319.4	307.0	294.8	284.2	273.4	259.7	246.7	235.8	..	..	..
Regular Reserves	ZBUJ	254.9	247.6	241.6	234.9	224.9	212.6	201.4	191.5	..	..	..
Naval Services	ZBUK	24.8	24.7	24.2	23.5	23.5	23.2	22.8	22.2	..	..	19.6
Army[4]	ZBUL	186.2	180.5	175.5	169.8	161.1	151.5	141.9	134.2	127.6	121.8	..
of which mobilised:	SNEO	0.2	0.1	0.3	0.2	0.3	0.4	0.1	0.2	0.3	0.1	–
Royal Air Force	ZBUM	43.9	42.4	41.9	41.5	40.2	37.7	36.4	35.0	34.4	33.4	..
of which mobilised:	SNEP	..	–	–	–	–	–	–	..	..	..	..
Volunteer Reserves	ZBUN	64.5	59.4	53.2	47.3	46.3	44.9	43.4	42.3	..	42.7	39.2
Royal Naval Reserve and Royal Marine Reserve	ZBUO	4.4	4.5	4.8	4.8	5.0	4.9	4.5	4.4	..	3.0	2.9
of which mobilised:	SNEQ	..	..	..	..	..	0.4	0.1	..	..	0.1	0.2
Territorial Army[2]	ZBUP	57.6	52.3	45.6	41.7	40.7	39.3	38.1	37.3	38.5	36.8	35.0
of which mobilised:	SNER	0.6	0.5	0.8	0.4	0.5	4.1	2.9	1.5	1.1	1.0	1.4
Royal Auxilliary Air Force	ZBUQ	2.5	2.6	2.7	1.6	1.5	1.5	1.4	1.4	1.4	1.3	1.3
of which mobilised:	SNES	..	–	–	–	0.1	0.8	–	..	0.1	0.2	0.1
Cadet Forces	ZBUR	150.2	151.0	154.5	151.0	152.3	155.6	155.6	153.1	..	150.5	150.4
Naval Service	ZBUS	25.9	24.5	24.1	23.8	23.8	23.2	22.6	21.9	..	18.2	18.6
Army[4]	ZBUT	73.9	74.6	77.4	75.4	75.8	78.7	80.5	80.9	81.7	81.9	82.7
Royal Air Force	ZBUU	50.5	51.9	53.0	51.8	52.7	53.7	52.5	50.3	51.0	50.4	49.5

1 See chapter text.

2 Due to ongoing validation of data from Joint Personnel Administration System, 2007 Reserve data for Army are as at March 2007.

3 The Royal Irish Regiment disbanded on 31 March 2008.

4 2008 Army Reserves data are as at 1 June.

Source: Ministry of Defence/DASA (Quad-Service): 0207 8078772

4.6 United Kingdom defence: civilian manpower strengths[1]
As at 1 April

Thousands: Full-time Equivalent

		1998	1999	2000	2001	2002	2003	2004	2005	2006	2007	2008
Ministry of Defence civilians												
MOD Head Office, HQ and centrally managed expenditure[2,3]												
Non-industrial	KDQE	22.2	21.5	19.7	19.1	20.0	21.2	22.7	24.0	24.6	19.8	19.6
Industrial	KDQF	1.1	1.0	0.9	0.9	0.8	0.7	0.6	0.7	0.8	0.8	0.7
Defence Logistics Organisation[3]												
Non-industrial	ZBTJ	..	..	19.7	17.8	17.3	16.4	16.5	16.5	14.1	..	..
Industrial	ZBTK	..	..	11.5	8.4	6.3	4.4	4.3	4.1	3.9	..	..
Defence Equipment & Support[3]												
Non-industrial	I6P5	..	..	..	..	..	..	..	..	..	17.3	15.2
Industrial	I6P6	..	..	..	..	..	..	..	..	..	3.6	2.8
Naval Service												
Non-industrial	KYCW	12.0	11.3	3.0	3.0	2.9	2.7	2.9	2.6	2.3	2.3	1.8
Industrial	KYCX	6.6	5.3	1.0	0.9	0.8	0.8	0.8	0.7	0.6	0.6	0.5
Royal Fleet Auxiliary	EQS9	2.4	2.4	2.4	2.4	2.4	2.5	2.3	2.3	2.3	2.4	2.3
Army												
Non-industrial	KDQK	21.7	21.6	16.3	16.4	16.0	16.0	14.7	14.5	13.4	12.7	12.2
Industrial	KDQL	12.1	10.6	5.8	5.7	5.5	5.4	5.6	5.5	5.2	5.3	5.0
Royal Air Force												
Non-industrial	KDQM	11.7	12.2	7.1	7.0	7.1	7.0	7.3	7.0	6.7	6.0	5.7
Industrial	KDQN	7.3	7.1	4.5	4.4	4.3	4.4	4.4	4.0	4.0	3.0	3.0
Level 1 Total	C7PE	97.1	94.1	91.9	86.0	83.6	81.5	82.2	82.0	78.1	73.8	69.1
Non-industrial	C7PF	67.6	66.6	65.8	63.4	63.4	63.3	64.1	64.7	61.3	58.1	54.7
Industrial	C7PG	27.1	25.1	23.7	20.2	17.8	15.7	15.7	15.0	14.5	13.3	12.1
Royal Fleet Auxiliary	EQT2	2.4	2.4	2.4	2.4	2.4	2.5	2.3	2.3	2.3	2.4	2.3
Locally engaged overseas	KDQA	15.2	14.9	14.8	13.3	14.1	13.8	15.4	15.7	15.1	14.2	11.2
Non-industrial	KDQT	6.7	6.7	6.7	6.3	6.5	6.5	7.3	..	..	..	..
Industrial	KDQU	8.4	8.1	8.2	7.0	7.6	7.4	8.1	..	..	..	..
Trading funds	GQHI	14.0	14.0	14.5	18.8	12.4	12.2	11.4	10.8	10.7	10.1	9.2
Level 0 Total	C7PH	126.3	123.0	121.3	118.2	110.1	107.6	109.0	108.5	103.9	98.0	89.5

1 See chapter text. Individuals on temporary and geographic (T&G) promotion are classed as non-industrial. From 2004, personnel who cannot be correctly allocated to Top Level Budgets (TLBs) are included with the Centre figures (numbering approx 200 in 2006).
2 The MOD Head Office, HQ and centrally managed expenditure budgetary area was formerly referred to as Centre.
3 At 1 April 2007, the Defence Logistics Organisation and the Defence Procurement Agency (formerly part of the MOD Head Office, HQ and centrally managed expenditure budgetary area) merged to form Defence Equipment & Support.

Source: Ministry of Defence/DASA (EPA): 01225 467144

4.7 Family accommodation and defence land holdings[1]
As at 1 April

Thousands and thousand hectares

		1998	1999	2000	2001	2002	2003	2004	2005	2006	2007	2008
Family accommodation (thousands)												
United Kingdom: Total	KDPA	67.3	65.5	64.8	59.2	55.8	53.8	52.8	51.9	51.8	51.1	51.2
Land holdings												
United Kingdom												
Land[2]	KDPF	220.0	220.2	219.9	224.3	222.4	221.4	221.3	222.1	222.0	222.0	221.7
Foreshore[2]	KDPH	18.6	18.6	18.6	18.6	18.6	18.6	18.6	18.6	18.6	18.6	18.6
Rights held	KDPJ	124.5	124.8	124.8	124.8	124.9	131.1	131.1	124.9	124.9	124.9	133.1
Defence land[3]												
Used for agricultural purposes	KDPL	103.5	114.5	92.2	98.6	91.8	103.0	100.5	106.3	..[3]	..[3]	..[3]
Used for grazing only	KDPM	59.6	65.5	50.3	66.6	60.0	70.2	68.3	71.0	..	..	..
Full agricultural use	KDPN	43.9	49.0	41.9	32.0	31.8	32.8	32.2	35.3	..	..	..

1 See chapter text.
2 Freehold and leasehold.
3 Following changes in the tenancies of agricultural land, these data are no longer available. Alternative data are being sought.

Sources: Ministry of Defence/Defence Estates Directorate of Operations;
Housing : 01480 52151;
Ministry of Defence/Defence Estates: 0121 311 2140

Defence

4.8 Location of United Kingdom service personnel[1]
As at 1 July

Thousands

		1998	1999	2000	2001	2002	2003	2004	2005	2006	2007	2008[12]
UK Service personnel, Regular Forces:												
UK distribution[2,3]												
In United Kingdom[4]	KDOB	173.4	171.7	170.3	172.0	..	..	..	169.7	167.3	161.4	158.7
England	KDOC	144.6	144.3	143.0	144.1	..	..	..	145.0	142.1	141.4	140.3
Wales	KDOD	3.2	3.3	3.2	2.6	..	..	..	2.9	3.3	2.6	2.6
Scotland	KDOE	14.2	14.9	15.1	14.5	..	..	..	13.2	13.5	12.6	12.0
Northern Ireland	KDOF	11.0	9.0	8.4	9.4	..	..	..	7.0	6.8	4.8	3.7
Global location[2,3]												
United Kingdom	MKCN	165.0	161.0	163.1	162.8	..	..	..	169.7	167.3	161.4	158.7
Overseas	KDOG	43.1	47.1	43.0	40.9	..	..	..	29.2	28.5	28.0	27.6
Mainland European States[4,5]	KDOI	6.9	15.2	8.2	8.6	..	..	..	27.0	26.6	26.2	26.0
Germany[6]	KDOH	20.3	18.0	19.5	17.3	..	..	..	22.2	22.0	21.7	21.7
Balkans	MKCO	..	..	..	..	..	..	..	0.1	–	0.1	–
Mediterranean[7,8]	KDOM	1.2	1.3	1.1	2.3	..	..	..	..	..	..	..
Gibraltar	KDOJ	0.5	0.6	0.6	0.5	..	..	..	0.4	0.3	0.3	0.3
Cyprus	KDOL	3.6	3.6	3.5	3.5	..	..	..	3.2	3.0	3.0	2.8
Far East/Asia[9]	MKCT	0.3	0.3	1.0	0.3	..	..	..	0.3	0.3	0.2	0.3
Africa[10]	MKCP	..	..	..	–	..	..	..	0.6	0.6	0.5	0.5
North America	MKCQ	..	..	..	2.5	..	..	..	0.7	0.7	0.7	0.7
Central/South America	MKCR	..	..	..	–	..	..	..	0.1	0.1	0.1	0.1
Falkland Islands	MKCS	..	..	..	0.8	..	..	..	0.3	0.3	0.3	0.1
Other locations, including unallocated	KDOQ	10.4	8.2	9.1	5.1	..	..	..	1.1	1.0	1.1	1.2
Locally entered service personnel:[11]												
United Kingdom	KDOS	2.1	2.0	2.1	2.3	2.6	2.6	2.6	2.1	2.2	2.4	2.7
Gibraltar	KDOT	0.4	0.4	0.3	0.4	0.4	0.4	0.4	0.4	0.4	0.4	0.4
Hong Kong	KDOV	..	..	..	..	..	..	..	..	..	..	..
Brunei	KDOW	0.9	0.8	0.8	0.8	0.8	0.8	0.7	0.8	0.8	0.8	0.8
India/Nepal	KDOX	0.5	0.5	0.5	0.4	0.3	0.4	0.4	0.3	0.3	0.1	–
Total	KDOK	4.0	3.7	3.7	3.9	4.2	4.1	4.1	3.3	3.7	3.7	3.9

1 See chapter text.
2 Prior to 2003, figures for UK distribution and global location are collated from seperate sources. Comparison is therefore not possible between the two sets of UK personnel figures.
3 Includes personnel within the UK whose location is unknown.
4 Includes the Balkans until 2002.
5 Post 2002 Mainland European States figure includes Germany, Balkans, Mediterranean, Gibraltar and Cyprus.
6 Prior to 1996, figures for the Federal Republic of Germany and Mainland European States were combined.
7 Includes Med Near East and Middle East until 2002.
8 Post 2002 Mediterranean figure is not shown separately but is included in Mainland European States figure.
9 Prior to 1997 figures include personnel serving in Hong Kong.
10 Post 2002 Africa figure includes Middle East.
11 Including trained Gurkhas.
12 All data for 2008 are provisional.

Source: Ministry of Defence/DASA (Quad-Service): 0207 8078772

4.9 United Kingdom regular forces: deaths

Numbers and rates per thousand

		1999	2000	2001	2002	2003	2004	2005	2006	2007	2008
Deaths											
Total	SNIA	142	147	142	147	177	170	160	191	204	137
Male	SNIB	139[1]	143	139	138	170	164[1]	152[1]	184[1]	195[1]	129
Female	SNIC	3	4	3	9	7	6	8	7	9	8
Rates per 100,000 strength[2]											
All	SNIH	66.3	71.0	69.0	71.8	83.4	81.0	79.0	90.0[1]	105.4	71.7
Navy	SNII	60.0	62.9	79.9	67.4	89.8	91.2	68.8	84.9[1]	68.9	108.0
Army	SNIJ	73.7	78.7	70.7	82.8	82.9	77.9	83.5	95.1[1]	128.6	72.0
RAF	SNIK	48.7	61.7	49.4	52.2	73.0	61.1	71.4	84.0[1]	68.5	33.4

1 Denotes where data has been updated from previously published information.
2 Rates have been age and gender standardised to the 2006 Armed Forces population. Following data validation on Gurkhas, they are now included in the numbers of deaths and the standardised rates provided in Table 4.9. Also included for the first time are non-regular Service Personnel who died whilst on Operations.

Source: Ministry of Defence/DASA (Health Information): 01225 467538

4.10 Strength of uniformed United Kingdom medical staff[1]
As at 1 April

Numbers

		1998	1999	2000	2001	2002	2003	2004	2005	2006	2007[8]	2008[9]
Qualified doctors:[2]												
Naval Service	KDMA	210	210	210	220	220	230	240	260	260	290	283
Army[3]	KDMB	440	450	460	470	490	550	600	610	650	550	598
Royal Air Force	KDMC	210	200	180	180	180	190	200	220	230	220	229
All Services	KDMD	850	860	860	870	890	970	1 040	1 090	1 140	1 060	1 110
Qualified dentists:[2]												
Naval Service	KDME	60	60	60	60	60	60	60	60	60	50	55
Army[3]	KDMF	140	140	140	150	140	150	150	150	140	130	132
Royal Air Force	KDMG	80	80	80	80	70	70	80	70	70	60	63
All Services	KDMH	280	290	280	290	280	270	290	280	270	240	250
Support staff:[4]												
Naval Service[5]	KDMI	990	970	1 000	1 030	1 010	1 060	1 110	1 110	1 120	1 130	1 278
Nursing services[5]	ZBTL	..	200	210	210	220	250	280	290	300	300	295
Support[5]	ZBTM	..	770	790	820	790	810	840	820	820	830	983
Army[3]	KDMJ	3 090	3 120	3 210	3 260	3 320	3 410	3 560	..	..	3 000	4 071
Nursing services[3,4,6]	ZBTN	..	520	570	610	650	710	770	770	800	790	962
Support[3]	ZBTO	..	2 600	2 640	2 650	2 670	2 700	2 800	..	..	2 210	3 109
Royal Air Force	KDMK	1 190	1 360	1 460	1 480	1 500	1 600	1 680	1 660	1 550	1 340	1 375
Nursing services[7]	ZBTP	..	330	400	420	450	470	480	510	480	490	437
Support	ZBTQ	..	1 030	1 060	1 070	1 050	1 130	1 200	1 160	1 070	850	938
All Services	KDML	5 230	5 540	5 760	5 800	5 930	6 180	6 440	..	..	..	..

1 See chapter text. Includes staff employed at units (including ships) and in hospitals.

2 The Medical and Dental Officers are trained only and exclude Late Entry Personnel. For 2007 includes all those individuals who hold a basic registrable qualification but may not necessarily be fully trained in their speciality. "Qualified" Doctors and Dentists refers to personnel who hold a basic registrable qualification, but may not necessarily have completed their career directed professional training, and as such may not necessarily be fully trained in their speciality.

3 Due to a change in source data, Army figures prior to 2005 cannot be verified.

4 Includes all members of the Nursing Services/Nursing Corps. From 1999, figures for support staff have been split so that nurses are separate from other support staff. From 2007, includes all medical support staff which the Defence Medical Services Department collects in its tri-service return.

5 From 2007, includes trained and untrained.

6 The 2006 Nursing Services figure is trained and untrained. Coldioro with Nursing trades in the QARANC and all trained Officers in QARANC. From 2007, includes trained and untrained.

7 From 2007, includes trained and untrained.

8 Figures from 2007 provided by DMSD.

9 2008 support figures include all support staff both trained and untrained.

Source: DASA DMSD: 0207 2181429

4.11 United Kingdom defence services and the civilian community[1]

Numbers

		1998	1999	2000	2001	2002	2003	2004	2005	2006	2007	2008
Military Search and rescue operations at home												
Call outs: total	GPYC	1 898	1 912	1 941	1 763	1 684	1 714	1 638	1 702	1 875	1 973	2 083
Royal Navy helicopters	GPXO	463	499	499	502	436	424	453	478	497	592	586
Royal Air Force helicopters	GPXP	1 257	1 235	1 278	1 115	1 122	1 173	1 079	1 114	1 258	1 258	1 377
Contractorised and other helicopters	GPXQ	20	–	–	–	–	–	–	–	1	–	–
Royal Air Force Nimrod aircraft	GPXR	71	65	71	54	46	37	37	37	32	21	29
Other fixed wing aircraft[2]	GPXS	2	–	1	1	1	–	2	–	1	–	–
HM ships and auxilliary vessels[2]	KCMG	3	–	–	–	–	–	–	–	–	–	–
Royal Air Force mountain rescue teams	KCMH	82	113	92	91	79	80	67	73	86	102	91
Persons moved: total	KCMI	1 243	1 204	1 316	1 182	1 224	1 273	1 412	1 384	1 463	1 767	1 607
Persons moved by rescue service												
Royal Navy helicopters	GPXT	283	355	360	386	314	320	416	380	479	507	516
Royal Air Force helicopters	GPXU	937	832	934	781	900	922	978	907	968	1 219	1 062
Royal Air Force mountain rescue teams	GPXV	12	17	22	15	10	31	17	97	16	41	29
Other	GPXW	11	–	–	–	–	–	1	–	–	–	–
Persons moved by type of assistance												
Rescue[3]	GPXX	317	307	276	281	343	280	494	408	384	582	450
Medrescue[4]	GPXY	667	640	713	629	654	779	672	778	830	946	869
Medevac[5]	GPXZ	209	216	241	228	201	174	195	143	175	198	219
Recovery[6]	GPYA	43	32	29	36	21	25	33	31	43	24	40
Airlift[7]	GPYB	7	9	57	8	5	15	18	24	31	17	29
Search and rescue incidents: total	KCMM	1 697	1 714	1 781	1 608	1 544	1 600	1 504	1 584	1 703	1 803	1 941

Source: Ministry of Defence/DASA (Equipment & Personnel Analysis): 01225 468594

		1998 /99	1999 /00	2000 /01	2001 /02	2002 /03	2003 /04	2004 /05	2005 /06	2006 /07	2007 /08
Fishery protection											
Vessels boarded	KCMO	1 879	1 716	1 603	1 464	1 375	1 709	1 747	1 371	1 335	1 309

Source: Fisheries Protection - Ministry of Defence

1 See chapter text.
2 Not permanently on stand-by.
3 Rescue: Moving an uninjured person from a hostile to a benign environment.
4 Medrescue: Moving an injured casualty from a hostile environment to a medical facility.

5 Medtransfer (formerly Medevac): Moving a sick person between medical facilities such as a hospital or occasionally to move transplant organs.
6 Recovery: Moving people declared dead on scene or confirmed dead on arrival by a qualified doctor.
7 Transfer (formerly Airlift): Moving military personnel, or their families, on compassionate grounds.

Population and vital statistics

Chapter 5

Population and vital statistics

This section begins with a summary of population figures for the UK and constituent countries for 1851 to 2026 and for Great Britain from 1801 (Table 5.1). Table 5.2 analyses the components of population change. Table 5.3 gives details of the national sex and age structures for years up to the present date, with projected figures up to the year 2026. Legal marital condition of the population is shown in Table 5.4. The distribution of population at regional and local levels is summarised in Table 5.5.

In the main, historical series relate to census information, while mid-year estimates, which make allowance for under-enumeration in the census, are given for the recent past and the present (from 1961 onwards).

Population

(Tables 5.1 to 5.3)

Figures shown in these tables relate to the population enumerated at successive censuses (up to 1951), mid-year estimates (from 1961 to 2007) and population projections (up to 2026). Further information can be found on the Office for National Statistics (ONS) website (www.statistics.gov.uk/popest).

Population projections are 2006-based and were published by ONS on 23 October 2007. Further information can be found at: www.statistics.gov.uk/cci/nugget.asp?id=1352

Definition of resident population

The estimated resident population of an area includes all people who usually live there, whatever their nationality. Members of HM and US Armed Forces in England and Wales are included on a residential basis wherever possible. HM Forces stationed outside England and Wales are not included. Students are taken to be resident at their term time address.

The projections of the resident population of the UK and constituent countries were prepared by the National Statistics Centre for Demography within ONS, in consultation with the Registrars General, as a common framework for use in national planning in a number of different fields. New projections are made every second year on assumptions regarding future fertility, mortality and migration which seem most appropriate on the basis of the statistical evidence available at the time. The population projections in Tables 5.1

to 5.3 are based on the estimates of the population of the UK at mid-2006 made by the Registrars General.

Marital condition (de jure): estimated population

(Table 5.4)

This table shows population estimates by marital status.

Geographical distribution of the population

(Table 5.5)

The population enumerated in the censuses for 1911 to 1951, and the mid-year population estimates for later years, are provided for standard regions of the UK, for metropolitan areas, for broad groupings of local authority districts by type within England and Wales, and for some of the larger cities. Projections of future sub-national population levels are prepared from time to time by the Registrar General, but are not shown in this publication.

Migration into and out of the UK

(Tables 5.7 to 5.9)

A migrant is defined as a person who changes his or her country of usual residence for a period of at least a year, so that the country of destination effectively becomes the country of usual residence.

The main source of international migration data is the International Passenger Survey (IPS). This is a continuous voluntary sample survey that provides information on passengers entering and leaving the UK by the principal air, sea and tunnel routes. Being a sample survey, the IPS is subject to some uncertainty; therefore it should be noted that international migration estimates, in particular the difference between inflow and outflow, may be subject to large sampling errors. The IPS excludes routes between the Channel Islands and Isle of Man and the rest of the world.

The IPS data are supplemented with three types of additional information in order to provide a full picture of total international migration:

1. The IPS is based on intentions to migrate and intentions are liable to change. Adjustments are made for visitor switchers (those who intend to stay in the UK or abroad for less than one year but subsequently stay for longer and become migrants) and for migrant switchers (those who intend to stay in the UK or abroad for one year or more but then return earlier so are no longer migrants). These adjustments are primarily based on IPS data but,

for years prior to 2001, Home Office data on short-term visitors who were subsequently granted an extension of stay for a year or longer for other reasons have been incorporated.

2. Home Office data on applications for asylum and dependants of asylum seekers entering the UK are used to estimate inflows of asylum seekers and dependants not already captured by the IPS. In addition, Home Office data on removals and refusals are used to estimate outflows of failed asylum seekers not identified by the IPS.

3. Migration flows between the UK and the Irish Republic are added to these data, as the IPS did not cover this route until recently and the quality of these data are still being assessed. Migration flows are obtained mainly from the Quarterly National Household Survey and are agreed between the Irish Central Statistics Office and ONS.

The international migration estimates in Table 5.7 are derived from all these sources and represent total international migration. The estimates in Tables 5.8 and 5.9 are based on the International Passenger Survey only (without the three adjustments outlined above).

Grants for settlement in the UK

(Table 5.10)

This table presents in geographic regions the statistics of individual countries of nationality, arranged alphabetically within each region. The figures are on a different basis from those derived from IPS (Tables 5.8 and 5.9) and relate only to people subject to immigration control. Persons granted settlements are allowed to stay indefinitely in the UK. They exclude temporary migrants such as students and generally relate only to non-EEA nationals. Settlement can occur several years after entry to the country.

Applications received for asylum in the UK, excluding dependants

(Table 5.11)

This table shows statistics of applications for asylum in the UK. Figures are shown for the main applicant nationalities by geographic region. The basis of assessing asylum applications, and hence of deciding whether to grant asylum in the UK, is the 1951 United Nations Convention on Refugees.

Marriages

(Table 5.12)

The figures in this table relate to marriages solemnised in the constituent countries of the UK. They take no account of the growing trend towards marrying abroad.

Divorces

(Tables 5.13 and 5.14)

A marriage may be either dissolved following a petition for divorce and the granting of a decree absolute, or annulled, following a petition for nullity and the awarding of a decree of nullity. The first group of decrees are known as dissolutions of marriage and the second as annulments of marriage. In Table 5.13 the term 'divorce' includes both types of decrees, although strictly speaking, it should refer only to dissolutions.

Births

(Tables 5.15 to 5.17)

Live births: For England and Wales, figures relate to the number of births occurring in a period; for Scotland and Northern Ireland, figures relate to births registered in a period. By law, births must be registered within 42 days in England and Wales, within 21 days in Scotland, and within 42 days in Northern Ireland. In England and Wales, where a birth is registered later than the legal time period, and too late to be included in the count for the year of occurrence, it will be included in the count for the following year.

All data for England and Wales and for Scotland include births occurring in those countries to mothers not usually resident in them. Data for Northern Ireland, and hence UK, prior to 1981 include births occurring in Northern Ireland to non-resident mothers; from 1981, such births are excluded.

Deaths

(Tables 5.19 and 5.21)

The figures relate to the number of deaths registered during each calendar year.

Infant and maternal mortality

(Table 5.20)

On 1 October 1992 the legal definition of a stillbirth was altered from a baby born dead after 28 completed weeks

Population and vital statistics

gestation or more, to one born after 24 completed weeks of gestation or more. The 258 stillbirths of 24 to 27 weeks gestation that occurred between 1 October and 31 December 1992 are excluded from this table.

Life tables

(Table 5.22)

The current set of interim life tables are constructed from the estimated populations in 2005–07 and corresponding data on births, infant deaths and deaths by individual age occurring in those years.

The estimates used in these interim life tables are the estimates, or revised estimates, issued on the following dates:

Mid-year population estimates	England	Wales	Scotland	Northern Ireland
2004	August 2007	August 2007	July 2007	July 2005
2005	August 2007	August 2007	July 2007	October 2006
2006	August 2007	August 2007	July 2007	July 2007
2007	August 2008	August 2008	July 2008	July 2008

Adoptions

(Tables 5.23)

The figures shown in this table relate to the date the adoption was entered in the Adopted Children Register. Figures based on the date of the court order are available for England and Wales in the volume *Marriage, divorce and adoption statistics 2006* (no. 34 in the FM2 series) available on the Office for National Statistics website (www.ons.gov.uk) or from the ONS enquiry point telephone number shown at the foot of the table.

5.1 Population summary: by country and sex

Thousands

	United Kingdom			England and Wales			Wales	Scotland			Northern Ireland		
	Persons	Males	Females	Persons	Males	Females	Persons	Persons	Males	Females	Persons	Males	Females
Enumerated population:													
Census figures													
1801	..	..	..	8 893	4 255	4 638	587	1 608	739	869	..	..	..
1851	22 259	10 855	11 404	17 928	8 781	9 146	1 163	2 889	1 376	1 513	1 442	698	745
1901	30 237	18 492	19 745	32 528	15 729	16 799	2 013	4 472	2 174	2 298	1 237	590	647
1911	42 082	20 357	21 725	36 070	17 446	18 625	2 421	4 761	2 309	2 452	1 251	603	648
1921[1]	44 027	21 033	22 994	37 887	18 075	19 811	2 656	4 882	2 348	2 535	1 258	610	648
1931[1]	46 038	22 060	23 978	39 952	19 133	20 819	2 593	4 843	2 326	2 517	1 243	601	642
1951	50 225	24 118	26 107	43 758	21 016	22 742	2 599	5 096	2 434	2 662	1 371	668	703
1961	52 709	25 481	27 228	46 105	22 304	23 801	2 644	5 179	2 483	2 697	1 425	694	731
Resident population:													
mid-year estimates													
	DYAY	BBAB	BBAC	BBAD	BBAE	BBAF	KGJM	BBAG	BBAH	BBAI	BBAJ	BBAK	BBAL
1972	56 097	27 259	28 837	49 327	23 989	25 339	2 755	5 231	2 513	2 717	1 539	758	782
1973	56 223	27 332	28 891	49 459	24 061	25 399	2 773	5 234	2 515	2 719	1 530	756	774
1974	56 236	27 349	28 887	49 468	24 075	25 393	2 785	5 241	2 519	2 722	1 527	755	772
1975	56 226	27 361	28 865	49 470	24 091	25 378	2 795	5 232	2 516	2 716	1 524	753	770
1976	56 216	27 360	28 856	49 459	24 089	25 370	2 799	5 233	2 517	2 716	1 524	754	770
1977	56 190	27 345	28 845	49 440	24 076	25 364	2 801	5 226	2 515	2 711	1 523	754	769
1978	56 178	27 330	28 849	49 443	24 067	25 375	2 804	5 212	2 509	2 704	1 523	754	770
1979	56 240	27 373	28 867	49 508	24 113	25 395	2 810	5 204	2 505	2 699	1 528	755	773
1980	56 330	27 411	28 919	49 603	24 156	25 448	2 816	5 194	2 501	2 693	1 533	755	778
1981	56 357	27 412	28 946	49 634	24 160	25 474	2 813	5 180	2 495	2 685	1 540	757	700
1982	56 291	27 364	28 927	49 582	24 119	25 462	2 804	5 165	2 487	2 677	1 545	757	788
1983	56 316	27 371	28 944	49 617	24 133	25 484	2 803	5 148	2 479	2 669	1 551	759	792
1984	56 409	27 421	28 989	49 713	24 185	25 528	2 801	5 139	2 475	2 664	1 557	761	796
1985	56 554	27 489	29 065	49 861	24 254	25 606	2 803	5 128	2 470	2 658	1 565	765	800
1986	56 684	27 542	29 142	49 999	24 311	25 687	2 811	5 112	2 462	2 649	1 574	768	805
1987	56 804	27 599	29 205	50 123	24 371	25 752	2 823	5 099	2 455	2 644	1 582	773	809
1988	56 916	27 652	29 265	50 254	24 434	25 820	2 841	5 077	2 444	2 633	1 585	774	812
1989	57 076	27 729	29 348	50 408	24 510	25 898	2 855	5 078	2 443	2 635	1 590	776	814
1990	57 237	27 819	29 419	50 561	24 597	25 964	2 862	5 081	2 444	2 637	1 596	778	818
1991	57 439	27 909	29 530	50 748	24 681	26 067	2 873	5 083	2 445	2 639	1 607	783	824
1992	57 585	27 977	29 608	50 876	24 739	26 136	2 878	5 086	2 445	2 640	1 623	792	831
1993	57 714	28 039	29 675	50 986	24 793	26 193	2 884	5 092	2 448	2 644	1 636	798	837
1994	57 862	28 108	29 754	51 116	24 853	26 263	2 887	5 102	2 453	2 649	1 644	802	842
1995	58 025	28 204	29 821	51 272	24 946	26 326	2 889	5 104	2 453	2 650	1 649	804	845
1996	58 164	28 287	29 877	51 410	25 030	26 381	2 891	5 092	2 447	2 645	1 662	810	851
1997	58 314	28 371	29 943	51 560	25 113	26 446	2 895	5 083	2 442	2 641	1 671	816	856
1998	58 475	28 458	30 017	51 720	25 201	26 519	2 900	5 077	2 439	2 638	1 678	819	859
1999	58 684	28 578	30 106	51 933	25 323	26 610	2 901	5 072	2 437	2 635	1 679	818	861
2000	58 886	28 690	30 196	52 140	25 438	26 702	2 907	5 063	2 432	2 631	1 683	820	862
2001	59 113	28 832	30 281	52 360	25 574	26 786	2 910	5 064	2 434	2 630	1 689	824	865
2002	59 323	28 964	30 359	52 572	25 704	26 868	2 920	5 055	2 432	2 623	1 697	829	868
2003	59 557	29 109	30 449	52 797	25 841	26 956	2 931	5 057	2 435	2 623	1 703	833	870
2004	59 846	29 278	30 568	53 057	25 995	27 062	2 946	5 078	2 446	2 632	1 710	836	874
2005	60 238	29 497	30 741	53 419	26 197	27 223	2 954	5 095	2 456	2 639	1 724	844	880
2006	60 587	29 694	30 893	53 729	26 371	27 358	2 966	5 117	2 469	2 647	1 742	853	888
2007	60 975	29 916	31 059	54 072	26 569	27 503	2 980	5 144	2 486	2 659	1 759	862	897
Resident population:													
projections (mid-year)[2]													
	C59J	C59K	C59L	C59M	C59N	C59O	C59P	C59Q	C59R	C59S	C59T	C59U	C59V
2011	62 761	30 893	31 868	55 744	27 482	28 262	3 038	5 206	2 520	2 685	1 812	890	921
2016	64 975	32 088	32 887	57 837	28 610	29 226	3 113	5 270	2 557	2 713	1 868	921	947
2021	67 191	33 252	33 938	59 943	29 717	30 226	3 186	5 326	2 587	2 739	1 922	949	973
2026	69 260	34 313	34 946	61 931	30 737	31 194	3 248	5 363	2 605	2 758	1 966	972	994
2031	71 100	35 243	35 857	63 727	31 646	32 081	3 296	5 374	2 609	2 765	1 999	988	1 011

1 Figures for Northern Ireland are estimated. The population at the Census of 1926 was 1 257 thousand (608 thousand males and 649 thousand females).

2 These projections are 2006-based. See chapter text for more detail.

Sources: Office for National Statistics: 01329 444661; General Register Office for Scotland; Northern Ireland Statistics and Research Agency

Population and vital statistics

5.2 Population changes: by country

Thousands

	Population[1] at start of period	Average annual change				
		Overall annual change	Births	Deaths[2]	Natural change	Net migration and other changes
United Kingdom						
1901 - 1911	38 237	385	1 091	624	467	-82
1911 - 1921	42 082	195	975	689	286	-92
1921 - 1931	44 027	201	824	555	268	-67
1931 - 1951	46 038	213	793	603	190	22
1951 - 1961	50 225	258	839	593	246	12
1961 - 1971	52 807	312	962	638	324	-12
1971 - 1981	55 928	42	736	666	69	-27
1981 - 1991	56 357	108	757	655	103	5
1991 - 2001	57 439	161	731	631	100	61
2001 - 2007	59 113	310	710	591	119	191
2011 - 2021	62 761	443	802	551	252	191
England and Wales						
1901 - 1911	32 528	354	929	525	404	-50
1911 - 1921	36 070	182	828	584	244	-62
1921 - 1931	37 887	207	693	469	224	-17
1931 - 1951	39 952	193	673	518	155	38
1951 - 1961	43 758	244	714	516	197	47
1961 - 1971	46 196	296	832	560	272	23
1971 - 1981	49 152	48	638	585	53	-5
1981 - 1991	49 634	111	664	576	89	23
1991 - 2001	50 748	155	647	556	92	63
2001 - 2007	52 360	285	634	520	114	171
2011 - 2021	55 744	420	722	484	238	182
Scotland						
1901 - 1911	4 472	29	131	76	54	-25
1911 - 1921	4 761	12	118	82	36	-24
1921 - 1931	4 882	-4	100	65	35	-39
1931 - 1951	4 843	13	92	67	25	-12
1951 - 1961	5 096	9	95	62	34	-25
1961 - 1971	5 184	5	97	63	34	-30
1971 - 1981	5 236	-6	70	64	6	-11
1981 - 1991	5 180	-7	66	63	3	-10
1991 - 2001	5 083	-2	60	60	-1	-1
2001 - 2007	5 064	27	57	56	1	26
2011 - 2021	5 206	12	56	52	3	9
Northern Ireland						
1901 - 1911	1 237	1	31	23	8	-6
1911 - 1921	1 251	1	29	22	7	-6
1921 - 1931	1 258	-2	30	21	9	-11
1931 - 1951	1 243	6	28	18	10	-4
1951 - 1961	1 371	6	30	15	15	-9
1961 - 1971	1 427	11	33	16	17	6
1971 - 1981	1 540	-	28	17	11	-11
1981 - 1991	1 543	6	27	16	12	-5
1991 - 2001	1 607	8	24	15	9	-
2001 - 2007	1 689	17	24	15	9	8
2011 - 2021	1 812	11	25	14	10	1

1 Census enumerated population up to 1951; mid-year estimates of resident population from 1961 to 2006 and mid-2006-based projections of resident population thereafter.
2 Including deaths of non-civilians and merchant seamen who died outside the country. These numbered 577 000 in 1911-1921 and 240 000 in 1931-1951 for England and Wales; 74 000 in 1911-1921 and 34 000 in 1931-1951 for Scotland; and 10 000 in 1911-1926 for Northern Ireland.

Sources: Office for National Statistics: 01329 444661;
General Register Office for Scotland;
Northern Ireland Statistics and Research Agency

5.3 Age distribution of the resident population: by sex and country

Thousands

| | | United Kingdom | | | | | | | | | | | | | | | |
| | | Population enumerated in Census | | | Estimated mid-year resident population | | | | | | | | Projected mid-year resident population[1] | | | |
		1901	1931	1951	1971	1981	1991[2]	2001[3]	2003	2004	2005	2006	2007	2011	2016	2021	2026
Persons: All ages	KGUA	38 237	46 038	50 225	55 928	56 357	57 439	59 114	59 557	59 846	60 238	60 587	60 975	62 761	64 975	67 191	69 260
Under 1	KGUK	938	712	773	899	730	790	663	680	705	716	732	756	794	799	802	790
1 - 4	KABA	3 443	2 818	3 553	3 654	2 726	3 077	2 819	2 706	2 686	2 713	2 765	2 837	3 104	3 191	3 217	3 188
5 - 9	KGUN	4 106	3 897	3 689	4 684	3 677	3 657	3 735	3 650	3 608	3 554	3 490	3 424	3 515	3 915	4 006	4 035
10 - 14	KGUO	3 934	3 746	3 310	4 232	4 470	3 485	3 890	3 896	3 867	3 819	3 751	3 704	3 499	3 523	3 922	4 013
15 - 19	KGUP	3 826	3 989	3 175	3 862	4 735	3 719	3 678	3 856	3 921	3 957	3 996	4 016	3 827	3 570	3 593	3 992
20 - 29	KABB	6 982	7 865	7 154	7 968	8 113	9 138	7 499	7 400	7 496	7 691	7 880	8 107	8 787	8 888	8 431	8 198
30 - 44	KABC	7 493	9 717	11 125	9 797	10 956	12 125	13 405	13 506	13 460	13 419	13 302	13 141	12 699	12 691	13 492	14 132
45 - 59	KABD	4 639	7 979	9 558	10 202	9 540	9 500	11 168	11 412	11 507	11 616	11 744	11 728	12 295	13 094	12 986	12 398
60 - 64	KGUY	1 067	1 897	2 422	3 222	2 935	2 888	2 884	2 949	3 027	3 114	3 240	3 483	3 746	3 450	3 842	4 293
65 - 74	KBCP	1 278	2 461	3 689	4 764	5 195	5 067	4 947	5 001	5 028	5 046	5 029	5 058	5 519	6 375	6 591	6 742
75 - 84	KBCU	470	844	1 555	2 159	2 677	3 119	3 296	3 398	3 431	3 420	3 416	3 424	3 539	3 827	4 362	5 135
85 and over	KGVD	61	113	224	485	603	873	1 130	1 104	1 111	1 174	1 243	1 298	1 436	1 653	1 947	2 342
School ages (5-15)	KBWU	..	13 120	7 649	9 704	9 086	7 818	8 381	8 334	8 254	8 159	8 041	7 917	7 745	8 106	8 668	8 850
Under 18	KGUD	..	10 557	13 248	15 798	14 472	13 120	13 357	13 259	13 219	13 176	13 120	13 111	13 139	13 494	14 133	14 420
Pensionable ages[5]	KFIA	2 387	4 421	6 828	9 123	10 035	10 557	10 845	11 012	11 117	11 232	11 344	11 562	12 184	12 493	12 900	13 431
Males: All ages	KGWA	18 492	22 060	24 118	27 167	27 412	27 909	28 832	29 109	29 278	29 497	29 694	29 916	30 893	32 088	33 252	34 313
Under 1	KGWK	471	361	397	461	374	400	338	346	362	367	374	387	406	409	410	404
1 - 4	KBCV	1 719	1 423	1 818	1 874	1 400	1 572	1 445	1 384	1 376	1 389	1 416	1 453	1 585	1 630	1 643	1 628
5 - 9	KGWN	2 052	1 967	1 885	2 401	1 889	1 871	1 913	1 870	1 847	1 819	1 785	1 750	1 798	1 998	2 045	2 060
10 - 14	KGWO	1 972	1 892	1 681	2 175	2 295	1 784	1 993	1 998	1 985	1 962	1 924	1 898	1 795	1 807	2 007	2 053
15 - 19	KGWP	1 898	1 987	1 564	1 976	2 424	1 905	1 879	1 989	2 018	2 030	2 060	2 069	1 975	1 842	1 854	2 054
20 - 29	KBCW	3 293	3 818	3 509	4 024	4 103	4 578	3 744	3 709	3 773	3 878	3 978	4 116	4 483	4 563	4 330	4 210
30 - 44	KBCX	3 597	4 495	5 461	4 938	5 513	6 045	6 645	6 695	6 669	6 655	6 597	6 522	6 313	6 335	6 789	7 157
45 - 59	KBUU	2 215	3 753	4 493	4 970	4 711	4 732	5 534	5 646	5 691	5 745	5 804	5 786	6 060	6 450	6 392	6 116
60 - 64	KGWY	490	894	1 061	1 507	1 376	1 390	1 412	1 440	1 479	1 522	1 584	1 701	1 824	1 679	1 870	2 079
65 - 74	KBWL	565	1 099	1 560	1 999	2 264	2 272	2 308	2 347	2 365	2 380	2 379	2 398	2 636	3 052	3 153	3 230
75 - 84	KBWM	196	335	617	716	922	1 146	1 308	1 369	1 392	1 400	1 413	1 432	1 535	1 716	1 991	2 357
85 and over	KGXD	23	36	70	126	141	212	312	312	321	350	379	403	483	608	770	965
School ages (5-15)	KBWV	..	6 711	3 895	4 982	4 666	4 001	4 294	4 273	4 233	4 185	4 122	4 054	3 969	4 148	4 431	4 525
Under 18	KGWD	..	3 630	6 753	8 108	7 430	6 711	6 845	6 799	6 780	6 756	6 727	6 721	6 733	6 910	7 231	7 376
Pensionable ages[5]	KFIB	785	1 471	2 247	2 841	3 327	3 630	3 928	4 028	4 078	4 130	4 171	4 233	4 654	5 376	5 913	6 173
Females: All ages	KGYA	19 745	23 978	26 107	28 761	28 946	29 530	30 281	30 449	30 568	30 741	30 893	31 059	31 868	32 887	33 938	34 946
Under 1	KGYK	466	351	376	437	356	387	324	331	343	349	357	368	388	390	392	386
1 - 4	KBWN	1 724	1 397	1 735	1 779	1 327	1 505	1 375	1 322	1 310	1 324	1 349	1 383	1 519	1 561	1 574	1 560
5 - 9	KGYN	2 054	1 930	1 804	2 283	1 788	1 786	1 822	1 781	1 761	1 735	1 705	1 674	1 717	1 917	1 962	1 976
10 - 14	KGYO	1 962	1 854	1 629	2 057	2 175	1 701	1 897	1 897	1 882	1 857	1 827	1 806	1 704	1 716	1 915	1 960
15 - 19	KGYP	1 928	2 002	1 611	1 887	2 311	1 815	1 799	1 867	1 903	1 927	1 936	1 947	1 852	1 728	1 739	1 939
20 - 29	KBWO	3 690	4 047	3 644	3 945	4 009	4 560	3 755	3 691	3 723	3 813	3 902	3 990	4 304	4 325	4 101	3 989
30 - 44	KBWP	3 895	5 222	5 663	4 859	5 442	6 080	6 760	6 811	6 792	6 764	6 706	6 620	6 386	6 356	6 703	6 975
45 - 59	KBWR	2 424	4 226	5 065	5 231	4 829	4 769	5 634	5 766	5 816	5 871	5 940	5 942	6 235	6 645	6 594	6 282
60 - 64	KGYY	577	1 003	1 361	1 715	1 559	1 498	1 473	1 509	1 548	1 591	1 656	1 782	1 922	1 770	1 972	2 215
65 - 74	KBWS	713	1 361	2 127	2 765	2 931	2 795	2 640	2 654	2 662	2 666	2 650	2 660	2 883	3 323	3 438	3 512
75 - 84	KBWT	274	509	937	1 443	1 756	1 972	1 987	2 029	2 040	2 020	2 002	1 992	2 005	2 111	2 372	2 778
85 and over	KGZD	38	77	154	359	462	661	817	792	789	825	864	895	953	1 045	1 177	1 378
School ages (5-15)	KBWW	..	6 409	3 753	4 722	4 421	3 817	4 087	4 061	4 022	3 974	3 919	3 863	3 776	3 958	4 237	4 326
Under 18	KGYD	..	6 927	6 495	7 690	7 042	6 409	6 512	6 460	6 439	6 419	6 393	6 390	6 406	6 585	6 903	7 044
Pensionable ages[5]	KFIC	1 601	2 950	4 580	6 282	6 708	6 927	6 917	6 984	7 039	7 102	7 172	7 329	7 531	7 117	6 986	7 258

5.3 Age distribution of the resident population: by sex and country

continued

Thousands

		England — Estimated mid-year resident population							Projected population[1]			England code	Wales — Estimated mid-year resident population							Projected population[1]			Wales code
		1991[2]	2001[3]	2003[4]	2004[4]	2005[4]	2006	2007	2011	2026			1991[2]	2001[3]	2003[4]	2004[4]	2005[4]	2006	2007	2011	2026	
Persons: All ages	KCCI	47 875	49 450	49 866	50 111	50 466	50 763	51 092	52 706	58 682	KERY	2 873	2 910	2 931	2 946	2 954	2 966	2 980	3 038	3 248	
Under 1	KCCJ	660	558	576	597	606	620	641	677	681	KFAC	38	32	31	32	32	33	34	35	34	
1 - 4	KCCK	2 560	2 366	2 275	2 262	2 289	2 335	2 398	2 639	2 741	KFBX	153	136	129	127	126	127	130	139	139	
5 - 9	KCCL	3 019	3 121	3 055	3 020	2 976	2 922	2 869	2 966	3 452	KFCA	186	185	180	178	175	172	167	164	182	
10 - 14	KCCM	2 865	3 238	3 250	3 225	3 185	3 130	3 092	2 925	3 418	KFCB	177	196	197	195	193	189	186	175	186	
15 - 19	KCCN	3 067	3 045	3 203	3 261	3 297	3 334	3 354	3 195	3 391	KFCC	187	186	196	199	200	202	204	194	186	
20 - 29	KCEG	7 651	6 307	6 232	6 315	6 483	6 633	6 816	7 420	7 008	KFCD	415	336	334	340	348	359	372	401	356	
30 - 44	KCEH	10 147	11 257	11 369	11 337	11 318	11 230	11 102	10 770	12 097	KFCE	583	608	608	606	599	590	579	547	608	
45 - 59	KCEQ	7 920	9 327	9 522	9 591	9 675	9 777	9 758	10 241	10 486	KFCF	486	572	582	586	589	592	590	605	568	
60 - 64	KCEW	2 399	2 395	2 445	2 509	2 586	2 697	2 904	3 117	3 580	KFCG	154	154	161	166	171	177	188	204	218	
65 - 74	KCGD	4 222	4 113	4 155	4 175	4 189	4 171	4 192	4 585	5 576	KFCH	284	264	268	270	271	273	276	306	362	
75 - 84	KCJG	2 626	2 764	2 850	2 875	2 865	2 860	2 865	2 955	4 289	KFCI	164	183	187	188	186	186	185	189	286	
85 and over	KCKJ	739	959	936	942	996	1 055	1 102	1 214	1 964	KFCK	45	59	59	60	63	67	70	78	125	
School ages (5-15)	KCWX	6 439	6 985	6 960	6 895	6 817	6 719	6 617	6 502	7 552	KFCL	397	420	417	413	407	401	393	375	404	
Under 18	KCWY	10 840	11 146	11 089	11 064	11 036	10 997	10 995	11 068	12 326	KFCM	662	662	654	651	646	641	637	625	651	
Pensionable ages[5]	KEAA	8 827	9 055	9 188	9 273	9 370	9 462	9 645	10 161	11 175	KFEB	573	584	595	602	608	615	627	665	732	
Males: All ages	KEAB	23 291	24 166	24 419	24 563	24 758	24 926	25 114	25 995	29 134	KFEI	1 391	1 409	1 423	1 432	1 439	1 445	1 454	1 487	1 603	
Under 1	KEAC	336	285	296	306	310	317	328	346	348	KFEJ	20	16	16	16	17	17	17	18	17	
1 - 4	KEAD	1 307	1 212	1 163	1 159	1 172	1 196	1 228	1 348	1 400	KFEK	78	69	66	65	65	65	67	71	71	
5 - 9	KEAE	1 545	1 599	1 564	1 546	1 522	1 493	1 466	1 517	1 762	KFEL	95	95	92	91	90	88	85	84	93	
10 - 14	KEAF	1 467	1 658	1 667	1 657	1 638	1 606	1 584	1 500	1 750	KFFA	91	101	101	100	99	97	96	90	95	
15 - 19	KECA	1 572	1 558	1 654	1 679	1 691	1 720	1 729	1 650	1 746	KFFN	95	94	100	102	103	104	105	99	95	
20 - 29	KECB	3 835	3 155	3 126	3 182	3 270	3 349	3 463	3 785	3 594	KFHA	207	166	166	170	176	181	189	206	185	
30 - 44	KECC	5 064	5 600	5 658	5 639	5 637	5 591	5 533	5 372	6 132	KFHB	289	297	296	295	292	287	282	267	309	
45 - 59	KECD	3 957	4 624	4 715	4 748	4 791	4 839	4 821	5 063	5 198	KFHW	242	283	287	288	290	291	289	295	274	
60 - 64	KECE	1 159	1 176	1 197	1 228	1 267	1 320	1 418	1 518	1 741	KFQO	74	75	79	82	84	87	93	100	105	
65 - 74	KECF	1 900	1 928	1 958	1 972	1 984	1 981	1 995	2 194	2 678	KFQV	128	124	127	128	129	130	132	147	174	
75 - 84	KECG	970	1 103	1 154	1 172	1 179	1 190	1 205	1 289	1 972	KFUK	60	73	75	76	77	77	78	83	133	
85 and over	KECH	181	267	267	274	298	324	344	411	814	KFUL	11	16	16	17	19	20	22	26	52	
School ages (5-15)	KECI	3 295	3 578	3 569	3 536	3 497	3 444	3 388	3 331	3 862	KFUV	204	215	214	212	209	206	202	193	207	
Under 18	KECJ	5 545	5 712	5 686	5 675	5 658	5 638	5 635	5 672	6 306	KFVE	339	340	336	335	332	329	327	321	333	
Pensionable ages[5]	KECK	3 050	3 298	3 379	3 419	3 461	3 494	3 544	3 894	5 148	KFVF	198	212	218	221	224	227	231	256	339	
Females: All ages	KEJV	24 584	25 284	25 448	25 548	25 708	25 837	25 978	26 711	29 549	KFVL	1 482	1 502	1 508	1 514	1 515	1 521	1 526	1 550	1 645	
Under 1	KEJW	324	273	280	291	296	303	312	331	332	KFYW	19	15	15	15	16	16	16	17	16	
1 - 4	KEJX	1 253	1 154	1 112	1 103	1 117	1 139	1 170	1 291	1 341	KFZJ	75	66	63	62	61	62	63	68	68	
5 - 9	KEKP	1 474	1 522	1 490	1 474	1 454	1 428	1 403	1 450	1 690	KGCK	91	90	88	87	85	84	81	80	89	
10 - 14	KEKQ	1 399	1 580	1 583	1 569	1 547	1 523	1 507	1 425	1 669	KGCM	86	95	95	95	94	92	91	85	91	
15 - 19	KEKR	1 495	1 487	1 549	1 582	1 606	1 615	1 626	1 545	1 646	KGCN	91	92	95	97	97	98	99	94	91	
20 - 29	KEKS	3 816	3 152	3 106	3 133	3 213	3 284	3 353	3 635	3 414	KGCO	208	170	167	170	172	178	183	195	171	
30 - 44	KENR	5 083	5 657	5 711	5 699	5 682	5 638	5 570	5 397	5 965	KGCP	294	312	312	311	307	303	297	280	299	
45 - 59	KEOQ	3 964	4 702	4 808	4 843	4 885	4 938	4 937	5 179	5 289	KGGZ	244	289	295	298	299	301	300	310	293	
60 - 64	KEOZ	1 239	1 219	1 248	1 280	1 319	1 377	1 485	1 599	1 839	KGIY	80	78	82	84	87	90	96	104	113	
65 - 74	KEQJ	2 323	2 185	2 197	2 203	2 206	2 190	2 198	2 391	2 898	KGKR	156	141	141	142	142	143	144	158	189	
75 - 84	KEQK	1 656	1 661	1 696	1 703	1 686	1 670	1 660	1 666	2 316	KGTQ	104	110	112	112	110	108	107	106	153	
85 and over	KEQL	558	692	669	667	697	731	758	803	1 150	KGTZ	34	43	42	42	44	47	49	52	73	
School ages (5-15)	KEQM	3 143	3 406	3 392	3 359	3 320	3 275	3 229	3 171	3 690	KGVG	194	204	203	201	198	195	191	183	198	
Under 18	KEQN	5 295	5 434	5 403	5 389	5 377	5 358	5 359	5 396	6 020	KGVH	323	323	318	317	314	311	310	304	318	
Pensionable ages[5]	KEQO	5 777	5 757	5 809	5 854	5 908	5 968	6 100	6 267	6 027	KGVK	375	372	377	380	383	387	395	408	393	

5.3 Age distribution of the resident population: by sex and country

continued   Thousands

		Scotland										Northern Ireland								
		Estimated mid-year resident population							Projected population[1]			Estimated mid-year resident population							Projected population[1]	
		1991[2]	2001[3]	2003	2004	2005	2006	2007	2011	2026		1991	2001[3]	2003	2004	2005	2006	2007	2011	2026
Persons: All ages	KGVP	5 083	5 064	5 057	5 078	5 095	5 117	5 144	5 206	5 363	KIOY	1 607	1 689	1 703	1 710	1 724	1 742	1 759	1 812	1 966
Under 1	KHAQ	66	52	52	54	54	55	57	57	52	KIOZ	26	22	21	22	23	23	24	25	23
1 - 4	KHCT	258	224	212	210	211	213	218	228	214	KIPA	106	93	89	87	88	89	91	97	95
5 - 9	KHDN	320	306	294	290	285	279	273	271	278	KIPN	131	123	121	120	119	117	115	113	124
10 - 14	KHDQ	313	323	320	319	315	308	303	281	285	KIPP	129	132	129	128	126	125	124	118	124
15 - 19	KHDT	337	318	324	328	327	328	330	314	294	KIPQ	128	130	133	133	132	131	128	124	121
20 - 29	KHDU	820	630	614	617	630	649	671	700	606	KIPR	253	225	221	224	230	239	249	265	228
30 - 44	KHDV	1 080	1 163	1 150	1 140	1 124	1 107	1 086	1 019	1 032	KIPS	315	376	378	378	377	375	374	364	396
45 - 59	KHFK	853	979	1 008	1 025	1 042	1 058	1 060	1 104	992	KIPT	241	290	301	305	310	316	321	345	352
60 - 64	KHOZ	265	262	265	270	273	280	301	331	376	KIPU	70	74	78	81	84	87	90	93	120
65 - 74	KHTU	441	447	452	455	457	456	457	482	612	KIPV	120	123	126	127	128	130	132	147	191
75 - 84	KHUO	259	272	281	286	286	287	290	306	428	KIPW	69	77	81	82	83	83	84	89	132
85 and over	KHUQ	70	89	86	85	91	95	98	111	194	KIPX	19	23	24	24	25	26	27	33	59
School ages (5-15)	KHVV	697	694	679	672	664	653	642	611	621	KIPY	285	282	278	274	271	268	265	256	273
Under 18	KIMT	1 150	1 098	1 074	1 067	1 059	1 050	1 047	1 019	1 003	KIQL	467	451	443	437	435	432	432	427	440
Pensionable ages[5]	KIMU	912	944	958	968	975	983	1 001	1 048	1 163	KIQM	246	262	271	275	280	284	290	310	361
Males: All ages	KIMV	2 445	2 434	2 435	2 446	2 456	2 469	2 486	2 520	2 605	KIQN	783	824	833	836	844	853	862	890	972
Under 1	KIMW	34	26	26	28	28	28	29	29	27	KIQO	13	11	11	11	12	12	13	13	12
1 - 4	KIMX	132	115	108	107	107	109	112	117	109	KIQP	54	48	46	45	45	46	47	49	48
5 - 9	KIMY	164	156	151	149	146	143	140	139	142	KIQQ	67	63	62	62	61	60	59	58	63
10 - 14	KIMZ	161	166	164	163	161	157	155	144	145	KIQR	66	68	66	65	64	64	63	61	64
15 - 19	KINA	171	161	166	168	168	169	169	161	150	KIQS	66	66	68	68	68	67	66	64	62
20 - 29	KINB	410	311	306	309	317	328	339	356	312	KIQT	127	113	111	112	116	121	126	136	119
30 - 44	KINC	535	563	556	550	542	534	524	495	516	KIQU	156	185	186	185	185	184	183	178	200
45 - 59	KIND	415	483	496	503	511	517	517	533	474	KIQV	118	144	149	151	153	156	158	169	170
60 - 64	KINE	124	125	126	129	131	135	146	160	176	KIQW	32	35	38	39	41	42	44	45	57
65 - 74	KINR	192	200	204	207	208	209	210	225	287	KIRJ	53	56	57	58	59	60	61	69	92
75 - 84	KINS	91	103	108	111	112	113	116	126	192	KIRK	26	30	31	32	32	33	33	37	60
85 and over	KINT	16	23	23	23	25	27	29	35	75	KIRL	5	6	7	7	7	8	8	10	24
School ages (5-15)	KINU	357	356	348	344	340	334	328	313	317	KIRM	146	145	142	141	139	138	136	131	139
Under 18	KINV	588	562	550	546	543	538	536	522	512	KIRN	239	231	227	225	223	222	222	219	225
Pensionable ages[5]	KINW	299	327	336	341	345	349	354	386	521	KIRO	83	92	95	97	99	101	103	117	165
Females: All ages	KINX	2 639	2 630	2 623	2 632	2 639	2 648	2 659	2 685	2 758	KIRP	824	865	870	874	880	888	897	921	994
Under 1	KINY	32	26	25	26	26	27	28	28	25	KIRQ	13	10	10	11	11	11	12	12	11
1 - 4	KINZ	126	109	104	103	103	104	106	112	105	KIRR	52	45	43	42	43	43	44	47	46
5 - 9	KIOA	157	149	143	141	139	136	134	133	136	KIRS	64	60	59	58	58	57	56	55	61
10 - 14	KIOB	153	157	156	156	154	151	148	137	140	KIRT	63	65	63	62	62	61	60	57	61
15 - 19	KIOC	166	156	158	160	159	160	160	153	143	KIRU	62	64	65	65	64	64	62	60	59
20 - 29	KIOO	411	319	307	308	314	321	332	344	295	KISH	126	113	110	111	114	118	123	129	108
30 - 44	KIOP	545	600	595	590	583	573	562	524	515	KISI	159	191	193	192	192	191	190	185	196
45 - 59	KIOQ	437	496	512	521	531	541	542	571	518	KISJ	123	146	152	154	157	160	163	175	182
60 - 64	KIOR	141	137	139	141	142	145	155	171	200	KISK	38	38	40	42	43	45	46	48	63
65 - 74	KIOS	249	246	248	248	249	248	247	257	326	KISL	67	68	68	69	69	69	70	77	100
75 - 84	KIOT	168	169	173	175	174	174	174	180	236	KISM	44	47	49	50	50	51	51	52	72
85 and over	KIOU	54	66	63	62	65	68	70	76	119	KISN	14	17	17	17	18	18	19	22	36
School ages (5-15)	KIOV	340	339	331	328	324	319	314	298	304	KISO	139	138	135	134	132	130	129	124	134
Under 18	KIOW	562	536	524	520	516	512	511	497	491	KISP	228	220	215	213	212	210	210	208	215
Pensionable ages[5]	KIOX	612	617	622	627	630	634	646	662	642	KISQ	163	170	175	178	181	183	187	193	196

1 2006 based national population projections . See explanatory notes at beginning of chapter for further details.
2 Data for mid 1991 for UK, England and Wales and Scotland were revised in light of the results of the 2001 Census.
3 Data for mid-2001 was revised as a result of local authority population studies.
4 England & Wales population estimates for mid-2003 to mid-2005 were revised in August 2007 to take account of improved estimates of international migration.
5 The pensionable age population is that over state retirement age. These figures take account of the forthcoming changes in state retirement age between April 2010 and March 2020 from 65 for men and 60 for women to 65 for both sexes; and a further increase to 66 for both sexes between April 2024 and March 2026.

Sources: Office for National Statistics: 01329 444661; General Register Office for Scotland; General Register Office for Northern Ireland

Population and vital statistics

5.4 Marital condition (*de jure*)[1]: estimated population: by age and sex
England and Wales

Thousands

		Males								Females							
		1991[2]	2001	2002[3]	2003[3]	2004[3]	2005[3]	2006	2007	1991[2]	2001	2002[3]	2003[3]	2004[3]	2005[3]	2006	2007
All ages:																	
	Single KRPL	11 131	12 270	12 408	12 550	12 714	12 893	13 078	13 279	KUBS 9 824	10 917	11 035	11 167	11 310	11 494	11 673	11 853
	Married KRPM	11 636	11 090	11 043	10 995	10 941	10 923	10 881	10 851	KVCC 11 833	11 150	11 094	11 033	10 980	10 943	10 893	10 851
	Widowed KRPN	727	733	730	726	722	719	716	715	KVCD 2 951	2 745	2 709	2 669	2 628	2 588	2 548	2 511
	Divorced KRPO	1 187	1 482	1 524	1 571	1 617	1 662	1 696	1 724	KVCE 1 459	1 975	2 031	2 087	2 144	2 198	2 244	2 289
Age groups:																	
0 - 14:	Single KRPP	4 939	5 036	4 999	4 967	4 941	4 912	4 880	4 872	KVCF 4 720	4 796	4 763	4 726	4 696	4 670	4 648	4 644
15 - 19:	Single KRPQ	1 659	1 645	1 698	1 749	1 778	1 792	1 822	1 832	KVCG 1 554	1 560	1 587	1 631	1 667	1 693	1 706	1 718
	Married KRPR	8	5	5	4	3	2	2	2	KVCH 32	16	13	12	11	10	7	7
	Widowed KRPS	–	1	1	1	–	–	–	–	KVCI –	1	1	1	–	–	–	–
	Divorced KRPT	–	1	1	1	–	–	–	–	KVCJ –	1	1	–	–	–	–	–
20 - 24:	Single KRPU	1 717	1 501	1 530	1 568	1 632	1 693	1 741	1 813	KVCK 1 421	1 390	1 427	1 459	1 491	1 539	1 591	1 637
	Married KRPV	242	74	73	74	75	73	67	64	KVCL 490	178	170	166	163	157	146	136
	Widowed KRPW	–	1	1	1	1	1	1	1	KVCM 1	1	1	1	2	2	1	1
	Divorced KRPX	12	3	3	3	3	3	3	3	KVCN 29	8	8	8	8	8	7	6
25 - 34:	Single KRPY	1 652	2 227	2 229	2 230	2 245	2 292	2 343	2 383	KVCO 1 135	1 770	1 788	1 811	1 846	1 906	1 961	2 000
	Married KRPZ	2 028	1 391	1 311	1 237	1 173	1 125	1 068	1 027	KVCP 2 488	1 768	1 671	1 584	1 506	1 452	1 386	1 326
	Widowed KRQA	2	3	3	3	3	3	2	2	KVCQ 8	10	9	8	7	7	7	7
	Divorced KRQB	237	136	129	124	118	111	103	96	KVCR 312	231	217	206	193	182	169	158
35 - 44:	Single KRQC	477	963	1 027	1 080	1 126	1 173	1 219	1 259	KVEH 280	692	749	801	853	903	955	1 004
	Married KRQD	2 632	2 494	2 499	2 488	2 466	2 452	2 419	2 385	KVEI 2 760	2 649	2 653	2 638	2 623	2 597	2 564	2 525
	Widowed KRQE	11	12	12	12	11	11	11	10	KVEJ 34	36	35	33	32	31	30	29
	Divorced KRQF	384	411	420	427	433	436	431	422	KVEK 444	558	570	579	588	590	585	574
45 - 54:	Single KRQG	251	419	432	450	473	499	530	563	KVEL 144	256	271	288	310	334	363	397
	Married KUAR	2 347	2 511	2 432	2 383	2 356	2 348	2 355	2 365	KVEM 2 322	2 548	2 477	2 428	2 401	2 391	2 398	2 413
	Widowed KUBA	31	37	35	34	32	31	30	29	KVEN 118	111	105	99	96	92	90	87
	Divorced KUBB	290	448	451	461	474	489	504	518	KVEO 332	557	565	576	591	609	630	654
55 - 59:	Single KUBC	101	128	141	150	158	164	170	170	KVEP 69	74	81	86	91	96	102	104
	Married KUBD	1 050	1 156	1 238	1 278	1 288	1 285	1 271	1 201	KVEQ 982	1 125	1 212	1 256	1 271	1 271	1 260	1 197
	Widowed KUBE	34	34	36	36	37	37	36	34	KVER 136	112	115	114	111	109	106	98
	Divorced KUBF	95	174	194	208	219	228	234	231	KVES 107	210	235	255	269	281	290	288
60 - 64:	Single KUBG	104	97	97	100	104	108	114	124	KVET 80	62	61	62	63	65	69	75
	Married KUBH	997	980	977	991	1 013	1 039	1 077	1 150	KVEU 908	906	910	932	958	988	1 029	1 110
	Widowed KUBI	63	50	49	48	47	47	48	51	KVEV 250	178	172	167	163	160	159	162
	Divorced KUBJ	70	125	131	138	147	156	168	186	KVEW 82	151	158	169	180	193	210	234
65 - 74:	Single KUBK	150	155	154	153	152	151	149	150	KMGN 176	130	126	123	120	117	113	111
	Married KUBL	1 574	1 569	1 581	1 595	1 606	1 614	1 610	1 620	KMGO 1 317	1 322	1 336	1 356	1 373	1 389	1 393	1 410
	Widowed KUBM	229	188	183	178	174	170	165	162	KMGP 879	697	675	655	633	611	584	563
	Divorced KUBN	74	139	148	158	168	178	186	196	KMGQ 107	177	190	204	218	232	243	257
75 and over:	Single KUBO	81	99	101	103	106	109	111	114	KMGR 246	188	182	177	173	169	166	163
	Married KUBP	759	909	928	944	962	984	1 011	1 038	KMGS 536	639	651	661	673	689	709	728
	Widowed KUBQ	357	407	411	414	417	419	422	425	KMGT 1 526	1 598	1 597	1 590	1 583	1 576	1 571	1 564
	Divorced KUBR	25	44	48	51	56	61	66	71	KMGU 46	81	86	90	96	103	110	118

1 Data for 2002 to 2007 has been updated to include marriages abroad.
2 Mid-1991 marital status estimates are revised in light of the 2001 Census.
3 Mid-2002 to Mid-2005 marital status estimates for England and Wales have been updated to include the latest revised estimates that take into account improved estimates of international migration.

Source: Office for National Statistics: 01329 444661

5.5 Geographical distribution of the population

Thousands

		Population enumerated in Census			Mid-year population estimates								
		1911	1931	1951	1971	1991	2001	2002[1]	2003[1]	2004[1]	2005[1]	2006	2007
United Kingdom	KIUR	42 082	46 074	50 225	55 928	57 439	59 113	59 323	59 557	59 846	60 238	60 587	60 975
Great Britain	KISR	40 831	44 795	48 854	54 388	55 831	57 424	57 627	57 855	58 136	58 514	58 846	59 216
England	KKOJ	33 650	37 359	41 159	46 412	47 875	49 450	49 652	49 866	50 111	50 466	50 763	51 092
Standard Regions													
North	KKNA	2 729	2 938	3 009	3 152	3 073	3 028	3 029	3 033	3 037	3 045	3 052	3 061
Yorkshire and Humberside	KKNB	3 896	4 319	4 567	4 902	4 936	4 977	5 002	5 028	5 064	5 108	5 142	5 177
East Midlands	KKNC	2 467	2 732	3 118	3 652	4 011	4 190	4 222	4 254	4 291	4 328	4 364	4 400
East Anglia	KKND	1 191	1 231	1 381	1 688	2 068	2 181	2 195	2 220	2 242	2 268	2 287	2 311
South East	KKNE	11 613	13 349	14 877	17 125	17 511	18 566	18 646	18 706	18 783	18 936	19 069	19 216
South West	KKNF	2 818	2 984	3 479	4 112	4 688	4 943	4 973	5 005	5 042	5 087	5 124	5 178
West Midlands	KKNG	3 277	3 743	4 423	5 146	5 230	5 281	5 295	5 312	5 327	5 351	5 367	5 382
North West	KKNH	5 659	6 062	6 305	6 634	6 357	6 285	6 290	6 309	6 325	6 344	6 357	6 367
Government Office Regions													
North East	JZBU	..	..	..	2 679	2 587	2 540	2 541	2 541	2 542	2 550	2 556	2 564
North West (including Merseyside)	JZBV	..	..	..	7 108	6 843	6 773	6 778	6 800	6 820	6 840	6 853	6 864
Yorkshire and The Humber	JZBX	..	..	..	4 902	4 936	4 977	5 002	5 028	5 064	5 108	5 142	5 177
East Midlands	JZBY	..	..	..	3 652	4 011	4 190	4 222	4 254	4 291	4 328	4 364	4 400
West Midlands	JZBZ	..	..	..	5 146	5 230	5 281	5 295	5 312	5 327	5 351	5 367	5 382
South West	JZCA	..	..	..	4 112	4 688	4 943	4 973	5 005	5 042	5 087	5 124	5 178
East of England	JZCB	..	..	..	4 454	5 121	5 400	5 433	5 475	5 511	5 563	5 607	5 661
London	JZCC	..	..	..	7 529	6 829	7 322	7 362	7 364	7 389	7 456	7 512	7 557
South East	JZCD	..	..	..	6 830	7 629	8 023	8 047	8 087	8 125	8 185	8 238	8 309
Wales	KKNI	2 421	2 593	2 599	2 740	2 873	2 910	2 920	2 931	2 946	2 954	2 966	2 980
Scotland	KGJB	4 761	4 843	5 096	5 236	5 083	5 064	5 055	5 057	5 078	5 095	5 117	5 144
Northern Ireland[4]	KGJC	1 251	1 280	1 371	1 540	1 607	1 689	1 697	1 703	1 710	1 724	1 742	1 759
Greater London	KKNJ	7 161	8 110	8 197	7 529	6 829	7 322	7 362	7 364	7 389	7 456	7 512	7 557
Inner London[2]	KISS	4 998	4 893	3 679	3 060	2 599	2 859	2 886	2 891	2 907	2 944	2 973	3 000
Outer London[2]	KITF	2 162	3 217	4 518	4 470	4 230	4 463	4 475	4 473	4 482	4 512	4 539	4 557
Metropolitan areas of England and Wales	KITG	9 716	10 770	11 365	11 862	11 085	10 888	10 907	10 930	10 956	11 010	11 049	11 086
Tyne and Wear	KGJN	1 105	1 201	1 201	1 218	1 124	1 087	1 087	1 085	1 083	1 086	1 088	1 089
West Yorkshire	KGJP	1 852	1 939	1 985	2 090	2 062	2 083	2 094	2 103	2 119	2 142	2 161	2 181
South Yorkshire	KGJO	963	1 173	1 253	1 331	1 289	1 266	1 270	1 273	1 279	1 288	1 293	1 299
West Midlands	KGJQ	1 780	2 143	2 547	2 811	2 619	2 568	2 574	2 578	2 582	2 594	2 600	2 604
Greater Manchester	KGJR	2 638	2 727	2 716	2 750	2 554	2 516	2 518	2 528	2 534	2 543	2 554	2 562
Merseyside	KGJS	1 378	1 587	1 663	1 662	1 438	1 368	1 364	1 362	1 359	1 357	1 354	1 350
Principal Metropolitan Cities[2]	KITH	3 154	3 906	3 915	3 910	3 415	3 344	3 356	3 364	3 382	3 417	3 441	3 467
Newcastle	KGJT	267	286	292	312	275	266	267	267	267	270	270	272
Leeds	KGJX	446	483	505	749	707	716	720	723	729	741	750	761
Sheffield	KGJV	455	512	513	579	520	513	514	513	517	522	526	530
Birmingham	KGKF	526	1 003	1 113	1 107	1 005	985	989	992	996	1 003	1 007	1 010
Manchester	KGKJ	714	766	703	554	433	423	426	431	436	445	452	458
Liverpool	KGKM	746	856	789	610	476	442	441	439	437	437	436	435
Other metropolitan districts[2]	KITI	6 562	6 864	7 450	7 952	7 670	7 544	7 551	7 565	7 574	7 593	7 608	7 619
Non-metropolitan districts of England and Wales	KITJ	19 194	21 072	24 196	29 761	32 834	31 239	31 383	31 572	31 766	32 000	32 201	32 449
Non-metropolitan cities[2,3]	KITK	..	–	–	4 715	..	–	–	–	–	..	..	..
Incl. Kingston-upon-Hull	KKNZ	278	314	299	288	263	250	250	251	253	255	256	257
Leicester	KKOA	227	239	285	285	281	283	282	282	283	286	290	293
Nottingham	KKNX	260	269	308	302	279	269	272	275	279	283	286	289
Bristol	KKNV	357	397	443	433	392	390	391	394	397	406	410	416
Plymouth	KITL	207	215	225	249	251	241	242	242	244	246	248	251
Stoke-on-Trent	KKOD	235	277	275	265	249	240	239	239	239	239	240	239
Cardiff	KKOB	182	224	244	291	297	310	311	310	312	314	318	321
Newport	IFX3	84	89	106	137	135	138	139	139	139	140	140	140
Industrial districts[2,3]	KITM	..	–	–	6 486	..	–	–	–	–	–	–	–
New Towns[2,3]	KITN	..	–	–	1 895	..	–	–	–	–	–	–	–
Resort, port and retirement districts[2,3]	KITO	..	–	–	3 184	–	–	–	–	–	–	–	–
Urban and mixed urban/rural districts[2,3]	KITP	..	–	–	8 821	–	–	–	–	–	–	–	–
Remoter, mainly rural districts[2,3]	KITQ	..	–	–	4 661	–	–	–	–	–	–	–	–
City of Edinburgh local government district	KGKU	320	439	467	478	436	449	448	448	455	458	464	468
City of Glasgow local government district	KGKT	784	1 088	1 090	983	629	579	577	577	578	579	581	582
Belfast[4]	KGKV	387	438	444	–	293	277	274	272	269	268	267	268

1 Mid 2002 to mid 2005 population estimates for the UK and England & Wales have been updated to include the latest revised estimates that take improved estimates of international migration into account.

2 Details of the classification by broad area type are given in recent issues of the ONS annual reference volume *Key Population and Vital Statistics; local and health authority areas* (Series VS). The ten broad area types include all local authorities in England and Wales.

3 The breakdown of non-metropolitan districts by area type has not been provided from mid-2001 onwards. This is because the effect of boundary changes due to the major local government reorganisation on 1 April 1995 and 1 April 1996 (particularly in Wales) make the comparison of 2001 data with data for earlier years invalid.

4 1931 figures shown for Northern Ireland and the City of Belfast relate to the 1937 Census.

Sources: Office for National Statistics: 01329 444661;
General Register Office for Scotland;
Northern Ireland Statistics and Research Agency

Population and vital statistics

5.6

Population: by ethnic group and age, January - December 2007
United Kingdom

	0 to 4	5 to 9	10 to 14	15 to 19	20 to 24	25 to 29	30 to 34	35 to 44	45 to 59	60 to 74	75 and over	All ages (=100%) (thousands)
White[1]												
British	6	5	6	7	6	6	6	15	20	15	8	49 082
Other	4	4	4	4	9	12	11	17	17	12	6	3 127
Mixed												
White and Black Caribbean	17	16	17	14	10	7	4	9	4	1	0	229
White and Black African	21	16	10	9	6	8	6	12	9	2	1	90
White and Asian	24	18	12	11	7	6	4	10	5	2	1	165
Other Mixed	17	12	10	9	10	8	9	14	7	3	1	158
Asian												
Indian	7	6	6	6	9	11	11	15	18	9	2	1 174
Pakistani	11	10	9	10	10	10	9	14	12	5	1	936
Bangladeshi	12	12	9	8	9	11	12	11	9	5	1	343
Other Asian	9	7	7	7	8	9	12	19	15	5	1	464
Black												
Black Caribbean	7	6	6	7	7	7	6	20	18	11	4	633
Black African	13	10	9	8	7	9	10	21	10	3	0	774
Black Other	14	13	7	8	5	9	5	22	7	7	2	67
Chinese	5	5	4	6	15	15	12	17	16	4	1	247
Other	8	7	6	6	9	12	11	19	14	5	2	902
All[2]	6	6	6	7	7	6	6	15	19	14	7	60 145

1 Respondents in Northern Ireland who state that their ethnicity is white are not asked this question.

2 Includes those who did not state their ethnic origin and those in Northern Ireland who stated that their ethnicity was white.

Source: Office for National Statistics, Annual Population Survey

5.7

Total international migration estimates: citizenship[1,2]
United Kingdom

Citizenship by country of next or last residence

Thousands[3]

	All citizenships	British	Non-British	European Union[4]	Commonwealth Old	Commonwealth New[5]	Other foreign[6]
Inflow							
	C58E	C58H	C58K	C58N	C58Q	C58T	C58W
2000	479	99	379	63	56	91	169
2001	479	110	370	57	65	84	164
2002	513	97	416	59	63	92	201
2003	508	99	409	64	62	105	177
2004	586	88	498	128	73	141	155
2005	563	96	466	149	62	117	137
2006	591	81	510	167	62	139	142
2007	577	75	502	197	45	130	131
Outflow							
	C58F	C58I	C58L	C58O	C58R	C58U	C58X
2000	321	161	160	57	32	15	55
2001	306	158	149	49	32	19	49
2002	358	185	174	52	42	16	64
2003	361	191	171	50	42	17	62
2004	342	195	147	42	33	19	52
2005	359	185	174	54	37	23	59
2006	400	207	194	66	42	24	61
2007	340	171	169	68	31	26	43
Balance							
	C58G	C58J	C58M	C58P	C58S	C58V	C58Y
2000	158	−62	220	6	24	76	114
2001	173	−48	221	8	33	65	115
2002	154	−87	242	7	21	77	137
2003	147	−91	238	14	20	88	115
2004	244	−107	351	85	40	122	104
2005	204	−89	293	95	25	94	78
2006	191	−126	316	100	20	115	81
2007	237	−96	333	128	13	103	88

1 The1998-2005 were revised, following changes to the weightings used to gross up the IPS data, in November 2007. Therefore they may not agree with previously published estimates.

2 Based mainly on data from the IPS. Includes adjustments for (1) those whose intended length of stay changes so that their migrant status changes; (2) asylum seekers and their dependants not identified by the IPS; and (3) flows between the UK and the Republic of Ireland.

3 Estimates of international migration flows are shown rounded to the nearest thousand, rather than nearest hundred, as they are considered less reliable at the more detailed level.

4 European Union estimates are for the EU15 (Austria, Belgium, Denmark, Finland, France, Germany, Greece, Republic of Ireland, Italy, Luxembourg, Netherlands, Portugal, Spain and Sweden) from 1998- 2003, EU25 (EU15 and Czech Republic, Estonia, Hungary, Latvia, Lithuania, Malta, Poland,Cyprus, Slovakia and Slovenia). from 2004-2006, and for the EU27 (EU25 plus Bulgaria and Romania) from 2007. British citizens are excluded from all EU citizenship groupings and are shown separately.

5 For 2004 onwards, the New Commonwealth excludes Malta and Cyprus.

6 For 2004 onwards, Other foreign excludes the eight Central and Eastern European member states that joined the EU in May 2004. For 2007 other foreign excludes Bulgaria and Romania which joined the EU in January 2007.

Source: Office for National Statistics: 01329 444645

5.8 Estimates of migration into and out of the United Kingdom by usual occupation[1,2] and sex

Thousands

	Total			Professional and managerial			Manual and clerical			Not gainfully employed[3]		
	Persons	Males	Females	Persons	Males	Females	Persons	Males	Females	Persons	Males	Females
Inflow												
	KGOA	KGOB	KGOC	KGOD	KGOE	KGOF	KGOG	KGOH	KGOI	KGOJ	KGOK	KGOL
1991	255	117	138	76	47	28	53	22	31	127	48	79
1992	207	95	112	59	37	22	42	16	26	106	42	65
1993	204	97	108	63	40	23	41	20	21	100	37	63
1994	243	121	121	79	47	32	54	30	24	110	44	65
1995	235	125	111	83	55	28	44	19	25	108	51	57
1996	261	124	137	86	51	35	55	24	31	120	50	71
1997	273	137	136	89	57	33	42	23	19	141	57	84
1998	318	160	158	112	65	47	71	35	35	136	60	76
1999	354	181	173	131	77	54	75	40	35	148	63	84
2000	359	188	171	162	98	64	64	33	31	133	57	76
2001	372	187	185	138	77	62	77	39	38	157	72	85
2002	386	200	186	139	78	62	83	45	38	163	77	87
2003	427	211	215	146	76	71	92	46	46	189	90	99
2004	518	261	257	175	102	73	132	66	65	212	92	119
2005	496	273	223	168	97	71	145	90	55	184	86	98
2006	529	280	249	154	82	72	136	79	57	239	120	119
2007	527	286	241	168	99	69	136	79	57	223	108	115
Outflow												
	KGPA	KGPB	KGPC	KGPD	KGPE	KGPF	KGPG	KGPH	KGPI	KGPJ	KGPK	KGPL
1991	247	124	123	87	50	37	51	29	21	110	46	64
1992	235	117	118	85	51	33	49	24	25	101	41	60
1993	223	117	106	73	39	33	46	25	21	105	53	52
1994	197	96	102	57	33	24	50	24	26	90	38	52
1995	198	105	93	64	43	21	43	23	20	91	39	52
1996	223	109	114	87	54	32	48	23	24	89	31	58
1997	232	125	107	88	59	29	50	23	26	94	43	51
1998	206	103	103	82	48	34	42	22	21	82	33	48
1999	245	132	114	97	60	38	69	32	37	79	41	39
2000	278	154	124	128	80	48	59	36	23	90	37	53
2001	250	135	115	102	66	36	60	30	30	88	39	49
2002	305	161	144	123	79	45	80	40	40	102	42	59
2003	314	165	149	108	60	49	103	59	44	102	46	57
2004	310	152	158	114	65	49	73	40	33	123	47	76
2005	328	187	141	137	88	50	83	47	37	108	53	55
2006	369	208	162	125	77	48	119	73	46	126	58	68
2007	318	178	139	112	65	48	101	60	42	104	54	50
Balance												
	KGRA	KGRB	KGRC	KGRD	KGRE	KGRF	KGRG	KGRH	KGRI	KGRJ	KGRK	KGRL
1991	8	-7	16	-11	-3	-8	2	-8	10	17	3	14
1992	-28	-22	-6	-26	-14	-12	-7	-8	1	5	–	5
1993	-19	-20	2	-9	–	-10	-5	-5	–	-4	-15	11
1994	45	26	20	22	14	8	4	6	-2	20	6	13
1995	37	19	18	18	11	7	1	-4	6	17	12	5
1996	37	15	22	-1	-3	2	7	–	7	31	18	13
1997	40	12	29	1	-2	3	-7	-1	-7	47	14	33
1998	113	57	55	30	17	13	28	13	15	54	27	27
1999	109	49	60	34	18	16	6	8	-2	69	23	46
2000	82	35	47	34	18	16	5	-3	8	43	20	23
2001	122	52	70	36	11	25	17	9	8	70	33	36
2002	81	39	42	16	-1	17	3	5	-2	62	34	27
2003	113	47	67	38	16	22	-11	-13	2	86	44	42
2004	208	109	99	61	37	24	58	26	32	89	45	43
2005	168	86	82	31	9	21	61	43	18	76	34	43
2006	160	72	87	29	5	24	17	6	11	113	62	51
2007	209	108	101	55	34	21	34	19	15	119	54	65

1 See chapter text.
2 The 1991-2005 estimates were revised, following changes to the weightings used to gross up the IPS data, in November 2007. Therefore the above figures may not agree with estimates published before then.
3 Includes housewives, students, children and retired persons.

Source: Office for National Statistics: 01329 444645

5.9 Estimates of migration into and out of the United Kingdom[1] by citizenship and country of last or next residence

Thousands

	All citizens	British citizens						European Union citizens[1] (excluding British)			
	All residences Total	Total	European Union[1]	Old Commonwealth	New Commonwealth[2]	United States of America	Other countries[3]	Total	European Union[1]	Other Europe[3]	Other countries[4]

Inflow

	KEZR	KGLA	KGLB	KGLC	KGLD	KGLE	KGLF	KGLG	KGLH	KGLI	KGLJ
1991	255	110	38	27	19	9	16	33	30	–	3
1992	207	94	46	19	10	8	11	25	23	–	2
1993	204	86	31	21	13	9	12	26	23	–	2
1994	243	111	44	20	14	15	18	31	28	1	3
1995	235	86	31	15	12	12	16	42	37	–	5
1996	261	97	32	19	16	13	18	55	50	1	4
1997	273	90	34	20	11	7	18	62	57	–	4
1998	318	104	28	29	15	16	17	70	64	–	5
1999	354	115	30	37	15	13	20	59	54	–	5
2000	359	99	28	29	14	8	20	59	52	–	6
2001	372	110	26	34	18	10	22	53	50	–	3
2002	386	97	30	23	10	9	25	55	50	2	3
2003	427	99	37	25	11	10	15	61	54	1	6
2004	518	84	21	23	15	9	16	106	99	–	6
2005	496	91	35	24	14	8	11	118	110	2	7
2006	529	77	32	16	7	4	18	136	129	1	7
2007	527	71	25	18	9	5	15	172	161	4	6

Outflow

	KEZS	KGMA	KGMB	KGMC	KGMD	KGME	KGMF	KGMG	KGMH	KGMI	KGMJ
1991	247	141	47	43	16	13	22	32	23	2.0	6
1992	235	137	45	35	13	17	27	17	14	–	3
1993	223	130	45	35	12	17	21	24	21	–	3
1994	197	111	35	29	11	15	21	23	19	–	4
1995	198	122	39	35	10	18	20	20	16	–	4
1996	223	143	53	38	16	16	20	24	18	–	6
1997	232	135	41	38	13	16	27	32	27	1.0	4
1998	206	114	37	36	8	15	19	26	21	1.0	4
1999	245	115	37	41	8	14	14	47	41	–	6
2000	278	141	41	48	9	19	24	46	39	1.0	6
2001	250	133	41	47	7	15	22	40	34	1.0	5
2002	305	164	68	44	10	18	24	42	38	–	4
2003	314	170	71	55	9	13	22	42	33	3.0	5
2004	310	184	68	62	12	16	27	34	30	1.0	3
2005	328	174	74	62	6	10	22	47	42	1.0	4
2006	369	196	71	69	10	16	30	59	52	–	7
2007	318	159	54	60	7	12	27	65	57	2.0	5

Balance

	KEZT	KGNA	KGNB	KGNC	KGND	KGNE	KGNF	KGNG	KGNH	KGNI	KGNJ
1991	8	−30	−8	−16	3	−3	−5	–	6	−2	−3
1992	−28	−43	1	−16	−3	−9	−16	8	10	–	−1
1993	−19	−44	−14	−14	1	−8	−9	2	3	–	–
1994	45	–	10	−10	2	–	−3	8	10	1	−2
1995	37	−36	−8	−21	2	−6	−4	22	22	–	1
1996	37	−46	−21	−20	–	−3	−3	31	32	1	−1
1997	40	−45	−7	−18	−2	−9	−9	30	30	−1	1
1998	113	−10	−10	−6	7	1	−2	44	43	−1	1
1999	109	–	−8	−4	7	−2	6	12	13	–	−1
2000	82	−42	−14	−19	6	−11	−3	13	14	−1	
2001	122	−23	−15	−13	11	−5	–	13	16	−1	−2
2002	81	−66	−37	−21	–	−9	1	13	11	2	−1
2003	113	−70	−34	−29	2	−2	−7	19	21	−3	1
2004	208	−100	−47	−39	3	−7	−11	72	69	−1	3
2005	168	−83	−39	−38	8	−2	−12	72	67	1	3
2006	160	−119	−39	−53	−3	−12	−12	78	78	1	–
2007	209	−88	−29	−42	2	−7	−12	107	104	2	1

The 1991-2005 estimates were revised following changes to the weightings used to gross up the IPS data, in November 2007. Therefore the above figures may not agree with previous estimates published before then.

1 EU estimates are for the EU15 (Austria, Belgium, Denmark, Finland, France, Germany, Greece, the Irish Republic, Italy, Luxembourg, Netherlands, Portugal, Spain and Sweden) from 1991-2003, EU25 (EU15 and A8 groupings plus Malta and Cyprus) form 2004 -2006 and for the EU27 (EU25 plus Bulgaria and Romania) from 2007.

2 From 2004 onwards, the New Commonwealth excludes Malta and Cyprus.

3 From 2004 onwards these categories exclude the A8 Central and Eastern countries that joined the EU in 2004. From 2007 these categories exclude the A2 countries (Bulgaria and Romania) that joined the EU in 2007.

4 From 2004 onwards Other countries excludes Malta and cyprus.

5.9 Estimates of migration into and out of the United Kingdom[1] by citizenship and country of last or next residence

continued

Thousands

	Commonwealth[1] citizens								Other foreign citizens[3]				
	Total	Australia	Canada	New Zealand	South Africa	Indian[2] sub-continent	Other African Common-wealth	Other count-ries	Total	Euro-pean Union[4]	Other Europe[5]	United States of America	Other count-ries
Inflow													
	KGLK	KGLL	KGLM	KGLN	KTDK	IBH3	KGLQ	IBH4	KGLU	KGLV	KGLW	KGLX	KGLY
1991	61	11	4	6	1	16	8	15	51	6	7	14	26
1992	47	9	2	6	–	12	6	13	41	2	7	9	23
1993	48	10	3	5	2	13	5	10	44	2	11	11	19
1994	48	9	2	6	1	10	8	13	52	5	14	11	22
1995	56	12	5	6	2	11	4	16	52	2	10	11	29
1996	59	14	3	7	4	15	6	11	49	–	7	15	27
1997	75	14	5	7	5	20	6	20	45	–	7	11	27
1998	88	24	5	13	11	13	10	12	56	4	7	18	27
1999	101	27	2	12	12	22	14	12	79	3	18	15	43
2000	113	22	6	11	13	30	13	18	89	2	11	13	63
2001	120	30	4	9	13	31	17	17	89	1	13	12	63
2002	121	20	4	9	20	33	22	11	113	2	11	16	84
2003	142	21	5	7	20	46	24	18	124	2	22	17	84
2004	204	24	5	8	30	77	38	21	125	1	12	14	98
2005	172	22	4	11	23	74	24	13	115	3	13	14	85
2006	193	29	6	8	16	95	17	21	122	9	13	15	86
2007	169	16	4	8	13	89	17	21	115	5	11	15	84
Outflow													
	KGMK	KGML	KGMM	KGMN	KTDL	IBH5	KGMQ	IBH7	KGMU	KGMV	KGMW	KGMX	KGMY
1991	33	7	4	5	–	4	3	10	41	2	3	17	20
1992	28	6	2	5	1	3	3	8	53	1	12	20	21
1993	32	8	2	4	1	4	4	8	38	2	3	17	16
1994	28	6	2	4	1	4	2	9	35	1	10	8	16
1995	27	6	1	4	2	2	2	10	30	–	5	9	16
1996	29	8	2	3	2	3	2	10	27	1	7	5	14
1997	36	7	1	5	5	4	2	13	29	3	5	9	13
1998	30	9	1	3	4	3	2	7	35	2	7	9	18
1999	38	11	2	6	4	2	1	11	45	–	9	14	21
2000	43	12	3	8	5	3	2	10	48	3	11	9	24
2001	44	15	3	6	5	4	2	9	33	1	9	7	16
2002	52	18	6	9	5	5	2	7	47	2	12	16	18
2003	53	19	2	8	9	5	2	8	48	2	12	8	26
2004	50	17	4	5	7	4	3	12	42	5	2	8	28
2005	59	15	4	8	9	13	2	7	49	1	7	14	28
2006	65	17	5	7	13	11	3	8	50	3	7	11	29
2007	56	17	2	5	9	15	3	6	37	4	5	6	23
Balance													
	KGNK	KGNL	KGNM	KGNN	KTDM	IBH6	KGNQ	IBH8	KGNU	KGNV	KGNW	KGNX	KGNY
1991	28	5	–	2	1	12	5	5	10	4	4	–3	6
1992	19	3	–	1	–1	9	3	4	–13	1	–5	–11	2
1993	16	2	1	1	1	8	2	2	7	–	9	–5	3
1994	20	3	1	2	–	5	6	3	17	4	4	3	7
1995	29	5	4	2	–	9	2	6	22	2	5	2	13
1996	30	7	1	4	2	12	4	1	22	–1	–	10	13
1997	39	7	4	2	1	16	4	7	16	–2	2	3	14
1998	59	15	3	10	7	10	8	6	21	2	1	9	9
1999	63	16	–	5	8	20	13	1	34	3	8	2	21
2000	70	10	4	2	9	26	10	8	41	–1	–	4	38
2001	76	15	1	3	8	27	14	8	56	–	3	6	47
2002	69	2	–1	–	15	29	21	4	66	–	–1	–	66
2003	89	2	3	–1	11	41	23	10	76	–1	10	9	57
2004	153	7	1	3	23	74	35	10	83	–4	10	7	71
2005	113	7	1	3	14	61	22	7	66	2	7	1	57
2006	128	13	2	1	3	84	14	12	72	5	6	4	57
2007	112	–	2	4	4	74	14	15	78	1	6	10	61

The 1991 - 2005 estimates were revised following changes to the weightings used to gross up the IPS data, in November 2007. Therefore the above data may not agree with previous estimates published before then.
1 From 2004 onwards, the Commonwealth excludes Malta and Cyprus.
2 Indian sub-contitent consists of Bangladesh, India, Sir Lanka and Pakistan.
3 From 2004 onwards Other foreign citizens excludes the A8 Central and Eastern European countries (Czech Republic, Estonia, Hungary, Latvia, Lithuania, Poland, Slovakia and Slovenia) that joined the EU in 2004. From 2007 Other foreign citizens exlcudes the A2 countries (Bulagria and Romania) that joined the EU in 2007.

4 European Union estimates are for the EU15 (Austria, Belgium, Denmark, Finland, France, Germany, Greece, the Irish Republic, Italy, Luxembourg, Netherlands, Portugal, Spain and Sweden) from 1991-2003, EU25 (EU15 and A8 groupings plus Malta and Cyprus) from 2004-2006 and for the EU27 (EU25 plus Bulgaria and Romania) from 2007.
5 From 2004 onwards Other Europe excludes the 8 Central and Eastern European countries that joined the EU in 2004. From 2007 these categories exclude the A2 countries that joined the EU in 2007.

Source: Office for National Statistics: 01329 444645

Population and vital statistics

5.10 Grants of settlement by country of nationality[1,2]
United Kingdom

Number of persons

Geographical region and country of nationality		2005	2006	2007[7,8]
Grand Total	KGFA	179 120	134 445	124 855
Europe[1]				
Accession States				
Bulgaria	KGFW	1 225	4 250	..
Romania	KGGB	955	1 610	..
Total Accession States	EL2O	2 180	5 860	..
Remainder of Europe				
Albania	I4UK	1 015	1 185	1 220
Croatia	LQMA	625	180	175
Russia	LQLX	1 795	1 375	1 310
Serbia & Montenegro[3]	LQMC	6 805	2 070	1 400
Turkey	KGFT	5 330	3 040	2 545
Ukraine	LQLY	1 195	850	865
Other former USSR	LQLZ	1 015	630	855
Other former Yugoslavia	LQMD	385	290	225
Other Europe	KOSO	470	110	65
Total Remainder of Europe	EL2P	18 630	9 715	8 660
Total Europe[1]	KOSP	20 810	15 580	8 660
Americas				
Argentina	KGGF	145	125	155
Barbados	KGGG	120	130	80
Brazil	KGGH	645	850	865
Canada	KGGI	1 215	1 125	1 015
Chile	KGGJ	50	105	80
Colombia	KGGK	1 555	855	590
Guyana	KGGM	235	165	140
Jamaica	KGGN	2 780	2 900	2 440
Mexico	KGGO	140	220	185
Peru	KGGP	220	200	145
Trinidad and Tobago	KGGQ	505	375	405
USA	KGGR	4 350	3 845	3 310
Venezuela	KGGT	155	145	150
Other Americas	KOSR	1 790	1 055	885
Total Americas	KGGU	13 905	12 085	10 435
Africa				
Algeria	KGGV	940	735	750
Angola	KOSS	1 695	965	1 590
Congo (Dem. Rep.)[4]	KOST	2 960	1 345	2 055
Egypt	KGGW	615	510	485
Ethiopia	KGGX	735	505	635
Ghana	KGGY	2 880	2 870	2 560
Kenya	KGHA	2 690	1 670	1 575
Libya	KGHB	360	260	185
Mauritius	KGHC	860	675	715
Morocco	KGHD	390	390	360
Nigeria	KGHE	5 310	4 440	3 965
Sierra Leone	KGHF	3 420	1 145	725
Somalia	KGHG	8 255	2 125	2 845
South Africa	KGHH	9 385	5 665	5 805
Sudan	KGHI	730	400	365
Tanzania	KGHJ	700	480	360
Tunisia	KGHK	135	195	175

Geographical region and country of nationality		2005	2006	2007[7,8]
Africa (continued)				
Uganda	KGHL	1 065	670	530
Zambia	KGHM	830	460	495
Zimbabwe	KGHN	4 520	3 415	4 280
Other Africa	KOSU	5 600	3 320	3 595
Total Africa	KGHO	54 080	32 240	34 050
Asia				
Indian sub-continent				
Bangladesh	KGHP	3 085	2 850	3 330
India	KGHQ	16 720	11 190	14 865
Pakistan	KGHR	9 185	10 960	10 825
Total Indian sub-continent	KGHS	28 990	25 005	29 020
Middle East				
Iran	KGHT	2 055	1 035	1 755
Iraq	KGHU	4 675	7 285	7 020
Israel	KGHV	590	340	370
Jordan	KGHW	310	150	150
Kuwait	KGHX	70	20	20
Lebanon	KGHY	535	265	450
Saudi Arabia	KGHZ	70	60	30
Syria	KGIA	295	220	200
Yemen	KOSV	410	315	325
Other Middle East	KOSW	380	110	330
Total Middle East	KGIB	9 395	9 795	10 655
Remainder of Asia				
Afghanistan	I4UL	9 215	7 395	3 165
China[5]	KGIC	4 215	3 320	3 440
Hong Kong[6]	KOSX	805	1 060	785
Indonesia	KGID	300	250	225
Japan	KGIE	1 540	1 255	925
Malaysia	KGIF	1 945	1 785	1 635
Nepal	I4UM	3 610	6 940	4 155
Philippines	KGIG	14 710	6 315	8 485
Singapore	KGIH	290	205	240
South Korea	KOTE	815	620	565
Sri Lanka	KGII	5 475	3 080	2 440
Thailand	KGIJ	1 945	2 425	1 605
Other Asia	KOSZ	490	600	625
Total Remainder of Asia	KGIL	45 355	35 245	28 280
Total Asia	KGIM	83 740	70 045	67 955
Oceania				
Australia	KGIN	3 740	2 645	2 215
New Zealand	KGIO	2 505	1 405	1 280
Other Oceania	KOTA	90	165	125
Total Oceania	KGIP	6 335	4 215	3 615
British Overseas citizens	KGIQ	95	60	35
Nationality unknown	KGIS	160	220	100
Grand Total	KGFA	179 120	134 445	124 855

1 Members of the European Economic Area prior to 2005 and Swiss nationals are excluded throughout the period covered.
2 Data also excludes dependants of EEA and Swiss nationals in confirmed relationships granted permanent residence.
3 Serbia and Montenegro continue to be counted together due to the use of a single (Federal Republic of Yugoslavia) passport.
4 Formerly known as Zaire.
5 Includes Taiwan.
6 Hong Kong (Special Administrative Region of China) includes British overseas territories citizens and stateless persons from Hong Kong and British Nationals (overseas).
7 Excludes nationals of Bulgaria and Romania from 1 January 2007.
8 Provisional.

Source: Home Office: 020 8760 8291

5.11 Applications[1] received for asylum in the United Kingdom, excluding dependants, by country of nationality

Number of principal applicants

		1999[2]	2000[2]	2001	2002	2003	2004	2005	2006	2007[5]
Europe										
Albania	LQME	1 310	1 490	1 065	1 150	595	295	175	155	165
Macedonia	PTDW	90	65	755	310	60	15	5	–	25
Moldova	VQHP	180	235	425	820	380	170	115	45	30
Russia	ZAEQ	685	1 000	450	450	295	280	190	130	115	80
Serbia & Montenegro[3]	ZAFA	11 465	6 070	3 230	2 265	815	290	155	70	–
Turkey	KEAW	2 850	3 990	3 695	2 835	2 390	1 230	755	425	210
Ukraine	ZAER	775	770	445	365	300	120	55	50	40
E U Accession States[4]	GH5T	7 415	5 985	3 455	4 455	875	370	130	95	25
Other Former USSR	ZAES	875	1 050	485	615	520	315	265	220	155
Other Europe	ZAEU	2 630	2 230	210	130	70	35	30	35	95
Total Europe	KEAZ	28 280	22 880	14 215	13 235	6 295	3 025	1 810	1 210	825
Americas										
Colombia	KEBZ	1 000	505	365	420	220	120	70	60	30
Ecuador	KYDB	610	445	255	315	150	35	10	15	10
Jamaica	PTDX	180	310	525	1 310	965	455	325	215	240
Other Americas	PTDY	240	155	170	240	230	130	100	95	115
Total Americas	KECT	2 025	1 420	1 315	2 290	1 560	740	505	385	390
sub Saharan Africa										
Algeria	KOTB	1 385	1 635	1 140	1 060	550	490	255	225	260
Angola	KECU	545	800	1 015	1 420	850	400	145	95	95
Burundi	PTDZ	780	620	610	700	650	265	90	35	25
Cameroon	VQHU	245	355	380	615	505	360	290	260	160
Congo	PTEA	450	485	540	600	320	150	65	45	25
Dem. Rep. Congo	KEEH	1 240	1 030	1 370	2 215	1 540	1 475	1 080	570	370
Eritrea	PTEC	565	505	620	1 180	950	1 105	1 760	2 585	1 810
Ethiopia	KECW	455	415	610	700	640	540	385	200	90
Gambia	DMMA	30	50	65	130	95	100	90	110	100
Ghana	KECX	195	285	190	275	325	355	230	130	120
Ivory Coast	DMLZ	190	445	275	315	390	280	210	170	100
Kenya	KOTC	485	455	305	350	220	145	100	95	115
Liberia	C53K	65	55	115	450	740	405	175	50	40
Nigeria	KECY	945	835	810	1 125	1 010	1 090	1 025	790	780
Rwanda	ZAEV	820	760	530	655	260	75	40	20	15
Sierra Leone	KOTD	1 125	1 330	1 940	1 155	380	230	135	125	85
Somalia	KECZ	7 495	5 020	6 420	6 540	5 090	2 585	1 760	1 845	1 615
Sudan	KEEE	280	415	390	655	930	1 305	885	670	330
Tanzania	DMMC	80	60	80	40	30	20	20	15	20
Uganda	KEEG	420	740	480	715	705	405	205	165	130
Zimbabwe	GRFS	230	1 010	2 140	7 655	3 295	2 065	1 075	1 650	1 800
Other sub Saharan Africa	PTEB	400	615	555	845	895	910	615	480	440
Total sub Saharan Africa	KEEJ	18 435	17 920	20 590	29 390	20 370	14 745	10 640	10 340	8 510
Middle East										
Iran	KEEK	1 320	5 610	3 420	2 630	2 875	3 455	3 150	2 375	2 210
Iraq	KEEL	1 800	7 475	6 680	14 570	4 015	1 695	1 415	945	1 825
Libya	GH5U	115	155	140	200	145	160	125	90	45
Syria	GH5V	95	140	110	70	110	350	330	160	155
Other Middle East	ZAEX	835	1 035	915	850	825	870	715	735	825
Total Middle East	KEGY	4 165	14 415	11 265	18 315	7 970	6 525	5 730	4 305	5 060
Asia & Oceania										
Afghanistan	DMLY	3 975	5 555	8 920	7 205	2 280	1 395	1 580	2 400	2 500
Bangladesh	ZAEY	530	795	510	720	735	510	425	440	540
China	KEGZ	2 625	4 000	2 390	3 675	3 450	2 365	1 730	1 945	2 100
India	KEIL	1 365	2 120	1 850	1 865	2 290	1 405	940	680	510
Pakistan	KEIM	2 615	3 165	2 860	2 405	1 915	1 710	1 145	965	1 030
Sri Lanka	KEIN	5 130	6 395	5 510	3 130	705	330	395	525	990
Vietnam	VQIB	105	180	400	840	1 125	755	380	90	165
Other Asia & Oceania	PTEE	1 120	1 025	1 040	915	655	375	320	275	740
Total Asia & Oceania	KEJO	17 465	23 230	23 480	20 755	13 150	8 850	6 915	7 315	8 570
Other and Nationality not known	KEJP	785	450	160	150	55	70	105	55	75
Grand Total	KEJQ	71 160	80 315	71 025	84 130	49 405	33 960	25 710	23 610	23 430

Source: Home Office: 020 8760 8349

1 Figures rounded to the nearest 5.
2 May exclude some cases lodged at Local Enforcement Offices between January 1999 and March 2000.
3 Serbia (Inc Kosovo) and Montenegro counted separately under 'Other Europe' from 2007.
4 EU Accession States: Bulgaria, Cyprus, Czech Republic, Estonia, Hungary, Latvia, Lithuania, Malta, Poland, Romania, Slovakia and Slovenia. Figures between 1998 and 2000 exclude Malta but include Cyprus (Northerm part of).
5 Provisional figures.

Population and vital statistics

5.12 Marriages: by previous marital status, sex, age and country

Numbers

		1997	1998	1999	2000	2001	2002	2003	2004	2005	2006	2007
United Kingdom[1]												
Marriages	KKAA	310 218	304 797	301 083	305 912	286 129	293 021	308 623	313 551	286 826	277 611	270 000
Persons marrying per 1,000 resident population	KKAB	10.6	10.4	10.3	10.4	9.7	9.9	10.4	10.5	9.5	9.2	8.9
Previous marital status												
Single men[2]	KKAC	216 237	214 005	211 820	213 777	202 690	206 196	217 534	221 477	201 791	197 137	193 720
Divorced men	KKAD	85 625	82 977	81 750	84 771	76 852	80 040	84 011	85 210	78 537	74 262	70 318
Widowers	KKAE	8 356	7 815	7 513	7 364	6 587	6 785	7 078	6 864	6 498	6 212	5 965
Single women[2]	KKAF	216 776	215 399	213 246	215 865	205 048	208 385	219 828	224 344	205 569	201 384	197 337
Divorced women	KKAG	85 648	82 016	80 816	83 166	74 807	78 182	82 181	82 559	75 120	70 256	66 986
Widows	KKAH	7 794	7 382	7 021	6 881	6 274	6 454	6 614	6 648	6 137	5 971	5 680
First marriage for both partners	KMGH	181 135	180 404	178 759	180 020	171 912	174 374	184 661	188 517	173 123	170 410	168 309
First marriage for one partner	KMGI	70 743	68 596	67 548	69 602	63 914	65 833	68 040	68 787	61 114	57 701	54 449
Remarriage for both partners	KMGJ	58 340	55 797	54 776	56 290	50 303	52 814	55 922	56 247	52 589	49 500	47 245
Males												
Under 21 years	KKAI	5 126	5 173	5 234	5 019	4 625	4 396	4 340	4 233	3 262	2 821	2 576
21-24	KKAJ	36 875	32 723	29 390	28 467	25 840	26 293	27 155	27 223	22 355	20 768	19 771
25-29	KKAK	97 345	94 696	90 412	85 870	78 687	74 858	75 580	74 873	67 943	66 234	65 953
30-34	KKAL	70 904	71 096	72 129	73 809	70 657	72 592	75 892	75 705	68 453	64 688	61 326
35-44	KKAM	58 292	59 838	62 114	68 019	65 242	69 747	75 695	79 510	74 343	72 416	70 183
45-54	KKAN	26 472	26 118	26 581	28 791	26 122	27 801	30 387	31 851	30 737	30 800	30 387
55 and over	KKAO	15 204	15 153	15 223	15 937	14 956	17 334	19 574	20 156	19 733	19 884	19 807
Females												
Under 21 years	KKAP	17 254	16 793	16 082	15 938	13 874	13 194	13 510	12 878	9 113	8 110	7 343
21-24	KKAQ	59 549	54 645	50 350	48 578	45 687	45 789	47 400	46 891	39 482	36 955	35 241
25-29	KKAR	97 932	97 181	94 703	92 753	85 647	82 892	84 066	84 714	79 579	78 478	78 507
30-34	KKAS	58 589	59 349	60 446	62 478	59 859	62 279	65 979	66 508	61 047	57 899	54 880
35-44	KKAT	47 267	47 721	50 136	54 697	52 209	56 997	61 682	65 007	60 969	59 248	57 175
45-54	KKAU	21 038	20 708	20 822	22 621	20 459	22 187	24 721	25 846	24 982	25 041	25 077
55 and over	KKAV	8 589	8 400	8 544	8 847	8 394	9 683	11 265	11 707	11 654	11 880	11 780
England and Wales[1]												
Marriages	KKBA	272 536	267 303	263 515	267 961	249 227	255 596	270 109	273 069	247 805	239 454	231 450
Persons marrying per 1,000 resident population	KKBB	10.6	10.3	10.1	10.3	9.5	9.7	10.2	10.3	9.3	8.9	8.6
Previous marital status												
Single men[2]	KKBC	188 268	186 329	184 266	186 113	175 721	179 121	189 470	191 956	173 413	169 248	165 490
Divorced men	KKBD	76 839	74 029	72 617	75 378	67 678	70 506	74 397	75 129	68 672	64 777	60 750
Widowers	KKBE	7 429	6 945	6 632	6 470	5 828	5 969	6 242	5 984	5 720	5 429	5 210
Single women[2]	KKBF	188 457	187 391	185 328	187 717	177 506	180 675	191 170	194 348	176 505	172 803	168 350
Divorced women	KKBG	77 098	73 330	71 971	74 092	66 120	69 234	73 071	72 875	65 915	61 435	58 110
Widows	KKBH	6 981	6 582	6 216	6 152	5 601	5 687	5 868	5 846	5 385	5 216	4 990
First marriage for both partners	KMGK	156 907	156 539	155 027	156 140	148 642	151 014	160 283	163 007	148 405	145 995	143 440
First marriage for one partner	KMGL	62 911	60 642	59 540	61 550	55 943	57 768	60 074	60 290	53 108	50 061	46 970
Remarriage for both partners	KMGM	52 718	50 122	48 948	50 271	44 642	46 814	49 752	49 772	46 292	43 398	41 040
Males												
Under 21 years	KKBI	4 574	4 608	4 629	4 536	4 160	3 952	3 885	3 803	2 883	2 521	2 310
21-24	KKBJ	31 907	28 389	25 424	24 764	22 436	22 961	23 802	23 873	19 430	18 002	17 200
25-29	KKBK	84 644	82 135	78 364	74 367	67 934	64 619	65 568	64 701	58 066	56 607	56 090
30-34	KKBL	62 265	62 323	63 212	64 611	61 409	62 998	66 060	65 510	58 830	55 595	52 260
35-44	KKBM	51 654	52 812	54 528	59 834	56 872	61 196	66 364	69 364	64 394	62 539	60 010
45-54	KKBN	23 688	23 385	23 676	25 470	22 949	24 336	26 785	27 830	26 679	26 508	26 040
55 and over	KKBO	13 804	13 651	13 682	14 379	13 467	15 534	17 645	17 988	17 523	17 682	17 540
Females												
Under 21 years	KKBP	15 439	15 065	14 379	14 421	12 467	11 916	12 270	11 667	8 182	7 286	6 630
21-24	KKBQ	51 766	47 446	43 691	42 265	39 746	39 968	41 567	40 962	34 185	32 082	30 460
25-29	KKBR	85 352	84 399	82 250	80 312	73 799	71 540	72 790	73 072	68 062	67 090	66 620
30-34	KKBS	51 405	51 982	52 721	54 649	51 865	53 970	57 348	57 592	52 369	49 611	46 740
35-44	KKBT	41 838	42 245	44 199	48 245	45 672	49 984	54 103	56 660	52 758	51 032	48 840
45-54	KKBU	18 938	18 575	18 572	20 083	18 071	19 535	21 858	22 648	21 811	21 688	21 630
55 and over	KKBV	7 798	7 591	7 703	7 986	7 607	8 683	10 173	10 468	10 438	10 659	10 530

5.12 Marriages: by previous marital status, sex, age and country

continued

Numbers

		1997	1998	1999	2000	2001	2002	2003	2004	2005	2006	2007
Scotland												
Marriages	KKCA	29 611	29 668	29 940	30 367	29 621	29 826	30 757	32 154	30 881	29 898	29 866
Persons marrying per 1,000 resident population	KKCB	11.7	11.7	11.8	12.0	11.7	11.8	12.2	12.7	12.1	11.7	11.6
Previous marital status												
Single men[2]	KKCC	20 994	20 987	21 052	21 201	20 737	20 671	21 477	22 526	21 421	20 912	20 851
Divorced men	KKCD	7 845	7 934	8 142	8 427	8 238	8 475	8 574	8 930	8 796	8 330	8 361
Widowers	KKCE	772	747	746	739	646	680	706	698	664	656	654
Single women[2]	KKCF	21 303	21 241	21 308	21 608	21 223	21 180	21 974	22 884	21 991	21 460	21 482
Divorced women	KKCG	7 621	7 754	7 949	8 141	7 825	8 008	8 157	8 622	8 244	7 802	7 793
Widows	KKCH	687	673	683	618	573	638	626	648	646	636	591
First marriage for both partners	KEZV	17 751	17 677	17 680	17 864	17 468	17 426	18 232	19 039	18 221	17 922	18 005
First marriage for one partner	KEZW	6 795	6 874	7 000	7 081	7 024	6 999	6 987	7 332	6 970	6 528	6 323
Remarriage for both partners	KEZX	5 065	5 117	5 260	5 422	5 129	5 401	5 538	5 783	5 690	5 448	5 538
Males												
Under 21 years	KKCI	406	421	490	364	371	367	361	336	304	228	211
21-24	KKCJ	3 494	3 147	2 853	2 720	2 489	2 395	2 507	2 501	2 120	2 012	1 840
25-29	KKCK	9 495	9 439	9 031	8 536	7 949	7 468	7 219	7 365	6 981	6 795	6 902
30-34	KKCL	6 911	6 988	7 179	7 419	7 464	7 692	7 752	7 992	7 516	6 935	6 744
35-44	KKCM	5 649	5 945	6 470	7 018	7 215	7 328	8 007	8 553	8 390	8 234	8 357
45-54	KKCN	2 459	2 412	2 575	2 060	2 816	3 033	3 213	3 503	3 588	3 772	3 805
55 and over	KKCO	1 197	1 316	1 342	1 350	1 317	1 543	1 698	1 904	1 982	1 922	2 007
Females												
Under 21 years	KKCP	1 302	1 289	1 322	1 171	1 111	996	1 007	954	724	635	554
21-24	KKCQ	5 568	5 248	4 778	4 581	4 343	4 171	4 199	4 358	3 772	3 473	3 325
25-29	KKCR	9 574	9 764	9 539	9 495	8 994	8 520	8 321	8 528	8 339	8 230	8 500
30-34	KKCS	5 927	6 036	6 433	6 463	6 618	6 832	7 110	7 235	7 016	6 511	6 289
35-44	KKCT	4 722	4 726	5 150	5 633	5 712	6 115	6 583	7 163	7 083	7 003	7 063
45-54	KKCU	1 844	1 900	1 994	2 279	2 147	2 322	2 589	2 821	2 862	2 975	3 016
55 and over	KKCV	674	705	724	745	696	870	948	1 095	1 085	1 071	1 119
Northern Ireland												
Marriages	KKDA	8 071	7 826	7 628	7 584	7 281	7 599	7 757	8 328	8 140	8 259	8 687
Persons marrying per 1,000 resident population	KKDB	9.7	9.3	9.1	9.0	8.6	9.0	9.1	9.7	9.4	8.0	9.9
Previous marital status												
Single men[2]	KKDC	6 975	6 689	6 502	6 463	6 232	6 404	6 587	6 995	6 957	6 977	7 379
Divorced men	KKDD	941	1 014	991	966	936	1 059	1 040	1 151	1 069	1 155	1 207
Widowers	KKDE	155	123	135	155	113	136	130	182	114	127	101
Single women[2]	KKDF	7 016	6 767	6 610	6 540	6 319	6 530	6 684	7 112	7 073	7 121	7 505
Divorced women	KKDG	929	932	896	933	862	940	953	1 062	961	1 019	1 083
Widows	KKDH	126	127	122	111	100	129	120	154	106	119	99
First marriage for both partners	KEZY	6 477	6 188	6 052	6 016	5 802	5 934	6 146	6 471	6 497	6 493	6 864
First marriage for one partner	KEZZ	1 037	1 080	1 008	971	947	1 066	979	1 165	1 036	1 112	1 156
Remarriage for both partners	KFBI	557	558	568	597	532	599	632	692	607	654	667
Males												
Under 21 years	KKDI	146	144	115	119	94	77	94	94	75	72	55
21-24	KKDJ	1 474	1 187	1 113	983	915	937	846	849	805	754	731
25-29	KKDK	3 206	3 122	3 017	2 967	2 804	2 771	2 793	2 807	2 896	2 832	2 961
30-34	KKDL	1 728	1 785	1 738	1 779	1 784	1 902	2 080	2 203	2 107	2 158	2 322
35-44	KKDM	989	1 081	1 116	1 167	1 155	1 223	1 324	1 593	1 559	1 643	1 816
45-54	KKDN	325	321	330	361	357	432	389	518	470	520	542
55 and over	KKDO	203	186	199	208	172	257	231	264	228	280	260
Females												
Under 21 years	KKDP	513	439	381	346	296	282	233	257	207	189	159
21-24	KKDQ	2 215	1 951	1 881	1 732	1 598	1 650	1 634	1 571	1 525	1 400	1 456
25-29	KKDR	3 006	3 018	2 914	2 946	2 854	2 832	2 955	3 114	3 178	3 158	3 387
30-34	KKDS	1 257	1 331	1 292	1 366	1 376	1 477	1 521	1 681	1 662	1 771	1 851
35-44	KKDT	707	750	787	819	825	898	996	1 184	1 128	1 213	1 272
45-54	KKDU	256	233	256	259	241	330	274	377	309	378	431
55 and over	KKDV	117	104	117	116	91	130	144	144	131	150	131

1 Figures for 2007 are rounded and provisional. Final unrounded figures will be available in spring 2010.
2 Single men and single women are those who have never been married.

Sources: Office for National Statistics: 01329 444110;
General Register Office for Scotland;
Northern Ireland Statistics and Research Agency

5.13 Divorce: by duration of marriage, age of wife and country

Numbers

		1997	1998	1999	2000	2001	2002	2003	2004	2005	2006	2007
United Kingdom												
Decrees absolute granted[1,2,5]												
Number	ZBRL	161 087	160 057	158 746	154 628	156 814	160 726	166 737	167 138	155 052	148 141	144 220
Duration of marriage												
0-4 years	ZBRM	33 719	33 087	31 047	28 933	28 306	28 591	28 781	28 746	26 549	25 005	24 704
5-9 years	ZBRN	45 040	44 243	43 357	41 621	42 360	42 924	43 558	42 855	39 070	37 116	35 772
10-14 years	ZBRO	29 085	29 706	30 270	30 166	30 849	31 257	32 564	31 775	29 007	27 647	26 446
15-19 years	ZBRP	20 211	20 078	20 147	19 902	20 568	21 881	23 119	23 898	22 593	21 244	20 894
20 years and over	ZBRQ	33 020	32 935	33 916	34 000	34 729	36 073	38 713	39 844	37 824	37 116	36 397
Not stated	ZBRR	12	8	9	6	2	..	2	20	9	13	7
Age of wife at marriage												
16-19 years	ZBRS	28 987	27 627	25 440	23 505	22 558	22 107	22 367	20 948	18 507	16 707	15 430
20-24 years	ZBRT	72 971	71 416	69 509	66 215	66 282	66 264	67 070	65 671	58 829	55 085	52 438
25-29 years	ZBRU	33 452	34 195	35 585	36 009	37 418	39 116	41 464	42 544	40 143	38 812	38 315
30-34 years	ZBRV	12 968	13 719	14 420	14 892	15 842	17 374	18 658	19 729	19 366	19 419	19 294
35-39 years	ZBRW	6 155	6 571	6 848	6 993	7 417	8 070	8 742	9 456	9 275	9 261	9 663
40-44 years	ZBRX	3 375	3 360	3 557	3 568	3 778	4 104	4 404	4 550	4 703	4 677	4 784
45 years and over	ZBRY	3 094	3 086	3 291	3 352	3 429	3 572	3 917	4 093	4 042	3 985	4 081
Not stated	ZBRZ	85	83	96	94	90	119	115	147	187	195	215
Age of wife at divorce												
16-24 years	ZBSA	7 371	6 758	5 671	5 115	4 874	4 998	5 092	4 885	4 388	3 739	3 492
25-29 years	ZBSB	28 814	26 968	24 120	21 280	19 635	18 340	17 633	16 972	14 870	14 216	13 772
30-34 years	ZBSC	37 257	36 795	36 052	34 356	34 194	33 555	32 774	30 754	26 431	23 641	21 911
35-39 years	ZBSD	30 641	31 688	32 605	32 588	33 997	35 050	36 465	35 894	32 722	30 567	28 765
40-44 years	ZBSE	22 246	22 810	23 614	23 879	25 579	27 564	30 154	31 372	30 359	29 412	28 990
45 years and over	ZBSF	34 662	34 947	36 578	37 311	38 442	41 102	44 498	47 108	46 085	46 352	47 071
Not stated	ZBSG	96	91	106	99	93	117	121	153	197	214	219
Divorces in which there were[3,4]												
No children aged under 16	ZBSH	..	..	..	..	..	..	..	..	..	..	..
One or more children aged under 16	ZBSI	..	..	..	..	..	..	..	..	..	..	..
England and Wales												
Decrees absolute granted[1,2]												
Number	KKEA	146 689	145 214	144 556	141 135	143 818	147 735	153 490	153 399	141 750	132 562	128 534
Rate per 1,000 married couples	KKEB	13.0	12.9	12.9	12.7	12.9	13.4	14.0	14.1	13.0	12.2	12.0
Duration of marriage												
0-4 years	KKEC	31 767	31 136	29 307	27 474	26 987	27 344	27 511	27 389	25 345	23 427	23 039
5-9 years	KKED	41 260	40 239	39 676	38 206	39 079	39 730	40 599	39 779	36 161	33 864	32 522
10-14 years	KKEE	26 215	26 698	27 384	27 459	28 176	28 592	29 831	29 086	26 394	24 680	23 496
15-19 years	KKEF	18 027	17 934	18 072	17 870	18 603	19 784	20 923	21 591	20 363	18 792	18 266
20 years and over	KKEG	29 408	29 199	30 108	30 120	30 971	32 285	34 624	35 554	33 478	31 786	31 204
Not stated	KKEH	12	8	9	6	2	–	2	–	9	13	7
Age of wife at marriage												
16-19 years	KKEI	25 579	24 276	22 486	20 930	20 218	19 828	20 063	18 709	16 519	14 478	13 273
20-24 years	KKEJ	66 167	64 453	62 853	59 874	60 211	60 353	61 057	59 548	53 041	48 550	45 929
25-29 years	KKEK	31 022	31 533	32 867	33 282	34 759	36 387	38 722	39 575	37 103	35 177	34 675
30-34 years	KKEL	12 094	12 788	13 507	13 972	14 890	16 339	17 567	18 545	18 134	17 834	17 637
35-39 years	KKEM	5 767	6 153	6 432	6 562	6 956	7 623	8 249	8 912	8 755	8 560	8 880
40-44 years	KKEN	3 156	3 135	3 331	3 378	3 559	3 841	4 154	4 274	4 421	4 318	4 393
45 years and over	KKEO	2 904	2 876	3 080	3 137	3 225	3 364	3 678	3 836	3 773	3 645	3 747
Age of wife at divorce												
16-24 years	KKEP	6 871	6 298	5 318	4 839	4 643	4 808	4 867	4 658	4 216	3 525	3 273
25-29 years	KKEQ	26 435	24 586	22 173	19 650	18 231	17 227	16 539	15 867	13 905	13 182	12 653
30-34 years	KKER	33 967	33 446	32 837	31 420	31 489	30 982	30 345	28 368	24 381	21 409	19 865
35-39 years	KKES	27 715	28 605	29 663	29 820	31 164	32 282	33 519	33 013	29 864	27 479	25 665
40-44 years	KKET	20 125	20 521	21 325	21 469	23 190	25 017	27 610	28 558	27 570	26 128	25 548
45 years and over	KKEU	31 564	31 750	33 231	33 931	35 099	37 419	40 608	42 935	41 805	40 826	41 523
Not stated	KKEV	12	8	9	6	2	–	2	–	9	13	7
Divorces in which there were[3]												
No children aged under 16	ZBSJ	66 019	64 738	65 258	64 359	64 541	66 738	69 681	71 382	88 349	62 667	62 497
One or more children aged under 16	ZBSK	80 670	80 476	79 298	76 776	79 277	80 997	83 809	82 017	75 340	69 895	66 037

5.13 Divorce: by duration of marriage, age of wife and country
continued

Numbers

		1997	1998	1999	2000	2001	2002	2003	2004	2005	2006	2007
Scotland												
Decrees absolute granted[2]												
Number	KKFA	12 222	12 384	11 864	11 143	10 631	10 826	10 928	11 227	10 940	13 014	12 773
Rate per 1,000 married couples	KKFB	11.0	11.3	10.9	10.3	9.7	10.0	10.2	10.5	10.3	12.3	12.2
Duration of marriage												
0-4 years	KKFC	1 793	1 766	1 588	1 304	1 159	1 128	1 141	1 204	1 089	1 444	1 526
5-9 years	KKFD	3 224	3 360	3 095	2 890	2 721	2 689	2 450	2 536	2 403	2 759	2 659
10-14 years	KKFE	2 385	2 456	2 368	2 168	2 163	2 183	2 222	2 173	2 113	2 418	2 345
15-19 years	KKFF	1 804	1 729	1 686	1 622	1 562	1 705	1 773	1 810	1 789	2 033	2 100
20 years and over	KKFG	3 016	3 073	3 127	3 159	3 026	3 121	3 342	3 504	3 546	4 360	4 143
Not stated	ZBSL	–	–	–	–	–	–	–	–	–	–	–
Age of wife at marriage												
16-19 years	ZBSM	2 749	2 654	2 374	2 043	1 839	1 845	1 816	1 753	1 557	1 764	1 700
20-24 years	ZBSN	5 714	5 744	5 453	5 142	4 873	4 823	4 869	4 892	4 721	5 373	5 141
25-29 years	KKFJ	2 151	2 314	2 333	2 318	2 233	2 316	2 307	2 462	2 515	3 075	2 999
30-34 years	KKFK	791	824	829	805	827	895	958	1 025	1 065	1 387	1 404
35-39 years	KKFL	360	382	379	378	401	407	432	489	455	619	699
40-44 years	KKFM	199	198	208	170	193	235	219	252	252	325	336
45 years and over	KKFN	173	185	192	193	175	186	212	221	232	312	298
Not stated	KKFO	85	83	96	94	90	119	115	133	143	159	196
Age of wife at divorce												
16-24 years	KKFP	426	377	301	232	182	180	191	192	148	190	199
25-29 years	KKFQ	2 021	1 957	1 597	1 330	1 109	974	884	869	777	877	938
30-34 years	KKFR	2 736	2 767	2 642	2 381	2 215	2 174	1 943	1 918	1 837	1 655
35-39 years	KKFS	2 489	2 582	2 450	2 298	2 311	2 281	2 388	2 278	2 304	2 544	2 445
40-44 years	KKFT	1 819	1 951	1 929	1 999	1 963	2 110	2 106	2 341	2 330	2 751	2 801
45 years and over	KKFU	2 667	2 687	2 848	2 810	2 760	2 990	3 297	3 496	3 596	4 650	4 542
Not stated	KKFV	84	83	97	93	91	117	119	133	144	165	193
Divorces in which there were[3,4]												
No children aged under 16	KKFW	..	..	..	..	..	..	..	..	..	..	..
One or more children under 16	KKFX	..	..	..	..	..	..	..	..	..	..	..
Northern Ireland												
Decrees absolute granted:[2,5]												
Number	ZBSO	2 176	2 459	2 326	2 350	2 365	2 165	2 319	2 512	2 362	2 565	2 913
Duration of marriage												
0-4 years	ZBSP	159	185	152	155	160	119	129	153	115	134	139
5-9 years	ZBSQ	556	644	586	525	560	505	509	540	506	493	591
10-14 years	ZBSR	485	552	518	539	510	482	511	516	500	549	605
15-19 years	ZBSS	380	415	389	410	403	392	423	497	441	419	528
20 years and over	ZBST	596	663	681	721	732	667	747	786	800	970	1 050
Not stated[5]	EK8B	–	–	–	–	–	–	–	20	–	..	..
Age of wife at marriage												
16-19 years	ZBSU	659	697	580	532	501	434	488	486	431	465	457
20-24 years	ZBSV	1 090	1 219	1 203	1 199	1 198	1 088	1 144	1 231	1 067	1 162	1 368
25-29 years	ZBSW	279	348	385	409	426	413	435	507	525	560	641
30-34 years	ZBSX	83	107	84	115	125	140	133	159	163	198	253
35-39 years	ZBSY	28	36	37	53	60	40	61	55	65	82	84
40-44 years	ZBSZ	20	27	18	20	26	28	31	24	30	34	55
45 years and over	ZBTA	17	25	19	22	29	22	27	36	37	28	36
Not stated[6]	EK8C	–	–	–	–	–	–	–	14	44	36	19
Age of wife at divorce												
16-24 years	ZBTB	74	83	52	44	49	10	34	35	24	24	20
25-29 years	ZBTC	358	425	350	300	295	139	210	236	188	157	181
30-34 years	ZBTD	554	582	573	555	490	399	486	468	409	395	391
35-39 years	ZBTE	457	521	492	470	522	487	558	603	554	544	655
40-44 years	ZBTF	302	338	360	411	426	437	438	473	459	533	641
45 years and over	ZBTG	431	510	499	570	583	693	593	677	684	876	1 006
Not stated[6]	EK8D	–	–	–	–	–	–	–	20	44	36	19
Divorces in which there were[3]												
No children aged under 16	ZBTH	1 573	1 807	1 649	1 051	1 054	972	1 050	1 218	982	662	1 372
One or more children aged under 16	ZBTI	603	652	677	1 299	1 311	1 193	1 269	1 282	1 380	1 903	1 541
Not stated[6]	EK8E	–	–	–	–	–	–	–	12	–	..	..

1 Data for 2007 are provisional.
2 Includes decrees of nullities.
3 Children of the family as defined by the Matrimonial Causes Act 1973.
4 Data not available in Scotland.
5 Marital estimates are not available for Northern Ireland - no divorce rate for
  UK/Northern Ireland.
6 Due to some incomplete records.

Sources: Office for National Statistics: 01329 444410;
General Register Office for Scotland;
Northern Ireland Statistics and Research Agency

5.14 Divorce proceedings: by country

Numbers

		1997	1998	1999	2000	2001	2002	2003	2004	2005	2006	2007
United Kingdom												
Dissolution of marriage[1,4]												
Decree absolute/decree granted	ZBXR	160 733	159 688	158 418	154 273	156 562	160 528	166 536	166 937	154 879	147 989	144 071
On grounds of:												
Adultery	ZBXS	38 652	37 302	35 545	34 082	33 452	33 389	33 844	32 586	28 411	25 293	23 355
Behaviour	ZBXT	68 546	68 685	67 851	65 687	66 818	68 499	70 866	70 879	66 824	63 782	62 238
Desertion	ZBXU	956	828	748	722	718	727	697	675	612	516	461
Separation (2 years and consent)	ZBXV	39 398	39 627	40 368	39 763	40 699	42 579	44 012	44 819	41 433	36 917	33 612
Separation(5 years)	ZBXW	12 552	12 697	13 389	13 653	14 575	15 076	16 831	17 714	17 101	15 297	13 192
Combination of more than one ground and other	ZBXX	629	549	517	366	300	258	286	264	498	601	325
Separation[2]												
1 year and consent	IE9T	..	..	..	..	..	..	..	..	..	1 456	3 003
2 years	IE9U	..	..	..	..	..	..	..	..	..	4 127	4 127
Decree absolute/decree granted to:												
the wife	ZBXY	111 910	111 555	109 824	106 957	107 345	108 104	114 664	113 970	105 008	100 003	96 749
the husband	ZBXZ	48 393	47 764	48 236	47 069	49 015	52 251	51 691	52 793	49 725	47 847	47 205
both	ZBYA	430	369	358	247	202	173	181	174	146	139	119
Nullity of marriage												
Decree absolute/decree granted	ZBYB	354	369	328	355	252	198	201	201	173	152	149
England and Wales												
Dissolution of marriage[4]												
Petitions filed[3]	KKGA	163 769	165 870	162 137	157 809	172 341	177 224	173 265	167 340	151 824	148 564	137 465
Decree nisi granted[3]	KKGM	148 310	144 231	143 446	143 729	163 146	170 980	168 037	166 334	150 917	145 242	143 153
Decree absolute granted	KKGN	146 339	144 851	144 233	140 783	143 568	147 538	153 294	153 199	141 583	132 418	128 393
On grounds of:												
Adultery	KKGB	37 592	36 319	34 584	33 310	32 839	32 829	33 331	32 035	27 992	24 936	23 125
Behaviour	KKGC	65 047	65 257	64 816	63 182	64 768	66 480	68 944	68 859	65 169	62 234	61 004
Desertion	KKGD	912	790	713	680	689	681	665	654	593	499	451
Separation (2 years and consent)	KKGE	32 638	32 394	33 482	32 820	33 703	35 476	36 931	37 543	34 388	31 794	31 268
Separation(5 years)	KKGF	9 592	9 616	10 193	10 498	11 355	11 896	13 239	13 933	13 196	12 628	12 220
Combination of more than one ground and other	ZBYC	558	475	445	293	214	176	184	175	245	327	325
Decree absolute granted to:												
the wife	ZBYD	102 173	101 583	100 469	98 227	98 992	102 676	106 208	105 381	96 855	90 587	87 362
the husband	ZBYE	43 739	42 902	43 413	42 311	44 378	44 694	46 915	47 651	44 583	41 702	40 928
both	ZBYF	427	366	351	245	198	168	171	167	145	129	103
Nullity of marriage												
Petitions filed[3]	KKGO	485	505	549	452	492	443	463	495	440	406	352
Decree nisi granted[3]	KKGR	248	281	495	274	160	216	204	308	260	240	190
Decree absolute granted	KKGS	350	363	323	352	250	197	196	200	167	144	141
Judicial separation												
Petitions filed[4]	KKGT	1 078	916	882	650	1 078	1 001	826	745	697	613	502
Decrees granted[4]	KKGW	589	519	696	540	925	560	467	419	387	353	329

5.14 Divorce proceedings: by country
continued

		1997	1998	1999	2000	2001	2002	2003	2004	2005	2006	2007
Scotland												
Dissolution of marriage[1]												
Decree granted	ZBYG	12 220	12 383	11 860	11 142	10 631	10 825	10 927	11 226	10 939	13 013	12 771
On grounds of:												
Adultery	ZBYH	909	832	770	610	473	428	401	413	327	263	131
Behaviour	ZBYI	3 081	3 005	2 611	2 099	1 639	1 656	1 537	1 546	1 344	1 215	875
Desertion	ZBYJ	33	28	18	34	24	42	23	15	17	15	7
Separation (2 years and consent)	ZBYK	5 773	6 121	5 908	5 878	5 943	6 101	6 016	6 122	5 989	4 014	971
Separation(5 years)	ZBYL	2 424	2 397	2 553	2 521	2 552	2 598	2 950	3 130	3 262	1 923	182
Separation[2]												
1 year and consent	IE9T	..	..	..	..	..	..	..	..	..	1 456	3 003
2 years	IE9U	..	..	..	..	..	..	..	..	..	4 127	4 127
Decree granted to[2]												
the wife	ZBYM	8 266	8 328	7 770	7 190	6 775	6 800	6 926	6 938	6 653	7 750	7 528
the husband	ZBYN	3 954	4 055	4 090	3 952	3 856	4 025	4 001	4 288	4 286	5 263	5 245
Nullity of marriage												
Decree granted	ZBYO	2	1	4	1	–	1	1	1	1	1	2
Northern Ireland												
Dissolution of marriage												
Petitions filed	ZBYP	2 808	2 760	2 414	3 005	2 869	2 929	3 192	2 808	3 299	3 098	3 010
Decree nisi granted	ZBYQ	2 532	2 904	2 393	2 456	2 615	2 454	2 616	2 697	2 594	2 607	2 985
Decree absolute granted	ZBYR	2 174	2 454	2 325	2 348	2 363	2 165	2 315	2 512	2 357	2 558	2 907
On grounds of:												
Adultery	ZBYS	151	151	191	162	140	132	112	138	92	94	99
Behaviour	ZBYT	418	423	424	406	411	363	385	474	311	333	359
Desertion	ZBYU	11	10	17	8	5	3	9	6	2	2	3
Separation (2 years and consent)	ZBYV	991	1 112	978	1 065	1 053	1 002	1 065	1 154	1 056	1 109	1 373
Separation(5 years)	ZBYW	536	684	643	634	668	582	642	651	643	746	790
Combination of more than one ground and other	ZBYX	67	74	72	73	86	83	102	89	253	274	283
Decree absolute granted to:												
the wife	ZBYY	1 473	1 644	1 585	1 540	1 578	1 405	1 530	1 651	1 500	1 666	1 859
the husband	ZBYZ	698	807	733	806	781	755	775	854	856	882	1 032
both	ZBZA	3	3	7	2	4	5	10	7	1	10	16
Nullity of marriage												
Petitions filed	ZBZB	7	5	1	2	1	5	4	8	9	–	5
Decree nisi granted	ZBZC	2	6	2	5	2	2	5	3	3	3	4
Decree absolute granted	ZBZD	2	5	1	2	2	–	4	–	5	7	6
Judicial separation												
Petitions filed	ZBZE	70	64	50	54	40	27	35	18	3	7	2
Decrees granted	ZBZF	34	40	31	23	25	15	22	12	4	8	12

1 The terms petition filed, decree nisi granted, decree absolute and judicial separation are not used in Scotland. Decree absolute granted to 'both' and 'Combination of more than one ground and other' are not procedures used in Scotland.

2 New categories introduced with effect from 4 May 2006 by the Family Law (Scotland) Act 2006. These replace the two 'non-cohabitation' categories (non-cohabiation is a category that is used in Scotland only) of 2 years with consent and 5 years.

3 Data supplied by Ministry of Justice (12 February 2008) see Judicial and Court Statistics.

4 2007 data are provisional.

Sources: Office for National Statistics: 01329 444410;
General Register Office for Scotland;
Northern Ireland Statistics and Research Agency;
Ministry of Justice (England & Wales);
Scottish Courts Administration;
Northern Ireland Courts Administration

Population and vital statistics

5.15 Births:[1] by country and sex

| | Live births | | | | Rates | | | | |
	Total	Male	Female	Sex ratio[2]	Crude birth rate[3]	General fertility rate[4]	TFR[5]	Still-births[6]	Still-birth rate[6]
United Kingdom[7]									
1900 - 02	1 095	558	537	1 037	28.6	115.1	..	..	..
1910 - 12	1 037	528	508	1 039	24.6	99.4	..	..	..
1920 - 22	1 018	522	496	1 052	23.1	93.0	..	..	..
1930 - 32	750	383	367	1 046	16.3	66.5	..	..	..
1940 - 42	723	372	351	1 062	15.0	..	1.89	..	..
1950 - 52	803	413	390	1 061	16.0	73.7	2.21	..	..
1960 - 62	946	487	459	1 063	17.9	90.3	2.80	18.6	19.2
1970 - 72	880	453	427	1 064	15.8	82.5	2.36	11.3	12.7
1980 - 82	735	377	358	1 053	13.0	62.5	1.83	5.0	6.8
1990 - 92	790	405	385	1 051	13.8	63.7	1.81	3.6	4.6
2000 - 02	672	345	328	1 052	11.4	54.7	1.64	3.6	5.4
	BBCA	KBCZ	KBCY	KMFW	KBCT	KBCS	KBCR	KBCQ	KMFX
1997	726.6	372	354	1 051	12.6	59.6	1.72	3.9	5.3
1998	716.9	367	350	1 052	12.3	58.8	1.71	3.9	5.4
1999	700.0	359	341	1 056	11.9	57.3	1.68	3.7	5.3
2000	679.0	348	331	1 051	11.5	55.4	1.64	3.6	5.3
2001	669.1	343	326	1 050	11.3	54.3	1.63	3.6	5.3
2002	668.8	343	326	1 054	11.3	54.2	1.64	3.8	5.6
2003	695.6	357	339	1 052	11.7	56.2	1.71	4.0	5.7
2004	716.0	368	348	1 055	12.0	57.7	1.77	4.1	5.7
2005	722.5	370	353	1 050	12.0	57.8	1.78	3.9	5.3
2006	748.6	383	366	1 047	12.4	59.7	1.84	4.0	5.3
2007	772.2	397	376	1 056	13.8	61.5	1.90	4.0	5.2
England and Wales									
1900 - 02	932	475	458	1 037	28.6	114.7	..	..	..
1910 - 12	884	450	433	1 040	24.5	98.6	..	..	..
1920 - 22	862	442	420	1 051	22.8	91.1	..	..	..
1930 - 32	632	323	309	1 047	15.8	64.4	..	27.0	..
1940 - 42	607	312	295	1 057	15.6	61.3	1.81	22.0	..
1950 - 52	683	351	332	1 058	15.6	72.1	2.16	16.0	..
1960 - 62	812	418	394	1 061	17.6	88.9	2.77	15.6	18.9
1970 - 72	764	394	371	1 061	15.6	81.4	2.31	9.7	12.5
1980 - 82	639	328	311	1 053	12.9	61.8	1.81	4.3	6.7
1990 - 92	698	358	340	1 051	13.8	63.8	1.82	3.2	4.5
2000 - 02	598	307	292	1 052	11.4	55.2	1.65	3.2	5.4
	BBCB	KMFY	KMFZ	KMGA	KMGB	KMGC	KMGD	KMGE	KMGF
1997	643.1	330	314	1 051	12.5	60.0	1.73	3.4	5.3
1998	635.9	326	310	1 051	12.3	59.2	1.72	3.4	5.3
1999	621.9	319	303	1 055	12.0	57.8	1.70	3.3	5.3
2000	604.4	310	295	1 050	11.6	55.9	1.65	3.2	5.3
2001	594.6	305	290	1 050	11.4	54.7	1.63	3.2	5.3
2002	596.1	306	290	1 055	11.3	54.7	1.65	3.4	5.6
2003	621.5	318	303	1 051	11.8	56.8	1.73	3.6	5.8
2004	639.7	328	311	1 054	12.1	58.2	1.78	3.7	5.7
2005	645.8	331	315	1 049	12.1	58.3	1.79	3.5	5.4
2006	669.6	342	327	1 047	12.5	60.2	1.86	3.6	5.4
2007	690.0	354	336	1 057	12.8	62.0	1.92	3.6	5.2

5.15 Births:[1] by country and sex

continued

Thousands

	Live births				Rates				
	Total	Male	Female	Sex ratio[2]	Crude birth rate[3]	General fertility rate[4]	TFR[5]	Still-births[6]	Still-birth rate[6]
Scotland									
1900 - 02	132	67	65	1 046	29.5	120.6	..	..	..
1910 - 12	123	63	60	1 044	25.9	107.4	..	..	..
1920 - 22	125	64	61	1 046	25.6	105.9	..	..	..
1930 - 32	93	47	45	1 040	19.1	78.8	..	..	..
1940 - 42	89	46	43	1 051	18.5	73.7	..	4.0	..
1950 - 52	91	47	44	1 060	17.9	81.4	2.41	2.0	..
1960 - 62	102	53	50	1 060	19.7	97.8	2.98	2.2	20.8
1970 - 72	84	43	41	1 057	16.1	83.3	2.46	1.1	13.5
1980 - 82	68	35	33	1 051	13.1	62.2	1.80	0.4	6.3
1990 - 92	66	34	32	1 052	13.0	59.2	1.68	0.4	5.7
2000 - 02	52	27	26	1 046	10.3	48.6	1.48	0.3	5.6
	BBCD	KMEU	KMEV	KMEW	KMEX	KMEY	KMEZ	KMFM	KMFN
1997	59.4	31	29	1 055	11.7	54.4	1.58	0.3	5.3
1998	57.3	29	28	1 060	11.3	52.7	1.55	0.4	6.1
1999	55.1	28	27	1 050	10.9	50.9	1.51	0.3	5.2
2000	53.1	27	26	1 051	10.5	49.2	1.48	0.3	5.6
2001	52.5	27	26	1 041	10.4	48.8	1.49	0.3	5.7
2002	51.3	26	25	1 047	10.1	48.1	1.48	0.3	5.4
2003	52.4	27	26	1 054	10.4	49.4	1.54	0.3	5.6
2004	54.0	28	26	1 060	10.6	51.0	1.60	0.3	5.8
2005	54.4	28	26	1 068	10.7	51.5	1.62	0.3	5.3
2006	55.7	28	27	1 046	10.9	52.8	1.67	0.3	5.3
2007	57.8	30	28	1 057	11.2	54.8	1.73	0.3	5.6
Northern Ireland[7]									
1900 - 02	..	..	..	..	..	..	..	..	..
1910 - 12	..	..	..	..	..	..	..	..	..
1920 - 22	31	16	15	1 048	24.2	105.9	..	..	..
1930 - 32	26	13	12	1 047	20.5	78.8	..	..	..
1940 - 42	27	14	13	1 078	20.8	73.7	..	..	..
1950 - 52	29	15	14	1 066	20.9	81.4	..	..	..
1960 - 62	31	16	15	1 068	22.5	111.5	3.47	0.7	22.0
1970 - 72	31	16	15	1 074	20.4	105.7	3.13	0.5	14.3
1980 - 82	28	14	13	1 048	18.0	87.5	2.59	0.2	8.4
1990 - 92	26	13	13	1 051	16.1	74.8	2.15	0.1	4.6
2000 - 02	22	11	11	1 054	12.8	58.8	1.78	0.1	5.0
	BBCE	KMFO	KMFP	KMFQ	KMFR	KMFS	KMFT	KMFU	KMFV
1997	24.1	12	12	1 048	14.4	66.4	1.93	0.1	5.4
1998	23.7	12	12	1 039	14.1	65.0	1.90	0.1	5.1
1999	23.0	12	11	1 084	13.7	62.9	1.86	0.1	5.7
2000	21.5	11	10	1 070	12.8	58.7	1.75	0.1	4.3
2001	22.0	11	11	1 058	13.0	59.7	1.80	0.1	5.1
2002	21.4	11	11	1 035	12.6	58.1	1.77	0.1	5.7
2003	21.6	11	10	1 081	12.7	59.0	1.81	0.1	5.0
2004	22.3	11	11	1 059	13.0	60.6	1.87	0.1	5.0
2005	22.3	11	11	1 032	12.9	60.4	1.87	0.1	4.0
2006	23.3	12	11	1 066	13.4	62.5	1.94	0.1	3.8
2007	24.5	13	12	1 049	13.9	65.1	2.02	0.1	4.2

1 See chapter text.
2 Males per 1,000 females (calculated using whole numbers).
3 Rate per 1,000 population (calculated using whole numbers).
4 Rate per 1,000 women aged 15 - 44.
5 Total fertility rate is the average number of children which would be born to a woman if she experienced the age-specific fertility rates of the period in question throughout her child-bearing life span. UK figures for the years 1970-72 and earlier are estimates.
6 On 1 October 1992 the legal definition of a stillbirth was changed from a baby born dead after 28 completed weeks gestation or more to one born

dead after 24 completed weeks gestation or more. Between 1 October and 31 December 1992 in the UK there were 258 babies born dead between 24 and 27 completed weeks gestation (216 in England and Wales, 35 in Scotland and 7 in Northern Ireland). If these babies were included in the stillbirth figures given, the stillbirth rate would be 4.7 for the UK and England and Wales, while Scotland and Northern Ireland stillbirth rate would remain as stated.
7 From 1981, data for the United Kingdom and Northern Ireland have been revised to exclude births in Northern Ireland to non-residents of Northern Ireland.

Sources: Office for National Statistics: 01329 444410;
General Register Office for Scotland;
Northern Ireland Statistics and Research Agency

5.16 Birth occurrence inside and outside marriage by age of mother

Thousands

	Inside marriage						Outside marriage					
	All ages	Under 20	20 - 24	25 - 29	Over 30	Mean[1] age (Years)	All ages	Under 20	20 - 24	25 - 29	Over 30	Mean[1] age (Years)
United Kingdom[2]												
	KKEY	KKEZ	KKFY	KKFZ	KKGX	KKGY	KKGZ	KKIC	KKID	KKIE	KKIF	KKIG
1961	890	55	273	280	282	27.7	54	13	17	10	13	25.5
1971	828	70	301	271	185	26.4	74	24	25	13	12	23.8
1981	640	36	193	231	180	27.3	91	30	33	16	13	23.4
1987	598	18	153	235	192	28.1	178	48	68	37	26	23.9
1988	589	16	144	234	195	28.2	198	51	76	42	29	24.1
1989	570	14	130	228	198	28.4	207	49	79	46	32	24.3
1990	576	13	121	233	209	28.6	223	51	83	53	37	24.5
1991	556	10	109	224	213	28.9	236	50	87	58	41	24.8
1992	540	9	98	216	218	29.1	241	46	86	62	46	25.1
1993	520	8	87	204	221	29.3	242	44	84	64	50	25.4
1994	510	7	78	194	231	29.6	240	41	80	65	55	25.7
1995	486	6	69	180	232	29.8	246	42	79	66	60	25.9
1996	473	6	61	170	237	30.1	260	45	80	69	66	26.0
1997	460	6	55	159	240	30.3	267	47	79	71	71	26.1
1998	447	6	51	149	243	30.5	270	49	77	70	74	26.2
1999	428	6	47	136	239	30.7	272	49	77	68	77	26.3
2000	411	5	44	126	237	30.9	268	47	77	66	78	26.4
2001	401	5	44	116	236	30.9	268	45	77	64	82	26.7
2002	397	5	44	109	239	31.1	272	44	80	62	85	26.7
2003	407	5	44	110	248	31.2	289	45	86	65	92	26.8
2004	413	4	44	110	255	31.3	303	46	90	69	97	26.9
2005	412	4	43	111	254	31.4	310	47	93	72	98	26.9
2006	422	3	43	115	260	31.4	327	48	99	78	102	26.9
2007	429	3	42	119	265	31.5	343	47	104	85	106	27.1
Great Britain												
	KKIH	KKII	KKIJ	KKIK	KKIL	KKIM	KKIN	KKIO	KKIP	KKIQ	KKIR	KKIS
1961	859	53	264	270	272	27.7	53	13	17	10	13	25.5
1971	797	68	293	261	176	26.4	73	24	25	13	12	23.8
1981	614	34	186	223	171	27.2	89	29	32	16	13	23.3
1987	574	17	147	227	184	28.0	174	46	66	36	25	23.4
1988	566	16	138	226	186	28.2	194	49	74	42	29	23.6
1989	549	13	125	220	190	28.4	202	48	77	45	32	24.2
1990	554	12	116	225	201	28.6	218	49	81	52	36	24.6
1991	535	10	105	216	205	28.9	231	48	85	57	41	24.8
1992	520	9	94	208	210	29.1	235	45	84	61	46	25.1
1993	500	7	84	196	213	29.3	236	42	82	62	49	25.4
1994	492	7	75	188	222	29.6	235	41	78	63	53	25.7
1995	468	6	66	173	223	29.8	240	40	77	65	59	25.9
1996	455	6	59	163	227	30.1	254	44	78	68	65	26.0
1997	442	6	53	152	231	30.3	261	46	76	69	69	26.2
1998	430	6	49	143	233	30.5	263	48	74	68	73	26.3
1999	412	6	46	131	230	30.7	265	48	74	67	76	26.4
2000	396	5	43	121	228	30.9	261	46	74	65	77	26.5
2001	386	5	43	112	227	30.9	261	44	75	62	80	26.6
2002	383	5	43	105	230	31.1	265	43	77	61	84	26.7
2003	393	4	43	106	239	31.2	281	44	83	64	90	26.9
2004	399	4	43	106	245	31.3	295	45	88	67	95	26.9
2005	398	4	42	107	245	31.4	302	45	90	70	97	26.9
2006	407	3	42	111	251	31.4	318	46	96	76	100	26.9
2007	414	3	41	114	255	31.5	334	46	101	83	104	27.1

1 The mean ages presented in this table are unstandardised and therefore take no account of the age structure of the population.

2 From 1981, data for the United Kingdom have been revised to exclude births in Northern Ireland to non-residents of Northern Ireland.

Sources: Office for National Statistics: 01329 444410; General Register Office for Scotland; Northern Ireland Statistics and Research Agency

5.17 Live births: by age of mother and country

Numbers

	All ages	Under 20	20 - 24	25 - 29	30 - 34	35 - 39	40 - 44	45 and over
United Kingdom								
All live births[1,2]								
	KMBZ	KMDV	KMDW	KMDX	KMDY	KMDZ	KMES	KMET
1997	726 622	52 851	133 257	229 429	212 162	84 508	13 731	618
1998	716 888	54 822	127 230	218 072	212 876	88 729	14 453	640
1999	699 976	54 921	124 036	204 808	208 986	91 272	15 210	695
2000	679 029	52 059	120 305	191 583	202 893	95 400	16 032	708
2001	669 123	50 157	121 664	179 776	202 017	97 379	17 271	831
2002	668 777	49 165	123 844	171 852	203 261	101 379	18 273	968
2003	695 549	49 874	129 867	175 473	210 071	109 038	20 233	933
2004	715 996	50 752	134 614	179 050	213 620	114 852	22 107	975
2005	722 549	50 396	135 891	183 513	211 076	116 902	23 518	1 176
2006	748 563	51 066	142 171	192 800	212 333	123 867	24 999	1 288
2007	772 245	50 515	145 725	204 276	214 020	129 599	26 633	1 420
Age-specific fertility rates[3]								
	KMBY	KMBR	KMBS	KMBT	KMBU	KMBV	KMBW	KMBX
1997	59.6	30.2	74.9	104.2	89.8	39.1	7.1	0.3
1998	58.8	30.8	73.6	101.4	90.4	40.0	7.4	0.3
1999	57.3	30.7	71.8	98.0	89.4	40.2	7.6	0.4
2000	55.4	29.2	68.7	93.9	87.7	41.0	7.8	0.4
2001	54.3	27.9	68.0	91.5	88.0	41.3	8.2	0.4
2002	54.2	27.0	68.0	91.3	89.7	42.6	8.4	0.5
2003	50.2	26.7	70.2	95.4	94.6	45.9	9.1	0.5
2004	57.7	26.7	71.5	97.3	99.2	48.6	9.7	0.5
2005	57.8	26.2	70.4	97.4	100.5	50.0	10.6	0.6
2006	59.7	26.4	72.0	100.1	104.6	53.4	10.6	0.6
2007	61.5	25.9	72.3	103.5	109.8	56.6	11.2	0.7
England and Wales								
All live births								
	KGSH	KGSA	KGSB	KGSC	KGSD	KGSE	KGSF	KGSG
1997	643 095	46 372	118 589	202 792	187 528	74 900	12 332	582
1998	635 901	48 285	113 537	193 144	188 499	78 881	12 980	575
1999	621 872	48 375	110 722	181 931	185 311	81 281	13 617	635
2000	604 441	45 846	107 741	170 701	180 113	84 974	14 403	663
2001	594 634	44 189	108 844	159 926	178 920	86 495	15 499	761
2002	596 122	43 467	110 959	153 379	180 532	90 449	16 441	895
2003	621 469	44 236	116 622	156 931	187 214	97 386	18 205	875
2004	639 721	45 094	121 072	159 984	190 550	102 228	19 884	909
2005	645 835	44 830	122 145	164 348	188 153	104 113	21 155	1 091
2006	669 601	45 509	127 828	172 642	189 407	110 509	22 512	1 194
2007	690 013	44 805	130 784	182 570	191 124	115 380	24 041	1 309
Age-specific fertility rates[3]								
	KGSP	KGSI	KGSJ	KGSK	KGSL	KGSM	KGSN	KGSO
1997	60.0	30.2	76.0	104.3	89.8	39.4	7.3	0.3
1998	59.2	30.9	74.9	101.5	90.6	40.4	7.5	0.3
1999	57.8	30.9	73.0	98.3	89.6	40.6	7.7	0.4
2000	55.9	29.3	70.0	94.3	87.9	41.4	8.0	0.4
2001	54.7	28.0	69.0	91.7	88.0	41.5	8.4	0.5
2002	54.7	27.0	69.1	91.5	89.9	43.0	8.6	0.5
2003	56.8	26.9	71.1	95.8	94.9	46.4	9.3	0.5
2004	58.2	26.9	72.8	97.6	99.6	48.8	9.9	0.5
2005	58.3	26.3	71.6	97.9	100.7	50.3	10.8	0.6
2006	60.2	26.6	73.2	100.6	104.8	53.8	10.8	0.6
2007	62.0	26.0	73.5	104.0	110.2	56.9	11.4	0.7

Population and vital statistics

5.17 Live births: by age of mother and country

continued

Numbers

	All ages	Under 20	20 - 24	25 - 29	30 - 34	35 - 39	40 - 44	45 and over
Scotland								
All live births[1]								
	KGTH	KGTA	KGTB	KGTC	KGTD	KGTE	KGTF	KGTG
1997	59 440	4 835	10 607	18 782	17 455	6 740	936	19
1998	57 319	4 802	9 804	17 477	17 207	6 893	1 027	43
1999	55 147	4 755	9 440	16 011	16 722	7 034	1 096	41
2000	53 076	4 599	8 962	14 676	16 233	7 395	1 133	29
2001	52 527	4 444	9 121	13 763	16 206	7 701	1 224	40
2002	51 270	4 195	9 267	12 694	16 038	7 727	1 267	47
2003	52 432	4 155	9 626	12 725	16 085	8 310	1 432	39
2004	53 957	4 172	9 950	13 131	16 085	8 912	1 631	50
2005	54 386	4 171	10 008	13 229	15 962	9 179	1 694	66
2006	55 690	4 130	10 399	13 876	15 878	9 535	1 775	58
2007	57 781	4 305	10 913	14 917	15 622	10 035	1 849	83
Age-specific fertility rates[3]								
	KGTP	KGTI	KGTJ	KGTK	KGTL	KGTM	KGTN	KGTO
1997	54.4	31.0	65.5	97.4	83.9	34.0	5.3	0.1
1998	52.7	30.6	62.8	94.3	83.2	34.1	5.7	0.3
1999	50.9	30.3	61.0	90.4	82.0	34.3	5.9	0.2
2000	49.2	29.3	57.6	86.5	81.3	35.6	6.0	0.2
2001	48.8	28.4	57.8	85.1	82.2	36.9	6.3	0.2
2002	48.1	26.8	58.3	83.3	83.6	37.1	6.4	0.3
2003	49.4	26.3	60.1	86.5	86.8	40.0	7.1	0.2
2004	51.0	26.1	61.8	89.4	90.3	43.3	7.9	0.3
2005	51.5	26.2	60.9	88.6	93.2	45.4	8.1	0.3
2006	52.8	25.8	61.9	90.2	97.1	47.8	8.4	0.3
2007	54.8	26.9	63.6	93.1	100.1	51.3	8.8	0.4
Northern Ireland								
All live births[2]								
	KMDM	KMDF	KMDG	KMDH	KMDI	KMDJ	KMDK	KMDL
1997	24 087	1 644	4 061	7 855	7 179	2 868	463	17
1998	23 668	1 735	3 889	7 451	7 170	2 955	446	22
1999	22 957	1 791	3 874	6 866	6 953	2 957	497	19
2000	21 512	1 614	3 602	6 206	6 547	3 031	496	16
2001	21 962	1 524	3 699	6 087	6 891	3 183	548	30
2002	21 385	1 502	3 619	5 779	6 691	3 203	565	26
2003	21 648	1 483	3 619	5 817	6 772	3 342	596	19
2004	22 318	1 486	3 592	5 935	6 985	3 712	592	16
2005	22 328	1 395	3 738	5 936	6 961	3 610	669	19
2006	23 272	1 427	3 944	6 282	7 048	3 823	712	36
2007	24 451	1 405	4 028	6 789	7 274	4 184	741	30
Age-specific fertility rates[2,3]								
	KMDU	KMDN	KMDO	KMDP	KMDQ	KMDR	KMDS	KMDT
1997	66.4	26.4	71.1	124.2	109.2	46.6	8.8	0.3
1998	65.0	27.8	69.6	119.0	108.4	47.2	8.2	0.4
1999	62.9	28.6	70.6	112.3	105.6	46.1	8.9	0.4
2000	58.7	25.6	66.0	103.9	100.4	46.2	8.5	0.3
2001	59.7	23.9	67.5	105.1	106.0	48.0	9.1	0.6
2002	58.1	23.3	66.0	102.9	104.2	48.2	9.2	0.5
2003	59.0	22.9	65.5	106.8	107.0	50.2	9.8	0.3
2004	60.6	23.0	62.8	109.8	112.6	56.1	9.5	0.3
2005	60.4	21.7	63.2	108.6	114.8	55.0	10.2	0.3
2006	62.5	22.5	63.6	112.0	119.2	58.2	10.8	0.6
2007	65.1	22.5	62.6	116.1	124.6	64.2	11.1	0.5

1 The 'All ages' figure for Scotland includes births to mothers whose age was not known. There were 128 such births in 1996, 66 in 1997, 66 in 1998, 48 in 1999, 49 in 2000, 28 in 2001, 35 in 2002, 60 in 2003, 26 in 2004, 77 in 2005, 39 in 2006 and 57 in 2007.
2 From 1981 data for the United Kingdom and Northern Ireland have been revised to exclude births in Northern Ireland to non residents in Northern Ireland.
3 The rates for women of all ages, under 20, and 45 and over are based upon the populations of women aged 15-44, 15-19 and 45 respectively.

Sources: Office for National Statistics: 01329 444410;
General Register Office for Scotland;
Northern Ireland Statistics and Research Agency

5.18 Legal abortions[1]: by age for residents

Numbers

	All ages	Under 15	15	16 - 19	20 - 24	25 - 29	30 - 34	35 - 39	40 - 44	45 and over	Not stated
England and Wales											
	C53Z	C542	C543	C544	C545	C546	C547	C548	C549	C54A	C54B
1986	147 619	924	2 970	33 819	45 316	28 656	18 005	12 977	4 521	409	22
1987	156 191	907	2 858	35 167	49 256	31 243	18 960	12 639	4 757	390	14
1988	168 298	859	2 709	37 928	54 067	34 584	20 000	12 681	5 047	412	11
1989	170 463	803	2 580	36 182	54 880	36 604	21 284	12 713	5 020	388	9
1990	173 900	873	2 549	35 520	55 281	38 770	22 431	12 956	5 104	404	12
1991	167 376	886	2 272	31 130	52 678	38 611	23 445	13 035	4 901	408	10
1992	160 501	905	2 095	27 589	49 052	38 430	23 870	13 252	4 844	452	12
1993	157 846	964	2 119	25 806	46 846	38 139	24 690	13 885	4 889	494	14
1994	156 539	1 080	2 166	25 223	44 871	38 081	25 507	14 156	5 008	440	7
1995	154 315	946	2 324	24 945	43 394	37 254	25 759	14 352	4 868	457	16
1996	167 916	1 098	2 547	28 790	46 356	39 311	28 228	16 118	5 027	428	13
1997	170 145	1 020	2 414	29 947	44 960	40 159	28 892	16 858	5 413	482	..
1998	177 871	1 103	2 656	33 236	45 766	40 366	30 449	18 174	5 576	511	34
1999	173 701	1 066	2 537	32 807	45 004	38 492	29 139	18 341	5 755	502	58
2000	175 542	1 048	2 700	33 218	47 099	37 852	28 735	18 589	5 794	459	48
2001	176 364	1 066	2 592	33 431	48 267	36 506	28 782	19 146	6 094	456	24
2002	175 932	1 075	2 658	32 985	48 359	35 795	28 503	19 450	6 531	457	119
2003	181 582	1 171	2 796	34 247	51 201[2]	36 018	28 749	19 868	7 032	500	–
2004	185 415	1 034	2 722	35 386	52 701[2]	37 759	28 064	19 820	7 422	507	–
2005	186 416	1 083	2 703	35 313	53 342	38 330	27 836	19 782	7 459	568	–
2006	193 737	1 042	2 948	37 296	55 340	40 396	28 153	20 074	7 825	663	–
2007	198 499	1 171	3 205	39 579	56 963	41 704	27 257	19 976	7 915	729	–
Scotland											
	C54C	C54D	C54E	C54F	C54G	C54H	C54I	C54J	C54K	C54L	EVH4
1986	9 611	74	236	2 526	2 984	1 740	1 080	702	247	22	–
1987	9 449	70	210	2 415	2 991	1 728	1 082	695	241	17	–
1988	10 111	65	217	2 526	3 299	1 965	1 105	662	257	15	–
1989	10 191	53	209	2 554	3 199	1 967	1 225	704	266	14	–
1990	10 198	54	185	2 536	3 235	2 061	1 157	698	253	19	–
1991	11 046	77	203	2 567	3 479	2 247	1 443	740	262	28	–
1992	10 791	73	173	2 368	3 383	2 283	1 444	798	252	17	–
1993	11 059	92	193	2 297	3 365	2 443	1 489	889	262	29	–
1994	11 371	78	214	2 311	3 480	2 427	1 640	876	315	30	–
1995	11 131	79	233	2 168	3 395	2 437	1 606	885	295	33	–
1996	11 957	87	234	2 360	3 569	2 595	1 798	957	330	27	–
1997	12 087	85	204	2 429	3 438	2 644	1 849	1 091	322	25	–
1998	12 458	73	213	2 703	3 419	2 740	1 801	1 148	339	22	–
1999	12 145	69	182	2 629	3 351	2 548	1 807	1 178	358	23	–
2000	11 979	93	181	2 608	3 349	2 400	1 765	1 174	381	28	–
2001	12 114	66	210	2 718	3 461	2 317	1 816	1 126	377	23	–
2002	11 840	79	194	2 646	3 447	2 165	1 731	1 166	382	29	1
2003	12 267	71	242	2 781	3 673	2 224	1 725	1 112	411	28	–
2004	12 349	103	206	2 887	3 666	2 250	1 652	1 171	382	32	2
2005	12 597	94	247	2 962	3 765	2 331	1 682	1 094	397	25	–
2006	13 110	91	273	3 086	3 967	2 433	1 614	1 205	413	28	–
2007	13 635	97	273	3 162	4 098	2 715	1 630	1 216	407	37	..

1 Refers to therapeutic abortions notified in accordance with the Abortion Act 1967.
2 Records with missing ages were assigned to the 20 - 24 age group.

Sources: Department of Health;
Notifications (to the Chief Medical Officer for Scotland) of abortions performed;
under the Abortion Act 1967: ISD Scotland

Population and vital statistics

5.19 Deaths: by sex and age[1]

Numbers

	All ages[2]	Under 1 year	1-4	5-9	10-14	15-19	20-24	25-34	35-44	45-54	55-64	65-74	75-84	85 and over
United Kingdom														
Males														
1900 - 02	340 664	87 242	37 834	8 429	4 696	7 047	8 766	19 154	24 739	30 488	37 610	39 765	28 320	6 563
1910 - 12	303 703	63 885	29 452	7 091	4 095	5 873	6 817	16 141	21 813	28 981	37 721	45 140	29 397	7 283
1920 - 22	284 876	48 044	19 008	6 052	3 953	5 906	6 572	13 663	19 702	29 256	40 583	49 398	34 937	7 801
1930 - 32	284 249	28 840	11 276	4 580	2 890	5 076	6 495	12 327	16 326	29 376	47 989	63 804	45 247	10 022
1940 - 42	314 643	24 624	6 949	3 400	2 474	4 653	4 246	11 506	17 296	30 082	57 076	79 652	59 733	12 900
1950 - 52	307 312	14 105	2 585	1 317	919	1 498	2 289	5 862	11 074	27 637	53 691	86 435	79 768	20 131
1960 - 62	318 850	12 234	1 733	971	871	1 718	1 857	3 842	8 753	26 422	63 009	87 542	83 291	26 605
1970 - 72	335 166	9 158	1 485	1 019	802	1 778	2 104	3 590	7 733	24 608	64 898	105 058	82 905	30 027
1980 - 82	330 495	4 829	774	527	652	1 999	1 943	3 736	6 568	19 728	54 159	105 155	98 488	31 936
1990 - 92	312 521	3 315	623	372	396	1 349	2 059	4 334	6 979	15 412	40 424	87 849	106 376	43 032
2000 - 02	288 261	2 065	365	233	326	1 032	1 502	4 270	7 181	15 370	32 328	66 808	98 363	58 419
	KHUA	KHUB	KHUC	KHUD	KHUE	KHUF	KHUG	KHUH	KHUI	KHUJ	KHUK	KHUL	KHUM	KHUN
1996	306 466	2 575	484	268	369	1 087	1 689	4 709	6 807	15 777	35 078	81 746	102 546	53 331
1997	301 713	2 414	465	301	366	1 134	1 738	4 558	6 678	15 770	33 910	78 121	101 817	54 441
1998	299 655	2 315	465	297	361	1 145	1 651	4 782	6 893	15 836	33 673	75 608	101 066	55 563
1999	299 235	2 323	459	260	333	1 088	1 548	4 647	6 930	15 862	33 181	73 457	101 327	57 820
2000	291 337	2 136	390	263	305	1 068	1 595	4 491	7 168	15 458	32 661	69 707	98 398	57 697
2001	287 942	2 052	358	230	369	1 106	1 518	4 459	7 275	15 668	32 135	66 257	98 041	58 474
2002	289 083	2 050	382	224	327	1 071	1 575	4 345	7 362	15 222	32 509	65 140	99 387	59 489
2003	289 185	2 047	356	228	308	1 013	1 586	4 041	7 530	14 692	32 895	63 520	100 900	60 069
2004	278 918	2 033	345	206	282	975	1 484	3 831	7 454	14 510	31 660	60 760	98 466	56 912
2005	277 349	2 117	339	194	312	1 022	1 449	3 660	7 454	14 241	31 645	58 828	95 641	60 447
2006	274 201	2 078	328	213	299	1 008	1 482	3 712	7 485	14 406	32 012	56 319	92 532	62 327
2007	274 883	2 106	379	200	270	979	1 491	3 711	7 423	14 045	31 994	55 338	91 488	65 459
Females														
1900 - 02	322 058	68 770	36 164	8 757	5 034	6 818	8 264	18 702	21 887	25 679	34 521	42 456	34 907	10 099
1910 - 12	289 608	49 865	27 817	7 113	4 355	5 683	6 531	15 676	19 647	24 481	32 813	46 453	37 353	11 828
1920 - 22	274 772	35 356	17 323	5 808	4 133	5 729	6 753	14 878	18 121	24 347	34 026	48 573	45 521	14 203
1930 - 32	275 336	21 072	9 995	3 990	2 734	4 721	5 931	12 699	15 373	24 695	39 471	59 520	56 250	18 886
1940 - 42	296 646	17 936	5 952	2 743	2 068	4 180	5 028	11 261	14 255	23 629	42 651	70 907	71 377	24 658
1950 - 52	291 597	10 293	2 098	880	625	1 115	1 717	5 018	8 989	18 875	37 075	75 220	92 848	36 844
1960 - 62	304 871	8 887	1 334	627	522	684	811	2 504	6 513	16 720	36 078	73 118	105 956	51 117
1970 - 72	322 968	6 666	1 183	654	459	718	900	2 110	5 345	15 594	36 177	75 599	109 539	68 024
1980 - 82	330 269	3 561	585	355	425	733	772	2 099	4 360	12 206	32 052	72 618	117 760	82 743
1990 - 92	328 218	2 431	485	259	255	520	714	1 989	4 340	9 707	25 105	61 951	115 467	104 994
2000 - 02	317 356	1 586	283	188	208	446	536	1 877	4 426	10 270	20 549	47 324	101 650	128 012
	KIUA	KIUB	KIUC	KIUD	KIUE	KIUF	KIUG	KIUH	KIUI	KIUJ	KIUK	KIUL	KIUM	KIUN
1996	332 430	1 921	366	220	217	488	599	2 170	4 229	10 290	21 476	58 156	110 215	122 083
1997	330 804	1 863	336	221	236	489	587	1 953	4 320	10 451	21 103	55 947	108 777	124 521
1998	327 937	1 744	339	221	233	511	554	2 015	4 316	10 441	20 819	54 048	106 703	125 993
1999	330 241	1 736	346	195	244	487	567	1 963	4 359	10 400	20 963	52 098	106 323	130 560
2000	319 242	1 677	288	181	215	468	573	1 975	4 488	10 477	20 620	49 138	102 052	127 090
2001	316 451	1 639	299	218	200	447	557	1 895	4 475	10 354	20 479	47 138	101 135	127 615
2002	318 962	1 488	280	181	229	456	556	1 838	4 380	10 080	20 707	46 094	102 503	130 170
2003	322 900	1 639	309	182	237	441	563	1 869	4 506	9 870	20 974	45 374	105 182	131 754
2004	305 873	1 626	279	160	201	480	572	1 765	4 486	9 463	20 500	43 118	100 775	122 448
2005	305 615	1 555	256	153	216	450	557	1 684	4 432	9 492	20 655	41 839	98 338	125 988
2006	298 023	1 659	303	151	201	437	520	1 604	4 434	9 474	20 855	40 290	92 877	125 218
2007	299 797	1 627	266	137	212	423	522	1 575	4 398	9 487	21 026	39 685	90 822	129 617

5.19 Deaths: by sex and age[1]
continued

	All ages[2]	Under 1 year	1-4	5-9	10-14	15-19	20-24	25-34	35-44	45-54	55-64	65-74	75-84	85 and over
England and Wales														
Males														
1900 - 02	288 886	76 095	32 051	7 066	3 818	5 611	7 028	15 869	21 135	26 065	31 600	33 568	23 835	5 144
1910 - 12	257 253	54 678	24 676	5 907	3 348	4 765	5 596	13 603	18 665	24 820	32 217	38 016	24 928	6 036
1920 - 22	240 605	39 796	15 565	5 151	3 314	4 901	5 447	11 551	17 004	25 073	34 639	42 025	29 685	6 455
1930 - 32	243 147	23 331	9 099	3 844	2 435	4 354	5 580	10 600	14 041	25 657	41 581	54 910	39 091	8 624
1940 - 42	268 876	19 393	5 616	2 834	2 051	3 832	3 156	9 484	14 744	25 983	50 058	68 791	51 779	11 158
1950 - 52	266 879	11 498	2 131	1 087	778	1 248	1 947	4 990	9 489	23 815	46 948	75 774	69 496	17 677
1960 - 62	278 369	10 157	1 444	812	742	1 523	1 624	3 278	7 524	22 813	54 908	77 000	73 180	23 364
1970 - 72	293 934	7 818	1 259	860	677	1 524	1 788	3 079	6 637	21 348	56 667	92 389	73 365	26 522
1980 - 82	290 352	4 168	657	452	555	1 716	1 619	3 169	5 590	16 909	47 144	92 485	87 338	28 551
1990 - 92	275 550	2 926	545	325	338	1 157	1 757	3 717	6 057	13 258	34 977	77 063	94 672	38 757
2000 - 02	253 706	1 836	323	200	282	862	1 244	3 619	6 104	13 184	27 696	58 114	87 481	52 761
	KHVA	KHVB	KHVC	KHVD	KHVE	KHVF	KHVG	KHVH	KHVI	KHVJ	KHVK	KHVL	KHVM	KHVN
1996	269 825	2 285	436	237	308	908	1 405	4 027	5 861	13 546	30 111	71 459	91 164	48 078
1997	266 164	2 160	421	268	327	970	1 468	3 915	5 718	13 565	29 110	68 275	90 659	49 308
1998	264 202	2 058	415	254	309	962	1 404	4 111	5 886	13 606	28 947	65 989	90 048	50 213
1999	263 166	2 080	408	221	289	905	1 265	3 978	5 918	13 633	28 532	64 017	89 963	51 957
2000	256 698	1 902	345	227	263	898	1 328	3 849	6 135	13 355	28 003	60 801	87 449	52 143
2001	253 608	1 818	329	192	320	927	1 276	3 830	6 184	13 424	27 599	57 638	87 238	52 833
2002	254 390	1 831	329	198	286	912	1 310	3 665	6 255	13 011	27 807	56 584	88 493	53 709
2003	254 433	1 827	310	203	263	852	1 348	3 478	6 440	12 697	28 291	55 064	89 596	54 064
2004	245 208	1 809	303	174	252	833	1 257	3 281	6 360	12 417	27 117	52 709	87 367	51 329
2005	243 870	1 877	297	166	272	856	1 217	3 146	6 362	12 158	27 292	51 019	84 661	54 547
2006	240 888	1 863	292	187	261	844	1 212	3 132	6 315	12 256	27 551	48 881	81 912	56 182
2007	240 780	1 882	339	182	226	797	1 218	3 138	6 264	11 893	27 508	47 830	80 573	58 930
Females														
1900 - 02	269 432	60 090	30 674	7 278	4 010	5 265	6 497	15 065	18 253	21 474	28 424	35 307	29 118	7 977
1910 - 12	242 079	42 642	23 335	5 883	3 519	4 522	5 256	12 742	16 363	20 611	27 571	38 489	31 363	9 782
1920 - 22	229 908	29 178	14 174	4 928	3 456	4 719	5 533	12 244	15 142	20 580	28 633	41 010	38 439	11 871
1930 - 32	233 915	16 929	8 013	3 338	2 293	3 969	5 039	10 716	13 022	21 190	33 798	50 844	48 531	16 234
1940 - 42	253 702	14 174	4 726	2 265	1 695	3 426	4 198	9 470	12 093	20 413	36 814	60 987	61 891	21 550
1950 - 52	252 176	8 367	1 727	732	520	893	1 365	4 131	7 586	16 161	31 875	65 087	81 154	32 579
1960 - 62	266 849	7 409	1 103	527	444	591	700	2 147	5 576	14 389	31 083	63 543	93 548	45 789
1970 - 72	284 181	5 677	1 020	562	396	620	806	1 814	4 585	13 417	31 222	65 817	96 952	61 293
1980 - 82	290 026	3 064	511	301	365	635	670	1 821	3 740	10 420	27 606	63 023	103 676	74 194
1990 - 92	288 851	2 161	420	227	217	455	625	1 718	3 765	8 347	21 466	53 783	101 752	93 914
2000 - 02	279 482	1 412	251	168	182	382	455	1 629	3 805	8 893	17 659	40 734	89 387	114 525
	KIVA	KIVB	KIVC	KIVD	KIVE	KIVF	KIVG	KIVH	KIVI	KIVJ	KIVK	KIVL	KIVM	KIVN
1996	293 182	1 704	331	181	189	425	517	1 882	3 672	18 314	50 462	97 316	109 348	
1997	291 888	1 664	300	183	206	428	503	1 711	3 734	9 055	18 053	48 553	96 009	111 489
1998	289 233	1 547	301	185	207	432	466	1 768	3 705	9 077	17 872	46 742	94 281	112 650
1999	290 366	1 555	308	168	219	399	484	1 707	3 773	8 999	17 949	44 958	93 360	116 487
2000	281 179	1 497	257	160	191	403	504	1 702	3 853	9 108	17 722	42 318	89 651	113 813
2001	278 890	1 449	272	198	171	386	472	1 665	3 858	8 984	17 608	40 639	89 036	114 152
2002	280 966	1 337	240	160	204	391	467	1 597	3 767	8 689	17 807	39 645	90 213	116 449
2003	284 718	1 479	278	159	209	370	485	1 636	3 884	8 554	18 001	39 001	92 694	117 968
2004	269 042	1 462	251	140	173	410	494	1 536	3 855	8 139	17 649	37 041	88 404	109 488
2005	269 123	1 371	222	134	189	379	478	1 481	3 805	8 175	17 797	35 913	86 309	112 870
2006	261 711	1 505	267	135	169	381	444	1 382	3 802	8 098	17 948	34 502	81 210	111 868
2007	263 265	1 456	235	121	192	357	453	1 360	3 787	8 072	18 166	33 903	79 411	115 752

Population and vital statistics

5.19 Deaths: by sex and age[1]

continued

	All ages[2]	Under 1 year	1-4	5-9	10-14	15-19	20-24	25-34	35-44	45-54	55-64	65-74	75-84	85 and over
Scotland														
Males														
1900 - 02	40 224	9 189	4 798	1 083	672	1 069	1 292	2 506	2 935	3 591	4 597	4 531	3 117	834
1910 - 12	35 981	7 510	3 935	962	595	826	910	1 969	2 469	3 325	4 356	5 113	3 182	813
1920 - 22	34 649	6 757	2 847	710	489	747	791	1 616	2 128	3 314	4 785	5 624	3 928	911
1930 - 32	32 476	4 426	1 771	610	365	568	706	1 352	1 848	2 979	5 095	6 906	4 839	1 010
1940 - 42	36 384	3 973	1 011	449	321	668	888	1 643	2 090	3 348	5 728	8 556	6 317	1 337
1950 - 52	32 236	1 949	349	175	105	200	265	693	1 267	3 151	5 574	8 544	8 094	1 871
1960 - 62	32 401	1 578	222	121	102	146	185	456	1 013	2 986	6 682	8 505	7 980	2 425
1970 - 72	32 446	944	168	119	93	178	233	396	875	2 617	6 641	10 176	7 383	2 624
1980 - 82	31 723	451	80	56	71	206	233	423	776	2 280	5 601	10 152	8 804	2 591
1990 - 92	29 421	287	57	34	40	137	230	485	744	1 730	4 402	8 611	9 311	3 353
2000 - 02	27 526	165	30	23	30	119	196	523	882	1 775	3 781	7 038	8 535	4 430
	KHWA	KHWB	KHWC	KHWD	KHWE	KHWF	KHWG	KHWH	KHWI	KHWJ	KHWK	KHWL	KHWM	KHWN
1996	29 223	206	41	23	46	139	212	556	755	1 845	4 087	8 259	8 926	4 128
1997	28 305	186	32	22	27	114	208	521	788	1 794	3 876	7 909	8 791	4 037
1998	28 132	183	37	34	39	134	200	524	843	1 796	3 828	7 746	8 585	4 183
1999	28 605	161	31	23	33	138	215	545	818	1 820	3 773	7 569	8 908	4 571
2000	27 511	173	33	24	28	115	198	512	842	1 716	3 789	7 224	8 523	4 334
2001	27 324	155	22	27	35	131	179	510	902	1 820	3 751	6 950	8 433	4 409
2002	27 743	167	34	17	27	111	211	546	901	1 789	3 804	6 940	8 648	4 548
2003	27 832	146	35	15	31	122	186	469	893	1 634	3 787	6 797	8 994	4 723
2004	26 775	160	29	21	23	105	181	449	889	1 676	3 629	6 507	8 733	4 373
2005	26 522	159	33	19	30	106	150	385	882	1 654	3 478	6 352	8 691	4 583
2006	26 251	145	21	18	21	112	206	461	938	1 697	3 567	5 966	8 353	4 746
2007	26 895	154	25	13	31	127	207	461	908	1 685	3 572	6 082	8 547	5 083
Females														
1900 - 02	39 891	7 143	4 477	1 162	747	1 058	1 246	2 625	2 732	3 130	4 485	5 273	4 305	1 508
1910 - 12	36 132	5 854	3 674	981	618	836	910	2 149	2 473	2 909	3 960	5 636	4 588	1 552
1920 - 22	34 449	5 029	2 602	687	489	711	889	1 947	2 266	2 828	4 157	5 587	5 443	1 814
1930 - 32	32 377	3 319	1 602	527	339	568	666	1 508	1 812	2 731	4 380	6 630	6 178	2 117
1940 - 42	33 715	2 852	921	373	283	595	656	1 382	1 672	2 528	4 630	7 674	7 613	2 536
1950 - 52	31 525	1 432	284	115	84	185	293	714	1 127	2 188	4 204	8 157	9 310	3 431
1960 - 62	30 559	1 107	170	80	63	72	87	287	762	1 897	4 115	7 752	9 991	4 177
1970 - 72	30 978	694	118	69	46	73	74	231	608	1 769	4 036	7 823	10 112	5 324
1980 - 82	32 326	337	49	37	44	74	73	213	493	1 456	3 565	7 781	11 333	6 871
1990 - 92	31 747	190	45	20	29	49	72	218	458	1 093	2 966	6 630	11 079	8 898
2000 - 02	30 235	123	24	14	21	50	64	199	493	1 110	2 341	5 326	9 785	10 685
	KIWA	KIWB	KIWC	KIWD	KIWE	KIWF	KIWG	KIWH	KIWI	KIWJ	KIWK	KIWL	KIWM	KIWN
1996	31 448	159	24	31	21	49	67	218	453	1 172	2 573	6 206	10 256	10 219
1997	31 189	130	23	28	21	43	71	199	496	1 128	2 480	5 985	10 164	10 421
1998	31 032	137	26	28	19	55	68	198	485	1 106	2 416	5 955	9 913	10 626
1999	31 676	115	26	20	17	65	58	201	467	1 128	2 431	5 837	10 198	11 113
2000	30 288	132	20	10	21	46	56	222	510	1 086	2 324	5 512	9 875	10 474
2001	30 058	135	20	16	21	47	71	189	480	1 111	2 361	5 235	9 695	10 677
2002	30 360	103	32	15	20	58	65	185	489	1 134	2 339	5 232	9 784	10 904
2003	30 640	119	24	18	20	57	64	181	489	1 062	2 446	5 194	9 977	10 989
2004	29 412	106	19	15	22	52	62	179	492	1 065	2 291	4 924	9 924	10 261
2005	29 225	125	27	11	18	55	58	163	506	1 073	2 316	4 841	9 620	10 412
2006	28 842	103	26	11	17	40	58	170	497	1 090	2 351	4 722	9 303	10 454
2007	29 091	118	26	11	14	50	52	166	490	1 124	2 311	4 732	9 083	10 914

5.19

Deaths: by sex and age[1]

continued

Numbers

	All ages[2]	Under 1 year	1-4	5-9	10-14	15-19	20-24	25-34	35-44	45-54	55-64	65-74	75-84	85 and over
Northern Ireland														
Males														
1900 - 02	11 554	1 958	985	280	206	367	446	779	669	832	1 413	1 666	1 368	585
1910 - 12	10 469	1 697	841	222	152	282	311	569	679	836	1 148	2 011	1 287	434
1920 - 22	9 622	1 491	596	191	150	258	334	496	570	869	1 159	1 749	1 324	435
1930 - 32	8 626	1 083	406	126	90	154	209	375	437	740	1 313	1 988	1 317	388
1940 - 42	9 383	1 258	322	117	102	153	202	379	462	751	1 290	2 305	1 637	405
1950 - 52	8 197	658	105	55	36	50	77	179	318	671	1 169	2 117	2 178	583
1960 - 62	8 080	499	67	38	27	49	48	108	216	623	1 419	2 037	2 131	816
1970 - 72	8 786	396	58	40	32	76	83	115	221	643	1 590	2 493	2 157	881
1980 - 82	8 420	211	37	20	26	77	92	144	202	539	1 414	2 346	2 393	795
1990 - 92	7 550	102	21	13	18	55	73	132	178	423	1 044	2 175	2 393	922
2000 - 02	7 029	64	13	11	14	50	62	128	195	411	851	1 656	2 347	1228
	KHXA	KHXB	KHXC	KHXD	KHXE	KHXF	KHXG	KHXH	KHXI	KHXJ	KHXK	KHXL	KHXM	KHXN
1996	7 418	84	7	8	15	40	72	126	191	386	880	2 028	2 456	1 125
1997	7 244	68	12	11	12	50	62	122	172	411	924	1 937	2 367	1 096
1998	7 321	74	13	9	13	49	47	147	164	434	898	1 873	2 433	1 167
1999	7 464	82	20	16	11	45	68	124	194	409	876	1 871	2 456	1 292
2000	7 128	61	12	12	14	55	69	130	191	387	869	1 682	2 426	1 220
2001	7 010	79	7	11	14	48	63	119	189	424	785	1 669	2 370	1 232
2002	6 950	52	19	9	14	48	54	134	206	422	898	1 616	2 246	1 232
2003	6 920	74	11	10	14	39	52	94	197	361	817	1 659	2 310	1 282
2004	6 935	64	13	11	7	37	46	101	205	417	914	1 544	2 366	1 210
2005	6 957	81	9	9	10	60	82	129	210	429	875	1 457	2 289	1 317
2006	7 062	70	15	8	17	52	64	119	232	453	894	1 472	2 267	1 399
2007	7 208	70	15	5	13	55	66	112	251	467	914	1 426	2 368	1 446
Females														
1900 - 02	12 735	1 537	1 013	317	277	495	521	1 012	902	1 075	1 612	1 876	1 484	614
1910 - 12	11 397	1 369	808	249	218	325	365	785	811	961	1 282	2 328	1 402	494
1920 - 22	10 415	1 149	547	193	188	299	331	687	713	939	1 236	1 976	1 639	518
1930 - 32	9 044	824	380	125	102	184	226	475	539	774	1 293	2 046	1 541	535
1940 - 42	9 229	910	305	105	90	159	174	409	490	688	1 207	2 246	1 873	572
1950 - 52	7 896	494	87	33	21	37	59	173	276	526	996	1 976	2 384	834
1960 - 62	7 463	371	61	20	15	21	24	70	175	434	880	1 823	2 417	1 151
1970 - 72	7 809	295	45	23	17	25	20	65	152	408	919	1 959	2 475	1 407
1980 - 82	7 917	160	26	17	17	23	29	65	127	329	881	1 813	2 752	1 678
1990 - 92	7 620	80	20	12	9	16	17	53	117	267	672	1 538	2 636	2 182
2000 - 02	7 638	50	9	7	5	13	17	49	129	266	548	1 263	2 479	2 802
	KIXA	KIXB	KIXC	KIXD	KIXE	KIXF	KIXG	KIXH	KIXI	KIXJ	KIXK	KIXL	KIXM	KIXN
1996	7 800	58	11	8	7	14	15	70	104	277	589	1 488	2 643	2 516
1997	7 727	69	13	10	9	18	13	43	90	268	570	1 409	2 604	2 611
1998	7 672	60	12	8	7	24	20	49	126	258	531	1 351	2 509	2 717
1999	8 199	66	12	7	8	23	25	55	119	273	583	1 303	2 765	2 960
2000	7 775	48	11	11	3	19	13	51	125	283	574	1 308	2 526	2 803
2001	7 503	55	7	4	8	14	14	41	137	259	510	1 264	2 404	2 786
2002	7 636	48	8	6	5	7	24	56	124	257	561	1 217	2 506	2 817
2003	7 542	41	7	5	8	14	14	52	133	254	527	1 179	2 511	2 797
2004	7 419	58	9	5	6	18	16	50	139	259	560	1 153	2 447	2 699
2005	7 267	59	7	8	9	16	21	40	121	244	542	1 085	2 409	2 706
2006	7 470	51	10	5	15	16	18	52	135	286	556	1 066	2 364	2 896
2007	7 441	53	5	5	6	16	17	49	121	291	549	1 050	2 328	2 951

1 See chapter text.
2 In some years the totals include a small number of persons whose age was not stated.

Sources: Office for National Statistics: 01329 444410;
General Register Office for Scotland;
Northern Ireland Statistics and Research Agency

5.20 Infant and maternal mortality[1]
(i) - By country. (ii) - Infant mortality by country, type of death and sex

| | Deaths of Infants under 1 year of age per thousand live births | | | | | | | | | | | | Maternal deaths per thousand live births[3] | | | |
| | United Kingdom | | | England and Wales[2] | | | Scotland | | | Northern Ireland | | | United Kingdom | England and Wales | Scotland | Northern Ireland |
	Total	Males	Females	Total	Males	Females	Total	Males	Females	Total	Males	Females				
1900 - 02	142	156	128	146	160	131	124	136	111	113	123	103	4.71	4.67	4.74	6.03
1910 - 12	110	121	98	110	121	98	109	120	97	101	110	92	3.95	3.67	5.65	5.28
1920 - 22	82	92	71	80	90	69	94	106	82	86	95	77	4.37	4.03	6.36	5.62
1930 - 32	67	75	58	64	72	55	84	94	73	75	83	66	4.54	4.24	6.40	5.24
1940 - 42	59	66	51	55	62	48	77	87	66	80	89	70	3.29	2.74	4.50	3.79
1950 - 52	30	34	26	29	33	25	37	42	32	40	45	36	0.88	0.79	1.09	1.09
1960 - 62	22	25	19	22	24	19	26	30	22	27	30	24	0.36	0.36	0.37	0.43
1970 - 72	18	20	16	18	20	15	19	22	17	22	24	20	0.17	0.17	0.17	0.12
1980 - 82	12	13	10	11	13	10	12	13	10	13	15	12	0.09	0.09	0.14	0.06
1990 - 92	7	8	6	7	8	6	7	8	6	7	8	6	0.07	0.07	0.10	-
2000 - 02	5	6	5	5	6	5	5	6	5	5	6	5	0.07	0.06	0.12	0.05
	KKAW	KKAX	KKAY	KKAZ	KKBW	KKBX	KKBY	KKBZ	KKCW	KKCX	KKCY	KKCZ	KKDW	KKDX	KKDY	KKDZ
1996	6.1	6.8	5.4	6.1	6.9	5.4	6.2	6.7	5.5	5.8	6.7	4.8	0.07	0.07	0.10	0.04
1997	5.8	6.4	5.3	5.9	6.5	5.3	5.3	6.1	4.5	5.6	5.5	5.8	0.06	0.06	0.07	–
1998	5.7	6.3	5.0	5.7	6.4	5.0	5.6	6.2	4.9	5.6	6.1	5.1	0.07	0.07	0.09	0.04
1999	5.8	6.4	5.1	5.8	6.5	5.1	5.0	5.7	4.3	6.4	6.8	5.9	0.05	0.05	0.13	–
2000	5.6	6.1	5.0	5.6	6.1	5.1	5.7	6.4	5.1	5.1	5.5	4.6	0.07	0.06	0.15	–
2001	5.5	6.0	5.0	5.4	5.9	4.9	5.5	5.8	5.2	6.1	7.0	5.2	0.07	0.07	0.11	0.09
2002	5.2	5.9	4.5	5.2	5.9	4.5	5.3	6.4	4.1	4.7	4.8	4.6	0.06	0.06	0.10	0.05
2003	5.3	5.7	4.9	5.3	5.7	4.9	5.1	5.4	4.7	5.2	6.5	3.9	0.10	0.07	0.10	0.14
2004	5.0	5.5	4.6	5.0	5.5	4.6	4.9	5.8	4.0	5.3	5.4	5.2	0.07	0.07	0.11	0.04
2005	5.1	5.7	4.5	5.0	5.7	4.4	5.2	5.7	4.8	6.1	7.0	5.3	0.06	0.06	0.07	0.04
2006	5.0	5.4	4.5	5.0	5.4	4.6	4.5	5.1	3.8	5.2	5.8	4.5	0.07	0.06	0.13	0.13
2007	4.8	5.3	4.3	4.8	5.3	4.3	4.7	5.2	4.2	4.9	5.5	4.4	0.07	0.07	0.14	–

5.20

Infant and maternal mortality[1]
(i) - By country. (ii) - Infant mortality by country, type of death and sex

continued

Deaths per thousand live births

		1997	1998	1999	2000	2001	2002	2003	2004	2005	2006	2007
Total												
United Kingdom:												
Stillbirths[4]	KHNQ	5.3	5.4	5.3	5.3	5.3	5.6	5.7	5.7	5.3	5.3	5.2
Perinatal[4]	KHNR	8.3	8.3	8.2	8.1	8.0	8.3	8.5	8.3	8.0	7.9	7.7
Neonatal	KHNS	3.9	3.8	3.9	3.9	3.6	3.5	3.6	3.4	3.5	3.5	3.3
Post neonatal	KHNT	2.0	1.9	1.9	1.7	1.8	1.7	1.7	1.6	1.6	1.5	1.5
England and Wales:												
Stillbirths[4]	KHNU	5.3	5.3	5.3	5.3	5.3	5.6	5.7	5.7	5.4	5.4	5.2
Perinatal[4]	KHNV	8.3	8.2	8.2	8.2	8.0	8.3	8.5	8.4	8.0	8.0	7.7
Neonatal	KHNW	3.9	3.8	3.9	3.9	3.6	3.6	3.6	3.5	3.4	3.5	3.3
Post neonatal	KHNX	2.0	1.9	1.9	1.7	1.9	1.7	1.7	1.6	1.6	1.5	1.5
Scotland:												
Stillbirths[4]	KHNY	5.3	6.1	5.2	5.6	5.7	5.4	5.6	5.8	5.3	5.3	5.6
Perinatal[4]	KHNZ	7.8	8.7	7.6	8.4	8.5	7.6	8.0	8.1	7.7	7.4	7.8
Neonatal	KHOA	3.2	3.6	3.3	4.0	3.8	3.2	3.4	3.1	3.5	3.5	3.3
Post neonatal	KHOB	2.1	2.0	1.7	1.8	1.7	2.1	1.7	1.9	1.7	1.5	1.5
Northern Ireland:												
Stillbirths[4]	KHOC	5.4	5.1	5.7	4.3	5.1	5.7	4.9	5.0	4.0	3.8	4.1
Perinatal[4]	KHOD	8.2	8.1	10.0	7.3	8.5	8.9	8.0	8.0	8.1	7.1	6.9
Neonatal	KHOE	4.2	3.9	4.8	3.8	4.5	3.5	3.9	3.6	4.9	4.1	3.2
Post neonatal	KHOF	1.4	1.7	1.6	1.3	1.6	1.2	1.3	1.7	1.3	1.4	1.7
Males												
United Kingdom:												
Perinatal[4]	KHOG	8.7	8.8	8.7	8.7	8.6	8.9	8.8	8.8	8.3	8.3	8.1
Neonatal	KHOH	4.2	4.2	4.3	4.2	4.0	4.0	3.9	3.8	3.9	3.9	3.6
Infant mortality	KHOI	6.4	6.3	6.4	6.1	6.0	5.9	5.7	5.5	5.7	5.5	5.3
England and Wales:												
Perinatal[4]	KHOK	8.7	8.8	8.6	8.7	8.5	8.9	8.9	8.8	8.4	8.3	8.1
Neonatal	KHOL	4.2	4.3	4.3	4.2	3.9	4.0	3.8	3.8	3.8	3.8	3.6
Infant mortality	KHOM	6.5	6.4	6.5	6.1	5.9	5.9	5.7	5.5	5.7	5.4	5.3
Scotland:												
Perinatal[4]	KHOO	8.1	9.6	8.4	9.5	9.2	7.9	8.4	8.8	7.6	7.7	8.4
Neonatal	KHOP	3.4	4.0	3.8	4.5	4.0	3.7	3.6	3.6	3.8	4.0	3.5
Infant mortality	KHOQ	6.1	6.2	5.7	6.4	5.8	6.4	5.4	5.8	5.7	5.6	5.2
Northern Ireland:												
Perinatal[4]	KHOS	8.5	8.9	10.5	8.0	9.8	10.0	8.2	8.2	9.2	7.5	7.2
Neonatal	KHOT	4.3	4.4	5.5	4.2	5.3	3.8	4.6	3.7	5.5	5.0	3.4
Infant mortality	KHOU	5.5	6.1	6.8	5.5	7.0	4.8	6.5	5.4	7.0	5.8	5.5
Females												
United Kingdom:												
Perinatal[4]	KHOW	7.9	7.7	7.8	7.5	7.4	7.7	8.2	7.9	7.6	7.5	7.3
Neonatal	KHOX	3.5	3.3	3.4	3.5	3.3	3.1	3.4	3.1	3.1	3.2	3.0
Infant mortality	KHOY	5.3	5.0	5.1	5.0	5.0	4.5	4.9	4.6	4.5	4.5	4.3
England and Wales:												
Perinatal[4]	KHPA	7.9	7.7	7.8	7.6	7.3	7.7	8.2	8.0	7.6	7.6	7.4
Neonatal	KHPB	3.6	3.3	3.5	3.5	3.2	3.1	3.4	3.1	3.0	3.2	3.0
Infant mortality	KHPC	5.3	5.0	5.1	5.1	4.9	4.5	4.9	4.6	4.4	4.6	4.3
Scotland:												
Perinatal[4]	KHPE	7.5	7.9	6.7	7.2	7.8	7.2	7.7	7.3	7.9	7.1	7.3
Neonatal	KHPF	2.9	3.2	2.8	3.5	3.5	2.6	3.1	2.5	3.2	2.9	3.0
Infant mortality	KHPG	4.5	4.9	4.3	5.1	5.2	4.1	4.7	4.0	4.8	3.8	4.2
Northern Ireland:												
Perinatal[4]	KHPI	8.0	7.3	9.5	6.5	7.0	7.8	7.8	7.8	6.9	6.6	6.5
Neonatal	KHPJ	4.0	3.4	4.1	3.4	3.6	3.1	3.2	3.5	4.2	3.1	3.0
Infant mortality	KHPK	5.8	5.1	5.9	4.6	5.2	4.6	3.9	5.2	5.3	4.5	4.4

1 See chapter text.
2 From 1937 to 1956 death rates are based on the births to which they relate
  in the current and preceding years.
3 Deaths in pregnancy and childbirth.
4 Deaths per 1,000 live and stillbirths. See chapter introduction.

Sources: Office for National Statistics;
General Register Office for Scotland;
General Register Office (Northern Ireland)

5.21 Death rates by sex and age[1]
United Kingdom

Rates per 1,000 population

	All ages	0-4	5-9	10-14	15-19	20-24	25-34	35-44	45-54	55-64	65-74	75-84	85 and over
Males													
1900 - 02	18.4	57.0	4.1	2.4	3.7	5.0	6.6	11.0	18.6	35.0	69.9	143.6	289.6
1910 - 12	14.9	40.5	3.3	2.0	3.0	3.9	5.0	8.0	14.9	29.8	62.1	133.8	261.5
1920 - 22	13.5	33.4	2.9	1.8	2.9	3.9	4.5	6.9	11.9	25.3	57.8	131.8	259.1
1930 - 32	12.9	22.3	2.3	1.5	2.6	3.3	3.5	5.7	11.3	23.7	57.9	134.2	277.0
1940 - 42	..	..	..	..	..	..	..	..	..	..	..	..	..
1950 - 52	12.6	7.7	0.7	0.5	0.9	1.4	1.6	3.0	8.5	23.2	55.2	127.6	272.0
1960 - 62	12.5	6.4	0.5	0.4	0.9	1.1	1.1	2.5	7.4	22.2	54.4	123.4	251.0
1970 - 72	12.4	4.6	0.4	0.4	0.9	1.0	1.0	2.4	7.3	20.9	52.9	116.3	246.1
1980 - 82	12.1	3.2	0.3	0.3	0.8	0.9	0.9	1.9	6.3	18.2	46.7	107.1	224.9
1990 - 92	11.2	2.0	0.2	0.2	0.7	0.9	1.0	1.8	4.6	14.2	38.6	93.0	201.4
2000 - 02	10.0	1.4	0.1	0.2	0.5	0.8	1.0	1.6	4.0	10.4	28.9	75.2	187.7
	KHZA	KHZB	KHZC	KHZD	KHZE	KHZF	KHZG	KHZH	KHZJ	KHZK	KHZL	KHZM	KHZN
1996	10.8	1.6	0.1	0.2	0.6	0.9	1.0	1.7	4.2	12.3	35.2	86.0	199.6
1997	10.6	1.5	0.2	0.2	0.6	1.0	1.0	1.7	4.1	11.8	33.9	83.2	196.7
1998	10.5	1.5	0.1	0.2	0.6	0.9	1.1	1.7	4.1	11.6	33.0	81.8	193.6
1999	10.5	1.5	0.1	0.2	0.6	0.9	1.0	1.7	4.1	11.2	32.2	80.9	195.7
2000	10.1	1.4	0.1	0.2	0.6	0.8	1.0	1.6	4.0	10.7	30.3	76.8	187.9
2001	9.9	1.3	0.1	0.2	0.6	0.8	1.0	1.6	4.0	10.4	28.6	74.8	186.9
2002	9.9	1.4	0.1	0.2	0.5	0.8	1.0	1.6	4.0	10.1	27.8	74.1	188.2
2003	9.9	1.4	0.1	0.1	0.5	0.8	1.0	1.6	3.9	9.9	27.0	73.6	191.7
2004	9.5	1.4	0.1	0.1	0.5	0.7	0.9	1.6	3.8	9.3	25.5	70.6	176.3
2005	9.5	1.4	0.1	0.1	0.5	0.7	0.9	1.6	3.7	9.3	24.8	68.7	187.8
2006	9.2	1.3	0.1	0.2	0.5	0.7	0.9	1.6	3.7	9.1	23.7	65.5	164.5
2007	9.2	1.3	0.1	0.1	0.5	0.7	0.9	1.6	3.6	9.0	23.1	63.9	162.5
Females													
1900 - 02	16.3	47.9	4.3	2.6	3.5	4.3	5.8	9.0	14.4	27.9	59.3	127.0	262.6
1910 - 12	13.3	34.0	3.3	2.1	2.9	3.4	4.4	6.7	11.5	23.1	50.7	113.7	234.0
1920 - 22	11.9	26.9	2.8	1.9	2.8	3.4	4.1	5.6	9.3	19.2	45.6	111.5	232.4
1930 - 32	11.5	17.7	2.1	1.5	2.4	2.9	3.3	4.6	8.3	17.6	43.7	110.1	246.3
1940 - 42	..	..	..	..	..	..	..	..	..	..	..	..	..
1950 - 52	11.2	6.0	0.5	0.4	0.7	1.0	1.4	2.3	5.3	12.9	35.5	98.4	228.8
1960 - 62	11.2	4.9	0.3	0.3	0.4	0.5	0.8	1.8	4.5	11.0	30.8	87.3	218.5
1970 - 72	11.3	3.6	0.3	0.2	0.4	0.4	0.6	1.6	4.5	10.5	27.5	76.7	196.1
1980 - 82	11.4	2.3	0.2	0.2	0.3	0.4	0.5	1.3	3.9	9.9	24.8	67.2	179.5
1990 - 92	11.1	1.5	0.1	0.2	0.3	0.3	0.4	1.1	2.9	8.4	22.1	58.7	157.2
2000 - 02	10.5	1.1	0.1	0.1	0.2	0.3	0.4	1.0	2.6	6.4	17.9	51.1	157.3
	KHZO	KHZP	KHZQ	KHZR	KHZS	KHZT	KHZU	KHZV	KHZW	KHZX	KHZY	KHZZ	KHZI
1996	11.1	1.2	0.1	0.1	0.3	0.3	0.5	1.1	2.7	7.3	21.0	56.4	159.4
1997	11.0	1.2	0.1	0.1	0.3	0.3	0.4	1.1	2.7	7.1	20.5	55.2	160.3
1998	11.0	1.2	0.1	0.1	0.3	0.3	0.4	1.0	2.7	7.0	20.2	54.4	159.8
1999	11.0	1.2	0.1	0.1	0.3	0.3	0.4	1.0	2.7	6.9	19.6	54.2	163.7
2000	10.5	1.1	0.1	0.1	0.3	0.3	0.5	1.0	2.7	6.6	18.5	51.6	155.8
2001	10.4	1.1	0.1	0.1	0.2	0.3	0.4	1.0	2.6	6.4	17.8	50.8	155.8
2002	10.5	1.0	0.1	0.1	0.2	0.3	0.4	1.0	2.6	6.2	17.4	51.0	160.3
2003	10.6	1.2	0.1	0.1	0.2	0.3	0.4	1.0	2.6	6.1	17.1	51.8	166.4
2004	10.0	1.1	0.1	0.1	0.2	0.3	0.4	1.0	2.4	5.8	16.2	49.3	155.2
2005	10.0	1.1	0.1	0.1	0.2	0.3	0.4	0.9	2.5	5.9	15.8	48.2	160.1
2006	9.6	1.1	0.1	0.1	0.2	0.3	0.4	0.9	2.4	5.7	15.2	46.4	144.9
2007	9.7	1.1	0.1	0.1	0.2	0.3	0.4	0.9	2.3	5.7	14.9	45.6	144.8

1 See chapter text.

Sources: Office for National Statistics;
General Register Office for Scotland;
Northern Ireland Statistics and Research Agency

5.22 Interim life tables, 2005-07

Age(x)	United Kingdom				England and Wales			
	Males		Females		Males		Females	
	l_x	e^0_x	l_x	e^0_x	l_x	e^0_x	l_x	e^0_x
0 years	100 000	77.2	100 000	81.5	100 000	77.4	100 000	81.7
5 years	99 355	72.7	99 477	76.9	99 356	72.9	99 478	77.1
10 years	99 298	67.7	99 434	71.9	99 300	68.0	99 435	72.1
15 years	99 223	62.8	99 377	67.0	99 227	63.0	99 379	67.2
20 years	98 981	57.9	99 266	62.0	99 000	58.2	99 271	62.2
25 years	98 627	53.1	99 132	57.1	98 670	53.4	99 141	57.3
30 years	98 232	48.3	98 963	52.2	98 292	48.5	98 976	52.4
35 years	97 711	43.5	98 729	47.3	97 798	43.8	98 748	47.5
40 years	97 051	38.8	98 369	42.5	97 171	39.0	98 401	42.7
45 years	96 135	34.2	97 800	37.7	96 294	34.4	97 845	37.9
50 years	94 761	29.6	96 885	33.1	94 970	29.8	96 957	33.2
55 years	92 614	25.3	95 449	28.5	92 891	25.4	95 558	28.7
60 years	89 405	21.1	93 309	24.1	89 759	21.2	93 469	24.3
65 years	84 346	17.2	90 005	19.9	84 839	17.3	90 251	20.0
70 years	76 869	13.6	84 917	15.9	77 494	13.7	85 305	16.0
75 years	66 023	10.4	77 044	12.3	66 793	10.5	77 583	12.4
80 years	50 841	7.7	64 700	9.1	51 684	7.7	65 362	9.2
85 years	32 518	5.6	47 253	6.5	32 242	5.6	47 939	6.5
90 years	15 761	3.9	27 108	4.5	16 245	4.0	27 673	4.5

Age(x)	Scotland				Northern Ireland			
	Males		Females		Males		Females	
	l_x	e^0_x	l_x	e^0_x	l_x	e^0_x	l_x	e^0_x
0 years	100 000	74.8	100 000	79.7	100 000	76.2	100 000	81.2
5 years	99 373	70.3	99 476	75.1	99 270	71.7	99 455	76.6
10 years	99 315	65.3	99 435	70.2	99 211	66.8	99 402	71.7
15 years	99 229	60.3	99 381	65.2	99 108	61.8	99 322	66.7
20 years	98 893	55.5	99 231	60.3	98 696	57.1	99 197	61.8
25 years	98 351	50.8	99 066	55.4	98 159	52.4	99 047	56.9
30 years	97 801	46.1	98 863	50.5	97 682	47.6	98 886	52.0
35 years	96 981	41.5	98 550	45.6	97 126	42.9	98 648	47.1
40 years	95 993	36.9	98 062	40.9	96 372	38.2	98 272	42.3
45 years	94 692	32.3	97 366	36.1	95 368	33.6	97 711	37.5
50 years	92 914	27.9	96 210	31.5	93 758	29.1	96 763	32.8
55 years	90 179	23.7	94 443	27.1	91 451	24.8	95 275	28.3
60 years	86 225	19.6	91 831	22.8	88 207	20.6	93 010	23.9
65 years	79 979	16.0	87 656	18.7	82 566	16.8	89 804	19.7
70 years	71 219	12.6	81 260	15.0	75 297	13.1	84 803	15.7
75 years	59 118	9.7	72 100	11.6	64 304	9.9	76 798	12.1
80 years	43 421	7.2	58 702	8.6	48 564	7.3	64 281	8.9
85 years	26 260	5.3	40 966	6.2	30 111	5.3	46 991	6.2
90 years	11 671	3.9	22 128	4.3	13 673	3.7	25 954	4.2

Note Column l_x shows the number who would survive to exact **age**(x), out of 100,000 born, who were subject throughout their lives to the death rates experienced in the three-year period indicated. Column e^0_x is 'the expectation of life', that is, the average future lifetime which would be lived by a person aged exactly x if likewise subject to the death rates experienced in the three-year period indicated. See introductory notes.

Source: Office for National Statistics: 01329 444681

Population and vital statistics

5.23 Adoptions by date of entry in Adopted Children Register: by sex, age and country

Numbers and Percentages

	All ages		Under 1		1-4		5-9		10-14		15-17	
	Numbers	Percentages	Numbers	Percentages	Numbers	Percentages	Numbers	Percentages	Numbers	Percentages	Numbers	Percentages
United Kingdom **Persons**												
	VOXI	VOXJ	VOXK	VOXL	VOXM	VOXN	VOXO	VOXP	VOXQ	VOXR	VOXS	VOXT
2002	6 239	100	313	5	2 737	44	1 937	31	999	16	253	4
2003	5 426	100	212	4	2 481	46	1 716	32	789	15	228	4
2004	6 116	100	274	5	2 843	46	1 856	30	847	14	269	4
2005	6 151	100	242	4	3 127	51	1 757	29	798	13	228	4
2006	5 539	100	216	4	2 788	50	1 608	29	696	13	226	4
2007	5 224	100	163	3	2 761	53	1 400	27	672	13	205	4
Males												
	VOXU	VOXV	VOXW	VOXX	VOXY	VOXZ	VOYA	VOYB	VOYC	VOYD	VOYE	VOYF
2002	3 140	100	176	6	1 425	45	935	30	488	16	116	4
2003	2 634	100	104	4	1 224	46	844	32	351	13	111	4
2004	3 051	100	145	5	1 426	47	936	31	418	14	126	4
2005	3 072	100	121	4	1 566	51	910	30	370	12	105	3
2006	2 708	100	97	4	1 377	51	806	30	314	12	113	4
2007	2 614	100	83	3	1 392	53	714	27	314	12	103	4
Females												
	VOYG	VOYH	VOYI	VOYJ	VOYK	VOYL	VOYM	VOYN	VOYO	VOYP	VOYQ	VOYR
2002	3 099	100	137	4	1 312	42	1 002	32	511	16	137	4
2003	2 792	100	108	4	1 257	45	872	31	438	16	117	4
2004	3 065	100	129	4	1 417	46	920	30	456	15	143	5
2005	3 079	100	121	4	1 561	51	847	28	428	14	122	4
2006	2 831	100	119	4	1 411	50	802	28	382	13	113	4
2007	2 610	100	80	3	1 369	52	686	26	358	14	102	4
England and Wales[1] **Persons**												
	GQTP	GQTQ	GQTR	GQTS	GQTT	GQTU	GQTV	GQTW	GQTX	GQTY	GQTZ	GQUA
2002	5 680	100	287	5	2 532	45	1 748	31	900	16	213	4
2003	4 818	100	183	4	2 260	47	1 503	31	683	14	189	4
2004	5 562	100	253	5	2 627	47	1 651	30	786	14	245	4
2005	5 565	100	222	4	2 906	52	1 555	28	683	12	199	4
2006	4 980	100	197	4	2 592	52	1 406	28	585	12	195	4
2007	4 637	100	151	3	2 510	54	1 206	26	576	12	171	4
Males												
	GQUB	GQUC	GQUD	GQUE	GQUF	GQUG	GQUH	GQUI	GQUJ	GQUK	GQUL	GQUM
2002	2 871	100	160	6	1 324	46	846	29	443	15	98	3
2003	2 339	100	91	4	1 115	48	737	32	301	13	95	4
2004	2 777	100	132	5	1 327	48	831	30	373	13	114	4
2005	2 791	100	112	4	1 461	52	808	29	320	11	90	3
2006	2 446	100	95	4	1 282	52	707	29	267	11	94	4
2007	2 315	100	77	3	1 253	54	618	27	270	12	89	4
Females												
	GQUN	GQUO	GQUP	GQUQ	GQUR	GQUS	GQUT	GQUU	GQUV	GQUW	GQUX	GQUY
2002	2 809	100	127	5	1 208	43	902	32	457	16	115	4
2003	2 479	100	92	4	1 145	46	766	31	382	15	94	4
2004	2 785	100	121	4	1 300	47	820	29	413	15	131	5
2005	2 774	100	110	4	1 445	52	747	27	363	13	109	4
2006	2 534	100	102	4	1 310	52	699	28	318	13	101	4
2007	2 322	100	74	3	1 257	54	588	25	306	13	82	4

5.23 Adoptions by date of entry in Adopted Children Register: by sex, age and country

continued

Numbers and Percentages

	All ages		Under 1		1-4		5-9		10-14		15-17	
	Numbers	Percentages	Numbers	Percentages	Numbers	Percentages	Numbers	Percentages	Numbers	Percentages	Numbers	Percentages

Scotland[1]
Persons

	GQUZ	GQVA	GQVB	GQVC	GQVD	GQVE	GQVF	GQVG	GQVH	GQVI	GQVJ	GQVK
2002	385	100	13	3	143	37	130	34	73	19	26	7
2003	468	100	25	5	153	33	170	36	88	19	32	7
2004	393	100	21	5	144	37	143	36	67	17	18	5
2005	439	100	18	4	162	37	155	35	81	18	23	5
2006	418	100	16	4	153	37	150	36	73	17	26	6
2007	440	100	9	2	198	45	141	32	65	15	27	6

Males

	GQVL	GQVM	GQVN	GQVO	GQVP	GQVQ	GQVR	GQVS	GQVT	GQVU	GQVV	GQVW
2002	193	100	8	4	75	39	60	31	37	19	13	7
2003	228	100	11	5	78	34	85	37	43	19	11	5
2004	200	100	13	7	67	34	77	39	34	17	9	5
2005	217	100	9	4	80	37	79	36	36	17	13	6
2006	194	100	2	1	72	37	78	40	25	13	17	9
2007	229	100	4	2	115	50	70	31	30	13	10	4

Females

	GQVX	GQVY	GQVZ	GQWA	GRFK	GRFL	GRFM	GRFN	GRFO	GRFP	GRFQ	GRFR
2002	192	100	5	3	68	35	70	36	36	19	13	7
2003	240	100	14	6	75	31	85	35	45	19	21	9
2004	193	100	8	4	77	40	66	34	33	17	9	5
2005	222	100	9	4	82	37	76	34	45	20	10	5
2006	224	100	14	6	81	36	72	32	48	22	9	4
2007	211	100	5	2	83	39	71	34	35	17	17	8

Northern Ireland
Persons

	VOYS	VOYT	VOYU	VOYV	VOYW	VOYX	VOYY	VOYZ	VOZA	VOZB	VOZC	VOZD
2002	174	100	13	7	62	36	59	34	26	15	14	8
2003	140	100	4	3	68	49	43	31	18	13	7	5
2004	161	100	–	2	72	43	62	38	21	12	6	4
2005	147	100	2	4	59	38	47	32	34	21	5	4
2006	141	100	2	2	44	31	52	36	38	27	5	4
2007	147	100	3	2	53	36	53	36	31	21	7	5

Males

	VOZE	VOZF	VOZG	VOZH	VOZI	VOZJ	VOZK	VOZL	VOZM	VOZN	VOZO	VOZP
2002	76	100	8	11	26	34	29	38	8	11	5	7
2003	67	100	2	3	31	46	22	33	7	10	5	7
2004	74	100	–	–	32	43	28	38	11	15	3	4
2005	64	100	–	–	25	39	23	36	14	22	2	3
2006	68	100	–	–	23	35	21	29	22	32	2	3
2007	70	100	2	3	24	34	26	37	14	20	4	6

Females

	VOZQ	VOZR	VOZS	VOZT	VOZU	VOZV	VOZW	VOZX	VOZY	VOZZ	VPAA	VPVD
2002	98	100	5	5	36	37	30	31	18	18	9	9
2003	73	100	2	3	37	51	21	29	11	15	2	3
2004	87	100	–	–	40	46	34	39	10	11	3	3
2005	83	100	2	2	34	41	24	29	20	24	3	4
2006	73	100	3	4	20	27	31	42	16	22	3	4
2007	77	100	1	1	29	38	27	35	17	22	3	4

1 England & Wales: number of persons aged over 17 (counted into 'All ages')

Year	Persons	Male	Female
2006	5	1	4
2007	23	8	15

Scotland: number of persons aged over 17 (counted into 15-17 age group)

Year	Persons	Male	Female
2002	4	1	3
2003	4	3	1
2004	3	-	3
2006	5	5	-

Sources: Office for National Statistics: 01329 444410;
General Register Office for Scotland;
Northern Ireland Statistics and Research Agency

Education

Chapter 6

Education

Educational establishments in the UK are administered and financed in several ways. Most schools are controlled by local authorities, which are part of the structure of local government, but some are 'assisted', receiving grants direct from central government sources and being controlled by governing bodies which have a substantial degree of autonomy. Completely outside the public sector are non maintained schools run by individuals, companies or charitable institutions.

For the purposes of UK education statistics, schools fall under the following broad categories:

Mainstream state schools
(In Northern Ireland, grant-aided mainstream schools)

These schools work in partnership with other schools and local authorities and they receive funding from local authorities. Since 1 September 1999, the categories (typically in England) are:

Community – schools formerly known as 'county' plus some former grant-maintained (GM) schools

Foundation – most former GM schools

Voluntary Aided – schools formerly known as 'aided' and some former GM schools

Voluntary Controlled – schools formerly known as 'controlled'

Non-maintained mainstream schools
These consist of:

(a) Independent schools

Schools which charge fees and may also be financed by individuals, companies or charitable institutions. These include Direct Grant schools, where the governing bodies are assisted by departmental grants and a proportion of the pupils attending them do so free or under an arrangement by which local authorities meet tuition fees. City Technology Colleges (CTCs) and Academies (applicable in England only) are also included as independent schools.

(b) Non-maintained schools

Run by voluntary bodies who may receive some grant from central government for capital work and for equipment, but their current expenditure is met primarily from the fees charged to the local authorities for pupils placed in schools.

Special schools

Special schools provide education for children with Special Educational Needs (SEN) (In Scotland, Record of Needs or a Coordinated Support Plan), who cannot be educated satisfactorily in an ordinary school. Maintained special schools are run by local authorities, while non-maintained special schools are financed as described at (b) above.

Pupil Referral Units

Pupil Referral Units (PRUs) operate in England and Wales and provide education outside of a mainstream or special school setting, to meet the needs of difficult or disruptive children.

Schools in Scotland are categorised as Education Authority, Grant-aided, Opted-out/Self-governing (these three being grouped together as 'Publicly funded' schools), Independent schools and Partnership schools.

The home government departments dealing with education statistics are:

Department for Children, Schools and Families (DCSF)

Department for Innovation, Universities and Skills (DIUS)

Welsh Assembly Government (WAG)

Scottish Government (SG)

Northern Ireland Department of Education (DENI)

Northern Ireland Department for Employment and Learning (DELNI)

Each of the home education departments in Great Britain, along with the Northern Ireland Department of Education, have overall responsibility for funding the schools sectors in their own country.

Up to March 2001, further education (FE) courses in FE sector colleges in England and in Wales were largely funded through grants from the respective FE funding councils. In April 2001, however, the Learning and Skills Council (LSC) took over the responsibility for funding the FE sector in England, and the National Council for Education and Training for Wales (part of Education and Learning Wales – ELWa) did so for Wales.

The LSC in England is also responsible for funding provision for FE and some non-prescribed higher education in FE sector colleges; it also funds some FE provided by local authority maintained and other institutions referred to as 'external institutions'. In Wales, the National Council – ELWa, funds FE provision made by FE institutions via a third party or sponsored arrangements. The Scottish Further Education Funding Council (SFEFC) funds FE colleges in Scotland, while the Department for Employment and Learning funds FE colleges in Northern Ireland.

Higher education (HE) courses in higher education establishments are largely publicly funded through block grants from the HE funding councils in England and Scotland, the Higher Education Council – ELWa in Wales, and the Department for Employment and Learning in Northern Ireland. In addition, some designated HE (mainly HND/HNC Diplomas and Certificates of HE) is also funded by these sources. The FE sources mentioned above fund the remainder.

Statistics for the separate systems obtained in England, Wales, Scotland and Northern Ireland are collected and processed separately in accordance with the particular needs of the responsible departments. Since 1994/95 the Higher Education Statistics Agency (HESA) has undertaken the data collection for all higher education institutions (HEIs) in the UK. This includes the former Universities Funding Council (UFC) funded UK universities previously collected by the Universities Statistical Record. There are some structural differences in the information collected for schools, FE and HE in each of the four home countries and in some tables the GB/UK data presented are amalgamations from sources that are not entirely comparable.

Stages of education

There are five stages of education: early years, primary, secondary, FE and HE, and education is compulsory for all children between the ages of 5 (4 in Northern Ireland) and 16. The non-compulsory fourth stage, FE, covers non-advanced education, which can be taken at further (including tertiary) education colleges, HE institutions (HEIs) and increasingly in secondary schools. The fifth stage, HE, is study beyond GCE A levels and their equivalent which, for most full-time students, takes place in universities and other HEIs.

Early years education

Children under 5 attend a variety of settings including state nursery schools, nursery classes within primary schools and, in England and Wales, reception classes within primary schools, as well as settings outside the state sector such as voluntary pre-schools or privately run nurseries. In recent years there has been a major expansion of early years education, and the *Education Act 2002* extended the National Curriculum for England to include the foundation stage. The foundation stage was introduced in September 2000, and covered children's education from the age of 3 to the end of the reception year, when most are just 5 and some almost 6 years old. The Early Years Foundation Stage (EYFS), came into force in September 2008, and is a single regulatory and quality framework for the provision of learning, development and care for children in all registered early years settings between birth and the academic year in which they turn 5.

Children born in Scotland between March and December are eligible for early years education at the time the Pre-School Education and Day Care Census is carried out. In Scotland, early years education is called ante-pre-school education for those aged 3 to 4 years old, and pre-school education for those aged 4.

Primary education

The primary stage covers three age ranges: nursery (under 5), infant (5 to 7 or 8) and junior (up to 11 or 12) but in Scotland and Northern Ireland there is generally no distinction between infant and junior schools. Most public sector primary schools take both boys and girls in mixed classes. It is usual to transfer straight to secondary school at age 11 (in England, Wales and Northern Ireland) or 12 (in Scotland), but in England some children make the transition via middle schools catering for various age ranges between 8 and 14. Depending on their individual age ranges middle schools are classified as either primary or secondary.

Secondary education

Public provision of secondary education in an area may consist of a combination of different types of school, the pattern reflecting historical circumstance and the policy adopted by the local authority. Comprehensive schools largely admit pupils without reference to ability or aptitude and cater for all the children in a neighbourhood, but in some areas they co exist with grammar, secondary modern or technical schools. In 2005/06, 88 per cent of secondary pupils in England attended comprehensive schools while all secondary schools in Wales are comprehensive schools. The majority of education authority secondary schools in Scotland are comprehensive in character and offer six years of secondary education; however in remote areas there are several two-year and four-year secondary schools. In Northern Ireland, post-primary education is provided by grammar schools and non-selective secondary schools. In England, the Specialist Schools Programme helps schools, in partnership with private sector sponsors and supported by additional government funding, to establish distinctive identities through their chosen specialisms and achieve their targets to raise standards. Specialist schools have a special focus on their chosen subject area but must meet the National Curriculum requirements and deliver a broad and balanced education to all pupils. Any maintained secondary school in England can apply to be designated as a specialist school in one of ten specialist areas: arts, business & enterprise, engineering, humanities, languages, mathematics & computing, music, science, sports and technology. Schools can also combine any two specialisms.

Academies, operating in England, are publicly funded independent local schools that provide free education. They are all ability schools established by sponsors from business, faith or voluntary groups working with partners from the local community. The DCSF Secretary of State announced in July 2007, that all new academies (that is, not including those with a signed agreement although they could if they wished), would be required to follow the National Curriculum programmes of study in English, mathematics, science and information and communication technology (ICT). This is different to the previous model whereby academies had to teach English, mathematics, science and ICT to all pupils and the curriculum had to be broad and balanced.

Special schools

Special schools (day or boarding) provide education for children who require specialist support to complete their education, for example because they have physical or other difficulties. Many pupils with special educational needs are educated in mainstream schools. All children attending special schools are offered a curriculum designed to overcome their learning difficulties and to enable them to become self-reliant. Since December 2005, special schools have also been able to apply for the Special Educational Needs (SEN) specialism, under the Specialist Schools Programme. They can apply for a curriculum specialism, but not for both the SEN and a curriculum specialism.

Further education

The term further education may be used in a general sense to cover all non advanced courses taken after the period of compulsory education, but more commonly it excludes those staying on at secondary school and those in higher education, that is, courses in universities and colleges leading to qualifications above GCE A Level, Scottish Certificate of Education (SCE) Higher Grade, GNVQ/NVQ level 3, and their equivalents. Since 1 April 1993, sixth

form colleges in England and Wales have been included in the further education sector.

Higher education

Higher education is defined as courses that are of a standard that is higher than GCE A level, the Higher Grade of the SCE/National Qualification, GNVQ/NVQ level 3 or the Edexcel (formerly BTEC) or SQA National Certificate/ Diploma. There are three main levels of HE course:

(i)   Postgraduate courses leading to higher degrees, diplomas and certificates (including postgraduate certificates of education (PGCE) and professional qualifications) which usually require a first degree as entry qualification.

(ii)   Undergraduate courses which includes first degrees, first degrees with qualified teacher status, enhanced first degrees, first degrees obtained concurrently with a diploma, and intercalated first degrees (where first degree students, usually in medicine, dentistry or veterinary medicine, interrupt their studies to complete a one-year course of advanced studies in a related topic).

(iii)   Other undergraduate courses which includes all other higher education courses, for example HNDs and Diplomas in HE.

As a result of the *Further and Higher Education Act 1992*, former polytechnics and some other HEIs were designated as universities in 1992/93. Students normally attend HE courses at HEIs, but some attend at FE colleges. Some also attend institutions which do not receive public grant (such as the University of Buckingham) and these numbers are excluded from the tables, however, the University of Buckingham is included in Table 6.10.

6.1 Number of schools by type and establishments of further and higher education
Academic years

Numbers

		1995[1]/96	2002[1]/03	2003[1]/04	2004[1]/05	2005[1]/06	2006[1]/07	2007/08
United Kingdom:								
Public sector mainstream								
Nursery[2,3]	KBFK	1 486	3 394	3 438	3 425	3 349	3 326	3 273
Primary[4]	KBFA	23 441	22 638	22 509	22 343	22 156	21 968	21 768
Secondary[5,6,7]	KBFF	4 478	4 302	4 281	4 261	4 244	4 232	4 209
of which 6th form colleges	KPGM	..	..	..	..	..	..	..
Non-maintained mainstream[8]	KBFU	2 485	2 362	2 498	2 445	2 455	2 486	2 527
Special - all	KBFP	1 560	1 473	1 465	1 436	1 416	1 391	1 378
maintained	KPVX	1 456	1 369	1 362	1 329	1 311	1 285	1 264
non maintained	KPGO	104	104	103	107	105	106	114
Pupil referral units	KXEP	315	390	457	478	481	489	506
Universities (including Open University)[9,10,11]	KAHG	114	110	112	117	119	120	120
All other further and higher education institutions	KJPQ	611	526	522	530	523	507	489
Higher education institutions	KPVY	68	60	57	50	47	48	45
Further education institutions	KSNY	543	466	465	480	476	459	444
of which 6th form colleges	KPGP	110	103	102	102	102	96	95
England:								
Public sector mainstream								
Nursery	KBAK	547	475	468	456	453	446	445
Primary	KBAA	18 480	17 861	17 762	17 642	17 504	17 361	17 205
Secondary[5,6,7]	KBAF	3 609	3 454	3 435	3 416	3 405	3 399	3 383
of which 6th form colleges	KPGS	..	..	..	..	..	..	..
Non-maintained maintream[8]	KBAU	2 251	2 162	2 304	2 252	2 263	2 286	2 329
Special - all	KBAP	1 263	1 160	1 148	1 122	1 105	1 078	1 065
maintained	KPGT	1 191	1 088	1 078	1 049	1 033	1 006	993
non maintained	KPGU	72	72	70	73	72	72	72
Pupil referral units	KXEQ	291	360	420	447	449	448	455
Universities (including Open University)[9,10]	KAHM	92	88	89	95	96	98	98
All other further and higher education institutions	KJPR	503	426	423	431	425	411	406
Higher education institutions	KPXA	50	45	43	36	34	34	33
Further education institutions	KPWC	453	381	380	395	391	377	373
of which 6th form colleges	KPGV	110	103	102	102	102	96	95
Wales:								
Public sector mainstream								
Nursery	KBBK	52	37	34	34	33	31	28
Primary	KBBA	1 681	1 602	1 588	1 572	1 555	1 527	1 509
Secondary[6]	KBBF	228	227	227	227	224	224	222
of which 6th form colleges	KPGY	..	..	..	..	..	..	..
Non-maintained	KBBU	62	59	60	58	56	66	66
Special (Maintained)	KBBP	54	43	43	43	43	44	44
Pupil referral units	KZBF	24	30	31	31	32	41	51
Universities[9,11]	KAHS	7	7	8	7	7	7	7
All other further and higher education institutions	KJQP	33	29	28	28	28	28	26
Higher education institutions	KSNZ	7	6	5	5	5	5	4
Further education institutions	KPGZ	26	23	23	23	23	23	22
Scotland:								
Public sector mainstream								
Nursery[2]	KBDK	796	2 782	2 836	2 836	2 763	2 750	2 702
Primary	KBDA	2 332	2 258	2 248	2 217	2 194	2 184	2 169
Secondary	KBDF	405	386	386	386	385	381	378
Non-maintained	KBDU	151	119	117	118	117	116	115
Special - all	KBDP	196	223	227	226	223	224	226
maintained	KYCZ	164	191	194	192	190	190	184
non-maintained	KYDA	32	32	33	34	33	34	42
Universities[9]	KAHX	13	13	13	13	14	13	13
All other further and higher education institutions	KJRA	56	53	53	53	52	50	49
Higher education institutions	KPWE	9	7	7	7	6	7	6
Further education institutions	KPHB	47	46	46	46	46	43	43
Northern Ireland:								
Grant aided mainstream								
Nursery[3]	KBEK	91	100	100	99	100	99	98
Primary[4]	KBEA	948	917	911	912	903	896	885
Secondary	KBEF	236	235	233	232	230	228	226
Non-maintained	KBEU	21	22	17	17	19	18	17
Special (Maintained)	KBEP	47	47	47	45	45	45	43
Universities	KIAD	2	2	2	2	2	2	2
Colleges of education	KIAE	2	2	2	2	2	2	2
Further education colleges	KIAG	17	16	16	16	16	16	6

1 Includes revised data.

2 Nursery schools figures for Scotland prior to 1998/99 only include data for Local Authority pre-schools. Data thereafter include partnership pre-schools. From 2005/06, figures exclude pre-school education centres not in partnership with the Local Authority.

3 Excludes voluntary and private pre-school education centres in Northern Ireland (366 in total in 2007/08).

4 From 1995/96, includes Preparatory Departments in Northern Ireland Grammar Schools (17 in total in 2007/08).

5 Time series revised to show State-funded secondary schools (i.e. including City Technology Colleges (CTCs) and Academies in England, previously included in the 'Non-maintained' category). In 2007/08, there were 5 CTCs and 83 Academies in England.

6 Excludes sixth form colleges in England and Wales which were reclassified as further education colleges on 1 April 1993.

7 Includes Specialist schools in England, operational from September of the first year shown (2,799 in total in 2007/08).

8 Revised to exclude CTCs and Academies - see footnote 5.

9 Includes former polytechnics and colleges which became universities as a result of the Further and Higher Education Act 1992.

10 Includes the members of the University of London separately.

11 Includes the members of the University of Wales separately.

Source: Education Departments: 01325 391266

6.2 Full-time and part-time pupils in school[1] by age and sex[2]
United Kingdom
All schools at January[3]

Thousands

		1998	1999	2000	2001	2002	2003	2004	2005	2006	2007[4]	2008[5]
Age at previous 31 August[6]												
Number (thousands)												
England[7]	KBIA	8 261	8 310	8 346	8 374	8 369	8 367	8 335	8 274	8 216	8 149	8 102
Wales	KBIB	513	513	512	512	511	509	506	501	495	490	485
Scotland	KBIC	850	844	874	882	876	874	866	851	850	845	829
Northern Ireland[2]	KBID	352	352	349	348	346	345	341	337	333	329	326
United Kingdom	KBIE	9 975	10 020	10 081	10 116	10 102	10 095	10 048	9 963	9 893	9 813	9 742
Boys and girls												
2 - 4[8]	KBIF	1 149	1 154	1 184	1 187	1 180	1 189	1 145	1 138	1 130	1 139	1 160
5[9] - 10	KBIG	4 668	4 661	4 629	4 597	4 537	4 489	4 403	4 378	4 321	4 264	4 212
11	KBIH	746	762	783	771	783	791	784	758	756	739	730
12 - 14	KBII	2 182	2 211	2 256	2 297	2 320	2 343	2 355	2 369	2 344	2 309	2 265
15	KBIK	701	706	705	732	737	751	775	764	777	786	783
16	KBIL	288	283	285	287	298	290	314	304	304	314	320
17	KBIM	217	218	213	219	223	217	238	226	235	234	242
18 and over	KBIN	24	25	27	27	23	24	32	27	26	28	30
Boys												
14	KBIO	368	367	381	384	391	401	394	402	407	404	391
15	KBIP	358	361	359	374	377	384	394	390	397	401	401
16	KBIQ	140	137	138	139	145	140	150	146	146	150	154
17	KBIR	104	104	101	105	107	104	112	107	111	110	114
18 and over	KBIS	13	13	14	15	13	13	17	14	15	15	16
Girls												
14	KBIT	350	352	364	365	373	384	378	384	388	385	373
15	KBIU	343	345	346	358	360	368	379	375	380	385	382
16	KBIV	149	146	147	148	153	150	161	159	159	164	165
17	KBIW	113	114	111	114	116	113	124	119	123	124	128
18 and over	KBIX	11	11	13	12	11	11	15	12	12	13	14

1 From 1 April 1993 excludes 6th form colleges in England and Wales which were reclassified as further education colleges.

2 In Northern Ireland, a gender split is not collected by age but is available by year group and so this is used as a proxy.

3 In Scotland, as at the previous September.

4 Includes revised figures.

5 Provisional.

6 1 July for Northern Ireland and 31 December for non-maintained primary and secondary schools pupils in Scotland and age at census date in January for pre-school education in Scotland.

7 From 1992, figures for independent schools in England include pupils aged less than 2.

8 Includes the so-called "rising 5s" (i.e. those pupils who become 5 during the autumn term).

9 In Scotland, includes some 4-year-olds.

Source: Education Departments: 01325 391266

6.3 Number of pupils and teachers, and pupil:teacher ratios:[1] by school type
United Kingdom
At January[2]

Numbers

		2003	2004	2005[3]	2006[3]	2007[3,4]	2008[3,5]
All schools or departments							
Total							
Pupils (thousands)							
Full-time and full-time							
equivalent of part-time	KBCA	9 852.2	9 812.6	9 686.7	9 613.9	9 527.6	9 459.8
Teachers[6] (thousands)	KBCB	561.6	561.4	562.6	568.6	570.1	575.8
Pupils per teacher[6]:							
United Kingdom	KBCC	17.6	17.6	17.3	17.0	16.8	16.5
England	KBCD	17.9	17.8	17.5	17.2	17.1	16.8
Wales	KBCE	18.0	18.0	18.0	17.6	17.6	17.5
Scotland	KBCF	14.9	15.0	14.3	13.8	13.1	12.8
Northern Ireland	KBCG	16.3	16.5	16.5	16.7	16.8	16.7
Public sector mainstream schools or departments							
Nursery							
Pupils (thousands)							
Full-time and full-time							
equivalent of part-time	KBFM	84.8	83.9	29.1	29.1	29.4	29.0
Teachers[6] (thousands)	KBFN	3.6	3.5	1.7	1.7	1.7	1.7
Pupils per teacher[6]	KBFO	23.6	23.7	17.6	17.3	17.7	17.3
Primary[7]							
Pupils (thousands)							
Full-time and full-time							
equivalent of part-time	KBFB	5 021.9	4 953.9	4 896.6	4 831.9	4 778.8	4 747.6
Teachers[6] (thousands)	KBFD	228.9	224.9	224.2	226.6	226.3	227.5
Pupils per teacher[6]	KBFE	21.9	22.0	21.8	21.3	21.1	20.9
Secondary[8,9]							
Pupils (thousands)							
Full-time and full-time							
equivalent of part-time	KBFG	3 994.0	4 014.1	4 001.9	3 987.1	3 941.3	3 872.8
Teachers[6] (thousands)	KBFH	243.3	243.8	246.6	248.5	247.6	248.0
Pupils per teacher[6]	KBFI	16.4	16.5	16.2	16.0	15.9	15.6
Special schools							
Pupils (thousands)							
Full-time and full-time							
equivalent of part-time	KPGE	104.5	102.2	100.4	99.5	99.4	99.3
Teachers[6] (thousands)	KPGG	17.0	16.9	16.8	17.0	17.0	17.1
Pupils per teacher[6]	KPGI	6.1	6.1	6.0	5.9	5.9	5.8

1 'All schools' pupil: teacher ratios exclude Pupil Referral Units and non-maintained special schools.
2 In Scotland, as at the previous September.
3 Excluding nursery school figures for Scotland as FTE pupils numbers are not available.
4 Includes revised figures.
5 Provisional.
6 Figures of teachers and of pupil/teacher ratios take account of the full-time equivalent of part-time teachers.

7 Includes preparatory departments attached to grammar schools in Northern Ireland.
8 Includes voluntary grammar schools in Northern Ireland.
9 For 2007/08, State-funded secondary schools (i.e. including City Technology Colleges (CTCs) and Academies in England, which were previously included under 'Non-maintained').

Source: Education Departments: 01325 391266

6.4 Full-time and part-time pupils with special educational needs (SEN) or nearest equivalent)[1], 2007/08[2] United Kingdom

By type of school

Thousands and percentages

	United Kingdom	England[3]	Wales	Scotland	Northern Ireland
All schools					
Total pupils	9 748.4	8 102.2	484.6	829.3	332.4
SEN pupils[4] with statements	261.8	223.6	14.9	10.3	13.0
Incidence (%)[5]	2.7	2.8	3.1	1.2	3.9
State-funded schools[6]					
Nursery[7]					
Total pupils[8]	157.6	37.4	1.8	106.1	12.4
SEN pupils[4] with statements[9]	1.1	0.3	-	0.8	0.1
Incidence (%)[5]	0.7	0.7	0.5	0.7	0.6
Placement (%)[10]	0.4	0.1	0.1	7.6	0.5
Primary[11]					
Total pupils	4 892.0	4 087.8	261.6	375.9	166.6
SEN pupils[4] without statements[12]	830.8	739.9	49.7	14.1	27.1
SEN pupils[4] with statements	70.9	59.1	4.8	2.4	4.5
SEN Pupils[4] with statements-incidence (%)[5]	1.4	1.4	1.8	0.6	2.7
SEN Pupils[4] with statements-placement (%)[10]	27.1	26.4	32.3	23.5	35.0
Secondary[13]					
Total pupils	3 953.4	3 289.0	206.9	309.6	147.9
SEN pupils[4] without statements[12]	642.5	584.4	30.9	10.3	16.9
SEN pupils[4] with statements	80.1	67.3	5.6	3.0	4.2
SEN Pupils[4] with statements - incidence (%)[5]	2.0	2.0	2.7	1.0	2.8
SEN Pupils[4] with statements - placement (%)[10]	30.6	30.1	37.7	29.6	32.1
Special[14,15]					
Total pupils	100.2	84.8	4.0	6.7	4.6
SEN pupils[4] with statements	94.5	82.4	4.0	3.9	4.2
Incidence (%)[5]	94.3	97.2	100.0	57.5	91.0
Placement (%)[10]	36.1	36.9	27.1	37.5	32.3
Pupil referral units[14]					
Total pupils	16.7	16.1	0.6	..	..
SEN pupils[4] with statements	2.1	1.9	0.1	..	..
Incidence (%)[5]	12.3	12.1	18.5	..	..
Placement (%)[10]	0.8	0.9	0.8	..	..
Other schools					
Independent					
Total pupils	622.6	582.4	9.6	29.8	0.8
SEN pupils[4] with statements	8.4	8.1	0.3	-	..
Incidence (%)[5]	1.3	1.4	3.2	0.1	..
Placement (%)[10]	3.2	3.6	2.0	0.3	..
Non-maintained special[14]					
Total pupils	5.8	4.7	..	1.1	..
SEN pupils[4] with statements	4.7	4.5	..	0.2	..
Incidence (%)[5]	80.9	97.3	..	14.1	..
Placement (%)[10]	1.8	2.0	..	1.6	..

1 Scotland no longer has Special Educational Needs as the Education (Additional Support for Learning) (Scotland) Act 2004 (the Act) replaces the system for assessment and recording of children and young people with special educational needs. Nursery schools include the number of children registered for pre-school education with Additional Support Needs with a Coordinated Support Plan. Primary and secondary schools include pupils with a Record of Needs or a Coordinated Support Plan, including some who also had an individualised educational Programme (IEP).

2 Provisional.

3 Includes new codes for recording SEN status following the introduction of a new SEN Code of Practice from January 2002.

4 Or nearest equivalent.

5 Incidence of pupils - the number of pupils with statements within each school type expressed as a proportion of the total number of pupils on roll in each school type.

6 Grant-Aided schools in Northern Ireland.

7 Includes 6,535 pupils in Voluntary and Private Pre-School Centres in Northern Ireland funded under the Pre-School Expansion Programme which began in 1998/99.

8 In Scotland, pre-school registrations for places funded by the local authority, in centres providing pre-school education as a local authority centre or in partnership with the local authority only. Children are counted once for each centre they are registered with.

9 For Scotland, number of children registered for pre-school education and Additional Support Needs with a Coordinated Support Plan are likely to be an undercount as only centres that returned the full census form were asked about Coordinated Support Plans, and of those who were asked, not all completed them. Out of 2,702 centres, 713 did not provide this information.

10 Placement of pupils - the number of pupils with statements within each school type expressed as a proportion of the number of pupils with statements in all schools.

11 Includes nursery classes (except for Scotland, where they are included with Nursery schools) and reception classes in Primary schools.

12 For Scotland, those with IEP only used for the 'without statement' category.

13 City Technology Colleges (CTCs) and Acadamies in England, previously included with Independent schools are included with State-funded secondary schools, therefore figures are not directly comparable with previous years.

14 England and Wales figures exclude dually registered pupils, where applicable.

15 Including general and hospital special schools.

Source: Education Departments: 01325 391266

6.5 GCE, GCSE and SCE/NQ[1] and vocational qualifications obtained by pupils and students

United Kingdom

Percentages and thousands

	Pupils in their last year of compulsory education[2]					Pupils/students in education[3]	
						% achieving GCE A Levels and equivalent[4,5]	Population
	5 or more grades A*-C[6]	1-4 grades A*-C[6]	Grades D-G[7] only	No graded results	Total (=100%) (Thousands)	2 or more passes[8]	aged 17 (thousands)
2000/01							
All	51.0	24.1	19.4	5.5	729.7	37.4	717.9
Males	45.7	24.6	23.1	6.5	372.1	33.4	366.6
Females	56.5	23.6	15.5	4.4	357.6	41.6	351.3
2001/02							
All	52.5	23.7	18.4	5.4	732.5	37.4	739.0
Males	47.2	24.3	22.0	6.4	374.0	33.0	379.8
Females	58.0	23.1	14.6	4.3	358.5	42.0	359.2
2002/03							
All	53.5	23.1	18.2	5.2	750.2	38.4	771.2
Males	48.3	23.6	21.8	6.3	382.7	33.9	397.2
Females	58.8	22.7	14.4	4.1	367.6	43.2	374.0
2003/04							
All	54.2	22.7	18.8	4.4	772.0	39.2	769.5
Males	49.2	23.1	22.4	5.3	392.6	34.7	395.8
Females	59.3	22.2	15.0	3.4	379.4	44.0	373.7
2004/05							
All	57.0	22.1	17.9	3.0	759.1	38.3	788.5
Males	52.1	22.8	21.4	3.7	385.5	33.8	405.2
Females	62.1	21.4	14.2	2.3	373.5	43.1	383.4
2005/06							
All	59.0	21.4	16.9	2.7	773.8	37.3	807.3
Males	54.3	22.1	20.3	3.3	394.2	32.7	415.5
Females	63.9	20.6	13.5	2.1	379.6	42.1	391.8
2006/07[9]							
All	61.3	20.1	17.0	1.6	778.2	45.2	791.6
Males	56.9	20.6	20.5	2.1	395.8	39.5	407.8
Females	65.8	19.5	13.4	1.2	382.4	51.2	383.8

1 From 1999/00, National Qualifications (NQ) were introduced in Scotland but are not all shown until 2001/01. NQs include Standard Grades, Intermediate 1 & 2 and Higher Grades. The figures for Higher Grades combine the new NQ Higher and the old SCE Higher and include Advanced Highers.

2 Pupils aged 15 at the start of the acadamic year, pupils in Year S4 in Scotland. From 2004/05, pupils at the end of Key Stage 4 in England.

3 Pupils in schools and students in further education institutions generally aged 16-18 at the start of the academic year in England, Wales and Northern Ireland as a percentage of the 17 year old population. Data from 2002/03 for Wales and Northern Ireland however, relate to schools only. Pupils in Scotland generally sit Highers one year earlier than those sitting A levels in the rest of the UK, and the figures relate to the results of the pupils in Year S5/S6.

4 Figures, other than for Scotland, include Vocational Certificates of Education (VCE) and, previously, Advanced level GNVQ which is equivalent to 2 GCE A level or AS equivalents.

5 2 AS levels or 2 Highers/1Advanced Higher or 1 each in Scotland, count as 1 A level pass.

6 Standard Grades 1-3/Intermediate 2 A-C/Intermediate 1 A in Scotland.

7 Grades D-G at GCSE and Scottish Standard Grades 4-6/Intermediate 1 B and C/Access 3 (pass).

8 3 or more SCE/NQ Higher Grades/2 or more Advanced Highers/1 Advanced Higher with 2 or more Higher Passes in Scotland.

9 Provisional.

Source: Education Departments: 01325 391266

73

Education

6.6 Students in further[1] education: by country, mode of study,[2] sex and age,[3] during 2006/07

United Kingdom (home and overseas students)

Thousands

	United Kingdom		England[4]		Wales		Scotland[5]		Northern Ireland	
	Full-time	Part-time	Full-time	Part-time	Full-time	Part-time	Full-time	Part-time	Full-time	Part-time
All										
Age under 16	5.5	66.7	3.6	8.3	0.4	4.5	1.4	44.4	0.2	9.4
16	320.5	67.5	289.6	38.2	13.9	2.9	9.0	13.7	8.0	12.7
17	274.9	70.5	245.4	42.9	11.6	3.4	9.7	15.1	8.2	9.0
18	134.6	79.1	115.3	55.7	6.1	5.2	7.6	12.3	5.6	5.9
19	50.6	67.2	42.4	49.0	2.5	4.4	3.6	9.9	2.2	3.9
20	27.2	62.0	22.7	47.2	1.4	3.8	2.2	8.0	1.0	3.0
21	19.4	61.4	16.3	48.3	0.9	3.9	1.7	6.4	0.6	2.8
22	15.2	62.3	13.1	50.0	0.7	3.9	1.2	5.8	0.3	2.6
23	13.4	64.3	11.5	52.0	0.6	3.9	1.0	5.5	0.3	2.9
24	12.1	65.8	10.6	53.4	0.4	4.1	0.8	5.5	0.2	2.8
25	11.1	67.2	9.7	55.2	0.4	3.9	0.8	5.5	0.1	2.7
26	10.8	68.2	9.6	56.2	0.3	4.0	0.7	5.4	0.1	2.6
27	9.4	63.9	8.4	52.9	0.3	3.7	0.6	5.0	0.1	2.3
28	8.2	58.4	7.3	48.2	0.3	3.5	0.5	4.6	0.1	2.1
29	7.6	54.9	6.9	45.6	0.3	3.2	0.5	4.4	-	1.8
30+	124.6	1 601.6	114.6	1 275.0	3.6	128.6	5.6	152.8	0.8	45.3
Unknown	1.3	12.5	1.2	10.2	-	2.3	-	-	-	-
All ages	1 046.6	2 593.6	928.2	1 988.2	43.6	189.2	47.0	304.3	27.8	111.9
Males										
Age under 16	3.2	36.5	2.1	4.7	0.2	2.6	0.8	23.0	0.1	6.3
16	159.9	34.6	143.3	20.1	7.1	1.4	4.8	6.6	4.7	6.4
17	133.5	36.8	118.5	22.7	5.6	1.9	4.8	8.0	4.7	4.2
18	67.4	40.2	58.0	27.1	3.0	2.7	3.4	7.8	2.9	2.7
19	27.5	34.3	23.1	23.9	1.3	2.2	1.7	6.3	1.3	1.9
20	14.8	29.8	12.4	21.9	0.8	1.9	1.0	4.6	0.6	1.3
21	10.2	27.4	8.7	21.2	0.5	1.8	0.8	3.2	0.3	1.1
22	7.6	26.3	6.6	21.0	0.3	1.7	0.5	2.6	0.2	1.0
23	6.6	26.4	5.8	21.4	0.3	1.6	0.4	2.4	0.1	1.0
24	5.9	26.5	5.3	21.5	0.2	1.7	0.3	2.3	0.1	1.0
25	5.3	27.1	4.7	22.3	0.1	1.6	0.3	2.2	0.1	0.9
26	5.2	27.5	4.8	22.8	0.1	1.7	0.3	2.1	-	1.0
27	4.4	25.9	4.0	21.6	0.1	1.5	0.2	2.0	-	0.8
28	3.7	23.4	3.4	19.4	0.1	1.4	0.2	1.8	-	0.7
29	3.5	21.8	3.2	18.1	0.1	1.3	0.2	1.7	-	0.7
30+	55.7	575.2	52.6	457.1	1.1	46.8	1.6	55.3	0.3	16.0
Unknown	1.1	7.0	1.1	6.0	-	0.9	-	-	-	-
All Ages	515.4	1 026.7	457.4	772.9	21.1	74.6	21.4	132.0	15.5	47.2
Females										
Age under 16	2.4	30.1	1.5	3.7	0.2	1.9	0.6	21.5	0.1	3.2
16	160.6	32.9	146.3	18.0	6.8	1.5	4.2	7.1	3.3	6.3
17	141.4	33.7	126.9	20.2	6.0	1.6	5.0	7.1	3.5	4.8
18	67.2	38.8	57.3	28.6	3.0	2.5	4.2	4.5	2.7	3.2
19	23.2	32.9	19.3	25.1	1.1	2.2	1.9	3.6	0.9	2.0
20	12.5	32.3	10.3	25.3	0.6	1.9	1.2	3.3	0.4	1.7
21	9.2	34.1	7.6	27.1	0.4	2.1	0.9	3.1	0.2	1.7
22	7.6	36.0	6.5	29.0	0.3	2.3	0.7	3.2	0.2	1.6
23	6.8	37.8	5.8	30.6	0.3	2.3	0.6	3.1	0.1	1.8
24	6.2	39.2	5.3	31.9	0.3	2.4	0.5	3.2	0.1	1.7
25	5.8	40.2	5.0	32.9	0.2	2.3	0.5	3.3	0.1	1.7
26	5.6	40.6	4.9	33.4	0.2	2.4	0.4	3.3	0.1	1.6
27	5.1	38.0	4.5	31.3	0.2	2.2	0.4	3.0	0.1	1.5
28	4.5	35.0	3.9	28.8	0.2	2.1	0.4	2.8	0.1	1.4
29	4.1	33.2	3.7	27.5	0.2	1.9	0.3	2.7	-	1.1
30+	68.9	1 026.5	62.0	817.9	2.5	81.8	4.0	97.5	0.5	29.3
Unkown	0.2	5.5	0.1	4.2	-	1.4	-	-	-	-
All ages	531.2	1 566.9	470.8	1 215.3	22.6	114.6	25.6	172.3	12.2	64.7

1 Further education (FE) institution figures are whole year counts. Higher education (HE) institution figures are based on the HESA 'standard registration' count.

2 Full-time includes sandwich. Part-time comprises both day and evening, including block release and open/distance learning.

3 Ages as at 31 August 2006 (1 July in Northern Ireland and 31 December in Scotland).

4 FE institution figures for England include LSC funded students only.

5 Figures for Scotland FE colleges are vocational course enrolments rather than headcounts.

Source: Education Departments/DIUS: 01325 391266

6.7 Students in further education:[1] by country, mode of study,[2] sex and area[3] 2006/07

United Kingdom - Home and overseas students

Thousands

	United Kingdom		England[4]		Wales		Scotland[5]		Northern Ireland	
	Full-time	Part-time	Full-time	Part-time	Full-time	Part-time	Full-time	Part-time	Full-time	Part-time
All persons										
Health, Public Services and Care	115.8	373.3	104.4	298.8	-	-	8.3	65.7	3.1	8.8
Science and Mathermatics	61.3	47.8	57.9	32.7	-	-	1.3	5.0	2.1	10.1
Agriculture, Horticulture and Animal Care	24.3	39.3	22.7	29.2	-	-	1.3	9.4	0.3	0.7
Engineering and Manufacturing Technologies	54.3	110.3	46.9	78.3	-	0.1	5.0	25.5	2.3	6.4
Construction, Planning and the Built Environment	54.3	79.9	43.8	55.9	-	-	4.6	16.6	5.9	7.4
Information & Communication Technology	57.8	360.1	53.1	289.9	-	-	2.8	55.8	1.9	14.4
Retail and Commercial Enterprise	71.3	101.7	67.9	84.0	-	-	0.1	5.5	3.2	12.2
Leisure,Travel and Tourism	63.6	87.3	57.0	55.6	-	-	4.5	30.6	2.1	1.1
Arts, Media and Publishing	119.1	132.1	111.5	107.4	-	-	4.7	20.5	2.9	4.2
History, Philosophy and Theology	14.9	19.9	14.7	19.3	-	-	-	-	0.2	0.5
Social Sciences	19.3	9.2	18.5	7.3	-	-	-	-	0.8	1.9
Languages, Literature and Culture	30.5	170.8	27.5	127.1	-	3.3	2.8	25.0	0.2	15.4
Education and Training	4.6	90.2	4.3	74.9	-	-	-	-	0.3	15.3
Preparation for Life and Work	171.2	530.4	170.6	526.4	-	-	-	-	0.6	4.1
Business Adimnstration & Law	64.1	159.7	58.8	128.7	-	0.1	3.6	21.5	1.7	9.4
Other subjects[6] / Unknown	120.1	281.7	68.6	72.7	43.6	185.7	8.0	23.3	-	-
All subjects	1 046.6	2 593.6	928.2	1 988.2	43.6	189.2	47.0	304.3	27.8	111.9
Males										
Health, Public Services and Care	30.5	89.2	29.0	64.9	-	-	1.3	22.6	0.2	1.6
Science and Mathematics	28.1	15.4	26.8	9.7	-	-	0.5	2.1	0.8	3.6
Agriculture, Horticulture and Animal Care	11.4	18.9	10.6	13.0	-	-	0.7	5.8	0.2	0.2
Engineering and Manufacturing Technologies	50.9	95.5	43.9	68.3	-	0.1	4.7	21.4	2.3	5.7
Construction, Planning and the Built Environment	52.2	74.5	42.1	52.5	-	-	4.3	15.2	5.8	6.8
Information & Communication Technology	43.0	137.2	39.5	110.9	-	-	1.9	20.9	1.5	5.5
Retail and Commercial Enterprise	11.3	29.9	10.8	23.0	-	-	0.1	4.5	0.4	2.5
Leisure, Travel and Tourism	36.7	45.7	33.3	33.7	-	-	2.3	11.4	1.1	0.6
Arts Media and Publishing	55.6	38.5	51.8	30.1	-	-	2.2	6.8	1.6	1.6
History, Philosophy and Theology	6.5	6.7	6.5	6.5	-	-	-	-	0.1	0.2
Social Sciences	7.8	2.5	7.5	1.8	-	-	-	-	0.3	0.7
Languages, Literature and Culture	10.6	59.9	9.4	42.9	-	1.1	1.1	9.5	0.1	6.4
Education and Training	1.7	25.8	1.4	18.7	-	-	-	-	0.2	7.1
Preparation for Life and Work	85.7	226.6	85.3	224.3	-	-	-	-	0.4	2.3
Business Administration & Law	30.3	51.5	28.8	42.3	-	-	0.9	6.8	0.5	2.3
Other Subjects[6]/Unknown	53.1	108.9	30.7	30.4	21.1	73.4	1.3	5.1	-	-
All subjects	515.4	1 026.7	457.4	772.9	21.1	74.6	21.4	132.0	15.5	47.2
Females										
Health, Public Services and Care	85.4	284.1	75.4	233.9	-	-	7.0	43.0	2.9	7.1
Science and Mathematics	33.2	32.5	31.1	23.0	-	-	0.8	3.0	1.3	6.5
Agriculture, Horticulture and Animal Care	12.8	20.3	12.1	16.2	-	-	0.6	3.6	0.1	0.5
Engineering and Manufacturing Technologies	3.5	14.8	3.1	10.0	-	-	0.3	4.1	-	0.7
Construction, Planning and the Built Environment	2.1	5.4	1.7	3.4	-	-	0.3	1.4	0.1	0.6
Information & Communication Technology	14.8	222.8	13.6	179.0	-	-	0.8	34.9	0.4	8.9
Retail and Commercial Enterprise	60.0	71.8	57.1	61.1	-	-	-	1.0	2.8	9.7
Leisure, Travel and Tourism	26.8	41.6	23.7	21.9	-	-	2.2	19.2	1.0	0.5
Arts, Media and Publishing	63.5	93.6	59.7	77.3	-	-	2.5	13.7	1.3	2.6
History, Philosophy and Theology	8.4	13.2	8.2	12.9	-	-	-	-	0.1	0.3
Social Sciences	11.5	6.7	10.9	5.4	-	-	-	-	0.5	1.2
Language, Literature and Culture	19.9	110.9	18.1	84.2	-	2.3	1.7	15.5	0.2	9.0
Education and Training	2.9	64.4	2.8	56.2	-	-	-	-	0.1	8.2
Preparation for Life and Work	85.5	303.8	85.3	302.1	-	-	-	-	0.2	1.7
Business Administration & Law	33.8	108.3	30.0	86.5	-	-	2.6	14.7	1.2	7.1
Other subjects[6]/Unknown	67.1	172.8	37.9	42.3	22.5	112.3	6.7	18.2	-	-
All subjects	531.2	1 566.9	470.8	1 215.3	22.6	114.6	25.6	172.3	12.2	64.7

1 Further education (FE) institution figures are whole year counts. Higher education (HE) institution figures are based on the HESA 'standard registration' count.

2 Full-time includes sandwich. Part-time comprises both day and evening including block release and open/distance learning.

3 Data are shown by sector subject area and not directly comparable with previous years prior to 2005/06.

4 FE institution figures for England include LSC funded students only.

5 Figures for Scotland FE colleges are vocational course enrolments rather than headcounts.

6 For UK HE institutions, includes the previous subject groups not allocated to specific sector subject areas, i e. medicine & dentistry, subjects allied to medicine, biological, veterinary, physical, mathematical and computer sciences and creative arts & design.

Source: Education Departments/DIUS: 01325 391266

Education

6.8 Students in higher[1] education by level, mode of study,[2] sex and age,[3] 2006/07[4],[5]
United Kingdom (home and overseas students)

Thousands

| | Postgraduate level | | | | | | First degree | | Other undergraduate | | Total higher education[6] | |
| | PhD and equivalent | | Masters and others | | Total Postgraduate | | | | | | | |
	Full-time	Part-time	Full-time	Part-time	Full-time	Part-time	Full-time	Part-time	Full-time	Part-time	Full-time	Part-time
All												
Age under 16	-	-	-	-	-	-	-	-	-	0.5	-	0.5
16	-	-	-	-	-	-	0.3	-	0.5	3.3	0.8	3.4
17	-	-	-	-	-	-	9.9	0.2	4.1	2.6	14.0	2.8
18	-	-	-	-	-	-	178.7	1.8	20.7	7.9	199.5	9.8
19	-	-	0.1	0.1	0.1	0.1	239.4	4.9	25.2	13.3	264.8	18.3
20	0.1	-	1.7	0.4	1.8	0.4	241.9	7.2	19.5	14.9	263.3	22.5
21	0.7	-	17.3	2.0	18.0	2.0	159.2	9.3	13.6	14.3	190.9	25.7
22	2.8	0.1	28.5	6.1	31.3	6.2	75.5	9.4	9.8	13.5	116.7	29.2
23	4.9	0.2	28.2	10.2	33.1	10.5	40.3	8.6	8.0	14.4	81.4	33.5
24	6.4	0.9	22.2	12.3	28.6	13.2	24.9	7.9	6.4	15.1	59.9	36.2
25	5.9	2.6	16.4	12.7	22.3	15.3	17.5	7.7	5.4	15.5	45.2	38.5
26	4.9	3.2	12.7	12.8	17.6	16.0	13.6	7.6	4.8	15.7	36.0	39.3
27	4.1	3.0	10.1	12.4	14.3	15.3	10.5	7.0	4.2	15.1	28.9	37.5
28	3.2	2.5	7.7	11.2	10.9	13.7	8.1	6.3	3.6	13.5	22.6	33.5
29	2.8	2.4	6.5	10.5	9.3	12.8	6.7	5.7	3.2	12.8	19.1	31.4
30+	16.2	32.6	40.4	184.2	56.6	216.8	68.7	124.5	44.9	332.6	170.4	674.7
Unknown	-	0.1	0.1	0.9	0.1	1.0	0.1	0.2	0.1	5.3	0.3	6.4
All ages	52.1	47.4	191.8	275.8	243.9	323.3	1 095.4	208.2	174.0	510.3	1 513.8	1 043.1
Males												
Age under 16	-	-	-	-	-	-	-	-	-	0.2	-	0.2
16	-	-	-	-	-	-	0.1	-	0.2	1.4	0.4	1.5
17	-	-	-	-	-	-	4.4	0.1	1.7	1.2	6.2	1.3
18	-	-	-	-	-	-	79.2	0.8	8.9	4.3	88.2	5.2
19	-	-	-	-	-	-	108.1	2.3	11.1	7.1	119.3	9.5
20	-	-	0.8	0.1	0.9	0.1	110.4	3.5	8.2	7.6	119.5	11.2
21	0.4	-	7.1	0.7	7.5	0.7	76.6	4.5	5.8	6.8	89.9	12.1
22	1.6	-	12.2	2.5	13.8	2.5	38.4	4.6	4.1	5.8	56.2	13.0
23	2.8	0.1	12.8	4.1	15.6	4.2	20.6	3.9	3.2	5.6	39.4	13.8
24	3.5	0.5	10.5	4.9	14.0	5.4	12.6	3.5	2.4	5.6	29.0	14.5
25	3.1	1.5	7.9	5.1	11.1	6.6	8.3	3.2	2.0	5.5	21.4	15.3
26	2.6	1.8	6.3	5.1	8.9	6.9	6.3	2.9	1.7	5.5	16.9	15.3
27	2.2	1.6	5.2	5.1	7.4	6.7	4.7	2.8	1.5	5.5	13.5	14.9
28	1.7	1.4	4.0	4.7	5.7	6.0	3.6	2.4	1.2	4.8	10.5	13.2
29	1.5	1.3	3.5	4.5	5.1	5.8	2.8	2.1	1.0	4.6	8.9	12.5
30+	9.3	17.5	21.1	79.8	30.4	97.3	22.4	44.8	11.7	112.6	64.5	255.0
Unknown	-	-	-	0.3	-	0.4	0.1	0.1	-	1.8	0.1	2.2
All ages	28.8	25.8	91.5	117.0	120.3	142.8	498.6	81.3	64.7	185.8	683.8	410.6
Females												
Age under 16	-	-	-	-	-	-	-	-	-	0.3	-	0.3
16	-	-	-	-	-	-	0.2	-	0.3	1.9	0.4	1.9
17	-	-	-	-	-	-	5.4	0.1	2.4	1.4	7.8	1.5
18	-	-	-	-	-	-	99.4	1.0	11.8	3.6	111.3	4.6
19	-	-	0.1	-	0.1	-	131.3	2.5	14.1	6.2	145.5	8.8
20	-	-	0.9	0.3	0.9	0.3	131.5	3.7	11.3	7.3	143.8	11.3
21	0.3	-	10.1	1.3	10.5	1.3	82.6	4.8	7.8	7.5	100.9	13.6
22	1.2	-	16.3	3.6	17.5	3.7	37.1	4.8	5.8	7.7	60.4	16.2
23	2.1	0.1	15.4	6.1	17.5	6.2	19.7	4.7	4.8	8.8	42.0	19.7
24	2.9	0.4	11.7	7.3	14.6	7.8	12.3	4.4	4.0	9.5	30.9	21.7
25	2.8	1.1	8.5	7.6	11.2	8.7	9.2	4.6	3.4	9.9	23.8	23.2
26	2.3	1.4	6.3	7.7	8.7	9.1	7.3	4.7	3.1	10.2	19.1	24.0
27	1.9	1.4	5.0	7.3	6.9	8.7	5.8	4.2	2.7	9.7	15.4	22.6
28	1.6	1.1	3.7	6.5	5.2	7.6	4.6	3.9	2.4	8.8	12.1	20.3
29	1.2	1.1	3.0	5.9	4.2	7.0	3.9	3.6	2.1	8.2	10.2	18.8
30+	6.9	15.1	19.3	104.5	26.3	119.5	46.3	79.7	33.3	220.0	105.9	419.7
Unknown	-	-	-	0.6	-	0.6	0.1	0.1	-	3.5	0.2	4.2
All ages	23.3	21.7	100.3	158.9	123.6	180.5	596.8	126.8	109.3	324.5	830.0	632.6

1 Includes Open University students. Part-time figures include dormant modes, those writing up at home and on sabbaticals.

2 Full-time includes sandwich. Part-time comprises both day and evening, including block release and open/distance learning.

3 Ages as at 31 August 2006 (1 July in Northern Ireland and 31 December in Scotland).

4 Figures for higher education (HE) institutions are based on the HESA 'standard registration' count. Figure for further education (FE) institutions are whole year enrolments.

5 FE institution figures for England include Learning and Skills Council (LSC) funded students only.

6 Includes data for HE students in FE institutions in Wales which cannot be split by level.

Source: Education Departments: 01325 391266

76

6.9 Students in higher[1] education by level, mode of study[2], sex and subject group[3], 2006/07[3,4]

United Kingdom - Home and overseas students

Thousands

	PhD and equivalent		Masters and others		Total Postgraduate		First degree		Other undergraduate		Total higher education[5]	
	Full-time	Part-time	Full-time	Part-time	Full-time	Part-time	Full-time	Part-time	Full-time	Part-time	Full-time	Part-time
All persons												
Medicine & Dentistry	3.6	4.3	3.4	8.6	7.1	12.9	42.6	0.1	0.4	0.2	50.0	13.3
Subjects Allied to Medicine	2.4	3.3	8.1	33.3	10.6	36.6	85.1	31.1	66.0	74.2	161.6	141.9
Biological Sciences	8.3	4.9	7.6	10.2	15.9	15.0	105.2	17.6	4.0	6.9	125.1	39.5
Vet. Science, Agriculture & related	0.7	0.5	1.4	1.3	2.1	1.7	10.9	0.5	3.2	3.1	16.2	5.4
Physical Sciences	7.5	3.6	6.0	3.9	13.5	7.5	49.7	6.2	1.2	6.0	64.4	19.7
Mathematical and Computing Sciences	4.3	2.7	12.4	9.9	16.6	12.6	74.8	13.7	8.7	19.0	100.2	45.3
Engineering & Technology	7.8	4.7	15.1	13.1	23.0	17.8	71.6	10.9	8.2	16.0	102.7	44.7
Architecture, Building & Planning	0.8	0.8	4.8	9.1	5.6	9.9	26.9	7.7	3.6	9.7	36.1	27.3
Social Sciences (inc Law)	5.5	5.5	31.1	26.7	36.6	32.2	155.6	30.6	8.7	38.2	200.9	101.0
Business & Administrative Studies	2.2	3.3	41.2	59.0	43.3	62.2	141.7	19.1	18.0	43.7	203.0	125.0
Mass Communication & Documentation	0.4	0.4	5.2	4.3	5.6	4.8	33.2	1.7	2.3	1.6	41.1	8.1
Languages	3.0	2.9	6.8	5.6	9.8	8.4	74.2	8.8	2.3	36.8	86.3	54.1
Historical and Philosophical Studies	3.0	3.9	4.7	7.8	7.7	11.6	51.9	12.9	0.5	18.6	60.1	43.1
Creative Arts & Design	1.2	1.5	9.1	6.1	10.3	7.6	115.6	5.0	16.8	13.8	142.7	26.4
Education[6]	1.1	4.9	34.0	67.9	35.1	72.8	41.9	9.9	4.3	54.3	81.4	136.9
Other subjects[7]	0.1	0.2	0.1	2.4	0.2	2.6	5.8	26.5	3.6	81.6	9.6	110.8
Unknown[5,8]	-	-	0.8	6.8	0.8	6.8	8.7	5.9	22.2	86.6	32.3	100.8
All subjects	52.1	47.4	191.8	275.8	243.9	323.3	1 095.4	208.2	174.0	510.3	1 513.8	1 043.1
of which overseas students	24.9	17.1	100.4	42.2	125.2	59.2	126.0	0.0	14.2	22.1	205.5	91.2
Males												
Medicine and Dentistry	1.5	2.3	1.4	3.9	2.9	6.2	17.5	0.1	-	0.1	20.4	6.3
Subjects Allied to Medicine	1.0	1.2	2.7	8.7	3.7	9.9	18.7	4.9	8.1	10.3	30.5	25.1
Biological Sciences	3.1	2.0	2.9	3.2	5.9	5.2	39.2	4.8	2.1	2.5	47.2	12.5
Vet. Science, Agriculture & related	0.3	0.2	0.7	0.7	1.0	0.9	3.3	0.1	1.3	1.5	5.5	2.5
Physical Sciences	4.8	2.4	3.4	2.2	8.1	4.6	29.2	3.6	0.6	3.1	37.9	11.2
Mathematical and Computing Sciences	3.3	2.1	9.7	7.5	12.9	9.6	57.4	10.2	7.2	11.5	77.5	31.3
Engineering & Technology	6.2	3.7	12.2	10.7	18.3	14.4	60.4	9.7	7.1	14.4	85.9	38.5
Architecture, Building & Planning	0.5	0.5	2.9	5.6	3.4	6.2	18.7	5.9	2.8	7.3	24.9	19.4
Social Sciences (inc Law)	2.8	2.8	13.4	10.7	16.2	13.6	61.9	10.4	2.5	10.1	80.6	34.0
Business & Administrative Studies	1.3	2.1	22.2	31.3	23.4	33.4	73.7	8.7	8.7	18.3	105.8	60.3
Mass Communication & Documentation	0.2	0.2	1.9	1.3	2.0	1.5	14.5	0.6	1.4	0.6	17.9	2.8
Languages	1.3	1.1	2.2	1.7	3.5	2.9	21.9	2.3	1.1	14.1	26.4	19.3
Historical and Philosophical Studies	1.7	2.3	2.3	4.0	3.9	6.2	24.8	5.1	0.2	6.6	29.0	17.9
Creative Arts & Design	0.6	0.8	3.6	2.4	4.2	3.2	45.4	1.8	7.1	4.4	56.6	9.4
Education[6]	0.4	1.9	9.9	19.7	10.3	21.6	6.8	1.4	1.0	13.9	18.1	36.9
Other subjects[7]	0.1	0.1	0.1	1.2	0.1	1.3	2.2	10.0	1.9	31.6	4.2	42.9
Unknown[5,8]	-	-	0.2	2.1	0.2	2.1	3.2	1.9	11.7	35.6	15.4	40.2
All subjects	28.8	25.8	91.5	117.0	120.3	142.8	498.6	81.3	64.7	185.8	683.8	410.6
of which overseas students	14.7	9.9	53.8	23.7	68.5	33.6	63.6	5.1	6.9	9.6	138.9	48.3
Females												
Medicine & Dentistry	2.2	2.1	2.0	4.7	4.1	6.8	25.1	0.1	0.3	0.1	29.6	6.9
Subjects Allied to Medicine	1.4	2.1	5.4	24.6	6.8	26.7	66.4	26.2	57.9	63.8	131.1	116.8
Biological Sciences	5.3	2.9	4.8	6.9	10.0	9.8	66.0	12.8	1.9	4.3	77.9	26.9
Vet. Science, Agriculture & related	0.4	0.2	0.7	0.6	1.1	0.9	7.6	0.4	1.9	1.7	10.7	2.9
Physical Sciences	2.7	1.3	2.6	1.7	5.4	3.0	20.5	2.6	0.6	2.9	26.5	8.5
Mathematical and Computing Sciences	1.0	0.7	2.7	2.4	3.7	3.0	17.5	3.5	1.5	7.5	22.7	14.0
Engineering & Technology	1.7	0.9	3.0	2.4	4.6	3.4	11.1	1.2	1.0	1.6	16.8	6.2
Architecture, Building & Planning	0.3	0.3	1.8	3.5	2.2	3.7	8.2	1.8	0.8	2.4	11.2	7.9
Social Sciences (inc Law)	2.7	2.7	17.7	16.0	20.4	18.7	93.8	20.2	6.1	28.1	120.4	67.0
Business & Administrative Studies	0.9	1.2	19.0	27.7	19.9	28.8	68.0	10.5	9.3	25.4	97.1	64.7
Mass Communication & Documentation	0.2	0.2	3.4	3.0	3.6	3.2	18.7	1.0	1.0	1.0	23.3	5.2
Languages	1.8	1.7	4.6	3.8	6.4	5.6	52.3	6.6	1.3	22.7	59.9	34.8
Historical and Philosophical Studies	1.3	1.6	2.5	3.8	3.8	5.4	27.1	7.7	0.3	12.1	31.2	25.2
Creative Arts & Design	0.6	0.8	5.5	3.6	6.1	4.4	70.3	3.2	9.7	9.3	86.1	17.0
Education[6]	0.7	2.9	24.1	48.2	24.8	51.1	35.1	8.5	3.4	40.4	63.3	100.0
Other subjects[7]	-	0.1	0.1	1.2	0.1	1.3	3.6	16.5	1.7	50.0	5.4	67.8
Unknown[5,8]	-	-	0.6	4.7	0.6	4.7	5.6	4.0	10.5	51.0	16.9	60.5
All subjects	23.3	21.7	100.3	158.9	123.6	180.5	596.8	126.8	109.3	324.5	830.0	632.6
of which overseas students	10.2	7.1	46.6	18.5	56.8	25.6	62.4	4.8	7.4	12.5	126.5	43.0

1 Higher Education Statistics Agency (HESA) higher education institutions include Open University students. Part-time figures include dormant modes, those writing up at home and on sabbaticals.
2 Full-time includes sandwich. Part-time comprises both day and evening, including block release and open/distance learning.
3 Figures for higher education (HE) institutions are based on the HESA 'standard registration' count. Figures for further education (FE) institutions are whole year enrolments.
4 FE institution figures for England include Learning and Skills Council (LSC) funded students only.

5 Includes data for HE students in FE institutions in Wales which cannot be split by level.
6 Including ITT and INSET.
7 Includes Combined and general categories.
8 Includes data for HE students in FE institutions in England, which cannot be split by subject group.

Source: Education Departments: 01325 391266

Education

6.10 Students[1,2] obtaining higher education qualifications[3]: by level, sex and subject group, 2006/07

United Kingdom

Thousands

| | Postgraduate | | | | | |
	PhD and equivalent	Masters and Other	Total	First Degree	Sub-degree[4]	Total higher education
All persons						
Subject group						
Medicine & Dentistry	1.7	3.8	5.5	8.3	0.2	14.0
Subjects Allied to Medicine	1.0	10.4	11.4	30.5	42.5	84.4
Biological Sciences	2.6	6.8	9.4	29.1	4.5	43.0
Vet. Science, Agriculture & related	0.3	1.2	1.4	2.8	1.3	5.6
Physical Sciences	2.4	4.0	6.4	12.5	2.3	21.2
Mathematical & Computer Sciences	1.2	9.1	10.3	22.1	7.7	40.1
Engineering & Technology	2.4	10.9	13.3	19.9	5.5	38.6
Architecture, Building & Planning	0.2	5.5	5.8	7.6	3.6	16.9
Social Studies (inc Law)	1.7	27.7	29.5	46.7	14.5	90.8
Business & Administrative Studies	0.7	40.1	40.8	43.7	13.1	97.7
Mass Communication & Documentation	0.1	4.5	4.7	9.2	1.5	15.3
Languages	1.0	5.6	6.6	19.9	4.9	31.4
Historical and Philosophical Studies	1.0	4.9	5.9	15.9	3.5	25.3
Creative Arts & Design	0.4	7.3	7.7	32.2	6.7	46.6
Education[5]	0.7	42.7	43.4	13.4	15.4	72.3
Combined, general	0.1	0.1	0.2	5.5	2.4	8.0
All subjects	17.5	184.7	202.2	319.3	129.6	651.1
Males						
Subject group						
Medicine and Dentistry	0.8	1.6	2.4	3.4	-	5.9
Subjects Allied to Medicine	0.4	2.7	3.0	5.6	5.5	14.2
Biological Sciences	1.1	2.1	3.1	10.1	1.9	15.1
Vet. Science, Agriculture & related	0.1	0.6	0.7	0.9	0.6	2.1
Physical Sciences	1.6	2.1	3.6	7.0	1.2	11.8
Mathematical & Computer Sciences	0.9	6.9	7.8	16.7	5.7	30.2
Engineering & Technology	1.9	8.7	10.6	16.8	4.9	32.3
Architecture, Building & Planning	0.2	3.2	3.4	5.4	2.5	11.3
Social Studies (inc Law)	0.9	11.7	12.6	18.1	4.2	34.9
Business & Administrative Studies	0.5	20.7	21.2	21.3	6.1	48.5
Mass Communication & Documentation	-	1.5	1.5	3.8	0.7	6.1
Languages	0.4	1.7	2.1	5.5	1.8	9.4
Historical and Philosophical Studies	0.6	2.4	2.9	7.2	1.2	11.4
Creative Arts & Design	0.2	2.8	3.0	12.2	2.9	18.0
Education[5]	0.3	11.9	12.1	2.0	4.0	18.2
Combined, general	0.1	-	0.1	2.3	0.9	3.3
All subjects	9.8	80.6	90.4	138.2	44.2	272.8
Females						
Subject group						
Medicine & Dentistry	0.9	2.2	3.1	4.9	0.1	8.1
Subjects Allied to Medicine	0.6	7.8	8.4	24.9	37.0	70.2
Biological Sciences	1.6	4.7	6.2	19.0	2.6	27.9
Vet. Science, Agriculture & related	0.1	0.6	0.7	2.0	0.8	3.5
Physical Sciences	0.8	1.9	2.8	5.5	1.1	9.4
Mathematical & Computer Sciences	0.3	2.2	2.5	5.4	2.0	9.9
Engineering & Technology	0.5	2.1	2.6	3.1	0.6	6.3
Architecture, Building & Planning	0.1	2.3	2.3	2.2	1.0	5.6
Social Studies (inc Law)	0.8	16.1	16.9	28.6	10.4	55.8
Business & Administrative Studies	0.3	19.4	19.7	22.4	7.0	49.1
Mass Communication & Documentation	0.1	3.1	3.1	5.4	0.7	9.2
Languages	0.6	4.0	4.6	14.5	3.1	22.1
Historical and Philosophical Studies	0.4	2.5	3.0	8.6	2.3	13.8
Creative Arts & Design	0.2	4.5	4.7	20.1	3.8	28.6
Education[5]	0.4	30.9	31.3	11.3	11.4	54.0
Combined, general	-	-	0.1	3.2	1.5	4.8
All subjects	7.7	104.1	111.9	181.1	85.3	378.3

1 Includes students on Open University courses.
2 Includes students qualifying on all modes of study.
3 Includes higher education (HE) qualifications in HE institutions in the UK only. Excludes qualifications from the private sector, except for the University of Buckingham who returned data to HESA in 2006/07, and HE qualifications in further education FE institutions.

4 Excludes students who successfully completed courses for which formal qualifications are not awarded.
5 Includes ITT and INSET.

Source: Education Departments: 01325 391266

6.11 Qualified teachers: by type of school and sex[1]

Thousands

	Public sector mainstream schools		Non-maintained mainstream schools	All special schools	Total[6]
	Nursery[2,3,4] and primary	Secondary[5]			
All full-time teachers					
United Kingdom					
1990/91[7]	208.8	233.1	44.9	19.0	505.7
1995/96[7,8]	211.8	222.1	48.6	17.2	499.7
2000/01[9,10]	211.2	225.7	52.3	16.5	505.7
2001/02	211.2	227.1	52.8	16.3	507.3
2002/03[11]	210.5	229.7	53.6	19.8	513.6
2003/04	210.6	229.7	55.8	19.8	516.0
2004/05	208.5	232.5	56.3	19.9	517.2
2005/06[12]	208.4	233.8	57.2	20.4	519.8
2006/07[13]	207.0	234.4	58.7	20.5	520.6
of which:					
England and Wales[1]	177.0	200.4	55.9	17.7	450.9
Scotland	22.4	24.2	2.7	2.1	51.4
Northern Ireland	7.6	9.8	0.1	0.7	18.2
Full-time male teachers					
United Kingdom					
1990/91[7]	37.7	120.7	20.6	5.9	184.9
1995/96[7,8]	35.5	107.9	21.1	5.4	169.8
2000/01[9,10]	32.1	102.9	21.3	5.0	161.3
2001/02	31.8	102.6	21.5	4.9	160.8
2002/03[11]	31.7	101.6	21.6	5.9	160.8
2003/04	31.7	101.5	22.7	5.9	161.9
2004/05	31.2	101.6	22.9	5.9	161.6
2005/06[12]	31.0	100.8	23.5	6.0	161.3
2006/07[13]	30.7	99.9	23.9	6.1	160.6
of which:					
England and Wales[1]	27.7	85.9	22.8	5.4	141.8
Scotland	1.7	10.3	1.1	0.5	13.5
Northern Ireland	1.3	3.7	-	0.1	5.2
Full-time female teachers					
United Kingdom					
1990/91[7]	171.1	112.3	24.3	13.1	320.8
1995/96[7,8]	176.3	114.2	27.4	11.8	329.9
2000/01[9,10]	179.1	122.8	30.9	11.6	344.4
2001/02	179.4	124.5	31.2	11.4	346.5
2002/03[11]	178.8	128.2	32.0	13.9	352.8
2003/04	178.9	128.2	33.0	13.9	354.0
2004/05	177.3	130.9	33.4	14.0	355.6
2005/06[12]	175.8	133.1	33.7	14.3	356.8
2006/07[13]	174.6	134.5	34.8	14.4	358.3
of which:					
England and Wales[1]	149.3	114.5	33.1	12.2	309.1
Scotland	19.1	13.9	1.6	1.6	36.2
Northern Ireland	6.2	6.1	0.1	0.6	13.0
All full time equivalents (FTE) of part-time teachers					
United Kingdom					
1990/91	..	..	..	..	30.0
1995/96[7,8]	19.1	17.7	8.9	1.5	47.2
2000/01[9,10]	21.9	16.7	10.2	1.6	50.4
2001/02	23.4	17.4	10.4	1.8	53.0
2002/03[11]	23.8	17.8	11.1	1.7	54.4
2003/04	26.4	19.5	11.4	1.9	59.3
2004/05	27.5	20.6	11.5	1.9	61.4
2005/06[12]	30.1	21.5	11.6	2.0	65.2
2006/07[13]	31.1	22.1	11.8	2.1	67.1

1 Public sector teachers numbers in England & Wales have been provided from the 618G survey and gender split has been calculated by using the proportions from the Database of Teacher Records (DTR).

2 From 2005/06, data for Scotland include only centres providing pre-school education as a local authority centre or in partnership with the local authority. Figures are not therefore directly comparable with previous years.

3 From 2005/06, for Scotland pre-school education centres, the total full-time equivalent (FTE) of General Teaching Council of Scotland (GTC) registered staff has been provided within the 'full-time' section only because information on full time/part-time split is not available. Teachers are counted once for each centre they work for, so the number of teachers contains some double counting. However, as each centre calculates the teacher's FTE as the time they spend working in that centre, the FTE should not be double-counted. Full-time/part-time figures for 2004/05 are estimates based on the headcount of all GTC registered staff.

4 For Scotland pre-school education centres FTE staff, a gender split is not available. Gender figures for 2004/05 are estimates based on the headcount of all GTC registered staff.

5 From 1993/94 excludes sixth form colleges in England and Wales which were reclassified as further education colleges on 1 April 1993.

6 Excludes Pupil Referral Units (PRUs).

7 Figures for non-maintained mainstream schools refer to Great Britain.

8 Includes 1994/95 data for Northern Ireland.

9 Includes 1999/00 pre-school data for Scotland.

10 Includes 2001/02 data for Northern Ireland.

11 Includes 2001/02 pre-school and 2003/04 school data for Scotland.

12 Includes revised data.

13 Provisional.

Source: Education Departments: 01325 391266

Labour market

Chapter 7

Labour market

Labour Force Survey

(Tables 7.1 to 7.3, 7.6, 7.9, 7.10 to 7.11, 7.13 and 7.16 to 7.18)

The impact of Census 2001 on LFS data

(Tables 7.1 to 7.3, 7.6, 7.9, 7.10 to 7.11, 7.16 to 7.18)

The first results of the 2001 Census, published on 30 September 2002, showed that previous estimates of the total UK population were about one million too high. Estimates of employment and unemployment levels from the Labour Force Survey (LFS) released before 30 October 2002 were therefore too high, with rates also affected. This led to the LFS needing to reweight its estimates to the new population figures.

Top-level seasonally adjusted interim reweighed figures were published in the 2003 edition of *Annual Abstract of Statistics*. LFS estimates for the UK, used in this chapter, continue to show seasonally adjusted data for these tables, in line with other headline publications. These figures are not directly comparable to the non -seasonally adjusted figures published in the *Annual Abstract of Statistics before 2003*.

Since 2003, the LFS aggregate estimates (that is, the key labour market indicators, for example, the levels and rates of employment, unemployment and economic inactivity) have been interim reweighted every year. Interim reweighting applies adjustments to the aggregate results to reflect how the latest available LFS household population estimates compare with those used for weighting the microdata. This amounts to an approximation of the effect that a full reweighting of the microdata would have.

A full reweighting exercise was carried out in 2007–08 and the results were published on 14 May 2008. The microdatasets were weighted to the latest (2007/08) population estimates whereas previously they were based on population totals published in 2003. For the previous reweighting exercise the microdata were weighted to Census 2001 population estimates published in spring 2003. In autumn 2003 these estimates were revised but it was too late to incorporate them into the reweighting without significantly delaying the project. Therefore, it was decided that the weights already produced using the spring 2003 estimates would be retained and that projections from the pre-revised Census would then be used to weight subsequent datasets until 2007.

Up-to-date population estimates that are in line with the revised Census figures have been used in the latest reweighting project. Analysis of the 2007 reweighted microdata produced aggregates at the UK level that are

approximately 900,000 above the estimates produced from the datasets weighted to the 2003 population totals. The changes in the estimates are primarily due to overall differences between the 2003 and 2007 population totals used to weight the data. However, the underlying weighting methodology was changed for the 2007 reweighting exercise, which is another factor that has contributed to changes in the reweighted estimates.

For more information on the reweighting exercise, see 'Labour Force Survey: reweighting and seasonal adjustment review 2008' available at: www.statistics.gov.uk/CCI/article. asp?ID=2011 and 'Labour Force Survey: Interim reweighting 2008 available at: www.statistics.gov.uk/cci/article. asp?id=2061

Background

The LFS is the largest regular household survey in the UK LFS interviews are conducted continuously throughout the year. In any three-month period, a nationally representative sample of approximately 102,000 people aged 16 or over in around 52,000 households are interviewed. Each household is interviewed five times, at three-monthly intervals. The initial interview is done face-to-face by an interviewer visiting the address. The other interviews are done by telephone wherever possible. The survey asks a series of questions about respondents' personal circumstances and their labour market activity. Most questions refer to activity in the week before the interview.

The concepts and definitions used in the LFS are agreed by the International Labour Organisation (ILO) – an agency of the United Nations. The definitions are used by European Union member countries and members of the Organisation for Economic Co-operation and Development (OECD).

Labour Market

The LFS was carried out every two years from 1973 to 1983. The ILO definition was first used in 1984. This was also the first year in which the survey was conducted on an annual basis with results available for every spring quarter (representing an average of the period from March to May). The survey moved to a continuous basis in spring 1992 in Great Britain and in winter 1994/95 in Northern Ireland, with average quarterly results published four times a year for seasonal quarters: spring (March to May), summer (June to August), autumn (September to November) and winter (December to February). From April 1998, results are published 12 times a year for the average of three consecutive months.

The LFS collects information on a sample of the population. To convert this information to give estimates for the population the data must be grossed, This is achieved by calculating weighting factors (often referred to simply as weights) which can be applied to each sampled individual in such a way that the weighted-up results match estimates or projections of the total population in terms of age distribution, sex, and region of residence.

Strengths and limitations of the LFS

The LFS produces coherent labour market information on the basis of internationally standard concepts and definitions. It is a rich source of data on a wide variety of labour market and personal characteristics. It is the most suitable source for making comparisons between countries. The LFS is designed so that households interviewed in each three month period constitute a representative sample of UK households. The survey covers those living in private households and nurses in National Health Service accommodation. Students living in halls of residence have been included since 1992 as information about them is collected at their parents' address.

However the LFS has its limitations. It is a sample survey and is therefore subject to sampling variability. The survey does not include people living in institutions such as hostels or residential homes. 'Proxy' reporting (when members of the household are not present at the interview, another member of the household answers the questions on their behalf) can affect the quality of information on topics such as earnings, hours worked, benefit receipt and qualifications. Around one-third of interviews are conducted 'by proxy', usually by a spouse or partner but sometimes by a parent or other near relation.

Sampling variability

Survey estimates are prone to *sampling variability*. The easiest way to explain this concept is by example. In the September to November 1997 period, International Labour Organisation (ILO) unemployment in Great Britain (seasonally adjusted) stood at 1,847,000. If we drew another sample for the same period we could get a different result, perhaps 1,900,000 or 1,820,000.

In theory, we could draw many samples, and each would give a different result. This is because each sample would be made up of different people who would give different answers to the questions. The spread of these results is the sampling variability. Sampling variability is determined by a number of factors including the sample size, the variability of the population from which the sample is drawn and the sample design. Once we know the sampling variability we can calculate a range of values about the sample estimate that represents the expected variation with a given level of assurance. This is called a confidence interval. For a 95 per cent confidence interval we expect that in 95 per cent of the samples (19 times out of 20) the confidence interval will

contain the true value that would be obtained by surveying the entire population. For the example given above, we can be 95 per cent confident that the true value was in the range 1,791,000 to 1,903,000.

Unreliable estimates

Very small estimates have relatively wide confidence intervals making them unreliable. For this reason, ONS does not publish LFS estimates below 10,000.

Non-response

Non-response can introduce bias to a survey, particularly if the people not responding have characteristics that are different from those who do respond. The LFS has a response rate of around 80 per cent to the first interview, and over 90 per cent of those who are interviewed once go on to complete all five interviews. These are relatively high levels for a household survey. Any bias from non-response is minimised by *weighting* the results.

Weighting (or grossing) converts sample data to represent the full population. In the LFS, the data are weighted separately by age, sex and area of residence to population estimates based on the census. Weighting also adjusts for people not in the survey and thus minimises non-response bias.

LFS concepts and definitions

Discouraged workers – a sub-group of the economically inactive population, defined as those neither in employment nor unemployed (on the ILO measure) who said they would like a job and whose main reason for not seeking work was because they believed there were no jobs available.

Economically active – people aged 16 and over who are either in employment or ILO unemployed.

Economic activity rate – the percentage of people aged 16 and over who are economically active.

Economically inactive – people who are neither in employment nor unemployed. This group includes, for example, all those who were looking after a home or retired.

Employment – people aged 16 or over who did at least one hour of paid work in the reference week (whether as an employee or self-employed); those who had a job that they were temporarily away from (on holiday, for example); those on government-supported training and employment programmes (from spring 1983); and those doing unpaid family work (from spring 1992).

Employees – the division between employees and self-employed is based on survey respondents' own assessment of their employment status.

Full Time – the classification of employees, self-employed and unpaid family workers in their main job as full-time or part-time is on the basis of self-assessment. Up until autumn 1995, people who were on government work-related training programmes are classified as full-time or part-time according to whether their usual hours of work per week were over 30 or 30 and under; from winter 1995/96 onwards, the full-time/part-time classification for this group has been changed to self-assessment, in line with the other groups outlined above. People on government-supported training and employment programmes who are at college in the survey reference week are classified, by convention, as part-time.

Government-supported training and employment programmes – comprise all people aged 16 and over participating in one of the government's employment and training programmes (Youth Training, Training for Work and Community Action), together with those on similar programmes administered by Training and Enterprise Councils in England and Wales, or Local Enterprise Companies in Scotland.

Hours worked – respondents to the LFS are asked a series of questions enabling the identification of both their usual hours and their actual hours. Total hours include overtime (paid and unpaid) and exclude lunch-breaks.

Unemployment – Unemployment figures from the LFS, which are based upon the ILO definition, were re-labelled 'unemployment' rather than 'ILO unemployment' in January 2003. This emphasises that the LFS figures provide the official and only internationally comparable measure of unemployment in the UK. For more details see: www.statistics.gov.uk/cci/nugget.asp?id=251

The ILO measure of unemployment used throughout this publication refers to people without a job who were available to start work in the two weeks following their LFS interview and who had either looked for work in the four weeks prior to interview or were waiting to start a job they had already obtained. This definition of unemployment is in accordance with that adopted by the 13th International Conference of Labour Statisticians, further clarified at the 14th ICLS, and promulgated by the ILO in its publications.

Unemployment (rate) – the percentage of economically active people who are unemployed on the ILO measure.

Unemployment (duration) – defined as the shorter of the following two periods:

- duration of active search for work

- length of time since employment

Part-time – see full-time.

Second jobs – jobs which LFS respondents hold in addition to a main full-time or part-time job.

Self-employment – See Employees.

Temporary employees – in the LFS these are defined as those employees who say that their main job is non-permanent in one of the following ways: fixed period contract; agency temping; casual work; seasonal work; other temporary work.

Unpaid family workers – the separate identification from spring 1992 of this group in the LFS is in accordance with international recommendations. The group comprises persons doing unpaid work for a business they own or for a business that a relative owns.

Distribution of workforce

(Table 7.4)

Claimant unemployed – those people who were claiming unemployment-related benefits (contributions or income related Jobseeker's Allowance and/or National Insurance credits) at Jobcentre Plus local offices on the day of the monthly count. The seasonally adjusted claimant unemployment series allows for all relevant changes which, unless adjusted for, would distort comparisons over time.

Workforce jobs (formerly workforce in employment) – comprises employee jobs, self-employment jobs (from the LFS), HM Forces and government-supported trainees.

HM Forces (provided by Ministry of Defence) – represent the total number of UK service personnel, male and female, in HM Regular. Full Time Reserve personnel, mobilised reservists, the Ghurkhas and the Home Service battalions of the Royal Irish Regiment, wherever serving and including those on leave.

Self-employed jobs – estimates are based on the results of the Labour Force Survey. The Northern Ireland estimates are not seasonally adjusted.

Government-supported trainees – include all participants on government training and employment programmes who are receiving some work experience on their placement but who do not have a contract of employment (those with a contract are included in the employee jobs series). The numbers are not subject to seasonal adjustment.

International Employment Comparisons

(Table 7.7)

All employment rates for European Union (EU) countries published by Eurostat (including the rate for the UK) are based on the population aged 15–64. The rates for Canada and Japan are also based on the population aged 15–64, but the rate for the US is for those aged 16–64. The employment rate for the UK published by ONS is based on the working age population aged 16–64 (men) and 16–59 (women) and therefore takes into account both the current school leaving age and state pension ages.

The unemployment rate published by Eurostat for most EU countries (but not for the UK), are calculated by extrapolating from the most recent LFS data using monthly registered unemployment data. A standard population basis (15–74) is used by Eurostat except for Spain and the UK (16–74). The unemployment rate for the US is based on those aged 16 and over, but the rates for Canada and Japan are for those aged 15 and over. All unemployment rates are seasonally adjusted.

The unemployment rate for the UK published by Eurostat is based on the population aged 16–74 while the unemployment rate for the UK published by ONS is based on those aged 16 and over. There are other minor definitional differences.

Jobseekers allowance claimant count

(Tables 7.14 and 7.15)

This is a count of all those people who are claiming Jobseeker's Allowance (JSA) at Jobcentre Plus local offices. People claiming JSA must declare that they are:

- out of work

- capable of work

- available for work

- actively seeking work

during the week in which the claim is made.

All people claiming JSA on the day of the monthly count are included in the claimant count, irrespective of whether they are actually receiving benefits. Also see Table 10.6 in the Social protection chapter.

Labour disputes

(Table 7.19)

These figures exclude details of stoppages involving fewer than ten workers or lasting less than one day except any in which the aggregate number of working days lost is 100 or more. There may be some under-recording of small or short stoppages; this would have much more effect on the total of stoppages than of working days lost. Some stoppages which affected more than one industry group have been counted under each of the industries but only once in the totals. Stoppages have been classified using the *Standard Industrial Classification (SIC) 2003*.

The figures for working days lost and workers involved have been rounded and consequently the sum of the constituent items may not agree with the totals. Classifications by size are based on the full duration of stoppages where these continue into the following year. Working days lost per thousand employees are based on the latest available mid-year (June) estimates of employee jobs.

Earnings

(Tables 7.20 to 7.25)

The total gross remuneration employees receive before any statutory deductions (tax, national insurance). Income in kind and pension funds are excluded.

Annual Survey of Hours and Earnings

(Tables 7.20, 7.21, 7.24 and 7.25)

The Annual Survey of Hours and Earnings (ASHE) replaced the New Earnings Survey (NES) in 2004. The ASHE includes improvements to the coverage of employees and to the weighting of earnings estimates. The data variables collected remain broadly the same, although an improved questionnaire was introduced for the 2005 survey. The change in methodology means that statistics on pay and hours published from the ASHE, including the calculation of ONS's low pay statistics, are discontinuous with previous NES surveys.

To improve coverage and make the survey more representative, supplementary information was collected for the 2004 ASHE survey on businesses not registered for Value Added Tax (VAT) and for people who changed or started new jobs between sample selection and the survey reference period. The 2004 ASHE results are therefore discontinuous with the results for 2003, for which no supplementary information was collected. However, for 2004 two sets of results are available; the headline results that include supplementary information and results that exclude this information. These second set of results are given solely for comparison to earlier results.

The ASHE methodology includes imputation and weighting, the main impact of these changes when applied to existing NES data for 1997 to 2003 are:

- to increase the estimates of the level of average weekly pay over estimates published from the NES

- for males the increase in estimates of earnings is more than the increase for females. In particular this affects hourly pay excluding overtime, which is used in the calculation of ONS's preferred measure of the gender pay gap. The estimate of hourly pay for males is increased more then the estimate for females, which widens the estimate of the gap between male and female hourly pay

- estimates of the level of earnings for people working in London are increased more than estimates for other regions. This widens the estimate of the difference in pay between London and other regions of the UK

For information about methodological changes to the 2007 ASHE survey see: www.statistics.gov.uk/downloads/theme_labour/ASHE/ChangeInASHE07.pdf

Average Earnings Index

(Tables 7.22 and 7.23)

The Average Earnings Index (AEI) is designed to measure changes in the level of earnings, that is, wage inflation in Great Britain. Average earnings are calculated as the total wages and salaries paid by firms, divided by the number of employees paid. Like all indices, changes are measured against a base year, whose index value is set to 100. The current base year is 2000 for Tables 7.22 and 7.23.

Users should note that the data contained in Table 7.23 of the *Annual Abstract of Statistics* since 2003 are not comparable with that published up until 2002. Table 7.23 now shows the set of 20 industry sectors that better reflect the current state of the economy, and supersedes the previous set of 26 industry sectors. The new series are available in the format of excluding bonus index, including bonus index, and an annual percentage change for including and excluding bonuses. An article covering the reasons for the change can be found at: www.statistics.gov.uk/labour

The AEI is published monthly in the ONS Labour Market Statistics First Release. The main indicator of growth, the headline

rate, is based on the annual change in the seasonally adjusted index values for the latest three months compared with the same period a year ago. The use of a three-month average reduces the level of volatility seen in the data on a month-on-month basis.

Strengths of the AEI

The AEI, based on monthly survey data, is a timely indicator of changes in the level of earnings.

Limitations of the AEI

The index is not adjusted for any changes in the composition of the workforce such as changes in the share of full-time and part-time workers, or in the share of skilled and unskilled workers. Similarly, the index does

not account for changes in the number of hours worked, or any temporary factors that affect earnings.

The sample of the Monthly Wages and Salaries Survey on which the AEI is based is not designed to provide information on the level of earnings. The sample is not completely representative of the economy as firms with fewer than 20 employees are excluded, as are the earnings of self-employed persons.

The AEI only covers earnings in Great Britain as earnings information is not collected for Northern Ireland and regional data are not available.

Trade unions

(Table 7.26)

The statistics relate to all organisations of employees known to Certification Officer with head offices in the UK that fall within the appropriate definition of a trade union in the Trade Union and Labour Relations (Consolidation) Act 1992. Included in the data are home and overseas membership figures of contributory and non-contributory members. Employment status of members is not provided and the figures may therefore include some people who are self-employed, unemployed or retired.

The membership part of this table was revised in 2001, so that statistics presented here are on a consistent basis with the Great Britain table produced by the Certification Officer in his Annual Report and with tables produced in the annual Trade Union membership article published by the Department for Business, Enterprise & Regulatory Reform (BERR).

7.1 Labour force summary:[1] by sex
United Kingdom
At Quarter 2 each year[2]. Seasonally adjusted

Thousands and percentages

	All aged 16 and over					Percentages			
	Total[3]	Total economically active	Total in employment	Total unemployed	Economically inactive	Economic activity rate 16-59/64[4]	Employment rate all aged 16 and over[5]	Employment rate 16-59/64[6]	Unemployment rate[7]
All Persons									
	MGSL	MGSF	MGRZ	MGSC	MGSI	MGSO	MGSR	MGSU	MGSX
1998	45 720	28 583	26 795	1 791	17 137	78.4	58.6	73.4	6.3
1999	45 937	28 840	27 167	1 743	17 065	78.7	59.2	74.0	6.0
2000	46 194	29 069	27 483	1 600	17 084	78.8	59.5	74.4	5.5
2001	46 502	29 176	27 710	1 470	17 291	78.6	59.6	74.4	5.0
2002	46 787	29 433	27 921	1 521	17 317	78.6	59.7	74.5	5.2
2003	47 087	29 659	28 186	1 468	17 382	78.7	59.9	74.6	5.0
2004	47 448	29 867	28 485	1 439	17 524	78.5	60.0	74.7	4.8
2005	47 871	30 170	28 774	1 438	17 653	78.5	60.1	74.7	4.8
2006	48 268	30 686	29 030	1 687	17 531	79.0	60.2	74.6	5.5
2007	48 668	30 821	29 222	1 662	17 800	78.8	60.0	74.6	5.4
2008	49 059	31 190	29 443	1 685	17 816	79.1	60.0	74.5	5.4
Male									
	MGSM	MGSG	MGSA	MGSD	MGSJ	MGSP	MGSS	MGSV	MGSY
1998	21 992	15 685	14 597	1 076	6 308	84.3	66.4	78.4	6.9
1999	22 110	15 795	14 767	1 060	6 298	84.4	66.8	78.8	6.7
2000	22 249	15 860	14 909	959	6 365	84.4	67.0	79.2	6.0
2001	22 430	15 883	15 026	882	6 525	83.9	67.0	79.3	5.6
2002	22 600	15 988	15 099	914	6 591	83.8	66.8	79.0	5.7
2003	22 775	16 187	15 262	890	6 562	84.1	67.0	79.2	5.5
2004	22 978	16 217	15 405	845	6 731	83.6	67.1	79.3	5.2
2005	23 214	16 352	15 535	837	6 835	83.4	66.9	79.0	5.1
2006	23 438	16 606	15 662	978	6 804	83.7	66.9	78.8	5.9
2007	23 668	16 742	15 813	950	6 899	83.6	66.8	78.8	5.7
2008	23 891	16 928	15 894	990	6 934	83.7	66.5	78.5	5.8
Female									
	MGSN	MGSH	MGSB	MGSE	MGSK	MGSQ	MGST	MGSW	MGSZ
1998	23 728	12 899	12 198	715	10 829	72.1	51.4	68.1	5.4
1999	23 827	13 046	12 400	683	10 767	72.6	52.0	68.8	5.2
2000	23 945	13 209	12 573	641	10 719	72.9	52.5	69.3	4.9
2001	24 072	13 292	12 684	589	10 766	72.9	52.7	69.3	4.4
2002	24 186	13 445	12 823	607	10 726	73.1	53.0	69.6	4.5
2003	24 311	13 472	12 925	579	10 819	72.9	53.1	69.7	4.3
2004	24 469	13 650	13 080	593	10 793	73.1	53.5	69.9	4.3
2005	24 657	13 819	13 239	601	10 818	73.3	53.7	70.0	4.4
2006	24 830	14 080	13 367	709	10 728	74.0	53.8	70.0	5.0
2007	25 001	14 079	13 409	712	10 901	73.6	53.7	69.9	5.1
2008	25 168	14 262	13 549	695	10 882	74.1	53.8	70.2	4.9

1 See chapter text. In August 2007, ONS published the mid-year population estimates for 2006. These estimates have now been incorporated into the LFS estimates from 2001 onwards. Further details can be found at http://www.statistics.gov.uk/cci/article.asp?id=1919

2 The Labour Force Survey has now moved to calendar quarters from May 2006. More information can be found on page 5 of the Concepts and Definitions.pdf by following this link:- www.statistics.gov.uk/downloads/theme_labour/Concepts_Definitions_HQS.pdf

3 Population aged 16 and over in private households and student halls of residence.

4 Economically active of working age as a percentage of all persons of working age (men 16-64, women 16-59).

5 Total employed as a percentage of all persons aged 16 and over.

6 Total employed of working age as a percentage of all persons of working age (men 16-64, women 16-59).

7 Total unemployed as a percentage of all economically active.

Sources: Labour Force Survey, Office for National Statistics;
Helpline: 01633 456901

Labour Market

7.2 Employment status: full-time, part-time and temporary employees[1]
United Kingdom
At Quarter 2 each year[2]. Seasonally adjusted

Thousands

	All in employment[3]					Total employment[3]		Employees[3]		Self-employed[3]			
	Total	Employees	Self employed	Unpaid family workers	Government supported training and employment programmes[4]	Full-time	Part-time	Full-time	Part-time	Full-time	Part-time	Workers with second jobs[5]	Temporary employees
All Persons													
	MGRZ	MGRN	MGRQ	MGRT	MGRW	YCBE	YCBH	YCBK	YCBN	YCBQ	YCBT	YCBW	YCBZ
1998	26 795	23 182	3 347	100	167	20 074	6 721	17 338	5 844	2 612	735	1 212	1 734
1999	27 167	23 603	3 306	101	158	20 343	6 825	17 671	5 932	2 566	741	1 242	1 686
2000	27 483	23 975	3 256	109	143	20 517	6 966	17 883	6 092	2 531	725	1 178	1 691
2001	27 710	24 183	3 296	98	133	20 723	6 987	18 047	6 136	2 582	714	1 140	1 651
2002	27 921	24 386	3 337	95	103	20 809	7 112	18 173	6 213	2 565	772	1 150	1 587
2003	28 186	24 427	3 565	95	100	20 915	7 271	18 116	6 311	2 730	834	1 116	1 516
2004	28 485	24 645	3 618	97	124	21 131	7 354	18 265	6 381	2 789	830	1 073	1 509
2005	28 774	24 929	3 636	96	115	21 484	7 290	18 596	6 333	2 811	825	1 058	1 445
2006	29 030	25 098	3 738	97	97	21 642	7 388	18 712	6 386	2 864	874	1 053	1 479
2007	29 222	25 204	3 806	102	110	21 801	7 422	18 844	6 360	2 891	915	1 097	1 500
2008	29 443	25 407	3 826	101	110	21 938	7 505	18 969	6 438	2 911	915	1 122	1 399
Male													
	MGSA	MGRO	MGRR	MGRU	MGRX	YCBF	YCBI	YCBL	YCBO	YCBR	YCBU	YCBX	YCCA
1998	14 597	12 021	2 437	31	107	13 303	1 294	11 055	967	2 170	267	512	787
1999	14 767	12 216	2 415	35	102	13 408	1 359	11 207	1 009	2 135	280	522	788
2000	14 909	12 429	2 357	36	88	13 540	1 370	11 394	1 035	2 082	275	489	770
2001	15 026	12 484	2 423	33	86	13 625	1 402	11 415	1 070	2 148	275	459	759
2002	15 099	12 559	2 444	33	63	13 606	1 493	11 430	1 129	2 131	313	480	721
2003	15 262	12 566	2 604	34	58	13 691	1 570	11 388	1 178	2 259	345	461	697
2004	15 405	12 634	2 659	39	73	13 776	1 629	11 413	1 222	2 313	346	456	709
2005	15 535	12 768	2 666	35	67	13 887	1 649	11 517	1 251	2 322	344	455	681
2006	15 662	12 857	2 710	38	58	13 975	1 688	11 579	1 279	2 355	356	452	677
2007	15 813	12 950	2 762	39	61	14 068	1 745	11 650	1 301	2 379	384	454	699
2008	15 894	13 011	2 780	37	67	14 072	1 822	11 643	1 368	2 393	387	461	641
Female													
	MGSB	MGRP	MGRS	MGRV	MGRY	YCBG	YCBJ	YCBM	YCBP	YCBS	YCBV	YCBY	YCCB
1998	12 198	11 161	910	69	60	6 771	5 427	6 283	4 878	442	468	700	948
1999	12 400	11 387	892	67	55	6 935	5 466	6 465	4 923	430	461	720	899
2000	12 573	11 547	898	73	56	6 977	5 596	6 489	5 058	449	450	689	921
2001	12 684	11 699	873	65	47	7 099	5 586	6 633	5 066	434	440	681	892
2002	12 823	11 827	893	63	40	7 203	5 620	6 743	5 084	434	459	670	866
2003	12 925	11 861	961	60	42	7 224	5 701	6 729	5 133	471	490	656	819
2004	13 080	12 011	960	58	51	7 355	5 726	6 852	5 159	476	484	617	800
2005	13 239	12 161	970	61	48	7 598	5 642	7 079	5 082	489	481	603	763
2006	13 367	12 241	1 027	59	39	7 667	5 700	7 133	5 108	510	518	602	802
2007	13 409	12 254	1 044	63	49	7 732	5 677	7 194	5 060	512	532	643	801
2008	13 549	12 396	1 047	64	42	7 866	5 683	7 327	5 070	518	529	661	758

1 See chapter text. In August 2007, ONS published the mid-year population estimates for 2006. These estimates have now been incorporated into the LFS estimates from 2001 onwards. Further details can be found at http://www.statistics.gov.uk/cci/article.asp?id=1919

2 The Labour Force Survey has now moved to calendar quarters from May 2006. More information can be found on page 5 of the Concepts and Definitions.pdf by following this link:- www.statistics.gov.uk/downloads/theme_labour/Concepts_Definitions_HQS.pdf

3 People whose main job is full or part-time and based on respondents' self assessment.

4 Those on employment and training programmes are classified as in employment. Some of those on programmes may consider themselves to be employees or self employed so appear in other categories.

5 Second jobs reported in LFS in addition to person's main full or part-time job.

Sources: Labour Force Survey, Office for National Statistics;
Helpline: 01633 456901

7.3 Employment: by sex and age[1]
United Kingdom
At Quarter 2 each year[2]. Seasonally adjusted

Thousands and percentages

	All aged 16 and over	16-59/64	16-17	18-24	25-34	35-49	50-64 (m) 50-59 (f)	65+ (m) 60+ (f)
Thousands								
All Persons								
	MGRZ	YBSE	YBTO	YBTR	YBTU	YBTX	MGUW	MGUZ
2002	27 921	27 034	659	3 381	6 509	10 430	6 055	887
2003	28 186	27 240	652	3 415	6 362	10 591	6 221	946
2004	28 485	27 486	642	3 528	6 283	10 742	6 293	998
2005	28 774	27 705	607	3 539	6 297	10 885	6 379	1 070
2006	29 030	27 863	559	3 618	6 261	10 975	6 451	1 167
2007	29 222	27 996	534	3 657	6 254	11 039	6 513	1 226
2008	29 443	28 120	525	3 663	6 285	11 065	6 583	1 323
Male								
	MGSA	YBSF	YBTP	YBTS	YBTV	YBTY	MGUX	MGVA
2002	15 099	14 801	321	1 773	3 566	5 559	3 582	297
2003	15 262	14 932	316	1 802	3 473	5 659	3 682	330
2004	15 405	15 068	309	1 868	3 417	5 743	3 731	337
2005	15 535	15 175	293	1 879	3 432	5 781	3 790	361
2006	15 662	15 272	260	1 912	3 423	5 845	3 832	390
2007	15 813	15 407	257	1 943	3 443	5 879	3 885	407
2008	15 894	15 452	260	1 935	3 444	5 871	3 943	443
Female								
	MGSB	YBSG	YBTQ	YBTT	YBTW	YBTZ	MGUY	MGVB
2002	12 823	12 232	338	1 608	2 943	4 871	2 473	591
2003	12 925	12 309	336	1 612	2 889	4 932	2 539	616
2004	13 080	12 419	333	1 660	2 866	4 998	2 562	661
2005	13 239	12 530	315	1 660	2 865	5 104	2 589	709
2006	13 367	12 591	299	1 706	2 838	5 130	2 619	776
2007	13 409	12 589	277	1 714	2 812	5 160	2 627	820
2008	13 549	12 669	265	1 729	2 841	5 195	2 640	880
Percentages[3]								
All Persons								
	MGSR	MGSU	YBUA	YBUD	YBUG	YBUJ	YBUM	YBUP
2002	59.7	74.5	43.6	67.5	79.6	81.9	68.2	8.5
2003	59.9	74.6	42.7	66.5	79.5	82.1	69.6	8.9
2004	60.0	74.7	41.2	66.9	79.7	82.2	70.0	9.4
2005	60.1	74.7	38.6	65.6	80.2	82.4	70.4	9.9
2006	60.2	74.6	35.5	65.5	80.1	82.3	70.8	10.7
2007	60.0	74.6	33.7	64.8	80.3	82.3	71.3	11.0
2008	60.0	74.5	33.1	63.8	80.3	82.4	71.9	11.7
Male								
	MGSS	MGSV	YBUB	YBUE	YBUH	YBUK	YBUN	YBUQ
2002	66.8	79.0	41.4	70.7	88.0	88.3	70.3	7.7
2003	67.0	79.2	40.3	69.8	87.6	88.7	71.6	8.4
2004	67.1	79.3	38.7	70.1	87.4	89.0	72.0	8.5
2005	66.9	79.0	36.3	68.8	88.1	88.5	72.4	9.0
2006	66.9	78.8	32.3	68.3	88.1	88.7	72.3	9.6
2007	66.8	78.8	31.5	67.6	88.7	88.8	72.6	9.9
2008	66.5	78.5	31.9	65.9	87.9	88.6	73.0	10.5
Female								
	MGST	MGSW	YBUC	YBUF	YBUI	YBUL	YBUO	YBUR
2002	53.0	69.6	45.9	64.3	71.3	75.7	65.4	8.9
2003	53.1	69.7	45.1	63.1	71.6	75.6	66.8	9.3
2004	53.5	69.9	43.9	63.7	72.1	75.6	67.2	9.9
2005	53.7	70.0	41.0	62.3	72.3	76.4	67.8	10.5
2006	53.8	70.0	39.0	62.8	72.2	76.1	68.5	11.3
2007	53.7	69.9	36.0	62.0	72.0	75.9	69.6	11.8
2008	53.8	70.2	34.3	61.5	72.8	76.3	70.2	12.4

1 See chapter text. In August 2007, ONS published the mid-year population estimates for 2006. These estimates have now been incorporated into the LFS estimates from 2001 onwards. Further details can be found at http://www.statistics.gov.uk/cci/article.asp?id=1919

2 The Labour Force Survey has now moved to calendar quarters from May 2006. More information can be found on page 5 of the Concepts and Definitions.pdf by following this link:- www.statistics.gov.uk/downloads/theme_labour/Concepts_Definitions_HQS.pdf

3 Total in employment as a percentage of all persons in the relevant group.

Sources: Labour Force Survey, Office for National Statistics;
Helpline: 01633 456901

7.4 Distribution of the workforce:[1,2] by sex
At mid-June each year. Seasonally adjusted

Thousands

		1998	1999	2000	2001	2002	2003	2004	2005	2006	2007	2008
United Kingdom												
Claimant count	BCJD	1 347.8	1 248.1	1 088.4	969.9	946.6	933.0	853.3	862.1	944.7	863.3	902.4
Males	DPAE	1 029.4	955.0	831.6	739.6	717.1	700.3	636.2	639.7	697.3	630.6	663.3
Females	DPAF	318.4	293.1	256.8	230.3	229.6	232.8	217.1	222.1	247.4	232.7	239.1
Workforce jobs	DYDC	28 824	29 127	29 554	29 890	30 064	30 350	30 671	31 012	31 257	31 471	31 661
Males	KAMS	15 327	15 663	15 772	15 992	16 002	16 245	16 376	16 487	16 662	16 773	16 908
Females	KAMT	13 497	13 464	13 782	13 898	14 061	14 105	14 296	14 525	14 596	14 698	14 753
HM Forces	KAMU	219	218	217	214	214	223	218	210	204	198	193
Males	KAMV	203	201	199	196	197	203	199	191	185	180	176
Females	KAMW	17	17	18	18	18	19	19	18	18	18	18
Self-employment jobs	DYZN	3 691	3 688	3 579	3 604	3 674	3 883	3 964	3 943	4 056	4 169	4 181
Males	KAMZ	2 639	2 642	2 552	2 593	2 637	2 785	2 863	2 840	2 879	2 953	2 961
Females	KANA	1 052	1 046	1 027	1 012	1 037	1 097	1 101	1 103	1 177	1 216	1 220
Employees jobs	BCAJ	24 783	25 091	25 639	25 973	26 085	26 152	26 381	26 763	26 933	27 051	27 232
Males	KANC	12 409	12 740	12 948	13 142	13 114	13 201	13 249	13 398	13 559	13 609	13 739
Females	KAND	12 374	12 351	12 691	12 831	12 971	12 951	13 132	13 365	13 374	13 442	13 493
of whom												
Total, production and construction industries	KANF	5 525	5 382	5 349	5 194	4 952	4 749	4 594	4 475	4 423	4 377	4 378
Total, all manufacturing industries	KANG	4 208	4 059	3 959	3 805	3 599	3 410	3 246	3 102	2 975	2 911	2 867
Government-supported trainees	KANH	131	131	119	99	90	92	108	96	65	53	54
Males	KANI	76	81	73	62	55	55	65	58	38	31	32
Females	KANJ	55	50	46	38	36	37	44	38	27	21	22
Great Britain												
Claimant count	DPAG	1 290.3	1 197.3	1 046.3	930.5	910.2	898.5	822.5	833.2	916.8	839.0	874.7
Males	ZSDP	984.6	915.7	799.6	709.7	689.3	673.9	612.8	618.0	676.4	612.3	641.8
Females	ZSDQ	305.7	281.6	246.8	220.8	220.9	224.6	209.8	215.1	240.4	226.7	232.9
Workforce jobs	KANQ	28 103	28 394	28 804	29 127	29 289	29 561	29 870	30 186	30 423	30 632	30 810
Males	KANR	14 937	15 267	15 366	15 580	15 588	15 822	15 946	16 044	16 214	16 327	16 454
Females	KANS	13 167	13 126	13 438	13 547	13 702	13 739	13 924	14 142	14 209	14 305	14 355
HM Forces	BCAH	219	218	217	214	214	223	218	210	204	198	193
Males	KANU	203	201	199	196	197	203	199	191	185	180	176
Females	KANV	17	17	18	18	18	19	19	18	18	18	18
Self-employment jobs	KANW	3 598	3 592	3 480	3 500	3 572	3 774	3 851	3 820	3 933	4 055	4 059
Males	KANX	2 563	2 565	2 470	2 506	2 553	2 695	2 770	2 738	2 780	2 862	2 863
Females	KANY	1 035	1 027	1 011	994	1 019	1 079	1 081	1 082	1 153	1 193	1 196
Employee jobs	KANZ	24 169	24 465	24 997	25 321	25 419	25 478	25 699	26 067	26 227	26 332	26 507
Males	KAOA	12 105	12 429	12 630	12 821	12 788	12 873	12 917	13 062	13 215	13 258	13 386
Females	KAOB	12 065	12 036	12 367	12 500	12 631	12 605	12 782	13 005	13 012	13 074	13 120
of whom												
Total, production and construction industries	KAOC	5 383	5 239	5 205	5 052	4 813	4 616	4 464	4 344	4 290	4 239	4 242
Total, all manufacturing industries	KAOD	4 101	3 954	3 856	3 704	3 501	3 318	3 157	3 015	2 888	2 823	2 778
Government-supported trainees	KAOE	117	120	110	92	84	86	102	90	58	46	51
Males	KAOF	67	73	67	57	50	51	60	53	33	27	29
Females	KAOG	50	47	43	35	34	35	42	36	25	19	21

Note. Because the figures have been rounded independently totals may differ from the sum of the components. Also the totals may include some employees whose industrial classification could not be ascertained.

1 The data in this table have not been adjusted to reflect the 2001 Census population data. See chapter text.

2 There is a discontinuity in the employee jobs series between December 2005 and September 2006 due to improvements to the annual benchmark. Further information can be found at:
http://www.statistics.gov.uk/statbase/product.asp?vlnk=9765

Sources: Employment, Earnings and Innovations Division, Office for National Statistics;
Customer Helpline: 01633 456776

7.5 Employee jobs: by industry[1,2,3]
Standard Industrial Classification 2003
At June each year. Not seasonally adjusted

Thousands

		SIC 2003	United Kingdom						Great Britain				
			2004	2005	2006	2007	2008		2004	2005	2006	2007	2008
All sections	KAOH	A - O	26 349	26 735	26 908	27 030	27 211	LMAB	25 669	26 041	26 204	26 312	26 486
Index of production and construction industries	KAOI	C - F	4 583	4 462	4 411	4 365	4 367	LMAH	4 452	4 333	4 278	4 228	4 231
Index of production industries	KAOJ	C - E	3 413	3 258	3 136	3 087	3 049	LMAF	3 320	3 166	3 044	2 994	2 955
of which, manufacturing industries	KAOK	D	3 245	3 102	2 976	2 913	2 869	KAPQ	3 156	3 015	2 889	2 825	2 780
Service industries	KAOL	G - O	21 530	22 023	22 256	22 411	22 574	LMAJ	20 994	21 472	21 697	21 842	21 998
Agriculture, hunting and forestry and fishing	KAOM	A/B	237	249	241	254	269	KAPS	222	236	229	242	257
Agriculture hunting and forestry	KPHI	A	229	244	234	247	262	KOVW	215	231	222	235	250
Agriculture hunting & related activities	KPHJ	01	219	234	225	238	251	KOVX	206	221	213	226	239
Fishing	KPHK	B	7	5	7	7	7	KOVY	7	5	7	7	7
Mining and quarrying	KPHL	C	58	57	58	59	58	KOVZ	56	55	56	57	56
Mining and quarrying of energy producing materials	KPHM	CA	35	34	35	35	35	KOWA	35	34	35	35	35
Mining	KAPG	10/12	..	..	..	..	..	KOWB	9	7	6	7	..
Extraction of crude petroleum	KPHN	11	..	..	..	..	..	KOWC	25	27	29	30	..
Mining and quarrying except of energy producing materials	KPHO	CB(13/14)	23	23	22	23	24	KOWD	22	21	20	21	22
Energy and water supply industries	KAOO	C/E	168	156	160	174	180	LMAM	163	151	155	169	175
Manufacturing	KPHP	D	3 245	3 102	2 976	2 913	2 869	LMAD	3 156	3 015	2 889	2 825	2 780
Manufacture of food products Beverages and tobacco	KPHQ	DA	443	428	418	415	413	LMAN	424	409	400	396	395
Of food	KPHR	151 to 158	..	..	..	..	..	KOWH	375	364	356	354	352
Of beverages and tobacco	KPHS	159/16	..	..	..	..	..	KOWI	48	45	44	43	43
Manufacture of textiles and textile products	KPHT	DB	142	123	107	98	94	KOWJ	135	118	103	94	91
Of textiles	KPHU	17	95	84	74	68	65	KOWK	90	81	71	66	63
Of made-up textile articles except apparel	KPHV	174	..	..	..	..	..	KOWL	29	27	25	24	23
Of textiles excluding made-up textile	KPHW	Rest of 17	..	..	..	..	..	KOWM	61	54	46	42	40
Of wearing apparel,dressing and dyeing of fur	KPHX	18	47	39	33	30	29	KOWN	45	38	31	28	28
Manufacture of leather and leather products including footwear	KPHY	DC	12	11	11	10	9	KOWO	12	11	11	10	8
Of leather and leather goods	KPHZ	191/192	..	..	..	..	..	KOWP	6	5	7	5	4
Of footwear	KPIA	193	..	..	..	..	..	KOWQ	6	5	5	4	4
Manufacture of wood and wood products	KPIB	DD(20)	83	81	77	80	78	LMAP	79	77	73	75	73
Manufacture of pulp paper and paper products, publishing and printing	KPIC	DE	412	400	381	367	353	LMAQ	406	394	375	362	348
Of pulp paper and paper products	KPID	21	82	77	71	67	65	KOWT	80	76	70	66	64
Publishing printing and reproduction of recorded media	KPIE	22	330	322	310	300	288	KOWU	326	318	306	296	284
Manufacture of coke refined petroleum products and nuclear fuel	KPIF	DF(23)	24	23	23	24	24	KOWV	23	23	22	24	24
Manufacture of chemicals, chemical products and man-made fibres	KPIG	DG(24)	210	199	193	186	181	LMAR	207	196	190	182	178
Manufacture of rubber and plastics	KPIH	DH(25)	212	203	196	186	182	LMAS	205	196	189	179	175
Manufacture of other non-metallic mineral products	KPII	DI(26)	118	111	107	105	105	KOWZ	112	105	101	99	98
Manufacture of basic metals and fabricated metal products	KPIJ	DJ	417	398	387	381	374	KOXA	409	391	380	373	366
Of basic metals	KPIK	27	81	74	73	69	68	KOXB	81	73	72	69	67
except machinery	KPIL	28	335	325	314	311	307	KOXC	328	317	307	304	299

7.5
continued

Employee jobs: by industry[1,2,3]
Standard Industrial Classification 2003
At June each year. Not seasonally adjusted

Thousands

		SIC 2003	United Kingdom						Great Britain				
			2004	2005	2006	2007	2008		2004	2005	2006	2007	2008
Manufacture of Machinery and Equipment not elsewhere classified	KPIM	DK(29)	285	280	270	275	276	LMAU	279	273	263	268	269
Manufacture of electrical and optical equipment	KPIN	DL	351	333	315	306	296	LMAV	341	324	306	297	287
Of office machinery and computers	KPIO	30	33	30	26	22	21	KOXF	30	28	24	20	19
Of electrical machinery and apparatus	KPIP	31	127	122	117	115	110	KOXG	123	118	113	111	106
Of electric motors etc control apparatus and insulated cable	KPIQ	311 to 313	..	..	..	..	..	KOXH	66	63	61	60	58
Of accumulators, primary cells, batteries, lamps and electrical equipment	KPIR	314 to 316	..	..	..	..	..	KOXI	58	56	52	51	48
Radio television and communication equipment	KPIS	32	74	66	61	58	55	KOXJ	72	64	59	56	54
Of electronic components	KPIT	321	..	..	..	..	..	KOXK	29	27	24	24	22
Of radio TV and telephone apparatus, sound and video recorders	KPIU	322/323	..	..	..	..	..	KOXL	42	37	35	33	32
Of medical precision and optical equipment, watches	KPIV	33	118	116	111	112	110	KOXM	116	114	109	110	108
Manufacture of transport equipment	KPIW	DM	343	329	316	310	315	LMAW	333	320	306	301	306
Of motor vehicles and trailers	KPIX	34	196	184	172	159	159	KOXO	193	180	168	156	155
Of other transport equipment	KPIY	35	146	146	144	151	157	KOXP	140	139	138	145	150
Manufacturing not elsewhere classified	KPIZ	DN(36/37)	197	182	175	171	169	KOXQ	193	178	170	164	163
Electricity gas and water supply	KPJA	E	110	99	102	115	122	KOXR	107	96	99	112	119
Electricity gas steam and hot water supply	KPJB	40	..	..	..	..	..	KOXT	82	73	73	83	89
Collection purification and distribution of water	KPJC	41	..	..	..	..	..	KOXU	25	24	26	29	30
Construction	KPJD	F(45)	1 169	1 204	1 275	1 278	1 319	LMAY	1 133	1 166	1 234	1 234	1 275
Services	KPJE	G - O	21 530	22 023	22 256	22 411	22 574	KOXX	20 994	21 472	21 697	21 842	21 998
Wholesale and retail trade; Repair of motor vehicles, motorcycles and personal household goods	KPJF	G (50 - 52)	4 562	4 597	4 554	4 553	4 583	LMAZ	4 445	4 478	4 432	4 429	4 455
Sale maintenance and repair of motor vehicles, retail of automotive fuel	KPJG	50	561	565	566	564	561	KOXZ	546	550	549	547	543
Sale of motor vehicles, motorcycles and parts, motorcycle repair and sale of automotive fuel	KPJH	501/503 - 505	..	..	..	..	..	KOYA	379	380	374	373	369
Maintenance and repair of motor vehicles	KPJI	502	..	..	..	..	..	KOYB	168	169	175	174	174
Wholesale trade and commission trade except motor vehicles	KPJJ	51	1 119	1 131	1 126	1 139	1 151	KOYC	1 095	1 108	1 102	1 115	1 129
Wholesale on a fee of contract basis	KPJK	511	..	..	..	..	..	KOYD	60	61	66	70	76
Wholesale agricultural raw materials and live animals	KPJL	512	..	..	..	..	..	KPLD	23	22	19	19	19
Wholesale food beverages & tobacco	KPJM	513	..	..	..	..	..	KPLE	188	190	195	195	196
Wholesale household goods	KPJN	514	..	..	..	..	..	KPLF	267	274	272	274	273
Wholesale of non-agricultural intermediate products waste & scrap	KPJO	515	..	..	..	..	..	KPLG	232	232	230	238	241
Wholesale machinery eqpt. & supplies	KPJP	516	..	..	..	..	..	KPLH	230	238	232	232	236
Other wholesale	KPJQ	517	..	..	..	..	..	KPLI	95	91	89	86	87
Retail trade except of motor vehicles and motorcycles;repair of personal and household goods	KPJR	52	2 882	2 901	2 862	2 851	2 871	KPLJ	2 804	2 820	2 781	2 767	2 783
Non-specialised stores selling mainly food beverages & tobacco	KPJS	5211/5221-4,5227	..	..	..	..	..	KPLK	1 120	1 140	1 119	1 109	1 125
Other non-specialised stores second hand shops & sales not in stores	KPJT	5212/525-526	..	..	..	..	..	KPLL	360	353	337	329	336

7.5

Employee jobs: by industry[1,2,3]
Standard Industrial Classification 2003
continued   At June each year. Not seasonally adjusted

Thousands

		SIC 2003	United Kingdom						Great Britain				
			2004	2005	2006	2007	2008		2004	2005	2006	2007	2008
Alcoholic & other beverages, tobacco	KPJU	5225 to 5226	..	..	..	..	..	KPLM	54	49	46	41	39
Pharmaceutical & medical goods cosmetics & toilet articles	KPJV	523	..	..	..	..	..	KPLN	99	103	105	107	111
Clothing footwear & leather goods	KPJW	5242/5243	..	..	..	..	..	KPLO	409	415	416	428	424
Textile furniture lighting equipment electrical household appliances radio and TV paints glass hardware and household goods not elsewhere classified	KPJX	5241/5244-46	..	..	..	..	..	KPLP	304	299	291	293	282
Books newspapers and stationery, other retail in specialised stores	KPJY	5247/5248	..	..	..	..	..	KPLQ	432	435	444	438	446
Repair of personal and household goods	KPJZ	527	..	..	..	..	..	KPLR	26	26	22	22	20
Hotels and restaurants	KPKA	H	1 839	1 855	1 840	1 826	1 835	LMBA	1 798	1 813	1 797	1 783	1 793
Hotels camp sites short-stay accom.	KPKB	551/552	..	..	..	..	..	KPLT	379	387	383	388	392
Restaurants	KPKC	553	..	..	..	..	..	KPLU	594	614	634	628	635
Bars	KPKD	554	..	..	..	..	..	KPLV	558	552	542	536	517
Canteens and catering	KPKE	555	..	..	..	..	..	KPLW	267	261	238	231	249
Transport, storage and communication	KPKF	I	1 570	1 594	1 588	1 582	1 596	KPLX	1 542	1 565	1 559	1 551	1 565
Land transport, transport via pipelines	KPKG	60	519	534	547	549	558	KPLY	505	521	533	535	544
Transport via railways	KPKH	601	..	..	..	..	..	KPLZ	50	53	52	54	54
Other land transport and via pipelines	KPKI	602/603	..	..	..	..	..	KPMA	456	468	481	479	490
Water transport	KPKJ	61	17	19	18	17	17	KPMB	17	18	17	16	16
Air transport	KPKK	62	85	88	90	90	85	KPMC	85	88	89	92	85
Supporting and auxiliary transport activities, activities of travel agents	KPKL	63	440	453	443	452	462	KPMD	435	447	438	446	456
Travel agencies and tour operators	KPKM	633	..	..	..	..	..	KPME	133	120	107	104	106
Post and telecommunications	KPKN	64	509	500	491	474	473	LMBC	500	491	482	465	464
National post and courier activities	KPKO	641	..	..	..	..	..	KPMG	275	275	266	255	260
Telecommunications	KPKR	6420	..	..	..	..	..	KPMJ	225	216	216	209	204
Financial intermediation	KPKS	J	1 073	1 062	1 059	1 064	1 049	LMBD	1 056	1 044	1 040	1 045	1 030
Financial intermediation except insurance and pension funding	KPKT	65	621	609	603	595	580	KPML	609	596	590	582	567
Insurance and pension funding except compulsory social security	KPKU	66	197	183	181	183	180	KPMM	196	181	179	180	178
Activities auxiliary to financial intermediation	KPKV	67	255	271	274	287	289	KPMN	252	267	271	283	285
Except insurance and pension funding	KPKW	671	..	..	..	..	..	KPMO	123	136	138	149	150
Auxiliary to insurance and pension funding	KPKX	672	..	..	..	..	..	KPMP	129	131	133	134	135
Real estate renting & business activities	KPKY	K	4 129	4 336	4 533	4 698	4 766	KPMQ	4 065	4 268	4 462	4 625	4 689
Real estate activities	KPKZ	70	409	449	451	450	453	LMBE	402	441	443	442	445
Activities with own property, letting of own property	KPLA	701/702	..	..	..	..	..	KPMS	236	252	249	241	249
Activities on a fee or contract basis	KPLB	703	..	..	..	..	..	KPMT	166	189	194	200	196

7.5 Employee jobs: by industry[1,2,3]
Standard Industrial Classification 2003

At June each year. Not seasonally adjusted

Thousand

			United Kingdom						Great Britain			
		SIC 2003	2004	2005	2006	2007	2008		2004	2005	2006	2007	2008
Renting of machinery and equipment without operator & of personal & household goods	KPLC	71	153	157	160	157	156	KPMU	150	155	158	155	154
Construction and civil engineering machinery	KOUU	7132	..	..	..	..	..	KPMV	41	42	45	45	46
All other goods and equipment	KOUV	Rest of 71	..	..	..	..	..	KPMW	109	113	113	110	108
Computer and related equipment	KOUW	72	488	493	525	542	548	KPMX	482	486	518	535	540
Research and development	KOUX	73	101	104	108	109	108	KPMY	100	103	106	108	106
Other business activities	KOUY	74	2 978	3 133	3 289	3 440	3 501	KPMZ	2 930	3 083	3 238	3 386	3 444
Legal, accounting, book-keeping & auditing activities	KOUZ	741	..	..	..	..	..	KPNA	840	889	962	1 005	1 027
Legal activities	KOVA	7411	..	..	..	..	..	KPNB	254	260	280	294	292
Accounting, book-keeping auditing, tax consultancy	KOVB	7412	..	..	..	..	..	KPNC	194	203	218	226	238
Market research business and consultancy activities	KOVC	7413/7414	..	..	..	..	..	KPND	291	316	355	377	389
Management activities of holding companies[4]	KOVD	7415	..	..	..	..	..	KPNE	101	110	109	108	108
Architectural engineering activities and related technical consultancy, technical testing	KOVE	742/743	..	..	..	..	..	KPNF	340	347	374	394	410
Advertising	KOVF	744	..	..	..	..	..	KPNG	80	84	81	87	83
Industrial cleaning	KOVG	747	..	..	..	..	..	KPNH	414	436	449	449	455
Public administration and defence, compulsory social security	KOVH	L(75)	1 492	1 516	1 514	1 509	1 474	LMBG	1 431	1 456	1 454	1 450	1 415
Education	KOVI	M(80)	2 299	2 348	2 384	2 401	2 420	LMBH	2 230	2 274	2 311	2 328	2 348
Health and social work	KOVJ	N	3 178	3 298	3 345	3 364	3 421	LOJV	3 070	3 188	3 233	3 249	3 305
Human health, veterinary activities	KOVK	851/852	..	..	..	..	..	KPNL	2 027	2 103	2 100	2 095	2 123
Social work activities	KOVL	853	..	..	..	..	..	KPNM	1 043	1 084	1 133	1 153	1 182
Other community social and personal service activities, private households with employed persons, extra-territorial organisations and bodies	KOVM	O	1 388	1 417	1 440	1 414	1 431	LMBK	1 357	1 385	1 408	1 382	1 398
Sewage and refuse disposal; sanitation	KOVN	90	100	104	108	110	109	KPNO	97	101	105	106	106
Activities of membership organisations	KOVO	91	212	215	225	215	208	KPNP	204	206	217	207	200
Recreational cultural and sporting activities	KOVP	92	762	779	783	771	789	KPNQ	747	764	767	755	773
Motion picture video radio TV news agencies and entertainment activities	KOVQ	921 to 924	..	..	..	..	..	KPNR	224	222	222	218	232
Other service activities, private households with employed persons, extra territorial organisations	KOVT	93/95/99	314	318	325	319	325	KPNU	309	313	320	314	320
Washing, dry cleaning of textile and fur products	KOVU	9301	..	..	..	..	..	KPNV	42	40	43	40	38
Hairdressing, other beauty treatment, physical and well-being activities	KOVV	9302/9304	..	..	..	..	..	KPNW	105	114	122	122	122

Note. Because the figures have been rounded independently totals may differ from the sum of the components. Also the totals may include some employees whose industrial classification could not be ascertained.

1 See chapter text. The data in this table have not been adjusted to reflect the 2001 Census population data.

2 All figures have been revised. For further information see: http://www.statistics.gov.uk/cci/article.asp?id=1340

3 There is a discontinuity in the employee jobs series between December 2005 and September 2006 due to improvements to the annual benchmark. Further information can be found at: http://www.statistics.gov.uk/Stat-base/Product.asp?vlnk=9765

4 Head office and holding company local units were reclassified to Class 74.15 (within Section K) from December 2003 as a result of the SIC 2003 update.

Sources: Department of Manpower Services (Northern Ireland);; Employment, Earnings and Innovations Division, ONS: 01633 456776

7.6 Weekly hours worked: by sex[1,2]
United Kingdom
At Quarter 2 each year[3]. Seasonally adjusted

Hours

	All workers' weekly hours[4,5]		Average actual weekly hours of work[5]		
	Total (millions)	Average	Full-time employment[4,6]	Part-time employment[6]	Second jobs[7]
All Persons					
	YBUS	YBUV	YBUY	YBVB	YBVE
1998	884.8	33.1	38.5	15.2	9.1
1999	892.7	32.9	38.2	15.3	9.1
2000	894.8	32.6	37.9	15.5	9.1
2001	903.5	32.7	37.9	15.6	9.4
2002	901.0	32.3	37.5	15.6	9.4
2003	904.6	32.2	37.4	15.6	9.3
2004	912.1	32.1	37.3	15.6	9.3
2005	923.7	32.2	37.3	15.7	9.5
2006	928.5	32.0	37.1	15.6	9.4
2007	936.1	32.1	37.2	15.6	9.5
2008	940.7	32.0	37.1	15.6	9.7
Male					
	YBUT	YBUW	YBUZ	YBVC	YBVF
1998	562.4	38.6	40.5	14.9	9.7
1999	564.0	38.3	40.2	15.1	9.8
2000	564.2	37.9	39.8	15.3	9.9
2001	567.0	37.8	39.7	15.3	10.3
2002	561.9	37.3	39.3	15.1	10.3
2003	564.3	37.0	39.2	15.3	10.1
2004	569.0	37.0	39.2	15.6	10.3
2005	572.2	36.9	39.1	15.6	10.3
2006	573.6	36.7	38.9	15.5	10.1
2007	580.2	36.8	39.0	15.5	10.6
2008	580.8	36.6	39.0	15.4	10.8
Female					
	YBUU	YBUX	YBVA	YBVD	YBVG
1998	322.4	26.5	34.5	15.3	8.6
1999	328.6	26.5	34.5	15.4	8.6
2000	330.6	26.3	34.2	15.5	8.5
2001	336.5	26.5	34.3	15.7	8.8
2002	339.1	26.5	34.1	15.7	8.8
2003	340.3	26.4	34.0	15.7	8.8
2004	343.1	26.3	33.9	15.6	8.5
2005	351.5	26.6	34.0	15.8	8.9
2006	354.9	26.6	34.0	15.7	8.9
2007	355.9	26.6	33.9	15.6	8.8
2008	359.9	26.6	33.8	15.6	8.9

1 See chapter text. In August 2007, ONS published the mid-year population estimates for 2006. These estimates have now been incorporated into the LFS estimates from 2001 onwards. Further details can be found at http://www.statistics.gov.uk/cci/article.asp?id=1919

2 Average hours actually worked in the reference week which includes hours worked in second jobs.

3 The Labour Force Survey has now moved to calendar quarters from May 2006. More information can be found on page 5 of the Concepts and Definitions.pdf by following this link:- www.statistics.gov.uk/downloads/theme_labour/Concepts_Definitions_HQS.pdf

4 Main and second job.

5 Includes both paid and unpaid overtime.

6 People whose main job is full-time or part-time and based on respondents' self assessment.

7 Second jobs reported in the LFS in addition to persons' main full time job.

Sources: Labour Force Survey, Office for National Statistics;
Helpline: 01633 456901

Labour Market

7.7 International comparisons
Employment and unemployment rates[1,2]

		2006 Q1	2006 Q2	2006 Q3	2006 Q4	2007 Q1	2007 Q2	2007 Q3	2007 Q4	2008 Q1	2008 Q2	2008 Q3	2008 Q4
EUROSTAT Employment rates													
Austria	YXSN	68.2	70.0	71.9	70.6	70.3	71.5	72.5	71.3	71.0	72.3	72.8	72.2
Belgium	YXSO	60.3	60.4	61.2	62.1	61.7	61.6	62.1	62.7	62.6	62.0	62.6	62.4
Bulgaria	A495	55.5	59.1	60.3	59.8	59.7	61.6	62.7	62.9	62.6	63.9	65.0	64.3
Cyprus	A4AC	68.2	69.5	70.4	70.4	69.8	71.2	71.3	71.5	70.2	71.1	71.0	71.1
Czech Republic	A4AD	64.8	65.3	65.4	65.6	65.5	66.0	66.3	66.5	66.1	66.6	66.7	66.8
Denmark	YXSP	76.5	76.9	78.2	77.9	76.7	77.3	77.1	77.4	77.0	78.4	78.6	78.3
Estonia	A4AE	67.4	68.8	67.9	68.1	68.6	69.7	70.2	69.1	69.5	69.8	70.4	69.6
Finland	YXSQ	67.7	69.9	70.8	69.0	68.3	71.3	71.7	69.9	69.5	72.3	72.1	70.3
France	YXSR	63.2	63.8	64.4	63.9	63.8	64.6	65.1	64.9	64.8	65.2	65.7	65.0
Germany	YXSS	66.4	67.4	68.1	68.3	68.4	69.1	69.9	70.0	70.0	70.3	71.3	71.3
Greece	YXST	60.4	61.0	61.5	61.0	60.8	61.5	61.8	61.5	61.3	62.2	62.2	61.7
Hungary	A4AF	56.7	57.3	57.6	57.6	56.9	57.6	57.7	57.1	57.6	56.5	57.3	56.5
Ireland	YXSU	68.0	68.1	69.6	68.7	68.5	68.9	69.9	69.0	68.6	68.1	68.0	65.6
Italy	YXSV	57.9	58.9	58.4	58.5	57.9	58.9	59.1	58.7	58.3	59.2	59.0	58.5
Latvia	A4AG	64.3	65.5	68.0	67.4	66.4	67.6	69.0	70.3	69.6	69.5	69.0	66.5
Lithuania	A4AH	63.0	63.7	64.2	63.5	63.9	65.4	66.1	64.4	63.9	64.6	65.0	63.8
Luxembourg	YXSW	63.6	63.6	63.6	63.6	63.9	63.6	64.7	64.4	62.8	64.4	63.9	62.6
Malta	A4AI	53.6	53.6	53.9	53.4	53.9	55.2	54.9	54.5	54.7	55.2	56.1	54.9
Netherlands	YXSX	73.5	74.2	74.7	75.0	75.0	76.0	76.5	76.4	76.4	77.2	77.5	77.6
Poland	A4AJ	52.6	53.9	55.6	55.7	55.4	56.8	57.8	58.1	58.0	58.9	60.0	60.0
Portugal	YXSY	67.6	68.1	68.2	67.6	67.4	67.6	68.1	68.1	68.1	68.6	68.1	67.9
Romania	A494	57.2	59.6	60.9	57.4	57.2	59.6	60.5	57.9	57.7	59.7	60.5	58.3
Slovak Republic	A4AK	58.3	59.3	59.9	60.2	60.1	60.4	60.7	61.6	61.3	61.7	63.1	62.9
Slovenia	A4AL	65.9	67.1	67.2	66.0	66.0	68.3	69.0	67.7	67.1	68.3	70.1	68.8
Spain	YXSZ	64.0	64.7	65.2	65.2	65.1	65.8	66.0	65.5	65.1	65.0	64.5	62.8
Sweden	YXTA	71.5	73.1	74.7	73.2	72.7	74.3	75.7	74.0	73.4	74.8	75.7	73.4
United Kingdom	ANZ6	71.5	71.4	71.8	71.6	71.1	71.2	71.6	71.9	71.6	71.6	71.5	71.3
Total EU[3]	A496	63.6	64.5	65.1	64.8	64.6	65.4	66.0	65.7	65.5	66.0	66.4	65.8
Eurozone[3]	YXTC	63.8	64.7	65.1	65.0	64.9	65.7	66.1	65.9	65.7	66.2	66.5	65.9
National Statistical Offices Employment Rates													
Canada	IUUK	71.3	73.4	74.0	73.0	72.1	74.0	74.6	73.7	72.6	74.3	74.5	73.3
Japan	YXTF	69.1	70.4	70.3	70.1	69.7	71.3	70.8	70.9	70.0	71.3	70.8	70.9
United Kingdom	MGSU	74.7	74.6	74.6	74.5	74.3	74.5	74.6	74.8	74.8	74.7	74.4	74.1
United States	YXTE	71.9	71.9	72.0	72.2	72.1	71.8	71.6	71.5	71.6	71.4	70.8	69.9

		2008 Feb	2008 Mar	2008 Apr	2008 May	2008 Jun	2008 Jul	2008 Aug	2008 Sep	2008 Oct	2008 Nov	2008 Dec	2009 Jan	2009 Feb	2009 Mar
EUROSTAT Unemployment rates															
Austria	ZXDS	3.9	3.8	3.6	3.5	3.6	3.7	3.8	3.9	4.0	4.0	4.2	4.3	4.5	4.5
Belgium	ZXDI	7.0	6.8	6.7	6.6	6.9	7.2	7.4	7.2	7.1	6.9	6.9	7.1	7.2	7.3
Bulgaria	A492	6.3	6.1	6.0	5.8	5.6	5.4	5.3	5.2	5.1	5.0	5.3	5.3	5.6	5.9
Cyprus	A4AN	3.7	3.7	3.6	3.6	3.6	3.7	3.7	3.8	3.8	4.0	4.3	4.4	4.6	4.9
Czech Republic	A4AO	4.5	4.4	4.3	4.3	4.3	4.3	4.3	4.3	4.4	4.5	4.7	4.9	5.2	5.5
Denmark	ZXDJ	3.1	3.0	3.0	3.1	3.1	3.2	3.3	3.4	3.7	3.9	4.3	4.7	5.1	5.7
Estonia	A4AP	4.2	4.0	3.8	4.0	4.7	5.8	6.4	6.7	6.9	7.4	8.4	9.1	10.0	11.1
Finland	ZXDU	6.3	6.3	6.2	6.3	6.3	6.4	6.4	6.5	6.6	6.6	6.7	6.9	7.1	7.4
France	ZXDN	7.6	7.6	7.6	7.6	7.7	7.7	7.8	7.9	8.0	8.2	8.3	8.4	8.6	8.8
Germany	ZXDK	7.6	7.4	7.4	7.4	7.3	7.2	7.2	7.1	7.1	7.1	7.2	7.3	7.4	7.6
Greece	ZXDL	7.8	7.8	7.5	7.5	7.5	7.5	7.5	7.5	7.8	7.8	7.8	..	..	..
Hungary	A4AQ	7.7	7.6	7.6	7.7	7.8	7.8	7.9	7.9	7.8	8.0	8.3	8.4	8.8	9.2
Ireland	ZXDO	4.8	5.2	5.2	5.5	6.0	6.3	6.6	7.1	7.6	8.2	8.7	9.4	10.0	10.6
Italy	ZXDP	6.6	6.6	6.8	6.8	6.8	6.7	6.7	6.7	6.9	6.9	6.9	..	..	..
Latvia	A4AR	6.1	6.1	6.1	6.2	6.4	7.0	7.5	8.1	9.3	10.3	11.5	13.2	14.6	16.1
Lithuania	A4AS	4.4	4.3	4.3	4.6	5.1	5.8	6.4	6.6	7.2	8.4	9.7	11.6	13.6	15.5
Luxembourg	ZXDQ	4.4	4.4	4.7	4.8	4.9	5.0	5.0	5.1	5.1	5.3	5.5	5.7	5.9	6.1
Malta	A4AT	5.9	5.8	5.9	6.0	6.0	5.9	5.9	5.7	5.9	6.1	6.0	6.3	6.5	6.7
Netherlands	ZXDR	2.8	2.8	2.8	2.9	2.8	2.7	2.7	2.7	2.7	2.7	2.7	2.7	2.7	2.8
Poland	A4AU	7.6	7.4	7.3	7.3	7.1	7.0	6.9	6.8	6.8	6.9	7.0	7.2	7.5	7.7
Portugal	ZXDT	7.7	7.6	7.6	7.6	7.7	7.7	7.8	7.8	7.8	7.9	8.0	8.2	8.4	8.5
Romania	A48Z	5.8	5.8	5.8	5.8	5.8	5.7	5.7	5.7	5.8	5.8	5.8	..	..	..
Slovak Republic	A4AV	10.2	9.9	9.9	9.8	9.6	9.3	9.1	9.0	9.1	9.2	9.3	9.6	10.0	10.5
Slovenia	A4AW	4.7	4.5	4.4	4.5	4.5	4.4	4.3	4.1	4.2	4.2	4.1	4.3	4.6	5.0
Spain	ZXDM	9.2	9.5	10.0	10.5	10.9	11.4	11.8	12.4	13.2	13.9	14.7	15.7	16.5	17.4
Sweden	ZXDV	5.9	5.8	5.8	5.7	5.7	5.8	6.1	6.4	6.7	7.0	7.0	7.3	7.6	8.0
United Kingdom	ZXDW	5.1	5.2	5.2	5.3	5.5	5.7	5.8	6.0	6.1	6.3	6.4	6.6	..	..
Total EU[3]	A493	6.8	6.7	6.8	6.8	6.9	7.0	7.0	7.1	7.3	7.4	7.6	7.8	8.1	8.3
Eurozone[3]	ZXDH	7.2	7.2	7.3	7.4	7.4	7.5	7.6	7.7	7.8	8.0	8.2	8.4	8.7	8.9
National Statistical Offices Unemployment Rates															
Canada	ZXDZ	5.9	6.1	6.0	6.1	6.2	6.1	6.2	6.2	6.3	6.4	6.6	7.2	7.7	8.0
Japan	ZXDY	3.9	3.8	4.0	4.0	4.1	4.0	4.1	4.0	3.8	4.0	4.3	4.2	4.4	..
United Kingdom	MGSX	5.2	5.3	5.2	5.4	5.5	5.7	5.8	6.0	6.1	6.3	6.5	6.7	7.1	..
United States	ZXDX	4.8	5.1	5.0	5.5	5.6	5.8	6.2	6.2	6.6	6.8	7.2	7.6	8.1	8.5

1 See chapter text.
2 The UK employment rate as published by the Office for National Statistics is seasonally adjusted. All other employment and unemployment rates are not seasonally adjusted.

3 The "Total EU" series consists of all 27 EU countries. The Eurozone series consists of the following EU countries: Austria, Belgium, Cyprus, Finland, France, Germany, Greece, Ireland, Italy, Luxembourg, Malta, Netherlands, Portugal, Slovenia and Spain.

Sources: Office for National Statistics; Eurostat; StatsBLS; StatCan; Stat.go.JP;
Labour Market Statistics Helpline: 01633 456901

7.8 Civil Service employment by department[1]
Great Britain

Full-time equivalents, not seasonally adjusted

		2007 Q4	2008 Q1	2008 Q2	2008 Q3	2008 Q4
Attorney General's Departments	GB3F	9 550	9 520	9 540	9 700	9 610
Cabinet Office	BBGD	1 270	1 220	1 240	1 220	1 250
Other Cabinet Office Agencies	GB3G	1 090	1 090	1 020	1 050	1 180
HM Treasury	GB3H	1 140	1 140	1 120	1 180	1 160
Chancellor's other departments	GB3I	4 810	4 660	1 610	1 630	1 680
Charity Commission	GB3J	460	440	450	460	450
Communities and Local Government	YEGA	5 350	5 270	5 220	5 190	5 170
Ministry of Justice	GB3K	83 380	83 350	83 620	83 610	84 230
Culture, Media and Sport	DMTC	600	560	580	560	560
Defence	BCDW	80 250	77 800	77 120	76 790	75 910
Education and Skills (former)	LNFW	–	–	–	–	–
Children, Schools and Families	I44Z	3 290	3 170	3 090	3 090	3 180
Innovation, Universities and Skills	I452	1 850	1 880	1 890	1 830	1 860
Environment, Food and Rural Affairs	LNFX	11 580	10 970	10 720	10 770	10 840
Export Credits Guarantee Department	GB3L	240	220	210	200	210
Foreign and Commonwealth	BCDK	6 030	5 890	5 880	5 870	5 920
Health	BAKR	3 520	3 550	3 550	3 550	3 610
Food Standards Agency	H6NX	790	780	770	760	760
Meat Hygiene Service	H6NY	1 270	1 230	1 150	1 100	1 050
HM Revenue and Customs	GB3M	88 420	87 850	86 290	84 930	85 580
Home Office	BCDL	25 220	24 730	24 820	24 830	24 600
International Development	DMUA	1 660	1 610	1 610	1 590	1 600
Northern Ireland Office	BBGG	130	120	120	120	120
Office for Standards in Education	GB3N	2 480	2 460	2 400	2 510	2 490
Security and Intelligence Services	GB3O	5 070	5 090	5 130	5 270	5 350
Business, Enterprise and Regulatory Reform	BCDQ	8 490	8 650	8 710	8 750	8 840
Transport	BCDR	18 910	18 530	18 860	18 780	18 630
Work and Pensions	LNGA	107 960	105 830	106 270	106 980	107 110
Central Governments Departments Total	GB3P	474 820	467 620	466 120	465 400	466 160
Scottish Government	GB3Q	15 820	16 050	16 260	16 220	16 250
Welsh Assembly	GB3R	5 720	5 970	5 890	5 880	5 890
TOTAL	BCDX	496 360	489 640	488 270	487 560	488 300

1 Numbers are rounded to the nearest ten.

Source: Office for National Statistics

7.9 Unemployment: number by sex and age group[1]
United Kingdom

At Quarter 2 each year[2]. Seasonally adjusted

Thousands

	All aged 16 and over	16-59/64	16-17	18-24	25-34	35-49	50-64 (m) 50-59 (w)	65+ (m) 60+ (w)
All Persons								
	MGSC	YBSH	YBVH	YBVN	YCGM	YCGS	MGVL	MGVO
2002	1 521	1 499	162	388	342	387	221	22
2003	1 468	1 450	176	400	318	343	213	18
2004	1 439	1 422	173	402	299	353	195	17
2005	1 438	1 421	177	432	285	338	190	17
2006	1 687	1 661	179	514	341	419	208	27
2007	1 662	1 633	196	517	305	393	223	28
2008	1 685	1 662	188	526	327	405	216	23
Male								
	MGSD	YBSI	YBVI	YBVO	YCGN	YCGT	MGVM	MGVP
2002	914	905	93	243	193	227	150	10
2003	890	880	99	244	182	211	145	..
2004	845	837	99	231	185	185	137	..
2005	837	829	101	261	160	183	125	..
2006	978	967	105	309	190	229	134	11
2007	950	937	109	312	161	205	149	13
2008	990	980	102	331	182	218	147	11
Female								
	MGSE	YBSJ	YBVJ	YBVP	YCGO	YCGU	MGVN	MGVQ
2002	607	594	69	145	149	160	71	12
2003	579	570	78	156	137	132	67	..
2004	593	585	74	171	114	168	57	..
2005	601	592	76	172	125	154	65	..
2006	709	693	74	205	151	191	73	16
2007	712	697	86	205	143	188	74	15
2008	695	683	86	196	145	187	69	12

1 See chapter text. In August 2007, ONS published the mid-year population estimates for 2006. These estimates have now been incorporated into the LFS estimates from 2001 onwards. Further details can be found at http://www.statistics.gov.uk/cci/article.asp?id=1919

2 The LFS has now moved to calendar quarters from May 2006. More information is on page 5 of the Concepts and Definitions.pdf :
www.statistics.gov.uk/downloads/theme_labour/Concepts_Definitions_HQS.pdf
Source: Labour Force Survey, Office for National Statistics; Helpline: 01633 456901

7.10 Unemployment: percentage by sex and age group[1,2]
United Kingdom
At Quarter 2 each year[3]. Seasonally adjusted

Percentages

	All aged 16 and over	16-59/64	16-17	18-24	25-34	35-49	50-64 (m) 50-59 (w)	65+ (m) 60+ (w)
All Persons								
	MGSX	YBTI	YBVK	YBVQ	YCGP	YCGV	MGXE	MGXH
2001	5.0	5.1	18.6	10.1	4.9	3.6	3.3	1.7
2002	5.2	5.3	20.0	10.3	5.0	3.6	3.5	2.4
2003	5.0	5.1	21.4	10.6	4.8	3.1	3.3	1.9
2004	4.8	4.9	21.5	10.2	4.6	3.2	3.0	1.7
2005	4.8	4.9	21.9	10.9	4.3	3.0	2.9	1.6
2006	5.5	5.6	24.0	12.5	5.2	3.7	3.1	2.3
2007	5.4	5.5	27.3	12.4	4.6	3.4	3.3	2.3
2008	5.4	5.6	25.9	12.5	4.9	3.5	2.9	1.7
Male								
	MGSY	YBTJ	YBVL	YBVR	YCGQ	YCGW	MGXF	MGXI
2001	5.6	5.6	21.6	11.2	5.3	3.7	4.0	..
2002	5.7	5.8	22.3	12.1	5.1	3.9	4.0	3.2
2003	5.5	5.6	23.6	12.0	4.9	3.6	3.8	..
2004	5.2	5.3	24.4	11.0	5.2	3.1	3.6	..
2005	5.1	5.2	24.8	12.2	4.5	3.1	3.2	..
2006	5.9	6.0	28.3	14.1	5.3	3.8	3.4	2.7
2007	5.7	5.7	30.9	13.8	4.5	3.4	3.7	3.2
2008	5.8	5.9	28.2	14.5	5.0	3.6	3.5	2.3
Female								
	MGSZ	YBTK	YBVM	YBVS	YCGR	YCGX	MGXG	MGXJ
2001	4.4	4.6	15.6	8.9	4.3	3.5	2.2	..
2002	4.5	4.6	17.6	8.2	4.8	3.2	2.8	2.1
2003	4.3	4.4	19.0	8.9	4.5	2.6	2.6	..
2004	4.3	4.5	18.6	9.4	3.8	3.3	2.2	..
2005	4.4	4.5	19.0	9.4	4.2	2.9	2.4	..
2006	5.0	5.2	19.7	10.7	5.0	3.6	2.7	2.0
2007	5.1	5.3	23.8	10.8	4.9	3.5	2.7	1.8
2008	4.9	5.1	23.6	10.2	4.9	3.5	2.3	1.4

Note: Where figure denoted as .. it is not shown as it is based on a small sample size and is subject to a margin of uncertainty.

1 See chapter text. In August 2007, ONS published the mid-year population estimates for 2006. These estimates have now been incorporated into the LFS estimates from 2001 onwards. Further details can be found at http://www.statistics.gov.uk/cci/article.asp?id=1919

2 Total unemployment as a percentage of all economically active persons in the relevant age group.

3 The Labour Force Survey has now moved to calendar quarters from May 2006. More information can be found on page 5 of the Concepts and Definitions.pdf by following this link:- www.statistics.gov.uk/downloads/theme_labour/Concepts_Definitions_HQS.pdf

Sources: Labour Force Survey, Office for National Statistics; Helpline: 01633 456901

7.11 Duration of unemployment: by sex[1,2]
United Kingdom
At Quarter 2 each year[3]. Seasonally adjusted

Thousands

		1998	1999	2000	2001	2002	2003	2004	2005	2006	2007	2008
All Persons												
All unemployed[4]	MGSC	1 791	1 743	1 600	1 470	1 521	1 468	1 439	1 438	1 687	1 662	1 685
Duration of unemployment												
Less than 6 months	YBWF	981	984	920	877	980	950	927	911	1 025	1 002	994
6 months & less than 1 year	YBWG	253	268	240	218	219	206	228	215	302	264	276
1 year or more	YBWH	557	491	441	375	322	312	284	311	360	396	415
1 year or more as % of total	YBWI	*31.1*	*28.2*	*27.5*	*25.5*	*21.2*	*21.3*	*19.8*	*21.7*	*21.3*	*23.8*	*24.6*
Male												
All unemployed[4]	MGSD	1 076	1 060	959	882	914	890	845	837	978	950	990
Duration of unemployment												
Less than 6 months	MGYK	519	535	501	482	539	539	506	485	545	527	540
6 months & less than 1 year	MGYM	160	166	140	132	147	132	141	138	177	155	162
1 year or more	MGYO	397	360	318	268	228	218	198	213	255	269	288
1 year or more as % of total	YBWJ	*36.9*	*33.9*	*33.2*	*30.4*	*24.9*	*24.5*	*23.4*	*25.5*	*26.1*	*28.3*	*29.1*
Female												
All unemployed[4]	MGSE	715	683	641	589	607	579	593	601	709	712	695
Duration of unemployment												
Less than 6 months	MGYL	462	449	419	394	441	410	421	426	479	475	454
6 months & less than 1 year	MGYN	93	102	100	87	72	74	86	77	125	109	114
1 year or more	MGYP	160	131	122	107	94	94	87	98	105	127	127
1 year or more as % of total	YBWK	*22.4*	*19.2*	*19.1*	*18.3*	*15.5*	*16.3*	*14.6*	*16.4*	*14.7*	*17.9*	*18.3*

1 All aged 16 and over. See chapter text.
2 In August 2007, ONS published the mid-year population estimates for 2006. These estimates have now been incorporated into the LFS estimates from 2001 onwards. Further details can be found at http://www.statistioo.gov.uk/cci/article asp?id=1919
3 The Labour Force Survey has now moved to calendar quarters from May 2006. More information can be found on page 5 of the Concepts and Definitions.pdf by following this link:- www.statistics.gov.uk/downloads/theme_labour/Concepts_Definitions_HQS.pdf
4 Totals include people who did not state their duration of unemployment.

Sources: Labour Force Survey, Office for National Statistics;
Helpline: 01633 456901

7.12 Claimant count:[1] by age and duration
Computerised claims only
United Kingdom. Seasonally adjusted

Thousands

		2002	2003	2004	2005	2006	2007	2008
Annual averages								
Males								
All ages								
All durations	AGNG	708.3	693.0	630.7	635.0	694.0	628.5	661.2
Up to 6 months	AGXK	457.4	451.2	408.8	423.4	438.6	405.2	473.6
Over 6 and up to 12 months	ELNP	124.2	127.1	113.7	113.3	136.5	111.1	105.9
All over 12 months	ELON	126.7	114.7	108.2	98.2	119.0	112.3	81.7
All over 24 months	IKBS	50.7	37.6	34.6	33.1	34.5	33.9	21.4
Aged 18 to 24								
All durations	JLGC	168.1	171.9	161.8	174.6	195.5	176.7	189.8
Up to 6 months	JLGD	141.0	143.8	134.3	143.6	155.0	145.7	163.8
Over 6 and up to 12 months	JLGE	23.8	24.5	23.3	25.9	33.1	25.3	22.0
All over 12 months	JLGF	3.3	3.6	4.2	5.0	7.5	5.8	4.0
All over 24 months	JLGH	0.3	0.4	0.5	0.6	0.9	1.1	1.0
Aged 25 to 49								
All durations	AGMA	421.8	404.8	362.3	357.4	387.5	352.5	374.3
Up to 6 months	JLHG	254.9	248.0	221.3	225.9	228.9	211.5	249.2
Over 6 and up to 12 months	JLHH	80.9	82.9	72.9	70.4	83.4	69.6	67.8
All over 12 months	JLHI	86.1	73.8	68.1	61.2	75.2	71.4	57.2
All over 24 months	JLHK	29.2	17.0	14.1	14.2	15.2	14.5	11.5
Aged 50 and over								
All durations	JLHL	118.4	116.3	106.7	103.0	111.0	99.3	97.2
Up to 6 months	JLHM	61.6	59.4	53.2	53.9	54.7	48.0	60.6
Over 6 and up to 12 months	JLHN	19.6	19.7	17.5	17.0	20.0	16.3	16.1
All over 12 months	JLHO	37.3	37.2	35.9	32.0	36.3	35.0	20.5
All over 24 months	JLHQ	21.1	20.2	19.9	18.3	18.4	18.2	8.9
Females								
All ages								
All durations	JLGI	226.8	230.1	214.7	220.0	245.9	231.8	238.2
Up to 6 months	JLGK	163.6	166.3	153.2	159.2	171.5	164.2	181.0
Over 6 and up to 12 months	JLGJ	35.5	37.2	34.9	35.6	43.6	37.5	34.3
All over 12 months	JLGL	27.6	26.5	26.7	25.2	30.8	30.1	22.9
All over 24 months	JLGN	9.7	8.1	8.0	7.9	8.4	8.4	5.8
Aged 18 to 24								
All durations	JLGO	75.0	77.3	74.0	79.1	90.2	85.2	88.1
Up to 6 months	JLGP	62.9	64.9	61.5	65.3	72.2	70.7	76.0
Over 6 and up to 12 months	JLGQ	10.4	10.6	10.4	11.4	14.7	12.0	10.2
All over 12 months	JLGR	1.8	1.8	2.1	2.3	3.3	2.5	1.9
All over 24 months	JLGT	0.2	0.3	0.3	0.4	0.5	0.5	0.5
Aged 25 to 49								
All durations	JLHR	111.4	112.1	102.1	101.9	111.8	105.1	109.5
Up to 6 months	JLHS	76.7	77.3	69.0	70.3	73.6	69.3	77.5
Over 6 and up to 12 months	JLHT	18.5	19.9	18.2	17.7	21.3	18.8	17.7
All over 12 months	JLHU	16.2	14.9	14.9	13.8	16.9	17.0	14.3
All over 24 months	JLHW	4.7	3.1	2.9	3.0	3.3	3.2	2.9
Aged 50 and over								
All durations	JLHX	40.4	40.7	38.7	39.1	44.0	41.4	40.6
Up to 6 months	JLHY	24.1	24.1	22.7	23.5	25.6	24.1	27.5
Over 6 and up to 12 months	JLHZ	6.6	6.8	6.3	6.5	7.8	6.8	6.4
All over 12 months	JLIA	9.7	9.8	9.7	9.1	10.6	10.6	6.7
All over 24 months	JLIC	4.0	4.7	4.8	4.5	4.7	4.7	2.4

1 Count of claimants of unemployment-related benefits.

Source: Office for National Statistics: 01633 456901

7.13 Unemployment rates: by region[1,2,3]

At Quarter 2 each year[4]. Seasonally adjusted[5]

Percentages

		1998	1999	2000	2001	2002	2003	2004	2005	2006	2007	2008
North East	YCNC	8.3	9.6	8.9	7.5	6.5	6.1	5.5	6.8	6.1	6.3	7.5
North West	YCND	6.9	6.3	5.3	5.3	5.6	5.0	4.5	4.4	5.3	5.8	6.3
Yorkshire and The Humber	YCNE	7.3	6.3	6.1	5.5	5.3	5.1	4.6	4.8	5.8	5.5	6.1
East Midlands	YCNF	4.9	5.3	4.8	5.0	4.6	4.3	4.3	4.3	5.5	5.0	5.7
West Midlands	YCNG	5.9	7.0	6.1	5.5	5.7	5.6	5.5	4.6	5.6	6.7	6.3
East	YCNH	4.9	4.3	3.6	3.6	3.7	3.9	3.8	3.9	5.0	4.6	4.6
London	YCNI	8.6	7.4	7.4	6.2	6.8	7.2	7.0	7.1	7.8	7.4	6.9
South East	YCNJ	4.4	3.9	3.3	3.2	3.9	4.0	3.7	3.8	4.7	4.3	4.2
South West	YCNK	4.8	4.5	4.3	3.5	3.7	3.4	3.7	3.2	3.8	4.0	3.8
Wales	YCNM	7.0	7.5	6.1	6.1	5.7	4.5	4.2	4.5	5.6	5.5	4.9
Scotland	YCNN	7.4	7.1	7.0	6.2	6.3	5.3	6.0	5.5	5.5	4.7	4.2
Northern Ireland	ZSFB	6.9	7.6	6.7	6.1	5.6	5.2	5.2	5.0	4.3	3.8	4.2

1 Total unemployed as a percentage of all economically active persons.
2 All aged 16 and over. See chapter text.
3 In August 2007, ONS published the mid-year population estimates for 2006. These estimates have now been incorporated into the LFS estimates from 2001 onwards. Further details can be found at http://www.statistics.gov.uk/cci/article.asp?id=1919
4 The Labour Force Survey has now moved to calendar quarters from May 2006. More information can be found on page 5 of the Concepts and Definitions.pdf by following this link:- www.statistics.gov.uk/downloads/theme_labour/Concepts_Definitions_HQS.pdf
5 Previously not seasonally adjusted data was shown.

Sources: Labour Force Survey, Office for National Statistics;
Helpline: 01633 456901

7.14 Claimant count rates: by region[1]

Seasonally adjusted annual averages

Percentages

		1998	1999	2000	2001	2002	2003	2004	2005	2006	2007	2008
United Kingdom	BCJE	4.5	4.1	3.6	3.1	3.1	3.0	2.7	2.7	2.9	2.7	2.8
North East	DPDM	7.0	7.0	6.2	5.6	5.1	4.5	4.0	3.9	4.1	4.0	4.3
North West	IBWC	5.0	4.6	4.1	3.7	3.5	3.3	2.9	2.9	3.3	3.1	3.4
Yorkshire and the Humber	DPBI	5.4	5.0	4.3	3.9	3.6	3.3	2.8	2.9	3.3	3.0	3.3
East Midlands	DPBJ	3.9	3.6	3.3	3.1	2.9	2.8	2.5	2.5	2.8	2.6	2.8
West Midlands	DPBN	4.5	4.4	4.0	3.7	3.5	3.5	3.3	3.4	3.9	3.7	3.8
East	DPDP	3.2	2.9	2.4	2.0	2.1	2.1	2.0	2.1	2.3	2.1	2.2
London	DPDQ	5.1	4.4	3.7	3.3	3.5	3.6	3.5	3.4	3.4	3.0	2.9
South East	DPDR	2.6	2.3	1.8	1.5	1.6	1.7	1.6	1.6	1.8	1.6	1.7
South West	DPBM	3.4	3.0	2.5	2.0	1.9	1.9	1.6	1.6	1.8	1.6	1.7
England	VASQ	4.3	3.9	3.4	3.0	2.9	2.9	2.6	2.6	2.9	2.6	2.8
Wales	DPBP	5.4	5.0	4.4	3.9	3.5	3.3	3.0	3.0	3.1	2.8	3.1
Scotland	DPBQ	5.3	5.0	4.5	3.9	3.8	3.7	3.4	3.2	3.3	2.8	2.8
Northern Ireland	DPBR	7.3	6.3	5.3	4.9	4.4	4.2	3.6	3.3	3.2	2.8	3.2
Great Britain	DPAJ	4.4	4.0	3.5	3.1	3.0	3.0	2.7	2.7	2.9	2.7	2.8

1 The number of unemployment-related benefit claimants as a percentage of the estimated total workforce (the sum of claimants, employee jobs, self-employed, participants on work-related government training programmes and HM Forces) at mid-year. Excluded are claimants under 18, consistent with current coverage. See chapter text.

Source: Office for National Statistics: 01633 456901

Labour Market

7.15 Claimant count:[1] by region
Seasonally adjusted

Thousands

	North East	North West	Yorkshire and the Humber	East Midlands	West Midlands	East	London	South East	South West	England	Wales	Scotland	Great Britain	Northern Ireland	United Kingdom
	DPDG	IBWA	DPAX	DPAY	DPBC	DPDJ	DPDK	DPDL	DPBB	IBWK	DPBE	DPBF	DPAG	DPBG	BCJD
1993 Jan	146.2	348.3	247.5	185.2	286.2	229.5	464.6	325.2	222.6	2 454.4	131.4	245.3	2 832.0	105.5	2 937.5
Apr	148.0	345.2	246.5	183.6	285.1	228.2	469.5	321.4	220.0	2 446.6	130.3	243.2	2 821.0	104.5	2 925.5
Jul	148.5	338.0	240.9	180.8	278.7	223.5	466.3	314.0	214.4	2 404.4	129.3	241.2	2 775.6	102.5	2 878.1
Oct	147.5	331.1	237.8	177.8	271.5	216.6	460.4	306.6	208.4	2 356.8	127.8	236.6	2 722.1	101.8	2 823.9
1994 Jan	145.6	325.1	233.7	174.7	262.3	210.0	451.4	296.7	203.6	2 302.3	126.7	236.0	2 665.8	100.2	2 766.0
Apr	141.6	314.5	227.4	170.7	252.0	200.4	440.4	280.9	194.5	2 221.7	123.3	231.7	2 577.4	98.9	2 676.3
Jul	139.1	304.2	222.7	166.3	242.3	191.0	428.1	268.1	188.1	2 148.8	119.0	227.4	2 496.3	97.2	2 593.5
Oct	136.0	291.7	215.9	160.1	230.5	180.5	415.4	251.1	178.9	2 059.0	112.9	218.1	2 391.1	93.8	2 484.9
1995 Jan	133.0	280.1	210.6	153.2	218.5	172.3	401.4	237.9	171.4	1 977.5	108.3	209.3	2 296.0	91.3	2 387.3
Apr	130.0	270.8	206.8	148.1	211.0	167.1	395.0	229.7	166.0	1 923.8	106.2	200.3	2 231.0	88.6	2 319.6
Jul	128.2	266.1	204.6	145.3	206.9	165.0	390.2	225.1	162.5	1 892.8	106.7	195.3	2 195.9	87.6	2 283.5
Oct	126.4	260.9	200.7	142.3	201.3	160.7	383.2	219.1	159.4	1 852.7	105.4	193.5	2 152.9	85.8	2 238.7
1996 Jan	123.1	255.8	197.0	140.0	196.5	157.2	376.8	213.3	155.6	1 814.6	104.0	193.2	2 112.5	85.9	2 198.4
Apr	121.7	254.9	195.7	137.7	194.2	153.5	367.9	207.6	152.3	1 785.1	104.6	194.9	2 085.0	86.1	2 171.1
Jul	116.9	248.2	188.8	131.8	187.6	146.8	357.5	198.9	146.8	1 722.5	101.8	191.9	2 017.0	86.4	2 103.4
Oct	110.5	238.4	181.1	124.9	177.8	138.5	341.6	185.5	137.9	1 635.0	98.2	186.3	1 920.7	81.7	2 002.4
1997 Jan	101.0	218.5	166.4	111.8	160.1	123.5	312.6	163.3	126.0	1 483.2	90.3	173.8	1 747.3	71.1	1 818.4
Apr	95.2	201.3	154.7	102.4	147.3	110.6	284.9	144.4	112.1	1 352.9	82.5	162.2	1 597.6	65.0	1 662.6
Jul	92.4	188.9	148.2	95.0	138.0	102.5	264.3	131.0	100.7	1 261.0	78.1	153.6	1 492.7	61.4	1 554.1
Oct	90.4	177.6	142.0	87.6	131.7	94.3	246.4	120.4	93.0	1 183.4	73.6	146.5	1 403.5	60.6	1 464.1
1998 Jan	87.6	170.6	137.2	82.8	126.1	88.5	234.3	112.3	88.7	1 128.1	70.9	141.6	1 340.6	59.9	1 400.5
Apr	84.1	165.4	134.1	79.9	122.3	85.2	229.4	108.0	85.1	1 093.5	69.3	138.7	1 301.5	57.9	1 359.4
Jul	81.8	163.7	133.3	80.0	121.4	83.7	225.2	105.5	84.1	1 078.7	68.6	139.4	1 286.7	57.3	1 344.0
Oct	82.1	160.9	130.9	79.9	121.4	82.0	219.3	102.5	81.8	1 060.8	68.1	136.9	1 265.8	56.1	1 321.9
1999 Jan	82.6	159.5	129.5	79.0	122.6	80.3	214.5	101.2	81.2	1 050.4	67.8	135.6	1 253.8	55.9	1 309.7
Apr	82.5	157.2	127.0	78.2	123.1	79.1	207.8	98.8	78.4	1 032.1	67.1	133.9	1 233.1	55.0	1 288.1
Jul	80.3	153.8	122.4	75.9	120.2	76.6	202.2	94.4	74.9	1 000.7	63.8	130.2	1 194.7	50.0	1 244.7
Oct	76.7	150.0	118.3	73.6	115.9	73.6	196.5	91.1	71.4	967.1	61.0	126.1	1 154.2	46.5	1 200.7
2000 Jan	75.7	145.7	114.6	73.2	112.1	70.3	189.4	87.2	68.0	936.2	59.3	123.2	1 118.7	44.2	1 162.9
Apr	73.6	139.9	108.9	70.0	108.1	66.9	181.6	81.3	63.8	894.1	57.8	119.0	1 070.9	42.4	1 113.3
Jul	72.0	135.4	104.9	68.7	107.2	62.5	172.0	77.5	61.1	861.3	57.1	115.1	1 033.5	41.2	1 074.7
Oct	69.5	131.0	102.5	67.7	106.5	60.7	165.0	74.3	58.1	835.3	56.4	111.7	1 003.4	41.3	1 044.7
2001 Jan	66.2	127.4	99.9	66.6	104.0	57.2	158.2	69.7	54.9	804.1	54.9	108.8	967.8	40.8	1 008.6
Apr	63.2	124.9	97.6	65.1	100.8	54.8	151.8	66.1	53.6	777.9	52.4	105.3	935.6	39.9	975.5
Jul	61.4	121.5	95.1	63.0	97.4	53.7	151.0	65.1	52.1	760.3	49.8	102.4	912.5	39.3	951.8
Oct	61.5	121.4	93.2	61.6	95.7	54.3	156.3	65.9	51.1	761.0	49.2	104.2	914.4	38.6	953.0
2002 Jan	60.9	121.3	91.4	60.6	95.4	55.4	163.1	68.6	51.1	767.8	48.1	104.3	920.2	38.0	958.2
Apr	59.2	119.4	89.4	59.4	93.6	56.4	166.2	71.0	50.9	765.5	47.5	104.4	917.4	37.5	954.9
Jul	58.5	118.1	89.1	58.6	93.4	57.5	167.3	72.3	50.1	764.9	46.8	101.9	913.6	36.4	950.0
Oct	55.9	116.1	87.6	57.9	93.7	57.2	167.6	72.3	49.3	757.6	46.7	100.1	904.4	35.1	939.5
2003 Jan	54.8	115.9	87.0	58.0	94.3	57.4	168.6	72.9	48.9	757.8	46.3	100.2	904.3	35.0	939.3
Apr	53.5	112.7	84.1	58.8	94.7	58.5	171.3	75.6	48.6	757.8	45.2	99.1	902.1	34.0	936.1
Jul	52.6	112.5	84.2	59.9	94.9	58.7	171.7	76.4	49.1	760.0	45.0	100.6	905.6	34.6	940.2
Oct	51.1	108.7	81.6	58.8	94.2	57.3	170.2	76.0	47.4	745.3	43.1	98.9	887.3	34.7	922.0
2004 Jan	49.8	104.6	78.3	56.2	93.0	56.7	167.8	75.0	45.3	726.7	42.0	97.0	865.7	33.5	899.2
Apr	47.5	101.3	75.6	53.7	89.7	56.0	165.5	72.3	42.7	704.3	41.4	94.4	840.1	31.8	871.9
Jul	45.4	96.7	71.6	51.1	86.7	54.6	162.0	68.5	40.4	677.0	39.5	90.0	806.5	29.9	836.4
Oct	45.1	96.5	71.1	50.9	86.0	55.0	158.8	69.2	40.6	673.2	39.2	89.5	801.9	29.6	831.5
2005 Jan	44.0	94.4	70.1	50.8	85.7	55.1	158.8	68.4	40.9	668.2	38.9	87.4	794.6	29.1	823.3
Apr	44.9	98.0	73.2	52.1	88.0	56.4	162.1	69.7	41.5	685.9	39.6	86.1	811.7	28.6	840.3
Jul	46.1	102.2	76.1	54.5	97.1	58.9	162.4	71.6	42.5	711.4	41.7	84.9	838.1	28.6	866.7
Oct	47.4	105.9	79.9	56.5	99.2	60.2	166.0	73.7	43.0	731.8	42.8	85.8	860.0	28.2	888.2
2006 Jan	47.4	109.0	84.0	58.7	102.5	62.1	168.1	78.2	44.1	754.1	43.8	84.1	883.0	28.3	911.3
Apr	49.6	115.2	87.0	62.4	109.2	65.6	167.7	81.1	48.2	786.0	45.4	88.3	919.6	28.1	947.7
Jul	50.4	117.2	88.3	62.6	109.9	65.9	168.6	83.8	49.3	796.0	44.3	88.5	929.2	27.9	957.1
Oct	51.4	117.9	88.9	63.2	109.7	67.5	166.2	82.9	49.2	796.9	44.0	87.2	928.2	27.8	956.0
2007 Jan	51.2	115.4	85.9	61.8	109.5	66.0	159.1	78.1	47.4	774.4	42.3	81.4	898.4	26.1	924.5
Apr	50.1	111.5	83.3	60.2	104.4	63.3	151.2	74.6	44.6	743.2	41.3	79.0	863.5	25.1	888.6
Jul	49.1	108.9	80.7	58.3	100.7	60.6	143.7	70.9	42.2	715.1	40.3	74.8	830.2	23.6	853.8
Oct	48.0	107.6	77.7	55.9	99.5	57.7	136.5	67.6	39.8	690.3	39.7	72.6	802.6	23.5	826.1
2008 Jan	47.2	105.2	75.3	52.5	94.8	55.4	131.0	64.9	37.9	664.2	38.5	68.5	771.2	23.7	794.9
Apr	48.5	108.3	77.5	54.1	96.0	56.4	129.1	66.4	39.1	675.4	40.2	70.2	785.8	24.5	810.3
Jul	51.5	116.0	84.7	59.0	102.6	60.8	133.8	73.2	44.4	726.0	43.9	75.7	845.6	26.8	872.4
Oct	59.1	131.4	98.4	68.2	115.8	70.1	144.9	86.9	53.6	828.4	50.5	86.3	965.2	31.0	996.2

1 The figures are based on the number of claimants receiving unemployment related benefits and are adjusted for seasonality and discontinuities to be consistent with current coverage. See chapter text.

The latest national and regional seasonally adjusted claimant count figures are provisional and subject to revision in the following month.

Source: Office for National Statistics: 01633 456901

7.16 Economic activity: by sex and age[1]
United Kingdom
At Quarter 2 each year[2]. Seasonally adjusted — Thousands and percentages

	All aged 16 and over	16-59/64	16-17	18-24	25-34	35-49	50-64 (m) 50-59 (w)	65+ (m) 60+ (w)
Thousands								
All Persons								
	MGSF	YBSK	YBZL	YBZO	YBZR	YBZU	YBZX	YCAD
2002	29 433	28 528	810	3 777	6 870	10 821	6 249	904
2003	29 659	28 712	826	3 787	6 687	10 947	6 466	947
2004	29 867	28 838	805	3 927	6 581	11 061	6 465	1 028
2005	30 170	29 095	807	3 969	6 569	11 201	6 549	1 076
2006	30 686	29 507	744	4 109	6 616	11 375	6 662	1 179
2007	30 821	29 586	718	4 156	6 562	11 429	6 722	1 235
2008	31 190	29 844	729	4 202	6 621	11 498	6 795	1 346
Male								
	MGSG	YBSL	YBZM	YBZP	YBZS	YBZV	YBZY	YCAE
2002	15 988	15 685	416	2 011	3 768	5 780	3 710	302
2003	16 187	15 848	418	2 035	3 674	5 869	3 853	339
2004	16 217	15 869	405	2 108	3 591	5 908	3 857	348
2005	16 352	15 991	407	2 139	3 581	5 965	3 899	361
2006	16 606	16 206	370	2 196	3 611	6 056	3 973	400
2007	16 742	16 329	354	2 252	3 611	6 087	4 025	413
2008	16 928	16 472	363	2 274	3 638	6 103	4 094	456
Female								
	MGSH	YBSM	YBZN	YBZQ	YBZT	YBZW	YBZZ	YCAF
2002	13 445	12 843	394	1 766	3 103	5 042	2 539	602
2003	13 472	12 864	408	1 752	3 013	5 078	2 613	608
2004	13 650	12 969	400	1 819	2 989	5 152	2 608	681
2005	13 819	13 104	400	1 830	2 988	5 236	2 651	715
2006	14 080	13 301	374	1 913	3 005	5 319	2 690	779
2007	14 079	13 257	364	1 904	2 950	5 342	2 697	822
2008	14 262	13 372	365	1 927	2 983	5 396	2 701	890
Percentages[3]								
All Persons								
	MGWG	MGSO	YCAG	YCAJ	YCAM	YCAP	MGWP	MGWS
2002	63.0	78.6	53.7	75.7	83.8	85.1	70.5	8.6
2003	63.0	78.7	54.2	74.0	83.4	84.9	72.4	9.0
2004	63.0	78.5	51.7	74.7	83.4	84.8	71.9	9.6
2005	63.1	78.5	51.3	73.7	83.6	84.9	72.4	10.0
2006	63.6	79.0	47.4	74.6	84.6	85.4	73.1	10.8
2007	63.4	78.8	45.2	73.8	84.3	85.2	73.6	11.1
2008	63.6	79.1	45.8	73.3	84.8	85.6	74.3	11.9
Male								
	MGWH	MGSP	YCAH	YCAK	YCAN	YCAQ	MGWQ	MGWT
2002	70.8	83.8	53.7	80.5	92.7	92.0	72.9	7.8
2003	71.2	84.1	53.3	79.1	92.5	92.1	75.1	8.7
2004	70.7	83.6	50.7	79.3	91.9	91.7	74.5	8.8
2005	70.5	83.4	50.6	78.5	91.9	91.4	74.6	9.0
2006	70.9	83.7	45.9	78.7	93.0	92.0	75.1	9.9
2007	70.8	83.6	43.4	78.5	93.1	91.9	75.3	10.0
2008	70.9	83.7	44.5	77.6	93.1	92.1	75.9	10.9
Female								
	MGWI	MGSQ	YCAI	YCAL	YCAO	YCAR	MGWR	MGWU
2002	55.6	73.1	53.6	70.9	75.0	78.4	67.2	9.1
2003	55.5	72.9	55.0	68.8	74.5	78.0	68.8	9.1
2004	55.8	73.1	52.7	70.0	75.1	78.1	68.5	10.2
2005	56.1	73.3	52.1	68.8	75.4	78.5	69.4	10.6
2006	56.8	74.0	49.0	70.5	76.3	78.9	70.3	11.4
2007	56.4	73.6	47.2	69.0	75.5	78.6	71.4	11.8
2008	56.7	74.1	47.2	68.7	76.5	79.2	71.9	12.5

1 See chapter text. In August 2007, ONS published the mid-year population estimates for 2006. These estimates have now been incorporated into the LFS estimates from 2001 onwards. Further details can be found at http://www.statistics.gov.uk/cci/article.asp?id=1919

2 The Labour Force Survey has now moved to calendar quarters from May 2006. More information can be found on page 5 of the Concepts and Definitions.pdf by following this link:- www.statistics.gov.uk/downloads/theme_labour/Concepts_Definitions_HQS.pdf

3 Total economically active as a percentage of all persons in the relevant age group.

Sources: Labour Force Survey, Office for National Statistics; Helpline. 01633 456901

Labour Market

7.17 Economically inactive: by sex and age[1]
United Kingdom
At Quarter 2 each year[2]. Seasonally adjusted

Thousands and percentages

	All aged 16 and over	16-59/64	16-17	18-24	25-34	35-49	50-64 (m) 50-59 (w)	65+ (m) 60+ (w)
Thousands								
All Persons								
	MGSI	YBSN	YCAS	YCAV	YCAY	YCBB	MGWA	MGWD
2002	17 317	7 751	700	1 212	1 330	1 891	2 619	9 566
2003	17 382	7 769	699	1 333	1 332	1 941	2 464	9 612
2004	17 524	7 892	752	1 330	1 306	1 984	2 521	9 632
2005	17 653	7 960	766	1 413	1 291	1 997	2 494	9 693
2006	17 531	7 836	825	1 396	1 205	1 952	2 458	9 695
2007	17 800	7 957	869	1 474	1 222	1 988	2 405	9 842
2008	17 816	7 872	862	1 534	1 183	1 939	2 355	9 944
Male								
	MGSJ	YBSO	YCAT	YCAW	YCAZ	YCBC	MGWB	MGWE
2002	6 591	3 026	359	486	295	504	1 381	3 565
2003	6 562	2 987	365	538	299	504	1 280	3 575
2004	6 731	3 116	393	549	317	537	1 320	3 615
2005	6 835	3 185	398	585	315	560	1 328	3 651
2006	6 804	3 152	436	595	273	530	1 319	3 651
2007	6 899	3 203	462	617	267	536	1 323	3 695
2008	6 934	3 200	454	657	269	525	1 297	3 734
Female								
	MGSK	YBSP	YCAU	YCAX	YCBA	YCBD	MGWC	MGWF
2002	10 726	4 725	341	725	1 035	1 387	1 237	6 002
2003	10 819	4 782	334	795	1 033	1 436	1 184	6 037
2004	10 793	4 776	359	780	988	1 447	1 201	6 017
2005	10 818	4 775	368	828	976	1 437	1 166	6 043
2006	10 728	4 683	390	800	932	1 422	1 139	6 044
2007	10 901	4 754	407	857	955	1 452	1 083	6 147
2008	10 882	4 672	408	877	914	1 414	1 058	6 210
Percentages[3]								
All Persons								
	YBTC	YBTL	LWEX	LWFA	LWFD	LWFG	LWFJ	LWFM
2002	37.0	21.4	46.3	24.3	16.2	14.9	29.5	91.4
2003	37.0	21.3	45.8	26.0	16.6	15.1	27.6	91.0
2004	37.0	21.5	48.3	25.3	16.6	15.2	28.1	90.4
2005	36.9	21.5	48.7	26.3	16.4	15.1	27.6	90.0
2006	36.4	21.0	52.6	25.4	15.4	14.6	26.9	89.2
2007	36.6	21.2	54.8	26.2	15.7	14.8	26.4	88.9
2008	36.4	20.9	54.2	26.7	15.2	14.4	25.7	88.1
Male								
	YBTD	YBTM	LWEY	LWFB	LWFE	LWFH	LWFK	LWFN
2002	29.2	16.2	46.3	19.5	7.3	8.0	27.1	92.2
2003	28.8	15.9	46.7	20.9	7.5	7.9	24.9	91.3
2004	29.3	16.4	49.3	20.7	8.1	8.3	25.5	91.2
2005	29.5	16.6	49.4	21.5	8.1	8.6	25.4	91.0
2006	29.1	16.3	54.1	21.3	7.0	8.0	24.9	90.1
2007	29.2	16.4	56.6	21.5	6.9	8.1	24.7	90.0
2008	29.1	16.3	55.5	22.4	6.9	7.9	24.1	89.1
Female								
	YBTE	YBTN	LWEZ	LWFC	LWFF	LWFI	LWFL	LWFO
2002	44.4	26.9	46.4	29.1	25.0	21.6	32.8	90.9
2003	44.5	27.1	45.0	31.2	25.5	22.0	31.2	90.9
2004	44.2	26.9	47.3	30.0	24.9	21.9	31.5	89.8
2005	43.9	26.7	47.9	31.2	24.6	21.5	30.6	89.4
2006	43.2	26.0	51.0	29.5	23.7	21.1	29.7	88.6
2007	43.6	26.4	52.8	31.0	24.5	21.4	28.6	88.2
2008	43.3	25.9	52.8	31.3	23.5	20.8	28.1	87.5

1 See chapter text. In August 2007, ONS published the mid-year population estimates for 2006. These estimates have now been incorporated into the LFS estimates from 2001 onwards. Further details can be found at http://www.statistics.gov.uk/cci/article.asp?id=1919

2 The Labour Force Survey has now moved to calendar quarters from May 2006. More information can be found on page 5 of the Concepts and Definitions.pdf by following this link:- www.statistics.gov.uk/downloads/theme_labour/Concepts_Definitions_HQS.pdf

3 Total economically inactive as a percentage of all persons in the relevant age group.

Sources: Labour Force Survey, Office for National Statistics; Helpline: 01633 456901

7.18 Economically inactive:[1,2] by reason and sex
United Kingdom
At Quarter 2 each year[3]. Seasonally adjusted

Thousands and percentages

| | Economic inactivity by reason: | | | | | | | by: | | All economically inactive |
	Student	Looking after family/home	Temporary sick	Long-term sick	Discouraged workers[4]	Retired	Other	Does not want a job	Wants a job	

Thousands

All Persons

	BEDZ	BEEC	BEBK	BEBN	YCFO	BEEI	BEEL	YBVZ	YBWC	YBSN
2001	1 515	2 394	193	2 209	34	591	792	5 530	2 198	7 728
2002	1 516	2 386	179	2 232	32	583	821	5 499	2 252	7 751
2003	1 655	2 402	195	2 109	38	567	805	5 622	2 147	7 769
2004	1 712	2 344	193	2 165	35	596	847	5 864	2 028	7 892
2005	1 804	2 343	191	2 145	34	618	825	5 873	2 088	7 960
2006	1 821	2 313	191	2 077	37	584	813	5 750	2 086	7 836
2007	1 920	2 348	198	2 034	34	609	813	5 869	2 088	7 957
2008	1 969	2 295	181	1 997	39	590	801	5 709	2 163	7 872

Male

	BEEX	BEAQ	BEDI	BEDL	YCFP	BEDR	BEDU	YBWA	YBWD	YBSO
2001	737	180	92	1 240	21	403	315	2 076	910	2 987
2002	750	182	88	1 244	22	395	345	2 085	941	3 026
2003	827	180	89	1 149	20	387	336	2 069	918	2 987
2004	871	187	95	1 180	23	408	352	2 255	861	3 116
2005	899	192	101	1 188	22	423	361	2 338	847	3 185
2006	909	195	96	1 137	27	430	358	2 253	900	3 152
2007	964	207	90	1 137	19	444	342	2 316	887	3 203
2008	993	195	88	1 113	22	432	357	2 272	929	3 200

Female

	BEBL	BEBO	BEEG	BEEJ	YCFQ	BEEP	BEES	YBWB	YBWE	YBSP
2001	777	2 214	102	970	13	188	477	3 454	1 287	4 741
2002	766	2 205	91	988	11	188	476	3 414	1 311	4 725
2003	828	2 222	105	959	18	180	469	3 553	1 229	4 782
2004	842	2 157	98	985	12	188	495	3 609	1 167	4 776
2005	905	2 151	90	958	12	195	465	3 535	1 240	4 775
2006	912	2 118	95	940	10	154	455	3 497	1 187	4 683
2007	956	2 141	108	897	15	165	472	3 553	1 201	4 754
2008	976	2 100	93	883	17	159	445	3 437	1 234	4 672

Percentages[5]

All Persons

	BEDJ	BEDM	BEDP	BEDS	BEDV	BEDY	BEEB	BEEE	BEBM	BEAR
2001	19.6	31.0	2.5	28.6	0.4	7.7	10.3	71.6	28.4	100
2002	19.6	30.8	2.3	28.8	0.4	7.5	10.6	70.9	29.1	100
2003	21.3	30.9	2.5	27.1	0.5	7.3	10.4	72.4	27.6	100
2004	21.7	29.7	2.4	27.4	0.4	7.5	10.7	74.3	25.7	100
2005	22.7	29.4	2.4	26.9	0.4	7.8	10.4	73.8	26.2	100
2006	23.2	29.5	2.4	26.5	0.5	7.5	10.4	73.4	26.6	100
2007	24.1	29.5	2.5	25.6	0.4	7.7	10.2	73.8	26.2	100
2008	25.0	29.2	2.3	25.4	0.5	7.5	10.2	72.5	27.5	100

Male

	BEEH	BEEK	BEEN	BEEQ	BEET	BEEW	BEEZ	BEAS	BEGT	BEBP
2001	24.7	6.0	3.1	41.5	0.7	13.5	10.5	69.5	30.5	100
2002	24.8	6.0	2.9	41.1	0.7	13.1	11.4	68.9	31.1	100
2003	27.7	6.0	3.0	38.5	0.7	12.9	11.2	69.3	30.7	100
2004	27.9	6.0	3.1	37.9	0.7	13.1	11.3	72.4	27.6	100
2005	28.2	6.0	3.2	37.3	0.7	13.3	11.3	73.4	26.6	100
2006	28.8	6.2	3.0	36.1	0.9	13.6	11.4	71.5	28.5	100
2007	30.1	6.5	2.8	35.5	0.6	13.9	10.7	72.3	27.7	100
2008	31.0	6.1	2.7	34.8	0.7	13.5	11.2	71.0	29.0	100

Female

	BEGZ	BEHC	BEHF	BEHI	BEHL	BEHO	BEBQ	BEHR	BEHU	BEGW
2001	16.4	46.7	2.1	20.4	0.3	4.0	10.1	72.8	27.2	100
2002	16.2	46.7	1.9	20.9	0.2	4.0	10.1	72.3	27.7	100
2003	17.3	46.5	2.2	20.1	0.4	3.8	9.8	74.3	25.7	100
2004	17.6	45.2	2.1	20.6	0.3	3.9	10.4	75.6	24.4	100
2005	18.9	45.0	1.9	20.1	0.3	4.1	9.7	74.0	26.0	100
2006	19.5	45.2	2.0	20.1	0.2	3.3	9.7	74.7	25.3	100
2007	20.1	45.0	2.3	18.9	0.3	3.5	9.9	74.7	25.3	100
2008	20.9	44.9	2.0	18.9	0.4	3.4	9.5	73.6	26.4	100

1 All persons aged 16-59 (women) / 16-64 (men). See chapter text.

2 In August 2007, ONS published the mid-year population estimates for 2006. These estimates have now been incorporated into the LFS estimates from 2001 onwards. Further details can be found at http://www.statistics.gov.uk/cci/article.asp?id=1919

3 The Labour Force Survey has now moved to calendar quarters from May 2006. More information can be found on page 5 of the Concepts and Definitions.pdf by following this link:- www.statistics.gov.uk/downloads/theme_labour/Concepts_Definitions_HQS.pdf

4 People whose reason for not seeking work was that they believed no jobs were available.

5 Reasons for inactivity as a percentage of all economically inactive.

Sources: Labour Force Survey, Office for National Statistics;
Helpline: 01633 456901

7.19
Labour disputes: by industry[1]
United Kingdom
Standard Industrial Classification 2003

Thousands and numbers

		2001	2002	2003	2004	2005	2006	2007
Working days lost through all stoppages in progress (thousands)	KBBZ	525	1 323	499	905	157	755	1 041
Analysis by industry								
Mining, quarrying, electricity, gas and water	DMME	25	..	..	5	6	12	..
Manufacturing	BBFX	43	21	63	31	16	18	16
Construction	DMMG	10	17	14	..	2	15	2
Transport, storage and communication	BBFY	107	96	126	44	33	41	657
Public administration and defence	BBFZ	216	488	138	437	23	627	325
Education	BBGA	43	376	131	379	43	31	31
Health and social work	BBGB	73	148	15	4	..	5	5
Other community, social and personal services	DMML	4	107	10	4	6	2	4
All other industries and services	DMMM	4	70	2	2	29	5	2
Analysis by number of working days lost in each stoppage								
Under 250 days	KBFC	9	7	6	7	5	7	6
250 and under 500 days	KBFJ	11	8	6	5	4	8	6
500 and under 1,000 days	KBFL	15	15	13	12	7	8	11
1,000 and under 5,000 days	KBFY	59	47	69	51	80	66	50
5,000 and under 25,000 days	KBFZ	140	104	46	59	61	69	76
25,000 and under 50,000 days	KBGS	72	122	112	–	–	–	..
50,000 days and over	KBGT	220	1 021	248	770	..	597	892
Working days lost per 1 000 employees all industries and services	KBHA	20	51	19	34	6	28	38
Workers directly and indirectly involved (thousands)	KBHB	180	943	151	293	93	713	745
Analysis by industry								
Mining, quarrying, electricity, gas and water	DMMN	3	..	..	1	6	1	..
Manufacturing	DMMO	17	10	18	14	3	11	13
Construction	DMMP	3	17	2	..	1	2	1
Transport, storage and communications	DMMQ	69	33	52	12	13	14	399
Public administration and defence	DMMR	46	171	56	207	15	654	317
Education	DMMS	34	388	15	55	43	28	9
Health and social work	DMMT	6	144	3	1	..	2	2
Other community, social and personal services	DMMU	1	103	3	3	6	1	2
All other industries and services	DMMV	1	76	1	1	5	2	2
Analysis by duration of stoppage								
Not more than 5 days	KBHM	98	828	78	222	89	705	357
Over 5 but not more than 10 days	KBHN	43	57	23	47	3	5	288
Over 10 but not more than 20 days	KBJQ	4	3	31	1	1	2	6
Over 20 but not more than 30 days	KBJR	–	1	..	3	..	1	94
Over 30 but not more than 50 days	KBJS	6	1	..	..	1	–	..
Over 50 days	KBJT	30	55	20	20	–	–	..
Numbers of stoppages in progress: total	KBLG	194	146	133	130	116	158	142
Analysis by industry								
Mining, quarrying, electricity, gas and water	DMMW	3	2	1	3	2	2	..
Manufacturing	DMMX	32	33	43	30	19	25	22
Construction	DMMY	9	3	4	1	3	5	4
Transport, storage and communications	DMMZ	94	51	45	46	42	30	55
Public administration and defence	DMNA	22	20	12	19	13	18	20
Education	DMNB	16	16	15	16	22	53	21
Health and social work	DMNC	12	14	7	4	1	4	12
Other community, social and personal services	DMND	10	11	9	12	5	8	11
All other industries and services	DMNE	9	12	4	4	10	13	7
Analysis of number of stoppages by duration								
Not more than 5 days	KBNH	162	118	113	111	102	126	119
Over 5 but not more than 10 days	KBNI	15	16	10	10	8	19	12
Over 10 but not more than 20 days	KBNJ	7	3	5	4	3	10	6
Over 20 but not more than 30 days	KBNK	1	3	1	2	..	1	1
Over 30 but not more than 50 days	KBNL	4	1	1	1	3	2	2
Over 50 days	KBNM	5	5	3	2	..	..	2

1 See chapter text.

Source: Labour Market Statistics, Office for National Statistics: 01633 456721

7.20 Average earnings and hours of full-time employees by industry division:[1] by sex

United Kingdom

At April. Standard Industrial Classification 2003

	Agriculture, Hunting and Forestry	Fishing	Mining and Quarrying	Manufacturing	Electricity, Gas and Water Supply	Construction	Wholesale and Retail Trade; repair of motor vehicles, cycles, personal and household goods
All employees							
	C9EG	C9EI	C9EK	C9EM	C9EO	C9EP	C9EQ
2005	364.7	440.6	657.9	508.0	612.2	524.6	425.2
2006[2]	_379.9_	_450.7_	_753.4_	_526.8_	_625.8_	_554.2_	_447.5_
	379.7	445.1	749.9	524.2	624.8	553.4	445.6
2007	425.7	375.3	761.9	538.0	626.5	571.8	463.5
2008	439.0	409.7	802.9	562.7	696.6	592.9	482.2
Total hours worked	C5TJ	C5TK	C5TL	C5TV	C5TW	C5TX	C5U3
2005	43.7	43.1	43.5	40.6	39.3	43.0	40.3
2006[2]	44.1	_42.3_ 42.2	42.6	40.7	40.3	43.1	_40.3_ 40.4
2007	44.1	43.9	44.1	40.9	39.6	42.9	40.3
2008	43.4	44.1	43.6	41.0	39.7	43.3	40.3
Hourly earnings excluding overtime	C9HV	C9HX	C9HZ	C9I3	C9I5	C9I7	C9IA
2005	8.27	10.14	15.56	12.50	15.33	12.15	10.57
2006[2]	8.53	_10.72_ 10.60	_18.17_ 18.08	_12.94_ 12.87	_15.23_ 15.19	_12.82_ 12.80	_11.12_ 11.07
2007	9.64	8.18	17.75	13.14	15.61	13.29	11.53
2008	10.09	8.99	18.82	13.69	17.30	13.67	12.00
Male employees							
	C9FZ	C9F4	C9F6	C9F8	C9FA	C9FC	C9FE
2005	381.9	445.7	675.4	533.8	647.3	537.6	469.5
2006[2]	395.2	_433.6_ 428.2	_787.6_ 783.4	_553.0_ 551.4	_668.8_ 666.5	_570.0_ 569.8	_493.3_ 491.1
2007	409.2	322.8	772.7	566.6	662.2	585.9	509.6
2008	..	355.1	828.6	590.2	745.2	608.2	531.8
Total hours worked	C5W8	C5WE	C5WH	C5WK	C5WN	C5WQ	C5WT
2005	44.7	43.4	44.4	41.2	39.9	43.5	41.2
2006[2]	_44.9_ 45.0	_43.3_ 43.2	43.6	41.3	41.1	43.6	41.3
2007	44.7	44.7	45.1	41.4	40.1	43.4	41.2
2008	44.0	44.8	44.6	41.5	40.2	43.8	41.3
Hourly earnings excluding overtime	C9IS	C9IU	C9IW	C9IY	C9J2	C9J4	C9J6
2005	8.46	10.13	15.72	12.98	15.96	12.30	11.42
2006[2]	_8.71_ 8.70	_10.01_ 9.91	_18.66_ 18.55	_13.42_ 13.38	_15.90_ 15.89	_13.04_ 13.02	_12.00_ 11.94
2007	9.93	6.65	17.69	13.67	16.29	13.45	12.39
2008	10.52	7.40	19.11	14.19	18.29	13.85	12.93
Female employees							
	C9G6	C9G8	C9GA	C9GC	C9GE	C9GG	C9GI
2005	287.6	–	552.5	404.3	490.2	411.5	343.2
2006[2]	316.1	–	_581.4_ 580.3	_420.9_ 415.9	_490.7_ 486.5	_419.3_ 415.7	_364.1_ 361.8
2007	329.0	–	691.0	421.7	494.1	449.0	377.2
2008	324.2	..	651.5	447.4	526.8	464.8	392.1
Total hours worked	C7NN	C7NP	C7NR	C7NT	C7NV	C7OA	C7OC
2005	39.0	42.2	38.1	38.4	37.3	38.0	38.5
2006[2]	_40.6_ 40.5	–	37.7	38.6	37.8	38.6	38.7
2007	40.7	–	38.0	38.6	37.8	38.1	38.4
2008	40.7	–	38.3	38.8	38.0	38.6	38.5
Hourly earnings excluding overtime	C9JO	C9JQ	C9JS	C9JU	C9JW	C9JY	C9K2
2005	7.35	–	14.54	10.51	13.13	10.82	8.92
2006[2]	_7.77_ 7.78	–	15.54	_10.93_ 10.80	_12.98_ 12.87	_18.87_ 10.78	_9.45_ 9.39
2007	8.04	–	18.21	10.93	13.05	11.77	9.83
2008	7.93	–	17.01	11.56	13.85	12.05	10.21

7.20
Average earnings and hours of full-time employees by industry division:[1] by sex
United Kingdom
At April. Standard Industrial Classification 2003

	Hotels and restaurants	Transport, Storage and Communication	Financial Inter-mediation	Real Estate, Renting and Business	Public Administration and Defence; compulsory social security	Educa-tion	Health and Social work	Other community, social and personal service activities
All employees								
	C9ER	C9ES	C9ET	C9EU	C9EV	C9EW	C9EX	C9EY
2005	323.5	508.0	701.3	589.3	525.0	518.6	503.2	503.8
2006[2]	344.0	526.5	723.0	616.0	540.4	533.1	518.4	525.9
	343.3	523.4	719.7	612.8	536.6	532.2	515.9	524.1
2007	361.8	543.4	760.3	624.6	555.1	544.8	527.7	511.7
2008	375.9	567.6	806.9	651.8	583.4	568.8	542.6	524.9
Total hours worked								
	C5U4	C5U5	C5U6	C5U7	C5U8	C5V5	C5V8	C5VU
2005	40.9	42.9	36.0	39.1	39.2	35.5	38.7	40.0
2006[2]	41.0	42.2	36.1	39.3	39.2	35.6	38.6	39.9
		42.3						
2007	41.0	42.3	36.2	39.2	39.4	35.7	38.4	39.5
2008	41.2	42.4	36.2	39.5	39.5	35.7	38.7	39.7
Hourly earnings excluding overtime								
	C9IC	C9IE	C9IG	C9II	C9IK	C9IM	C9IO	C9IQ
2005	7.93	11.89	19.54	15.14	13.28	14.64	12.99	12.65
2006[2]	8.39	12.56	20.07	15.75	13.72	15.03	13.44	13.28
	8.38	12.47	19.96	15.67	13.63	14.99	13.38	13.23
2007	8.84	12.89	21.07	15.99	14.03	15.32	13.76	12.99
2008	9.13	13.44	22.35	16.62	14.68	15.70	14.01	13.28
Male employees								
	C9FO	C9FQ	C9FS	C9FU	C9FW	C9FY	C9G2	C9G4
2005	357.2	527.7	872.4	654.9	583.6	568.4	669.5	563.6
2006[2]	381.7	544.3	888.2	683.7	593.0	589.9	695.6	582.8
	381.4	541.8	884.9	681.6	589.4	589.2	692.7	582.5
2007	402.1	561.4	928.9	690.7	617.7	599.3	695.9	564.1
2008	419.5	584.2	977.0	720.7	644.2	629.1	699.6	573.7
Total hours worked								
	C5WW	C5WZ	C7MU	C7MW	C7NF	C7NH	C7NJ	C7NL
2005	41.8	43.8	36.2	39.9	40.1	36.5	39.7	41.1
2006[2]	41.8	43.2	36.3	40.2	40.0	36.6	39.5	40.7
		43.3						40.8
2007	41.9	43.3	36.3	40.0	40.2	36.7	39.4	40.4
2008	42.0	43.3	36.4	40.3	40.3	36.6	39.6	40.6
Hourly earnings excluding overtime								
	C9J8	C9JA	C9JC	C9JE	C9JG	C9JI	C9JK	C9JM
2005	8.56	12.12	24.19	16.52	14.43	15.64	16.91	13.83
2006[2]	9.14	12.71	24.54	17.14	14.76	16.21	17.64	14.44
	9.13	12.63	24.43	17.08	14.68	16.18	17.56	14.42
2007	9.62	13.05	25.65	17.36	15.28	16.43	17.70	14.05
2008	10.00	13.58	26.96	18.03	15.89	17.05	17.58	14.21
Female employees								
	C9GK	C9GM	C9HJ	C9HL	C9HN	C9HP	C9HR	C9HT
2005	282.4	432.8	500.0	472.8	440.2	484.0	440.3	417.9
2006[2]	296.8	463.3	524.2	494.3	463.4	495.7	451.4	441.8
	295.9	458.1	519.6	490.2	460.0	494.8	448.9	438.3
2007	310.4	474.2	551.3	502.2	466.2	508.2	462.9	431.8
2008	321.4	501.7	585.9	527.4	493.9	528.8	482.8	450.9
Total hours worked								
	C7OE	C7OG	C7OI	C7OK	C7OM	C7OO	C7OQ	C7OS
2005	39.7	39.3	35.7	37.6	37.9	34.8	38.4	38.4
2006[2]	40.0	38.7	35.9	37.7	38.1	34.9	38.3	38.7
						35.0	38.2	
2007	39.8	38.7	36.0	37.6	38.2	35.0	38.0	38.2
2008	40.2	39.0	36.0	38.0	38.4	35.2	38.3	38.4
Hourly earnings excluding overtime								
	C9K4	C9K6	C9K8	C9KG	C9KI	C9KK	C9KS	C9KU
2005	7.12	10.99	14.00	12.59	11.57	13.92	11.49	10.90
2006[2]	7.42	12.02	14.62	13.14	12.14	14.22	11.83	11.51
	7.39	11.89	14.48	13.03	12.07	14.19	11.77	11.41
2007	7.80	12.27	15.33	13.34	12.20	14.54	12.21	11.32
2008	8.00	12.86	16.29	13.95	12.84	14.78	12.63	11.80

1 See chapter text. Employees on adult rates whose pay for the survey period was not affected by absence.

2 In 2006 additional methodology was introduced. Therefore the bottom data is comparable with 2007, whilst the top data is comparable with earlier years (where the two figures are equal, only one appears).

Sources: Annual Survey of Hours and Earnings;
Office for National Statistics: 01633 819024

7.21 Average earnings and hours of full-time employees:[1] by sex
United Kingdom
At April

£ and numbers

	All Industries				Manufacturing industries			
	Average weekly earnings	Total hours worked (numbers)	Average hourly earnings		Average weekly earnings	Total hours worked (numbers)	Average hourly earnings	
			including overtime	excluding overtime			including overtime	excluding overtime
All employees								
	C7Q5	C7QX	C7Q7	C7Q9	C7PU	C7QL	C7PV	C7PW
2003	487.1	39.5	12.32	12.34	476.5	40.9	11.65	11.62
2004[2]	506.1	39.5	12.80	12.84	493.1	41.0	12.03	12.01
	498.2	37.5	12.60	12.63	485.0		11.83	11.80
2005	516.5	39.4	13.11	13.15	508.0	40.6	12.51	12.50
2006[3]	537.5	39.4	13.63	13.68	526.8	40.7	12.94	12.94
	535.0		13.56	13.61	524.2		12.87	12.87
2007	550.3	39.4	13.97	14.00	538.0	40.9	13.16	13.14
2008	574.3	39.5	14.53	14.53	562.7	41.0	13.72	13.69
Male employees								
	C7QA	C7QZ	C7QC	C7QE	C7PX	C7QT	C7PY	C7PZ
2003	539.3	40.8	13.21	13.28	503.2	41.5	12.13	12.12
2004[2]	557.4	40.8	13.67	13.76	519.4	41.6	12.50	12.49
	548.1		13.44	13.51	511.2		12.30	12.28
2005	568.1	40.6	13.98	14.05	533.8	41.2	12.97	12.98
2006[3]	592.0	40.7	14.56	14.64	553.0	41.3	13.40	13.42
	589.8		14.50	14.58	551.4		13.36	13.38
2007	605.0	40.7	14.88	14.95	566.6	41.4	13.67	13.67
2008	631.2	40.8	15.49	15.54	590.2	41.5	14.21	14.19
Female employees								
	C7QF	C7SA	C7QH	C7QJ	C7Q2	C7QV	C7Q3	C7Q4
2003	400.7	37.4	10.71	10.70	372.8	38.7	9.64	9.62
2004[2]	422.1	37.5	11.26	11.27	388.1	38.7	10.02	10.02
	416.8		11.11	11.12	380.8		9.83	9.84
2005	435.7	37.4	11.64	11.65	404.3	38.4	10.52	10.51
2006[3]	453.0	37.5	12.06	12.10	420.9	38.6	10.91	10.93
	450.0		11.99	12.02	415.9		10.78	10.80
2007	463.7	37.4	12.40	12.42	421.7	38.6	10.93	10.93
2008	485.5	37.6	12.91	12.88	447.4	38.8	11.53	11.56

1 See chapter text. Employees on adult rates whose pay for the survey period was not affected by absence.

2 For 2004, two sets of figures are shown. The first does not include supplementary information and therefore is comparable with earlier years. The second includes supplementary information and so is discontinuous with previous years (where the two figures are equal, only one appears).

3 In 2006 additional methodology was introduced. Therefore the bottom data is comparable with 2007, whilst the top data is comparable with earlier years (where the two figures are equal, only one appears).

Sources: Annual Survey of Hours and Earnings;
Office for National Statistics: 01633 819024

7.22 Average earnings index:[1] all employees by main industrial sectors
Great Britain
Analyses by industry based on Standard Industrial Classification 1992

Indices (2000=100)

Not seasonally adjusted

	Annual averages	Jan-uary	Feb-ruary	March	April	May	June	July	August	Sept-ember	Oct-ober	Nov-ember	Dec-ember
Whole economy (Divisions 01 - 93) LNMM													
2006	126.4	127.2	131.6	133.2	124.1	124.5	126.4	125.2	123.5	123.7	123.9	124.6	129.4
2007	131.5	133.3	138.8	137.8	128.0	129.0	130.5	129.7	128.7	128.8	128.2	130.2	134.4
2008	136.0	138.4	144.4	144.1	132.5	133.0	134.9	134.3	132.8	132.9	132.7	133.5	138.5
Manufacturing industries (Divisions 15 - 37) LNMN													
2006	126.2	121.9	125.5	133.0	126.8	124.1	125.2	125.5	124.4	125.6	126.5	126.1	130.0
2007	130.7	125.9	130.1	137.8	130.8	129.6	130.4	131.1	127.9	128.6	130.0	130.8	135.6
2008	134.6	130.5	134.1	143.6	135.4	134.1	133.5	134.4	131.5	132.2	133.3	133.7	138.6
Production industries (Divisions 10 - 41) LNMO													
2006	126.0	121.7	125.2	133.0	126.9	124.1	125.6	125.3	124.0	125.2	126.0	125.9	129.4
2007	130.9	125.7	129.7	138.8	131.0	129.7	131.0	131.3	127.9	128.8	130.0	131.1	135.2
2008	135.1	130.6	134.1	145.1	136.1	134.5	134.7	135.0	131.8	132.8	133.6	134.1	138.6
Service industries (Divisions 50 - 93) LNMP													
2006	126.5	128.6	133.4	133.5	123.5	124.6	126.6	125.1	123.5	123.3	123.4	124.2	129.1
2007	131.7	135.3	141.4	137.8	127.5	129.0	130.6	129.5	129.1	128.7	127.9	129.8	133.9
2008	136.7	140.7	147.7	144.8	132.2	133.1	135.4	134.6	133.5	133.0	132.8	133.7	138.6
Private sector services (Divisions 50-99) JJGF													
2006	125.2	129.2	135.1	135.3	121.5	121.6	125.1	123.0	121.0	120.8	121.0	121.7	127.3
2007	130.7	136.7	144.6	139.8	125.5	126.1	129.1	128.1	127.0	126.8	125.7	127.1	131.9
2008	135.7	142.2	151.4	147.6	130.1	130.2	134.3	132.9	131.0	130.7	130.6	130.5	136.6

Seasonally adjusted

	Annual averages	Jan-uary	Feb-ruary	March	April	May	June	July	August	Sept-ember	Oct-ober	Nov-ember	Dec-ember
Whole economy (Divisions 01 - 93) LNMQ													
2006	126.5	123.3	124.6	125.1	125.7	126.1	127.1	126.7	126.9	127.5	128.1	128.2	129.0
2007	131.5	129.4	130.2	129.4	130.1	130.8	131.2	131.5	132.4	132.9	132.5	133.8	133.8
2008	136.1	134.3	135.1	135.2	134.9	135.3	135.8	136.2	136.6	137.0	137.3	137.5	138.1
Manufacturing industries (Divisions 15 - 37) LNMR													
2006	126.4	124.0	124.7	124.7	125.9	125.2	126.3	125.8	127.5	128.3	128.4	128.1	128.0
2007	130.8	128.4	129.1	128.9	130.0	130.5	131.2	131.2	131.1	131.4	131.7	132.7	133.3
2008	134.8	133.2	133.2	134.6	133.9	134.8	134.4	134.8	135.0	135.3	135.6	135.9	136.3
Production industries (Divisions 10 - 41) LNMS													
2006	126.0	123.8	124.2	124.3	125.8	125.1	125.9	125.4	127.1	127.7	128.0	127.7	127.6
2007	130.7	128.1	128.7	129.2	129.8	130.2	131.1	131.3	131.2	131.4	131.9	132.9	133.3
2008	135.1	133.3	133.3	135.2	134.4	135.1	134.8	135.2	135.3	135.7	136.0	136.3	136.8
Service industries (Divisions 50 - 93) LNMT													
2006	126.7	123.1	124.5	125.7	125.7	126.4	127.2	126.9	126.8	127.6	128.3	128.5	129.3
2007	131.8	129.6	130.6	129.5	130.3	131.2	131.4	131.7	132.7	133.5	133.1	134.1	134.0
2008	136.8	134.7	135.4	135.9	135.6	135.8	136.3	136.8	137.2	137.7	138.2	138.4	139.0
Private sector services (Divisions 50-93) JJGH													
2006	125.6	121.6	123.3	124.7	124.6	125.2	126.5	125.8	125.7	126.5	127.4	127.5	128.5
2007	131.1	128.9	130.1	128.5	129.5	130.3	130.5	131.1	132.1	133.0	132.2	133.6	133.3
2008	136.0	134.0	134.8	135.4	134.8	135.0	135.8	136.1	136.5	136.9	137.4	137.5	138.2

1 See chapter text.

Source: Office for National Statistics: 01633 819024

7.23

Average earnings index:[1] all employee jobs: by industry
Great Britain
Not seasonally adjusted

Indices (2000=100)

	Agriculture, forestry and fishing	Mining and quarrying	Food products, beverages and tobacco	Textiles, leather and clothing	Chemicals and man-made fibres	Basic metals and metal products	Engineering and allied industries	Other manufacturing	Electricity, gas and water supply	Construction
Excluding bonuses										
SIC 1992										
	JVUZ	JVVA	JVVB	JVVC	JVVD	JVVE	JVVF	JVVG	JVVH	JVVI
2007	127.4	139.1	128.6	125.4	127.2	130.8	133.0	132.2	121.3	130.6
2008	128.2	148.7	132.8	125.0	130.5	136.0	136.3	135.5	125.3	134.1
2006 May	140.2	128.1	128.4	123.2	122.0	126.9	126.3	125.9	118.3	127.2
Jun	141.4	128.4	127.8	124.0	123.0	129.5	126.5	126.9	118.2	127.9
Jul	137.2	128.7	128.3	122.8	121.6	128.4	126.4	126.5	118.7	128.2
Aug	139.9	129.0	128.2	120.1	122.5	127.9	126.2	127.1	116.2	126.7
Sep	135.7	131.0	128.1	122.1	124.3	129.3	127.7	127.7	114.6	128.5
Oct	130.3	131.3	128.2	122.0	125.1	129.2	128.8	127.8	113.0	129.5
Nov	123.8	131.7	127.7	122.4	123.9	129.9	129.1	128.8	116.6	130.0
Dec	130.5	134.7	130.0	124.4	125.2	127.9	128.6	128.6	114.9	129.3
2007 Jan	129.5	133.1	126.7	124.2	123.2	128.0	129.6	128.7	114.3	130.6
Feb	121.7	132.5	125.2	125.6	124.9	129.4	130.6	129.8	115.1	129.7
Mar	129.8	134.0	125.4	123.5	125.6	130.0	132.6	131.4	118.9	131.5
Apr	133.3	139.6	127.5	123.0	125.0	130.3	133.3	131.7	118.6	129.8
May	132.0	140.4	130.2	124.2	127.6	128.4	133.0	131.3	122.2	129.5
Jun	124.5	141.7	128.0	129.1	128.7	131.6	133.6	132.3	122.9	130.2
Jul	124.9	140.3	128.2	127.6	127.8	130.8	134.3	132.6	124.4	131.6
Aug	127.7	141.6	128.8	127.8	127.1	130.9	132.8	132.2	121.5	129.3
Sep	126.6	140.3	129.1	126.4	126.6	131.5	133.1	133.2	122.5	130.8
Oct	128.1	142.3	130.3	126.6	129.2	132.8	134.2	134.4	124.3	131.3
Nov	126.3	140.8	130.3	124.4	129.5	133.5	134.5	134.7	127.3	132.0
Dec	125.0	143.2	133.2	122.2	131.0	132.5	134.3	134.2	123.3	131.0
2008 Jan	125.4	145.4	129.3	125.2	127.9	135.0	134.3	133.7	122.3	131.3
Feb	126.2	145.9	130.0	123.8	129.6	134.7	134.5	134.9	122.5	133.1
Mar	129.1	141.0	133.1	122.6	129.4	133.0	136.7	135.4	121.3	130.8
Apr	127.5	150.6	131.6	125.5	130.0	135.9	136.7	135.4	123.3	133.1
May	127.5	150.7	133.0	123.2	130.6	135.6	136.5	136.0	124.3	132.8
Jun	128.9	152.4	132.5	126.1	131.4	136.6	136.5	136.1	125.9	134.5
Jul	126.2	150.0	132.4	126.9	131.4	137.1	137.2	135.1	127.2	135.6
Aug	126.6	148.8	133.2	126.0	129.5	136.2	136.4	134.6	125.7	133.1
Sep	127.4	150.4	133.0	126.6	130.3	136.5	135.0	135.6	127.4	136.1
Oct	130.1	148.5	134.2	127.8	130.9	137.1	137.0	136.1	127.5	136.3
Nov	131.3	149.0	134.0	127.8	130.4	138.7	137.9	136.9	128.0	136.2
Dec	132.1	151.5	136.6	119.0	134.8	135.3	137.2	136.6	127.7	135.8
Percentage change on the year										
	JVVT	JVVU	JVVV	JVVW	JVVX	JVVY	JVVZ	JVWA	JVWB	JVWC
2007 May	−5.8	9.5	1.4	0.8	4.5	1.1	5.3	4.3	3.2	1.9
Jun	−11.9	10.4	0.1	4.1	4.6	1.6	5.6	4.3	4.0	1.8
Jul	−8.9	9.0	−	3.9	5.1	1.9	6.2	4.8	4.8	2.7
Aug	−8.7	9.7	0.4	6.4	3.8	2.3	5.2	4.0	4.6	2.0
Sep	−6.7	7.1	0.7	3.5	1.9	1.7	4.2	4.4	6.9	1.8
Oct	−1.7	8.4	1.7	3.8	3.3	2.8	4.2	5.1	10.0	1.4
Nov	2.0	7.0	2.0	1.7	4.5	2.8	4.2	4.6	9.2	1.6
Dec	−4.2	6.3	2.5	−1.8	4.7	3.6	4.5	4.4	7.2	1.3
2008 Jan	−3.2	9.2	2.1	0.8	3.8	5.5	3.6	3.9	7.0	0.6
Feb	3.7	10.2	3.9	−1.4	3.8	4.2	3.0	3.9	6.4	2.6
Mar	−0.5	5.3	6.1	−0.7	3.0	2.3	3.1	3.0	2.0	−0.5
Apr	−4.3	7.9	3.2	2.0	4.0	4.3	2.5	2.9	4.0	2.6
May	−3.4	7.4	2.2	−0.8	2.5	5.6	2.7	3.6	1.7	2.5
Jun	3.6	7.6	3.5	−2.3	2.1	3.8	2.2	2.9	2.4	3.3
Jul	1.0	6.9	3.2	−0.5	2.8	4.8	2.2	1.9	2.3	3.1
Aug	−0.9	5.1	3.5	−1.5	1.9	4.1	2.7	1.9	3.4	2.9
Sep	0.7	7.2	3.1	0.1	2.9	3.8	1.4	1.8	4.0	4.0
Oct	1.5	4.3	3.0	0.9	1.3	3.2	2.1	1.3	2.6	3.8
Nov	4.0	5.8	2.8	2.7	0.7	3.9	2.5	1.6	0.5	3.2
Dec	5.7	5.8	2.5	−2.6	2.9	2.1	2.1	1.8	3.6	3.7

7.23
Average earnings index:[1] all employee jobs: by industry
Great Britain
continued   Not seasonally adjusted

Indices (2000=100)

	Wholesale trade	Retail trade and repairs	Hotels and restaurants	Transport, storage and communication	Financial interm-ediation	Real estate renting and business activities	Public admini-stration	Education	Health and social work	Other services
Excluding bonuses										
SIC 1992										
	JVVJ	JVVK	JVVL	JVVM	JVVN	JVVO	JVVP	JVVQ	JVVR	JVVS
2007	127.2	122.3	140.3	130.0	128.6	133.7	130.7	134.0	142.7	126.0
2008	131.3	126.9	144.1	133.6	133.2	139.5	135.3	138.4	149.7	133.3
2006 May	120.9	120.0	133.1	127.5	126.5	127.3	127.9	127.1	137.2	122.3
Jun	122.1	118.5	132.1	127.9	125.7	128.0	128.4	127.6	138.7	124.6
Jul	122.0	119.2	134.0	126.8	125.8	128.0	128.5	128.8	138.7	123.0
Aug	122.1	120.1	134.1	126.8	125.6	128.1	127.2	131.6	137.7	122.7
Sep	122.4	120.5	134.7	128.3	124.9	128.3	128.4	132.2	137.7	121.4
Oct	123.6	120.5	136.2	127.0	126.3	129.3	128.2	131.3	137.8	121.2
Nov	124.4	118.7	136.1	127.4	125.8	129.4	128.8	130.9	139.4	122.3
Dec	125.3	119.7	139.8	128.0	125.8	130.1	131.4	131.4	139.2	123.3
2007 Jan	124.8	122.0	135.9	127.7	127.1	130.9	129.2	130.4	139.8	124.1
Feb	125.0	119.6	137.2	127.7	127.5	131.5	129.6	130.2	139.3	123.1
Mar	126.3	120.9	138.1	128.2	126.3	132.5	129.4	130.5	139.8	122.7
Apr	126.8	123.7	137.6	129.0	127.7	132.6	130.2	132.6	141.0	123.3
May	127.0	122.7	140.6	130.0	128.6	133.9	130.2	132.5	142.0	125.8
Jun	127.5	122.2	141.0	131.0	129.0	134.0	130.0	132.8	142.8	127.9
Jul	128.0	122.4	141.4	130.6	129.2	134.2	130.0	133.8	142.0	127.8
Aug	126.9	124.1	142.4	131.4	128.6	134.5	131.6	136.2	142.8	128.1
Sep	127.2	123.5	141.4	130.4	129.2	133.9	131.3	137.3	143.2	127.3
Oct	128.0	122.8	141.4	130.3	129.8	134.9	130.8	135.9	144.5	126.4
Nov	128.4	122.1	142.8	131.4	130.3	135.3	132.1	137.5	148.8	127.2
Dec	130.1	122.1	143.5	132.6	130.2	136.5	133.4	138.8	146.9	128.2
2008 Jan	129.4	125.7	141.2	131.0	130.7	137.0	133.4	134.7	146.2	129.7
Feb	129.9	123.9	141.8	131.5	131.5	137.9	134.3	134.7	145.9	129.0
Mar	131.0	126.3	146.9	132.8	133.1	137.7	133.5	134.8	146.7	130.9
Apr	130.9	127.3	144.4	133.5	133.5	138.8	135.3	136.6	149.1	130.3
May	131.2	127.2	145.8	133.6	133.1	138.8	134.7	136.6	148.1	132.5
Jun	131.1	127.2	144.0	134.1	134.5	139.8	134.9	136.6	149.3	134.3
Jul	130.9	126.8	144.0	134.0	134.4	140.4	135.1	137.9	150.8	137.3
Aug	130.8	127.8	146.4	133.5	133.7	140.3	134.7	139.5	153.6	135.8
Sep	131.7	128.5	143.6	134.2	133.1	139.9	135.0	141.1	151.1	134.1
Oct	132.5	128.0	144.5	135.2	133.1	140.9	135.0	140.3	151.2	134.3
Nov	132.7	126.5	141.7	134.6	134.1	141.4	139.0	144.9	151.8	135.0
Dec	133.1	127.6	145.1	135.7	133.9	141.5	138.7	143.4	153.0	137.0
Percentage change on the year										
	JVWD	JVWE	JVWF	JVYJ	JVYK	JVYL	JVYM	JVYN	JVYO	JVYP
2007 May	5.0	2.3	5.6	2.0	1.7	5.2	1.8	4.2	3.5	2.8
Jun	4.4	3.1	6.8	2.5	2.7	4.7	1.3	4.1	2.9	2.7
Jul	5.0	2.7	5.5	3.0	2.7	4.8	1.2	3.9	2.4	3.9
Aug	4.0	3.3	6.2	3.6	2.4	5.0	3.4	3.5	3.7	4.4
Sep	3.9	2.5	4.9	1.7	3.5	4.3	2.2	3.8	4.0	4.8
Oct	3.6	1.9	3.8	2.6	2.8	4.3	2.0	3.5	1.8	4.3
Nov	3.2	2.8	4.9	3.1	3.6	4.6	2.6	5.0	6.7	4.1
Dec	3.9	2.0	2.6	3.6	3.5	4.9	1.6	5.7	5.5	4.0
2008 Jan	3.7	3.0	3.9	2.6	2.8	4.6	3.2	3.3	4.6	4.5
Feb	4.0	3.6	3.3	2.9	3.2	4.8	3.6	3.4	4.7	4.7
Mar	3.8	4.5	6.4	3.5	5.4	3.9	3.1	3.4	5.0	6.7
Apr	3.2	2.9	4.9	3.4	4.6	4.7	3.9	3.0	5.8	5.6
May	3.3	3.6	3.7	2.7	3.5	3.7	3.5	3.1	4.3	5.3
Jun	2.8	4.1	2.1	2.3	4.2	4.4	3.7	2.8	4.6	5.0
Jul	2.2	3.6	1.9	2.6	4.1	4.7	3.9	3.0	6.2	7.5
Aug	3.1	3.0	2.8	1.6	3.9	4.4	2.4	2.4	7.6	6.0
Sep	3.6	4.1	1.5	2.9	3.0	4.5	2.8	2.8	5.6	5.4
Oct	3.6	4.3	2.1	3.8	2.5	4.4	3.2	3.3	4.6	6.3
Nov	3.3	3.7	−0.7	2.5	2.9	4.6	5.2	5.4	2.1	6.1
Dec	2.3	4.5	1.1	2.3	2.9	3.7	3.9	3.3	4.2	6.8

7.23
continued

Average earnings index:[1] all employee jobs: by industry
Great Britain
Not seasonally adjusted

Indices (2000=100)

	Agriculture, forestry and fishing	Mining and quarrying	Food products, beverages and tobacco	Textiles, leather and clothing	Chemicals and man-made fibres	Basic metals and metal products	Engineering and allied industries	Other manufacturing	Electricity, gas and water supply	Construction
Including bonuses										
SIC 1992										
	JVUF	JVUG	JVUH	JVUI	JVUJ	JVUK	JVUL	JVUM	JVUN	JVUO
2007	129.0	144.4	122.0	131.7	123.6	138.6	135.0	128.2	126.1	129.3
2008	132.2	154.8	127.3	130.1	126.0	143.0	137.8	133.1	132.8	129.2
2006 May	137.3	130.3	122.0	124.4	112.9	130.2	126.7	122.3	121.3	123.0
Jun	139.0	128.8	122.5	125.6	115.4	131.8	127.0	124.1	129.6	125.8
Jul	134.5	126.8	122.5	125.4	114.8	135.2	127.4	123.6	119.2	125.1
Aug	137.2	126.6	120.4	121.8	114.7	130.4	126.3	124.0	115.6	121.6
Sep	133.0	130.6	125.1	122.7	117.8	135.6	127.6	121.9	114.4	125.1
Oct	127.6	130.2	121.6	125.1	116.5	139.6	129.6	122.6	114.3	125.1
Nov	121.2	136.8	121.4	125.5	114.5	133.2	130.5	123.4	116.5	127.8
Dec	138.2	135.7	125.7	131.2	123.5	138.2	132.3	127.3	115.1	133.8
2007 Jan	127.6	137.7	117.9	128.1	116.0	132.0	130.7	123.9	114.3	126.7
Feb	120.0	141.5	119.4	130.4	120.1	135.3	138.2	126.3	115.7	128.3
Mar	135.4	177.0	128.3	134.4	152.2	135.1	141.1	134.6	136.2	135.9
Apr	133.6	147.6	125.4	126.7	124.8	140.2	134.6	127.1	124.3	125.9
May	134.9	140.1	121.2	127.7	119.1	137.5	134.0	128.1	126.4	126.6
Jun	124.9	144.1	119.1	133.9	123.1	143.0	133.6	128.0	135.8	128.3
Jul	125.3	139.0	121.0	137.2	120.0	141.9	134.3	129.9	130.2	128.2
Aug	130.8	138.3	119.9	134.7	118.6	134.8	132.3	125.5	122.9	124.2
Sep	128.4	143.0	122.6	136.6	120.1	135.4	132.3	125.5	124.9	130.0
Oct	128.7	138.6	121.2	131.4	119.8	140.6	133.9	127.6	126.9	126.8
Nov	128.8	143.0	120.0	130.6	121.5	138.8	135.4	129.4	130.7	132.5
Dec	129.3	143.3	128.5	128.8	127.8	148.6	139.1	132.1	125.0	138.3
2008 Jan	130.3	143.7	119.6	135.2	121.1	142.3	134.2	128.6	125.1	126.7
Feb	127.7	149.6	126.5	127.6	125.0	142.0	139.9	130.5	125.9	127.2
Mar	134.2	197.8	132.2	132.7	150.0	142.0	148.4	142.1	140.8	132.5
Apr	130.6	159.0	125.5	128.5	140.0	145.9	137.0	132.5	134.1	126.3
May	130.0	151.1	134.2	126.3	120.4	140.0	137.2	132.2	131.6	127.8
Jun	131.1	159.6	126.7	131.4	121.9	142.0	136.8	132.2	141.9	129.5
Jul	128.1	152.8	128.3	130.1	122.5	144.2	136.6	134.0	134.2	129.2
Aug	129.3	144.7	124.7	127.3	118.8	142.5	134.5	130.1	129.2	125.7
Sep	130.6	151.8	129.4	130.3	120.3	141.3	133.9	130.8	132.7	131.2
Oct	131.3	145.9	125.5	132.7	121.0	144.6	136.2	132.0	132.3	128.6
Nov	131.8	148.4	124.0	130.5	121.1	143.7	137.0	133.6	133.5	130.0
Dec	151.3	152.6	131.5	128.7	130.5	145.1	141.4	138.7	131.8	135.2
Percentage change on the year										
	JVYQ	JVYR	JVYS	JVYT	JVYU	JVYV	JVYW	JVYX	JVYY	JVYZ
2007 May	−1.7	7.5	−0.7	2.6	5.6	5.6	5.8	4.7	4.2	2.9
Jun	−10.2	11.9	−2.8	6.6	6.6	8.5	5.2	3.1	4.8	2.0
Jul	−6.8	9.6	−1.2	9.4	4.5	5.0	5.5	5.1	9.2	2.5
Aug	−4.7	9.3	−0.4	10.6	3.4	3.4	4.8	1.2	6.4	2.2
Sep	−3.5	9.5	−2.0	11.3	2.0	−0.1	3.7	2.9	9.2	3.9
Oct	0.8	6.5	−0.3	5.0	2.8	0.7	3.3	4.1	11.1	1.4
Nov	6.2	4.6	−1.2	4.0	6.1	4.2	3.8	4.9	12.2	3.7
Dec	−6.5	5.6	2.2	−1.9	3.5	7.6	5.1	3.8	8.7	3.4
2008 Jan	2.1	4.3	1.4	5.5	4.4	7.8	2.6	3.7	9.4	−
Feb	6.5	5.8	5.9	−2.1	4.0	5.0	1.3	3.3	8.8	−0.9
Mar	−0.8	11.8	3.0	−1.3	−1.5	5.1	5.2	5.6	3.3	−2.5
Apr	−2.2	7.7	0.1	1.4	12.2	4.1	1.8	4.2	7.9	0.3
May	−3.7	7.9	10.7	−1.1	1.1	1.8	2.4	3.2	4.1	1.0
Jun	5.0	10.7	6.4	−1.9	−0.9	−0.7	2.4	3.3	4.5	1.0
Jul	2.3	9.9	6.1	−5.2	2.0	1.6	1.7	3.2	3.1	0.8
Aug	−1.1	4.6	4.0	−5.4	0.1	5.8	1.7	3.6	5.1	1.2
Sep	1.8	6.1	5.6	−4.6	0.2	4.3	1.2	4.3	6.2	0.9
Oct	2.0	5.3	3.6	1.0	1.0	2.8	1.7	3.4	4.3	1.4
Nov	2.4	3.8	3.3	−0.1	−0.3	3.5	1.2	3.2	2.1	−1.9
Dec	17.0	6.5	2.3	−0.1	2.1	−2.4	1.7	5.0	5.4	−2.2

7.23
continued

Average earnings index:[1] all employee jobs: by industry
Great Britain
Not seasonally adjusted

Indices (2000=100)

	Wholesale trade	Retail trade and repairs	Hotels and restaurants	Transport, storage and communication	Financial interm- ediation	Real estate renting and business activities	Public admini- stration	Education	Health and social work	Other services
Including bonuses										
SIC 1992										
	JVUP	JVUQ	JVUR	JVUS	JVUT	JVUU	JVUV	JVUW	JVUX	JVUY
2007	132.6	123.7	143.8	131.5	130.2	129.5	131.2	133.8	142.6	129.5
2008	137.0	126.8	147.7	134.4	136.7	134.4	135.9	138.3	149.5	139.2
2006 May	120.2	119.7	138.4	139.0	103.4	122.3	127.7	126.8	137.0	125.4
Jun	123.0	120.8	134.7	138.2	113.2	124.7	129.1	127.3	138.5	124.9
Jul	123.9	121.3	136.5	127.5	103.4	124.9	131.2	128.7	138.5	123.9
Aug	121.3	119.0	136.9	124.6	99.3	122.2	130.1	131.3	137.4	123.2
Sep	121.9	119.6	137.6	124.6	96.7	122.3	128.6	131.9	137.4	121.6
Oct	124.6	120.2	139.4	122.9	97.7	122.6	128.6	130.9	137.6	120.6
Nov	126.6	118.0	140.7	124.4	100.4	122.7	129.1	130.7	139.2	123.5
Dec	133.9	118.9	145.5	130.8	113.5	129.5	134.7	131.2	139.2	126.7
2007 Jan	129.1	120.5	139.3	125.5	195.0	125.3	128.9	130.0	139.8	126.8
Feb	133.7	120.0	142.5	127.5	243.1	127.4	129.6	129.9	139.5	125.1
Mar	140.6	128.4	146.3	129.7	176.0	134.4	129.3	130.3	140.5	129.2
Apr	129.9	126.4	139.3	126.3	105.1	127.5	130.4	132.3	140.7	127.8
May	128.8	124.1	145.8	140.9	108.0	127.2	130.3	132.1	141.7	127.8
Jun	132.3	126.3	142.5	145.2	106.4	130.0	131.1	132.4	142.5	132.4
Jul	130.2	126.7	142.6	129.0	104.3	132.1	130.4	133.8	141.8	133.0
Aug	129.0	122.8	144.6	130.7	102.7	129.9	134.4	135.8	142.5	131.0
Sep	131.1	122.4	143.0	127.9	106.4	128.1	131.1	136.9	143.1	129.3
Oct	130.4	123.6	143.8	127.7	99.0	128.1	130.6	135.9	144.2	128.4
Nov	135.4	121.0	145.8	130.0	103.9	128.7	133.0	137.5	148.6	129.9
Dec	140.4	122.3	150.4	137.0	113.1	135.0	135.6	138.9	146.8	133.0
2008 Jan	138.3	123.7	144.2	129.5	196.9	131.3	134.1	134.4	145.8	135.2
Feb	143.2	125.3	149.1	132.5	250.2	132.1	134.4	134.7	145.6	136.3
Mar	149.5	134.3	153.3	135.7	185.8	141.7	133.4	134.7	146.7	139.4
Apr	134.6	128.8	147.0	132.2	104.6	133.3	135.5	136.3	148.8	138.6
May	133.6	127.7	151.6	143.2	109.2	131.9	134.6	136.3	147.9	135.3
Jun	136.0	128.2	146.2	144.9	119.3	134.8	134.7	136.4	149.1	139.6
Jul	134.8	127.0	146.2	131.6	110.5	137.9	137.2	138.0	150.6	143.5
Aug	132.0	125.1	148.4	132.3	109.8	133.5	137.2	139.1	153.5	140.5
Sep	132.1	124.5	145.3	130.2	113.8	132.2	135.1	140.9	150.8	138.2
Oct	133.3	126.0	146.1	131.2	107.6	133.1	134.5	140.1	150.9	140.5
Nov	136.7	124.1	145.3	131.4	106.4	133.0	139.6	144.8	151.8	139.4
Dec	139.9	126.4	150.0	138.0	126.2	138.4	140.3	143.7	152.9	144.1
Percentage change on the year										
	JVZA	JVZB	JVZC	JVZD	JVZE	JVZF	JVZG	JVZH	JVZI	JVZJ
2007 May	7.2	3.7	5.4	1.4	4.5	4.0	2.0	4.2	3.4	1.9
Jun	7.6	4.6	5.8	5.1	−6.0	4.2	1.6	4.0	2.9	6.0
Jul	5.1	4.5	4.5	1.2	0.9	5.7	−0.6	3.9	2.4	7.3
Aug	6.3	3.2	5.6	4.9	3.4	6.4	3.3	3.4	3.7	6.3
Sep	7.6	2.3	4.0	2.7	10.0	4.8	2.0	3.8	4.1	6.3
Oct	4.6	2.8	3.2	3.9	1.3	4.5	1.6	3.8	4.8	6.5
Nov	7.0	2.5	3.6	4.6	3.5	4.9	3.1	5.2	6.7	5.1
Dec	4.8	2.9	3.4	4.8	−0.3	4.3	0.6	5.9	5.5	5.0
2008 Jan	7.1	2.6	3.5	3.2	1.0	4.8	4.0	3.4	4.4	6.6
Feb	7.1	4.4	4.6	3.9	2.9	3.7	3.7	3.7	4.4	8.9
Mar	6.3	4.6	4.8	4.6	5.6	5.4	3.1	3.3	4.4	7.9
Apr	3.6	2.0	5.5	4.6	−0.5	4.5	3.9	3.1	5.8	8.4
May	3.7	2.9	3.9	1.7	1.1	3.7	3.3	3.2	4.3	5.9
Jun	2.8	1.5	2.6	−0.2	12.1	3.7	2.7	3.0	4.6	5.4
Jul	3.5	0.3	2.5	2.0	6.0	4.4	5.2	3.2	6.2	7.9
Aug	2.3	1.9	2.6	1.2	6.9	2.7	2.1	2.5	7.7	7.2
Sep	0.7	1.7	1.6	1.8	6.9	3.2	3.0	2.9	5.4	6.8
Oct	2.3	1.9	1.6	2.7	8.7	3.9	2.9	3.1	4.7	9.4
Nov	1.0	2.5	−0.3	1.1	2.4	3.3	4.9	5.3	2.2	7.3
Dec	−0.3	3.4	−0.3	0.7	11.6	2.5	3.5	3.4	4.2	8.4

1 See chapter text.

Source: Office for National Statistics: 01633 819024

7.24 Gross weekly and hourly earnings of full-time employees:[1] by sex
United Kingdom
At April

£

	Gross weekly earnings					Gross hourly earnings				
	Lowest decile	Lower quartile	Median	Upper quartile	Highest decile	Lowest decile	Lower quartile	Median	Upper quartile	Highest decile
All employees										
	C5U9	C5UC	C5UF	C5UI	C5UL	C5UO	C5UR	C5UU	C5V2	C5UX
2003	222.7	288.0	404.0	572.6	794.2	5.68	7.23	10.07	14.82	21.27
2004[2]	231.9	301.3	422.8	595.0	827.3	5.91	7.54	10.56	15.41	22.18
	230.3	298.0	419.2	590.6	814.4	5.84	7.45	10.44	15.32	21.83
2005	235.4	305.3	431.2	611.6	850.5	6.00	7.68	10.77	15.91	22.86
2006[3]	244.1	316.2	446.4	632.5	886.2	6.24	7.96	11.20	16.46	23.63
	243.8	315.2	443.6	630.5	881.6		7.93	11.12	16.39	23.49
2007	252.9	325.8	457.6	650.5	907.1	6.47	8.22	11.47	16.87	24.17
2008	261.8	338.4	478.6	676.1	946.8	6.66	8.50	11.97	17.56	25.02
Male employees										
	C5UA	C5UD	C5UG	C5UJ	C5UM	C5UP	C5US	C5UV	C5V3	C5UY
2003	246.6	320.3	444.6	622.8	881.9	6.00	7.68	10.75	15.83	23.17
2004[2]	254.5	333.3	463.0	647.8	916.8	6.21	7.99	11.23	16.42	24.08
	250.0	329.4	460.0	640.5	900.7	6.13	7.89	11.10	16.25	23.67
2005	255.6	335.4	471.0	666.0	939.1	6.27	8.08	11.42	16.88	24.74
2006[3]	264.9	347.1	487.1	689.9	985.5	6.50	8.39	11.83	17.50	25.79
	264.5	346.0	484.3	687.5	980.5		8.37	11.76	17.38	25.64
2007	274.0	358.0	498.3	706.0	1 008.1	6.73	8.65	12.09	17.89	26.40
2008	283.0	371.3	521.2	736.0	1 054.1	6.95	8.94	12.62	18.64	27.43
Female employees										
	C5UB	C5UE	C5UH	C5UK	C5UN	C5UQ	C5UT	C5UW	C5V4	C5UZ
2003	201.3	251.6	343.0	490.2	645.7	5.30	6.63	9.07	13.28	18.33
2004[2]	210.8	265.3	360.8	515.5	678.8	5.53	6.96	9.57	13.96	19.19
	209.3	262.3	356.7	510.0	673.9	5.50	6.91	9.42	13.82	18.96
2005	217.5	271.6	371.4	532.8	704.7	5.71	7.16	9.85	14.45	20.01
2006[3]	226.6	282.2	385.8	554.1	728.5	5.99	7.44	10.24	15.04	20.48
	226.3	282.1	383.3	550.0	724.9	5.98	7.42	10.16	14.92	20.39
2007	233.5	289.8	394.8	565.4	749.0	6.18	7.67	10.48	15.33	20.95
2008	240.5	302.4	412.0	589.6	776.2	6.36	7.94	10.92	15.97	21.60

1 See chapter text. Employees on adult rates whose pay for the survey period was not affected by absence.

2 For 2004, two sets of figures are shown. The first does not include supplementary information and therefore is comparable with earlier years. The second includes supplementary information and so is discontinuous with previous years (where the two figures are equal, only one appears).

3 In 2006 additional methodology was introduced. Therefore the bottom data is comparable with 2007, whilst the top data is comparable with earlier years (where the two figures are equal, only one appears).

Sources: Annual Survey of Hours and Earnings; Office for National Statistics: 01633 819024

7.25 Median earnings by age group of full-time employees:[1] by sex, 2008
United Kingdom
At April

£ and numbers

	Median gross weekly pay excluding overtime	Median gross weekly overtime	Median weekly hours (numbers)		Median gross hourly earnings excluding overtime
			Total	Overtime	
All employees					
16 to 17	175.9	..	39.0	..	4.60
18 to 21	262.4	27.6	39.0	3.4	6.74
22 to 29	386.0	41.4	37.5	3.6	10.11
30 to 39	508.3	60.6	37.5	4.3	13.33
40 to 49	507.7	64.9	37.5	4.7	13.29
50 to 59	479.1	58.9	37.5	4.4	12.53
60+	408.8	54.6	38.0	4.8	10.56
All ages	453.5	54.5	37.5	4.1	11.87
Male employees					
16 to 17	172.5	..	39.7	..	4.51
18 to 21	268.8	36.0	40.0	4.0	6.83
22 to 29	395.7	49.6	39.1	4.1	10.11
30 to 39	530.2	70.3	39.0	5.0	13.69
40 to 49	559.0	78.7	39.1	5.5	14.37
50 to 59	526.4	72.0	38.9	5.2	13.54
60+	429.0	60.7	39.0	5.0	10.89
All ages	486.0	66.4	39.0	5.0	13.60
Female employees					
16 to 17	179.6	..	37.5	..	4.90
18 to 21	253.9	18.0	37.5	2.1	6.62
22 to 29	377.6	28.3	37.5	2.6	10.11
30 to 39	472.8	38.1	37.3	2.9	12.78
40 to 49	425.0	33.4	37.0	2.7	11.56
50 to 59	409.0	28.5	37.0	2.6	11.08
60+	365.0	29.4	37.0	2.6	9.78
All ages	402.5	30.7	37.1	2.6	10.91

1 See chapter text. Employees on adult rates whose pay for the survey period was not affected by absence.

Sources: Annual Survey of Hours and Earnings, Office for National Statistics; 01633 819024

7.26 Trade unions[1]
United Kingdom
Year ending 31st March[2]

Percentages

		2000 /01	2001 /02	2002 /03	2003 /04	2004 /05	2005 /06	2006 /07	2007 /08
Number of trade unions	KCLB	237	226	216	213	206	193	192	193
Analysis by number of members:									
Under 100 members	KCLC	18.60	22.10	19.00	20.70	19.90	17.60	17.70	17.10
100 and under 500	KCLD	20.70	18.10	18.50	18.80	17.50	20.70	18.20	19.20
500 and under 1,000	KCLE	9.30	9.30	11.60	10.30	10.70	9.30	9.90	10.90
1,000 and under 2,500	KCLF	14.30	12.40	10.20	10.80	11.70	13.00	12.50	11.40
2,500 and under 5,000	KCLG	9.70	9.30	11.60	10.80	10.70	10.90	11.50	12.40
5,000 and under 10,000	KCLH	5.10	5.30	4.20	4.70	5.30	5.70	6.30	6.20
10,000 and under 15,000	KCLI	1.70	1.80	2.80	3.30	2.40	2.10	1.60	1.60
15,000 and under 25,000	KCLJ	4.20	5.30	6.00	4.20	4.90	4.10	4.70	4.10
25,000 and under 50,000	KCLK	7.60	6.60	6.50	7.00	7.30	7.80	8.90	8.30
50,000 and under 100,000	KCLL	2.10	2.70	2.30	1.90	2.40	1.60	1.60	1.00
100,000 and under 250,000	KCLM	2.10	2.20	2.30	2.80	2.40	2.60	2.60	3.10
250,000 and over	KCLN	4.60	4.90	5.10	4.70	4.90	4.70	4.70	4.70
All sizes	KCLP	100	100	100	100	100	100	100	100
Membership									
Analysis by size of union:									
Under 100 members	KCLQ	—	—	—	—	—	—	—	—
100 and under 500	KCLR	0.20	0.20	0.20	0.20	0.10	0.10	0.10	0.10
500 and under 1,000	KCLS	0.20	0.20	0.20	0.20	0.20	0.20	0.20	0.20
1,000 and under 2,500	KCLT	0.70	0.60	0.50	0.50	0.50	0.60	0.50	0.50
2,500 and under 5,000	KCLU	1.10	1.00	1.20	1.10	1.00	1.00	1.00	1.10
5,000 and under 10,000	KCLV	1.20	1.10	0.90	0.90	1.10	1.20	1.20	1.20
10,000 and under 15,000	KCLW	0.70	0.60	0.90	1.10	0.80	0.60	0.50	0.50
15,000 and under 25,000	KCLX	2.30	2.90	3.30	2.20	2.50	1.90	2.20	2.00
25,000 and under 50,000	KCLY	7.80	6.60	6.30	6.70	6.90	7.10	8.10	7.40
50,000 and under 100,000	KCLZ	3.80	4.60	4.00	3.10	4.40	2.60	2.70	1.80
100,000 and under 250,000	KCMA	10.00	9.80	9.60	10.20	9.00	10.60	10.60	12.20
250,000 and over	KCMB	72.10	72.40	73.00	73.90	73.30	74.10	72.90	73.00
All sizes	KCMC	100	100	100	100	100	100	100	100
Total membership (thousands)	KCMD	7 897 519	7 779 393	7 750 990	7 735 983	7 559 062	7 473 000	7 602 842	7 627 693

1 See chapter text.
2 Data derived from trade union annual returns with periods which ended between October and September each year. The majority, however, ended in December. In the case of year 2004/05, for example, the data derived from annual returns with periods which ended between October 2004 and September 2005 - approximately 73% ended in December.

Source: Certification Office

Personal income, expenditure and wealth

Chapter 8

Personal income, expenditure and wealth

Distribution of total incomes

(Table 8.1)

The information shown in Table 8.1 comes from the Survey of Personal Incomes for the financial years 2003/04, 2004/05, 2005/06 and 2006/07. This is an annual survey that covers approximately 540,000 individuals across the whole of the UK. It is based on administrative data held by HM Revenue and Customs (HMRC) offices on individuals who could be liable to tax.

The table relates only to those individuals who are taxpayers. The distributions cover only incomes as computed for tax purposes and above a level which for each year corresponds approximately to the single person's allowance. Incomes below these levels are not shown because the information about them is incomplete.

Investment income from which tax has been deducted at source is not always known to local tax offices. Estimates of missing bank and building society interest and dividends from UK companies are included in these tables. The missing investment income is distributed, in a manner consistent with information from the Expenditure and Food Survey and the National Accounts, to individuals for whom there is no investment income already reported by the tax office.

Superannuation contributions are estimated and included in total income. They have been distributed among earners in the Survey of Personal Incomes sample by a method consistent with information about the number of employees who are contracted in or out of the State Earnings Related Pension Scheme and the proportion of their earnings contributed.

When comparing results of these surveys across years, it should be noted that the Survey of Personal Incomes is not a longitudinal survey. However, sample sizes have increased in recent years to increase precision.

Average incomes of households

(Table 8.2)

Original income is the total income in cash of all the members of the household before receipt of state benefits or the deduction of taxes. It includes income from employment, self-employment, investment income and occupational pensions. Gross income is original income plus cash benefits received from government (retirement pensions, child benefit, etc). Disposal income is the income available for consumption. It is equal to gross income less direct taxes which include income tax, national insurance contributions, and council tax. By further allowing for taxes paid on goods and services purchased, such as VAT, an estimate of post-tax income is derived. These income figures are derived from estimates made by the Office for National Statistics, based largely on information from the Expenditure and Food Survey (EFS), and published each on the Office for National Statistics website.

For the purposes of Table 8.2, a retired household is defined as one where the combined income of retired members amounts to at least half the total gross income of the household, where a retired person is defined as anyone who describes themselves as 'retired' or anyone over the minimum NI pension age describing themselves as 'unoccupied' or 'sick or injured but not intending to seek work'.

Children are defined as persons aged under 16 or aged between 16 and 18, unmarried and receiving full-time non-advanced further education.

Expenditure and Food Survey

(Tables 8.3 to 8.5)

The Expenditure and Food Survey (EFS) is a sample survey of 11,484 private households in the UK, with an achieved response of around 6,200 private households. The survey was introduced in April 2001 as a result of the amalgamation of the Family Expenditure and National Food Surveys (FES and NFS). The EFS sample is representative of all regions of the UK and of different types of households. The survey is continuous with interviews spread evenly over the year to ensure that estimates are not biased by seasonal variation. The survey results show how households spend their money – how much goes on food, clothing and so on – and how spending patterns vary depending upon income, household composition, and regional location of households. From January 2006, the survey has been conducted on a calendar year basis; therefore the latest results refer to the January to December 2007 period.

One of the main purposes of the EFS is to define the 'basket of goods' for the Retail Price Index (RPI) and the Consumer Price Index (CPI). The RPI has a vital role in the up rating of state pensions and welfare benefits, while the CPI is a key instrument of the Government's monetary policy. Information from the survey is also a major source for estimates of household expenditure in the UK National Accounts. In addition, many other government departments use EFS data as a basis for policy making, for example in the areas of housing and transport. The Department for Environment, Food and Rural Affairs (Defra) uses EFS data to report on trends in food consumption and nutrient intake within the UK. Users of the EFS outside government include independent research institutes, academic researcher and business and market researchers. Like all surveys based on a sample of the population, its results are subject to sampling variability and potentially to some bias due to non-response. The results of the survey are published in an annual report, the latest being *Family Spending 2008* edition. The report includes a list of definitions used in the survey, items on which information is collected and a brief account of the fieldwork procedure.

8.1 Distribution of total income before and after tax
United Kingdom
Years ending 5 April

	2003/2004 Annual Survey	£ million				2004/05 Annual Survey	£ million		
	Number of individuals (Thousands)	Total income before tax	Total tax	Total income after tax		Number of individuals (Thousands)	Total income before tax	Total tax	Total income after tax
Lower limit of range of income					**Lower limit of range of income**				
All incomes[1]	28 500	624 900	110 600	514 300	All incomes[1]	30 300	691 000	123 000	568 000
Income before tax (£)					Income before tax (£)				
4 615	498	2 390	8	2 380	4 745	329	1 600	4	1 600
5 000	1 090	6 000	93	5 900	5 000	1 110	6 090	80	6 010
6 000	2 710	19 100	636	18 400	6 000	2 760	19 500	600	18 900
8 000	2 660	23 900	1 570	22 300	8 000	2 950	26 500	1 600	24 900
10 000	2 570	28 300	2 500	25 800	10 000	2 760	30 300	2 580	27 700
12 000	2 430	31 600	3 400	28 200	12 000	2 470	32 100	3 350	28 700
14 000	2 270	33 900	4 130	29 800	14 000	2 280	34 200	4 080	30 100
16 000	1 000	00 700	4 450	29 300	16 000	2 050	34 800	4 520	30 300
18 000	1 730	32 900	4 610	28 300	18 000	1 790	34 100	4 720	29 300
20 000	5 710	139 400	21 800	117 500	20 000	6 000	146 000	22 700	124 000
30 000	3 360	124 500	22 800	101 700	30 000	4 090	152 000	27 300	125 000
50 000	1 110	73 600	19 300	54 200	50 000	1 270	83 700	21 600	62 100
100 000	256	34 000	10 800	23 200	100 000	300	40 000	12 600	27 400
200 000 and over	95	41 600	14 400	27 200	200 000 and over	111	49 500	17 300	32 200
Income after tax (£)					Income after tax (£)				
4 615	545	2 620	10	2 610	4 745	364	1 770	5	1 770
5 000	1 220	6 820	116	6 710	5 000	1 220	6 830	98	6 730
6 000	3 190	23 500	955	22 500	6 000	3 270	24 100	902	23 200
8 000	3 270	31 900	2 470	29 400	8 000	3 600	34 800	2 510	32 300
10 000	3 160	38 600	3 920	34 700	10 000	3 280	40 000	3 920	36 000
12 000	2 890	42 600	5 120	37 500	12 000	2 920	43 000	5 050	37 900
14 000	2 400	42 400	5 660	36 800	14 000	2 540	43 700	5 730	38 000
16 000	2 090	41 300	5 910	35 400	16 000	2 180	43 200	6 090	37 100
18 000	1 720	38 400	5 840	32 600	18 000	1 850	41 400	6 210	35 200
20 000	4 900	141 600	23 300	118 300	20 000	5 320	154 000	25 100	129 000
30 000	2 280	106 000	22 800	83 200	30 000	2 840	131 000	27 100	104 000
50 000	601	55 700	16 300	39 400	50 000	681	63 200	18 300	44 800
100 000	119	23 800	7 930	15 800	100 000	143	28 400	9 420	19 000
200 000 and over	45	29 600	10 200	19 300	200 000 and over	53	35 500	12 500	23 000

8.1
continued

Distribution of total income before and after tax
United Kingdom
Years ending 5 April

	2005/06 Annual Survey					2006/07 Annual Survey			
	Number of individuals (Thousands)	£ million				Number of individuals (Thousands)	£ million		
		Total income before tax	Total tax	Total income after tax			Total income before tax	Total tax	Total income after tax
Lower limit of range of income					**Lower limit of range of income**				
All incomes[1]	31 100	756 000	138 000	618 000	All incomes[1]	31 800	810 000	150 000	661 000
Income before tax (£)					Income before tax (£)				
4 895	112	555	-	555	-	-	-	-	-
5 000	1 040	5 750	62	5 690	5 035	919	5 090	43	5 050
6 000	2 540	18 000	522	17 500	6 000	2 440	17 200	451	16 800
8 000	2 920	26 200	1 450	24 800	8 000	2 920	26 200	1 330	24 900
10 000	2 810	30 900	2 500	28 400	10 000	2 790	30 600	2 390	28 200
12 000	2 550	33 100	3 380	29 700	12 000	2 570	33 400	3 310	30 100
14 000	2 340	35 000	4 140	30 900	14 000	2 400	36 000	4 180	31 800
16 000	2 100	35 700	4 610	31 100	16 000	2 140	36 300	4 630	31 700
18 000	1 880	35 700	4 930	30 800	18 000	1 970	37 300	5 110	32 200
20 000	6 200	152 000	23 400	128 000	20 000	6 530	160 000	24 600	135 000
30 000	4 540	170 000	29 900	140 000	30 000	4 900	184 000	32 000	152 000
50 000	1 500	98 800	25 000	73 700	50 000	1 670	110 000	27 400	82 600
100 000	366	49 300	15 300	34 000	100 000	406	54 700	16 700	38 000
200 000 and over	144	66 000	22 900	43 000	200 000 and over	170	79 700	27 400	52 300
Income after tax (£)					Income after tax (£)				
4 895	129	636	1	636	-	-	-	-	-
5 000	1 160	6 500	77	6 420	5 035	1 040	5 800	55	5 750
6 000	3 000	22 000	767	21 300	6 000	2 860	20 900	656	20 200
8 000	3 590	34 600	2 300	32 300	8 000	3 550	34 000	2 090	31 900
10 000	3 390	41 100	3 890	37 200	10 000	3 410	41 200	3 770	37 500
12 000	3 020	44 300	5 120	39 200	12 000	3 120	45 600	5 160	40 500
14 000	2 650	45 600	5 940	39 600	14 000	2 710	46 700	5 990	40 700
16 000	2 260	44 600	6 270	38 300	16 000	2 370	46 800	6 530	40 200
18 000	1 850	41 300	6 140	35 100	18 000	1 920	42 700	6 320	36 400
20 000	5 630	163 000	26 400	137 000	20 000	5 980	173 000	28 000	145 000
30 000	3 310	152 000	30 700	121 000	30 000	3 650	168 000	33 200	134 000
50 000	817	75 500	21 600	53 900	50 000	914	83 800	23 600	60 200
100 000	188	37 100	12 100	24 900	100 000	220	43 300	13 900	29 400
200 000 and over	69	47 900	16 800	31 100	200 000 and over	82	58 600	20 200	38 300

1 See chapter text. All figures have been independently rounded.

Sources: Survey of Personal Incomes;
Board of HM Revenue & Customs:020 7438 7055

Personal income, expenditure and wealth

8.2

Average incomes of households before and after taxes and benefits,[1] 2006/07
United Kingdom

	Retired households		Non-retired households								
	1 adult	2 or more adults	1 adult	2 adults	3 or more adults	1 adult with children	2 adults with 1 child	2 adults with 2 children	2 adults with 3 or more children	3 or more adults with children	All house-holds
Number of households in the population (thousands)	3 291	3 234	3 638	5 260	2 172	1 441	1 847	2 176	812	965	24 836
Average per household (£ per year)											
Original income	5 020	13 047	22 053	42 649	48 549	11 698	43 084	48 056	41 866	44 947	30 080
Gross income	12 387	22 800	24 153	44 681	51 476	19 331	45 778	51 141	48 062	50 704	34 661
Disposable income	10 970	19 522	18 545	34 050	40 410	16 988	35 412	39 270	38 272	41 237	27 370
Post-tax income	8 951	15 400	15 379	28 081	32 862	13 526	29 485	32 464	31 920	33 193	22 420

1 See chapter text. Figures taken from the article "Effects of taxes and bene-fits on household income, 2006/07", published on the National Statistics website www.statistics.gov.uk/taxesbenefits

Source: Office for National Statistics: 01633 455951

8.3

Sources of gross household income[1]
United Kingdom

		1996 /97	1997 /98	1998[2] /99	1999 /00	2000 /01	2001[3] /02	2002 /03	2003 /04	2004 /05	2005 /06	2006[4,5]	2007
Weighted number of households (thousands)	GH92	24 310	24 560	24 660	25 330	25 030	24 450	24 350	24 670	24 430	24 800	25 440	25 350
Number of households supplying data	KPDA	6 420	6 410	6 630	7 100	6 640	7 470	6 930	7 050	6 800	6 790	6 650	6 140
Average weekly household income by source (£)													
Wages and salaries	KPCB	256.30	280.20	309.20	315.40	336.70	369.30	373.90	383.90	409.70	414.80	428.20	444.90
Self-employment	KPCC	37.50	32.90	37.20	46.00	44.50	43.10	44.50	49.80	49.00	50.80	55.20	53.50
Investments	KPCD	17.70	18.70	18.80	21.80	20.00	20.00	18.80	16.70	16.50	19.50	20.90	23.20
Annuities and pensions (other than social security benefits)	KPCE	26.00	28.90	30.30	32.80	35.00	37.00	39.90	40.90	41.70	45.50	44.40	47.60
Social security benefits[6]	KPCF	54.10	55.00	55.80	58.00	60.10	64.50	68.50	72.50	76.90	78.00	79.40	83.30
Other sources	KPCH	5.30	5.20	5.70	5.90	6.20	6.70	6.70	6.40	6.90	7.40	6.50	7.00
Total[7]	KPCI	396.90	420.80	457.00	479.90	502.50	540.60	552.30	570.30	600.70	615.90	634.70	659.40
Sources of household income as a percentage of total household income													
Wages and salaries	KPCJ	65	67	68	66	67	68	68	67	68	67	67	67
Self-employment	KPCK	9	8	8	10	9	8	8	9	8	8	9	8
Investments	KPCL	4	4	4	5	4	4	3	3	3	3	3	4
Annuities and pensions (other than social security benefits)	KPCM	7	7	7	7	7	7	7	7	7	7	7	7
Social security benefits[6]	KPCN	14	13	12	12	12	12	12	13	13	13	13	13
Other sources	KPCP	1	1	1	1	1	1	1	1	1	1	1	1
Total[7]	KPCQ	100	100	100	100	100	100	100	100	100	100	100	100

1 See chapter text.
2 Based on weighted data from 1998/99.
3 From 2001/02 onwards, weighting is based on the population estimates from the 2001 census.
4 From 2006 the survey has moved onto a calendar year basis.
5 From 1998/99 to 2005/06, the figures shown are based on weighted data using non-response weights based on the 1991 Census and population figures from the 1991 and 2001 Census. From 2006, figures shown on weighted data using updated weigths, with non-response weights and population figures based on the 2001 Census.

6 Excluding housing benefit and council tax benefit (rates rebate in Northern Ireland) and their predecessors in earlier years.
7 Does not include imputed income from owner-occupied and rent-free occupancy.

Sources: Expenditure and Food Survey and Family Expenditure Survey;
Office for National Statistics;
01633 455282

8.4 Household expenditure based on FES classification[1]
United Kingdom

		1996 /97	1997 /98	1998[2] /99	1999 /00	2000 /01	2001[3] /02	2002 /03	2003 /04	2004 /05	2005 /06	2006[4,5]	2007
Weighted number of households (thousands)	GH92	24 310	24 560	24 660	25 330	25 030	24 450	24 350	24 670	24 430	24 800	25 440	25 350
Number of households supplying data	KPDA	6 420	6 410	6 630	7 100	6 640	7 470	6 930	7 050	6 800	6 790	6 650	6 140

Average weekly household expenditure on commodities and services (£)

		1996 /97	1997 /98	1998[2] /99	1999 /00	2000 /01	2001[3] /02	2002 /03	2003 /04	2004 /05	2005 /06	2006[4,5]	2007
Housing (NET)[6]	KPEV	49.10	51.50	57.20	57.00	63.90	65.90	66.70	69.90	76.70	80.90	83.20	92.00
Fuel and power	KPEW	13.40	12.70	11.70	11.30	11.90	11.70	11.70	12.00	12.50	13.90	15.80	17.20
Food and non-alcoholic drinks	KPEX	55.20	55.90	58.90	59.60	61.90	61.90	64.30	64.90	67.30	67.90	69.60	71.40
Alcoholic drink	KPEY	12.40	13.30	14.00	15.30	15.00	14.30	14.80	14.70	14.80	14.80	14.70	14.70
Tobacco	KPEZ	6.10	6.10	5.80	6.00	6.10	5.50	5.40	5.50	5.00	4.50	4.70	4.60
Clothing and footwear	KCWC	18.30	20.00	21.70	21.00	22.00	22.30	22.00	22.40	23.50	22.40	22.60	21.60
Household goods	KCWH	26.70	26.90	29.60	30.70	32.60	33.00	33.80	35.10	35.60	33.50	34.00	34.60
Household services	KCWI	16.40	17.90	18.90	18.90	22.00	23.60	23.30	24.90	26.30	27.10	26.40	26.50
Personal goods and services	KCWJ	11.60	12.50	13.30	13.90	14.70	14.90	15.20	16.20	16.00	16.90	17.50	17.80
Motoring	KCWK	41.20	46.60	51.70	52.60	55.10	57.90	61.70	62.40	62.60	63.80	61.10	62.00
Fares and other travel costs	KCWL	7.50	8.10	8.30	9.20	9.50	9.30	9.70	9.60	9.50	11.10	11.00	10.90
Leisure goods	KCWM	15.20	16.40	17.80	18.50	19.70	19.60	20.50	21.40	21.40	19.40	19.40	20.10
Leisure services	KCWN	34.00	38.80	41.90	43.90	50.60	51.90	53.60	55.00	59.60	63.00	65.30	61.70
Miscellaneous	KCWO	2.20	2.00	1.20	1.40	0.70	1.90	2.00	1.90	2.00	2.20	2.10	1.90
Total	KCWP	309.10	328.80	352.20	359.40	385.70	393.90	404.70	415.70	432.90	441.40	447.40	456.80

Expenditure on commodity or service as a percentage of total expenditure

		1996 /97	1997 /98	1998[2] /99	1999 /00	2000 /01	2001[3] /02	2002 /03	2003 /04	2004 /05	2005 /06	2006[4,5]	2007
Housing (NET)[6]	KPFH	16	16	16	16	17	17	16	17	18	18	19	20
Fuel and power	KPFI	4	4	3	3	3	3	3	3	3	3	4	4
Food and non-alcoholic drinks	KPFJ	18	17	17	17	16	16	16	16	16	15	16	16
Alcoholic drink	KPFK	4	4	4	4	4	4	4	4	3	3	3	3
Tobacco	KPFL	2	2	2	2	2	1	1	1	1	1	1	1
Clothing and footwear	KPFM	6	6	6	6	6	6	5	5	5	5	5	5
Household goods	KCWQ	9	8	8	9	8	8	8	8	8	8	8	8
Household services	KCWR	5	5	5	5	6	6	6	6	6	6	6	6
Personal goods and services	KCWS	4	4	4	4	4	4	4	4	4	4	4	4
Motoring	KCWT	13	14	15	15	14	15	15	15	14	14	14	14
Fares and other travel costs	KCWU	2	2	2	3	2	2	2	2	2	3	2	2
Leisure goods	KCWV	5	5	5	5	5	5	5	5	5	4	4	4
Leisure services	KCWW	11	12	12	12	13	13	13	13	14	14	15	13
Miscellaneous	KPFR	1	1	–	–	–	–	–	–	–	–	–	–
Total	KPFS	100	100	100	100	100	100	100	100	100	100	100	100

1 Data are based on the Family Expenditure Survey (FES) classification and not the Expenditure and Food Survey (EFS) standard classification: Classification of Individual Consumption by Purpose (COICOP). This has been done to preserve an historical time-series, as COICOP data are only available from 2001/02.

2 From 1998/99 figures shown are based on weighted data, including children's expenditure. Weighting is based on the population figures from the 1991 and 2001 Censuses.

3 From 2001/02 onwards, weighting is based on population estimates from the 2001 census.

4 From 2006 the survey has moved onto a calendar year basis.

5 From 1998/99 to 2005/06, the figures shown are based on weighted data using non-response weights based on the 1991 Census and population figures from the 1991 and 2001 Census. From 2006, figures shown are based on weighted data using updated weights, with non-response weights and population figures based on the 2001 Census.

6 An improvement to the implation of mortgage intrest payments has been implemented for 2006 and 2007 data which should lead to more accurate figures. This will lead to a slight discontinuity. An error was discovered in the derivation of mortgage capital repayments which was leading to double counting. This has been amended for the 2006 and 2007 data.

Sources: Expenditure and Food Survey and Family Expenditure Survey;
Office for National Statistics;
01633 455282

8.5 Percentage of households with certain durable goods
United Kingdom

		1996 /97	1997 /98	1998[1] /99	1999 /00	2000 /01	2001[2] /02	2002 /03	2003 /04	2004 /05	2005 /06	2006[4,5]	2007
Weighted number of households (thousands)	GH92	24 310	24 560	24 660	25 330	25 030	24 450	24 350	24 670	24 430	24 800	25 440	25 350
Number of households supplying data	KPDA	6 420	6 410	6 630	7 100	6 640	7 470	6 930	7 050	6 800	6 790	6 650	6 140
Car/van	KPDB	69	70	72	71	72	74	74	75	75	74	74	75
One	KPDC	43	44	44	43	44	44	44	44	42	46	43	44
Two	KPDD	22	21	23	21	22	23	25	25	27	23	25	25
Three or more	KPDE	5	5	5	6	6	6	6	6	6	5	6	6
Central heating, full or partial	KPDF	87	89	89	90	91	92	93	94	95	94	95	95
Washing machine	KPDG	91	91	92	91	92	93	94	94	95	95	96	96
Tumble dryer	J803	51	51	51	52	53	54	56	57	58	58	59	57
Fridge/freezer or deep freezer	KPDI	91	90	92	91	94	95	96	96	96	97	97	97
Dishwasher	GPTL	20	22	23	23	25	27	29	31	33	35	37	37
Microwave	J804	75	77	79	80	84	86	87	89	90	91	91	91
Telephone	KPDL	93	94	95	95	93	94	94	92	93	92	91	89
Mobile phone	GH96	16	20	27	44	47	64	70	76	78	79	79	78
Home computer	KPDM	27	29	33	38	44	49	55	58	62	65	67	70
Video recorder	KPDN	82	84	85	86	87	90	90	90	88	86	82	75
DVD player	J805	..	..	..	..	..	..	31	50	67	79	83	86
CD player	J806	59	63	68	72	77	80	83	86	87	88	87	86
Digital television service[3]	GH97	19	26	28	32	40	43	45	49	58	65	70	77
Internet connection	ZBUZ	..	..	10	19	32	39	45	49	53	55	58	61

1 Based on weighted data from 1998/99.
2 From 2001/02 onwards, weighting is based on the population estimates from the 2001 census.
3 Includes digital, satellite and cable receivers.
4 From 2006 the survey has moved onto a calendar year basis.
5 From 1998/99 to 2005/06, the figures shown are based on weighted data using non-response weights based on the 1991 Census and population figures from the 1991 and 2001 Census. From 2006, figures shown are based on weighted data using updated weights, with non-response weights and population figures based on the 2001 Census.

Sources: Expenditure and Food Survey and Family Expenditure Survey;
Office for National Statistics;
01633 455282

Health

Chapter 9

Health

Deaths: analysed by cause

(Table 9.6)

All figures in this table for England and Wales represent the number of deaths **occurring** in each calendar year. All data for Scotland and Northern Ireland relate to the number of deaths **registered** during each calendar year. From 2001, all three constituent countries of the UK are coding their causes of death using the latest, tenth, revision of the International Statistical Classification of Diseases and Related Health Problems (ICD-10). All cause of death information from 2001 (also for 2000 for Scotland) presented in this table is based on the revised classification.

To assist users in assessing any discontinuities arising from the introduction of the revised classification, bridge-coding exercises were carried out on all deaths registered in 1999 in England and Wales and also in Scotland. For further information about ICD-10 and the bridge-coding carried out by the Office for National Statistics, see the ONS Report: 'Results of the ICD-10 bridge-coding study, England and Wales, 1999', *Health Statistics Quarterly* 14 (2002), pages 75–83 or see the website at: *www. ons.gov.uk*

For information on the Scottish bridge-coding exercise, consult the Annual Report of the General Register Office for Scotland or see their website at: *www.gro-scotland.gov.uk*. No bridge-coding exercise was conducted for Northern Ireland.

Neonatal deaths and homicide and assault

For England and Wales, neonatal deaths (those at age under 28 days) are included in the number of total deaths but excluded from the cause figures. This has particular impact on the totals shown for the chapters covered by the ranges P and Q, 'Conditions originating in the perinatal period' and 'Congenital malformations, deformations and chromosomal abnormalities'. These are considerably lower than the actual number of deaths because it is not possible to assign an underlying cause of death from the neonatal death certificate used in England and Wales.

Also, for England and Wales only, the total number shown for Homicide and assault, X85–Y09, will not be a true representation because the registration of these deaths is often delayed by adjourned inquests.

Occupational ill-health

(Tables 9.8 and 9.9)

There are a number of sources of data on the extent of occupational or work-related ill health in Great Britain. For some potentially severe lung diseases caused by exposures which are highly unlikely to be found in a non-occupational setting, it is useful to count the number of death certificates issued each year. This is also true for *mesothelioma*, a cancer affecting the lining of the lungs and stomach, for which the number of cases with non-occupational causes is likely to be larger (although still a minority). **Table 9.9** shows the number of deaths for *mesothelioma* and *asbestosis* (linked to exposure to asbestos), *pneumoconiosis* (linked to coal dust or silica), *byssinosis* (linked to cotton dust) and some forms of *allergic alveolitis* (including farmer's lung). For asbestos-related diseases the figures are derived from a special register maintained by the Health and Safety Executive (HSE).

Most conditions which can be caused or made worse by work can also arise from other factors. The remaining sources of data on work-related ill health rely on attribution of individual cases of illness to work causes. In The Health and Occupation Reporting Network (THOR), this is done by specialist doctors – either occupational physicians or those working in particular disease specialisms (covering musculoskeletal, psychological, respiratory, skin, audiological and infectious disease). **Table 9.8** presents data from THOR for the last three years. It should be noted that not all cases of occupational disease will be seen by participating specialists; for example, the number of deaths due to *mesothelioma* (shown in Table 9.9) is known to be greater than the number of cases reported to THOR.

Injuries at work

(Table 9.10)

The appropriate 'responsible person' is required to report injuries arising from workplace activities to HSE or the local authority under the Reporting of Injuries, Diseases and Dangerous Occurrences Regulations 1995 (RIDDOR 95). This includes fatal injuries, non-fatal major injuries, as defined by the Regulations, and other injuries causing incapacity for work for more than three days. As of 1 April 2001, reports are to be made to an Incident Centre (ICC), based at Caerphilly.

HSE gets to know about virtually all workplace fatalities. However, it is known that employers and others do not report all non-fatal reportable injuries. To estimate the level of under-reporting by employers, HSE places questions each year with the Labour Force Survey (LFS), asking respondents if they have suffered a workplace injury in the past year.

The results from the latest LFS show that in Great Britain employers report around 54 per cent of reportable injuries (2006/07). When compared to the previous year, these results also indicate a drop of in the non-fatal injury rate of 3 per cent. The self-employed report between 5 and 10 per cent of reportable non-fatal injuries.

9.1 Ambulance Staff by Type : by country

Headcount

		2004	2005	2006[1]	2007	2008
England						
Qualified ambulance staff:						
Total Amubulance Staff	JF83	26 902	28 180	28 648	28 471	30 518
Manager	JF85	789	773	614	598	685
Emergency care practitioner	JF87	..	..	438	646	705
Paramedic	JF89	7 536	8 311	8 222	8 241	9 203
Ambulance Technician	JF8B	..	..	6 902	7 543	6 858
Ambulance Personnel	JF8D	8 947	9 033	..	..	..
Support to Ambulance Staff						
Trainee Ambulance Technician	JF8F	..	..	1 829	1 147	1 258
Trainee Ambulance Personnel	JF8H	2 047	2 201	..	..	..
Wales						
Qualified ambulance staff:						
Total Amubulance Staff	JF84	1 354	1 401	1 458	1 397	1 413
Manager	JF86	144	136	125	99	89
Emergency care practitioner	JF88	..	..	..	2	4
Paramedic	JF8A	668	749	804	818	847
Ambulance Technician	JF8C	..	..	..	477	462
Ambulance Personnel	JF8E	385	385	489	..	..
Support to Ambulance Staff						
Trainee Ambulance Technician	JF8G	..	..	..	1	11
Trainee Ambulance Personnel	JF8I	157	131	40	..	..
Scotland						
Total Ambulance staff	JHQ3	2 779	2 883	..	3 372	3 379
Paramedic	JHQ4	1 023	1 153	..	1 247	1 269
Technician	JHQ5	982	899	..	1 010	989
Driver/chauffeur	JHQ6	53	55	..	103	91
Care assistant	JHQ7	722	776	..	931	948
Other	JHQ8	–	–	..	81	82
Northern Ireland						
Total Ambulance staff	JHQ9	867	889	934	988	1 038
Emergency Medical Technicians and Paramedics	JHR2	687	722	753	557	621
Other/Patient care services	JHR3	122	126	121	339	328
Ambulance officers	JHR4	45	28	48	79	89
Manager	JHR5	11	12	12	11	..

Note: In 2006 ambulance staff were collected under new, more detailed, occupational codes. As a result, qualified totals and support to ambulance staff totals are not directly comparable with previous years.

1 Scottish ambulance service 2006 data is unavailable.

Sources: The NHS Information Centre for health and social care;
Welsh Assembly Government;
ISD Scotland;
Department of Health, Social services and Public Safety Northern Ireland

9.2 Hospital and primary care services
Scotland

			1997 /98	1998 /99	1999 /00	2000 /01	2001 /02	2002 /03	2003 /04	2004 /05	2005 /06	2006 /07
Hospital and community services												
In-patients:[1,2]												
Average available staffed beds	KDEA	Thousands	36.8	35.2	33.5	32.1	30.9	29.8	28.9	28.1	27.4	26.8
Average occupied beds:												
All departments	KDEB	"	29.5	28.2	26.9	25.8	25.1	24.2	23.2	22.5	22.1	21.7
Psychiatric and learning disability	KDEC	"	10.0	9.1	8.3	7.6	7.0	6.4	5.9	5.5	5.2	4.9
Discharges or deaths[3]	KDED	"	992	991	980	972	969	959	989	1 003	1 014	1 036
Outpatients:[2,4]												
New cases	KDEE	"	2 715	2 734	2 766	2 749	2 728	2 731	2 750	2 718	2 763	2 818
Total attendances	KDEF	"	6 331	6 424	6 451	6 382	6 254	6 193	6 147	5 983	6 066	6 030
Medical and dental staff:[5,6]	JYXO	Numbers	9 018	9 081	9 273	9 325	9 644	10 256	10 407	10 658	10 871	11 201
Whole-time	KDEG	"	7 024	7 057	7 185	7 216	7 530	8 115	8 349	8 612	8 796	9 201
Part-time	KDEH	"	1 510	1 550	1 632	1 648	1 681	1 697	1 636	1 630	1 670	1 607
Honorary	JYXN	"	521	506	495	495	468	468	437	431	418	411
Professional and technical staff:[6,7]												
Whole-time	KDEI	"	10 740	10 884	11 261	11 261	11 705	12 265	12 942	13 258	13 750	14 323
Part-time	KDEJ	"	4 738	4 928	5 218	5 483	5 852	6 273	6 708	6 968	7 440	7 990
Nursing and midwifery staff:[6,8]												
Whole-time	KDEK	"	32 218	32 156	32 356	32 401	33 334	34 294	34 939	35 338	36 093	37 104
Part-time	KDEL	"	29 736	29 178	29 242	29 131	29 004	29 015	29 354	29 484	29 688	29 995
Administrative and clerical staff:[6,9]												
Whole-time	KDEM	"	14 707	14 564	14 541	14 710	15 361	16 200	17 260	17 806	18 434	18 907
Part-time	KDEN	"	7 174	7 265	7 456	7 677	8 075	8 630	9 307	9 943	10 707	11 375
Domestic, transport, etc, staff:[6,10]												
Whole-time	KDEO	"	8 187	8 090	7 972	7 848	7 625	7 768	8 234	8 305	8 516	8 697
Part-time	KDEP	"	13 082	12 716	12 424	12 272	11 522	11 915	12 588	12 324	12 545	12 675
Primary care services												
Medical services												
Doctors (GPs) on the list:[11]												
Performer(Principal)GPs[12]	KDET	Numbers	3 666	3 702	3 710	3 761	3 769	3 805	3 782	3 801	3 807	3 826
Performer (Salaried) GPs[13]	KDEU	"	85	88	99	108	114	155	188	267	330	408
Average number of patients per												
Performer (principal)GP[14]	KDEV	"	1 462	1 449	1 441	1 423	1 418	1 404	1 421	1 418	1 416	1 414
Payments to doctor[15]	KDEW	£ million	356.4	365.9	377.5	404.7	429.6	467.5	519.0	628.4	701.0	699.8
Pharmaceutical services[16]												
Prescriptions dispensed	KDEX	Millions	58.52	60.36	62.34	65.56	69.13	71.83	74.66	76.74	79.03	81.89
Payments to pharmacists (gross)	KDEY	£ million	627.2	693.7	731.0	788.6	868.9	946.3	988.0	993.7	1 043.0	1 063.9
Average gross cost per												
prescription	KDEZ	£	10.7	11.5	11.7	12.0	12.6	13.2	13.2	12.9	13.2	13.0
Dental services												
Dentists on list[17]	KDFA	Numbers	1 739	1 786	1 808	1 808	1 844	1 869	1 882	1 900	1 936	2 009
Number of courses of treatment												
completed	KDFB	Thousands	3 578	3 530	3 338	3 389	3 359	3 420	3 359	3 375	3 348	3 387
Payments to dentists (gross)	KDFC	£ million	154.9	157.5	160.6	162.9	165.1	172.3	170.4	173.5	179.0	188.3
Payments by patients	KDFD	"	45.9	47.4	48.8	50.6	52.3	54.7	53.3	53.9	54.1	46.0
Payments out of public funds	KDFE	"	109.0	110.1	111.8	112.3	112.9	117.6	117.1	119.6	124.9	142.6
Average gross cost per course	KDFF	£	35.6	37.2	37.6	38.0	38.4	39.7	39.7	40.4	41.3	41.9
General ophthalmic services Number of Eye Exams given[18,19]	KDFG	Thousands	656	657	850	861	877	907	920	935	960	1 573
Number of pairs of glasses												
supplied[20]	KDFH	"	488	485	494	439	463	458	450	457	457	443
Payments out of public funds												
for sight testing and dispensing[21]	KDFK	£ million	..	..	..	..	..	34.9	35.5	37.8	39.4	65.5

1 Excludes joint user and contractual hospitals.
2 In year to 31 March.
3 Includes transfers out and emergency inpatients treated in day bed units.
4 Including attendances at accident and emergency consultant clinics.
5 As at 30 September. Figures exclude officers holding honorary locum appointments. Part-time includes maximum part-time appointments. There is an element of double counting of "heads" in this table as doctors can hold more than one contract. For example, they may hold contracts of different type, eg part time and honorary. Doctors holding two or more contracts of the same type, eg part time, are not double counted. Doctors, whose sum of contracts amounts to whole time, are classed as such. Figures have been revised due to coding changes.
6 The change in both collection and presentation of workforce data due to changes to staff groupings under Agenda for Change has inevitably meant that the amount of historical trend analysis of data is limited, though still available for some high level groupings.
7 As at 30 September. Comprises Therapeutic, Healthcare science, Technical and Pharmacy staff.
8 As at 30 September. Includes Health Care Assistants. Figures post 2003 have been amended due to a coding error resulting in some staff previously in this group being moved to the admin and clerical group.

9 As at 30 September. Comprises Senior Management and Administrative and Clerical staff. Figures for 2003 onwards have been amended due to the inclusion of some staff previously in the nursing and midwifery staff group
10 As at 30 September. Comprises Ambulance, Works, Ancillary and Trades.
11 At 1 October for 1995/96 -2003/04 and 30 Sept for 2004-05 onwards. Source www.isdscotland.org/workforce
12 Performer GPs only (known prior to 2004/05 as Unrestricted and restricted principals).
13 For 1995/06-2003/04 this group comprises salaried GPs plus associates, assistants and 'other' GPs. Terminology changed with the introduction of the new GMS contract in April 2004.
14 Average number of registered patients for Performer (Principal) GPs only. Note this is based only on GP headcount, not Whole Time Equivalence (WTE). and does not take account of the fact that a significamt number of non-principal/partner GPs also provide services to patients. Source : ISD Primary Medical Services Information Team.
15 Total expenditure on General Medical Services/Primary Medical Services Source: NHS Scotland Costs Book "R390" tables, www.isdscotland.org/costs Note, the contractual arrangements for payments to many general practises changed with the introduction of the new GMS contract in April 2004.
16 For prescriptions dispensed in calendar year by all community pharmacists (including stock orders), dispensing doctors and appliance suppliers. Gross total excludes patient charges.
17 Comprises of non-salaried GDS principal dentists only as at 31 March.
18 Figures represent sight tests paid for by health boards, hospital eye service referrals and GOD(s) ST (v) claimants.
19 Free NHS eye examinations were extended to all on 1st April 2006.
20 Does not include hospital eye service.
21 OPTIX, the electronic system for recording ophtalmic payment information, was introduced in 2002. Information for previous years is now not centrally available from ISD

Sources: ISD Scotland, NHS National Services Scotland;
0131 275 7777

9.3 Hospital and general health services
Northern Ireland

			1999	2000	2001	2002	2003	2004	2005	2006	2007	2008
Hospital services[1]												
In-patients:												
Beds available[2]	KDGA	Numbers	8 639	8 571	8 419	8 301	8 347	8 323	8 238	8 049	7 895	..
Average daily occupation of beds	KDGB	Percentages	*81.5*	*82.0*	*83.3*	*84.3*	*84.1*	*84.2*	*83.6*	*83.2*	*82.5*	..
Discharges or deaths[3]	KDGC	Thousands	332	333	328	327	332	337	343	359	370	..
Out-patients:[4]												
New cases	KDGD	"	984	994	997	992	1 014	1 027	1 043	1 081	1 120	..
Total attendances	KDGE	"	2 111	2 114	2 131	2 122	2 161	2 175	2 221	2 233	2 287	..
General health services												
Medical services[1]												
Doctors (principals) on the list[5,6]	KDGF	Numbers	1 054	1 066	1 073	1 076	1 076	1 078	1 084	1 100	1 127	..
Number of patients per doctor	KDGG	"	1 678	1 661	1 651	1 652	1 658	1 663	1 655	1 631	1 626	..
GrossPayments to doctors[7]	KDGH	£ thousand	78 604	82 471	84 664	88 194	96 894	..	..	..	..	..
Pharmaceutical services[8]												
Prescription forms dispensed	KDGI	Thousands	13 454	13 666	14 277	14 622	15 158	15 283	15 860	16 393	17 280	..
Number of prescriptions	KDGJ	"	23 249	23 985	24 705	25 501	26 656	27 401	28 417	29 599	30 864	..
Gross Cost[9]	KDGK	£ thousand	266 535	278 405	303 489	327 045	362 401	382 789	390 763	408 771	425 440	..
Charges[10]	KDGL	"	8 183	8 499	9 074	9 597	9 798	10 262	10 676	11 298	11 943	..
Net Cost[9]	KDGM	"	258 353	269 906	294 415	317 448	352 602	372 527	380 087	397 473	413 497	..
Average gross cost per prescription[9]	KDGN	£	11.46	11.61	12.28	12.82	13.60	13.97	13.75	13.81	13.78	..
Dental services[8,11]												
Dentists on the list[5]	KDGO	Numbers	632	661	673	689	696	720	722	751	763	..
Number of courses of paid treatment	KDGP	Thousands	1 086	1 113	1 126	1 123	1 107	1 086	1 084	1 064	1 002	..
Gross cost	KDGQ	£ thousand	58 712	61 237	64 454	66 201	66 910	67 294	69 480	65 172	68 775	..
Patients	KDGR	Thousands	14 358	15 302	16 041	930	919	907	910	900	859	..
Contributions (Net cost)	KDGS	£ thousand	44 354	46 152	48 413	49 376	50 282	50 498	52 308	50 068	53 301	..
Average gross cost per paid treatment	KDGT	£	54	55	57	59	60	62	64	61	69	..
Ophthalmic services[8]												
Number of sight tests given[12]	KDGU	Thousands	305	307	326	334	346	347	360	368	385	..
Number of optical appliances supplied[13]	KDGV	"	178	181	187	190	192	189	194	196	200	..
Cost of service (gross)[14]	KDGW	£ thousand	11 509	12 035	12 738	13 473	13 981	14 395	15 868	16 280	16 970	..
Health and social services[15]												
Medical and dental staff:												
Whole-time	KDGZ	Numbers	2 231	2 224	2 281	2 411	2 607	2 749	2 948	3 152	3 254	3 280
Part-time	KDHA	"	1 014	580	597	626	620	627	562	556	589	605
Nursing and midwifery staff:												
Whole-time	KDHB	"	10 135	9 926	9 828	10 248	10 729	11 137	11 416	11 477	11 641	11 542
Part-time	KDHC	"	8 813	7 591	7 814	8 395	8 706	8 887	9 047	9 107	9 362	9 318
Administrative and clerical staff:												
Whole-time	KDHD	"	7 230	7 373	7 536	7 966	8 370	8 846	9 047	9 113	8 782	8 351
Part-time	KDHE	"	2 910	2 972	3 136	3 372	3 609	3 858	4 190	4 249	4 261	4 242
Professional and technical staff:												
Whole-time	KDHF	"	3 177	3 642	3 762	3 975	4 163	4 528	4 695	4 772	4 954	4 632
Part-time	KDHG	"	1 226	1 283	1 369	1 499	1 616	1 731	1 827	2 032	2 093	2 365
Social services staff(excluding casual home helps):												
Whole-time	KDHH	"	3 319	3 017	3 127	3 284	3 461	3 716	3 777	3 893	4 024	4 454
Part-time	KDHI	"	2 358	868	911	986	1 105	1 207	1 297	1 429	2 061	2 835
Ancillary and other staff:												
Whole-time	KDHJ	"	3 426	3 506	3 472	3 426	3 418	3 470	3 725	3 836	3 861	3 870
Part-time	KDHK	"	3 913	4 508	4 925	5 125	5 420	5 588	5 498	5 904	5 685	4 766
Cost of services (gross)[14]	KDHL	£ thousand	1 422 920	1 576 657	1 639 283	1 868 538	2 113 453	..	..	..	..	..
Payments by recipients	KDHM	Thousands	65 533	71 411	78 478	88 860	87 999	..	..	..	..	..
Payments out of public funds	KDHN	£ thousand	1 357 387	1 505 246	1 560 805	1 779 678	2 025 454	..	..	..	..	..

1 Financial Year.
2 Average available beds in wards open overnight during the year.
3 Includes transfers to other hospitals.
4 Includes consultant outpatient clinics and Accident and Emergency departments.
5 At beginning of period for Dentists. Doctors numbers at 2002 (Oct), 2003 (Nov), 2004, 2005 & 2006 (Oct).
6 From 2003 onwards (UPE's).
7 These costs refer to the majority of non-cash limited services: further expenditure under GMS is allocated through HSS Boards on a cash limited basis. Change between 2002 and 2003 is due to advance payments being made in relation to the new GMS contract introduced in April 2004.
8 From 1995 onwards figures are taken from financial year.
9 Gross cost is defined as net ingredient costs plus on-cost, fees and other payments.
10 Excludes amount paid by patients for pre-payment certificates.
11 Due to changes in the Dental Contract which came into force in October 1990 dentists are paid under a combination of headings relating to Capitation and Continuing Care patients. Prior to this, payment was simply on an item of service basis.

12 Excluding sight tests given in hospitals and under the school health service and in the home.
13 Relates to the number of vouchers supplied and excludes repair/replace spectacles.
14 Figures relate to the costs of the hospital, community health and personal social services, and have been estimated from financial year data.
15 Workforce figures until 1999 refer to 31st December and are taken from the Trust and Board payroll system. Figures from 2000 onwards are at 30th September and are taken from the Trust and Board Human Resource Management Systems. Some figures for 2000 have been revised. Figures for 2000 onwards exclude all home helps and all agency /bank staff Figures include Ambulance and Works staff in the Ancillary & Other Staff category and from 2008 this category also includes staff grouped as 'Generic' who are multidisciplinary staff. Due to Agenda for Change new grade codes have been gradually introduced which have resulted in some staff moving between categories. This will be seen from 2007 onwards. Backward comparison of the workforce is therefore not advisable as definitions differ.

Sources: Central Services Agency Northern Ireland: 028 9053 2975; Dept of Health, Social Services & Public Safety Northern Ireland: 028 9052 2509;

(Figures on Hospital Services: 028 9052 2800)

9.4 Health services: workforce summary
England
As at 30 September each year

headcount

		1999	2000	2001	2002	2003	2004	2005	2006	2007	2008
Total	JHR6	1 098 348	1 118 958	1 167 166	1 224 934	1 283 901	1 331 857	1 366 030	1 338 779	1 331 109	1 368 693
Total employed staff (exc. GP retainers)	JHR7	1 097 376	1 117 841	1 166 016	1 223 824	1 282 930	1 331 087	1 365 388	1 338 140	1 330 544	1 368 186
Professionally qualified clinical staff (excl retainers)	JHR8	540 792	552 936	574 646	603 077	633 375	660 706	679 157	674 621	681 246	701 324
All doctors	JHR9	94 953	97 436	100 319	104 460	109 964	117 806	122 987	126 251	128 210	133 662
All doctors (excl retainers)[1]	JHS2	93 981	96 319	99 169	103 350	108 993	117 036	122 345	125 612	127 645	133 155
Consultants (including directors of public health	JHS3	23 321	24 401	25 782	27 070	28 750	30 650	31 993	32 874	33 674	34 910
Registrars	JHS4	12 682	12 730	13 220	13 770	14 619	16 823	18 006	18 808	30 759	35 042
Other doctors in training	JHS5	18 845	19 192	19 572	21 145	22 701	24 874	26 305	27 461	16 024	14 136
Hospital practioners and clinical assistants (non-dental specialities)[6]	JHS6	6 006	5 621	5 362	4 863	4 451	4 045	3 587	3 077	2 848	2 761
Other medical and dental staff	JHS7	9 146	9 744	9 910	10 183	10 330	10 604	10 739	11 100	11 333	11 854
GPs (excl retainers)[2]	JHS8	29 987	30 252	30 685	31 182	32 593	34 085	35 302	35 369	35 855	37 213
GPs excluding retaners and registrars	JHS9	28 467	28 593	28 802	29 202	30 358	31 523	32 738	33 091	33 364	34 010
GP Providers	JHT2	27 681	27 791	27 938	28 117	28 646	28 781	29 340	27 691	27 342	27 347
Other GPs	JHT3	786	802	864	1 085	1 712	2 742	3 398	5 400	6 022	6 663
GP registrars[8]	JHT4	1 520	1 659	1 883	1 980	2 235	2 562	2 564	2 278	2 491	3 203
GP retainers	JHT5	972	1 117	1 150	1 110	971	770	642	639	565	507
Total qualified nursing staff[3]	JHT6	329 637	335 952	350 381	367 520	386 359	397 515	404 161	398 335	399 597	408 160
Qualified nursing, midwifery & health visiting staff	JHT7	310 142	316 752	330 535	346 537	364 692	375 371	381 257	374 538	376 737	386 112
GP pratice nurses[2,4]	JHT8	19 495	19 200	19 846	20 983	21 667	22 144	22 904	23 797	22 860	22 048
Total qualified scientific, therapeutic & technical staff[5]	JHT9	102 391	105 910	110 241	116 598	122 066	128 883	134 534	134 498	136 976	142 558
Qualified Allied Health Professions	JHU2	53 105	54 788	57 001	59 415	62 189	65 515	67 841	67 483	68 687	71 301
Other qualified scientific, therapeutic & technical staff	JHU3	49 286	51 122	53 240	57 183	59 877	63 368	66 693	67 015	68 289	71 257
Qualified ambulance staff[7]	JHU4	14 783	14 755	14 855	15 609	15 957	17 272	18 117	16 176	17 028	17 451
Support to clinical staff	JHU5	296 619	307 225	325 890	344 524	360 666	368 285	376 219	357 877	346 596	355 010
Support to doctors & nursing staff	JHU6	249 216	257 136	271 978	287 098	298 752	303 630	310 441	291 098	281 894	286 254
Support to scientific, therapeutic & technical staff	JHU7	40 465	41 800	44 602	48 030	52 230	55 025	55 715	54 307	53 259	55 689
Support to ambulance staff	JHU8	6 938	8 289	9 310	9 396	9 684	9 630	10 063	12 472	11 443	13 067
NHS infrastructure support	JHU9	171 205	173 733	179 783	189 274	199 808	211 489	220 387	209 387	207 778	219 064
Central functions	JHV2	73 996	77 628	81 439	85 706	92 257	99 831	105 565	101 860	100 177	105 354
Hotel, property & estates	JHV3	72 922	70 849	70 920	71 274	72 230	73 932	75 431	70 776	71 102	73 797
Manager & senior manager	JHV4	24 287	25 256	27 424	32 294	35 321	37 726	39 391	36 751	36 499	39 913
Other non-medical staff or unknown classification	JHV5	2 427	877	1 224	657	657	497	435	410	409	353
Other GP pratice staff[2]	JHV6	86 333	83 070	84 473	86 292	88 424	90 110	89 190	95 845	94 515	92 436

1 All doctors excluding GP retainers.

2 In order to avoid double counting these staff are excluded from the all doctors totals, as they are predominantly GPs that work part time in hospitals (applies to headcount data only).

3 GP Data as at 1 October 1999 and 30 September 2000 - 2008.

4 Nursing and midwifery figures exclude students on training courses leading to a first qualification as a nurse or midwife.

5 Headcount Pratice Nurse figures are estimated for 1999 based on the 1997 FTE to headcount ratio.

6 To make the census data comparable with the Review Body for Nursing Staff and Other Health Professionals definitions, qualified Allied Health Speech & Language Therapists (previously these were included in Other Qualified ST &T staff). For comparability historical data has been reassigned to match the revised definition.

7 In 2006 ambulance staff were collected under new, more detailed, occupation codes. As a result, qualified totals and support to ambulance staff totals are not directly comparable with previous years.

8 GP Registrar count for 2008 represents an improvement in data collection processes and comparisons with previous years should be treated with caution.

Note: Enhanced validation processes have led to the removal of duplicate records from the non-medical census (from 2006 onwards). Although percentages were small (less than 1%), comparisons with years prior to this need to be treated with caution. This only effects headcount.

Source: NHS Information centre for health and social care

9.5 Health service: workforce summary
Wales

Wte and numbers

		2003	2004	2005	2006	2007
Directly employed NHS staff[1]:						
Medical and dental staff[2]						
Hospital medical staff	JHV7	3 911	4 381	4 546	..	5 182
Of which consultants	JHV8	1 377	1 503	1 584	..	1 820
Community/Public health medical staff	JHV9	82	78	79	..	98
Hospital dental staff	JHW2	126	142	138	..	149
Of which consultants	JHW3	40	46	43	..	49
Community/Public health dental staff	JHW4	89	115	97	..	89
Total	JHW5	4 208	4 715	4 859	..	5 520
Nursing, midwifery and health visiting staff[3]	JHW6	26 697	27 407	28 152	27 901	28 060
of which qualified	JHW7	19 514	20 126	20 698	20 980	21 443
Scientific, therapeutic and technical staff	JHW8	8 709	9 394	9 699	10 242	10 654
Health care assistants and other support staff	JHW9	8 158	8 305	8 584	9 904	9 015
Administration and estates staff	JHX2	13 456	14 677	15 421	16 417	16 031
Ambulance staff	JHX3	1 269	1 347	1 394	1 444	1 377
Other[4]	JHX4	143	159	163	161	170
Unknown	JHX5	4	–	–	–	80
Total	JHX6	62 644	66 004	68 272	..	70 907
Family Practitioners:						
General medical practitioners[5]	JHX7	1 822	1 816	1 849	1 882	1 936
GP Registrars	JHX8	110	115	103	152	165
GP retainers	JHX9	70	70	70	61	73
General dental practitioners[6]	JHY2	1 003	1 026	1 027	1 087	1 141
Ophthalmic medical practitioners[7]	JHY3	35	34	33	25	27
Ophthalmic opticians	JHY4	594	638	640	648	681

Source: Welsh Assembly Government

1 Whole-time equivalent at 30 September. The majority of the information on NHS staff has been obtained as a by-product of personnel systems. Some staff may be undergoing temporary regrading at the time and these staff are excluded from the figures.

2 Excludes locum staff.

3 Excludes pre-registration learners.

4 Health Authority professional advisors and staff on general payments, eg Macmillan and Marie Curie nurses.

5 Numbers at 1 October. All practitioners excluding GP registrars, GP Retainers and locums.

6 Numbers at 31 March. Number of performers (dentists) on an open contract recorded by Local Health Boards on the Dental Practice Division's Payments Online system Data for 2006 are not comparable with previous years.

7 Numbers at 31 December.

9.6 Deaths: by cause
International Statistical Classification of Diseases, Injuries and Causes of Death[1]
Tenth Revision 2001

Numbers

	ICD-10 code	England and Wales				
		2003	2004	2005	2006	2007
Total deaths		538 254	512 541	512 692	502 599	504 052
Deaths from natural causes	A00-R99	519 297	493 835	494 054	482 745	484 350
Certain infectious and parasitic diseases	A00-B99	4 763	5 009	6 141	7 632	8 169
Intestinal infectious diseases	A00-A09	1 063	1 382	2 221	3 630	4 225
Respiratory and other tuberculosis including late effects	A15-A19,B90	451	388	406	432	335
Meningococcal infection	A39	118	72	86	52	75
Viral hepatitis	B15-B19	209	197	205	205	223
AIDS (HIV - disease)	B20-B24	224	209	230	235	256
Neoplasms	C00-D48	139 360	138 062	138 454	138 777	140 080
Malignant neoplasms	C00-97	135 955	134 856	135 252	135 635	136 804
Malignant neoplasm of oesophagus	C15	6 427	6 298	6 490	6 495	6 424
Malignant neoplasm of stomach	C16	5 285	5 098	4 927	4 562	4 587
Malignant neoplasm of colon	C18	9 152	9 130	9 076	8 954	8 854
Malignant neoplasm of rectum and anus	C20-C21	3 982	3 917	3 995	3 870	3 795
Malignant neoplasm of pancreas	C25	6 242	6 294	6 509	6 584	6 845
Malignant neoplasm of trachea, bronchus and lung	C33-C34	28 765	28 328	28 792	29 332	29 660
Malignant neoplasm of skin	C43	1 585	1 597	1 622	1 649	1 825
Malignant neoplasm of breast	C50	11 276	11 031	11 121	11 011	10 727
Malignant neoplasm of cervix uteri	C53	951	957	911	831	820
Malignant neoplasm of prostate	C61	9 166	9 169	9 042	9 057	9 230
Leukaemia	C91-C95	3 916	3 828	3 910	3 859	3 935
Diseases of the blood and blood-forming organs and certain disorders involving the immune mechanism	D50-D89	1 065	1 014	1 096	1 013	1 029
Endocrine, nutritional and metabolic diseases	E00-E90	8 016	7 519	7 433	7 153	7 214
Diabetes mellitus	E10-E14	6 316	5 837	5 677	5 490	5 433
Mental and behavioural disorders	F00-F99	14 846	14 299	14 563	14 863	16 582
Vascular and unspecified dementia	F01,F03	13 401	12 756	12 995	13 289	14 040
Alcohol abuse (inc. alcoholic psychosis)	F10	469	538	523	545	533
Drug dependence and non-dependent abuse of drugs	F11-F16,F18-F19	655	718	762	739	781
Diseases of the nervous system and sense organs	G00-H95	15 793	14 645	15 253	15 218	16 375
Meningitis (including meningococcal)	G00-G03	229	182	187	164	164
Alzheimer's disease	G30	5 055	4 821	4 914	4 901	5 697
Diseases of the circulatory system	I00-I99	205 508	190 603	183 997	174 637	170 338
Ischaemic heart diseases	I20-I25	99 790	92 528	88 271	82 619	79 910
Cerebrovascular diseases	I60-I69	57 808	52 899	50 772	48 389	46 597
Diseases of the respiratory system	J00-J99	75 138	69 213	72 517	68 599	68 974
Influenza	J10-J11	77	25	44	17	31
Pneumonia	J12-J18	34 400	30 649	31 443	28 674	28 152
Bronchitis, emphysema and other chronic obstructive pulmonary diseases	J40-J44	25 765	23 204	24 230	23 319	23 727
Asthma	J45-J46	1 284	1 243	1 186	1 082	1 033
Diseases of the digestive system	K00-K93	24 948	24 912	25 213	25 786	25 670
Gastric and duodenal ulcer	K25-K27	3 678	3 495	3 266	3 145	2 833
Chronic liver disease	K70,K73-K74	5 844	5 824	5 873	6 250	6 326
Diseases of the skin and subcutaneous tissue	L00-L99	1 661	1 670	1 788	1 812	1 822
Diseases of the musculo-skeletal system and connective tissue	M00-M99	4 634	4 393	4 378	4 238	4 304
Rheumatoid arthritis and juvenile arthritis	M05-M06,M08	907	794	835	743	734
Osteoporosis	M80-M81	1 583	1 478	1 416	1 390	1 509
Diseases of the genito-urinary system	N00-N99	9 120	9 397	10 231	10 722	11 301
Diseases of the kidney and ureter	N00-N29	4 135	4 024	3 967	3 988	4 386
Complications of pregnancy, childbirth and the puerperium	O00-O99	45	46	36	41	47
Certain conditions originating in the perinatal period (excluding neonatals)[1]	P00-P96	207	213	205	160	180
Congenital malformations, deformations and chromasomal abnormalities (excluding neonatals)[1]	Q00-Q99	1 299	1 274	1 292	1 214	1 235
Congenital malformations of the nervous system	Q00-Q07	142	116	123	117	124
Congenital malformations of the circulatory system	Q20-Q28	540	527	535	484	527
Symptoms, signs and abnormal clinical and laboratory findings not elsewhere classified	R00-R99	12 894	11 566	11 457	10 880	11 030
Senility without mention of psychosis (old age)	R54	11 394	9 905	9 785	9 169	9 195
Sudden infant death syndrome	R95	136	148	164	143	170
Deaths from external causes	V01-Y89	16 693	16 497	16 411	17 509	17 000
All accidents	V01-X59,Y85,Y86	10 979	10 735	11 053	11 824	11 883
Land transport accidents	V01-V89	2 943	2 693	2 697	2 990	2 919
Accidental falls	W00-W19	2 732	2 915	3 006	3 226	3 318
Accidental poisonings	X40-X49	835	927	910	1 072	1 207
Suicide and intentional self-harm	X60-X84,Y87.0	3 270	3 306	3 172	3 331	3 165
Homicide and assault[1]	X85 Y09,Y87.1	318	363	326	342	370
Event of undetermined intent	Y10-Y34, Y87.2	1 776	1 685	1 486	1 616	1 161

9.6
continued

Deaths: by cause
International Statistical Classification of Diseases, Injuries and Causes of Death[1]
Tenth Revision 2001

Numbers

	ICD-10 code	Scotland				
		2003	2004	2005	2006	2007
Total deaths		58 472	56 187	55 747	55 093	55 986
Deaths from natural causes	A00-R99	56 161	53 759	53 535	52 856	53 683
Certain infectious and parasitic diseases	A00-B99	660	688	719	791	949
Intestinal infectious diseases	A00-A09	85	104	99	128	164
Respiratory and other tuberculosis including late effects	A15-A19,B90	59	52	49	43	41
Meningococcal infection	A39	5	8	4	6	8
Viral hepatitis	B15-B19	23	20	16	20	22
AIDS (HIV - disease)	B20-B24	33	16	31	19	21
Neoplasms	C00-D48	15 412	15 336	15 408	15 360	15 570
Malignant neoplasms	C00-C97	15 116	15 047	15 135	15 084	15 274
Malignant neoplasm of oesophagus	C15	776	801	798	765	786
Malignant neoplasm of stomach	C16	579	615	590	552	506
Malignant neoplasm of colon	C18	966	917	966	922	899
Malignant neoplasm of rectum and anus	C20-21	368	383	367	390	394
Malignant neoplasm of pancreas	C25	641	615	603	567	713
Malignant neoplasm of trachea, bronchus and lung	C33-34	3 893	3 923	4 009	4 062	4 115
Malignant neoplasm of skin	C43	146	151	158	158	164
Malignant neoplasm of breast	C50	1 149	1 093	1 151	1 112	1 067
Malignant neoplasm of cervix uteri	C53	120	102	127	92	105
Malignant neoplasm of prostate	C61	786	802	765	779	793
Leukaemia	C91-C95	367	352	351	362	348
Diseases of the blood and blood-forming organs and certain disorders involving the immune mechanism	D50-D89	148	111	118	113	111
Endocrine, nutritional and metabolic diseases	E00-E90	958	972	988	1 018	980
Diabetes mellitus	E10-E14	709	760	745	751	726
Mental and behavioural disorders	F00-F99	2 637	2 670	2 454	2 817	3 117
Vascular and unspecified dementia	F01,F03	1 997	1 955	1 835	2 101	2 446
Alcohol abuse (inc. alcoholic psychosis)	F10	356	421	343	378	321
Drug dependence and non-dependent abuse of drugs	F11-F16,F18-F19	228	238	217	293	310
Diseases of the nervous system and sense organs	G00-H95	1 303	1 254	1 306	1 333	1 555
Meningitis (including meningococcal)	G00-G03	19	25	18	15	16
Alzheimer's disease	G30	354	399	415	452	549
Diseases of the circulatory system	I00-I99	22 102	20 837	20 060	18 771	18 579
Ischaemic heart diseases	I20-I25	11 441	10 778	10 331	9 532	9 343
Cerebrovascular diseases	I60-I69	6 497	6 155	5 789	5 466	5 333
Diseases of the respiratory system	J00-J99	7 454	6 743	7 093	7 183	7 362
Influenza	J10-J11	15	3	11	2	5
Pneumonia	J12-J18	2 859	2 399	2 483	2 513	2 444
Bronchitis, emphysema and other chronic obstructive pulmonary diseases	J40-J44	3 014	2 752	2 857	2 848	2 901
Asthma	J45-J46	98	94	100	82	112
Diseases of the digestive system	K00-K93	3 215	3 065	3 221	3 208	3 076
Gastric and duodenal ulcer	K25-K27	316	305	230	262	206
Chronic liver disease	K70,K73-K74	1 170	1 044	1 152	1 162	1 080
Diseases of the skin and subcutaneous tissue	L00-L99	131	131	127	130	131
Diseases of the musculo-skeletal system and connective tissue	M00-M99	369	350	326	354	395
Rheumatoid arthritis and juvenile arthritis	M05-M06,M08	103	107	109	108	139
Osteoporosis	M80-M81	70	52	47	40	64
Diseases of the genito-urinary system	N00-N99	1 056	965	1 063	1 112	1 149
Diseases of the kidney and ureter	N00-N29	670	574	617	578	598
Complications of pregnancy, childbirth and the puerperium	O00-O99	7	6	4	7	8
Certain conditions originating in the perinatal period	P00-P96	149	151	164	139	157
Congenital malformations, deformations and chromasomal abnormalities	Q00-Q99	172	134	159	151	150
Congenital malformations of the nervous system	Q00-Q07	23	21	15	25	22
Congenital malformations of the circulatory system	Q20-Q28	63	53	58	46	47
Symptoms, signs and abnormal clinical and laboratory findings not elsewhere classified	R00-R99	388	340	325	369	394
Senility without mention of psychosis (old age)	R54	236	193	210	206	221
Sudden infant death syndrome	R95	43	28	20	27	31
Deaths from external causes	V01-Y89	2 311	2 428	2 212	2 237	2 303
All accidents	V01-X59,Y85,Y86	1 326	1 390	1 284	1 264	1 289
Land transport accidents	V01-V89	357	325	293	326	294
Accidental falls	W00-W19	668	690	676	642	658
Accidental poisonings	X40-X49	30	57	48	70	63
Suicide and intentional self-harm	X60-X84,Y87.0	560	606	547	542	517
Homicide and assault	X85-Y09,Y87.1	101	121	80	115	88
Event of undetermined intent	Y10-Y34, Y87.2	234	229	216	223	321

9.6
continued

Deaths: by cause
International Statistical Classification of Diseases, Injuries and Causes of Death[1]
Tenth Revision 2001

Numbers

		Northern Ireland				
	ICD-10 code	2003	2004	2005	2006	2007
Total deaths		14 462	14 354	14 224	14 532	14 649
Deaths from natural causes	A00-R99	13 912	13 711	13 463	13 679	13 876
Certain infectious and parasitic diseases	A00-B99	157	149	162	188	184
Intestinal infectious diseases	A00-A09	13	16	16	39	35
Respiratory and other tuberculosis including late effects	A15-A19,B90	11	13	4	7	10
Meningococcal infection	A39	4	5	1	1	3
Viral hepatitis	B15-B19	-	1	2	4	4
AIDS (HIV - disease)	B20-B24	2	-	5	-	-
Neoplasms	C00-D48	3 882	3 835	3 826	3 959	3 992
Malignant neoplasms	C00-C97	3 757	3 757	3 735	3 848	3 870
Malignant neoplasm of oesophagus	C15	154	138	162	161	161
Malignant neoplasm of stomach	C16	165	180	161	159	161
Malignant neoplasm of colon	C18	313	286	293	280	319
Malignant neoplasm of rectum and anus	C20-C21	103	94	99	99	96
Malignant neoplasm of pancreas	C25	173	152	173	194	205
Malignant neoplasm of trachea, bronchus and lung	C33-C34	810	837	824	850	863
Malignant neoplasm of skin	C43	40	36	43	48	56
Malignant neoplasm of breast	C50	291	320	307	300	311
Malignant neoplasm of cervix uteri	C53	31	37	20	29	16
Malignant neoplasm of prostate	C61	217	241	222	212	235
Leukaemia	C91-C95	85	95	92	91	94
Diseases of the blood and blood-forming organs and certain disorders involving the immune mechanism	D50-D89	37	34	36	31	39
Endocrine, nutritional and metabolic diseases	E00-E90	246	248	302	281	299
Diabetes mellitus	E10-E14	190	189	224	197	210
Mental and behavioural disorders	F00-F99	341	370	408	418	514
Vascular and unspecified dementia	F01,F03	284	298	316	335	405
Alcohol abuse (inc, alcoholic psychosis)	F10	52	68	86	79	94
Drug dependence and non-dependent abuse of drugs	F11-F16,F18-F19	3	2	2	1	5
Diseases of the nervous system and sense organs	G00-H95	481	487	484	557	588
Meningitis (including meningococcal)	G00-G03	3	1	2	1	5
Alzheimer's disease	G30	224	251	207	265	291
Diseases of the circulatory system	I00-I99	5 448	5 272	5 002	4 879	4 838
Ischaemic heart diseases	I20-I25	2 843	2 775	2 708	2 556	2 494
Cerebrovascular diseases	I60-I69	1 531	1 435	1 307	1 326	1 325
Diseases of the respiratory system	J00-J99	2 082	1 950	1 921	1 982	1 992
Influenza	J10-J11	4	1	-	1	1
Pneumonia	J12-J18	1 025	909	895	895	859
Bronchitis, emphysema and other chronic obstructive pulmonary diseases	J40-J44	660	609	596	616	639
Asthma	J45-J46	32	44	32	35	28
Diseases of the digestive system	K00-K93	587	691	584	646	711
Gastric and duodenal ulcer	K25-K27	77	70	60	57	53
Chronic liver disease	K70,K73-K74	156	189	150	171	193
Diseases of the skin and subcutaneous tissue	L00-L99	15	19	20	21	26
Diseases of the musculo-skeletal system and connective tissue	M00-M99	93	66	95	79	76
Rheumatoid arthritis and juvenile arthritis	M05-M06,M08	26	15	28	36	25
Osteoporosis	M80-M81	16	10	12	11	12
Diseases of the genito-urinary system	N00-N99	327	364	351	359	381
Diseases of the kidney and ureter	N00-N29	225	252	210	219	232
Complications of pregnancy, childbirth and the puerperium	O00-O99	3	1	1	3	-
Certain conditions originating in the perinatal period	P00-P96	62	64	81	54	50
Congenital malformations, deformations and chromasomal abnormalities	Q00-Q99	69	61	82	84	61
Congenital malformations of the nervous system	Q00-Q07	12	10	10	9	8
Congenital malformations of the circulatory system	Q20-Q28	16	17	20	19	19
Symptoms, signs and abnormal clinical and laboratory findings not elsewhere classified	R00-R99	82	100	108	138	125
Senility without mention of psychosis (old age)	R54	63	70	71	98	95
Sudden infant death syndrome	R95	-	-	2	1	4
Deaths from external causes	V01-Y89	550	643	761	853	773
All accidents	V01-X59,Y85,Y86	364	448	492	525	499
Land transport accidents	V01-V89	120	161	175	184	172
Accidental falls	W00-W19	44	63	99	117	112
Accidental poisonings	X40-X49	30	17	40	22	37
Suicide and intentional self-harm	X60-X84,Y87.0	132	128	186	249	215
Homicide and assault	X85-Y09,Y87.1	30	32	32	30	30
Event of undetermined intent	Y10-Y34, Y87.2	12	18	27	42	27

1 See chapter text.

Sources: Office for National Statistics;
General Register Office, Scotland;
Northern Ireland Statistics and Research Agency

9.7 Notifications of infectious diseases: by country

Numbers

		1997	1998	1999	2000	2001	2002	2003	2004	2005	2006	2007
United Kingdom												
Measles	KHQD	4 844	4 540	2 951	2 865	2 661	3 675	2 726	2 703	2 326	4 016	3 869
Mumps	KWNN	2 264	1 917	2 000	3 367	3 433	2 333	4 565	20 742	66 541	15 963	10 101
Rubella	KWNO	4 205	4 064	2 575	2 064	1 782	2 002	1 525	1 548	1 327	1 407	1 254
Whooping cough	KHQE	3 669	1 902	1 461	866	1 059	1 051	509	619	679	645	1 203
Scarlet fever	KHQC	4 639	4 708	2 956	2 544	2 320	2 749	3 252	2 642	2 075	2 653	2 477
Dysentery	KHQG	2 427	1 934	1 630	1 613	1 495	1 167	1 144	1 301	1 346	1 241	1 383
Food poisoning	KHQH	105 579	105 060	96 866	98 076	95 752	81 562	79 073	78 812	78 959	79 407	80 889
Typhoid and Paratyphoid fevers	KHQB	249	252	278	205	254	183	277	282	300	390	341
Hepatitis	KWNP	3 601	3 781	4 365	4 530	4 419	5 035	5 203	5 054	5 246	5 290	5 306
Tuberculosis	KHQI	6 367	6 605	6 701	7 100	7 204	7 239	6 978	7 259	8 017	8 083	7 461
Malaria	KWNQ	1 549	1 163	1 038	1 166	1 118	866	820	634	700	637	445
England and Wales[1]												
Measles	KHRD	3 962	3 728	2 438	2 378	2 250	3 187	2 488	2 356	2 089	3 705	3 670
Mumps	KWNR	1 914	1 587	1 691	2 162	2 741	1 997	4 204	16 367	56 256	12 841	7 196
Rubella	KWNS	3 260	3 208	1 954	1 653	1 483	1 660	1 361	1 287	1 155	1 221	1 082
Whooping cough	KHRE	2 989	1 577	1 139	712	888	883	409	504	594	550	1 089
Scarlet fever	KHRC	3 569	3 339	2 086	1 933	1 756	2 159	2 553	2 201	1 678	2 166	1 948
Dysentery	KHRG	2 274	1 813	1 538	1 494	1 388	1 087	1 047	1 203	1 237	1 122	1 217
Food poisoning	KHRH	93 901	93 932	86 316	86 528	85 468	72 649	70 895	70 311	70 407	70 603	72 382
Typhoid and Paratyphoid fevers	KHRB	241	243	276	204	250	175	275	280	298	386	334
Viral hepatitis	KWNT	3 186	3 183	3 424	3 541	3 388	3 859	4 004	3 932	4 109	4 007	3 857
Tuberculosis[2]	KHRJ	5 859	6 087	6 144	6 572	6 714	6 753	6 518	6 723	7 628	7 621	6 989
Malaria	KWNU	1 476	1 110	1 005	1 128	1 081	847	791	609	679	614	426
Total meningitis	KHRO	2 345	2 072	2 094	2 432	2 623	1 545	1 472	1 267	1 381	1 494	1 251
Meningococcal meningitis	KHRP	1 220	1 152	1 145	1 164	1 020	706	646	554	579	618	557
Meningococcal septicaemia	KWNV	1 440	1 509	1 822	1 614	1 238	842	732	691	721	657	673
Ophthalmia neonatorum	KHRI	224	198	163	176	115	91	102	85	87	100	83
Scotland												
Measles	KHSE	762	700	434	395	315	399	181	257	186	259	168
Mumps	KWNW	282	251	216	199	155	259	181	3 595	5 698	2 917	2 741
Rubella	KWNX	818	745	548	349	234	292	130	222	141	153	146
Whooping cough	KHSF	545	225	214	93	106	99	60	87	51	67	98
Scarlet fever	KHSD	645	883	438	301	281	376	395	213	208	274	315
Dysentery	KHSH	124	103	82	95	85	73	83	90	103	112	156
Food poisoning	KHSI	10 144	9 186	8 517	9 263	8 640	7 693	6 910	6 835	6 918	7 335	7 186
Typhoid and Paratyphoid fevers	KHSB	6	6	2	1	3	4	2	2	1	3	4
Viral hepatitis	KWNY	359	490	863	943	1 008	1 165	1 159	1 063	1 002	1 235	1 397
Tuberculosis[3]	KHSL	433	457	496	469	442	418	422	463	389	414	409
Malaria	KWUC	57	30	20	27	24	17	28	20	20	18	15
Meningococcal infection	KWUD	271	313	329	301	256	175	117	147	139	140	150
Erysipelas	KHSC	95	66	64	41	39	41	28	28	17	25	20
Northern Ireland												
Measles	KHTD	120	112	79	92	96	89	57	90	56	52	31
Mumps	KHTR	68	79	93	1 006	537	77	180	780	4 556	205	164
Rubella	KHTQ	127	111	73	62	65	50	34	39	31	33	26
Whooping cough	KHTE	135	100	108	61	65	69	40	28	28	28	16
Scarlet fever	KHTC	425	486	432	310	283	214	304	228	186	213	214
Dysentery	KHTG	29	18	10	24	22	7	14	8	7	7	10
Food poisoning	KHTH	1 534	1 942	2 033	2 285	1 644	1 220	1 268	1 666	1 409	1 469	1 321
Typhoid and Paratyphoid fevers	KHTB	2	3	–	–	1	4	–	–	1	1	3
Infective hepatitis	KHTO	56	108	78	46	23	11	40	59	74	48	52
Tuberculosis	KHTI	75	61	61	59	48	68	38	73	68	48	63
Malaria	KWUE	16	23	13	11	13	2	1	5	2	6	4
Acute encephalitis/meningitis	KHTM	91	64	99	130	97	98	78	64	66	58	36
Meningococcal septicaemia	KWUF	56	87	145	123	90	98	76	82	66	75	42
Gastro-enteritis (children under 2 years)	KHTP	896	1 371	1 121	1 205	1 106	882	867	697	736	718	762

1 The figures show the corrected number of notifications, incorporating revisions of diagnosis, either by the notifying medical practitioner or by the medical superintendent of the infectious diseases hospital. Cases notified in Port Health Authorities are included.

2 Formal notifications of new cases only. The figures exclude chemoprophylaxis.

3 Figures include cases of tuberculosis not notified before death.

Sources: Health Protection Scotland;
Communicable Disease Surveillance Centre (Northern Ireland);
Health Protection Agency, Centre for Infections, IM&T Dept: 020 8200 6868

9.8 Estimated number of cases of work-related disease reported by specialist physicians to THOR[1]

Great Britain

Numbers

	All physicians				Disease specialist				Occupational physicians			
	2004	2005	2006	2007	2004	2005	2006	2007	2004	2005	2006	2007
Musculoskeletal disorders					MOSS				OPRA			
Upper limb	4 189	3 654	3 328	2 391	1 534	1 521	1 503	1 049	2 655	2 133	1 825	1 342
Spine/ back	2 028	1 761	1 348	1 243	394	447	392	297	1 634	1 314	956	946
Lower limb	580	441	406	487	175	122	158	150	405	319	248	337
Other	252	221	204	149	29	33	55	28	223	188	149	121
Total number of diagnoses	7 161	6 205	5 347	4 394	2 181	2 204	2 131	1 608	4 980	4 001	3 216	2 786
Total number of individuals[2]	6 879	5 932	5 160	4 226	2 063	2 064	2 036	1 521	4 816	3 868	3 124	2 705
Mental ill health					SOSMI				OPRA			
Stress/ anxiety/ depression	6 440	6 063	5 648	5 467	1 804	1 751	1 423	1 014	4 636	4 312	4 225	4 453
Other	869	912	908	803	663	702	660	507	206	210	248	296
Total number of diagnoses	7 309	6 975	6 556	6 270	2 467	2 453	2 083	1 521	4 842	4 522	4 473	4 749
Total number of individuals[2]	6 801	6 396	5 916	5 753	2 282	2 223	1 975	1 421	4 519	4 173	3 941	4 332
Respiratory disease					SWORD				OPRA			
Asthma	555	492	596	306	386	374	451	250	169	118	145	56
Malignant mesothelioma	830	762	653	873	819	754	637	872	11	8	16	1
Benign pleural disease	1 132	1 496	1 293	968	1 120	1 481	1 281	968	12	15	12	-
Other	837	906	564	592	567	620	506	424	270	286	58	54
Total number of diagnoses	3 342	3 656	3 106	2 739	2 892	3 229	2 875	2 514	450	427	231	225
Total number of individuals[2]	3 249	3 609	3 059	2 711	2 799	3 207	2 829	2 486	450	402	230	225
Skin disease					EPIDERM				OPRA			
Contact dermatitis	2 374	2 285	2 406	1 780	1 750	1 698	1 810	1 365	624	587	596	415
Skin neoplasia	616	434	760	614	615	434	760	614	1	-	-	-
Other	325	361	390	223	215	176	295	154	110	185	95	69
Total number of diagnoses	3 315	3 080	3 556	2 617	2 580	2 308	2 865	2 133	735	772	691	484
Total number of individuals[2]	3 281	3 045	3 507	2 589	2 546	2 275	2 828	2 106	735	770	679	483
Audiological disease					OSSA				OPRA			
Sensorineural hearing loss	291	315	264	..	33	53	28	..	258	262	236	..
Other	41	48	31	..	12	22	15	..	29	26	16	..
Total number of diagnoses	332	363	295	..	45	75	43	..	287	288	252	..
Total number of individuals[2]	321	340	280	..	34	54	28	..	287	286	252	..
Infections					SIDAW				OPRA			
Diarrhoeal diseases	916	1 429	1 408	..	915	1 396	1 408	..	1	33	-	..
Other	192	149	168	..	123	121	165	..	69	28	3	..
Total number of diagnoses	1 108	1 578	1 576	..	1 038	1 517	1 573	..	70	61	3	..
Total number of individuals[2]	1 108	1 578	1 576	..	1 038	1 517	1 573	..	70	61	3	..

1 THOR: The Health and Occupation Reporting Network (formerly know as ODIN) comprises of the following schemes: MOSS: Musculoskeletal Occupation Surveillance Scheme; SOSMI: Surveillance of Occupational Stress and Mental Illness; SWORD: Surveillance or Work-related and Occupational Respiratory Disease; EPIDERM: Occupational Skin Disease Surveillance by Dermatologists; OSSA: Occupational Surveillance Scheme for Audiologists; SIDAW: Surveillance of Infectious Disease at Work.

2 Individuals may have more than one diagnosis.

Sources: Health and Safety Executive: 0151 951 4842; statisticsrequestteam@hse.gsi.gov.uk

Health

9.9 Deaths due to occupationally related lung disease
Great Britain

		1996	1997	1998	1999	2000	2001	2002	2003	2004	2005	2006
Asbestosis (without mesothelioma)[1,3]	KADY	196	191	165	171	186	233	234	235	266	301	324
Mesothelioma[2]	KADZ	1 322	1 367	1 541	1 615	1 633	1 862	1 868	1 887	1 979	2 047	2 056
Pneumoconiosis (other than asbestosis)	KAEA	223	230	268	321	279	240	271	231	214	194	167
Byssinosis	KAEB	3	5	5	6	4	2	–	3	4	3	5
Farmer's lung and other occupational allergic alveolitis	KAEC	1	5	8	9	7	7	6	7	5	13	10
Total	KAED	1 745	1 798	1 987	2 122	2 109	2 344	2 373	2 362	2 467	2 548	2 562

1 By definition every case of asbestosis is due to asbestos; the association with mesothelioma is also very strong, though there is thought to be a low natural background incidence.

2 For the inclusion into the Mesothelioma register the cause of death on the death certificate must mention the word Mesothelioma.

3 For inclusion into the Asbestosis register the cause of death on the death certificate must mention the word Asbestosis.

Sources: Office for National Statistics; Health and Safety Executive: 0151 951 4842; statisticsrequestteam@hse.gsi.gov.uk

9.10 Injuries to workers:[1] by industry and severity of injury
Great Britain

As reported to all enforcing authorities

				Fatal				Major				Over 3 Days[2]		
		Section	SIC (92)	2005/06	2006/07	2007/08		2005/06	2006/07	2007/08		2005/06	2006/07	2007/08
Agriculture, hunting, forestry and fishing[3]	KSYS	A,B	01,02,05	34	36	39	KSZN	538	488	591	KTAZ	893	863	1 094
Energy and water supply industries	KSYT	C,E	10-14,40/41	5	10	9	KSZO	402	397	401	KTBH	1 344	1 366	1 295
Mining and quarrying	KSYU	C	10-14	4	9	5	KSZP	220	196	201	KTBI	589	615	615
Mining and quarrying of energy producing materials	KSON	CA	10-12	2	7	3	KSZQ	128	117	128	KTBJ	362	385	442
Mining and quarrying except energy producing materials	KSOO	CB	13/14	2	2	2	KSZR	92	79	73	KTBK	227	230	173
Electricity, gas and water supply	KSOP	E	40/41	1	1	4	KSZS	182	201	200	KTBL	755	751	680
Manufacturing	KSOQ	D	15-37	45	36	35	KSZT	5 525	5 200	5 176	KTBM	24 220	21 968	20 720
of food products; beverages and tobacco	KSOR	DA	15/16	4	3	3	KSZU	1 060	927	914	KTBN	5 987	5 281	4 836
of textile and textile products	KSOS	DB	17/18	2	–	1	KSZV	132	131	100	KTBO	525	441	447
of leather and leather products	KSOT	DC	19	–	–	–	KSZW	8	5	3	KTBP	30	24	27
of wood and wood products	KSOU	DD	20	4	3	1	KSZX	231	228	271	KTBQ	690	702	714
of pulp, paper and paper products; publishing and printing	KSOV	DE	21/22	1	2	2	KSZY	311	340	322	KTBR	1 520	1 330	1 222
of coke, refined petroleum products and nuclear fuel	KSOW	DF	23	–	1	–	KSZZ	22	23	10	KTBS	52	50	58
of chemicals, chemical products and man-made fibres	KSOX	DG	24	3	2	2	KTAE	261	222	248	KTBT	1 063	985	943
of rubber and plastic products	KSOY	DH	25	4	–	4	KTAF	388	368	385	KTBU	1 747	1 530	1 345
of other non-metallic mineral products	KSOZ	DI	26	7	2	2	KTAG	280	268	292	KTBV	1 171	994	921
of basic metals and fabricated metal products	KSYV	DJ	27/28	5	10	10	KTAH	1 220	1 206	1 222	KTBW	3 921	3 873	3 773
of machinery and equipment not elsewhere classified	KSYW	DK	29	2	7	1	KTAI	313	322	367	KTBX	1 415	1 387	1 462
of electrical and optical equipment	KSYX	DL	30-33	–	1	3	KTAJ	187	197	191	KTBY	1 021	944	898
of transport equipment	KSYY	DM	34/35	5	3	2	KTAK	474	473	476	KTBZ	2 541	2 391	2 122
Manufacturing not elsewhere classified	KSYZ	DN	36/37	8	2	4	KTAL	638	490	375	KTCA	2 537	2 036	1 952
Construction	KSZA	F	45	60	79	72	KTAM	4 472	4 457	4 467	KTCB	8 384	7 915	8 148
Total service industries	KSZB	G-Q	50-99	73	86	74	KTAN	19 280	19 196	18 528	KTCC	85 427	83 687	78 655
Wholesale and retail trade, and repairs	KSZC	G	50-52	16	7	17	KTAO	3 759	3 671	3 489	KTCD	15 020	14 206	13 652
Hotel and restaurants	KSZD	H	55	3	4	1	KTAP	1 190	1 099	1 206	KTCE	4 068	4 102	4 154
Transport, storage and communication[4]	KSZE	I	60-64	20	34	20	KTAQ	3 541	3 362	3 443	KTCF	22 035	20 746	19 227
Financial intermediation	KSZF	J	65-67	1	–	–	KTAR	250	277	285	KTCG	747	736	759
Real estate, renting and business activities	KSZG	K	70-74	19	9	12	KTAS	2 573	2 489	2 393	KTCH	7 182	7 227	6 546
Public administration and defence	KSZH	L	75	2	6	10	KTAT	3 393	3 438	1 812	KTCI	16 873	16 565	11 284
Education	KSZI	M	80	1	4	1	KTAU	1 073	1 186	1 885	KTCJ	2 679	2 989	4 706
Health and social work	KSZJ	N	85	2	4	3	KTAV	2 334	2 428	2 573	KTCK	13 812	14 133	14 312
Other community, social and personal services activities	KSZK	O-Q	90-99	9	18	10	KTAW	1 167	1 246	1 442	KTCL	3 011	2 983	4 015
All industries	KSZM			217	247	229	KTAY	30 217	29 738	29 163	KTCN	120 268	115 799	109 912

1 See chapter text.

2 Injuries causing incapacity for normal work for more than 3 days.

3 Excludes sea fishing.

4 Injuries arising from shore based services only. Excludes incidents reported under merchant shipping legislation.

Sources: Health and Safety Executive (HSE): 0151 951 4842; statisticsrequestteam@hse.gsi.gov.uk

Social protection

Chapter 10

Social protection

(Tables 10.2 to 10.11, 10.13 and 10.15 to 10.19)

Tables 10.2 to 10.6, 10.9 to 10.11 and 10.13 to 10.19 give details of contributors and beneficiaries under the National Insurance and Industrial Injury Acts, supplementary benefits and war pensions.

There are four classes of National Insurance Contributions (NICs):

Class 1   Earnings-related contributions paid on earnings from employment. Employees pay primary Class 1 contributions and employers pay secondary Class 1 contributions. Payment of Class 1 contributions builds up entitlement to contributory benefits which include Basic State Pension; Additional State Pension (State Earnings Related Pension Scheme SERPS and from April 2002, State Second Pension, S2P); Contribution Based Jobseeker's Allowance; Bereavement Benefits; and Incapacity Benefit.

Primary class 1 contributions stop at State Pension age, but not Class 1 secondary contributions paid by employers.

There are reduced contribution rates where the employee contracts out of S2P (previously SERPS). They still receive a Basic State Pension but an Occupational or Personal Pension instead of the Additional State Second Pension.

Class 2   Flat rate contributions paid by the self-employed whose profits are above the small earnings exception. Payment of Class 2 contributions builds up entitlement to the contributory benefits, which include Basic State Pension, Bereavement Benefits, Maternity Allowance and Incapacity Benefit, but not Additional State Second Pension or Contribution Based Jobseeker's Allowance (JSA).

Class 2 contributions stop at State Pension age.

Class 3   Flat rate voluntary contributions, which can be paid by someone whose contribution record is insufficient. Payment of Class 3 contributions builds up entitlement to contributory benefits which include Basic State Pension and Bereavement Benefits.

Class 4   Profit-related contributions paid by the self-employed in addition to Class 2 contributions. Class 4 contributions stop at State Pension age. Under some circumstances people who are not in employment do not have to make voluntary contributions to accrue a qualifying year for Basic State Pension.

Home Responsibilities Protection

Home Responsibilities Protection (HRP) helps to protect the basic State Pension of those precluded from regular employment because they are caring for children or a sick or disabled person at home. To be entitled to HRP, a person must have been precluded from regular employment for a full tax year. HRP reduces the amount of qualifying years a person would otherwise need for a Basic State Pension.

National Insurance Credits

In addition to paying, or being treated as having paid contributions, a person can be credited with National Insurance. Contribution credits help to protect people's rights to State Retirement Pension and other Social Security Benefits.

A person is likely to be entitled to contributions credits if they are: a student in full-time education or training, in receipt of Jobseeker's Allowance, unable to work due to sickness or disability, entitled to Statutory Maternity Pay or Statutory Adoption Pay, or they have received Carer's Allowance.

Credits are automatically awarded for men aged 60 to 65 provided they are not liable to pay Class 1 or 2 NICs, and to young people for the tax years containing their 16th, 17th and 18th birthdays.

Jobseeker's Allowance

(Table 10.6)

Jobseeker's Allowance (JSA) replaced Unemployment Benefit and Income Support for unemployed claimants on 7 October 1996. It is a unified benefit with two routes of entry: contribution-based, which depends mainly on National Insurance contributions, and income-based, which depends mainly on a means test. Some claimants can qualify by either route. In practice they receive income-based JSA but have an underlying entitlement to the contribution-based element.

Sickness Benefit, Invalidity Benefit and Incapacity Benefit

(Tables 10.7 and 10.8)

Incapacity Benefit replaced Sickness Benefit and Invalidity Benefit from 13 April 1995. The first condition for entitlement to these contributory benefits is that the claimants are incapable of work because of illness or disablement. The second is that they satisfy the contribution conditions, which depend on contributions paid as an employed (Class 1) or self-employed person (Class 2). Under Sickness and Invalidity Benefits the contribution conditions were automatically treated as satisfied if a person was incapable of work because of an industrial accident or prescribed disease. Under Incapacity Benefit those who do not satisfy the contribution conditions do not have them treated as satisfied. Class 1A contributions paid by employers are in respect of the benefit of cars provided for the private use of employees, and the free fuel provided for private use. These contributions do not provide any type of benefit cover.

Since 6 April 1983, most people working for an employer and paying National Insurance contributions as employed persons receive Statutory Sick Pay (SSP) from their employer when they are off work sick. SSP was payable for a maximum of eight weeks until 5 April 1986, and 28 weeks thereafter. People who do not work for an employer, and employees who are excluded from the SSP scheme, or those who have run out of SSP before reaching the maximum of 28 weeks and are still sick, can claim benefit. Any period of SSP is excluded from the tables.

Spells of incapacity of three days or less do not count as periods of interruption of employment and are excluded from the tables. Exceptions are where people are receiving regular weekly treatment by dialysis or treatment by radiotherapy, chemotherapy or plasmapheresis where two days in any six consecutive days make up a period of interruption of employment, and those whose incapacity for work ends within three days of the end of SSP entitlement.

At the beginning of a period of incapacity, benefit is subject to three waiting days, except where there was an earlier spell of incapacity of more than three days in the previous eight weeks. Employees entitled to SSP for less than 28 weeks and who are still sick can get Sickness Benefit or Incapacity Benefit Short Term (Low) until they reach a total of 28 weeks provided they satisfy the conditions.

After 28 weeks of SSP and/or Sickness Benefit (SB), Invalidity Benefit (IVB) was payable up to pension age for as long as the incapacity lasted. From pension age, IVB was paid at the person's State Pension rate, until entitlement ceased when SP was paid, or until deemed pension age (70 for a man, 65 for a woman). People who were on Sickness or Invalidity Benefit on 12 April 1995 were automatically transferred to Incapacity Benefit, payable on the same basis as before.

For people on Incapacity Benefit under State Pension age there are two short-term rates: the lower rate is paid for the first 28 weeks of sickness and the higher rate for weeks 29 to 52. From week 53 the Long Term rate Incapacity Benefit is payable. The Short Term rate Incapacity Benefit is based on State Pension entitlement for people over State Pension age and is paid for up to a year if incapacity began before pension age.

The long-term rate of Incapacity Benefit applies to people under State Pension age who have been sick for more than a year. People with a terminal illness, or who are receiving the higher rate care component of Disability Living Allowance, will get the Long Term rate. The Long Term rate is not paid for people over pension age.

Under Incapacity Benefit, for the first 28 weeks of incapacity, people previously in work will be assessed on the 'own occupation' test – the claimant's ability to do their own job. Otherwise, incapacity will be based on a personal capability assessment, which will assess ability to carry out a range of work-related activities. The test will apply after 28 weeks of incapacity or from the start of the claim for people who did not previously have a job. Certain people will be exempted from this test.

The tables exclude all men aged over 65 and women aged over 60 who are in receipt of State Pension, and all people over deemed pension age (70 for a man and 65 for a woman), members of the armed forces, mariners while at sea, and married women and certain widows who have chosen not to be insured for sickness benefit. The tables include a number of individuals who were unemployed prior to incapacity.

The Short Term (Higher) and Long Term rates of Incapacity Benefit are treated as taxable income. There were transitional provisions for people who were on Sickness or Invalidity Benefit on 12 April 1995. They were automatically transferred to Incapacity Benefit, payable on the same basis as before. Former IVB recipients continue to get Additional Pension entitlement, but frozen at 1994 levels. Also their IVB is not subject to tax. If they were over State Pension age on 12 April 1995 they may get Incapacity Benefit for up to five years beyond pension age.

Child Benefits

(Table 10.9)

Child Benefit (CB) is paid to those responsible for children (aged under 16) or qualifying young people. The latter includes:

a) a person under the age of 19 in full-time non-advanced education or (from April 2006) on certain approved vocational training programmes

b) a person who is aged 19 who began their course of full-time, non-advanced education or approved training before reaching age 19 (note: those reaching 19 up to 9 April 2006 ceased to qualify on their 19th birthdays)

c) a person who has reached the age of 16 until the 31 August following their 16th birthday

d) a person aged 16 or 17 who has left education and training who is registered with the Careers service or with Connexions and is awaiting a placement in employment or training for the limited period of up to 20 weeks from the date they left education or training

Entitlement for a qualifying young person continues until the terminal date following the date they leave full-time education or approved training. The terminal dates are at the end of August, November, February and May (there is a slight variation for Scotland). Entitlement is also maintained for a person who is entered for external examinations connected with their course throughout the period between a person leaving education or training and completing those examinations.

Entitlement in all cases ceases when a person reaches the age of 20.

Guardian's Allowance is an additional allowance for people bringing up a child because one or both of their parents has died. They must be getting Child Benefit (CB) for the child.

The table shows the number of families in the UK in receipt of CB. The numbers shown in the table are estimates based on a random 5 per cent sample of awards current at 31 August, and are therefore subject to sampling error. The figures take no account of new claims, or revisions to claims that were received or processed after 31 August, even if they are backdated to start before 31 August.

Family Credit/ Working Families' Tax Credit

(Table 10.10)

Working Families' Tax Credit (WFTC) replaced Family Credit from 5 October 1999.

Family Credit was, and Working Families' Tax Credit is, available to families with at least one adult in remunerative work for at least 16 hours per week and who is responsible for at least one child under 16 (under 19 if in full-time education up to A-level or equivalent standard). The rate of payment of WFTC depends on the number of such children and expenditure incurred on eligible childcare. It is also higher if the worker works for at least 30 hours per week, or if there are disabled children or severely disabled adults in the family. It is tapered away above an income threshold. Further details can be obtained from HM Revenue & Customs.

Child and Working Tax Credits (New Tax Credits)

(Table 10.11)

Child and Working Tax Credits (CTC and WTC) replaced Working Families' Tax Credit (WFTC) from 6th April 2003. CTC and WTC are claimed by individuals, or jointly by couples, whether or not they have children.

CTC provides support to families for the children (up to the 31 August after their 16th birthdays) and the 'qualifying' young people (in full-time non-advanced education until their 19th birthdays) for which they are responsible. It is paid in addition to CB.

WTC tops up the earnings of families on low or moderate incomes. People working for at least 16 hours a week can claim it if they: (a) are responsible for at least one child or qualifying young person, (b) have a disability which puts them at a disadvantage in getting a job or, (c) in the first year of work, having returned to work aged at least 50 after a period of at least six months receiving out-of-work benefits. Other adults also qualify if they are aged at least 25 and work for at least 30 hours a week.

Widow's Benefit and Bereavement Benefit

(Table 10.12 and 10.13)

Widow's Benefit is payable to women widowed on or after 11 April 1988 and up to and including 8 April 2001. There are three types of Widow's Benefits: Widow's Payment, Widowed Mother's Allowance and Widow's Pension. Women widowed before 11 April 1988 continue to receive Widow's Benefit based on the rules that existed before that date. Bereavement Benefit was introduced on 9 April 2001 as a replacement for Widow's Benefit, payable to both men and women widowed on or after 9 April 2001. There are three types of Bereavement Benefits available: Bereavement Payment, Widowed Parent's Allowance and Bereavement Allowance.

Government expenditure on social services and housing

(Table 10.20 to 10.25)

The tables of general government expenditure on social services and housing in the UK comprise a summary table followed by separate tables for each of the social services and housing categories. The definition of government expenditure used in the tables is consistent with Table 5.2.4S of the *Blue Book* 2008 edition, and covers both current and capital expenditure of central government (including the National Insurance Fund) and local authorities.

The figures in the tables have been compiled based on the United Nations Classification of the Functions of Government (COFOG) and are consistent with the European System of Accounts 1995 (ESA95). The format of the tables was revised in the 2007 edition. As such they may not be comparable with earlier editions of the *Annual Abstract of Statistics*, which were based on information supplied directly by government departments. This information from government departments is generally no longer available and, as such, the tables are compiled under the categories of National Accounts.

Useful links

National Accounts Blue Book: www.statistics.gov.uk/cci/article.asp?id=2055

UN CoFoG classification: http://unstats.un.org/unsd/cr/registry/regcst.asp?Cl=4

The main categories of expenditure now used are:

Final Consumption Expenditure – The expenditure on goods and services that are used for the direct satisfaction of individual needs or the collective needs of members of the community as distinct from their purchase for use in the productive process. It may be contrasted with actual final consumption, which is the value of goods consumed but not necessarily purchased by that sector.

Compensation of Employees – Total remuneration payable to employees in cash or in kind. Includes the value of social contributions payable by the employer

Net Procurement – current expenditure less receipts for sales and charges.

Gross Capital Formation – acquisition less disposals of fixed assets and the improvement of land.

Subsidies – current unrequited payments made by general government or the European Union to enterprises. Those made on the basis of a quantity or value of goods or services are classified as 'subsidies on products'. Other subsidies based on levels of productive activity (for example, numbers employed) are designated ,Other subsidies on production.

Capital Transfers – transfers which are related to the acquisition or disposal of assets by the recipient or payer. They may be in cash or kind, and may be imputed to reflect the assumption or forgiveness of debt.

Non-produced financial or non financial assets – assets produced either through production or otherwise of a non-financial nature.

Non-market capital consumption – output of own account production of goods and services provided free or at price that are not economically significant. Non-market output is produced mainly by the general government and Non-profit Institutions Serving Household sectors.

Education

(Table 10.21)

Table 10.21 includes expenditure by the education departments, local education authorities and the University Grants Committee on education in schools, training colleges, technical institutions and universities. Compensation of employees' figures are based on revenue outturn returns produced by Department for Communities and Local Government, Welsh Assembly Government and the Scottish Government.

National Health Service

(Table 10.22)

Table 10.22 includes expenditure by central government on hospital and community health, family practitioner and other health services. The figures are based on departmental expenditure reported to HM Treasury.

Welfare services

(Table 10.23)

Personal social services: this table covers local authority and central government expenditure on such things as the aged, handicapped, homeless, child care, care of mothers and young children, mental health, domestic help, etc.

Social protection

Social security

(Table 10.24)

Table 10.24 comprises both benefits under the Social Security schemes and non-contributory benefits and allowances, administered by the Department for Work and Pensions (DWP). Benefits paid overseas are also included, as are unfunded social benefits such as voluntary employer social contributions. The analysis by type of Income Support is not exact; the estimates are derived from average numbers in receipt of benefit and average amounts paid. War pensions which are now administered by the Ministry of Defence are included in this table. Child and Working Tax Credits (NTCs) replaced Working Families' Tax Credit (WFTC) from 6 April 2003 and are administered by the HMRC.

Housing

(Table 10.25)

The table shows government expenditure on housing. It includes expenditure made by the central and local government sectors, but excludes expenditure by public corporations. The Housing Revenue Account is classified as a quasi-public corporation, so that most of its current and capital expenditure and income is included in the corporate rather than government sector. All overhead and administration expenses are included in final current expenditure. Non-capitalised support for public corporations and other market bodies relating to housing is recorded as subsidies. Capital transfers are paid mainly by local government to individuals for repair and improvement of privately owned housing. Current transfers paid include insurance premiums. Gross capital formation includes that of the council houses administered by the Housing Revenue Account. This is net of any sales of housing either through Right to Buy or Large Scale Voluntary Transfers. Housing benefit in the form of rent rebates and rent allowances is not included in the table, as they are regarded as forms of social security.

10.1 National Insurance Fund
(Great Britain and Northern Ireland)
Years ended 31 March

£ million

		1999 /00	2000 /01	2001 /02	2002 /03	2003 /04	2004 /05	2005 /06	2006 /07	2007 /08
Receipts										
Opening balance	KJFB	12 625	14 909	19 868	24 177	27 267	27 816	29 804	34 940	39 245
Contributions	JXVM	51 852	55 627	58 050	59 658	59 827	62 863	67 786	69 599	77 224
State Scheme Premiums[1]	C59W	..	..	..	194	147	115	117	76	79
Grant from Consolidated Fund	KOTF	2	..	..	..	..	..	..	..	..
Compensation for SSP/SMP	KJQM	625	688	710	775	1 346	1 470	1 392	1 197	1 919
Transfers from Great Britian	KOTG	230	200	110	350	260	270	185	630	452
Income from										
investments	KJFE	724	884	1 146	1 457	1 292	1 288	1 399	1 867	2 452
Other receipts	KJFF	127	112	67	80	82	72	66	54	56
Redundancy receipts	KIBQ	21	23	22	24	28	32	38	43	37
Total	JYJO	66 206	72 442	79 972	86 716	90 249	93 926	100 787	108 406	121 464
Expenditure										
Total benefits	JYJP	50 026	50 960	54 550	54 201	56 255	58 572	61 304	63 695	67 443
Jobseeker's Allowance										
(Contributory)	LUQW	475	449	478	519	512	455	497	493	435
Incapacity	JYXL	7 206	6 982	7 074	7 104	7 116	6 910	7 028	7 009	6 945
Maternity	KETY	40	46	57	70	128	153	128	180	250
Bereavement Benefits	KEWU	1 020	1 008	1 132	1 142	1 033	946	903	826	760
Guardian's allowances and										
Child's special allowance[2]	KJFK	2	2	2	2	2	1	2	2	2
Retirement pensions[3]	JYJV	41 157	42 350	45 677	45 240	47 339	49 979	52 578	55 053	58 921
Pensioners' lump										
sum payments	KAAW	126	123	131	124	125	128	168	131	131
Other payments	KAAZ	19	21	29	27	34	30	33	40	61
Administration	KABE	847	1 197	873	1 280	1 794	1 521	1 464	1 473	1 430
Transfers to Northern										
Ireland	KABF	230	200	110	350	260	270	185	630	452
Redundancy payments	KIBR	174	195	232	255	243	222	295	248	215
Personal Pensions	C59X	..	..	..	3 336	3 847	3 508	2 566	3 076	2 557
Total	JYJU	51 297	52 574	55 795	59 449	62 433	64 123	65 847	69 161	72 158
Accumulated funds	KABH	14 909	19 868	24 177	27 267	27 816	29 804	34 940	39 245	49 306

1 State Scheme Premiums are payable in respect of employed persons who cease to be covered, in certain circumstances, by a contracted out pension scheme.
2 Includes Child's special allowance for Northern Ireland.
3 Includes personal pensions up to 2001/02.

Sources: HM Revenue and Customs: 01702 367480; Department for Work and Pensions: 01253 856123 Ext 62436

10.2 Persons[1] who paid National Insurance contributions[2,3] in a tax year:[4] by sex
United Kingdom

Millions

		Total				Men				Women		
		2004 /05	2005 /06	2006 /07		2004 /05	2005 /06	2006 /07		2004 /05	2005 /06	2006 /07
Total	KABI	28.60	28.84	28.33	KEYF	15.71	15.80	15.55	KEYP	12.90	13.03	12.78
Class 1	KABJ	25.25	25.57	25.17	KEYG	13.34	13.49	13.31	KEYQ	11.91	12.08	11.86
Not contracted out[5]	KABK	16.95	17.38	17.68	KEYH	9.37	9.64	9.83	KEYR	7.58	7.74	7.85
Contracted out	KABL	7.06	7.00	6.41	KEYI	3.45	3.34	3.01	KEYS	3.62	3.66	3.41
Mixed contracted in/out[6]	KABM	1.24	1.20	1.08	KEYJ	0.53	0.52	0.48	KEYT	0.71	0.68	0.61
Class 1 Reduced rate (including standard rate)	KABO	0.06	0.04	0.03	KEYL	..	–	–	KEYV	0.06	0.04	0.03
Class 2 exclusively[7]	KABP	2.37	2.35	2.37	KEYM	1.81	1.77	1.77	KEYW	0.57	0.58	0.60
Mixed Class 1 and Class 2	KABQ	0.68	0.70	0.68	KEYN	0.45	0.46	0.44	KEYX	0.22	0.24	0.24
Class 3 exclusively[8]	KABR	0.17	0.13	0.08	KEYO	0.07	0.06	0.04	KEYY	0.09	0.08	0.04
Mixed Class 1 and Class 3	I6CF	0.06	0.03	0.01	I6CI	0.01	0.01	–	I6CL	0.04	0.02	0.01
Mixed Class 2 and Class 3	I6CG	0.02	0.01	–	I6CJ	0.01	0.01	–	I6CM	0.01	–	..
Mixed Class 1, 2 and 3	I6CH	..	..	..	I6CK	..	..	..	I6CN	..	..	..

1 Based on all persons making contributions and not only if they have a qualifying year.
2 Estimates obtained from DWP Information Directorate: Lifetime Labour Market Data Tabulation Tool which uses a 1% sample of the National Insurance Recording System (NIRS2) summer 2008 extract.
3 Components may not sum to totals as a result of rounding.
4 The tax year commences on 6 April and ends on 5 April the following year.
5 Includes those persons with an Appropriate Personal Pension (such persons pay contributions at the not contracted out rate but then receive a rebate paid directly to their scheme).
6 Not included in the above rows.
7 Persons who paid a mixture of Class 2 contributions and others are not included in this category.
8 Persons who paid a mixture of Class 3 contributions and others are not included in this category.

Source: HM:Revenue and Customs:020 7147 3045

Social protection

10.3 National Insurance contributions
United Kingdom

	Employee's standard contibutions[1]		Employer's standard contributions[1]	
	not contracted-out rate	contracted-out rate[2]	not contracted-out rate	contracted-out rate[3]

Class 1

Weekly earnings

2002/03
Below 75.00 (LEL)	-	-	-	-
75.00-89.00 (PT/ST)		See note 4		See note 5
89.01-585.00 (UEL)	10.0%	8.4%	11.8%	8.3%
Above 585.00 (UEL)	£49.60	£41.44	11.8%	11.8%

2003/04
Below 77.00 (LEL)	-	-	-	-
77.00-89.00 (PT/ST)		See note 4		See note 5
89.01-595.00 (UEL)	11.0%	9.4%	12.8%	9.3%
	£55.66	£47.37		
Above 595.00 (UEL)	1%	1%	12.8%	12.8%

2004/05
Below 79.00 (LEL)	-	-	-	-
79.00-91.00 (PT/ST)		See note 4		See note 5
91.01-610.00 (UEL)	11.0%	9.4%	12.8%	9.3%
	£57.09	£48.59		
Above 610.00(UEL)	1.0%	1.0%	12.8%	12.8%

2005/06
Below 82.00 (LEL)	-	-	-	-
82.00-94.00 (PT/ST)		See note 4		See note 5
94.01-630.00 (UEL)	11.0%	9.4%	12.8%	9.3%
	£58.96	£50.38		
Above 630.00(UEL)	1.0%	1.0%	12.8%	12.8%

2006/07
Below 84.00 (LEL)	-	-	-	-
84.00-97.00 (PT/ST)		See note 4		See note 5
97.01-645.00 (UEL)	11.0%	9.4%	12.8%	9.3%
	£60.28	£51.51		
Above 645.00(UEL)	1.0%	1.0%	12.8%	12.8%

2007/08
Below 87.00 (LEL)	-	-	-	-
87.00-100.00 (PT/ST)		See note 4		See note 6
100.01-670.00 (UEL)	11.0%	9.4%	12.8%	9.1%
	£62.70	£53.58		
Above 670.00(UEL)	1.0%	1.0%	12.8%	12.8%

2008/09
Below 90.00 (LEL)	-	-	-	-
90.00-105.00 (PT/ST)		See note 4		See note 6
105.01-770.00 (UEL)	11.0%	9.4%	12.8%	9.1%
	£73.15	£62.51		
Above 770.00(UEL)	1.0%	1.0%	12.8%	12.8%

	2002/03	2003/04	2004/05	2005/06	2006/07	2007/08	2008/09
Class 2							
Flat rate weekly	£2.00	£2.00	£2.05	£2.10	£2.10	£2.20	£2.30
Small earnings exception[7] (per annum)	£4,025	£4,095	£4,215	£4,345	£4,465	£4,635	£4,825
Class 3							
Flat-rate voluntary weekly contributions	£6.85	£6.95	£7.15	£7.35	£7.55	£7.80	£8.10
Class 4 (Self-employed; profit-related)							
Rate on profits between LPL and UPL	7.0%	8.0%	8.0%	8.0%	8.0%	8.0%	8.0%
Rate on profits above UPL	..	1.0%	1.0%	1.0%	1.0%	1.0%	1.0%
Lower profits limit (LPL)	£4,615	£4,615	£4,745	£4,895	£5,035	£5,225	£5435
Upper profits limit (UPL)	£30,420	£30,940	£31,720	£32,760	£33,540	34,840	£40040

Note: LEL: Lower Earnings Limit; UEL: Upper Earnings Limit. PT: Primary Threshold; ST: Secondary Threshold.

1 Married women opting to pay contributions at the reduced rate at 3.85% before 2003-04 and 4.85% from 2003-04 earn no entitlement to contributory National Insurance benefits as a result of these contributions. No women have been allowed to exercise this option since 1977, but around 70,000 women who have been continually married or widowed and in the labour market since that time have retained their right to pay the reduced rate.

2 The contracted-out rebate for employees' contributions is applied only between LEL and UEL. Earnings below LEL are charged at the appropriate not contracted-out rate (which depends on total earnings). Earnings above the UEL are not subject to employee NICs before 2003-04.

3 The rates shown only apply to Contracted-Out Salary Related schemes (COSR).

Earnings below the LEL and above the UEL are charged at the appropriate not-contracted out rate. The employers' contracted-out rate applies only between the LEL and the UEL.

4 The contracted-out rebate for primary contributions is 1.6% of earnings between the LEL and the UEL for all forms of contracting-out.

5 The contracted-out rebate for secondary contributions is 3.5% of earnings between the LEL and the UEL up to 2006-07.

6 Since 2007-08 the contracted-out rebate for secondary contributions is 3.7% of earnings between the LEL and UEL.

7 If earnings from self-employment are below this annual limit and the contributor applies for and is granted a small earnings exception Class 2 contributions need not be paid. Class 2 or 3 contributions may be paid voluntarily.

Source: HM Revenue and Customs: 020 7147 3045

10.4 Weekly rates of principal social security benefits[1]
Great Britain
At April

£

		1998	1999	2000	2001	2002	2003	2004	2005	2006	2007	2008
Jobseeker's Allowance:												
Personal allowances												
Single												
Aged under 18[2]	KXDH	30.30	30.95	31.45	31.95	32.50	32.90	33.50	33.85	34.60	35.65	47.95
Aged 18 - 24	KXDJ	39.85	40.70	41.35	42.00	42.70	43.25	44.05	44.50	45.50	46.85	47.95
Aged 25 or over	KXDK	50.35	51.40	52.20	53.05	53.95	54.65	55.65	56.20	57.45	59.15	60.50
Lone parent												
Aged under 18 - usual rate	F92E	..	..	31.45	31.95	32.50	32.90	33.50	33.85	34.60	35.65	47.95
Aged under 18 - higher rate payable in specific circumstances	F92F	..	..	41.35	42.00	42.70	43.25	44.05	44.50	45.50	46.85	47.95
Aged 18 or over	F92G	..	..	52.20	53.05	53.95	54.65	55.65	56.20	57.45	59.15	60.50
Couple												
Both aged under 18[3]	KXDL	30.30	30.95	31.45	31.95	32.50	32.90	33.50	33.85	34.60	35.65	47.95
Both under 18, one disabled	KXDI	39.85	40.70	41.35	42.00	42.70	43.25	44.05	44.50	45.50	46.85	47.95
Both under 18, with a child	F92H	..	..	62.35	63.35	64.45	65.30	66.50	67.15	68.65	70.70	72.35
One under 18, one 18 - 24[3]	KXDI	39.85	40.70	41.35	42.00	42.70	43.25	44.05	44.50	45.50	46.85	47.95
One under 18, one 25+[3]	F92I	..	..	52.20	53.05	53.95	54.65	55.65	56.20	57.45	59.15	60.50
Both aged 18 or over	KXDM	79.00	80.65	81.95	83.25	84.65	85.75	87.30	88.15	90.10	92.80	94.95
Dependant children and young people												
Aged under 11 - 16	KXDN	17.30	20.20	26.60	31.45	33.50	38.50	42.27	43.88	45.58	47.45	52.59
Aged 16 - 18	KXDP	30.30	30.95	31.75	32.25	34.30	38.50	42.27	43.88	45.58	47.45	52.59
Invalidity allowance[4]												
High rate	KJND	13.60	14.05	14.20	14.65	14.90	15.15	15.55	16.05	16.50	17.10	17.75
Middle rate	KJNE	8.60	8.90	9.00	9.30	9.50	9.70	10.00	10.30	10.60	11.00	11.40
Low rate	KJNF	4.30	4.45	4.50	4.65	4.75	4.85	5.00	5.15	5.30	5.50	5.70
Increase for dependants												
Adult	KJNG	38.70	39.95	40.40	41.75	42.45	43.15	44.35	45.70	46.95	48.65	50.55
Each child[5]	KJNH	11.30	11.35	11.35	11.35	11.35	11.35	11.35	11.35	11.35	11.35	11.35
Incapacity Benefit:												
Short term (Lower) Under pension age	KOSB	48.80	50.35	50.90	52.60	53.50	54.40	55.90	57.65	59.20	61.35	63.75
Increase for adult dependant	KOSC	30.20	31.15	31.50	32.55	33.10	33.65	34.60	35.65	36.60	37.90	39.40
Short term (Lower) Over pension age	KOSD	62.05	64.05	64.75	66.90	68.05	69.20	71.15	73.35	75.35	78.05	81.10
Increase for adult dependant	KOSE	37.20	38.40	38.80	40.10	42.45	41.50	42.65	43.95	45.15	46.80	48.65
Short term (Higher)	KOSF	57.70	59.55	60.20	62.20	63.25	64.35	66.15	68.20	70.05	72.55	75.40
Increase for dependants:												
Adult	KOSG	30.20	31.15	31.50	32.55	33.10	33.65	34.60	35.65	36.60	37.90	39.40
Child[5]	KOSH	11.30	11.35	11.35	11.35	11.35	11.35	11.35	11.35	11.35	11.35	11.35
Long term	KOSI	64.70	66.75	67.50	69.75	70.95	72.15	74.15	76.45	78.50	81.35	84.50
Increase for dependants:												
Adult	KOSJ	38.70	39.95	40.40	41.75	42.45	43.15	44.35	45.70	46.95	48.65	50.55
Child[5]	KOSK	11.30	11.35	11.35	11.35	11.35	11.35	11.35	11.35	11.35	11.35	11.35
Incapacity age addition:[6]												
Higher rate	KOSL	13.60	14.05	14.20	14.65	14.90	15.15	15.55	16.05	16.50	17.10	17.75
Lower rate	KOSM	6.80	7.05	7.10	7.35	7.45	7.60	7.80	8.05	8.25	8.55	8.90
Attendance Allowance:												
Higher rate	KJNI	51.30	52.95	53.55	55.30	56.25	57.20	58.80	60.60	62.25	64.50	67.00
Lower rate	KJNJ	34.30	35.40	35.80	37.00	37.65	38.30	39.35	40.55	41.65	43.15	44.85
Carer's Allowance												
Standard Rate	J8T6	..	..	..	..	..	43.15	44.35	45.70	46.95	48.65	50.55
Disability Living Allowance:												
Care component												
Higher rate	KXDC	51.30	52.95	53.55	55.30	56.25	57.20	58.80	60.60	62.25	64.50	67.00
Middle rate	KXDD	34.30	35.40	35.80	37.00	37.65	38.30	39.35	40.55	41.65	43.15	44.85
Lower rate	KXDE	13.60	14.05	14.20	14.65	14.90	15.15	15.55	16.05	16.50	17.10	17.75
Mobility component												
Higher rate	KXDF	35.85	37.00	37.40	38.65	39.30	39.95	41.05	42.30	43.45	45.00	46.75
Lower rate	KXDG	13.60	14.05	14.20	14.65	14.90	15.15	15.55	16.05	16.50	17.10	17.75

10.4
Weekly rates of principal social security benefits[1]
Great Britain

At April

£

		1998	1999	2000	2001	2002	2003	2004	2005	2006	2007	2008
Maternity Benefit:												
Maternity allowances for insured women[7]												
Higher rate	KOSN	57.70	59.55	60.20	..	..	..	..	..	..	..	..
Lower rate[8]	KJNL	50.10	51.70	52.25	..	..	..	..	..	..	..	..
Standard rate[9]	GPTJ	..	..	..	62.20	75.00	100.00	102.80	106.00	108.85	112.75	117.18
Threshold[10]	GPTK	..	..	..	30.00	30.00	30.00	30.00	30.00	30.00	30.00	30.00
Guardian's Allowance	KJNN	11.30	11.35	11.35	11.35	11.35	11.55	11.85	12.20	12.50	12.95	13.45
Widow's Benefit:												
Widow's pension	KJNO	64.70	66.75	67.50	72.50	75.50	77.45	79.60	82.05	84.25	87.30	90.70
Widowed mother's allowance	KJNP	64.70	66.75	67.50	72.50	75.50	77.45	79.60	82.05	84.25	87.30	90.70
Addition for each child[5]	KJNQ	11.30	11.35	11.35	11.35	11.35	11.35	11.35	11.35	11.35	11.35	11.35
Bereavement Benefit:												
Bereavement allowance	WMPF	..	..	..	72.50	75.50	77.45	79.60	82.05	84.25	87.30	90.70
Widowed parent's allowance	WMOZ	..	..	..	72.50	72.50	77.45	79.60	82.05	84.25	87.30	90.70
Addition for each child[5]	WMPA	..	..	..	11.35	11.35	11.35	11.35	11.35	11.35	11.35	11.35
State Pension contributory:[11]												
Single person	KJNR	64.70	66.75	67.50	72.50	75.50	77.45	79.60	82.05	84.25	87.30	90.70
Married couple	KJNS	103.40	106.70	107.90	115.90	120.70	122.80	127.25	131.20	134.75	139.60	145.05
State Pension non contributory:												
Man or woman	KJNT	38.70	39.95	40.40	43.40	45.20	45.45	47.65	49.15	50.50	52.30	54.35
Married woman	KJNU	23.15	23.90	24.15	24.95	27.00	27.70	28.50	29.40	30.20	31.30	32.50
Industrial Injuries Benefit:												
Disablement pension at 100 per cent rate	KJNW	104.70	108.10	109.30	112.90	114.80	116.80	120.10	123.80	127.10	131.70	136.80
Widow's or widower's pension	KJNX	..	..	..	..	..	..	..	..	..	..	..
Child Benefit:												
First child	KJOA	11.45	14.40	15.00	15.50	15.75	16.05	16.50	17.00	17.45	18.10	18.80
Subsequent children	KETZ	9.30	9.60	10.00	10.35	10.55	10.75	11.05	11.40	11.70	12.10	12.55
Family Credit[12]												
(maximum awards payable):[13]												
Families with 1 child												
Birth to September following 11th birthday	KJOB	61.15	64.95	..	..	..	..	..	..	..	..	..
From September following 11th birthday to September following 16th birthday	KJOC	69.25	70.70	..	..	..	..	..	..	..	..	..
From September following 16th birthday to day before 19th birthday	KJOD	74.20	75.95	..	..	..	..	..	..	..	..	..
Increase for each additional child												
Birth to September following 11th birthday	KJOF	12.35	15.15	..	..	..	..	..	..	..	..	..
From September following 11th birthday to September following 16th birthday	KJOG	20.45	20.90	..	..	..	..	..	..	..	..	..
From September following 16th birthday to day before 19th birthday	KJOH	25.40	25.95	..	..	..	..	..	..	..	..	..
War pension:												
Ex-private (100 per cent assessment)	KJOJ	111.10	114.70	116.00	116.00	119.80	121.79	123.90	127.38	130.20	133.60	138.34
War widow	KJOK	83.90	86.60	87.55	86.74	89.55	91.00	92.69	95.27	98.09	101.43	105.09

10.4

Weekly rates of principal social security benefits[1]
Great Britain

continued   At April

£

		1998	1999	2000	2001	2002	2003	2004	2005	2006	2007	2008
Income Support:												
Personal allowances[14]												
Single												
aged 16-17 usual rate	KJOW	30.30	30.95	31.45	31.95	32.50	32.90	33.50	33.85	34.60	35.65	47.95
aged 16-17 higher rate in specific circumstances	KABS	39.85	40.70	41.35	42.00	42.70	43.25	44.05	44.50	45.50	46.85	47.95
aged 18-24	KJOX	39.85	40.70	41.35	42.00	42.70	43.25	44.05	44.50	45.50	46.85	47.95
aged 25 or over	KJOY	50.35	51.40	52.20	53.05	53.95	54.65	55.65	56.20	57.45	59.15	60.50
Couple												
both aged under 18[2]	KJOZ	..	..	31.45	31.95	32.50	32.90	33.50	33.85	34.60	35.65	47.95
both aged under 18, one disabled	F92J	..	..	41.35	42.00	42.70	43.25	44.05	44.50	45.50	46.85	47.95
both aged under 18, with a child	F92K	..	..	62.35	63.35	64.45	65.30	66.50	67.15	68.65	70.70	72.35
One aged under 18, one 18-24[2]	F92L	..	..	41.35	42.00	42.70	43.25	44.05	44.50	45.50	46.85	47.95
One aged under 18, one 25+[2]	F92M	..	..	52.20	53.05	53.95	54.65	55.65	56.20	57.45	59.15	60.50
Both aged 18 or over	KJPA	79.00	80.65	81.95	83.25	84.65	85.75	87.30	88.15	90.10	92.80	94.95
Lone parent												
aged 16-17 usual rate	KJPB	30.30	30.95	31.45	31.95	32.50	32.90	33.50	33.85	34.60	35.65	47.95
aged 16-17 higher rate in specific circumstances	KABT	39.85	40.70	41.35	42.00	42.70	43.25	44.05	44.50	45.50	46.85	47.95
aged 18 or over	KJPC	50.35	51.40	52.20	53.05	53.95	54.65	55.65	56.20	57.45	59.15	60.50
Dependant children and young people[14]												
From 1997 to 1999												
Birth to September following 11th birthday	KXDQ	17.30	20.20	..	..	..	..	..	..	..	..	..
From September following 11th birthday to September following 16th	KXDR	25.35	25.90	..	..	..	..	..	..	..	..	..
From September following 16th birthday to day before 19th	KXDS	30.30	30.95	..	..	..	..	..	..	..	..	..
Dependant children and young people - from 2000												
Birth to September following 16th birthday	WMOD	..	..	26.60	31.45	33.50	38.50	42.27	43.88	45.58	47.45	52.59
From September following 16th birthday to day before 19th	WMOP	..	..	31.75	32.25	34.30	38.50	42.27	43.88	45.58	47.45	52.50
Pension Credit[15]												
Standard minimum guarantee:												
single	C59Y	..	..	..	..	..	102.10	105.45	109.45	114.05	119.05	124.05
couple	C59Z	..	..	..	..	..	155.80	160.95	167.05	174.05	181.70	189.35
Additional amount for severe disability												
single	C5A2	..	..	..	..	..	42.95	44.15	45.50	46.75	48.45	50.35
couple (one qualifies)	C5A3	..	..	..	..	..	42.95	44.15	45.50	46.75	48.45	50.35
couple (both qualifies)	C5A4	..	..	..	..	..	85.90	88.30	91.00	93.50	96.90	100.70
Additional amount for carers	C5A8	..	..	..	..	..	25.10	25.55	25.80	26.35	27.15	27.75
savings credit												
threshold single	C5A9	..	..	..	..	..	77.45	79.60	82.05	84.25	87.30	91.20
threshold couple	C5AA	..	..	..	..	..	123.80	127.25	131.20	134.75	139.60	145.80
maximum single	C5AB	..	..	..	..	..	14.79	15.51	16.44	17.88	19.05	19.71
maximum couple	C5AC	..	..	..	..	..	19.20	20.22	21.51	23.58	25.26	26.13

1 See chapter text.
2 Persons under 18 are entitled to the appropriate adult rate.
3 From 12 April 1999 the personal allowance for couples where both members are not yet 18 or one of the couples is aged 18 or over depends on the couple's circumstances. They may be entitled to a couple allowance or a single person's allowance dependant on certain criteria.
4 Incapacity benefit, introduced from 13 April 1995, has replaced sickness benefit and invalidity benefit.
5 The rate of child dependency increase is adjusted where it is payable for the eldest child for whom child benefit (ChB) is also paid. The weekly rate in such cases is reduced by the difference (less £3.65) between the ChB rates for the eldest and subsequent children.
6 The rate of age addition depends on age at date of onset of incapacity: higher rate for under age 35 and lower rate for age 35-44.
7 Following a EU Directive, employee's maternity benefit is aligned with the state benefit they would receive if off work sick.
8 Women who were either not employed or self-employed received the lower rate.

9 New Standard rate introduced from April 2000.
10 MA Earnings Threshold introduced April 2000.
11 Retirement pensioners over 80 receive 25p addition.
12 Family credit was replaced by In-work Families with Child or Working Child Tax Credit awards. Some children have protected rights. Further information is available from the Department for Work and Pensions.
13 Maximum award does not include the 30 hour credit.
14 In addition to personal allowances, a claimant may also be entitled to premiums. The types of premiums are family, lone parent, pensioner, higher pensioner, disability, severe disability and disabled child.
15 Pension Credit replaced Minimum Income Guarantee (MIG) for Income Support for those aged 60 and over on 6th Ocotober 2003.

Sources: Department for Work and Pensions;
Information and Analysis Directorate : 0191 225 7373;
HM Revenue and Customs: 020 7438 7370;
Ministry of Defence/DASA (Pay & Pensions): 020 7218 4271

10.5 Social Security Acts: number of persons receiving benefit[1]
Great Britain

At any one time

Thousands

		1999	2000	2001	2002	2003	2004	2005	2006	2007	2008
Persons receiving:											
Jobseeker's Allowance[2,3]	JYXM	1 105.80	1 037.01	909.15	877.38	885.78	777.40	800.66	895.88	807.27	787.87
Incapacity benefit[3]	KXDT	1 557.10	2 352.52	2 420.88	2 471.14	2 494.89	2 508.77	2 490.85	2 449.99	2 417.71	2 382.00
Severe Disablement Allowance	J8T2	..	375.56	374.45	336.48	320.76	305.94	292.87	280.01	267.61	255.56
Attendance Allowance[4]	KXDU	1 243.80	1 556.10	1 570.90	1 290.77	1 315.64	1 377.35	1 419.42	1 465.59	1 507.50	1 546.68
Disability Living Allowance[4]	KXDW	2 061.30	2 193.10	2 306.40	2 424.35	2 547.09	2 644.28	2 729.72	2 799.16	2 881.83	2 973.54
Carers' Allowance	J8T3	..	..	..	..	..	421.18	441.03	453.54	464.67	480.73
Child Benefit[5]	J8T4	..	7 305.0	7 297.1	7 296.1	7 297.5	7 301.3	7 311.4	7 365.4	7 449.6	..
Widows' Benefits	KJHF	267.60	265.11	254.97	223.41	191.50	163.43	138.96	117.65	96.89	77.90
Bereavement Benefits	VQAA	..	..	..	41.49	47.68	51.18	55.24	57.66	58.54	59.85
National Insurance											
State pension contributory:											
Males	KJHH	3 956.30	4 039.40	4 083.90	4 149.16	4 211.37	4 275.67	4 336.81	4 374.18	4 432.31	4 520.56
Females	KJHL	6 886.30	6 928.00	6 959.70	6 972.20	7 037.15	7 117.78	7 197.92	7 245.71	7 391.10	7 529.40
Total	KJHG	10 842.60	10 967.40	11 043.60	11 121.35	11 248.52	11 393.45	11 534.73	11 619.89	11 823.40	12 049.96
State pension non contributory:											
Males	KJHI	5.10	5.20	5.10	5.26	5.37	5.39	5.34	5.36	5.68	6.23
Females	KJHJ	18.80	18.00	18.20	18.06	17.73	17.31	16.74	16.58	17.34	18.80
Total	KJHK	23.90	23.20	23.30	23.32	23.10	22.70	22.08	21.94	23.03	25.03
Industrial Injuries Disablement											
Pensions assessments[6]	KJHN	278.20	274.60	275.40	273.70	267.13	266.48	267.12	266.45	264.88	261.99
Reduced Earnings Allowance/											
Retirement Allowance assessments[7]	KEYC	153.50	82.90	82.60	81.00	76.22	74.81	73.15	71.38	69.36	67.19
Income Support (Excluding MIG)[8]	KABV	3 814.40	2 237.13	2 260.63	2 238.76	2 236.38	2 192.64	2 139.78	2 114.77	2 117.70	2 091.52
Minimum Income Guaranteed	J8T5	..	1 607.48	1 714.37	1 737.53	1 777.79	12.09	10.98	10.27	10.65	10.74
Pension Credit[8]	C5AP	..	..	..	..	..	2 490.76	2 682.73	2 717.39	2 733.50	2 719.14
Housing Benefit and Council Tax Benefit[9,10]											
Housing Benefit Total	EW3X	4 313.10	4 033.30	3 874.40	3 812.60	3 796.40	3 879.40	3 957.10	3 990.00	4 031.81	..
Social Landlord[11]	KABY	2 518.50	3 218.40	3 131.10	3 093.80	3 081.67	3 135.49	3 165.89	3 152.25	3 108.73	..
Private Landlord	KABZ	1 794.60	815.00	743.30	718.83	714.75	743.93	790.93	837.79	923.07	..
Council tax benefit[12]	KJPO	5 166.10	4 830.10	4 673.40	4 601.73	4 627.78	4 800.22	4 959.69	5 049.97	5 076.94	..
War pensions[13]	KADG	306.06	295.67	284.33	272.78	260.79	247.59	235.30	223.85	212.54	201.27

1 See chapter text. Figures as at May each year unless otherwise stated. Taken from DWP 100% Work and Pensions Longitudinal Study (WPLS) data.

2 JSA statistics have been completely revised since the last issue following improvements to the methodology in compiling the statistics. A paper detailing the improvements can be found at: http://www.dwp.gov.uk/asd/asd1/improvements_to_JSA.pdf

3 Totals include 'credits only' cases.

4 AA and DLA figures based on WPLS data from 2002. Prior to 2002 a consistent series for caseload, based on WPLS levels, has been created by combining older information, available from the previously published 5% sample data, with the WPLS data.

5 Figures for Child Benefit in 2008 are delayed due to extraction system updates.

6 Figures for IIDB include those receiving both IIDB and REA, at March.

7 Figures show REA only from 2000, at March.

8 Pension Credit replaced MIG on 6th October 2003 and extended Income Support entitlement to customers aged 60+. MIG claimants have been excluded from the IS figures in order to keep the series consistent.

9 In order to produce more up to date and accurate data, we are currently changing our data sources for HB/CTB. In the transition period there will be no new figures available for the publication and May 2007 will continue to be the latest.

10 Housing Benefit figures excludes any Extended Payment cases.

11 Social landlord figures include registered social landlord tenants.

12 Figure excludes Second Adult Rebate Claims.

13 Includes overseas cases. As at end of March.

Sources: Department for Work and Pensions; Information and Analysis Directorate : 0191 225 7373; HM Revenue and Customs: 020 7438 7370; Ministry of Defence/DASA (Pay & Pensions): 020 7218 4271

10.6 Jobseeker's Allowance[1,2,3,4] claimants: by benefit entitlement
Great Britain
As at May

Thousands

		2002	2003	2004	2005	2006	2007	2008
All Persons								
All with benefit - total	KXDX	790.4	797.9	699.6	728.3	812.0	730.8	718.0
Contribution-based JSA only	KXDY	155.3	160.4	131.0	139.5	134.6	113.6	127.8
Contribution based JSA & income-based JSA	KXDZ	18.5	18.1	13.5	13.5	13.0	11.9	12.8
Income-based JSA only payment	KXEA	616.6	619.4	555.1	575.3	664.5	605.3	577.4
No benefit in payment	KXEB	87.0	87.9	77.8	72.4	83.9	76.4	69.9
Total	KXEC	877.4	885.8	777.4	800.7	895.9	807.4	788.0
Males								
All with benefit - total	KXED	606.2	605.6	527.2	545.3	606.8	537.8	529.9
Contribution-based JSA only	KXEE	110.8	114.1	93.8	99.5	95.8	79.6	90.6
Contribution based JSA & income-based JSA	KXEF	16.7	15.9	12.3	12.6	12.0	10.7	11.7
Income-based JSA only payment	KXEG	478.7	475.6	421.1	433.2	498.9	447.5	427.6
No benefit in payment	KXEH	59.5	60.3	52.7	49.8	56.6	51.7	46.7
Total	KXEI	665.7	665.9	580.0	595.1	663.4	589.6	576.7
Females								
All with benefit - total	KXEJ	184.2	192.3	172.4	182.9	205.3	193.0	188.1
Contribution-based JSA only	KXEK	44.5	46.3	37.2	40.0	38.7	34.0	37.2
Contribution based JSA & income-based JSA	KXEL	1.8	2.2	1.2	0.8	1.0	1.2	1.2
Income-based JSA only payment	KXEM	137.9	143.8	134.0	142.1	165.5	157.8	149.8
No benefit in payment	KXEN	27.5	27.6	25.0	22.6	27.2	24.8	23.2
Total	KXEO	211.7	219.8	197.4	205.5	232.5	217.8	211.3

1 See chapter text. Jobseeker's Allowance (JSA) has two routes of entry: contribution-based which depends mainly upon national insurance contributions and income-based which depends mainly on a means test. Some claimants can qualify by either route. In practice they receive income-based JSA but have an underlying entitlement to the contribution-based element.
2 JSA statistics have been completely revised since the last issue following improvements to the methodology in compiling the statistics. A paper detailing the improvements can be found at: http://www.dwp.gov.uk/asd/asd1/improvements_to_JSA.pdf

3 Figures are given at May each year and have been derived by applying 5% proportions to 100% totals taken from the DWP 100% Work and Pensions Longitudinal Study (WPLS).
4 Figures are rounded to the nearest hundred and quoted in thousands. They not sum due to rounding.

Sources: Department for Work and Pensions; Information and Analysis Directorate: 0191 225 7373

Social protection

10.7 Sickness, Invalidity and Incapacity Benefit[1,2,3] claimants: by sex, age and duration of spell

Great Britain and Overseas. At end of May

Thousands

		2003	2004	2005	2006	2007	2008
Males							
All durations: All ages	KJJA	1 525.02	1 517.62	1 492.38	1 455.52	1 428.65	1 399.58
Under 20	KJJB	21.81	22.04	21.45	19.95	18.66	17.25
20-29	KJJC	138.54	142.68	143.24	141.80	146.07	149.47
30-39	KJJD	254.30	253.32	245.61	233.70	224.29	215.51
40-49	KJJE	311.85	318.04	320.77	319.77	320.24	319.22
50-59	KJJF	472.03	463.37	451.93	439.54	418.26	404.76
60-64	KJJG	326.45	318.12	309.36	300.73	301.10	293.33
65 and over	KJJH	0.05	0.05	0.04	0.02	0.03	0.04
Over six months: All ages	KJJI	1 359.53	1 359.08	1 347.43	1 323.20	1 291.32	1 267.06
Under 20	KJJJ	13.40	13.78	13.51	12.85	11.70	10.90
20-29	KJJK	105.72	110.85	114.57	115.21	117.83	121.90
30-39	KJJL	217.05	217.81	213.91	205.36	195.22	188.25
40-49	KJJM	278.53	285.90	290.72	291.36	289.94	289.71
50-59	KJJN	434.04	427.06	418.60	409.46	387.76	374.75
60-64	KJJO	310.75	303.64	296.10	288.93	288.85	281.25
65 and over	KJJP	0.03	0.04	0.02	0.02	0.03	0.30
Females							
All durations: All ages	KJJQ	969.44	990.84	998.20	994.33	988.93	982.33
Under 20	KJJR	21.49	21.48	20.51	18.92	17.86	16.79
20-29	KJJS	100.78	105.02	108.61	109.73	114.42	117.91
30-39	KJJT	177.70	177.91	173.45	167.36	162.39	156.95
40-49	KJJU	262.20	270.90	276.62	279.32	283.45	285.84
50-59	KJJV	407.24	415.52	418.99	418.99	410.80	404.82
60 and over	KJJW	0.03	0.02	0.02	0.02	0.02	0.02
Over six months: All ages	KJJX	858.03	880.52	894.57	896.33	885.69	881.59
Under 20	KJJY	12.35	12.40	12.10	11.13	10.20	9.55
20-29	KJJZ	79.63	84.02	88.98	90.99	93.60	97.24
30-39	KJKA	154.19	154.95	152.48	148.00	142.28	137.59
40-49	KJKB	234.71	243.52	250.11	253.50	255.99	258.74
50-59	KJKC	377.12	385.61	390.88	392.69	383.60	378.27
60 and over	KJKD	0.03	0.02	0.02	0.02	0.02	0.20
Unknown Gender							
All durations	EW44	0.44	0.31	0.26	0.15	0.13	0.12
Over 6 months	EW45	0.21	0.16	0.13	0.10	0.09	0.09

Definitions and conventions. Caseload figures are rounded to the nearest ten and displayed in thousands. Totals may not sum due to rounding.

1 See chapter text. Figures are given at May each year and are based on 100% Work and Pensions Longitudinal Study (WPLS) data.
2 Figures include overseas cases.
3 Table includes Incapacity Benefit ONLY claimants and not those claiming Severe Disablement Allowance (SDA).

Sources: Department for Work and Pensions;
Information and Analysis Directorate: 0191 225 7373

10.8 Sickness, Invalidity and Incapacity Benefit: days of certified incapacity

Great Britain analysis by age at end of period[1]

Years starting on first Monday in April[2]

Millions

		1992 /93	1993 /94	1994[3] /95	1995 /96	1996 /97	1997 /98	1998 /99	1999 /00	2000 /01	2001 /02	2002 /03
Age at 31 March[4]												
Males: All ages	KJKH	445.5	468.8	507.9	596.2	576.3	563.5	538.6	526.7	531.7	536.1	540.3
Under 20	KJKI	1.5	1.6	1.8	3.4	3.1	3.5	3.7	3.3	2.6	3.5	5.4
20 - 29	KJKJ	24.5	27.0	30.4	43.7	42.4	43.2	41.7	38.3	38.9	40.4	44.3
30 - 39	KJKK	41.4	46.6	56.0	72.3	73.9	77.7	78.2	75.8	81.3	84.0	85.1
40 - 49	KJKL	64.6	72.7	78.9	98.5	98.5	97.7	97.6	98.0	103.9	106.0	106.8
50 - 59	KJKM	121.7	129.8	141.4	172.0	170.7	172.2	170.0	161.9	165.9	168.5	168.1
60 - 64	KJKN	102.4	107.3	112.6	127.9	127.8	126.7	124.3	126.0	125.8	120.2	116.3
65 and over	KJKO	80.4	83.9	86.8	78.4	59.9	41.7	23.0	23.4	13.3	13.4	14.4
Females: All ages	KJKP	190.7	211.4	237.5	279.5	285.8	292.8	294.8	315.0	325.1	338.7	344.6
Under 20	KJKQ	2.1	2.4	2.6	4.8	4.1	4.4	4.5	4.0	3.5	3.9	5.4
20 - 29	KJKR	22.1	22.1	23.9	31.9	32.0	32.1	31.3	30.7	30.3	32.3	34.4
30 - 39	KJKS	28.5	32.7	37.6	48.0	49.8	51.4	53.4	54.9	58.9	59.9	61.3
40 - 49	KJKT	46.6	51.5	58.9	72.1	74.0	75.8	77.1	79.1	82.8	88.9	89.8
50 - 59	KJKU	71.3	79.1	88.4	101.0	107.5	115.3	120.0	134.3	142.2	145.9	146.0
60 and over	KJKV	20.1	23.6	26.1	21.7	18.4	13.8	8.4	12.0	7.3	7.9	7.7

1 See chapter text. The end of the statistical year up to 1993/94 was the Saturday before the first Monday in April.
2 Up to and including 1994/95 years start first Monday in April. The 1995/96 year started 13 April and ended 31 March. From 1996/97 years start 1 April.
3 The statistical year for 1994/95 was extended to 12 April 1995, the day before the introduction of the new Incapacity Benefit which replaced Sickness and Invalidity Benefit.
4 Until 1995/96 then at 1 March.

Sources: Department for Work and Pensions;
Taken from 1% extract;
Information and Analysis Directorate: 0191 225 7373

10.9 Child benefits[1,2]

Thousands

		Great Britain As at 31 December				United Kingdom As at 31 August							
		1997[3]	1998[3]	1999		2000	2001	2002	2003	2004	2005	2006	2007
Families receiving allowances:													
Total	KJMU	6 956	6 976	7 102	VOWX	7 340	7 335	7 336	7 342	7 353	7 375	7 441	7 530
With 1 child	KJMV	..	..	3 015	VOWY	3 128	3 143	3 162	3 189	3 219	3 260	3 329	3 414
2 children	KJMW	..	..	2 822	VOWZ	2 898	2 891	2 894	2 890	2 885	2 882	2 884	2 893
3 children	KJMX	..	..	943	VOXA	977	970	954	942	931	920	917	911
4 children	KJMY	..	..	241	VOXB	251	247	242	239	235	233	231	231
5 or more children	KJMZ	..	..	82	VOXC	86	84	83	82	82	80	80	81
Families receiving Guardian's Allowance	VOXG	2.3	2.3	2.3	VOXH	2.5	2.3	2.5	2.6	2.9	2.8	3.2	3.3

1 See chapter text.
2 Data for 2008 unavailable at time of printing.
3 Figures provided by Child Benefit Centre Management Information Statistics as a new scan was being developed.

Source: HM Revenue and Customs: 020 7147 3021

10.10 Family Credit/ Working Families' Tax Credit[1,2]

Thousands

		Great Britain As at 31 December						United Kingdom As at 30 November			
		1994	1995	1996	1997	1998		1999	2000	2001	2002
Families in receipt:											
Total	KJTO	578.0	646.5	716.7	751.4	779.7	ZCMK	965.3	1 167.8	1 293.7	1 377.3
Two-parent families: total	KJTP	324.6	356.9	390.2	388.0	383.4	ZCML	467.6	565.9	617.2	639.8
With 1 child	KJTQ	80.1	89.7	98.6	96.6	95.4	ZCMM	116.8	144.8	151.6	159.0
2 children	KJTR	122.4	135.1	146.1	144.4	141.7	ZCMN	178.4	220.1	243.5	252.7
3 children	KJTS	76.4	83.4	91.1	91.4	89.1	ZCMO	107.8	129.2	142.9	147.3
4 children or more children	ZIYM	45.8	48.6	54.4	55.6	57.3	ZCMP	64.6	71.8	79.2	80.8
One-parent families: total	KJTW	253.4	289.6	326.5	363.4	396.3	ZIYI	497.8	601.8	676.5	737.6
With 1 child	KJTX	133.8	152.2	170.4	189.3	203.4	ZIYJ	259.6	313.7	349.5	381.2
2 children	KJTY	86.0	99.1	111.2	121.8	136.1	ZIYK	169.6	207.6	238.7	261.6
3 or more children	KJTZ	33.5	38.3	45.0	52.3	56.9	ZIYL	68.6	80.5	88.3	94.8

1 See chapter text. Family Credit was replaced by Working Families Tax Credit (WFTC) in October 1999. The WFTC figures for December 1999 include Family Credit awards made before October 1999 and still current (both FC and WFTC awards last for 26 weeks).
2 WFTC was replaced by Child Credit and Working Tax Credit on 6th April 2003. See table 10.11.

Sources: Board of Inland Revenue: 020 7438 7370;
Department for Work and Pensions;
Information and Analysis Directorate: 0191 225 7373

10.11 In-work families with Child Tax Credit or Working Tax Credit awards
United Kingdom
As at December

Thousands

		2003[1]	2004	2005	2006	2007	2008
In-work families with positive award:	C5PF	4 423	4 519	4 538	4 526	4 541	4 630
With children	C5PG	4 208.0	4 261.0	4 218.0	4 204.0	4 189.0	4 205.0
Receiving Working Tax Credit and Child Tax Credit	C5PH	1 548.0	1 492.0	1 497.0	1 596.0	1 650.0	1 763.0
Receiving Child Tax Credit only	C5PI	2 660.0	2 769.0	2 721.0	2 608.0	2 539.0	2 442.0
Without children							
Working Tax Credit only	C5PL	215.0	258.0	320.0	323.0	352.0	426.0

1 Child and Working Tax Credits replaced Working Families' Tax Credit on 6th April 2003. Figures for 2003 are based on awards current at 5th January 2004. All other figures at December each year. See chapter text.

Source: HM Revenue and Customs: 020 7147 3083

10.12 Widows' Benefit (excluding bereavement payment[1,2,3]): by type of benefit Great Britain

Number in receipt of widows benefit as at May 2008

Thousands

		2003	2004	2005	2006	2007	2008
All Widows' Benefit (excluding bereavement allowance)							
All ages	KJGA	191.50	163.40	139.00	117.70	96.89	77.90
Unknown Age	EW4O	0.10	–	–	–	0.02	–
18 - 24	EW4P	–	–	–	–	–	–
25 - 29	EW4Q	0.30	0.20	0.10	0.10	0.04	0.02
30 - 34	EW4R	1.70	1.20	0.80	0.50	0.32	0.20
35 - 39	EW4S	5.10	3.90	2.90	2.10	1.53	1.08
40 - 44	EW4T	9.10	7.50	6.10	4.90	3.93	3.04
45 - 49	EW4U	16.30	13.20	11.00	9.10	7.58	6.26
50 - 54	EW4V	40.60	33.30	26.90	21.80	17.69	14.42
55 - 59	EW4W	90.90	77.70	66.90	57.30	45.78	36.86
60 - 64	EW4X	27.40	26.40	24.30	21.80	20.01	16.01
Widowed parents' allowance - with dependant children							
All ages	KJGG	34.2	28.2	23.2	19.0	15.6	12.6
Unknown Age	EW4Y	0.1	–	–	–	–	–
18 - 24	EW4Z	–	–	–	–	–	–
25 - 29	EW52	0.30	0.20	0.10	0.10	0.03	0.02
30 - 34	EW53	1.60	1.10	0.80	0.50	0.31	0.19
35 - 39	EW54	4.90	3.80	2.80	2.10	1.49	1.05
40 - 44	EW55	8.40	7.00	5.70	4.60	3.75	2.92
45 - 49	EW56	9.30	7.80	6.70	5.60	4.71	3.87
50 - 54	EW57	6.60	5.70	4.80	4.10	3.58	3.10
55 - 59	EW58	2.70	2.30	2.00	1.80	1.57	1.33
60 - 64	EW59	0.30	0.30	0.30	0.20	0.17	0.13
Widowed parents' allowance - without dependant children							
All ages	KJGM	1.80	1.40	1.10	0.80	0.69	0.54
Unknown Age	EW5A	–	–	–	–	–	–
18 - 24	EW5B	–	–	–	–	–	–
25 - 29	EW5C	–	–	–	–	–	–
30 - 34	EW5D	–	–	–	–	0.01	0.01
35 - 39	EW5E	0.20	0.10	0.10	0.10	0.04	0.03
40 - 44	EW5F	0.40	0.30	0.20	0.20	0.13	0.09
45 - 49	EW5G	0.50	0.40	0.30	0.20	0.21	0.17
50 - 54	EW5H	0.50	0.30	0.30	0.20	0.17	0.13
55 - 59	EW5I	0.30	0.20	0.20	0.10	0.11	0.10
60 - 64	EW5J	0.10	–	–	–	0.02	0.01
Age -related bereavement allowance							
All ages	KJGS	124.30	110.10	96.60	84.00	70.13	57.37
Unknown Age	EW5K	–	–	–	–	0.01	–
18 - 24	EW5L	–	–	–	–	–	–
25 - 29	EW5M	–	–	–	–	–	–
30 - 34	EW5N	–	–	–	–	–	–
35 - 39	EW5O	–	–	–	–	–	–
40 - 44	EW5P	0.20	0.20	0.20	0.10	0.06	0.03
45 - 49	EW5Q	6.60	5.10	4.00	3.30	2.66	2.23
50 - 54	EW5R	32.80	26.70	21.40	17.20	13.75	11.08
55 - 59	EW5S	73.50	66.30	59.00	50.90	40.57	32.61
60 - 64	EW5T	11.20	11.90	12.00	12.50	13.08	11.42
Bereavement allowance (Not age related)							
All ages	KJGW	31.30	23.70	18.10	13.90	10.47	7.39
Unknown Age	EW5U	–	–	–	–	–	–
18 - 24	EW5V	–	–	–	–	–	–
25 - 29	EW5W	–	–	–	–	–	–
30 - 34	EW5X	–	–	–	–	–	–
35 - 39	EW5Y	–	–	–	–	–	–
40 - 44	EW5Z	–	–	–	–	–	–
45 - 49	EW62	–	–	–	–	–	–
50 - 54	EW63	0.80	0.60	0.50	0.30	0.20	0.11
55 - 59	EW64	14.40	8.80	5.60	4.40	3.53	2.82
60 - 64	EW65	16.00	14.20	12.00	9.10	6.74	4.45

1 Definitions and Conventions: "-" Nil or Negligible; "." Not applicable; Caseload figures are rounded to the nearest hundred and displayed in thousands.

2 Caseload (Thousands) All Claimants of Widows Benefit are female. No new claims for WB have been accepted since April 2001 when it was replaced by Bereavement Benefit.

3 Figures include overseas cases.

Sources: DWP Information Directorate: Work and Pensions Longitudinal Study 100% data;
Information and Analysis Directorate: 0191 225 7373

10.13 Bereavement Benefit[1,2] (excluding bereavement payment): by sex, type of benefit and age of widow/er

Great Britain.

Thousands

		Males				Females		
		2006	2007	2008		2006	2007	2008
All Bereavement Benefit (excluding bereavement allowance)								
All ages	WLSX	17.97	17.77	17.82	WLTC	39.69	40.77	42.04
18 - 24	EVW9	..	..	..	EVY2	0.09	0.07	0.08
25 - 29	EVX2	0.05	0.05	0.06	EVY3	0.49	0.53	0.53
30 - 34	EVX3	0.33	0.28	0.25	EVY4	1.67	1.63	1.66
35 - 39	EVX4	1.20	1.15	1.11	EVY5	3.82	4.05	4.31
40 - 44	EVX5	2.60	2.50	2.50	EVY6	6.49	7.01	7.33
45 - 49	EVX6	3.46	3.61	3.69	EVY7	8.14	8.92	9.54
50 - 54	EVX7	3.43	3.47	3.51	EVY8	8.32	8.65	9.10
55 - 59	EVX8	3.70	3.43	3.33	EVY9	10.67	9.90	9.49
60 - 64	EVX9	3.20	3.29	3.36	EVZ2	..	..	..
Widowed parents' allowance - with dependant children								
All ages	WLUD	11.05	11.27	11.51	WLUH	24.40	26.86	29.18
18 - 24	EVZ3	..	..	..	EW24	0.09	0.07	0.08
25 - 29	EVZ4	0.05	0.05	0.06	EW25	0.47	0.52	0.52
30 - 34	EVZ5	0.33	0.28	0.25	EW26	1.65	1.61	1.64
35 - 39	EVZ6	1.20	1.14	1.11	EW27	3.77	4.01	4.27
40 - 44	EVZ7	2.58	2.48	2.49	EW28	6.41	6.93	7.25
45 - 49	EVZ8	2.94	3.13	3.26	EW29	6.31	7.23	7.99
50 - 54	EVZ9	2.25	2.36	2.48	EW2A	4.04	4.61	5.29
55 - 59	EW22	1.24	1.29	1.32	EW2B	1.67	1.89	2.14
60 - 64	EW23	0.46	0.53	0.54	EW2C	..	..	..
Widowed parents' allowance without dependant children								
All ages	WLVK	0.06	0.05	0.04	WMMR	0.37	0.34	0.32
18 - 24	EW2D	..	..	..	EW2M	..	..	..
25 - 29	EW2E	..	..	..	EW2N	0.01	0.01	0.01
30 - 34	EW2F	..	..	..	EW2O	0.03	0.02	0.02
35 - 39	EW2G	0.01	0.01	..	EW2P	0.05	0.05	0.04
40 - 44	EW2H	0.02	0.02	0.01	EW2Q	0.08	0.08	0.08
45 - 49	EW2I	0.02	0.01	0.01	EW2R	0.08	0.08	0.09
50 - 54	EW2J	0.01	0.01	0.01	EW2S	0.07	0.06	0.05
55 - 59	EW2K	0.01	0.01	..	EW2T	0.04	0.04	0.04
60 - 64	EW2L	..	..	..	EW2U	..	..	..
Age-related bereavement allowance								
All ages	WMOB	1.87	1.71	1.59	WMOC	6.58	6.17	5.76
18 - 24	EW2V	..	..	..	EW36	..	..	..
25 - 29	EW2W	..	..	..	EW37	..	..	..
30 - 34	EW2X	..	..	..	EW38	..	..	..
35 - 39	EW2Y	..	..	..	EW39	..	..	..
40 - 44	EW2Z	..	..	..	EW3A	..	..	..
45 - 49	EW32	0.50	0.46	0.42	EW3B	1.75	1.61	1.46
50 - 54	EW33	1.17	1.10	1.03	EW3C	4.21	3.97	3.76
55 - 59	EW34	0.20	0.15	0.14	EW3D	0.62	0.58	0.54
60 - 64	EW35	..	..	..	EW3E	..	..	..
Bereavement allowance (not age related)								
All ages	WMOX	4.98	4.74	4.68	WMOY	8.34	7.39	6.77
18 - 24	EW3F	..	..	..	EW3O	..	..	..
25 - 29	EW3G	..	..	..	EW3P	..	..	..
30 - 34	EW3H	..	..	..	EW3Q	..	..	..
35 - 39	EW3I	..	..	..	EW3R	..	..	..
40 - 44	EW3J	..	..	..	EW3S	..	..	..
45 - 49	EW3K	..	..	..	EW3T	..	..	..
50 - 54	EW3L	..	..	..	EW3U	..	..	..
55 - 59	EW3M	2.24	1.98	1.86	EW3V	8.34	7.39	6.77
60 - 64	EW3N	2.74	2.76	2.81	EW3W	..	..	..

1 Figures include overseas cases.
2 Figures are given at May each year and are taken from the DWP 100% Work and Pensions Longitudinal Study (WPLS).

Source: DWP Information Directorate: 0191 225 7874

10.14 Contributory and non-contributory retirement pensions:[1,2] by sex and age of claimant

Great Britain and Overseas. At May each year.

Thousands and percentages

		2004	2005	2006	2007	2008
Men:						
Age-groups:						
65-69	KJSB	1 354.30	1 364.10	1 341.50	1 332.77	1 350.61
Percentage	KJSC	*31.60*	*31.40*	*30.60*	*30.03*	*29.84*
70-74	KJSD	1 140.30	1 150.00	1 160.10	1 177.96	1 205.70
Percentage	KJSE	*26.60*	*26.50*	*26.50*	*26.54*	*26.63*
75-79	KJSF	875.00	887.10	903.00	918.47	932.17
Percentage	KJSG	*20.40*	*20.40*	*20.60*	*20.70*	*20.59*
80-84	KJSH	593.70	593.30	596.90	604.74	614.77
Percentage	KJSI	*13.90*	*13.70*	*13.60*	*13.63*	*13.58*
85-89	KJSJ	221.40	246.40	273.10	296.36	317.90
Percentage	KJSK	*5.20*	*5.70*	*6.20*	*6.68*	*7.02*
90 and over	KJSL	95.50	100.20	103.60	106.13	105.33
Percentage	KJSM	*2.20*	*2.30*	*2.40*	*2.39*	*2.33*
Unknown age	EW3Y	0.80	1.10	1.20	1.45	0.19
Percentage	EW3Z	*–*	*–*	*–*	*–*	*..*
Total all ages	KJSA	4 281.10	4 342.20	4 379.50	4 437.99	4 526.79
Women:						
Age-groups:						
60-64	KJSO	1 451.30	1 498.70	1 524.00	1 628.19	1 695.88
Percentage	KJSP	*20.30*	*20.80*	*21.00*	*21.98*	*22.47*
65-69	KJSQ	1 452.70	1 464.20	1 453.10	1 456.08	1 484.80
Percentage	KJSR	*20.40*	*20.30*	*20.00*	*19.65*	*19.67*
70-74	KJSS	1 319.20	1 314.50	1 312.70	1 322.14	1 343.22
Percentage	KJST	*18.50*	*18.20*	*18.10*	*17.85*	*17.80*
75-79	KJSU	1 156.70	1 158.60	1 165.50	1 168.86	1 170.01
Percentage	KJSV	*16.20*	*16.10*	*16.00*	*15.78*	*15.50*
80-84	KJSW	973.90	951.60	933.30	923.70	919.11
Percentage	KJSX	*13.60*	*13.20*	*12.90*	*12.47*	*12.18*
85-89	KJSY	473.10	511.00	552.70	587.91	621.15
Percentage	KJSZ	*6.60*	*7.10*	*7.60*	*7.94*	*8.23*
90 and over	KJTA	307.20	314.90	319.40	319.90	313.66
Percentage	KJTB	*4.30*	*4.40*	*4.40*	*4.32*	*4.16*
Unknown age	EW42	1.10	1.30	1.50	1.67	0.37
Percentage	EW43	*–*	*–*	*–*	*–*	*..*
Total all ages	KJSN	7 135.10	7 214.70	7 262.30	7 408.44	7 548.20

1 See chapter text.
2 Caseloads include both contributory and non-contributory state pensioners.

Sources: Department for Work and Pensions;
Work and Pensions Longitudinal Study (WPLS);
Information and Analysis Directorate: 0191 225 7373

10.15 War pensions: estimated number of pensioners[1]
Great Britain

At 31 March each year

Thousands

		1998	1999	2000	2001	2002	2003	2004	2005	2006[2]	2007	2008
Disablement	KADH	259.16	248.93	240.76	231.62	221.80	212.18	201.55	191.75	182.80	173.85	165.17
Widows and dependants	KADI	58.49	55.85	54.92	52.71	50.98	48.61	46.04	43.55	41.05	38.69	36.10
Total	KADG	317.65	306.06	295.67	284.33	272.78	260.79	247.59	235.30	223.85	212.54	201.27

1 See chapter text. From 1914 war, 1939 war and later service.
2 The discontinuity between 2005 and 2006 is due to improvements in data processing.

Source: Ministry of Defence/DASA (Health Information): 01225 467801

10.16 Income support[1] (excluding MIG)[2] by statistical group[3]: number of claimants receiving weekly payment
Great Britain

Thousands[4]

		2003	2004	2005	2006	2007	2008
All income support claimants (excluding MIG)[5]	F8YY	2 236.4	2 192.6	2 139.8	2 114.8	2 117.7	2 091.5
Incapacity Benefits	F8YZ	1 215.1	1 205.2	1 193.8	1 183.2	1 184.7	1 182.5
Lone Parent	F8Z2	853.3	823.3	789.3	774.9	765.6	738.6
Carer	F8Z3	77.50	78.40	79.00	80.20	82.80	85.70
Others on Income Related Benefits	F8Z4	90.50	85.90	77.70	76.50	84.60	84.70

1 Figures are given at May each year and are taken from the DWP 100% Work and Pensions Longitudinal Study (WPLS).
2 Figures exclude MIG claimants. Pension Credit replaced MIG on 6th October 2003 and extended Income Support entitlements to customers aged 60 and over.
3 Statistical groups are defined as follows:
Incapacity Benefits- claimants aged under 60 on Incapacity Benefit or Severe Disablement Allowance;
Lone Parent - single claimants aged under 60 with dependants not in receipt of IB/SDA;
Carer- claimants aged under 60 entitled to Carer's Allowance;
Other Income Related Benefit- claimants not in one of the above categories.
4 Figures are rounded to the nearest hundred and quoted in thousands.
5 Totals may not sum due to rounding.

Sources: Department for Work and Pensions;
Information and Analysis Directorate: 0191 225 7373

10.17 MIG/Pension Credit[1,2]: number of claimants
Great Britain

End of May

Thousands[3]

		2003[4]	2004[5]	2005	2006	2007	2008
All Pension Credit	F8Z5	..	2 490.8	2 682.7	2 717.4	2 733.5	2 719.1
Guarantee Credit Only	F8Z6	..	735.0	767.3	775.6	805.7	882.1
Guarantee Credit Only and Savings Credit	F8Z7	..	1 269.5	1 321.7	1 343.2	1 330.1	1 246.2
Savings Credit	F8Z8	..	486.0	593.7	598.6	597.7	590.8
(Residual)[6] MIG Case	F8Z9	1 777.8	0.3	–	–	–	–

1 Source: DWP 100% Work and Pensions Longitudinal study (WPLS).
2 Pension Credit was introduced on 6th October 2003 and replaced Monthly Income Guarantee (Income Support for people aged 60 or over). The vast majority of people who were in receipt of MIG transferred to PC in October 2003.
3 Figures are rounded to the nearest hundred and expressed in thousands.
4 Columns 2002 - 2003 represent MIG caseloads.
5 Columns 2004 onwards represent Pension Credit Caseloads.
6 When MIG was replaced by Pension Credit in October 2003 some cases continued to be MIG cases. These were cases where the partner aged under 60 continued as the claimant. These cases are minimal and are reducing each quarter.

Sources: Department for Work and Pensions;
Information and Analysis Directorate: 0191 225 7373

10.18 Income support: average weekly amounts of benefit[1,2]
Great Britain
As at May

£ per week

		2003	2004	2005	2006	2007	2008
All income support claimants (excluding MIG)[3]	F8ZF	91.07	91.14	85.81	83.41	82.29	82.35
Incapacity benefits[4]	F8ZG	76.10	77.70	76.93	78.12	79.78	81.55
Lone Parent[4]	F8ZH	116.52	114.96	102.85	94.88	89.70	87.37
Carer[4]	F8ZI	76.63	76.78	72.42	70.40	69.97	69.28
Others on income related benefits[4]	F8ZJ	64.43	64.25	62.69	62.62	62.33	62.87

1 Figures are given at May each year and are taken from the DWP 100% Work and Pensions Longitudinal Study (WPLS).

2 Average amounts are rounded to the nearest penny.

3 Figures exclude MIG claimants. Pension Credit replaced MIG on 6 October 2003 and extended Income Support entitlement to customers aged 60 and over.

4 Statistical groups are defined as follows:
Incapacity Benefits- claimants under 60 on incapacity benefit or Severe Disablement Allowance;
Lone Parent- single claimants aged under 60 with dependants not in receipt of IB/SDA;
Carer- claimants aged under 60 entitled to Carer's Allowance;
Other Income Related Benefit- claimants not in one of the above categories.

Sources: Department for Work and Pensions; Information and Analysis Directorate: 0191 225 7373

10.19 MIG/Pension Credit: average weekly amounts of benefit[1,2]
Great Britain
As at May

£ per week[3]

		2003[4]	2004[5]	2005	2006	2007	2008
All Pension Credit	F8ZA	..	42.30	43.62	46.75	50.04	52.69
Guarantee Credit Only	F8ZB	..	71.91	75.43	79.56	83.74	85.07
Guarantee Credit and Savings Credit	F8ZC	..	37.51	39.87	43.11	46.11	48.29
Savings Credit only	F8ZD	..	10.03	10.83	12.39	13.36	13.62
(Residual) MIG Case[6]	F8ZE	50.37	47.49	68.89	110.60	110.49	111.05

1 Figures are given in each May from 2000 - 2005 and are taken from the DWP 100% Work and Pensions Longitudinal Study (WPLS).

2 Pension Credit was introduced on 6th October 2003 and replaced Minimum Income Guarantee (Income Support for people aged 60 or over).

3 Average amounts are shown as pounds per week and rounded to the nearest penny.

4 Columns 2002-2003 represent MIG average amounts.

5 Columns 2004 onwards represent Pension Credit Average amounts.

6 When pension credit replaced MIG in October 2003 some cases continued to be MIG cases. These were cases where a partner aged under 60 continued as the claimant. These cases are minimal and are reducing each quarter.

Sources: Department for Work and Pensions; Information and Analysis Directorate: 0191 225 7373

10.20 Summary of government expenditure on social services and housing[1]
Years ended 31 March

£ million

		1999 /00	2000 /01	2001 /02	2002 /03	2003 /04	2004 /05	2005 /06	2006 /07
Final Consumption Expenditure									
Education	QYWZ	43 044	46 933	52 752	57 475	61 983	65 653	68 530	75 002
Health	QYXA	52 901	57 362	62 727	69 065	75 585	83 989	90 394	96 889
Personal social services	GB7F	12 659	13 717	15 033	17 232	19 930	21 922	23 239	24 217
Social benefits	GG5O	106 998	110 417	121 098	126 345	135 571	141 612	145 616	150 614
Housing	QYXD	6 168	6 387	6 590	7 236	10 802	11 222	12 294	13 707
Total government expenditure	GH2K	221 770	234 816	258 200	277 353	303 871	324 398	341 630	361 059
Total government expenditure on social services and housing as a percentage of GDP	GGN7	24.1	24.4	25.6	26.1	27.0	27.2	27.8	27.4

1 See chapter text.

Source: Office for National Statistics: 0207 014 2125

10.21 Summary of Government expenditure on education[1]
Years ended 31 March

£ million

		1999 /00	2000 /01	2001 /02	2002 /03	2003 /04	2004 /05	2005 /06	2006 /07
Education									
Final consumption expenditure									
Current expenditure									
Compensation of employees									
Local Authorities[2]									
Nursery and primary schools	G8ZX	8 396	9 092	10 079	10 740	11 955	13 132	13 879	14 638
Secondary schools	G8ZY	7 991	8 652	9 592	10 356	11 570	13 115	13 891	14 651
Special schools	G8ZZ	858	929	1 030	1 164	1 145	1 362	1 746	1 842
Central Government									
Northern Ireland wages and salaries	HMPM	666	709	769	841	928	959	997	1 251
Other wages and salaries[3]	GB7H	275	297	463	529	610	661	703	872
Total Central Government expenditure	MMTF	941	1 006	1 232	1 370	1 538	1 620	1 700	2 123
Tertiary Education & Other Education[4]	G922	3 284	3 569	3 840	4 127	3 728	2 553	2 524	2 332
Total Compensation of employees	QYSA	21 470	23 248	25 773	27 757	29 936	31 782	33 446	35 586
Net procurement									
Local Government Net procurement[5]	QTKJ	5 839	6 154	6 407	7 620	7 785	8 418	9 741	10 726
Central Government Net procurement[6]	QTLN	1 560	1 737	1 623	1 787	1 933	2 020	2 186	2 445
Nursery/Primary schools									
secondary schools									
Tertiary education									
Total	QYSB	7 399	7 891	8 030	9 407	9 718	10 438	10 670	13 171
Non-market capital consumption	QYSD	1 108	1 142	1 200	1 248	1 305	1 409	1 568	1 778
Total final consumption expenditure	QYSE	29 846	32 116	34 711	38 039	40 640	43 580	69 985	50 535
Other current transfers	QZNU	11 061	12 123	14 315	15 407	17 050	17 862	17 321	18 531
Gross capital formation	QYVD	1 843	2 188	2 863	2 753	2 936	3 094	3 853	4 766
Non-produced non-financial assets	QYWM	−167	−151	−187	−191	−206	−217	−229	−240
Capital transfers	QZKJ	000	492	758	1 094	1 244	1 285	1 907	2 040
Total Central Government Expediture	G924	15 584	17 411	20 623	22 239	24 519	25 690	26 769	30 705
Total Local Government Expediture	G925	27 460	29 522	32 129	35 236	37 464	39 963	43 318	44 927
Total government expenditure	QYWZ	43 044	46 933	52 752	57 475	61 983	65 653	68 536	75 632
Total government education expenditure as a percentage of GDP	GGN8	4.7	4.9	5.2	5.4	5.5	5.5	5.7	5.8

1 See chapter text.
2 Based on pay figures published by Dept for Communities and Local Government , Scottish Executive and National Assembly for Wales.
3 Includes wages/salaries for Scotland, Wales and Non-Departmental Public Bodies (NDPBs).
4 Includes Higher, Further, Adult and Continuing education.
5 Net of VAT.
6 Includes Central Government Net Procurement on NDPBs, Scotland, Wales, Northern Ireland and Education in Healthcare.

Sources: Office for National Statistics: 0207 014 2125; Department for Communities and Local Government; Scottish Government; Welsh Assembly Government

Social protection

10.22 Summary of Government expenditure on Health[1]
Years ended 31 March

£ million

		1999 /00	2000 /01	2001 /02	2002 /03	2003 /04	2004 /05	2005 /06	2006 /07
Final Consumption expenditure[2]									
Current expenditure[3]									
Compensation of employees	QWWQ	26 560	28 794	31 470	34 954	38 140	42 574	45 069	46 430
non-market capital consumption	QYOB	1 492	1 593	1 574	1 680	1 787	1 884	2 113	2 342
other	QTLP	22 413	23 954	26 155	28 407	31 218	34 446	40 712	42 383
Total Final consumption expenditure	QYOT	50 465	54 341	59 199	65 041	71 145	78 904	87 126	91 155
Subsidies	CBRA	–	28	34	33	21	21	21	38
other current transfers	QZMR	931	1 277	1 312	1 171	1 220	1 248	1 658	1 452
Grosss capital formation	QYVE	1 440	1 643	2 067	2 581	3 049	3 727	3 215	4 063
Non produced non financial assets	QYWN	–	–	–	–	–	–	–	–
Capital transfers	HMSF	65	73	115	239	150	89	169	181
total outlays	QYXA	52 901	57 362	62 727	69 065	75 585	83 989	90 394	96 889
Total NHS expenditure as a percentage of GDP	GGN9	5.8	5.9	6.2	6.5	6.7	7.1	7.2	7.3

1 See chapter text.
2 Figures are based on Departmental Expenditure reported to HM Treasury Statistics database.
3 Includes expenditure by Dept. of Health, NHS Trusts, Scottish Government, Welsh Assembly Government and Northern Ireland Executive.

Source: Office for National Statistics: 0208 014 2125

10.23 Summary of Government expenditure on personal social services[1]
Years ended 31 March

£ million

		1999 /00	2000 /01	2001 /02	2002 /03	2003 /04	2004 /05	2005 /06	2006 /07
Personal social services									
Central government Current Expenditure									
Compensation of employees	ADQ7	282	318	331	376	462	482	508	541
Net Procurement	ADR2	252	311	343	532	489	667	410	395
Total	GB7D	534	629	674	908	951	1 149	918	936
Local Authorities Current Expenditure									
Compensation of employees	CFCR	5 735	5 760	5 936	6 385	6 960	7 506	7 959	8 278
Net Procurement	QWSB	6 326	7 259	8 349	9 859	11 934	13 165	14 244	14 863
Total	GB7E	12 061	13 019	14 285	16 244	18 894	20 671	22 203	23 141
Capital Expenditure	GDZU	64	69	74	80	85	102	118	140
Total Final Consumption Expenditure	GB7F	12 659	13 717	15 033	17 232	19 930	21 922	23 239	24 217
Total government expenditure as a percentage of GDP	GGO2	1.4	1.4	1.5	1.6	1.8	1.8	1.9	1.8

1 See chapter text.

Source: Office for National Statistics: 0208 014 2125

10.24 Summary of Government expenditure on social security benefits[1] and administration

Years ended 31 March

£ million

		2000 /01	2001 /02	2002 /03	2003 /04	2004 /05	2005 /06	2006 /07	2007 /08
Social benefits									
Social security benefits in cash									
National Insurance fund									
Retirement pensions	CSDG	38 923	42 157	44 590	46 699	48 968	51 579	53 766	57 775
Widows and Guardians allowances	CSDH	980	1 099	1 093	1 006	923	873	792	725
Unemployment Benefit	CSDI	−1	−	−2	−1	−	−3	−	−
Jobseeker's Allowance	CJTJ	435	470	520	507	445	486	474	390
Incapacity Benefit	CUNL	6 677	6 678	6 839	6 779	6 673	6 635	6 563	6 565
Maternity Benefit	CSDL	45	56	69	125	150	164	175	246
Statutory sick pay	CSDQ	29	22	18	72	75	80	85	..
Statutory maternity pay	GTKZ	635	665	737	1 261	1 339	1 295	1 303	..
Payment in lieu of benefits foregone	GTKV	−	−	−	−	−	−	−	..
Total national insurance fund benefits	ACHH	47 723	51 147	53 864	56 471	58 657	61 109	63 158	
Redundancy fund benefit	GTKN	168	205	280	240	186	253	205	..
Maternity fund benefit	GTKO	−	−	−	−	−	−	−	−
Social fund benefit	GTLQ	1 784	1 883	1 925	2 159	2 200	2 249	2 279	2 334
Benefits paid to overseas residents	FJVZ	1 176	1 262	1 357	1 445	1 522	1 607	1 724	..
Total social security benefits in cash	QYRJ	50 851	54 497	57 426	60 296	62 489	65 218	67 366	71 395
Total unfunded social benefits[2]:	QYJT	12 445	13 728	14 539	15 962	15 676	18 083	19 365	..
Social assistance benefits in cash									
War pensions and allowances[3]	CSDD	1 201	1 200	1 186	1 089	1 068	1 009	983	1 016
Income Support	CSDE	13 076	14 100	14 527	15 106	16 356	15 506	15 616	..
Income tax credits and reliefs	RYCQ	4 654	5 745	6 711	9 485	11 566	12 938	14 316	15 642
Child benefit	EKY3	8 532	8 795	8 955	9 414	9 565	9 756	10 132	..
Non-contributory job seekers allowance	EKY4	2 442	2 124	2 118	2 062	1 780	1 890	2 082	..
Care allowances	EKY5	2 955	5 096	5 214	5 445	5 714	6 218	6 487	..
Disability benefits	EKY6	6 021	7 310	7 863	8 389	8 900	9 376	9 997	..
Other benefits	EKY7	4 360	4 387	3 924	4 473	4 554	5 574	4 222	..
Benefits paid to overseas residents	RNNF	54	55	48	48	48	48	48	..
Total social assistance benefits in cash	NZGO	43 295	48 812	50 546	55 522	59 597	62 315	63 883	..
Total social benefits	NMDR	106 591	117 037	122 511	131 822	138 217	145 616	150 614	159 265
Administration[4]	KJEE	3 826	4 061	3 834	3 772	3 774	−	−	..
Total benefits and administration	GG5O	110 417	121 098	126 345	135 571	141 612	145 616	150 614	..
Total government benefit expenditure as a percentage of GDP	GGO3	11.5	11.2	11.9	12.0	11.9	11.7	11.4	..

1 See chapter text. Figures are based on table 5.2.4s of the Blue Book 2007. They are not fully comparable with earlier editions of the Annual Abstract.
2 Includes Civil & Defence, voluntary employer social contributions, teachers & NHS inflationary pensions increase payments.
3 From 2002/03 War Pensions are administered by the Ministry of Defence.
4 Figures published by HM Treasury in Public Expenditure Statistical Analyses. A separate figure for administration is no longer published.

Sources: Office for National Statistics: 0208 014 2125; Department for Work and Pensions; HM Treasury

Social protection

10.25 Summary of Government expenditure on housing[1]
Years ended 31 March

£ million

		1999 /00	2000 /01	2001 /02	2002 /03	2003 /04	2004 /05	2005 /06	2006 /07
Housing									
Final consumption expenditure									
Compensation of employees	QYSV	748	776	851	985	1 077	1 172	1 359	1 599
Other current expenditure on goods and services	QYSW	709	935	1 068	1 295	3 023	2 940	3 636	4 195
Capital consumption	QYSY	1 117	1 181	1 301	1 407	1 454	1 632	1 563	1 596
Total	QYSZ	2 574	2 892	3 220	3 687	5 554	5 744	6 558	7 390
Subsidies	QYVP	798	759	613	611	495	302	478	554
Other current transfers	QZNY	30	42	129	93	539	119	227	249
Gross Fixed Capital Formation	QYVH	312	434	497	552	1 184	1 408	1 458	1 598
Non-produced financial assets	QYWQ	–	–	–	–	–	–	–	–
Capital transfers	GVFX	2 454	2 260	2 131	2 293	3 030	3 649	3 573	3 916
Total government expenditure	QYXD	6 168	6 387	6 590	7 236	10 802	11 222	12 294	13 707
Total public sector housing expenditure as a percentage of GDP	GGO4	0.7	0.7	0.7	0.7	1.0	1.0	1.0	1.0

1 See chapter text.

Source: Office for National Statistics: 0208 014 2125

Crime and Justice

Chapter 11

Crime and Justice

There are differences in the legal and judicial systems of England and Wales, Scotland and Northern Ireland which make it impossible to provide tables covering the UK as a whole in this section. These differences concern the classification of offences, the meaning of certain terms used in the statistics, the effects of the several Criminal Justice Acts and recording practices.

Recorded crime statistics

(Table 11.3)

Crimes recorded by the police provide a measure of the amount of crime committed. The statistics are based on counting rules, revised with effect from 1 April 1998, which are standard for all the police forces in England, Wales and Northern Ireland and now include all indictable and triable-either-way offences together with a few summary offences which are closely linked to these offences. The new rules have changed the emphasis of measurement more towards one crime per victim, and have also increased the coverage of offences. These changes have particularly impacted on the offence groups of violence against the person, fraud and forgery, drugs offences and other offences.

For a variety of reasons many offences are either not reported to the police or not recorded by them. The changes in the number of offences recorded do not necessarily provide an accurate reflection of changes in the amount of crime committed.

In order to further improve the consistency of recorded crime statistics and to take a more victim oriented approach to crime recording, the National Crime Recording Standard (NCRS) was introduced across all forces in England, Wales and Northern Ireland from 1 April 2002. Some police forces implemented the principles of NCRS in advance of its introduction across all forces. The NCRS had the effect of increasing the number of offences recorded by the police.

Similarly, the Scottish Crime Recording Standard (SCRS) was introduced by the eight Scottish police forces with effect from 1 April 2004. This means that no corroborative evidence is required initially to record a crime-related incident as a crime if so perceived by the victim. Again, the introduction of this new recording standard was expected to increase the numbers of minor crimes recorded by the police, such as minor crimes of vandalism and minor thefts and offences of petty assault and breach of the peace. However, it was expected that the SCRS would not have much impact on the figures for the more serious crimes such as serious assault, sexual assault, robbery or housebreaking.

The Sexual Offences Act 2003 introduced in May 2004 altered the definition and coverage of sexual offences. In particular, it redefined indecent exposure as a sexual offence, which is likely to account for much of the increase in sexual offences.

Further information is available from *Crime in England and Wales 2007/2008* (Home Office, Sian Nicholas, Chris Kershaw and Alison Walker, editors).

Court proceedings and police cautions

(Tables 11.4 to 11.8, 11.13 to 11.17, 11.20 to 11.22)

The statistical basis of the tables of court proceedings is broadly similar in England and Wales, Scotland and Northern Ireland; the tables show the number of persons found guilty, recording a person under the heading of the principal offence of which they were found guilty, excluding additional findings of guilt at the same proceedings. A person found guilty at a number of separate court proceedings is included more than once.

The statistics on offenders cautioned in England and Wales cover only those who, on admission of guilt, were given a formal caution by, or on the instructions of, a senior police officer as an alternative to prosecution. Written warnings by the police for motor offences and persons paying fixed penalties for certain motoring offences are excluded. Formal cautions are not issued in Scotland. There are no statistics on cautioning available for Northern Ireland.

The Crime and Disorder Act 1998 created provisions in relation to reprimands and final warnings, new offences and orders which have been implemented nationally since 1 June 2000. They replace the system of cautioning for offenders aged under 18. Reprimands can be given to first-time offenders for minor offences. Any further offending results in either a final warning or a charge.

For persons proceeded against in Scotland, the statistics relate to the High Court of Justiciary, the sheriff courts and the district courts. The High Court deals with serious solemn (that is, Jury) cases and has unlimited sentencing power. Sheriff courts are limited to imprisonment of 3 years for solemn cases, or 3 months (6 months when specified in legislation for second or subsequent offences and 12 months for certain statutory offences) for summary (that is, non-Jury) cases. District courts deal only with summary cases and are limited to 60 days imprisonment and level 4 fines. Stipendiary magistrates sit in Glasgow District Court and have the summary sentencing powers of a sheriff.

In England and Wales, indictable offences are offences which are:

- *triable only on indictment*. These offences are the most serious breaches of the criminal law and must be tried at the Crown Court. 'Indictable-only' offences include murder, manslaughter, rape and robbery

- *triable either way*. These offences may be tried at the Crown Court or a magistrates' court

The Criminal Justice Act 1991 led to the following main changes in the sentences available to the courts in England and Wales:

- introduction of combination orders

- introduction of the 'unit fine scheme' at magistrates' courts

- abolishing the sentence of detention in a young offender institution for 14-year-old boys and changing the minimum and maximum sentence lengths for 15 to 17-year-olds to 10 and 12 months respectively, and

- abolishing partly suspended sentences of imprisonment and restricting the use of a fully suspended sentence

The Criminal Justice Act 1993 abolished the 'unit fine scheme' in magistrates' courts, which had been introduced under the Criminal Justice Act 1991.

A *charging standard for assault* was introduced in England and Wales on 31 August 1994 with the aim of promoting consistency between the police and prosecution on the appropriate level of charge to be brought.

The Criminal Justice and Public Order Act 1994 created several new offences in England and Wales, mainly in the area of public order, but also including male rape (there is no statutory offence of male rape in Scotland, although such a crime may be charged as serious assault). The Act also:

- extended the provisions of section 53 of the Children and Young Persons Act 1993 for 10 to 13-year-olds

- increased the maximum sentence length for 15 to 17-year-olds to 2 years

- increased the upper limit from £2,000 to £5,000 for offences of criminal damage proceeded against as if triable only summarily

- introduced provisions for the reduction of sentences for early guilty pleas, and

- increased the maximum sentence length for certain firearm offences

Provisions within the Crime (Sentences) Act 1997 (as amended by the Powers of Criminal Courts Sentencing Act 2000) in England and Wales, and the Crime and Punishment (Scotland) Act 1997 in Scotland, included:

- an automatic life sentence for a second serious violent or sexual offence unless there are exceptional circumstances (this provision has not been enacted in Scotland)

- a minimum sentence of 7 years for an offender convicted for a third time of a class A drug trafficking offence unless the court considers this to be unjust in all the circumstances, and

- in England and Wales, the new section 38A of the Magistrates' Courts' Act 1980 extending the circumstances in which a magistrates' court may commit a person convicted of an offence triable-either-way to the Crown Court for sentence – it was implemented in conjunction with section 49 of the Criminal Procedure and Investigations Act 1996, which involves the magistrates' courts in asking defendants to indicate a plea before the mode of trial decision is taken and compels the court to sentence or commit for sentence any defendant who indicates a guilty plea

Under the Criminal Justice and Court Service Act 2000 new terms were introduced for certain orders. Community rehabilitation order is the new name for a probation order. A community service order is now known as a community punishment order. Finally, the new term for a combination order is community punishment and rehabilitation order. In April 2000 the secure training order was replaced by the detention and training order. Section 53 of the Children and Young Persons Act 1993 was repealed on 25 August 2000 and its provisions were transferred to sections 90 to 92 of the Powers of Criminal Courts (Sentencing) Act 2000. Reparation and action plan orders were implemented nationally from 1 June 2000. The drug treatment and testing order was introduced in England, Scotland and Wales from October 2000. The referral order was introduced in England, Scotland and Wales from April 2000. These changes are now reflected in Table 11.8.

The system of magistrates' courts and Crown Courts in Northern Ireland operates in a similar way to that in England and Wales. A particularly significant statutory development, however, has been the Criminal Justice (NI) Order 1996 which introduces a new sentencing regime into Northern Ireland, largely replicating that which was introduced into England and Wales by the Criminal Justice Acts of 1991 and 1993. The order makes many changes to both community and custodial sentences, while introducing new orders such as the combination order, the custody probation order, and orders for release on licence of sexual offenders.

Expenditure on penal establishments in Scotland

(Table 11.19)

The results shown in this table are reported on a cash basis for financial years 1996/97 to 2000/01 in line with funding arrangements. Financial year 2001/02 is reported on a resource accounting basis in line with the introduction of resource budgeting. Capital charges were introduced with resource accounting and budgeting.

11.1 Police force strength[1]: by country and sex
As at 31 March

Numbers

		1998	1999	2000	2001	2002	2003	2004	2005	2006	2007	2008
England and Wales												
Regular Police(FTE)												
Strength:												
Men	KERB	105 145	103 956	101 801	102 321	104 483	106 996	110 150	110 597	109 327	108 118	106 866
Women	KERC	19 611	19 885	20 155	21 155	22 784	24 430	26 956	28 898	30 307	31 914	32 861
Seconded:[2,3]												
Men	KERD	1 836	2 017	2 077	1 914	2 031	1 689	1 811	1 514	1 545	422	432
Women	KERE	222	238	307	292	305	251	284	222	203	60	70
Additional Officers:[4]												
Men	KERF	267	324	361	493	567	375	394	522	676	657	661
Women	KERG	514	582	519	509	564	709	969	1 042	1 213	1 203	1 471
Special constables												
Strength:[5]												
Men	KERH	11 977	10 860	9 623	8 630	8 014	7 718	7 645	8 074	8 829	9 327	9 719
Women	KERI	6 279	5 624	4 724	4 108	3 584	3 319	3 343	3 844	4 350	4 694	4 828
Scotland												
Regular police												
Strength:[6]												
Men	KERK	12 753	12 545	12 374	12 547	12 513	12 590	12 685	12 798	12 820	12 687	12 532
Women	KERL	2 227	2 265	2 325	2 602	2 738	2 897	2 898	3 203	3 401	3 547	3 689
Central service:[7]												
Men	KERM	85	88	95	87	116	131	166	195	171	153	219
Women	KERN	6	9	13	10	12	17	29	29	21	28	44
Seconded:[8]												
Men	KERO	101	85	130	140	133	166	192	216	200	195	196
Women	KERP	10	12	18	14	18	24	30	31	27	28	30
Additional regular police:												
Men	HFVM	88	85	80	83	80	79	88	79	85	107	106
Women	HFVN	9	6	4	5	12	10	13	21	15	12	14
Special constables												
Strength:												
Men	KERS	1 286	1 229	981	924	812	711	773	718	888	886	884
Women	KERT	437	422	355	336	307	280	328	437	432	471	510
Northern Ireland												
Regular police[9,10]												
Strength:												
Men	KERU	7 523	7 406	6 844	6 227	6 057	6 171	6 108	6 016	5 992	5 949	5 761
Women	KERV	933	987	966	1 009	1 080	1 266	1 418	1 547	1 534	1 600	1 653
Reserve[11]												
Strength:												
Men	KERW	3 469	3 199	2 962	2 629	2 223	1 983	1 824	1 431	1 424	1 212	1 119
Women	KERX	705	641	607	556	510	453	485	410	402	400	382

1 Figures for England and Wales excluding those on career breaks or maternity/paternity leave. From 1999, figures for Northern Ireland reflect the position at the end of the financial year, prior to this figures were as at 31 December.

2 Figures exclude secondments outside the police service in England and Wales (eg to the private sector or to law enforcement agencies overseas).

3 From 31 March 2007 onwards details of officers seconded to NCIS and NCS will no longer appear following the launch of Serious Organised Crime Agency (SOCA) in April 2006.

4 Figures include those officers on career breaks or maternity/paternity leave. Prior to 2003, these figures were not collected centrally.

5 Special constable figures are given as a headcount measure.

6 'Strength' is FTE police strength, only excluding special constables.

7 Instructors at Training Establishments, etc, formerly shown as secondments.

8 Includes Scottish Crime and Drug Enforcement Agency.

9 Does not include officers on secondment.

10 Also includes student officers.

11 Includes part-time reserve and full-time reserve, FTR -664 as at 31 March 2008 (618 males and 46 females). Con PT - 837 as at 31 March 2008 (501 males and 336 females).

Sources: Home Office: 020 7035 0289;
Scottish Government Justice Department: 0131 244 4253;
The Police Service of Northern Ireland: 028 9065 0222 ext 24070

Crime and justice

11.2 Prison Population[1] international comparisons

Country	2001	2002	2003	2004	2005	2006	2007	% change 2006-2007	Rate[16] per 100,000 population in 2007
England & Wales[5]	67 056	71 324	72 992	75 057	76 896	79 085	80 692	2	149
Northern Ireland[3]	910	1 026	1 160	1 274	1 301	1 433	1 468	2	83
Scotland[7]	6 137	6 404	6 524	6 805	6 792	7 111	7 291	3	142
Austria	6 915	7 511	7 816	9 000	8 767	8 780	8 887	1	107
Belgium[12]	8 544	8 605	9 308	9 245	9 375	9 635	10 008	4	94
Bulgaria[3]	8 971	8 994	9 422	10 066	10 871	11 436	11 058	-3	144
Croatia[3]	2 623	2 584	2 732	2 803	3 022	3 485	3 833	10	86
Cyprus	369	345	355	546	536	599	673	12	85
Czech Republic[6]	19 320	16 213	17 277	18 343	18 937	18 578	18 901	2	182
Denmark	3 150	3 439	3 577	3 762	4 132	3 759	3 406	-9	62
Estonia[3]	4 803	4 775	4 352	4 576	4 565	4 411	4 327	-2	322
Finland[6]	3 110	3 469	3 463	3 535	3 883	3 477	3 370	-3	64
France[10]	47 005	53 463	57 440	56 271	56 595	55 754	60 677	9	95
Germany[4]	80 333	74 904	81 176	81 166	80 410	78 581	75 719	-4	92
Greece[9]	8 343	8 284	8 555	8 760	9 589	10 113	10 700	6	96
Hungary[6]	17 275	17 838	16 507	16 543	15 720	14 821	14 353	-3	143
Iceland	110	107	112	115	119	119	115	-3	37
Ireland (Eire)[13]	3 025	3 028	2 986	3 083	3 022	3 080	3 325	8	76
Italy[6]	57 203	56 723	56 845	56 068	59 523	39 005	48 693	25	82
Latvia[3]	8 831	8 531	8 366	8 179	7 646	6 965	6 548	-6	287
Lithuania[3]	9 516	11 566	11 070	8 063	8 125	8 137	8 079	-1	239
Luxembourg	357	380	498	548	693	756	745	-1	155
Malta[11]	257	283	278	277	298	346	387	12	95
Netherlands	15 246	16 239	18 242	20 075	21 826	20 463	18 103	-12	110
Norway	2 666	2 662	2 914	2 975	3 097	3 164	3 280	4	69
Poland[5]	80 004	80 610	80 692	79 344	82 656	87 669	90 199	3	237
Portugal[6]	13 260	13 918	13 835	13 152	12 889	12 636	11 587	-8	109
Romania[6]	49 840	48 081	42 815	39 031	36 700	34 038	29 390	-14	137
Russian Federation[3]	925 072	980 151	877 393	847 004	763 115	823 451	871 693	6	613
Slovakia[6]	7 433	7 758	8 873	9 422	8 897	8 249	7 986	-3	148
Slovenia	1 155	1 120	1 099	1 126	1 132	1 301	1 336	3	66
Spain	46 962	50 994	55 244	59 224	61 269	64 120	66 400	4	148
Sweden[15]	6 089	6 506	6 755	7 332	7 054	7 175	6 770	-6	74
Switzerland[14]	5 137	4 937	5 214	5 977	6 137	5 888	5 715	-3	76
Turkey	61 336	60 091	64 051	71 148	54 296	67 795	85 865	27	122
Ukraine	198 885	198 946	198 386	193 489	179 519	165 716	154 055	-7	332
Australia[2]	22 458	22 492	23 555	24 171	25 353	25 790	27 224	6	130
Canada[8]	35 533	35 736	35 868	34 155	34 365	35 110	-	-	108
Japan[3]	61 242	65 508	69 502	73 734	76 413	79 052	81 255	3	63
Korea(Rep. of)[7]	62 235	61 084	58 945	57 184	52 403	46 721	46 313	-1	96
Mexico[6]	165 687	172 888	182 530	193 889	205 821	210 140	212 841	1	193
New Zealand[7]	5 887	5 738	6 059	6 556	7 100	7 595	7 959	5	188
South Africa[4]	170 959	178 998	189 748	187 640	187 394	150 302	161 639	8	339
U.S.A.[2]	1 961 247	2 033 331	2 081 580	2 129 802	2 186 230	2 245 189	2 299 116	2	762
European Union 27	581 419	592 331	607 522	609 873	620 099	601 513	611 078	2	123

1 At 1 September: number of prisoners, including pre-trial detainees/remand prisoners.
2 At 30 June.
3 At 1 January.
4 At 31 March.
5 At 31 August.
6 At 31 December.
7 Annual averages. Countries calculate these on the basis of daily, weekly or monthly figures.
8 Annual averages by financial year (e.g. 2006=1 April 2005-31 March 2006). Rate per 100,000 population reflects the position in 2006.
9 At 1 September (2001-03, 2005-06). At 16 December (2004). At 30 June (2007).
10 Metropolitan and overseas departments and territories.
11 At 1 September (2001-06). Annual average (2007).
12 At 1 March.
13 At 1 September (2001-06). At 26 October (2007).
14 At third Wednesday in March (2001). At first Wednesday in September (2002-07).
15 At 1 October.
16 Based on estimates of national population.

Sources: Ministries responsible for prisons, national prison administrations; national statistical offices, Council of Europe Annual Penal Statistics (SPACE); World Prison Population List and World Prison Brief; (International Centre for Prison Studies King's College, London)

11.3 Recorded crime statistics: by offence group[1]
England and Wales

Thousands

		1997	1998[2,3]		1998[3] /99	1999 /00	2000 /01	2001[4] /02	2002[4,6] /03	2003 /04	2004 /05	2005 /06	2006[8] /07	2007 /08
Violence against the person	BEAB	250.8	434.3	LQMP	502.8	581.0	600.9	650.3	845.1	967.2	1 048.1	1 059.6	1 046.4	961.2
Sexual offences[7]	BEAC	33.2	35.9	LQMQ	36.2	37.8	37.3	41.4	58.9	62.5	62.9	62.1	57.5	53.5
Burglary	BEAD	1 015.0	966.3	LQMR	953.2	906.5	836.0	878.5	890.1	820.0	680.4	645.1	622.0	583.7
Robbery	BEAE	63.1	63.8	LQMS	66.8	84.3	95.2	121.4	110.3	103.7	91.0	98.2	101.4	84.7
Theft and handling stolen goods (of which):	BEAF	2 164.9	2 172.4	LQMT	2 191.4	2 223.6	2 145.4	2 267.0	–	–	–	–	–	–
Offences against vehicles				I8RM	..	..	..	..	1 074.7	985.0	820.1	792.8	765.0	656.5
Other theft offences				I8RN	..	..	..	..	1 336.9	1 327.9	1 247.6	1 226.2	1 180.8	1 121.1
Fraud and forgery	BEAG	134.3	236.7	LQMU	279.5	334.8	319.3	314.9	331.1	319.6	280.1	232.8	199.7	155.4
Criminal damage	BEAH	877.0	866.5	LQMV	879.6	945.7	960.1	1 064.5	1 120.6	1 218.5	1 197.5	1 184.3	1 185.0	1 036.2
Drug offences[5]	LQMO	..	21.3	LQYT	135.9	121.9	113.5	121.4	143.3	143.5	145.8	178.5	194.2	229.0
Other offences[5]	BEAI	36.6	57.3	LQYU	63.6	65.7	63.2	65.7	64.0	65.7	64.0	75.6	75.7	69.3
Total	BEAA	4 598.3	4 943.7	LQYV	5 109.1	5 301.2	5 170.8	5 525.0	5 975.0	6 013.8	5 637.5	5 555.2	5 427.6	4 950.7

1 See chapter text.
2 Estimates.
3 Figures from this period are not directly comparable with data prior to 1998/99 and from 2002/03 onwards.
4 The National Crime Recording Standard (NCRS) was introduced in England and Wales from 1 April 2002. These figures are not directly comparable with those for earlier years. For more details about the inflationary effects of the NCRS on the 2001/02 and 2002/03 figures see chapter text. A detailed explanation for the NCRS can be accessed via the following Home Office Research Development and Statistics website http://www.homeoffice.gov.uk/rds/countrules.html

5 Prior to 1 April 1998 the offence of drug trafficking was included in the 'Other offences' group. From 1 April 1999, under the new counting rules, drug trafficking became part of a new 'Drug offences' group which, now also includes possession and other drug offences. For 1998/99 under the old counting rules, drug trafficking has been separated out and listed under drugs offences.
6 Includes the British Transport Police (BTP) from 2002/03 onwards.
7 The Sexual Offences Act 2003, introduced in May 2004, altered the definitions and coverage of sexual offences.
8 The offence groupings were revised in 2006/07 and backdated to 2002/03.

Source: Home Office: 020 7035 0307

11.4 Offenders found guilty: by offence group[1,2,3], England and Wales

Magistrates' courts and the Crown Court

Thousands

		1997	1998	1999	2000	2001	2002	2003	2004	2005	2006	2007
All ages[4]												
Indictable offences												
Violence against the person:	KJEJ	34.6	35.7	34.4	34.0	35.3	37.7	38.0	39.1	40.9	41.9	42.1
Murder	KESB	0.3	0.3	0.3	0.3	0.3	0.3	0.3	0.4	0.4	0.4	0.4
Manslaughter	KESC	0.3	0.3	0.3	0.3	0.3	0.3	0.2	0.3	0.3	0.2	0.2
Wounding	KESD	32.7	35.2	33.9	33.5	33.5	35.7	35.9	36.9	38.6	39.8	40.0
Other offences of violence against the person	KESE	1.3	1.3	1.3	1.3	1.2	1.4	1.5	1.3	1.3	1.2	1.5
Sexual offences	KESF	4.5	4.6	4.3	3.9	3.8	4.4	4.4	4.8	4.8	4.9	5.1
Burglary	KESG	31.7	30.8	29.3	26.2	24.8	26.7	25.7	24.3	23.0	23.0	23.8
Robbery	KESH	5.6	5.5	5.6	6.0	6.8	7.7	7.3	7.3	7.1	8.1	8.8
Theft and handling stolen goods	KESI	118.4	125.7	131.2	128.0	127.0	127.3	119.1	110.6	103.8	99.0	106.0
Fraud and forgery	KESJ	17.0	19.8	20.3	19.2	18.3	18.1	18.0	18.1	18.5	18.2	19.9
Criminal damage	KESK	10.5	10.9	10.9	10.2	10.7	11.0	11.2	11.7	11.7	12.7	12.5
Drugs	KBWX	40.7	48.8	48.7	44.6	45.6	49.0	51.2	54.5	39.1	39.6	44.6
Other offences (excluding motoring)	KESL	47.6	49.6	47.9	44.5	44.2	48.0	51.4	54.7	53.1	50.0	45.3
Motoring offences	KESM	9.5	9.0	8.1	7.6	7.7	8.2	8.7	8.0	6.6	5.9	5.4
Total	KESA	320.1	341.7	342.0	325.5	324.2	338.3	335.1	317.8	308.5	303.2	313.3
Summary offences												
Assaults	KESO	32.0	35.3	37.5	37.4	37.7	40.7	45.6	53.4	60.4	64.5	68.9
Betting and gaming	KESP	–	–	–	–	–	–	–	–	–	–	–
Offences with pedal cycles	KBWY	1.5	2.1	1.3	0.8	0.6	0.5	0.6	0.7	0.7	0.7	0.7
Other Highways Acts offences	KBWZ	3.2	3.1	2.9	2.7	2.4	2.2	1.9	1.8	2.0	2.1	1.7
Breach of local or other regulations	KESQ	6.4	5.8	6.5	5.0	4.3	3.9	3.4	3.1	2.6	1.9	1.6
Intoxicating Liquor Laws:												
Drunkenness	KESR	28.8	30.8	28.7	27.2	26.2	26.9	27.7	21.1	16.1	15.7	17.4
Other offences	KESS	0.6	0.6	0.5	0.4	0.3	0.4	0.7	0.8	1.0	1.2	1.0
Education Acts	KEST	3.7	5.0	5.1	5.1	5.6	5.8	5.8	6.5	6.4	7.4	8.4
Game Laws	KESU	0.3	0.4	0.3	0.2	0.2	0.3	0.2	0.2	0.4	–	0.1
Labour Laws	KESV	0.1	0.1	0.1	0.1	–	–	–	–	–	–	–
Summary offences of criminal damage and malicious damage	KESW	24.7	26.5	27.9	28.0	26.9	28.3	29.8	31.5	31.1	30.2	32.1
Offences by prostitutes	KESX	6.6	6.0	4.0	4.1	3.7	4.2	3.9	2.9	2.2	1.6	1.4
Railway offences	KESY	11.4	12.6	15.2	17.4	22.6	29.4	34.8	35.0	40.2	44.6	46.0
Revenue Laws	KESZ	143.5	174.7	165.8	175.0	146.9	167.8	172.5	175.5	130.5	104.4	104.8
Vagrancy Acts	KETB	2.0	2.2	2.7	3.3	3.2	3.3	3.8	2.9	2.2	2.2	2.0
Wireless Telegraphy Acts	KETC	77.0	76.6	55.8	105.7	83.8	96.6	79.9	89.3	105.0	115.6	121.0
Other summary offences	KETD	74.7	80.9	79.3	78.1	77.8	76.4	82.9	97.9	108.2	103.6	86.0
Motoring offences (summary)	KETA	649.3	665.2	632.9	607.5	583.3	595.8	662.6	707.9	667.1	622.5	611.1
Total	KESN	1 065.8	1 128.0	1 066.5	1 098.2	1 025.5	1 083.0	1 156.1	1 230.7	1 175.9	1 118.2	1 102.6
Persons aged 10 to under 18[5]												
Indictable offences												
Violence against the person:	KETF	5.9	5.9	6.2	6.4	6.9	6.9	6.6	6.9	7.4	7.5	7.7
Murder	KBXA	–	–	–	–	–	–	–	–	–	–	–
Manslaughter	KBXB	–	–	0.2	–	–	–	–	–	–	–	–
Wounding	KBXC	5.8	5.9	5.9	6.3	6.8	6.8	6.5	6.5	7.3	7.4	7.6
Other offences of violence against the person	KCAA	0.1	0.1	–	0.1	0.1	0.1	0.1	0.3	0.2	0.1	0.1
Sexual offences	KETG	0.5	0.5	0.5	0.5	0.5	0.6	0.4	0.6	0.6	0.5	0.5
Burglary	KETH	8.6	8.5	7.8	6.8	6.3	6.4	5.8	5.9	6.0	6.2	6.1
Robbery	KETI	2.3	2.2	2.0	2.2	2.8	2.8	2.6	3.0	3.1	3.7	4.1
Theft and handling stolen goods	KETJ	19.6	21.9	22.7	21.0	20.6	18.4	16.5	16.8	17.1	16.3	18.2
Fraud and forgery	KETK	0.8	1.0	1.1	1.0	1.0	1.2	0.8	0.8	0.7	0.6	0.7
Criminal damage	KETL	2.3	2.3	2.7	2.6	2.9	2.9	2.9	3.2	3.3	3.7	3.6
Drugs	KCAB	1.8	2.7	3.1	3.7	4.3	5.0	5.1	4.5	4.6	4.5	5.3
Other offences (excluding motoring)	KETM	4.2	4.2	4.3	4.4	4.4	4.4	4.3	4.6	4.5	4.1	4.2
Motoring	KETN	0.4	0.4	0.4	0.6	0.7	0.8	0.8	0.7	0.6	0.5	0.4
Total	KETE	46.4	49.7	50.6	49.2	50.3	49.1	46.0	47.0	47.8	47.6	50.9
Summary offences												
Offences with pedal cycles	KETP	0.2	0.3	0.3	0.2	0.2	0.2	0.2	0.2	0.3	0.2	0.2
Breach of local or other regulations	KETR	0.2	0.2	0.2	0.2	0.2	0.1	0.1	0.1	0.1	0.1	0.1
Summary offences of criminal damage and malicious damage	KETS	4.4	5.2	6.1	6.7	6.9	7.0	7.2	8.3	8.8	8.6	9.2
Railway offences	KETT	0.5	0.5	0.5	0.4	0.4	0.4	0.3	0.4	0.4	0.4	0.5
Other summary offences	KETU	16.6	19.4	20.0	20.2	20.8	20.6	20.9	23.1	24.0	24.7	26.8
Motoring offences (summary)	KCAC	10.8	11.3	12.6	14.5	16.7	17.1	17.8	17.0	14.8	12.1	9.9
Total	KETO	22.0	36.8	39.6	42.2	45.2	45.4	46.6	49.2	48.3	46.1	46.6

1 See chapter text.
2 Data provided on the principal offence basis.
3 Every effort is made to ensure that the figures presented are accurate and complete. However, it is important to note that these data have been extracted from large administrative data systems generated by the courts and police forces. As a consequence, care should be taken to ensure data collection processes and their inevitable limitations are taken into account when those data are used.
4 Includes 'Companies', etc .
5 Figures for persons aged 10 to under 18 are included in the totals above.

Sources: Office for Criminal Justice Reform: 020 7035 4955;
Evidence and Analysis

11.5 Offenders cautioned: by offence group[1,2,3]
England and Wales

Thousands

		1997	1998	1999	2000	2001	2002	2003	2004	2005	2006	2007
All ages[4]												
Indictable offences												
Violence against the person	KELB	23.6	23.5	21.2	19.9	19.5	23.6	28.8	36.6	51.0	57.3	52.3
Murder	KCAD	–	–	–	–	–	–	–	–	–	–	–
Manslaughter	KCAE	–	–	–	–	–	–	–	–	–	–	–
Wounding	KCAF	23.3	22.9	20.6	19.3	18.9	22.9	27.9	35.0	49.6	55.7	50.8
Other violence against the person	KCAG	0.4	0.6	0.6	0.6	0.6	0.7	0.9	1.2	1.4	1.5	1.6
Sexual offences	KELC	1.9	1.7	1.5	1.3	1.2	1.1	1.4	1.6	1.8	1.9	2.0
Burglary	KELD	9.4	8.4	7.7	6.6	6.4	5.8	5.6	5.6	6.5	7.7	7.0
Robbery	KELE	0.7	0.6	0.6	0.6	0.5	0.4	0.4	0.5	0.6	0.7	0.6
Theft and handling stolen goods	KELF	82.8	83.6	75.4	67.6	63.5	54.2	54.5	61.9	67.6	72.4	72.8
Fraud and forgery	KELG	7.2	7.4	7.2	6.2	5.8	5.3	5.5	6.0	6.9	8.0	8.6
Criminal damage	KELH	2.8	2.7	3.0	3.2	3.4	3.1	3.7	5.5	7.2	9.0	8.8
Drug offences	KCAI	56.0	58.7	49.4	41.1	39.4	44.9	45.7	32.6	34.4	37.4	43.0
Other offences	KELI	5.0	5.0	4.6	4.4	4.1	4.4	5.3	6.0	6.9	9.3	10.0
All offenders cautioned	KELA	189.4	191.7	170.6	150.9	143.9	142.9	150.7	156.3	182.9	203.7	205.1
Summary offences												
Assaults	KELK	9.1	..	17.0	17.2	18.2	17.3	19.8	26.1	40.8	64.6	72.6
Betting and gaming	KELL	–	–	–	–	–	–	–	–	–	–	–
Offences with pedal cycles	KCAK	0.9	0.8	0.6	0.3	0.2	0.1	0.1	0.3	0.3	0.3	0.3
Other Highways Acts offences	KCAL	0.8	0.8	0.7	0.4	0.3	0.2	0.3	0.3	0.2	0.3	0.3
Breach of local or other regulations	KELM	0.9	0.9	0.7	0.5	0.3	0.3	0.2	0.2	0.2	0.1	0.1
Intoxicating Liquor Laws: Drunkenness	KELN	25.7	22.8	20.3	18.1	16.6	16.2	18.1	13.5	8.6	5.8	6.1
Other offences	KELO	0.9	0.7	0.4	0.2	0.3	0.3	0.3	0.3	0.3	0.2	0.2
Education Acts	KELP	–	–	–	–	–	–	0.1	0.1	0.1	0.1	0.1
Game Laws	KELQ	0.1	0.1	0.1	–	–	–	–	–	–	–	–
Labour Laws	KELR	–	–	–	–	–	–	–	–	–	–	–
Summary offences of criminal damage and malicious damage	KELS	27.6	28.3	28.7	26.8	26.7	24.7	27.6	33.3	38.0	43.2	44.3
Offences by prostitutes	KELT	3.5	3.5	2.1	1.3	1.0	1.8	1.3	1.6	1.4	1.2	1.2
Railway offences	KELU	0.1	–	–	–	–	–	–	–	0.1	0.1	0.1
Revenue Laws	KELV	0.1	0.1	0.1	–	–	–	–	–	–	–	–
Vagrancy Acts	KELX	0.6	1.2	0.8	0.4	0.3	0.3	0.3	0.2	0.3	0.4	0.5
Wireless Telegraphy Acts	KELY	–	–	–	–	–	–	–	–	–	–	–
Other summary offences	KELZ	22.3	37.0	24.1	22.5	21.9	21.0	22.9	23.5	25.2	29.2	32.1
All offenders cautioned	KELJ	92.7	96.2	95.6	88.1	85.9	82.4	91.1	99.5	115.5	145.6	157.8
Persons aged 10 to under 18[5]												
Indictable offences												
Violence against the person	KEMB	9.6	9.5	8.5	8.3	8.7	9.3	11.0	13.6	16.5	16.6	13.9
Murder	KCAN	–	–	–	–	–	–	–	–	–	–	–
Manslaughter	KCAO	–	–	–	–	–	–	–	–	–	–	–
Wounding	KCAP	9.6	9.4	8.4	8.2	8.6	9.2	10.9	13.5	16.4	16.5	13.8
Other violence against the person	KCCE	–	0.1	0.1	0.1	0.1	0.1	0.1	0.1	0.1	0.1	0.1
Sexual offences	KEMC	0.7	0.6	0.6	0.5	0.5	0.4	0.5	0.5	0.6	0.6	0.7
Burglary	KEMD	7.5	6.7	6.1	5.4	5.3	4.6	4.4	4.2	4.6	5.0	4.5
Robbery	KEME	0.6	0.5	0.5	0.5	0.5	0.4	0.4	0.4	0.5	0.6	0.5
Theft and handling stolen goods	KEMF	40.9	44.0	39.6	36.9	35.2	28.1	28.3	33.1	36.8	39.4	39.7
Fraud and forgery	KEMG	1.4	1.6	1.7	1.5	1.3	1.1	1.0	1.0	1.1	1.3	1.4
Criminal damage	KEMH	1.8	1.7	1.9	2.1	2.3	1.9	2.3	3.1	3.9	4.7	4.5
Drug offences	KCCF	9.7	11.0	9.6	7.9	8.5	9.5	9.6	8.3	7.8	7.1	8.0
Other offences	KEMI	1.5	1.5	1.4	1.3	1.3	1.3	1.4	1.6	1.6	1.9	2.0
All offenders cautioned	KEMA	73.7	77.2	69.8	64.3	63.5	56.6	58.7	65.9	73.4	77.1	75.2
Summary offences												
Offences with pedal cycles	KEMK	0.5	0.4	0.3	0.2	0.1	0.1	0.1	0.2	0.2	0.2	0.2
Breach of local or other regulations	KEMM	0.3	0.3	0.2	0.2	0.1	0.1	0.1	0.1	0.1	0.1	0.1
Summary offences of criminal damage and malicious damage	KEMN	13.5	14.2	14.7	14.4	15.2	12.6	14.3	17.1	19.8	21.9	21.7
Railway offences	KEMO	0.1	–	–	–	–	–	–	–	–	–	–
Other summary offences	KEMP	16.4	17.7	19.0	18.4	19.1	17.1	18.8	21.7	25.1	29.6	30.2
All offenders cautioned	KEMJ	30.8	32.5	34.2	33.2	34.5	29.9	33.3	39.1	45.1	51.7	52.1

1 See chapter text.
2 Data provided on the principal offence basis.
3 Every effort is made to ensure that the figures presented are accurate and complete. However, it is important to note that these data have been extracted from large administrative data systems generated by police forces. As a consequence, care should be taken to ensure data collection processes and their inevitable limitations are taken into account when those data are used.
4 Includes 'Companies', etc.
5 Figures for persons aged 10 to under 18 are included in the totals above.

Sources: Office for Criminal Justice Reform: 020 7035 4955;
Evidence and Analysis

Crime and justice

11.6 Offenders found guilty of offences: by age and sex[1,2,3]
England and Wales

Magistrates' courts and the Crown Court

Thousands

		1997	1998	1999	2000	2001	2002	2003	2004	2005	2006	2007
Males												
Indictable offences												
All ages	KEFA	276.5	292.9	291.7	276.5	275.5	287.1	283.4	268.4	261.3	258.4	267.0
10 and under 15 years	KEFB	7.1	8.1	8.9	8.7	9.0	8.8	8.0	8.5	8.6	8.3	8.5
15 and under 18 years	KEFC	33.6	35.2	35.1	33.8	34.4	33.7	31.4	31.8	32.0	32.5	35.0
18 and under 21 years	KEFD	48.4	51.8	52.6	49.9	48.2	46.6	43.8	39.9	38.5	39.0	40.6
21 years and over	KEFE	187.3	197.9	195.0	184.0	183.9	198.0	200.2	188.2	182.2	178.7	182.9
Summary offences												
All ages	KEFF	880.9	929.0	886.6	881.0	826.6	866.4	937.1	990.0	931.2	877.7	851.5
10 and under 15 years	KEFG	3.0	3.9	5.1	5.8	6.2	6.1	6.1	6.7	7.2	7.0	7.5
15 and under 18 years	KEFH	25.9	28.5	30.3	32.2	34.5	34.6	35.3	36.4	34.6	32.3	31.9
18 and under 21 years	KEFI	91.0	96.3	94.8	93.0	92.2	94.7	99.9	98.2	89.4	85.1	80.5
21 years and over	KEFJ	761.0	800.3	756.5	750.0	693.6	731.0	795.8	848.8	800.1	753.4	731.8
Females												
Indictable offences												
All ages	KEFK	42.2	47.3	49.0	47.7	47.4	50.0	50.2	48.4	46.1	43.7	45.3
10 and under 15 years	KEFL	1.0	1.4	1.4	1.5	1.6	1.6	1.6	1.7	1.7	1.7	1.7
15 and under 18 years	KEFM	4.6	5.1	5.2	5.2	5.3	5.1	4.9	5.0	5.5	5.1	5.5
18 and under 21 years	KEFN	6.3	7.1	7.6	7.5	7.0	6.9	6.2	5.7	5.3	4.8	4.6
21 years and over	KEFO	30.4	33.7	34.7	33.5	33.5	36.5	37.5	35.9	33.6	32.1	33.4
Summary offences												
All ages	KEFP	174.9	188.3	171.0	208.3	190.2	208.7	210.5	231.2	236.6	233.9	244.2
10 and under 15 years	KEFQ	0.5	0.6	0.8	0.9	0.9	1.1	1.2	1.4	1.6	1.6	1.7
15 and under 18 years	KEFR	3.4	3.8	3.4	3.3	3.6	3.6	4.0	4.6	4.9	5.2	5.6
18 and under 21 years	KEFS	11.1	12.1	10.8	11.8	11.1	11.6	12.6	13.0	13.5	14.2	14.9
21 years and over	KEFT	160.0	171.7	155.4	192.3	174.7	192.4	192.7	212.1	216.6	212.9	221.9
Companies, etc												
Indictable offences	KEFU	1.3	1.5	1.3	1.3	1.3	1.2	1.4	1.1	1.1	1.0	1.1
Summary offences	KEFV	10.0	10.7	8.9	8.8	8.6	7.9	8.6	9.4	8.1	6.6	6.9

1 See chapter text.
2 These data are on the principal offence basis.
3 Every effort is made to ensure that the figures presented are accurate and complete. However, it is important to note that these data have been extracted from large administrative data systems generated by the courts and police forces. As a consequence, care should be taken to ensure data collection processes and their inevitable limitations are taken into account when those data are used.

Source: Office for Criminal Justice Reform: 020 7035 4955

11.7 Persons cautioned by the police: by age and sex[1,3,4]
England and Wales

Thousands

		1997	1998	1999	2000	2001	2002	2003	2004	2005	2006	2007
Males												
Indictable offences												
All ages	KEGA	143.3	142.9	126.1	109.7	103.8	104.4	109.8	110.0	129.9	147.6	148.5
10 and under 15 years[2]	KEGB	22.9	23.7	22.0	20.3	19.7	16.7	16.9	18.7	21.0	21.7	19.7
15 and under 18 years[2]	KEGC	32.0	32.0	28.7	25.0	24.5	23.3	24.1	25.9	28.0	30.2	30.0
18 and under 21 years	KEGD	25.2	25.7	22.7	20.1	18.5	18.9	19.4	16.7	19.8	22.9	23.7
21 years and over	KEGE	63.2	61.5	52.7	44.3	41.2	45.6	49.4	48.7	61.1	72.8	75.1
Summary offences												
All ages	KEGF	75.7	76.9	76.1	69.6	68.0	63.8	70.9	76.0	87.6	112.0	120.2
10 and under 15 years[2]	KEGG	9.9	10.6	11.7	12.0	12.7	10.3	10.9	12.6	15.5	17.9	17.8
15 and under 18 years[2]	KEGH	16.1	16.1	16.1	14.9	15.2	13.3	15.1	17.2	18.6	21.3	21.3
18 and under 21 years	KEGI	12.9	13.2	13.0	11.9	11.0	11.0	12.4	12.3	12.2	15.0	16.4
21 years and over	KEGJ	36.9	37.0	35.3	30.9	29.0	29.2	32.5	33.9	41.2	57.8	64.6
Females												
Indictable offences												
All ages	KEGK	46.0	48.8	44.5	41.2	40.1	38.5	41.0	46.3	53.0	56.2	56.6
10 and under 15 years[2]	KEGL	9.2	11.1	9.8	10.0	10.1	8.4	8.6	10.6	12.2	12.5	12.6
15 and under 18 years[2]	KEGM	9.5	10.3	9.3	9.0	9.3	8.3	9.1	10.7	12.2	12.7	13.0
18 and under 21 years	KEGN	5.7	5.9	5.7	5.2	4.9	4.8	4.9	5.2	5.8	6.2	6.3
21 years and over	KEGO	21.5	21.4	19.6	17.0	15.9	17.0	18.4	19.9	22.8	24.7	24.8
Summary offences												
All ages	KEGP	17.0	19.2	9.4	18.5	18.0	18.6	20.2	23.5	28.5	34.2	37.6
10 and under 15 years[2]	KEGQ	1.7	2.1	2.5	2.8	2.9	2.7	3.0	3.9	5.1	5.6	5.7
15 and under 18 years[2]	KEGR	3.2	3.7	3.9	3.7	3.8	3.6	4.3	5.4	6.2	7.1	7.3
18 and under 21 years	KEGS	2.3	2.6	2.7	2.5	2.3	2.4	2.7	2.9	3.3	4.1	4.7
21 years and over	KEGT	9.9	10.8	10.3	9.6	9.0	9.8	10.2	11.3	13.9	17.4	20.0

1 See chapter text.
2 From 1 June 2000 the Crime and Disorder Act 1998 came into force nationally and removed the use of cautions for persons under 18 and replaced them with reprimands and final warnings.
3 These data are on the principal offence basis.
4 Every effort is made to ensure that the figures presented are accurate and complete. However, it is important to note that these data have been extracted from large administrative data systems generated by police forces. As a consequence, care should be taken to ensure data collection processes and their inevitable limitations are taken into account when those data are used.

Source: Office for Criminal Justice Reform:020 7035 4955

11.8 Sentence or order passed on persons sentenced for indictable offences: by sex[1]
England and Wales

Magistrates' courts and the Crown Court

Percentages and thousands

		1997	1998	1999	2000	2001	2002	2003	2004	2005	2006	2007
Males												
Sentence or order												
Absolute discharge	KEJB	0.7	0.7	0.6	0.6	0.6	0.8	0.9	0.8	0.7	0.7	0.7
Conditional discharge	KEJC	15.5	15.3	15.0	14.1	13.4	12.4	13.0	12.2	11.9	11.3	12.2
Fine	KEJF	28.2	28.4	27.7	25.7	24.5	23.9	24.0	20.9	19.4	17.4	16.2
Community rehabilitation order	KEJD	10.0	10.0	10.1	10.1	10.7	10.6	10.1	9.5	5.6	0.8	0.5
Supervision order	KEJE	2.7	2.7	2.7	2.4	2.3	2.1	1.8	2.0	2.1	2.3	2.4
Community punishment order	KEJG	9.5	9.3	9.3	9.5	9.0	8.6	8.3	8.8	6.3	1.2	0.5
Attendance centre order	KEJH	1.8	1.7	1.8	1.5	1.2	0.7	0.6	0.6	0.6	0.6	0.6
Community punishment and rehabilitation order	KIJW	3.7	3.8	3.7	3.6	2.6	2.6	2.6	2.8	2.1	0.5	0.4
Curfew order	LUJP	0.1	0.2	0.3	0.5	0.7	1.1	1.6	2.7	2.3	1.3	1.3
Reparation order	SNFI	..	..	..	0.7	1.3	0.8	0.4	0.4	0.5	0.6	0.6
Action plan order	SNFJ	..	..	..	0.9	1.7	1.1	0.7	0.8	0.8	0.8	0.8
Drug treatment and testing order	SNFK	..	..	..	0.1	1.2	1.4	1.9	2.3	1.6	0.1	–
Referral order	SNFL	..	..	..	..	..	3.0	4.0	4.4	5.2	5.2	5.5
Community order[2]	GN7P	..	..	..	..	..	..	..	..	8.7	19.8	20.4
Suspended sentence order	KEJL	0.8	0.7	0.6	0.7	0.6	0.5	0.5	0.6	1.7	6.7	8.6
Imprisonment												
Sec 90-92	LUJQ	0.3	0.2	0.2	0.2	0.2	0.2	0.2	0.2	0.2	0.2	0.1
Detention and training order	LUJR	..	..	..	1.4	1.9	1.8	1.5	1.6	1.6	1.7	1.5
Young offender institution	KEJK	6.1	6.0	6.2	5.2	4.5	4.2	3.6	3.8	3.7	3.6	3.8
Unsuspended imprisonment	KEJM	17.9	18.2	18.7	19.9	20.0	20.9	20.6	21.5	21.2	20.4	19.9
Other sentence or order	KEJN	3.0	2.6	3.1	3.1	3.4	3.3	3.5	4.1	3.9	4.4	4.0
Total number of males (thousands) = 100 per cent	KEJA	275.4	292.4	291.3	277.1	274.6	285.6	282.3	267.5	259.4	258.4	265.8
Females												
Sentence or order												
Absolute discharge	KEKB	0.8	0.7	0.7	0.6	0.6	0.9	1.0	0.8	0.8	0.7	0.8
Conditional discharge	KEKC	29.4	28.7	26.9	24.9	23.9	22.0	22.5	21.8	20.7	20.1	20.8
Fine	KEKF	21.8	21.3	20.8	20.1	18.6	17.9	18.5	16.7	15.2	12.8	12.1
Community rehabilitation order	KEKD	19.1	19.1	19.4	19.6	19.1	19.2	17.0	15.4	9.0	1.4	0.5
Supervision order	KEKE	2.9	3.1	2.9	2.8	2.7	2.1	2.1	2.1	2.4	2.5	2.6
Community punishment order	KEKG	6.5	6.5	7.1	7.5	7.3	6.8	6.6	7.6	6.1	1.6	0.4
Attendance centre order	KEKH	1.0	0.9	0.9	0.8	0.6	0.4	0.3	0.3	0.3	0.5	0.3
Community punishment and rehabilitation order	KIJX	3.2	3.4	3.3	3.0	2.1	2.1	1.8	1.9	1.5	0.5	0.2
Curfew order	LUJT	0.1	0.1	0.3	0.4	0.6	0.8	1.4	2.2	2.3	1.1	1.1
Reparation order	SNFX	..	..	..	0.8	1.6	0.8	0.4	0.5	0.5	0.5	0.6
Action plan order	SNFZ	..	..	..	1.0	2.0	1.2	0.8	0.8	1.0	0.9	0.9
Drug treatment and testing order	SNGA	..	..	..	0.1	1.4	1.7	2.4	3.2	2.1	0.2	–
Referral order	SNGB	..	..	..	..	..	3.9	5.1	5.6	6.7	6.9	7.0
Community order[2]	GN7Q	..	..	..	..	..	..	..	..	9.9	23.3	24.5
Suspended sentence order	KEKL	1.6	1.5	1.3	1.3	1.2	1.1	1.0	1.3	2.5	7.8	9.6
Imprisonment												
Sec 90-92	LUJU	0.1	..	0.1	0.1	0.1	0.1	0.1	0.1	0.1	–	–
Detention and training order	LUJV	..	..	..	0.6	0.8	0.8	0.7	0.7	0.8	0.7	0.8
Young offender institution	KEKK	1.9	2.2	2.4	2.2	2.0	1.9	1.7	1.4	1.6	1.6	1.4
Unsuspended imprisonment	KEKM	9.4	10.0	11.0	11.5	12.1	12.7	12.8	13.2	12.6	12.8	12.4
Other sentence or order	KEKN	2.2	2.5	3.0	2.9	3.5	3.4	3.8	4.3	3.8	4.3	3.7
Total number of females (thousands) = 100 per cent	KEKA	42.1	47.2	49.0	47.8	47.3	49.9	50.2	48.3	46.1	43.7	45.4

1 See chapter text. Every effort is made to ensure that the figures presented are accurate and complete. However, it is important to note that these data have been extracted from large administrative data systems generated by the courts and police forces. As a consequence, care should be taken to ensure data collection processes and their inevitable limitations are taken into account when those data are used.

2 The community order was introduced on 4 April 2005 and applies to offences committed on or after that date.

Source: Office for Criminal Justice Reform: 020 7035 4955

11.9 Persons sentenced to life imprisonment or immediate custody: by sex and age
England and Wales

Number of Persons

		1997	1998	1999	2000	2001	2002	2003	2004	2005	2006	2007
Life imprisonment[1]												
Males												
All ages	I28G	346	380	465	446	484	536	489	548	594	531	471
10 - 17 years	I28D	24	11	26	19	28	21	11	15	27	16	23
18 - 20 years	I28E	29	25	38	9	27	21	47	24	50	46	70
21 years and over	I28F	293	344	401	418	429	494	431	509	517	469	378
Females												
All ages	I28K	21	14	19	21	19	19	24	22	31	16	21
10 - 17 years	I28H	3	1	3	2	1	1	–	1	1	–	3
18 - 20 years	I28I	2	–	2	1	3	2	4	2	4	2	3
21 years and over	I28J	16	13	14	18	15	16	20	19	26	14	15
All persons												
All ages	I28O	367	394	484	467	503	555	513	570	625	547	492
10 - 17 years	I28L	27	12	29	21	29	22	11	16	28	16	26
18 - 20 years	I28M	31	25	40	10	30	23	51	26	54	48	73
21 years and over	I28N	309	357	415	436	444	510	451	528	543	483	393
Immediate custody[2]												
Males												
All ages	JF7E	87 989	93 619	97 355	97 841	97 728	102 240	98 371	97 020	91 954	86 239	85 285
10 - 17 years	JF7F	6 751	6 870	7 218	6 949	7 119	6 865	5 765	5 866	5 463	5 669	5 277
18 - 20 years	JF7G	15 114	16 127	17 011	17 315	16 855	16 269	14 418	13 793	13 237	12 802	13 126
21 years and over	JF7H	66 124	70 622	73 126	73 577	73 754	79 106	78 188	77 361	73 254	67 768	66 882
Females												
All ages	JF7I	5 485	6 553	7 485	7 879	8 042	8 812	8 786	8 732	8 231	7 783	7 722
10 - 17 years	JF7J	305	335	406	444	448	529	424	443	498	453	466
18 - 20 years	JF7K	640	851	961	1 116	1 063	1 071	969	817	875	841	793
21 years and over	JF7L	4 540	5 367	6 118	6 319	6 531	7 212	7 393	7 472	6 858	6 489	6 463
All persons												
All ages	JF7M	93 474	100 172	104 840	105 720	105 770	111 052	107 157	105 752	100 185	94 022	93 007
10 - 17 years	JF7N	7 056	7 205	7 624	7 393	7 567	7 394	6 189	6 309	5 961	6 122	5 743
18 - 20 years	JF7O	15 754	16 978	17 972	18 431	17 918	17 340	15 387	14 610	14 112	13 643	13 919
21 years and over	JF7P	70 664	75 989	79 244	79 896	80 285	86 318	85 581	84 833	80 112	74 257	73 345

1 Includes detention under the Powers of Criminal Courts (Sentencing) Act 2000, Secs 90-92 (Childrens and Young Persons Act 1993, Secs 53(1) & (2) prior to Aug 2000) (persons aged 10-17), custody for life under the Powers of Criminal Courts (Sentencing) Act 2000, Secs 93 and 94 (1) (persons aged 18 - 20), mandatory life sentences under the Powers of Criminal Courts (Sentencing) Act 2000

Sec 109 (persons aged 18 and over) and immediate imprisonment (persons aged 21 and over). Indeterminate sentences for public protection under the Criminal Justice Act 2003 are excluded.

2 Excludes life and indeterminate sentences.

Source: Office for Criminal Justice Reform:020 8760 1404

11.10 Receptions and average population in custody
England and Wales

Numbers[1]

		1997	1998	1999	2000	2001	2002	2003	2004	2005	2006	2007
Receptions												
Type of inmate:												
Untried	KEDA	62 066	64 697	64 572	54 892	53 467	58 708	58 696	54 556	55 455	55 809	55 305
Convicted, unsentenced	KEDB	36 424	43 387	45 893	43 889	46 851	53 301	53 246	50 115	49 104	47 995	43 566
Sentenced	KEDE	87 168	91 282	93 965	93 671	91 978	94 807	93 495	95 161	92 452	90 038	91 736
Immediate custodial sentence	KEDF	80 832	85 908	90 238	91 195	90 523	93 615	92 245	93 326	90 414	88 134	90 261
Young offenders	KEDG	18 743	19 599	21 020	21 333	20 969	20 236	18 179	18 264	17 819	17 985	19 022
Up to 12 months	KEDH	11 867	12 942	14 330	14 639	14 234	12 891	11 850	11 855	11 610	11 526	12 295
12 months up to 4 years	KEDJ	5 949	5 921	5 904	5 877	5 856	6 355	5 412	5 426	5 243	5 317	5 530
4 years up to and including life	KEDL	927	736	786	817	879	990	917	983	966	1 142	1 197
Adults	KFBO	62 089	66 309	69 218	69 862	69 554	73 379	74 066	75 062	72 595	70 149	71 239
Up to 12 months	KEDV	38 702	42 513	45 662	46 759	46 146	47 870	48 962	49 814	48 190	45 768	46 706
12 months up to 4 years	KEDW	17 546	18 100	17 751	17 290	17 116	18 313	17 968	17 988	17 397	16 970	17 233
4 years up to and including life	KEDX	5 841	5 696	5 805	5 813	6 292	7 196	7 136	7 260	7 008	7 411	7 300
Committed in default of payment												
of a fine	KEDY	6 336	5 374	3 727	2 476	1 455	1 192	1 250	1 835	1 876	1 904	1 475
Young offenders	KEEA	555	568	366	216	138	110	116	155	162	118	92
Adults	KAFQ	5 781	4 806	3 361	2 260	1 317	1 082	1 134	1 680	1 714	1 786	1 383
Non-criminal prisoners	KEDM	3 204	3 290	3 271	3 153	4 630	2 674	3 142	3 669	3 668	4 734	3 888
Immigration Act 1971	KEDN	2 122	2 348	2 443	2 455	4 035	2 093	2 457	3 041	3 093	4 073	3 347
Others	KEDO	1 082	942	828	698	595	581	685	628	575	661	541
Average population												
Total in custody	KEDP	61 114	65 298	64 771	64 602	66 301	70 861	73 038	74 657	75 979	78 150	80 395
Total in prison service establishments	KFBQ	61 114	65 298	64 771	64 602	66 301	70 778	73 038	74 657	75 979	78 127	80 216
Police cells[2]	KFBN	–	–	–	–	–	83	–	–	–	22	179
Untried	KEDQ	8 453	8 157	7 947	7 098	6 924	7 727	7 862	7 735	8 088	8 293	8 273
Convicted, unsentenced	KEDR	3 678	4 411	4 571	4 177	4 314	5 064	5 060	4 750	4 806	4 967	4 560
Sentenced	KEDU	48 413	52 176	51 691	52 685	54 051	57 222	59 007	61 071	61 991	63 504	65 963
Immediate custodial sentence	KFBR	48 272	52 045	51 596	52 620	54 006	57 184	58 959	61 012	61 925	63 429	65 533
Young offenders	KFBS	7 821	8 490	8 336	8 435	8 558	8 777	8 421	8 290	8 239	8 535	9 188
Determinate sentence	I7IJ	7 707	8 363	8 197	8 288	8 408	8 616	8 262	8 123	8 030	8 141	8 502
Indeterminate sentence	I7IL	114	127	139	147	150	161	159	167	209	394	683
Adults	KFCO	40 451	43 556	43 261	44 185	45 448	48 408	50 536	52 721	53 686	54 894	56 776
Determinate sentence	I7IK	36 838	39 733	39 183	39 779	40 768	43 411	45 278	47 264	47 914	47 885	47 850
Indeterminate sentence	I7IM	3 613	3 823	4 078	4 406	4 680	4 997	5 258	5 457	5 772	7 009	8 850
Committed in default of payment												
of a fine	KFCS	141	131	95	64	45	37	48	59	71	82	79
Young offenders	KFEW	13	15	9	4	6	2	3	4	3	3	3
Adults	KFEX	128	116	86	59	39	35	45	54	68	79	76
Non-criminal prisoners	KEEB	572	554	558	641	1 012	847	1 107	1 100	1 087	1 355	1 420
Immigration Act 1971	KEEC	485	474	485	576	955	777	1 041	1 033	1 022	1 288	1 348
Others	KEED	87	79	73	63	57	69	67	68	65	65	72
Accommodation[3]	I7IQ	56 329	61 253	62 369	63 436	63 757	64 232	66 104	67 576	69 443	70 585	73 618

1 The components do not always add up to the totals as they have been rounded independently.
2 Mostly untried prisoners.
3 In use Certified Normal Accommodation at 30 June every year.

Source: Ministry of Justice: 020 7210 0638

11.11 Prison population serving sentences: by age and offence[1,2]
England and Wales

Numbers

	15 - 17	18 - 20	21 - 24	25 - 29	30 - 39	40 - 49	50 - 59	60 and over	Total
At 30 June 2002									
Offences									
Males									
Total	1 986	5 821	9 722	10 196	15 415	6 630	2 832	1 365	53 967
Violence against the person	336	1 187	1 942	1 937	3 490	1 769	749	267	11 678
Sexual offences	58	167	262	406	1 347	1 241	996	794	5 270
Burglary	396	1 130	2 159	2 331	2 379	448	58	15	8 917
Robbery	503	1 285	1 647	1 390	1 865	443	66	10	7 208
Theft, handling, fraud and forgery	302	570	1 055	1 105	1 416	480	213	62	5 203
Drugs offences	43	431	1 255	1 763	3 142	1 496	495	129	8 754
Other offences	275	875	1 195	1 103	1 555	640	205	73	5 921
Offences not known	72	174	207	162	222	113	50	15	1 016
Females									
Total	103	356	596	662	1 030	439	134	19	3 339
Violence against the person	27	67	73	85	163	84	33	6	538
Sexual offences	-	1	-	1	11	6	3	1	23
Burglary	9	37	58	54	68	12	1	-	239
Robbery	19	63	89	65	60	14	3	1	314
Theft, handling, fraud and forgery	22	56	103	139	168	68	20	4	581
Drugs offences	8	94	206	256	474	216	60	6	1 319
Other offences	12	32	52	50	73	34	9	1	262
Offences not known	6	7	16	13	13	5	4	-	63
At 30 June 2003									
Offences									
Males									
Total	1 724	5 740	10 112	10 441	16 304	7 252	2 975	1 413	55 962
Violence against the person	310	1 257	2 112	2 068	3 733	1 932	780	290	12 482
Sexual offences	42	183	310	390	1 376	1 353	1 023	838	5 514
Burglary	289	919	2 003	2 204	2 555	527	71	11	8 579
Robbery	436	1 370	1 910	1 546	2 022	514	69	12	7 879
Theft, handling, fraud and forgery	291	543	1 020	1 060	1 437	472	201	45	5 069
Drugs offences	43	452	1 256	1 791	3 215	1 579	528	127	8 993
Other offences	271	884	1 329	1 218	1 760	787	263	69	6 581
Offences not known	42	133	172	164	205	89	40	21	865
Females									
Total	57	305	670	702	1 100	492	123	28	3 477
Violence against the person	10	61	91	66	155	82	32	7	506
Sexual offences	-	-	2	1	11	7	3	2	26
Burglary	1	24	64	60	77	12	2	-	240
Robbery	21	60	105	100	93	24	4	-	407
Theft, handling, fraud and forgery	10	56	117	128	199	70	18	11	609
Drugs offences	6	73	226	271	453	253	54	8	1 343
Other offences	7	27	58	66	108	39	6	-	311
Offences not known	2	3	8	10	5	4	4	-	36
At 30 June 2004									
Offences									
Males									
Total	1 706	5 585	10 095	10 738	17 021	7 858	3 013	1 508	57 523
Violence against the person	326	1 353	2 247	2 272	3 965	2 107	799	304	13 373
Sexual offences	55	193	329	424	1 433	1 416	1 030	865	5 747
Burglary	242	855	1 807	2 141	2 662	608	71	11	8 397
Robbery	449	1 254	1 865	1 691	2 127	583	70	17	8 056
Theft, handling, fraud and forgery	272	502	903	1 045	1 479	573	180	63	5 017
Drugs offences	51	471	1 383	1 789	3 258	1 615	537	150	9 256
Other offences	286	848	1 390	1 249	1 895	868	284	87	6 900
Offences not known	25	108	171	126	202	87	41	10	769
Females									
Total	58	300	632	727	1 056	507	152	20	3 453
Violence against the person	15	70	98	89	192	95	36	9	603
Sexual offences	-	-	3	3	8	7	4	2	27
Burglary	6	19	59	83	56	22	3	-	247
Robbery	8	65	93	90	114	20	2	-	392
Theft, handling, fraud and forgery	11	28	100	140	171	67	25	1	543
Drugs offences	6	78	197	245	392	246	65	6	1 235
Other offences	11	37	75	72	108	44	13	2	361
Offences not known	2	3	8	7	15	7	4	-	46

11.11
continued

Prison population serving sentences: by age and offence[1,2]
England and Wales

Numbers

	15 - 17	18 - 20	21 - 24	25 - 29	30 - 39	40 - 49	50 - 59	60 and over	Total
At 30 June 2005									
Offences									
Males									
Total	1 782	5 595	9 937	10 969	16 843	8 731	3 256	1 594	58 707
Violence against the person	366	1 493	2 553	2 553	4 015	2 402	840	319	14 541
Sexual offences	65	186	397	505	1 436	1 552	1 084	922	6 147
Burglary	285	719	1 559	1 947	2 570	669	78	17	7 844
Robbery	422	1 307	1 819	1 705	2 035	649	83	15	8 035
Theft, handling, fraud and forgery	240	433	858	1 074	1 449	650	238	55	4 997
Drugs offences	76	491	1 332	1 834	3 263	1 741	544	148	9 429
Other offences	310	870	1 306	1 245	1 902	987	360	99	7 079
Offences not known	18	96	113	106	173	81	29	19	635
Females									
Total	55	269	614	680	1 073	585	179	24	3 479
Violence against the person	23	68	109	85	190	114	40	9	638
Sexual offences	-	2	3	4	12	8	7	3	39
Burglary	4	18	50	62	79	23	3	-	239
Robbery	16	59	61	82	102	20	3	-	343
Theft, handling, fraud and forgery	4	35	105	119	202	88	27	3	583
Drugs offences	3	54	195	255	366	268	84	9	1 234
Other offences	5	30	84	68	117	56	14	-	374
Offences not known	-	3	7	5	5	8	1	-	29
At 30 June 2006									
Offences									
Males									
Total	1 014	5 718	9 612	11 349	16 828	9 349	3 511	1 719	59 898
Violence against the person	381	1 563	2 616	2 977	4 109	2 609	935	348	15 537
Sexual offences	67	213	452	560	1 497	1 683	1 118	971	6 561
Burglary	275	707	1 363	1 838	2 554	715	97	15	7 563
Robbery	486	1 413	1 739	1 674	1 975	706	91	16	8 100
Theft, handling, fraud and forgery	200	451	830	1 093	1 598	707	214	54	5 147
Drugs offences	68	492	1 232	1 913	3 153	1 829	623	174	9 484
Other offences	327	835	1 326	1 231	1 838	1 040	406	129	7 129
Offences not known	12	43	55	64	105	60	28	10	378
Females									
Total	50	271	551	707	1 094	604	189	39	3 506
Violence against the person	11	75	111	101	205	118	48	9	678
Sexual offences	1	3	2	2	8	13	5	3	37
Burglary	7	13	39	63	80	24	2	-	228
Robbery	17	48	67	76	86	18	2	-	315
Theft, handling, fraud and forgery	3	30	97	171	232	106	24	7	671
Drugs offences	4	62	158	217	354	253	88	17	1 163
Other offences	7	36	61	72	120	67	19	3	385
Offences not known	1	5	5	4	9	5	1	-	30
At 30 June 2007									
Offences									
Males									
Total	1 827	6 354	9 860	11 653	16 606	10 092	3 823	1 973	62 188
Violence against the person	402	1 772	2 927	3 183	4 337	2 846	1 063	399	16 929
Sexual offences	73	276	487	675	1 555	1 909	1 202	1 112	7 287
Burglary	281	817	1 334	1 865	2 492	812	109	13	7 723
Robbery	495	1 558	1 855	1 716	1 928	774	96	14	8 437
Theft, handling, fraud and forgery	194	426	677	1 044	1 478	711	246	67	4 844
Drugs offences	71	546	1 285	1 858	3 002	1 908	689	210	9 569
Other offences	294	908	1 237	1 242	1 731	1 087	401	152	7 051
Offences not known	17	51	59	69	83	47	18	5	348
Females									
Total	56	280	475	662	1 011	610	202	49	3 345
Violence against the person	20	99	113	111	170	117	47	11	687
Sexual offences	-	1	3	7	16	15	4	2	48
Burglary	2	11	28	56	76	23	1	-	197
Robbery	13	54	53	78	82	27	2	1	311
Theft, handling, fraud and forgery	7	29	68	128	211	111	37	10	601
Drugs offences	3	42	124	201	335	230	90	19	1 044
Other offences	9	45	75	76	115	77	20	6	423
Offences not known	2	-	10	5	6	10	2	-	35

1 The data presented in this table are drawn from administrative IT systems. Where figures in the table have been rounded to the nearest whole number, the rounded components do not always add to the totals, which are calculated and rounded independently. Reconciliation exercises with published Home Office figures may demonstrate differences due to rounded components. A programme of work is currently being undertaken to audit the quality of the data and to identify priorities for improvements.
2 Excludes persons committed in default of payment of a fine.

Source: Ministry of Justice: 020 7210 8500

11.12 Expenditure on prisons
England and Wales

Operating cost and total capital employed, years ending 31 March   £ thousand

		2001 /02	2002 /03	2003 /04	2004 /05	2005 /06	2006 /07	2007 /08
Expenditure								
Staff costs	KWUV	1 138 400	1 259 502	1 364 193	1 439 882	1 498 446	1 586 126	1 646 757
Accommodation costs	KXCO	193 100	200 000	194 000	185 400	150 270	138 322	144 170
Other operating costs	KXCP	706 100	756 198	653 007	694 618	528 529	498 913	511 688
Depreciation	KXCQ	128 100	132 600	129 600	143 800	7 974	11 044	12 135
Cost of capital	KXCR	284 900	292 700	164 400	170 300	279	905	−610
Total expenditure	KXCS	2 450 600	2 641 000	2 505 200	2 634 000	2 185 498	2 235 310	2 314 140
Income								
Contributions from industries	KXCT	−11 600	−10 100	−11 000	−10 600	−11 154	−7 698	−7 079
Other operating income	KXCU	−13 100	−15 500	−21 000	−38 400	−41 323	−45 411	−43 566
Income from Other Government Departments[1]	GDPM	−180 600	−210 200	−368 000	−381 500	−302 549	−245 917	−205 524
Total income	KXCV	−205 300	−235 800	−400 000	−430 500	−355 026	−299 026	−256 169
Net operating costs	KXCW	2 245 300	2 405 200	2 105 200	2 203 500	1 830 472	1 936 284	2 057 971
Total capital employed	KXCX	4 859 600	4 821 500	5 228 600	5 116 700	5 716	−52 207	−42 577

1 Income from the Youth Justice Board (a non-departmental public body of the Home Office) for the provision of juvenile custody within the Prison Service, Department for Education and Skills for the provision of education services and Department of Health and PCTs for the provision of healthcare.

Source: NOMS Agency: 020 7217 5213

11.13 Crimes and offences recorded by the police: by crime group[1]
Scotland

Thousands

		1998 /99	1999 /00	2000 /01	2001 /02	2002 /03	2003 /04	2004[4] /05	2005 /06	2006 /07	2007 /08
Non-sexual crimes of violence against the person	BEBC	19.8	15.8	14.9	15.7	16.1	15.1	14.7	13.8	14.1	12.9
Serious assault, etc[2]	KAFS	6.7	7.3	6.9	7.5	7.6	7.5	7.8	7.2	7.5	6.9
Robbery	KAFU	5.0	4.9	4.3	4.6	4.6	4.2	3.7	3.6	3.6	3.1
Other	KAFV	3.0	3.6	3.6	3.5	3.8	3.5	3.2	3.0	3.0	3.0
Crimes involving indecency	BEBD	7.1	5.8	5.8	6.0	6.6	6.8	7.3	6.6	6.8	6.6
Rape and attempted rape[1]	OXBQ	0.8	0.8	0.7	0.8	0.9	1.0	1.1	1.2	1.1	1.1
Indecent assault[1]	OXBR	1.3	1.1	1.0	1.2	1.4	1.4	1.5	1.5	1.7	1.7
Lewd and indecent behaviour	KAFY	2.9	2.3	2.4	2.4	2.8	2.6	2.8	2.7	2.6	2.6
Other	KAFZ	2.1	1.7	1.6	1.6	1.6	1.7	1.9	1.2	1.4	1.3
Crimes involving dishonesty	BEBE	276.9	275.6	253.3	242.8	224.8	211.0	210.4	187.8	183.7	166.7
Housebreaking[3]	KAGB	55.8	52.9	47.7	45.5	40.6	36.4	35.0	31.3	30.6	25.4
Theft by opening lockfast places	KAGC	12.1	11.6	10.6	8.2	7.8	7.4	7.9	8.3	7.4	6.4
Theft from a motor vehicle (OLP)	EPI4	39.5	38.0	32.0	32.7	30.4	26.8	20.4	16.5	16.1	15.2
Theft of a motor vehicle	KAGD	29.3	28.9	25.6	23.1	20.9	17.6	15.6	14.0	15.0	12.1
Shoplifting	KAGE	30.8	32.1	32.3	31.6	28.3	27.9	28.5	28.2	28.8	29.2
Other theft	KAGF	80.1	81.2	76.6	76.0	73.2	72.5	77.6	72.1	70.2	64.6
Fraud	KAGG	18.4	20.6	20.0	17.4	15.8	15.3	18.3	11.1	9.3	8.4
Other	KAGH	11.1	10.3	8.4	8.4	7.9	7.0	7.1	6.3	6.4	5.3
Fire-raising, vandalism, etc	BEBF	77.6	81.2	85.8	95.0	97.7	103.8	128.5	127.9	129.7	118.0
Fire-raising	KAGJ	2.5	2.3	2.4	2.9	3.8	4.2	4.7	4.9	5.0	4.6
Vandalism, etc	KAGK	75.2	78.9	83.4	92.0	93.8	99.6	123.9	123.0	124.8	113.4
Other crimes	BEBG	52.6	57.1	58.9	66.8	73.2	77.5	77.2	81.9	84.9	81.3
Crimes against public justice	KAGM	17.7	18.4	18.6	20.9	22.7	25.8	25.6	27.7	32.1	31.4
Handling offensive weapons[2]	KAFT	7.1	8.1	8.1	9.0	9.4	9.3	9.5	9.6	10.1	0.0
Drugs	KAGN	32.8	30.4	32.1	36.0	40.9	42.3	41.8	44.2	42.4	40.7
Other	KAGO	0.1	0.1	0.1	0.1	0.2	0.2	0.2	0.3	0.4	0.3
Total crimes	KAGQ	434.1	435.5	418.5	426.2	418.3	414.2	438.1	417.8	419.3	385.5
Miscellaneous offences	BEBH	153.2	151.9	154.8	163.4	169.6	181.0	214.3	219.5	232.4	224.3
Minor assault	KAGS	51.6	54.6	54.1	55.4	55.0	57.4	73.7	72.3	78.2	73.5
Breach of the peace	KAGT	71.7	71.3	70.2	72.7	74.7	77.9	90.0	89.6	93.4	90.3
Drunkenness	KAGU	8.4	7.6	7.8	7.8	7.3	7.5	7.2	7.0	6.7	6.7
Other	KAGV	21.6	18.4	22.8	27.6	32.6	38.2	43.4	50.6	54.2	53.7
Motor vehicle offences	BEBI	367.2	347.5	340.1	362.5	350.1	435.0	424.3	380.5	375.1	347.7
Dangerous and careless driving	KAGX	15.8	13.2	12.0	12.2	12.7	12.0	13.1	13.0	13.6	13.0
Drunk driving	KAGY	10.6	10.9	10.8	11.5	11.8	11.6	11.1	11.3	11.7	10.7
Speeding	KAGZ	119.7	123.4	113.9	126.8	117.2	199.2	210.1	167.7	162.9	137.2
Unlawful use of a motor vehicle	KAHA	76.0	80.7	84.3	94.6	99.5	99.5	76.7	75.1	73.1	73.7
Vehicle defect offences	KAHB	63.8	48.0	46.8	45.5	46.5	37.2	27.0	23.9	21.2	22.3
Other	KAHC	81.3	71.2	73.3	77.9	66.9	75.4	86.3	89.4	92.6	90.8
Total offences	KAHD	520.5	499.4	496.1	532.0	524.1	615.9	638.6	600.0	607.4	571.9
Total crimes and offences	BEBB	954.6	934.9	913.5	952.4	937.8	1 030.1	1 076.7	1 017.7	1 026.6	957.4

1 See chapter text.
2 Includes murder, attempted murder, culpable homicide and serious assault.
3 Includes dwellings, non-dwellings and other premises.
4 The introduction of the Scottish Crime Recording Standard on 1 April 2004 has increased the number of minor crimes recorded, such as minor crimes of theft, vandalism, petty assault and breach of the peace.

Source: The Scottish Government Justice Department: 0131 244 2635

Crime and justice

11.14 Persons with a charge proved: by crime group[1]
Scotland

Numbers

		1997/98	1998/99	1999/00	2000/01	2001/02	2002/03	2003/04	2004/05	2005/06	2006/07	2007[3]/08
Non-sexual crimes of violence	KEHC	2 039	2 000	2 003	1 976	2 092	2 381	2 596	2 427	2 455	2 441	2 723
Homicide	KEHD	104	92	105	100	103	99	131	143	111	118	129
Serious assault, etc	KEHE	1 039	1 036	1 053	1 089	1 171	1 360	1 475	1 374	1 560	1 480	1 721
Robbery	KEHG	666	652	659	603	627	682	689	610	509	527	539
Other violence	KEHH	230	220	186	184	191	240	301	300	275	316	334
Crimes of indecency	KEHI	1 329	1 280	790	633	614	562	666	810	853	862	785
Rape and attempted rape	HFVU	55	58	48	52	67	55	58	70	61	58	48
Indecent assault	KEHJ	91	83	84	60	48	65	93	87	84	81	116
Lewd and libidinous practices	KEHK	343	320	302	256	298	273	297	321	319	312	247
Other indecency	KEHL	840	819	356	265	201	169	218	332	389	411	374
Crimes of dishonesty	KEHM	25 272	24 726	22 652	20 571	21 536	21 700	19 887	19 665	18 045	18 447	17 736
Housebreaking	KEHN	3 174	3 071	2 860	2 676	2 672	2 752	2 508	2 373	2 074	2 025	1 868
Theft by opening lockfast places	KEHO	1 940	1 770	1 614	1 504	1 478	1 448	1 288	1 194	951	911	942
Theft of motor vehicle	KEHP	2 006	1 882	1 536	1 426	1 386	1 486	1 268	1 099	985	1 028	932
Shoplifting	KEHQ	7 313	7 559	7 753	7 345	8 366	8 826	8 123	8 427	8 162	8 548	8 407
Other theft	KEHR	5 866	5 796	5 026	4 303	4 234	3 783	3 521	3 551	3 187	3 303	3 138
Fraud	KEHS	1 992	1 920	1 595	1 448	1 479	1 459	1 444	1 355	1 245	1 180	1 165
Other dishonesty	KEHT	2 981	2 728	2 268	1 869	1 921	1 946	1 735	1 666	1 441	1 452	1 284
Fire-raising, vandalism, etc	KEHU	4 871	4 591	3 979	3 942	4 051	4 212	4 759	5 024	4 998	5 437	5 350
Fire-raising	KEHV	112	125	102	109	125	147	169	192	192	251	223
Vandalism, etc	KEHW	4 759	4 466	3 877	3 833	3 926	4 065	4 590	4 832	4 806	5 186	5 127
Other crime	KEHX	14 551	13 698	12 888	12 558	13 823	13 954	15 453	16 800	16 968	19 833	20 191
Crime against public justice	KFBK	5 096	4 776	4 589	4 929	5 257	5 048	5 290	5 767	5 753	7 206	8 028
Handling offensive weapons	KEHF	2 173	2 033	2 118	2 340	2 633	2 771	2 875	3 447	3 500	3 550	3 418
Drugs offences	KFBL	7 236	6 861	6 158	5 279	5 913	6 111	7 258	7 555	7 606	8 874	8 477
Other	KFBM	46	28	23	10	20	24	30	31	109	203	268
Total crimes	KEHB	48 062	46 295	42 312	39 680	42 116	42 809	43 361	44 726	43 319	47 020	46 785
Miscellaneous offences	KEHZ	42 051	35 024	29 505	28 651	30 152	32 062	34 536	37 492	39 679	42 278	41 143
Common assault	KEIA	12 441	11 677	10 749	10 270	10 823	11 745	12 317	13 574	14 427	15 441	15 460
Breach of the peace	KEIB	19 355	17 156	14 023	13 031	13 950	14 384	15 050	16 172	16 901	18 111	17 410
Drunkenness	KEIC	937	626	454	430	374	370	418	311	293	261	235
Other miscellaneous offences	KEID	9 318	5 565	4 279	4 920	5 005	5 563	6 751	7 435	8 058	8 465	8 038
Motor vehicle offences	KEIE	55 456	51 638	51 603	40 264	44 821	47 956	50 622	47 515	45 203	45 065	45 148
Dangerous and careless driving	KEIF	4 577	3 764	3 431	2 561	3 319	3 628	4 118	3 810	3 621	3 773	3 963
Drunk driving	KEIG	8 173	7 290	7 366	6 265	6 538	9 508	8 158	8 001	7 970	8 066	7 812
Speeding[2]	KEIH	12 220	12 971	15 293	9 427	9 988	9 832	12 700	13 546	12 273	13 434	14 114
Unlawful use of vehicle	KEII	20 052	18 662	16 950	15 987	18 553	19 192	19 563	16 696	14 711	13 449	13 569
Vehicle defect offences	KEIJ	3 198	2 470	2 075	1 302	1 252	1 510	1 859	1 791	1 653	1 709	2 298
Other motor vehicle offences	KEIK	7 236	6 481	6 488	4 722	5 171	4 286	4 224	3 671	4 975	4 634	3 392
Total offences	KEHY	101 272	90 879	85 792	73 526	79 482	84 963	90 253	85 007	84 882	87 343	86 291
Total crimes and offences	KEHA	149 334	137 174	128 104	113 206	121 598	127 772	133 614	129 733	128 201	134 363	133 076

1 See chapter text. Data as at 28 April 2009.
2 Includes motorway and clearway offences.

3 Figures for 2007-08 for some categories dealt with by the High Court - including homicide, rape and major drug cases - may be underestimated slightly due to late recording of disposals on SCRO.

Source: Scottish Government Justice Department: 0131 244 2229

11.15 Persons with a charge proved: by court procedure[1],[2]
Scotland

Numbers

		1997/98	1998/99	1999/00	2000/01	2001/02	2002/03	2003/04	2004/05	2005/06	2006/07	2007/08
Court procedure												
High Court[3]	KEIQ	1 105	1 043	1 174	1 092	1 125	1 194	1 217	974	882	858	804
Sheriff Court	KEIU	78 668	74 484	70 541	65 714	72 021	80 117	80 155	80 866	79 956	85 185	85 096
District Court[4],[5]	KEIV	57 388	50 784	46 052	38 422	38 484	41 516	47 144	47 891	47 358	48 319	47 176
Stipendiary Magistrate Court[4]	KEIW	8 406	6 646	5 652	3 365	5 455	..	..	..	..	..	..
Total called to court[6]	KEIZ	145 569	132 957	123 420	108 595	117 089	122 827	128 519	129 733	128 201	134 363	133 076

1 See chapter text.
2 All figures are now reported as financial years.
3 Including cases remitted to the High Court from the Sheriff Court. Figure for 2007/08 may be an underestimate due to late recording of disposals on the Scottish Criminal History System.

4 District Court figures from 2002/03 include the Stipendiary Magistrate Court.
5 Figure for 2007/08 includes Justice of the Peace courts in Lothian & Borders from 10 March 2008.
6 Includes court type not known.

Source: Scottish Government Justice Department: 0131 244 2229

11.16 Persons with charge proved: by main penalty[1,2]
Scotland

Numbers

Main penalty		1997/98	1998/99	1999/00	2000/01	2001/02	2002/03	2003/04	2004/05	2005/06	2006/07	2007/08
Restriction of liberty order[3]	ZBRE	..	106	196	152	166	656	879	1 097	1 136	1 179	1 151
Supervised attendance order[4]	ZBRF	56	31	37	5	11	13	18	33	99	112	129
Drug treatment and testing order[5]	OEWA	..	..	5	117	286	409	610	713	758	865	817
Absolute discharge	KEXA	508	403	368	364	415	385	435	403	401	411	427
Admonition or caution	KEXB	14 367	13 442	12 188	11 203	11 702	12 360	12 934	13 744	14 175	15 967	15 955
Probation	KEXC	6 278	6 824	6 542	6 654	7 708	8 451	8 137	8 623	8 785	8 612	8 984
Remit to children's hearing	KEXD	208	176	120	116	158	230	196	221	260	313	259
Community service order	KEXE	5 237	4 811	4 254	4 272	4 323	4 719	4 298	4 849	5 195	5 305	5 593
Fine	KEXF	102 617	91 393	84 255	70 683	76 217	78 541	84 327	83 237	80 723	83 445	81 742
Compensation order	KEXG	1 288	1 238	1 151	1 076	1 142	1 347	1 767	1 695	1 471	1 375	1 313
Insanity, hospital, guardianship order	KYAN	154	125	136	116	103	101	129	95	115	65	20
Prison	KEXI	11 028	10 635	10 609	10 430	11 437	12 427	11 960	12 307	12 153	13 449	13 530
Young offenders' institution	KEXJ	3 804	3 749	3 546	3 394	3 407	3 162	2 801	2 685	2 902	3 241	3 130
Detention of child	KEXM	24	24	13	13	14	25	24	20	24	24	26
Total persons with charge proved[6]	KEXO	145 569	132 957	123 420	108 595	117 089	122 827	128 549	129 733	128 201	134 363	133 076

1 See chapter text.
2 All figures are now reported as financial years.
3 A community sentence introduced by Section 5 of the Crime and Punishment (Scotland) Act 1995 and available on a pilot basis to 3 Scottish sheriff courts since August 1998. This sentence was made available to High Court, Sheriff Courts and Stipendiary Magistrates court from 1 May 2002.
4 The pilot scheme under the Crime and Punishment (S) Act 1995, where fines for 16 & 17 year olds were replaced by supervised attendance orders, was discontinued in December 1999. The majority of supervised attendance orders recorded from the year 2000-01 onwards were disposals relating to the breach of an existing order.

5 Drug treatment and testing orders are new measures made available on a pilot basis to the High Court and to Sheriff Courts for residents in Glasgow (from October 1999), Fife (from July 2000) and Aberdeen/Aberdeenshire (from December 2001). They are now available to all Sheriff courts and the High Court.
6 Totals from 2002/03 include a small number of cases where penalty is unknown.

Source: Scottish Government Justice Department: 0131 244 2229

11.17 Persons with charge proved[1]: by age and sex
Scotland

Numbers

		1997/98	1998/99	1999/00	2000/01	2001/02	2002/03	2003/04	2004/05	2005/06	2006/07	2007/08
Males	KEWA	124 691	114 884	106 654	92 919	100 874	104 312	107 932	108 460	107 801	113 465	112 349
Under 16	KEWB	134	112	75	56	80	129	96	107	133	121	155
16 to 20	KEWC	29 163	27 399	24 671	21 973	23 701	23 948	23 454	23 098	24 051	25 513	24 254
21 to 30	KEWD	48 751	43 599	40 048	35 251	38 441	39 405	40 053	39 336	38 078	40 389	41 076
Over 30	KEWE	45 643	42 857	41 047	34 957	38 362	40 811	44 324	45 913	45 536	47 440	46 864
Age not known	KEWF	1 000	917	813	682	290	19	5	6	3	2	–
Females	KEWG	20 158	17 405	16 188	15 302	15 871	18 160	20 120	20 775	20 039	20 598	20 477
Under 16	KEWH	14	2	5	10	4	5	17	18	8	9	3
16 to 20	KEWI	3 314	3 252	3 089	2 768	2 742	2 840	2 927	2 891	2 929	3 255	3 287
21 to 30	KEWJ	8 004	6 872	6 219	5 833	6 200	6 843	7 494	7 652	7 387	7 397	7 355
Over 30	KEWK	8 411	6 971	6 614	6 448	6 854	8 468	9 680	10 214	9 715	9 935	9 832
Age not known	KEWL	415	308	261	243	71	4	2	–	–	2	–
Males and Females	KEWM	144 851	132 298	122 858	108 279	116 768	122 484	128 068	129 253	127 848	134 069	132 835
Under 16	KEWN	148	114	80	66	84	134	113	125	141	130	158
16 to 20	KEWO	32 477	30 652	27 761	24 746	26 444	26 790	26 381	25 989	26 981	28 768	27 541
21 to 30	KEWP	56 757	50 473	46 272	41 094	44 652	46 252	47 556	46 993	45 468	47 786	48 434
Over 30	KEWQ	54 054	49 829	47 665	41 437	45 226	49 285	54 011	56 140	55 255	57 381	56 702
Age not known	KEWR	1 415	1 230	1 080	936	363	23	7	6	3	4	–
Companies	KEWS	718	659	562	316	320	343	451	480	353	294	241
Total persons with charge proved[2]	KEWT	145 569	132 957	123 420	108 595	117 089	122 827	128 519	129 733	128 201	134 363	133 076

1 See chapter text.
2 Includes sex unknown.

Source: Scottish Government Justice Department: 0131 244 2229

11.18 Penal establishments: average daily population and receptions
Scotland

Numbers

		1998/99	1999/00	2000/01	2001/02	2002/03	2003/04	2004/05	2005/06	2006/07	2007/08
Average daily population											
Male	KEPB	5 830	5 765	5 676	5 929	6 193	6 307	6 447	6 523	6 830	7 005
Female	KEPC	199	210	207	257	282	314	332	334	353	371
Total	KEPA	6 029	5 975	5 883	6 186	6 475	6 621	6 779	6 857	7 183	7 376
Analysis by type of custody											
Remand	KEPD	971	976	881	1 019	1 247	1 246	1 216	1 242	1 567	1 560
Persons under sentence: total	KEPE	5 056	4 997	5 001	5 165	5 226	5 375	5 561	5 614	5 615	5 815
Adult prisoners	KEPF	4 347	4 317	4 346	4 537	4 624	4 802	5 001	4 989	4 970	5 130
Young offenders	KEPI	708	679	655	628	601	573	560	625	645	685
Persons recalled from supervision/licence[1]	KEPN	78	100	145	202	250	310	356	400	519	614
Others[1]	KEPO	21	28	36	37	6	6	5	1	–	–
Persons sentenced by court martial[1]	KEPP	–	2	–	–	–	–	1	–	–	–
Civil prisoners[1]	KEPQ	1	1	1	1	2	–	1	1	1	1
Receptions to penal establishments											
Remand	KEPR	15 713	14 626	14 062	15 725	19 198	18 963	18 892	19 593	23 181	22 491
Male	KEPS	14 527	13 450	13 042	14 402	17 455	17 111	17 085	17 796	21 129	20 256
Female	KEPT	1 186	1 176	1 020	1 323	1 743	1 852	1 807	1 797	2 052	2 235
Persons under sentence: total	KEPU	22 376	20 336	19 136	18 953	20 084	19 357	18 584	19 477	20 403	18 227
Male	KEPV	20 952	19 125	17 953	17 755	18 779	18 013	17 272	18 161	19 018	17 011
Female	KEPW	1 424	1 211	1 183	1 198	1 305	1 344	1 312	1 316	1 385	1 216
Imprisoned: Adults:											
directly	KEPX	9 887	9 217	8 943	9 470	10 571	10 255	10 299	10 746	11 684	11 846
in default of fine[2]	KEPY	7 907	7 030	6 450	5 882	6 081	6 063	5 404	5 442	5 265	3 208
Sentenced to young offenders' institution:											
directly	KEQA	2 824	2 582	2 436	2 312	2 207	1 949	1 908	2 170	2 286	2 359
in default of fine[2]	KEQB	1 606	1 328	1 116	1 109	1 016	825	694	771	698	402
Persons recalled from supervision/licence[3]	JYYD	152	179	191	180	209	265	279	348	470	412
Persons sentenced by court martial	KEQH	2	3	2	2	3	1	5	–	–	1
Civil prisoners[2]	KEQI	10	17	10	8	11	10	7	4	4	11

1 Persons recalled from supervision/licence and others are included in persons under sentence. Persons sentenced by court martial and civil prisoners are not included in persons under sentence.

2 Includes in default of compensation orders.
3 Now covers all recalls from supervised release orders.

Source: The Scottish Government Justice Department: 0131 244 8740

11.19 Expenditure on penal establishments[1]
Scotland

Years ended 31 March

£ thousand

		1997/98	1998/99	1999/00	2000/01	2001/02	2002/03	2003/04	2004/05	2005/06	2006/07	2007/08
Departmental Expenditure												
Manpower and Associated Services	KPHC	137 890	144 660	170 347	160 242	172 490	168 593	169 784	181 931	200 742	199 854	206 298
Prisoner and Associated Costs	KPHD	16 313	18 891	22 930	23 501	24 652	23 363	51 070	42 767	28 582	41 821	29 408
Capital Expenditure	KPHE	22 136	23 697	28 918	24 283	24 955	36 519	34 617	72 812	70 406	81 818	53 564
Gross Expenditure	KPHF	176 339	187 248	222 195	208 026	222 097	228 475	255 471	297 510	299 730	323 493	289 270
Less Receipts	KPHG	2 810	8 160	6 668	8 380	8 194	3 485	3 298	3 312	2 872	2 178	2 034
Net Departmental Expenditure	KPHH	173 529	179 088	215 527	199 646	213 903	224 990	252 173	294 198	296 858	321 315	287 236
Plus Annually Managed Expenditure Capital Charges	DSJI	..	..	..	..	31 341	40 432	41 728	48 497	52 840	41 816	59 498
Total Net Expenditure	DSNX	173 529	179 088	215 527	199 646	245 244	265 422	293 901	342 695	349 698	363 131	346 734

1 See chapter text.

Source: The Scottish Government Justice Department: 0131 244 2225

11.20
Recorded crime statistics: by offence group[1]
Northern Ireland

Thousands

		Old counting rules				New counting rules									
		1995	1996	1997		1998 /99	1999 /00	2000 /01	2001 /02	2002 /03	2003 /04	2004 /05	2005 /06	2006 /07	2007 /08
Violence against the person	RVCP	5.2	5.6	5.2	RVCQ	18.5	21.4	21.4	26.1	28.5	29.0	29.3	31.0	31.8	29.6
Sexual offences	RVCR	1.7	1.7	1.4	RVCS	1.6	1.3	1.2	1.4	1.5	1.8	1.7	1.7	1.8	1.8
Burglary	RVCT	16.5	16.1	14.3	RVCU	15.5	16.1	15.8	17.1	18.7	16.4	13.4	12.8	11.6	11.7
Robbery	RVCV	1.5	1.7	1.7	RVCW	1.4	1.4	1.8	2.2	2.5	2.0	1.5	1.7	1.6	1.1
Theft	RVCX	33.5	32.8	29.5	RVCY	35.4	37.0	36.9	41.7	41.9	35.7	31.1	29.5	27.8	24.7
Fraud and forgery	RVCZ	4.9	4.1	3.8	RVDA	6.8	7.9	8.0	8.6	8.8	6.3	5.2	5.1	4.5	2.8
Criminal damage	RVDB	3.8	4.8	4.7	RVDC	27.7	31.2	32.3	40.0	36.6	32.4	31.4	34.8	36.3	30.9
Offences against the state	RVDD	0.3	0.4	0.5	RVDE	0.6	0.7	0.8	1.2	1.8	1.3	1.2	1.3	1.3	1.1
Other notifiable offences	RVDF	1.5	1.2	1.1	RVDG	1.7	2.1	1.7	1.4	2.4	3.2	3.3	5.3	4.5	4.7
of which drug offences	RVDH	1.4	1.1	1.0	RVDI	1.4	1.7	1.5	1.1	1.9	2.6	2.6	2.9	2.4	2.7
Total	RVDR	68.8	68.5	62.2	RVDS	109.1	119.1	119.9	139.8	142.5	128.0	118.1	123.2	121.1	108.5

1 See chapter text.

Source: The Police Service of Northern Ireland

11.21
Persons found guilty at all courts: by offence group[1]
Northern Ireland

Numbers

		1996	1997	1998	1999	2000	2001	2002	2003	2004	2005	2006
Violence against the person	KYCT	1 597	1 594	1 596	1 699	1 858	1 621	1 790	1 965	2 012	2 009	2 296
Sexual offences	KEVG	184	130	128	90	130	112	84	108	137	136	161
Burglary	KYDW	801	715	847	703	703	496	595	602	620	557	532
Robbery	KYBX	161	166	134	129	122	121	152	192	159	135	149
Theft	KYBY	2 765	2 596	2 342	1 995	2 111	1 831	1 695	1 803	1 819	1 819	1 728
Fraud and forgery	KYBZ	467	491	426	476	403	398	362	314	359	330	333
Criminal damage	KYCA	1 076	1 163	1 043	931	1 060	917	957	1 034	1 094	1 168	1 295
Offences against the state	KYCB	147	165	198	178	174	158	215	274	252	270	348
Other indictable[2]	KYCC	899	739	936	943	700	495	453	527	636	722	793
Total indictable[3]	KYCD	8 097	7 759	7 450	7 144	7 261	6 149	6 303	6 819	7 088	7 146	7 635
Summary[4]	KYCE	4 402	4 435	4 062	3 598	3 967	3 735	3 453	3 514	3 622	3 575	3 645
Motoring[5]	KYCF	18 177	18 770	15 369	15 782	15 390	14 466	14 344	16 342	17 215	15 534	15 083
All offences	KYCG	30 676	30 964	26 881	26 524	26 618	24 350	24 100	26 675	27 925	26 255	26 363

1 See chapter text.
2 1998 and 1999 figures include 'dangerous driving' (a triable-either-way offence).
3 From 2000, includes 'indictable-only' motoring offences.

4 Excludes motoring offences.
5 Prior to 2000, includes all motoring offences (except for note 2 above). From 2000, includes summary and triable-either-way motoring offences.

Source: Northern Ireland Office: 028 9052 7157

11.22
Juveniles found guilty at all courts:[1] by offence group
Northern Ireland

Numbers

		1996	1997	1998	1999	2000	2001	2002	2003	2004	2005	2006
Violence against the person	KYCH	75	49	97	73	77	66	82	75	78	146	152
Sexual offences	KAHF	4	8	12	12	4	1	6	5	7	9	8
Burglary	KYCI	137	124	108	117	125	73	77	89	66	113	81
Robbery	KYCJ	13	18	4	7	15	8	14	10	6	8	11
Theft	KYCK	338	334	304	227	254	244	212	173	183	291	202
Fraud and forgery	KYCL	14	11	4	10	2	9	3	7	2	6	7
Criminal damage	KYCM	121	136	139	102	143	152	132	162	129	241	240
Offences against the state	KYCN	6	10	11	12	8	10	20	26	18	19	40
Other indictable[2]	KYCO	24	10	20	17	10	12	7	19	22	46	44
Total indictable[3]	KYCP	732	700	699	577	638	575	553	566	511	879	785
Summary[4]	KYCQ	182	198	187	163	180	203	194	174	135	296	258
Motoring[5]	KYCR	58	57	98	97	82	102	89	94	76	280	230
All offences	KYCS	972	955	984	837	900	880	836	834	722	1 455	1 273

1 See chapter text. For the purpose of criminal proceedings, prior to 30 August 2005, a juvenile refers to a person aged 10 years or more but under 17. From 30 August 2005, the youth justice system was extended to include those under the age of 18. The number of juveniles convicted in 2005 and 2006 refers to those aged 10 years or more but under 18.

2 1998 and 1999 figures include 'dangerous driving'.
3 From 2000, includes 'indictable-only' motoring offences.
4 Excludes motoring offences.
5 Prior to 2000 includes all motoring offences (except for note 2 above). From 2000, includes summary and triable-either-way motoring offences.

Source: Northern Ireland Office: 028 9052 7157

Crime and justice

11.23 Disposals given to those convicted by court
Northern Ireland

Numbers

		1996	1997	1998	1999	2000	2001	2002	2003	2004	2005	2006
Magistrates court - all offences												
Prison[1]	KYAO	1 003	989	996	1 278	1 356	1 048	1 107	1 133	1 101	977	1 018
Custody Probation Order[1]	EOG9	..	..	..	..	..	..	..	7	7	9	12
Young offenders centre	KYAP	443	430	326	243	191	209	288	395	456	416	366
Training school[2]	KYAQ	147	148	136	13	..	..	..	..	..	..	..
Juvenile Justice Centre order[2]	OEUX	..	..	..	22	78	72	58	48	50	50	35
Total immediate custody	KYAR	1 593	1 567	1 458	1 556	1 625	1 329	1 453	1 583	1 614	1 452	1 431
Prison suspended	KYAS	1 722	1 506	1 025	1 080	1 247	1 215	1 278	1 407	1 469	1 584	1 692
YOC suspended	KYAT	444	461	139	104	93	77	100	201	372	375	335
Attendance centre	KYAU	91	66	55	14	20	37	84	91	108	127	132
Probation/supervision[3]	KYAV	1 134	1 155	1 473	1 246	1 096	1 070	1 005	974	991	977	1 045
Community service order	KYAW	591	561	622	678	726	587	643	623	647	628	597
Combination order	OEUZ	..	..	38	7	48	24	36	96	78	106	133
Fine[4]	KYAX	20 614	21 313	17 956	18 076	17 716	16 439	15 968	17 546	18 520	17 231	17 311
Recognizance	KYAY	1 203	1 267	1 134	1 089	1 357	810	912	1 091	913	853	693
Conditional discharge	KYAZ	1 679	1 597	1 538	1 439	1 286	1 559	1 497	1 526	1 524	1 326	1 093
Absolute discharge	KYBA	509	424	303	223	242	209	163	201	183	148	129
Youth conference order[5]	GGL8	..	..	..	..	..	..	..	..	21	74	304
Community responsibility order	GGL9	..	..	..	..	..	..	..	..	1	32	71
Reparation order	J8FR	..	..	..	..	..	..	..	..	..	..	1
Other	KYBC	15	8	123	221	57	61	104	215	190	122	61
Total	KYBD	29 595	29 925	25 864	25 733	25 513	23 417	23 243	25 554	26 631	25 035	25 028
Crown court - all offences												
Prison[1]	KYBE	469	475	520	386	521	407	410	238	259	248	318
Custody Probation Order[1]	EOH2	..	..	..	..	..	..	..	331	332	370	416
Young offenders centre	KYBF	106	111	63	67	32	42	23	51	47	41	38
Training school[2]	KYBG	–	4	2	–	..	..	..	..	..	..	..
Juvenile Justice Centre order[2]	VQEV	..	..	–	–	–	–	2	–	–	–	1
Total immediate custody	KYBH	575	590	585	453	553	449	435	620	638	659	773
Prison suspended	KYBI	253	220	199	185	313	262	220	240	262	260	267
YOC suspended	KYBJ	71	60	49	41	48	37	35	50	72	45	42
Attendance centre	KYBK	–	–	–	–	–	–	1	–	–	–	1
Probation/supervision[3]	KYBL	49	47	70	43	68	48	49	63	93	79	91
Community service order	KYBM	54	37	33	24	29	45	25	27	33	31	32
Combination order	ZAEP	..	..	13	6	7	5	18	34	33	40	22
Fine[4]	KYBN	39	40	25	20	40	38	32	49	108	57	51
Recognizance	KYBO	7	10	7	–	4	11	12	8	6	9	8
Conditional discharge	KYBR	30	31	23	17	38	36	20	24	45	28	33
Absolute discharge	KYBS	–	1	6	–	3	–	6	1	1	6	4
Youth conference order[5]	GGM2	..	..	..	..	..	..	..	..	–	–	5
Community responsibility order	GGM3	..	..	..	..	..	..	..	..	–	–	–
Reparation order	J8FS	..	..	..	..	..	..	..	..	..	..	–
Other	KYBU	3	3	7	2	2	2	4	5	3	6	6
Total	KYBV	1 081	1 039	1 017	791	1 105	933	857	1 121	1 294	1 220	1 335

1 Custody Probation Orders cannot be separately identified from 'prison' sentences from 1998 to 2002. Thus during this timeframe, figures for prison include custody probation orders.

2 The Juvenile Justice Centre order replaced the training school order from 31st January 1999.

3 Supervision orders were abolished with the introduction of the Criminal Justice (Children) Northern Ireland Order 1998.

4 From 2000, fine incorporates 'fine plus disqualification' and 'fine plus penalty points'.

5 Refers to the number of youth conference orders completed.

Source: Northern Ireland Office: 028 9052 7157

11.24 Prisons and Young Offenders Centres
Northern Ireland
Receptions and average population

Numbers

		1997	1998	1999	2000	2001	2002	2003	2004	2005	2006	2007
Receptions:												
Reception of untried prisoners	KEOA	2 188	2 284	2 497	2 197	1 922	2 337	2 439	2 440	2 776	3 193	2 929
Reception of sentenced prisoners:												
Imprisonment under sentence of immediate custody[1]	KEOB	1 062	949	963	1 001	791	916	1 032	975	966	1 075	1 123
Imprisonment in default of payment of a fine	KEOC	1 513	1 530	1 423	1 261	1 090	990	1 143	1 296	1 437	1 569	1 425
Total	KEOD	2 575	2 479	2 386	2 262	1 881	1 906	2 175	2 271	2 403	2 644	2 548
Reception into Young Offender Centres:												
Detention under sentence of immediate custody	KEOE	331	347	346	282	252	315	268	287	222	229	247
Detention in default of payment of a fine	KEOF	366	385	417	389	303	250	310	351	377	382	299
Total	KEOG	697	732	763	671	555	565	578	638	599	611	546
Other receptions[2]	KEOL	42	70	38	56	58	57	117	106	134	24	38
Daily average population:												
Unconvicted[3]	KEON	376	383	377	317	272	347	393	456	450	531	531
Convicted[4]	KEOP	1 256	1 124	867	751	638	679	767	818	851	902	935
Total	KEOM	1 632	1 507	1 244	1 068	910	1 026	1 160	1 274	1 301	1 433	1 466

1 Includes those detained under Section 73 of the Children and Young Persons (NI) Act 1968.

2 Non-criminal prisoners including those imprisoned for non-payment of maintenance, non-payment of debt, contempt of court or are being held under the terms of an Immigration Act.

3 Prisoners on remand or awaiting trial and prisoners committed by civil process.

4 Includes those sentenced to immediate custody and fine defaulters.

Sources: The Northern Ireland Prison Population in 2007;
Northern Ireland Office: 028 9052 7534

Lifestyles

Chapter 12

Lifestyles

Expenditure by the Department for Culture, Media and Sport

(Table 12.1)

The figures in this table are taken from the department's Annual Report and are outturn figures for each of the headings shown (later figures are the estimated outturn). The department's planned expenditure for future years is also shown.

International tourism and holidays abroad

(Tables 12.8 and 12.9)

The figures in these tables are compiled using data from the International Passenger Survey. A holiday abroad is a visit made for holiday purposes. Business trips and visits to friends and relatives are excluded.

Domestic tourism

(Table 12.10)

The figures in this table are compiled using data from the United Kingdom Tourism Survey (UKTS) and represent trips of one or more nights away from home. The UKTS changed survey methodology in 2000 and 2005. Data from 1995 to 1999 were reworked to allow comparisons to be made with 2000–2004 data. 2004 data should be used and interpreted with caution. 2005 data is not comparable with previous years.

Attendances at leisure and cultural activities

(Table 12.11)

The definitions used in this table differ from those normally used to define regular attendees by the Department for Culture, Media and Sport.

Gambling

(Table 12.12)

The National Lottery figures in this table are the latest figures at the time of going to press which have been released by The National Lottery Commission, and represent ticket sales (money staked) for each of the games which comprise the lottery. The figures have been adjusted to real terms using the Retail Prices Index.

The National Lottery commenced on 19 November 1994, with the first instant ticket being sold in March 1995. Various other games have been started since, the latest shown in the table being the Euromillions game. The sum of the individual games may not agree exactly with the figures for total sales. Total sales also include the Easy Play games which commenced in 1998, but were dropped in 1999.

The other gambling figures in this table are obtained from the Gambling Commission (formerly the Gaming Board) and HM Revenue and Customs. The figures have been adjusted to real terms using the Retail Prices Index.

The money staked at bingo clubs refers to licensed clubs only.

12.1 Expenditure by the Department for Culture, Media and Sport[1]

£ million

	Museums, galleries and libraries[2]	The arts (England)	Sports (UK)	Architect-ure and the Historic Environ-ment (England)	The Royal Parks (UK)	Tourism (UK)	Broad-casting and media (UK)	Admin-istration and research	Gambling and the National Lottery[3]	Comme-morative services (Queen's Golden Jubilee)	Regional Cultural Consortiu-ms	Unallocat-ed Provision	Total Resource Budget
	GQIF	KWFP	KWFQ	KWFR	LQYY	KWFS	KWFT	GQIG	SNKA	SNKB	GLZ8	GLZ9	GM22
2000/01	407	239	52	137	24	48	2 490	29	801	–	–	–	4 228
2001/02	302	254	67	133	42	68	2 337	33	897	–	–	–	4 134
2002/03	424	286	123	142	26	73	2 571	38	698	6	–	–	4 386
2003/04	446	329	66	153	26	53	2 489	42	712	–	–	–	4 315
2004/05	442	367	106	162	27	50	2 552	42	654	–	2	–	4 404
2005/06	512	407	121	146	31	51	2 572	49	825	–	2	5	4 720
2006/07	557	388	137	181	19	55	2 832	55	689	–	2	–	4 913
2007/08[4]	624	425	177	174	20	56	2 824	58	805	–	2	–	5 165
2008/09[5]	624	401	152	182	20	54	3 007	53	732	–	–	–	5 223

1 See chapter text.
2 Includes museums and galleries (England), libraries (UK) and museums library archives (UK) and culture online.
3 DCMS and Treasury undertook a complete overhaul of the way Lottery expenditure is recorded. For classification of the functions of the government (COFOG) purposes each lottery distrubution body is recorded separately, the exercise offered an opportunity to remove erroneously recorded data.
4 Data is estimated.
5 Data are forecasts.

Source: Department for Culture, Media and Sport: 020 7211 6121

12.2 Employment in tourism
United Kingdom

Non seasonally adjusted. At June each year

Thousands

	Hotels and other tourist accommodation	Restaurants, bars and canteens	Transport	Travel agents, tour operators	Recreation services	Rest of the economy	All tourism related industries	Of which: Employee jobs	Of which: Self-employment jobs
	EUR7	EUR8	EUR9	EUS2	EUS3	EUS4	EUS5	EUS6	EUS7
2000	230.0	556.1	132.2	135.2	73.2	205.2	1 331.9	1 214.4	117.5
2001	229.2	578.9	136.7	146.5	76.6	212.6	1 380.5	1 261.6	119.0
2002	225.4	601.1	135.5	140.0	82.1	213.6	1 397.7	1 277.9	119.8
2003	228.5	616.3	137.6	134.3	81.2	215.2	1 413.1	1 294.2	119.0
2004	238.0	634.0	136.1	144.0	87.2	217.2	1 456.4	1 326.8	129.6
2005	234.7	635.9	138.7	131.8	89.9	219.8	1 450.9	1 330.8	120.2
2006	235.4	631.3	143.6	117.9	93.3	221.6	1 443.1	1 316.2	126.9
2007	243.2	624.4	142.4	114.1	92.7	223.6	1 440.4	1 308.1	132.4
2008	245.1	627.4	144.9	121.2	99.7	225.4	1 463.7	1 317.7	146.0

Sources: Department for Culture, Media and Sport: 020 7211 6451; using data from Labour Force Survey, Office for National Statistics

Lifestyles

12.3 Employment in creative industries
Great Britain

Thousands

	Advertising	Architecture	Crafts	Design and designer fashion	Film, video and photography	Music and the visual and performing arts	Publishing	Software computer games and electronic publishing	Television and radio	Art/antiques	All
	EUS8	EUS9	EUT2	EUT3	EUT4	EUT5	EUT6	EUT7	EUT8	EUT9	EUU2
1999	200.9	101.5	96.8	93.5	61.9	255.7	317.0	488.6	92.5	20.8	1 729.3
2000	206.0	102.6	111.3	98.5	67.5	224.3	283.9	544.6	109.8	20.9	1 769.4
2001	220.5	103.4	115.1	103.0	75.5	224.6	293.3	567.7	104.1	20.9	1 828.1
2002	215.4	102.9	114.1	115.0	68.9	240.8	286.8	556.7	108.8	21.4	1 830.7
2003	213.8	103.1	108.7	113.2	74.3	245.8	305.2	581.2	110.9	22.5	1 878.8
2004	200.0	102.6	112.9	110.4	65.5	232.3	274.3	593.9	110.6	22.5	1 825.0
2005	223.4	108.2	95.5	115.5	63.8	236.3	253.3	596.8	108.7	22.9	1 824.4
2006	230.3	111.3	99.3	118.7	57.5	257.2	269.7	631.3	109.4	21.7	1 906.3
2007	247.2	120.7	109.7	130.7	65.4	262.8	275.8	640.9	103.4	21.8	1 978.2

*Sources: Creative Industries Economic Estimates Statistical Bulletin;
Department for Culture, Media and Sport*

12.4 Cinema statistics[1,2]
United Kingdom

	Sites (numbers)	Screens (numbers)	Total number of admissions[3] (millions)	Gross box office takings[4] (£ million)	Revenue per admission[3] (£)	Revenue per screen (£ thousand)
	JMHX	JMHY	JMHZ	JMIA	JMIB	JMIC
1999	751	2 825	139.1	549.7	3.95	194.6
2000	754	3 017	142.5	572.8	4.02	189.9
2001	766	3 248	155.9	645.0	4.14	198.6
2002	775	3 402	175.9	755.3	4.29	222.0
2003	776	3 433	167.3	742.0	4.44	216.1
2004	773	3 475	171.3	769.6	4.49	221.4
2005	771	3 486	164.7	770.3	4.68	221.0
2006	783	3 569	156.6	762.1	4.87	213.5
2007	775	3 596	162.4	821.0	5.05	228.3
2008	772	3 661	164.2	850.0	5.18	232.2

1 See chapter text.
2 Includes Isle of Man and the Channel Islands.
3 Admissions are based on all cinemas taking advertising.
4 Box office takings are for UK only.

Source: CAA/Nielsen EDI

12.5 Films
United Kingdom

Numbers and £ million

	Production of UK films		Expenditure on feature films (Current prices)		
	Films produced in the UK (numbers)	Production costs (1998 prices)	UK box office	Video rental	Video retail[1]
	KWGD	KWGE	KWHU	KWHV	KWHW
1997	116	558.0	489	369	784
1998	88	487.0	547	437	896
1999	100	570.0	563	408	878
2000	98	793.0	583	444	1 100
2001	96	..	645	465	1 417
2002	119	550.0	755	476	1 895
2003	173	1 158.0	742	450	2 244
2004	133	812.0	770	461	2 478
2005	131	577.0	770	399	2 317
2006	134	842.0	762	340	2 161
2007	117	747.0	821	297	2 353

1 In 2005 the British Video Association changed its methodology for producing market value which has necessitated a change to historical figures quoted.

Source: UK Film Council

12.6 Box office top 20 films released in the UK and Republic of Ireland 2004-2007

Rank	2004[1] Film	Box office gross £m	Rank	2005[2] Film	Box office gross £m
1	Shrek 2	48.10	1	Harry Potter and the Goblet of Fire[3]	48.59
2	Harry Potter and the Prisoner of Azkaban	46.08	2	The Chronicles of Narnia: The lion, the witch and the wardrobe[3]	43.64
3	Bridget Jones: The Edge of Reason	36.00	3	Star Wars: Revenge of the Sith	39.43
4	The Incredibles	32.27	4	Charlie and the Chocolate Factory	37.46
5	Spider-Man 2	26.72	5	Wallace & Gromit: The Curse of the Were-Rabbit	32.00
6	The Day After Tomorrow	25.21	6	War of the Worlds	30.65
7	Shark Tale	22.82	7	King Kong[3]	30.04
8	Troy	18.00	8	Meet the Fockers	28.93
9	I, Robot	17.98	9	Madagascar	22.65
10	Scooby-Doo Too	16.49	10	Hitch	17.39
11	Van Helsing	15.15	11	Nanny McPhee	16.49
12	Lemony Snicket's A Series of Unfortunate Events	13.26	12	Batman Begins	16.42
13	Starsky & Hutch	12.60	13	Pride & Prejudice	14.57
14	The Last Samurai	11.90	14	Mr & Mrs Smith	13.59
15	The Bourne Supremacy	11.56	15	Wedding Crashers	13.16
16	The Passion of Christ	11.08	16	Fantastic Four	12.71
17	School of Rock	10.50	17	Ocean's Twelve	12.58
18	The Village	10.31	18	Robots	12.48
19	Lost in Translation	10.06	19	The Hitchhiker's Guide to the Galaxy	10.67
20	Dodge Ball: A True Underdog Story	10.03	20	Valliant	8.52

Rank	2006[4] Film	Box office gross £m	Rank	2007[6] Film	Box office gross £m
1	Casino Royale[5]	55.48	1	Harry Potter and the Order of the Phoenix	49.43
2	Pirates of the Caribbean: Dead Man's Chest	52.52	2	Pirates of the Caribbean: At World's End	40.65
3	The Da Vinci Code	30.42	3	Shrek the Third	38.74
4	Ice Age II	29.60	4	The Simpsons	38.66
5	Borat: Cultural Learnings	24.11	5	Spider-Man 3	33.55
6	Night at the Museum[5]	20.77	6	The Golden Compass[7]	26.00
7	X-Men 3	19.22	7	I Am Legend[7]	25.52
8	Happy Feet[5]	18.86	8	Ratatouille	24.80
9	Cars	16.45	9	The Bourne Ultimatum	23.72
10	Superman Returns	16.12	10	Transformers	23.50
11	Mission: Impossible 3	15.45	11	Mr Bean's Holiday	22.11
12	The Devil Wears Prada	14.02	12	Hot Fuzz	20.99
13	Chicken Little	13.51	13	Enchanted	16.78
14	Over the Hedge	13.22	14	Stardust	15.02
15	The Departed[5]	12.80	15	300	14.22
16	The Holiday	12.34	16	Die Hard 4.0	13.89
17	Flushed Away[5]	11.13	17	Ocean's Thirteen	13.15
18	The Break Up	10.38	18	Hairspray	12.58
19	Walk the Line	10.36	19	Fantastic Four: Rise of the Silver Surfer	12.38
20	Brokeback Mountain	10.08	20	St Trinian's[7]	12.04

1 Box office cumulative total up to 27 February 2005.
2 Box office cumulative total up to 19 February 2006.
3 Films were still being exhibited on 19 February 2006.
4 Box office cumulative total up to 4 March 2007.
5 Films were still being exhibited on 4 March 2007.
6 Box office cumulative total up to 2 March 2008.
7 Films were still being exhibited on 2 March 2008.

Source: Nielsen EDI, RSU

12.7 Activities undertaken by visitors from overseas during visit: by region 2007
Great Britain

Percentages

	London	North East	North West	Yorkshire	West Midlands	East Midlands	East of England	South West	South East	Scotland	Wales
Shopping for clothes/accessories	70	60	60	63	51	52	53	64	60	70	47
Shopping (eg fashion, design, home, antiques)	68	71	57	68	49	50	52	55	62	67	37
Visiting castles, churches, monuments, historic houses	57	35	33	64	37	33	37	61	56	78	54
Going to a pub	49	67	57	60	56	64	52	58	40	67	61
Museums, art galleries	51	24	30	42	26	16	30	44	35	45	34
Visiting parks or gardens	48	20	25	39	30	22	36	37	45	46	32
Socialising with the locals	30	38	61	39	59	57	47	54	47	56	62
Exploring other locations	31	27	34	31	33	31	32	62	49	60	49
Walking in the countryside	12	26	24	37	33	32	27	58	45	52	50
Going to theatre, ballet, opera, concert	25	8	9	5	13	6	15	12	8	12	2
Visiting coastline, countryside	8	20	19	34	22	26	23	52	39	55	40
Sports activities	11	15	18	29	22	30	23	29	22	37	31
Nightclubs	12	39	21	8	16	12	12	7	7	13	6
Learning activites	8	12	10	4	3	4	6	20	17	8	8
Zoos, aquarium, other wildlife	7	1	7	12	12	6	3	10	8	7	4
Watching sport event	3	14	10	5	9	10	6	4	4	7	6
Going to a football match	3	17	6	5	9	5	6	2	1	1	6
Visiting literary, music, tv and film locations	3	4	1	8	2	5	6	5	1	4	2
Visiting a spa/beauty centre	2	1	4	5	3	4	3	6	2	4	1
Researching ancestry	2	3	0	4	2	1	1	1	3	4	5
Playing Golf	0	0	1	5	3	3	3	3	4	7	3
Cycling	1	4	0	2	2	2	3	7	2	2	1

Source: Visit Britain

Lifestyles

12.8 International tourism[1]

Thousands and £ million

	Visits to the UK by overseas residents (thousands)	Spending in the UK by overseas residents		Visits overseas by UK residents (thousands)	Spending overseas by UK residents	
		Current prices	Constant 1995 prices		Current prices	Constant 1995 prices
	GMAA	GMAK	CQPR	GMAF	GMAM	CQPS
1998	25 745	12 671	11 573	50 872	19 489	21 847
1999	25 394	12 498	11 133	53 881	22 020	24 676
2000	25 209	12 805	11 102	56 837	24 251	27 281
2001	22 835	11 306	9 528	58 281	25 332	27 710
2002	24 180	11 737	9 641	59 377	26 962	29 311
2003	24 715	11 855	9 451	61 424	28 550	28 677
2004	27 755	13 047	10 146	64 194	30 285	30 444
2005	29 970	14 248	10 714	66 441	32 154	30 954
2006	32 713	16 002	11 641	69 536	34 411	30 904
2007	32 778	15 960	11 389	69 450	35 013	32 483
2008	32 010	16 440	11 403	68 820	36 620	32 472

1 See chapter text.

Sources: International Passenger Survey, Office for National Statistics;
01633 456032

12.9 Holidays abroad:[1] by destination

Percentages

		1971	1981	1991	2001	2002	2003	2004	2005	2006	2007	2008
Spain[2]	JTKC	34.3	29.8	21.3	27.9	28.5	29.8	28.4	27.2	27.8	26.5	26.6
France	JTKD	15.9	18.1	25.8	18.3	19.0	18.1	17.3	16.6	15.9	16.7	16.7
Greece	JTKF	4.5	6.6	7.6	7.8	7.0	6.6	5.7	5.1	5.0	5.0	4.2
United States	JTKE	1.0	5.5	6.8	6.3	5.4	5.5	6.1	6.0	5.1	5.2	5.4
Italy	JTKG	9.2	5.0	3.5	4.3	4.6	5.0	5.0	5.4	5.4	5.6	5.2
Ireland	JTKI	–	3.7	3.0	4.1	4.1	3.7	3.8	3.8	4.0	3.3	3.2
Portugal	JTKH	2.6	4.0	4.8	3.6	4.0	4.0	3.5	3.6	3.7	4.1	4.8
Cyprus	JTKL	1.0	2.7	2.4	3.5	3.0	2.7	2.6	2.8	2.4	2.4	2.4
Netherlands	JTKK	3.6	2.6	3.5	2.6	2.8	2.6	2.6	2.5	2.7	2.4	2.1
Turkey	JTKJ	–	2.3	0.7	2.0	2.2	2.3	2.3	2.7	2.7	2.8	3.7
Belgium	JTKM	–	2.2	2.1	2.1	2.0	2.2	1.8	1.9	2.0	2.2	2.0
Germany	JTKN	3.4	1.2	2.7	1.4	1.5	1.2	1.6	1.7	1.7	2.0	1.9
Austria	JTKP	5.5	1.1	2.4	1.1	1.4	1.1	1.4	1.3	1.2	1.2	1.4
Malta	JTKO	–	1.0	1.7	1.0	1.0	1.0	1.0	1.1	1.0	0.9	0.9
Other countries	JTKQ	19.0	14.2	11.8	13.8	13.6	14.2	16.8	18.4	20.0	19.6	19.5

1 See chapter text.
2 Excludes the Canary Islands prior to 1981.

Sources: International Passenger Survey, Office for National Statistics;
01633 456032

12.10 Domestic tourism[1]
United Kingdom

	Number of trips (millions)	Number of nights spent (millions)	Expenditure at current prices (£ million)	Average nights spent (numbers)	Average expenditure per trip (£)
	GQGY	GQGZ	GQHA	GQHB	GQHC
1999	173.1	568.6	25 635	3.3	148.1
2000	175.4	576.4	26 133	3.3	149.0
2001	163.1	529.6	26 094	3.2	160.0
2002	167.3	531.9	26 699	3.2	159.6
2003	151.0	490.5	26 482	3.2	175.4
2004[2]	126.6	408.9	24 357	3.2	192.4
2005[3]	138.7	442.3	22 667	3.2	163.4
2006	126.3	400.1	20 965	3.2	165.9
2007	123.5	394.4	21 238	3.2	172.0
2008	117.7	378.4	21 107	3.2	179.3

1 See chapter text.
2 There were concerns that data for 2004 was not truly representative of the United Kingdom population. Data for 2004 should be used and interpreted with caution.

3 The UKTS underwent a methodological change in 2005 and results should not be compared with previous years. The survey did not run between Jan-April 2005, as a result full-year estimates were made using Jan-April 2003 data.

Source: United Kingdom Tourism Survey, VisitBritain: 020 8563 3317

12.11 Attendance at leisure and cultural activities[1]
Great Britain
At Spring
Percentages

		1997/98	1998/99	1999/00	2000/01	2001/02	2002/03	2003/04	2004/05	2005/06	2006/07	2007/08
Attendance by men at:												
Cinema	JSPR	55	57	57	57	57	62	59	64	59	59	64
Plays	JSPS	20	19	21	21	20	22	23	23	25	25	32
Art galleries and exhibitions	JSPT	20	20	21	22	22	23	24	24	27	26	29
Classical music	JSPU	11	10	11	11	12	12	13	12	15	15	18
Ballet	JSPV	4	4	4	4	4	5	5	5	5	5	7
Opera	JSPW	6	6	6	6	5	6	6	6	7	7	8
Contemporary dance	JSPX	4	3	3	3	3	3	5	4	4	5	7
Taking part in sporting events - regularly[2]	EU5X	..	..	50	53	50	51	51	54	54	54	55
Watching sporting events	JSPY	87	86	85	81	76	76	74	77	75	70	65
Pop/rock concerts	C3Q8	..	..	..	..	..	25	26	25	29	30	37
Attendance by women at:												
Cinema	JSQA	54	57	55	54	56	60	62	63	61	61	64
Plays	JSQB	25	24	25	24	26	26	27	27	33	32	37
Art galleries and exhibitions	JSQC	22	22	22	22	23	24	24	25	30	29	30
Classical music	JSQD	13	13	12	12	13	13	14	14	17	17	18
Ballet	JSQE	8	8	8	8	8	9	10	10	12	12	14
Opera	JSQF	7	7	7	7	7	7	8	8	10	9	10
Contemporary dance	JSQG	5	5	5	5	6	6	7	7	9	8	11
Taking part in sporting events - regularly[2]	EU5Y	..	..	38	40	39	41	41	40	43	43	45
Watching sporting events	JSQH	67	66	66	58	56	57	55	62	61	55	47
Pop/rock concerts	C3Q9	..	..	..	..	..	21	23	24	26	28	34
Attendance by all persons at:												
Cinema	JSQJ	55	57	56	55	56	61	61	63	60	60	64
Plays	JSQK	22	22	23	23	23	24	25	25	29	29	35
Art galleries and exhibitions	JSQL	21	21	22	22	22	23	24	25	29	27	30
Classical music	JSQM	12	12	12	11	12	13	13	13	16	16	18
Ballet	JSQN	6	6	6	6	6	7	8	7	9	9	11
Opera	JSQO	6	6	6	6	6	7	8	7	9	8	9
Contemporary dance	JSQP	5	4	4	4	5	5	6	5	7	7	9
Taking part in sporting events - regularly[2]	EU5Z	..	..	44	46	44	46	46	47	48	49	50
Watching sporting events	JSQQ	77	76	75	69	66	66	64	69	68	62	55
Pop/rock concerts	C3QA	..	..	..	..	..	23	25	24	27	29	36

1 Percentage of resident population aged 15 and over attending 'these days'. See chapter text.
2 From 2002 the question asked to the respondent was changed.

Source: Target Group Index, BMRB International: 020 8433 4166

12.12 Gambling[1]
United Kingdom

£ million[2] and numbers

		1997/98	1998/99	1999/00	2000/01	2001/02	2002/03	2003/04	2004/05	2005/06	2006/07	2007/08
Money staked on gambling												
National Lottery - Total[3]	C229	6 325	5 809	5 450	5 315	5 029	4 670	4 614	4 757	5 000	4 911	4 966
Lotto including on-line	C3PU	5 408	5 064	4 641	4 416	4 038	3 479	3 225	3 225	3 021	2 858	2 752
Instants[4]	C3PV	917	744	612	590	606	592	641	729	804	943	1 109
Thunderball	C3PW	..	..	197	257	254	287	351	343	355	329	309
Lottery Extra[7]	C3PX	..	..	..	51	131	90	78	77	57	12	–
HotPicks	C3PY	..	..	..	..	..	222	244	219	228	222	210
Euromillions	C3Q2	..	..	..	..	..	..	15	104	427	464	476
Daily Play	C3Q3	..	..	..	..	..	..	45	59	54	49	50
Dream Numbers[8]	I67H	..	..	..	..	..	..	..	..	..	59	59
Lotteries (excluding the National Lottery)[5]	C3Q4	144	179	114	114	114	134	127	141	139	164	170
Bingo clubs	C3Q5	1 170	1 159	1 179	1 190	1 221	1 256	1 381	1 783	1 826	1 820	1 620
Football pools	C3Q6	400	286	221	185	151	124	112	109	90	88	..
Off-course betting[6]	C3Q7	7 869	7 916	7 996	7 689	9 969	17 985	32 265	44 971	44 437	36 553	..
Number operating in GB:												
Casinos	JE55	115	116	118	117	122	126	131	138	140	138	144
Bingo clubs	JE56	818	751	727	705	688	699	696	676	657	634	675
Gaming machines	JE57	250 000	250 000	250 000	250 000	255 000	255 000	250 000	244 000	235 000	234 000	261 000
Society Lotteries	JE58	614	634	646	657	678	651	644	647	660	651	562
on-course bookmakers[9]	JE59	..	..	..	..	..	..	..	..	..	..	579
off-course bookmakers[9]	JE5A	..	..	..	..	..	..	..	..	..	..	801
Betting shops[9]	JE5B	..	..	..	..	..	..	..	..	..	..	8 800

1 See chapter text.
2 Adjusted to real terms using the Retail Prices Index.
3 Includes Easy Play tickets which are not shown separately.
4 From 2003/04 includes Inter-active games.
5 From 2002/03 includes Hotspot lotteries.
6 From 2001/02 includes Fixed Odds Betting Terminals.

7 Discontinued July 2006.
8 Started July 2006.
9 The Gambling Commission started regulating the betting industry on 1 September 2007, the number of betting shops is an ABB estimate.

Sources: National Lottery Commission;
Gambling Commission: 0121 230 6666;
Department for Culture, Media and Sport: 020 7211 6451

Environment

Chapter 13

Environment

Environmental Taxes

(Table 13.1)

In 2007, government revenue from environmental taxes was £38 billion. As a proportion of Gross Domestic Product (GDP) this amounts to 2.7 per cent, and as a proportion of total taxes and social contributions, environmental taxes were 7.4 per cent in 2007. These proportions are lower than in previous years because growth in the economy and total taxes and social contributions has exceeded that of environmental taxes.

Air emissions

(Table 13.2 to 13.8)

Emissions of air pollutants arise from a wide variety of sources. The National Atmospheric Emissions Inventory (NAEI) is prepared annually for the Government and the devolved administrations by AEA Energy and Environment, with the work being co-ordinated by the Department for Food and Rural Affairs (Defra). Information is available for a range of point sources, including the most significant polluters. However, a different approach has to be taken for diffuse sources, such as transport and domestic emissions, where this type of information is not available and estimates for these are derived from statistical information and from research on emission factors for stationary and mobile sources. Although for any given year considerable uncertainties surround the emission estimates for each pollutant, trends over time are likely to be more reliable.

UK national emission estimates are updated annually and any developments in methodology are applied retrospectively to earlier years. Adjustments in the methodology are made to accommodate new technical information and to improve international comparability.

Three different classification systems are used in the tables presented here: a National Accounts basis (Table 13.2); the format required by the Inter-governmental Panel on Climate Change (IPCC) (Table 13.3); and the National Communications (NC) categories (Tables 13.5-13.7).

The NC source categories are detailed below, together with details of the main sources of these emissions:

Energy supply total: power stations, petroleum refining, manufacture of solid fuels and other energy industries, fossil fuel exploration, production, transport and offshore oil – venting and flaring.

Business total: iron and steel combustion, other industrial combustion and miscellaneous industrial and commercial combustion.

Transport total: road transport (passenger cars, light duty vehicles, buses, HGVs, mopeds, motorcycles) and gasoline evaporation from vehicles, tyre and brake wear.

Other transport: civil aviation (domestic cruise, take off and landing cycles); railway locomotives; railway – stationary combustion; shipping; national navigation; fishing vessels; and other mobile sources including agricultural machinery, gardening, construction and aircraft support equipment and mobile industrial equipment powered by diesel or petrol engines.

Residential total: residential plant, household and gardening (mobile).

Agriculture total: stationary combustion, manure liquid systems, manure solid storage and dry lot, other manure management, direct soil emission, and field burning of agricultural wastes.

Industrial process total: industrial process sinter production, iron and steel – flaring, nitric acid production, adipic acid production and metal production.

Solvent and other product use: paint application, degreasing and dry cleaning, chemical products, manufacture and processing wood impregnation, and tyre manufacture.

Land-use change: emissions from managed and unmanaged forests, and forest and grassland conversion.

Waste management total: treatment of domestic, industrial and other waste, including landfill and waste incineration.

Atmospheric emissions on a National Accounts basis

(Table 13.2)

The National Accounts figures in Table 13.2 differ from those on an IPCC basis in that they include estimated emissions from fuels purchased by UK resident households and companies either at home or abroad. These include emissions from UK international shipping and aircraft operators, and exclude emissions in the UK resulting from the activities of non-residents.

Greenhouse gases include carbon dioxide, methane, nitrous oxide, hydro-fluorocarbons, perfluorocarbons and sulphur hexafluoride which are expressed in thousand tonnes of carbon dioxide equivalent.

Acid rain precursors include sulphur dioxide, nitrogen oxides and ammonia which are expressed as thousand tonnes of sulphur dioxide equivalent.

Estimated total emissions of greenhouse gases on an IPCC basis

(Table 13.3)

The IPCC classification is used to report greenhouse gas emissions under the UN Framework Convention on Climate Change (UNFCCC) and includes land use change and all emissions from domestic aviation and shipping, but excludes international marine and aviation bunker fuels. Estimates of the relative contribution to global warming of the main greenhouse gases, or classes of gases, are presented weighted by their global warming potential.

Greenhouse gas emissions bridging table

(Table 13.4)

National Accounts measure to UNFCCC measure

There are a number of formats for the reporting and recording of atmospheric emissions data, including those used by the Department of Energy and Climate Control (DECC) for reporting greenhouse gases under UNFCCC and the Kyoto Protocol, and for reporting air pollutant emissions to the UN Economic Commission for Europe (UNRECE), which differ from the National Accounts consistent measure published by the Office for National Statistics (ONS).

Differences between the National Accounts measure and those for reporting under UNFCCC and the Kyoto Protocol, following the guidance of the IPCC, are shown in Table 13.4.

Emissions of carbon dioxide

(Table 13.5)

Carbon dioxide is the main man-made contributor to global warming. The UK contributes about 2 per cent to global man-made emissions which, according to the IPCC, was estimated to be 38 billion tonnes of carbon dioxide in 2004. Carbon dioxide accounted for about 85 per cent of the UK's man-made greenhouse gas emissions in 2007.

Emissions of methane

(Table 13.6)

Weighted by global warming potential, methane accounted for about 8 per cent of the UK's greenhouse gas emissions in 2007. Methane emissions, excluding those from natural sources, were 53 per cent below 1990 levels. In 2007, the main sources of methane were landfill sites (41 per cent of total) and agriculture (38 per cent). Emissions from landfill have reduced by 59 per cent and emissions from agriculture by 17 per cent since 1990.

Emissions of nitrous oxide

(Table 13.7)

Weighted by global warming potential, nitrous oxide emissions accounted for about 5 per cent of the UK's man made greenhouse gas emissions in 2007. Nitrous oxide emissions fell by 47 per cent between 1990 and 2007. The largest reductions were in emissions from adipic acid production between 1998 and 1999. This leaves agriculture as the main source, accounting for over two-thirds of emissions, mainly from agricultural soils.

Annual Rainfall

(Table 13.9)

Regional rainfall is derived by the Met Office's National Climate Information Centre for the National Hydrological Monitoring Programme at the Centre for Ecology and Hydrology. These monthly area rainfalls are based initially on a subset of rain gauges (circa 350) but are updated after four to five months with figures using the majority of the UK's rain gauge network.

The regions of England shown in this table correspond to the original nine English regions of the National Rivers Authority (NRA). The NRA became part of the Environment Agency on its creation in April 1996. The figures in this table relate to the country of Wales, not the Environment Agency Welsh Region.

UK Weather Summary

(Table 13.10)

For 2008, initial averages use data available from about 180 observing sites available on 1 January 2009. They represent an initial assessment of the weather that was experienced across the UK during 2008 and how it compares with the 1961 to 1990 average.

Enviroment

For all other years, final averages use quality controlled data from the UK climate network of observing stations. They show the Met Office's best assessment of the weather that was experienced across the UK during the years and how it compares with the 1961 to 1990 average. The columns headed 'Anom' (anomaly) show the difference from, or percentage of, the 1961 to 1990 long-term average.

Biological and chemical quality of rivers and canals

(Table 13.11)

The chemical quality of river and canal waters is monitored in a series of separate national surveys in England, Wales and Northern Ireland. The General Quality Assessment Headline Indicator (GQAHI) and General Quality Assessment (GQA) schemes are used in surveys to provide a rigorous and objective method for assessing the basic chemical quality of rivers and canals. In England the GQAHI survey is based on two determinants: dissolved oxygen and ammoniacal nitrogen, in previous years this assessment included biochemical oxygen demand however in 2007 this was removed from the assessment and the historic data recalculated. In Wales and Northern Ireland the GQA assessment is based on three determinants: dissolved oxygen, biochemical oxygen demand and ammoniacal nitrogen. The GQA grades river stretches into six categories (A-F) of chemical quality, and these in turn have been grouped into four broader groups: good (classes A and B), fair (C and D), poor (E) and bad (F)

To provide a more comprehensive picture of the health of rivers and canals, biological testing has also been carried out. The biological grading is based on the monitoring of tiny animals (invertebrates) which live in or on the bed of the river. Research has shown that there is a relationship between species composition and water quality. Using a procedure known as the River Invertebrate Prediction and Classification System, species groups recorded at a site were compared with those which would be expected to be present in the absence of pollution, allowing for the different environmental characteristics in different parts of the country. Two different summary statistics (known as ecological quality indices) were calculated and then the biological quality was assigned to one of six bands based on a combination of these two statistics.

It should be noted that the monitoring network only covers selected stretches which the Environment Agency are required to monitor. In England and Wales 32,000 km of river network are monitored out of an estimated total river length of 150,000 km. No canals are classified in Northern Ireland.

Biological and chemical quality of rivers and canals Scotland

(Table 13.12)

Scotland's previous classification schemes focused on describing the pollution levels of the water environment. As required by the Water Framework Directive, the new classification scheme for surface waters now assesses:

- the quality of the aquatic ecosystems within rivers, lochs, estuaries and coastal waters

- the extent to which they have been adversely affected by the full range of pressures on the water environment – from water resources and physical habitat to pollution and invasive non-native species

This new scheme which started in 2007 assesses the condition of each river, loch, estuary and coastal water and assigns it a 'status' from high, good, moderate, poor to bad.

The results on the current condition of our rivers, lochs, estuaries, coasts and ground waters are based primarily on monitoring data collected during 2007. However, as the new monitoring programmes have only been in place for one year, the Scottish Environment Protection Agency (SEPA) has supplemented the limited new monitoring data with data from previous assessments (where relevant and available). This is to ensure the classification results reflect the best current understanding of the status of the water environment. As more monitoring data are collected, SEPA expects its confidence in classification to progressively increase over the next five years.

Prior to 2007, river and canal water quality was based on the Scottish River Classification Scheme of 20 June 1997, which combined chemical, biological, nutrient and aesthetic quality using the following classes: excellent (A1), good (A2), fair (B), poor (C) and seriously polluted (D). The figures in the table are rounded to the nearest 10 km and may not sum to totals.

During 2000 a new digitised river network (DRN) was developed, based on 1:50,000 ordnance survey data digitised by the Institute of Hydrology. The DRN ensures consistency between all SEPA areas and includes the Scottish Islands which were not previously covered. Data based on this network were published for the first time in the 2004 edition of *Annual Abstract of Statistics* and are not consistent with data published previously. The DRN includes:

- All mainland and island rivers with a catchment area of 10 km2 or more. This is known as the 'baseline network'

- Mainland and island stream stretches with a catchment of less than 10 km² which are classified as fair, poor or seriously polluted and have been monitored. These are added to the baseline network to give a 'classification network'

It is intended that future emphasis will be placed on the baseline network, which will be the reportable network for the purposes of the European Commission Water Framework Directive. Efforts to improve the quality of the downgraded smaller streams will continue, but once this has been sustainably achieved, their monitoring may be reduced. Many of these streams are the subject of current attention because of their influence on the quality of larger classification network rivers.

Using the DRN scheme, data for every routine sampling point are automatically applied to an identified river stretch of predetermined length. The loss in total river length in moving to the DRN (that is despite the first time inclusion of island rivers) arises mainly from the exclusion from classification of thousands of small remote headwater streams which were never monitored, but assumed to be of excellent quality. The smaller reduction in length of downgraded waters arises mainly from using 1:50,000 maps for the DRN; in the former system lengths were hand measured from 1:10,000 maps, so more minor channel bends were included.

Reservoir stocks in England and Wales

(Table 13.13)

Data are collected for a network of major reservoirs (or reservoir groups) in England and Wales for the National Hydrological Monitoring Programme at the Centre for Ecology and Hydrology. Figures of usable capacity are supplied by the Water PLCs and the Environment Agency at the start of each month and are aggregated to provide an index of the total reservoir stocks for England and Wales.

Water industry expenditure

(Table 13.14)

The table is informed by the annual and regulatory accounts of water and sewerage companies and water companies of England and Wales. The elements that make up operating expenditure are as follows: manpower costs, other costs of employment, power, agencies, associated companies, Environment Agency charges, bulk supply imports, general and support, customer services, scientific services, other business activities, local authority rates, water charges, local authority sewerage agencies, materials and consumables, hired and contracted services, charge for bad and doubtful

debts, depreciation, infrastructure renewals expenditure, infrastructure renewals accrual, exceptional items and other operating costs. Capital expenditure figures are the addition to tangible fixed assets including management and general expenditure but excluding infrastructure renewals expenditure. Adopted assets at nil cost are also included.

Water pollution incidents

(Table 13.15)

The Environment Agency responds to complaints and reported incidents of pollution in England and Wales. Each incident is then logged and categorised according to its severity. The category describes the impact of each incident on water, land and air. The impact of an incident on each medium is considered and reported separately. If no impact has occurred for a particular medium, the incident is reported as a category 4. Before 1999, the reporting system was used only for water pollution incidents; thus the total number of substantiated incidents was lower, as it did not include incidents not relating to the water environment.

Bathing waters

(Table 13.16)

Under the EC Bathing Water Directive 76/160/EEC, 11 physical, chemical and microbiological parameters are measured including total and faecal coliforms which are generally considered to be the most important indicators of the extent to which water is contaminated by sewage. The mandatory value for total coliforms is 10,000 per 100 ml, and for faecal coliforms 2,000 per 100 ml. For a bathing water to comply with the coliform standards, the Directive requires that at least 95 per cent of samples taken for each of these parameters over the bathing season are less than or equal to the mandatory values. In the UK a minimum of 20 samples are normally taken at each site. In practice this means that where 20 samples are taken, a maximum of only one sample may exceed the mandatory value for the bathing water to comply, and where less than 20 samples are taken none may exceed the mandatory value for the bathing water to comply.

The bathing water season is from mid-May to end-September in England and Wales, but shorter in Scotland and Northern Ireland. Bathing waters which are closed for the season are excluded for that year.

The table shows Environment Agency regions for England and Wales, the boundaries of which are based on river catchment areas and not county borders. In particular, the figures shown for Wales are the Environment Agency Welsh Region, the boundary of which does not coincide with the boundary of Wales.

Surface and groundwater abstractions

(Table 13.17)

Significant changes in the way data is collected and/or reported were made in 1991 (due to the Water Resources Act 1991) and 1999 (commission of National Abstraction Licensing Database). Figures are therefore not strictly comparable with those in previous/intervening years. From 1999, data have been stored and retrieved from one system nationally and are therefore more accurate and reliable. Some regions report licensed and actual abstracts for financial rather than calendar years. As figures represent an average for the whole year expressed as daily amounts, differences between amounts reported for financial and calendar years are small.

Under the Water Act 2003, abstraction of less than 20 m3/day became exempt from the requirement to hold a licence as of 1 April 2005. As a result over 22,000 licences were deregulated, mainly for agricultural or private water supply purposes. However, due to the small volumes involved, this has had a minimal affect on the estimated licensed and actual abstraction totals.

The following changes have occurred in the classification of individual sources:

Spray irrigation: this category includes small amounts of non-agricultural spray irrigation

Mineral washing: from 1999 this was not reported as a separate category; licences for 'Mineral washing' are now contained in 'Other industry'

Private water supply: this was shown as separate category from 1992 and includes private abstractions for domestic use and individual households

Fish farming, cress growing, amenity ponds: includes amenity ponds, but excludes miscellaneous from 1991

Estimates of remaining recoverable oil and gas reserves

(Table 13.18)

Only a small proportion of the estimated remaining recoverable reserves of oil and gas are known with any degree of certainty. The latest oil and gas data for 2007 shows that the upper range of total UK oil reserves was estimated to be around 2.8 billion tonnes, while UK gas reserves were around 1979 billion cubic metres. Of these, proven reserves of oil were 0.5 billion tonnes and proven reserves of gas were 343 billion cubic metres. Compared with a year earlier, proven reserves were 5.6 per cent lower for oil and 16.7 per cent

lower for gas. The monetary value of oil reserves increased from £120.9 billion in 2006 to £177.9 billion in 2007, a rise of 47.1 per cent reflecting rising oil prices. At £68.3 billion, the value of gas reserves decreased by 1.6 per cent from £69.4 billion between 2006 and 2007.

Municipal waste disposal

(Table 13.19)

Municipal waste includes household and non-household waste that is collected and disposed of by local authorities. It includes regular household collections, specific recycling collections, special collections of bulky items, waste received at civic amenity sites, and waste collected from non-household sources that come under the control of local authorities.

Amounts of different materials from household sources collected for recycling

(Table 13.20)

Household recycling includes those materials collected for recycling, composting or reuse by local authorities and those collected from household sources by 'private/voluntary' organisations where this material comes under the possession or control of local authorities. It includes residual waste from the household stream which was diverted for recycling by sorting or further treatment.

'Bring sites' are facilities where members of the public can bring recyclable materials (such as paper, glass, cans, textiles, shoes, etc). These are often located at supermarkets or similar locations, but exclude civic amenity sites.

'Civic Amenity sites' refers to household waste collected at sites provided by local authorities for the disposal of excess household and garden waste free of charge, as required by the Refuse Disposal (Amenity) Act 1978. These are also known as Household Waste Recycling Centres.

Noise incidents

(Table 13.21)

The table shows trends in the number of incidents reported by local authority Environmental Health Officers (EHO). The figures are from those authorities making returns and are calculated per million people based on the population of the authorities making returns. Environmental health has changed from calculating complaints per million of population to incidents per million of the population in 2004/05. The reason for asking about incidents is to better reflect both the local noise environment and investigatory workloads during the reporting year, while avoiding the double counting which occurs with complaints (that is, multiple complaints about the same incident). This change is reflected in the data, which shows a drop in numbers across all categories.

Most complaints about traffic noise are addressed to highways authorities or Department for Transport (DfT) Regional Directors, and will not necessarily be included in the figures. Similarly, complaints about noise from civil aircraft are generally received by aircraft operators, the airport companies, the DfT or Civil Aviation Authority. Complaints about military flying are dealt with either by Station Commanding Officers or by Ministry of Defence headquarters. It is also true that railway noise will be reported elsewhere. Thus the figures in this table will not necessarily include these complaints and are likely to be considerably understated. Therefore, the information reported to the EHO is considered to give, at best, only a very approximate indication of the trend in noise complaints from these sources.

Over time some of the categories shown in this table have changed. These have included, up until 1996/97, Section 62 of the Control of Pollution Act 1974 which covered noise in the streets; it primarily included the chimes of ice-cream vendors and the use of loudspeakers other than for strictly defined purposes. From 1997/98, all complaints about noise in the street are included with 'vehicles machinery and equipment in streets'. From 1997/98, complaints about roadworks are included with 'vehicles machinery and equipment in streets'.

Material flows

(Table 13.22)

Economy-wide material flow accounts record the total mass of natural resources and products that are used by the UK economy, either directly in the production and distribution of products and services, or indirectly through the movement of materials which are displaced in order for production to take place.

The direct movement of materials into the economy derives primarily from domestic extraction, that is from biomass (agricultural harvest, timber, fish and animal grazing), fossil fuel extraction (such as coal, crude oil and natural gas) and mineral extraction (metal ores, industrial minerals such as pottery clay, and construction material such as crushed rock, sand and gravel). This domestic extraction is supplemented by the imports of products, which may be of raw materials such as unprocessed agricultural products, but can also be of semi-manufactured or finished products. In a similar way the

UK produces exports of raw materials, semi-manufactured and finished goods which can be viewed as inputs to the production and consumption of overseas economies.

Indirect flows of natural resources consist of the unused material resulting from domestic extraction, such as mining and quarrying overburden and the soil removed during construction and dredging activities. They also include the movement of used and unused material overseas which is associated with the production and delivery of imports. Water, except for that included directly in products, is excluded.

There are three main indicators used to measure inputs. The Direct Material Input measures the input of used materials into the economy, that is all materials which are of economic value and are used in production and consumption activities (including the production of exports). Domestic Material Consumption measures the total amount of material directly used in the economy, that is it includes imports but excludes exports. The Total Material Requirement (TMR) measures the total material basis of the economy, that is the total primary resource requirements of all the production and consumption activities. It includes not only the direct use of resources for producing exports, but also indirect flows from the production of imports and the indirect flows associated with domestic extraction. Although TMR is widely favoured as a resource use indicator, the estimates of indirect flows are less reliable than those for materials directly used by the economy, and the indicator therefore needs to be considered alongside other indicators.

13.1 Government revenues from environmental taxes
United Kingdom

£ million

		1998	1999	2000	2001	2002	2003	2004	2005	2006	2007
Energy											
Duty on hydrocarbon oils	GTAP	20 996	22 391	23 041	22 046	22 070	22 476	23 412	23 346	23 448	24 512
including											
Unleaded petrol[1]	GBHE	9 897	11 952	11 527	1 922	–	–	–	–	–	–
Leaded petrol/LRP[2]	GBHL	2 984	1 630	1 116	655	102	70	67	20	15	13
Ultra low sulphur petrol	ZXTK	–	–	972	10 198	12 548	12 025	12 086	11 645	11 274	11 213
Diesel[3]	GBHH	7 088	1 274	23	66	–	–	–	–	–	–
Ultra low sulphur diesel	GBHI	806	7 338	9 051	8 560	9 129	9 562	10 281	10 802	11 203	12 017
VAT on duty	CMYA	3 674	3 918	4 032	3 858	3 862	3 933	4 097	4 086	4 103	4 290
Fossil fuel levy	CIQY	181	104	56	86	32	–	–	–	–	–
Gas levy	GTAZ	32	–	–	–	–	–	–	–	–	–
Climate change levy	LSNT	–	–	–	585	825	828	756	747	711	690
Hydro-benefit	LITN	32	35	42	46	44	44	40	10	–	–
Road vehicles											
Vehicle excise duty	CMXZ	4 631	4 873	4 606	4 102	4 294	4 720	4 763	4 762	5 010	5 384
Other environmental taxes											
Air passenger duty	CWAA	823	884	940	824	814	781	856	896	961	1 883
Landfill tax	BKOF	333	430	461	502	541	607	672	733	804	877
Aggregates levy	MDUQ	–	–	–	–	218	340	339	327	331	339
Total environmental taxes	JKVW	**30 702**	**32 635**	**33 178**	**32 049**	**32 695**	**33 729**	**34 924**	**34 907**	**35 358**	**37 975**
Environmental taxes as a % of:											
Total taxes and social contributions	JKVX	9.7	9.7	9.3	8.6	8.7	8.5	8.3	7.7	7.2	7.4
Gross domestic product	JKVY	3.5	3.5	3.4	3.1	3.0	3.0	2.9	2.8	2.7	2.7

1 Unleaded petrol includes superunleaded petrol.
2 Lead Replacement Petrol (the alternative to 4-Star leaded petrol introduced in 2000) is lead-free.
3 Duty incentives have concentrated production on ultra low sulphur varieties.

Sources: ONS, Department for Business Enterprise & Regulatory Reform; environment.accounts@ons.gsi.gov.uk

13.2 Atmospheric emissions on a National Accounts basis[1], 2006
United Kingdom

Thousand tonnes CO2 equivilent

	Greenhouse gases[1]	Acid rain precursors[2]	Emissions affecting air quality							
			PM10[3]	CO[4]	NMVOC[5]	Benzene	Butadiene	Lead	Cadmium (tonnes)	Mercury (tonnes)
Agriculture	50 563	553	21.609	46.700	82.8	0.234	0.083	0.391	0.033	0.030
Mining and quarrying	26 759	92	13.236	35.400	95.8	0.437	0.015	0.294	0.074	0.022
Manufacturing	113 754	385	32.263	603.900	321.3	2.269	0.472	75.913	2.015	3.576
Electricity, gas and water supply	201 374	639	11.939	80.300	45.8	0.480	0.006	10.304	0.868	2.264
Construction	12 306	47	8.877	55.500	60.8	0.234	0.111	0.380	0.044	0.019
Wholesale and retail trade	19 810	53	6.191	70.700	55.0	0.262	0.168	12.286	0.095	0.034
Transport and communication	96 271	762	50.982	145.000	50.4	3.132	0.823	3.587	2.571	0.155
Other business services	7 300	14	1.898	46.100	4.3	0.105	0.040	0.114	0.037	0.003
Public administration	8 530	40	1.875	41.300	4.6	0.266	0.051	0.492	0.029	0.040
Education, health and social work	8 618	13	0.828	11.800	2.1	0.051	0.008	0.389	0.020	0.036
Other services	27 514	39	1.425	94.300	28.5	2.033	0.189	0.160	0.055	1.294
Households	151 658	256	37.829	1 098.900	247.1	7.082	0.630	4.574	0.344	0.156
Total	**724 455**	**2 892**	**188.953**	**2 330.000**	**998.5**	**16.586**	**2.595**	**108.883**	**6.184**	**7.600**
of which, emissions from road transport	128 533	391	32.979	998.500	104.400	2.623	1.450	2.1	0.418	0.004

1 Carbon dioxide, methane, nitrous oxide, hydro-fluorocarbons, perfluorocarbons and sulphur hexafluoride expressed as thousand tonnes of carbon dioxide equivalent.
2 Sulphur dioxide, nitrogen oxides and ammonia expressed as thousand tonnes of sulphur dioxide equivalent.
3 PM10 is particulate matter arising from various sources including fuel combustion quarrying and construction, and formation of 'secondary' particles in the atmosphere from reactions involving other pollutants sulphur dioxide, nitrogen oxides, ammonia and NMVOCs.
4 Carbon monoxide.
5 Non-methane Volatile Compounds, including benzene and 1,3-butadiene.

Source: AEA Energy & Environment, ONS

13.3 Estimated emissions of greenhouse gases on an IPCC basis[1,2,3,6,7]
United Kingdom

Million tonnes (Carbon dioxide equivalent[4])

		1990	1995	1996	1997	1998	1999	2000	2001	2002	2003	2004	2005	2006	2007
Net CO_2 emissions/removals	JZCK	592.9	553.1	575.3	551.6	553.6	543.0	551.1	562.5	544.9	556.2	555.9	553.2	551.1	542.6
Methane(CH_4)	GXDO	104.3	91.0	88.6	83.8	79.4	74.2	69.7	63.7	60.7	54.7	52.9	51.0	50.4	48.9
Nitrous oxide(N_2O)	GXDP	64.6	53.7	53.0	54.1	53.5	42.9	41.9	39.5	37.7	37.1	37.6	36.4	34.9	34.2
Hydrofluorocarbons(HFCs)	JZCN	11.4	15.6	16.9	19.5	17.6	11.1	10.0	10.7	11.0	11.4	10.0	10.1	10.0	9.6
Perfluorocarbons(PFCs)	JZCO	1.4	0.5	0.5	0.4	0.4	0.4	0.5	0.4	0.3	0.3	0.3	0.3	0.3	0.2
Sulphur hexafluoride(SF_6)	JZCP	1.0	1.2	1.3	1.2	1.3	1.4	1.8	1.4	1.5	1.3	1.1	1.1	0.9	0.8
Kyoto greenhouse gas basket[5]	F92X	773.0	714.1	734.7	709.8	705.4	672.7	674.7	678.2	656.4	661.1	658.6	652.8	647.9	636.6

1 Net emissions weighted by global warming potential. Emissions inventories based on the methodology developed by the Intergovernmental Panel on Climate Change (IPCC) are used to report UK emissions to the Climate Change Convention.
2 See chapter text.
3 Figures for each individual gas include the Land use, Land-Use Change and Forestry sector (LULUCF) but exclude emissions from UK overseas territories.
4 Emissions are presented as carbon dioxide equivalent in line with international reporting and carbon trading. To convert Carbon Dioxide into carbon equivalents, divide figures by 44 /12.

5 Kyoto basket total differs slightly from sum of individual pollutants above as the basket uses a narrower definition for the Land Use Change and Forestry sector, and includes emissions from UK Overseas Territories.
6 The entire time series is revised each year to take account of methodological improvements in the UK emissions inventory.
7 Figures shown do not include any adjustment for the effect of the EU Emissions Trading Scheme (EUETS), which was introduced in 2005.

Sources: AEA Energy & Environment;
Department for Energy and Climate Change: 0300 060 4000

13.4 Greenhouse gas emissions bridging table
National Accounts measure to UNFCC[1] measure

Thousand tonnes CO2 equivilent

		1990	1995	1999	2000	2001	2002	2003	2004	2005	2006
Greenhouse gases - CO2,CH4,N2O,HFC,PFCs and SF6[2]											
National Accounts measure	JKRU	809 034	754 034	727 332	732 433	740 044	720 803	729 880	734 743	734 875	724 455
less											
Bunker emissions[3]	A43J	22 633	27 166	34 362	36 402	36 330	34 685	35 175	38 761	41 324	42 817
CO2 from biomass[4]	A43K	2 980	5 240	6 411	6 573	7 261	7 507	8 352	9 349	9 198	9 433
Cross boundary adjustment[5]	A43L	13 082	12 910	16 541	17 432	21 317	23 848	25 677	27 336	27 342	18 167
plus											
Crown Dependancies[6]	EQ44	296	305	331	291	289	271	227	216	228	255
Landuse change / forestry[7]	A43M	2 912	1 194	−284	−413	−543	−1 107	−1 141	−1 888	−2 058	−1 991
UNFCC Reported[8,9] (exc. overseas territories)	A43N	773 547	710 218	670 065	671 905	674 881	653 927	659 761	657 625	655 181	652 302

1 United Nations Framework Convention on Climate Change.
2 Carbon dioxide, methane, nitrous oxide, hydrofluorocarbons, perfluorocarbon and sulphur hexafluoride expressed as thousand tonnes of carbon dioxide equivalent.
3 Bunker emissions include IPCC memo items International Aviation (source no. 126) and international Shipping (source no. 127).
4 Emissions arising from wood, straw, biogases and poultry litter combustion for energy production.
5 Emissions generated by UK households and businesses transport and travel abroad, net of emissions generated by non-residents travel and transport in the UK.
6 Includes emissions of crown dependancies; Guernsey, Jersey, Isle of Man.

The total used for assessing progress against the Kyoto Protocol target differs slightly from the sum of greenhouse gases reported above in the table due to differences in the coverage of land use change and forestry Cayman Islands, Falkland Islands and Montserrat.
7 Emissions from deforestation, soils and changes in forest and other woody biomass.
8 Excludes emissions from overseas territories. The UK's base year for the Kyoto target of a 12.5 per cent reduction by 2008-12 is the sum of 1990 emissions for Co2, CH4, and N2O and from 1995 emissions for HFC, PFC and SF6.
9 A link to Defra's Greenhouse Gas Inventory report can be found at http://www.airquality.co.uk/archive/reports/cat07/0809291432_DA_ghgi-report _2006_main_text_Issue_1r.pdf

Source: AEA Energy & Environment, DECC, ONS

13.5 Estimated emissions[1] of carbon dioxide (CO_2)
United Kingdom

Million tonnes as CO_2

		1970	1980	1990	1996	1997	1998	1999	2000	2001	2002	2003	2004	2005	2006	2007
By source NC category																
Energy Supply Total	I6AH	260.3	262.0	243.1	214.1	199.0	203.2	192.4	202.6	213.1	210.2	217.5	215.7	216.3	219.1	215.2
Business Total	I6AI	204.2	131.4	108.5	105.2	103.4	102.4	103.4	103.6	103.6	93.4	95.0	93.0	92.4	90.5	88.1
Transport Total	I6AJ	71.3	90.1	122.6	127.0	128.2	127.0	127.8	126.7	126.4	128.4	129.3	130.8	131.9	133.6	134.9
Public	I6AK	23.7	19.7	13.5	14.2	13.8	12.6	12.4	11.7	12.1	10.3	10.1	11.1	11.0	10.5	9.6
Residential Total	I6AL	96.2	84.4	79.8	92.3	85.2	87.2	86.3	87.0	89.2	85.9	86.8	88.4	84.6	81.3	77.6
Agriculture Total	I6AM	6.2	5.2	5.2	5.3	5.2	5.1	5.1	4.7	4.8	4.8	4.7	4.6	4.5	4.3	4.1
Industrial Process Total	I6AN	21.0	14.2	16.2	15.4	15.6	15.5	15.4	14.6	13.3	12.4	13.3	13.7	13.8	13.1	14.3
Land-use change	I6AO	–	–	2.9	1.0	0.7	0.1	−0.2	−0.3	−0.4	−1.0	−1.0	−1.8	−1.9	−1.8	−1.8
Waste treatment	I6AP	1.4	1.4	1.2	0.9	0.5	0.5	0.5	0.5	0.5	0.5	0.5	0.5	0.5	0.4	0.4
Total	I6AQ	684.3	608.4	592.9	575.3	551.6	553.6	543.0	551.1	562.5	544.9	556.2	556.0	553.2	551.1	542.5

1 See chapter text. Data are for the UK and exclude overseas territories.

Source: Department for Energy and Climate Change: 0300 060 4000

Environment

13.6 Estimated emissions[1] of methane (CH$_4$)
United Kingdom

Thousand tonnes

		1990	1996	1997	1998	1999	2000	2001	2002	2003	2004	2005	2006	2007
By source NC category														
Energy Supply Total	I6AR	1 371.3	1 017.5	968.9	882.6	789.7	724.5	696.1	685.2	547.6	534.5	482.1	450.1	397.0
Business Total	I6AS	15.8	16.3	16.4	16.1	15.9	15.6	14.5	13.3	14.1	13.8	13.6	13.6	13.4
Transport Total	I6AT	33.5	24.1	22.1	20.2	18.3	16.3	14.3	12.6	11.1	9.9	8.8	8.0	7.3
Public	I6AU	1.3	1.5	1.4	1.3	1.2	1.1	1.2	1.0	1.0	1.1	1.1	1.0	0.9
Residential Total	I6AV	69.0	41.5	38.4	39.9	42.7	32.5	29.2	24.2	22.6	21.8	19.9	20.6	22.1
Agriculture Total	I6AW	1 054.1	1 034.1	1 024.0	1 022.2	1 016.3	979.9	922.0	912.6	913.5	915.3	892.7	891.7	874.0
Industrial Process	I6AX	11.4	11.0	9.5	7.6	6.8	6.3	5.7	5.4	6.7	6.5	5.9	5.8	6.4
Land Use Change	I6AY	0.8	1.0	1.2	0.9	0.8	1.2	1.5	1.3	1.2	1.2	1.0	1.4	1.5
Waste Management	I6AZ	2 409.0	2 072.5	1 908.5	1 791.0	1 640.7	1 541.5	1 349.4	1 235.4	1 088.5	1 016.2	1 005.0	1 005.5	1 003.8
Total	I6B2	4 966.0	4 219.5	3 990.4	3 781.8	3 532.5	3 318.9	3 034.0	2 891.1	2 606.4	2 520.1	2 430.0	2 397.8	2 326.4

1 See chapter text. Data are for the UK and exclude overseas territories.

Source: Department for Energy and Climate Change: 0300 060 4000

13.7 Estimated emissions[1] of nitrous oxide (N$_2$O)
United Kingdom

Thousand tonnes

		1990	1995	1996	1997	1998	1999	2000	2001	2002	2003	2004	2005	2006	2007
By source NC Category															
Energy Supply Total	I6A7	6.7	5.6	5.4	4.9	5.1	4.7	5.1	5.4	5.4	5.4	5.2	5.4	5.6	5.1
Business Total	I6A8	5.1	4.7	4.6	4.4	4.3	4.3	4.2	4.3	4.1	4.1	4.1	4.1	4.2	4.2
Transport Total	I6A9	4.8	8.6	6.4	6.5	6.6	6.6	6.5	6.3	6.1	5.9	5.8	5.6	5.5	5.4
Public Total	I6AA	0.2	0.1	0.1	0.1	0.1	0.1	0.1	0.1	–	–	–	–	–	–
Residential Total	I6AB	0.9	0.7	0.8	0.7	0.7	0.7	0.6	0.6	0.5	0.5	0.5	0.4	0.4	0.4
Agriculture Total	I6AC	107.2	101.9	102.4	105.5	102.5	100.7	96.6	91.0	92.6	90.4	89.9	88.6	85.0	82.1
Industrial Processes Total	I6AD	79.7	48.2	47.9	48.5	49.4	17.5	18.1	15.7	8.8	9.3	11.7	9.2	7.8	9.1
Land-use change	I6AE	–	–	–	–	–	–	–	–	–	–	–	–	–	–
Waste Management Total	I6AF	3.5	3.5	3.6	3.9	4.0	3.8	4.0	4.1	4.1	4.1	4.1	4.1	4.2	4.2
Total	I6AG	208.3	173.2	171.1	174.6	172.7	138.3	135.1	127.4	121.6	119.7	121.4	117.5	112.7	110.5

1 See chapter text. Data are for the UK and exclude overseas territories.

Source: Department for Energy and Climate Change: 0300 060 4000

13.8 Road Transport Emissions by Pollutant
United Kingdom

Thousand tonnes

		1995	1996	1997	1998	1999	2000	2001	2002	2003	2004	2005	2006
Pollutant													
Greenhouse gases[1]	I6BZ	114 711	119 589	122 189	122 294	123 951	123 399	123 495	126 182	126 202	127 451	127 989	128 533
of which													
Carbon dioxide	I6C2	111 986	116 509	118 744	118 480	119 776	118 960	118 791	121 200	121 064	122 149	122 654	123 109
Methane	I6C3	479	453	418	384	350	312	273	242	214	189	169	154
Nitrous oxide	I6C4	2 246	2 627	3 027	3 430	3 824	4 128	4 431	4 740	4 924	5 113	5 166	5 270
Acid rain precursors[2]	I6C5	846	819	778	738	689	622	569	526	484	454	418	391
of which													
Sulphur dioxide	I6C6	52	38	28	23	14	6	3	3	3	3	2	2
Nitrogen oxides	I6C7	777	759	727	692	652	592	542	499	460	431	397	373
Ammonia	I6C8	17	22	23	23	23	24	24	23	22	20	18	16
PM10	I6C9	54	52	49	46	45	40	39	38	37	36	34	33
Carbon monoxide	I6CA	4 199	4 019	3 691	3 371	3 040	2 533	2 154	1 878	1 617	1 385	1 140	999
NMVOCs	I6CB	638	564	510	442	382	308	253	214	178	147	121	104
Benzene	I6CC	29	26	23	20	17	6	5	5	4	3	3	3
1,3-Butadiene	I6CD	7	7	6	5	5	4	3	3	2	2	2	1

1 Greenhouse gases are made up of carbon dioxide, methane & nitrous oxide. Weight in carbon dioxide equivalent.
2 Acid rain precursors are made of sulphur dioxide, nitrogen & ammonia. Weight in sulphur dioxide equivalent.

Sources: AEA Energy & Environment;
Office for National Statistics;
environment.accounts@ons.gsi.gov.uk

13.9 Annual rainfall: by region
United Kingdom

Region[1]		1971 - 2000[4] rainfall average (= 100%) millimetres	*Annual rainfall as a percentage of the 1971-2000 average*										
			1998	1999	2000	2001	2002	2003	2004	2005	2006	2007	2008[3]
United Kingdom	J8G4	1 084	117	114	123	97	118	83	112	100	108	110	120
North West	J8G5	1 176	118	111	132	94	121	85	116	96	114	110	128
Northumbria	J8G6	831	123	106	132	106	124	80	120	111	101	105	135
Severn Trent	J8G7	759	115	120	132	104	119	81	110	92	103	123	121
Yorkshire	J8G8	814	115	110	136	99	125	82	114	96	110	115	129
Anglian	J8G9	603	119	113	129	124	118	86	115	89	102	118	117
Thames	J8GA	700	117	111	137	116	128	81	103	79	106	118	116
Southern	J8GB	782	110	105	148	114	129	85	97	79	101	106	107
Wessex	J8GC	866	115	118	136	100	132	83	98	89	100	113	117
South West	J8GD	1 208	118	113	128	92	121	78	99	90	92	110	109
England	J8GE	819	117	113	133	105	123	82	109	91	103	114	120
Wales[2]	J8GF	1 373	121	116	133	98	119	83	108	95	107	108	121
Scotland	J8GG	1 440	116	116	113	91	112	84	117	110	114	109	120
Northern Ireland	J8GH	1 111	113	111	110	81	127	84	98	96	104	99	115

1 The regions of England shown in this table correspond to the original nine English regions of the National Rivers Authority (NRA); the NRA became part of the Environment Agency upon its creation in April 1996.
2 The figures in this table relate to the country of Wales, not the Environment Agency Welsh Region.

3 Data from July 2008 are provisional and subject to revision.
4 1971-2000 averages have been derived using Met Office 5km gridded rainfall.
Sources: The Met Office;
Centre for Ecology and Hydrology: 01491 838800

13.10 UK Annual Weather Summary

	Max Temp		Min Temp		Mean Temp		Sunshine		Rainfall	
	Actual (degrees celsius)	Anomaly (degrees celsius)	Actual (degrees celsius)	Anomaly (degrees celsius)	Actual (degrees celsius)	Anomaly (degrees celsius)	Actual (hours/ day)	Anomaly (%)	Actual (mm)	Anomaly (%)
	WLRL	WLRM	WLRO	WLRP	WLRR	WLRS	WLRX	WLRY	WLSH	WLSI
1988	12.2	0.3	5.4	0.6	8.8	0.5	1 324.3	99.0	1 131.2	102.9
1989	13.1	1.2	5.5	0.7	9.3	1.0	1 563.8	116.9	1 018.5	92.6
1990	13.1	1.2	5.8	0.9	9.4	1.1	1 490.7	111.4	1 172.8	106.7
1991	12.1	0.3	5.1	0.2	8.6	0.3	1 302.0	97.3	998.2	90.8
1992	12.3	0.4	5.2	0.4	8.7	0.4	1 290.8	96.5	1 186.8	107.9
1993	11.8	−0.1	5.0	0.1	8.4	..	1 218.6	91.1	1 121.1	102.0
1994	12.4	0.5	5.5	0.6	8.9	0.6	1 366.9	102.2	1 184.7	107.7
1995	13.0	1.1	5.4	0.6	9.2	0.9	1 588.5	118.7	1 023.7	93.1
1996	11.7	−0.1	4.7	−0.1	8.2	−0.2	1 403.5	104.9	916.6	83.4
1997	13.1	1.3	5.8	1.0	9.4	1.1	1 430.3	106.9	1 024.0	93.1
1998	12.6	0.8	5.8	1.0	9.1	0.8	1 268.4	94.8	1 265.1	115.1
1999	13.0	1.1	5.9	1.0	9.4	1.1	1 419.4	106.1	1 237.2	112.5
2000	12.7	0.8	5.6	0.8	9.1	0.8	1 367.5	102.2	1 335.6	121.5
2001	12.4	0.6	5.3	0.5	8.8	0.5	1 411.9	105.5	1 049.9	95.5
2002	13.0	1.1	6.0	1.2	9.5	1.2	1 304.0	97.5	1 280.5	116.5
2003	13.5	1.6	5.6	0.7	9.5	1.2	1 587.4	118.7	901.5	82.0
2004	13.0	1.2	6.0	1.2	9.5	1.2	1 361.4	101.8	1 210.1	110.1
2005	13.1	1.2	5.9	1.1	9.5	1.1	1 399.2	104.6	1 083.0	98.4
2006	13.4	1.5	6.1	1.3	9.7	1.4	1 495.9	111.8	1 175.9	106.8
2007	13.3	1.4	6.0	1.1	9.6	1.3	1 450.7	108.4	1 197.1	108.8
2008	12.6	0.8	5.5	0.7	9.0	0.7	1 418.4	106.0	1 303.9	118.0

Anomalies are with respect to the 1961-90 averaging period.
Source: Met Office

Environment

13.11 Biological[1] and chemical[2] water quality of rivers and canals[3]
England, Wales and Northern Ireland

Percentage of river surveyed (%)

		Percentage of river surveyed (%)						Percentage of total	
		Good		Fair					
	Years	A	B	C	D	Poor E	Bad F	Good or fair	Poor or bad
Biological quality									
North East	1990	35.8	28.9	12.4	7.3	10.0	5.6	84.4	15.6
	2007	49.0	24.1	12.1	7.4	6.7	0.8	92.6	7.4
North West	1990	14.4	26.2	18.7	6.2	14.1	20.3	65.6	34.4
	2007	23.5	40.3	15.3	10.1	9.1	1.7	89.2	10.8
Midlands	1990	10.6	25.4	27.8	19.4	11.4	5.4	83.2	16.8
	2007	23.8	36.0	23.6	9.1	5.2	2.3	92.4	7.6
Anglian	1990	13.1	37.2	36.5	9.2	2.7	1.3	96.0	4.0
	2007	37.3	46.0	11.1	5.5	-	0.2	99.8	0.2
Thames	1990	25.9	30.2	24.4	9.4	6.7	3.4	89.9	10.1
	2007	35.9	28.6	22.7	7.4	4.5	0.9	94.6	5.4
Southern	1990	37.3	30.1	24.4	6.3	1.8	-	98.2	1.8
	2007	54.2	27.8	14.2	2.4	1.5	-	98.5	1.5
South West	1990	42.4	35.8	14.6	4.0	2.8	0.5	96.7	3.3
	2007	67.2	25.6	6.7	0.4	0.1	-	99.9	0.1
England[4]	1990	25.0	30.4	21.9	9.0	7.7	6.0	86.4	13.6
	2007	39.6	32.8	15.7	6.6	4.4	1.1	94.6	5.4
Wales	1990	37.2	41.3	14.3	5.4	1.6	0.2	98.3	1.7
	2007	35.0	51.9	11.3	1.2	0.7	-	99.3	0.7
Northern Ireland	1991	32.6	43.5	18.9	4.6	0.4	-	99.6	0.4
	2007	20.1	39.0	28.1	10.8	2.0	-	98.0	2.0
Chemical quality									
North East	1990	39.3	29.0	11.5	7.7	10.5	2.0	87.5	12.5
	2007	67.5	14.5	11.9	3.8	2.3	-	97.7	2.3
North West	1990	36.8	21.4	17.3	10.2	10.9	3.5	85.6	14.4
	2007	66.9	15.6	9.3	4.4	3.7	0.2	96.1	3.9
Midlands	1990	19.0	30.0	23.7	14.2	12.8	0.3	86.9	13.1
	2007	43.2	30.0	14.8	7.0	5.0	0.1	95.0	5.0
Anglian	1990	4.1	25.6	38.6	18.8	12.2	0.8	87.0	13.0
	2007	19.9	35.8	26.4	9.9	7.6	0.3	92.1	7.9
Thames	1990	17.6	35.3	21.9	11.3	13.6	0.3	86.1	13.9
	2007	49.1	27.2	12.0	7.7	4.1	-	95.9	4.1
Southern	1990	27.1	29.8	26.3	11.4	5.5	-	94.5	5.5
	2007	28.9	36.4	23.2	6.7	4.6	0.2	95.2	4.8
South West	1990	46.8	30.8	11.5	7.0	3.9	-	96.1	3.9
	2007	73.8	15.3	6.6	2.0	1.9	0.5	97.6	2.4
England[4]	1990	25.5	29.7	21.6	11.9	10.4	1.0	88.7	11.3
	2007	52.3	23.8	13.8	5.7	4.1	0.2	95.7	4.3
Wales	1990	51.9	34.4	7.6	3.7	1.6	0.8	97.6	2.4
	2007	79.7	15.7	1.8	1.0	1.6	0.2	98.2	1.8
Northern Ireland	1991	6.1	38.1	40.5	10.3	3.8	1.1	95.0	5.0
	2007	28.3	46.6	19.1	3.3	2.5	0.2	97.3	2.7

1 Based on the River Invertebrate Prediction and Classification System (RIV-PACS).
2 Based on the General Quality Assessment Headline Indicator (GQAHI) scheme for England, and the General Quality Assessment (GQA) scheme for Wales.
3 See chapter text.
4 Figures for the English regions will not add to the national figure for England because a small amount of river lengths which are located along the border between England and Wales are counted in both the national figures for England and Wales.

Sources: Environment Agency;
Environment and Heritage Service, Northern Ireland

13.12
Chemical and biological water quality [1]
Scotland

Kilometres and percentages

	Excellent A1	Good A2	Unclassified assumed good	Fair B	Poor C	Seriously polluted D	Total	Good or fair[2]	Poor or seriously polluted
	DZ38	DZ39	DZ3A	DZ3B	DZ3C	DZ3D	DZ3E	DZ3F	DZ3G
2001	3 870	6 320	11 960	2 340	930	80	25 510	96	4
2002	5 280	8 660	7 990	2 560	900	60	25 440	96	4
2003	6 820	9 540	5 900	2 370	750	50	25 440	97	3
2004	7 660	10 610	3 810	2 590	720	50	25 430	97	3
2005	8 000	12 050	2 130	2 470	720	50	25 430	97	3
2006	7 860	12 330	2 080	2 430	700	40	25 430	97	3

	High	Good	Moderate	Poor	Bad	Good	Moderate	Poor	Bad
							Ecological potential[3]		

River length surveyed (km)

	J8SC	J8SD	J8SF	J8SH	J8SJ	J8SE	J8SG	J8SI	J8SK
2007	1 074	9 077	8 613	3 311	910	1 145	37	533	418

Lake area surveyed (sqkm)

	J8SL	J8SM	J8SO	J8SQ	J8SS	J8SN	J8SP	J8SR	J8ST
2007	173	198	187	52	20	230	11	122	–

Transitional water area surveyed (sqkm)

	JDB5	JDB6	JDB7	JDB8	JDB9
2007	558	202	216	11	6

Coastal water area surveyed (sqkm)

	JDC2	JDC3	JDC4	JDC5	JDC6
2007	33 265	9 396	5 041	7	..

1 See chapter text.
2 Classes A1, A2, B and unclassified.
3 Ecological potential is used to classify artificial and heavily modified water bodies.

Source: Scottish Environment Protection Agency: 01786 457700

13.13
Reservoir stocks in England and Wales:[1] by month

Percentages

		1998	1999	2000	2001	2002	2003	2004	2005	2006	2007	2008
January	JTAS	90.5	95.8	95.8	94.8	86.5	95.1	79.9	91.2	85.9	92.2	89.8
February	JTAT	93.1	97.0	95.9	94.4	93.7	95.0	93.8	92.3	88.7	93.7	95.7
March	JTAU	92.3	96.5	97.4	95.0	95.5	92.1	92.1	92.1	91.2	96.7	95.6
April	JTAV	96.9	96.9	95.1	95.5	94.5	92.3	94.4	93.6	96.2	95.2	97.3
May	JTAW	97.0	97.0	97.0	96.7	91.9	88.6	94.7	95.0	93.4	91.9	95.1
June	JTAX	93.8	95.4	95.7	91.9	97.0	93.1	90.5	93.0	94.4	91.1	92.6
July	JTAY	95.1	92.0	93.7	85.1	94.9	87.0	84.8	85.6	88.4	94.4	90.6
August	JTAZ	93.4	82.6	88.5	80.7	91.1	81.1	78.5	77.9	77.2	93.5	92.0
September	JTBA	88.3	76.9	83.2	77.9	85.9	69.9	82.4	71.5	70.7	88.3	92.5
October	JTBB	86.6	79.7	88.0	77.0	77.3	60.4	84.2	67.4	67.8	86.1	90.9
November	JTBC	93.3	81.7	95.1	85.5	82.9	53.0	87.5	77.2	80.0	81.2	93.7
December	JTBD	93.1	84.9	96.7	87.9	91.8	60.9	86.2	83.8	89.8	82.4	93.1

1 Reservoir stocks are the percentage of useable capacity based on a representative selection of reservoirs; the percentages relate to the beginning of each month.

Sources: Water PLCs;
Environment Agency;
Centre for Ecology and Hydrology: 01491 838800

Environment

13.14 Water industry expenditure[1]
England and Wales

		1997 /98	1998 /99	1999 /00	2000 /01	2001 /02	2002 /03	2003 /04	2004 /05	2005 /06	2006 /07	2007 /08
Operating expenditure												
Water supply	KQQX	2 339.3	2 386.1	2 448.1	2 391.0	2 426.9	2 544.2	2 676.5	2 690.7	2 942.7	3 118.6	3 244.9
Sewerage services	KQQY	1 854.6	1 971.3	2 069.8	2 087.1	2 167.6	2 265.2	2 319.4	2 499.3	2 708.1	2 876.2	3 049.0
Capital expenditure												
Water supply	KQSX	1 467.2	1 294.1	1 290.0	935.0	1 132.5	1 347.1	1 346.4	1 309.0	1 282.5	1 681.7	1 883.6
Sewerage	KQSY	455.2	507.5	488.5	352.0	362.4	507.2	617.6	601.4	476.1	585.3	584.4
Sewage treatment and disposal	KQSZ	1 296.3	1 374.5	1 440.8	1 040.9	996.0	1 066.2	1 235.6	1 185.6	1 046.2	1 289.6	1 542.3

1 See chapter text.

Source: Office of Water Services: 0121 625 1300

13.15 Water pollution incidents[1,3]
United Kingdom

		1997	1998		1999[2]	2000[2]	2001[2]	2002[2]	2003[2]	2004[2]	2005[2]	2006[2]	2007[2]
Categories 1 to 3													
Environment Agency Regions													
North West	JZIA	2 160	2 201	MKDB	1 668	1 757	1 734	1 805	1 534	1 091	1 056	913	932
North East	JZIB	2 404	1 993	MKDC	1 828	1 822	1 952	1 789	1 971	1 692	1 448	1 132	993
Midlands	JZKR	4 411	4 061	MKDD	2 804	3 106	2 862	2 843	2 464	1 955	1 890	1 914	1 671
Anglian	JZKS	2 411	2 163	MKDE	1 726	1 369	1 606	1 716	1 616	1 418	1 290	1 223	1 327
Thames	JZKT	1 917	1 819	MKDF	1 208	1 379	1 510	1 630	1 447	1 211	1 203	1 159	1 023
Southern	JZKU	1 174	1 138	MKDG	1 317	1 540	1 585	1 511	1 543	1 218	955	1 020	887
South West	JZKV	2 847	2 603	MKDH	2 463	2 294	2 292	1 929	1 882	1 689	1 744	1 539	1 343
Welsh	JZKW	2 247	1 885	MKDI	1 360	1 395	1 475	1 287	1 356	1 309	1 260	1 202	1 193
England and Wales	JZKX	19 571	17 863	MKDJ	14 374	14 662	15 016	14 510	13 813	11 583	10 846	10 102	9 369
Scotland[3]	JZKY	3 356	2 329	MKDK	2 306	2 345	1 829	1 409	1 708	1 480	1 377	1 641	1 782
Northern Ireland	JZKZ	1 826	1 644	MKDL	1 507	1 705	1 546	1 510	1 551	1 227	1 174	1 133	1 292
By category in England and Wales													
Category 1	MKCW	194	128	MKDM	90	77	118	82	94	114	99	86	70
Category 2	MKCX	1 354	1 238	MKDN	863	758	860	784	685	594	562	519	452
Category 3	MKCY	18 023	16 497	MKDO	13 421	13 827	14 038	13 644	13 034	10 875	10 185	9 497	8 847
Category 4[2,4]	MKCZ	..	..	MKDP	16 548	21 744	18 706	15 370	15 813	13 613	12 658	11 932	11 339
Total substantiated incidents[4]	MKDA	19 571	17 863	MKDQ	30 922	36 406	33 722	29 880	29 626	25 196	23 504	22 034	20 708

1 See chapter text. Substantiated incidents to water, unless otherwise specified.

2 From 1999, categories 1-3 do not include all substantiated incidents to water. An additional category (Category 4) was introduced which includes all incidents which were substantiated, but which had no impact on the water environment. Therefore, data are not comparable to previous years.

3 Data for all years refer to financial years.

4 Category 4 and Total substantiated incidents include incidents to other media (air, land), which did not involve the water environment.

Sources: Environment Agency;
Scottish Environment Protection Agency;
Environment and Heritage Service, Nothern Ireland

13.16 Bathing water:[1] by region
United Kingdom

Compliance with EC Bathing Water Directive coliform standards during the bathing season

		Identified bathing waters (numbers)						Numbers complying						Percentage complying
		2004	2005	2006	2007	2008		2004	2005	2006	2007	2008		2008
Coastal bathing waters														
Environment Agency Regions														
United Kingdom	GPKA	556	559	561	567	587	GPKN	543	550	559	547	563	GPLA	96
North East	GPKB	55	55	55	55	54	GPKO	53	53	54	52	53	GPLB	98
North West	GPKC	34	34	33	32	33	GPKP	33	32	33	29	30	GPLC	91
Anglian	GPKE	38	39	39	39	38	GPKR	38	39	39	39	38	GPLE	100
Thames	GPKF	8	8	8	8	8	GPKS	8	8	8	8	8	GPLF	100
Southern	GPKG	79	79	78	81	81	GPKT	78	79	78	81	80	GPLG	99
South West	GPKH	190	190	191	190	191	GPKU	187	189	191	187	181	GPLH	95
England	GPKI	404	405	404	405	405	GPKV	397	400	403	396	390	GPLI	96
Wales	GPKJ	78	80	80	80	81	GPKW	78	80	79	78	80	GPLJ	99
Scotland	GPKL	58	58	61	59	77	GPKY	54	55	61	52	70	GPLL	91
Northern Ireland	GPKM	16	16	16	23	24	GPKZ	14	15	16	21	23	GPLM	96
Inland bathing waters														
United Kingdom	JTIG	11	11	11	11	12	JTIH	11	11	10	11	11	JTII	92

1 See chapter text.

Sources: Environment Agency;
Scottish Environment Protection Agency;
Environment and Heritage Service, Northern Ireland

13.17 Estimated abstractions from all surface and groundwater sources: by purpose[1]
England and Wales

Megalitres per day

		1996	1997	1998	1999	2000	2001	2002	2003	2004	2005	2006
Public water supply	JZLA	17 453	16 820	16 765	16 255	16 990	16 231	16 938	16 920	17 210	17 370	17 004
Spray irrigation	JZLB	369	292	282	325	291	259	248	315	225	226	277
Agriculture (excl spray irrigation)[4]	JZLC	136	108	111	142	152	108	120	132	122	60	48
Electricity supply industry[2]	JZLD	31 294	33 307	34 587	29 490	31 546	32 263	35 447	31 378	30 568	30 021	32 160
Other industry[3]	JZLE	4 960	4 352	4 964	5 428	5 433	4 772	4 883	6 623	6 585	6 339	6 519
Mineral washing	JZLF	250	297	223	..	..	..	..	..	..	..	..
Fish farming, cress growing, amenity ponds	JYXG	4 338	4 211	5 495	4 867	4 709	4 657	3 215	3 077	4 068	3 654	3 622
Private water supply	JZLG	171	162	175	91	102	92	54	61	30	26	37
Other	JZLH	531	408	289	526	559	108	77	86	77	60	86
Total	JZLI	59 503	59 957	62 891	57 123	59 782	58 489	60 981	58 593	58 885	57 757	59 752

1 See chapter text.
2 Increased electricity supply abstraction from 2002 due to increased production from power station in Anglian Region and two new licences issued in Southern Region.
3 Three abstraction licences re-assigned to other industry from electricty supply in Midlands Region (2003).
4 Reduction in agricultural abstraction due to deregulation of licences with effect from 1 April 2005.

Source: Environment Agency

13.18 Estimates of remaining recoverable oil and gas reserves
United Kingdom

		1998	1999	2000	2001	2002	2003	2004	2005	2006	2007
Oil (Million tonnes)											
Reserves											
Proven	JKOV	685	665	630	605	593	571	533	516	479	452
Probable	JKOW	575	455	380	350	327	286	283	300	298	328
Proven plus Probable	JKOX	1 260	1 120	1 010	955	920	857	816	816	776	780
Possible	JKOY	540	545	480	475	425	410	512	451	478	399
Maximum	JKOZ	1 800	1 665	1 490	1 430	1 344	1 267	1 328	1 267	1 254	1 179
Range of undiscovered resources											
Lower	JKNY	275	250	225	205	272	323	396	346	438	379
Upper	JKNZ	2 550	2 600	2 300	1 930	1 770	1 826	1 830	1 581	1 637	1 577
Range of total reserves											
Lower[1]	JKOA	960	915	855	810	865	894	929	862	917	831
Upper[2]	JKOB	4 350	4 265	3 790	3 360	3 115	3 093	3 158	2 848	2 892	2 756
Expected level of reserves[3]											
Opening stocks	JKOC	1 675	1 535	1 370	1 235	1 160	1 192	1 180	1 212	1 162	1 215
Extraction[5]	JKOD	132	137	106	117	117	106	95	95	77	77
Other volume changes	JKOE	−8	−28	−9	42	149	94	127	35	130	21
Closing stocks	JKOF	1 535	1 370	1 235	1 160	1 192	1 180	1 212	1 162	1 215	1 159
Life expectancy[4] (years)	JKOG	12	10	10	10	10	11	13	14	16	15
Gas (billion cubic metres)											
Reserves											
Proven	JKOH	755	760	735	695	628	590	531	481	412	343
Probable	JKOI	585	500	460	445	369	315	296	247	272	304
Proven plus Probable	JKOJ	1 340	1 260	1 195	1 140	998	905	826	728	684	647
Possible	JKOK	455	490	430	395	331	336	343	278	283	293
Maximum	JKOL	1 795	1 750	1 630	1 535	1 329	1 241	1 169	1 006	967	940
Range of undiscovered resources											
Lower	JKOM	440	355	325	290	238	279	293	226	301	280
Upper	JKON	1 595	1 465	1 440	1 680	1 386	1 259	1 245	1 035	1 049	1 039
Range of total reserves											
Lower[1]	JKOO	1 195	1 115	1 060	985	866	869	824	707	713	623
Upper[2]	JKOP	3 390	3 215	3 065	3 215	2 714	2 500	2 415	2 041	2 016	1 979
Expected level of reserves[3]											
Opening stocks	JKOQ	1 885	1 780	1 615	1 520	1 430	1 235	1 184	1 120	954	985
Extraction[5]	JKOR	−89	−99	−108	−104	−102	−102	−95	−86	−78	−71
Other volume changes	JKOS	−16	−66	13	14	−93	51	31	−80	109	13
Closing stocks	JKOT	1 780	1 615	1 520	1 430	1 235	1 184	1 120	954	985	927
Life expectancy[4] (years)	JKOU	20	16	14	14	12	12	12	11	13	13

1 The lower end of the range of total reserves has been calculated as the sum of proven reserves and the lower end of the range of undiscovered reserves.

2 The upper end of the range of total reserves is the sum of proven, probable and possible reserves and the upper end of the range of undiscovered reserves.

3 Expected reserves are the sum of proven reserves, probable reserves and the lower end of the range of undiscovered reserves.

4 Based on expected level of reserves at year end and current extraction rates (source: ONS).

5 Negative extraction is shown here for the purposes of the calculation only. Of itself, extraction should be considered as a positive value.

Sources: Office for National Statistics and Department of Energy and Climate Change;
environment.accounts@ons.gsi.gov.uk

13.19 Municipal waste disposal: by method
United Kingdom

Thousand tonnes

		2000/01	2001/02	2002/03	2003/04	2004/05	2005/06	2006/07	2007/08
England									
Household									
Disposed	I6EB	22 270	22 327	22 092	20 927	19 873	18 658	17 799	16 553
Recycled/composted	I6EC	2 809	3 197	3 740	4 521	5 785	6 796	7 976	8 735
Total	I6ED	25 079	25 524	25 832	25 448	25 658	25 454	25 775	25 287
Non Household									
Disposed	I6EE	2 342	2 656	2 730	2 650	2 795	2 289	2 408	2 250
Recycled/composted	I6EF	636	724	832	1 016	1 167	1 003	961	969
Total	I6EG	2 978	3 380	3 562	3 666	3 962	3 292	3 369	3 219
Total Municipal Waste									
Disposed	I6EH	24 612	24 983	24 822	23 577	22 668	20 947	20 207	18 803
Recycled/composted	I6EI	3 445	3 921	4 572	5 537	6 952	7 799	8 937	9 703
Total	I6EJ	28 057	28 905	29 394	29 114	29 619	28 745	29 144	28 506
Wales									
Household									
Disposed	I6EK	1 314	1 330	1 309	1 271	1 298	1 210	1 153	1 044
Recycled/composted	I6EL	90	126	179	252	286	332	419	499
Total	I6EM	1 404	1 456	1 488	1 522	1 585	1 542	1 572	1 543
Non Household									
Disposed	I6EN	223	244	238	227	213	204	132	150
Recycled/composted	I6EO	25	18	43	71	131	152	130	105
Total	I6EP	248	262	281	298	344	356	262	255
Total Municipal Waste									
Disposed	I6EQ	1 537	1 573	1 547	1 498	1 511	1 414	1 285	1 194
Recycled/composted	I6ER	115	144	222	323	418	484	549	604
Total	I6ES	1 652	1 718	1 769	1 820	1 928	1 898	1 834	1 798
Scotland									
Household									
Disposed	I6ET	2 405	2 472	2 477	2 375	2 276	2 221	2 127	2 022
Recycled/composted	I6EU	122	149	206	330	522	665	879	979
Total	I6EV	2 527	2 621	2 683	2 705	2 798	2 886	3 006	3 001
Non Household									
Disposed	I6EW	662	619	602	545	584	508	332	309
Recycled/composted	I6EX	22	27	60	66	125	265	99	103
Total	I6EY	684	646	663	611	709	773	431	412
Total Municipal Waste									
Disposed	I6EZ	3 067	3 091	3 079	2 920	2 860	2 729	2 459	2 331
Recycled/composted	I6F2	145	176	267	397	647	930	978	1 082
Total	I6F3	3 211	3 267	3 345	3 317	3 506	3 658	3 437	3 414

		1999/00	2001	2002	2003	2004/05	2005/06	2006/07	2007/08
Northern Ireland									
Household									
Disposed	I6F4	776	785	813	786	746	702	679	632
Recycled/composted	I6F5	55	94	90	112	173	235	260	296
Total	I6F6	831	879	902	898	919	937	939	928
Non Household									
Disposed	I6F7	..	..	119	116	114	111	108	117
Recycled/composted	I6F8	..	..	2	13	18	15	12	10
Total	I6F9	159	135	121	129	132	126	125	133
Total Municipal Waste									
Disposed	I6FA	..	..	932	902	860	813	792	749
Recycled/composted	I6FB	..	..	92	125	191	250	272	312
Total	I6FC	1 004	1 056	1 023	1 027	1 051	1 064	1 064	1 061

Sources: Department for Environment, Food and Rural Affairs 08459 33 55 77;
Welsh Assembly Government 029 2046 6151;
Scottish Environment Protection Agency 01786 457700;
Northern Ireland Environment Agency 028 9056 9427

13.20 Amounts of different materials from household sources collected for recycling by collection method 2007/08[1]

United Kingdom

Thousand tonnes

	Paper & Card	Glass	Compost	Scrap Metal & White Goods	Textiles	Cans	Plastics	Co-Mingled	Other	Total
England[2]										
Kerbside collection	1 123	471	2 045	30	11	64	32	1 525	15	5 317
Bring site collection	208	364	16	2	40	9	20	31	7	697
Civic Amenity site collection	238	63	1 124	565	33	8	14	3	539	2 587
Private/voluntary collection schemes[3]	30	4	4	1	29	1	1	4	167	241
Total	**1 599**	**902**	**3 189**	**598**	**113**	**83**	**66**	**1 563**	**728**	**8 841**
Wales										
Kerbside collection	85	37	85	2	1	9	13	-	29	260
Bring site collection	17	16	4	-	3	1	1	-	1	42
Civic Amenity site collection	16	5	59	38	2	-	3	-	64	187
Private/voluntary collection schemes[3]	1	-	6	-	-	-	-	-	2	10
Total	**119**	**58**	**155**	**41**	**5**	**10**	**17**	**-**	**95**	**499**
Scotland										
Kerbside collection	114	31	187	7	-	4	4	74	20	441
Bring site & Civic Amenity collection	46	44	60	39	12	2	2	14	118	337
Private/voluntary collection schemes[3]	-	-	29	-	-	-	-	-	21	50
Total	**160**	**75**	**276**	**46**	**12**	**6**	**6**	**88**	**159**	**828**
Northern Ireland										
Kerbside collection	77	7	57	-	-	4	9	-	4	155
Bring site collection	1	6	-	-	1	-	-	-	-	8
Civic Amenity site collection	10	7	57	22	2	-	1	-	34	99
Total	**87**	**20**	**114**	**23**	**3**	**4**	**10**	**-**	**38**	**262**

1 See chapter text.
2 Total amount of household waste collected for recycling is greater than that sent for recycling as some material is subsequently rejected during sorting or by the reprocessor.
3 Includes household waste collected from municipal parks, community skips and other methods of capture for recycling/composting.

Sources: Department for Environment Food and Rural Affairs 08459 33 55 77;
Welsh Assembly Government 029 2046 6151;
Scottish Environment Protection Agency 01786 457700;
Northern Ireland Environment Agency 028 9056 9427

13.21 Noise incidents[1] received by Environmental Health Officers[2]

England, Wales and Northern Ireland[3]

Number per million people

		2001 /02	2002 /03	2003 /04	2004 /05	2005 /06	2006 /07	2007 /08
Not controlled by the Environmental Protection Act 1990:								
Road traffic	JZLJ	37	36	32	..	..	..	..
Aircraft	JZLK	101	104	120	..	..	..	..
Railway	JTHH	12	18	21	..	..	..	..
Total	JUZR	150	158	173	..	..	..	..
Controlled by the Environmental Protection Act 1990:								
Industrial/commercial premises	JZLN	1 273	1 315	1 480	1 260	936	1 021	1 132
Industrial	EAC3	..	301	284	219	192	176	159
Commercial/leisure[4]	EAC4	..	1 014	1 196	1 041	744	845	973
Construction/Demolition sites	SNLE	347	325	335	343	220	246	284
Domestic premises	JZLP	5 540	5 573	5 973	5 903	4 186	4 329	4 648
Vehicles, machinery and equipment in streets	JZLQ	372	377	346	330	180	205	211
Traffic	I4SR	..	..	..	..	116	154	139
Miscellaneous[5]	EAC2	..	..	..	433	267	414	443
Total	JZLR	7 532	7 590	8 134	8 269	5 905	6 369	6 857

1 From 2004/05 Data reported is for incidents per million where previously complaints per million was reported.
2 See chapter text.
3 Before 2005/06 data is for England and Wales only.
4 Includes railway noise and airports (non aircraft).
5 From 2004/05 includes 'traffic' which consists of commercial vehicles, cars motorbikes, fixed-wing aircraft in flight and helicopters in flight. From 2005/06 this data is recorded separately as 'traffic'.

Sources: The Chartered Institute of Environmental Health;
020 7827 6322

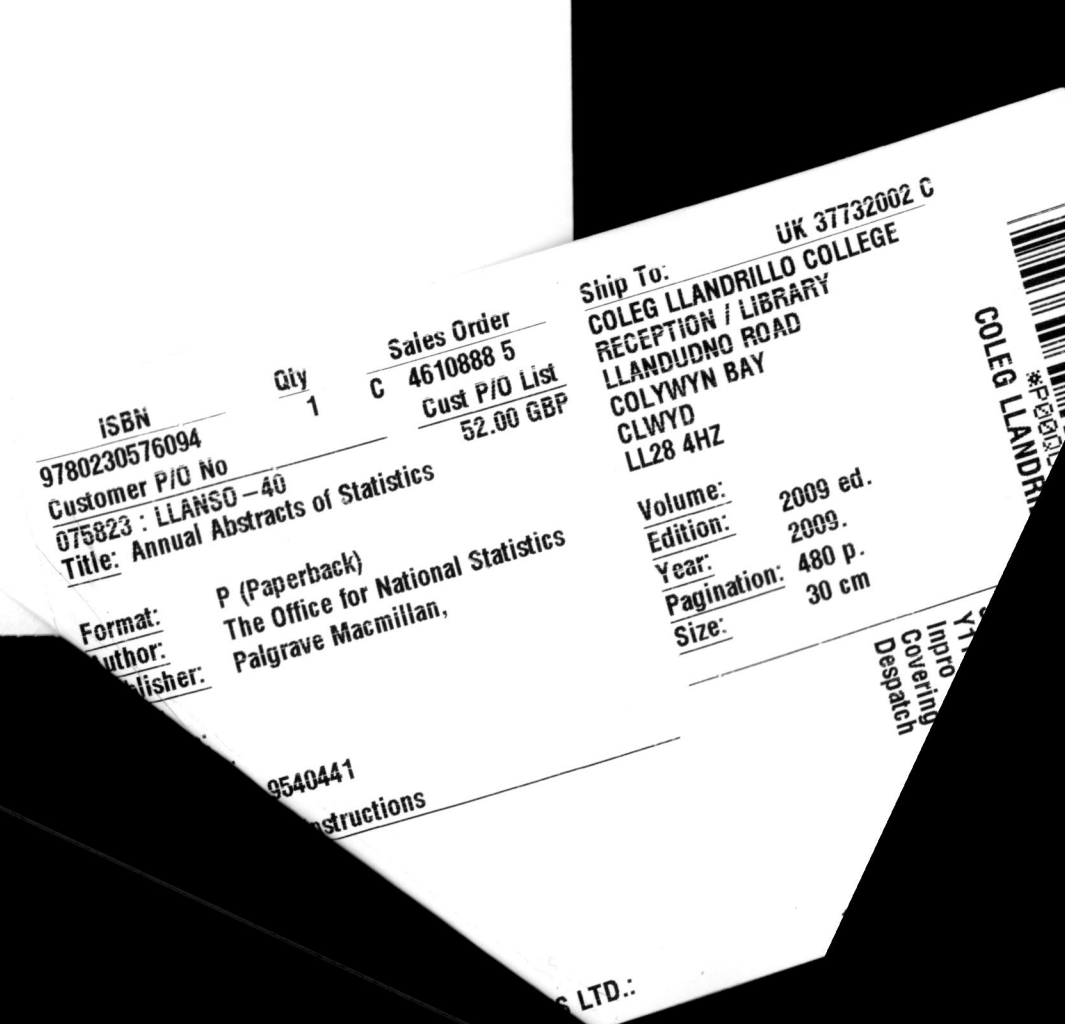

ISBN	Qty	Sales Order
	1	C 4610888 5

9780230576094

Customer P/O No
075823 : LLANSO –40
Title: Annual Abstracts of Statistics

Cust P/O List
52.00 GBP

Format:
Author:
Publisher:

P (Paperback)
The Office for National Statistics
Palgrave Macmillan,

Ship To:
COLEG LLANDRILLO COLLEGE
RECEPTION / LIBRARY
LLANDUDNO ROAD
COLYWYN BAY
CLWYD
LL28 4HZ

Volume:	2009 ed.
Edition:	2009.
Year:	480 p.
Pagination:	30 cm
Size:	

Inpro
Covering
Despatch

9540441

...structions

S LTD.:

13.22 Material flows[1]
United Kingdom

Million tonnes

		1970	1975	1980	1985	1990	1995	2000	2001	2002	2003	2004	2005	2006	2007
Domestic extraction															
Biomass															
Agricultural harvest	JKUN	42	38	47	47	46	47	51	45	51	48	49	47	45	43
Timber	JKUO	3	3	4	5	6	8	8	8	8	8	8	8	8	8
Animal grazing	JKUP	49	49	49	48	47	45	43	43	43	43	43	43	43	43
Fish	JKUQ	1	1	1	1	1	1	1	1	1	1	1	1	1	1
Total	JKUR	96	92	101	100	101	100	102	97	102	100	101	100	98	95
Minerals															
Ores	JKUS	12	5	1	1	–	–	–	–	–	–	–	–	–	–
Clay	JKUT	38	33	25	23	21	18	15	14	14	14	15	14	13	13
Other industrial minerals	JKUU	14	11	11	11	11	10	8	9	8	9	8	8	8	8
Sand and gravel	JKUV	122	131	110	112	128	106	106	105	98	95	102	99	97	98
Crushed stone	JKUW	156	169	150	160	212	200	176	183	173	170	175	169	171	179
Total	JKUX	342	349	298	307	373	334	305	311	293	288	300	290	290	299
Fossil fuels															
Coal	JKUY	149	129	130	94	94	53	31	32	30	28	25	20	19	17
Natural gas	JKUZ	17	54	55	37	42	71	108	106	104	103	96	88	80	72
Crude oil	JKVA	–	2	80	128	92	130	126	117	116	106	95	85	76	77
Total	JKVB	166	184	266	259	228	254	266	254	250	237	217	193	175	166
Total domestic extraction	JKVC	603	625	664	665	702	688	673	663	645	625	618	584	563	560
Imports															
Biomass	JKVD	38	33	30	31	38	40	42	46	47	49	50	50	50	50
Minerals	JKVE	30	32	24	34	41	50	51	54	55	55	60	58	59	63
Fossil fuels	JKVF	123	111	74	76	89	73	83	99	95	102	127	137	148	146
Other products	JKVG	6	7	14	15	19	23	34	34	32	34	36	35	35	37
Total	JKVH	197	184	141	157	187	188	210	232	228	240	273	280	292	296
Exports															
Biomass	JKVI	3	5	8	11	13	15	17	13	15	19	18	19	20	20
Minerals	JKVJ	17	20	26	22	25	39	44	43	42	44	48	48	50	50
Fossil fuels	JKVK	23	19	60	102	67	103	115	118	120	104	98	88	83	80
Other products	JKVL	5	7	8	11	12	17	21	21	20	21	21	21	21	22
Total	JKVM	47	51	101	146	117	173	198	194	197	189	185	177	174	173
Domestic Material Consumption	JKVU	753	758	704	677	772	703	686	701	677	677	706	687	680	683
(domestic extraction + imports - exports)															
of which:															
Biomass	G9A8	131	119	123	120	125	126	127	130	134	130	133	131	128	125
Minerals	G9A9	355	361	296	319	389	346	312	322	307	298	312	300	299	312
Fossil fuels	G9AA	267	277	279	233	250	224	233	236	224	236	246	242	239	232
Indirect flows															
From domestic extraction,[2] excluding soil erosion	JKVN	577	577	635	627	693	633	566	572	564	549	547	519	487	488
Of which:															
Unused biomass	JKVO	25	23	32	35	37	37	40	35	40	38	39	38	36	34
Fossil fuels	JKVP	169	204	289	274	309	276	230	241	225	209	204	178	149	151
Minerals and ores	JKVQ	185	155	120	120	144	116	97	95	101	100	104	101	99	100
Soil excavation and dredging	JKVR	197	195	195	199	203	203	198	202	199	202	201	202	203	203
From production of raw materials and semi-natural products imported	JKVS	394	395	368	423	457	527	614	711	648	671	692	752	792	761
Other indicators															
Physical Trade Balance (imports - exports)[3]	DZ76	150	133	40	11	70	14	13	38	32	52	88	103	117	123
Direct material input (Domestic extraction + imports)	JKVT	801	809	805	822	889	876	884	895	874	866	892	864	855	856
Total material requirement (Direct material input + indirect flows)	JKVV	1 771	1 781	1 809	1 872	2 039	2 036	2 064	2 179	2 086	2 086	2 130	2 135	2 134	2 105

1 See chapter text. Components may not sum to totals due to rounding.
2 Indirect flows from domestic extraction relate to unused material which is
  moved during extraction, such as overburden from mining and quarrying.
3 A positive physical trade balance indicates a net import of material into the
  UK. This calculation of the PTB differs from the National Accounts formula
  (exports - imports) because flows of materials and products are considered
  the inverse of the flows of money recorded in the National Accounts.

Sources: Office for National Statistics;
environment.accounts@ons.gsi.gov.uk

Housing

Chapter 14

Housing

Permanent dwellings

(Table 14.1, 14.3)

Local housing authorities include the Commission for the New Towns and New Towns Development Corporations, Communities Scotland and the Northern Ireland Housing Executive. The figures shown for housing associations include dwellings provided by housing associations other than the Communities Scotland and the Northern Ireland Housing Executive and provided or authorised by government departments for the families of police, prison staff, the Armed Forces and certain other services.

Mortgage possession actions by region

(Table 14.6)

The table shows mortgage possession actions in the county courts of England and Wales and excludes a small number of mortgage actions in the High Court.

A claimant begins an action for an order for possession of a property by issuing a claim in the county court, either by using the Possession Claim Online system or locally through a county court.

In mortgage possession cases, the usual procedure is for the claim being issued to be given a hearing date before a district judge. The court, following a judicial hearing, may grant an order for possession immediately. This entitles the claimants to apply for a warrant to have the defendant evicted. However, even where a warrant for possession is issued, the parties can still negotiate a compromise to prevent eviction.

Frequently, the court grants the claimant possession but suspends the operation of the order. Provided the defendant complies with the terms of suspension, which usually require the defendant to pay the current mortgage instalments plus some of the accrued arrears, the possession order cannot be enforced.

The mortgage possession figures do **not** indicate how many houses have actually been repossessed through the courts. Repossessions can occur without a court order being made while not all court orders result in repossession.

A new mortgage pre-action protocol (MPAP), approved by the Master of the Rolls, was introduced for possession claims in the county courts with effect from 19 November 2008. The

MPAP gives clear guidance on what the courts expect lenders and borrowers to have done prior to a claim being issued. Evidence from administrative records from Quarter 4, 2008 suggests that this date coincided with a fall of around 50 per cent in the daily and weekly numbers of new mortgage repossession claims being issued in the courts.

It therefore seems highly likely that the launch of the MPAP has led to a fall in the number of new claims being issued since introduction of MPAP (19 November to 31 December 2008).

Mortgage possession orders are typically made (where necessary) around eight weeks after the corresponding claims are issued. For this reason, the impact of the MPAP is yet to have visible effect on the statistics on possession orders made.

At this early stage is not clear to what extent the launch of the MPAP has led to a permanent fall in the numbers of new mortgage possession claims being issued, as opposed to some merely being postponed. This will become clearer as statistics for 2009 become available.

Households in temporary accommodation under homelessness provisions

(Table 14.9)

This comprises households in accommodation arranged by local authorities pending enquiries or after being accepted as owed a main homeless duty under the Housing Act 1996 Act (includes residual cases awaiting re-housing under the 1985 Housing Act). Excludes 'homeless at home' cases.

14.1 Stock of dwellings: [1,2] by tenure and country

Thousands

		1997	1998	1999	2000	2001	2002	2003	2004	2005	2006	2007
England[3]												
Owner occupied	JUTY	14 111	14 308	14 518	14 701	14 838	14 942	15 088	15 210	15 312	15 390	15 449
Rented	JUUC	6 511	6 470	6 410	6 374	6 369	6 395	6 393	6 426	6 493	6 601	6 739
Local Authority	JUTZ	3 401	3 309	3 178	3 012	2 812	2 706	2 457	2 335	2 166	2 086	1 987
Privately	JUUA	2 125	2 121	2 086	2 089	2 133	2 197	2 285	2 389	2 525	2 673	2 866
Registered Social Landlords	JUUB	985	1 040	1 146	1 273	1 424	1 492	1 651	1 702	1 802	1 842	1 886
All dwellings	JUUD	20 622	20 778	20 927	21 075	21 207	21 337	21 481	21 636	21 805	21 990	22 189
Wales[4]												
Owner occupied	JUUE	891	888	915	903	905	932	925	946	951	955	968
Rented	JUUI	352	363	343	364	370	350	364	352	356	359	356
Local Authority	JUUF	204	201	197	193	188	183	177	162	158	156	154
Privately	JUUG	100	112	94	117	127	110	130	125	133	137	135
Registered Social Landlords	JUUH	48	50	52	54	55	57	57	65	65	66	67
All dwellings	JUUJ	1 243	1 251	1 259	1 267	1 274	1 282	1 290	1 298	1 306	1 314	1 323
Scotland[5]												
Owner occupied	JUUK	1 366	1 400	1 435	1 472	1 446	1 479	1 514	1 544	1 555	1 570	1 587
Rented	JUUO	899	883	869	849	861	853	835	825	833	838	841
Local Authority	JUUL	630	608	583	557	553	531	416	389	374	362	347
Privately	JUUM	154	154	155	155	169	179	180	184	208	225	233
Registered Social Landlords	JUUN	115	121	131	137	139	143	238	251	251	251	261
All dwellings	JUUP	2 266	2 283	2 303	2 322	2 307	2 332	2 349	2 369	2 389	2 408	2 427
Northern Ireland[6]												
Owner occupied	JUUQ	434	446	455	488	–	481	491	501	505	508	523
Rented	JUUU	183	180	180	185	–	187	188	183	193	198	190
Local Authority	JUUR	142	137	131	129	–	120	113	100	102	99	97
Privately	JUUS	26	27	32	37	–	47	54	61	68	76	69
Registered Social Landlords	JUUT	15	16	17	19	–	20	21	22	22	23	24
All dwellings	JUUV	618	626	636	674	–	668	679	684	698	706	713
United Kingdom[7]												
Owner occupied	JUVY	16 751	16 996	17 279	17 494	17 677	17 834	18 018	18 201	18 323	18 423	18 527
Rented	JUWC	7 970	7 915	7 816	7 787	7 785	7 785	7 779	7 785	7 875	7 996	8 126
Local Authority	JUVZ	4 421	4 282	4 120	3 919	3 682	3 540	3 163	2 986	2 800	2 703	2 585
Privately	JUWA	2 402	2 413	2 361	2 393	2 466	2 533	2 649	2 759	2 934	3 111	3 303
Registered Social Landlords	JUWB	1 147	1 220	1 335	1 475	1 637	1 712	1 967	2 040	2 140	2 182	2 238
All dwellings	JUWD	24 721	24 913	25 095	25 281	25 462	25 619	25 799	25 987	26 198	26 418	26 652

1 For detailed definitions of all tenures, see Definitions of housing terms in Housing Statistics home page.

2 April data for census years are based on census output.

3 Series from 1992 to 2001 for England has been adjusted so that 2001 total dwellings estimate matches the 2001 census. Estimates from 2002 are based on local authority and Registered Social Landlord dwelling counts, and the Labour force survey (LFS). Estimates may not be strictky comparable between periods.

4 Information from 1997 onwards uses information from the Labour Force Survey (LFS) Wales.

5 Estimates up to 2000 are based on the 1991 Census. Estimates from 2001 onwards are based on the 2001 General Register Of scotland (GROS) dwelling counts and Scottish Household Survey (SHS) tenure splits are not strictly comparable.

6 To include estimates for vacant dwellings, stock figures in Northern Ireland Statistics 2006/07 table 1.3 have been apportioned according the % of occupied dwellings for each of the tenures given in table 1.4.

7 UK totals from 2002 are derived by summing country totals at 31st March. For 1991-2001 Scotland and Northern Ireland stock levels from the year before is added to the UK total. Data for earlier years are less reliable and definitions may not be consistent throughout the series. Components may not sum to totals due to rounding.

Sources: Communities and Local Government;
Welsh Assembly Government;
Scottish Executive;
Department for Social Development (Northern Ireland)

14.2 Type Of Accommodation by Tenure [1] 2007 Great Britain

Weighted Percentages

	Type of accommodation[2]						
	Detached House	Semi-detached house	Terraced	All Houses	Purpose-built flat or maisonette	Converted flat maisonette/rooms	All flats
Owner-occupied							
Owned outright	37	34	21	92	7	1	8
Owned with mortgage	25	34	31	91	7	2	9
All owners	30	34	27	91	7	2	9
Rented from social sector							
Council[3]	1	24	30	55	43	2	45
Housing association[4]	2	22	33	56	39	5	44
All rented from social sector	1	23	31	56	41	3	44
Rented privately[6]							
Unfurnished[5]	15	24	33	72	16	12	28
Furnished	2	14	34	49	29	22	51
Private renters[6]	11	22	33	66	19	15	34
All Tenures	**23**	**31**	**28**	**82**	**15**	**3**	**18**

1 Results for 2007 include longitudinal data.

2 Tables for type of accommodation exclude households living in caravans.

3 Council includes local authority.

4 Since 1996, housing associations are more correctly described as Registered Social Landlords (RSLs).

5 Unfurnished includes the answer 'partly furnished'.

6 Tenants whose accommodation goes with the job of someone in the household have been allocated to 'rented privately'. Squatters are also included.

Source: General Household Survey, Office for National Statistics

14.3 Permanent dwellings completed:[1] by tenure and country

Numbers

	United Kingdom				England and Wales			
	All dwellings	Local authorities[2]	Private enterprise	Registered Social Landlords[3][4]	All dwellings	Local authorities[2]	Private enterprise	Registered Social Landlords[3][4]
	KAAD	KAAE	KAAF	KAAG	KAAH	KAAI	KAAJ	KAAK
1980	242 017	88 534	131 989	21 494	214 934	78 539	116 179	20 216
1981	206 915	68 554	118 647	19 714	180 147	58 633	104 069	17 445
1982	181 894	40 091	128 088	13 715	159 407	33 544	113 893	11 970
1983	207 496	39 161	151 638	16 697	181 391	31 625	134 901	14 865
1984	220 414	37 573	165 555	17 286	191 112	31 338	145 263	14 511
1985	205 938	30 420	161 828	13 690	178 284	24 359	142 020	11 905
1986	214 471	25 377	175 905	13 189	187 710	20 496	156 056	11 158
1987	226 167	21 833	191 250	13 084	198 732	17 435	169 895	11 402
1988	242 233	21 448	207 423	13 362	214 156	16 921	185 733	11 502
1989	221 494	19 323	187 542	14 629	190 990	15 332	163 344	12 314
1991/92	191 849	10 027	160 664	21 158	165 553	7 447	139 583	18 523
1992/93	178 872	4 433	144 367	30 072	152 452	2 706	123 045	26 701
1993/94	185 960	3 611	145 914	36 435	157 813	1 726	122 779	33 308
1994/95	197 169	2 970	156 547	37 652	168 301	997	133 002	34 302
1995/96	198 212	3 045	156 696	38 471	164 581	954	130 891	32 736
1996/97	185 654	1 538	153 165	30 951	156 334	474	128 682	27 178
1997/98	190 748	1 519	160 675	28 554	157 987	325	134 327	23 335
1998/99	178 289	865	154 557	22 867	147 994	207	127 633	20 154
1999/00	183 982	317	160 491	23 174	150 502	58	132 326	18 118
2000/01	175 220	382	152 590	22 248	141 588	226	124 030	17 332
2001/02	173 933	225	153 312	30 396	138 139	131	123 195	14 813
2002/03	182 901	301	163 994	18 606	146 049	205	131 979	13 865
2003/04	190 219	207	171 996	18 016	152 254	207	137 959	14 088
2004/05	205 890	131	183 771	21 988	164 385	131	147 118	17 136
2005/06	214 934	326	190 619	23 989	171 655	326	152 820	18 509
2006/07	218 644	255	191 739	26 650	177 010	249	154 669	22 092
2007/08[5]	214 112	347	185 272	28 493	175 650	319	151 902	23 429

	Scotland				Northern Ireland			
	All dwellings	Local authorities[2]	Private enterprise	Registered Social Landlords[3]	All dwellings	Local authorities[2]	Private enterprise[6]	Registered Social Landlords[3]
	BLFI	BAEZ	BLFK	BLFO	BLGI	BAFA	BLGK	BLGO
1979	23 782	4 755	15 175	3 852	7 312	3 507	3 574	231
1980	20 611	7 488	12 242	881	6 456	2 563	3 568	325
1981	20 011	7 062	11 021	1 928	6 827	3 082	3 557	188
1982	16 423	3 733	11 523	1 167	7 033	3 032	3 606	395
1983	17 929	3 492	13 166	1 271	9 698	4 093	4 971	634
1984	18 838	2 647	14 115	2 076	10 464	3 594	6 177	693
1985	18 411	2 828	14 435	1 148	10 770	3 235	6 940	595
1986	18 637	2 301	14 870	1 466	10 197	2 580	7 082	535
1987	17 707	2 634	13 904	1 169	9 795	1 764	7 451	580
1988	18 272	2 815	14 179	1 278	9 931	1 715	7 511	705
1989	20 190	2 283	16 287	1 620	10 283	1 708	7 911	664
1991/92	19 161	1 619	15 528	2 014	7 318	971	5 553	794
1992/93	19 520	778	15 563	3 179	7 559	002	5 759	808
1993/94	21 256	997	17 407	2 852	7 083	907	5 642	534
1994/95	22 249	1 107	18 195	2 947	7 212	877	5 859	476
1995/96	24 226	709	18 640	4 877	8 990	1 325	6 750	915
1996/97	20 486	106	17 331	3 049	9 166	860	7 373	933
1997/98	22 541	114	17 938	4 489	10 181	1 080	8 371	730
1998/99	20 635	120	18 762	1 753	9 638	538	8 140	960
1999/00	24 196	69	19 024	5 103	10 399	190	9 117	1 092
2000/01	23 434	112	18 004	5 318	11 668	44	10 512	1 112
2001/02	23 598	65	18 054	5 479	13 487	29	12 072	1 386
2002/03	23 361	94	18 572	4 695	14 415	2	13 387	1 026
2003/04	23 749	–	20 079	3 670	14 511	–	13 954	557
2004/05	25 740	–	21 720	4 020	15 760	–	14 940	830
2005/06	25 870	–	21 170	4 700	17 410	–	16 630	780
2006/07	24 060	10	20 830	3 230	17 580	–	16 250	1 330
2007/08	25 740	30	21 620	4 090	12 730	–	11 750	970

1 See chapter text.
2 Including the Commission for the New Towns Development Corporations, Communities Scotland, the Northern Ireland Housing Executive.
3 Dwellings provided by housing associations other than Communities Scotland and the Northern Ireland Housing Trust and provided or authorised by government departments for families of police, prison staff, the armed forces and certain other services.
4 Includes non-registered social landlords.

5 Provisional.
6 Northern Ireland private enterprise completions are statistically adjusted to correct, as far as possible, the proven under recording of private sector completions in NI. This calculation has been revised for 2007/08, as such the figures and not comparable with previous years.

Sources: Communities and Local Government;
Scottish Government;
Welsh Assembly Government;
Department for Social Development, Northern Ireland

14.4 Stock of dwellings: Estimated annual gains and losses
England

Thousands of dwellings

		1997 /98	1998 /99	1999 /00	2000[2] /01	2001 /02	2002 /03	2003 /04	2004 /05	2005 /06	2006 /07	2007 /08
Dwelling stock at start of financial year	GRWM	20 622	20 778	20 927	21 075	21 207	21 337	21 481	21 636	21 805	21 992	22 191
Gains to dwelling stock:												
Housebuilding completions	GRWN	149.6	138.6	141.4	133.1	129.8	137.7	144.0	155.9	163.4	167.6	167.0
Conversions (net gain)[1]	GRWO	2.8	4.2	3.5	2.8	..	..	..	..	..	..	..
Change of use	GRWP	11.6	15.9	13.9	10.1	..	..	..	..	..	..	..
Non-permanent dwellings additions	GRWQ	0.2	0.2	0.3	0.3	..	..	..	..	..	..	..
Losses from dwelling stock:												
Slum clearance (non LA owned dwelling demolished)	GRWR	1.3	1.3	1.4	1.7	..	..	..	..	..	..	..
Other demolitions[1]	GRWS	12.8	13.2	15.8	18.3	..	..	..	..	..	..	..
Change of use	GRWT	0.7	1.4	0.8	0.7	..	..	..	..	..	..	..
Non-permanent dwelling losses	GRWU	0.1	0.2	0.1	0.3	..	..	..	..	..	..	..
New gain in year	GRWV	149.3	143.0	140.9	125.3	130.5	143.7	154.8	169.5	186.6	199.0	207.5
Adjustment[3]	VQDN	6.6	6.6	6.6	6.6	..	..	..	..	..	..	..
Dwelling stock at end of financial year	GRWW	20 778	20 927	21 075	21 207	21 337	21 481	21 636	21 805	21 992	22 191	22 399

1 Conversion figures prior to 1997/98 include change of use.
2 Figures for 2000/01 conversions, change of use and non permanent dwellings are based on reported figures and do not include estimates for missing returns.

3 Series has been adjusted so that the 2000/01 estimates matches the 2001 Census.

Source: Communities and Local Government - 020 7944 4178

14.5 Housebuilding completions: by number of bedrooms

Percentages

		1997 /98	1998 /99	1999 /00	2000 /01	2001[1] /02	2002[1] /03	2003[1] /04	2004[1] /05	2005[1] /06	2006[1] /07	2007[1] /08
England												
1 bedroom	JUWJ	7	7	7	7	7	6	8	10	10	11	11
2 bedrooms	JUWK	27	27	26	27	25	29	33	38	42	42	44
3 bedrooms	JUWL	38	36	35	34	31	30	29	28	27	27	26
4 or more bedrooms	JUWM	28	30	32	32	37	34	30	23	21	20	19
All houses and flats	JUWN	100	100	100	100	100	100	100	100	100	100	100
Wales[2]												
1 bedroom	JUWO	4	3	5	5	4	6	6	7	9	11	10
2 bedrooms	JUWP	24	21	19	18	19	18	20	21	27	28	30
3 bedrooms	JUWQ	46	46	43	42	39	35	37	35	35	33	33
4 or more bedrooms	JUWR	26	30	34	34	38	41	37	37	30	28	27
All houses and flats	JUWS	100	100	100	100	100	100	100	100	100	100	100

1 Figures for 2001/02 onwards for England only are based on just NHBC figures, so there is some degree of variability owing to partial coverage.
2 Figures for all years for Wales are based on the reports of local authority building inspectors and the National House Building Council (NHBC). It does not include information from private approved inspector.

Sources: Communities and Local Government;
Welsh Assembly Government

14.6 County Court mortgage possession actions:[1] by region

Thousands

		1998	1999	2000	2001	2002	2003	2004	2005	2006	2007	2008
Claims issued												
England and Wales	JURS	84.8	77.9	70.4	65.9	63.2	65.9	77.3	114.8	131.2	137.7	142.6
North East	JURT	4.3	4.0	4.0	3.5	3.2	3.1	3.4	5.5	7.1	8.1	8.5
North West	JURU	14.2	14.1	12.7	12.1	11.1	10.0	10.6	15.3	19.2	21.7	23.1
Yorkshire and the Humber	JURV	8.2	8.8	7.8	7.1	6.1	5.9	6.6	10.1	12.0	13.8	14.7
East Midlands	JURW	6.4	6.5	5.7	5.2	4.7	4.8	5.8	8.6	10.2	10.8	11.4
West Midlands	JURX	8.1	8.5	8.2	7.5	6.8	7.3	8.6	12.2	14.8	16.2	16.4
East	JURY	8.5	6.8	6.2	5.6	5.5	6.4	7.8	11.2	12.0	12.4	12.7
London	JURZ	11.4	8.7	7.0	7.6	8.7	10.5	13.4	21.1	21.9	20.1	19.5
South East	JUSA	11.2	9.9	9.0	8.4	8.3	9.3	11.4	16.5	17.4	17.0	17.2
South West	JUSB	7.3	5.7	4.9	4.4	4.3	4.5	5.4	7.8	8.5	8.6	9.4
England	JUSC	79.4	72.9	65.4	61.3	58.7	61.7	72.9	108.3	123.0	128.5	132.9
Wales	JUSD	5.4	5.0	5.0	4.6	4.5	4.2	4.3	6.5	8.2	9.2	9.7
Northern Ireland	JUSE	..	1.9	1.7	1.6	1.6	1.7	2.2	2.6	2.5	..	..
Suspended orders[1]												
England and Wales	JUSF	40.8	32.9	31.1	29.4	25.1	24.5	26.6	38.1	44.6	44.2	53.7
North East[2]	JUSG	2.3	2.0	2.0	1.8	1.4	1.3	1.3	1.9	2.6	7.0	8.1
North West	JUSH	6.5	6.2	5.7	5.5	4.9	4.0	3.8	5.0	6.7	7.2	8.7
Yorkshire and the Humber	JUSI	4.3	3.9	3.6	3.4	2.5	2.3	2.4	3.5	4.3	..	..
East Midlands[3]	JUSJ	3.1	2.8	2.5	2.5	1.9	1.8	2.1	2.9	3.4	9.0	10.9
West Midlands[3]	JUSK	3.8	3.7	3.7	3.7	2.9	2.9	3.1	4.3	5.2	..	..
East[4]	JUSL	3.9	2.8	2.6	2.3	2.2	2.3	2.7	3.8	4.0	9.2	11.2
London	JUSM	5.3	3.3	2.7	2.7	2.8	3.3	4.0	6.5	6.9	6.1	7.6
South East	JUSN	5.8	4.0	3.8	3.5	3.1	3.3	3.8	5.4	5.9	..	..
South West	JUSO	3.0	2.3	2.2	1.9	1.6	1.7	1.9	2.7	2.9	2.6	3.5
England	JUSP	38.0	30.9	28.7	27.3	23.2	22.8	25.1	36.0	41.9	41.2	50.0
Wales	JUSQ	2.8	2.0	2.3	2.1	1.9	1.7	1.5	2.2	2.7	3.0	3.7
Northern Ireland	JUSR	..	0.3	0.2	0.2	0.2	0.3	0.4	0.5	0.4	..	..
Orders made												
England and Wales	JUSS	25.3	23.0	19.9	18.6	16.7	16.5	20.1	32.8	46.0	51.6	60.6
North East[2]	JUST	1.2	1.3	1.2	1.2	0.9	0.8	0.9	1.4	2.5	8.1	9.4
North West	JUSU	3.7	4.3	4.0	3.7	3.2	2.6	2.7	4.1	6.5	7.9	9.9
Yorkshire and the Humber	JUSV	3.1	2.7	2.4	2.3	1.8	1.6	1.7	2.8	4.2	..	..
East Midlands[3]	JUSW	1.7	2.0	1.6	1.6	1.4	1.2	1.5	2.6	3.8	10.1	12.8
West Midlands[3]	JUSX	2.4	2.3	2.1	2.2	1.8	1.7	2.2	3.3	5.0	..	..
East[4]	JUSY	2.6	1.9	1.6	1.4	1.3	1.5	2.0	3.2	4.4	11.1	12.5
London	JUSZ	3.5	2.5	1.8	1.9	2.2	2.7	3.8	6.6	8.3	8.0	8.2
South East	JUTA	3.4	2.6	2.2	1.9	1.9	2.2	2.9	4.6	5.7	..	..
South West	JUTB	2.1	1.8	1.3	1.1	1.0	1.0	1.4	2.3	2.9	3.2	3.8
England	JUTC	23.6	21.4	18.3	17.2	15.4	15.4	19.0	31.0	43.3	48.4	56.6
Wales	JUTD	1.7	1.6	1.6	1.4	1.3	1.1	1.1	1.8	2.7	3.2	4.0
Northern Ireland	JUTE	..	0.7	0.6	0.7	0.5	0.6	0.7	0.9	0.9	..	..

Note In 1999 the data extraction method changed. From 1999 the data are collected electronically from Caseman, the main administrative system in the county courts. Previously they were collected from Stats Module, a manual form completed monthly by all county courts.

1 Where the court grants the claimant possession but suspends the operation of the order. Provided the defendant complies with the terms of suspension, which usually require the defendant to pay the current mortgage plus some of the accrued arrears, the possession order cannot be enforced.

2 Orders figures for North East in 2007 & 2008 include those for Yorkshire and the Humber.

3 Orders figures for the Midlands in 2007 & 2008 include those for the West Midlands.

4 Orders figures for the East in 2007 & 2008 include those for South East.

Sources: Ministry of Justice 020 3334 3090;
Northern Ireland Court Service: 028 9032 8594

14.7 Mortgages
United Kingdom

		1998	1999	2000	2001	2002	2003	2004	2005	2006	2007	2008
Mortgages[1] (Thousands)	JUTH	10 821	10 987	11 177	11 251	11 368	11 452	11 515	11 608	11 746	11 852	11 667
Arrears and repossessions[1] (Thousands)												
Loans in arrears at end-period												
By 6-12 months	JUTI	74	57	48	43	34	31	30	39	35	41	72
By over 12 months	JUTJ	35	30	21	20	17	13	11	15	16	15	30
Properties repossessed in period	JUTK	34	30	23	18	12	9	8	15	21	26	40
Type of mortgage for house purchase[2] (Percentages)												
Standard repayment	JUTL	40.0	41.0	53.0	64.0	80.0	79.0	77.0	67.0	62.0	58.0	60.0
Endowment	JUTM	35.0	29.0	22.0	13.0	6.0	5.0	5.0	4.0	7.0	9.0	10.0
Other[3]	JUTN	22.0	25.0	18.0	16.0	9.0	11.0	11.0	22.0	24.0	26.0	24.0

1 Estimates cover only members of the Council of Mortgage Lenders; these account for 98 per cent of all mortgages outstanding.
2 Includes new mortgages advanced by building societies, banks and other major lenders. Includes sitting tenants.
3 Includes interest only, PEP/ISA and pension.

4 Figures are estimates of arrears on first charge loans held by CML members. They do not include arrears relating relating to other secured lending or to firms that are not CML members.
5 Figures are subject to revision as better information about rates of growth and performance in different parts of the market is received, or lenders report for the first time or re-submit earlier figures.

Source: Council of Mortgage Lenders

14.8 Sales and transfers of local authority dwellings
Great Britain

Thousands

		1996 /97	1997 /98	1998 /99	1999 /00	2000 /01	2001 /02	2002 /03	2003 /04	2004 /05	2005 /06	2006 /07	2007 /08
Right to buy sales	JUQV	45.0	58.1	56.0	66.8	71.3	66.6	78.5	94.1	74.7	41.6	26.1	19.2
Large scale voluntary transfers[1]	JUQW	29.9	21.1	36.9	88.7	111.4	100.8	102.5	104.6	67.9	81.7	82.7	117.2
Other sales and transfers[2]	JUQX	3.0	3.4	2.7	3.3	2.4	1.6	1.4	0.6	0.5	0.3	3.7	0.3
Total sales and transfers	JUQY	77.9	82.6	95.5	158.8	185.2	168.9	182.4	199.4	143.1	123.6	105.6	136.6

1 Except for 2003 large scale and voluntary transfers are included in other sales and transfers for Wales.
2 Excludes new town and Scottish Homes sales and transfers.

Sources: Communities and Local Government;
Welsh Assembly Government;
Scottish Government

14.9 Households in Temporary Accommodation[1]
Great Britain

As at 31st March of each year

Households

		1998 /99	1999 /00	2000 /01	2001 /02	2002 /03	2003 /04	2004 /05	2005 /06	2006 /07	2007 /08
Bed and breakfast hotels	JUWF	7 062	9 254	11 436	13 404	13 654	8 985	9 100	7 288	6 253	5 731
Hostels/women's refuges	JUWG	11 567	12 068	12 273	11 128	11 707	12 753	12 205	10 979	9 580	8 026
Social sector accommodation[2]	JXVN	20 686	23 510	27 826	30 310	31 719	31 821	31 295	27 758	23 463	24 756
Private sector accommodation and other[3]	JXVO	21 934	25 067	28 533	30 391	38 715	52 456	58 129	61 086	58 586	50 809
All accommodation[4]	JUWI	61 393	70 100	80 334	85 665	96 015	107 146	111 960	108 092	99 436	89 908

1 Households in temporary accommodation arranged by the local authority pending enquiries, or after being accepted as owed a main duty under homelessness legislation. Excludes 'homeless at home' cases who have remained in their existing accommodation after acceptance but have the same rights to suitable alternative housing as those in accommodation arranged directly by authorities.
2 Local authorities' and Registered Social Landlords' own stock.

3 Includes private sector properties leased by social sector landlords, households placed directly with a private sector landlord and other accommodation. From 2002 some self-contained B&B Annexe-style units, previously recorded under B&B have been more appropriately attributed to private sector accommodation.
4 Includes 'homeless at home' for Wales.

Sources: Communities and Local Government;
Welsh Assembly Government;
Scottish Government

Transport and communications

Chapter 15

Transport and communications

Road data

(Tables 15.4, 15.5, 15.6 and 15.7)

Traffic estimates are disaggregated for roads in urban and rural areas rather than between built-up and non built-up roads. The urban/rural split of roads is largely determined by whether roads lie within the boundaries of urban areas with a population of 10,000 or more with adjustments in some cases for major roads at the boundary.

Traffic estimates are based on the results of many 12-hour manual counts in every year, which are grossed up to estimates of annual average daily flows using expansion factors based on data from automatic traffic counters on similar roads. These averages are needed so that traffic in off-peak times, at weekends and in the summer and winter months (when only special counts are undertaken) can be taken into account when assessing the traffic at each site. For this purpose roads are sorted into 22 groupings and this allows a better match of manual count sites with automatic count sites. These groupings are based on a detailed analysis of the results from all the individual automatic count sites and take into account regional groupings, road category (that is both the urban/rural classification of the road and the road class) and traffic flow levels. The groupings range from lightly-trafficked, rural minor roads in holiday areas such as Cornwall and Devon, to major roads in central London.

Road class

(Tables 15.5 and 15.6)

Urban major and minor roads, from 1993 onwards, are defined as being within an urban area with a population of more than 10,000 people, based on the 2001 urban settlements. The definition for urban settlement can be found on the CLG web site at:

www.communities.gov.uk/planningandbuilding/planningbuilding/planningstatistics/urbanrural

Rural major and minor roads, from 1993 onwards, are defined as being outside an urban settlement.

National Travel Survey data

(Tables 15.1, 15.11)

TThe National Travel Survey (NTS) is designed to provide a databank of personal travel information for Great Britain. It has been conducted as a continuous survey since July 1988, following ad hoc surveys since the mid-1960s. The survey is designed to identify long-term trends and is not suitable for monitoring short-term trends.

In 2006, a weighting strategy as introduced to the NTS and applied retrospectively to data back to 1995. The weighting methodology adjusts for non-response bias and also adjusts for the drop-off in the number of trips recorded by respondents during the course of the travel week. All results now published for 1995 onwards are based on weighted data, and direct comparisons cannot be made to earlier years or previous publications.

During 2005, over 8,400 households provided details of their personal travel by filling in travel diaries over the course of a week. The drawn sample size from 2002 was nearly trebled compared with previous years following recommendations in a National Statistics Review of the NTS. This enables most results to be presented on a single year basis from 2002.

Travel included in the NTS covers all trips by British residents within Great Britain for personal reasons, including travel in the course of work. A trip is defined as a one-way course of travel having a single main purpose. It is the basic unit of personal travel defined in the survey. A round trip is split into two trips, with the first ending at a convenient point about half-way round as a notional stopping point for the outward destination and return origin. A stage is that portion of a trip defined by the use of a specific method of transport or of a specific ticket (a new stage being defined if either the mode or ticket changes). The main mode of a trip is that used for the longest stage of the trip. With stages of equal length, the mode of the latest stage is used. Walks of less than 50 yards are excluded.

Travel details provided by respondents include trip purpose, method of travel, time of day and trip length. The households also provided personal information, such as their age, sex, working status, driving licence holding, and details of the cars available for their use.

Because estimates made from a sample survey depend on the particular sample chosen, they generally differ from the true values of the population. This is not usually a problem when considering large samples (such as all car trips in Great Britain), but it may give misleading information when considering data from small samples even after weighting.

The most recent editions of all NTS publications are available on the DfT website at: www.dft.gov.uk/transtat/personaltravel. Bulletins of key results are published annually. The most recent bulletin is *National Travel Survey: 2007*.

Households with regular use of cars

(Table 15.12)

The mid-year estimates of the percentage of households with regular use of a car or van are based on combined data from the NTS, the Expenditure and Food Survey (previously the Family Expenditure Survey) and the General Household Survey (GHS). The method for calculating these figures was changed slightly for 2006, to incorporate weighted data from the NTS and the GHS. Figures for 2005 have also been revised to incorporate weighted data. Results by area type are based on weighted data from the NTS only.

Continuing Survey of Road Goods Transport

(Tables 15.3, 15.18, 15.19)

The estimates are derived from the Continuing Survey of Road Goods Transport (CSRGT) which is based on a sample of about 350 heavy goods vehicles each week. The samples are drawn from the computerised vehicle licence records held by the Driver and Vehicle Licensing Agency. Questionnaires are sent to the registered keepers of the sampled vehicles asking for a description of the vehicle and its activity during the survey week. The estimates are grossed to the vehicle population and, at the overall national level, have a 2 per cent margin of error (at 95 per cent confidence level). Further details and results are published in *Road Freight Statistics 2007* available at: www.dft.gov.uk/pgr/statistics/datatablespublications/freight/goodsbyroad/

Methodological changes

A key component of National Statistics outputs is a programme of quality reviews carried out at least every five years to ensure that such statistics are fit for purpose and that their quality and value continue to improve. A quality review of the Department for Transport's road freight surveys, including the CSRGT, was carried out in 2003. A copy of the report can be accessed at:

www.statistics.gov.uk/nsbase/methods_quality/quality_review/downloads/NSQR30FinalReport.doc

The quality review made a number of recommendations about the CSRGT. The main methodological recommendation was that, to improve the accuracy of survey estimates, the sample

strata should be amended to reflect current trends in vehicle type, weight and legislative groups. These new strata are described more fully in Appendix C of the survey report. For practical and administrative reasons, changes were also made to the sample selection methodology (see Appendix B of the report). These changes have resulted in figures from 2004 not being fully comparable with those for 2003 and earlier years. Detailed comparisons should therefore be made with caution.

Activity at civil aerodromes

(Table 15.27)

Figures exclude Channel Island and Isle of Man airports. Other covers local pleasure flights, scheduled service, positioning flights and non-transport charter flights for reward (for example: aerial survey work, crop dusting and delivery of empty aircraft). Non-commercial covers test and training flights, private, aeroclub, military and official flights, and business aviation, etc.

Postal services and television licences

(Table 15.30)

The letters posted category includes printed papers, newspapers, postcards and sample packets. Airmail includes letters without special charge for air transport. Business reply and freepost is now known as Response Services.

15.1 Trips per person per year: by sex, main mode and trip purpose[1], 2006
Great Britain

Numbers

Males

	Car	Walk	Bus and coach	Rail[2]	Other[3]	All modes
Social/entertainment	154	44	11	5	12	226
Shopping	123	49	13	2	6	193
Other escort	82	10	2	0	1	95
Other personal business	66	22	5	1	4	99
Commuting	131	15	11	13	14	185
Education	20	27	10	2	6	64
Escort education	17	8	0	0	0	25
Business	37	3	0	2	2	45
Holiday/day trip	28	2	2	1	5	38
Other, including just walk	0	43	0	0	0	44
All purpose (=100%) (number)	659	225	53	27	50	1014
Base						
Unweighted Base(Trips)	114,000	40,000	9,000	4,000	8,000	175,000

Females

	Car	Walk	Bus and coach	Rail[2]	Other[3]	All modes
Social/entertainment	165	48	13	4	9	239
Shopping	149	60	26	3	5	243
Other escort	82	13	2	0	1	99
Other personal business	71	29	8	1	3	111
Commuting	87	19	14	9	5	135
Education	18	26	10	1	3	60
Escort education	34	25	1	0	1	62
Business	19	4	1	1	1	26
Holiday/day trip	30	3	2	1	3	39
Other, including just walk	1	45	0	0	0	46
All purposes (numbers)	657	272	77	22	32	1060
Base						
Unweighted Base(Trips)	119,000	52,000	14,000	4,000	6,000	194,000

All persons

	Car	Walk	Bus and coach	Rail[2]	Other[3]	All modes
Social/entertainment	160	46	12	5	11	233
Shopping	136	55	20	2	6	219
Other escort	82	12	2	0	1	97
Other personal business	69	26	6	1	3	105
Commuting	109	17	12	11	10	160
Education	19	27	10	2	5	62
Escort education	26	17	1	0	0	44
Business	28	3	1	2	1	35
Holiday/daytrip	29	2	2	1	4	38
Other, including just walk	1	44	0	0	0	45
All purposes (numbers)	658	249	65	24	40	1037
Base						
Unweighted Base(Trips)	233,000	92,000	22,000	0,000	14,000	369,000

1 Main mode is that used for the longest part of the trip.
2 Includes London Underground.
3 Includes bicycles, two-wheeled motor vehicles, motorcaravans, taxis/ mini-cabs, domestic air travel and other private and public transport.

Source: National Travel Survey, Department for Transport 020 7944 3097

15.2 Retail Prices Index: transport components: 1997-2007
Great Britain

Indices (1997=100)

| | All items | Motor vehicles | | | | | Rail fares | Bus fares |
		Purchase	Maintenance	Petrol and oil	Tax and insurance	All motor[1]		
	ENX3	ENX4	ENX5	ZCFV	ENX6	ZCFW	ZCFX	ENX7
1997	100.0	100.0	100.0	100.0	100.0	100.0	100.0	100.0
1998	103.4	98.9	104.1	105.0	108.8	103.1	104.1	103.3
1999	105.0	94.7	108.2	113.8	117.6	105.6	107.9	107.0
2000	108.1	89.6	112.7	128.8	130.2	109.7	109.8	111.3
2001	110.0	88.3	118.2	122.2	137.0	109.1	114.0	116.0
2002	111.9	86.6	124.3	118.3	139.1	108.2	116.6	119.6
2003	115.1	84.1	131.7	122.6	145.1	109.6	118.6	124.6
2004	118.5	81.5	139.7	129.4	145.8	110.7	123.1	131.0
2005	121.9	77.3	148.2	140.8	143.9	111.4	128.1	139.6
2006	125.8	75.2	157.2	148.5	145.7	113.1	133.2	141.6
2007	131.2	73.2	165.3	152.6	152.4	114.5	140.0	149.7

1 The RPI all motor index includes purchase of a vehicle, maintenance, petrol and oil and tax and insurance.

Source: Consumer Prices and Inflation Division, ONS: 020 7944 4442

15.3 Domestic freight transport: by mode
Great Britain

		1997	1998	1999	2000	2001	2002	2003	2004	2005	2006	2007
Goods moved (billion tonnes kilometres)												
Petroleum products												
Road[1]	ZBZP	5.8	5.2	5.0	6.4	5.8	5.2	5.5	5.7	5.5	5.6	5.1
Rail[2]	ZBZQ	..	1.6	1.5	1.4	1.2	1.2	1.2	1.2	1.2	1.5	1.6
Water[3]	ZBZR	38.3	45.2	48.6	52.7	43.5	51.7	46.9	46.9	47.2	37.8	36.4
of which: coastwise	ZBZS	33.8	36.4	33.3	26.0	23.1	24.2	23.3	26.6	30.3	22.7	25.0
Pipeline	ZBZT	11.2	11.7	11.6	11.4	11.5	10.9	10.5	10.7	10.8	10.8	10.2
All modes	ZBZU	55.3	63.7	66.7	71.9	62.0	69.0	64.1	64.5	64.7	55.8	53.3
Coal and coke												
Road[1]	ZBZV	2.7	2.0	2.2	1.5	2.1	1.5	1.5	1.2	1.5	1.3	1.6
Rail[2]	ZBZW	4.4	4.5	4.8	4.8	6.2	5.7	5.8	6.7	8.3	8.8	7.7
Water[3]	ZBZX	0.6	0.5	0.5	0.2	0.5	0.3	0.5	0.3	0.4	0.5	0.5
All modes	ZBZY	7.7	7.0	7.5	6.5	8.8	7.5	7.9	8.5	10.2	10.4	9.8
Other traffic												
Road[1]	ZBZZ	148.9	153.1	150.5	151.5	150.6	152.7	154.7	155.6	156.4	159.7	166.4
Rail[2]	ZCAA	12.5	11.2	11.9	11.9	12.0	11.7	11.9	12.5	12.2	11.8	11.9
Water[3]	ZCAB	9.20	11.20	9.60	14.60	14.80	15.20	13.50	12.30	13.30	13.49	13.90
All modes	ZCAC	170.6	175.5	172.0	178.0	177.4	179.6	180.0	180.4	181.9	185.0	192.2
All traffic												
Road[1]	ZCBD	157.4	160.0	157.7	159.4	158.5	159.4	161.7	162.5	163.4	166.7	173.1
Rail[2]	KCTB	16.9	17.3	18.2	18.1	19.4	18.5	18.9	20.4	21.7	21.9	21.2
Water[3]	ZCAD	48.10	56.90	58.70	67.40	58.80	67.20	60.90	59.45	60.87	51.85	50.80
Pipeline	KCTE	11.2	11.7	11.6	11.4	11.5	10.9	10.5	10.7	10.8	10.8	10.2
All modes	KCTF	233.6	246.2	246.2	256.3	248.2	256.0	252.0	253.0	256.8	251.3	255.3
Percentage of all traffic												
Road[1]	ZCAE	67	65	64	62	64	62	64	64	64	66	68
Rail[2]	ZCAF	7	7	7	7	8	7	7	8	8	9	8
Water[3]	ZCAG	21	23	24	26	24	26	24	23	24	21	20
Pipeline	ZCAH	5	5	5	4	5	4	4	4	4	4	4
All modes	ZCAI	100	100	100	100	100	100	100	100	100	100	100
Goods lifted (million tonnes)												
Petroleum products												
Road[1]	ZCAJ	73	61	61	75	74	59	64	67	70	69	71
Rail[2]	ZCAK	..	..	..	..	..	..	..	..	..	..	..
Water[3]	ZCAL	69	76	72	72	60	67	64	63	66	57	56
of which: coastwise	ZCAM	52	55	52	40	34	36	35	38	42	34	35
Pipeline	ZCAN	148	153	155	151	151	146	141	158	168	159	146
All modes[4]	ZCAO	290	290	288	298	285	272	269	288	304	285	274
Coal and coke												
Road[1]	ZCAP	37	26	28	22	21	17	22	14	21	17	24
Rail[2]	ZCAQ	50	45	36	35	40	34	35	43	48	49	43
Water[3]	ZCAR	4	3	3	3	3	2	2	1	2	2	2
All modes	ZCAS	91	70	75	60	64	53	59	67	72	68	69
Other traffic												
Road[1]	ZCAT	1 630	1 640	1 575	1 596	1 587	1 658	1 667	1 782	1 777	1 854	1 906
Rail[2]	ZCAU	55	57	61	60	55	53	54	57	58	59	59
Water[3]	ZCAV	69	70	70	62	68	70	67	63	65	66	68
All modes	ZCAW	1 754	1 767	1 706	1 718	1 710	1 781	1 788	1 902	1 901	1 980	2 032
All traffic												
Road[1]	KCTG	1 740	1 727	1 664	1 693	1 682	1 734	1 753	1 863	1 868	1 940	2 001
Rail[2]	KCTH	105	102	97	96	94	87	89	100[6]	105[7]	108[7]	102[8]
Water[3]	ZCAX	142.0	149.0	144.0	137.0	131.0	139.0	133.0	127.0	133.0	126.0	126.0
Pipeline	KCTK	148.0	153.0	155.0	151.0	151.0	146.0	141.0	158.0	168.0	159.0	146.0
All modes	KCTL	2 135	2 131	2 060	2 077	2 058	2 106	2 116	2 249	2 275	2 333	2 376
Percentage of all traffic												
Road[1]	ZCAY	81	81	81	82	82	82	83	83	82	83	84
Rail[2]	ZCAZ	5	5	5	5	5	4	4	4	5	5	4
Water[3]	ZCBA	7	7	7	7	6	7	6	6	6	5	5
Pipeline	ZCBB	7	7	8	7	7	7	7	7	7	7	6
All modes	ZCBC	100	100	100	100	100	100	100	100	100	100	100

1 All goods vehicles, including those up to 3.5 tonnes gross vehicle weight.
2 Figures for rail are for financial years e.g 1997/98 etc.
3 Figures for water are for UK traffic.
4 Excludes rail.
5 See footnote 2 Table 4.4 - TSGB publication.
6 See footnote 6 Table 4.1 - TSGB publication.
7 There is a break in the series between 2003-04 and 2004-05, due to a change in the method of data collection.
8 There is a break in the series between 2006 07 and 2007 08 because coal data was not supplied by GB Railfreight prior to 2007-08.

Sources: Department for Transport;
Rail: 020 7944 4977;
Road 020 7944 4261;
Water: 020 7944 3087;
Pipeline : 020 7215 2718;
Sources - Rail : ORR;
Pipeline : Department for Business Enterprise and Regulatory Reform

15.4 Passenger transport by mode
Great Britain

Billion passenger kilometres		1997	1998	1999	2000	2001	2002	2003	2004	2005	2006	2007
Road												
Buses and coaches	GRXK	44	45	46	47	47	47	47	48	48	50	50
Cars, vans and taxis	GRXG	632	636	642	640	654	677	673	678	674	686	689
Motor cycles	GRXH	4	4	5	5	5	5	6	6	6	6	6
Pedal cycles	GRXI	4	4	4	4	4	4	5	4	4	5	4
All road	GRXJ	685	689	697	695	710	733	731	736	733	746	749
Rail[1]	KCTN	42	44	46	47	47	48	49	50	52	55	59
Air	KCTM	7.0	7.0	7.0	8.0	8.0	8.0	9.0	10.0	10.0	10.0	9.5
All modes[2]	GRXM	733	740	751	749	765	790	789	796	794	811	817
Percentages												
Road												
Buses and coaches	GRXN	6	6	6	6	6	6	6	6	6	6	6
Cars, vans and taxis	GRXO	86	86	86	85	85	86	85	85	85	85	84
Motor cycles	GRXP	1	1	1	1	1	1	1	1	1	1	1
Pedal cycles	GRXQ	1	1	1	1	1	1	1	–	1	1	1
All road	GRXR	93	93	93	93	93	93	93	92	92	92	92
Rail[1]	ZCBJ	6	6	6	6	6	6	6	6	7	7	7
Air	ZCBK	1.0	1.0	1.0	1.0	1.0	1.0	1.0	1.0	1.0	1.0	1.2
All modes[2]	GRXU	100	100	100	100	100	100	100	100	100	100	100

1 Financial years. National Rail, urban metros and modern trams.
2 Excluding travel by water.

Sources: Bus & coach: 020 7944 3076;
Car, m/cycle & pedal cycle: 020 7944 3097;
Rail: 020 7944 3076;
Air: 020 7944 3088;
Rail : ORR Air : CAA

15.5 Motor vehicle traffic: by road class: 1996-2006
Great Britain

Billion vehicle kilometres

		1997	1998	1999	2000[1]	2001[2]	2002	2003	2004	2005	2006[6]	2007
Motorways	JSZV	82.1	85.7	87.8	88.4	90.8	92.6	93.0	96.6	97.0	99.4	100.6
Rural 'A' roads[3]												
Trunk[5]	JSZW	62.5	63.3	64.7	64.2	65.9	64.6	61.5	59.7	58.0	59.2	58.6
Principal[5]	JSZX	64.1	65.4	66.0	65.8	67.4	71.8	77.7	81.6	83.3	84.4	84.9
All rural 'A' roads	JSZY	126.6	128.7	130.7	130.0	133.3	136.4	139.3	141.3	141.3	143.6	143.5
Urban 'A' roads[4]												
Trunk[5]	JSZZ	13.8	13.8	14.0	14.0	7.6	7.4	6.7	6.0	5.5	5.6	5.4
Principal[5]	JTAA	67.1	67.5	67.9	67.7	74.2	74.8	75.1	76.8	76.2	76.9	75.9
All urban 'A' roads	JTAB	80.9	81.3	81.9	81.7	81.8	82.2	81.7	82.8	81.7	82.5	81.3
All Major Roads	I45C	289.6	295.7	300.4	300.0	305.9	311.2	314.0	320.7	320.1	325.5	325.4
Minor roads												
Minor rural roads	JTAC	60.0	60.4	61.3	61.5	61.6	64.5	64.4	65.9	66.8	69.3	72.0
Minor urban roads	JTAD	100.7	102.4	105.3	105.5	106.9	110.8	111.9	112.0	112.5	112.7	115.5
All minor roads	JTAE	160.7	162.8	166.6	167.0	168.5	175.3	176.4	177.9	179.3	182.0	187.5
All roads	JTAF	450.3	458.5	467.0	467.1	474.4	486.5	490.4	498.6	499.4	507.5	513.0

1 The decline in the use of cars and taxis in 2000 was due to the fuel dispute.
2 Figures affected by the impact of Foot and Mouth disease during 2001.
3 Rural roads; Major and minor roads, from 1993 onwards, are defined as being outside an urban area. (see definition below).
4 Urban roads; Major and minor roads, from 1993 onwards, are defined as within an urban area with a population of 10,000 or more. These are based on the 2001 urban settlements. The definition for 'urban settlement' is in Urban and Rural area definitions: a user guide which can be found on the Department for Communities and Local Government web site at: http:/www.communities.gov.uk/publications/planningandbuilding/urbanrural
5 Figures for trunk and principal 'A' roads in England, from 2001 onwards are affected by the detrunking programme.

Source: Department for Transport: 020 7944 3095

Transport and communications

15.6 Public road length:[1] by road type
Great Britain

Kilometres

		1997	1998	1999	2000	2001	2002	2003	2004	2005	2006[6]	2007
Trunk motorway	JSZD	3 333	3 376	3 404	3 422	3 431	3 433	3 432	3 478	3 466	3 503	3 518
Principal motorway	JSZE	45	44	45	45	45	45	46	46	54	53	41
Rural 'A' roads[2]:												
Trunk[3]	JSZF	10 690	10 585	10 611	10 627	10 607	9 973	9 027	8 641	8 239	8 277	8 258
Principal[3]	JSZG	24 636	24 783	24 852	24 866	24 915	25 559	26 498	26 889	27 312	27 336	27 346
All rural 'A' roads	JSZH	35 326	35 369	35 463	35 493	35 522	35 532	35 525	35 530	35 550	35 612	35 603
Urban 'A' roads[4]:												
Trunk[3]	JSZI	1 108	1 096	1 087	1 074	762	705	587	506	444	446	425
Principal[3]	JSZJ	9 923	9 931	10 019	10 040	10 370	10 436	10 539	10 632	10 663	10 696	10 714
All urban 'A' roads	JSZK	11 031	11 027	11 106	11 114	11 132	11 141	11 127	11 138	11 107	11 143	11 139
Minor rural roads[5]:												
B roads	JSZL	24 594	24 586	24 579	24 570	24 562	24 554	24 547	24 640	24 639	24 574	24 795
C roads	JSZM	73 312	73 405	73 500	73 593	73 688	73 783	73 878	73 363	73 581	73 548	73 480
Unclassified	JSZN	110 915	111 132	111 350	111 568	111 787	112 006	112 231	109 561	109 426	115 250	115 365
All minor rural roads	JSZO	208 820	209 123	209 429	209 731	210 037	210 343	210 656	207 565	207 646	213 371	213 641
Minor urban roads[5]:												
B roads	JSZP	5 618	5 622	5 626	5 630	5 633	5 638	5 641	5 538	5 550	5 445	5 470
C roads	JSZQ	10 966	10 986	11 009	11 031	11 054	11 076	11 098	10 859	10 878	10 921	10 942
Unclassified	JSZR	112 754	113 093	113 432	113 772	114 114	114 456	114 816	113 520	113 757	114 355	114 524
All minor urban roads	JSZS	129 338	129 701	130 068	130 433	130 803	131 169	131 556	129 917	130 186	130 721	130 936
All major roads	GG5B	49 735	49 816	50 018	50 074	50 130	50 152	50 130	50 192	50 176	50 310	50 302
All minor roads[5]	JSZT	338 158	338 825	339 496	340 163	340 838	341 512	342 212	337 482	337 832	344 092	344 577
All roads	JSZU	387 893	388 641	389 515	390 237	390 969	391 663	392 342	387 674	388 008	394 402	394 879

1 A number of minor revisions have been made to the lengths of major roads from 1993 onwards.
2 Rural roads: Major and minor roads, from 1993 onwards, are defined as being outside an urban area.
3 Figures for trunk and principal 'A' roads in England, from 2001 onwards, are affected by the detrunking programme.
4 Urban roads: Major and minor roads, from 1993 onwards, are defined as within an urban area with a population of 10,000 or more. These are based on the 2001 urban settlements. The definition for 'urban settlement' is in Urban and rural area definitions : a user guide can be found on the Department for Communities and Local Government web site at : http//www.communities.gov.uk/publications/planningandbuilding/urbanrural
5 New information from 2004 and from 2006 has enabled better estimates of minor road lengths to be made.
6 Data for minor roads in 2006 have been revised.

Sources: National Road Traffic Survey; Department for Transport 020 7944 3095

15.7 Road traffic: by type of vehicle
Great Britain

Billion vehicle kilometres

		1997	1998	1999	2000[1]	2001[2]	2002	2003	2004	2005	2006	2007
Cars and taxis	JTAH	365.8	370.6	377.4	376.8	382.8	392.9	393.1	398.1	397.2	402.6	404.1
Motor cycles etc.	JTAI	4.0	4.1	4.5	4.6	4.8	5.1	5.6	5.2	5.4	5.2	5.6
Larger buses and coaches	JTAJ	5.2	5.2	5.3	5.2	5.2	5.2	5.4	5.2	5.2	5.4	5.7
Light vans[3]	JTAK	48.6	50.8	51.6	52.3	53.7	55.0	57.9	60.8	62.6	65.2	68.2
Goods vehicles[4]:												
2 axles rigid	JTAL	11.0	11.1	11.6	11.7	11.5	11.6	11.7	11.7	11.5	11.3	11.1
3 axles rigid	JTAM	1.6	1.9	1.7	1.7	1.8	1.8	1.8	1.9	1.9	1.9	2.0
4 or more axles rigid	JTAN	1.5	1.6	1.5	1.5	1.5	1.5	1.6	1.6	1.7	1.7	1.8
3 and 4 axles artic	JTAO	3.2	3.0	3.0	2.7	2.5	2.3	2.2	2.2	2.0	1.9	1.8
5 axles artic	JTAP	7.1	7.3	7.2	6.7	6.4	6.4	6.2	6.5	6.4	6.6	6.6
6 or more axles artic	JTAQ	2.5	2.9	3.3	4.1	4.5	4.8	5.0	5.4	5.5	5.7	6.1
All	JTAR	26.9	27.7	28.1	28.2	28.1	28.3	28.5	29.4	29.0	29.1	29.4
All motor vehicles	JURA	450.3	458.5	467.0	467.1	474.4	486.5	490.4	498.6	499.4	507.5	513.0
Pedal cycles	JURB	4.1	4.0	4.1	4.2	4.2	4.4	4.5	4.2	4.4	4.6	4.2

1 The decline in the use of cars and taxis in 2000 was due to the fuel dispute.
2 Figures affected by the impact of Foot and Mouth disease during 2001.
3 Not exceeding 3,500 kgs gross vehicle weight.
4 Over 3,500 kgs gross vehicle weight.

Sources: National Road Traffic Survey; Department for Transport 020 7944 3095

15.8 Motor vehicles currently licenced
Great Britain
At end of year

Thousands

| | Private and light goods | | | | | | | | | | Body type cars | |
| | | | Motor cycles, scooters and mopeds | Public transport vehicles[1] | Goods vehicles | Special machines/ special conces- sionary[1] | Other vehicles | Crown and exempt vehicles[1] | Special vehicles group | All vehicles | All | Percent- age of company cars |
	Private cars	Other vehicles										
	BMBJ	BMBK	BMBB	BMBE	BMBD	KSBY	BMBF	BMBL	KSBZ	BMBI	ZCGR	ZCGS
1998	22 115	2 362	684	80	412	243	84	1 558	47	27 538	23 293	10.4
1999	22 785	2 427	760	84	415	241	83	1 573	47	28 368	23 975	10.0
2000	23 196	2 469	825	86	418	233	81	1 590	46	28 898	24 406	10.3
2001	23 899	2 544	882	89	422	233	76	1 602	45	29 747	25 126	9.7
2002	24 543	2 622	941	92	425	243	79	1 855	46	30 557	25 782	9.0
2003	24 985	2 730	1 005	96	426	258	78	1 887	47	31 207	26 240	8.4
2004	25 754	2 900	1 060	100	434	–	82	1 929	50	32 259	27 028	8.5
2005	26 208	3 019	1 075	103	433	–	81	1 978	51	32 897	27 520	8.8
2006	26 508	3 137	1 094	107	446	–	86	1 991	54	33 369	27 830	8.7
2007	26 878	3 261	1 133	109	446	..	86	2 043	56	33 957	..	..
2008	27 021	3 303	1 160	111	436	..	85	2 091	..	34 206	..	..

1 The 'Special concession' vehicles form part of the 'Crown and exempt' taxation class from 2002.

Source: Department for Transport 020 7944 3077

15.9 New vehicle registrations by taxation class
Great Britain

Thousands

		1998	1999	2000	2001	2002	2003	2004	2005	2006	2007	2008
Cars	BMAA	2 123.5	2 100.4	2 174.9	2 426.4	2 528.9	2 497.1	2 437.5	2 266.2	2 241.7	2 191.4	1 891.9
Other Vehicles	BMAE	244.5	241.6	254.9	278.0	286.9	323.5	347.2	337.0	338.4	348.0	296.4
Motor Cycles, Scooters and Mopeds	BMAL	143.3	168.4	182.9	177.5	162.3	157.3	133.7	132.1	131.9	143.0	138.4
Goods	BBJY	49.1	48.3	50.4	49.0	44.9	48.4	48.0	51.3	47.9	41.2	47.0
Buses	BBJZ	7.4	8.0	7.5	7.1	7.7	8.4	8.1	8.9	7.6	9.1	8.3
Other Vehicles[1]	I8B3	157.0	174.0	176.0	169.0	192.0	189.0	204.0	218.0	219.0	265.0	..
All Vehicles	BBKD	2 740.3	2 765.8	2 870.9	3 136.6	3 229.5	3 231.9	3 185.3	3 021.4	2 913.6	2 996.9	2 672.2

1 Includes three wheelers, special machines, special concessionary, special
vehicles and crown and exempt vehicles.

Source: Department for Transport: 020 7944 3077

231

15.10 Driving test pass rates: by sex and type of vehicle licence
Great Britain

Percentages

		1989 /90	1991 /92	1998 /99	2000 /01	2001 /02	2002 /03	2003 /04	2004 /05	2005 /06	2006 /07	2007 /08
Males												
Motorcycle	JTRB	72	69	69	68	67	66	67	66	66	67	68
Car	JTRC	58	57	51	48	47	47	46	46	46	46	47
Bus	JTTG	–	–	48	47	46	44	46	46	43	43	50
Lorry	JTTH	–	–	52	53	50	50	49	47	45	46	46
All males	JTTI	–	–	–	51	50	49	48	47	47	48	49
Females												
Motorcycle	JTTJ	68	63	63	56	55	54	53	53	52	54	56
Car	JTTK	47	46	42	40	40	40	40	39	40	41	41
Bus	JTTL	–	–	47	45	40	40	45	46	47	49	53
Lorry	JTTM	–	–	50	53	47	46	48	45	45	47	48
All females	JTTN	–	–	–	41	41	40	40	40	40	41	42
All												
Motorcycle	JTTO	–	–	68	66	66	65	65	64	64	65	67
Car	JTTP	–	–	46	44	43	43	43	42	42	43	44
Bus	JTTQ	–	–	48	48	45	44	46	44	43	44	50
Lorry	JTTR	–	–	52	54	56	49	49	46	45	46	46
All persons	JTTS	–	–	–	46	46	45	44	43	44	44	45

Source: Driving Standards Agency - info.rsis@dsa.gov.uk

15.11 Full car driving licence holders by sex and age[1]
Great Britain

Percentages and millions

	All aged 17+	17-20	21-29	30-39	40-49	50-59	60-69	70 and over	Estimated number of licence holders (millions)
All adults									
1975/76	48	28	59	67	60	50	35	15	19.4
1985/86	57	33	63	74	71	60	47	27	24.3
1989/91	64	43	72	77	78	67	54	32	27.8
1992/94	67	48	75	82	79	72	57	33	29.3
1995/97[2]	69	43	74	81	81	75	63	38	30.3
1998/00	71	41	75	84	83	77	67	39	31.4
	GB9O	C98J	C98K	C98L	C98M	C98N	C98O	C98P	C98Q
2004	70	27	65	82	83	80	72	46	32.2
2005	72	32	66	82	84	82	74	51	33.3
2006	72	34	67	82	84	82	76	50	33.7
2007	71	38	66	81	83	82	75	52	33.8
Males									
1975/76	69	36	78	85	83	75	58	32	13.4
1985/86	74	37	73	86	87	81	72	51	15.1
1989/91	80	52	82	88	89	85	78	58	16.7
1992/94	81	54	83	91	88	88	81	59	17.0
1995/97[2]	81	50	80	88	89	89	83	65	17.2
1998/00	82	44	80	89	91	88	83	65	17.4
	GB9P	C98R	C98S	C98T	C98U	C98V	C98W	C98X	C98Y
2004	79	30	68	87	89	90	86	72	17.7
2005	81	37	69	86	90	90	88	73	18.1
2006	81	37	71	86	89	91	90	76	18.4
2007	80	41	69	86	88	90	87	75	18.4
Females									
1975/76	29	20	43	48	37	24	15	4	6.0
1985/86	41	29	54	62	56	41	24	11	9.2
1989/91	49	35	64	67	66	49	33	15	11.1
1992/94	54	42	68	73	70	57	37	16	12.2
1995/97[2]	57	36	67	74	73	62	45	21	13.1
1998/00	60	38	69	78	76	67	53	22	14.0
	GB9Q	C98Z	C992	C993	C994	C995	C996	C997	C998
2004	61	24	62	77	77	71	58	28	14.5
2005	63	27	62	77	79	73	61	35	15.2
2006	63	31	63	78	79	74	63	31	15.3
2007	63	34	62	76	78	74	63	36	15.4

1 See chapter text.
2 Figures for 1995 onwards are based on weighted data.

Source: National Travel Survey, Department for Transport 020 7944 3097

15.12 Households with regular use of cars[1]
Great Britain

	No car	One car	Two cars	Three or more cars	Total (millions)
	ZCGA	ZCGB	ZCGC	ZCGD	ZCGE
1996	30	45	21	4	23.0
1997	30	45	21	5	23.1
1998	28	44	23	5	23.3
1999	28	44	22	5	23.4
2000	27	45	23	5	23.6
2001	26	45	23	5	23.9
2002	26	44	24	5	24.1
2003	26	44	25	5	24.4
2004	25	44	25	5	24.6
2005	25	44	25	5	24.8
2006	24	44	26	6	24.8

	No car	One car	Two or more cars	Total
Government Office Regions, 2006[1,2]				
Great Britain	24	44	32	100
North East	31	45	23	100
North West	27	43	31	100
Yorkshire and The Humber	25	45	30	100
East Midlands	19	45	36	100
West Midlands	23	42	36	100
East	17	42	41	100
London	36	46	18	100
South East	18	43	39	100
South West	17	45	37	100
England	24	44	33	100
Wales	22	45	33	100
Scotland	29	45	26	100
Northern Ireland	24	41	34	100

	No car	One car	Two or more cars	Total
Area type, 2006				
Great Britain	25	43	32	100
London	43	41	16	100
Metropolitan areas	31	42	27	100
Other urban areas with population:				
Over 250,000	27	44	29	100
25,000 - 250,000	23	44	32	100
10,000 - 25,000	22	46	32	100
3,000 - 10,000	19	42	40	100
Rural areas	10	38	51	100

1 Includes cars and light vans normally available to the household.
2 Based on combined survey data sources - Family Expenditure Survey, ONS, General Household Survey, ONS, National Survey DfT.

Sources: Office for National Statistics; Department for Transport 020 7944 3097

15.13 Vehicles with current licences[1]
Northern Ireland

Numbers

		1997	1998	1999	2000	2001[3]	2002	2003[4]	2004	2005	2006	2007
Private light goods, etc	KNKA	575 923	584 706	608 316	615 180	644 968	666 731	711 913	737 198	765 061	800 969	840 621
Motorcycles, Scooters and mopeds	KNKB	10 932	11 663	13 087	14 116	15 205	17 598	23 820	24 533	25 998	27 083	28 150
Public road passenger vehicles[2]:												
Taxis,buses,coaches	KNKD	..	..	..	..	..	..	..	..	..	..	..
Buses, coaches (9 seats or more)	KNKE	2 144	2 175	2 204	2 266	2 315	2 322	2 353	2 378	2 566	2 670	2 865
Total	KNKC	2 144	2 175	2 204	2 266	2 315	2 322	2 353	2 378	2 566	2 670	2 865
General (HGV) goods vehicles:	KNKF	18 172	18 312	17 075	17 864	19 415	20 244	22 100	23 062	23 517	24 806	25 785
Agricultural tractors and engines, etc[3]	KNKM	6 378	5 906	5 505	5 048	4 901	5 731	7 503	8 674	9 584	10 586	12 817
Other	KNKN	1 188	1 193	1 446	1 287	1 366	1 347	1 671	1 794	1 898	2 039	2 125
Vehicles exempt from duty:												
Government owned	KNKP	3 705	3 785	4 032	3 822	6 427	6 383	6 172	6 116	6 367	7 315	9 655
Other:												
Ambulances	KNKQ	389	425	417	452	318	299	325	355	355	388	378
Fire engines	KNKR	291	285	286	290	181	174	170	178	179	166	155
Other exempt[4]	KNKS	64 447	66 981	68 277	70 405	72 209	73 648	76 715	78 973	81 874	82 655	85 738
Total	KNKO	68 832	71 476	73 012	74 969	79 135	80 504	83 382	85 622	88 775	90 524	95 926
Total	KNKT	683 569	695 431	720 645	730 730	767 305	794 477	852 742	883 261	917 399	958 677	1 008 289

1 Licences current at 31 December.
2 Tax class change from 'Hackney' to 'Bus' with effect from July 2005. Only Vehicles with 9 or more seats are included in 'Bus' class. Vehicles with 8 seats or less previously recorded in ' Hackney ' class moved into 'Private Light Goods' class.
3 Taxation classes have been revised
4 New Tax Class 36 introduced.

Source: Driver and Vehicle Agency: 028 7034 6903

15.14 New vehicle registrations
Northern Ireland

Numbers

		1997	1998	1999	2000	2001	2002	2003	2004	2005	2006	2007
Private cars	KNLA	83 968	91 141	89 078	84 973	88 592	83 402	87 506	85 190	86 366	91 224	97 346
Motorcycles	KNLB	3 376	4 307	5 310	6 010	5 591	5 596	6 804	4 601	4 648	4 289	4 477
Public road passenger vehicles	KNLC	714	486	568	565	451	439	609	467	621	677	629
Goods vehicles:												
General haulage vehicles:												
Under 3.5 tonnes	KNLH	8 468	10 107	11 054	12 617	13 274	12 007	11 492	11 090	12 300	13 457	13 855
3.5 tonnes and over	KNLJ	3 521	3 572	3 697	3 502	4 534	3 669	4 059	3 987	3 768	4 080	3 676
Agricultural tractors[1]	KNLM	1 364	971	987	1 313	301	1	9	2	2	8	–
Vehicles exempt from duty	KNLR	10 882	10 718	11 081	10 789	12 126	12 515	11 907	12 881	13 987	13 031	14 083
General haulage and special types	JTAG	..	..	..	..	..	15	12	11	16	32	46
Total	KNLS	112 296	121 302	121 777	119 769	124 869	117 644	122 398	118 229	121 708	126 798	134 112

1 Agricultural tractors driven on public roads. From April 2001 tractors were exempt.

Source: Driver and Vehicle Agency : 028 7034 6903

15.15 Local bus services: passenger journeys by area: 1997/98-2007/08[1]

Millions

		1997 /98	1998 /99	1999 /00	2000 /01	2001 /02	2002 /03	2003 /04	2004 /05	2005 /06	2006 /07	2007 /08
Great Britain	ZCET	4 430	4 350	4 376	4 420	4 455	4 550	4 681	4 737	4 791	5 097	5 164
London	KILS	1 281	1 266	1 294	1 347	1 422	1 527	1 692	1 802	1 881	1 993	2 090
English Metropolitan Counties	KILT	1 292	1 256	1 213	1 203	1 196	1 182	1 162	1 128	1 111	1 141	1 121
English other areas	KILU	1 286	1 286	1 297	1 292	1 263	1 255	1 233	1 210	1 204	1 336	1 319
All outside London	ZCES	3 149	3 084	3 082	3 073	3 033	3 023	2 989	2 935	2 910	3 104	3 074
England	ZCER	3 859	3 808	3 804	3 842	3 881	3 964	4 087	4 140	4 196	4 470	4 530
Scotland	KILV	448	424	455	458	466	471	478	479	477	506	513
Wales	KILW	122	118	117	119	108	115	116	118	118	122	122

1 Previous years figures have been revised.

Source: Department for Transport 020 7944 3076

15.16 Local bus services: fare indices: by area
Current prices

Indices (1995=100)

		1997 /98	1998 /99	1999 /00	2000 /01	2001 /02	2002 /03	2003 /04	2004 /05	2005 /06	2006 /07	2007 /08
Great Britain	KNEU	112.1	117.1	121.8	126.4	130.6	134.5	139.2	146.5	157.5	159.0	167.6
London	KNEP	109.4	113.8	117.2	117.3	115.5	114.8	116.9	126.8	139.7	151.5	159.5
English Metropolitan Counties	KILD	112.8	117.9	123.5	128.6	135.5	140.7	146.7	153.3	166.0	168.3	178.3
English other areas	KILE	112.0	117.3	122.6	129.2	136.1	142.4	149.0	155.9	166.2	159.5	168.0
All outside London	ZCEQ	112.9	118.2	123.2	129.0	135.1	140.4	146.0	152.3	162.2	160.7	169.1
England	ZCEP	111.5	116.4	121.4	125.8	130.3	134.3	139.4	147.2	159.4	160.1	169.1
Scotland	KILF	116.2	121.2	124.1	129.1	131.1	133.8	136.1	140.0	143.9	151.0	155.7
Wales	KILG	109.6	116.0	121.9	128.4	135.7	142.3	147.2	153.7	159.9	169.7	177.8
Retail Prices Index (1995=100)	KNEV	106.5	109.9	111.6	114.9	116.6	119.1	122.4	126.2	129.5	134.4	139.9

Source: Department for Transport 020 7944 4139

15.17 Road accident casualties: by road user type and severity
Great Britain

Numbers

		1997	1998	1999	2000	2001	2002	2003	2004	2005	2006	2007
Child pedestrians[1]:												
Killed	ZCDH	138	103	107	107	107	79	74	77	63	71	57
Killed or seriously injured	KIJS	3 954	3 737	3 457	3 226	3 144	2 828	2 381	2 339	2 134	2 025	1 899
All severities	ZCDI	18 407	17 971	16 876	16 184	15 819	14 231	12 544	12 234	11 250	10 131	9 527
Adult pedestrians[3]:												
Killed	ZCDJ	835	803	760	750	712	688	695	589	604	602	585
Killed or seriously injured	KIJT	6 925	6 592	6 221	6 112	5 745	5 644	5 422	5 005	4 847	4 894	4 900
All severities	ZCDK	26 223	25 827	24 806	24 481	23 463	23 258	22 531	21 404	20 725	19 774	19 676
Child pedal cyclists[1]:												
Killed	ZCDL	33	32	36	27	25	22	18	25	20	31	13
Killed or seriously injured	KIJU	1 016	915	950	758	674	594	595	577	527	503	522
All severities	ZCDM	7 899	6 930	7 290	6 260	5 451	4 809	4 769	4 682	4 286	3 765	3 633
Adult pedal cyclists[3]:												
Killed	ZCDN	150	126	135	98	111	107	95	109	127	115	122
Killed or seriously injured	KIJV	2 542	2 345	2 172	1 954	1 951	1 801	1 776	1 697	1 787	1 898	1 994
All severities	ZCDO	16 181	15 326	14 834	13 630	12 974	11 712	11 643	11 366	11 637	11 911	12 050
Motorcyclists[4] and passengers:												
Killed	ZCDP	509	498	547	605	583	609	693	585	569	599	588
Killed or seriously injured	ZCDQ	6 446	6 442	6 908	7 374	7 305	7 500	7 652	6 648	6 508	6 484	6 737
All severities	BMDH	24 492	24 610	26 192	28 212	28 810	28 353	28 411	25 641	24 824	23 326	23 459
Car drivers and passengers:												
Killed	ZCDS	1 795	1 696	1 687	1 665	1 749	1 747	1 769	1 671	1 675	1 612	1 432
Killed or seriously injured	ZCDT	23 191	21 676	20 368	19 719	19 424	18 728	17 291	16 144	14 617	14 254	12 967
All severities	ZCDU	211 448	210 474	205 735	206 799	202 802	197 425	188 342	183 858	178 302	171 000	161 433
Bus/coach drivers and passengers:												
Killed	ZCDV	14	18	11	15	14	19	11	20	9	19	12
Killed or seriously injured	KCUZ	601	631	611	578	562	551	500	488	363	426	455
All severities	ZCDW	9 439	9 839	10 252	10 088	9 884	9 005	9 068	8 820	7 920	7 253	7 079
LGV drivers and passengers:												
Killed	ZCDX	64	67	65	66	64	70	72	62	54	52	58
Killed or seriously injured	ZCDY	928	949	867	813	811	780	765	631	587	564	494
All severities	ZCDZ	7 476	7 672	7 124	7 007	7 304	7 007	6 897	6 166	6 048	5 914	5 340
HGV drivers and passengers:												
Killed	ZCEA	45	60	52	55	54	63	44	47	55	39	52
Killed or seriously injured	ZCEB	573	560	540	571	500	524	429	406	395	383	363
All severities	ZCEC	3 302	3 444	3 484	3 597	3 388	3 178	3 061	2 883	2 843	2 530	2 476
All road users[5]:												
Killed	BMDC	3 599	3 421	3 423	3 409	3 450	3 431	3 508	3 221	3 201	3 172	2 943
Killed or seriously injured	ZCEE	46 583	44 255	42 545	41 564	40 560	39 407	37 215	34 351	32 155	31 845	30 720
All severities	BMDA	327 803	325 212	320 310	320 283	313 309	302 605	290 607	280 840	271 017	258 404	247 780

1 Casualities aged 0 - 15.
2 Killed and seriously injured.
3 Casualties aged 16 and over.
4 Includes mopeds and scooters.
5 Includes other motor or non-motor vehicle users, and unknown road user
   type and casualty age.

Source: Department for Transport 020 7944 6595

15.18
Freight transport by road: goods moved by goods vehicles over 3.5 tonnes[1]
Great Britain

Billion tonne kilometres

		1997	1998	1999	2000	2001	2002	2003	2004[2]	2005[2]	2006[2]	2007[2]
By mode of working												
Mainly public haulage	KNND	112.2	114.3	110.9	113.0	114.7	110.6	114.3	110.8	109.7	112.1	115.6
Mainly own account	KNNC	37.4	37.6	38.3	37.5	34.7	39.2	37.4	41.4	43.0	43.5	45.9
All modes	KNNB	149.6	151.9	149.2	150.5	149.4	149.8	151.7	152.2	152.7	155.6	161.5
By gross weight of vehicle												
Rigid vehicles:												
Over 3.5 tonnes to 17 tonnes	ZCIL	19.2	17.8	17.9	15.8	13.1	11.9	10.1	9.1	8.1	7.2	5.8
Over 17 tonnes to 25 tonnes	ZCIM	4.7	4.2	4.3	4.8	5.7	6.3	6.8	7.9	8.3	8.6	9.5
Over 25 tonnes	ZCIN	14.3	14.7	15.3	15.4	15.6	17.3	18.3	18.9	20.3	20.8	22.5
All rigids	ZCIO	38.1	36.6	37.5	36.0	34.5	35.6	35.2	35.9	36.7	36.6	37.8
Articulated vehicles:												
Over 3.5 tonnes to 33 tonnes	ZCIP	14.3	14.4	14.0	14.0	12.8	9.9	8.8	7.0	6.3	6.1	5.6
Over 33 tonnes	ZCIQ	97.1	100.9	97.7	100.4	102.1	104.4	107.7	109.4	109.7	112.9	118.1
All articulated vehicles	ZCIR	111.4	115.3	111.7	114.4	114.9	114.3	116.5	116.4	116.0	119.0	123.7
All vehicles												
Over 3.5 tonnes to 25 tonnes	ZCIS	24.3	22.5	22.7	21.3	19.3	18.7	17.3	17.3	16.7	16.3	15.7
Over 25 tonnes	KNNG	125.2	129.4	126.5	129.2	130.1	131.1	134.4	134.9	136.0	139.3	145.8
All weights	ZCIT	149.6	151.9	149.2	150.5	149.4	149.8	151.7	152.2	152.7	155.6	161.5
By commodity												
Food, drink and tobacco	ZCIU	40.8	42.5	41.5	44.3	41.4	43.1	42.2	41.7	40.6	42.0	45.1
Wood, timber and cork	ZCIV	3.5	3.6	3.8	3.7	3.9	3.8	4.1	4.5	4.7	4.1	3.3
Fertiliser	ZCIW	1.3	1.2	1.4	1.2	1.2	1.2	1.2	0.8	1.1	0.8	0.9
Crude minerals	ZCIX	13.6	13.3	12.7	12.4	13.0	13.9	13.8	14.1	14.8	15.4	16.0
Ores	ZCIY	1.7	1.1	1.3	1.2	1.2	1.1	1.2	1.4	1.7	1.4	1.8
Crude materials	ZCIZ	2.1	2.6	2.6	2.6	2.3	2.7	2.3	3.3	2.4	2.7	2.6
Coal and coke	ZCJA	2.7	2.0	2.2	1.5	2.1	1.5	1.5	1.2	1.5	1.3	1.6
Petrol and petroleum products	ZCJB	5.8	5.2	5.0	6.4	5.8	5.2	5.5	5.7	5.5	5.7	5.1
Chemicals	ZCJC	8.2	7.9	7.4	6.8	7.2	6.5	6.8	6.3	7.6	6.2	7.0
Building materials	ZCJD	11.1	10.7	10.6	10.6	11.7	10.9	12.0	12.1	10.9	11.5	11.6
Iron and steel products	ZCJE	7.9	7.7	6.8	6.8	5.7	5.3	5.4	5.4	5.2	4.7	6.4
Other metal products	ZCJF	1.5	1.7	1.7	1.7	1.4	1.5	1.5	1.9	2.1	2.1	2.0
Machinery and transport equipment	ZCJG	8.4	9.1	8.7	9.1	8.9	8.5	8.7	8.9	9.3	9.4	9.5
Miscellaneous manufactures	ZCJH	14.2	15.9	15.7	15.1	15.4	16.2	15.8	16.3	15.5	16.3	16.4
Miscellaneous articles	ZCJI	26.8	27.5	27.9	27.1	28.2	28.4	29.5	28.8	29.8	31.7	32.2
All commodities	ZCJJ	149.6	151.9	149.2	150.5	149.4	149.8	151.7	152.2	152.7	155.6	161.5

1 Rigid vehicles or articulated vehicles (tractive unit and trailer) with gross vehicle weight over 3.5 tonnes.
2 Figures for 2004 onwards are not fully comparable with those for 2003 and earlier years. Detailed comparisons should therefore be made with caution.

Source: Department for Transport 020 7944 3180

15.19 Freight transport by road: goods lifted by goods vehicles over 3.5 tonnes[1]
Great Britain

Million tonnes

		1997	1998	1999	2000	2001	2002	2003	2004[2]	2005[2]	2006[2]	2007[2]
By mode of working												
Mainly public haulage	ZCJK	1 044	1 041	991	1 038	1 052	1 019	1 053	1 101	1 079	1 127	1 145
Mainly own account	ZCJL	599	589	576	556	529	608	590	643	667	685	724
All modes	ZCJM	1 643	1 630	1 567	1 593	1 581	1 627	1 643	1 744	1 746	1 813	1 869
By gross weight of vehicle												
Rigid vehicles:												
Over 3.5 tonnes to 17 tonnes	ZCJN	294	268	254	229	203	188	159	160	135	130	109
Over 17 tonnes to 25 tonnes	ZCJO	120	106	86	87	86	90	100	113	118	120	130
Over 25 tonnes	ZCJP	380	401	408	424	443	491	506	539	559	598	629
All rigids	ZCJQ	793	776	748	741	733	768	765	812	812	849	868
Articulated vehicles:												
Over 3.5 tonnes to 33 tonnes	ZCJR	124	125	113	107	97	81	69	60	51	50	50
Over 33 tonnes	ZCJS	726	729	706	746	751	778	809	872	883	914	952
All articulated vehicles	ZCJT	850	854	819	852	848	859	878	932	934	964	1 001
All vehicles												
Over 3.5 tonnes to 25 tonnes	ZCJU	419	382	346	325	294	283	265	277	257	256	245
Over 25 tonnes	ZCJV	1 224	1 248	1 221	1 268	1 287	1 343	1 378	1 467	1 489	1 557	1 624
All weights	ZCJW	1 643	1 630	1 567	1 593	1 581	1 627	1 643	1 744	1 746	1 813	1 869
By commodity												
Food, drink and tobacco	ZCJX	342	346	333	346	321	339	333	351	339	360	373
Wood, timber and cork	ZCJY	26	27	28	26	28	28	32	42	36	30	29
Fertiliser	ZCJZ	10	9	11	10	9	11	12	7	14	7	9
Crude minerals	ZCKA	329	327	297	308	298	333	327	364	370	380	390
Ores	ZCKB	25	18	20	16	16	17	21	22	23	19	22
Crude materials	ZCKC	17	20	20	18	20	21	19	25	22	23	23
Coal and coke	ZCKD	37	26	28	22	21	17	22	14	21	17	24
Petrol and petroleum products	ZCKE	73	61	61	75	74	59	64	67	70	69	71
Chemicals	ZCKF	53	53	47	49	50	41	47	46	53	48	48
Building materials	ZCKG	156	161	159	165	165	167	165	185	169	180	175
Iron and steel products	ZCKH	55	54	48	49	44	39	41	43	42	41	47
Other metal products	ZCKI	16	18	17	16	14	14	16	19	19	21	20
Machinery and transport equipment	ZCKJ	71	73	67	69	70	68	66	70	76	79	83
Miscellaneous manufactures	ZCKK	90	96	91	97	97	105	98	111	109	112	113
Miscellaneous articles	ZCKL	343	342	340	328	353	367	379	378	384	426	440
All commodities	ZCKM	1 643	1 630	1 567	1 593	1 581	1 627	1 643	1 744	1 746	1 813	1 869

1 Rigid vehicles or articulated vehicles (tractive unit and trailer) with gross vehicle weight over 3.5 tonnes.

2 Figures for 2004 onwards are not fully comparable with those for 2003 and earlier years. Detailed comparison should therefore be made with caution.

Source: Department for Transport 020 7944 3180

15.20 Rail systems summary

		1997 /98	1998 /99	1999 /00	2000 /01	2001 /02	2002 /03	2003 /04	2004 /05	2005 /06	2006 /07	2007 /08
Passenger journeys (millions)												
National Rail network[1]	ZCKN	846	892	931	957	960	976	1 012	1 045	1 082	1 151	1 232
London Underground	KNOE	832	866	927	970	953	942	948	976	970	1 040	1 096
Docklands Light Railway	ZCKO	21	28	31	38	41	46	48	50	54	64	67
Glasgow Underground	ZCKP	14	15	15	14	14	13	13	13	13	13	14
Tyne and Wear Metro[2]	ZCKQ	35	34	33	33	33	37	38	37	36	38	40
Blackpool trams[3]	EL9L	5	4	4	4	5	4	4	4	4	3	3
Manchester Metrolink[4]	ZCKS	14	13	14	17	18	19	19	20	20	20	20
Midland Metro[5]	ZCKR	–	–	5	5	5	5	5	5	5	5	5
Croydon Tramlink[6]	GEOE	–	–	–	15	18	19	20	22	23	25	27
Sheffield Supertram	ZCKT	9	10	11	11	11	12	12	13	13	14	15
Nottingham NET[7]	C3MI	–	–	–	–	–	–	–	8	10	10	10
All rail	ZCKU	1 776	1 862	1 971	2 065	2 059	2 072	2 119	2 193	2 229	2 383	2 529
All light rail	GENZ	98	104	113	138	146	154	160	172	177	192	201
Passenger revenue (£ million at current prices)												
National Rail network	KNDL	2 821	3 089	3 368	3 413	3 548	3 663	3 901	4 158	4 493	5 012	5 555
London Underground	KNOA	899	977	1 058	1 129	1 151	1 138	1 161	1 241	1 309	1 417	1 525
Docklands Light Railway	ZCKV	14	20	22	29	32	36	37	40	46	54	62
Glasgow Underground	ZCKW	9	9	10	10	10	10	10	11	11	13	13
Tyne and Wear Metro	ZCKX	22	23	24	24	25	29	31	33	34	38	32
Blackpool trams	EL9M	5	4	4	4	5	5	4	4	4	5	4
Manchester Metrolink	ZCKZ	14	..	..	18	20	20	21	22	23	24	22
Midland Metro	ZCKY	–	–	..	3	4	5	5	5	6	6	4
Croydon Tramlink	GEOF	–	–	–	12	13	15	16	18	19	20	15
Sheffield Supertram	ZCLA	6	6	7	7	8	10	9	11	10	13	11
Nottingham NET	C3MJ	–	–	–	–	–	–	..	6	7	8	7
All rail	ZCLB	3 790	3 789	4 493	4 650	4 815	4 931	5 197	5 550	5 963	6 609	7 251
All light rail	GEOA	70	69	63	108	117	130	135	151	161	180	171
Passenger kilometres (millions)												
National Rail network	KNDZ	34 700	36 280	38 472	38 179	39 141	39 678	40 906	41 762	43 211	46 218	49 007
London Underground	KNOI	6 479	6 716	7 171	7 470	7 451	7 367	7 340	7 606	7 586	7 947	8 352
Docklands Light Railway	ZCLC	103	144	172	200	207	232	235	245	257	301	326
Glasgow Underground	ZCLD	45	47	47	46	44	43	43	43	42	42	46
Tyne and Wear Metro	ZCLE	249	238	230	229	238	275	284	283	279	295	313
Blackpool trams	EL9N	..	..	13	13	15	14	11	12	11	10	9
Manchester Metrolink	ZCLG	88	117	126	152	161	167	169	204	206	208	210
Midland Metro	ZCLF	–	–	50	56	50	50	54	52	54	51	51
Croydon Tramlink	GEOG	–	–	–	96	99	100	105	112	117	128	141
Sheffield Supertram	ZCLH	34	35	37	38	39	40	42	44	44	42	44
Nottingham NET	C3MK	–	–	–	–	–	–	2	37	42	43	44
All rail	ZCLI	41 698	43 577	46 318	46 479	47 446	47 965	49 191	50 401	51 849	55 285	58 544
All light rail	GEOB	519	581	675	830	854	920	945	1 033	1 052	1 120	1 185
Route kilometres open for passenger traffic (numbers)												
National Rail network[8]	ZCLJ	15 024	15 038	15 038	15 042	15 042	15 042	14 883	14 328	14 356	14 353	14 484
London Underground	ZCLK	392	392	408	408	408	408	408	408	408	408	408
Docklands Light Railway	ZCLM	22	22	26	26	26	26	26	26	30	31	55
Glasgow Underground	ZCLN	11	11	11	11	11	11	11	11	10	10	10
Tyne and Wear Metro	ZCLO	59	59	59	59	78	78	78	78	78	78	78
Blackpool trams	EL9O	18	18	18	18	18	18	18	18	18	18	18
Manchester Metrolink	ZCLQ	31	31	39	39	39	39	39	39	39	39	42
Midland Metro	ZCLP	–	–	20	20	20	20	20	20	20	20	20
Croydon Tramlink	GEOH	–	–	–	28	28	28	28	28	28	28	28
Sheffield Supertram	ZCLR	29	29	29	29	29	29	29	29	29	29	29
Nottingham NET	C3ML	–	–	–	–	–	–	14	14	15	14	14
All rail	ZCLS	15 586	15 600	15 648	15 680	15 699	15 699	15 554	14 999	15 032	15 028	15 186
All light rail	GEOC	170	170	202	230	249	249	263	263	268	267	294
Stations served (numbers)												
National Rail network	ZCLT	2 495	2 499	2 503	2 508	2 508	2 508	2 507	2 508	2 510	2 520	2 516
London Underground	KNOO	269	269	274	274	274	274	274	274	274	273	268
Docklands Light Railway	ZCLU	29	29	34	34	34	34	34	34	38	34	39
Glasgow Underground	ZCLV	15	15	15	15	15	15	15	15	15	15	15
Tyne and Wear Metro	ZCLW	46	46	46	46	58	58	58	58	59	59	60
Blackpool trams	EL9P	124	124	124	124	124	124	124	124	124	121	121
Manchester Metrolink	ZCLY	26	26	36	36	36	37	37	37	37	37	37
Midland Metro	ZCLX	–	–	23	23	23	23	23	23	23	23	23
Croydon Tramlink	GEOI	–	–	–	38	38	38	38	38	39	39	38
Sheffield Supertram	ZCLZ	46	47	47	47	48	48	48	48	48	48	48
Nottingham NET	C3MM	–	–	–	–	–	–	23	23	23	23	23
All rail	ZCLL	3 050	3 055	3 102	3 146	3 145	3 159	3 181	3 182	3 190	3 192	3 188
All light rail	GSOC	286	287	325	363	376	377	400	400	406	399	404

1 Franchised train operating companies from Feb 1996 after privatisation.
2 Tyne & Wear Metro extension to Sunderland opened in March 2002.
3 Blackpool Trams shown as a self-contained system.
4 Transfer of 20 stations from the rail network to Manchester Metrolink.
5 Midland Metro opened in 1999.
6 Croydon Tramlink opened in 2000.
7 Nottingham Express Transit opened in March 2004.
8 Break in series due to change in methodology.

*Sources: Department for Transport: 020 7944 3076/8874;
Network Rail, former Railtrack,ORR, TfL, light rail operators and PTEs*

Transport and communications

15.21 National railways freight: 1997/98-2007/08
Great Britain

Billion tonne kilometres

		1997/98	1998[1]/99	1999/00	2000/01	2001/02	2002[2]/03	2003[2]/04	2004[2]/05	2005[2]/06	2006[2]/07	2007/08
Freight moved by commodity												
Coal	ZCGG	4.4	4.5	4.8	4.8	6.2	5.7	5.8	6.7	8.3	8.6	7.7
Metals	ZCGH	..	2.1	2.2	2.1	2.4	2.7	2.6	2.6	2.2	2.0	1.8
Construction	ZCGI	..	2.1	2.0	2.4	2.8	2.5	2.7	2.9	2.9	2.7	2.8
Oil and petroleum	ZCGJ	..	1.6	1.5	1.4	1.2	1.2	1.2	1.2	1.2	1.5	1.6
Other traffic	ZCGK	12.5	7.1	7.6	7.4	6.7	6.6	6.8	7.0	7.1	7.1	7.2
All traffic	VOXD	16.9	17.3	18.2	18.1	19.4	18.5	18.9	20.4	21.7	21.9	21.2

Million tonnes

		1997/98	1998/99	1999/00	2000/01	2001/02	2002/03	2003/04	2004[4]/05	2005[4]/06	2006[4]/07	2007[7]/08
Freight lifted by commodity												
Coal	ZCGL	50.3	45.3	35.9	35.3	39.5	34.0	35.2	43.3	47.6	48.7	43.3
Metals	ZCGM	..	..	..	..	..	..	..	..	..	..	..
Construction	ZCGN	..	..	..	..	..	..	..	..	..	..	..
Oil and petroleum	ZCGO	..	..	..	..	..	..	..	..	..	..	..
Other traffic	ZCGP	55.1	56.8	60.6	60.3	54.5	53.0	53.7	56.8	57.7	59.5	59.1
All traffic	VOXE	105.400	102.100	96.500	95.600	93.900	87.000	88.900	100.100	105.300	108.211	102.403

1 Revised series on new basis from 1998/99.
2 Goods moved data from 2002/03 onwards have been revised since the last TSGB publication.
3 Break in series from 1999/2000.
4 Goods lifted data from 2004/05 onwards have been revised since the last TSGB publication.
5 Break in series with most of the increase due to changes in the data collection method.
6 Break in the series from 2005/06 as some GB Railfreight tonnes lifted now included.
7 Break in series from 2007/08 as GB Railfreight coal data now included.

Source: Rail :ORR : 020 7944 8874

15.22 Railways: permanent way and rolling stock
Northern Ireland
At end of year

Numbers

		1997	1998	1999	2000	2001	2002	2003	2004	2005	2006	2007
Length of road open for traffic[1] (Km)	KNRA	335	335	335	356	334	334	334	299	299	299	299
Length of track open for traffic (Km)												
Total	KNRB	506	526	526	547	480	480	480	445	445	445	445
Running lines	KNRC	464	484	484	505	464	464	464	427	427	427	427
Sidings (as single track)	KNRD	42	42	42	42	16	16	16	18	18	18	18
Locomotives												
Diesel-electrics	KNRE	6	5	6	6	6	6	5	6	5	5	5
Passenger carrying vehicles												
Total	KNRF	112	120	105	105	106	100	100	102	124	125	128
Rail motor vehicles:												
Diesel-electric, etc	KNRG	30	28	30	30	29	28	28	28	70	85	84
Trailer carriages:												
Total locomotive hauled	KNRH	28	38	21	21	25	22	22	22	22	22	22
Ordinary coaches	KNRI	26	36	19	19	23	20	20	20	20	20	20
Restaurant cars	KNRJ	2	2	2	2	2	2	2	2	2	2	2
Rail car trailers	KNRK	54	54	54	54	52	50	50	52	32	18	22
Rolling stock for maintenance and repair	KNRT	41	26	18	18	18	18	39	46	48	48	48

1 The total length of railroad open for traffic irrespective of the number of tracks comprising the road.

Sources: Department for Regional Development; Northern Ireland: 028 9054 0800

15.23 Operating statistics of railways
Northern Ireland

		Unit	1997	1998	1999	2000	2001	2002	2003	2004	2005	2006	2007
Maintenance of way and works													
Material used:													
Ballast	KNSA	Thousand m^2	51.3	38.5	40.0	47.0	80.0	40.0	130.0	70.0	90.0	30.0	15.0
Rails	KNSB	Thousand tonnes	0.4	2.5	3.0	3.5	2.5	1.0	4.5	1.0	3.2	1.0	1.0
Sleepers	KNSC	Thousands	5.1	32.0	30.0	40.0	50.0	5.0	40.0	28.0	45.0	2.0	5.0
Track renewed	KNSD	Km	2.4	22.5	7.0	29.0	15.0	5.0	25.8	2.0	29.0	1.0	–
New Track laid	KPGD	Km	–	–	–	21.0	–	–	–	–	–	–	–
Engine kilometres													
Total[1]	KNSE	Thousand Km	4 100	4 100	4 100	4 100	4 056	4 056	4 170	4 110	3 610	3 900	3 900
Train kilometres:													
Total	KNSF	"	3 670	3 670	3 670	3 670	3 626	3 626	3 704	3 610	3 610	3 900	3 900
Coaching	KNSG	"	3 666	3 666	3 666	3 666	3 622	3 622	3 700	3 610	3 610	3 900	3 900
Freight	KNSH	"	4	4	4	4	4	4	4	–	–	–	–

1 Including shunting, assisting, light, departmental, maintenance and repair.

Sources: Department for Regional Development;
Northern Ireland: 028 9054 0800

15.24 Main output of United Kingdom airlines

Available tonne kilometres (millions)

		1998	1999	2000	2001	2002	2003	2004	2005	2006	2007	2008
All services	KNTA	40 021	42 002	43 370	42 070	40 550	42 784	43 883	48 186	50 391	54 181	53 348
Percentage growth on previous year	KNTB	*12.5*	*5.0*	*3.6*	*–2.4*	*–4.3*	*5.5*	*2.6*	*9.8*	*4.4*	*7.5*	*–1.6*
Scheduled services	KNTC	29 756	31 815	32 938	31 866	30 433	31 513	32 422	36 937	38 590	40 971	41 241
Percentage growth on previous year	KNTD	*12.3*	*6.9*	*3.5*	*–3.3*	*–4.5*	*3.6*	*2.9*	*13.9*	*4.5*	*6.2*	*0.7*
Non-scheduled services	KNTE	10 265	10 186	10 440	10 505	10 117	11 271	11 461	11 249	11 801	13 209	12 077
Percentage growth on previous year	KNTF	*13.3*	*–0.7*	*4.1*	*0.6*	*–3.7*	*11.4*	*1.7*	*–1.8*	*4.3*	*11.9*	*–8.6*

Source: Civil Aviation Authority: 020 7453 6246

15.25 Air traffic between the United Kingdom and abroad[1]

Thousands

		1998	1999	2000	2001	2002	2003	2004	2005	2006	2007	2008
Flights												
United Kingdom airlines												
Scheduled services	KNUA	443.7	480.9	520.3	536.7	531.3	517.7	546.5	584.2	596.3	621.9	601.7
Non-scheduled services	KNUB	218.7	212.6	216.2	208.5	218.6	211.0	198.6	200.6	209.6	207.1	193.4
Overseas airlines[2]												
Scheduled services	KNUC	426.4	467.6	467.6	496.8	487.5	487.0	544.2	584.5	629.5	656.9	686.7
Non-scheduled services	KNUD	34.8	31.7	31.7	26.0	36.7	27.1	28.8	33.7	28.4	27.2	24.3
Total	KNUE	1 123.6	1 192.8	1 235.8	1 268.0	1 274.1	1 242.8	1 318.1	1 403.0	1 463.8	1 513.1	1 506.1
Passengers carried												
United Kingdom airlines												
Scheduled services	KNUF	46 747.7	50 148.5	54 522.8	53 591.7	54 360.0	56 476.7	63 216.1	69 106.2	72 196.4	76 959.9	76 636.5
Non-scheduled services	KNUG	31 616.6	32 603.8	33 185.9	34 009.1	33 935.7	33 385.6	32 195.7	30 179.4	29 725.5	28 524.0	25 906.9
Overseas airlines[2]												
Scheduled services	KNUH	42 554.5	46 628.0	46 627.9	51 107.8	51 317.6	54 504.0	60 278.0	67 634.9	74 670.8	79 820.1	83 176.7
Non-scheduled services	KNUI	4 569.7	4 156.5	4 156.5	3 966.1	3 956.3	3 947.1	4 068.3	4 169.1	4 107.7	3 803.3	3 417.0
Total	KNUJ	125 488.5	133 536.8	138 493.1	142 674.7	143 569.6	148 313.4	159 758.1	171 089.6	180 700.4	189 107.3	189 137.1

1 Excludes travel to and from the Channel Islands.
2 Includes airlines of overseas UK Territories.

Source: Civil Aviation Authority: 020 7453 6246

15.26 Operations and traffic on scheduled services: revenue traffic
United Kingdom airlines[1]

		Unit	1998	1999	2000	2001	2002	2003	2004	2005	2006	2007	2008
All services													
Aircraft stage flights:													
Number	KNFA	Numbers	797 682	835 031	878 582	921 556	911 518	895 095	926 498	1 016 354	1 037 729	1 052 799	1 056 298
Average length	KNFB	Kilometres	1 111.0	1 134.0	1 156.0	1 138.0	1 149.0	1 215.0	1 227.0	1 304.0	1 349.0	1 400.0	1 427.9
Aircraft-kilometres flown	KNFC	Millions	886.0	947.0	1 016.0	1 049.0	1 047.0	1 088.0	1 137.0	1 325.0	1 400.0	1 474.0	1 508.3
Passengers uplifted	KNFD	"	62.0	65.0	70.0	70.0	72.0	76.0	83.0	94.0	98.0	102.0	104.7
Seat-kilometres used	KNFE	"	151 969.0	160 336.0	170 469.0	158 651.0	156 494.0	164 806.0	173 722.0	200 460.0	213 442.0	227 720.0	232 591.6
Cargo uplifted:[2]	KNFF	Tonnes	831 436.0	860 291.0	897 184.0	742 705.0	768 736.0	800 645.0	842 912.0	921 412.0	946 365.0	941 421.0	97 979.1
Tonne-kilometres used:		Millions											
Passenger	KNFH	"	14 755.0	15 518.0	16 507.0	15 258.0	15 035.0	15 419.0	15 580.0	15 044.0	16 090.0	17 246.0	17 717.7
Freight	KNFI	"	4 663.0	4 925.0	5 160.0	4 548.0	4 941.0	5 187.0	5 297.0	5 998.0	6 213.0	6 199.0	6 283.8
Mail	KNFJ	"	178	153	179	102	57	55	75	90	99	112	99
Total	KNFG	"	19 596.0	20 596.0	21 846.0	19 908.0	20 032.0	20 660.0	20 952.0	21 133.0	22 402.0	23 557.0	24 100.5
Domestic services													
Aircraft stage flights:													
Number	KNFK	Numbers	352 936	354 864	353 525	365 881	359 400	345 954	373 858	394 069	399 438	383 591	369 499
Average length	KNFL	Kilometres	333	337	344	350	350	357	360	374	371	367	469
Aircraft-kilometres flown	KNFM	Millions	118.0	120.0	121.0	128.0	126.0	123.0	135.0	147.0	148.0	140.0	173.3
Passengers uplifted	KNFN	"	17	17	18	18	20	21	22	23	23	22	21
Seat-kilometres used	KNFO	"	6 948.0	7 184.0	7 542.0	7 645.0	8 322.0	8 904.0	9 263.0	9 795.0	9 800.0	9 449.0	8 951.5
Cargo uplifted:[2]	KNFP	Tonnes	31 879	25 964	24 644	19 498	16 755	17 248	14 862	10 015	8 498	7 099	6 125
Tonne-kilometres used:		Millions											
Passenger	KNFR	"	593.0	610.0	640.0	649.0	703.0	738.0	757.0	784.0	759.0	733.0	720.2
Freight	KNFS	"	6.0	6.0	6.0	4.0	4.0	3.0	3.0	3.0	2.0	2.0	1.8
Mail	KNFT	"	6.0	4.0	4.0	4.0	3.0	3.0	3.0	–	1.0	1.0	0.1
Total	KNFQ	"	605.0	620.0	650.0	656.0	709.0	744.0	762.0	787.0	762.0	735.0	722.1
International services													
Aircraft stage flights:													
Number	KNFU	Numbers	444 746	480 167	525 057	555 675	552 118	549 141	552 640	622 285	638 291	669 208	686 799
Average length	KNFV	Kilometres	1 729.0	1 723.0	1 704.0	1 656.0	1 670.0	1 758.0	2 148.0	1 893.0	1 960.0	1 993.0	1 994.4
Aircraft-kilometres flown	KNFW	Millions	769	827	895	921	921	965	1 002	1 178	1 251	1 333	1 371
Passengers uplifted	KNFX	"	45.0	48.0	52.0	52.0	52.0	56.0	61.0	71.0	75.0	80.0	83.8
Seat-kilometres used	KNFY	"	145 022.0	153 153.0	162 927.0	151 006.0	148 172.0	155 903.0	164 459.0	190 666.0	203 642.0	218 271.0	223 640.1
Cargo uplifted:[2]	KNFZ	Tonnes	799 557	834 327	872 540	723 206	751 975	783 397	828 051	911 398	937 868	934 323	973 665
Tonne-kilometres used:		Millions											
Passenger	KNJX	"	14 162.0	14 908.0	15 867.0	14 610.0	14 332.0	14 681.0	14 824.0	14 260.0	15 331.0	16 513.0	16 997.5
Freight	KNJY	"	4 657	4 919	5 154	4 544	4 937	5 184	5 294	5 995	6 383	6 197	6 282
Mail	KNJZ	"	172.0	149.0	176.0	98.0	54.0	51.0	72.0	90.0	99.0	111.0	98.9
Total	KNJW	"	18 991.0	19 976.0	21 197.0	19 252.0	19 322.0	19 916.0	20 190.0	20 345.0	21 813.0	22 822.0	23 378.4

1 Includes services of British Airways and other UK private companies.
2 Cargo has re-defined as freight and mail.

Source: Civil Aviation Authority: 020 7453 6246

15.27 Activity at civil aerodromes
United Kingdom[1]

Thousands and tonnes

		1999	2000	2001	2002	2003	2004	2005	2006	2007	2008
Movement of civil aircraft (thousands)											
Commercial											
Transport	KNQC	1 959	2 045	2 095	2 094	2 160	2 277	2 406	2 451	2 494	2 407
Other[2]	KNQD	159	159	150	120	117	116	120	129	124	113
Total	KNQB	2 118	2 204	2 245	2 214	2 277	2 393	2 526	2 580	2 609	2 520
Non-commercial[3]	KNQE	1 263	1 186	1 207	1 100	1 186	1 135	1 129	1 059	1 033	964
Total	KNQA	3 381	3 390	3 452	3 314	3 463	3 528	3 655	3 639	3 637	3 484
Passengers handled											
Terminal	KNQG	168 363	179 885	181 231	188 761	199 950	215 681	228 214	235 139	240 722	235 359
Transit	KNQH	1 156	1 167	1 087	1 054	990	950	984	1 016	963	735
Total	KNQF	169 519	181 052	182 318	189 815	200 940	216 631	229 198	236 155	241 685	236 094
Commercial freight handled[4] (tonnes)											
Set down	KNQJ	1 135 065	1 174 635	1 093 142	1 124 026	1 172 552	1 267 411	1 282 724	1 277 177	1 316 359	1 274 539
Picked up	KNQK	1 053 902	1 139 292	1 052 379	1 071 407	1 035 680	1 103 539	1 080 620	1 038 261	1 009 414	1 007 616
Total	KNQI	2 188 967	2 313 927	2 145 521	2 195 433	2 208 232	2 370 950	2 363 344	2 315 438	2 325 773	2 282 155
Mail handled											
Set down	KNQM	92 974	101 743	98 690	90 738	86 415	108 481	102 344	91 535	102 027	111 002
Picked up	KNQN	114 752	123 352	117 389	99 747	93 096	112 424	110 576	98 391	105 755	123 014
Total	KNQL	207 726	225 095	216 079	190 485	179 511	220 905	212 920	189 926	207 790	234 016

1 Figures exclude Channel Island and Isle of Man Airports.
2 Local pleasure flights for reward (eg aerial survey work, crop dusting and delivery of empty aircraft) and empty positioning flights.
3 Test and Training flights, Other flights by Air Transport Operators, Aero-club, Private, Official, Military & Business Aviation.

4 With effect from 2001, passengers, freight and mail handled exclude traffic carried on air taxi operations.

Source: Civil Aviation Authority: 020 7453 6258

15.28 Household digital television[1]: by type of service[2,3]
United Kingdom[1]

Percentages

	Total digital television	Digital satellite	Digital terrestrial	Digital cable
	IM6S	IM6T	IM6U	IM6V
1999	2.2	14.4	0.5	12.4
2000	15.5	17.6	2.8	13.6
2001	30.9	22.4	4.5	14.8
2002	38.5	25.0	5.2	14.5
2003	43.2	28.6	5.9	13.4
2004	53.0	29.1	14.1	13.5
2005	61.9	31.3	20.3	13.2
2006	69.7	33.1	25.3	13.2
2007	79.6	35.7	33.0	13.0
2008	87.1	36.6	37.9	12.5

1 Multichannel take-up on main sets.
2 Data are at the end of the first quarter in each year.
3 GfK research from Q1 2007 onwards, previous years use platform operator data, research and Ofcom estimates.

Source: Ofcom: 020 7981 3000

15.29 Telephones and The Internet

Call Revenue (All Operators)

	Business call revenue (£s millions)				Residential call revenue (£s millions)			
	UK Geographic calls	International calls	Calls to mobiles	Other calls[1]	UK Geographic calls	International calls	Calls to mobiles	Other calls[1]
	IM6A	IM6B	IM6C	IM6D	IM6E	IM6F	IM6G	IM6H
2006	669	243	776	273	902	325	954	983
2007	594	255	688	185	870	307	977	807
2006 Q4	159	59	196	..	238	84	252	229
2007 Q1	156	62	181	51	228	78	234	229
Q2	151	62	174	49	207	76	236	200
Q3	147	64	170	47	213	76	249	190
Q4	140	67	163	38	222	77	258	188

Call Volumes (All Operators)

	Business call volumes (millions of minutes)				Residential call volumes (millions of minutes)			
	UK Geographic calls	International calls	Calls to mobiles	Other calls[1]	UK Geographic calls	International calls	Calls to mobiles	Other calls[1]
	IM6I	IM6J	IM6K	IM6L	IM6M	IM6N	IM6O	IM6P
2006	34 466	3 040	7 420	19 702	71 912	2 722	8 320	45 499
2007	32 114	3 235	6 998	11 549	64 844	2 872	7 421	33 065
2006 Q4	8 557	758	1 888	3 787	17 828	717	2 040	10 045
2007 Q1	8 225	777	1 772	3 087	17 490	728	1 946	9 702
Q2	8 134	824	1 758	2 910	15 986	676	1 881	8 293
Q3	8 033	814	1 752	2 963	15 511	688	1 816	8 322
Q4	7 722	820	1 716	2 589	15 857	780	1 778	6 748

Selected lines with Carrier Pre-Selection (000's) / Exchange line numbers (All operators)

	CPS lines[2]	WLR lines[3]	Business (000's)	Residential (000's)
	IM6W	IM6X	IM6Q	IM6R
2006	6 315	4 193	10 062	23 542
2007	24 026	17 406	40 986	93 864
2006 Q4	6 315	4 193	10 062	23 542
2007 Q1	6 213	4 227	10 091	23 568
Q2	6 138	4 285	10 302	23 503
Q3	5 782	4 366	10 294	23 388
Q4	5 893	4 528	10 299	23 405

Data taken from the Telecommunications Market Data Update Q4 2007.

Source: Ofcom Tel: 020 7981 3000

1 Includes freephone, special services, premium rate, directory enquiries and all other call types.
2 Allows usage of any service provide through a BT line.
3 Service which any other operator takes control of all connections made through a telephone line and connects subscription fee from the subscribers.

15.29
continued
Telephones and The Internet

Selected uses of the Internet, United Kingdom: by age, 2008[1]

	16-24	25-44	45-54	55-64	65 plus	All
Finding information about goods or services	77	87	86	85	75	84
Sending/receiving emails	91	87	85	86	89	87
Using services related to travel and accommodation	50	65	68	71	61	63
Internet banking	43	57	46	44	34	49
Looking for information - education, training, courses	44	37	26	16	..	31
Reading or downloading online news, magazines	54	50	46	42	35	48
Looking for a job or sending job application	35	33	18	11	..	25
Seeking health-related information	22	39	36	35	26	34
Downloading software	55	38	30	25	25	37
Selling of goods or services	17	24	17	14	..	19
Consulting the Internet with the purpose of learning	43	33	31	23	19	32

Internet purchases by adults, United Kingdom

	2006	2007	2008
Travel, accommodation or holidays	51	46	48
Clothes or sports goods	37	38	42
Films, music	53	51	41
Household goods	24	39	40
Books, magazines or newspapers	37	35	37
Tickets for events	35	33	37
Electronic equipment	25	20	26
Computer software and upgrades	29	21	22
Food and groceries	20	20	19
Computer hardware	22	17	12
Shares, financial services or insurance	24	9	11
Lotteries or betting	7	6	10
Other goods and services	11	8	8

Households with access to the Internet, Great Britain and United Kingdom, 2002 to 2008[2]

	Great Britain				United Kingdom			
	Year	Per cent	Number of Households	Percentage change on previous year	Year	Per cent	Number of Households	Percentage change on previous year
	2002	46	11.02m	-	2002	-	-	-
	2003	50	11.88m	8	2003	-	-	-
	2004	51	12.16m	2	2004	-	-	-
	2005	55	13.26m	9	2005	-	-	-
	2006	57	13.93m	5	2006	57	14.26m	-
	2007	61	14.94m	7	2007	61	15.23m	7
	2008	65	16.05m	7	2008	65	16.46m	8

1 The most popular activity of recent Internet users was sending or receiving emails at 87 per cent. This proved to be the most popular activity for the oldest age group and the youngest age group. While the youngest age group was often the most likely to be involved in Internet activities, it was the least likely to use the Internet for services related to travel and accommodation (50 per cent), and seeking health related information (22 per cent).

2 The survey is conducted in the first quarter of each year but should not be confused with being quarterly figures as they relate to use at a point in time.

Sources: Office for National Statistics; Omnibus survey, Internet Access 2008; 01633 456769

15.30 Postal services and television licences[1]
United Kingdom

	Price of first class stamp (p)	Volume of first class stamped mail delivered (million items)	Total first class mail delivered (million items)	Price of second class stamp (p)	Volume of second class stamped mail delivered (million items)	Total second class mail delivered (million items)	Domestic parcels (million)	International parcels (million)
	IM7A	IM7B	IM7C	IM7D	IM7E	IM7F	IM7G	IM7H
2004 Q4	28	523	1 564	21	528	2 674	9.8	0.7
2005 Q1	28	434	1 369	21	305	2 381	7.8	0.5
Q2	30	385	1 359	21	268	2 292	8.9	0.5
Q3	30	402	1 354	21	277	2 102	7.9	0.6
Q4	30	516	1 499	21	536	2 413	10.2	0.8
2006 Q1	30	399	1 280	21	284	2 059	8.6	0.5
Q2	32	396	1 292	23	267	1 978	9.0	0.6
Q3	32	340	1 217	23	242	1 811	9.0	0.5
Q4	32	479	1 377	23	507	2 146	11.8	0.8
2007 Q1	32	365	1 189	23	272	1 786	9.6	0.6
Q2	34	342	1 185	24	244	1 696	11.1	0.6
Q3	34	320	1 118	24	229	1 560	9.8	0.6
Q4	34	412	1 250	24	457	1 852	12.4	0.8
2008 Q1	34	373	1 195	24	282	1 664	10.5	0.7
Q2	36	317	1 092	27	238	1 490	10.8	0.7
Q3	36	259	997	27	205	1 362	9.7	0.9

		1998	1999	2000	2001	2002[3]	2003	2004	2005	2006	2007	2008[3]
Letters, etc posted (millions)	KMRA	18 350	18 878	19 711	20 076	20 648	21 979	22 837	24 341	24 880	24 089	23 705
of which:												
Registered and insured	KMRB	28.7	31.6	30.2	32.3	36.1	38.5	41.4	45.3	45.3	44.7	46.6
Airmail (Commonwealth and foreign)	KMRC	658.4	693.2	672.3	659.2	600.7	541.6	512.0	457.9	502.2	541.0	470.3
Business reply and freepost items	KMRD	524.7	503.6	475.3	487.4	486.2	434.4	397.7	401.1	402.3	373.7	349.1
Postal orders												
Total issued (thousands)[2]	KMRH	31 907	30 289	30 153	30 931	29 150	28 666	28 888	29 344	20 489	19 714	16 650
Television licences (thousands)												
In force on 31 March	KMQL	21 723	22 240	22 625	22 839	23 157	23 486	23 899	24 162	24 419	24 546	24 740
of which:												
Colour	KMQM	21 344	21 944	22 413	22 684	23 040	23 392	23 824	24 103	24 370	24 505	24 706

1 See chapter text.
2 Excluding those issued on HM ships, in many British possessions and in other places abroad. Up to 1998 includes Postal Orders issued Overseas and by Ministry of Defence.
3 53 week year rather than 52 week standard.

Sources: Royal Mail Group : 0207 2502890;
Capita Business Services Limited: 0117 302 1088;
Post Office Limited: 0207 3207424

National accounts

Chapter 16

National accounts

National accounts

(Tables 16.1 to 16.22)

The tables which follow are based on those in the *Blue Book* 2008 Edition. Some of the figures are provisional and may be revised later; this applies particularly to the figures for 2006 and 2007.

The accounts are based on the European System of Accounts 1995 (ESA95). The *Blue Book* contains an introduction to the system of the UK accounts outlining some of the main concepts and principles of measurement used. It explains how key economic indicators are derived from the sequence of accounts and how the figures describing the whole economy are broken-down by sector and by industry. A detailed description of the structure for the accounts is provided in a separate Office for National Statistics publication *United Kingdom National Accounts: Concepts, Sources and Methods* (TSO 1998). Further information on the financial accounts is given in the *Financial Statistics Explanatory Handbook*.

In the tables in this chapter on national income, analyses by industry are based, as far as possible, on the Standard Industrial Classification Revised 2003. The principal aggregate measured in these tables is the Gross Domestic Product (GDP). This is a concept of the value of the total economic activity taking place in UK territory. It can be viewed as incomes earned, as expenditures incurred, or as production. Adding all primary incomes received from the rest of the world and deducting all primary incomes payable to non-residents produces Gross National Income (GNI) (previously known as Gross National Product). This is a concept of the value of all incomes earned by UK residents.

ESA95, the internationally compatible accounting framework, provides a systematic and detailed description of the UK economy. It includes the sector accounts which provide, by institutional sector, a description of the different stages of the economic process from production through income generation, distribution and use of income to capital accumulation and financing; and the input–output framework, which describes the production process in more detail. It contains all the elements required to compile such aggregate measures as GDP, GNI and saving.

Gross Domestic Product and Gross National Income

(Tables 16.1, 16.2, 16.3)

Table 16.1 shows the main national accounts aggregates, both at current prices and chained volume measures.

Table 16.2 shows the various money flows which generate the GDP and GNI. The output approach to GDP shows the total output of goods and services, the use of goods and services in the production process (intermediate consumption) and taxes and subsidies on products. The expenditure approach to GDP shows consumption expenditure by households and government, gross capital formation and expenditure on UK exports by overseas purchasers. The sum of these items overstates the amount of income generated in the UK by the value of imports of goods and services. This item is therefore subtracted to produce GDP at market prices.

The income approach to GDP shows gross operating surplus, mixed income and compensation of employees (previously known as income from employment). Taxes are added and subsidies are deducted to produce the total of the income based components at market prices.

Table 16.2 also shows the primary incomes received from the rest of the world, which are added to GDP, and primary incomes payable to non-residents, which are deducted from GDP, to arrive at GNI. Primary income comprises compensation of employees, taxes less subsidies on production, and property and entrepreneurial income.

Table 16.3 shows the expenditure approach to the chained volume measure of GDP. When looking at the change in the economy over time the main concern is usually whether more goods and services are actually being produced now than at some time in the past. Over time changes in current price GDP show changes in the monetary value of the components of GDP and, as these changes in value can reflect changes in both price and volume, it is difficult to establish how much of an increase in the series is due either to increased activity in the economy or to an increase in the price level. As a result, when looking at the real growth in the economy over time, it is useful to look at volume estimates of GDP. In chained volume series, volume measures for each year are produced in prices of the previous year. These volume measures are then 'chain-linked' together to produce a continuous time series.

Industrial analysis

(Tables 16.4, 16.5)

The analysis of gross value added by industry at current prices shown in Table 16.4 reflects the estimates based on the

Standard Industrial Classification, revised 2003 (SIC2003). The table is based on current price data reconciled through the input–output process for 1992 to 2006. The estimates are valued at basic prices, that is, the only taxes included in the price will be taxes paid as part of the production process, such as business rates, and not any taxes specifically levied on the production of a unit of output, for example VAT. Table 16.5 shows chained volume measures of gross value added at basic prices by industry. Chained volume measures of gross value added (output approach) provides the lead indicator of economic change in the short term. The output analysis of gross value added is estimated in terms of change and expressed in index number form. It is therefore inappropriate to show as a statistical adjustment any divergence of an output measure of GDP derived from other measures of GDP. Such an adjustment does, however, exist implicitly.

Sector analysis – Distribution of income accounts and capital account

(Tables 16.6 to 16.13)

The National Accounts accounting framework includes the sector accounts which provide, by institutional sector, a description of the different stages of the economic process, from production through income generation, distribution and use of income to capital accumulation and financing.

Tables 16.6 to 16.12 show the allocation of primary income account and the secondary distribution of income account for the non-financial corporations, financial corporations, government and households sectors. Additionally, Table 16.12 shows the use of income account for the households sector and Table 16.13 provides a summary of the capital account. The full sequence of accounts is shown in the *Blue Book*.

The allocation of primary income account shows the resident units and institutional sectors as recipients rather than producers of primary income. It demonstrates the extent to which operating surpluses are distributed to the owners of the enterprises. The resources side of the allocation of primary income accounts includes the components of the income approach to measurement of GDP. The balance of this account is the gross balance of primary income (B.5g) for each sector, and if the gross balance is aggregated across all sectors of the economy the result is *Gross National Income*.

The secondary distribution of income account describes how the balance of income for each sector is allocated by redistribution; through transfers such as taxes on income, social contributions and benefits and other current transfers. The balancing item of this account is Gross Disposable Income (GDI) (B.6g). For the households sector, the chained volume measure of GDI is shown as real household disposable income.

Table 16.12 shows, for the households sector, the use of disposable income where the balancing item is saving (B.8g). For the non-financial corporations sector the balancing item of the secondary distribution of income account, gross disposable income (B.6g) is equal to saving (B.8g).

The summary capital account (Table 16.13) brings together the saving and investment of the several sectors of the economy. It shows saving, capital transfers, gross capital formation and net acquisition of non-financial assets for each of the four sectors.

Household and non-profit institutions serving households consumption expenditure at current market prices and chained volume measures

(Tables 16.14 to 16.17)

Household and non-profit institutions serving households (NPISH) consumption expenditure is a major component of the expenditure measure of GDP, both at current prices (Table 16.2) and chained volume measures (Table 16.3).

Household final consumption expenditure includes the value of income-in-kind and imputed rent of owner-occupied dwellings, but excludes business expenditure allowed as deductions in computing income for tax purposes. It includes expenditure on durable goods, for instance motor cars, which from the point of view of the individual might more appropriately be treated as capital expenditure. The only exceptions are the purchase of land and dwellings and costs incurred in connection with the transfer of their ownership and expenditure on major improvements by occupiers, which are treated as personal capital expenditure.

The estimates of household consumption expenditure include purchases of second-hand as well as new goods, *less* the proceeds of sales of used goods.

The most detailed figures are published quarterly in *Consumer Trends* (available as a web-only publication on the Office for National Statistics website: www.statistics.gov.uk).

Change in inventories (previously known as value of physical increase in stocks and work in progress)

(Table 16.18)

This table gives a broad analysis by industry and, for manufacturing industry, by asset, of the value of entries less withdrawals and losses of inventories (stocks).

Gross fixed capital formation

(Table 16.19 to 16.22)

Gross fixed capital formation comprises expenditure on the replacement of, and additions to, fixed capital assets located in the UK, including all ships and aircraft of UK ownership.

16.1 United Kingdom national and domestic product[1]
Main aggregates
At current prices and chained volume measures, reference year 2003

Indices (2003=100) and £ million

		2000	2001	2002	2003	2004	2005	2006	2007	2008
INDICES (2003=100)										
VALUES AT CURRENT PRICES										
Gross domestic product at current market prices ("money GDP")	YBEU	85.7	89.7	94.4	100.0	105.3	109.9	116.0	122.9	126.6
Gross value added at current basic prices	YBEX	85.2	89.4	94.3	100.0	105.3	109.9	116.0	122.9	127.5
CHAINED VOLUME MEASURES										
Gross domestic product at market prices	YBEZ	93.0	95.3	97.3	100.0	102.8	104.9	107.8	111.1	111.9
Gross national disposable income at market prices	YBFP	90.7	93.9	97.1	100.0	102.8	104.2	106.1	110.6	112.7
Gross value added at basic prices	CGCE	93.4	95.5	97.2	100.0	102.7	104.9	107.9	111.1	111.9
PRICES										
Implied deflator of GDP at market prices	YBGB	92.2	94.1	97.0	100.0	102.5	104.8	107.5	110.6	113.1
VALUES AT CURRENT PRICES (£ million)										
Gross measures (before deduction of fixed capital consumption) at current market prices										
Gross Domestic Product ("money GDP")	YBHA	976 533	1 021 828	1 075 564	1 139 746	1 200 595	1 252 505	1 321 860	1 400 526	1 442 921
Employment, property and entrepreneurial income from the rest of the world (receipts *less* payments)	YBGG	1 962	9 425	18 286	17 523	17 830	21 872	10 097	8 606	..
Subsidies (receipts) *less* taxes (payments) on products from/to the rest of the world	-QZOZ	−4 098	−3 920	−2 890	−2 596	−1 234	−4 260	−4 496	−4 731	..
Other subsidies on production from/to the rest of the world	-IBJL	292	298	519	..	..	..	..	..	..
Gross National Income (GNI)	ABMX	974 732	1 027 915	1 091 479	1 155 265	1 217 783	1 273 525	1 330 681	1 419 319	1 474 243
Current transfers from the rest of the world (receipts *less* payments)	-YBGF	−6 016	−3 182	−6 500	−7 843	−9 645	−11 052	−10 657	−11 943	..
Gross National Disposable Income	NQCO	968 716	1 024 733	1 084 979	1 147 422	1 208 138	1 262 473	1 320 024	1 407 459	1 402 424
Adjustment to current basic prices										
Gross Domestic Product (at current market prices)	YBHA	976 533	1 021 828	1 075 564	1 139 746	1 200 595	1 252 505	1 321 860	1 400 526	1 442 921
Adjustment to current basic prices (*less* taxes *plus* subsidies on products)	-NQBU	−112 248	−114 234	−118 470	−124 738	−132 362	−137 347	−144 658	−153 147	−148 642
Gross Value Added (at current basic prices)	ABML	864 285	907 594	957 094	1 015 008	1 068 574	1 115 121	1 177 232	1 247 379	1 294 279
Net measures (after deduction of fixed capital consumption) at current market prices	-NQAE	−111 251	−115 796	−121 914	−125 507	−135 098	−138 530	−147 898	−154 940	..
Net domestic product	NHRK	865 282	906 032	953 650	1 014 143	1 065 411	1 113 985	1 174 002	1 242 899	..
Net national income	NSRX	863 481	912 119	969 565	1 029 662	1 082 599	1 135 005	1 182 823	1 249 717	..
Net national disposable income	NQCP	857 465	908 937	963 065	1 021 819	1 072 954	1 123 953	1 172 166	1 237 774	..
CHAINED VOLUME MEASURES (Reference year 2003, £ million)										
Gross measures (before deduction of fixed capital consumption) at market prices										
Gross Domestic Product	ABMI	1 059 658	1 085 745	1 108 508	1 139 746	1 171 178	1 195 276	1 229 196	1 266 347	1 275 299
Terms of trade effect ("Trading gain or loss")	YBGJ	−10 361	−11 125	−3 696	−	690	−8 676	−9 628	−4 066	..
Real gross domestic income	YBGL	1 049 297	1 074 620	1 104 812	1 139 746	1 171 868	1 186 600	1 219 568	1 262 331	..
Real employment, property and entrepreneurial income from the rest of the world (receipts *less* payments)	YBGI	2 103	9 901	18 775	17 523	17 411	20 732	9 323	7 768	..
Subsidies (receipts) *less* taxes (payments) on production from/to the rest of the world	-QZPB	−4 392	−4 118	−2 967	−2 596	−1 205	−4 038	−4 151	−4 270	..
Other subsidies on production from/to the rest of the world	-IBJN	359	611	533	592	578	3 230	2 973	2 656	..
Gross National Income (GNI)	YBGM	1 047 337	1 081 003	1 121 154	1 155 265	1 188 652	1 206 524	1 227 713	1 268 485	..
Real current transfers from the rest of the world (receipts *less* payments)	-YBGP	−6 448	−3 342	−6 673	−7 843	−9 419	−10 476	−9 840	−10 779	..
Gross National Disposable Income	YBGO	1 040 885	1 077 665	1 114 481	1 147 422	1 179 233	1 196 048	1 217 873	1 268 712	1 293 408
Adjustment to basic prices										
Gross Domestic Product (at market prices)	ABMI	1 059 658	1 085 745	1 108 508	1 139 746	1 171 178	1 195 276	1 229 196	1 266 347	1 275 299
Adjustment to basic prices (*less* taxes *plus* subsidies on products)	-NTAQ	−112 020	−116 584	−121 657	−124 738	−128 532	−130 433	−133 633	−138 328	..
Gross Value Added (at basic prices)	ABMM	947 927	969 279	986 849	1 015 008	1 042 646	1 064 843	1 095 563	1 127 574	1 135 940
Net measures (after deduction of fixed capital consumption) at market prices	-CIHA	−114 678	−118 027	−123 357	−125 508	−133 307	−134 030	−139 661	−143 385	..
Net national income at market prices	YBET	932 606	962 937	997 724	1 029 712	1 055 449	1 072 818	1 088 486	1 123 509	..
Net national disposable income at market prices	YBEY	926 150	959 613	991 053	1 021 869	1 046 030	1 062 342	1 078 646	1 112 730	..

1 See chapter text.

Source: Office for National Statistics: 020 7014 2083

16.2 United Kingdom gross domestic product and national income[1]
Current prices

£ million

		2000	2001	2002	2003	2004	2005	2006	2007	2008
Gross domestic product: Output										
Gross value added, at basic prices										
Output of goods and services	NQAF	1 777 360	1 861 011	1 939 534	2 040 175	2 138 303	2 257 351	2 384 827	..	..
less intermediate consumption	-NQAJ	-913 075	-953 417	-982 440	-1 025 167	-1 069 729	-1 142 230	-1 207 595	..	..
Total Gross Value Added	ABML	864 285	907 594	957 094	1 015 008	1 068 574	1 115 121	1 177 232	1 247 379	1 294 279
Value added taxes (VAT) on products	QYRC	64 189	67 097	71 059	77 335	81 540	83 382	87 679	92 000	..
Other taxes on products	NSUI	54 086	52 845	53 945	54 813	58 307	59 167	62 869	66 704	..
less subsidies on products	-NZHC	-6 027	-5 708	-6 534	-7 410	-7 836	-5 198	-5 994	-5 383	..
Gross Domestic Product at market prices	YBHA	976 533	1 021 828	1 075 564	1 139 746	1 200 595	1 252 505	1 321 860	1 400 526	1 442 921
Gross domestic product: Expenditure										
Final consumption expenditure										
Actual individual consumption										
Household final consumption expenditure	ABPB	616 558	647 778	680 964	714 608	747 502	780 265	814 659	859 980	891 002
Final consumption expenditure of NPISH	ABNV	23 531	25 111	26 422	27 668	28 748	30 402	32 209	34 409	37 550
Individual government final consumption expenditure	NNAQ	109 297	118 458	130 816	143 954	148 944	160 456	173 115	182 802	193 258
Total actual individual consumption	NQEO	749 386	791 347	838 202	886 230	925 194	971 123	1 019 983	1 077 191	1 121 810
Collective government final consumption expenditure	NQEP	72 675	76 126	81 761	88 865	102 825	108 182	112 554	113 239	122 356
Total final consumption expenditure	ABKW	822 061	867 473	919 963	975 095	1 028 019	1 079 305	1 132 537	1 190 430	1 244 166
Households and NPISH	NSSG	640 089	672 889	707 386	742 276	776 250	810 667	846 868	894 389	928 552
Central government	NMBJ	110 829	118 778	130 348	142 658	152 563	161 800	173 905	179 131	192 660
Local government	NMMT	71 143	75 806	82 229	90 161	99 206	106 838	111 764	116 910	122 954
Gross capital formation										
Gross fixed capital formation	NPQX	167 172	171 782	180 551	186 700	200 672	211 318	227 920	247 823	240 722
Changes in inventories	ABMP	5 271	6 189	2 909	3 983	4 695	4 973	4 322	7 379	1 422
Acquisitions less disposals of valuables	NPJO	3	396	214	-37	-37	-377	285	374	614
Total gross capital formation	NQFM	172 446	178 367	183 674	190 646	205 330	215 914	232 527	255 576	242 758
Exports of goods and services	KTMW	269 819	276 866	280 536	290 677	303 392	331 028	376 384	370 049	417 032
less imports of goods and services	-KTMX	-287 793	-300 878	-308 609	-316 672	-336 146	-373 742	-419 588	-417 346	-461 030
External balance of goods and services	KTMY	-17 974	-24 012	-28 073	-25 995	-32 754	-42 714	-43 204	-47 297	-43 998
Statistical discrepancy between expenditure components and GDP	RVFD	–	–	–	–	–	–	–	1 817	-5
Gross Domestic Product at market prices	YBHA	976 533	1 021 828	1 075 564	1 139 746	1 200 595	1 252 505	1 321 860	1 400 526	1 442 921
Gross domestic product: Income										
Operating surplus, gross										
Non-financial corporations										
Public non-financial corporations	NRJT	7 176	6 879	6 586	7 200	7 038	8 928	9 872	9 890	..
Private non-financial corporations	NRJK	182 115	183 157	188 444	201 091	214 851	222 175	236 916	254 156	259 884
Financial corporations	NQNV	10 996	12 965	27 125	33 218	32 460	32 300	36 628	46 049	61 979
Adjustment for financial services	-NSRV	-33 465	-33 648	-41 136	-45 370	-50 165	-51 922	-53 065	-57 536	..
General government	NMXV	9 542	9 796	10 289	10 807	11 429	12 174	12 931	14 523	15 441
Households and non-profit institutions serving households	QWLS	49 172	53 000	55 647	60 984	65 182	68 632	71 963	79 843	76 392
Total operating surplus, gross	ABNF	259 001	265 797	288 091	313 300	330 960	344 209	368 310	404 660	422 038
Mixed income	QWLT	56 931	61 282	64 967	68 324	72 816	74 858	78 908	83 614	85 673
Compensation of employees	HAEA	532 179	564 194	587 396	616 893	648 099	682 205	715 496	745 405	770 530
Taxes on production and imports	NZGX	135 358	137 507	143 117	150 665	158 587	162 059	171 518	180 262	..
less subsidies	-AAXJ	-6 936	-6 952	-8 007	-9 436	-9 990	-11 055	-12 307	-12 079	..
Statistical discrepancy between income components and GDP	RVFC	–	–	–	–	–	–	–	-1 421	209
Gross Domestic Product at market prices	YBHA	976 533	1 021 828	1 075 564	1 139 746	1 200 595	1 252 505	1 321 860	1 400 526	1 442 921

16.2 United Kingdom gross domestic product and national income[1]
Current prices
continued

		2000	2001	2002	2003	2004	2005	2006	2007	2008
Gross Domestic Product at market prices	YBHA	976 533	1 021 828	1 075 564	1 139 746	1 200 595	1 252 505	1 321 860	1 400 526	1 442 921
Compensation of employees										
receipts from the rest of the world	KTMN	1 032	1 087	1 121	1 116	931	974	1 058	1 159	1 221
less payments to the rest of the world	-KTMO	−882	−1 021	−1 054	−1 057	−1 425	−1 584	−1 803	−1 824	−1 840
Total	KTMP	150	66	67	59	−494	−610	−745	−665	−619
less Taxes on products paid to the rest of the world										
plus Subsidies received from the rest of the world	-QZOZ	−4 098	−3 920	−2 890	−2 596	−1 234	−4 260	−4 496	−4 731	..
Other subsidies on production	-IBJL	292	298	519	..	..	..	..	..	..
Property and entrepreneurial income										
receipts from the rest of the world	HMBN	131 902	137 447	120 543	122 069	137 382	185 765	237 448	290 399	271 299
less payments to the rest of the world	-HMBO	−130 090	−128 088	−102 324	−104 605	−119 058	−163 283	−226 606	−269 162	−237 551
Total	HMBM	1 812	9 359	18 219	17 464	18 324	22 482	10 842	21 237	33 748
Gross National Income at market prices	ABMX	974 732	1 027 915	1 091 479	1 155 265	1 217 783	1 273 525	1 330 681	1 419 319	1 474 243

1 See chapter text.

Source: Office for National Statistics: 020 7014 2083

16.3 United Kingdom gross domestic product[1]
Chained volume measures, reference year 2003

£ million

		2000	2001	2002	2003	2004	2005	2006	2007	2008
Gross domestic product: expenditure approach										
Final consumption expenditure										
Actual individual consumption										
Household final consumption expenditure	ABPF	647 796	668 482	693 124	714 608	736 857	751 288	766 378	789 682	800 541
Final consumption expenditure of non-profit institutions serving households	ABNU	27 536	27 567	27 576	27 668	27 198	27 212	28 289	29 485	29 802
Individual government final consumption expenditure	NSZK	111 763	114 159	117 238	120 288	..	..	..	..	..
Total actual individual consumption	YBIO	806 541	830 840	860 237	886 230	912 715	929 549	947 894	975 182	..
Collective government final consumption expenditure	NSZL	80 972	82 620	85 437	88 865	92 012	93 801	95 549	96 450	..
Total final consumption expenditure	ABKX	887 499	913 470	945 687	975 095	1 004 727	1 023 350	1 043 443	1 071 632	..
Gross capital formation										
Gross fixed capital formation	NPQR	173 710	178 203	184 701	186 700	195 782	200 187	212 146	226 469	219 524
Changes in inventories	ABMQ	4 648	5 577	2 289	3 982	4 371	4 814	4 575	6 448	993
Acquisitions less disposals of valuables	NPJP	−28	342	183	−37	−42	−354	290	535	1 231
Total gross capital formation	NPQU	178 660	184 462	187 374	190 646	200 111	204 647	217 011	234 572	..
Gross domestic final expenditure	YBIK	1 066 206	1 098 000	1 133 077	1 165 741	1 204 838	1 227 997	1 260 454	1 305 134	1 313 296
Exports of goods and services	KTMZ	274 338	282 607	285 433	290 677	304 699	329 491	365 818	350 660	350 937
Gross final expenditure	ABME	1 340 692	1 380 763	1 418 530	1 456 418	1 509 537	1 557 487	1 626 272	1 655 794	1 664 233
less imports of goods and services	-KTNB	−282 018	−295 491	−309 982	−316 672	−338 359	−362 211	−397 076	−391 090	−388 933
Statistical discrepancy between expenditure components and GDP	GIXS	−	−	−	−	−	−	−	1 643	−3
Gross Domestic Product at market prices	ABMI	1 059 658	1 085 745	1 108 508	1 139 746	1 171 178	1 195 276	1 229 196	1 266 347	1 275 299
of which External balance of goods and services	KTNC	−7 680	−12 884	−24 549	−25 995	−33 660	−32 720	−31 258	−40 430	−37 996

1 See chapter text.

Source: Office for National Statistics: 020 7014 2083

16.4 Gross value added at current basic prices: by industry[1,2]
United Kingdom

£ million

		2000	2001	2002	2003	2004	2005	2006	2007	2008
Agriculture, hunting, forestry and fishing	EWSH	8 532	8 333	9 007	9 806	10 600	7 422	7 865	..	..
Production										
Mining and quarrying										
Mining and quarrying of energy producing materials										
Mining of coal	QTOQ	607	545	538	472	398	323	314	309	..
Extraction of mineral oil and natural gas	QTOR	22 174	20 825	19 911	19 451	20 321	25 265	29 776	29 831	..
Other mining and quarrying	QTOS	1 784	1 750	1 469	1 519	1 841	2 081	2 112	2 291	..
Total mining and quarrying	EWSL	24 565	23 120	21 918	21 442	22 560	27 669	32 202		..
Manufacturing										
Food; beverages and tobacco	QTOU	19 963	20 655	20 834	21 408	21 979	21 826	22 143	22 996	..
Textiles and textile products	QTOV	5 813	5 343	4 818	4 282	4 240	3 977	3 944	3 887	..
Leather and leather products	QTOW	747	645	590	462	474	424	418	429	..
Wood and wood products	QTOX	2 294	2 332	2 479	2 655	2 790	3 052	3 200	3 603	..
Pulp, paper and paper products; publishing and printing	QTOY	20 187	20 129	20 008	19 780	19 378	19 315	19 246	19 530	..
Coke, petroleum products and nuclear fuel	QTOZ	2 336	2 488	2 435	2 377	2 439	2 529	2 506	2 636	..
Chemicals, chemical products and man-made fibres	QTPA	15 040	16 077	16 083	16 149	17 321	17 246	18 847	18 874	..
Rubber and plastic products	QTPB	7 609	7 656	7 569	7 516	7 380	7 563	7 928	7 929	..
Other non-metal mineral products	QTPC	4 965	5 033	5 296	5 417	5 528	5 193	5 469	5 718	..
Basic metals and fabricated metal products	QTPD	15 903	15 525	14 897	14 774	15 678	16 402	16 400	17 312	..
Machinery and equipment not elsewhere classified	QTPE	12 346	12 256	12 085	12 146	12 381	12 525	13 901	14 876	..
Electrical and optical equipment	QTPF	20 337	18 347	16 468	15 545	15 661	16 117	15 908	15 730	..
Transport equipment	QTPG	15 987	16 091	16 178	15 903	15 652	15 932	16 305	16 805	..
Manufacturing not elsewhere classified	QTPH	6 477	6 643	6 567	6 429	6 361	6 491	6 938	7 403	..
Total manufacturing	EWSP	150 009	149 223	146 308	144 845	147 261	148 591	153 155	..	..
Electricity, gas and water supply	EWST	15 798	15 660	16 052	16 405	16 672	16 667	18 870	..	..
Total production	QTPK	190 367	188 000	184 277	182 690	186 494	192 928	204 225	208 855	..
Construction	EWSX	45 626	50 526	54 684	59 522	63 955	68 019	73 993	..	..
Service industries										
Wholesale and retail trade (including motor trade); repair of motor vehicles, personal and household goods	QTPM	103 409	110 250	113 778	120 520	127 411	130 952	136 071	142 402	..
Hotels and restaurants	QTPN	25 605	26 927	28 638	30 120	31 290	31 969	33 765	36 645	..
Transport, storage and communication										
Transport and storage	QTPO	42 476	43 184	44 501	47 022	49 576	50 203	50 491	53 434	..
Communication	QTPP	26 726	27 317	28 562	29 566	30 253	30 307	30 537	31 892	..
Total	EWTF	69 201	70 502	73 064	76 587	79 828	80 510	81 027	..	..
Financial intermediation	QTPR	44 990	48 202	63 368	71 530	75 042	79 356	91 011	95 398	..
Adjustment for financial services (FISIM)	-NSRV	–33 465	–33 648	–41 136	–45 370	–50 165	–51 922	–53 065	–57 536	..
Real estate, renting and business activities										
Letting of dwellings including imputed rent of owner occupiers	QTPS	57 261	61 352	64 249	69 298	76 166	80 155	84 809	90 065	..
Other real estate, renting and business activities	QTPT	131 098	142 688	150 598	162 906	170 882	179 180	188 835	212 540	..
Total	QTPU	188 359	204 040	214 847	232 204	247 048	259 335	273 644	302 605	..
Public administration and defence (PAD)	EWTN	42 712	45 025	47 528	51 302	55 393	60 096	63 033	..	..
Education	QTPW	48 111	51 675	55 099	58 328	61 814	66 186	69 345	73 105	..
Health and social work	QTPX	55 282	59 549	64 492	70 593	74 417	78 497	81 883	86 689	..
Other social and personal services, private households with employees and extra-territorial organisations	EWTV	42 086	44 561	48 312	51 804	55 283	59 852	61 368	..	..
Total service industries	QTPZ	619 756	660 729	709 122	762 988	807 529	846 753	891 148	950 333	..
All industries	ABML	864 285	907 594	957 094	1 015 008	1 068 574	1 115 121	1 177 232	1 247 379	1 294 279

1 See chapter text. Components may not sum to totals as a result of rounding.

2 Because of differences in the annual and monthly production inquiries, estimates of current price output and value added by industry derived from the current price input-output supply-use balances are not consistent with the equivalent measures of constant price growth given in Table 16.5. These differences do not affect GDP totals. For further information see "Experimental Constant Price Input-Output Supply-Use Balances: An approach to improving the quality of the national accounts" Nadim Ahmad, *Economic Trends*, July 1999 (No. 548).

Source: Office for National Statistics: 020 7014 2083

16.5 Gross value added at basic prices: by industry[1,2,3,4]
Chained volume indices
United Kingdom

Indices (2003=100)

	Weight per 1000[1]		2000	2001	2002	2003	2004	2005	2006	2007	2008
	2003										
Agriculture, hunting, forestry and fishing	9.9	GDQA	100.1	91.1	101.7	100.0	99.8	105.1	107.9	103.2	103.3
Production											
Mining and quarrying											
Mining and quarrying of energy producing materials											
Mining of coal	0.6	CKZP	112.5	112.9	105.9	100.0	85.9	67.2	64.4	58.3	62.2
Extraction of mineral oil and natural gas	25.1	CKZO	113.5	107.1	105.8	100.0	91.5	82.4	75.1	73.3	69.9
Other mining and quarrying	2.0	CKZQ	86.4	81.5	98.8	100.0	102.1	112.6	119.2	128.2	99.5
Total mining and quarrying	27.7	CKYX	111.0	104.9	105.3	100.0	92.1	84.2	78.0	76.7	72.0
Manufacturing											
Food; beverages and tobacco	23.8	CKZA	98.4	98.9	101.7	100.0	102.0	103.6	102.9	101.8	99.7
Textiles and textile products	6.3	CKZB	122.1	105.7	99.6	100.0	91.2	90.0	89.9	87.3	88.0
Leather and leather products	0.7	CKZC	139.0	128.2	116.5	100.0	73.6	67.0	70.2	71.3	67.7
Wood and wood products	2.7	CKZD	98.0	97.9	98.6	100.0	105.3	101.2	98.8	103.0	95.9
Pulp, paper and paper products; publishing and printing	23.2	CKZE	102.0	101.6	101.8	100.0	99.0	95.0	94.3	93.8	91.7
Coke, petroleum products and nuclear fuel	2.9	CKZF	113.0	106.9	109.2	100.0	107.8	111.0	105.4	109.6	113.9
Chemicals, chemical products and man-made fibres	18.4	CKZG	93.3	98.4	99.2	100.0	103.6	106.5	110.0	108.6	109.0
Rubber and plastic products	9.0	CKZH	106.2	103.2	99.1	100.0	98.3	97.2	101.3	100.7	95.2
Other non-metallic mineral products	5.8	CKZI	96.0	96.8	95.8	100.0	106.2	106.2	109.1	108.7	103.4
Basic metals and fabricated metal products	17.8	CKZJ	103.0	100.2	101.3	100.0	102.7	103.6	105.1	105.9	101.5
Machinery and equipment not elsewhere classified	13.9	CKZK	102.4	104.4	98.8	100.0	105.9	109.3	116.1	120.6	119.2
Electrical and optical equipment	21.3	CKZL	127.0	119.6	103.9	100.0	102.2	98.0	98.3	99.8	95.3
Transport equipment	18.1	CKZM	99.9	98.4	95.4	100.0	105.3	105.2	111.3	110.4	107.4
Manufacturing not elsewhere classified	7.6	CKZN	100.5	98.9	100.1	100.0	100.2	100.7	101.7	102.3	96.9
Total manufacturing	171.0	CKYY	103.9	102.5	100.3	100.0	102.2	102.0	103.8	104.0	101.3
Electricity, gas and water supply	18.2	CKYZ	95.0	97.7	98.3	100.0	101.0	100.7	100.1	101.2	101.0
Total production	217.6	CKYW	103.9	102.3	100.7	100.0	100.9	99.8	100.5	100.6	97.8
Construction	56.7	GDQB	89.5	91.6	95.2	100.0	103.4	104.5	105.5	108.2	108.5
Service industries											
Wholesale and retail trade (including motor trade); repair of motor vehicles, personal and household goods	125.5	GDQC	89.0	91.5	96.6	100.0	104.1	105.2	108.0	111.2	110.4
Hotels and restaurants	33.3	GDQD	92.2	94.5	97.2	100.0	101.7	103.9	109.4	112.3	112.6
Transport, storage and communication											
Transport and storage	49.8	GDQF	100.8	99.9	101.3	100.0	104.5	108.8	111.7	114.1	114.8
Communication	31.3	GDQG	84.3	94.4	93.4	100.0	102.5	107.6	109.8	115.3	118.7
Total	81.0	GDQH	93.8	97.6	98.0	100.0	103.7	108.3	111.0	114.6	116.3
Financial intermediation	48.5	GDQI	85.4	89.4	93.4	100.0	104.2	109.2	117.4	126.9	134.1
Adjustment for financial services (FISIM)	–38.1	GDQJ	81.7	86.3	89.2	100.0	113.0	123.3	138.8	162.8	..
Real estate, renting and business activities											
Letting of dwellings, including imputed rent of owner occupiers	77.8	GDQL	96.5	97.4	98.3	100.0	100.4	101.1	102.6	103.1	103.9
Other real estate, renting and business activities	160.4	GDQK	89.6	95.2	95.5	100.0	106.6	113.5	121.4	128.9	130.8
Total	238.3	GDQM	91.6	95.9	96.3	100.0	104.7	109.8	115.8	121.2	122.7
Public administration and defence (PAD)[4]	55.6	GDQO	91.2	92.5	95.1	100.0	101.1	101.6	101.9	102.0	100.7
Education	58.7	GDQP	96.0	97.1	99.1	100.0	99.4	99.8	99.3	99.1	100.0
Health and social work[4]	62.3	GDQQ	89.0	92.4	96.2	100.0	103.7	106.1	108.7	112.7	117.0
Other social and personal services, private households with employees and extra-territorial organisations	51.0	GDQR	93.5	97.0	99.2	100.0	99.3	100.5	102.2	102.1	103.8
Total service industries	715.8	GDQS	91.1	94.3	96.6	100.0	103.2	106.3	110.2	114.1	115.8
All industries	1 000.0	CGCE	93.4	95.5	97.2	100.0	102.7	104.9	107.9	111.1	111.9

1 See chapter text. The weights are in proportion to total gross value added (GVA) in 2003 and are used to combine the industry output indices to calculate the totals for 2004 and 2005. For 2003 and earlier, totals are calculated using the equivalent weight for the previous year (eg totals for 2002 use 2001 weights).

2 As GVA is expressed in index number form, it is inappropriate to show as a statistical adjustment any divergence from the other measures of GDP. Such an adjustment does, however, exist implicitly.

3 See footnote 2 to Table 16.4.

4 The GVA for PAD, education and Health and social work in this table follows the SIC(92) and differs from that used in Table 2.3 in *United Kingdom National Accounts* (the *Blue Book*) which is based on Input-Output groups. The administration costs of the NHS are included in PAD in this table but are included in Health and social work in Table 2.3.

Source: Office for National Statistics: 020 7014 2083

16.6 Non-financial corporations[1]
Allocation of primary income account[2]
United Kingdom. ESA95 sector S.11

£ million

		2000	2001	2002	2003	2004	2005	2006	2007	2008
Resources										
Operating surplus, gross	NQBE	189 291	190 036	195 030	208 291	221 889	231 103	246 788	264 245	268 226
Property income, received										
Interest	EABC	14 598	13 177	9 330	9 727	14 145	17 389	24 562	29 461	22 318
Distributed income of corporations	EABD	26 631	36 868	32 210	..	..	..	..	..	..
Reinvested earnings on direct foreign investment	HDVR	20 118	22 950	26 893	12 492	22 713	33 199	36 426	49 474	50 296
Attributed property income of insurance policy-holders	FAOF	489	280	302	..	..	..	..	..	..
Rent	FAOG	117	117	118	..	..	..	..	..	..
Total	FAKY	61 667	74 102	67 229	73 070	80 467	98 171	106 500	118 886	110 554
Total resources	FBXJ	250 958	264 138	262 259	281 361	302 356	329 274	353 288	383 131	378 780
Uses										
Property income, paid										
Interest	EABG	30 405	30 661	29 045	29 592	34 937	39 338	45 229	55 310	50 455
Distributed income of corporations	NVCS	83 202	100 810	91 868	..	..	..	..	..	..
Reinvested earnings on direct foreign investment	HDVB	7 348	1 699	1 614	3 955	6 325	4 983	16 802	15 331	11 775
Rent	FBXO	1 319	1 896	1 853	..	..	..	..	..	..
Total	FBXK	123 265	137 950	119 879	128 885	136 074	152 442	168 741	172 402	170 536
Balance of primary incomes, gross	NQBG	127 693	126 188	142 380	152 476	166 282	176 832	184 547	210 729	208 244
Total uses	FBXJ	250 958	264 138	262 259	281 361	302 356	329 274	353 288	383 131	378 780
After deduction of fixed capital consumption	-DBGF	−66 420	−68 362	−70 547	−72 598	−75 559	−77 278	−80 360	−83 565	..
Balance of primary incomes, net	FBXQ	61 273	57 826	71 833	79 878	90 723	99 554	104 187	113 074	..

1 See chapter text.
2 Before deduction of fixed capital formation.

Source: Office for National Statistics: 020 7014 2014

16.7 Non-financial corporations[1]
Secondary distribution of income account
United Kingdom. ESA95 sector S.11

£ million

		2000	2001	2002	2003	2004	2005	2006	2007	2008
Resources										
Balance of primary incomes, gross	NQBG	127 693	126 188	142 380	152 476	166 282	176 832	184 547	210 729	208 244
Social contributions										
Imputed social contributions	NSTJ	4 175	4 357	4 575	4 229	3 810	3 535	3 425	3 508	4 148
Current transfers other than taxes, social contributions and benefits										
Non-life insurance claims	FCBP	4 456	4 565	7 789	..	..	..	..	..	..
Miscellaneous transfers	NRJY	622	619	616	..	..	..	..	..	..
Total	NRJB	5 847	3 836	5 543	6 124	6 550	7 261	8 368	4 220	4 930
Total resources	FCBR	137 715	134 381	152 498	162 829	176 642	187 628	196 340	218 457	217 322
Uses										
Current taxes on income, wealth etc.										
Taxes on income	FCBS	24 497	23 177	24 038	23 702	27 368	33 602	37 183	38 269	37 982
Social benefits other than social transfers in kind	NSTJ	4 175	4 357	4 575	4 229	3 810	3 535	3 425	3 508	4 148
Current transfers other than taxes, social contributions and benefits										
Net non-life insurance premiums	FCBY	4 456	4 565	7 789	..	..	..	..	..	..
Miscellaneous current transfers	FDBI	413	411	422	434	446	..	..	..	..
Total, other current transfers	FCBX	6 315	4 220	5 876	6 462	6 973	7 749	8 842	4 708	5 418
Gross Disposable Income	NRJD	102 728	102 627	118 009	128 436	138 491	142 742	146 890	171 972	169 774
Total uses	FCBR	137 715	134 381	152 498	162 829	176 642	187 628	196 340	218 457	217 322
After deduction of fixed capital consumption	-DBGF	−66 420	−68 362	−70 547	−72 598	−75 559	−77 278	−80 360	−83 565	..
Disposable income, net	FCCF	36 308	34 265	47 462	55 838	62 932	65 464	66 530	74 338	..

1 See chapter text.

Source: Office for National Statistics: 020 7014 2014

16.8 General government[1]
Allocation of primary income account
United Kingdom. ESA95 sector S.13 Unconsolidated

£ million

		2000	2001	2002	2003	2004	2005	2006	2007	2008
Resources										
Operating surplus, gross	NMXV	9 542	9 796	10 289	10 807	11 429	12 174	12 931	14 523	15 441
Taxes on production and imports, received										
Taxes on products										
Value added tax (VAT)	NZGF	59 998	63 525	68 258	74 603	79 761	81 416	85 591	89 698	88 909
Taxes and duties on imports excluding VAT										
Import duties	NMXZ	–	–	–	–	–	–	–	–	..
Taxes on imports excluding VAT and import duties	NMBT	–	–	–	–	–	..	..	..	..
Taxes on products excluding VAT and import duties	NMYB	51 956	50 745	52 001	52 858	56 137	56 906	60 540	64 309	60 357
Total taxes on products	NVCC	111 941	114 267	120 252	127 453	135 898	138 322	146 126	154 007	149 268
Other taxes on production	NMYD	17 083	17 565	18 113	18 517	18 853	19 706	20 831	21 543	22 347
Total taxes on production and imports, received	NMYE	129 024	131 832	138 365	145 970	154 751	158 028	166 957	175 550	171 615
less Subsidies, paid										
Subsidies on products	-NMYF	–3 791	–3 953	–4 672	–5 311	–5 111	–5 198	–5 994	–5 591	–5 532
Other subsidies on production	-LIUF	–574	–662	–954	–1 434	–1 562	–2 449	–3 093	–3 470	–3 419
Total	-NMRL	–4 365	–4 615	–5 626	–6 745	–6 673	–7 647	–9 087	–8 920	..
Property income, received										
Total Interest	NMYL	7 403	7 359	6 683	7 131	6 804	6 458	7 109	8 125	8 170
Distributed income of corporations	NMYM	5 480	4 710	3 290	3 027	2 763	2 866	2 541	3 126	3 079
Property income attributed to insurance policy holders	NMYO	54	24	22	19	19	27	25	24	19
Rent										
from sectors other than general government	NMYR	1 289	1 919	1 901	1 565	1 182	1 229	1 226	1 233	1 162
Total	NMYU	14 226	14 012	11 892	11 742	10 768	10 580	10 901	12 508	12 430
Total resources	NMYV	148 427	151 025	154 920	161 774	170 275	173 135	181 702	193 520	190 535
Uses										
Property income, paid										
Total interest	NRKB	30 585	27 911	25 410	26 913	27 013	29 469	30 392	34 232	..
Total	NMYY	30 585	27 911	25 410	26 913	27 013	29 469	30 392	34 176	36 396
Balance of primary incomes, gross	NMZH	117 842	123 114	129 510	134 861	143 262	143 666	151 310	159 344	154 139
Total uses	NMYV	148 427	151 025	154 920	161 774	170 275	173 135	181 702	193 520	190 535
After deduction of fixed capital consumption	-NMXO	–9 542	–9 796	–10 289	–10 807	–11 429	–12 174	–12 931	–14 523	..
Balance of primary incomes,net	NMZI	108 300	113 318	119 221	124 054	131 833	131 492	138 379	145 270	..

1 See chapter text.

Source: Office for National Statistics: 020 7014 2122

16.9 General government[1]
Secondary distribution of income account
United Kingdom. ESA95 sector S.13 Unconsolidated

£ million

		2000	2001	2002	2003	2004	2005	2006	2007	2008
Resources										
Balance of primary incomes, gross	NMZH	117 842	123 114	129 510	134 861	143 262	143 666	151 310	159 344	154 139
Current taxes on income, wealth etc.										
Taxes on income	NMZJ	140 002	147 264	142 842	144 234	154 127	172 498	192 812	200 213	206 121
Other current taxes	NVCM	20 287	22 068	23 664	26 016	28 001	29 444	30 906	32 719	34 030
Total	NMZL	160 289	169 332	166 506	170 250	182 128	201 942	223 718	232 932	240 151
Social contributions										
Actual social contributions										
Employers' actual social contributions	NMZM	36 397	38 460	38 780	45 067	49 202	52 769	56 024	58 723	63 146
Employees' social contributions	NMZN	27 293	28 725	29 568	34 376	38 835	41 768	44 378	45 587	48 168
Social contributions by self- and non-employed persons	NMZO	2 049	2 183	2 318	2 595	2 727	2 825	2 930	3 013	2 873
Total	NMZP	65 739	69 368	70 666	82 038	90 764	97 362	103 332	107 323	114 187
Imputed social contributions	NMZQ	7 395	7 577	8 348	6 456	6 219	7 383	7 289	7 933	7 830
Total	NMZR	73 134	76 945	79 014	88 494	96 983	104 745	110 621	115 256	122 017
Other current transfers										
Non-life insurance claims	NMZS	403	353	400	296	338	328	366	277	321
Current transfers within general government	NMZT	66 187	72 522	77 592	85 224	94 720	101 369	110 407	113 210	118 370
Current international cooperation	NMZU	2 084	4 568	3 112	3 570	3 673	3 726	3 674	3 676	4 966
Miscellaneous current transfers										
from sectors other than general government	NMZX	447	460	502	562	721	728	612	583	561
Other current transfers	NNAA	69 111	77 815	81 526	89 632	99 452	106 151	115 059	117 746	124 218
Total resources	NNAB	420 376	447 206	456 556	483 237	521 825	556 504	600 708	625 278	640 525
Uses										
Social benefits other than social transfers in kind	NNAD	120 163	129 591	136 801	146 066	154 332	161 425	167 053	178 376	190 126
Other current transfers										
Net non-life insurance premiums	NNAE	403	353	400	296	338	328	366	277	321
Current transfers within general government	NNAF	66 187	72 522	77 592	85 224	94 720	101 369	110 407	113 210	118 370
Current international cooperation	NNAG	2 181	2 190	2 362	2 433	3 080	3 255	3 632	3 930	4 196
Miscellaneous current transfers										
to sectors other than general government	NNAI	20 913	22 131	27 351	30 275	31 178	34 355	34 695	35 878	36 739
Of which: GNP based fourth own resource	NMFH	4 379	3 858	5 335	6 772	7 549	8 732	8 521	8 323	8 423
Other current transfers	NNAN	89 674	97 108	107 625	118 208	129 316	139 307	149 100	153 295	159 626
Gross Disposable Income	NNAO	209 679	219 605	211 254	218 121	237 253	254 750	283 480	292 496	289 626
Total uses	NNAB	420 376	447 206	456 556	483 237	521 825	556 504	600 708	625 278	640 525
After deduction of fixed capital consumption	-NMXO	-9 542	-9 796	-10 289	-10 807	-11 429	-12 174	-12 931	-14 523	..
Disposable income, net	NNAP	200 137	209 809	200 965	207 314	225 824	242 576	270 549	278 697	..

1 See chapter text.

Source: Office for National Statistics: 020 7014 2122

16.10 Households and non-profit institutions serving households[1]
Allocation of primary income account
United Kingdom. ESA95 sectors S.14 and S.15

£ million

		2000	2001	2002	2003	2004	2005	2006	2007	2008
Resources										
Operating surplus, gross	QWLS	49 172	53 000	55 647	60 984	65 182	68 632	71 963	79 843	76 392
Mixed income, gross	QWLT	56 931	61 282	64 967	68 324	72 816	74 858	78 908	83 614	85 673
Compensation of employees										
Wages and salaries	QWLW	462 505	491 044	508 681	527 689	548 899	573 932	599 461	627 978	651 550
Employers' social contributions	QWLX	69 824	73 216	78 782	89 263	98 706	107 663	115 290	116 762	118 361
Total	QWLY	532 329	564 260	587 463	616 952	647 605	681 595	714 751	744 740	769 911
Property income										
Interest	QWLZ	35 488	31 957	26 658	27 251	34 550	40 007	42 706	53 595	46 144
Distributed income of corporations	QWMA	43 755	49 894	43 787	45 248	45 862	50 704	47 957	44 429	44 292
Attributed property income of insurance policy holders	QWMC	53 081	53 277	52 104	55 008	54 623	64 028	66 640	71 872	75 195
Rent	QWMD	105	105	106	108	110	110	112	110	115
Total	QWME	132 429	135 233	122 655	127 615	135 145	154 849	157 415	170 006	165 746
Total resources	QWMF	770 861	813 775	830 732	873 875	920 748	979 934	1 023 037	1 078 203	1 097 722
Uses										
Property income										
Interest	QWMG	36 968	33 752	30 512	32 001	43 207	46 739	49 046	67 339	55 876
Rent	QWMH	215	215	216	220	224	224	228	234	239
Total	QWMI	37 183	33 967	30 728	32 221	43 431	46 963	49 274	67 573	56 115
Balance of primary incomes, gross	QWMJ	733 678	779 808	800 004	841 654	877 317	932 971	973 763	1 010 630	1 041 607
Total uses	QWMF	770 861	813 775	830 732	873 875	920 748	979 934	1 023 037	1 078 203	1 097 722
After deduction of										
fixed capital consumption	-QWLL	−30 518	−32 908	−36 043	−36 903	−42 561	−43 387	−48 789	−52 077	..
Balance of primary incomes, net	QWMK	703 160	746 900	763 961	804 751	834 808	889 714	925 140	957 795	..

1 See chapter text.

Source: Office for National Statistics: 020 7014 2131

16.11 Households and non-profit institutions serving households[1]
Secondary distribution of income account
United Kingdom. ESA95 sectors S.14 and S.15

£ million

		2000	2001	2002	2003	2004	2005	2006	2007	2008
Resources										
Balance of primary incomes, gross	QWMJ	733 678	779 808	800 004	841 654	877 317	932 971	973 763	1 010 630	1 041 607
Imputed social contributions	RVFH	476	502	530	505	499	506	514	518	524
Social benefits other than social transfers in kind	QWML	162 833	171 814	182 673	193 596	198 680	211 686	225 891	226 684	247 057
Other current transfers										
Non-life insurance claims	QWMM	15 713	11 723	17 327	13 890	17 479	17 199	20 346	14 842	17 254
Miscellaneous current transfers	QWMN	27 520	29 080	33 041	34 687	34 845	37 840	38 708	39 618	40 094
Total	QWMO	43 233	40 803	50 368	48 577	52 324	55 039	59 054	54 460	57 348
Total resources	QWMP	940 220	992 927	1 033 575	1 084 332	1 128 820	1 200 202	1 259 222	1 292 292	1 346 536
Uses										
Current taxes on income, wealth etc										
Taxes on income	QWMQ	105 299	111 888	112 171	113 087	119 591	130 200	139 969	151 913	154 039
Other current taxes	NVCO	19 427	21 166	22 788	25 174	27 077	28 422	29 831	31 608	32 883
Total	QWMS	124 726	133 054	134 959	138 261	146 668	158 622	169 800	183 521	186 922
Social contributions										
Actual social contributions										
Employers' actual social contributions	QWMT	57 288	60 296	64 805	77 571	87 675	95 732	103 551	104 289	105 339
Employees' social contributions	QWMU	58 807	60 599	62 458	66 490	70 451	78 540	84 129	84 907	90 833
Social contributions by self and non-employed	QWMV	2 049	2 183	2 318	2 595	2 727	2 825	2 930	3 013	2 873
Total	QWMW	118 144	123 078	129 581	146 656	160 853	177 097	190 610	195 798	..
Imputed social contributions	QWMX	12 536	12 920	13 977	11 692	11 031	11 931	11 739	12 473	13 022
Total	QWMY	130 680	135 998	143 558	158 348	171 884	189 028	202 349	204 682	212 067
Social benefits other than social transfers in kind	QWMZ	948	977	1 006	987	988	1 000	1 010	1 014	1 020
Other current transfers										
Net non-life insurance premiums	QWNA	15 713	11 723	17 327	13 890	17 479	17 199	20 346	14 842	17 254
Miscellaneous current transfers	QWNB	10 865	11 081	11 458	11 930	12 462	13 442	13 274	13 532	13 826
Total	QWNC	26 578	22 804	28 785	25 820	29 941	30 641	33 620	28 374	31 080
Gross Disposable Income[2]	QWND	657 288	700 094	725 267	760 916	779 339	820 911	852 443	874 701	915 447
Total uses	QWMP	940 220	992 927	1 033 575	1 084 332	1 128 820	1 200 202	1 259 222	1 292 292	1 346 536
After deduction of fixed capital consumption	-QWLL	−30 518	−32 908	−36 043	−36 903	−42 561	−43 387	−48 789	−52 077	..
Disposable income, net	QWNE	626 770	667 186	689 224	724 013	736 830	777 654	803 820	819 368	..

1 See chapter text.
2 Gross household disposable income revalued by the implied households and NPISH's final consumption expenditure deflator. For more details see table 6.1.4 on page 217 in *United Kingdom National Accounts* (the *Blue book*).

Source: Office for National Statistics: 020 7014 2131

16.12 Households and non-profit institutions serving households[1]
Use of disposable income account
United Kingdom. ESA95 sectors S.14 and S.15

£ million and percentages

		2000	2001	2002	2003	2004	2005	2006	2007	2008
Resources										
Disposable income, gross	QWND	657 288	700 094	725 267	760 916	779 339	820 911	852 443	874 701	915 447
Adjustment for the change in net equity of households in pension funds	NSSE	14 154	16 038	17 784	21 377	29 468	32 888	31 714	39 816	31 656
Total resources	NSSF	671 442	716 132	743 051	782 293	808 807	853 799	884 157	914 517	947 103
Uses										
Final consumption expenditure										
Individual consumption expenditure	NSSG	640 089	672 889	707 386	742 276	776 250	810 667	846 868	894 389	928 552
Saving, gross	NSSH	31 353	43 243	35 665	40 017	32 557	43 132	37 289	20 128	18 551
Total uses	NSSF	671 442	716 132	743 051	782 293	808 807	853 799	884 157	914 517	947 103
Saving ratio (percentages)	RVGL	4.7	6.0	4.8	5.1	4.0	5.1	4.2	2.2	2.0

1 See chapter text.

Source: Office for National Statistics: 020 7014 2131

16.13 The sector accounts: key economic indicators[1]
United Kingdom

£ million and indices (2003=100)

		2000	2001	2002	2003	2004	2005	2006	2007	2008
Net lending/borrowing by:										
Non-financial corporations	EABO	−4 614	−6 366	10 549	22 971	30 983	22 285	27 728	36 780	41 908
Financial corporations	NHCQ	−26 988	−22 123	4 386	13 451	18 477	5 036	−3 275	21 964	56 010
General government	NNBK	13 168	6 546	−20 389	−37 206	−39 959	−41 239	−34 739	−37 107	−75 807
Households and NPISH's	NSSZ	−6 436	1 044	−12 477	−12 091	−29 533	−17 731	−33 643	−56 382	−40 715
Rest of the world	NHRB	24 084	19 784	17 725	16 841	23 136	31 188	44 056	37 761	20 988
Private non-financial corporations										
Gross trading profits										
Continental shelf profits	CAGJ	21 458	20 397	18 742	..	..	..	..	..	..
Others	CAED	152 682	151 364	160 068	173 584	182 976	185 873	195 399	217 755	214 863
Rental of buildings	FCBW	11 747	12 394	12 904	13 891	16 097	16 936	17 350	18 011	18 930
less Holding gains of inventories	-DLQZ	−2 941	438	−2 856	−4 266	−2 786	−4 058	−3 444	−6 644	−9 323
Gross operating surplus	NRJK	182 115	183 157	188 444	201 091	214 851	222 175	236 916	254 156	259 884
Households and NPISH										
Household gross disposable income	QWND	657 288	700 094	725 267	760 916	779 339	820 911	852 443	874 701	915 447
Implied deflator of household and NPISH individual consumption expenditure indicies (2003=100)	YBFS	94.8	96.7	98.2	100.0	101.6	104.1	106.6	109.2	111.8
Real household disposable income:										
Chained volume measures (Reference year 2003)	RVGK	693 322	724 114	738 900	760 916	767 096	788 338	799 898	801 135	818 624
Indices (2003=100)	OSXR	91.1	95.2	97.1	100.0	100.8	103.6	105.1	105.3	107.6
Gross saving	NSSH	31 353	43 243	35 665	40 017	32 557	43 132	37 289	20 128	18 551
Households total resources	NSSJ	780 730	834 590	873 867	926 247	957 751	1 014 255	1 057 272	1 097 319	1 140 361
Saving ratio (percentages)	RVGL	*4.7*	*6.0*	*4.8*	*5.1*	*4.0*	*5.1*	*4.2*	*2.2*	*2.0*

1 See chapter text.

Source: Office for National Statistics: 020 7014 2083

16.14 Household final consumption expenditure: by purpose[1]
Current market prices
United Kingdom

£ million

		2000	2001	2002	2003	2004	2005	2006	2007	2008
Durable goods										
Furnishings, household equipment and routine maintenance of the house	LLIJ	18 006	19 275	20 470	21 595	22 316	22 976	23 622	24 960	25 079
Health	LLIK	1 997	2 109	2 411	2 604	2 467	2 368	2 650	2 713	2 710
Transport	LLIL	33 291	35 864	36 574	38 016	38 643	38 361	39 047	40 886	37 707
Communication	LLIM	601	636	644	810	850	900	900	927	1 005
Recreation and culture	LLIN	14 878	15 970	16 471	17 752	19 058	20 180	21 012	21 441	21 702
Miscellaneous goods and services	LLIO	3 403	3 750	4 204	4 284	4 739	4 636	5 283	5 507	5 754
Total durable goods	UTIA	72 176	77 604	80 774	85 061	88 073	89 421	92 514	96 434	93 957
Semi-durable goods										
Clothing and footwear	LLJL	34 759	36 092	38 351	40 389	42 114	42 999	44 178	45 841	46 587
Furnishings, household equipment and routine maintenance of the house	LLJM	11 677	12 400	13 361	13 932	13 502	13 396	13 987	13 788	13 294
Transport	LLJN	2 772	2 783	3 112	3 423	3 048	3 444	3 438	3 567	4 249
Recreation and culture	LLJO	20 405	21 606	23 910	26 009	26 544	26 659	26 671	26 985	27 318
Miscellaneous goods and services	LLJP	2 018	2 427	2 886	3 356	3 477	3 278	3 448	3 658	3 382
Total semi-durable goods	UTIQ	71 631	75 308	81 620	87 109	88 685	89 776	91 722	93 839	94 830
Non-durable goods										
Food & drink	ABZV	58 628	59 804	61 310	63 174	64 830	67 187	69 410	77 144	84 993
Alcohol & tobacco	ADFL	24 617	25 158	25 966	27 297	28 101	28 437	30 061	30 947	31 120
Housing, water, electricity, gas and other fuels	LLIX	22 265	23 076	23 444	24 241	27 439	29 375	33 936	35 824	41 582
Furnishings, household equipment and routine maintenance of the house	LLIY	2 786	2 972	3 169	3 338	3 879	3 873	4 091	4 095	4 029
Health	LLIZ	3 268	3 613	3 855	3 938	4 457	4 525	4 491	4 601	4 859
Transport	LLJA	19 987	19 391	19 129	20 072	21 161	24 183	25 089	26 359	29 202
Recreation and culture	LLJB	12 959	13 107	13 392	13 507	13 976	14 359	14 879	15 305	15 660
Miscellaneous goods and services	LLJC	9 463	9 884	11 272	12 602	13 187	13 276	14 208	15 579	16 270
Total non-durable goods	UTII	153 973	157 005	161 537	168 169	177 030	185 215	196 165	209 854	227 715
Total goods	UTIE	297 780	309 917	323 931	340 339	353 788	364 412	380 401	400 127	416 502
Services										
Clothing and footwear	LLJD	720	730	741	766	682	760	824	847	920
Housing, water, electricity, gas and other fuels	LLJE	85 785	92 829	97 794	104 810	110 605	117 947	125 760	133 758	138 727
Furnishings, household equipment and routine maintenance of the house	LLJF	3 206	3 327	3 448	3 601	3 772	4 084	3 791	3 685	3 904
Health	LLJG	3 943	4 254	4 512	4 793	5 105	5 413	5 603	6 184	6 090
Transport	LLJH	37 002	38 397	41 332	43 058	45 604	48 180	50 923	52 912	55 678
Communication	LLJI	12 755	13 521	14 031	14 844	15 944	16 308	16 532	17 089	17 261
Recreation and culture	LLJJ	21 912	22 769	25 349	27 118	29 263	31 218	32 528	34 736	35 588
Education	ADIE	9 534	9 409	9 381	9 610	11 094	11 762	12 432	13 703	14 100
Restaurants and hotels	ADIF	68 557	71 620	76 426	78 902	82 476	84 808	86 729	90 549	93 248
Miscellaneous goods and services	LLJK	68 423	71 481	73 456	74 609	77 229	83 414	87 259	93 679	95 142
Total services	UTIM	311 837	328 337	346 470	362 111	381 774	403 894	422 381	447 142	460 658
Final consumption expenditure in the UK by resident and non-resident households (domestic concept)	ABQI	609 617	638 254	670 401	702 450	735 562	768 306	802 782	847 269	877 160
Final consumption expenditure outside the UK by UK resident households	ABTA	21 654	22 907	24 435	26 314	27 550	29 028	30 389	31 702	33 325
less Final consumption expenditure in the UK by households resident in the rest of the world	CDFD	−14 713	−13 383	−13 872	−14 156	−15 610	−17 069	−18 512	−18 991	−19 483
Final consumption expenditure by UK resident households in the UK and abroad (national concept)	ABPB	616 558	647 778	680 964	714 608	747 502	780 265	814 659	859 980	891 002

1 See chapter text. Additional detail is published in *Consumer Trends* and table A7 of *UK Economic Accounts*, available from the National Statistics website *www.statistics.gov.uk/statbase/Product.asp?vlnk=1904*.

Source: Office for National Statistics: 020 7014 2116

16.15 Household final consumption expenditure: by purpose[1]
Chained volume measures, reference year 2003

United Kingdom

£ million

		2000	2001	2002	2003	2004	2005	2006	2007	2008
Durable goods										
Furnishings, household equipment and routine maintenance of the house	LLME	18 442	19 542	20 603	21 595	21 974	22 325	22 753	23 212	22 492
Health	LLMF	2 455	2 337	2 421	2 604	2 361	2 239	2 519	2 535	2 490
Transport	LLMG	31 680	35 100	36 057	38 016	38 962	39 617	40 792	42 622	40 622
Communication	LLMH	536	582	640	810	824	957	1 030	1 298	1 681
Recreation and culture	LLMI	11 243	13 344	14 911	17 752	21 053	25 553	30 063	36 478	44 580
Miscellaneous goods and services	LLMJ	3 618	3 932	4 360	4 284	4 636	4 493	4 821	4 791	4 656
Total durable goods	UTIC	67 366	74 551	78 825	85 061	89 810	95 184	101 978	110 936	116 521
Semi-durable goods										
Clothing and footwear	LLNG	30 969	33 712	37 727	40 389	43 400	45 405	47 006	49 275	52 145
Furnishings, household equipment and routine maintenance of the house	LLNH	11 473	12 221	13 215	13 932	13 507	13 679	14 364	14 079	13 430
Transport	LLNI	2 856	2 880	3 172	3 423	2 989	3 279	3 167	3 237	3 729
Recreation and culture	LLNJ	19 175	20 339	23 040	26 009	27 340	27 997	28 461	28 685	29 406
Miscellaneous goods and services	LLNK	2 053	2 438	2 920	3 356	3 489	3 196	3 315	3 408	3 072
Total semi-durable goods	UTIS	66 478	71 563	80 058	87 109	90 725	93 556	96 313	98 684	101 782
Non-durable goods										
Food & drink	ADIP	61 944	61 048	62 143	63 174	64 473	65 855	66 499	70 628	71 521
Alcohol & tobacco	ADIS	26 704	26 497	26 884	27 297	27 861	27 735	28 463	28 816	28 232
Housing, water, electricity, gas and other fuels	LLMS	23 189	23 958	23 881	24 241	26 157	25 521	24 932	24 446	24 451
Furnishings, household equipment and routine maintenance of the house	LLMT	2 666	2 878	3 101	3 338	4 033	4 025	4 108	4 027	3 852
Health	LLMU	3 397	3 686	3 895	3 938	4 473	4 583	4 577	4 618	4 791
Transport	LLMV	19 114	19 550	19 825	20 072	20 058	21 132	20 826	21 254	20 462
Recreation and culture	LLMW	13 657	13 537	13 681	13 507	13 794	14 102	14 282	14 493	14 297
Miscellaneous goods and services	LLMX	9 248	9 586	11 124	12 602	13 335	13 550	14 997	15 990	16 567
Total non-durable goods	UTIK	159 677	160 597	164 482	168 169	174 184	176 503	178 684	184 272	184 173
Total goods	UTIG	292 390	306 198	323 179	340 339	354 719	365 243	376 975	393 892	402 476
Services										
Clothing and footwear	LLMY	805	790	775	766	658	696	721	707	744
Housing, water, electricity, gas and other fuels	LLMZ	102 168	102 778	104 106	104 810	106 095	106 834	109 156	109 443	109 538
Furnishings, household equipment and routine maintenance of the house	LLNA	3 821	3 718	3 646	3 601	3 562	3 661	3 251	3 011	3 037
Health	LLNB	4 612	4 683	4 665	4 793	5 005	5 195	5 187	5 562	5 373
Transport	LLNC	43 153	40 971	42 611	43 058	43 872	44 357	45 288	45 537	46 169
Communication	LLND	12 167	13 877	14 158	14 844	15 837	16 547	16 787	17 901	18 436
Recreation and culture	LLNE	25 101	25 960	26 216	27 118	28 381	29 166	28 948	29 709	29 565
Education	ADMJ	11 489	10 692	10 091	9 610	10 591	10 717	10 832	11 001	10 532
Restaurants and hotels	ADMK	76 252	76 434	78 303	78 902	80 651	80 051	78 868	79 518	78 706
Miscellaneous goods and services	LLNF	69 846	72 526	73 631	74 609	74 702	77 207	78 887	80 539	83 189
Total services	UTIO	348 641	352 299	358 149	362 111	369 354	374 431	377 925	382 928	385 289
Final consumption expenditure in the UK by resident and non-resident households (domestic concept)	ABQJ	639 565	657 752	681 082	702 450	724 073	739 674	754 900	776 820	787 765
Final consumption expenditure outside the UK by UK resident households	ABTC	24 189	24 897	26 376	26 314	27 994	27 675	28 339	29 590	29 337
less Final consumption expenditure in the UK by households resident in the rest of the world	CCHX	−16 038	−14 164	−14 292	−14 156	−15 210	−16 061	−16 861	−16 728	−16 561
Final consumption expenditure by UK resident households in the UK and abroad (national concept)	ABPF	647 796	668 482	693 124	714 608	736 857	751 288	766 378	789 682	800 541

1 See chapter text. Additional detail is published in *Consumer Trends* and table A7 of *UK Economic Accounts*, available from the National Statistics website *www.statistics.gov.uk/statbase/Product.asp?vlnk=1904*.

Source: *Office for National Statistics: 020 7014 2116*

16.16 Individual consumption expenditure: by households, NPISHs and general government[1] Current market prices

United Kingdom. Classified by function (COICOP/COPNI/COFOG)[2]

£ million

		2000	2001	2002	2003	2004	2005	2006	2007	2008
FINAL CONSUMPTION EXPENDITURE OF HOUSEHOLDS										
Food and non-alcoholic beverages	ABZV	58 628	59 804	61 310	63 174	64 830	67 187	69 410	77 144	84 993
Food	ABZW	51 905	52 742	53 984	55 507	56 667	58 690	60 627	67 125	74 790
Non-alcoholic beverages	ADFK	6 723	7 062	7 326	7 667	8 163	8 497	8 783	10 019	10 203
Alcoholic beverages and tobacco	ADFL	24 617	25 158	25 966	27 297	28 101	28 437	30 061	30 947	31 120
Alcoholic beverages	ADFM	10 395	10 700	11 344	12 027	13 035	13 065	13 924	14 927	15 024
Tobacco	ADFN	14 222	14 458	14 622	15 270	15 066	15 372	16 137	16 020	16 096
Clothing and footwear	ADFP	35 479	36 822	39 092	41 155	42 796	43 759	45 002	46 688	47 507
Clothing	ADFQ	31 048	32 103	33 927	35 689	36 770	37 609	38 419	39 765	40 433
Footwear	ADFR	4 431	4 719	5 165	5 466	6 026	6 150	6 583	6 923	7 074
Housing, water, electricity, gas and other fuels	ADFS	108 050	115 905	121 238	129 051	138 044	147 322	159 696	169 582	180 309
Actual rentals for housing	ADFT	23 595	25 302	25 828	27 610	29 205	30 142	32 716	34 648	35 205
Imputed rentals for housing	ADFU	54 378	59 581	63 279	68 458	72 179	78 179	82 388	87 729	92 007
Maintenance and repair of the dwelling	ADFV	10 512	11 340	12 306	12 615	13 956	13 538	13 287	14 233	14 124
Water supply and miscellaneous dwelling services	ADFW	5 033	5 059	5 222	5 438	5 831	6 279	6 820	7 228	7 760
Electricity, gas and other fuels	ADFX	14 532	14 623	14 603	14 930	16 873	19 184	24 485	25 744	31 213
Furnishings, household equipment and routine maintenance of the house	ADFY	35 675	37 974	40 448	42 466	43 469	44 329	45 491	46 528	46 306
Furniture, furnishings, carpets and other floor coverings	ADFZ	13 758	14 362	15 591	16 789	17 168	17 309	17 702	18 813	18 597
Household textiles	ADGG	4 465	4 636	5 086	5 452	5 299	4 916	5 146	5 423	5 094
Household appliances	ADGL	5 156	5 758	5 715	5 578	6 028	6 391	6 704	6 729	6 698
Glassware, tableware and household utensils	ADGM	4 231	4 609	4 710	4 701	3 870	4 210	4 122	3 494	3 495
Tools and equipment for house and garden	ADGN	2 722	2 977	3 355	3 589	4 006	4 090	4 445	4 739	4 835
Goods and services for routine household maintenance	ADGO	5 343	5 632	5 991	6 357	7 098	7 413	7 372	7 330	7 587
Health	ADGP	9 208	9 976	10 778	11 335	12 029	12 306	12 744	13 498	13 659
Medical products, appliances and equipment	ADGQ	5 265	5 722	6 266	6 542	6 924	6 893	7 141	7 314	7 569
Out-patient services	ADGR	2 178	2 344	2 422	2 553	2 747	2 909	2 983	3 460	3 315
Hospital services	ADGS	1 765	1 910	2 090	2 240	2 358	2 504	2 620	2 724	2 775
Transport	ADGT	93 052	96 435	100 147	104 569	108 456	114 168	118 497	123 724	126 836
Purchase of vehicles	ADGU	33 291	35 864	36 574	38 016	38 643	38 361	39 047	40 886	37 707
Operation of personal transport equipment	ADGV	37 059	37 028	38 816	40 507	42 848	47 205	49 059	50 867	55 134
Transport services	ADGW	22 702	23 543	24 757	26 046	26 965	28 602	30 391	31 971	33 995
Communication	ADGX	13 356	14 157	14 675	15 654	16 794	17 208	17 432	18 016	18 266
Postal services	CDEF	873	870	878	890	961	1 017	1 005	1 045	924
Telephone & telefax equipment	ADWO	601	636	644	810	850	900	900	927	1 005
Telephone & telefax services	ADWP	11 882	12 651	13 153	13 954	14 983	15 291	15 527	16 044	16 337
Recreation and culture	ADGY	70 154	73 452	79 122	84 386	88 841	92 416	95 090	98 467	100 268
Audio-visual, photographic and information processing equipment	ADGZ	17 034	17 580	18 051	19 408	20 603	21 234	20 927	20 611	20 151
Other major durables for recreation and culture	ADHL	3 944	4 325	4 672	5 126	5 271	5 711	6 019	6 148	6 606
Other recreational items and equipment; flowers, garden and pets	ADHZ	18 636	20 216	22 475	23 894	24 349	24 769	25 723	27 366	28 369
Recreational and cultural services	ADIA	20 272	21 034	23 555	25 278	27 313	28 830	30 272	32 138	33 328
Newspapers, books and stationery	ADIC	10 268	10 297	10 369	10 680	11 305	11 872	12 149	12 204	11 814
Package holidays[3]	ADID	–	–	–	–	–	–	–	–	–
Education										
Education services	ADIE	9 534	9 409	9 381	9 610	11 094	11 762	12 432	13 703	14 100
Restaurants and hotels	ADIF	68 557	71 620	76 426	78 902	82 476	84 808	86 729	90 549	93 248
Catering services	ADIG	59 019	62 449	66 701	68 839	72 399	74 294	75 501	78 249	80 094
Accommodation services	ADIH	9 538	9 171	9 725	10 063	10 077	10 514	11 228	12 300	13 154
Miscellaneous goods and services	ADII	83 307	87 542	91 818	94 851	98 632	104 604	110 198	118 423	120 548
Personal care	ADIJ	13 883	14 626	16 444	18 181	19 538	20 022	21 020	22 623	22 990
Personal effects not elsewhere classified	ADIK	4 748	5 455	6 140	6 462	6 819	6 647	7 652	7 986	8 292
Social protection	ADIL	8 643	8 963	9 219	9 501	8 745	8 918	9 452	10 136	11 230
Insurance	ADIM	22 238	25 423	25 456	24 373	23 345	25 407	25 100	28 367	29 396
Financial services not elsewhere classified	ADIN	27 706	26 990	28 384	29 977	33 173	35 758	39 289	41 657	40 582
Other services not elsewhere classified	ADIO	6 089	6 085	6 175	6 357	7 012	7 852	7 685	7 654	8 058
Final consumption expenditure in the UK by resident and non-resident households (domestic concept)	ABQI	609 617	638 254	670 401	702 450	735 562	768 306	802 782	847 269	877 160
Final consumption expenditure outside the UK by UK resident households	ABTA	21 654	22 907	24 435	26 314	27 550	29 028	30 389	31 702	33 325
less Final consumption expenditure in the UK by households resident in the rest of the world	CDFD	–14 713	–13 383	–13 872	–14 156	–15 610	–17 069	–18 512	–18 991	–19 483
Final consumption expenditure by UK resident households in the UK and abroad (national concept)	ABPB	616 558	647 778	680 964	714 608	747 502	780 265	814 659	859 980	891 002

16.16

continued

Individual consumption expenditure: by households, NPISHs and general government[1] Current market prices

United Kingdom. Classified by function (COICOP/COPNI/COFOG)[2]

£ million

		2000	2001	2002	2003	2004	2005	2006	2007	2008
FINAL CONSUMPTION EXPENDITURE OF UK RESIDENT HOUSEHOLDS										
Final consumption expenditure of UK resident households in the UK and abroad	ABPB	616 558	647 778	680 964	714 608	747 502	780 265	814 659	859 980	891 002
FINAL INDIVIDUAL CONSUMPTION EXPENDITURE OF NPISH										
Final individual consumption expenditure of NPISH	ABNV	23 531	25 111	26 422	27 668	28 748	30 402	32 209	34 409	37 550
FINAL INDIVIDUAL CONSUMPTION EXPENDITURE OF OF GENERAL GOVERNMENT										
Health	QYOT	53 236	58 032	63 388	69 888	76 855	83 579	85 331	..	..
Recreation and culture	QYSU	3 898	4 049	4 335	4 513	4 272	..	..	..	..
Education	QYSE	31 521	33 900	37 535	39 876	42 727	11 058	47 235	..	..
Social protection	QYSP	18 055	19 441	22 464	25 517	28 028	..	..	..	..
Housing	QYXO	–	–	–	..	..	..	..	..	..
Final individual consumption expenditure of general government	NNAQ	109 297	118 458	130 816	143 954	148 944	160 456	173 115	182 802	193 258
Total, individual consumption expenditure/ actual individual consumption	NQEO	749 386	791 347	838 202	886 230	925 194	971 123	1 019 983	1 077 191	1 121 810

1 See chapter text.

2 "Purpose" or "function" classifications are designed to indicate the "socio-economic objectives" that institutional units aim to achieve through various kinds of outlays. COICOP is the Classification of Individual Consumption by Purpose and applies to households. COPNI is the Classification of the Purposes of Non-Profit Institutions Serving Households and COFOG the Classification of the Functions of Government. The introduction of ESA95 coincides with the redefinition of these classifications and data will be available on a consistent basis for all European Union member states.

3 Package holidays data are dispersed between components (transport etc).

Source: Office for National Statistics: 020 7014 2116

16.17 Individual consumption expenditure: by households, NPISHs and general government[1] Chained volume measures, reference year 2003

United Kingdom. Classified by function (COICOP/COPNI/COFOG)[2]

£ million

		2000	2001	2002	2003	2004	2005	2006	2007	2008
FINAL CONSUMPTION EXPENDITURE OF HOUSEHOLDS										
Food and non-alcoholic beverages	ADIP	61 944	61 048	62 143	63 174	64 473	65 855	66 499	70 628	71 521
Food	ADIQ	55 255	53 992	54 835	55 507	56 240	57 305	57 969	61 282	62 255
Non-alcoholic beverages	ADIR	6 725	7 063	7 312	7 667	8 233	8 550	8 530	9 346	9 266
Alcoholic beverages and tobacco	ADIS	26 704	26 497	26 884	27 297	27 861	27 735	28 463	28 816	28 232
Alcoholic beverages	ADIT	10 476	10 831	11 516	12 027	13 204	13 331	14 005	15 056	14 888
Tobacco	ADIU	16 341	15 716	15 380	15 270	14 657	14 404	14 458	13 760	13 344
Clothing and footwear	ADIW	31 744	34 485	38 499	41 155	44 058	46 101	47 727	49 982	52 889
Clothing	ADIX	27 394	29 827	33 315	35 689	37 924	39 688	40 823	42 816	45 531
Footwear	ADIY	4 360	4 660	5 185	5 466	6 134	6 413	6 904	7 166	7 358
Housing, water, electricity, gas and other fuels	ADIZ	125 299	126 749	127 979	129 051	132 252	132 355	134 088	133 889	133 989
Actual rentals for housing	ADJA	27 345	27 418	27 084	27 610	27 933	27 644	29 071	28 877	28 721
Imputed rentals for housing	ADJB	65 704	66 495	67 872	68 458	69 438	70 672	71 154	71 518	72 147
Maintenance and repair of the dwelling	ADJC	11 675	12 139	12 702	12 615	13 581	12 793	12 115	12 400	11 673
Water supply and miscellaneous dwelling services	ADJD	5 386	5 379	5 424	5 438	5 537	5 429	5 521	5 505	5 553
Electricity, gas and other fuels	ADJE	15 149	15 277	14 891	14 930	15 763	15 817	16 227	15 589	15 895
Furnishings, household equipment and routine maintenance of the house	ADJF	36 305	38 310	40 552	42 466	43 076	43 690	44 476	44 329	42 811
Furniture, furnishings, carpets and other floor coverings	ADJG	14 514	14 860	15 896	16 789	16 751	16 425	16 419	16 795	15 775
Household textiles	ADJH	4 361	4 534	5 043	5 452	5 202	4 944	5 283	5 618	5 289
Household appliances	ADJI	4 922	5 549	5 566	5 578	6 059	6 527	7 033	6 886	6 801
Glassware, tableware and household utensils	ADJJ	4 266	4 655	4 717	4 701	3 866	4 317	4 231	3 554	3 464
Tools and equipment for house and garden	ADJK	2 590	2 856	3 238	3 589	4 136	4 293	4 611	4 837	4 886
Goods and services for routine household maintenance	ADJL	5 708	5 859	6 092	6 357	7 062	7 184	6 899	6 639	6 596
Health	ADJM	10 421	10 697	10 980	11 335	11 839	12 017	12 283	12 715	12 654
Medical products, appliances and equipment	ADJN	5 819	6 020	6 315	6 542	6 834	6 822	7 096	7 153	7 281
Out-patient services	ADJO	2 528	2 560	2 492	2 553	2 712	2 829	2 780	3 130	2 976
Hospital services	ADJP	2 082	2 122	2 173	2 240	2 293	2 366	2 407	2 432	2 397
Transport	ADJQ	96 209	98 485	101 621	104 569	105 881	108 385	110 073	112 650	110 982
Purchase of vehicles	ADJR	31 680	35 100	36 057	38 016	38 962	39 617	40 792	42 622	40 622
Operation of personal transport equipment	ADJS	39 124	39 225	40 668	40 507	40 508	41 553	40 907	40 790	40 240
Transport services	ADJT	25 913	24 214	24 965	26 046	26 411	27 215	28 374	29 238	30 120
Communication	ADJU	12 698	14 452	14 796	15 654	16 661	17 504	17 817	19 199	20 117
Postal services	CCGZ	916	901	906	890	932	1 034	1 120	1 293	1 294
Telephone & telefax equipment	ADQF	536	582	640	810	824	957	1 030	1 298	1 681
Telephone & telefax services	ADQG	11 264	12 978	13 254	13 954	14 905	15 513	15 667	16 608	17 142
Recreation and culture	ADJV	68 038	72 552	77 597	84 386	90 568	96 818	101 754	109 365	117 848
Audio-visual, photographic and information processing equipment	ADJW	13 022	14 690	16 301	19 408	23 041	27 358	30 782	36 317	43 900
Other major durables for recreation and culture	ADJX	4 182	4 560	4 817	5 126	5 117	5 419	5 678	5 835	6 256
Other recreational items and equipment; flowers, gardens and pets	ADJY	17 455	18 980	21 642	23 894	24 842	25 541	26 943	28 519	29 586
Recreational and cultural services	ADJZ	23 206	24 049	24 333	25 278	26 522	26 995	26 977	27 537	27 768
Newspapers, books and stationery	ADKM	11 181	10 910	10 756	10 680	11 046	11 505	11 374	11 157	10 338
Package holidays[3]	ADMI	–	–	–	–	–	–	–	–	–
Education										
Education services	ADMJ	11 489	10 692	10 091	9 610	10 591	10 717	10 832	11 001	10 532
Restaurants and Hotels	ADMK	76 252	76 434	78 303	78 902	80 651	80 051	78 868	79 518	78 706
Catering services	ADML	65 644	66 815	68 462	68 830	70 766	70 248	68 896	68 974	67 697
Accommodation services	ADMM	10 610	9 620	9 843	10 063	9 885	9 803	9 972	10 544	11 009
Miscellaneous goods and services	ADMN	84 709	88 415	92 015	94 851	96 162	98 446	102 020	104 728	107 484
Personal care	ADMO	14 251	14 719	16 526	18 181	19 451	19 747	21 035	22 020	22 099
Personal effects not elsewhere classified	ADMP	4 922	5 607	6 289	6 462	6 730	6 481	7 134	7 132	6 981
Social protection	ADMQ	10 357	10 058	9 760	9 501	8 416	8 062	8 013	8 259	8 775
Insurance	ADMR	23 526	25 453	24 880	24 373	22 633	23 523	24 125	24 935	25 295
Financial services not elsewhere classified	ADMS	24 666	25 875	28 040	29 977	32 391	33 760	35 338	36 247	38 169
Other services not elsewhere classified	ADMT	7 336	6 827	6 536	6 357	6 545	6 870	6 377	6 135	6 165
Final consumption expenditure in the UK by resident and non-resident households (domestic concept)	ABQJ	639 565	657 752	681 082	702 450	724 073	739 674	754 900	776 820	787 765
Final consumption expenditure outside the UK by UK resident households	ABTC	24 189	24 897	26 376	26 314	27 994	27 675	28 339	29 590	29 337
less Final consumption expenditure in the UK by households resident in the rest of the world	CCHX	–16 038	–14 164	–14 292	–14 156	–15 210	–16 061	–16 861	–16 728	–16 561
Final consumption expenditure by UK resident households in the UK and abroad (national concept)	ABPF	647 796	668 482	693 124	714 608	736 857	751 288	766 378	789 682	800 541

16.17
continued

Individual consumption expenditure: by households, NPISHs and general government[1] Chained volume measures, reference year 2003

United Kingdom. Classified by function (COICOP/COPNI/COFOG)[2]

£ million

		2000	2001	2002	2003	2004	2005	2006	2007	2008
FINAL CONSUMPTION EXPENDITURE OF UK RESIDENT HOUSEHOLDS										
Final consumption expenditure of UK resident households in the UK and abroad	ABPF	647 796	668 482	693 124	714 608	736 857	751 288	766 378	789 682	800 541
FINAL INDIVIDUAL CONSUMPTION EXPENDITURE OF NPISH										
Final individual consumption expenditure of NPISH	ABNU	27 536	27 567	27 576	27 668	27 198	27 212	28 289	29 485	29 802
FINAL INDIVIDUAL CONSUMPTION EXPENDITURE OF GENERAL GOVERNMENT										
Health	EMOA	58 517	61 019	63 272	65 611	68 758	..	..	..	..
Recreation and culture	QYXK	4 051	3 968	4 470	4 717	..	..	..	..	..
Education	EMOB	36 876	37 100	37 535	37 732	37 944	..	..	..	..
Social protection	QYXM	23 454	23 645	24 864	25 843	27 213	27 203	27 347	27 602	..
Housing	QYXN	–	–	–	–	..	..	..	..	..
Final individual consumption expenditure of general government	NSZK	111 763	114 159	117 238	120 288	..	..	..	..	..
Total, individual consumption expenditure/ actual individual consumption	YBIO	806 541	830 840	860 237	886 230	912 715	929 549	947 894	975 182	..

1 See chapter text.
2 "Purpose" or "function" classifications are designed to indicate the "soci-economic objectives" that institutional units aim to achieve through various kinds of outlays. COICOP is the Classification of Individual Consumption by Purpose and applies to households. COPNI is the Classification of the Purposes of Non-Profit Institutions Serving Households (NPISH) and COFOG the Classification of the Functions of Government. The introduction of ESA95 coincides with the redefinition of these classifications and data will be available on a consistent basis for all European Union member states.
3 Package holidays data are dispersed between components (transport etc).

Source: Office for National Statistics: 020 7014 2116

16.18

Change in inventories[1,2]
Chained volume measures, reference year 2003

United Kingdom

Reference year 2003, £ million

	Mining and quarrying	Manufacturing industries				Electricity, gas and water supply	Distributive trades		Other industries[4]	Change in inventories
		Materials and fuel	Work in progress	Finished goods	Total		Wholesale[3]	Retail[3]		
	FADO	FBID	FBIE	FBIF	DHBH	FADP	FAJM	FBYH	DLWV	ABMQ
1999	−325	503	−259	−430	−157	−167	1 743	1 722	3 464	5 803
2000	−263	543	358	418	1 318	202	1 939	1 480	−283	4 648
2001	87	−513	369	160	17	16	887	1 113	3 458	5 577
2002	−37	−496	−149	−372	−1 017	−132	788	1 716	971	2 289
2003	−66	−198	−650	−138	−986	−13	407	1 241	3 399	3 982
2004	−47	33	−592	−278	−837	8	304	1 000	3 943	4 371
2005	14	43	1 093	314	1 450	586	978	−412	2 198	4 814
2006	−14	265	1 152	395	1 812	222	490	677	1 388	4 575
2007	−105	377	−479	453	351	−275	72	1 862	4 542	6 448
2008	−65	−825	−468	−347	−1 640	855	826	−218	1 237	993

1 See chapter text. Estimates are given to the nearest £ million but cannot be regarded as accurate to this degree.
2 Components may not sum to totals due to rounding.
3 Wholesaling and retailing estimates exclude the motor trades.
4 Quarterly alignment adjustment included in this series.

Source: Office for National Statistics 020 7014 2083

16.19 Gross fixed capital formation at current purchasers' prices: by broad sector and type of asset[1,2]

United Kingdom. Total economy

£ million

		2000	2001	2002	2003	2004	2005	2006	2007	2008
Private sector										
New dwellings, excluding land	DFDF	25 604	27 085	31 455	34 804	40 927	43 845	49 273	51 745	45 910
Other buildings and structures	EQBU	31 966	32 730	33 580	35 366	33 227	36 372	38 047	44 001	..
Transport equipment	EQBV	12 859	13 897	15 637	14 708	13 135	13 818	14 199	14 714	..
Other machinery and equipment and cultivated assets	EQBW	61 236	58 062	53 498	50 228	55 138	56 347	58 339	64 735	..
Intangible fixed assets	EQBX	4 048	4 285	4 674	4 894	5 258	5 594	..	..	..
Costs associated with the transfer of ownership of non-produced assets	EQBY	11 174	12 697	15 399	16 385	20 739	19 940	24 611	26 400	14 211
Total	EQBZ	146 887	148 756	154 243	156 385	170 025	177 123	..	..	..
Public non-financial corporations										
New dwellings, excluding land	DEER	1 421	2 387	2 837	3 509	3 235	3 574	4 049	3 899	4 089
Other buildings and structures	DEES	1 775	1 854	2 304	2 236	1 493	2 111	1 830	1 587	..
Transport equipment	DEEP	178	171	110	126	193	334	181	175	..
Other machinery and equipment and cultivated assets	DEEQ	600	628	787	1 037	1 042	16 478	986	1 629	..
Intangible fixed assets	DLXJ	551	397	556	623	737	754	769	802	..
Costs associated with the transfer of ownership of non-produced assets	DLXQ	−2 171	−2 254	−2 764	−5 674	−5 440	−2 675	−2 375	−2 032	−1 112
Total	FCCJ	2 354	3 183	3 830	1 857	1 260	20 576	5 440	5 774	7 435
General government										
New dwellings, excluding land	DFHW	369	334	207	149	137	71	9	31	..
Other buildings and structures	EQCH	9 434	10 348	11 678	14 693	15 866	18 884	20 930	22 508	..
Transport equipment	EQCI	540	588	567	758	1 011	610	500	499	..
Other machinery and equipment and cultivated assets	EQCJ	1 699	2 239	2 867	3 176	3 652	−12 438	2 480	2 484	..
Intangible fixed assets	EQCK	367	334	358	384	400	304	418	339	..
Costs associated with the transfer of ownership of non-produced assets	EQCL	−182	−310	−225	1 349	2 153	−340	−670	−651	..
Total	NNBF	12 227	13 533	15 452	20 509	23 219	7 091	23 667	25 542	33 019
Total gross fixed capital formation	NPQX	167 172	171 782	180 551	186 700	200 672	211 318	227 920	247 823	240 722

1 See chapter text.
2 Components may not sum to totals due to rounding.

Source: Office for National Statistics: 020 7014 2083

16.20 Gross fixed capital formation at current purchasers' prices: by type of asset[1,2]

United Kingdom. Total economy

£ million

		2000	2001	2002	2003	2004	2005	2006	2007	2008
Tangible fixed assets										
New dwellings, excluding land	DFDK	27 394	29 806	34 499	38 462	44 299	47 490	53 331	55 647	50 013
Other buildings and structures	DLWS	43 175	44 932	47 562	52 295	50 586	57 367	60 807	68 096	..
Transport equipment	DLWZ	13 577	14 656	16 314	15 592	14 339	14 762	14 880	15 392	15 020
Other machinery and equipment and cultivated assets	DLXI	63 535	60 929	57 152	54 441	59 832	60 387	61 805	68 798	68 134
Total	EQCQ	147 081	150 323	155 527	160 790	169 056	180 006	190 823	209 130	..
Intangible fixed assets	DLXP	10 670	11 326	12 614	13 850	14 164	14 387	15 531	16 045	16 823
Costs associated with the transfer of ownership of non-produced assets	DFBH	8 821	10 133	12 410	12 060	17 452	16 925	21 566	24 053	..
Total gross fixed capital formation	NPQX	167 172	171 782	180 551	186 700	200 672	211 318	227 920	247 823	240 722

1 See chapter text.
2 Components may not sum to totals due to rounding.

Source: Office for National Statistics: 020 7014 2083

16.21 Gross fixed capital formation: by broad sector and type of asset[1,2,3]
Chained volume measures, reference year 2003
United Kingdom. Total economy

£ million

		2000	2001	2002	2003	2004	2005	2006	2007	2008
Private sector										
New dwellings, excluding land	DFDP	31 041	31 318	33 748	34 804	38 302	38 380	41 650	42 824	38 211
Other buildings and structures	EQCU	33 206	33 251	33 406	35 366	32 131	35 033	36 567	42 194	..
Transport equipment	EQCV	12 713	13 863	15 708	14 708	13 090	13 598	13 807	14 223	..
Other machinery and equipment and cultivated assets	EQCW	53 869	54 140	52 405	50 228	56 659	57 925	61 053	67 107	..
Intangible fixed assets	EQCX	10 702	11 228	11 680	12 843	13 023	13 072	13 881	14 091	..
Costs associated with the transfer of ownership of non-produced assets	EQCY	16 293	16 173	17 369	16 385	19 603	16 809	18 437	17 440	9 422
Total	EQCZ	158 347	160 569	164 304	164 334	172 808	174 817	185 395	199 693	..
Public non-financial corporations										
New dwellings, excluding land	DEEW	1 552	2 521	2 898	3 509	3 161	3 423	3 807	3 479	3 546
Other buildings and structures	DEEX	1 939	1 961	2 342	2 236	1 426	1 928	1 575	1 303	..
Transport equipment	DEEU	186	180	114	126	193	326	179	174	..
Other machinery and equipment and cultivated assets	DEEV	516	588	765	1 037	1 063	16 172	1 018	1 638	..
Intangible fixed assets	EQDE	586	415	572	623	714	711	703	701	..
Costs associated with the transfer of ownership of non-produced assets	EQDF	−3 093	−2 825	−3 092	−5 674	−5 561	−2 812	−1 869	−1 487	−823
Total	EQDG	1 695	2 424	3 019	1 857	996	19 748	5 413	5 772	..
General government										
New dwellings, excluding land	DFID	404	354	213	149	135	69	9	27	..
Other buildings and structures	EQDI	10 513	11 107	12 115	14 693	14 877	16 506	17 397	17 597	..
Transport equipment	EQDJ	606	672	696	758	809	751	813	826	..
Other machinery and equipment and cultivated assets	EQDK	1 424	2 063	2 801	3 176	3 757	−11 905	3 045	3 158	..
Intangible fixed assets	EQDL	219	196	211	384	397	294	394	313	..
Costs associated with the transfer of ownership of non-produced assets	EQDM	−542	−548	−261	1 349	2 004	−93	−321	−199	..
Total	EQDN	12 665	13 980	15 740	20 509	21 978	5 621	21 338	22 737	27 527
Total gross fixed capital formation	NPQR	173 710	178 203	184 701	186 700	195 782	200 187	212 146	226 469	219 524

1 See chapter text.
2 For the years before 2003, the total differs from the sum of their components.
3 Components may not sum to totals due to rounding.

Source: Office for National Statistics: 020 7014 2083

16.22 Gross fixed capital formation: by type of asset[1,2,3]
Chained volume measures, reference year 2003
United Kingdom. Total economy

£ million

		2000	2001	2002	2003	2004	2005	2006	2007	2008
Tangible fixed assets										
New dwellings, excluding land	DFDV	32 888	34 172	36 839	38 462	41 598	41 872	45 466	46 306	41 770
Other buildings and structures	EQDP	45 780	46 413	47 913	52 295	48 434	53 467	55 539	61 094	..
Transport equipment	DLWJ	13 489	14 698	16 414	15 592	14 092	14 675	14 799	15 211	14 188
Other machinery and equipment and cultivated assets	DLWM	55 774	56 780	55 971	54 441	61 479	62 192	65 116	72 252	70 473
Total	EQDS	148 509	152 571	157 257	160 790	165 602	172 205	180 921	195 763	..
Intangible fixed assets	EQDT	11 445	11 742	12 371	13 850	14 134	14 077	14 978	15 123	15 520
Costs associated with the transfer of ownership of non-produced assets	DFDW	12 810	12 960	14 097	12 060	16 046	13 904	16 247	16 319	..
Total gross fixed capital formation	NPQR	173 710	178 203	184 701	186 700	195 782	200 187	212 146	226 469	219 524

1 See chapter text.
2 For the years before 2003, the total differs from the sum of their components.
3 Components may not sum to totals due to rounding.

Source: Office for National Statistics: 020 7014 2083

Prices

Chapter 17

Prices

Producer price index numbers

(Tables 17.1 and 17.2)

The producer price indices (PPIs) were published for the first time in August 1983, replacing the former wholesale price indices. Full details of the differences between the two indices were given in an article published in *British Business*, 15 April 1983. The producer price indices are calculated using the same general methodology as that used by the wholesale price indices.

The high level index numbers in Tables 17.1 and 17.2 are constructed on a net sector basis. That is to say, they are intended to measure only transactions between the sector concerned and other sectors. Within sector transactions are excluded. Index numbers for the whole of manufacturing are thus not weighted averages of sector index numbers.

The index numbers for selected industries in Tables 17.1 and 17.2 are constructed on a gross sector basis, that is, all transactions are included in deriving the weighting patterns, including sales within the same industry.

All the index numbers are compiled exclusive of Value Added Tax (VAT). Excise duties on cigarettes, manufactured tobacco and alcoholic liquor are included, as is the duty on hydrocarbon oils.

The indices relate to the average prices for a year. The movement in these prices are weighted to reflect the relative importance of the composite products in a chosen year (known as the base year), currently 2005.

Since July 1995, PPIs have been published fully reclassified to the 1992 version of the Standard Industrial Classification (SIC).

Further details are available from the National Statistics website: www.statistics.gov.uk/ppi.

Purchasing power of the pound

(Table 17.3)

Changes in the internal purchasing power of a currency may be defined as the 'inverse' of changes in the levels of prices; when prices go up, the amount which can be purchased with a given sum of money goes down. Movements in the internal purchasing power of the pound are based on the consumers' expenditure deflator (CED) prior to 1962 and on the General index of retail prices (RPI) from January 1962 onwards. The

CED shows the movement in prices implied by the national accounts estimates of consumers' expenditure valued at current and at constant prices, while the RPI is constructed directly by weighting together monthly movements in prices according to a given pattern of household expenditure derived from the Expenditure and Food Survey. If the purchasing power of the pound is taken to be 100p in a particular month (quarter, year), the comparable purchasing power in a subsequent month (quarter, year) is:

$$100 \quad \times \quad \frac{\text{earlier period price index}}{\text{later period price index}}$$

where the price index used is the CED for years 1946–1961 and the RPI for periods after 1961.

Consumer prices index

(Table 17.4)

The Consumer Prices Index (CPI) is the main UK domestic measure of inflation for macro-economic purposes. Like the RPI (see below) it measures the average change from month to month in the prices of consumer goods and services purchased in the UK, but there are differences in coverage and methodology. A detailed description of these differences is given in the paper entitled 'The New Inflation Target: the Statistical Perspective'. This paper is available at: www.statistics.gov.uk/StatBase/Product.asp?vlnk=10913.

Since 10 December 2003, the Government inflation target for the UK has been defined in terms of the CPI measure of inflation. Prior to that the CPI had been published in the UK as the Harmonised Index of Consumer Prices (HICP); the two shall remain one and the same index.

The HICPs are calculated in each member state of the European Union (EU), according to rules specified in a series of European regulations developed by the EU statistical office in conjunction with the EU Member States. The HICPs are used to compare inflation rate across the EU. Since January 1999 it has also been used by the European Central Bank (ECB) as the measure of price stability across the euro area. Additional

information on HICPs is available at: www.statistics.gov.uk/hicp

Further details on the CPI are available from the Office for National Statistics website at: www.statistics.gov.uk/cpi

Retail prices index

(Table 17.5)

The Retail Prices Index (RPI) is the most familiar general purpose measure of inflation in the UK, measuring the percentage changes month by month in the average level of prices of the goods and services purchased by the great majority of households in the UK. The uses of the RPI include indexation of pensions, state benefits and index-linked gilts. The expenditure pattern on which the index is based is revised each year using information from the Expenditure and Food Survey. The expenditure of certain higher income households and households of retired people dependent mainly on social security benefits is excluded.

The index covers a large and representative selection of more than 650 separate goods and services, for which price movements are regularly measured in around 150 locations throughout the country. Around 120,000 separate price quotations are used in compiling the index.

Further details are available from the Office for National Statistics website: www.statistics.gov.uk/rpi

Tax and price index (TPI)

(Table 17.6)

The purpose and methodology of the TPI were described in an article in the August 1979 issue (No. 310) of *Economic Trends*. The TPI measures the change in gross taxable income needed for taxpayers to maintain their purchasing power, allowing for changes in retail prices. The TPI thus takes account of the changes to direct taxes (and employees' National Insurance (NI) contributions) facing representative cross-section of taxpayers as well as changes in the RPI.

When direct taxation or employees' NI contributions change, the TPI will rise by less than or more than the RPI according to the type of changes made. Between Budgets, the monthly increase in the TPI is normally slightly larger than that in the RPI, since all the extra income needed to offset any rise in retail prices is fully taxed.

Index numbers of agricultural prices

(Tables 17.7 and 17.8)

The indices of producer prices of agricultural products are currently based on the calendar year 2000. They are designed to provide short-term and medium-term indications of movements in these prices. All annual series are base-weighted Laspeyres type, using value weights derived from the *Economic Accounts for Agriculture* prepared for the Statistical Office of the European Union. Prices are measured exclusive of VAT. For Table 17.7, it has generally been necessary to measure the prices of materials (inputs) ex-supplier. For Table 17.8, it has generally been necessary to measure the prices received by producers (outputs) at the first marketing stage. The construction of the indices enables them to be combined with similar indices for other member countries of the EU to provide an overall indication of trends within the Union which appears in the Union's Eurostat series of publications.

Index numbers at a more detailed level and for earlier based series are available from the Department for Environment, Food and Rural Affairs, SSP, Room 146 Foss House, Kingspool 1–2 Peasholme Green, York, YO1 7PX, tel: +44 (0)1904 455249.

17.1 Producer price index of materials and fuels purchased: by all manufacturing and selected industries SIC(92)[1]

United Kingdom: Annual averages

Indices (2005=100)

			2001	2002	2003	2004	2005	2006	2007	2008
Net sector										
Materials and fuel purchased by manufacturing industry[2]	RNNK	6292000050	92.2	88.0	88.5	90.5	100.0	109.5	112.8	137.4#
Materials	PLKX	6292000010	94.2	89.9	90.5	92.3	100.0	107.3	111.5	134.7#
Fuels[2]	RNNL	6292000060	70.1	67.6	66.6	71.9	100.0	130.7	122.7	159.6
Materials and fuels purchased by manufacturing industry-seasonally adjusted[2]	RNPE	6292008950	98.8	94.4	95.7	99.5	111.0	121.8r	125.9#	..
Materials and fuels purchased by manufacturing industry other than food, beverages, petroleum and tobacco[2]	RNNQ	6292990050	99.4	94.6	93.3	93.8	100.0	106.9	109.3	127.4p
Materials	RWCJ	6292990010	102.6	97.6	96.1	96.1	100.0	104.5	108.0	124.1
Fuel[2]	RNNS	6292990060	70.2	67.8	66.7	72.0	100.0	130.8	123.2	159.8
Materials and fuels purchased by manufacturing industries other than food, beverages, petroleum and tobacco-seasonally adjusted[2]	RNPF	6292998950	99.4	94.7	93.3	93.9	100.0	107.0	109.4	127.3#
Gross sector[3]										
All manufacturing	RBBO	6192000000	94.7	92.6	93.3	95.1	100.0	105.7	109.1	122.0#
Other mining and quarrying products[4]	RABE	6112140000	97.8	93.2	95.9	95.2	100.0	105.3	106.5	121.7p
Manufacture of food products	RBBQ	6192151600	95.4	94.6	96.6	98.9	100.0	104.2	109.1	126.6p
Food products and beverages	RABF	6112150000	96.9	96.0	96.7	97.7	100.0	103.1	106.6	121.7p
Tobacco products	RABG	6112160000	91.4	92.5	96.5	99.8	100.0	105.3	111.1	129.3#
Manufacture of textiles	RBBR	6192171800	98.7	96.6	96.8	96.7	100.0	103.4	104.0	111.9p
Textiles	RABH	6112170000	97.0	95.2	97.2	96.6	100.0	103.6	105.8	121.2p
Wearing apparel	RABI	6112180000	95.1	92.7	93.5	94.6	100.0	105.8	112.5	129.0#
Manufacture of leather	RBBS	6192190000	99.3	97.5	97.9	97.8	100.0	103.2	104.6	114.4p
Manufacture of wood and wood products	RBBT	6192200000	96.8	94.2	93.8	96.1	100.0	104.7	113.3	121.0p
Manufacture of pulp, paper, publishing and printing	RBBU	6192212200	99.4	97.7	97.1	97.4	100.0	104.7	106.6	114.3p
Pulp and paper products	RABL	6112210000	102.4	99.1	97.2	96.9	100.0	106.2	108.2	117.8p
Printed matter and recording material	RABM	6112220000	97.9	96.9	97.2	97.7	100.0	103.7	105.5	111.9p
Manufacture of coke	RBBV	6192230000	60.1	58.2	62.1	71.6	100.0	116.8	120.3	169.5p
Manufacture of chemical products	RBBW	6192240000	93.0	91.5	93.4	94.5	100.0	106.7	107.7	121.8#
Manufacture of rubber products	RBBX	6192250000	94.9	93.5	94.0	95.4	100.0	107.1	112.2	123.3p
Manufacture of other non-metallic mineral products	RBBY	6192260000	94.8	93.9	94.5	95.6	100.0	104.1	105.3	121.3p
Manufacture of basic metals	RBBZ	6192272800	83.6	82.0	84.3	92.9	100.0	111.8	120.3	134.9#
Basic metals	RABV	6112270000	102.8	101.0	102.8	99.6	100.0	103.0	111.2	123.5p
Fabricated metal products	RABW	6112280000	92.1	90.1	91.9	93.4	100.0	105.7	109.6	122.6p
Manufacture of machinery and equipment not elsewhere classified	RBCA	6192290000	98.9	97.2	97.6	97.7	100.0	102.9	104.6	114.7p
Manufacture of electrical and optical equipment	RBCB	6192303300	117.5	111.8	104.4	99.5	100.0	103.2	102.7	107.6p
Office machinery and computers	RABY	6112300000	133.1	121.9	109.2	101.5	100.0	101.0	97.4	100.8p
Electrical machinery and apparatus not elsewhere classified	RACB	6112310000	103.8	100.9	97.8	96.9	100.0	106.2	108.5	115.4p
Radio, television and communication equipment	RACC	6112320000	117.0	112.8	106.2	100.5	100.0	102.0	101.4	105.4p
Medical, precision, optical instruments and clocks	RACD	6112330000	116.2	112.6	105.3	99.5	100.0	103.0	102.2	107.6p
Manufacture of transport equipment	RBCC	6192343500	97.4	95.6	96.0	96.7	100.0	104.1	107.1	113.7p
Motor vehicles, trailers and semi-trailers	RACE	6112340000	96.6	95.5	96.0	96.7	100.0	103.7	106.8	113.8p
Other transport equipment	RACF	6112350000	99.3	95.9	95.8	96.7	100.0	105.1	108.0	113.5p
Manufacturing not elsewhere classified	RBCD	6192363700	93.5	92.3	93.4	95.7	100.0	105.8	109.8	118.3p
Electricity including Climate Change Levy	RCVR	7167850000	75.5	72.5	70.0	74.7	100.0	135.9	138.2	166.2
Gas including Climate Change Levy	RCVW	7167860000	60.7	58.9	61.0	67.1	100.0	123.8	99.8	140.8
Collected and purified water	PQNB	7167870000	78.1	79.5	82.2	87.1	100.0	110.1	118.2	126.2

1 See chapter text.
2 These indices include the Climate Change Levy which was introduced in April 2001.
3 The Climate Change Levy is excluded from the detailed industry input index.
4 These indices include the Aggregates Levy which was introduced in April 2002.

Source: Office for National Statistics: 01633 815783

17.2 Producer price index of output: by all manufacturing and selected industries SIC(92)[1]

United Kingdom: Annual averages

Indices (2005=100)

			2001	2002	2003	2004	2005	2006	2007	2008
Net sector										
Output of manufactured products	PLLU	7209200000	95.8	95.8	96.8	98.2	100.0	102.2	104.8	112.5p
All manufacturing excluding duty	PVNP	7209200010	96.1	96.1	97.1	98.3	100.0	102.2	104.6	112.3p
All manufacturing excluding duty - seasonally adjusted	PVNQ	7209200890	99.7	99.8	101.2	103.7	106.8	109.7	113.0	..
Products of manufacturing industries other than the food, beverages, petroleum and tobacco manufacturing industries - not seasonally adjusted	PLLV	7209299000	98.0	98.0	98.6	99.1	100.0	101.8	103.7	108.6p
All manufacturing excluding food, beverages, tobacco and petroleum - seasonally adjusted	PLLW	7209299890	99.4	99.3	100.6	102.5	104.7	107.1	109.7	..
Gross sector										
Manufactured products excluding duty	POKE	7109200000	92.4	92.1	93.6	96.2	100.0	103.3	106.6	117.3
Manufactured products excluding food, drink, tobacco and petroleum	POKF	7109299000	95.1	95.0	96.0	97.8	100.0	102.7	105.9	111.8
Other mining and quarrying products[2]	ROFV	7112148000	83.9	96.8	99.6	99.7	100.0	101.9	105.5	120.7
Food products, beverages and tobacco excluding duty	POKH	7111151600	95.1	96.4	97.6	99.4	100.0	101.8	106.4	117.2
Food products, beverages and tobacco including duty	RBGA	7111151680	94.7	95.9	97.1	99.1	100.0	101.9	106.4	116.6
Food products and beverages including duty	RPUN	7112150080	95.6	96.6	97.6	99.5	100.0	101.6	106.1	116.9
Food products excluding beverages	RBGD	7112159900	95.9	96.8	97.8	99.6	100.0	101.5	106.1	117.9
Alcoholic beverages including duty	RPUX	7113159080	94.0	95.5	..	..	100.0	101.9	104.9	..
Tobacco products including duty	RPUS	7112160080	87.7	90.0	92.8	96.2	100.0	104.1	109.1	113.9
Textiles and textile products	POKI	7111171800	99.7	99.2	98.8	98.5	100.0	101.1	102.0	103.6
Textiles	POKZ	7112170000	98.7	98.5	98.3	98.0	100.0	101.3	102.4	104.4
Wearing apparel: Furs	POLA	7112100000	102.0	100.0	100.0	00.6	100.0	100.7	101.1	101.8
Leather and leather products	POKJ	7111190000	98.4	98.6	98.8	98.7	100.0	101.7	102.7	103.3
Wood and wood products	POKK	7111200000	92.6	92.7	93.9	96.1	100.0	102.5	111.4	116.1
Pulp, paper and paper products, recorded media and printing services	POKL	7111212200	95.7	96.3	98.0	99.1	100.0	101.7	103.6	106.7
Pulp, paper and paper products	POLD	7112210000	103.2	102.4	102.2	101.5	100.0	101.6	105.0	108.6
Printed matter and recorded media	POLE	7112220000	93.3	94.3	96.6	98.3	100.0	101.8	103.2	106.1
Chemicals, chemical, products and manmade fibres	POKN	7111240000	94.3	94.6	96.9	98.0	100.0	103.4	105.7	117.2
Rubber and plastic products	POKO	7111250000	95.7	95.8	95.8	96.3	100.0	103.0	104.3	109.1
Other non-metallic mineral products	POKP	7111260000	90.5	93.2	95.5	96.9	100.0	103.4	108.5	114.0
Base metals and fabricated metal products	POKQ	7111272800	87.6	87.3	88.4	93.5	100.0	105.4	111.1	118.8
Base metals	POLJ	7112270000	80.9	78.9	99.2	113.1	126.6	141.5	154.9	..
Fabricated metal products, except machinery and equipment	POLK	7112280000	90.0	90.4	91.3	94.4	100.0	102.6	106.8	113.1
Machinery and equipment not elsewhere classified	POKR	7111290000	95.6	96.4	96.4	97.5	100.0	102.0	105.5	109.0
Electrical and optical equipment	POKS	7111343500	111.6	106.1	103.0	100.5	100.0	101.2	101.1	102.9
Office machinery and computers	POLM	7112300000	165.9	142.5	127.0	108.9	100.0	95.0	87.8	85.1
Electrical machinery and apparatus not elsewhere classified	POLN	7112310000	95.6	96.1	96.2	97.5	100.0	104.4	107.7	111.4
Radio, television and communication equipment and apparatus	POLO	7112320000	130.2	117.7	110.6	104.8	100.0	98.5	94.2	91.2
Medical precision and optical instruments, watches and clocks	POLP	7112330000	97.2	98.4	99.3	99.4	100.0	100.7	100.8	103.8
Transport equipment	POKT	7111343500	96.6	96.9	97.3	98.2	100.0	101.5	102.5	106.8
Motor vehicles, trailers and semi-trailers	POLQ	7112340000	99.0	98.7	98.3	98.7	100.0	100.9	101.0	105.0
Other transport	POLR	7112350000	92.0	93.3	95.3	97.2	100.0	102.5	105.3	110.1
Furniture: other manufactured goods not elsewhere classified	POLS	7112360000	97.4	97.9	100.5	100.3	100.0	100.9	102.9	106.4

1 See chapter text.
2 These indices include the Aggregates Levy which was introduced in April 2002. These indices do not feed into Net Sector output (PLLU).

Source: Office for National Statistics: 01633 815783

17.3 Internal purchasing power of the pound[1,2]
United Kingdom

Pence

	Year in which purchasing power was 100p																			
	1989	1990	1991	1992	1993	1994	1995	1996	1997	1998	1999	2000	2001	2002	2003	2004	2005	2006	2007	2008
	BAMV	BAMW	BASX	CZVM	CBXX	DOFX	DOHR	DOLM	DTUL	CDQG	JKZZ	ZMHO	IKHI	FAUI	SEZH	C687	E9AO	GB4Y	HT4R	J5TL
1989	100	109	116	120	122	125	129	133	137	141	144	148	150	153	157	162	167	172	179	186
1990	91	100	106	110	112	114	118	121	125	129	131	135	137	140	144	148	152	157	164	170
1991	86	94	100	104	105	108	112	114	118	122	124	128	130	132	136	140	144	148	155	161
1992	83	91	96	100	102	104	108	110	114	118	119	123	125	127	131	135	139	143	149	155
1993	82	90	95	98	100	102	106	109	112	116	118	121	123	125	129	133	136	141	147	153
1994	80	88	93	96	98	100	103	106	109	113	115	118	120	122	126	130	133	137	143	149
1995	77	85	90	93	94	97	100	102	106	109	111	114	116	118	122	125	129	133	139	144
1996	75	83	87	91	92	94	98	100	103	107	108	112	113	115	119	122	126	130	135	141
1997	73	80	85	88	89	92	95	97	100	103	105	108	110	112	115	119	122	126	131	136
1998	71	77	82	85	86	88	92	94	97	100	102	105	106	108	111	115	118	122	127	132
1999	70	76	81	84	85	87	90	92	95	98	100	103	105	107	110	113	116	120	125	130
2000	68	74	78	81	83	85	88	90	92	96	97	100	102	103	106	110	113	116	121	126
2001	66	73	77	80	81	83	86	88	91	94	95	98	100	102	105	108	111	114	119	124
2002	65	72	76	79	80	82	85	87	89	92	94	97	98	100	103	106	109	112	117	122
2003	64	70	74	76	78	79	82	84	87	90	91	94	96	97	100	103	106	109	114	118
2004	62	68	72	74	75	77	80	82	84	87	89	91	93	94	97	100	103	106	111	115
2005	60	66	70	72	73	75	78	80	82	85	86	89	90	92	94	97	100	103	108	112
2006	58	64	67	70	71	73	75	77	80	82	83	86	87	89	92	94	97	100	104	108
2007	56	61	65	67	68	70	72	74	76	79	80	82	84	85	88	90	93	96	100	104
2008	54	59	62	64	65	67	69	71	73	76	77	79	81	82	84	87	89	92	96	100

1 See chapter text. These figures are calculated by taking the inverse ratio of
  the respective annual averages of the Retail Prices Index (RPI).
2 To find the purchasing power of the pound in 1995, given that it was 100
  pence in 1990, select the column headed 1990 and look at the 1995 row.
  The result is 85 pence.

Source: Office for National Statistics: 020 7533 5874

17.4 Consumer Prices Index:[1] detailed figures by division
United Kingdom

Indices (2005=100)

	Food and non-alcoholic beverages	Alcoholic beverages and tobacco	Clothing and footwear	Housing, water, electric-ity, gas & other fuels	Furniture, household equipment & routine mainte-nance	Health	Transport	Commun-ication	Recreation and culture	Education	Restaur-ants and hotels	Miscell-aneous goods and services	CPI (overall index)
COICOP Division	01	02	03	04	05	06	07	08	09	10	11	12	
Weights 2006	102	44	65	108	73	24	155	25	147	17	134	106	1000
	D7BU	D7BV	D7BW	D7BX	D7BY	D7BZ	D7C2	D7C3	D7C4	D7C5	D7C6	D7C7	D7BT
2006 Sep	103.6	103.7	96.4	111.5	100.6	103.6	102.9	99.6	98.6	107.9	103.8	104.7	103.0
Oct	104.2	103.9	96.6	112.7	99.0	104.2	101.5	100.4	98.6	117.8	104.2	105.0	103.2
Nov	105.1	103.4	97.2	113.7	100.0	104.1	101.1	100.3	98.7	117.8	104.5	105.0	103.4
Dec	105.4	103.0	96.0	114.5	103.3	104.2	102.8	99.9	99.2	117.8	104.7	104.9	104.0
2007 Jan	104.4	104.5	92.0	114.9	98.3	104.8	102.1	99.0	98.3	117.8	104.9	105.1	103.2
Feb	105.4	105.1	91.9	115.1	99.6	104.9	102.8	98.1	98.4	117.8	105.2	105.8	103.7
Mar	106.0	105.6	92.8	115.0	102.9	104.8	103.1	98.1	98.2	117.8	105.7	106.2	104.2
Apr	106.2	107.0	93.7	115.7	100.7	105.5	104.5	97.2	98.3	117.8	106.3	105.8	104.5
May	106.7	106.8	93.7	115.0	101.8	105.8	106.1	96.6	98.0	117.8	106.6	105.7	104.8
Jun	107.3	107.1	93.6	114.5	104.0	106.1	106.8	96.1	97.6	117.8	106.9	105.8	105.0
Jul	105.5	106.9	89.8	114.3	99.7	106.6	108.0	94.8	97.0	117.8	107.2	106.1	104.4
Aug	106.1	107.0	91.1	114.0	100.3	106.8	108.6	97.2	97.5	117.8	107.4	105.6	104.7
Sep	107.4	107.1	92.5	114.0	102.1	107.1	105.7	96.6	97.6	122.9	107.6	105.8	104.8
Oct	109.1	106.8	92.5	114.3	100.8	107.5	106.6	96.2	97.7	133.2	107.9	106.4	105.3
Nov	110.1	106.4	92.9	114.6	101.6	107.3	107.0	96.3	97.6	133.2	108.0	106.6	105.6
Dec	111.1	105.7	92.2	114.7	104.2	107.6	108.7	96.2	98.0	133.2	108.3	106.8	106.2
2008 Jan	110.8	106.9	87.5	115.4	100.0	108.1	108.6	95.8	97.0	133.2	100.3	106.8	105.5
Feb	111.3	108.1	87.6	119.1	101.3	108.2	109.1	94.3	97.2	133.2	108.7	107.1	106.3
Mar	111.8	108.2	87.9	119.5	103.5	108.4	110.3	94.2	96.8	133.2	109.2	107.5	106.7
Apr	113.2	111.5	87.8	122.0	102.1	108.9	110.8	94.4	97.3	133.2	110.4	108.3	107.6
May	115.1	112.0	87.8	122.3	103.5	109.0	112.7	94.3	97.3	133.2	110.8	108.5	108.3
Jun	117.5	111.9	86.5	122.5	105.9	109.3	114.6	94.9	97.6	133.2	111.1	108.6	109.0
Jul	118.4	111.4	83.8	123.0	102.6	110.1	116.6	94.1	96.9	133.2	111.6	109.0	109.0
Aug	120.0	111.8	84.9	125.6	103.4	110.3	116.5	94.3	97.3	133.2	111.7	109.2	109.7
Sep	119.6	111.7	86.8	131.1	105.1	110.2	113.8	94.1	97.8	136.2	112.2	109.4	110.3
Oct	120.1	111.4	86.3	131.6	104.0	110.4	111.3	94.1	97.4	144.6	112.5	109.6	110.0
Nov	121.8	110.6	86.3	131.5	104.7	111.0	108.4	94.8	97.6	144.6	112.5	110.1	109.9
Dec	122.7	110.4	82.7	131.1	105.0	109.9	108.9	92.9	96.8	144.6	112.2	109.6	109.5

Percentage change on a year earlier

	D7G8	D7G9	D7GA	D7GB	D7GC	D7GD	D7GE	D7GF	D7GG	D7GH	D7GI	D7GJ	D7G7
2007 Jan	3.9	3.5	−4.1	11.2	0.5	3.8	0.9	−1.8	−0.3	14.0	3.3	3.1	2.7
Feb	4.4	4.2	−4.2	11.1	1.2	3.7	1.4	−2.8	−1.0	14.0	3.3	3.6	2.8
Mar	5.6	4.4	−3.9	10.1	2.7	3.7	1.6	−2.8	−0.7	14.0	3.4	3.7	3.1
Apr	6.0	4.5	−2.8	7.9	2.2	3.2	1.5	−3.7	−0.8	14.0	3.8	2.4	2.8
May	5.0	4.2	−3.6	5.7	2.5	3.1	2.5	−3.2	−0.8	14.0	3.5	2.2	2.5
Jun	4.8	3.4	−3.2	4.3	3.8	3.4	3.2	−3.9	−1.1	14.0	3.7	1.8	2.4
Jul	2.8	3.4	−2.6	3.5	1.6	3.4	2.4	−5.0	−1.4	14.0	3.6	2.0	1.9
Aug	3.0	3.1	−3.5	2.8	1.2	3.3	2.6	−2.0	−0.9	14.0	3.6	1.1	1.8
Sep	3.7	3.2	−4.0	2.3	1.5	3.4	2.7	−3.0	−1.0	13.9	3.7	1.0	1.8
Oct	4.7	2.7	−4.3	1.4	1.8	3.2	5.1	−4.2	−0.9	13.2	3.5	1.3	2.1
Nov	4.8	2.9	−4.4	0.8	1.7	3.1	5.8	−4.0	−1.1	13.2	3.4	1.6	2.1
Dec	5.4	2.7	−3.9	0.2	0.9	3.3	5.8	−3.8	−1.3	13.2	3.4	1.9	2.1
2008 Jan	6.1	2.2	−4.9	0.4	1.7	3.1	6.4	−3.2	−1.4	13.2	3.3	1.5	2.2
Feb	5.6	2.9	−4.7	3.5	1.7	3.1	6.2	−3.9	−1.2	13.2	3.3	1.2	2.5
Mar	5.5	2.5	−5.3	3.9	0.5	3.5	7.0	−4.0	−1.5	13.2	3.3	1.2	2.5
Apr	6.6	4.2	−6.3	5.4	1.4	3.3	6.1	−2.9	−1.0	13.2	3.8	2.3	3.0
May	7.8	4.9	−6.3	6.3	1.7	3.0	6.2	−2.4	−0.8	13.2	3.9	2.6	3.3
Jun	9.5	4.5	−7.5	7.0	1.8	3.0	7.3	−1.3	–	13.2	3.9	2.7	3.8
Jul	12.3	4.3	−6.7	7.6	2.8	3.3	8.0	−0.7	−0.1	13.2	4.1	2.8	4.4
Aug	13.0	4.4	−6.7	10.1	3.2	3.2	7.3	−3.0	−0.2	13.2	4.0	3.4	4.7
Sep	11.3	4.3	−6.2	15.0	2.9	2.9	7.6	−2.7	0.2	10.8	4.3	3.4	5.2
Oct	10.1	4.4	−6.7	15.2	3.1	2.6	4.3	−2.2	−0.2	8.6	4.2	3.0	4.5
Nov	10.6	4.0	−7.1	14.8	3.0	3.5	1.3	−1.5	–	8.6	4.1	3.3	4.1
Dec	10.4	4.4	−10.3	14.3	0.8	2.1	0.1	−3.4	−1.2	8.6	3.6	2.6	3.1
2009 Jan	..	..	..	..	..	..	..	..	..	..	..	..	3.0
Feb	..	..	..	..	..	..	..	..	..	..	..	..	3.2
Mar	..	..	..	..	..	..	..	..	..	..	..	..	2.9
Apr	..	..	..	..	..	..	..	..	..	..	..	..	2.3

1 See chapter text. Prior to 10 December 2003, the consumer prices index (CPI) was published in the UK as the harmonised index of consumer prices (HICP).

Source: Office for National Statistics: 020 7533 5874

Prices

17.5 Retail Prices Index[1]
United Kingdom

Indices (13 January 1987=100)

| | All items (RPI) | All items excluding | | | | | Food and catering | Alcohol and tobacco | Housing and household expenditure | Personal expenditure | Travel and leisure | Consumer durables | All items excluding mortgage interest payments & indirect taxes (RPIY)[3] |
		mortgage interest payments (RPIX)	mortgage interest payments and depreciation	housing	food	seasonal food[2]							
Weights													
	CZGU	CZGY	DOGZ	CZGX	CZGV	CZGW	CBVV	CBVW	CBVX	CBVY	CBVZ	CBWA	
2000	1 000	960	924	805	882	982	170	95	355	101	279	126	
2001	1 000	954	914	795	884	982	169	97	362	96	276	125	
2002	1 000	964	924	801	886	980	166	99	363	94	278	126	
2003	1 000	961	919	797	891	983	160	98	365	92	285	126	
2004	1 000	961	914	791	889	981	160	97	367	93	283	121	
2005	1 000	950	901	776	890	981	159	96	387	89	269	122	
2006	1 000	950	906	778	895	983	155	96	392	90	267	117	
2007	1 000	945	895	762	895	981	152	95	408	83	262	109	
2008	1 000	940	885	746	889	980	158	86	417	83	256	104	
Annual averages													
	CHAW	CHMK	CHON	CHAZ	CHAY	CHAX	CHBS	CHBT	CHBU	CHBV	CHBW	CHBY	CBZW
2000	170.3	167.7	166.4	161.3	175.1	171.4	156.7	210.3	176.2	137.2	170.3	108.0	159.9
2001	173.3	171.3	169.5	163.7	178.0	174.3	162.2	216.9	180.0	135.7	172.0	105.0	163.7
2002	176.2	175.1	172.5	166.0	181.1	177.2	164.8	222.3	184.6	133.2	174.2	101.9	167.5
2003	181.3	180.0	176.2	168.9	186.7	182.4	167.9	228.0	194.3	133.2	177.0	99.8	172.0
2004	186.7	184.0	179.1	170.9	192.8	187.9	170.0	233.6	207.4	131.5	178.1	97.7	175.5
2005	192.0	188.2	182.6	173.7	198.7	193.3	172.9	239.8	219.4	131.0	179.2	95.3	179.4
2006	198.1	193.7	187.8	178.3	205.2	199.5	176.9	247.1	231.8	131.7	181.1	94.0	184.8
2007	206.6	199.9	193.3	183.2	213.9	207.9	184.3	256.2	248.1	132.9	183.8	93.3	190.8
2008	214.8	208.5	201.9	191.3	221.2	216.0	198.5	266.7	258.6	132.4	189.0	91.6	199.2
Monthly figures													
2005 Dec	194.1	190.2	184.5	175.5	201.0	195.5	174.1	241.6	224.5	131.9	179.0	97.0	181.5
2006 Jan	193.4	189.4	183.7	174.5	200.3	194.8	174.1	242.5	223.0	129.1	179.4	92.4	180.7
Feb	194.2	190.1	184.4	175.2	201.0	195.6	174.9	242.8	224.0	130.0	179.9	93.5	181.4
Mar	195.0	190.8	185.2	176.0	202.0	196.4	174.3	243.8	225.8	131.1	180.0	95.1	182.2
Apr	196.5	192.3	186.7	177.0	203.8	198.0	174.2	245.8	228.3	131.7	181.6	93.6	183.2
May	197.7	193.6	187.8	178.2	204.9	199.1	176.1	246.8	230.0	132.7	182.1	94.3	184.5
Jun	198.5	194.2	188.4	178.9	205.7	199.8	176.8	248.3	231.6	132.6	181.9	94.7	185.2
Jul	198.5	194.2	188.3	178.7	205.6	199.9	177.1	248.3	231.5	129.4	183.3	91.8	185.2
Aug	199.2	194.9	188.9	179.3	206.4	200.7	177.6	249.1	232.6	131.3	183.3	93.0	186.0
Sep	200.1	195.3	189.2	179.6	207.4	201.5	178.1	249.2	235.9	133.0	181.2	94.8	186.4
Oct	200.4	195.5	189.3	179.7	207.5	201.7	179.1	249.7	237.3	133.4	179.6	93.7	186.7
Nov	201.1	196.2	190.0	180.4	208.2	202.4	180.2	249.6	238.7	133.7	179.8	94.5	187.5
Dec	202.7	197.4	191.2	181.7	210.1	204.1	180.6	249.4	242.7	132.9	181.0	96.7	188.6
2007 Jan	201.6	196.1	189.8	180.0	208.9	203.0	180.0	251.3	240.6	130.1	180.8	91.1	187.3
Feb	203.1	197.1	190.7	181.1	210.4	204.4	181.2	252.4	243.0	131.3	181.4	92.1	188.4
Mar	204.4	198.3	191.9	182.4	211.7	205.7	182.1	253.8	245.3	132.5	181.6	95.1	189.5
Apr	205.4	199.3	192.9	182.7	212.8	206.8	182.7	256.8	245.7	133.8	183.1	93.5	190.0
May	206.2	200.0	193.6	183.4	213.6	207.5	183.6	257.0	246.5	134.0	184.3	94.4	190.7
Jun	207.3	200.7	194.1	184.0	214.7	208.6	184.5	257.5	248.9	133.9	184.5	95.8	191.4
Jul	206.1	199.4	192.7	182.2	213.7	207.6	182.7	257.6	247.2	131.2	184.7	91.0	190.1
Aug	207.3	200.1	193.3	182.9	215.0	208.7	183.5	257.9	249.4	132.2	185.2	91.9	190.9
Sep	208.0	200.8	193.8	183.5	215.5	209.4	185.2	258.2	251.3	133.7	183.7	93.7	191.6
Oct	208.9	201.6	194.6	184.3	216.2	210.2	187.3	257.7	251.9	134.1	184.7	92.8	192.3
Nov	209.7	202.4	195.4	185.1	216.9	211.0	188.8	257.3	253.0	134.3	185.4	93.2	193.2
Dec	210.9	203.5	196.6	186.3	218.0	212.2	190.2	256.9	254.8	134.0	186.8	94.8	194.4
2008 Jan	209.8	202.7	195.7	185.2	216.8	211.1	190.2	258.0	252.6	130.7	186.7	89.8	193.5
Feb	211.4	204.3	197.3	187.0	218.5	212.8	191.0	260.2	255.5	132.0	187.2	91.2	195.2
Mar	212.1	205.3	198.5	188.2	219.2	213.5	191.7	261.2	256.0	133.0	188.0	92.6	196.3
Apr	214.0	207.2	200.4	189.6	221.1	215.3	193.7	267.9	258.0	133.4	188.9	91.7	197.5
May	215.1	208.7	201.9	191.2	221.9	216.3	196.0	268.9	258.3	133.5	190.7	92.7	199.0
Jun	216.8	210.4	203.7	193.2	223.3	218.0	199.2	269.1	260.2	132.8	192.9	94.4	200.8
Jul	216.5	210.0	203.3	192.8	222.7	217.7	200.6	268.7	258.3	130.9	194.1	90.2	200.4
Aug	217.2	210.6	204.0	193.5	223.2	218.4	202.4	269.2	260.2	132.1	192.6	90.8	201.2
Sep	218.4	211.8	205.4	194.8	224.7	219.7	202.3	269.6	264.3	133.7	191.0	92.6	202.4
Oct	217.7	211.1	204.8	194.0	223.8	218.9	203.1	269.7	264.2	133.3	188.5	91.3	201.7
Nov	216.0	210.2	204.1	193.2	221.3	217.0	205.5	268.8	261.6	133.6	184.3	91.6	200.8
Dec	212.9	209.2	203.3	192.4	217.5	213.7	206.2	268.7	254.5	130.1	183.1	90.8	201.9

1 See chapter text.
2 Seasonal food is defined as items of food the prices of which show significant seasonal variations. These are fresh fruit and vegetables, fresh fish, eggs and home-killed lamb.

3 There are no weights available for RPIY.

Source: Office for National Statistics: 020 7533 5874

17.6 Tax and Price Index[1]
United Kingdom

Tax and Price Index: (January 1988=100)

DQAB

	1994	1995	1996	1997	1998	1999	2000	2001	2002	2003	2004	2005	2006	2007	2008
January	132.1	137.2	141.6	143.6	147.1	150.5	152.7	156.7	156.5	161.4	166.9	172.1	175.9	183.3	190.7
February	132.9	138.2	142.3	144.2	147.9	150.8	153.7	157.6	157.0	162.3	167.6	172.8	176.7	184.8	192.3
March	133.4	138.8	143.0	144.6	148.4	151.2	154.6	157.8	157.7	163.0	168.4	173.7	177.4	186.1	192.9
April	135.3	140.3	141.7	143.8	149.7	151.2	155.7	156.3	158.6	164.9	168.9	174.1	178.3	186.3	192.2
May	135.8	141.0	142.0	144.4	150.6	151.7	156.3	157.4	159.1	165.2	169.7	174.5	179.5	187.1	193.4
June	135.8	141.2	142.1	145.0	150.5	151.7	156.7	157.6	159.1	165.0	170.0	174.7	180.3	188.2	195.1
July	135.1	140.4	141.5	145.0	150.1	151.1	156.1	156.5	158.8	165.0	170.0	174.7	180.3	187.0	194.8
August	135.8	141.3	142.2	146.0	150.8	151.5	156.1	157.2	159.3	165.4	170.6	175.1	181.0	188.2	195.5
September	136.1	142.0	143.0	146.9	151.5	152.3	157.3	157.8	160.6	166.3	171.3	175.6	181.9	188.9	196.7
October	136.4	141.2	143.0	147.1	151.6	152.6	157.2	157.5	160.9	166.4	171.8	175.8	182.2	189.8	196.0
November	136.5	141.2	143.1	147.2	151.5	152.8	157.7	156.8	161.2	166.5	172.2	176.1	182.8	190.6	194.3
December	137.2	142.1	143.6	147.6	151.5	153.4	157.8	156.6	161.5	167.3	173.1	176.6	184.4	191.8	191.2

Retail Prices Index: (January 1988=100)

CHAW

	1994	1995	1996	1997	1998	1999	2000	2001	2002	2003	2004	2005	2006	2007	2008
January	141.3	146.0	150.2	154.4	159.5	163.4	166.6	171.1	173.3	178.4	183.1	188.9	193.4	201.6	209.8
February	142.1	146.9	150.9	155.0	160.3	163.7	167.5	172.0	173.8	179.3	183.8	189.6	194.2	203.1	211.4
March	142.5	147.5	151.5	155.4	160.8	164.1	168.4	172.2	174.5	179.9	184.6	190.5	195.0	204.4	212.1
April	144.2	149.0	152.6	156.3	162.6	165.2	170.1	173.1	175.7	181.2	185.7	191.6	196.5	205.4	214.0
May	144.7	149.6	152.9	156.9	163.5	165.6	170.7	174.2	176.2	181.5	186.5	192.0	197.7	206.2	215.1
June	144.7	149.8	153.0	157.5	163.4	165.6	171.1	174.4	176.2	181.3	186.8	192.2	198.5	207.3	216.8
July	144.0	149.1	152.4	157.5	163.0	165.1	170.5	173.3	175.9	181.3	186.8	192.2	198.5	206.1	216.5
August	144.7	149.9	153.1	158.5	163.7	165.5	170.5	174.0	176.4	181.6	187.4	192.6	199.2	207.3	217.2
September	145.0	150.6	153.8	159.3	164.4	166.2	171.7	174.6	177.6	182.5	188.1	193.1	200.1	208.0	218.4
October	145.2	149.8	153.8	159.5	164.5	166.5	171.6	174.3	177.9	182.6	188.6	193.3	200.4	208.9	217.7
November	145.3	149.8	153.9	159.6	164.4	166.7	172.1	173.6	178.2	182.7	189.0	193.6	201.1	209.7	216.0
December	146.0	150.7	154.4	160.0	164.4	167.3	172.2	173.4	178.5	183.5	189.9	194.1	202.7	210.9	212.9

Percentage changes on one year earlier[1]

	1995	1996	1997	1998	1999	2000	2001	2002	2003	2004	2005	2006	2007	2008

Tax and Price Index[1]

	1995	1996	1997	1998	1999	2000	2001	2002	2003	2004	2005	2006	2007	2008
January	3.9	3.2	1.4	2.4	2.3	1.5	2.6	−0.1	3.1	3.4	3.1	2.2	4.2	4.0
February	4.0	3.0	1.3	2.6	2.0	1.9	2.5	−0.4	3.4	3.3	3.1	2.3	4.6	4.1
March	4.0	3.0	1.1	2.6	1.9	2.2	2.1	−0.1	3.4	3.3	3.1	2.1	4.9	3.7
April	3.7	1.0	1.5	4.1	1.0	3.0	0.4	1.5	4.0	2.4	3.1	2.4	4.5	3.2
May	3.8	0.7	1.7	4.3	0.7	3.0	0.7	1.1	3.8	2.7	2.8	2.9	4.2	3.4
June	4.0	0.6	2.0	3.8	0.8	3.3	0.6	1.0	3.7	3.0	2.8	3.2	4.4	3.7
July	3.9	0.8	2.5	3.5	0.7	3.3	0.3	1.5	3.9	3.0	2.8	3.2	3.7	4.2
August	4.1	0.6	2.7	3.3	0.5	3.0	0.7	1.3	3.8	3.1	2.6	3.4	4.0	3.9
September	4.3	0.7	2.7	3.1	0.5	3.3	0.3	1.8	3.5	3.0	2.5	3.6	3.8	4.1
October	3.5	1.3	2.9	3.1	0.7	3.0	0.2	2.2	3.4	3.2	2.3	3.6	4.2	3.3
November	3.4	1.3	2.9	2.9	0.9	3.2	−0.6	2.8	3.3	3.4	2.3	3.8	4.3	1.9
December	3.6	1.1	2.8	2.6	1.3	2.9	−0.8	3.1	3.6	3.5	2.0	4.4	4.0	−0.3

Retail Prices Index

	1995	1996	1997	1998	1999	2000	2001	2002	2003	2004	2005	2006	2007	2008
January	3.3	2.9	2.8	3.3	2.4	2.0	2.7	1.3	2.9	2.6	3.2	2.4	4.2	4.1
February	3.4	2.7	2.7	3.4	2.1	2.3	2.7	1.0	3.2	2.5	3.2	2.4	4.6	4.1
March	3.5	2.7	2.6	3.5	2.1	2.6	2.3	1.3	3.1	2.6	3.2	2.4	4.8	3.8
April	3.3	2.4	2.4	4.0	1.6	3.0	1.8	1.5	3.1	2.5	3.2	2.6	4.5	4.2
May	3.4	2.2	2.6	4.2	1.3	3.1	2.1	1.1	3.0	2.8	2.9	3.0	4.3	4.3
June	3.5	2.1	2.9	3.7	1.3	3.3	1.9	1.0	2.9	3.0	2.9	3.3	4.4	4.6
July	3.5	2.2	3.3	3.5	1.3	3.3	1.6	1.5	3.1	3.0	2.9	3.3	3.8	5.0
August	3.6	2.1	3.5	3.3	1.1	3.0	2.1	1.4	2.9	3.2	2.8	3.4	4.1	4.8
September	3.9	2.1	3.6	3.2	1.1	3.3	1.7	1.7	2.8	3.1	2.7	3.6	3.9	5.0
October	3.2	2.7	3.7	3.1	1.2	3.1	1.6	2.1	2.6	3.3	2.5	3.7	4.2	4.2
November	3.1	2.7	3.7	3.0	1.4	3.2	0.9	2.6	2.5	3.4	2.4	3.9	4.3	3.0
December	3.2	2.5	3.6	2.8	1.8	2.9	0.7	2.9	2.8	3.5	2.2	4.4	4.0	0.9

1 See chapter text.

Source: Office for National Statistics: 020 7533 5874

Prices

17.7 Index of purchase prices of the means of agricultural production[1]
United Kingdom
Annual averages

		Weights	1998	1999	2000	2001	2002	2003	2004	2005	2006	2007	2008
Goods and services currently consumed[2]	C3FU	100	99.5	98.1	100.0	104.3	103.7	106.5	113.5	115.9	121.0	133.6	169.4
Seeds	C3FV	3.3	119.2	109.0	100.0	109.2	105.5	116.0	110.3	107.9	110.0	153.5	146.8
Energy, lubricants	C3FW	8.1	75.1	82.4	100.0	96.7	92.4	100.5	108.8	137.4	154.4	162.0	221.3
Fuels for heating	C3FX	1.0	61.6	66.6	100.0	95.5	87.2	104.5	118.3	158.9	185.0	203.2	277.5
Motor fuel	C3FY	5.1	66.7	77.8	100.0	96.7	91.6	100.7	110.3	143.4	157.6	159.7	233.0
Electricity	C3FZ	1.8	104.8	102.9	100.0	96.9	96.2	96.5	98.9	110.7	132.0	150.1	166.7
Lubricants	C3G2	0.2	88.5	98.1	100.0	101.2	106.2	112.7	113.1	113.1	113.1	113.1	113.1
Fertilisers and soil improvers	C3G3	9.1	95.3	93.3	100.0	115.8	110.3	119.0	130.5	143.3	151.4	170.5	381.3
Straight nitrogen	C3G4	3.9	87.0	82.9	100.0	129.1	120.2	133.1	148.5	168.7	181.8	188.8	371.8
Compound fertilisers	C3G5	4.6	101.9	101.3	100.0	106.7	103.0	109.1	118.4	126.0	130.4	160.0	406.8
Other fertiliser (mainly lime and chalk)	C3G6	0.4	95.9	96.7	100.0	100.5	104.0	103.4	103.8	105.6	109.1	115.2	121.4
Plant protection products	C3G7	1.2	108.2	105.8	100.0	96.8	95.8	94.9	97.8	101.7	104.0	106.3	108.5
Animal feedstuffs	C3G8	26.4	106.5	99.1	100.0	107.4	103.5	104.9	111.6	103.0	108.1	132.7	169.8
Feed wheat	C3G9	2.2	113.8	110.7	100.0	110.9	97.3	106.5	119.4	97.6	111.9	156.2	210.9
Whole barley	C3GA	2.1	108.5	111.5	100.0	101.8	89.5	103.2	112.8	97.8	108.8	157.1	192.3
Whole oats	C3GB	0.2	98.0	104.7	100.0	97.8	90.7	85.1	94.3	94.6	102.6	125.8	154.3
Maize glutten feed	C3GC	0.4	95.3	100.2	100.0	110.0	102.9	122.9	123.8	110.1	124.6	165.8	179.9
Oilcake	C3GD	2.1	91.9	83.5	100.0	109.4	100.4	109.5	112.0	100.0	100.6	127.0	174.6
White fish meal	C3GE	0.4	137.9	93.2	100.0	115.1	134.7	129.1	120.3	126.6	182.6	173.7	175.4
Other straight feedstuffs	C3GF	3.3	98.2	91.8	100.0	114.1	109.3	109.9	115.1	109.8	109.1	142.3	168.5
All straight feedstuffs	C3GG	10.6	104.1	97.1	100.0	109.7	101.3	108.2	114.9	102.9	110.5	146.3	184.8
Feedstuffs non-concentrates	C3GH	0.1	104.1	97.1	100.0	109.7	101.3	108.2	114.9	102.9	110.5	146.3	184.8
Compound feedstuffs for:	C3GI	15.8	108.1	100.4	100.0	105.8	104.9	102.7	109.4	103.1	106.5	123.6	159.7
Cattle and calves	C3GJ	6.2	105.0	99.9	100.0	106.4	105.9	102.5	108.1	103.9	105.4	121.0	153.6
Pigs	C3GK	3.5	112.8	101.9	100.0	105.9	103.3	101.0	107.7	100.2	105.3	122.9	155.6
Poultry	C3GL	5.0	108.7	100.6	100.0	105.9	104.5	104.9	112.8	104.5	109.7	129.4	173.9
Sheep	C3GM	1.1	108.3	98.0	100.0	102.2	106.2	99.4	105.9	101.6	101.5	113.8	143.5
Maintenance and repair of plant	C3GN	7.9	93.4	96.6	100.0	104.3	109.4	116.0	122.5	130.3	137.8	143.4	151.6
Maintenance and repair of buildings	C3GO	3.6	98.5	97.7	100.0	101.9	105.1	108.3	113.4	118.1	125.1	134.2	142.9
Veterinary services	C3GP	3.2	101.1	101.2	100.0	98.6	97.8	101.6	104.6	103.9	111.1	112.6	108.4
Other goods and services	C3GQ	31.2	98.5	99.9	100.0	102.5	105.5	105.2	114.0	114.5	115.5	120.0	123.8
Goods and services contributing to investment in agriculture	C3GR	100	99.8	100.2	100.0	99.0	100.0	101.5	104.4	108.7	111.7	115.4	119.9
Materials	C3GS	71.5	101.6	101.7	100.0	97.3	97.0	97.5	99.4	103.4	105.3	107.3	110.6
Machinery and other equipment	C3GT	28.4	97.7	99.2	100.0	97.4	95.7	95.1	96.1	103.8	108.2	114.2	121.5
Machinery and plant for cultivation	C3GU	8.0	97.7	99.1	100.0	99.6	98.6	98.7	103.8	109.4	111.0	116.4	124.5
Machinery and plant for harvesting	C3GV	14.3	98.4	100.0	100.0	92.3	88.8	88.2	87.3	97.9	105.4	113.3	122.5
Farm machinery and installations	C3GW	6.0	96.1	97.5	100.0	106.3	108.2	106.8	107.0	110.2	111.2	113.4	115.4
Tractors	C3GX	28.6	101.6	102.4	100.0	96.8	98.4	101.4	106.1	110.5	111.8	111.8	114.8
Other vehicles	C3GY	14.5	109.1	105.1	100.0	98.3	96.7	94.4	92.4	88.6	86.7	84.9	80.7
Buildings	C3GZ	19.5	95.6	96.6	100.0	103.3	107.8	112.1	118.1	123.7	130.9	140.0	148.7
Engineering and soil improvement operations	C3H2	9.0	94.8	96.9	100.0	101.4	107.2	110.3	113.3	118.0	118.8	125.4	132.6

1 See chapter text.
2 The sum of the percentages of categories included does not add up to 100% due to the exclusion of some minor categories.

Source: Department for Environment, Food and Rural Affairs: 01904 455249

17.8 Index of producer prices of agricultural products[1]
United Kingdom
Annual averages

Indices (2000=100)

		Weights	1998	1999	2000	2001	2002	2003	2004	2005	2006	2007	2008
All products[2]	C3H6	100	107.0	103.6	100.0	108.3	103.3	109.9	113.3	109.7	114.2	129.5	155.9
All crop products	C3H7	40.2	111.7	109.0	100.0	112.0	104.0	110.7	115.1	108.6	118.2	144.0	164.4
Cereals (including cereal seeds)	C3H8	13.3	113.8	111.0	100.0	107.8	95.0	105.2	114.2	99.1	110.5	163.7	206.3
Wheat for:													
breadmaking	C3H9	1.1	122.8	112.9	100.0	109.6	101.4	110.6	120.8	102.1	107.4	172.6	219.8
other milling	C3HA	1.5	116.0	110.9	100.0	107.5	92.9	104.1	116.8	96.6	108.6	177.1	207.6
feeding	C3HB	6.4	114.0	110.5	100.0	110.5	96.7	105.6	117.6	98.2	112.0	154.1	211.1
Barley for:													
feeding	C3HC	2.5	109.2	112.9	100.0	102.6	89.1	103.7	110.8	98.7	108.4	159.8	187.7
malting	C3HD	1.4	115.1	108.9	100.0	104.8	96.5	107.1	101.6	104.5	112.8	199.1	216.5
Oats for:													
milling	C3HE	0.1	104.9	109.9	100.0	109.8	89.0	90.7	96.3	104.9	113.8	149.6	168.8
feeding	C3HF	0.2	97.0	106.1	100.0	98.5	91.2	86.7	94.4	96.3	104.3	130.5	156.4
Potatoes:	C3HG	4.5	138.8	143.5	100.0	131.0	90.0	105.6	140.3	109.2	141.7	161.1	167.9
early	C3HH	0.4	100.7	51.9	100.0	114.5	73.0	90.0	124.8	98.0	131.8	102.1	139.3
main crop	C3HI	4.1	141.1	151.5	100.0	132.5	90.6	106.0	141.6	109.7	143.1	166.5	170.4
Industrial crops	C3HJ	4.3	118.4	103.4	100.0	111.9	114.4	120.3	121.6	114.3	118.3	124.6	164.0
Oilseed rape (non set-aside)	C3HK	1.2	140.0	102.0	100.0	119.2	121.2	140.3	136.1	112.9	134.5	158.8	272.5
Sugar beet	C3HL	2.2	111.4	108.7	100.0	107.3	114.8	112.1	115.4	117.1	112.6	87.6	90.5
Fresh vegetables	C3HM	7.7	105.2	99.2	100.0	113.6	112.7	125.5	113.7	120.3	129.7	143.5	140.2
Cauliflowers	C3HN	0.4	87.9	82.4	100.0	103.9	117.7	119.8	102.4	127.1	123.2	166.2	134.4
Lettuce	C3HO	0.7	98.6	102.9	100.0	129.2	128.6	151.5	130.2	140.7	151.7	150.2	168.2
Tomatoes	C3HP	0.7	91.8	100.3	100.0	100.1	107.8	135.6	99.8	117.7	124.3	120.0	107.5
Carrots	C3HQ	0.7	125.4	119.3	100.0	166.5	150.4	157.2	144.7	170.5	184.2	208.9	216.9
Cabbage	C3HR	0.4	94.5	94.2	100.0	123.0	109.8	119.7	109.3	122.6	133.1	161.7	160.0
Beans	C3HS	0.2	107.8	102.8	100.0	124.3	118.0	119.1	128.7	127.2	172.5	188.6	176.1
Onions	C3HT	0.5	165.8	104.7	100.0	128.6	126.7	136.1	138.8	113.1	150.8	196.7	149.6
Mushrooms	C3HU	1.3	98.9	98.1	100.0	91.0	95.9	100.6	94.4	83.4	81.3	70.9	70.7
Fresh fruit	C3HV	1.9	105.4	100.0	100.0	99.0	113.9	124.2	112.4	120.1	114.6	126.7	142.2
Dessert apples	C3HW	0.3	110.5	104.3	100.0	109.8	111.3	124.6	120.7	116.4	122.5	140.4	152.2
Dessert pears	C3HX	0.1	110.4	108.7	100.0	128.7	124.8	115.3	114.6	115.0	123.0	122.9	159.8
Cooking apples	C3HY	0.2	150.9	100.7	100.0	105.6	109.4	152.1	142.5	118.8	129.7	144.1	175.8
Strawberries	C3HZ	0.7	93.7	102.4	100.0	94.5	121.7	124.4	97.1	111.8	106.5	113.2	126.3
Raspberries	C3I2	0.2	114.3	104.9	100.0	102.9	128.9	125.7	114.3	152.9	133.4	158.6	153.4
Seeds (excluding cereal seeds)	C3I3	0.5	98.6	97.7	100.0	104.0	95.7	113.6	112.9	114.1	113.1	113.1	113.1
Flowers and plants	C3I4	5.9	103.1	105.3	100.0	105.3	106.8	107.9	105.3	105.6	108.8	115.3	119.5
Other crop products	C3I5	0.7	98.7	97.0	100.0	106.0	98.9	108.6	109.7	110.8	110.6	114.0	113.6
Animals and animal products	C3I6	59.8	103.9	99.9	100.0	105.8	102.7	109.4	112.0	110.4	111.6	119.7	150.2
Animals for slaughter	C3I7	35.3	97.2	95.2	100.0	101.3	103.2	109.3	111.7	110.3	113.8	116.0	146.5
Calves	C3I8	0.1	149.4	115.1	100.0	94.2	120.2	143.9	140.8	108.3	131.5	135.9	168.3
Clean cattle	C3I9	9.7	95.0	101.7	100.0	100.8	103.8	106.7	113.4	114.6	123.9	125.9	161.9
Clean pigs	C3IA	7.0	85.8	83.4	100.0	103.6	98.7	109.0	109.3	109.8	110.9	114.3	133.7
Sows and boars	C3IB	0.2	81.1	81.0	100.0	107.4	94.0	103.2	123.9	124.1	126.1	99.8	161.5
Clean sheep and lambs	C3IC	5.2	97.1	90.2	100.0	101.3	118.5	132.5	131.4	122.9	125.5	111.7	142.6
Ewes and rams	C3ID	0.4	116.3	81.3	100.0	152.4	149.6	188.2	182.5	148.9	158.9	155.4	179.7
All poultry	C3IE	11.5	103.3	99.0	100.0	98.6	97.2	99.4	101.2	100.8	99.4	108.7	138.9
Chickens	C3IF	7.9	105.9	101.3	100.0	100.1	99.5	100.2	103.4	102.0	100.0	108.2	135.5
Turkeys	C3IG	2.9	91.3	90.0	100.0	94.4	89.5	97.8	95.0	94.7	94.0	108.6	149.3
Cows' milk	C3IH	20.1	114.4	108.3	100.0	113.7	101.0	106.4	109.0	109.0	106.0	122.4	153.1
Eggs	C3II	3.2	109.4	98.0	100.0	104.9	109.5	130.7	135.1	121.0	127.6	144.7	177.0
Other animal products:	C3IJ	1.1	108.0	103.0	100.0	107.7	100.0	107.4	110.4	107.5	93.5	115.2	139.5
Wool (clip)	C3IK	0.2	98.6	93.5	100.0	87.0	96.4	108.4	107.3	92.3	33.6	71.7	72.8

1 See chapter text.
2 The sum of the percentages of all the categories does not add up to 100% due to the exclusion of some minor categories.

Source: Department for Environment, Food and Rural Affairs: 01904 455249

17.9 Harmonised Indices of Consumer Prices (HICPs) International comparisons: EU countries

percentage change over 12 months

Per cent

		2006	2007	2008	2008 Mar	2008 Apr	2008 May	2008 Jun	2008 Jul	2008 Aug	2008 Sep	2008 Oct	2008 Nov	2008 Dec	2009 Jan	2009 Feb	2009 Mar
European Union countries																	
United Kingdom[1]	D7G7	2.3	2.3	3.6	2.5	3.0	3.3	3.8	4.4	4.7	5.2	4.5	4.1	3.1	3.0	3.2	2.9
Austria	D7SK	1.7	2.2	3.2	3.5	3.4	3.7	4.0	3.8	3.6	3.7	3.0	2.3	1.5	1.2	1.4	0.7
Belgium	D7SL	2.3	1.8	4.5	4.4	4.1	5.1	5.8	5.9	5.4	5.5	4.8	3.2	2.7	2.1	1.9	0.6
Bulgaria	GHY8	7.4	7.6	12.0	13.2	13.4	14.0	14.7	14.4	11.8	11.4	11.2	8.8	7.2	6.0	5.4	4.0
Cyprus	D7RO	2.2	2.2	4.4	4.4	4.3	4.6	5.2	5.3	5.1	5.0	4.8	3.1	1.8	0.9	0.6	0.9
Czech Republic	D7RP	2.1	3.0	6.3	7.1	6.7	6.8	6.6	6.8	6.2	6.4	5.7	4.1	3.3	1.4	1.3	1.7
Denmark	D7SM	1.9	1.7	3.6	3.3	3.4	3.6	4.2	4.4	4.8	4.5	3.8	2.8	2.4	1.7	1.7	1.6
Estonia	D7RQ	4.4	6.7	10.6	11.2	11.6	11.4	11.5	11.2	11.1	10.8	10.1	8.5	7.5	4.7	3.9	2.5
Finland	D7SN	1.3	1.6	..	3.6	3.3	4.1	4.3	4.3	4.6	4.7	4.4	3.5	3.4	..	..	..
France	D7SO	1.9	1.6	3.2	3.5	3.4	3.7	4.0	4.0	3.5	3.4	3.0	1.9	1.2	0.8	1.0	0.4
Germany	D7SP	1.8	2.3	2.8	3.3	2.6	3.1	3.4	3.5	3.3	3.0	2.5	1.4	1.1	0.9	1.0	0.4
Greece	D7SQ	3.3	3.0	4.2	4.4	4.4	4.9	4.9	4.9	4.8	4.7	4.0	3.0	2.2	2.0	1.8	1.5
Hungary	D7RR	4.0	7.9	6.0	6.7	6.8	6.9	6.6	7.0	6.4	5.6	5.1	4.1	3.4	2.4	2.9	2.8
Ireland	D7SS	2.7	2.9	3.1	3.7	3.3	3.7	3.9	3.6	3.2	3.2	2.7	2.1	1.3	1.1	0.1	-0.7
Italy	D7ST	2.2	2.0	3.5	3.6	3.6	3.7	4.0	4.0	4.2	3.9	3.6	2.7	2.4	1.4	1.5	1.1
Latvia	D7RS	6.6	10.1	15.3	16.6	17.4	17.7	17.5	16.5	15.6	14.7	13.7	11.6	10.4	9.7	9.4	7.9
Lithuania	D7RT	3.8	5.8	11.1	11.4	11.9	12.3	12.7	12.4	12.2	11.3	10.7	9.2	8.5	9.5	8.5	7.4
Luxembourg	D7SU	3.0	2.7	4.1	4.4	4.3	4.8	5.3	5.8	4.8	4.8	3.9	2.0	0.7	–	0.7	-0.3
Malta	D7RU	2.6	0.7	4.7	4.3	4.1	4.1	4.4	5.6	5.4	4.9	5.7	4.9	5.0	3.1	3.5	3.9
Netherlands	D7SV	1.7	1.6	2.2	1.9	1.7	2.1	2.3	3.0	3.0	2.8	2.5	1.9	1.7	1.7	1.9	1.8
Poland	D7RV	1.3	2.6	4.2	4.4	4.3	4.3	4.3	4.5	4.4	4.4	4.1	4.0	3.6	3.3	3.2	3.6	4.0
Portugal	D7SX	3.0	2.4	2.7	3.1	2.5	2.8	3.4	3.1	3.1	3.2	2.5	1.4	0.8	0.1	0.1	-0.6
Romania	GHY7	6.6	4.9	7.9	8.7	8.7	8.5	8.7	9.1	8.1	7.3	7.4	6.8	6.4	6.8	6.9	6.7
Slovakia	D7RW	4.3	1.9	3.9	3.6	3.7	4.0	4.3	4.4	4.4	4.5	4.2	3.9	3.5	2.7	2.4	1.8
Slovenia	D7RX	2.5	3.8	5.5	6.6	6.2	6.2	6.8	6.9	6.0	5.6	4.8	2.9	1.8	1.4	2.1	1.6
Spain	D7SY	3.6	2.8	4.1	4.6	4.2	4.7	5.1	5.3	4.9	4.6	3.6	2.4	1.5	0.8	0.7	-0.1
Sweden	D7SZ	1.5	1.7	3.3	3.3	3.2	3.7	4.0	3.8	4.1	4.2	3.4	2.4	2.1	2.0	2.2	1.9
EICP[2] EU 25 average[3]	D7RY	2.2	..	..	..	..	..	..	..	..	..	..	..	..	..	..	..
EICP[2] EU 27 average[3]	GJ2E	..	2.4	3.7	3.7	3.6	4.0	4.2	4.4	4.3	4.2	3.7	2.8	2.2	1.7	1.7	1.3

Note: Further information on HICP is available from the National Statistics Website: www.statistics.gov.uk/hicp.

1 Published as the Consumer Prices Index (CPI) in the UK (UK 2005=100, others 1996=100).

2 The EICP (European Index of Consumer Prices)is the official EU aggregate. It covers 15 member states until April 2004, 25 member states from May 2004, and 27 members from Jan 2007, the new member states being integrated using a chain index formula. The EU 25 annual average for 2004 is calculated from the EU 15 average from January to April and the EU 25 average from May to December.

3 The coverage of the European Union was extended to include Cyprus, Czech Republic, Estonia, Hungary, Latvia, Lithuania, Malta, Poland, Slovakia and Slovenia from 1 May 2004 and Bulgaria and Romania from 1 Jan 2007.

Sources: Statistical Office of the European Communities (Eurostat); Office for National Statistics: 01633 456900

Government finance

Chapter 18

Government finance

Public sector

(Tables 18.1 to 18.3 and 18.5)

In Table 18.1 the term public sector describes the consolidation of central government, local government and public corporations. General government is the consolidated total of central government and local government. The table shows details of the key public sector finances' indicators, consistent with the European System of Accounts 1995 (ESA95), by sub-sector.

The concepts in Table 18.1 are consistent with the format for public finances in the Economic and Fiscal Strategy Report (EFSR), published by HM Treasury on 11 June 1998, and the Budget. The public sector current budget is equivalent to net saving in national accounts plus capital tax receipts. Net investment is gross capital formation, plus payments less receipts of investment grants, less depreciation. Net borrowing is net investment less current budget. Net borrowing differs from the net cash requirement (see below) in that it is measured on an accruals basis whereas the net cash requirement is mainly a cash measure which includes some financial transactions. Table 18.2 shows the public sector key fiscal balances. The table shows the component detail of the public sector key fiscal balance by economic category. The tables are consistent with the Budget.

Table 18.3 shows public sector net debt. Public sector net debt consists of the public sector's financial liabilities at face value, minus its liquid assets – mainly foreign currency exchange reserves and bank deposits. General government gross debt (consolidated) in Table 18.3 is consistent with the definition of general government gross debt reported to the European Commission under the requirements of the Maastricht Treaty.

More information on the concepts in Table 18.1, 18.2 and 18.3 can be found in a guide to monthly public sector finance statistics, *GSS Methodology Series* No 12, the ONS First Releases *Public Sector Finances and Financial Statistics Explanatory Handbook*.

Table 18.6 shows the taxes and National Insurance contributions paid to central government, local government, and to the institutions of the European Union. The table is the same as Table 11.1 of the *National Accounts Blue Book*. More information on the data and concepts in the table can be found in Chapter 11 of the *Blue Book*.

Consolidated Fund and National Loans Fund

(Tables 18.4, 18.5 and 18.7)

The central government embraces all bodies for whose activities a Minister of the Crown, or other responsible person, is accountable to Parliament. It includes, in addition to the ordinary government departments, a number of bodies administering public policy, but without the substantial degree of financial independence which characterises the public corporations. It also includes certain extra-budgetary funds and accounts controlled by departments.

The government's financial transactions are handled through a number of statutory funds or accounts. The most important of these is the Consolidated Fund, which is the government's main account with the Bank of England. Up to 31 March 1968 the Consolidated Fund was virtually synonymous with the term 'Exchequer', which was then the government's central cash account. From 1 April 1968 the National Loans Fund, with a separate account at the Bank of England, was set up by the National Loans Act 1968. The general effect of this Act was to remove from the Consolidated Fund most of the government's domestic lending and the whole of the government's borrowing transactions, and to provide for them to be brought to account in the National Loans Fund.

Revenue from taxation and miscellaneous receipts, including interest and dividends on loans made from votes, continue to be paid into the Consolidated Fund.

After meeting the ordinary expenditure on Supply Services and the Consolidated Fund Standing Services, the surplus or deficit of the Consolidated Fund (Table 18.4), is payable into or met by the National Loans Fund. Table 18.4 also provides a summary of the transactions of the National Loans Fund. The service of the National Debt, previously borne by the Consolidated Fund, is now met from the National Loans Fund which receives: (a) interest payable on loans to the nationalised industries, local authorities and other bodies, whether the loans were made before or after 1 April 1968; and (b) the profits of the Issue Department of the Bank of England, mainly derived from interest on government securities, which were formerly paid into the Exchange Equalisation Account. The net cost of servicing the National Debt after applying these interest receipts and similar items is a charge on the Consolidated Fund as part of the standing services. Details of National Loans Fund loans outstanding are shown in Table 18.5. Details of borrowing and repayments of debt, other than loans from the National Loans Fund, are shown in Table 18.7.

Income tax

(Table 18.11, 18. 12)

Following the introduction of Independent Taxation from 1990/91, the Married Couple's Allowance was introduced. It is payable in addition to the Personal Allowance and between 1990/91 and 1992/93 went to the husband unless the transfer condition was met. The condition was that the husband was unable to make full use of the allowance himself and in that case he could transfer only part or all of the Married Couple's Allowance to his wife. In 1993/94 all or half of the allowance could be transferred to the wife if the couple had agreed beforehand. The wife has the right to claim half the allowance. The Married Couple's Allowance, and allowances linked to it, were restricted to 20 per cent in 1994/95 and to 15 per cent from 1995/96. From 2000/01 only people born before 6 April 1935 are entitled to Married Couple's Allowance.

The age allowance replaces the single allowance, provided the taxpayer's income is below the limits shown in the table. From 1989/90, for incomes in excess of the limits, the allowance is reduced by £1 for each additional £2 of income until the ordinary limit is reached (before it was £2 for each £3 of additional income). The relief is due where the taxpayer is aged 65 or over in the year of assessment.

The additional Personal Allowance could be claimed by a single parent (or by a married man if his wife was totally incapacitated) who maintained a resident child at his or her own expense. Widow's Bereavement Allowance was due to a widow in the year of her husband's death and in the following year provided the widow had not remarried before the beginning of that year. Both the additional Personal Allowance and the Widow's Bereavement Allowance were abolished from April 2000.

The Blind Person's Allowance may be claimed by blind persons (in England and Wales, registered as blind by a local authority) and surplus Blind Person's Allowance may be transferred to a husband or wife. Relief on life assurance premiums is given by deduction from the premium payable. From 1984/85, it is confined to policies made before 14 March 1984.

From 1993/94 until 1998/99 a number of taxpayers with taxable income in excess of the lower rate limit only paid tax at the lower rate. This was because it was only their dividend income and (from 1996/97) their savings income which took their taxable income above the lower rate limit but below the basic rate limit, and such income was chargeable to tax at the lower rate and not the basic rate.

In 1999/2000 the 10 per cent starting rate replaced the lower rate and taxpayers with savings or dividend income at the basic rate of tax are taxed at 20 per cent and 10 per cent respectively. Before 1999/2000 these people would have been classified as lower rate taxpayers.

Rateable values

(Table 18.13)

Major changes to local government finance in England and Wales took effect from 1 April 1990. These included the abolition of domestic rating (replaced by the Community Charge, then replaced in 1993 by the Council Tax), the revaluation of all non-domestic properties, and the introduction of the Uniform Business Rate. Also in 1990, a new classification scheme was introduced which has resulted in differences in coverage. Further differences are caused by legislative changes which have changed the treatment of certain types of property. There was little change in the total rateable value of non-domestic properties when all these properties were revalued in April 1995. Rateable values for offices fell and there was a rise for all other property types shown in the table.

With effect from 1 April 2000, all non-domestic properties were revalued. Overall there was an increase in rateable values of over 25 per cent compared to the last year of the 1995 list. The largest proportionate increase was for offices and cinemas, with all property types given in the table showing rises.

The latest revaluation affecting all non-domestic properties took effect from 1 April 2005. In this revaluation the overall increase in rateable values between 1 April of the first year of the new list and the same day on the last year of the 2000 list was 17 per cent. The largest proportionate increase was for theatres and music halls with, again, all property types in the table showing rises.

Local authority capital expenditure and receipts

(Table 18.17)

Authorities finance capital spending in a number of ways, including use of their own revenue funds, borrowing or grants and contributions from elsewhere. Until 31 March 2004, the capital finance system laid down in Part 4 of the Local Government and Housing Act 1989 (the '1989 Act') provided the framework within which authorities were permitted to finance capital spending from sources other than revenue – that is by the use of borrowing, long-term credit or capital receipts.

Government finance

Until 31 March 2004, capital spending could be financed by:

- revenue resources – either the General Fund Revenue Account, the Housing Revenue Account (HRA) or the Major Repairs Reserve – but an authority could not charge council tenants for spending on general services, or spending on council houses to local taxpayers

- borrowing or long-term credit as authorised by the credit approvals issued by central government. Credit approvals were normally accompanied by an element of Revenue Support Grant (RSG) covering most of the costs of borrowing

- grants received from central government

- contributions or grants from elsewhere – including the National Lottery and NDPBs such as Sport England, English Heritage and Natural England, as well as private sector partners, capital receipts (that is, proceeds from the sale of land, buildings or other fixed assets) and sums set aside as Provision for Credit Liabilities (PCL). This required the use of a credit approval, unless the authority was debt-free

From 1 April 2004, capital spending can be financed in the same ways, except that central government no longer issues credit approvals to allow authorities to finance capital spending by borrowing. However, it continues to provide financial support in the usual way, via RSG or HRA subsidy, towards some capital spending financed by borrowing that is Supported Capital Expenditure (Revenue). Authorities are now free to finance capital spending by self-financed borrowing within limits of affordability set, having regard to the 2003 Act and the CIPFA Prudential Code. The concept of PCL has not been carried forward into the new system, although authorities which were debt-free and had a negative credit ceiling at the end of the old system could still spend amounts of PCL built up under the old rules.

In 2007/08 capital expenditure of almost £3.1 billion (about 16 per cent) was financed by self-financed borrowing, an increase of 37 per cent from the amount financed in 2006/07. In 2001/02 credit approvals were the principal financing source for capital expenditure, accounting for 26 per cent of the total. By 2006/07, government grants accounted for 25 per cent of the total financing. Financing by government grant in 2007/08 was affected by the grant of £1.7 billion paid by the Department for Transport to the Greater London Authority (GLA) in respect of Metronet liabilities; this caused government grants to account for 34 per cent of the total financing for 2007/08.

Local authority financing for capital expenditure

(Table 18.18)

Capital spending by local authorities is mainly for buying, constructing or improving physical assets such as:

- buildings – schools, houses, libraries and museums, police and fire stations

- land – for development, roads, playing fields

- vehicles, plant and machinery – including street lighting and road signs

It also includes grants and advances made to the private sector or the rest of the public sector for capital purposes, such as advances to Registered Social Landlords

Local authority capital expenditure more than doubled between 2001/02 and 2007/08.

The underlying trend in capital expenditure (excluding an exceptional event) by local authorities in England increased by 12 per cent, from £16.3 billion in 2006/07 to £18.2 billion in 2007/08. The exceptional event was the payment by the Greater London Authority (Transport for London) of £1.7 billion to Metronet. The underlying trend was also affected by Liverpool's transfer of its housing stock to a registered social landlord, which had the effect of increasing expenditure in 2007/08 by £500 million.

New construction, conversion and renovation forms the major part of capital spending.

Excluding the GLA's repayment of Metronet liabilities in 2007/08, Education's share of capital expenditure fell from 23 per cent in 2003/04 to 20 per cent in 2007/08. Transport and Other services increased their share over the same period.

18.1 Sector analysis of key fiscal balances[1]
United Kingdom
Not seasonally adjusted

£ million[2]

		1998 /99	1999 /00	2000 /01	2001 /02	2002 /03	2003 /04	2004 /05	2005 /06	2006 /07	2007 /08	2008 /09
Surplus on current budget[3]												
Central Government	ANLV	12 472	24 401	26 756	13 812	−8 121	−17 590	−17 926	−13 762	−5 717	−5 941	−51 370
Local government	NMMX	−1 986	−4 507	−3 790	−3 909	−4 960	−3 332	−3 499	−5 099	−2 972	−2 352	..
General Government	ANLW	11 086	20 878	21 996	10 861	−11 103	−19 005	..	−18 657	−8 292	−13 273	..
Public corporations	FDDP	335	670	424	1 607	1 090	2 014	2 713	4 957	4 264	3 641	..
Public sector	ANMU	10 423	20 995	23 432	12 144	−11 320	−17 452	−19 288	−14 195	−4 823	−5 334	−52 298
Net investment[4]												
Central government	-ANNS	8 158	9 422	8 731	13 629	17 282	18 694	20 140	19 431	26 416	32 568	47 492
Local government	-ANNT	−313	−832	−1 882	−1 824	−3 595	−682	1 753	474	−13	−3 028	..
General Government	-ANNV	7 848	6 461	6 574	10 951	12 487	16 371	..	19 721	25 955	29 389	..
Public corporations	-ANNU	−1 084	−2 981	−2 192	−697	−1 160	−1 390	−1 584	3 693	−314	157	..
Public sector	-ANNW	5 955	5 501	5 125	11 901	13 804	15 707	20 575	23 461	25 969	29 315	37 660
Net borrowing[5]												
Central government	-NMFJ	−4 314	−14 979	−18 025	−183	25 403	36 284	38 066	33 193	32 133	38 509	98 862
Local government	-NMOE	1 816	3 134	2 490	2 081	1 074	189	3 775	5 296	2 630	215	3 054
General Government	-NNBK	−2 498	−11 845	−15 535	1 898	26 477	36 473	41 841	38 489	34 763	38 724	101 916
Public corporations	-CPCM	−1 890	−3 652	−2 565	−2 083	−1 309	−3 282	−1 927	−760	−3 886	−4 138	−199
Public sector	-ANNX	−4 468	−15 494	−18 307	−243	25 124	33 159	39 863	37 656	30 792	34 649	89 958
Net cash requirement												
Central government[6]	RUUX	−6 344	−10 664	−37 251	3 366	24 214	42 717	37 454	35 908	36 891	29 621	162 520
Local government	ABEG	−404	979	−611	−423	−2 715	−2 712	1 270	4 153	58	−723	4 184
General Government	RUUS	−6 748	−9 685	−37 862	2 943	21 499	40 005	38 724	40 061	36 949	28 898	..
Public corporations	ABEM	698	1 712	1 541	1 159	3 095	−1 539	−242	396	−1 792	−1 478	106
Public sector	RURQ	−6 145	−8 063	−36 538	4 078	24 562	38 448	38 421	40 396	35 110	21 572	59 902
Public sector debt												
Public sector net debt (£ billion)	RUTN	350.7	344.4	311.1	314.3	346.0	381.5	422.1	401.0	497.9	621.2	713.6
Public sector net debt as a percentage of GDP	RUTO	*38.4*	*35.6*	*30.7*	*29.7*	*30.8*	*32.2*	*34.1*	*35.4*	*36.0*	*43.1*	*50.9*

1 National accounts entities as defined under the European System of Accounts 1995 (ESA95) consistent with the latest national accounts. See chapter text.
2 Unless otherwise stated.
3 Net saving *plus* capital taxes.
4 Gross capital formation *plus* payments *less* receipts of investment grants *less* depreciation.

5 Net investment *less* surplus on current budget. A version of General government net borrowing is reported to the European Commision under the requirements of the Maastricht Treaty.
6 Central government net cash requirement (own account).

Source: Office for National Statistics: 020 7014 2124

Government finance

18.2 Public sector transactions and fiscal balances[1]
United Kingdom

£ million

		1998/99	1999/00	2000/01	2001/02	2002/03	2003/04	2004/05	2005/06	2006/07	2007/08	2008/09
Current receipts												
Taxes on income and wealth	ANSO	123 875	133 720	144 157	145 122	143 228	145 475	160 400	179 716	194 207	207 420	..
Taxes on production	NMYE	115 227	125 099	129 273	133 043	139 827	148 837	155 130	159 441	170 122	176 040	..
Other current taxes[2]	MJBC	17 688	18 916	19 696	21 569	23 194	25 795	27 422	28 808	30 313	31 926	..
Taxes on capital	NMGI	1 804	2 054	2 236	2 383	2 370	2 521	2 931	3 276	3 618	3 920	..
Social contributions	ANBO	54 746	56 935	62 068	63 162	63 529	75 148	80 408	85 335	90 933	95 510	..
Gross operating surplus	ANBP	16 822	16 949	16 669	16 907	17 106	18 428	19 097	21 907	23 419	24 097	..
Interest and dividends from private sector and Rest of World	ANBQ	5 283	4 368	6 226	4 898	4 606	4 659	6 044	6 696	6 228	8 162	..
Rent and other current transfers[3]	ANBS	891	1 037	2 036	2 427	2 470	2 036	1 964	1 969	1 870	1 795	..
Total current receipts	ANBT	336 336	359 078	382 361	389 511	396 330	422 899	453 396	487 148	520 692	548 846	..
Current expenditure												
Current expenditure on goods and services[4]	GZSN	159 443	172 299	185 875	198 935	217 512	236 743	256 639	274 231	288 380	302 077	..
Subsidies	NMRL	4 164	4 215	4 412	4 504	6 043	6 771	7 466	8 179	8 849	9 246	..
Social benefits	ANLY	106 585	105 555	108 010	118 269	122 636	130 802	136 860	142 380	147 430	157 271	..
Net current grants abroad[5]	GZSI	−1 018	−461	−380	−2 075	−824	−1 352	−637	−64	108	−133	..
Other current grants	NNAI	15 199	19 106	21 676	23 932	27 555	30 369	32 502	34 079	34 886	37 110	..
Interest and dividends paid to private sector and Rest of World	ANLO	29 289	25 297	26 400	22 495	21 453	22 839	24 990	26 870	28 649	31 280	..
Total current expenditure	ANLT	313 662	326 011	345 993	366 060	394 375	426 151	457 759	485 611	508 234	537 365	..
Saving, gross plus capital taxes	ANSP	22 674	33 067	36 368	23 451	1 955	−3 252	−4 363	1 537	12 458	11 481	..
Depreciation	-ANNZ	−12 436	−12 764	−13 107	−13 572	−14 459	−14 962	−15 757	−16 705	−17 836	−19 550	..
Surplus on current budget	ANMU	10 423	20 995	23 432	12 144	−11 320	−17 452	−19 288	−14 195	−4 823	−5 334	−52 298
Net investment												
Gross fixed capital formation[6]	ANSQ	14 061	14 150	13 283	17 308	20 125	21 079	25 644	27 859	28 989	34 002	..
Less depreciation	-ANNZ	−12 436	−12 764	−13 107	−13 572	−14 459	−14 962	−15 757	−16 705	−17 836	−19 550	..
Increase in inventories and valuables	ANSR	231	−472	−126	−10	−74	2 017	−239	−85	−138	−137	..
Capital grants to private sector and Rest of World	ANSS	4 942	4 371	3 875	7 958	7 564	10 142	11 046	12 452	15 337	14 463	..
Capital grants from private sector and Rest of World	-ANST	−367	−427	−756	−989	−1 091	−1 352	−972	−1 202	−1 380	−1 078	..
Total net investment	-ANNW	5 955	5 501	5 125	11 901	13 804	15 707	20 575	23 461	25 969	29 315	37 660
Net borrowing[7]	-ANNX	−4 468	−15 494	−18 307	−243	25 124	33 159	39 863	37 656	30 792	34 649	89 958
Financial transactions determining net cash requirement												
Net lending to private sector and Rest of World	ANSU	171	2 212	3 174	2 674	2 736	2 652	967	874	18	4 152	..
Net acquisition of UK company securities	ANSV	704	−310	949	−394	765	356	520	654	−2 269	−1 964	..
Accounts receivable/payable	ANSW	803	8 393	−17 163	2 210	−2 779	8 975	2 640	2 425	9 566	−9 541	..
Adjustment for interest on gilts	ANSX	−2 446	−1 294	−2 630	−361	−1 444	−1 186	−2 305	−2 749	−1 279	−4 625	..
Other financial transcations[8]	ANSY	−909	−1 576	−2 556	165	220	−5 483	−3 046	1 422	−1 533	−1 627	..
Public sector net cash requirement	RURQ	−6 145	−8 063	−36 538	4 078	24 562	38 448	38 421	40 396	35 110	21 572	59 902

1 See chapter text.
2 Includes domestic rates, council tax, community charge, motor vehicle duty paid by household and some licence fees.
3 ESA95 transactions D44, D45, D74, D75 and D72-D71: includes rent of land, oil royalties, other property income and fines.
4 Includes non-trading capital consumption.
5 Net of current grants received from abroad.
6 Including net acquisition of land.
7 Net investment *less* surplus on current budget.
8 Includes statistical discrepancy, finance leasing and similar borrowing, insurance technical reserves and some other minor adjustments.

Source: Office for National Statistics: 020 7014 2124

18.3 Public sector net debt[1]
United Kingdom

£ million

		2000/01	2001/02	2002/03	2003/04	2004/05	2005/06	2006/07	2007/08	2008/09
Central government sterling gross debt:										
British government stock										
Conventional gilts	BKPK	204 285	200 833	206 119	232 877	261 373	287 481	306 489	320 622	426 107
Index linked gilts	BKPL	70 316	70 417	75 966	78 982	86 749	98 654	113 090	132 404	154 038
Total	BKPM	274 601	271 250	282 085	311 859	348 122	386 135	419 579	453 026	580 145
Sterling Treasury bills	BKPJ	3 521	9 700	15 000	19 300	20 350	19 100	15 600	17 569	43 748
National savings	ACUA	62 611	62 275	63 087	66 522	68 504	73 365	78 929	84 789	97 340
Tax instruments	ACRV	491	478	376	407	350	308	353	428	1 121
Other sterling debt[2]	BKSK	30 230	28 276	32 711	35 032	32 279	36 481	41 261	39 370	57 627
Central government sterling gross debt total	BKSL	371 454	371 979	393 259	433 120	469 605	515 389	555 722	595 182	779 981
Central government foreign currency gross debt:										
US$ bonds	BKPG	4 924	2 107	–	1 632	1 587	1 730	1 530	1 509	–
ECU bonds	EYSJ	–	–	–	–	–	–	–	–	–
ECU/Euro Treasury notes	EYSV	2 486	1 225	–	–	–	–	–	–	–
Other foreign currency debt	BKPH	291	243	172	105	57	1	–	–	–
Central government foreign currency gross debt total	BKPI	7 701	3 575	172	1 738	1 644	1 731	1 530	1 509	–
Central government gross debt total	BKPW	379 155	375 554	393 431	434 858	471 249	517 120	557 252	596 691	779 981
Local government gross debt total	EYKP	52 522	52 566	51 353	50 547	53 300	60 114	62 425	66 371	67 458
less										
Central government holdings of local government debt	-EYKZ	–47 789	–47 530	–44 836	–41 540	–42 339	–46 664	–47 956	–50 364	–50 502
Local government holdings of central government debt	-EYLA	–31	–29	184	–510	–62	–62	–	–81	–2 959
General government gross debt (consolidated)	BKPX	383 857	380 561	399 764	443 355	482 148	530 508	571 721	612 617	793 978
Public corporations gross debt	EYYD	9 414	8 859	18 660	13 895	14 875	14 687	14 411	13 700	13 506
less:										
Central government holdings of public corporations debt	-EYXY	–4 714	–4 308	–4 171	–5 188	–5 740	–5 631	–4 984	–5 092	–4 879
Local government holdings of public corporations debt	-EYXZ	–124	–122	–121	–120	–121	–112	–103	–104	–101
Public corporations holdings of central government debt	-BKPZ	–6 414	–4 638	–4 928	–4 780	–5 080	–2 822	–2 255	–4 119	–3 947
Public corporations holdings of local government debt	-EYXV	–106	–60	–50	–84	–138	–79	–198	–39	–90
Public sector gross debt (consolidated)	BKQA	381 913	380 292	409 154	447 078	485 944	536 551	578 592	616 963	798 467
Public sector liquid assets:										
Official reserves	AIPD	30 423	28 055	26 387	25 266	25 813	27 835	26 631	29 561	..
Central government deposits[3]	BKSM	2 797	2 802	2 900	3 879	3 868	5 212	6 171	5 439	5 224
Other central government	BKSN	15 670	10 743	8 141	7 077	3 044	8 498	11 369	14 834	37 352
Local government deposits[3]	BKSO	11 522	13 698	14 797	16 797	18 718	20 993	23 740	28 327	21 773
Other local government short term assets	BKQG	5 719	5 990	6 061	5 573	5 057	5 381	4 709	4 946	4 420
Public corporations deposits[3]	BKSP	2 215	2 336	2 133	2 813	3 411	2 430	3 665	2 858	2 382
Other public corporations short term assets	BKSQ	1 212	1 180	1 586	2 845	2 457	2 453	2 378	2 254	2 166
Public sector liquid assets total	BKQJ	69 558	64 804	62 005	64 250	62 368	72 802	78 663	88 219	104 846
Public sector net debt	BKQK	311 143	314 257	346 034	381 502	422 065	461 616	497 912	621 173	743 644
as percentage of GDP[4]	RUTO	*30.7*	*29.7*	*30.8*	*32.2*	*34.1*	*35.4*	*36.0*	*43.1*	*50.9*

1 See chapter text.
2 Including overdraft with Bank of England.
3 Bank and building society deposits.
4 Gross domestic product at market prices from 12 months centred on the end of the month.

Source: Office for National Statistics: 020 7014 2124

18.4 Consolidated Fund and National Loans Fund:[1] revenue and expenditure; receipts and payments

United Kingdom, years ending 31 March

£ million

	Consolidated Fund														
	Revenue							Expenditure							Surplus (+) or deficit (-) of Consolidated Fund
	HM Revenue and Customs									Standing services					
	Total	Inland Revenue[1]	Customs and Excise	Vehicle excise duties	National non domestic rates	Interest and dividends	Other receipts	Total	Supply services	Service of national debt[2]	Northern Ireland	European community etc.	Contingencies Fund	Other expenditure[3]	
	1	2	3	4	5	6	7	8	9	10	11	12	13	14	15
	ACAA	EYJN	ACAC	ACAD	RUUD	ACAG	ACBC	ACAI	ACAJ	ACAK	ACAL	ACAM	ACAN	ACAO	ACAP
2004	301 011	153 699	119 726	4 816	13 468	516	8 786	345 938	322 672	15 201	–	7 301	501	261	–44 926
2005	329 708	170 130	121 109	4 865	17 326	389	15 889	368 821	342 414	17 654	–	8 910	–500	344	–39 116
2006	359 954	192 715	124 219	5 055	19 597	398	17 970	401 411	373 074	19 263	–	8 858	–	212	–41 456
2007	373 040	200 127	130 808	5 355	17 334	2 610	16 806	429 078	399 947	19 959	–	8 934	3	233	–56 035
2008	..	..	132 594	5 555	..	..	..	..	..	..	..	..	..	..	..
2003/04	293 052	145 555	115 660	4 712	16 580	352	10 193	335 274	313 072	14 501	–	7 494	1	203	–42 223
2004/05	313 323	158 974	120 924	4 752	15 990	578	12 105	351 237	325 541	16 966	–	8 460	–	267	–37 914
2005/06	336 031	178 707	120 845	5 001	17 762	351	13 365	382 230	355 429	18 323	–	8 139	–	340	–46 200
2006/07	369 841	195 598	125 846	5 108	19 698	2 340	21 251	400 394	371 574	19 895	–	8 685	3	232	–30 551
2007/08	378 538	205 681	132 043	5 398	..	953	15 530	427 567	398 160	19 390	–	9 786	6	224	–49 028
2004 Q1	90 045	46 381	28 541	1 196	7 439	263	6 225	81 330	77 537	2 557	–	2 186	–999	49	8 715
Q2	64 213	32 911	30 061	1 199	–	1	41	83 020	76 032	4 086	–	1 793	1 000	108	–18 808
Q3	72 074	38 847	29 840	1 239	1 316	29	803	87 069	81 009	3 884	–	2 124	–	53	–14 994
Q4	74 679	35 560	31 284	1 182	4 713	223	1 717	94 519	88 094	4 674	–	1 198	500	51	–19 839
2005 Q1	102 357	51 656	29 739	1 132	9 961	325	9 544	86 629	80 406	4 322	–	3 345	–1 500	55	15 727
Q2	67 425	36 762	29 379	1 242	–	3	39	94 409	86 970	4 426	–	1 883	1 000	132	–26 984
Q3	84 896	43 353	30 516	1 391	5 657	54	3 925	92 502	85 379	4 817	–	2 198	–	106	–7 606
Q4	75 030	38 359	31 475	1 100	1 708	7	2 381	95 281	89 659	4 089	–	1 484	–	51	–20 253
2006 Q1	108 680	60 233	29 475	1 268	10 397	287	7 020	100 038	93 421	4 991	–	2 574	–1 000	51	8 643
Q2	72 430	39 406	30 606	1 284	303	29	802	101 986	94 934	4 382	–	1 612	1 000	58	–29 555
Q3	79 869	47 921	30 571	1 348	–	–	29	99 192	91 420	5 588	–	2 132	–	49	–19 323
Q4	98 975	45 155	33 567	1 155	8 897	82	10 119	100 195	93 299	4 302	–	2 540	–	54	–1 221
2007 Q1	118 567	63 116	31 102	1 321	10 498	2 229	10 301	99 021	91 921	5 623	–	2 401	–997	71	19 548
Q2	75 241	38 704	32 917	1 394	–	89	2 137	106 166	99 627	4 005	–	1 478	1 000	56	–30 925
Q3	90 954	52 463	32 173	1 407	3 224	30	1 657	101 387	93 820	5 452	–	2 064	–	51	–10 433
Q4	88 278	45 844	34 616	1 233	3 612	262	2 711	122 504	114 579	4 879	–	2 991	–	55	–34 225
2008 Q1	124 065	68 670	32 337	1 364	..	572	9 025	97 510	90 134	5 054	–	3 253	–994	62	26 555
Q2	..	..	32 822	1 451	..	..	2 402	..	..	..	..	..	..	..	..
Q3	..	..	34 243	1 445	..	..	..	..	..	..	..	..	..	..	..
Q4	..	..	33 192	1 295	..	..	..	..	..	..	..	..	..	..	..

18.4 Consolidated Fund and National Loans Fund:[1] revenue and expenditure; receipts and payments

continued

United Kingdom, years ending 31 March

£ million

| | | National Loans Fund | | | | | | | | Other central government funds and accounts | | | |
| | | Receipts | | | | Payments | | | | | | | |
	Surplus (+) or deficit (-) of Consolidated Fund	Total receipts	Interest receipts and profits of note issue	Service of the national debt met from Consolidated Fund	Total payments	Service of national debt	CG Transactions with issue dept for asset revaluation	Net lending[4]	Borrowing required	Surplus (+) or deficit (-) of National Insurance Fund	Departmental balances and miscellaneous	Northern Ireland central government debt[1]	Central government net cash requirement
	16	17	18	19	20	21	22	23	24	25	26	27	28
	ACAP	ACAQ	RUUC	ACAK	ACAU	ACAV	RUUB	ACAW	ACAX	ACAY	ACAZ	ACBA	RUUW
2004	-44 926	22 659	7 455	15 201	23 242	22 658	-1	586	45 510	3 203	-890	-4	43 193
2005	-39 116	23 777	6 123	17 654	26 612	23 991	-	2 619	41 948	4 303	-2 779	-2	40 422
2006	-41 456	24 788	5 524	19 263	27 323	24 708	-	2 616	43 990	7 973	-3 592	3	39 612
2007	-56 035	25 425	5 466	19 959	27 144	25 898	-	1 246	57 758	7 593	16 391	4	33 778
2008	..	..	..	..	..	..	..	..	..	..	..	..	122 829
2003/04	-42 223	21 968	7 465	14 501	18 691	21 969	11	-3 289	38 947	2 270	-2 724	-10	39 391
2004/05	-37 914	23 673	6 705	16 966	24 245	23 672	-7	580	38 486	1 436	-1 484	-2	38 532
2005/06	-46 200	24 164	5 842	18 323	29 455	24 379	-	5 075	51 488	7 022	3 654	1	40 813
2006/07	-30 551	25 265	5 367	19 895	26 229	25 184	-	1 046	31 516	3 996	-9 546	3	37 069
2007/08	-49 028	25 014	..	19 390	28 077	25 486	..	2 589	52 093	10 536	9 007	4	32 582
2004 Q1	8 715	5 160	2 602	2 557	4 593	5 160	6	-572	-9 281	4 477	-13 009	-3	-752
Q2	-18 808	5 637	1 550	4 086	5 464	5 637	-4	-169	18 634	-1 212	6 089	-1	13 756
Q3	14 004	6 112	1 528	3 884	6 146	5 775	1	371	15 729	2 533	5 892		7 304
Q4	-19 839	6 450	1 775	4 674	7 039	6 086	-4	956	20 428	-2 595	138		22 885
2005 Q1	15 727	6 174	1 852	4 322	5 596	6 174	-	-578	-16 305	2 710	-13 603	-1	-5 413
Q2	-26 984	5 761	1 336	4 426	8 031	5 761	-	2 268	29 253	1 710	8 513	-	19 030
Q3	-7 606	6 183	1 365	4 817	6 793	6 359	-	434	8 215	532	-383	-1	8 065
Q4	-20 253	5 659	1 570	4 089	6 192	5 697	-	495	20 785	-649	2 694	-	18 740
2006 Q1	8 643	6 561	1 571	4 991	8 439	6 562	-	1 878	-6 765	5 429	-7 170	2	-5 022
Q2	-29 555	5 517	1 134	4 382	5 326	5 384	-	-59	29 364	1 952	4 152	1	23 261
Q3	-19 323	6 827	1 238	5 588	7 688	6 827	-	861	20 184	2 233	10 715	-	7 236
Q4	-1 221	5 883	1 581	4 302	5 870	5 935	-	-64	1 207	-1 641	-11 289	-	14 137
2007 Q1	19 548	7 038	1 414	5 623	7 345	7 038	-	308	-19 239	1 452	-13 124	2	-7 565
Q2	-30 925	5 280	1 274	4 005	4 772	5 753	-	-982	30 418	4 305	8 644	-	17 469
Q3	-10 433	6 734	1 283	5 452	8 251	6 734	-	1 518	11 951	1 628	6 964	2	3 361
Q4	-34 225	6 373	1 495	4 879	6 776	6 373	-	402	34 628	208	13 907	-	20 513
2008 Q1	26 555	6 627	..	5 054	8 278	6 626	..	1 651	-24 904	4 395	-20 508	2	-8 761
Q2	..	..	..	..	..	..	..	..	..	..	..	..	30 514
Q3	..	..	..	..	..	..	..	..	..	..	..	..	23 258
Q4	..	..	..	..	..	..	..	..	..	..	..	..	77 818

1 See chapter text.
2 Payment to National Loans Fund representing its payments for the service of the National Debt *less its receipts of interest on loans outstanding, etc.*
3 *Includes net issues to Contingencies Fund.*
4 *Minus sign indicates a net issue repayment.*

Sources: HM Treasury;
National Statistics 020 7014 2124

18.5 National Loans Fund: assets and liabilities[1]
United Kingdom
At 31 March each year

£ million

		1999	2000	2001	2002	2003	2004	2005	2006	2007
NATIONAL LOANS FUND[2]										
Total assets	KQKD	421 635.7	426 239.2	425 955.6	434 544.6	448 006.3	108 243.1	94 226.5	83 227.6	82 872.1
Total National Loans Fund loans outstanding[3]	KQKE	48 513.6	49 788.8	51 037.6	50 251.4	47 719.0	2 963.1	2 910.2	2 964.2	3 022.1
Loans to Public Corporations:										
Royal Mail Group plc	KQKF	..	..	500.0	500.0	550.0	500.0	500.0	500.0	500.0
Scottish Nuclear Ltd	KQKM	..	..	..	..	..	..	..	..	..
Railtrack	KTCR	..	..	..	..	..	..	..	..	..
European Passenger Services	KTCS	..	..	..	..	..	..	..	..	..
Civil Aviation Authority	KQKQ	365.7	342.5	92.5	9.8	8.8	8.2	7.6	11.0	10.1
British Railways Board	KQKS	546.2	518.7	481.3	..	..	..	..	..	..
British Waterways Board	KQKU	18.2	18.2	16.7	16.3	14.7	14.7	14.7	10.6	9.9
New Towns - Development Corporations and Commission	KQLD	8.0	8.0	8.0	8.0	7.9	7.9	7.9	7.9	7.9
Scottish Homes	KQLF	190.9	179.0	161.6	149.7	138.1	100.6	–	..	..
Housing Corporation (England)	KQLH	4.0	3.0	3.0	2.0	2.0	1.2	1.4	1.4	1.4
Housing for Wales	KQLI	..	..	..	..	..	..	..	..	..
Land Authority for Wales	KQLL	..	..	..	..	..	..	..	..	..
Scottish Enterprise	KQLM	..	..	..	..	..	..	..	..	..
Welsh Development Agency	KQLN	0.9	0.6	0.3	0.2	0.1	..	..	..	..
Land Registry Trading Fund	KPOF	..	..	..	..	..	..	..	..	..
Development Board for Rural Wales	KQLO	4.0	4.0	4.0	4.0	4.0	4.0	4.0	4.0	3.9
Royal Mint	KQLP	–	2.0	5.0	14.8	11.3	15.7	18.1	22.5	14.9
Crown Agents	KQLS	..	..	..	..	..	..	..	..	..
Her Majesty's Stationery Office	KQLT	..	..	..	..	..	..	..	..	..
Urban Development Corporations	KQLU	..	..	..	..	..	..	..	..	..
Harbour Authorities	KQLV	0.4	0.2	0.1	0.1	0.1	0.1	0.1	0.1	0.1
UK Atomic Energy Authority	KQLX	..	..	..	..	..	..	..	..	..
Ordnance Survey	GPVF	..	15.5	13.9	12.3	11.0	9.9	8.9	8.0	7.3
Central Office of Information	KJEI	..	..	..	..	..	..	..	..	..
Registers of Scotland	KZBB	5.1	4.5	4.0	3.7	3.6	3.5	3.3	3.2	3.1
East of Scotland Water Authority	KZBC	288.0	283.0	268.0	258.0	248.0	238.0	223.0	213.0	203.0
North of Scotland Water Authority	KZBD	242.0	236.5	236.5	236.5	231.5	231.5	226.5	226.5	226.5
West of Scotland Water Authority	KZBE	425.6	412.4	412.4	412.4	412.4	402.4	402.4	402.4	377.4
Loans to local authorities	KQLY	44 742.7	46 099.2	47 239.1	47 093.4	44 640.3	41 468.3	42 102.9	47 123.7	48 111.0
Loans to private sector:										
Housing associations	KGVS	0.5	0.5	0.5	..	..	..	..	..	..
Loans within central government:										
Northern Ireland Exchequer	KGVW	1 611.2	1 602.0	1 533.1	1 473.9	1 380.4	1 372.0	1 440.5	1 503.5	1 608.3
Married quarters for Armed Forces	KGVX	60.2	59.0	57.7	56.4	54.9	53.4	51.8	50.1	48.3
Other assets:										
Exchange Equalisation Account - Advances o/s	KGVZ	..	475.0	5 680.0	831.0	30.0	670.0	910.0	2 005.0	1 805.0
Subscriptions and contributions to international financial organisations:										
International Monetary Fund	KGXE	9 048.1	9 067.4	9 496.6	9 494.5	9 293.8	8 696.8	8 615.9	8 813.5	8 271.3
Gilt-Edged Official Operations Account -advances outstanding	KPUF	2 500.0	..	..	..	..	..	..	..	..
-surplus not paid to the National Loans Fund	KPUH	190.8	..	..	..	..	..	..	..	..
Borrowing included in national debt but not brought to account by 31 March	KGXF	317.9	281.6	405.9	417.5	467.1				
Other NLF Assets	GLX9	..	..	..	..	..	18 545.9	18 792.0	20 735.2	20 859.0
NLF Debtors	GLY2	..	..	..	..	..	899.0	895.5	1 586.0	803.6
Debt Management Account -advances outstanding	GPVG	..	15 000.0	35 000.0	35 000.0	28 000.0	35 000.0	20 000.0	–	..
Consolidated Fund liability	KCYI	361 065.3	351 626.3	324 335.5	338 550.2	362 496.5	395 161.4	436 345.0	483 836.2	519 312.1
Total liabilities										
National Loans Fund - Gross liabilities outstanding	KCYJ	421 635.7	426 239.2	425 955.6	434 544.6	448 006.3	503 404.5	530 571.5	567 063.8	602 184.2

1 See Chapter text.
2 From 2003-04 the NLF Account has been prepared on an Accruals basis. The figures from 2004 onwards reflect this accounting change.
3 Restated from 2004 onward. PWLB advances no longer included with NLF loans.

Source: HM Treasury: 020 7270 4761

18.6 Taxes paid by UK residents to general government and the European Union[1]
Total economy sector S.1

£ million

		1998 /99	1999 /00	2000 /01	2001 /02	2002 /03	2003 /04	2004 /05	2005 /06	2006 /07	2007 /08
Generation of income											
Uses											
Taxes on production and imports											
Taxes on products and imports											
Value added tax (VAT)											
Paid to central government	NZGF	53 738	58 688	60 746	64 735	69 087	76 638	79 978	81 497	87 739	89 878
Paid to the European Union	FJKM	4 105	3 451	4 172	3 592	2 518	2 574	1 905	1 964	2 288	2 571
Total	QYRC	57 845	62 127	64 908	68 322	71 599	79 201	81 869	83 421	89 855	92 433
Taxes and duties on imports excluding VAT											
Paid to EU: import duties	FJWE	2 042	2 049	2 103	2 024	1 893	1 957	2 207	2 264	2 332	2 462
Taxes on products excluding VAT and import duties											
Paid to central government											
Customs and Excise revenue											
Beer	GTAM	2 733	2 848	2 798	2 907	2 952	3 084	3 099	3 092	3 068	3 034
Wines, cider, perry & spirits	GTAN	3 301	3 652	3 814	4 068	4 430	4 526	4 790	4 784	4 846	5 181
Tobacco	GTAO	7 551	7 796	7 638	7 639	8 046	8 092	8 113	7 952	8 146	8 006
Hydrocarbon oils	GTAP	21 553	22 510	22 630	21 916	22 147	22 786	23 313	23 438	23 585	24 905
Betting, gaming & lottery	CJQY	1 527	1 500	1 517	1 317	977	898	876	884	961	961
Air passenger duty	CWAA	845	882	956	802	804	799	872	906	1 112	1 949
Insurance premium tax	CWAD	1 248	1 511	1 751	1 921	2 189	2 313	2 353	2 347	2 305	2 314
Landfill tax	BKOF	322	456	475	501	545	636	673	753	825	898
Other	ACDN	–	–	–	–	–	–	–	–	–	–
Fossil fuel levy	CIQY	164	84	52	92	9	–	–	–	–	–
Gas levy	GTAZ	–44	–	–	–	–	–	–	–	–	–
Stamp duties	GTBC	4 623	6 898	8 165	6 983	7 549	7 544	8 966	10 918	13 393	14 123
Camelot payments to National Lottery											
Distribution Fund	LIYH	1 665	1 593	1 542	1 520	1 382	1 311	1 354	1 397	1 366	1 349
Hydro-benefit	LITN	32	38	44	44	44	43	40	–	–	–
Aggregates Levy	MDUQ	–	–	–	–	293	341	326	323	324	340
Climate change levy	LSNT	–	–	–	822	813	816	750	741	696	705
Renewable energy obligations	EP89	–	–	–	–	265	375	368	381	389	..
Other taxes and levies	GCSP	–	–	–	–	–	–	–	–	–	–
Total paid to central government	NMBV	45 569	49 768	51 382	50 551	52 486	53 664	56 183	57 965	61 250	64 441
Paid to the European Union											
Sugar levy	GTBA	44	46	43	27	25	19	24	24	–	–
European Coal & Steel Community levy	GTBB	–	–	–	–	–	–	–	–	–	–
Total paid to the European Union	FJWG	44	46	43	27	25	19	24	24	–	–
Total taxes on products excluding VAT & import duties	QYRA	45 613	49 814	51 425	50 578	52 511	53 683	56 207	57 989	61 251	64 415
Total taxes on products and imports	NZGW	105 500	113 990	118 436	120 924	126 003	134 846	140 297	143 713	153 599	159 313
Production taxes other than on products											
Paid to central government											
Consumer Credit Act fees	CUDB	158	156	171	157	200	211	223	189	234	325
National non-domestic rates	CUKY	13 764	14 353	15 154	16 252	16 728	16 902	17 206	18 147	19 182	19 586
Old style non-domestic rates	NSEZ	130	123	132	131	136	167	268	294	326	369
Levies paid to CG levy-funded bodies	LITK	171	234	213	215	190	194	218	239	244	255
Motor vehicle duties paid by businesses	EKED	1 503	1 559	1 230	751	736	787	802	850	869	880
Regulator fees	GCSQ	61	86	105	95	94	99	85	74	71	75
Total	NMBX	15 787	16 511	17 005	17 601	18 084	18 360	18 802	19 793	20 926	21 490
Paid to local government											
Old style non-domestic rates	NMYH	131	144	150	161	176	181	167	187	207	229
Total production taxes other than on products	NMYD	15 918	16 655	17 155	17 762	18 260	18 541	18 969	19 980	21 119	21 717
Total taxes on production and imports, paid											
Paid to central government	NMBY	115 096	124 955	129 123	132 882	139 651	148 656	154 963	159 254	169 905	175 767
Paid to local government	NMYH	131	144	150	161	176	181	167	187	207	229
Paid to the European Union	FJWB	6 191	5 546	6 318	5 643	4 436	4 550	4 136	4 252	4 620	5 036
Total	NZGX	121 418	130 645	135 591	138 686	144 263	153 367	159 094	163 486	174 793	181 032

18.6

Taxes paid by UK residents to general government and the European Union[1]
Total economy sector S.1

continued

£ million

		1998/99	1999/00	2000/01	2001/02	2002/03	2003/04	2004/05	2005/06	2006/07	2007/08
Secondary distribution of income											
Uses											
Current taxes on income, wealth etc											
Taxes on income											
Paid to central government											
Household income taxes	DRWH	89 728	96 977	106 866	108 526	110 407	112 356	121 273	130 555	141 227	151 267
Petroleum revenue tax	DBHA	502	853	1 518	1 310	958	1 179	1 284	2 016	2 155	1 680
Windfall tax	EYNK	2 614	–	–	–	–	–	–	–	–	–
Other corporate taxes	BMNX	1 231	1 842	3 458	3 302	2 657	3 946	4 292	5 560	6 809	8 029
Total	NMCU	124 107	133 994	144 263	145 179	143 290	145 558	160 490	179 960	194 499	207 359
Other current taxes											
Paid to central government											
Motor vehicle duty paid by households	CDDZ	3 116	3 296	3 039	3 540	3 600	3 902	3 935	4 100	4 270	4 513
Old style domestic rates	NSFA	114	117	108	109	104	129	227	235	247	251
Licences	NSNP	8	8	2	–	–	–	–	–	–	–
National non-domestic rates paid by non-market sectors	BMNY	971	1 002	997	1 065	1 013	1 009	1 093	1 221	1 274	1 316
Passport fees	E8A6	41	89	113	139	153	198	237	285	346	..
Television licence fee	DH7A	2 179	2 286	2 064	2 183	2 287	2 391	2 508	2 623	2 734	..
Total	NMCV	6 429	6 798	6 325	7 036	7 155	7 634	8 019	8 484	8 902	9 341
Paid to local government											
Old style domestic rates	NMHK	62	68	76	80	85	103	141	149	157	173
Council tax	NMHM	12 037	12 918	14 155	15 371	16 809	18 913	20 194	21 226	22 340	23 398
Total	NMIS	12 099	12 986	14 231	15 451	16 894	19 016	20 335	21 375	22 497	23 571
Total	NVCM	18 528	19 784	20 554	22 487	24 051	26 650	28 354	29 859	31 397	33 042
Total current taxes on income, wealth etc											
Paid to central government	NMCP	130 536	140 792	150 586	152 215	150 447	153 192	168 509	188 444	203 401	216 700
Paid to local government	NMIS	12 099	12 986	14 231	15 451	16 894	19 016	20 335	21 375	22 497	23 571
Total	NMZL	142 635	153 778	164 817	167 666	167 341	172 208	188 844	209 819	225 895	240 882
Social contributions											
Actual social contributions											
Paid to central government											
(National Insurance Contributions)											
Employers' compulsory contributions	CEAN	29 779	31 705	35 212	35 816	35 476	41 459	44 576	47 302	50 420	53 832
Employees' compulsory contributions	GCSE	23 255	23 289	24 772	25 130	25 701	31 013	33 088	35 181	37 557	39 250
Self- and non-employed persons' compulsory contributions	NMDE	1 712	1 941	2 084	2 216	2 352	2 676	2 744	2 852	2 956	3 032
Total	AIIH	54 746	56 935	62 068	63 162	63 529	75 148	80 408	85 335	90 933	96 114
Capital account											
Changes in liabilities and net worth											
Other capital taxes											
Paid to central government											
Inheritance tax	GILF	1 763	2 017	2 184	2 346	2 323	2 486	2 881	3 226	3 508	3 814
Tax on other capital transfers	GILG	41	37	52	37	47	35	50	50	50	50
Development land tax and other	GCSV	–	–	–	–	–	–	–	–	–	–
Total	NMGI	1 004	2 054	2 236	2 383	2 370	2 521	2 931	3 276	3 618	3 920
Total taxes and compulsory social contributions											
Paid to central government	GCSS	302 182	324 736	344 015	350 642	355 995	379 517	406 811	436 309	467 857	492 501
Paid to local government	GCST	12 230	13 130	14 381	15 612	17 070	19 197	20 502	21 562	22 704	23 800
Paid to the European Union	FJWB	6 191	5 546	6 318	5 643	4 436	4 550	4 136	4 252	4 620	5 036
Total	GCSU	320 603	343 412	364 714	371 897	377 501	403 264	431 449	462 123	495 181	521 337
Total taxes and social contributions as percentage of GDP	GDWM	*36.7*	*37.3*	*37.8*	*36.9*	*35.5*	*35.8*	*36.2*	*37.3*	*36.8*	*36.6*

1 See chapter text.

Sources: HM Treasury;
Office for National Statistics: 020 7014 2129

18.7 Borrowing and repayment of debt[1]
United Kingdom
Years ending 31 March

£ million

		1998/99	1999/00	2000/01	2001/02	2002/03	2003/04	2004/05	2005/06	2006/07	2007/08
Borrowing											
Government securities: new issues	KQGA	12 048.0	26 426.5	25 789.8	43 433.4	54 068.9	53 220.9	57 290.5	80 668.9	66 233.4	64 197.4
National savings securities:											
National savings certificates	KQGB	3 028.7	1 962.7	3 086.2	2 580.7	2 434.3	1 940.4	1 696.4	1 206.8	1 464.7	2 524.9
Capital bonds	KQGC	469.6	35.4	29.0	40.9	107.3	65.0	25.2	34.3	20.7	31.6
Income bonds	KQGD	1 371.7	653.4	760.5	625.6	484.8	415.3	426.6	567.5	593.5	1 502.6
Deposit bonds	KQGE	..	..	..	..	..	−	..	..	..	..
British savings bonds	KQGF	..	..	..	..	..	..	..	..	..	..
Premium savings bonds	KQGG	3 652.8	3 449.4	3 296.0	3 859.6	4 604.5	7 530.1	5 737.8	7 817.5	8 432.5	6 573.2
Save As You Earn	KQGH	11.4	5.0	0.3	..	..	−	..	..	..	..
Yearly plan	KQGI	5.2	..	..	..	..	−	..	..	..	..
National savings stamps and gift tokens	KQGJ	..	..	..	..	..	−	..	..	..	..
National Savings Bank Investments	KQGK	1 085.0	901.6	955.3	864.9	1 012.4	809.9	817.5	643.6	558.4	535.7
Children's Bonus Bonds	KGVO	205.0	58.5	53.4	45.0	54.0	51.7	66.8	59.5	54.1	54.1
First Option Bonds	KIAR	1 001.8	34.3	..	..	..	..	..	..	..	..
Pensioners Guaranteed Income Bond	KJDW	201.0	590.7	687.2	603.5	662.9	274.2	323.9	142.7	216.4	371.3
Treasurer's account	KWNF	17.1	13.6	12.5	15.2	19.4	13.9	11.1	10.9	11.6	2.4
Individual Savings Account	ZAFC	..	257.8	265.9	397.8	405.6	335.4	276.4	261.3	1 015.1	1 394.2
Fixed Rate Savings Bonds	ZAFD	..	175.9	284.7	192.7	193.0	82.0	86.3	51.2	69.5	347.4
Guaranteed Equity Bonds	ECPU	..	..	..	27.2	274.8	227.9	317.1	81.4	62.1	56.0
Easy Access Savings Account	C3OM	..	..	..	..	..	126.9	903.5	608.6	513.2	933.4
Certificate of tax deposit	KQGL	66.4	121.4	76.5	77.6	59.6	145.2	114.8	110.6	100.2	163.7
Nationalised industries', etc temporary deposits	KQGM	39 962.4	40 343.3	56 106.6	62 150.0	55 395.1	47 958.6	25 022.0	22 039.1	35 224.0	51 365.0
Sterling Treasury bills (net receipt)	KQGO	3 546.2	..	..	..	..	−	..	..	..	..
ECU Treasury bills (net receipt)	KQGP	..	..	..	..	..	−	..	..	..	..
ECU Treasury notes (net receipt)	KDBB	..	721.1	..	..	..	..	..	..	..	..
Ways and means (net receipt)	KQGQ	183.6	5 599.0	12 126.0	12 095.3	3 899.9	22 700.2	..	..	23 428.0	12 810.5
Other debt : payable in sterling :											
Interest free notes	KQGR	2 130.9	373.5	972.7	1 427.2	754.0	1 213.2	662.3	1 858.9	1 049.9	97.2
Other debt : payable in external currencies	KHCY	..	..	..	..	..	1 792.5	..	..	..	..
Total receipts	KHCZ	68 986.8	81 723.1	104 502.6	128 436.6	124 430.5	138 903.3	93 778.2	116 162.8	139 047.3	142 960.6
Repayment of debt											
Government securities: redemptions	KQGS	18 575.5	19 815.8	33 722.2	43 642.3	42 109.9	35 087.4	25 130.1	17 456.5	62 406.9	32 940.2
Statutory sinking funds	KQGT	2.0	2.0	2.0	1.9	1.9	1.8	1.8	0.4	..	..
Terminable annuities:											
National Debt Commissioners	KQGU	..	..	..	..	..	..	..	..	..	..
National savings securities:											
National savings certificates	KQGV	3 449.0	2 405.2	4 546.8	4 177.7	4 146.7	2 769.1	1 979.6	1 107.4	1 172.1	1 201.9
Capital bonds	KQGW	888.3	324.2	375.0	175.9	155.9	116.9	121.1	159.2	137.4	184.0
Income bonds	KQGX	880.8	1 686.3	857.0	933.8	1 144.2	977.1	879.5	724.6	719.2	712.8
Deposit bonds	KQGY	84.2	70.2	71.1	45.4	369.9	4.4	..	..	..	..
Yearly Plan	KQGZ	120.0	141.8	18.4	4.5	3.0	2.0	..	..	0.8	4.9
British savings bonds	KQHA	..	..	..	..	..	..	..	..	..	..
Premium savings bonds	KQHB	1 398.4	1 923.8	1 872.6	1 942.9	2 343.3	2 967.4	3 492.4	3 289.2	4 279.8	4 952.3
Save As You Earn	KQHC	37.1	34.5	22.9	8.0	3.2	0.5	..	0.5	0.5	1.6
National savings stamps and gift tokens	KQHD	..	..	..	..	..	−	1.2	..	..	..
National Savings Bank Investments (repayments)	KQHE	2 027.0	1 886.3	1 654.1	1 415.8	1 350.1	1 342.7	1 554.0	1 153.3	1 172.4	976.8
Children's Bonus Bonds	KGVQ	183.2	69.3	95.0	114.5	92.6	79.8	84.5	95.8	105.7	108.5
First Option Bonds	KIAS	1 055.5	298.1	225.2	111.6	77.4	62.2	33.4	36.1	25.6	26.6
Pensioners Guaranteed Income Bond	KPOB	897.8	935.3	2 003.8	1 640.4	703.9	538.5	445.0	428.6	452.7	543.1
Treasurer's account	KWNG	13.7	16.4	13.9	16.5	16.9	14.2	16.2	18.3	11.7	47.1
Individual Savings Account	ZAFE	..	12.3	39.9	70.3	105.9	157.6	202.2	194.1	193.6	274.9
Fixed Rate Savings Bonds	ZAFF	..	2.8	62.1	110.1	133.6	153.1	92.1	105.0	77.2	104.2
Guaranteed Equity Bonds	JUWE	..	..	..	..	3.9	3.3	..	0.2	3.7	365.9
Easy Access Savings Account	C3ON	..	..	..	..	..	126.9	189.3	400.6	509.7	544.6
Certificates of tax deposit	KQHF	199.9	159.9	120.1	91.4	161.5	113.1	171.9	152.1	56.0	88.0
Tax reserve certificates	KQHG	..	..	..	..	..	..	..	..	..	..
Nationalised industries', etc temporary deposits	KQHH	41 776.9	41 089.4	56 004.0	63 127.9	55 695.6	47 757.7	25 949.5	21 943.1	35 686.5	48 265.0
Debt to the Bank of England	KPOC	..	..	..	..	..	..	..	..	..	..
Sterling Treasury bills (net repayment)	KQHJ	..	3 014.8	6 194.2	..	..	−	..	..	..	..
ECU Treasury bills (net repayment)	KJEG	..	2 492.9	..	..	..	−	..	..	..	..
ECU Treasury notes (net repayment)	KSPA	13.2	..	1 391.9	1 359.6	1 453.1	−	..	..	..	..
Ways and means (net repayment)	KQHK	..	..	..	..	..	−	9 760.2	36 207.3	..	..
Other debt: payable in sterling :											
Interest free notes	KQHL	850.5	246.4	458.2	1 723.3	1 393.3	990.5	300.4	222.3	586.4	474.4
Other	KQHM	..	..	..	..	..	..	..	..	..	..
Other debt : payable in external currencies	KQHN	92.0	98.1	1 835.6	2 838.1	1 960.3	47.0	46.5	98.9	52.4	−
Total payments	KQHO	72 545.0	76 725.8	111 586.0	123 551.9	113 426.1	93 313.2	70 450.9	83 793.5	107 650.3	91 816.8
Net borrowing	KQHP	..	4 997.3	..	4 884.7	11 004.4	45 590.1	23 327.3	32 369.3	31 397.0	51 143.8
Net repayment	KHDD	3 558.2	..	7 083.4	..	..	−	..	..	..	..

1 See chapter text.

Source: HM Treasury: 020 7270 4761

Government finance

18.8 Central government net cash requirement on own account (receipts and outlays on a cash basis)

£ million

| | Cash receipts | | | | | | | | Cash outlays | | | | |
| | HM Revenue and Customs | | | | | | | | | | | | |
	Total paid over [1]	Income tax [2]	Corpora- tion tax [2]	NICs [3]	V.A.T. [4]	Interest and dividends	Other receipts [5]	Total	Interest payments	Net acquisiti- on of company securities [6]	Net depart- mental outlays [7]	Total	Own account net cash requireme- nt
	1	2	3	4	5	6	7	8	9	10	11	12	13
	MIZX	RURC	ACCD	ABLP	EYOO	RUUL	RUUM	RUUN	RUUO	ABIF	RUUP	RUUQ	RUUX
1999	282 142	94 025	32 924	55 254	55 331	8 006	22 446	312 594	25 210	−387	285 286	310 109	−2 485
2000	305 547	103 118	33 003	59 274	58 509	9 009	46 078	360 634	23 890	−251	297 933	321 572	−39 062
2001	316 517	111 874	33 520	62 973	60 282	8 611	24 643	349 771	23 132	−661	324 633	347 104	−2 667
2002	315 987	111 559	28 866	63 992	63 000	6 954	25 310	348 251	19 343	–	347 612	366 955	18 704
2003	325 138	113 712	28 489	69 360	67 525	7 335	25 329	357 802	20 348	−39	379 418	399 727	41 925
2004	347 514	121 493	31 160	77 026	71 907	6 855	25 137	379 506	21 027	–	400 631	421 658	42 152
2005	372 567	130 818	37 820	83 612	73 012	6 549	26 341	405 457	22 434	–	421 021	443 455	37 998
2006	401 362	140 616	47 108	87 156	76 103	6 640	28 115	436 117	25 834	−347	448 131	473 618	37 501
2007	422 465	149 968	43 912	96 656	80 301	8 251	30 082	460 798	25 537	−2 340	470 169	493 366	32 568
2008	428 378	157 051	46 253	97 947	80 711	9 354	30 417	468 149	26 033	19 714	544 577	590 324	122 175
1999/00	291 280	96 032	34 322	56 354	56 395	8 637	22 660	322 577	24 320	−535	288 128	311 913	−10 664
2000/01	309 726	108 414	32 421	60 614	58 501	8 715	46 772	365 213	23 798	−81	304 245	327 962	−37 251
2001/02	314 959	111 028	32 041	63 168	61 026	7 843	25 001	347 803	22 126	−683	329 726	351 169	3 366
2002/03	317 174	111 102	29 268	64 553	63 451	7 425	24 725	349 324	19 687	−39	353 890	373 538	24 214
2003/04	331 133	116 194	28 077	72 457	69 075	7 172	25 348	363 653	21 251	–	385 119	406 370	42 717
2004/05	355 917	125 202	33 641	78 098	73 026	6 633	25 074	387 624	21 810	–	403 268	425 078	37 454
2005/06	382 067	133 519	41 829	85 522	72 856	6 393	27 022	415 482	23 121	−347	428 616	451 390	35 908
2006/07	406 337	147 134	44 308	87 274	77 360	6 754	27 359	440 450	26 279	–	451 062	477 341	36 891
2007/08	431 800	152 591	46 383	100 411	80 601	9 000	31 205	472 005	25 390	−2 340	478 576	501 626	29 621
2008/09	416 503	154 709	42 765	96 444	78 443	8 724	27 818	453 045	25 947	32 250	557 368	615 565	162 520
2006 Q4	96 813	28 713	12 993	20 470	21 058	1 932	7 622	106 367	5 734	–	115 138	120 872	14 505
2007 Q1	117 636	51 926	10 475	23 795	19 550	1 897	4 875	124 408	6 619	–	110 361	116 980	−7 428
Q2	96 004	29 417	8 015	25 932	20 123	1 864	8 203	106 071	5 959	−2 340	121 026	124 645	18 574
Q3	107 134	37 488	12 465	24 165	19 301	1 986	9 934	119 054	6 486	–	114 418	120 904	1 850
Q4	101 691	31 137	12 957	22 764	21 327	2 504	7 070	111 265	6 473	–	124 364	130 837	19 572
2008 Q1	126 971	54 549	12 946	27 550	19 850	2 646	5 998	135 615	6 472	–	118 768	125 240	−10 375
Q2	97 155	34 093	8 431	23 420	20 088	2 252	8 129	107 536	6 449	–	131 418	137 867	30 331
Q3	108 986	39 300	12 664	24 472	21 236	2 266	9 105	120 357	6 566	−255	150 435	156 746	36 389
Q4	95 266	29 109	12 212	22 505	19 537	2 190	7 185	104 641	6 546	19 969	143 956	170 471	65 830
2009 Q1	115 096	52 207	9 458	26 047	17 582	2 016	3 399	120 511	6 386	12 536	131 559	150 481	29 970

Relationships between columns 1+6+7=8; 9+10+11=12; 12-8=13.

1 Comprises payments into the Consolidated Fund and all payovers of NICS excluding those for Northern Ireland.

2 Income tax includes capital gains tax and is net of any tax credits treated by HM Revenue and Customs as tax deductions.

3 UK receipts net of personal pension rebates; gross of Statutory Maternity Pay and Statutory Sick Pay.

4 Payments into Consolidated Fund.

5 Including some elements of expenditure not separately identified.

6 Mainly comprises privatisation proceeds.

7 Net of certain receipts, and excluding on-lending to local authorities and public corporations.

Sources: HM Revenue & Customs;
Office for National Statistics

18.9 HM Revenue and Customs taxes and duties

£ million

		Net receipts by HM Revenue and Customs						
	Total[1],[6]	Income tax and Capital gains tax[2],[3]	Corporation tax[4]	Inheritance tax[6]	Stamp duties	Petroleum revenue tax[5]	Payments into Consolidated Fund[6]	Advance corporation tax
	MDXD	RURC	ACCD	ACCH	ACCI	ACCJ	ACAB	ACCN
2004	165 564	121 493	31 160	2 861	8 884	1 166	153 699	−32
2005	183 481	130 818	37 820	3 134	9 910	1 799	170 130	−73
2006	206 851	140 616	47 108	3 507	13 074	2 546	192 715	−21
2007	213 705	149 968	43 912	3 804	14 634	1 387	200 127	−
2008	218 626	157 051	46 253	3 169	9 491	2 662	202 283	−
2004/05	172 017	125 202	33 641	2 924	8 966	1 284	158 974	−33
2005/06	191 540	133 519	41 829	3 258	10 918	2 016	178 707	−84
2006/07	210 535	147 134	44 308	3 545	13 393	2 155	195 598	−4
2007/08	218 601	152 591	46 383	3 824	14 123	1 680	205 681	−
2008/09	210 869	154 709	42 765	..	7 992	2 566	193 539	..
2005 Q1	55 047	42 707	9 266	708	1 971	395	51 656	−6
Q2	39 965	28 884	7 766	799	2 285	231	36 762	−7
Q3	46 288	32 042	9 765	839	2 858	784	43 353	−8
Q4	42 181	27 185	11 023	788	2 796	389	38 359	−52
2006 Q1	63 106	45 408	13 275	832	2 979	612	60 233	−17
Q2	42 814	30 604	7 882	874	3 089	365	39 406	−2
Q3	53 944	35 891	12 958	887	3 419	789	47 921	−
Q4	46 987	28 713	12 993	914	3 587	780	45 155	−2
2007 Q1	66 790	51 926	10 475	870	3 298	221	63 116	−
Q2	42 352	29 417	8 015	937	3 727	256	38 704	−
Q3	55 460	37 488	12 405	1 054	3 998	455	52 463	−
Q4	49 103	31 137	12 957	943	3 611	455	45 844	−
2008 Q1	71 686	54 549	12 946	890	2 787	514	68 670	−
Q2	46 171	34 093	8 431	808	2 573	266	41 394	−
Q3	56 310	39 300	12 664	787	2 239	1 320	51 626	−
Q4	44 459	29 109	12 212	684	1 892	562	40 593	−
2009 Q1	63 929	52 207	9 458	..	1 288	418	59 926	..

1 The total is not always equal to the sum of the individual taxes due to rounding.
2 Income tax and Capital gains tax combined.
3 Figures for income tax treat payments of the personal tax credits as negative tax to the extent that the credits are less than or equal to the tax liability of the family. Payments exceeding this liability are treated as public expenditure.
4 Including net advance corporation tax receipts shown separately in the final column.

5 Including net advance petroleum revenue tax.
6 Payments into the consolidated fund are not directly comparable to receipts Over the year payments into the consolidated fund will always be lower than total receipts because the public expenditure element of payments of tax being recorded in receipts. Because the public expenditure element of payments of tax credits (both personal and company) are deducted from the payments into the consolidated fund but have no impact on receipts. In addition, there is a timing difference between payments taking value and hence paid over to the consolidated fund and being recorded in receipts.

Sources: HM Revenue and Customs; National Statistics

18.10 British government and government guaranteed marketable securities[1]
Nominal values of official and market holdings by maturity[2],[3]

At 31 March each year

£ million

		1998	1999	2000	2001	2002	2003	2004	2005	2006	2007	2008
Total holdings	KQMO	297 366	291 788	290 629	285 915	278 808	292 777	321 051	354 884	411 770	442 857	478 779
Up to 5 years	KQMP	86 094	95 112	95 131	92 090	92 780	106 074	88 678	110 839	122 496	119 872	117 620
Over 5 and up to 15 years	KQMQ	131 758	124 603	116 910	120 101	106 044	101 465	131 665	123 729	151 841	167 525	168 623
Over 15 years (including undated)	KQMR	79 515	72 074	78 587	73 724	79 984	85 238	97 500	117 350	134 485	152 529	192 536
Official holdings:[3]												
Total	HHAW	6 345	6 394	6 204	8 210	7 558	10 650	9 118	7 433	25 409	23 305	25 754
Up to 5 years	HHAY	2 499	2 600	2 849	4 652	3 928	4 797	3 321	2 770	8 222	7 328	7 120
Over 5 and up to 15 years	HHAZ	2 726	2 989	2 567	3 009	2 844	4 115	4 015	3 063	9 620	9 511	10 329
Over 15 years (including undated)	HHBA	1 120	805	788	549	786	1 738	1 540	1 562	7 530	6 420	8 304
Market holdings:												
Total	HHBB	291 021	285 394	284 425	277 705	271 250	282 127	311 933	347 451	386 361	419 552	453 025
Up to 5 years	HHBD	83 595	92 512	92 282	87 438	88 852	101 277	85 357	108 070	114 274	112 545	110 500
Over 5 and up to 15 years	HHBE	129 032	121 614	114 343	117 092	103 200	97 350	127 650	120 666	142 221	158 014	158 294
Over 15 years (including undated)	HHBF	78 395	71 269	77 800	73 175	79 198	83 500	95 960	115 788	126 955	146 109	184 231

1 The government guaranteed securities of nationalised industries only. A relatively small amount of other government guaranteed securities is excluded.
2 Securities with optional redemption dates are classified according to the final redemption date. The nominal value of index-linked British Government Stock has been raised by the amount of accrued capital uplift.

3 Official holdings were changed following the introduction of the central bank sector in the UK national accounts. These holdings now principally include those of the Debt Management Office and other government departments. The Issue and Banking Departments of the Bank of England are classified within the central bank sector and are therefore part of market holdings.

Source: Office for National Statistics: 020 7014 2124

18.11 Income tax: allowances and reliefs[1]
United Kingdom

£

Personal allowances		1998 /99	1999 /00	2000 /01	2001 /02	2002 /03	2003 /04	2004 /05	2005 /06	2006 /07	2007 /08	2008 /09
Personal allowance	KDZP	4 195	4 335	4 385	4 535	4 615	4 615	4 745	4 895	5 035	5 225	6 035
Married couple's (both partners under 65)[2]	KDZR	1 900	1 970	..	..	..	..	..	..	..	..	..
Age allowance:												
Personal (aged 65-74)	KSOH	5 410	5 720	5 790	5 990	6 100	6 610	6 830	7 090	7 280	7 550	9 030
Personal (aged 75 or over)	KSOI	5 600	5 980	6 050	6 260	6 370	6 720	6 950	7 220	7 420	7 690	9 180
Married couple's (either partner between 65-74 but neither partner 75 or over)[2,3]	KEDI	3 305	5 125	5 185	5 365	5 465	5 565	5 725	5 905	6 065	6 285	6 535
Married couple's (either partner 75 or over)[2]	KEIY	3 345	5 195	5 255	5 435	5 535	5 635	5 795	5 975	6 135	6 365	6 625
Minimum married couple's allowance	C58D	1 900	1 970	2 000	2 070	2 110	2 150	2 210	2 280	2 350	2 440	2 540
Income limit[4]	KEOO	16 200	16 800	17 000	17 600	17 900	18 300	18 900	19 500	20 100	20 900	21 800
Additional personal allowance[2]	KEPG	1 900	1 970	..	..	..	..	..	..	..	..	..
Widow's bereavement allowance	KEPH	1 900	1 970	..	..	..	..	..	..	..	..	..
Blind person's allowance												
Single or married (one spouse blind)	KSOJ	1 330	1 380	1 400	1 450	1 480	1 510	1 560	1 610	1 660	1 730	1 800
Married (both spouses blind)	KSOK	2 660	2 760	2 800	2 900	2 960	3 020	3 120	3 220	3 320	3 460	3 600
Life Assurance Relief												
Percentage of gross premium	KFDR	12.5 or Nil	12.5 or Nil	12.5 or Nil	12.5 or Nil	12.5 or Nil	12.5 or Nil	12.5 or Nil	12.5 or Nil	12.5 or Nil	12.5 or Nil	12.5 or Nil

1 See chapter text.
2 The allowance was restricted to 20 per cent in 1994-95, 15 per cent from 1995-96 and 10 per cent from 1999-00.
3 In the 2009-10 tax year all Married Couples Allowance claimants in this category will become 75 at some point during the year and will therefore be entitled to the higher amount of allowance, for those aged 75 and over.

4 If the total income, less allowable deductions of a taxpayer aged 65 or over exceeds the limit, the age-related allowances are reduced by £1 for each £2 of income over the aged income level until the basic levels of the personal and married couple's allowances are reached.

Source: HM Revenue & Customs: 020 7147 3045

18.12 Rates of Income tax
United Kingdom

	2000/01		2001/02		2002/03		2003/04		2004/05	
	Bands of taxable income (£)[1]	Rate of tax - Percentages	Bands of taxable income (£)[1]	Rate of tax - Percentages	Bands of taxable income (£)[1]	Rate of tax - Percentages	Bands of taxable income (£)[1]	Rate of tax - Percentages	Bands of taxable income (£)[1]	Rate of tax - Percentages
Starting rate[2]	1 - 1 520	10	1 - 1 880	10	1 - 1 920	10	1 - 1 960	10	1 - 2 020	10
Basic rate[3]	1 521 - 28400	22	1 881 - 29 400	22	1 921 - 29 900	22	1 961 - 30 500	22	2 021 - 31 400	22
Higher rate[4]	over 28 400	40	over 29 400	40	over 29 900	40	over 30 500	40	over 31 400	40

	2005/06		2006/07		2007/08		2008/09		2009/10	
	Bands of taxable income (£)[1]	Rate of tax - Percentages	Bands of taxable income (£)[1]	Rate of tax - Percentages	Bands of taxable income (£)[1]	Rate of tax - Percentages	Bands of taxable income (£)[1]	Rate of tax - Percentages	Bands of taxable income (£)[1]	Rate of tax - Percentages
Starting rate[2]	1 - 2 090	10	1 - 2 150	10	1 - 2 230	10	1 - 2 230	10[5]	1 - 2 440	10
Basic rate[3]	2 091 - 32 400	22	2 151 - 33 300	22	2 231 - 34 600	22	2 321 - 34 800	20	2 231 - 37 400	20
Higher rate[4]	over 32 400	40	over 33 300	40	over 34 600	40	over 34 800	40	over 37 400	40

1 Taxable income is defined as gross income for income tax purposes less any allowances and reliefs available at the taxpayer's marginal rate.
2 The starting rate also applies to savings and dividends.
3 The basic rate of tax on dividends is 10% and savings income is 20%.
4 The higher rate of tax on dividends is 32.5%.
5 From 2008/09 there is a 10% starting rate for savings income only. If non-savings income is above this limit the 10% rate does not apply.

Source: HM Revenue & Customs: 020 7147 3045

18.13 Local Authorities: gross loan debt outstanding[1]
At 31 March each year

£ billion

		2004	2005	2006	2007	2008
United Kingdom						
Total debt	KQBR	50.5	52.9	59.7	62.3	66.4
Public Works Loan Board	KQBS	41.3	42.4	47.1	47.9	50.7
Northern Ireland Consolidated Fund	KQBT	0.3	0.3	..	..	..
Other debt	KQBU	8.8	10.5	..	..	..
England						
Total debt	C3OO	37.7	40.1	46.1	48.6	52.4
of which Public Works Loan Board	C3OP	31.1	32.2	36.6	37.6	40.2
Wales						
Total debt	C3OQ	3.6	3.7	3.8	3.8	4.0
of which Public Works Loan Board	C3OR	3.1	3.1	3.3	3.1	3.2
Scotland						
Total debt	KQBX	8.8	8.7	9.4	9.5	9.7
of which Public Works Loan Board	KQBY	7.1	6.8	7.2	7.1	7.1
Northern Ireland						
Total debt	KQBZ	0.3	0.3	0.3	0.3	0.4
of which Northern Ireland Consolidated Fund	KQBT	0.3	0.3	..	..	..

1 The sums shown exclude inter-authority loans.

Sources: Communities and Local Government: 020 7944 4176;
Public Works Loan Board: 020 7862 6610;
Department of Finance and Personnel for Northern Ireland: 028 9185 8132

18.14 Rateable Values[1]
England and Wales
At 1 April each year

		1998	1999	2000	2001	2002	2003	2004	2005	2006	2007	2008
Number of properties (Thousands)												
Commercial	KMIN	1 223	1 219	1 223	1 230	1 234	1 236	1 239	1 234	1 245	1 258	1 267
Shops and cafes	KMIO	488	484	478	476	473	469	466	462	459	457	456
Offices	KMIP	257	258	261	269	273	279	284	287	296	304	311
Other	KMIQ	478	477	484	485	487	488	490	485	490	497	500
On-licensed premises	KMIR	59	60	61	61	60	60	60	66	65	65	64
Entertainment and recreational:	KMIS	81	80	79	79	80	80	80	78	79	81	81
Cinemas	KMIT	1	1	1	1	1	1	1	1	1	1	1
Theatres and music-halls	KMIU	1	1	1	1	1	1	1	1	1	1	1
Other	KMIV	80	79	76	76	77	77	78	76	78	80	80
Public utility	KMIW	9	9	8	8	8	8	8	8	8	8	8
Educational and cultural	KMIX	41	41	41	42	42	42	43	45	45	45	45
Miscellaneous	KMIY	56	61	67	70	70	72	74	74	77	80	81
Industrial	KMIZ	250	250	250	251	250	250	250	252	251	252	249
Total	KMIH	1 719	1 720	1 729	1 740	1 745	1 749	1 754	1 756	1 771	1 788	1 796
Value of assessments (£ million)												
Commercial	KMHG	19 733	19 652	26 320	27 255	27 622	27 713	27 878	33 013	33 548	33 566	33 427
Shops and cafes	KMHH	5 860	5 840	6 801	6 972	6 953	6 863	6 845	8 257	8 311	8 289	8 251
Offices	KMHI	5 624	5 575	8 625	9 191	9 388	9 555	9 591	10 840	10 904	10 724
Other	KMHJ	8 249	8 237	10 894	11 092	11 281	11 295	11 441	13 916	14 203	14 373	14 452
On-licensed premises	KMHK	980	997	1 311	1 347	1 345	1 334	1 320	1 667	1 652	1 615	1 589
Entertainment and recreational	KMHL	1 040	1 045	1 310	1 369	1 430	1 416	1 362	1 467	1 483	1 481	1 478
Cinemas	KMHM	39	45	79	92	104	106	96	117	115	110	101
Theatres and music-halls	KMHN	21	20	24	25	26	26	26	34	35	35	35
Other	KMHO	979	980	1 207	1 252	1 300	1 284	1 240	1 316	1 333	1 337	1 342
Public utility	KMHP	3 380	3 361	3 828	3 411	3 460	3 444	3 410	3 680	3 668	3 668	3 656
Educational and cultural	KMHQ	1 773	1 672	1 829	1 872	1 902	1 895	1 904	2 359	2 411	2 407	2 397
Miscellaneous	KMHR	1 464	1 439	2 142	2 172	2 220	2 218	2 022	2 582	2 646	2 687	2 694
Industrial	KMHS	5 540	5 463	6 249	6 202	6 157	6 034	5 935	6 651	6 575	6 453	6 314
Total	KMHA	33 909	33 649	42 985	43 626	44 136	44 053	43 831	51 419	51 983	51 878	51 555

1 See chapter text.

Source: HM Revenue & Customs: 020 7147 2941

18.15 Revenue expenditure of local authorities

£ million

	2005/06 outturn	2006/07 outturn	2007/08 outturn	2008/09 budget
England				
Education[1]	36 020	37 972	40 135	41 480
Highways and Transport	4 843	5 316	5 636	6 101
Social care[2]	17 359	18 108	18 587	19 478
Housing (excluding HRA)[3]	14 066	14 963	15 844	15 987
Cultural, environmental and planning	9 162	9 658	10 139	10 361
of which:				
Cultural	2 967	3 129	3 188	3 265
Environmental	4 248	4 524	4 832	5 205
Planning and development	1 947	2 005	2 119	1 890
Police	10 957	11 542	11 704	12 229
Fire	2 040	2 193	2 233	2 364
Courts	58	62	70	69
Central services	2 432	3 430	3 541	3 695
Other	206	128	360	328
Net current expenditure	97 142	103 341	108 249	112 094
Capital financing	2 473	2 993	3 004	3 570
Capital Expenditure charged to Revenue Account	891	1 103	1 095	1 234
Interest receipts	-1 214	-1 481	-1 862	-1 264
Pension Interest Costs	4 785	4 534	4 808	3 782
Other non-current expenditure[4]	3 194	3 350	3 449	3 561
Specific grants outside Aggregate External Finance (AEF)	-18 267	-19 643	-20 761	-19 817
Revenue expenditure	89 004	94 198	97 981	103 159
Specific and special grants inside AEF	-14 785	-41 741	-44 486	-42 133
Area Based Grant (ABG)	n/a	n/a	n/a	-2 731
Net revenue expenditure	74 219	52 457	53 494	58 295
Appropriation to/from reserves (excluding pension reserves)	816	974	1496	-1 204
Appropriation to/from Pension Reserves	-4 582	-6 025	-5 595	-4 704
Other adjustments	24	16	2	0
Budget requirement	70 477	47 422	49 398	52 387
Police grant	-4 353	-3 936	-4 028	-4 136
Revenue support grant	-26 663	-3 378	-3 105	-2 854
Redistributed business rates	-18 004	-17 506	-18 506	-20 506
General Greater London Authority Grant	-37	-38	-38	-48
Other items	-104	-111	-112	-85
Council tax requirement	21 315	22 453	23 608	24 759
Scotland				
Net revenue expenditure on general fund	10 603	10 708	11 023	12 298

18.15 Revenue expenditure of local authorities
continued

£ million

	2005/06 outturn	2006/07 outturn	2007/08 outturn	2008/09 budget
Wales[5]				
Education	2 121.8	2 213.0	2 325.6	2 401.0
Personal social services	1 164.7	1 253.6	1 302.9	1335.7
Housing[6]	674.6	716.7	759.4	763.4
Local environmental services[7]	318.9	353.9	356.4	383.7
Roads and transport	270.8	283.3	296.4	305.0
Libraries, culture, heritage, sport and recreation	248.3	259.9	267.4	269.8
Planning, economic development and community development	108.4	115.2	113.6	107.6
Council tax benefit and administration[8]	31.0	32.1	31.7	30.3
Debt financing costs: counties	272.4	278.0	289.0	311.3
Central administrative and other revenue expenditure: counties[9]	206.7	207.4	217.3	272.6
Total county and county borough council expenditure	5 417.4	5 713.1	5 959.8	6 180.5
Total police expenditure	557.9	601.4	623.3	643.4
Total fire expenditure	135.7	142.1	138.2	142.1
Total national park expenditure	17.0	15.8	17.8	16.8
Gross revenue expenditure	6 128.0	6 472.4	6 739.1	6 982.8
less specific and special government grants (except council tax benefit grant)	-1 473.5	-1 529.7	-1 630.2	-1 544.9
Net revenue expenditure	4 654.5	4 942.7	5 108.9	5 437.9
Putting to (+)/drawing from (-) reserves	13.5	24.6	97.0	49.3
Budget requirement	4 668.0	4 967.3	5 205.9	5 388.6
Plus discretionary non-domestic rate relief	2.5	2.6	2.5	2.4
less revenue support grant	-2 751.6	-2 951.8	-3 061.6	-3 104.6
less police grant	-235.0	-217.0	-225.0	-230.5
less re-distributed non-domestic rates income	-672.0	-730.0	-791.0	-868.0
Council tax requirement	1 012.0	1 071.2	1 130.8	1 187.9
of which:				
Paid by council tax benefit grant from the Department for Work and Pensions	170.1	177.2	184.6	184.9
Paid directly by council tax payers	841.9	894.0	946.2	1 003.0

1 Includes mandatory student awards and inter-authority education recoupment.

2 Includes supported employment.

3 Includes mandatory rent allowances and rent rebates.

4 Includes:
   (i) Gross expenditure on council tax benefit.
   (ii) Expenditure on council tax reduction scheme.
   (iii) Discretionary (non-domestic) rate relief.
   (iv) Flood defence payments to the Environment Agency.
   (v) Bad debt provision.

5 Service expenditure is shown excluding that financed by sales, fees and charges, but including that financed by specific and special government grants.

6 Includes housing benefit and private sector costs such as provision for the homeless. Includes rent rebates granted to HRA tenants which is 100% grant funded. Excludes council owned housing.

7 Includes cemeteries and crematoria, community safety, environmental health, consumer protection, waste collection/disposal and central services to the public such as birth registration and elections.

8 Excludes council tax benefit expednditure funded by the specific grant from the Department for Work and Pensions.

9 Includes agricultural services, coastal and flood defence and community councils. Also includes central administrative costs of corporate management, democratic representation and certain costs, such as those relating to back-year or additional pension contributions which should not be allocated to individual services, capital expenditure charged to the revenue account and is net of any interest expected to accrue on balances.

Sources: Communities and Local Government: 020 7944 4158; Scottish Government, Statistical Support for Local Government: 0131 245 7034; Welsh Assembly Government: 029 2082 5355

Government finance

18.16 Financing of revenue expenditure
England and Wales

Years ending 31 March

£ million

		1998/99	1999/00	2000/01	2001/02	2002/03	2003/04	2004/05	2005/06	2006/07	2007/08	2008/09[1]
England[2]												
Revenue expenditure[3]												
Cash £m	KRTN	50 189	53 651	57 329	61 952	65 898	75 244	79 303	84 422	88 172	92 386	98 455
Government grants												
Cash £m	KRTO	25 291	26 421	27 809	31 469	32 634	41 777	45 258	45 838	49 093	51 658	51 902
Percentage of revenue expenditure	KRTP	50	49	49	50	50	56	57	54	56	56	53
Redistributed business rates[4]												
Cash £m	KRTQ	12 531	13 619	15 407	15 144	16 639	15 611	15 004	18 004	17 506	18 506	20 506
Percentage of revenue expenditure	KRTR	25	25	27	24	25	21	19	21	20	20	21
Council tax												
Cash £m	KRTS	12 332	13 278	14 200	15 246	16 648	18 946	20 299	21 315	22 453	23 608	24 759
Percentage of revenue expenditure	KRTT	25	25	25	25	25	25	26	25	25	26	25
Wales												
Gross revenue expenditure[5]	ZBXH	3 246	3 424	3 605	4 350	4 709	5 243	5 786	6 128	6 472	6 739	6 983
General government grants[6]	ZBXI	2 009	2 093	2 234	2 345	2 541	2 743	2 817	2 987	3 169	3 287	3 335
Specific government grants[7]	ZBXG	84	80	94	601	779	1 005	1 381	1 473	1 530	1 630	1 545
Share of redistributed business rates	ZBXJ	612	656	638	697	643	660	672	672	730	791	868
Council tax income[8]	ZBXK	542	596	670	716	776	861	924	1 012	1 071	1 131	1 188
Other[9]	ZBXL	..	−1	−31	−10	−30	−25	−8	−16	−28	−100	47

1 Budget estimates.
2 Produced on a non-Financial Reporting Standard 17 (FRS17) basis.
3 The sum of government grants, business rates and local taxes does not normally equal revenue expenditure because of the use of reserves.
4 1993-94 to 2003-04 includes City of London Offset.
5 Gross revenue expenditure is total local authority expenditure on services, plus capital charges, but net of any income from sales, fees, and charges and other non-grant sources. It includes expenditure funded by specific grants. The figures have been adjusted to account for FRS17 pension costs.

6 Includes all unhypothecated grants, namely revenue support grant, police grant, council tax reduction scheme grant, transitional grant and the adjustment to reverse the transfer.
7 Comprises specific and supplementary grants, excluding police grant.
8 This includes community council precepts, and income covered by charge/council tax benefit grant, but excludes council tax reduction scheme.
9 This includes use of, or contributors to, local authority reserves and other minor adjustments.

Sources: Communities and Local Government: 020 7944 4158;
Welsh Assembly Government: 029 2082 5355

18.17 Capital expenditure and income
England

£ million

Financial year	Central government grants[1]	Other grants and contributions[2]	Use of usable capital receipts	BCA/SCE(R)Single Capital Pot	BCA/SCE(R)Separate Programme Element	Other borrowing and credit arrangements not supported by central government
	KRVM	I4V9	I4VA	I4VB	I4VC	I4VD
1998/99	1 160	485	1 223	1 048	1 286	..
1999/00	1 161	571	1 599	1 051	1 250	..
2000/01	1 298	762	1 592	2 271	945	..
2001/02	2 027	757	1 975	1 173	1 378	..
2002/03	2 474	716	2 426	2 281	935	..
2003/04	2 642	869	1 988	2 583	1 326	..
2004/05	3 196	1 080	2 647	2 959	704	1 061
2005/06	3 909	1 377	2 812	2 932	947	2 251
2006/07	4 083	1 344	2 628	2 734	630	2 291
2007/08	7 007	2 019	2 665	2 296	630	3 184

		Revenue financing of capital espenditure, of which:			
Financial year	Use of other resources [3]	Housing revenue account	Major repairs reserve	General Fund	Total resources used
	I4VE	I4VF	I4VG	I4VH	I4VI
1998/99	253	408	..	847	6 710
1999/00	231	327	..	808	6 998
2000/01	304	218	..	896	8 288
2001/02	387	1 505	..	825	10 028
2002/03	375	175	1 465	825	11 672
2003/04	262	212	1 388	1 055	12 326
2004/05	..	187	1 440	1 130	14 404
2005/06	..	238	1 327	1 004	16 797
2006/07	..	240	1 337	1 185	16 472
2007/08	..	208	1 180	1 205	20 395

1 Includes an exceptional item, £1.7 billion grant from DfT to GLA (TfL) for the £1.7 billion payment to Metronet.
2 Includes grants and contributions for private developers, Non-Departmental Public Bodies, National Lottery and European Structural Fund.

3 Use of monies set aside as provision for credit liabilities to finance capital expenditure (debt free authorities).
Source: Department for Communities and Local Government: 020 7944 4075

18.18 Local authority capital expenditure and receipts
England
Final outturn: Year ending 31 March   £ million

		2002 /03	2003 /04	2004 /05	2005 /06	2006 /07	2007 /08
Expenditure[1]							
Education	KRUD	2 287	2 780	3 087	3 492	3 442	3 711
Personal Social Services	KRUE	199	260	285	387	364	411
Transport[2]	KRUC	2 461	2 552	2 906	3 461	3 480	5 916
Housing[3]	KRUB	3 828	3 485	3 987	4 534	4 507	5 008
Arts and libraries	GEKZ	208	196	227	329	296	321
Agriculture and fisheries	GELA	65	72	66	93	96	85
Sport and recreation	KRUH	307	263	305	424	415	446
Other[4]	GELB	1 631	2 056	2 725	3 218	3 052	3 342
Fire and rescue	GELC	72	68	81	96	126	169
Police	GELD	408	513	561	606	531	550
Magistrates courts	GELE	40	37	46	1	–	..
Total	KRUR	11 508	12 282	14 276	16 641	16 307	19 958
Receipts[5]							
Education	KRUT	233	221	210	217	261	272
Personal social services	KRUV	75	74	75	85	85	100
Transport	KRUU	107	92	101	87	130	301
Housing	KRUS	3 474	3 622	3 193	2 179	1 769	1 696
Arts and libraries	GELF	22	5	10	7	10	13
Agriculture and fisheries	GELG	49	53	45	63	65	69
Sport and recreation	KRUX	21	7	11	48	51	78
Other[4]	GELH	975	1 145	931	987	1 172	1 316
Fire and rescue	GELI	10	18	6	8	9	20
Police	GELJ	70	78	71	96	117	126
Magistrates court	GELK	4	6	8	1	–	..
Total	KRVB	5 040	5 322	4 661	3 777	3 671	3 992

1 Includes aquisition of share and loan capital.
2 For 2008-08 Transport includes an exceptional item, the payment by the GLA (TfL) of £1.7 billion to Metronet.
3 For 2008-08 Housing includes an exceptional item, Liverpool's transfer of its housing stock to a registered social landlord which had the effect of increasing expenditure in 2007-08 by £500million.
4 Environmental services, consumer protection and employment services.
5 Includes disposal of share and loan capital and disposal of other investments.

Source: Department for Communities and Local Government: 020 7944 4075

18.19 Local authorities capital expenditure and receipts
Wales
Final outturn: Year ending 31 March   £ million

		2002 /03	2003 /04	2004 /05	2005 /06	2006 /07	2007 /08
Expenditure							
Education	IY8Q	96.9	115.9	143.8	161.1	185.8	189.8
Social services	IY8R	10.8	14.0	16.8	20.5	18.7	18.5
Transport	IY8S	109.9	127.4	141.2	203.4	214.0	237.6
Housing	IY8T	219.3	220.9	242.3	257.5	267.0	247.1
Local environmental services	IY8U	174.1	223.7	272.8	298.3	354.9	409.7
Law, order and protective services	IY8V	27.7	39.2	43.4	41.5	36.5	43.1
Total expenditure	IY8W	638.7	741.1	860.3	982.3	1 077.0	1 145.9
Receipts							
Education	IY8X	7.1	1.9	10.2	4.6	6.1	12.2
Social services	IY8Y	2.4	0.6	1.3	0.2	3.7	1.5
Transport	IY8Z	0.4	0.6	1.2	4.5	0.8	0.4
Housing	IY92	102.3	176.2	147.7	88.2	75.1	54.9
Local environmental services	IY93	49.4	70.2	55.3	69.5	131.1	100.0
Law, order and protective services	IY94	3.0	2.2	1.2	1.4	1.1	4.2
Total receipts	IY95	164.6	251.7	216.8	168.5	218.0	173.2

Source: Welsh Assembly Government:029 2082 5355

18.20 Expenditure of local authorities
Scotland
Years ending 31 March

£ thousand

		1998/99	1999/00	2000/01	2001/02	2002/03	2003/04	2004/05	2005/06	2006/07	2007/08
Out of revenue:[1] Total	KQTA	10 033 985	10 439 999	10 924 634	11 553 927	12 858 533	13 658 834	14 527 867	15 746 429	15 986 751	16 578 249
General Fund Services:	KQTB	7 021 038	7 429 626	7 884 168	8 428 217	9 290 268	10 139 679	10 964 598	12 021 453	12 143 056	12 653 585
Education	KQTC	2 649 170	2 855 945	3 037 780	3 283 827	3 533 853	3 872 786	4 180 675	4 406 876	4 596 832	4 747 148
Libraries, museums and galleries	KQTD	124 648	131 696	134 174	138 318	152 308	160 540	161 650	168 953	164 976	163 185
Social work	KQTE	1 394 142	1 519 191	1 632 843	1 793 732	2 173 752	2 400 652	2 621 134	2 808 040	2 994 486	3 192 214
Law, order and protective services	KQTF	952 940	1 006 000	1 047 034	1 088 791	1 130 693	1 226 067	1 306 085	1 501 854	1 469 644	1 506 432
Roads and Transport[2]	KQTG	546 945	527 018	564 738	506 326	601 454	611 721	635 329	673 167	625 341	633 828
Environmental services	KQTH	349 413	373 050	393 333	414 975	484 177	525 556	581 220	635 475	670 308	708 736
Planning	KQTI	179 078	198 285	194 771	223 414	265 315	282 572	299 182	351 617	366 803	372 445
Leisure and recreation	KQTJ	368 023	375 579	387 115	401 904	426 495	472 120	494 237	520 612	543 047	547 132
Other services	KQTL	430 790	435 155	465 612	572 136	515 661	585 425	681 288	948 167	702 554	782 035
Other general fund expenditure[3]	KQTM	25 889	7 707	26 768	4 794	6 560	2 240	3 798	6 692	9 065	430
Housing	KQTN	1 754 686	1 821 380	1 886 189	1 954 444	2 224 209	2 295 005	2 459 146	2 609 228	2 740 592	2 788 537
Trading services:	KQTO	79 644	87 321	80 355	61 899	74 062	92 782	106 445	103 461	102 336	100 104
Passenger transport	KQTR	121	336	162	343	427	441	282	353	355	315
Ferries	KQTS	8 930	9 709	10 005	9 650	11 493	11 768	13 759	14 308	18 400	31 007
Harbours, docks and piers	KQTT	15 697	15 000	10 881	10 912	12 222	13 405	12 407	11 995	8 495	8 312
Road bridges	KQTV	16 408	8 231	8 606	6 914	7 267	11 235	13 276	12 366	16 279	22 005
Slaughterhouses	KQTW	228	4	..	..	..	..	..	..	..	..
Markets	KQTX	13 161	14 106	23 844	16 657	17 995	14 824	15 353	17 447	16 793	18 461
Other trading services	KQTY	25 099	39 012	24 134	17 423	24 658	41 109	51 368	46 992	41 931	29 104
Loan charges:[4] Total	KQTZ	1 152 728	1 109 379	1 100 690	1 114 161	1 269 994	1 131 368	997 678	1 012 287	1 000 767	1 036 023
Allocated to :											
General Fund services	KMHV	710 371	701 515	708 822	739 351	738 870	772 852	772 648	792 404	782 002	806 806
Housing	KMHW	438 556	402 936	386 512	369 943	525 201	348 180	212 440	210 856	214 395	201 297
Trading services	KMHX	3 801	4 928	5 356	4 867	5 923	10 336	12 590	9 027	4 370	27 920
On capital works:[4] Total	KQUA	815 981	816 473	802 672	929 631	972 049	1 052 310	1 264 031	1 572 281	1 952 249	2 182 509
General Fund Services:	KQUB	541 769	557 119	538 843	610 485	662 869	767 122	1 006 150	1 160 818	1 462 620	1 652 425
Education	KQUC	125 341	136 508	127 781	143 268	157 439	172 227	199 387	310 054	402 865	464 827
Libraries, museums and galleries	KQUD	13 231	10 261	5 834	8 683	19 018	12 043	24 796	22 762	24 210	29 963
Social work	KQUE	22 554	22 097	21 539	31 359	30 116	31 966	33 450	37 877	50 327	65 449
Law, order and protective services	KQUF	37 727	37 132	35 761	39 901	53 268	65 477	65 154	51 146	60 287	68 680
Roads and Transport	KQUG	113 954	108 500	117 485	147 975	147 357	200 278	258 071	308 366	418 987	484 669
Environmental services	KQUH	18 397	14 936	17 944	16 396	17 957	20 567	40 773	55 020	43 104	101 325
Planning	KQUI	50 854	52 045	47 684	33 312	40 241	36 496	61 544	76 043	66 063	121 596
Leisure and recreation	KQUJ	40 926	52 365	44 516	39 240	50 558	71 486	74 116	83 681	98 275	136 029
Administrative buildings and equipment	KQUK	35 107	35 824	34 633	53 189	68 438	48 896	64 414	84 569	113 896	..
Other services	KQUL	83 678	87 451	85 666	97 162	78 477	107 686	184 445	131 300	184 606	179 887
Housing	KQUM	268 135	255 019	255 189	300 054	284 418	261 715	241 107	382 697	454 838	507 905
Trading Services:	KQUN	6 077	4 335	8 640	19 092	24 762	23 473	16 774	28 766	34 791	22 179
Ferries	KQUR	268	1 030	23	467	1	111	608	195	547	..
Harbours, docks and piers	KQUS	1 626	1 389	6 192	15 898	20 361	19 503	12 024	12 899	5 855	..
Airports	KQUT	..	..	607	663	1 031	609	572	663	798	..
Shipping, Airports, Transport piers & Ferry Terminals	J96X	..	..	..	..	..	..	..	..	..	18 654
Road bridges	KQUU	2 791	600	964	882	2 386	2 395	442	12 106	22 865	–
Slaughterhouses	KQUV	54	12	..	40	116	82	–	–	–	–
Other trading services	KMHY	1 338	1 304	854	1 142	867	773	3 128	2 903	4 726	3 525

1 Gross expenditure *less* inter-authority and inter-account transfers.
2 Including general fund support for transport (LA and NON-LA).
3 General fund contributions to Housing and Trading services (excluding transport), are also included in the expenditure figures for these services.
4 Expenditure out of loans, government grants and other capital receipts.

Source: Scottish Government, Statistical Support for Local Government: 0131 245 7034

18.21 Income of local authorities: classified according to source
Scotland

Years ending 31 March

£ thousand

		1997/98	1998/99	1999/00	2000/01	2001/02	2002/03	2003/04	2004/05	2005/06	2006/07	2007/08
Revenue account												
Non-Domestic Rates[1]	KQXA	1 326 129	1 437 646	1 440 522	1 662 691	1 553 926	1 718 104	1 804 423	1 895 941	1 897 073	1 883 769	1 859 727
Council tax	KPUC	70 405	1 146 366	1 193 693	1 273 316	1 363 399	1 459 212	1 532 071	1 614 808	1 720 305	1 811 577	1 889 913
Government grants												
Revenue Support Grant	KQXC	3 520 461	3 483 815	3 537 043	3 440 842	3 935 328	4 557 867	5 037 140	5 266 054	5 567 902	5 777 204	6 169 645
Council tax rebate grants	KPUD	260 424	274 940	275 789	279 459	285 131	293 606	307 733	344 899	354 067	359 159	354 030
Other grants and subsidies	KQXI	1 480 890	1 642 045	1 778 216	1 891 839	2 061 297	2 141 543	2 479 311	2 823 820	2 940 137	3 147 497	3 310 712
Sales	KQXJ	46 874	39 595	43 660	49 826	..	..	..	..	..	..	..
Fees and charges[2]	KQXK	1 625 952	1 668 223	1 682 385	1 776 455	1 789 428	1 954 337	1 785 672	1 845 161	1 951 315	2 039 217	2 125 114
Other income	KQXL	290 427	324 932	398 894	453 458	490 574	712 423	515 897	709 226	1 003 925	961 693	875 369
Capital account												
Sale of fixed assets	KQXM	327 569	335 037	303 582	149 504	165 016	207 388	222 844	355 069	366 302	451 353	513 913
Revenue contributions to capital	KQXP	149 423	204 982	213 564	210 912	147 760	239 778	212 533	219 593	247 693	199 749	173 668
Transfer from special funds	KMHZ	36 929	26 959	125 365	27 317	37 087	39 650	52 619	82 991	72 195	20 935	15 711
Other receipts[3]	KMGV	32 118	45 028	39 014	45 351	90 360	75 846	114 745	130 575	261 872	595 722	826 145

1 This is the Distributable Amount of Non-Domestic Rates.
2 From 2001-02 onwards, fees & charges incorporates sales.

3 Figures include public sector contributions from 2001-02 onwards.

Source: Scottish Government, Statistical Support for Local Government: 0131 245 7034

18.22 Income of local authorities from government grants[1]
Scotland

Year ending 31 March

£ thousand

		1998/99	1999/00	2000/01	2001/02	2002/03	2003/04	2004/05	2005/06	2006/07	2007/08
General fund services	KQYA	690 569	818 537	935 452	1 032 591	952 692	1 029 338	1 207 912	1 358 190	1 524 829	1 503 002
Education	KQYB	92 368	225 668	324 340	380 726	251 333	217 743	287 226	327 905	439 678	418 636
Libraries, museums and galleries	KQYC	627	507	634	1 137	5 359	1 517	763	818	1 394	1 523
Social work	KQYD	62 167	71 611	78 611	86 533	114 591	205 229	240 665	236 774	222 551	222 741
Law, order and protective services	KQYE	366 961	382 246	401 485	423 636	445 275	476 681	512 501	597 322	601 593	569 637
Roads and Transport[2]	KQYF	97 649	68 429	57 702	49 900	57 664	27 280	35 038	31 704	49 295	62 799
Environmental services	KQYG	89	71	301	2 272	5 407	18 120	39 971	45 338	55 173	59 112
Planning and Economic Development	KQYH	2 695	4 311	4 375	20 351	19 434	21 517	20 767	31 293	33 750	41 068
Leisure and recreation	KQYI	1 509	1 491	2 377	3 322	2 968	3 732	5 830	6 256	9 194	12 796
Other services	KQYK	66 504	64 203	65 627	64 714	50 661	57 519	65 151	80 780	112 201	114 690
Housing	KQYL	948 232	959 276	956 239	1 028 529	1 188 626	1 449 616	1 614 976	1 580 504	1 622 049	1 805 354
Trading services	KQYM	..	403	148	177	225	357	932	1 443	619	2 356
Grants not allocated to specific services[3]	KMGY	3 483 815	3 537 043	3 440 842	3 935 328	4 557 867	5 037 140	5 266 054	5 567 902	5 777 204	6 169 645
Total	KMGZ	5 122 616	5 315 259	5 332 681	5 996 625	6 699 410	7 516 451	8 089 874	8 508 039	8 924 701	9 480 357

1 Including grants for capital works.
2 The significant increase in 1998/99 is due to the different reporting of a grant in aid of expenditure on rail passenger services in the Strathclyde Passenger Transport area.
3 Revenue support grant.

Source: Scottish Government, Statistical Support for Local Government: 0131 245 7034

18.23 Expenditure of local authorities
Northern Ireland

Years ending 31 March

£ thousand

		1996 /97	1997 /98	1998 /99	1999 /00	2000 /01	2001 /02	2002 /03	2003 /04	2004 /05	2005 /06	2006 /07
Libraries, museums and art galleries	KQVB	10 956	13 928	14 571	19 900	23 097	24 181	32 728	30 062	30 481	33 516	28 655
Environmental health services:												
Refuse collection and disposal	KQVC	52 267	56 246	56 360	62 226	65 289	73 336	90 148	94 715	102 633	113 768	121 879
Public baths	KQVD	1 838	2 585	2 634	1 750	1 724	1 423	..	..	..	..	..
Parks, recreation grounds, etc	KQVE	111 884	115 302	118 396	158 304	170 999	184 406	194 224	193 617	205 734	221 298	198 314
Other sanitary services	KQVF	39 545	39 682	42 923	44 214	45 552	48 784	52 075	55 349	59 906	66 294	68 641
Housing (grants and small dwellings acquisition)	KQVG	489	545	358	37	28	27	12	21	18	10	15
Trading services:												
Cemeteries	KQVI	5 120	5 626	5 887	5 973	6 151	6 538	7 208	7 980	8 455	8 520	7 752
Other trading services (including markets, fairs and harbours)	KQVJ	8 672	7 016	10 779	9 366	7 209	7 769	18 281	17 489	18 776	19 596	15 240
Miscellaneous	KQVK	63 792	63 375	161 790	86 649	89 881	98 244	79 645	114 971	105 031	128 304	141 717
Total expenditure	KQVA	294 563	304 305	413 698	388 419	409 930	444 708	474 321	490 619	531 034	591 306	582 213
Total loan charges	KQVL	24 363	34 823	26 413	..	..	..	..	..	..	..	..

Source: Department of the Environment for Northern Ireland: 028 9025 6086

External trade and investment

Chapter 19

External trade and investment

External trade

(Table 19.1 and 19.3 to 19.6)

The statistics in this section are on a Balance of Payments (BoP) basis, compiled from information provided to HM Revenue and Customs (HMRC) by importers and exporters on an Overseas Trade Statistics (OTS) basis, which values exports 'f.o.b.' (free on board) and imports 'c.i.f.' (including insurance and freight). In addition to deducting these freight costs and insurance premiums from the OTS figures, coverage adjustments are made to convert the OTS data to a BoP basis. Adjustments are also made to the level of all exports and European Union (EU) imports to take account of estimated under-recording. The adjustments are set out and described in the annual *United Kingdom Balance of Payments Pink Book* (Office for National Statistics (ONS)). These adjustments are made to conform to the definitions in the 5th edition of the IMF Balance of Payments Manual.

Aggregate estimates of trade in goods, seasonally adjusted and on a BoP basis, are published monthly in the ONS First Release UK Trade. More detailed figures are available from time series data on the Office for National Statistics website (www.ons.gov.uk) and are also published in the Monthly Review of External Trade Statistics (Business Monitor MM24). Detailed figures for EU and non-EU trade on an OTS basis are published in *Overseas trade statistics: United Kingdom trade with the European Community and the world* (HMRC).

A fuller description of how trade statistics are compiled can be found in *Statistics on Trade in Goods* (Government Statistical Service Methodological Series) available at. www.statistics.gov. uk/STATBASE/Product.asp?vlnk=14943.

Overseas Trade Statistics

HM Revenue and Customs provide accurate and up to date information via the website: www.uktradeinfo.com
They also produce publications 'Overseas Trade Statistics'.

Import penetration and export sales ratios

(Table 19.2)

The ratios were first introduced in the August 1977 edition of *Economic Trends* in an article 'The Home and Export

Performance of United Kingdom Industries'. The article described the conceptual and methodological problems involved in measuring such variables as import penetration.

The industries are grouped according to the 1992 Standard Industrial Classification. The four different ratios are defined as follows:

Ratio 1:   percentage ratio of imports to home demand

Ratio 2:   percentage ratio of imports to (home demand plus exports)

Ratio 3:   percentage ratio of exports to total manufacturers' sales

Ratio 4:   percentage ratio of exports to (total manufacturers' sales plus imports)

Home demand is defined as total manufacturers' sales plus imports minus exports. This is only an approximate estimate as different sources are used for the total manufacturers' sales and the import and export data. Total manufacturers' sales are determined by the Products of the European Community inquiry, and import and export data are provided by HM Revenue and Customs.

Ratio 1 is commonly used to describe the import penetration of the home market. Allowance is made for the extent of a domestic industry's involvement in export markets by using Ratio 2; this reduces as exports increase.

Similarly, Ratio 3 is the measure normally used to relate exports to total sales by UK producers, and Ratio 4 makes an allowance for the extent that imports of the same product are coming into the UK.

International trade in services

(Tables 19.7 and 19.8)

These data relate to overseas trade in services and cover both production and non-production industries (excluding the public sector). In terms of types of services traded, this equates to trade in royalties, various forms of consultancy, computing and telecommunications services, advertising and market research and other business services. A separate inquiry covers the film and television industries. The surveys cover receipts from the provision of services to residents of other countries (exports) and payments to residents of other countries for services rendered (imports).

Sources of data

The International Trade in Services (ITIS) surveys (which consist of a quarterly component addressed to the largest businesses and an annual component for the remainder) are based on a sample of companies derived from the Inter-departmental Business Register. The companies are asked to show the amounts for their imports and exports against the geographical area to which they were paid or from which they were received – irrespective of where they were first earned.

The purpose of the ITIS survey is to record international transactions which impact on the UK's BoP; hence companies are asked to exclude from their earnings trade expenses such as the cost of services purchased abroad. Exports and imports of services are excluded where they are included within an invoice for the import or export of goods; in this case they will already be counted in the estimate for Trade in Goods. However, earnings from third country trade – that is, from arranging the sale of goods between two countries other than the UK and where the goods never physically enter the UK (known as merchanting) – are included. Earnings from commodity trading are also included. Together, these two comprise 'Trade Related Services'.

'Royalties' are the largest part of the total trade in services collected in the ITIS survey. These cover transactions for items such as printed matter, sound recordings, performing rights, patents, licences, trademarks, designs, copyrights, manufacturing rights, the use of technical 'know-how' and technical assistance.

Balance of payments

(Tables 19.9 to 19.12)

Tables 19.9 to 19.12 are derived from *United Kingdom Balance of Payments: The Pink Book* 2008 edition. The following general notes to the tables provide brief definitions and explanations of the figures and terms used. Further notes are included in the *Pink Book*.

Summary of Balance of Payments

The BoP consists of the current account, the capital account, the financial account and the International Investment Position (IIP). The current account consists of trade in goods and services, income and current transfers. Income consists of investment income and compensation of employees. The capital account mainly consists of capital transfers and the financial account covers financial transactions. The IIP covers balance sheet levels of UK external assets and liabilities. Every credit entry in the balance of payments accounts should, in theory, be matched by a corresponding debit entry so that total current, capital and financial account credits should be equal to, and therefore offset by, total debits. In practice there is a discrepancy termed net errors and omissions.

The current account

Trade in goods

The goods account covers exports and imports of goods. Imports of motor cars from Japan, for example, are recorded as debits in the trade in goods account, whereas exports of vehicles manufactured in the UK are recorded as credits. Trade in goods forms a component of the expenditure measure of Gross Domestic Product (GDP).

Trade in services

The services account covers exports and imports of services (for example, civil aviation). Passenger tickets for travel on UK aircraft sold abroad, for example, are recorded as credits in the services account, whereas the purchases of airline tickets from foreign airlines by UK passengers are recorded as debits. Trade in services, along with trade in goods, forms a component of the expenditure measure of GDP.

Income

The income account consists of compensation of employees and investment income and is dominated by the latter. Compensation of employees covers employment income from cross-border and seasonal workers which is less significant in the UK than in other countries. Investment income covers earnings (for instance, profits, dividends and interest payments and receipts) arising from cross-border investment in financial assets and liabilities. For example, earnings on foreign bonds and shares held by financial institutions based in the UK are recorded as credits in the investment income account, whereas earnings on UK company securities held abroad are recorded as investment income debits. Investment income forms a component of Gross National Income (GNI) but not GDP.

Current transfers

Current transfers are composed of central government transfers (for instance, taxes and payments to, and receipts from, the EU) and other transfers (for instance, gifts in cash or kind received by private individuals from abroad or receipts from the EU, where the UK government acts as an agent for the ultimate beneficiary of the transfer). Current transfers do not form a component either of GDP or of GNI. For example, payments to the UK farming industry under the EU Agricultural Guarantee Fund are recorded as credits in the current transfers account, while payments of EU agricultural levies by the UK farming industry are recorded as debits in the current transfers account.

Capital account

Capital account transactions involve transfers of ownership of fixed assets, transfers of funds associated with acquisition or disposal of fixed assets, and cancellation of liabilities by creditors without any counterparts being received in return. The main components are migrants transfers, EU transfers relating to fixed capital formation (regional development fund and agricultural guidance fund) and debt forgiveness. Funds brought into the UK by new immigrants would, for example, be recorded as credits in the capital account, while funds sent abroad by UK residents emigrating to other countries would be recorded as debits in the capital account. The size of capital account transactions are quite minor compared with the current and financial accounts.

Financial account

While investment income covers earnings arising from cross-border investments in financial assets and liabilities, the financial account of the balance of payments covers the flows of such investments. Earnings on foreign bonds and shares held by financial institutions based in the UK are, for example, recorded as credits in the investment income account, but the acquisition of such foreign securities by UK-based financial institutions are recorded as net debits in the financial account or portfolio investment abroad. Similarly, the acquisitions of UK company securities held by foreign residents are recorded in the financial account as net credits or portfolio investment in the UK.

International Investment Position

While the financial account covers the flows of foreign investments and financial assets and liabilities, the IIP records the levels of external assets and liabilities. While the acquisition of foreign securities by UK-based financial institutions are recorded in the financial account, as net debits, the total holdings of foreign securities by UK-based financial institutions are recorded as levels of UK external assets. Similarly, the holdings of UK company securities held by foreign residents are recorded as levels of UK liabilities.

Foreign direct investment

(Tables 19.13 to 19.18)

Direct investment refers to investment that adds to, deducts from or acquires a lasting interest in an enterprise operating in an economy other than that of the investor, the investor's purpose being to have an effective voice in the management of the enterprise. (For the purposes of the statistical inquiry, an effective voice is taken as equivalent to a holding of 10 per cent or more in the foreign enterprise.) Other investments in which the investor does not have an effective voice in the management of the enterprise are mainly portfolio investments and these are not covered here. Cross-border investment by public corporations or in property (which is regarded as direct investment in the national accounts) are not covered here, but are shown in the BoP. Similarly, foreign direct investment earnings data are shown net of tax in Tables 19.15 and 19.18 but are gross of tax in the BoP.

Direct investment is a financial concept and is not the same as capital expenditure on fixed assets. It covers only the money invested in a related concern by the parent company, and the concern will then decide how to use the money. A related concern may also raise money locally without reference to the parent company.

The investment figures are published on a net basis; that is, they consist of investments net of disinvestments by a company into its foreign subsidiaries, associate companies and branches.

Definitional changes from 1997

The new European System of Accounts (ESA(95)) definitions were introduced from the 1997 estimates. The changes were as follows:

i)   Previously for the measurement of direct investment, an effective voice in the management of an enterprise was taken as the equivalent of a 20 per cent shareholding. This is now 10 per cent.

ii) The Channel Islands (Jersey, Guernsey, etc.) and the Isle of Man have been excluded from the definition of the economic territory of the UK. Prior to 1987, these islands were considered to be part of the UK.

iii) Interest received or paid was replaced by interest accrued in the figures on earnings from direct investment. There is deemed to be little or no impact arising from this definitional change on the estimates.

New register sources available from 1998 have led to revisions for the figures from that year onwards. These sources gave an improved estimate of the population satisfying the criteria for foreign direct investment.

The definitional changes have been introduced from 1997 and the register changes from 1998. The data prior to these years have not been reworked in Tables 19.13 to 19.18. For clarity, the Offshore Islands are identified separately on the tables. The breaks in the series for the other definitional changes are not quantified but are relatively small. More detailed information on the effect of these changes appears in the business monitor MA4 – Foreign Direct Investment 2002, which was published in February 2003 and is available from the Office for National Statistics website.

Sources of data

The figures in Tables 19.13 to 19.18 are based on annual inquiries into foreign direct investment for 2007. These were sample surveys which involved sending around 1,250 forms to UK businesses investing abroad, and 2,250 forms to UK businesses in which foreign parents and associates had invested. The tables also contain some revisions to 2006 as a result of new information coming to light in the course of the latest surveys. Further details from the latest annual surveys, including analyses by industry and by components of direct investment, are available in business monitor MA4. Initial figures were published on the Office for National Statistics website in a First Release *Foreign Direct Investment 2007* in December 2008. Data for 2008 will be published in a First Release in December 2009, followed by the full business monitor MA4 in February 2009.

Country allocation

The analysis of inward investment is based on the country of ownership of the immediate parent company. Thus, inward investment in a UK company may be attributed to the country of the intervening overseas subsidiary, rather than the country of the ultimate parent. Similarly, the country analysis of outward investment is based on the country of ownership of the immediate subsidiary. As an example, to the extent that overseas investment in the UK is channelled through holding companies in the Netherlands, the underlying flow of investment from this country is overstated and the inflow from originating countries is understated.

Further information

More detailed statistics on foreign direct investment are available on request from Richard Tonkin, Office for National Statistics, International Transactions Branch, Room 2.354, Government Buildings, Cardiff Road, Newport, South Wales, United Kingdom, NP10 8XG. Telephone: +44 (0)1633 456082, fax: +44 (0)1633 812855, email Richard.tonkin@ons.gov.uk.

External trade and investment

19.1 Trade in goods[1]
United Kingdom

Balance of payments basis

£ million and indices (2003=100)

		1998	1999	2000	2001	2002	2003	2004	2005	2006	2007	2008
Value (£ million)												
Exports of goods	BOKG	164 056	166 166	187 936	189 093	186 524	188 320	190 874	211 608	243 635	220 858	251 088
Imports of goods	BOKH	185 869	195 217	220 912	230 305	234 229	236 927	251 774	280 197	319 947	310 612	343 964
Balance on trade in goods	BOKI	−21 813	−29 051	−32 976	−41 212	−47 705	−48 607	−60 900	−68 589	−76 312	−89 754	−92 876
Price index numbers												
Exports of goods	BQKR	100.9	98.8	99.9	98.3	98.2	100.0	100.0	104.6	107.8	109.2	125.9
Imports of goods	BQKS	102.4	100.8	104.2	103.3	100.7	100.0	99.4	103.7	107.5	109.0	123.1
Terms of trade[2]	BQKT	98.5	98.0	95.9	95.2	97.5	100.0	100.6	100.9	100.3	100.2	102.3
Volume index numbers												
Exports of goods	BQKU	85.8	88.6	99.3	101.5	100.3	100.0	101.5	111.0	125.2	110.4	110.6
Imports of goods	BQKV	76.4	81.5	89.1	93.8	98.2	100.0	106.9	114.6	127.5	122.3	119.8

1 See chapter text. Statistics of trade in goods on a balance of payments basis are obtained by making certain adjustments in respect of valuation and
coverage to the statistics recorded in the *Overseas Trade Statistics*. These
adjustments are described in detail in *The Pink Book 2008*.

2 Export price index as a percentage of the import price index.

Source: Office for National Statistics: 020 7014 2018

19.2 Import penetration and export sales ratios for products of manufacturing industry[1,2]

United Kingdom: Standard Industrial Classification 1992

Ratios

			2005	2006	2007
Ratio 1 Imports/Home Demand		SIC Division			
Other mining and quarrying	BBAM	14	212	182	162
Food products and beverages	BBAN	15	26	27	28
Tobacco products	BBAO	16	17	15	15
Textiles	BAZJ	17	77	77	79
Wearing apparel: Dressing and dyeing of fur	BAZK	18	104	107	110
Tanning and dressing of leather: Luggage, handbags, saddlery, harness and footwear	BBAP	19	109	111	112
Wood products of wood and cork (except furniture) articles of straw and plaiting materials	BBAQ	20	35	33	36
Pulp, paper and paper products	BBAR	21	42	44	44
Publishing, printing and reproduction of recorded media	BBAS	22	6	6	7
Chemicals and chemical products	BAZL	24	91	95	97
Rubber and plastic products	BBAT	25	35	37	39
Other non metallic mineral products	BBAU	26	25	26	26
Basic metals	BBAV	27	90	88	98
Fabricated metal products (except machinery and equipment)	BBAW	28	24	27	27
Machinery and equipment not elsewhere classified	BBAX	29	67	72	74
Office machinery and computers	BBAY	30	150	232	151
Electrical machinery not elsewhere classified	BBAZ	31	68	74	76
Radio, television and communication equipment and apparatus	BBBA	32	184	−619	104
Medical, precision and optical instruments, watches and clocks	BBBB	33	85	96	86
Motor vehicles, trailers and semi-trailers	BBBC	34	70	71	74
Other transport equipment	BBBD	35	77	117	99
Furniture and manufacturing not elsewhere classified	BBBE	36	60	72	74
Total	BAZY		59	66	62
Ratio 2 Imports/Home Demand plus Exports					
Other mining and quarrying	BBBH	14	64	63	60
Food products and beverages	BBBI	15	23	24	25
Tobacco products	BBBJ	16	12	12	13
Textiles	BAZN	17	56	56	58
Wearing apparel: Dressing and dyeing of fur	BAZO	18	84	85	87
Tanning and dressing of leather: Luggage, handbags, saddlery, harness and footwear	BBBK	19	87	88	88
Wood products of wood and cork (except furniture) articles of straw and plaiting materials	BBBL	20	33	31	35
Pulp, paper and paper products	BBBM	21	36	38	38
Publishing, printing and reproduction of recorded media	BBBN	22	5	5	6
Chemicals and chemical products	BAZP	24	46	45	50
Rubber and plastic products	BBBO	25	28	29	31
Other non metallic mineral products	BBBP	26	22	22	23
Basic metals	BBBQ	27	49	53	54
Fabricated metal products (except machinery and equipment)	BBBR	28	21	22	23
Machinery and equipment not elsewhere classified	BBBS	29	42	43	44
Office machinery and computers	BBBT	30	77	84	88
Electrical machinery not elsewhere classified	BBBU	31	44	46	47
Radio, television and communication equipment and apparatus	BBBV	32	70	73	71
Medical, precision and optical instruments, watches and clocks	BBBW	33	47	50	48
Motor vehicles, trailers and semi-trailers	BBBX	34	48	49	51
Other transport equipment	BBBY	35	42	50	49
Furniture and manufacturing not elsewhere classified	BBBZ	36	53	55	56
Total	BBBF		41	43	44

19.2

continued

Import penetration and export sales ratios for products of manufacturing industry[1,2]

United Kingdom: Standard Industrial Classification 1992

Ratios

			2005	2006	2007
Ratio 3 Exports/Sales		SIC Division			
Other mining and quarrying	BBCM	14	195	178	158
Food products and beverages	BBCN	15	15	15	16
Tobacco products	BBCO	16	35	25	18
Textiles	BAZR	17	62	62	63
Wearing apparel: Dressing and dyeing of fur	BAZS	18	121	136	160
Tanning and dressing of leather: Luggage, handbags, saddlery, harness and footwear	BBCP	19	157	168	180
Wood products of wood and cork (except furniture) articles of straw and plaiting materials	BBCQ	20	6	6	6
Pulp, paper and paper products	BBCR	21	22	22	22
Publishing, printing and reproduction of recorded media	BBCS	22	9	8	9
Chemicals and chemical products	BAZT	24	92	96	97
Rubber and plastic products	BBCT	25	27	28	30
Other non metallic mineral products	BBCU	26	18	19	19
Basic metals	BBCV	27	89	85	97
Fabricated metal products (except machinery and equipment)	BBCW	28	18	20	19
Machinery and equipment not elsewhere classified	BBCX	29	65	71	72
Office machinery and computers	BBCY	30	209	398	350
Electrical machinery not elsewhere classified	BBDK	31	63	71	72
Radio, television and communication equipment and apparatus	BBDL	32	206	421	110
Medical, precision and optical instruments, watches and clocks	BBDM	33	84	96	85
Motor vehicles, trailers and semi-trailers	BBDN	34	60	61	63
Other transport equipment	BBDO	35	78	115	99
Furniture and manufacturing not elsewhere classified	BBDP	36	48	52	56
Total	BBCK		52	61	53
Ratio 4 Exports/Sales plus Imports					
Other mining and quarrying	BBDS	14	70	65	63
Food products and beverages	BBDT	15	12	12	12
Tobacco products	BBDU	16	31	22	15
Textiles	BAZV	17	28	27	27
Wearing apparel: Dressing and dyeing of fur	BAZW	18	20	20	21
Tanning and dressing of leather: Luggage, handbags, saddlery, harness and footwear	BBDV	19	21	21	22
Wood products of wood and cork (except furniture) articles of straw and plaiting materials	BBDW	20	4	4	4
Pulp, paper and paper products	BBDX	21	14	14	14
Publishing, printing and reproduction of recorded media	BBDY	22	8	8	9
Chemicals and chemical products	BAZX	24	50	52	49
Rubber and plastic products	BBDZ	25	19	20	21
Other non-metallic mineral products	BBEA	26	14	15	14
Basic metals	BBEB	27	45	40	44
Fabricated metal products (except machinery and equipment)	BBEC	28	14	16	14
Machinery and equipment not elsewhere classified	BBED	29	38	41	41
Office machinery and computers	BBEE	30	49	64	42
Electrical machinery not elsewhere classified	BBEF	31	35	38	38
Radio, television and communication equipment and apparatus	BBEG	32	62	112	32
Medical, precision and optical instruments, watches and clocks	BBEH	33	45	48	44
Motor vehicles, trailers and semi-trailers	BBEI	34	31	31	31
Other transport equipment	BBEJ	35	45	57	50
Furniture and manufacturing not elsewhere classified	BBEK	36	22	24	24
Total	BBDQ		30	35	30

1 See chapter text.
2 Division 13 (Mining of metal ores) has not been published since 1995. Division 23 (Coke, refined petroleum products and nuclear fuel) and SIC 24610 (Manufacture of explosives) are excluded from the analysis. SIC 27100 (Basic iron and steel and ferro-alloys) is not incorporated in PRODCOM and therefore also does not form part of the analysis.

Source: Office for National Statistics: 01633 456746

19.3 United Kingdom exports: by commodity[1,2]
Seasonally adjusted

£ million

		1999	2000	2001	2002	2003	2004	2005	2006	2007	2008
0. Food and live animals	BOGG	5 925	5 827	5 491	5 693	6 478	6 461	6 552	6 770	7 374	8 726
of which:											
01. Meat and meat preparations	BOGS	657	642	428	516	606	667	729	754	839	1 173
02. Dairy products and eggs	BQMS	689	660	614	625	760	780	718	712	807	900
04 & 08. Cereals and animal feeding stuffs	BQMT	1 568	1 604	1 383	1 444	1 681	1 553	1 554	1 587	1 791	2 286
05. Vegetables and fruit	BQMU	437	403	401	433	475	507	515	586	606	696
1. Beverages and tobacco	BQMZ	4 022	4 081	4 139	4 300	4 401	4 116	4 095	4 175	4 395	5 012
11. Beverages	BQNB	3 004	3 065	3 218	3 320	3 478	3 354	3 481	3 715	4 093	4 563
12. Tobacco	BQOW	1 018	1 016	921	980	923	762	614	460	302	449
2. Crude materials	BQOX	2 087	2 447	2 422	2 645	3 069	3 565	3 746	4 621	5 196	6 258
of which:											
24. Wood, lumber and cork	BQOY	66	72	70	81	106	117	131	146	144	127
25. Pulp and waste paper	BQOZ	54	78	81	106	180	244	283	338	417	481
26. Textile fibres	BQPA	447	496	440	472	492	520	516	542	499	542
28. Metal ores	BQPB	518	759	810	928	1 193	1 604	1 713	2 418	2 898	3 665
3. Fuels	BOPN	9 929	17 057	16 386	16 000	16 558	17 885	21 496	25 301	24 700	34 846
33. Petroleum and petroleum products	ELBL	9 123	15 584	14 815	14 321	14 608	16 200	19 794	23 173	22 756	31 666
32, 34 & 35. Coal, gas and electricity	BOQI	806	1 473	1 571	1 679	1 950	1 685	1 702	2 128	1 944	3 180
4. Animal and vegetable oils and fats	BQPI	197	156	149	210	266	205	235	271	327	360
5. Chemicals	ENDG	23 071	24 992	27 514	28 386	31 373	32 009	33 388	37 179	30 091	43 877
of which:											
51. Organic chemicals	BQPJ	5 494	5 718	6 090	5 698	6 070	6 040	6 702	8 009	7 601	8 391
52. Inorganic chemicals	BQPK	1 137	1 491	1 636	1 367	1 460	1 543	1 555	2 143	2 830	2 823
53. Colouring materials	CSCE	1 534	1 555	1 521	1 583	1 627	1 630	1 635	1 602	1 672	1 827
54. Medicinal products	BQPL	6 279	7 217	9 067	10 103	11 897	12 325	12 320	13 786	14 507	17 310
55. Toilet preparations	CSCF	2 462	2 597	2 714	2 823	3 122	3 105	3 219	3 443	3 689	4 051
57 & 58. Plastics	BQQA	3 144	3 366	3 416	3 526	3 703	3 847	4 298	4 445	4 612	4 926
6. Manufactures classified chiefly by material	BQQB	20 302	22 673	22 781	21 837	23 119	24 458	26 492	27 664	29 378	32 557
of which:											
63. Wood and cork manufactures	BQQC	278	255	261	270	322	291	255	273	272	242
64. Paper and paperboard manufactures	BQQD	2 020	2 096	2 081	2 019	2 097	1 996	2 043	2 014	2 124	2 341
65. Textile manufactures	BQQE	3 020	3 051	3 022	2 847	2 956	2 847	2 647	2 680	2 589	2 598
67. Iron and steel	BQQF	2 576	2 848	2 879	2 916	3 319	4 245	5 183	5 131	6 016	6 867
68. Non-ferrous metals	BQQG	2 130	3 171	3 033	2 552	2 567	3 228	3 862	4 827	5 778	6 964
69. Metal manufactures	BQQH	3 553	3 595	3 853	3 660	3 766	3 856	4 066	4 520	4 665	5 071
7. Machinery and transport equipment[3]	BQQI	78 875	87 812	87 240	84 395	79 650	78 376	89 379	110 394	82 713	89 234
71 - 716, 72, 73 & 74. Mechanical machinery	BQQK	21 888	22 140	24 244	22 704	24 231	23 808	25 795	28 245	28 969	32 232
716, 75, 76 & 77. Electrical machinery	BQQL	36 012	42 681	41 997	38 706	30 651	28 624	37 120	55 336	24 215	25 325
78. Road vehicles	BQQM	15 077	15 604	13 845	16 316	17 474	18 489	19 439	19 334	21 114	22 551
79. Other transport equipment	BQQN	5 898	7 387	7 154	6 669	7 294	7 455	7 025	7 479	8 415	9 126
8. Miscellaneous manufactures[3]	BQQO	20 263	21 206	21 948	21 985	22 543	22 917	25 105	25 974	26 695	28 453
of which:											
84. Clothing	CSCN	2 804	2 722	2 578	2 507	2 708	2 729	2 712	2 877	3 100	3 307
85. Footwear	CSCP	532	514	484	452	426	419	470	522	541	624
87 & 88. Scientific and photographic	BQQQ	6 732	7 333	7 775	7 212	7 281	7 040	7 245	7 344	7 063	8 061
9. Other commodities and transactions	BOQL	1 495	1 685	1 023	1 073	863	882	1 120	1 286	1 189	1 765
Total United Kingdom exports	BOKG	166 166	187 936	189 093	186 524	188 320	190 874	211 608	243 635	220 858	251 088

1 See chapter text. The numbers on the left hand side of the table refer to the code numbers of the *Standard International Trade Classification,* Revision 3, which was introduced in January 1988.
2 Balance of payments consistent basis.
3 Sections 7 and 8 are shown by broad economic category in table G2 of the *Monthly Review of External Trade Statistics.*

Source: Office for National Statistics: 020 7014 2018

19.4 United Kingdom imports: by commodity[1,2]
Seasonally adjusted

£ million

		1999	2000	2001	2002	2003	2004	2005	2006	2007	2008
0. Food and live animals	BQQR	13 336	13 310	14 269	14 874	16 452	17 211	18 593	19 814	21 324	25 306
of which:											
01. Meat and meat preparations	BQQS	2 144	2 366	2 689	2 793	3 267	3 441	3 619	3 800	3 992	4 606
02. Dairy products and eggs	BQQT	1 167	1 165	1 245	1 291	1 501	1 609	1 700	1 808	1 837	2 290
04 & 08. Cereals and animal feeding stuffs	BQQU	1 719	1 762	1 957	1 985	2 219	2 307	2 363	2 497	2 918	3 818
05. Vegetables and fruit	BQQV	4 040	3 894	4 101	4 374	4 766	4 919	5 447	5 783	6 204	7 058
1. Beverages and tobacco	BQQW	4 451	4 350	4 216	4 501	4 735	4 939	5 102	5 199	5 423	5 868
11. Beverages	EGAT	3 064	2 910	2 854	3 028	3 237	3 474	3 625	3 701	3 942	4 354
12. Tobacco	EMAI	1 387	1 440	1 362	1 473	1 498	1 465	1 477	1 498	1 481	1 514
2. Crude materials	ENVB	4 861	5 816	5 921	5 420	5 525	5 716	6 129	7 116	8 663	9 609
of which:											
24. Wood, lumber and cork	ENVC	1 088	1 193	1 168	1 236	1 366	1 337	1 358	1 453	1 805	1 413
25. Pulp and waste paper	EQAH	510	763	606	488	489	480	477	512	503	597
26. Textile fibres	EQAP	413	412	393	361	337	339	314	298	315	338
28. Metal ores	EHAA	1 308	1 811	1 997	1 448	1 430	1 647	1 999	2 672	3 790	4 659
3. Fuels	BQAT	5 428	10 016	10 795	10 279	12 311	17 547	25 921	30 888	31 928	47 755
33. Petroleum and petroleum products	ENXO	4 675	9 048	9 525	9 213	11 232	15 307	21 989	25 967	26 787	37 315
32, 34 & 35. Coal, gas and electricity	BPBI	753	968	1 270	1 066	1 079	2 240	3 932	4 921	5 141	10 440
4. Animal and vegetable oils and fats	EHAB	568	491	521	538	614	622	641	771	898	1 408
5. Chemicals	ENGA	18 619	20 633	22 745	23 987	26 139	27 929	29 208	31 727	34 645	37 770
of which:											
51. Organic chemicals	EHAC	4 788	5 374	5 529	5 673	6 102	6 802	7 183	7 692	8 620	8 438
52. Inorganic chemicals	EHAE	1 056	1 046	1 171	1 070	1 094	1 367	1 507	2 123	2 679	2 581
53. Colouring materials	CSCR	956	1 002	975	952	1 003	1 060	1 072	1 090	1 164	1 222
54. Medicinal products	EHAF	4 124	4 714	6 149	7 288	8 189	8 372	8 504	9 158	9 943	11 049
55. Toilet preparations	CSCS	1 774	2 005	2 261	2 499	2 745	2 881	3 035	3 336	3 448	3 966
57 & 58. Plastics	EHAG	3 819	4 144	4 096	4 063	4 403	4 749	5 038	5 409	5 699	6 212
6. Manufactures classified chiefly by material	EHAH	26 930	29 232	30 165	28 735	29 906	32 299	33 469	37 615	39 792	41 893
of which:											
63. Wood and cork manufactures	EHAI	1 145	1 245	1 340	1 436	1 449	1 585	1 505	1 575	1 733	1 737
64. Paper and paperboard manufactures	EHAJ	4 321	4 407	4 864	4 582	4 747	4 841	4 820	5 037	5 248	5 443
65. Textile manufactures	EHAK	4 380	4 365	4 303	4 149	4 089	4 124	3 844	4 018	4 084	4 079
67. Iron and steel	EHAL	2 473	2 731	3 051	3 047	3 237	4 199	4 402	4 981	5 958	6 599
68. Non-ferrous metals	EHAM	2 942	3 711	3 780	3 222	3 320	3 616	3 923	6 185	6 230	6 410
69. Metal manufactures	EHAN	3 789	4 065	4 324	4 501	4 765	4 977	5 355	5 852	6 563	6 991
7. Machinery and transport equipment[3]	EHAO	90 183	102 420	105 386	107 556	101 473	103 882	117 118	139 828	117 726	120 856
71 - 716, 72, 73 & 74. Mechanical machinery	EHAQ	17 313	17 867	18 618	18 901	18 951	19 725	21 848	22 614	25 776	28 854
716, 75, 76 & 77. Electrical machinery	EHAR	42 423	53 631	50 842	49 917	43 656	45 495	55 535	75 087	46 006	47 628
78. Road vehicles	EHAS	24 000	23 117	26 289	28 449	29 921	30 734	31 436	32 674	36 590	33 794
79. Other transport equipment	EHAT	6 447	7 805	9 637	10 289	8 945	7 928	8 299	9 453	9 354	10 580
8. Miscellaneous manufactures[3]	EHAU	29 042	32 798	35 023	36 889	38 168	39 822	42 175	44 920	47 939	50 920
of which:											
84. Clothing	CSDR	7 483	8 495	9 119	9 804	10 323	10 646	11 303	11 847	12 310	13 220
85. Footwear	CSDS	2 041	2 001	2 236	2 365	2 375	2 447	2 563	2 699	2 659	2 846
87 & 88. Scientific and photographic	EHAW	6 170	7 273	7 620	7 044	7 049	7 255	7 414	7 655	7 572	8 425
9. Other commodities and transactions	BQAW	1 799	1 846	1 264	1 450	1 604	1 807	1 841	2 070	2 274	2 579
Total United Kingdom imports	BOKH	195 217	220 912	230 305	234 229	236 927	251 774	280 197	319 947	310 612	343 964

1 See chapter text. The numbers on the left hand side of the table refer to the code numbers of the *Standard International Trade Classification,* Revision 3, which was introduced in January 1988.
2 Balance of payments consistent basis.
3 Sections 7 and 8 are shown by broad economic category in table G2 of the *Monthly Review of External Trade Statistics.*

Source: Office for National Statistics: 020 7014 2018

19.5 United Kingdom exports: by area[1,2]
Seasonally adjusted

£ million

		1999	2000	2001	2002	2003	2004	2005	2006	2007	2008
European Union:[3]	LGCK	101 537	112 459	114 406	114 737	111 286	111 650	121 486	152 357	127 813	141 136
EMU members:	QAKW	92 359	102 138	104 202	103 908	100 631	100 595	109 506	136 061	114 537	126 102
Austria	CHMY	1 168	1 146	1 224	1 265	1 264	1 095	1 332	1 699	1 376	1 473
Belgium & Luxembourg	CHNQ	9 241	10 322	9 893	10 552	11 374	10 510	11 394	15 082	12 122	13 266
Finland	CHMZ	1 354	1 471	1 611	1 442	1 493	1 363	1 514	1 872	1 958	1 908
France	ENYL	16 907	18 577	19 249	18 757	18 885	18 562	19 931	28 693	18 103	18 067
Germany	ENYO	20 464	22 789	23 655	22 064	20 805	21 668	23 025	27 602	24 699	28 062
Greece	CHNT	1 181	1 267	1 156	1 234	1 286	1 408	1 367	1 469	1 350	1 649
Irish Republic	CHNS	10 783	12 372	13 835	15 422	12 224	14 134	16 294	17 480	17 801	19 104
Italy	CHNO	7 831	8 429	8 404	8 506	8 603	8 400	8 790	9 494	9 189	9 351
Netherlands	CHNP	13 632	15 167	14 599	14 011	13 597	12 029	12 716	16 522	15 115	19 697
Portugal	CHNU	1 712	1 660	1 579	1 518	1 453	1 580	1 698	2 374	1 481	1 640
Spain	CHNV	7 526	8 302	8 363	8 490	8 943	9 100	10 677	12 295	9 979	10 227
Non-EMU members:[3]	BQIA	9 178	10 321	10 204	10 829	10 655	11 055	11 980	16 296	13 276	15 034
of which:											
Bulgaria	WYUF	76	85	122	134	154	155	220	237	202	252
Czech Rep	FKML	733	927	1 075	1 031	1 003	978	1 080	1 526	1 401	1 547
Denmark	CHNR	2 054	2 315	2 267	2 729	2 180	2 042	2 314	3 715	2 182	2 599
Hungary	QALC	486	613	612	750	856	934	834	855	863	1 009
Poland	ERDR	1 169	1 299	1 297	1 318	1 462	1 417	1 653	2 705	2 372	3 010
Romania	WMDB	242	381	341	432	509	609	647	637	668	755
Sweden	CHNA	4 035	4 211	3 951	3 873	3 823	4 356	4 588	5 246	4 904	5 194
Other Western Europe:	HCJD	6 244	7 223	6 786	6 334	6 629	7 031	9 730	9 221	9 232	10 846
of which:											
Iceland	EPLW	159	193	150	131	141	167	179	188	198	189
Norway	EPLX	1 999	2 018	1 813	1 696	1 886	1 939	2 211	2 125	2 697	2 875
Switzerland	EPLV	2 768	3 061	3 496	3 080	2 786	2 842	4 985	4 189	3 808	4 701
Turkey	EOBA	1 198	1 800	1 150	1 287	1 638	1 903	2 160	2 426	2 283	2 580
North America:	HBZQ	27 582	33 714	33 408	32 261	32 924	32 764	35 010	36 929	36 367	39 416
of which:											
Canada	EOBC	2 532	3 487	3 203	3 107	3 239	3 340	3 277	3 894	3 291	3 282
Mexico	EPJX	577	675	681	704	687	629	638	747	801	911
USA	EOBB	24 040	29 276	29 244	28 197	28 672	28 589	30 916	32 098	32 113	34 924
Other OECD countries:	HCII	6 728	8 028	7 542	7 469	7 824	8 226	8 577	8 716	8 778	10 011
of which:											
Australia	EPMA	2 155	2 699	2 298	2 114	2 289	2 455	2 580	2 488	2 630	3 122
Japan	EOBD	3 300	3 672	3 673	3 583	3 710	3 863	3 900	4 109	3 866	3 933
New Zealand	EPMB	324	305	309	311	348	418	415	373	364	388
South Korea	ERDM	949	1 350	1 262	1 461	1 468	1 481	1 677	1 746	1 914	2 568
Oil exporting countries:	HDII	5 524	6 031	6 474	6 229	7 615	7 996	10 850	9 060	9 716	11 693
of which:											
Brunei	QALF	124	96	59	61	127	67	43	79	870	66
Dubai	QALI	790	966	1 012	940	1 383	2 019	4 656	2 829	1 927	2 718
Indonesia	FKMR	385	404	313	324	452	397	366	311	289	390
Kuwait	QATB	293	338	359	308	373	354	426	438	450	547
Nigeria	QATE	447	524	686	711	738	773	799	821	1 043	1 530
Saudi Arabia	ERDI	1 481	1 557	1 525	1 388	1 819	1 611	1 559	1 644	1 857	2 211
Rest of the World	HCHW	18 551	20 481	20 477	19 494	22 042	23 207	25 955	27 352	28 952	37 986
of which:											
Brazil	FKMO	739	775	808	880	825	789	836	918	1 108	1 704
China	ERDN	1 211	1 468	1 709	1 493	1 924	2 366	2 811	3 264	3 860	5 117
Egypt	QALL	539	498	452	463	458	667	543	577	686	951
Hong Kong	ERDG	2 312	2 673	2 683	2 411	2 481	2 630	3 087	2 864	2 726	3 702
India	ERDJ	1 450	2 058	1 772	1 755	2 284	2 234	2 798	2 693	2 968	4 164
Israel	ERDL	1 295	1 516	1 357	1 428	1 359	1 386	1 352	1 308	1 257	1 350
Malaysia	ERDK	934	907	1 029	877	1 028	991	1 088	877	975	1 142
Pakistan	FKMU	221	207	229	240	291	343	461	488	423	479
Philippines	FKMX	239	273	392	352	377	315	279	242	251	246
Russia	ERDQ	532	668	893	981	1 420	1 465	1 869	2 063	2 893	4 305
Singapore	ERDH	1 597	1 625	1 592	1 445	1 582	1 708	2 078	2 318	2 467	2 840
South Africa	EPME	1 281	1 413	1 534	1 597	1 766	1 874	2 073	2 184	2 244	2 675
Taiwan	ERDP	865	1 015	875	848	897	950	939	911	957	896
Thailand	ERDO	463	582	594	529	572	637	638	567	613	760

1 See chapter text.
2 Balance of payments consistent basis.
3 Includes Bulgaria and Romania after accession on 1 January 2007.

Source: Office for National Statistics: 020 7014 2018

External trade and investment

19.6 United Kingdom imports: by area[1,2]
Seasonally adjusted

£ million

		1999	2000	2001	2002	2003	2004	2005	2006	2007	2008
European Union:[3]	LGDC	109 622	117 644	126 973	136 931	137 404	142 523	158 163	183 748	169 799	180 322
EMU members	QAKX	99 645	106 146	114 724	123 716	123 224	126 804	139 541	157 276	149 719	157 346
Austria	CHNB	1 453	1 410	1 888	2 396	2 776	2 354	2 461	2 786	2 488	2 327
Belgium & Luxembourg	CHNY	10 156	10 927	12 159	13 201	13 205	13 846	15 155	18 183	15 820	17 178
Finland	CHNC	2 365	2 765	2 965	2 791	2 663	2 336	2 431	3 118	2 619	2 777
France	ENYP	18 410	18 644	20 127	20 798	20 389	20 133	21 984	26 376	21 896	23 154
Germany	ENYS	26 812	28 462	30 192	32 442	33 667	35 381	39 169	42 660	44 565	44 636
Greece	CHOB	408	459	476	555	613	637	703	789	640	663
Irish Republic	CHOA	8 705	10 261	12 141	13 176	9 920	10 131	10 411	10 770	11 338	12 286
Italy	CHNW	9 383	9 514	9 860	10 675	11 481	12 184	12 673	12 775	13 316	13 891
Netherlands	CHNX	13 768	15 380	15 395	16 143	16 692	18 196	20 436	22 275	23 079	25 715
Portugal	CHOC	1 822	1 735	1 625	1 761	1 966	1 928	2 018	3 054	1 506	1 738
Spain	CHOD	5 966	6 141	7 360	9 190	9 247	9 120	11 450	12 144	10 489	10 745
Non-EMU members:[3]	BQIB	9 977	11 498	12 249	13 215	14 180	15 719	18 622	26 472	20 080	22 976
of which:											
Bulgaria	WYUT	69	85	101	116	124	150	169	208	239	209
Czech Rep	FKMM	580	802	1 097	1 250	1 412	1 291	1 883	2 987	2 983	3 563
Denmark	CHNZ	2 341	2 630	2 922	3 595	3 399	3 357	4 393	6 439	3 444	3 905
Hungary	QALD	668	683	710	846	1 120	1 579	1 860	2 348	2 377	2 532
Poland	ERED	876	905	1 166	1 285	1 545	1 835	2 320	3 622	3 695	4 330
Romania	WMDC	253	336	448	522	679	786	803	861	938	762
Sweden	CHND	4 648	4 951	4 671	4 330	4 568	5 118	5 463	5 985	5 274	6 805
Other Western Europe:	HBTS	10 554	13 040	12 240	12 523	13 331	15 754	20 072	23 417	24 359	32 496
of which:											
Iceland	EPMW	282	365	281	289	296	355	346	402	415	458
Norway	EPMX	3 546	5 563	5 523	5 258	6 423	8 495	12 077	14 453	14 316	21 650
Switzerland	EPMV	5 341	5 485	4 544	4 595	3 759	3 447	3 884	4 372	4 746	5 264
Turkey	EOBU	1 204	1 450	1 669	2 164	2 619	3 250	3 510	3 946	4 632	4 885
North America:	HCRB	28 035	33 460	34 617	29 811	27 480	27 130	27 133	31 228	32 470	32 468
of which:											
Canada	EOBW	3 026	4 009	3 664	3 563	3 664	4 194	4 157	4 954	5 793	5 796
Mexico	EPJY	395	613	680	505	490	411	446	444	582	791
USA	EOBV	24 360	28 416	29 345	25 149	22 857	22 103	22 187	25 551	25 803	25 640
Other OECD countries:	HDJQ	13 805	15 717	14 154	13 017	12 989	13 644	14 424	13 633	13 870	15 171
of which:											
Australia	EPNA	1 338	1 543	1 776	1 688	1 789	1 868	2 100	2 107	2 245	2 386
Japan	EOBX	9 118	10 214	9 080	8 079	8 085	8 109	8 669	7 857	7 885	8 531
New Zealand	EPNB	565	544	542	522	552	584	592	600	667	745
South Korea	ERDY	2 784	3 416	2 756	2 728	2 563	3 083	3 063	3 069	3 073	3 509
Oil exporting countries:	HCPC	3 228	4 258	3 969	3 780	3 923	4 866	6 017	6 992	6 387	8 005
of which:											
Brunei	QALG	66	95	35	33	51	63	25	70	57	27
Dubai	QALJ	433	401	396	499	722	579	643	679	662	540
Indonesia	FKMS	931	1 081	1 128	1 006	875	918	839	958	925	1 184
Kuwait	QATC	121	314	296	271	313	396	367	741	696	1 096
Nigeria	QATF	112	89	65	90	83	106	152	206	271	912
Saudi Arabia	ERDU	783	977	933	677	715	1 158	1 714	1 232	821	673
Rest of the World	HCIF	29 973	36 793	38 352	38 167	41 800	47 857	54 388	60 929	63 727	75 502
of which:											
Brazil	FKMP	910	1 114	1 279	1 365	1 477	1 545	1 740	1 905	2 061	2 618
China	ERDZ	3 384	4 826	5 741	6 726	8 342	10 390	12 962	15 237	18 734	23 159
Egypt	QALM	255	411	406	416	432	495	349	662	538	638
Hong Kong	ERDS	4 909	5 917	5 754	5 561	5 500	5 761	6 602	7 338	6 939	8 074
India	ERDV	1 426	1 651	1 816	1 804	2 093	2 287	2 781	3 121	3 809	4 488
Israel	ERDX	996	1 025	939	880	861	920	1 002	965	1 045	1 156
Malaysia	ERDW	1 961	2 288	1 939	1 731	1 867	2 022	1 813	1 895	1 684	1 881
Pakistan	FKMV	318	363	421	472	519	554	487	511	512	630
Philippines	FKMY	983	1 155	1 155	944	713	655	712	742	717	629
Russia	EREC	1 324	1 496	2 047	1 950	2 454	3 506	5 010	5 740	5 248	6 923
Singapore	ERDT	2 348	2 395	2 067	1 959	2 672	3 379	3 828	3 756	4 247	4 008
South Africa	EPNE	1 636	2 553	2 841	2 685	2 949	3 272	3 937	3 904	3 060	4 734
Taiwan	EREB	2 626	3 561	2 784	2 385	2 198	2 341	2 226	2 339	2 418	2 597
Thailand	EREA	1 291	1 602	1 607	1 550	1 646	1 760	1 719	1 922	2 012	2 427

1 See chapter text.
2 Balance of payments consistent basis.
3 Includes Bulgaria and Romania after accession on 1 January 2007.

Source: Office for National Statistics: 020 7014 2018

19.7 Services supplied (exports) and purchased (imports)[1,2]: 2006

£ million

	Exports	Imports	Balances
Agricultural,Mining and On-site Processing services			
Agricultural	24	72	-48
Mining	83	15	68
Waste treatment and depollution	18	19	-1
Other on-site processing services	296	275	21
Business and Professional services			
Accountancy,auditing, bookkeeping and tax consul	1 328	359	970
Advertising	1 922	1 530	392
Management consulting	1 067	428	639
Public relations services	150	41	108
Recruitment	507	134	373
Other Business Management	1 245	803	442
Legal Services	2 589	535	2 055
Market research and public opinion polling	454	220	235
Operational leasing services	349	425	-76
Procurement	102	150	-48
Property management	73	27	47
Research and development	4 779	2 197	2 582
Services between related enterprises	5 910	3 426	2 484
Other business and professional services	1 507	630	877
Communications services			
Postal and courier	358	534	-177
Telecommunications	3 293	3 044	249
Computer services			
Computer	4 479	2 260	2 219
Information services			
News agency services	621	50	571
Publishing services	294	84	210
Other information provision services	1 185	245	940
Construction Goods and Services			
Construction in the UK	188	326	-138
Construction outside the UK	603	339	264
Financial services			
Financial	7 607	1 923	5 684
Insurance Services			
Auxiliary services	1 556	85	1 471
Freight Insurance - Claims	1		1
Freigh Insurance - Premiums		7	-7
Life insurance and pension funding - Claims			
Life insurance and pension funding - Premiums		5	-5
Reinsurance - Claims	12		12
Reinsurance - Premiums		23	-23
Other Direct insurance - Claims	26		26
Other Direct insurance - Premiums		155	-155
Merchanting and Other Trade related Services			
Merchanting	..		..
Other trade related services	..	389	..
Personal, Cultural and Recreational Services			
Audio-Visual and related services	198	66	132
Health services	17	10	7
Training and educational services	43	49	-6
Other personal, cultural and recreational services	338	159	180
Royalties and Licenses			
Use of Franchise and similar rights fees	1 629	1 896	-267
Other royalties and license fees	4 589	1 884	2 705
Purchases and sales of franchises and similar right	143	173	-29
Purchases and sales of other royalties and licenses	466	451	15
Technical services			
Architectural	177	22	156
Engineering	3 342	1 279	2 063
Surveying	148	41	107
Other technical services	1 441	432	1 009
Other Trade in Services			
Other Trade in services	2 289	1 163	1 126
World Total	**59 226**	**28 379**	**30 847**

1 Due to rounding, the sum of constituent items may not always equal the total shown.

2 Data excludes the following industries: Financial, Film and TV, Travel and Transport, Public Sector (including Education). Note (-) Denotes nil or less than £500,000. Note (..) Denotes disclosive data.

Source: Office for National Statistics: 01633 456644

External trade and investment

19.8 International trade in services:[1,2] by country, 2006

£ million

	Exports	Imports	Balances
European Union			
Austria	624	223	401
Belgium	1 156	638	518
Cyprus	69	73	-4
Czech Republic	149	85	64
Denmark	556	200	356
Estonia	23	7	16
Finland	616	104	513
France	2 785	2 662	123
Germany	3 724	3 132	592
Greece	217	126	91
Hungary	204	98	105
Irish Republic	3 899	1 184	2 715
Italy	1 484	996	488
Latvia	22	8	14
Lithuania	..	..	—
Luxembourg	650	178	471
Malta	21	13	7
Netherlands	4 000	1 199	2 800
Poland	175	147	28
Portugal	233	79	154
Slovakia	25	16	9
Slovenia	16	5	12
Spain	1 258	790	468
Sweden	719	761	-42
EU Institutions	..	..	
Total European Union	**22633**	**12732**	**9901**
EFTA			
Iceland	63	9	54
Liechtenstein	33	5	28
Norway	823	344	480
Switzerland	3 146	931	2 215
Total EFTA	**4 065**	**1 288**	**2 777**
Other European countries			
Russia	440	128	312
Channel Islands	734	264	470
Isle of Man	88	16	72
Turkey	144	157	-13
Rest of Europe	358	125	233
Europe Unallocated	1 814	935	879
Total Europe	**30 278**	**15 647**	**14 631**
Africa			
Nigeria	298	54	245
South Africa	428	137	291
Rest of Africa	784	243	541
Africa Unallocated	86	134	-48
Total Africa	**1 597**	**568**	**1 029**
America			
Brazil	195	85	110
Canada	571	313	257
Mexico	138	24	113
USA	13 825	6 173	7 652
Rest of America	2 350	984	1 366
America Unallocated	369	110	260
Total America	**17 448**	**7 689**	**9 759**

19.8 International trade in services:[1,2] by country, 2006

continued

£ million

	Exports	Imports	Balances
Asia			
China	281	134	147
Hong Kong	353	342	12
India	463	418	44
Indonesia	77	39	39
Israel	166	156	10
Japan	1 341	915	425
Malaysia	164	38	125
Pakistan	43	17	26
Phillippines	31	25	6
Saudi Arabia	1 400	530	870
Singapore	1 851	340	1 511
South Korea	303	47	255
Taiwan	170	46	124
Thailand	78	29	49
Rest of Asia	1 738	699	1 039
Asia Unallocated	302	243	59
Total Asia	**8 761**	**4 019**	**4 742**
Australiasia and Oceania			
Australia	814	304	510
New Zealand	102	29	73
Rest of Australia and Oceania	41	9	32
Oceania Unallocated	6	1	4
Total Australasia and Oceania	**962**	**343**	**619**
Rest of World Unallocated			
International organisations	..	..	..
	..	..	..
World Total	**59 220**	**28 370**	**30 847**
Economic Zones			
OECD	42 972	21 831	21 142
NAFTA	13 764	6 478	7 286
Central and Eastern Europe	824	479	345
OPEC	2 745	918	1 827
ASEAN	2 247	478	1 769
CIS	1 030	439	591
NICs1	2 677	776	1 902
Offshore Financial centres	5 376	1 903	3 473
ACP	1 428	586	843

1 Due to rounding, the sum of constituent items may not always equal the total shown.

2 Data excludes the following industries: Financial, Film and TV, Travel and Transport, Public Sector (including Education). Note (..) Denotes disclosive data. Note (-) Denotes nil or less than £500,000.

Source: Office for National Statistics: 01633 456644

321

External trade and investment

19.9 Summary of balance of payments,[1] 2008
United Kingdom

£ million

	Credits	Debits
1. Current account		
A. Goods and services	376 384	419 588
1. Goods	243 635	319 947
2. Services	132 749	99 641
2.1. Transportation	15 879	19 032
2.2. Travel	18 313	34 291
2.3. Communications	3 945	3 683
2.4. Construction	790	625
2.5. Insurance	4 132	979
2.6. Financial	33 832	10 267
2.7. Computer and information	6 806	2 729
2.8. Royalties and licence fees	7 471	5 166
2.9. Other business	37 389	19 333
2.10. Personal, cultural and recreational	2 136	856
2.11. Government	2 056	2 680
B. Income	238 506	228 409
1. Compensation of employees	1 058	1 803
2. Investment income	237 448	226 606
2.1 Direct investment	84 339	52 013
2.2 Portfolio investment	55 122	57 490
2.3 Other investment (including earnings on reserve assets)	97 987	117 103
C. Current transfers	18 223	30 147
1. General government	4 351	13 853
2. Other sectors	13 872	16 294
Total current account	**633 113**	**678 144**
2. Capital and financial accounts		
A. Capital account	4 024	3 049
1. Capital transfers	3 393	2 426
2. Acquisition/disposal of non-produced, non-financial assets	631	623
B. Financial account	615 463	573 588
1. Direct investment	80 539	47 155
Abroad		47 155
1.1. Equity capital		25 647
1.2. Reinvested earnings		47 795
1.3. Other capital[2]		−26 287
In United Kingdom	80 539	
1.1. Equity capital	56 005	
1.2. Reinvested earnings	22 930	
1.3. Other capital[3]	1 604	
2. Portfolio investment	152 609	138 588
Assets		138 588
2.1. Equity securities		19 615
2.2. Debt securities		118 973
Liabilities	152 609	
2.1. Equity securities	−11 469	
2.2. Debt securities	164 078	
3. Financial derivatives (net)		−7 449
4. Other investment	382 315	395 720
Assets		395 720
4.1 Trade credits		1 361
4.2 Loans		117 413
4.3 Currency and deposits		277 244
4.4 Other assets		−298
Liabilities	382 315	
4.1. Trade credits	−	
4.2. Loans	46 606	
4.3. Currency and deposits	334 478	
4.4. Other liabilities	1 231	
5. Reserve assets		−426
5.1. Monetary gold		−4
5.2. Special drawing rights		51
5.3. Reserve position in the IMF		−225
5.4. Foreign exchange		62
Total capital and financial accounts	**619 487**	**576 637**
Total current, capital and financial accounts	**1 252 600**	**1 254 781**
Net errors and omissions	2 181	

1 See chapter text.
2 Other capital transaction on direct investment abroad represents claims on affiliated enterprises less liabilities to affiliated enterprises.
3 Other capital transactions on direct investment in the United Kingdom represents liabilities to direct investors less claims on direct investors.

Source: Office for National Statistics

19.10 Summary of balance of payments: balances (credits less debits)[1]
United Kingdom

£ million

			Current account									
	Trade in goods	Trade in services	Total goods and services	Compensati-on of employees	Investment income	Total income	Current transfers	Current balance	Current balance as % of GDP[2]	Capital account	Financial account	Net errors & omissions
	LQCT	KTMS	KTMY	KTMP	HMBM	HMBP	KTNF	HBOG	AA6H	FKMJ	HBNT	HHDH
1954	−210	115	−95	−27	227	200	55	160	0.9	−13	−174	27
1955	−315	42	−273	−27	149	122	43	−108	−0.6	−15	34	89
1956	50	26	76	−30	203	173	2	251	1.2	−13	−250	12
1957	−29	121	92	−32	223	191	−5	278	1.3	−13	−313	48
1958	34	119	153	−34	261	227	4	384	1.7	−10	−411	37
1959	−116	118	2	−37	233	196	–	198	0.8	−5	−68	−125
1960	−404	39	−365	−35	201	166	−6	−205	−0.8	−6	−7	218
1961	−144	51	−93	−35	223	188	−9	86	0.3	−12	23	−97
1962	−104	50	−54	−37	301	264	−14	196	0.7	−12	−195	11
1963	−123	4	−119	−38	364	326	−37	170	0.6	−16	−30	−124
1964	−551	−34	−585	−33	365	332	−74	−327	−1.0	−17	392	−48
1965	−263	−66	−329	−34	405	371	−75	−33	−0.1	−18	49	2
1966	−111	44	−67	−39	358	319	−91	161	0.4	−19	22	−164
1967	−601	157	−444	−39	354	315	−118	−247	−0.6	−25	179	93
1968	−708	341	−367	−48	303	255	−119	−231	−0.5	−26	688	−431
1969	−214	392	178	−47	468	421	−109	490	1.0	−23	−794	327
1970	−18	457	437	−56	527	471	−89	819	1.6	−22	−818	21
1971	205	617	822	−63	454	391	−90	1 123	2.0	−23	−1 330	230
1972	−736	722	−14	−52	350	298	−142	142	0.2	−35	477	−584
1973	−2 573	907	1 666	−68	970	902	−336	−1 100	−1.5	−39	1 031	108
1974	−5 241	1 292	−3 949	−92	1 010	918	−302	−3 333	−4.0	−34	3 185	182
1975	−3 245	1 708	−1 537	−102	257	155	−313	−1 695	−1.6	−36	1 569	162
1976	−3 930	2 872	−1 058	−140	760	620	−534	−972	−0.8	−12	507	477
1977	−2 271	3 704	1 433	−152	−678	−830	−889	−286	−0.2	11	−3 286	3 561
1978	−1 534	4 215	2 681	−140	−300	−440	−1 420	821	0.5	−79	−2 655	1 913
1979	−3 326	4 573	1 247	−130	−342	−472	−1 777	−1 002	−0.5	−103	864	241
1980	1 329	4 414	5 743	−82	−2 268	−2 350	−1 653	1 740	0.8	−4	−2 157	421
1981	3 238	4 776	8 014	−66	−1 883	−1 949	−1 219	4 846	1.9	−79	−5 312	545
1982	1 879	4 261	6 140	−95	−2 336	−2 431	−1 476	2 233	0.8	6	−1 233	−1 006
1983	−1 618	5 406	3 788	−89	−1 050	−1 139	−1 391	1 258	0.4	75	−3 287	1 954
1984	−5 409	6 101	692	−94	−326	−420	−1 566	−1 294	−0.4	107	−7 130	8 317
1985	−3 416	8 499	5 083	−120	−2 609	−2 729	−2 924	−570	−0.2	185	−1 657	2 042
1986	−9 617	8 182	−1 435	−156	71	−85	−2 094	−3 614	−0.9	135	−122	3 601
1987	−11 698	8 604	−3 094	−174	−730	−904	−3 437	−7 435	−1.7	333	10 606	−3 504
1988	−21 553	6 388	−15 165	−64	−1 188	−1 252	−3 293	−19 710	−4.1	235	16 989	2 486
1989	−24 724	5 866	−18 858	−138	−2 309	−2 447	−4 228	−25 533	−4.9	270	13 614	11 649
1990	−18 707	6 643	−12 064	−110	−4 586	−4 696	−4 802	−21 562	−3.8	497	22 272	−1 207
1991	−10 223	6 312	−3 911	−63	−5 642	−5 705	−999	−10 615	−1.8	290	7 855	2 470
1992	−13 050	6 353	−6 697	−49	−1 037	−1 086	−5 228	−13 011	−2.1	421	16 311	−3 721
1993	−13 066	8 174	−4 892	35	−2 547	−2 512	−5 056	−12 460	−1.9	309	22 278	−10 127
1994	−11 126	8 161	−2 965	−170	1 521	1 351	−5 187	−6 801	−1.0	33	−3 240	10 008
1995	−12 023	11 165	−858	−296	−546	−842	−7 363	−9 063	−1.2	533	−1 717	10 247
1996	−13 722	14 312	590	93	−2 460	−2 367	−4 539	−6 316	−0.8	1 260	−940	5 996
1997	−12 342	16 801	4 459	83	241	324	−5 745	−962	−0.1	958	−7 294	7 298
1998	−21 813	15 003	−6 810	−10	11 813	11 803	−8 172	−3 179	−0.4	489	4 480	−1 790
1999	−29 051	15 562	−13 489	201	−1 244	−1 043	−7 322	−21 854	−2.4	747	29 505	−8 398
2000	−32 976	15 002	−17 974	150	1 812	1 962	−9 775	−25 787	−2.6	1 703	23 133	951
2001	−41 212	17 200	−24 012	66	9 359	9 425	−6 515	−21 102	−2.1	1 318	27 194	−7 410
2002	−47 705	19 632	−28 073	67	18 219	18 286	−8 870	−18 657	−1.7	932	24 204	−6 479
2003	−48 607	22 612	−25 995	59	17 464	17 523	−9 835	−18 307	−1.6	1 466	22 553	−5 712
2004	−60 900	28 146	−32 754	−494	18 324	17 830	−10 276	−25 200	−2.1	2 064	19 564	3 572
2005	−68 589	25 875	−42 714	−610	22 482	21 872	−11 849	−32 691	−2.6	1 503	30 581	607
2006	−76 312	33 108	−43 204	−745	10 842	10 097	−11 924	−45 031	−3.4	975	41 875	2 181
2007	−89 754	42 457	−47 297	−665	21 237	20 572	−13 602	−40 327	−2.9	2 566	39 712	−1 951
2008	−92 876	48 878	−43 998	−619	33 748	33 129	−13 624	−24 493	−1.7	3 505	19 657	1 331

1 See chapter text.
2 Using series YBHA: GDP at current market prices.

Source: Office for National Statistics

19.11 Balance of payments:[1] current account
United Kingdom

£ million

		1998	1999	2000	2001	2002	2003	2004	2005	2006	2007	2008
Credits												
Exports of goods and services												
Exports of goods	LQAD	164 056	166 166	187 936	189 093	186 524	188 320	190 874	211 608	243 635	220 858	251 088
Exports of services	KTMQ	69 228	76 525	81 883	87 773	94 012	102 357	112 518	119 420	132 749	149 191	165 944
Total exports of goods and services	KTMW	233 284	242 691	269 819	276 866	280 536	290 677	303 392	331 028	376 384	370 049	417 032
Income												
Compensation of employees	KTMN	840	960	1 032	1 087	1 121	1 116	931	974	1 058	1 159	1 221
Investment income	HMBN	102 551	100 733	131 902	137 447	120 543	122 069	137 382	185 765	237 448	290 399	271 299
Total income	HMBQ	103 391	101 693	132 934	138 534	121 664	123 185	138 313	186 739	238 506	291 558	272 520
Current transfers												
General government	FJUM	1 767	3 542	2 465	4 991	3 663	3 968	4 177	4 294	4 351	4 346	5 625
Other sectors	FJUN	10 682	8 510	8 018	8 926	8 571	8 079	9 590	13 106	13 872	9 731	10 126
Total current transfers	KTND	12 449	12 052	10 483	13 917	12 234	12 047	13 767	17 400	18 223	14 077	15 751
Total	HBOE	349 124	356 436	413 236	429 317	414 434	425 909	455 472	535 167	633 113	675 684	705 303
Debits												
Imports of goods and services												
Imports of goods	LQBL	185 869	195 217	220 912	230 305	234 229	236 927	251 774	280 197	319 947	310 612	343 964
Imports of services	KTMR	54 225	60 963	66 881	70 573	74 380	79 745	84 372	93 545	99 641	106 734	117 066
Total imports of goods and services	KTMX	240 094	256 180	287 793	300 878	308 609	316 672	336 146	373 742	419 588	417 346	461 030
Income												
Compensation of employees	KTMO	850	759	882	1 021	1 054	1 057	1 425	1 584	1 803	1 824	1 840
Investment income	HMBO	90 738	101 977	130 090	128 088	102 324	104 605	119 058	163 283	226 606	269 162	237 551
Total income	HMBR	91 588	102 736	130 972	129 109	103 378	105 662	120 483	164 867	228 409	270 986	239 391
Current transfers												
General government	FJUO	6 585	7 271	7 778	7 340	9 085	10 657	12 225	13 637	13 853	14 082	14 618
Other sectors	FJUP	14 036	12 103	12 480	13 092	12 019	11 225	11 818	15 612	16 294	13 597	14 757
Total current transfers	KTNE	20 621	19 374	20 258	20 432	21 104	21 882	24 043	29 249	30 147	27 679	29 375
Total	HBOF	352 303	378 290	439 023	450 419	433 091	444 216	480 672	567 858	678 144	716 011	729 796
Balances												
Trade in goods and services												
Trade in goods	LQCT	−21 813	−29 051	−32 976	−41 212	−47 705	−48 607	−60 900	−68 589	−76 312	−89 754	−92 876
Trade in services	KTMS	15 003	15 562	15 002	17 200	19 632	22 612	28 146	25 875	33 108	42 457	48 878
Total trade in goods and services	KTMY	−6 810	−13 489	−17 974	−24 012	−28 073	−25 995	−32 754	−42 714	−43 204	−47 297	−43 998
Income												
Compensation of employees	KTMP	−10	201	150	66	67	59	−494	−610	−745	−665	−610
Investment income	HMBM	11 813	−1 244	1 812	9 359	18 219	17 464	18 324	22 482	10 842	21 237	33 748
Total income	HMBP	11 803	−1 043	1 962	9 425	18 286	17 523	17 830	21 872	10 097	20 572	33 129
Current transfers												
General government	FJUQ	−4 818	−3 729	−5 313	−2 349	−5 422	−6 689	−8 048	−9 343	−9 502	−9 736	−8 993
Other sectors	FJUR	−3 354	−3 593	−4 462	−4 166	−3 448	−3 146	−2 228	−2 506	−2 422	−3 866	−4 631
Total current transfers	KTNF	−8 172	−7 322	−9 775	−6 515	−8 870	−9 835	−10 276	−11 849	−11 924	−13 602	−13 624
Total (Current balance)	HBOG	−3 179	−21 854	−25 787	−21 102	−18 657	−18 307	−25 200	−32 691	−45 031	−40 327	−24 493

1 See chapter text.

Source: Office for National Statistics

19.12 Balance of payments:[1] summary of international investment position, financial account and investment income

United Kingdom

£ billion

		1998	1999	2000	2001	2002	2003	2004	2005	2006	2007	2008
Investment abroad												
International investment position												
Direct investment	HBWD	309.8	438.3	618.8	616.9	637.2	691.1	678.1	705.9	733.6	913.9	1 036.2
Portfolio investment	HHZZ	703.8	838.3	906.1	937.4	844.0	935.8	1 092.3	1 361.2	1 531.1	1 686.2	1 751.3
Other investment	HLXV	1 098.4	1 097.3	1 379.7	1 521.9	1 545.2	1 813.7	2 118.1	2 714.7	2 917.3	3 750.7	4 316.7
Reserve assets	LTEB	23.3	22.2	28.8	25.6	25.5	23.8	23.2	24.7	22.9	26.7	36.3
Total	HBQA	2 135.4	2 396.1	2 933.4	3 101.9	3 051.9	3 464.5	3 911.7	4 806.6	5 204.9	6 377.5	7 140.5
Financial account transactions												
Direct investment	-HJYP	73.8	125.6	155.6	42.8	35.0	40.9	51.5	44.0	47.2	136.1	60.3
Portfolio investment	-HHZC	32.1	21.4	65.6	86.6	1.0	36.3	140.9	151.0	138.6	92.0	-132.0
Financial derivatives (net)	-ZPNN	3.0	-2.7	-1.6	-8.4	-1.0	5.4	7.9	-9.6	-7.4	19.0	-18.1
Other investment	-XBMM	30.0	41.5	241.7	170.7	70.4	260.4	325.3	501.2	395.7	747.1	-347.1
Reserve assets	-LTCV	-0.2	-0.6	3.9	-3.1	-0.5	-1.6	0.2	0.7	-0.4	1.2	-1.3
Total	-HBNR	138.7	185.2	465.2	288.5	105.0	341.4	525.8	687.4	573.6	995.4	-438.3
Investment income												
Direct investment	HJYW	29.9	33.1	45.0	46.7	51.5	55.1	63.3	79.2	84.3	90.3	77.7
Portfolio investment	HLYX	29.3	25.9	33.0	34.9	32.5	32.5	36.7	45.4	55.1	66.1	67.9
Other investment	AIOP	42.2	40.6	52.9	54.9	35.8	33.6	36.7	60.5	97.3	133.4	124.9
Reserve assets	HHCB	1.1	1.2	1.0	1.0	0.8	0.8	0.7	0.7	0.6	0.6	0.8
Total	HMBN	102.6	100.7	131.9	137.4	120.5	122.1	137.4	185.8	237.4	290.4	271.3
Investment in the UK												
International investment position												
Direct investment	HBWI	213.6	250.2	310.4	363.5	340.6	355.5	383.3	494.2	577.4	630.2	674.2
Portfolio investment	HLXW	739.9	933.2	1 067.6	1 013.2	925.3	1 082.9	1 227.6	1 457.5	1 704.3	1 918.2	1 981.4
Other investment	HLYD	1 350.3	1 400.9	1 651.6	1 861.9	1 906.0	2 143.2	2 520.8	3 103.0	3 293.8	4 126.4	4 551.3
Total	HBQB	2 303.8	2 584.3	3 029.5	3 238.5	3 171.9	3 581.6	4 131.7	5 054.7	5 575.5	6 674.7	7 206.9
Financial account transactions												
Direct investment	HJYU	45.1	55.1	80.6	37.3	16.8	16.8	31.2	97.8	80.5	98.2	52.4
Portfolio investment	HHZF	25.0	106.3	172.2	40.8	49.7	105.6	88.5	132.7	152.6	208.7	257.5
Other investment	XBMN	73.1	53.3	235.6	237.6	62.6	241.5	425.6	487.4	382.3	728.3	-728.5
Total	HBNS	143.2	214.7	488.3	315.7	129.2	364.0	545.3	718.0	615.5	1 035.1	-418.6
Investment income												
Direct investment	HJYX	8.6	17.0	27.4	21.4	16.0	21.9	27.6	36.2	52.0	44.8	11.9
Portfolio investment	HLZC	29.5	32.2	32.4	36.1	33.3	32.9	38.7	47.6	57.5	66.5	74.2
Other investment	HLZN	52.7	52.7	70.2	70.5	53.0	49.8	52.7	79.6	117.1	157.8	151.4
Total	HMBO	90.7	102.0	130.1	128.1	102.3	104.6	119.1	163.3	226.6	269.2	237.6
Net investment												
International investment position												
Direct investment	HBWQ	96.2	188.1	308.4	253.5	296.6	335.6	294.7	211.7	156.2	283.8	362.0
Portfolio investment	CGNH	-36.0	-94.9	-161.5	-75.7	-81.3	-147.0	-135.2	-96.3	-173.2	-232.0	-230.1
Other investment	CGNG	-251.9	-303.6	-271.9	-339.9	-360.8	-329.5	-402.7	-388.3	-376.5	-375.7	-234.6
Reserve assets	LTEB	23.3	22.2	28.8	25.6	25.5	23.8	23.2	24.7	22.9	26.7	36.3
Net investment position	HBQC	-168.4	-188.2	-96.2	-136.5	-120.0	-117.2	-220.0	-248.2	-370.7	-297.2	-66.4
Financial account transactions												
Direct investment	HJYV	-28.7	-70.5	-75.0	-5.5	-18.3	-24.1	-20.3	53.8	33.4	-38.0	-7.9
Portfolio investment	HHZD	-7.0	84.9	106.6	-45.7	48.7	69.4	-52.3	-18.3	14.0	116.7	389.5
Financial derivatives	ZPNN	-3.0	2.7	1.6	8.4	1.0	-5.4	-7.9	9.6	7.4	-19.0	18.1
Other investment	HHYR	43.1	11.8	-6.1	66.9	-7.7	-18.9	100.2	-13.8	-13.4	-18.8	-381.5
Reserve assets	LTCV	0.2	0.6	-3.9	3.1	0.5	1.6	-0.2	-0.7	0.4	-1.2	1.3
Net transactions	HBNT	4.5	29.5	23.1	27.2	24.2	22.6	19.6	30.6	41.9	39.7	19.7
Investment income												
Direct investment	HJYE	21.3	16.1	17.6	25.3	35.5	33.2	35.7	43.0	32.3	45.4	65.8
Portfolio investment	HLZX	-0.2	-6.4	0.5	-1.2	-0.8	-0.4	-2.0	-2.2	-2.4	-0.4	-6.3
Other investment	CGNA	-10.5	-12.2	-17.3	-15.7	-17.2	-16.1	-16.0	-19.0	-19.8	-24.4	-26.5
Reserve assets	HHCB	1.1	1.2	1.0	1.0	0.8	0.8	0.7	0.7	0.6	0.6	0.8
Net earnings	HMBM	11.8	-1.2	1.8	9.4	18.2	17.5	18.3	22.5	10.8	21.2	33.7

1 See chapter text.

19.13 Net outward foreign direct investment by United Kingdom companies:[1,2] by area and main country

£ million

		2003	2004	2005	2006	2007
Europe	GQBX	16 600	10 814	12 105	16 899	60 983
EU27	IY6N	13 417	11 917	13 337	4 038	53 042
Austria	CBJD	165	1 322	−301	−94	148
Belgium	HIIL	−1 241	−544	970	−4 356	1 127
Bulgaria	IY6O	..	−	11	−5	..
Cyprus	DG8D	−53	18	69	98	365
Czech Republic	DG8O	142	23	24	−160	128
Denmark	CAUW	−53	569	391	1 529	−69
Estonia	DG8E	4	21	2	3	−
Finland	CBJE	99	−37	707	106	275
France	CAUX	6 627	793	3 138	1 175	3 427
Germany	CAUY	1 552	−366	−479	3 186	1 634
Greece	CAUZ	229	−253	63	15	105
Hungary	DG8F	527	336	1 821	39	144
Irish Republic	CAVA	985	3 325	−1 181	5 161	4 269
Italy	CAVB	500	667	191	−397	1 752
Latvia	DG8G	..	1	−1	4	..
Lithuania	DG8H	..	1	−4	1	−
Luxembourg	HIIM	1 313	−1 022	−1 213	−14 131	8 879
Malta	DG8I	58	178	142	891	−2 132
Netherlands	CAVC	728	4 805	4 821	1 350	25 347
Poland	DG8J	4	182	150	397	599
Portugal	CAVD	900	444	603	314	529
Romania	IY6P	56	11	101	40	120
Slovakia	DG8K	−11	18	21	18	87
Slovenia	DG8L	37	−5	−5	14	9
Spain	CAVE	626	1 131	564	2 177	4 143
Sweden	CBJG	794	299	2 732	6 669	3 262
EFTA	CAVG	2 313	−6 667	547	6 926	3 309
of which						
Norway	CBJF	−274	367	−831	3	1 057
Switzerland	CBJH	2 591	−7 007	1 330	6 948	2 345
Other European Countries	IY6Q	870	5 564	−1 779	5 935	4 631
of which						
Russia	GLAA	2 030	1 831	349	−13	1 340
UK offshore islands	GLAC	−1 031	3 528	−2 341	5 023	2 088
The Americas	GQBZ	15 959	24 321	20 689	19 100	61 566
of which						
Bermuda	CBKZ	−2 613	6 242	653	908	1 958
Brazil	CBLA	786	386	48	354	721
Canada	CAVK	2 521	1 143	3 372	8 130	21 865
Chile	GQCA	290	675	790	25	106
Colombia	GQCB	78	225	−687	315	110
Mexico	GLAD	261	1 386	168	334	96
Panama	GLAE	58	12	27	7	−18
USA	CAVJ	19 300	9 732	15 041	−1 803	32 255
Asia	GQCI	3 601	7 689	5 399	7 992	9 214
Near and Middle East Countries	CBKF	82	486	398	1 219	1 912
of which						
Gulf Arabian countries[3]	GQCC	−85	293	577	329	343
Other Asian Countries	GQCD	3 518	7 203	5 001	6 773	7 302
of which						
China	HIIN	309	539	598	374	1 142
Hong Kong	CAVN	1 285	5 303	1 547	1 674	1 744
India	GLAF	193	274	616	104	667
Indonesia	GLAG	481	−289	−116	196	−134
Japan	CAVM	338	37	247	440	2 278
Malaysia	CBKN	277	428	244	241	263
Singapore	CBKQ	−449	−161	−508	2 621	−1 215
South Korea	GLAH	332	278	2 247	679	488
Thailand	GLAI	155	181	228	536	5
Australasia and Oceania	GQCE	−1 524	1 026	423	3 132	1 187
of which						
Australia	CBJO	−492	408	444	2 743	1 289
New Zealand	CBJP	−1 017	258	−56	405	−116
Africa	GQCF	3 454	5 863	5 843	−235	4 728
of which						
Kenya	GLAJ	58	47	73	62	96
Nigeria	CBJY	19	−44	−108	44	671
South Africa	CAVO	2 222	3 840	4 368	1 466	1 105
Zimbabwe	CBKD	37	91	18	8	5
World Total	CDQD	38 088	49 713	44 458	46 887	137 678
OECD	GQCG	37 030	18 355	35 305	21 276	117 119
Central and Eastern Europe[4]	GQCH	156	36	158	76	127

1 See chapter text. Net investment includes re-invested earnings.
2 Minus sign indicates net disinvestment abroad.
3 Includes Abu Dhabi, Bahrain, Dubai, Iraq, Kuwait, Oman, Other Gulf States, Qatar, Saudi Arabia and Yemen.

4 From 2003 includes Albania, Bosnia & Herzegovina, Bulgaria, Croatia, FYR of Macedonia, Romania and Serbia & Montenegro. Prior to 2003 Czech Republic, Estonia, Hungary, Latvia, Lithuania, Poland, Slovakia and Slovenia also included.

Source: ONS Foreign Direct Investments Surveys: 01633 456647; Bank of England

19.14 United Kingdom outward foreign direct international investment position: book value of net assets: by area and main country[1]

£ million

		2003	2004	2005	2006	2007
Europe	GQCJ	408 881	382 104	387 324	402 593	499 282
EU27	IY6R	355 045	348 576	339 692	314 481	383 301
Austria	CDLZ	3 339	4 102	4 005	2 402	2 709
Belgium	HIIO	8 662	7 828	13 492	4 380	6 971
Bulgaria	IY6S	81	22	53	46	49
Cyprus	DG8Q	80	64	59	561	681
Czech Republic	DG8R	954	793	823	523	696
Denmark	CDLP	3 021	5 256	5 090	7 782	6 816
Estonia	DG8S	21	78	7	−1	12
Finland	CDMA	588	695	2 465	1 287	2 341
France	CDLQ	31 460	35 313	47 348	36 327	39 729
Germany	CDLR	13 486	12 164	20 753	17 602	18 882
Greece	CDLS	460	456	625	562	684
Hungary	DG8T	1 722	1 506	2 491	1 795	1 873
Irish Republic	CDLT	29 989	29 059	26 824	26 432	25 831
Italy	CDLU	10 178	11 322	10 872	7 924	10 516
Latvia	DG8U	13	25	22	27	102
Lithuania	DG8V	16	22	16	6	11
Luxembourg	HIIP	79 208	81 709	97 260	62 355	72 334
Malta	DG8W	264	1 528	−459	2 399	3 147
Netherlands	CDLV	146 345	131 143	64 511	92 783	128 671
Poland	DG8X	2 900	2 316	1 974	2 519	2 180
Portugal	CDLW	973	1 664	2 702	3 167	3 538
Romania	IY6T	257	260	356	247	402
Slovakia	DG8Y	332	103	93	136	184
Slovenia	DG8Z	128	54	3	53	61
Spain	CDLX	9 460	11 318	25 604	25 233	31 057
Sweden	CDMD	11 108	9 776	12 702	17 935	23 824
EFTA	CDLY	27 187	14 468	12 933	12 637	17 102
of which						
Norway	CDMC	4 900	4 934	4 498	2 116	2 350
Switzerland	CDME	21 913	9 104	7 979	10 239	14 502
Other European Countries	IY6U	26 649	19 060	34 700	75 475	98 879
of which						
Russia	GQAA	777	1 627	1 814	6 054	7 192
UK offshore islands	GQAB	22 717	15 678	29 954	65 814	87 063
The Americas	GQCU	178 599	182 091	216 343	256 423	324 324
of which						
Bermuda	CDOA	1 554	7 561	10 604	13 889	14 469
Brazil	CDOB	2 532	3 922	3 220	2 824	3 789
Canada	CDML	8 537	8 922	12 812	19 188	46 890
Chile	GQCT	1 919	2 133	2 814	563	475
Colombia	GQCS	2 434	1 874	1 132	985	1 086
Mexico	GQAC	1 431	2 461	2 860	2 337	3 769
Panama	GQAD	153	132	166	..	113
USA	CDMM	150 021	140 321	164 405	180 629	211 955
Asia	GQCL	43 118	47 311	54 919	54 377	62 539
Near and Middle East Countries	CDNH	1 559	3 008	3 733	6 874	9 855
of which						
Gulf Arabian countries[2]	GQCM	1 211	2 062	3 013	4 756	6 262
Other Asian Countries	GQCR	41 559	44 303	51 187	47 503	52 684
of which						
China	HIIQ	1 809	1 882	2 685	2 228	2 727
Hong Kong	CDNN	17 221	19 165	20 432	22 256	25 387
India	GQAE	1 555	1 682	2 126	1 977	3 135
Indonesia	GQAF	1 309	1 178	1 168	982	919
Japan	CDMP	2 361	5 829	6 076	2 485	2 230
Malaysia	CDNQ	1 476	1 592	1 455	1 174	1 175
Singapore	CDNT	9 510	6 610	7 144	6 684	6 289
South Korea	GQAG	1 339	1 218	4 586	3 763	4 419
Thailand	GQAH	1 357	947	1 281	1 407	1 421
Australasia and Oceania	GQCN	17 486	16 888	16 694	12 665	14 147
of which						
Australia	CDMO	16 283	14 586	14 627	11 571	13 353
New Zealand	CDMQ	1 060	1 459	1 176	923	682
Africa	GQCQ	17 039	17 350	20 834	15 105	18 653
of which						
Kenya	GQAI	285	238	281	313	321
Nigeria	CDNA	1 028	950	924	1 011	1 330
South Africa	CDMR	11 250	10 964	13 733	8 255	9 095
Zimbabwe	CDNF	48	103	50	58	36
World Total	CDOO	665 123	645 744	696 113	741 163	918 946
OECD	GQCO	563 769	537 109	561 694	547 303	682 647
Central & Eastern Europe[3]	GQCP	560	534	640	515	687

1 See chapter text.
2 Includes Abu Dhabi, Bahrain, Dubai, Iraq, Kuwait, Oman, Other Gulf States, Qatar, Saudi Arabia and Yemen.
3 From 2003 includes Albania, Bosnia & Herzegovina, Bulgaria, Croatia, FYR of Macedonia, Romiania and Serbia & Montenegro. Prior to 2003 Czech

Republic, Estonia, Hungary, Latvia, Lithuania, Poland, Slovakia and Slovenia also included.

Sources: ONS Foreign Direct Investment Surveys: 01633 456647;
Bank of England

19.15 Net earnings from foreign direct investment abroad by United Kingdom companies:[1,2] by area and main country

£ million

		2003	2004	2005	2006	2007
Europe	GQCV	26 857	25 782	32 186	38 957	43 716
EU27	IY6V	23 114	20 708	23 904	28 337	33 457
Austria	CBLQ	317	296	301	186	244
Belgium	HIIR	324	653	818	875	1 310
Bulgaria	IY6W	..	–	9	3	–9
Cyprus	DG94	20	22	37	171	364
Czech Republic	DG95	165	110	108	–64	79
Denmark	CAWI	197	272	387	411	600
Estonia	DG96	9	3	..	11	5
Finland	CBLR	103	112	103	69	282
France	CAWJ	1 714	2 107	2 957	3 344	3 846
Germany	CAWK	1 592	2 328	2 685	2 189	2 687
Greece	CAWL	120	102	160	151	221
Hungary	DG97	241	202	295	83	95
Irish Republic	CAWM	2 197	2 461	2 835	2 525	3 048
Italy	CAWN	639	708	732	696	516
Latvia	DG98	–	–	..	5	3
Lithuania	DG99	–	–	–	–	2
Luxembourg	HIIS	1 500	2 191	4 006	7 626	7 953
Malta	DG9A	41	60	31	–185	–70
Netherlands	CAWO	11 691	6 651	5 344	7 251	9 122
Poland	DG9B	290	218	293	373	260
Portugal	CAWP	175	191	297	234	000
Romania	IY6X	10	19	26	43	78
Slovakia	DG9C	..	..	34	24	104
Slovenia	DG9D	..	..	17	5	11
Spain	CAWQ	576	694	1 023	918	837
Sweden	CBLT	959	1 271	1 395	1 395	1 602
EFTA	CAWS	1 761	2 382	3 334	3 759	4 981
of which						
Norway	CBLS	319	297	937	345	300
Switzerland	CBLU	1 441	2 084	2 396	3 411	4 367
Other European Countries	IY6Y	1 982	2 692	4 948	6 861	5 278
of which						
Russia	GQAJ	345	841	1 681	1 715	1 187
UK offshore islands	GQAK	1 332	1 602	3 017	4 580	3 571
The Americas	GQCX	17 586	21 113	26 585	26 461	26 481
of which						
Bermuda	CBNK	1 254	1 629	1 561	..	1 546
Brazil	CBNL	291	652	866	577	685
Canada	CAWW	1 055	1 340	1 895	1 769	1 812
Chile	GQCY	273	820	1 164	771	775
Colombia	GQCZ	234	379	414	274	190
Mexico	GQAL	207	485	536	531	522
Panama	GQAM	55	44	50	23	42
USA	CAWV	12 723	14 332	18 244	17 112	16 973
Asia	GQDA	5 108	8 001	10 975	11 621	11 526
Near and Middle East Countries	CBMS	461	692	1 053	1 430	2 566
of which						
Gulf Arabian countries[3]	GQDB	370	549	688	717	981
Other Asian Countries	GQDC	4 647	7 309	9 922	10 191	8 959
of which						
China	HIIT	278	370	580	445	515
Hong Kong	CAYB	1 083	2 541	3 553	3 786	4 244
India	GQAN	511	427	626	715	818
Indonesia	GQAO	184	155	226	336	102
Japan	CAWY	332	440	482	388	105
Malaysia	CBNA	477	525	508	494	596
Singapore	CBND	911	1 651	2 510	2 285	502
South Korea	GQAP	237	340	683	532	519
Thailand	GQAQ	160	159	171	–121	29
Australasia and Oceania	GQDD	2 022	3 623	3 157	3 065	3 590
of which						
Australia	CBMB	1 518	3 108	2 681	2 665	3 161
New Zealand	CBMC	478	279	359	388	383
Africa	GQDE	2 959	3 958	5 764	3 488	4 542
of which						
Kenya	GQAR	81	64	70	88	89
Nigeria	CBML	122	153	197	133	75
South Africa	CAWZ	1 693	2 706	3 768	1 620	2 270
Zimbabwe	CBMQ	43	87	16	10	7
World Total	GLAB	54 531	62 476	78 667	83 591	89 855
OECD	GQDF	41 353	43 453	52 138	55 675	61 885
Central & Eastern Europe[4]	GQDG	195	74	76	62	64

1 See chapter text. A minus sign indicates net losses.
2 Net earnings equal profits of overseas branches plus UK companies' receipts of interest and their share of profits of overseas subsidiaries and associates. Earnings are after deducting provisions for depreciation and withholding tax on profits, dividends and interest.

3 Includes Abu Dhabi, Bahrain, Dubai, Iraq, Kuwait, Oman, Other Gulf States, Qatar, Saudi Arabia and Yemen.
4 From 2003 includes Albania, Bosnia & Herzegovina, Bulgaria, Croatia, FYR of Macedonia, Romania and Serbia & Montenegro. Prior to 2003 Czech Republic, Estonia, Hungary, Latvia, Lithuania, Poland, Slovakia and Slovenia also included.

Source: ONS Foreign Direct Investments Survey: 01633 456647; Bank of England

19.16 Net inward foreign direct investment in the United Kingdom:[1,2] by area and main country

£ million

		2003	2004	2005	2006	2007
Europe	GQDH	7 013	29 901	80 087	53 837	48 696
EU27	IY6Z	5 505	26 384	71 034	47 698	37 818
Austria	CBOB	8	–31	171	–61	153
Belgium	HIIU	218	1 542	23	670	5
Bulgaria	IY72	..	..	..	..	..
Cyprus	DG9G	–	–	7	18	75
Czech Republic	DG9H	–	–	–	..	1
Denmark	CAYQ	321	–11	–1 246	13	313
Estonia	DG9I	–	–	–	–	..
Finland	CBOC	26	32	238	44	9
France	CAYR	414	1 703	9 643	2 356	–2 057
Germany	CAYS	1 437	11 131	7 279	5 566	18 826
Greece	CAYT	33	13	14	17	16
Hungary	DG9J	–	..	1	3	1
Irish Republic	CAYU	206	936	723	816	185
Italy	CAYV	–468	1 327	–42	282	283
Latvia	DG9K	..	–	..	..	..
Lithuania	DG9L	..	..	–	–	–
Luxembourg	HIIV	–105	–115	151	221	3 346
Malta	DG9M	–	–	1	2	6
Netherlands	CAYW	2 452	1 226	50 366	13 715	1 595
Poland	DG9N	–	–	1	50	–25
Portugal	CAYX	..	..	–6	9	124
Romania	IY73	..	–34	..	..	..
Slovakia	DG9O	..	..	..	..	..
Slovenia	DG9P	..	..	..	..	..
Spain	CAYY	518	..	3 297	23 457	14 875
Sweden	CBOE	406	–14	393	508	79
EFTA	CABB	1 408	3 016	8 050	5 321	9 331
of which						
Norway	CBOD	–179	–798	927	171	431
Switzerland	CBOF	1 411	3 488	7 405	4 786	8 685
Other European Countries	IY74	100	501	3	817	1 546
of which						
Russia	GQAS	..	..	..	..	..
UK offshore islands	GQAT	32	476	–60	733	1 426
The Americas	GQDJ	3 396	–4 792	17 422	17 242	30 942
of which						
Brazil	HP5A	4	..	6	..	2
Canada	CAZF	–325	683	1 632	3 509	847
USA	CAZE	2 676	–5 727	15 589	12 313	27 199
Asia	GQDK	–449	4 081	–4 168	11 806	11 126
Near and Middle East Countries	GQAU	–34	384	736	5 034	521
Other Asian Countries	GQAV	–415	3 697	–4 904	6 772	10 605
of which						
China	HP5B	2	–26	13	12	16
Hong Kong	GQAW	63	..	315	92	..
India	HP5C	7	–15	138	265	66
Japan	CAZH	–543	817	–5 575	3 726	5 803
Singapore	GQAX	–76	14	46	..	..
South Korea	GQAY	–20	193	175	–85	7
Australasia and Oceania	GQDL	310	1 420	3 396	1 869	412
of which						
Australia	CBOJ	309	1 412	3 396	1 479	265
New Zealand	CBOK	2	8	–	54	–45
Africa	GQAZ	7	–43	66	131	475
of which						
South Africa	CAZJ	21	–35	25	101	454
World Total	CBDH	10 276	30 566	96 803	84 885	91 651
OECD	GQBA	8 984	26 762	95 187	73 961	81 110
Central & Eastern Europe[3]	GQBB	4	–32	..	6	6

1 See chapter text. Net investment includes reinvested earnings.
2 A minus sign indicates net disinvestment in the UK.
3 From 2003 includes Albania, Bosnia & Herzegovina, Bulgaria, Croatia, FYR of Macedonia, Romiania and Serbia & Montenegro. Prior to 2003 Czech Republic, Estonia, Hungary, Latvia, Lithuania, Poland, Slovakia and Slovenia also included.

Sources: ONS Foreign Direct Investment Surveys: 01633 456647; Bank of England

19.17 United Kingdom inward foreign direct international investment position: book value of net liabilities: by area and main country[1]

At year end

£ million

		2003	2004	2005	2006	2007
Europe	GQDM	158 903	181 198	277 027	332 077	361 925
EU27	IY75	142 273	161 395	244 392	299 906	314 695
Austria	CDPF	349	366	561	848	969
Belgium	HIIW	1 987	4 338	4 481	5 609	3 925
Bulgaria	IY76	..	..	..	..	..
Cyprus	DG9S	67	78	100	162	437
Czech Republic	DG9T	9	6	3	..	8
Denmark	CDOV	2 086	2 359	1 404	4 344	5 353
Estonia	DG9U	–	–	..	..	..
Finland	CDPG	946	886	756	817	759
France	CDOW	36 565	41 100	56 309	59 998	54 120
Germany	CDOX	32 260	39 300	51 469	54 382	70 284
Greece	CDOY	86	100	103	121	165
Hungary	DG9V	9	12	9	12	12
Irish Republic	CDOZ	4 769	5 021	7 146	8 186	7 971
Italy	CDPA	4 580	6 708	6 122	4 482	4 640
Latvia	DG9W	..	–	..	..	..
Lithuania	DG9X	..	–	–	–	..
Luxembourg	HIIX	5 627	5 963	7 880	16 021	18 537
Malta	DG9Y	21	5	12	12	62
Netherlands	CDPB	46 876	47 579	95 579	119 843	113 462
Poland	DG9Z	10	7	21	96	74
Portugal	CDPC	115	113	111	122	222
Romania	IY77	..	..	..	..	..
Slovakia	DGA2	..	..	..	–	..
Slovenia	DGA3	..	..	..	..	9
Spain	CDPD	3 344	4 536	8 782	20 658	29 290
Sweden	CDPI	2 527	2 849	3 467	4 113	4 302
EFTA	CDPE	13 758	15 752	25 033	22 358	34 606
of which						
Norway	CDPH	831	242	1 085	969	1 348
Switzerland	CDPJ	12 439	14 685	21 624	19 033	31 149
Other European Countries	IY78	2 872	4 051	7 602	9 813	12 624
of which						
Russia	GQBC	..	..	..	..	179
UK offshore islands	GQBD	2 361	3 500	7 059	9 111	11 741
The Americas	GQDU	145 973	140 090	174 037	200 709	201 871
of which						
Brazil	HP5D	5	..	77	134	21
Canada	CDPM	11 176	12 108	15 587	19 369	20 528
USA	CDPN	130 512	122 069	149 759	170 880	167 610
Asia	GQDO	19 869	24 800	24 101	39 436	56 499
Near and Middle East Countries	GQBE	1 627	2 765	2 970	10 160	10 631
Other Asian Countries	GQBF	18 242	22 035	21 131	29 275	45 868
of which						
China	HP5E	102	119	111	99	193
Hong Kong	GQBG	..	..	..	..	..
India	HP5F	194	164	518	798	1 221
Japan	CDPQ	11 949	12 300	10 513	14 766	25 206
Singapore	GQBH	830	925	1 034	4 046	..
South Korea	GQBI	635	635	638	798	793
Australasia and Oceania	GQDP	14 336	16 804	12 537	7 623	9 096
of which						
Australia	CDPP	14 160	16 631	12 313	7 093	8 655
New Zealand	CDPR	158	153	224	428	433
Africa	GQBJ	560	530	510	469	1 362
of which						
South Africa	CDPS	387	296	186	130	868
World Total	CDPZ	339 641	363 422	488 212	580 313	630 753
OECD	GQBK	324 491	340 870	458 185	535 218	571 652
Central & Eastern Europe[2]	GQBL	34	..	..	..	93

1 See chapter text.
2 From 2003 includes Albania, Bosnia & Herzegovina, Bulgaria, Croatia, FYR of Macedonia, Romania and Serbia & Montenegro. Prior to 2003 Czech Republic, Estonia, Hungary, Latvia, Lithuania, Poland, Slovakia and Slovenia also included.

Sources: ONS Foreign Direct Investment Surveys 01633 456647; Bank of England

19.18 Net earnings from foreign direct investment in the United Kingdom:[1,2] by area and main country

£ million

		2003	2004	2005	2006	2007
Europe	GQDQ	10 158	12 676	17 592	27 447	25 254
EU27	IY79	9 010	11 330	15 278	22 919	22 913
Austria	CBOR	111	61	60	207	212
Belgium	HIIY	165	269	367	646	408
Bulgaria	IY7A	–	..	–	–	..
Cyprus	DGA6	24	20	24	44	66
Czech Republic	DGA7	–	–	–	..	1
Denmark	CBDL	305	311	326	204	298
Estonia	DGA8	–	–	–	–	..
Finland	CBOS	36	62	61	93	181
France	CBDM	2 743	3 842	5 121	5 329	3 063
Germany	CBDN	1 754	2 900	4 037	4 541	5 791
Greece	CBDO	4	–4	49	70	104
Hungary	DGA9	–	–	1	3	1
Irish Republic	CBDP	578	471	724	1 012	1 194
Italy	CBDQ	174	408	483	477	572
Latvia	DGB2	..	–	..	..	..
Lithuania	DGB3	–	..	1	1	–
Luxembourg	HIIZ	196	289	214	79	408
Malta	DGB4	–	–	–	3	7
Netherlands	CBDR	2 405	2 585	2 800	7 283	8 331
Poland	DGB5	–	–	1	8	6
Portugal	CBDS	49	47	30	48	54
Romania	IY7B	..	..	..	..	..
Slovakia	DGB6	..	..	5	5	3
Slovenia	DGB7	..	..	..	..	..
Spain	CBDT	298	37	773	2 536	1 610
Sweden	CBOU	167	21	182	316	594
EFTA	CBDW	822	849	1 495	3 366	£70
of which						
Norway	CBOT	–	–20	82	169	193
Switzerland	CBOV	794	819	1 320	2 933	–273
Other European Countries	IY7C	326	497	819	1 162	2 065
of which						
Russia	GQBM	..	..	..	..	7
UK offshore islands	GQBN	287	468	757	1 107	1 999
The Americas	GQDV	10 013	12 278	16 460	20 154	17 464
of which						
Brazil	HP5G	..	1	–4	–4	6
Canada	CBEA	639	1 021	1 348	1 458	–252
USA	CBDZ	9 054	10 981	14 156	16 828	15 351
Asia	GQDS	–781	168	937	2 710	701
Near and Middle East Countries	GQBO	114	188	354	564	490
Other Asian Countries	GQBP	–895	–19	583	2 145	212
of which						
China	HP5H	..	8	–63	–35	17
Hong Kong	GQBQ	–456	..	..	–597	..
India	HP5I	55	–2	65	132	139
Japan	CBEC	–538	608	1 089	1 956	–244
Singapore	GQBS	62	32	85	259	588
South Korea	GQBT	–54	23	72	104	125
Australasia and Oceania	GQDT	835	695	535	1 259	1 227
of which						
Australia	CBOZ	802	690	521	876	1 010
New Zealand	CBPA	4	5	13	46	25
Africa	GQBU	59	59	65	80	174
of which						
South Africa	CBED	50	26	25	31	97
World Total	CBEV	20 283	25 876	35 588	51 650	44 821
OECD	GQBV	19 715	25 471	33 927	47 476	39 097
Central & Eastern Europe[3]	GQBW	1	1	..	..	6

1 See chapter text. A minus sign indicates net losses.
2 Net earnings equal profits of UK branches plus overseas investors' receipts of interest and their share of the profits of UK subsidiaries and associates. Earnings are after deducting provisions for depreciation and withholding tax on profits and interest.
3 From 2003 includes Albania, Bosnia & Herzegovina, Bulgaria, Croatia, FYR of Macedonia, Romiania and Serbia & Montenegro. Prior to 2003 Czech Republic, Estonia, Hungary, Latvia, Lithuania, Poland, Slovakia and Slovenia also included.

Sources: ONS Foreign Direct Investment Surveys: 01633 456647; Bank of England

Research and development

Chapter 20

Research and development

Research and experimental development (R&D) is defined for statistical purposes as 'creative work undertaken on a systematic basis in order to increase the stock of knowledge, including knowledge of man, culture and society, and the use of this stock of knowledge to devise new applications'.

R&D is financed and carried out mainly by businesses, the Government, and institutions of higher education. A small amount is performed by non profit-making bodies. Gross Expenditure on R&D (GERD) is an indicator of the total amount of R&D performed within the UK: it has been approximately 2 per cent of GDP in recent years. Detailed figures are reported each year in a Statistical Bulletin (Formally First Release) published in March. Table 20.1 shows the main components of GERD.

ONS conducts an annual survey of expenditure and employment on R&D performed by Government, and of Government funding of R&D. The survey collects data on outturn and planning years. Until 1993 the detailed results were reported in the *Annual Review of Government Funded R&D*. From 1997 the results have appeared in the Science, Engineering and Technology (SET) Statistics published by the Department for Innovation, Universities and Skills (DIUS). Table 20.2 gives some broad totals for gross expenditure by Government (expenditure before deducting funds received by Government for R&D). Table 20.3 gives a breakdown of net expenditure (receipts are deducted).

ONS conducts an annual survey of R&D in business. Tables 20.4 and 20.5 give a summary of the main trends up to 2007. The latest set of results from the survey became available in a First Release dated 30 January 2009.

Revisions were made to the business data for the period 2001 to 2006 and were published at the same time as the 2007 Business Enterprise R&D (BERD) First Release on 30 January 2009. The format of this report was used as it covers all aspects of the R&D data published by ONS.

Statistics on expenditure and employment on R&D in Higher Education Institutions (HEIs) are based on information collected by Higher Education Funding Councils and the Higher Education Statistics Agency (HESA). In 1994 a new methodology was introduced to estimate expenditure on R&D in HEIs. This is based on the allocation of various Funding

Council Grants. Full details of the new methodology are contained in SET Statistics available on the DIUS website at: www.dius.gov.uk/science/science_funding/set_stats

The most comprehensive international comparisons of resources devoted to R&D appear in Main Science and Technology Indicators published by the Organisation for Economic Co-operation and Development (OECD). The Statistical Office of the European Union and the United Nations also compile R&D statistics based on figures supplied by member states.

To make international comparisons more reliable the OECD have published a series of manuals giving guidance on how to measure various components of R&D inputs and outputs. The most important of these is the Frascati Manual, which defines R&D and recommends how resources for R&D should be measured. The UK follows the Frascati Manual as far as possible.

For information on available aggregated data on Research and Development please contact Mark Pollard on 01633 456769 (email Mark.Pollard@ons.gsi.gov.uk).

20.1 Cost of research and development: by sector[1]
United Kingdom

£ million and percentages

	2001		2002		2003		2004		2005		2006		2007	
	£m	%	£m	%	£m	%	£m	%	£m	%	£m	%	%	£m
Sector carrying out the work														
Cash terms (£ million)														
Government	1 160	6	1 053	5	1 243	6	1 240	6	1 238	6	1 252	5	1 186	5
Research councils	674	4	713	4	825	4	930	5	1 051	5	1 061	5	1 052	4
Business enterprise	12 239	66	12 484	65	12 505	63	12 662	63	13 734	62	14 561	62	16 111	63
Higher education	4 149	22	4 618	24	4 785	24	5 004	25	5 580	25	6 022	26	6 517	26
Private non-profit	325	2	374	2	369	2	406	2	502	2	513	2	557	2
Total	18 547	100	19 243	100	19 727	100	20 242	100	22 106	100	23 410	100	25 423	100
Sector providing the funds														
Cash terms (£ million)														
Government	2 299	12	2 215	11	2 650	13	2 778	14	2 584	12	2 541	12	2 185	9
Research councils	1 512	8	1 713	9	1 947	10	2 084	10	2 574	12	2 709	12	3 253	13
Higher education funding councils	1 474	8	1 626	8	1 665	8	1 804	9	1 928	9	2 085	9	2 234	9
Higher education	184	1	208	1	218	1	229	1	266	1	288	1	308	1
Business enterprise[2]	8 499	46	8 384	44	8 287	42	8 914	44	9 580	43	10 776	45	11 864	47
Private non-profit	889	5	962	5	931	5	961	5	1 022	5	1 076	5	1 154	5
Abroad	3 691	20	4 135	22	4 029	20	3 472	17	4 152	19	3 935	17	4 426	17
Total	18 547	100	19 243	100	19 727	100	20 242	100	22 106	100	23 410	100	25 423	100

1 See chapter text.
2 Including research associations and public corporations.

Source: Office for National Statistics: 01633 456765

20.2 Gross central government expenditure on research and development[1]
United Kingdom

£ million

	2002/03		2003/04		2004/05		2005/06		2006/07		2007/08	
	Intra-mural	Extra-mural[2]	Intra-mural	Extra-mural[2]	Intra-mural	Extra-mural[2]	Intra-mural	Extra-mural[2]	Intra-mural	Extra-mural[2]	Intra-mural	Extra-mural[3]
Defence	288	2 502	380	2 364	357	2 283	365	2 223	361	1 851	279	1 941
Research councils	725	1 457	811	1 643	874	1 752	1 004	2 034	1 051	2 135	1 052	2 811
Higher education institutes	-	1 626	-	1 665	-	1 804	-	1 928	-	2 085	-	2 234
Other programmes	297	1 163	338	1 111	327	870	316	1 546	309	881	276	612
Total (excluding NHS)	1 310	6 748	1 529	6 783	1 558	6 709	1 685	7 731	1 721	6 952	1 607	7 598

1 See chapter text.
2 Extramural includes work performed overseas and excludes monies spent with other government departments.
3 2007/08 expenditure figure no longer includes VAT.

Source: Office for National Statistics: 01633 456765

20.3 Net central government expenditure on research and development:[1] by European Union objectives for research and development expenditure
United Kingdom

£ million

		1997 /98	1998 /99	1999 /00	2000 /01	2001 /02	2002 /03	2003 /04	2004 /05	2005 /06	2006 /07	2007 /08
Exploration and exploitation of the earth	KDVP	81.3	78.5	79.5	85.5	106.0	138.3	176.8	193.0	239.0	241.0	228.0
Infrastructure and general planning of land-use	KDVQ	98.9	103.5	104.4	102.4	100.3	101.0	118.7	88.0	70.0	89.0	117.0
Control of environmental pollution	KDVR	136.2	142.8	147.0	151.1	129.1	126.5	150.1	149.0	158.0	158.0	179.0
Protection and promotion of human health (ex NHS)	KDVS	444.8	450.1	519.5	530.6	571.6	597.8	1 163.7	1 227.3	1 258.0	1 394.0	1 471.0
Production, distribution and rational utilisation of energy	KDVT	41.0	28.0	29.0	31.9	36.8	40.3	28.4	35.0	21.0	43.0	56.0
Agricultural production and technology	KDVU	268.9	255.5	260.6	266.6	265.2	267.8	275.9	278.0	273.0	284.0	249.0
Industrial production and technology	KDVV	116.9	61.6	56.5	109.2	237.0	423.4	426.5	138.4	94.0	88.0	9.0
Social structures and relationships	KDVW	113.8	154.7	217.6	270.2	268.8	293.4	226.7	291.8	471.0	311.0	396.0
Exploration and exploitation of space	KDVX	164.4	142.5	142.7	146.3	139.8	155.5	168.6	168.9	192.0	153.0	177.0
Research financed from general university funds	KDVY	1 033.3	1 085.1	1 157.1	1 276.1	1 473.5	1 626.4	1 664.6	1 804.7	1 933.0	2 092.0	2 234.0
Non-oriented research	KDVZ	671.0	677.0	700.5	789.3	918.2	1 071.6	1 290.9	1 332.0	1 658.0	1 715.0	1 926.0
Other civil research[2]	KDWA	21.6	25.8	20.6	22.3	19.7	36.3	39.9	38.4	38.0	45.0	–
Defence	KDWB	2 317.2	2 144.2	2 275.9	2 245.1	2 063.0	2 739.7	2 682.2	2 582.7	2 528.0	2 132.0	2 150.0
Total (Excluding NHS)	KDWC	5 509.3	5 349.3	5 710.9	6 026.6	6 329.0	7 618.0	8 413.5	8 327.0	8 932.0	8 745.0	9 192.0

1 See chapter text.
2 Due to OECD changes to the NABS codes, from 2007 "Other Civil Research" no longer exists as a category.

Source: Office for National Statistics: 01633 456765

335

Research and development

20.4 Intramural expenditure on Business Enterprise research and development:[1] by industry

United Kingdom: At Current Prices and Constant 2007 Prices

£ million

		Total				Civil				Defence		
		2005	2006	2007		2005	2006	2007		2005	2006	2007
Current Prices												
Chemicals	KDWF	4 011	4 577	5 125	KDWP	..	..	..	KDWZ	..	..	..
Mechanical engineering	KDWG	978	997	1 101	KDWQ	458	464	609	KDXA	520	533	491
Electrical machinery	KJRT	1 274	1 273	1 246	KJTC	978	930	897	KJUL	296	343	348
Aerospace	KDWJ	2 169	1 832	2 070	KDWT	902	908	914	KDXD	1 267	924	1 156
Transport equipment	KDWK	892	913	1 110	KDWU	..	..	..	KDXE	..	..	..
Other manufacturing	KDWL	1 236	1 336	1 457	KDWV	1 146	1 266	1 358	KDXF	90	70	100
Manufacturing: Total	KDWE	10 560	10 928	12 109	KDWO	8 270	8 935	9 893	KDWY	2 290	1 991	2 216
Services	KDWM	2 949	3 430	3 775	KDWW	2 792	3 252	3 605	KDXG	157	178	169
Agriculture, hunting and forestry; fishing	HFRV	117	88	74	HFSA	..	88	74	MKFC	..	–	–
Extractive industries	HFRW	59	59	77	HFSB	59	59	77	MKFD	–	–	–
Electricity, gas and water supply	HFRX	15	21	35	HFSC	15	21	35	MKFE	–	–	–
Construction	HFRY	33	36	41	HFSE	..	36	41	MKFF	..	–	–
Other: Total	HFRU	225	205	227	HFRZ	225	205	227	MKFB	–	–	–
Total		13 734	14 561	16 111		11 288	12 392	13 726		2 446	2 169	2 385
2007 Prices												
Chemicals	HFXA	4 245	4 717	5 125	HFXJ	..	..	..	HFYO	..	..	..
Mechanical engineering	HFXB	1 036	1 028	1 101	HFXK	485	478	609	HFYP	550	549	491
Electrical machinery	HFXC	1 348	1 312	1 246	HFYH	1 035	958	897	HFYQ	313	353	348
Aerospace	HFXD	2 295	1 888	2 070	HFYI	955	936	914	HFYR	1 341	952	1 156
Transport equipment	HFXE	944	941	1 110	HFYJ	..	..	..	HFYS	..	..	..
Other manufacturing	HFXF	1 308	1 377	1 457	HFYK	1 213	1 305	1 358	HFYT	95	72	100
Manufacturing: Total	HFWZ	11 176	11 261	12 109	HFXI	8 753	9 208	9 893	HFYN	2 424	2 052	2 216
Services	HFXG	3 121	3 535	3 775	HFYL	2 955	3 352	3 605	HFYU	166	183	169
Agriculture, hunting and forestry: fishing	HFSG	124	90	74	HFSL	..	91	74	MKFH	..	..	–
Extractive industries	HFSH	63	61	77	HFSM	62	61	77	MKFI	–	–	–
Electricity, gas and water supply	HFSI	16	22	35	HFSN	16	22	35	MKFJ	–	–	–
Construction	HFSJ	35	37	41	HFSO	..	37	41	MKFK	..	..	–
Other: Total	HFSF	238	211	227	HFSK	238	211	227	MKFG	–	–	–
Total	HFWY	14 536	15 007	16 111	HFXH	11 947	12 771	13 726	HFYM	2 589	2 235	2 385

1 See chapter text.

Source: Office for National Statistics: 01633 456765

20.5 Sources of funds for research and development within Business Enterprises[1]

United Kingdom

£ million and percentages

		Total				Civil				Defence		
		2005	2006	2007		2005	2006	2007		2005	2006	2007
Cash terms (£ million)												
Government funds	KDYM	1 101	1 071	1 058	KDYU	156	161	168	KDZC	945	910	890
Overseas funds	KDYN	3 584	3 269	3 738	KDYV	2 656	2 693	3 090	KDZD	928	576	648
Mainly own funds	KDYO	9 049	10 221	11 314	KDYW	8 475	9 538	10 468	KDZE	573	683	847
Total	KDYL	13 734	14 561	16 111	KDYT	11 288	12 392	13 726	KDZB	2 446	2 169	2 385
Percentages												
Government funds	KDYQ	8	7	7	KDYY	1	1	1	KDZG	39	42	37
Overseas funds	KDYR	26	22	23	KDYZ	24	22	23	KDZH	38	27	27
Mainly own funds	KDYS	66	70	70	KDZA	75	77	76	KDZI	18	31	36
Total	KDYP	100	100	100	KDYX	100	100	100	KDZF	100	100	100

1 See chapter text.

Source: Office for National Statistics: 01633 456765

Agriculture, fisheries and food

Chapter 21

Agriculture, fisheries and food

Output and input

(Tables 21.1 and 21.2)

For both tables, output is net of VAT collected on the sale of non-edible products. Figures for total output include subsidies on products, but not other subsidies. Unspecified crops include turf, other minor crops and arable area payments for fodder maize. Eggs include the value of duck eggs and exports of eggs for hatching. Landlords' expenses are included within Farm maintenance, Miscellaneous expenditure and Depreciation of buildings and works. Also included within 'Other farming costs' are livestock and crop costs, water costs, insurance premia, bank charges, professional fees, rates, and other farming costs.

Other subsidies

Agri-Environment schemes include Environmentally and Nitrate Sensitive Areas, Countryside Stewardship, Countryside Premium, Tir Cymen, Tir Gofal, Moorland, Habitat, Farm Woodland and Organic Farming Schemes. Included in 'Other' subsidies are guidance premium for beef and sheep meat production, Pilot Beef and Sheep Extensification Scheme, non-agricultural horse grazing and farm accounts grant as well as historic data for fertiliser and lime grant and payments to small scale cereal producers.

Compensation of employees and interest charges

Total compensation of employees excludes the value of work done by farm labour on own account capital formation in buildings and work. 'Interest' relates to interest charges on loans for current farming purposes and buildings, less interest on money held on short-term deposit.

Rent

Rent paid (after deductions) is the rent paid on all tenanted land including 'conacre' land in Northern Ireland, less landlords' expenses and the benefit value of dwellings on that land. Rent received (after deductions) is the rent received by farming landowners from renting of land to other farmers, less landlords' expenses and the benefit value of dwellings on that land. Total net rent is the net rent flowing out of the agricultural sector paid to non-farming landowners, including that part of tenanted land in Northern Ireland. (Although there has been some updating of the technical procedures for calculating this figure, it corresponds with the previous net rent variable.)

Agricultural censuses and surveys

(Tables 21.3, 21.5 and 21.13)

The coverage for holdings includes all main and minor holdings for each country. Northern Ireland data are now based on all active farm business.

Estimated quantity of crops and grass harvested

(Table 21.4)

The estimated yields of sugar beet and hops are obtained from production figures supplied by British Sugar plc, and the main hop producers in England and Wales. In Great Britain potato yields are estimated in consultation with the British Potato Council.

Forestry

(Table 21.6)

Statistics for state forestry are from Forestry Commission and Forest Service management information systems. For private forestry in Great Britain, statistics on new planting and restocking are based on records of grant aid and estimates of planting undertaken without grant aid, and softwood production is estimated from a survey of the largest timber harvesting companies. Hardwood production is estimated from deliveries of roundwood to primary wood processors, data provided by trade associations and estimates provided by the Expert Group Timber and Trade Statistics.

Average weekly earnings and hours of agricultural and horticultural workers

(Tables 21.11 and 21.12)

Prior to 1998, data were collected from a monthly postal survey, which mainly covered male full-time workers. Between 1998 and 2002 the survey collected information on an annual basis via a telephone survey. The survey was reviewed in 2002 and it was concluded that the frequency of the survey should

be increased to four times per year to enable the production of more representative annual estimates. The annual sample size has been retained and has been split between four quarterly telephone surveys.

Results for other quarters can be found on the Department for Environment, Food and Rural Affairs (DEFRA) website at: www,defra.gov.uk

The survey covers seven main categories of workers and provides data which are used by the Agricultural Wages Board when considering wage claims and in considering the cost of labour in agriculture and horticulture.

Data on earnings represents the total earnings of regular full-time male workers aged 20 and over. Figures include all payments-in-kind, valued where applicable in accordance with the Agricultural Wages Order. The earnings and hours of hire farm managers are excluded. Part-time workers are defined as those working less than 39 basic hours per week. Casual workers are those employed on a temporary basis.

Fisheries

(Table 21.15)

Fishing fleet information is obtained from vessel registers maintained by DEFRA in England and Wales and the Scottish Executive Agriculture and Fisheries Department.

Estimated average household food consumption – 'Family Food' Expenditure and Food Survey

(Table 21.16)

The Expenditure and Food Survey (EFS) started in April 2001, having been preceded by the National Food Survey (NFS) and the Family Expenditure Survey (FES). Both surveys were brought into one to provide value for money without compromising data quality. The EFS is effectively a continuation of the FES extended to record quantities of purchases. Estimates from the NFS prior to 2000 have been adjusted by aligning estimates for the year 2000 with corresponding estimates from the FES. The survey is a voluntary sample survey of private households throughout the UK. The basic unit of the survey is the household which is defined as a group of people living at the same address and sharing common catering arrangements.

The survey is continuous, interviews being spread evenly over the year to ensure that seasonal effects are covered. Each household member over the age of seven keeps a diary of all their expenditure over a 2 week period. A simplified version of the diary is used by those aged between 7 and 15. The diaries record expenditure and quantities of purchases of food and drink rather than consumption of food and drink.

Items of food and drink are defined as either household or eating out and are recorded in the form the item was purchased not how it was consumed. 'Household' covers all food that is brought into the household. 'Eating out' covers all food that never enters the household, for example restaurant meals, school meals and snacks eaten on the hoof.

From 2006 the survey moved onto a calendar year basis (from the previous financial year basis) in preparation for its integration to the Integrated Household Survey (IHS) from January 2008.

In 2007 the Expenditure and Food Survey collected the diaries of 14,647 people within 6,141 households across the UK. The response rate for 2007 was 53 per cent in Great Britain and 54 per cent in Northern Ireland.

21.1 Production and income account at current prices[1]
United Kingdom

£ million

		1998	1999	2000	2001	2002	2003	2004	2005	2006	2007	2008[2]
Output[3]												
1.Total cereals:	C5X5	1 732.9	1 620.2	1 604.3	1 336.8	1 561.5	1 486.1	1 707.4	1 445.4	1 509.4	1 933.3	3 205.7
Wheat	KFKA	1 186.8	1 105.2	1 119.6	831.5	1 111.7	994.2	1 230.9	1 024.1	1 069.3	1 317.5	2 233.8
Rye	VQBG	2.8	1.8	1.5	1.8	1.2	1.4	1.6	1.3	1.4	1.5	1.4
Barley	KFKB	504.1	474.6	440.8	462.2	401.2	445.8	432.2	383.7	384.1	550.2	882.4
Oats and summer cereal mixtures	KFKC	38.8	37.9	41.6	40.8	46.5	43.9	41.8	35.4	53.7	63.1	86.7
Other cereals	VQBH	0.5	0.8	0.8	0.6	0.9	0.9	0.9	0.9	0.9	1.0	1.4
2.Total industrial crops	VQBI	848.2	783.3	699.4	773.8	859.7	812.2	798.4	806.0	733.9	771.3	1 150.5
Oilseeds	VQBJ	282.9	225.0	143.8	177.1	220.1	313.7	265.9	277.2	315.1	426.6	628.2
Oilseed rape	KFKG	262.6	194.8	139.0	171.5	217.4	303.7	256.7	261.2	307.2	422.3	617.8
Other oil seeds	KIBT	20.3	30.1	4.8	5.6	2.7	9.9	9.2	15.9	7.9	4.3	10.4
Sugar beet	KFKH	298.5	279.7	252.1	256.4	282.9	279.7	278.1	268.8	178.2	161.5	200.5
Other industrial crops	VQBK	266.8	278.7	303.4	340.3	356.7	218.8	254.4	260.0	240.6	183.2	321.9
Fibre plants	VQBL	2.6	2.3	1.3	1.7	1.0	1.8	1.2	0.9	0.9	0.4	1.0
Hops	KFKI	13.1	12.1	10.4	9.0	7.2	6.1	5.7	5.4	4.4	4.4	4.4
Others[4]	VQBM	251.1	264.2	291.7	329.6	348.4	210.9	247.5	253.7	235.3	178.3	316.5
3.Total forage plants	VQBO	71.0	75.9	80.9	103.4	90.3	103.7	93.3	94.9	85.9	106.3	110.8
4.Total vegetables and horticultural products	VQBP	1 627.6	1 667.5	1 561.1	1 612.6	1 591.1	1 672.6	1 621.5	1 690.3	1 748.8	1 848.3	1 897.0
5.Total potatoes (including seeds)	KFKO	629.4	749.0	463.7	682.1	485.0	526.9	674.0	514.9	622.9	662.3	755.4
6.Total fruit	KFKQ	258.8	256.9	280.0	239.8	251.2	310.3	315.8	388.1	382.8	452.5	516.5
7.Other crop products including seeds	VQBQ	39.4	42.0	37.7	37.5	25.5	31.6	31.0	52.0	47.9	44.3	43.1
8.Total crop output (Sum 1 to 7)	VQBR	5 207.2	5 194.8	4 679.3	4 785.0	4 864.2	4 943.3	5 241.4	4 991.5	5 131.6	5 818.2	7 679.1
9.Total livestock production	VQBS	4 694.3	4 326.7	4 363.6	4 260.8	4 574.4	4 823.2	4 839.1	4 934.7	5 059.6	5 220.4	6 510.0
Primarily for meat	KFLA	4 099.5	3 929.5	3 969.8	3 634.3	3 867.9	4 092.5	4 181.8	4 331.6	4 303.6	4 390.7	5 422.3
Cattle	KFKU	1 052.6	1 145.2	1 093.7	955.3	1 145.8	1 227.1	1 279.2	1 479.6	1 543.4	1 626.1	2 069.6
Pigs	KFKW	882.4	784.8	800.2	748.4	687.2	671.1	679.9	676.9	685.2	736.3	858.2
Sheep	VQBT	631.1	574.8	616.8	438.0	613.4	696.4	725.6	683.1	681.0	637.4	822.1
Poultry	KFXX	1 384.7	1 275.8	1 306.5	1 337.6	1 263.9	1 336.7	1 331.4	1 321.1	1 218.4	1 207.4	1 482.3
Other animals	KFKY	148.8	148.9	152.6	154.9	157.7	161.2	165.7	170.9	175.5	183.5	190.0
Gross fixed capital formation	KFLI	594.7	397.3	393.8	626.5	706.5	730.7	657.3	603.1	756.0	829.7	1 087.7
Cattle	KUJZ	296.9	206.9	192.9	371.3	392.2	447.7	337.4	354.5	483.6	522.6	734.9
Pigs	LUKB	5.7	6.9	5.6	5.3	7.4	7.0	7.6	6.2	8.0	5.3	8.2
Sheep	LUKA	155.3	56.7	63.9	122.5	177.5	145.8	176.4	111.5	133.3	153.0	181.4
Poultry	LUKC	136.8	126.8	131.4	127.4	129.3	130.1	135.9	130.8	131.1	148.7	163.2
10.Total livestock products	KFLF	3 068.0	2 963.1	2 711.4	3 088.2	2 834.3	3 030.7	3 037.7	3 009.5	2 918.1	3 286.1	4 027.0
Milk	KFLB	2 741.5	2 662.0	2 385.8	2 742.6	2 466.3	2 628.5	2 610.4	2 592.5	2 497.2	2 823.5	3 450.0
Eggs	KFLC	281.5	254.0	280.3	307.1	314.5	336.4	378.3	349.4	361.7	410.1	523.6
Raw wool	KFLD	23.9	21.4	22.7	17.2	19.1	20.8	20.1	19.5	11.5	11.8	12.2
Other animal products	KFLE	21.0	25.7	22.6	21.2	34.5	45.1	28.9	48.1	47.7	40.8	41.2
11.Total livestock output (9+10)	VQBV	7 762.3	7 289.8	7 075.0	7 348.9	7 408.7	7 853.9	7 876.8	7 944.2	7 977.7	8 506.5	10 537.1
12.Total other agricultural activities	LUOS	452 253	457 188	455 401	473 519	508 574	459 754	462 633	481 052	522 722	474 287	776
Agricultural services	LUKD	570.2	609.5	587.0	604.0	601.4	592.3	636.2	630.7	623.3	669.1	775.3
Leasing out quota	VQBW	119.1	116.5	51.2	28.1	42.8	40.2	82.0	9.7	0.9	0.4	0.4
13.Total inseparable non-agricultural activities	LUOT	214 027	273 476	370 184	367 736	450 749	480 252	573 382	712 489	810 993	889 723	759
14.Gross output at market prices (8+11+12+13)	LUOV	25 659	23 140	20 367	17 682	20 364	59 534	71 485	68 120	147 106	71 386	19 751
15.Total subsidies (less taxes) on product	LUOU	113 711	224 700	222 431	192 446	294 981	311 602	333 318	447 978	383 513	430 773	56
16.Output at basic prices (14+15)	KFLT	16 339.8	15 854.5	14 892.3	15 139.8	15 418.8	15 998.0	16 641.3	14 462.8	14 539.3	15 787.6	19 807.2
of which transactions within the agricultural industry												
Feed wheat	LUNQ	78.8	64.4	39.8	41.0	42.5	69.6	103.1	83.3	75.9	92.2	127.0
Feed barley	LUNR	163.6	147.9	136.9	148.5	146.9	148.6	147.9	140.2	148.2	200.0	265.5
Feed oats	LUNS	11.5	14.5	12.6	14.0	12.2	12.0	14.3	12.2	14.9	17.3	23.2
Seed potatoes	LUNT	12.7	28.8	6.9	14.0	12.1	4.0	9.2	12.5	16.0	8.5	13.4
Straw	LUNU	222.1	232.9	258.6	291.2	306.5	177.0	209.0	210.4	191.0	137.4	259.2
Contract work	LUNV	570.2	609.5	587.0	604.0	601.4	592.3	636.2	630.7	623.3	669.1	775.3
Leasing of quota	LUNW	119.1	116.5	51.2	28.1	42.8	40.2	82.0	9.7	0.9	0.4	0.4
Total capital formation in livestock	LUNX	594.7	397.3	393.8	626.5	706.5	730.7	657.3	603.1	756.0	829.7	1 087.7

21.1 Production and income account at current prices[1]
United Kingdom

continued

£ million

		1998	1999	2000	2001	2002	2003	2004	2005	2006	2007	2008[2]
Intermediate consumption												
17.Seeds	KFME	490.0	542.6	468.2	510.3	485.9	466.7	619.8	661.9	579.6	608.4	629.5
18.Energy	VQDO	598.3	621.9	697.9	683.3	647.0	600.0	669.1	779.0	832.6	897.7	1 225.6
Electricity	VQDQ	231.0	221.7	230.2	240.1	234.8	204.8	209.7	235.2	259.0	276.0	341.4
Fuels	VQDV	367.3	400.2	467.8	443.2	412.2	395.2	459.4	543.8	573.6	621.7	884.1
19.Fertilisers	KFMM	831.7	756.0	737.8	755.1	752.2	696.1	774.6	773.9	774.6	827.1	1 527.4
20.Pesticides	KFMN	653.7	621.0	579.4	526.2	531.2	501.1	576.1	547.2	518.0	566.6	655.9
21.Veterinary expenses	KCPC	288.0	270.0	255.8	241.2	250.1	253.4	279.1	280.3	285.9	304.5	284.0
22.Animal feed	KFMB	2 444.4	2 260.9	2 164.1	2 411.0	2 272.1	2 393.2	2 558.4	2 317.8	2 408.2	2 854.5	3 943.9
Compounds	LUNY	1 523.5	1 402.4	1 283.3	1 398.2	1 376.9	1 348.2	1 449.6	1 318.0	1 401.6	1 645.9	2 163.4
Straights	LUNZ	667.0	631.7	691.4	810.4	693.6	814.8	843.5	764.2	767.6	899.1	1 364.7
Feed purchased from other farms	LUOA	253.9	226.8	189.3	202.4	201.6	230.2	265.3	235.6	239.0	309.5	415.7
23.Total maintenance[5]	VQDW	1 023.1	1 013.4	939.0	980.6	957.0	967.9	1 012.1	993.6	1 013.6	1 085.6	1 145.6
Materials	KFMO	699.2	698.2	651.2	660.1	636.2	641.3	662.9	653.1	655.9	688.6	721.7
Buildings	KCPB	323.9	315.2	287.8	320.5	320.7	326.6	349.2	340.6	357.7	397.0	423.9
24.Agricultural services	LUOE	570.2	609.5	587.0	604.0	601.4	592.3	636.2	630.7	623.3	669.1	775.3
25.Other goods and services[5,6]	VQDX	2 251.3	2 265.8	2 083.4	2 032.0	2 061.6	2 122.5	2 362.0	2 341.1	2 320.6	2 381.9	2 804.0
26.Total intermediate consumption (Sum 17 to 25)	KCPM	9 150.6	8 960.9	8 512.7	8 743.7	8 558.4	8 593.2	9 487.6	9 325.3	9 356.5	10 195.3	12 991.2
27.Gross value added at market prices (14-26)	LUOG	4 929.2	4 680.0	4 367.9	4 646.4	4 918.6	5 428.8	4 986.2	4 929.2	5 103.2	5 536.5	6 760.0
28.Total consumption of Fixed Capital	KCPS	2 596.8	2 438.2	2 495.6	2 600.2	2 584.1	2 648.1	2 533.6	2 660.9	2 681.7	2 709.2	3 033.0
Equipment	KCPR	1 329.7	1 317.6	1 267.4	1 262.9	1 261.9	1 205.7	1 192.4	1 204.5	1 194.6	1 206.6	1 256.1
Buildings[5,7]	LUOH	681.5	701.3	691.2	686.4	689.5	692.3	673.9	675.7	685.3	696.4	707.1
Livestock	VQEA	585.6	419.3	537.0	650.8	632.8	750.0	667.2	780.7	801.8	806.2	1 069.9
Cattle	LUOI	314.8	208.2	281.1	348.4	353.2	441.2	363.6	489.6	501.4	502.2	720.1
Pigs	LUOK	8.4	7.7	8.0	6.1	7.8	7.7	8.6	7.3	7.3	6.1	8.8
Sheep	LUOJ	119.0	69.6	120.1	169.5	141.5	173.0	167.3	150.7	161.7	157.2	190.8
Poultry	LUOL	143.4	133.8	127.8	126.8	130.3	128.2	127.8	133.0	131.5	140.8	150.2
29.Net value added at market prices (27-28)	KCPT	2 332.3	2 241.8	1 872.3	2 046.2	2 334.4	2 780.7	2 452.6	2 268.3	2 421.4	2 827.2	3 727.0
30.Compensation of employees[8]	LUOR	1 975.0	2 028.3	1 900.1	1 949.9	1 965.4	1 915.2	2 004.2	2 217.6	2 272.0	2 365.3	2 527.2
31.Other taxes on production	VQEB	−88.9	−92.4	−92.2	−84.9	−80.6	−82.8	−96.5	−102.5	−99.3	−102.5	−106.6
32.Other subsidies on production	VQEC	379.2	470.1	462.1	695.7	722.7	782.6	778.0	2 805.1	2 931.9	2 941.5	3 182.4
Animal disease compensation	LUOM	8.3	11.9	19.1	13.0	23.9	25.2	18.9	19.2	16.7	21.6	27.9
Set-aside	LUON	87.7	170.0	127.3	180.1	142.5	176.7	129.5	–	..	..	..
Agri-environment schemes[9]	ZBXC	107.5	128.5	140.3	164.1	196.1	222.6	257.0	287.6	376.1	457.8	449.7
Other including Single Payment Scheme[10]	VQED	–	–	–	164.9	166.1	159.9	153.4	2 498.3	2 539.2	2 431.1	2 704.8
33.Net value added at factor cost	LUOQ	4 882.6	4 833.1	4 253.9	4 406.7	4 918.4	5 456.5	5 301.6	5 179.3	5 333.7	5 722.1	6 858.7
34.Rent	KCPV	250.1	239.6	224.5	250.5	253.7	268.6	241.2	216.0	234.2	286.6	249.3
Paid[11]	ZBXE	330.6	322.0	303.3	328.5	339.6	364.7	346.5	302.6	317.5	381.3	336.6
Received[12]	ZBXF	−80.5	−82.4	−78.8	−78.1	−85.9	−96.2	−105.2	−86.6	−83.4	−94.7	−87.2
35.Interest[13]	KCPU	673.0	588.1	598.8	527.7	451.6	427.1	490.7	529.6	523.1	633.5	625.2
Total income from farming (33-30-34-35)	KCQB	1 984.5	1 977.1	1 530.6	1 678.7	2 247.7	2 845.6	2 565.5	2 216.1	2 304.4	2 436.7	3 457.0

1 See chapter text.
2 Provisional.
3 Output is net of VAT collected on the sale of non-edible products. Figures for total output include subsidies on products, but not other subsidies.
4 Includes straw and minor crops.
5 Landlords' expenses are included within 'Total maintenance', 'Other goods and services' and 'Total consumption of Fixed Capital of buildings'.
6 Includes livestock and crop costs, water costs, insurance premiums, bank charges, professional fees, rates and other farming costs.
7 A more empirically based methodology for calculating landlords' consumption of fixed capital was introduced in 2000. The new series has been linked with the old one using a smoothing procedure for the transition year of 1996.
8 Excludes the value of work done by farm labour on own account capital formation in buildings and works.
9 Includes Environmentally and Nitrate Sensitive Areas, Countryside Stewardship and other management schemes, and Moorland, Habitat, Farm Woodland and Organic Farming Schemes.
10 Land area based schemes which replaced the Hill Livestock Compensatory Allowance Scheme in 2001. These are Tir Mynydd in Wales, Less Favoured Area Compensatory Scheme in Northern Ireland, Less Favoured Areas Support Scheme in Scotland and Hill Farm Allowance in England.
11 Rent paid on all tenanted land (including 'conacre' land in Northern Ireland) less landlords' expenses, landlords' consumption of fixed capital and the benefit value of dwellings on that land.
12 Rent received by farming landowners from renting of land to other farmers less landlords' expenses. This series starts in 1996 following a revision to the methodology of calculating net rent.
13 Interest charges on loans for current farming purposes and buildings and works less interest on money held on short term deposit.

Source: Department for Environment, Food and Rural Affairs: 01904 455080

21.2 Output and input volume indices[1]
United Kingdom

Indices (2000=100)

		1997	1998	1999	2000	2001	2002	2003	2004	2005	2006	2007
Outputs[2]												
1. Total cereals:	VQAN	97.7	95.0	92.1	100.0	79.9	96.8	91.1	92.9	89.0	88.0	80.9
Wheat	LUKH	89.5	92.4	89.0	100.0	70.1	96.1	86.5	93.2	89.8	88.7	79.4
Rye	VQAO	131.8	104.5	104.5	100.0	104.5	90.9	86.4	86.4	86.4	86.4	86.4
Barley	LUKI	120.1	102.2	100.8	100.0	103.6	95.6	99.8	90.4	86.1	82.2	80.2
Oats and summer cereal mixtures	LUKJ	90.8	92.1	84.2	100.0	97.1	117.9	116.8	97.6	82.8	113.7	111.0
Other cereals	VQAP	64.4	53.1	82.4	100.0	74.4	109.0	107.2	103.1	105.0	104.2	83.7
2. Total industrial crops:	VQAQ	111.9	113.5	117.6	100.0	93.3	105.7	109.3	105.7	103.9	96.9	89.7
Oil seeds	VQAR	139.2	145.7	167.0	100.0	100.3	124.1	153.3	139.9	168.0	163.1	178.4
Oilseed rape	VQAS	135.1	138.9	148.8	100.0	100.7	127.2	153.8	140.6	165.8	164.8	183.4
Other oil seeds	LUKN	248.8	335.5	708.3	100.0	90.2	42.7	138.1	121.3	208.6	114.5	45.1
Sugar beet	C5X4	122.1	110.2	116.6	100.0	91.8	105.3	101.0	99.6	95.7	81.5	82.9
Other industrial crops	VQAU	90.2	103.4	95.2	100.0	91.2	97.2	91.9	93.1	75.9	73.2	46.6
Fibre plants	VQAV	169.5	138.3	139.6	100.0	69.3	40.3	67.3	47.7	35.1	43.6	43.6
Hops	LUKP	192.5	131.9	112.4	100.0	94.3	94.5	72.4	72.4	61.9	51.1	51.1
Others[3]	VQAW	85.4	102.1	94.4	100.0	91.2	97.6	92.5	94.0	76.5	74.0	46.5
3. Total forage plants	VQAX	97.9	93.1	96.7	100.0	117.0	117.2	115.6	111.4	113.4	100.2	69.9
4. Total vegetables and horticultural Products:	VQAY	102.9	100.4	102.4	100.0	96.8	96.1	93.5	95.3	95.4	90.2	89.3
Fresh vegetables	LUKX	107.5	105.4	106.2	100.0	96.6	88.3	87.8	88.3	91.9	90.6	86.3
Plants and flowers	LUKZ	97.0	94.1	97.5	100.0	97.0	106.6	101.3	104.8	100.4	90.0	93.8
5. Total potatoes (including seeds)	LUKW	115.7	102.2	121.2	100.0	113.7	111.0	100.2	106.2	99.3	93.8	89.8
6. Total fruit	LUKY	81.3	103.9	108.2	100.0	105.8	99.8	109.7	130.0	148.5	149.7	168.9
7. Other crop products including seeds	VQAZ	98.5	91.3	101.8	100.0	101.2	69.0	83.0	84.6	123.6	116.3	108.5
8. Total crop output	VQBA	102.3	100.4	103.2	100.0	93.2	99.8	97.2	99.5	98.4	94.4	90.4
9. Total livestock production	VQBB	108.0	108.9	105.2	100.0	94.2	97.3	95.6	98.0	98.7	98.3	99.0
Mainly for meat processing	LULH	106.4	107.7	104.5	100.0	91.7	95.2	94.8	97.4	99.0	98.4	98.9
Cattle	LULC	98.5	101.2	103.1	100.0	88.6	102.7	105.9	104.5	111.7	116.2	119.8
Pigs	LULE	126.3	127.9	117.5	100.0	90.8	86.8	76.8	77.6	77.1	76.8	80.7
Sheep	LULD	98.4	104.2	104.1	100.0	71.8	81.8	83.5	88.5	89.4	85.8	87.0
Poultry	LULF	106.6	104.5	99.2	100.0	103.2	99.5	100.8	106.9	105.2	100.7	95.0
Other animals	LULG	100.5	100.6	100.0	100.0	99.7	99.8	99.3	99.1	99.6	99.0	99.3
Gross fixed capital formation	LULR	122.3	120.1	112.3	100.0	115.7	115.8	105.4	107.0	101.5	102.3	104.3
Cattle	LULN	114.9	112.0	112.7	100.0	115.8	110.6	109.2	101.8	103.6	103.1	99.9
Pigs	LULP	174.5	132.7	148.1	100.0	85.2	127.0	101.6	92.8	80.6	97.0	92.4
Sheep	LULO	188.3	196.0	147.5	100.0	155.6	173.6	119.9	148.2	115.8	124.0	149.9
Poultry	LULQ	108.5	102.3	96.7	100.0	95.7	95.3	95.0	98.0	93.9	92.7	96.1
10. Total livestock products	LULM	102.0	100.7	102.8	100.0	101.6	102.9	104.1	101.7	101.8	100.6	98.5
Milk	LULI	102.0	100.4	102.8	100.0	101.2	102.3	103.5	100.3	99.6	98.7	96.8
Eggs	LULJ	101.3	102.3	101.1	100.0	107.3	107.0	105.3	114.0	115.1	111.3	107.8
Raw wool	LULK	105.7	112.6	103.9	100.0	83.1	86.3	84.4	85.7	87.9	79.5	72.8
Other animal products	LULL	112.4	100.1	118.7	100.0	88.2	139.6	173.9	105.3	173.7	173.9	177.3
11. Total livestock output	VQBC	105.5	105.5	104.2	100.0	97.1	99.5	98.9	99.5	100.0	99.3	99.0
12. Total other agricultural activities	VQBD	111.0	110.6	116.2	100.0	99.0	100.7	98.7	109.8	96.2	92.2	90.0
Agricultural services	VQBE	94.0	99.1	105.9	100.0	102.9	102.5	100.9	106.3	103.6	100.5	98.2
Leasing out quota	VQBF	311.3	243.4	234.5	100.0	54.0	80.9	73.8	146.3	16.9	1.8	1.5
13. Total inseparable non-agricultural Activities	LULX	82.0	90.3	91.1	100.0	124.4	108.2	110.6	113.7	115.3	116.1	119.6

21.2 Output and input volume indices[1]
United Kingdom
continued

Indices (2000=100)

		1997	1998	1999	2000	2001	2002	2003	2004	2005	2006	2007
14.Gross output at market prices	VQEG	103.7	103.3	104.0	100.0	96.8	100.0	98.7	100.5	99.8	97.8	96.2
15.Total subsidies (less taxes) on product	VQEE	..	..	..	..	..	..	..	..	..	..	..
16.Output at basic prices	LULY	104.0	103.8	104.5	100.0	95.4	99.8	98.8	100.3	100.1	98.0	96.4
of which transactions within the agricultural industry												
Feed wheat	LULZ	146.4	174.7	145.6	100.0	95.8	103.2	162.8	220.7	216.4	176.8	157.5
Feed barley	LUMA	112.1	110.1	101.2	100.0	108.2	114.9	107.9	97.4	100.5	100.9	97.8
Feed oats	LUMB	75.0	92.1	108.6	100.0	103.3	101.7	109.7	109.5	96.1	106.4	105.1
Seed potatoes	LUMC	143.9	140.9	140.5	100.0	111.9	110.3	43.3	65.6	131.5	138.7	48.6
Straw	LUMD	84.4	102.9	93.9	100.0	89.8	95.8	89.9	90.9	71.3	67.9	40.0
Contract work	LUME	94.0	99.1	105.9	100.0	102.9	102.5	100.9	106.3	103.6	100.5	98.2
Leasing of quota	LUMF	311.3	243.4	234.5	100.0	54.0	80.9	73.8	146.3	16.9	1.8	1.5
Total capital formation in livestock	LUMG	122.3	120.1	112.3	100.0	115.8	115.9	105.5	107.1	101.6	102.3	104.4
Intermediate Consumption												
17.Seeds	LUMO	107.4	100.7	104.5	100.0	99.0	91.8	91.3	84.9	80.5	79.1	88.1
Cereals	LUMM	..	..	..	..	..	..	..	..	..	..	..
Other	LUMN	..	..	..	..	..	..	..	..	..	..	..
18.Energy	VQEH	103.3	108.3	101.6	92.8	94.0	93.4	79.4	82.0	76.5	..	..
Electricity	VQEI	104.0	113.7	108.1	100.0	108.2	110.3	89.6	86.6	81.7	74.2	78.7
Fuels	VQEJ	115.9	118.2	110.1	100.0	97.8	95.8	83.5	88.9	82.4	78.5	81.5
19.Fertilisers	VQEK	130.3	122.1	114.2	100.0	87.4	91.2	78.2	79.2	71.4	67.2	66.0
20.Pesticides	LUMQ	100.1	104.3	101.4	100.0	93.9	95.8	90.5	99.3	92.2	85.8	90.1
21.Veterinary expenses	LUMW	120.4	111.4	104.3	100.0	95.6	100.0	97.6	104.5	105.5	99.6	100.4
22.Animal feed	LUML	101.7	102.0	102.8	100.0	103.7	101.2	105.2	107.0	105.5	104.1	102.5
Compounds	LUMH	108.6	105.9	108.8	100.0	102.9	102.3	102.2	103.3	99.5	102.6	105.5
Straights	LUMI	84.6	88.9	89.3	100.0	104.7	96.4	106.8	109.0	111.0	102.7	94.8
Feed purchased from other farms	LUMJ	117.1	122.8	111.2	100.0	105.2	111.5	120.5	125.8	126.2	118.7	112.2
23.Total maintenance[4]	VQEL	121.4	113.0	110.6	100.0	102.0	96.1	92.4	92.8	86.0	83.5	83.3
Materials	LUMU	115.4	112.1	109.5	100.0	98.5	91.0	86.4	85.5	78.8	75.0	75.5
Buildings	LUMT	134.8	114.9	112.9	100.0	110.0	108.0	106.1	109.9	103.0	103.7	101.5
24.Agricultural services	VQEM	94.0	99.1	105.9	100.0	102.9	102.5	100.9	106.3	103.6	100.5	98.2
25.Other goods and services[4,5]	VQEO	125.0	116.3	112.2	100.0	93.6	93.7	99.2	105.4	98.3	93.9	93.8
26.Total intermediate consumption	LUNE	112.5	109.5	107.6	100.0	98.2	97.0	96.0	98.9	93.8	90.4	90.9
27.Gross value added at market prices	LUNF	88.9	92.3	97.2	100.0	94.2	105.5	103.6	103.3	112.1	113.4	107.1
28.Total consumption of Fixed Capital	LUNN	103.4	102.8	101.3	100.0	98.3	93.9	93.3	92.4	93.4	90.7	89.5
Equipment	LUNI	106.4	104.5	102.3	100.0	97.7	96.1	94.7	94.0	92.5	90.2	89.4
Buildings[4,6]	LUNG	107.7	107.0	104.3	100.0	101.3	103.2	100.5	98.1	94.8	96.7	95.7
Livestock	VQES	91.2	92.9	94.3	100.0	96.0	81.2	83.4	83.6	92.1	85.1	83.2
Cattle	LUNJ	87.0	86.4	88.1	100.0	86.4	76.0	81.0	81.5	92.2	81.8	79.3
Pigs	LUNL	121.2	129.9	117.3	100.0	67.9	98.9	79.0	78.7	67.7	67.1	69.4
Sheep	LUNK	82.9	85.1	95.1	100.0	120.7	78.7	78.0	78.7	86.2	86.7	84.8
Poultry	LUNM	102.8	110.3	105.0	100.0	98.0	98.8	96.2	94.7	98.2	95.5	95.9
29.Net value added at market prices	LUNO	75.0	81.6	92.4	100.0	88.9	120.9	117.3	117.8	138.6	146.8	132.8

1 See chapter text.
2 Output is net of VAT collected on the sale of non-edible products. Figures for total output include subsidies on products, but not other subsidies.
3 Includes straw and minor crops.
4 Landlords' expenses are included within 'Total maintenance', 'Other goods and services' and 'Total consumption of Fixed Capital of buildings'.

5 Includes livestock and crop costs, water costs, insurance premiums, bank charges, professional fees, rates, and other farming costs.
6 A more empirically based methodology for calculating landlords' depreciation was introduced in 2000. The new series has been linked with the old one using a smoothing procedure for the transition year of 1996.

Source: Department for Environment, Food and Rural Affairs: 01904 455080

21.3 Agriculture land-use
United Kingdom
Area at the June Survey[1]

Thousand hectares

		1998	1999	2000	2001	2002	2003	2004	2005	2006	2007	2008
Total agricultural area	BFAH	18 593	18 579	18 311	18 594	18 537	18 464	18 432	18 502	18 788	18 690	18 702
Crops	BFAA	4 972	4 709	4 665	4 493	4 604	4 475	4 589	4 437	4 415	4 439	4 740
Bare fallow[2]	BFAB	34	33	37	43	33	29	29	140	150	165	..
Uncropped arable land[3]	J8U3	..	..	..	..	..	..	..	..	..	..	195
Total tillage	KIJR	5 005	4 742	4 702	4 536	4 636	4 504	4 619	4 600	4 611	4 603	4 935
All grass under 5 years old	KFEM	1 301	1 226	1 226	1 205	1 243	1 200	1 246	1 193	1 137	1 176	1 141
Total arable land	KFEN	6 306	5 968	5 928	5 741	5 879	5 705	5 864	5 794	5 749	5 779	6 076
All grasses 5 years old and over	KFEO	5 364	5 449	5 364	5 584	5 519	5 683	5 620	5 711	5 967	5 965	6 036
Total tillage and grass	KFEP	11 671	11 417	11 292	11 325	11 397	11 388	11 485	11 505	11 716	11 744	12 112
Sole right rough grazing	BFAD	4 624	4 575	4 445	4 435	4 488	4 329	4 326	4 354	4 491	4 313	4 359
Set aside	DMNF	314	572	567	800	612	689	559	535	513	440	..
All other land on agricultural holdings including woodland	BFAE	777	789	780	801	806	820	825	872	874	954	993
Total land on agricultural holdings	BFAF	17 372	17 352	17 083	17 361	17 303	17 227	17 195	17 266	17 547	17 452	17 464
Common rough grazing (estimated)	BFAG	1 221	1 227	1 228	1 232	1 234	1 236	1 237	1 236	1 241	1 238	1 238
Crops	BFAA	4 972	4 709	4 665	4 493	4 604	4 475	4 589	4 437	4 415	4 439	4 740
Cereals	BFAJ	3 420	3 141	3 348	3 014	3 245	3 057	3 130	2 919	2 864	2 885	3 274
Wheat	BFAK	2 045	1 847	2 086	1 635	1 996	1 837	1 990	1 867	1 836	1 830	2 080
Barley	BFAL	1 255	1 179	1 128	1 245	1 101	1 076	1 007	938	881	898	1 032
Oats	BFAM	98	92	109	112	126	121	108	90	121	129	133
Mixed corn	BFAN	2	2	2	3	4	4	..	..	..	..	..
Rye[4]	BFAO	10	8	7	5	5	4	6	..	..	..	..
Triticale	DMNH	10	13	16	14	14	15	15	13	13	16	..
Rye, mixed corn and triticale	J8U4	22	23	25	21	23	23	25	24	25	27	27
Other arable crops (excluding potatoes)	DMNI	1 210	1 211	979	1 141	1 024	1 098	1 136	1 211	1 245	1 245	1 152
Oilseed rape	BFAP	506	417	332	404	357	460	498	519	568	674	598
Sugar beet not for stock feeding[4]	BFAQ	189	183	173	177	169	162	154	148	130	125	120
Hops[5]	DMNJ	3	3	2	2	2	2	2	1	1	..	..
Peas for harvesting dry and field beans	DMNK	213	202	208	275	249	235	242	239	231	161	148
Linseed	DMNL	99	209	71	31	12	32	30	45	36	13	16
Other crops	DMNM	200	197	192	214	204	201	203	252	278	272	269
Potatoes	BFAR	164	178	166	165	158	145	148	137	140	140	144
Horticultural	BFAV	177	179	172	173	176	176	175	170	166	169	170
Vegetables grown in the open	DMNN	123	126	119	120	124	125	125	121	119	121	122
Orchard fruit[6]	BFBG	28	28	28	28	26	25	24	23	23	23	24
Soft fruit	DMNO	10	9	10	9	9	9	9	9	10	9	10
Ornamentals	DMNP	14	13	14	14	15	14	15	14	12	13	13
Glasshouse crops	DMNQ	2	2	2	2	2	2	2	2	2	2	2

1 Includes estimates for minor holdings for all countries. See chapter text.
2 The area of bare fallow has shown an increase of 378% in 2006. The rise in the bare fallow area in England is believed to be due to the way the farmers have described their land following the introduction of the Single Payment Scheme.
3 Includes all uncropped arable land i.e. bare fallow and arable land not in production managed under GAEC12 conditions.
4 Figures are for England and Wales only.
5 Figures are for England only from 2005. From 2007 are included in Other Crops.
6 Includes non-commercial orchards.

Source: Agricultural Departments: 01904 455333

21.4

Estimated quantity of crops and grass harvested[1]
United Kingdom

Thousand tonnes

Agricultural crops		1998	1999	2000	2001	2002	2003	2004	2005	2006	2007	2008
Wheat	BADO	16 449	14 867	16 704	11 580	15 973	14 282	15 468	14 863	14 735	13 221	17 227
Barley (Winter and Spring) .	BADP	6 623	6 581	6 492	6 660	6 128	6 360	5 799	5 495	5 239	5 079	6 144
Oats	BADQ	586	541	640	621	753	749	626	532	728	712	784
Sugar beet[2]	BADR	10 002	10 584	9 079	8 335	9 559	9 168	8 850	8 687	7 400	7 525	..
Potatoes	BADS	6 422	7 131	6 636	6 649	6 966	5 918	6 316	5 979	5 727	5 564	..

		1998 /99	1999 /00	2000 /01	2001 /02	2002 /03	2003 /04	2004 /05	2005 /06	2006 /07	2007 /08	2008 /09
Horticultural crops												
Field vegetables												
Brussels sprouts	BADT	72.5	78.5	67.3	54.8	42.7	55.8	45.1	46.1	44.8	43.3	44.5
Cabbage (including savoys and spring greens)	BADU	308.9	295.2	273.2	295.4	255.2	245.6	290.9	262.7	254.8	216.3	234.2
Cauliflowers	BADV	191.7	172.4	156.1	107.4	116.5	126.3	168.3	133.2	123.7	122.1	118.5
Carrots	BADW	617.6	673.2	725.8	760.0	718.4	602.4	671.1	710.1	701.3	735.4	732.4
Turnips and swedes	BADX	117.5	123.3	132.1	141.8	103.9	96.5	97.0	103.1	105.7	106.2	105.3
Beetroot	BADY	69.5	63.4	67.1	68.6	56.3	58.8	53.1	51.0	57.3	56.8	55.0
Onions, dry bulb	BADZ	342.0	391.4	392.7	374.9	283.4	373.6	340.9	413.6	358.8	303.8	349.2
Peas, green for market (in pod weight)	BAEA	7.0	7.0	6.7	6.2	7.2	5.9	5.9	5.9	5.9	5.9	5.9
Peas, green for processing (shelled weight)	BAEB	152.0	143.1	184.5	161.0	169.3	167.6	131.1	129.0	124.4	97.8	153.0
Lettuce	BAEC	151.8	155.2	135.8	123.9	109.9	125.6	140.9	131.7	126.4	109.0	116.8
Protected crops												
Tomatoes	BAED	107.6	116.6	113.0	109.1	100.9	75.6	78.5	78.8	84.1	85.6	88.7
Cucumbers	BAEE	83.8	83.8	79.8	71.5	73.6	77.0	61.4	59.9	56.5	49.4	48.9
Lettuce	BAEF	20.6	19.9	18.7	20.9	16.0	16.6	10.4	8.1	8.2	7.8	7.4
Fruit												
Dessert apples	BFCD	97.8	133.9	101.3	104.4	84.0	69.0	92.2	118.0	129.3	106.2	118.4
Cooking apples	BFCE	85.9	112.4	107.5	107.4	95.3	74.9	78.2	100.1	111.5	136.9	124.5
Soft fruit	BFCF	60.1	65.9	65.6	64.6	67.1	79.9	86.0	105.4	107.7	124.1	136.4
Pears	BFBQ	26.3	22.7	26.6	38.5	34.2	29.6	22.7	23.4	28.4	20.6	19.8

1 See chapter text.
2 Figures are adjusted to constant 16% sugar content.

Source: Agricultural Departments: 01904 455332

345

Agriculture, fisheries and food

21.5 Cattle, sheep, pigs and poultry on agricultural holdings[1]
United Kingdom
At June each year

Thousands

		1998	1999	2000	2001	2002	2003	2004	2005	2006	2007	2008
Total cattle and calves[2]	BFCG	11 519	11 423	11 135	10 602	10 345	10 508	10 588	10 440	10 324	10 304	10 107
of which:												
dairy cows	BFCH	2 439	2 440	2 336	2 251	2 227	2 191	2 129	2 063	2 066	1 954	1 909
beef cows	BFCI	1 947	1 924	1 842	1 708	1 657	1 698	1 736	1 762	1 733	1 698	1 670
heifers in calf	BFCJ	787	763	718	701	728	679	690	638	645	..	..
Total sheep and lambs	BFCM	44 471	44 656	42 264	36 716	35 834	35 812	35 817	35 416	34 722	33 946	33 131
of which:												
ewes and shearlings	CKUQ	21 260	21 458	20 449	17 921	17 630	17 580	17 630	16 935	16 637	16 064	15 616
lambs under one year old	BFCP	22 138	22 092	20 857	17 769	17 310	17 322	17 238	17 488	17 058	16 855	16 574
Total pigs	BFCQ	8 146	7 284	6 482	5 845	5 588	5 046	5 159	4 862	4 933	4 834	4 714
of which:												
sows in pig and other sows for breeding	CKUU	675	603	537	527	483	442	449	403	401	398	365
gilts in pig	CKUR	103	85	73	71	74	73	66	67	67	57	55
Total fowls	KPSV	..	..	..	..	..	165 285	167 825	160 509	158 202	157 513	154 180
of which:												
table fowls including broilers	CKUT	98 244	101 625	105 689	112 531	105 137	116 738	119 888	111 475	110 672	109 794	109 859
laying fowls[3]	CKUV	29 483	29 258	28 687	29 895	28 778	29 274	29 655	29 544	28 632	27 321	25 940
growing pullets	CKUW	9 860	9 583	9 461	9 367	9 784	8 286	8 156	10 928	9 625	8 936	9 313

1 Includes estimates for minor holdings for all countries. See chapter text.
2 In 2007, cattle figures were sourced from the Cattle Tracing System (CTS) in England and Wales, the equivalent APHIS system in Northern Ireland and survey data in Scotland and are therefore not directly comparable with earlier years. To see comparable data for 2005-2007 please go to: http://statistics.defra.gov.uk/esg/statnot/june_uk.pdf
3 Excludes fowls laying eggs for hatching.

Sources: Department for Environment, Food and Rural Affairs;
Farming Statistics: 01904 455333

21.6 Forestry[1]
United Kingdom

		1980	1990	2000	2003	2004	2005	2006	2007	2008
Woodland area[2] - (Thousand hectares)										
United Kingdom	C5OF	2 175	2 400	2 793	2 807	2 816	2 825	2 829	2 837	2 841
England[3]	C5OG	948	958	1 103	1 110	1 114	1 119	1 121	1 124	1 127
Wales[3]	C5OI	241	248	289	285	286	286	285	285	285
Scotland[3]	C5OH	920	1 120	1 318	1 327	1 330	1 334	1 337	1 341	1 342
Northern Ireland	C5OJ	67	74	83	85	86	85	86	87	87
Forestry Commission/Forest Service	C5OK	946	956	886	848	842	838	832	827	821
Other[4]	C5OL	1 230	1 443	1 907	1 960	1 974	1 987	1 997	2 010	2 020
Conifer	C5OM	1 372	1 576	1 663	1 652	1 651	1 647	1 642	1 640	1 635
Broadleaved[5]	C5ON	804	824	1 131	1 155	1 165	1 178	1 187	1 197	1 207

		1997 /98	1998 /99	1999 /00	2000 /01	2001 /02	2002 /03	2003 /04	2004 /05	2005 /06	2006 /07	2007 /08
New Planting[6] - (Thousand hectares)												
United Kingdom	C5OO	16.9	17.0	17.9	18.7	14.4	13.5	12.4	11.9	8.7	10.7	7.5
England	C5OP	4.4	5.1	5.9	5.9	5.4	5.9	4.6	5.3	3.7	3.2	2.6
Wales	C5OR	0.5	0.6	0.7	0.4	0.3	0.3	0.5	0.5	0.5	0.4	0.2
Scotland	C5OQ	11.4	10.5	10.4	11.7	8.0	6.7	6.8	5.7	4.0	6.6	4.2
Northern Ireland	C5OS	0.6	0.7	0.8	0.7	0.7	0.6	0.5	0.4	0.6	0.5	0.6
Forestry Commission/Forest Service	C5OT	0.2	0.2	0.3	0.3	0.8	0.9	0.2	0.1	0.3	0.2	0.2
Other[7]	C5OU	16.7	16.8	17.6	18.4	13.6	12.6	12.1	11.8	8.4	10.4	7.4
Conifer	C5OV	7.0	6.6	6.5	4.9	3.9	3.7	2.9	2.1	1.1	2.1	0.9
Broadleaved	C5OW	9.9	10 4	11.4	13.8	10.5	9.8	9.5	9.8	7 6	8 5	6.7
Restocking[6] - (Thousand hectares)												
United Kingdom	C5OX	14.2	14.1	15.2	15.3	13.9	14.5	14.9	16.1	15.9	19.0	18.9
England	C5OY	4.4	4.1	3.9	4.0	3.4	3.4	3.2	2.8	3.2	2.8	3.5
Wales	C5P2	2.7	3.0	2.6	2.2	1.9	1.9	1.8	1.8	2.8	3.0	2.3
Scotland	C5OZ	6.3	6.3	8.0	8.0	7.8	8.5	8.9	10.4	9.0	12.4	12.6
Northern Ireland	C5P3	0.7	0.7	0.6	1.1	0.9	0.7	1.1	1.0	0.9	0.8	0.5
Forestry Commission/Forest Service	C5P4	8.5	8.5	8.8	8.9	9.2	9.1	9.9	10.6	10.4	11.0	10.4
Other[7]	C5P5	5.7	5.6	6.4	6.4	4.7	5.3	5.0	5.5	5.5	8.0	8.5
Conifer	C5P6	11.2	11.3	11.9	12.3	11.5	12.0	12.1	13.0	12.5	15.3	14.8
Broadleaved	C5P7	3.0	2.8	3.3	3.0	2.4	2.5	2.8	3.0	3.4	3.6	4.1

		1999	2000	2001	2002	2003	2004	2005	2006	2007
Wood Production (volume - Thousand green tonnes[8])										
United Kingdom	C5P8	7 960	8 080	8 140	8 250	8 880	9 030	9 070	9 000	9 520
Softwood total	C5PA	7 280	7 430	7 500	7 630	8 310	8 520	8 480	8 570	9 080
Forestry Commission/Forest Service	C5PB	4 730	4 850	4 600	4 650	4 820	4 890	4 580	4 580	4 650
Non-Forestry Commission/Forest Service	C5PC	2 550	2 580	2 900	2 980	3 500	3 620	3 900	3 980	4 420
Hardwood[9]	C5PD	670	650	630	620	560	510	590	440	440

1 See chapter text.
2 Areas as at 31 March.
3 For England, Wales and Scotland, 1980 woodland area figures are the published results from the 1979-1982 Census of Woodlands and Trees and figures for 1990 are adjusted to reflect subsequent changes. From 1998 onwards they are based on results from the 1995-1999 National Inventory of Woodlands and Trees, adjusted to reflect subsequent changes.
4 Includes private woodland and non-Forestry Commission / Forest Service public woodland.

5 Broadleaved includes coppice. For data based on 1979-82 Census, all scrub and other non-plantation woodland have been assumed to be broadleaved.
6 Figures shown are for the areas of new planting and restocking in the year to 31 March.
7 Includes grant aided planting on non-Forestry Commission/ Forest Service woodland and estimates for areas planted without the aid of grants.
8 Figures have been rounded to the nearest 10 thousand green tonnes.
9 Hardwood is timber from broadleaved species. Most hardwood production comes from non-FC/FS woodland; the figures are estimates based on reported deliveries to wood processing industries.

Source: Forest Service Agency;Forestry Commission: 0131 314 6171

Agriculture, fisheries and food

21.7 Sales for food of agricultural produce and livestock
United Kingdom

			1998	1999	2000	2001	2002	2003	2004	2005	2006	2007	2008
Cereals:		Thousand											
Wheat[1]	KCQK	tonnes	5 707	5 668	5 617	5 672	5 628	5 611	5 600	5 642	5 625	5 702	..
Barley	KCQL	"	5 548	5 280	5 363	5 714	5 771	5 438	5 418	4 962	4 971	4 904	..
Oats[2]	KCQM	"	272	266	261	287	312	322	321	343	373	420	..
Potatoes[3]	KCQN	"	5 997	6 209	6 129	6 605	6 803	6 560	6 449	5 868	5 674	5 816	..
Milk[4]:													
Utilised for liquid consumption	KCQO	Million litres	6 768	6 889	6 793	6 748	6 825	6 753	6 693	6 652	6 736	6 724	6 722
Utilised for manufacture	KCQP	"	6 807	6 973	6 628	6 902	7 056	7 271	6 827	6 568	6 343	6 085	5 809
Total available for domestic use[5]	KCQQ	"	13 975	14 234	13 730	13 940	14 100	14 290	13 765	13 485	13 346	13 151	12 853
		Million											
Hen eggs in shell	KCQR	dozens	774	738	712	753	747	730	773	772	743	720	755
Animals slaughtered:													
Cattle and calves:													
Cattle	KCQS	Thousands	2 297	2 217	2 275	2 072	2 184	2 188	2 290	2 302	2 593	2 616	2 588
Calves	KCQT	"	32	75	152	92	98	87	103	111	51	46	44
Total	KCQU	"	2 329	2 292	2 427	2 164	2 282	2 275	2 393	2 413	2 644	2 661	2 633
Sheep and lambs	KCQV	"	18 688	19 116	18 442	12 964	14 993	15 095	15 492	16 284	16 414	15 804	16 745
Pigs:													
Clean pigs	MBGD	"	15 872	14 350	12 370	10 446	10 260	9 133	9 150	8 971	8 900	9 274	9 193
Sows and boars	KCQZ	"	415	379	321	180	314	241	240	202	196	210	235
Total	KCRA	"	16 286	14 728	12 692	10 626	10 575	9 374	9 390	9 173	9 097	9 484	9 428
Poultry[6]	KCRB	Millions	857	863	843	866	862	882	882	903	880	867	853

Note: The figures for cereals and for animals slaughtered relate to periods of 52 weeks.

1 Flour millers' receipts of home-grown wheat.
2 Oatmeal millers' receipts of home-grown oats.
3 Total sales for human consumption in the UK. Figures for 2007 are provisional.
4 Data to 1994 sourced from the Milk Marketing Boards. Data from 1995 sourced from surveys run by the agricultural departments. 1994 includes two months of data sourced from the surveys run by the agricultural department.

5 The totals of liquid consumption and milk used for manufacture may not add up to the total available for domestic use because of adjustments for dairy wastage, stock changes and other uses, such as farmhouse consumption, milk fed to stock and on farm waste.
6 Total fowls, ducks, geese and turkeys.

Source: Department for Environment, Food and Rural Affairs: 01904 455332

21.8 Estimates of producers of organic and in-conversion livestock[1]
United Kingdom
At January each year

Thousand head

		2004	2005	2006	2007	2008
Cattle	IDR8	126.8	174.8	214.3	244.8	250.4
Sheep	IDR9	440.7	571.6	691.0	747.3	863.1
Pigs	IDS2	48.8	43.7	30.0	32.9	50.4
Poultry	IDS3	2 166.2	2 431.6	3 439.5	4 421.3	4 440.7
Goats	IDS4	0.7	0.5	0.5	0.6	0.5
Other Livestock	IDS5	1.0	1.2	1.5	4.3	3.4

1 Certification bodies record production data at various times of the year so figures should be treated with care as they will not represent an exact snapshot of organic livestock farming.

Sources: Department for Environment, Food and Rural Affairs; Organic Statistics Team: 01904 455558

21.9 Producers of organic and in-conversion livestock, Organic producers, growers, processors and importers

United Kingdom

Number of producers or businesses

		2004	2005	2006	2007	2008
Producers of organic and in-conversion livestock						
North East	IDZ2	49	44	54	46	58
North West	IDZ3	122	87	102	104	95
Yorkshire and Humberside	IDZ4	82	54	82	82	85
East Midlands	IDZ5	135	110	125	121	127
West Midlands	IDZ6	196	162	196	174	190
Eastern	IDZ7	99	69	86	91	76
South West	IDZ8	761	553	724	706	705
South East (including London)	IDZ9	220	162	201	179	188
England	IE22	1 664	1 241	570	1 503	1 524
Wales	IE23	469	402	502	493	580
Scotland	IE24	385	293	296	285	282
Northern Ireland	IE25	119	110	140	167	176
United Kingdom	IE26	2 637	2 046	2 508	2 448	2 562
		2004	2005	2006	2007	2008
Producers and growers businesses						
North East	IE27	74	83	101	116	137
North West	IE28	169	176	168	173	211
Yorkshire and Humberside	IE29	134	149	138	155	190
East Midlands	IE2A	218	237	221	236	276
West Midlands	IE2B	325	337	335	351	408
Eastern	IE2C	258	259	253	267	315
South West	IE2D	1 020	1 123	1 152	1 282	1 631
South East (including London)	IE2E	409	463	417	423	556
England	IE2F	2 607	2 827	2 785	3 003	3 724
Wales	IE2G	623	667	688	710	857
Scotland	IE2H	689	653	595	686	671
Northern Ireland	IE2I	153	174	217	240	254
United Kingdom	IE2J	4 072	4 321	4 285	4 639	5 506
Processors and/or importers businesses[1]						
North East	IE2K	31	19	28	45	53
North West	IE2L	130	107	143	159	180
Yorkshire and Humberside	IE2M	126	121	141	164	191
East Midlands	IE2N	191	154	195	210	241
West Midlands	IE2O	139	114	143	169	188
Eastern	IE2P	249	209	255	289	298
South West	IE2Q	353	242	380	450	509
South East (including London)	IE2R	450	387	484	516	579
England	IE2S	1 669	1 353	1 769	2 002	2 239
Wales	IE2T	112	85	112	125	149
Scotland	IE2U	174	152	197	225	231
Northern Ireland	IE2V	35	36	50	52	56
United Kingdom	IE2W	1 990	1 626	2 128	2 404	2 675

1 Processers and importers include abattoirs, bakers, stores and whole-salers. The recorded location depends on the address registered with the Sector Bodies and so larger businesses may be recorded at their head-quarters.

Sources: Department for Environment, Food and Rural Affairs;
Organic Statistics Team:01904 455558

Agriculture, fisheries and food

21.10 Organic and in-conversion land and land use
United Kingdom

Thousand hectares

		2004	2005	2006	2007	2008
Land, in-conversion						
North East	IDS6	6.8	4.6	6.6	6.9	4.8
North West	IDS7	2.6	2.5	3.2	1.8	3.3
Yorkshire and Humberside	IDS8	1.7	1.3	2.3	3.4	4.1
East Midlands	IDS9	1.6	1.2	2.4	2.1	3.1
West Midlands	IDT2	3.7	2.4	3.2	4.0	5.7
Eastern	IDT3	3.0	2.4	2.6	3.6	5.3
South West	IDT4	10.8	9.1	22.0	31.6	48.2
South East (including London)	IDT5	6.5	5.4	10.7	13.2	14.6
England	IDT6	36.8	28.8	53.2	66.5	89.0
Wales	IDT7	8.0	8.6	12.8	15.4	30.9
Scotland	IDT8	20.4	13.7	16.7	35.2	34.8
Northern Ireland	IDT9	0.8	1.6	3.2	4.0	3.2
United Kingdom	IDU2	66.0	52.7	86.0	121.1	157.9
Land, fully organic						
North East	IDU3	20.5	25.3	29.3	22.6	25.8
North West	IDU4	19.9	19.8	18.9	19.4	20.4
Yorkshire and Humberside	IDU5	8.1	8.6	9.0	9.0	9.6
East Midlands	IDU6	16.1	13.4	13.2	12.5	13.2
West Midlands	IDU7	25.5	26.8	27.0	26.3	28.2
Eastern	IDU8	9.7	10.3	11.8	10.8	12.7
South West	IDU9	86.2	90.5	94.0	93.4	106.3
South East (including London)	IDV2	34.3	34.9	35.2	35.8	42.5
England	IDV3	220.2	229.6	238.4	229.9	258.7
Wales	IDV4	50.2	55.6	58.0	63.5	65.1
Scotland	IDV5	351.9	331.6	231.2	200.1	193.1
Northern Ireland	IDV6	6.6	5.0	6.3	5.1	7.3
United Kingdom	IDV7	629.0	621.8	533.9	498.6	524.3

		2004	2005	2006	2007	2008
Land, in-conversion						
Cereals	IDV8	7.0	4.1	10.3	11.9	13.2
Other Crops	IDV9	1.9	2.7	3.5	3.4	3.5
Fruit and Nuts	IDW2	0.2	0.2	0.2	0.2	0.4
Vegetables (including potatoes)	IDW3	1.9	1.3	1.3	2.1	2.6
Herbs and ornamentals	IDW4	0.1	–	0.2	0.1	0.1
Temporary pasture	IDW5	12.7	10.4	15.9	22.9	34.2
Set aside	IDW6	2.3	1.3	1.4	1.1	..
Permanent pasture[1]	IDW7	38.1	27.2	47.5	72.1	93.6
Woodland	IDW8	0.7	0.6	3.5	4.2	5.6
Non cropping	IDW9	0.3	2.9	1.1	2.3	3.3
Other	IDX2	0.3	1.7	1.1	0.2	0.3
Unknown	IDX3	0.5	0.1	0.1	0.8	1.1
Total	IDX4	66.0	52.7	86.0	121.1	157.9
Land, fully organic						
Cereals	IDX5	35.4	35.1	37.4	35.5	38.4
Other Crops	IDX6	7.5	10.2	7.3	6.8	7.8
Fruit and Nuts	IDX7	1.4	1.5	1.5	1.6	1.6
Vegetables (including potatoes)	IDX8	11.7	12.7	12.4	13.5	14.3
Herbs and ornamentals	IDX9	0.2	0.2	0.6	0.6	0.5
Temporary pasture	IDY2	77.3	80.3	82.0	79.8	90.9
Set aside	IDY3	4.6	4.6	2.3	1.3	..
Permanent pasture[1]	IDY4	481.3	467.8	380.9	350.5	358.4
Woodland	IDY5	4.8	5.2	3.3	4.0	5.9
Non cropping	IDY6	0.9	1.3	2.4	4.0	4.7
Other	IDY7	3.0	2.4	3.2	0.4	..
Unknown	IDY8	0.8	0.4	0.4	0.6	1.8
Total	IDY9	629.0	621.8	533.9	498.6	524.3

1 Includes rough grazing.

Sources: Department for Environment, Food and Rural Affairs;
Organic Statistics Team: 01904 455558

21.11 Average weekly and hourly earnings and hours of full-time male agricultural workers[1]

England and Wales: At September each year

		2003	2004	2005	2006	2007	2008
Average weekly earnings (£)	LQML	352.88	380.75	422.15	359.48	359.62	351.52
95% confidence interval		(+/-£30.30)	(+/-£28.79)	(+/-£29.39)	(+/-£34.99)	(+/-£25.17)	(+/-£20.63)
Average weekly hours worked	LQMM	51.1	51.0	55.7	48.0	48.6	47.5
95% confidence interval		(+/-3.0)	(+/-2.8)	(+/-3.2)	(+/-3.1)	(+/-2.4)	(+/-1.9)
Average earnings/hours (£)	LQMN	6.91	7.46	7.58	7.48	7.40	7.09
95% confidence interval		(+/-£0.31)	(+/-£0.31)	(+/-£0.26)	(+/-£0.43)	(+/-£0.27)	(+/-£0.17)
Number of workers in the sample		72	94	76	50	68	52

1 See chapter text.

Source: Department for Environment, Food and Rural Affairs: 01904 455332

21.12 Average weekly and hourly earnings and hours of agricultural workers[1] : by type, aged 20 and over

England and Wales: At September 2008

	Full-time		Part-time		Casual		
	Male	Female	Male	Female	Male	Female	Managers
Average weekly earnings (£)	351.52	270.12	136.30	137.48	251.36	206.99	438.58
95% confidence interval	(+/-£20.63)	(+/-£18.56)	(+/-£26.26)	(+/-£25.93)	(+/-£16.38)	(+/-£30.16)	(+/-£30.73)
Average weekly hours worked	47.5	40.9	18.6	21.1	37.3	33.5	
95% confidence interval	(+/-1.9)	(+/-1.1)	(+/-2.9)	(+/-2.8)	(+/-1.6)	(+/-4.1)	
Average earnings/hour (£)	7.41	6.61	7.33	6.52	6.74	6.17	..
95% confidence interval	(+/-£0.17)	(+/-£0.26)	(+/-£0.42)	(+/-£0.42)	(+/-£0.23)	(+/-£0.24)	
Number of workers in the sample	52	48	25	17	49	19	25

1 See chapter text.

Source: Department for Environment, Food and Rural Affairs: 01904 455332

21.13 Workers employed in agriculture [1,2]: by type

United Kingdom

At June each year

Thousands

	Regular					Seasonal or casual			All			Salaried managers
		Full - time		Part - time								
	Total	Male	Female	Male	Female	Total	Male	Female	Total	Male	Female	
	BANC	BAMY	BAMZ	BANA	BANB	BANF	BAND	BANE	BANI	BANG	BANH	KAYG
1995	157.4	90.4	13.0	30.0	24.1	83.7	56.5	27.2	241.2	176.8	64.3	7.7
1996	156.4	89.2	12.6	31.2	23.4	81.5	55.6	25.8	237.9	176.0	61.9	7.8
1997	154.4	87.5	12.6	31.2	23.1	80.9	55.3	25.5	235.2	174.0	61.2	7.8
1998[3,4]	155.6	88.0	13.1	29.7	24.7	79.5	55.6	23.8	235.0	172.8	62.2	12.1
1999	144.7	82.7	11.9	27.5	22.6	73.0	51.8	21.2	217.7	162.0	55.6	13.8
2000	128.9	73.4	10.3	24.6	20.6	64.4	45.9	18.5	193.3	143.9	49.4	11.1
2001[5]	120.8	69.0	10.9	22.0	18.9	63.2	44.6	18.6	184.0	135.6	48.5	13.4
	123.5	70.3	11.2	22.5	19.4	64.1	45.4	18.8	187.6	138.2	49.4	14.1
2002	116.3	64.7	11.5	21.7	18.4	64.2	46.2	18.0	180.6	132.6	47.9	13.4
2003	108.4	60.4	10.0	21.0	17.0	62.6	44.8	17.8	170.9	126.2	44.8	12.7
2004 Jun	108.8	58.1	9.8	23.5	17.4	68.3	49.6	18.6	177.0	131.2	45.8	15.2
2005 Jun	109.2	57.2	10.3	24.5	17.2	65.1	46.4	18.7	174.3	128.1	46.2	15.7
2006 Jun	105.4	53.6	10.4	24.3	17.1	64.0	44.4	19.6	169.4	122.3	47.1	14.6
2007 Jun	107.8	52.2	10.3	28.0	17.3	58.9	41.0	17.9	166.6	121.2	45.5	15.4
2008 Jun	111.1	54.7	11.3	27.9	17.2	61.7	43.2	18.6	172.8	125.8	47.1	15.1

1 See chapter text. Includes estimates for minor holdings for all countries.
2 Figures exclude schoolchildren but include trainees employed under an official youth training scheme and paid at Agricultural Wages Board rates or above.
3 Results from 1998 onwards are not comparable with previous years, due to changes in the labour questions on the June Agricultural and Horticultural Census in England, Wales and Scotland.

4 From 1998, all farmers managing holdings for limited companies or other institutions in England and Wales were asked to classify themselves as salaried managers.
5 Due to an English register improvement only the top figure for 2001 is directly comparable with 2000, while the bottom figure for 2001 is only comparable with data from 2002.

Sources: Department for Environment, Food and Rural Affairs;
Farming Statistics: 01904 455332

21.14 Summary of UK fishing industry
United Kingdom

£ million (unless otherwise stated)

		1997	1998	1999	2000	2001	2002	2003	2004	2005	2006
GDP for fishing[1] current pricegross value added at basic prices	QTUF	412	399	406	398	377	374	376	389	399	468
Output index (chain volume measures)2003 = 100	EWAC	155.0	136.5	124.2	112.0	110.4	109.0	100.0	96.5	95.9	93.9
GDP for agriculture, forestry and fishing Current price gross value added at basic prices	QTOP	10 008	9 457	9 270	8 788	8 566	9 218	10 032	10 323	10 253	10 577
Output index (chain volume measures) 2003 = 100	GDQA	96.1	99.4	100.9	100.1	91.1	101.7	100.0	99.8	105.1	107.9
GDP at market prices Current price GDP at market prices	YBHA	830 094	879 102	928 730	976 533	1 021 828	1 075 564	1 139 746	1 200 595	1 252 505	1 321 860
Chain volume measures index 2003 = 100	YBEZ	83.5	86.5	89.5	93.0	95.3	97.3	100.0	102.8	104.9	107.8
Percentage contribution of GVA from fishing to GVA for agriculture, hunting, forestry & fishing Current prices		4.2%	4.4%	4.5%	4.4%	4.1%	3.7%	3.8%	3.9%	4.4%	3.8%
Current price gross value added for fishing[2] 2003=100	I3X3	109.6	106.1	108.0	105.9	100.3	99.5	100.0	103.5	106.1	124.6

		1998	1999	2000	2001	2002	2003	2004	2005	2006	2007
Fleet size at end of year[3] number of vessels	I3TC	8 271	8 039	7 818	7 721	7 578	7 096	7 022	6 716	6 752	6 763
Employment Number of fishermen	I3TD	17 889	16 896	15 649	14 958	14 205	13 122	13 453	12 831	12 934	12 729
Total landings by UK vessels[4] quantity ('000 tonnes)	I3TE	923.8	836.2	748.1	737.8	685.5	639.7	653.7	707.8	614.2	610.4
value	I3TF	661.5	587.6	550.3	574.4	545.6	528.3	513.0	513.0	610.3	644.8
Imports quantity ('000 tonnes)	I3TG	533.3	552.0	550.2	626.6	621.4	631.5	671.3	720.4	753.0	672.2
value[5]	I3TH	1 065.6	1 301.6	1 325.2	1 435.1	1 438.7	1 438.7	1 473.9	1 696.0	1 919.1	1 768.8
Exports quantity ('000 tonnes)	I3TI	376.9	351.4	364.9	391.0	389.1	479.5	477.8	461.4	416.3	431.3
value[5]	I3TJ	354.7	746.3	696.0	744.6	762.2	891.4	885.7	938.5	944.0	909.2

		1998	1999	2000	2001	2002	2003	2004	2005	2006	2007
Household consumption ('000 tonnes)[6])	I3TK	450.5	446.8	442.9	482.5	479.0	484.6	486.9	493.5	524.9	538.6
Population ('000 persons)	I3TL	58 475	58 684	58 886	59 113	59 322	59 554	59 834	60 209	60 349	60 763
Consumer expenditure on fish	I3TM	2 009	2 063	2 172	2 298	2 405	2 397	2 447	2 661	2 987	3 516
on food	I3TN	55 162	57 040	58 628	59 804	61 310	63 174	65 521	67 539	70 809	76 923
Fish as a % of food[7]	I3TO	3.6	3.6	3.7	3.8	3.9	3.8	3.7	3.9	4.2	4.6
Landed Price index 1987 = 100	I3TP	138.3	144.1	148.6	156.4	153.1	157.2	166.0	181.8	204.4	213.8
Retail Price Index[8]	I3TQ	135.7	147.8	151.0	153.4	157.9	156.3	153.6	154.2	163.9	175.9

1 GDP for fish includes landings abroad.
2 Year on year comparisons may be affected by changes in the industrial classification of some contributors. For most businesses data are appropriate to a single activity heading; where information covers a mixture of activities, the business is classified according to the main activity.
3 The number of vessels excludes those registered in the Channel Islands and the Isle of Man.
4 The quantity of landed fish is expressed in terms of liveweight. The figures relate to landings both into the UK and abroad.

5 Imports are valued at cost, including insurance and freight terms whereas exports are valued at free on board terms.
6 Data are derived from the National Food Survey prior to 2001, and from the Expenditure and Food Survey from 2001 onwards. Figures for 2001 onwards are based on financial year data.
7 Including non-alcoholic beverages.
8 The fish component of the RPI which includes canned and processed fish. The index is calculated on a monthly basis with January 1987 = 100.

Source: Fisheries Statistics Unit: 020 7272 8096

21.15 Fishing fleet[1]
United Kingdom
At 31 December each year

Numbers

		1998	1999	2000	2001	2002	2003	2004	2005	2006	2007	2008
By size												
10m and under	KSNF	5 487	5 409	5 273	5 227	5 287	5 113	5 092	4 833	4 896	4 521	4 520
10.01 - 12.19m	KSNG	628	577	547	536	514	486	465	449	445	446	439
12.20 - 17.00m	KSNH	491	468	467	442	409	405	393	387	384	378	379
17.01 - 18.29m	KSNI	154	154	131	143	129	121	115	112	111	110	106
18.30 - 24.38m	KSNJ	443	414	406	405	322	271	257	253	244	245	247
24.39 - 30.48m	KSNK	226	224	219	218	185	156	147	143	139	121	125
30.49 - 36.58m	KSNL	89	80	77	75	65	63	60	55	56	44	41
over 36.58m	KSNM	121	122	122	123	122	120	112	109	97	88	79
Total over 10m	KSNN	2 152	2 039	1 969	1 942	1 746	1 622	1 549	1 508	1 476	1 432	1 416
Total UK fleet[2]	KSNO	7 639	7 448	7 242	7 169	7 033	6 735	6 641	6 341	6 372	5 953	5 936
By segment												
Pelagic gears	KSNP	50	46	44	47	45	42	31	23	16	..	..
Beam trawl	KSNQ	123	114	111	116	113	162	102	96	93	..	..
Demersal, Seines and Nephrops	JZCI	1 318	1 235	1 208	1 158	969	853	852	812	785	..	..
Lines and Nets	KSNR	187	172	165	146	136	118	123	114	111	..	..
Shellfish: mobile	KSNS	241	243	211	229	228	191	166	155	151	..	..
Shellfish: fixed	KSNT	311	301	297	301	304	307	253	236	230	..	..
Distant water	KSNU	14	12	13	11	10	8	10	10	8	..	..
Under 10m	KSNV	6 027	5 916	5 709	5 713	5 773	5 587	5 395	4 276	4 191	..	..
Other: Mussel Dredgers	JZCJ	2	2	2	7	15	15	13	7	6	..	..
Total UK fleet[3]	KSNX	8 273	8 041	7 820	7 728	7 593	7 283	7 022	6 716	6 752	6 763	..

1 See chapter text.
2 Excluding Channel Islands and Isle of Man.
3 Including Channel Islands and Isle of Man.

Source: Department for Environment, Food and Rural Affairs: 01904 455332

21.16 Estimated household food consumption[1]

Grammes per person per week

		Great Britain						United Kingdom						
		1996	1997	1998	1999	2000		2001 /02	2002 /03	2003 /04	2004 /05	2005 /06	2006	2007
Liquid wholemilk[2] (ml)	KPQM	776	712	693	634	664	VQEW	599	555	585	484	460	477	420
Fully skimmed (ml)	KZBH	137	158	164	167	164	VQEX	160	166	154	158	159	163	173
Semi skimmed (ml)	KZBI	935	978	945	958	975	VQEZ	931	919	926	975	1 008	974	982
Other milk and cream (ml)	KZBJ	259	248	243	248	278	VQFA	333	350	358	366	385	395	397
Cheese	KPQO	111	109	104	104	110	VQFB	112	112	113	110	116	116	119
Butter	KPQP	39	38	39	37	39	VQFC	42	37	35	35	38	40	41
Margarine	KPQQ	36	26	26	20	21	VQFD	13	13	12	11	20	18	19
Low and reduced fat spreads	KZBK	79	77	69	71	68	VQFE	72	70	71	68	55	57	53
All other oils and fats (ml for oils)	KPQR	71	62	62	58	58	VQFF	70	70	68	68	70	69	68
Eggs (number)	KPQS	2	2	2	2	2	VQFG	2	2	2	2	2	2	2
Preserves and honey	KPQT	41	41	38	33	33	VQFH	35	34	33	34	35	34	33
Sugar	KPQU	144	128	119	107	105	VQFI	112	111	102	99	94	92	92
Beef and veal	KPQV	101	110	109	110	124	VQFJ	118	118	119	123	120	128	126
Mutton and lamb	KPQW	66	56	59	57	55	VQFK	51	51	49	50	53	54	55
Pork	KPQX	73	75	76	69	68	VQFL	61	61	56	56	52	55	54
Bacon and ham, uncooked	KPQY	77	72	76	68	71	VQFM	68	69	70	70	66	66	64
Bacon and ham, cooked (including canned)	KPQZ	33	41	40	39	41	VQFN	45	45	47	43	44	45	45
Poultry uncooked	JZCH	233	221	218	201	214	VQFO	206	199	200	197	212	207	208
Cooked poultry (not purchased in cans)	KYBP	23	33	33	35	39	VQFQ	43	44	11	10	12	12	12
Other cooked and canned meats	KPRB	62	52	49	48	51	VQFR	54	59	60	58	56	53	50
Offals	KPRC	7	7	5	5	5	VQFS	6	6	7	5	5	5	5
Sausages, uncooked	KPRD	63	63	60	58	60	VQFT	66	66	70	67	64	65	65
Other meat products	KPRE	207	209	216	221	239	VQFU	313	319	335	330	323	315	316
Fish, fresh and processed (including shellfish)	KPRF	72	70	70	70	67								
Canned fish	KPRG	31	31	29	31	32								
Fish and fish products, frozen	KPRH	50	46	46	42	44								
Fish, fresh chilled or frozen							VQAI	51	48	45	42	45	47	43
Other fish and fish products							VQAJ	105	106	111	115	122	123	122
Potatoes (excluding processed)	KPRI	805	745	715	673	707	VQFY	647	617	600	570	587	565	537
Fresh green vegetables	KPRJ	233	251	246	245	240	VQAK	229	231	228	225	235	221	224
Other fresh vegetables	KPRK	489	497	486	500	492	VQAL	502	505	505	536	567	566	566
Frozen potato products	KYBQ	113	106	111	113	120								
Other frozen vegetables	KPRL	94	94	88	87	80								
Potato products not frozen	JZCF	92	90	89	86	82								
Canned beans	KPRM	125	122	118	112	114								
Other canned vegetables (excl. potatoes)	KPRN	113	104	99	92	97								
Other processed vegetables (excl. potatoes)	LQZH	55	52	54	59	54								
All processed vegetables							VQAM	620	613	611	597	608	601	594
Apples	KPRO	175	179	181	169	180	VQGN	175	172	171	173	179	180	178
Bananas	KPRP	185	195	198	202	206	VQGO	203	208	211	217	225	226	230
Oranges	KPRQ	63	62	63	50	54	VQGP	55	62	64	57	59	55	59
All other fresh fruit	KPRR	263	276	274	290	304	VQGS	318	351	343	358	392	394	389
Canned fruit	KPRS	43	44	37	38	38	VQGT	40	39	40	38	36	39	35
Dried fruit, nuts and fruit and nut products	KPRT	36	35	34	30	35	VQGU	39	41	40	46	51	53	51
Fruit juices (ml)	KPRU	258	277	304	284	303	VQGX	327	333	322	280	350	366	340
Flour	KPRV	70	54	55	56	67	VQGY	55	61	52	55	60	54	54
Bread	KPRW	752	746	742	717	720	VQGZ	769	756	728	695	701	692	677
Buns, scones and teacakes	KPRX	47	43	41	40	43	VQHA	37	41	44	47	46	45	44
Cakes and pastries	KPRY	87	93	88	87	89	VQHB	139	122	120	117	122	120	115
Biscuits	KPRZ	150	138	137	132	141	VQHC	166	174	163	165	165	165	163
Breakfast cereals	KPSA	140	135	136	134	143	VQHE	133	132	134	131	135	135	130
Oatmeal and oat products	KPSB	13	16	11	13	15	VQHF	12	13	12	14	19	17	19
Other cereals and cereal products	JZCG	304	293	270	284	291	VQHG	345	366	360	354	378	378	387
Tea	KPSC	38	36	35	32	34	VQHK	34	34	31	31	33	30	30
Instant coffee	KPSD	13	11	12	11	11	VQHL	13	12	13	13	13	14	13
Canned soups	KPSE	72	70	71	67	71	VQHM	79	80	77	76	82	79	79
Pickles and sauces	KPSF	84	92	96	91	107	VQHN	121	123	121	120	125	128	129

1 See chapter text.
2 Including also school and welfare milk.

Sources: Expenditure and Food Survey;
Department for Environment Food and Rural Affairs: 01904 455067

Production

Chapter 22

Production

Annual Business Inquiry

(Table 22.1)

The Annual Business Inquiry (ABI) estimates cover all UK businesses registered for Value Added Tax (VAT) and/or Pay As You Earn (PAYE), classified to the 2003 Standard Industrial Classification (SIC(2003)) headings listed in the tables. The ABI obtains details on these businesses from the Office for National Statistics (ONS) Inter-Departmental Business Register (IDBR).

As with all its statistical inquiries, ONS is concerned to minimise the form-filling burden of individual contributors and as such the ABI is a sample inquiry. The sample was designed as a stratified random sample of about 66,500 businesses, the inquiry population is stratified by SIC(2003) and employment using the information from the register.

The inquiry results are grossed up to the total population, so that they relate to all active UK businesses on the IDBR for the sectors covered.

The results meet a wide range of needs for government, economic analysts and the business community at large. In official statistics the inquiry is an important source for the National Accounts and input-output tables, but also provides weights for the indices of production and producer prices. Inquiry results also enable the UK to meet statistical requirements of the European Union.

Manufacturers' sales by industry

(Table 22.2)

This table shows the total manufacturers' sales for products classified to SIC(2003) and collected under the Products of the European Community Inquiry since its introduction in 1993. Some data are not available for confidentiality reasons or where data have not been published for a given period. Detailed product sales data together with exports and imports data are available in ONS's *Product Sales and Trade* quarterly and annual reports (PRQ and PRA series).

Number of local units in manufacturing industries in 2003

(Table 22.3)

The table shows the number of local units (sites) in manufacturing by employment size-band. The classification breakdown

is at division level (2 digit) as classified to SIC(2003) held on the Inter-Departmental Business Register (IDBR). This register became fully operational in 1995 and combines information on VAT traders and PAYE employers in a statistical register comprising

2.1 million enterprises (businesses), representing nearly 99 per cent of economic activity. *UK Business: Activity, Size and Location* provides further details and contains detailed information on enterprises in the UK including size, classification and local units.

For further information on the IDBR see the Office for National Statistics website at: www.statistics.gov.uk/idbr

Production of primary fuels

(Table 22.4)

This table shows indigenous production of primary fuels. It includes the extraction or capture of primary commodities and the generation or manufacture of secondary commodities. Production is always gross; that is, it includes the quantities used during the extraction or manufacturing process. Primary fuels are coal, natural gas (including colliery methane), oil, primary electricity (that is, electricity generated by hydro, nuclear, wind and tide stations and also electricity imported from France through the interconnector) and renewables (includes solid renewables such as wood, straw and waste and gaseous renewables such as landfill gas and sewage gas). The figures are presented on a common basis, expressed in million tonnes of oil equivalent. Estimates of the gross calorific values used for converting the statistics for the various fuels to these are given in the *Digest of United Kingdom Energy Statistics* available at: www.berr.gov.uk/whatwedo/energy/statistics/publications/dukes/page45537.html

Total inland energy consumption

(Table 22.5)

This table shows energy consumption by fuel and final energy consumption by fuel and class of consumer. Primary energy consumption covers consumption of all primary fuels (defined above) for energy purposes. This measure of energy consumption includes energy that is lost by converting primary fuels into secondary fuels, that is, the energy lost burning coal to generate electricity or the energy used by refineries to separate crude oil into fractions, in addition to losses in distribution. The other common way of measuring energy consumption is to measure the energy content of the fuels supplied to consumers. This is called final energy consumption. It is net of fuel used by the energy industries, conversion, transmission and distribution losses. The figures are presented on a common basis, measured as energy supplied and expressed in million tonnes of oil equivalent. Estimates of the gross calorific values used for converting the statistics for the various fuels to these are given in the *Digest of United Kingdom Energy Statistics* available at:

www.berr.gov.uk/whatwedo/energy/statistics/publications/dukes/page45537.html

So far as practicable, the user categories have been grouped on the basis of the SIC(2003) although the methods used by each of the supply industries to identify end users are slightly different. Chapter 1 of the Digest of United Kingdom Energy Statistics gives more information on these figures.

Coal

(Table 22.6)

Since 1995, aggregate data on coal production have been obtained from the Coal Authority. In addition, main coal producers provide data in response to an annual Department of Energy and Climate Change (DECC) inquiry which covers production (deep-mined and opencast), trade, stocks and disposals. HM Revenue & Customs (HMRC) also provide trade data for solid fuels. DECC collects information on the use of coal from UK Iron and Steel Statistics Bureau, and consumption of coal for electricity generation is covered by data provided by the electricity generators.

Gas

(Table 22.7)

Production figures, covering the production of gas from the UK Continental Shelf offshore and onshore gas fields and gas obtained during the production of oil, are obtained from returns made under the DECC's Petroleum Production Reporting System. Additional information is used on imports and exports of gas and details from the operators of gas terminals in the UK to complete the picture.

Chapter 4 of the *Digest of United Kingdom Energy Statistics*, contains more detailed information on gas production and consumption in the UK.

DECC carry out an annual survey of gas suppliers to obtain details of gas sales to the various categories of consumer. Estimates are included for the suppliers with the smallest market share, since the DECC inquiry covers only the largest suppliers (that is, those known to supply more than 1,750 GWh per year).

Electricity

(Tables 22.8 to 22.10)

Tables 22.8 to 22.10 cover all generators and suppliers of electricity in the UK. The relationship between generation, supply, availability and consumption is as follows:

Electricity generated
less	electricity used on works
equals	electricity supplied (gross)
less	electricity used in pumping at pumped storage stations
equals	electricity supplied (net)
plus	imports (net of exports) of electricity
equals	electricity available
less	losses and statistical differences
equals	electricity consumed

In Table 22.8 'major power producers' are those generating companies corresponding to the old public sector supply system:

- AES Electric Ltd.
- Baglan Generation Ltd.
- Barking Power Ltd.
- British Energy plc
- Centrica Energy
- Coolkeeragh ESB Ltd.
- Corby Power Ltd.
- Coryton Energy Company Ltd.
- Derwent Cogeneration Ltd.
- Drax Power Ltd.
- EDF Energy plc
- E.ON UK plc
- Energy Power Resources Ltd.
- Immingham CHP
- International Power plc.
- Magnox Electricity Ltd.
- Premier Power Ltd.
- RGS Energy Ltd.
- Rocksavage Power Company Ltd.
- RWE Npower plc
- Scottish Power plc

Production

- Scottish and Southern Energy plc
- Seabank Power Ltd.
- SELCHP Ltd.
- Spalding Energy Company Ltd.
- Teesside Power Ltd.
- Uskmouth Power Company Ltd.
- Western Power Generation Ltd.

In Table 22.10 all fuels are converted to the common unit of million tonnes of oil equivalent, that is, the amounts of oil which would be needed to produce the output of electricity generated from those fuels.

More detailed statistics on energy are given in the *Digest of United Kingdom Energy Statistics*. Readers may wish to note that the production and consumption of fuels are presented using commodity balances. A commodity balance shows the flows of an individual fuel through from production to final consumption, showing its use in transformation and energy industry own use.

Oil and oil products

(Tables 22.11 to 22.13)

Data on the production of crude oil, condensates and natural gases given in Table 22.11 are collected by DECC direct from the operators of production facilities and terminals situated on UK territory, either onshore or offshore, that is, on the UK Continental Shelf. Data are also collected from the companies on their trade in oil and oil products. These data are used in preference to the foreign trade as recorded by HMRC in *Overseas Trade Statistics*.

Data on the internal UK oil industry (that is, on the supply, refining and distribution of oil and oil products in the UK) are collected by the UK Petroleum Industry Association. These data, reported by individual refining companies and wholesalers, and supplemented where necessary by data from other sources, provide the contents of Tables 22.12 and 22.13. The data are presented in terms of deliveries to the inland UK market. This is regarded as an acceptable proxy for actual consumption of products. The main shortcoming is that, while changes in stocks held by companies in central storage areas are taken into account, changes in the levels of stocks further down the retail ladder (such as stocks held on petrol station forecourts) are not. This is not thought to result in a significant degree of difference in the data.

Iron and steel

(Tables 22.14 to 22.16)

Iron and steel industry

The general definition of the UK iron and steel industry is based on groups 271 'ECSC iron and steel', 272 'Tubes', and 273 'Primary Transformation' of the UK SIC(92), except those parts of groups 272 and 273 which cover cast iron pipes, drawn wire, cold formed sections and Ferro alloys.

The definition excludes certain products which may be made by works within the industry, such as refined iron, finished steel castings, steel tyres, wheels, axles and rolled rings, open and closed die forgings, colliery arches and springs. Iron foundries and steel stockholders are also considered to be outside of the industry.

Statistics

The statistics for the UK iron and steel industry are compiled by the Iron and Steel Statistics Bureau (ISSB) Ltd from data collected from UK steel producing companies with the exception of trade data which is based on HMRC data.

Crude steel is the total of usable ingots, usable continuously cast semi-finished products and liquid steel for castings.

Production of finished products is the total production at the mill of that product after deduction of any material which is immediately scrapped.

Deliveries are based on invoiced tonnages and will include deliveries made to steel stockholders and service centres by the UK steel industry.

For more detailed information on definitions etc please contact ISSB Ltd on +44 (0)20 7343 3900.

Minerals

(Table 22.19)

Table 22.19 gives, separately for Great Britain and Northern Ireland, the production of minerals extracted from the ground. The figures for chemicals and metals are estimated from the quality of the ore which is extracted. The data come from an annual census of the quarrying industry which, for Great Britain, is conducted by ONS for Communities and Local Government and BERR.

Building materials

(Table 22.20)

Table 22.20 gives the production of a number of building materials which are closely associated with material extracted from the ground. The data come from surveys conducted by ONS on behalf of BERR.

Construction

(Tables 22.21 and 22.22)

Figures for the construction industry are based on SIC(2003).

The value of output represents the value of construction work done during the quarter in Great Britain and is derived from returns made by private contractors and public authorities with their own direct labour forces. The series (and the accompanying index of the volume of output) include estimates of the output of small firms and self-employed workers not recorded in the regular quarterly output inquiry.

The new orders statistics are collected from private contractors and analysed by the principal types of construction work involved. The series includes speculative work for eventual sale or lease undertaken on the initiative of the respondent where no formal contract or order is involved.

Engineering turnover and orders

(Tables 22.23 and 22.24)

The figures represent the output of UK-based manufacturers classified to subsections DK and DL of the SIC(2003). They are derived from the Monthly Production Inquiry (MPI) and include estimates for non-responders and for establishments which are not sampled.

Passenger cars

(Table 22.25)

The figures represent the output of UK-based manufacturers classified to class 34.10 (motor vehicles) of the SIC(2003). They are derived from the Motor Vehicle Production Inquiry (MVPI). This inquiry ceased at July 2007.

These figures include vehicles produced in the form of kits for assembly. The value of the kit must be 50 per cent or more of the value of a corresponding complete vehicle.

Drink and tobacco

(Tables 22.26 and 22.27)

Data for these tables are derived by HMRC from the systems for collecting excise duties. Alcoholic drinks and tobacco products become liable to duty when released for consumption in the UK. Figures for releases include both home-produced products and commercial imports. Production figures are also available for potable spirits distilled and beer brewed in the UK.

Alcoholic drink

(Table 22.26)

The figures for imported and other spirits released for home consumption include gin and other UK-produced spirits, for which a breakdown is not available.

Since June 1993 beer duty has been charged when the beer leaves the brewery or other registered premises. Previously duty was chargeable at an earlier stage (the worts stage) in the brewing process, and an allowance was made for wastage.

Made wine with alcoholic strength from 1.2 per cent to 5.5 per cent is termed 'coolers'. Included in coolers are alcoholic lemonade and similar products of appropriate strength. From 28 April 2002, duty on spirit-based 'coolers' (ready to drink products) is charged at the same rate as spirits per litre of alcohol. Made wine coolers include only wine based 'coolers' from this period.

Tobacco products

(Table 22.27)

Releases of cigarettes and other tobacco products tend to be higher in the period before a Budget. Products may then be stocked, duty paid, before being sold.

Production

22.1 Production and construction:[1] summary table
United Kingdom
Standard Industrial Classification 2003: Estimates for all firms

£ million

	Total turnover	Gross value added	Stocks and work in progress		Capital expenditure *less* disposals	Total employment costs
			At end of year	Change during year		

Standard Industrial Classification: Revised 2003

Production and construction
Sections C-F

2002	669 855	228 613	70 233	520	27 116	119 037
2003	678 072	228 976	67 044	1 845	25 663	118 540
2004	704 450	242 834	67 027	3 339	23 989	120 512
2005	743 738	255 974	70 536	4 038	27 292	123 310
2006	781 614	267 834	72 309	4 076	28 405	127 804

Production industries (Revised definitions)
Sections C-E

2002	529 380	178 828	50 261	−753	23 182	93 098
2003	527 180	175 826	49 122	−401	22 448	91 317
2004	546 426	187 199	48 831	1 180	20 598	92 423
2005	577 426	192 666	50 261	1 807	23 890	93 364
2006	606 630	200 705	51 041	2 761	25 104	95 393

Mining and quarrying
Section C

2002	32 950	19 279	882	30	4 813	2 682
2003	32 329	18 173	814	−29	4 420	2 782
2004	34 159	17 890	798	30	3 992	2 755
2005	43 633	23 485	1 045	143	6 230	3 117
2006	48 659	24 138	1 020	97	5 828	3 357

Mining and quarrying of energy producing materials
Subsection CA

2002	28 406	17 827	612	7	4 563	1 974
2003	27 506	16 682	506	−47	4 116	1 957
2004	29 012	16 163	492	12	3 680	1 975
2005	37 270	21 686	716	89	5 944	2 258
2006	42 449	22 364	689	85	5 551	2 489

Mining and quarrying except energy producing materials
Subsection CB

2002	4 544	1 452	271	23	249	708
2003	4 823	1 491	308	18	304	825
2004	5 147	1 728	307	17	312	780
2005	6 363	1 799	329	55	286	860
2006	6 209	1 774	331	12	277	869

Manufacturing (Revised definition)
Section D

2002	450 090	144 149	47 669	−667	13 237	86 691
2003	447 637	142 207	46 914	−371	12 677	84 597
2004	459 880	148 864	46 807	975	11 689	85 243
2005	472 235	146 913	47 805	1 488	11 322	85 432
2006	484 199	151 124	48 147	2 295	11 447	87 168

22.1 Production and construction:[1] summary table
United Kingdom
continued

Standard Industrial Classification 2003: Estimates for all firms

£ million

	Total turnover	Gross value added	Stocks and work in progress		Capital expenditure *less* disposals	Total employment costs
			At end of year	Change during year		

Standard Industrial Classification: Revised 2003

Manufacture of food; beverages and tobacco
Subsection DA

2002	76 764	20 721	7 557	53	2 161	10 416
2003	78 759	21 870	7 677	63	2 364	10 564
2004	81 985	22 516	7 846	177	1 966	10 632
2005	82 304	22 269	7 932	−40	2 115	11 098
2006	81 957	22 368	8 037	215	2 125	11 297

Manufacture of textile and textile products
Subsection DB

2002	12 203	4 480	1 881	41	307	2 894
2003	11 396	4 147	1 713	23	234	2 553
2004	10 840	3 825	1 639	7	117	2 333
2005	10 258	3 602	1 435	−10	118	2 283
2006	9 289	3 241	1 454	−23	120	1 999

Manufacture of leather and leather products
Subsection DC

2002	1 541	571	228	−3	18	275
2003	974	375	145	−1	11	198
2004	920	326	138	−6	20	197
2005	771	301	112	4	–	167
2006	760	291	112	9	−1	190

Manufacture of wood and wood products
Subsection DD

2002	7 016	2 459	658	37	186	1 626
2003	7 134	2 669	713	49	211	1 444
2004	7 421	2 958	702	6	177	1 662
2005	7 488	2 952	699	44	189	1 560
2006	7 519	2 711	661	42	151	1 670

Manufacture of pulp, paper and paper products; publishing and printing
Subsection DE

2002	45 317	19 294	2 651	104	1 477	10 927
2003	44 767	18 684	2 637	78	1 338	11 056
2004	45 924	19 413	2 750	−30	1 251	11 063
2005	44 188	18 382	2 392	55	1 516	10 928
2006	44 169	18 374	2 220	76	1 146	11 188

Manufacture of coke, refined petroleum products and nuclear fuel
Subsection DF

2002	24 255	2 502	1 287	190	473	1 099
2003	25 348	2 213	1 269	−13	604	1 160
2004	27 881	2 651	1 362	97	484	1 131
2005	29 719	2 621	1 702	458	512	1 386
2006	30 945	2 873	1 701	−1	292	1 200

22.1
Production and construction:[1] summary table
United Kingdom
continued
Standard Industrial Classification 2003: Estimates for all firms

£ million

	Total turnover	Gross value added	Stocks and work in progress		Capital expenditure *less* disposals	Total employment costs
			At end of year	Change during year		

Standard Industrial Classification: Revised 2003

Manufacture of chemicals, chemical products and man-made fibres
  Subsection DG

2002	48 759	15 847	6 208	−14	2 147	8 295
2003	49 779	15 700	6 190	−119	1 926	7 964
2004	51 375	17 240	5 941	−15	1 915	8 313
2005	60 460	18 070	6 407	−17	1 492	8 249
2006	62 020	18 985	6 574	438	1 735	8 141

Manufacture of rubber and plastic products
  Subsection DH

2002	19 637	7 536	1 769	27	690	4 694
2003	19 803	7 533	1 779	78	751	4 762
2004	20 790	7 799	1 878	116	579	4 960
2005	21 361	7 781	1 852	−25	475	4 841
2006	21 246	7 617	1 796	86	506	4 861

Manufacture of other non-metallic mineral products
  Subsection DI

2002	12 139	5 011	1 354	21	602	2 755
2003	12 573	5 315	1 321	11	579	2 779
2004	13 715	5 846	1 434	87	525	3 041
2005	12 562	5 240	1 392	76	633	2 889
2006	13 786	5 498	1 516	49	705	2 966

Manufacture of basic iron and of ferro-alloys
  Subsection DJ

2002	38 360	14 640	3 626	88	1 179	9 649
2003	38 125	14 623	3 744	216	1 121	9 584
2004	40 873	15 234	3 963	540	1 049	9 498
2005	43 300	15 417	4 339	302	879	9 787
2006	46 593	16 767	4 709	548	1 068	10 053

Manufacture of machinery and equipment not elsewhere specified
  Subsection DK

2002	32 247	11 841	4 118	−141	673	8 114
2003	32 078	11 785	4 913	134	644	7 914
2004	33 838	12 170	5 020	118	505	8 040
2005	34 591	12 251	5 021	95	500	8 057
2006	36 739	13 151	5 176	249	460	8 543

Manufacture of electrical and optical equipment
  Subsection DL

2002	53 048	15 960	6 107	−693	868	11 292
2003	46 638	15 302	5 228	−265	773	10 024
2004	41 545	15 206	5 210	160	703	9 389
2005	40 826	14 925	5 107	113	603	9 137
2006	40 721	15 270	4 826	76	674	9 257

22.1
continued

Production and construction:[1] summary table
United Kingdom
Standard Industrial Classification 2003: Estimates for all firms

£ million

	Total turnover	Gross value added	Stocks and work in progress		Capital expenditure *less* disposals	Total employment costs
			At end of year	Change during year		

Standard Industrial Classification: Revised 2003

Manufacture of transport equipment
Subsection DM

2002	61 550	16 925	8 581	−473	2 028	10 808
2003	63 338	15 838	7 975	−688	1 659	10 963
2004	64 870	16 963	7 198	−429	1 913	11 274
2005	66 290	16 689	7 637	365	1 940	11 409
2006	69 076	17 478	7 642	393	2 009	12 025

Manufacture not elsewhere classified
Subsection DN

2002	17 254	6 361	1 643	94	428	3 846
2003	16 923	6 153	1 608	61	463	3 633
2004	17 902	6 718	1 724	147	486	3 710
2005	18 117	6 413	1 780	68	351	3 641
2006	19 379	6 501	1 723	138	456	3 777

Electricity, gas and water supply
Section E

2002	10 011	15 300	1 700	116	5 132	3 725
2003	47 214	15 446	1 393	−1	5 351	3 938
2004	52 386	20 445	1 227	175	4 917	4 425
2005	61 557	22 268	1 411	175	6 338	4 814
2006	73 773	25 442	1 874	370	7 829	4 868

Construction
Section F

2002	140 475	49 785	19 973	1 272	3 934	25 939
2003	150 892	53 150	17 923	2 246	3 215	27 223
2004	158 025	55 636	18 195	2 159	3 391	28 088
2005	166 312	63 308	20 275	2 232	3 402	29 946
2006	174 984	67 129	21 267	1 316	3 301	32 411

1 See chapter text.

Source: Office for National Statistics: 01633 456592

Production

22.2 Manufacturers' sales: by industry[1]
United Kingdom
Standard Industrial Classification 2003

£ million

Industry	SIC (03)	2004	2005	2006	2007
Other mining and quarrying					
Quarrying of stone for construction	KSPF	14110	..	..	..	..
Quarrying of limestone, gypsum and chalk	KSPG	14120	..	..	..	..
Quarrying of slate	KSPH	14130	..	..	..	..
Operation of gravel and sand pits	KSPJ	14210	..	..	..	..
Mining of clays and kaolin	KSPK	14220	..	..	..	..
Mining of chemical and fertilizer minerals	KSPL	14300	..	..	..	..
Production of salt	KSPM	14400	..	..	..	..
Other mining and quarrying not elsewhere classified	KSPN	14500	46	52	42	37
Manufacture of food products and beverages					
Production and preserving of meat	KSPO	15110	3 927	4 166	4 319	4 320
Production and preserving of poultry meat	KSPP	15120	..	2 064	2 197	2 432
Bacon and ham production	KSPQ	15131	1 364	1 465	1 543	1 466
Other meat and poultry meat processing	KSPR	15139	3 993	4 174	3 976	4 189
Processing and preserving of fish and fish products	KSPS	15200	1 741	1 802	1 873	1 805
Processing and preserving of potatoes	KSPT	15310	1 233	..	1 286	1 336
Fruit and vegetable juice	KSPU	15320	567	586	712	775
Processing and preserving of fruit and vegetables not elsewhere classified	KSPV	15330	2 474	2 544	2 582	2 637
Crude oils and fats	KSPW	15410	399	446	372	397
Refined oils and fats	KSPX	15420	914	889	831	820
Margarine and similar edible fats	KSPY	15430	..	..	417	..
Operation of dairies	KTEH	15510	5 460	5 640	5 882	6 110
Ice cream	KSPZ	15520	..	467	432	438
Grain mill products	KSQA	15610	2 786	2 595	2 732	2 911
Starches and starch products	KSQB	15620	380	429	352	400
Prepared feeds for farm animals	KSPI	15710	2 419	2 151	2 365	2 685
Prepared pet foods	KSQC	15720	1 214	..	1 251	1 339
Bread; fresh pastry goods and cakes	KSQD	15810	4 407	4 186	4 367	4 596
Rusks and biscuits; preserved pastry goods and cakes	KSQE	15820	..	3 211	3 089	..
Sugar	KSQF	15830	1 133	1 077	1 056	1 045
Cocoa; chocolate and sugar confectionery	KSQG	15840	3 384	3 175	3 623	3 609
Macaroni, noodles, couscous and similar farinaceous products	KSQH	15850	..	..	468	..
Processing of tea and coffee	KSQI	15860	1 420	1 502	1 636	..
Condiments and seasonings	KSQJ	15870	1 129	1 129	1 235	1 217
Homogenised food preparations and dietetic foods	KSQK	15880	..	42	47	35
Manufacture of other food products not elsewhere classified	KSQL	15890	2 200	2 300	2 401	2 519
Distilled potable alcoholic beverages	KSQM	15910	2 216	..	..	..
Production of ethyl alcohol from fermented materials	KSQN	15920	..	..	..	..
Wines	KSQO	15930	52	..	..	..
Cider and other fruit wines	KSQP	15940	..	458	453	..
Other non-distilled fermented beverages	KSQQ	15950	–	–	–	..
Beer	KSQR	15960	4 072	3 805	3 896	3 578
Malt	KSQS	15970	255	239	242	..
Mineral waters and soft drinks	KSQT	15980	..	3 021	3 241	3 273
Manufacture of tobacco products					
Tobacco products	KSQU	16000	1 838	1 718	1 875	1 626
Manufacture of textiles					
Preparation and spinning of textile fibres	KSQV	17100	486	433	398	386
Textile weaving	KSQW	17200	690	626	593	578
Finishing of textiles	KSQX	17300	472	490	476	468
Soft furnishings	KSQY	17401	576	564	635	646
Canvas goods, sacks etc	KSQZ	17402	101	80	100	..
Household textiles	KSRA	17403	654	643	645	686
Carpets and rugs	KSRB	17510	690	711	770	773
Cordage, rope, twine and netting	KSRC	17520	76	84	76	85

22.2
Manufacturers' sales: by industry[1]
United Kingdom
continued Standard Industrial Classification 2003

£ million

Industry	SIC (03)	2004	2005	2006	2007
Manufacture of textiles continued					
Nonwovens and articles made from nonwovens, except apparel	KSRD	17530	149	150	160	169
Lace	KSRE	17541	16	19	15	..
Narrow fabrics	KSRF	17542	145	133	124	110
Other textiles not elsewhere classified	KSRG	17549	435	468	453	382
Knitted and crocheted fabrics	KSRH	17600	197	..	..	..
Knitted and crocheted hosiery	KSRI	17710	230	..	..	..
Knitted and crocheted pullovers, cardigans and similar	KSRJ	17720	219	193	176	155
Manufacture of wearing apparel; dressing and dyeing of fur					
Leather clothes	KSRK	18100	7	5	2	4
Workwear	KSRL	18210	263	225	220	198
Men's outerwear	KSRM	18221	249	182	158	167
Other women's outerwear	KSRN	18222	792	632	622	541
Men's underwear	KSRO	18231	171	..	102	63
Women's underwear	KSRP	18232	392	350	368	..
Hats	KSRQ	18241	35	..	31	28
Other wearing apparel and accessories	KSRR	18249	315	280	276	265
Dressing/dyeing of fur; articles of fur	KSRS	18300	4	4	3	3
Tanning and dressing of leather; manufacture of luggage, handbags, saddlery, harness and footwear					
Tanning and dressing of leather	KSRT	19100	..	..	..	200
Luggage, handbags and the like, saddlery and harness	KSRU	19200	140	128	127	132
Footwear	KSRV	19300	250	227	212	217
Manufacture of wood and of products of wood and cork, except furniture; manufacture of articles of straw and plaiting materials					
Sawmilling and planing of wood, impregnation of wood	KSRW	20100	752	786	834	994
Veneer sheets	KSRX	20200	801	790	838	874
Builders' carpentry and joinery	KSRY	20300	3 209	3 500	3 683	3 950
Wooden containers	KSRZ	20400	413	438	453	513
Other products of wood	KSSA	20510	380	408	373	437
Articles of cork, straw and plaiting materials	KSSB	20520	6	5	5	6
Manufacture of pulp, paper and paper products					
Paper and paperboard	KSSC	21120	2 775	2 787	2 798	2 759
Corrugated paper and paperboard, sacks and bags	KSSD	21211	551	513	543	603
Cartons, boxes, cases and other containers	KSSE	21219	3 100	2 899	2 881	3 050
Household and sanitary goods and toilet requisites	KSSF	21220	2 071	..	1 628	1 661
Paper stationery	KSSG	21230	580	581	555	..
Wallpaper	KSSH	21240	184	..	102	..
Manufacture of printed labels	EQ2T	21251	481	461	463	492
Manufacture of unprinted labels	EQ2U	21252	49	..	..	..
Manufacture of other articles of paper and paperboard not elsewhere classified	EQ2V	21259	292	228	203	380
Publishing, printing and reproduction of recorded media					
Publishing of books	KSSJ	22110	3 247	3 118	3 201	3 458
Publishing of newspapers	KSSK	22120	4 320	4 135	4 241	4 120
Publishing of journals and periodicals	KSSL	22130	7 303	7 632	7 544	7 304
Publishing of sound recordings	KSSM	22140	..	296	266	296
Other publishing	KSSN	22150	549	576	588	598
Printing of newspapers	KSSO	22210	235	..	..	193
Printing not elsewhere classified	KSSP	22220	9 148	8 859	8 576	8 993
Bookbinding and finishing	KSSQ	22230	414	422	365	353
Composition and plate-making	KSSR	22240	346	..	344	350
Other activities related to printing	KSSS	22250	819	712	652	687
Reproduction of sound recording	KSST	22310	209	242	128	65
Reproduction of video recording	KSSU	22320	272	197	123	..
Reproduction of computer media	KSSV	22330	..	26	..	6
Manufacture of chemicals and chemical products					
Industrial gases	KSSW	24110	528	525	565	599
Dyes and pigments	KSSX	24120	936	1 019	1 044	1 047
Other inorganic basic chemicals	KSSY	24130	1 090	1 165	1 169	1 211
Other organic basic chemicals	KSSZ	24140	5 825	5 740	7 169	7 101
Fertilizers and nitrogen compounds	KSTA	24150	786	863	846	945

22.2
continued

Manufacturers' sales: by industry[1]
United Kingdom
Standard Industrial Classification 2003

£ million

Industry	SIC (03)	2004	2005	2006	2007
Manufacture of chemicals and chemical products continued					
Plastics in primary forms	KSTB	24160	3 740	3 783	3 577	3 549
Synthetic rubber in primary forms	KSTC	24170	..	..	..	464
Pesticides and other agro-chemical products	KSTD	24200	470	433	424	393
Paints, varnishes and similar coatings, printing ink and mastic	KSTE	24300	2 776	2 673	2 706	2 822
Basic pharmaceutical products	KSTF	24410	734	895	1 057	797
Pharmaceutical preparations	KSTG	24420	8 761	9 568	9 731	10 960
Soap and detergents, cleaning and polishing preparations	KSTH	24510	1 805	1 661	1 646	1 753
Perfumes and toilet preparations	KSTI	24520	2 171	1 769	1 848	1 888
Explosives	KSTJ	24610	110	120	..	..
Glues and gelatines	KSTK	24620	400	438	460	382
Essential oils	KSTL	24630	..	504	564	..
Photographic chemical material	KSTM	24640	250	260	247	218
Prepared unrecorded media	KSTN	24650	..	..	31	27
Other chemical products not elsewhere classified	KSTO	24660	1 992	1 969	2 079	2 085
Man-made fibres	KSTP	24700	587	482	616	577
Manufacture of rubber and plastic products					
Rubber tyres and tubes	KSTQ	25110	569	..	551	..
Retreading and rebuilding of rubber tyres	KSTR	25120	99	..	..	..
Other rubber products	KSTS	25130	1 549	1 529	1 554	1 624
Plastic plates, sheets, tubes and profiles	KSTT	25210	3 755	4 202	4 348	4 389
Plastic packing goods	KSTU	25220	..	..	..	..
Builders' ware of plastic	KSTV	25230	4 478	4 393	4 344	4 230
Other plastic products	KSTW	25240	3 414	3 259	3 386	3 647
Manufacture of other non-metallic mineral products					
Flat glass	KSTX	26110	..	..	..	..
Shaping and processing of flat glass	KSTY	26120	1 026	1 044	1 050	1 084
Hollow glass	KSTZ	26130	638	632	560	525
Glass fibres	KSUA	26140	322	357	358	381
Manufacturing and processing of other glass including technical glassware	KSUB	26150	253	177	131	117
Ceramic household and ornamental articles	KSUC	26210	..	..	..	268
Ceramic sanitary fixtures	KSUD	26220	..	180	179	..
Ceramic insulators and insulating fittings	KSUE	26230	..	22	25	31
Other technical ceramic products	KSUF	26240	21	20	21	22
Other ceramic products	KSUG	26250	..	..	..	..
Refractory ceramic products	KSUH	26260	335	331	334	332
Ceramic tiles and flags	KSUI	26300	97	98	91	92
Bricks, tiles and construction products in baked clay	KSUJ	26400	656	650	652	614
Cement	KSUK	26510	763	..	860	963
Lime	KSUL	26520	..	78	..	..
Plaster	KSUM	26530	125	131	158	152
Concrete products for construction purposes	KSUN	26610	2 278	2 209	2 183	2 234
Plaster products for construction purposes	KSUO	26620	392	427	..	..
Ready mixed concrete	KSUP	26630	1 017	898	1 257	1 502
Mortars	KSUQ	26640	143	147	..	..
Fibre cement	KSUR	26650	85	96	..	101
Other articles of concrete, plaster and cement	KSUS	26660	116	100	87	81
Cutting, shaping and finishing of stone	KSUT	26700	386	..	435	453
Abrasive products	KSUU	26810	167	180	171	143
Other non-metallic mineral products not elsewhere classified	KSUV	26820	718	759	793	
Manufacture of basic metals					
Cast iron tubes	KSUW	27210	164	178	211	199
Steel tubes	KSUX	27220	1 053	1 254	1 498	1 690
Cold drawing	KSUY	27310	141	146	133	142

22.2
continued

Manufacturers' sales: by industry[1]
United Kingdom
Standard Industrial Classification 2003

£ million

Industry	SIC (03)	2004	2005	2006	2007
Manufacture of basic metals continued					
Cold rolling of narrow strip	KSUZ	27320	124	116	120	140
Cold forming or folding	KSVA	27330	..	..	..	..
Wire drawing	KSVB	27340	..	235	..	259
Precious metals production	KSVD	27410	247	280	302	322
Aluminium production	KSVE	27420	1 781	1 781	2 343	2 339
Lead, zinc and tin production	KSVF	27430	..	305	454	522
Copper production	KSVG	27440	786	685	..	652
Other non-ferrous metal production	KSVH	27450	638	755	981	1 306
Casting of iron	KSVI	27510	433	438	396	371
Casting of steel	KSVJ	27520	109	135	139	149
Casting of light metals	KSVK	27530	323	303	337	396
Casting of other non-ferrous metals	KSVL	27540	262	226	215	205
Manufacture of fabricated metal products, except machinery and equipment					
Metal structures and parts of structures	KSVM	28110	5 386	5 917	6 189	7 328
Builders' carpentry and joinery of metal	KSVN	28120	1 009	1 202	1 163	1 259
Tanks, reservoirs and containers of metal	KSVO	28210	294	313	373	421
Central heating radiators and boilers	KSVP	28220	652	805	..	..
Steam generators, except central heating hot water boilers	KSVQ	28300	..	..	..	..
Forging, pressing, stamping and roll forming of metal	KSVR	28400	1 965	2 056	2 057	2 135
Treatment and coating of metals	KSVS	28510	1 163	1 274	1 345	1 335
General mechanical engineering	KSVT	28520	2 798	2 933	3 429	3 732
Cutlery	KSVU	28610	25	21	24	23
Tools	KSVV	28620	805	755	735	757
Locks and hinges	KSVW	28630	597	566	547	567
Steel drums and similar containers	KSVX	28710	122	138	127	118
Light metal packaging	KSVY	28720	1 079	1 093	1 176	1 194
Wire products	KSVZ	28730	500	534	630	665
Fasteners, screw machine products, chain and spring	KSWA	28740	623	618	581	606
Other fabricated metal products not elsewhere classified	KSWB	28750	1 662	1 618	1 689	1 714
Manufacture of machinery and equipment not elsewhere classified					
Engines and turbines, except aircraft, vehicles and cycle engines	KSWC	29110	2 307	2 446	2 614	2 773
Pumps	KSWD	29121	1 157	1 220	1 233	1 412
Compressors	KSWE	29122	1 177	1 086	1 240	1 333
Taps and valves	KSWF	29130	1 164	1 237	1 269	1 423
Bearings, gears, gearing and driving elements	KSWG	29140	863	936	976	1 021
Furnaces and furnace burners	KSWH	29210	269	258	253	277
Lifting and handling equipment	KSWI	29220	2 948	3 101	3 165	3 261
Non-domestic cooling and ventilation equipment	KSWJ	29230	2 827	2 794	2 943	3 275
Other general purpose machinery not elsewhere classified	KSWK	29240	2 003	2 192	2 347	2 474
Agricultural tractors	KSWL	29310	739	658	698	748
Other agricultural and forestry machinery	KSWM	29320	510	497	547	565
Manufacture of portable hand held power tools	EQ2W	29410	146	148	..	..
Manufacture of other metal working machine tools	EQ2X	29420	529	544	553	622
Manufacture of other machine tools n.e.c.	EQ2Y	29430	271	252	300	296
Machinery for metallurgy	KSWO	29510	71	81	77	87
Machinery for mining	KSWP	29521	540	824	..	818
Earth-moving equipment	KSWQ	29522	..	1 287	1 429	1 854
Equipment for concrete crushing and screening and roadworks	KSWR	29523	..	..	..	940
Machinery for food, beverage and tobacco processing	KSWS	29530	683	644	647	774
Machinery for textile, apparel and leather production	KSWT	29540	106	94	93	91
Machinery for paper and paperboard production	KSWU	29550	200	160	..	135
Other special purpose machinery not elsewhere classified	KSWV	29560	1 721	1 614	1 584	1 707
Weapons and ammunition	KSWW	29600	2 094	107	94	73

22.2
continued

Manufacturers' sales: by industry[1]
United Kingdom
Standard Industrial Classification 2003

£ million

Industry	SIC (03)	2004	2005	2006	2007
Manufacture of machinery and equipment not elsewhere classified continued					
Electric domestic appliances	KSYR	29710	2 047	1 706	1 724	1 741
Non-electric domestic appliances	KSWX	29720	487	445	468	478
Manufacture of office machinery and computers					
Office machinery	KSWY	30010	367	446	412	313
Computers and other information processing equipment	KSWZ	30020	4 042	3 635	2 224	1 546
Manufacture of electrical machinery and apparatus not elsewhere classified					
Electric motors, generators and transformers	KSXA	31100	2 142	2 318	2 642	2 756
Electricity, distribution and control apparatus	KSXB	31200	2 410	2 398	2 426	2 682
Insulated wire and cable	KSXC	31300	989	928	1 103	1 093
Accumulators, primary cells and batteries	KSXD	31400	318	267	207	260
Lighting equipment and electric lamps	KSXE	31500	1 090	1 104	1 049	1 100
Electrical equipment for engines and vehicles not elsewhere classified	KSXF	31610	924	871	799	850
Other electrical equipment not elsewhere classified	KSXG	31620	1 670	1 773	1 887	1 865
Manufacture of radio, television and communication equipment and apparatus					
Electronic valves and tubes and other electronic components	KSXH	32100	2 995	2 710	2 450	2 304
Telegraph and telephone apparatus and equipment	KSXI	32201	941	883	1 005	828
Radio and electronic capital goods	KSXJ	32202	1 707	1 755	..	1 730
Television and radio receivers, sound or video recording etc	KSXK	32300	2 502	2 017	2 143	2 092
Manufacture of medical, precision and optical instruments, watches and clocks					
Medical and surgical equipment and orthopaedic appliances	KSXL	33100	2 262	2 510	2 599	2 771
Instruments and appliances for measuring, checking, testing etc	KSXM	33200	4 841	4 956	5 131	5 731
Industrial process control equipment	KSXN	33300	709	820	835	1 028
Optical instruments and photographic equipment	KSXO	33400	958	949	952	1 005
Watches and clocks	KSXP	33500	52	53	42	39
Manufacture of motor vehicles, trailers and semi-trailers					
Motor vehicles	KSXQ	34100	22 485	23 914	22 645	25 543
Bodies (coachwork) for motor vehicles (excluding caravans)	KSXR	34201	..	702	722	714
Trailers and semi-trailers	KSXS	34202	1 118	1 186	1 039	1 131
Caravans	KSXT	34203	593	..	..	..
Parts and accessories for motor vehicles and their engines	KSXU	34300	9 678	9 531	9 324	9 428
Manufacture of other transport equipment					
Building and repairing of ships	KSXV	35110	1 552	465	492	480
Building and repairing of pleasure and sporting boats	KSXW	35120	640	768	813	873
Railway and tramway locomotives and rolling stock	KSXX	35200	2 103	..	1 317	..
Aircraft and spacecraft	KSXY	35300	11 904	9 552	9 709	10 667
Motorcycles	KSXZ	35410	..	..	..	..
Bicycles	KSYA	35420	54	49	45	25
Invalid carriages	KSYB	35430	..	..	106	109
Other transport equipment not elsewhere classified.	KSYC	35500	83	..	..	..
Manufacture of furniture; manufacturing not elsewhere classified					
Chairs and seats	KSYD	36110	2 871	2 885	2 801	2 849
Other office and shop furniture	KSYE	36120	1 046	1 099	1 108	1 220
Other kitchen furniture	KSYF	36130	970	940	1 047	1 158
Other furniture	KSYG	36140	1 884	1 775	1 875	2 091
Mattresses	KSYH	36150	591	542	546	523
Striking of coins and medals	KSYI	36210	..	..	..	..
Jewellery and related articles not elsewhere classified	KSYJ	36220	385	338	444	434
Musical instruments	KSYK	36300	43	42	31	32
Sports goods	KSYL	36400	336	326	293	311
Games and toys	KSYM	36500	354	354	322	352
Imitation jewellery	KSYN	36610	25	31	35	37
Brooms and brushes	KSYO	36620	130	..	110	127
Miscellaneous stationers' goods	KSYP	36631	..	174	177	159
Other manufacturing not elsewhere classified	KSYQ	36639	390	423	419	447

1 See chapter text. PRODCOM data is published on the ONS website in the PRA and PRQ series of reports.

Source: Office for National Statistics: 01633 456746

22.3 Number of local units in manufacturing industries, March 2008[1]
United Kingdom
Standard Industrial Classification 2003 Division by Employment Sizeband

Numbers

					Employment size				
		0 - 4	5 - 9	10 - 19	20 - 49	50 - 99	100 - 249	250 - 499	500+	Total

Division

		0 - 4	5 - 9	10 - 19	20 - 49	50 - 99	100 - 249	250 - 499	500+	Total
15/16	Food products; beverages and tobacco	3 895	2 070	1 360	1 090	550	500	240	175	9 880
17	Textiles and textile products	2 860	830	545	420	195	105	20	5	4 980
18	Wearing apparel; dressing and dyeing of fur	2 455	690	380	235	80	25	5	0	3 870
19	Leather and leather products	430	140	80	65	25	15	0	0	755
20	Wood and wood products	5 485	1 480	965	545	160	70	15	0	8 720
21	Pulp, paper and paper products	940	275	255	320	165	160	35	5	2 155
22	Publishing, printing and reproduction of recorded media	20 065	3 895	2 330	1 490	550	325	95	50	28 800
23	Coke, refined petroleum products and nuclear fuel	160	50	25	20	20	15	15	10	315
24	Chemicals, chemical products and man-made fibres	1 885	580	495	530	335	245	110	55	4 235
25	Rubber and plastic products	3 015	1 330	1 180	1 020	500	330	70	15	7 460
26	Other non-metallic mineral products	3 515	1 020	670	565	265	180	40	10	6 265
27	Basic metals	800	270	230	250	145	100	30	15	1 840
28	Fabricated metal products, except machinery and equipment	17 420	4 940	3 480	2 475	850	335	60	15	29 575
29	Machinery and equipment not elsewhere classified	7 085	2 205	1 755	1 420	535	365	105	55	13 525
30	Office machinery and computers	775	140	75	75	30	25	10	10	1 140
31	Electrical machinery and apparatus not elsewhere classified	2 880	735	640	595	245	180	50	20	5 345
32	Radio, television and communication equipment and apparatus	1 695	365	250	270	105	90	35	15	2 825
33	Medical, precision and optical instruments, watches and clocks	2 935	880	710	580	255	140	55	15	5 570
34	Motor vehicles, trailers and semi-trailers	1 775	505	360	350	190	160	75	60	3 475
35	Other transport equipment	1 750	390	285	195	120	110	50	55	2 955
36/37	Manufacturing not elsewhere classified	12 750	3 170	1 640	985	315	180	45	15	19 100
Total manufacturing (15/37)		94 570	25 960	17 710	13 495	5 635	3 655	1 160	600	162 785

1 The data in this table is taken from the NS publication,
UK Business: Activity, Size and Location 2008.
The count of units refers to local units, i.e. individual sites, rather than
whole businesses. All counts have been rounded to avoid disclosure.

Source: Office for National Statistics: 01633 812293

22.4 Production of primary fuels[1]
United Kingdom

Million tonnes of oil equivalent

		1997	1998	1999	2000	2001	2002	2003	2004	2005	2006	2007
Coal	HFZQ	30.3	25.8	23.2	19.6	20.0	18.8	17.6	15.6	12.7	11.4	10.7
Petroleum[2]	HGCY	140.4	145.3	150.2	138.3	127.8	127.0	116.2	104.5	92.9	84.0	84.2
Natural Gas[3]	HGDB	85.9	90.2	99.1	108.4	105.9	103.6	102.9	96.4	88.2	80.0	72.1
Primary electricity[4]	HGDN	23.5	24.0	22.9	20.2	21.2	20.6	20.4	18.7	19.0	17.9	14.9
Renewable energy[5]	HGDO	1.9	2.1	2.2	2.3	2.5	2.8	3.0	3.1	3.7	3.7	4.0
Total Production	HGDP	282.1	287.2	297.7	288.7	277.4	272.9	260.2	238.4	216.5	197.0	185.9

1 See chapter text.
2 Includes crude oil, natural gas liquids and feedstocks.
3 Includes colliery methane.

4 Nuclear, natural flow hydro-electricity and generation at wind stations.
5 Includes solar and geothermal heat, solid renewable sources (wood, waste, etc), and gaseous renewable sources (landfill gas, sewage gas).

Source: Department of Energy and Climate Change: 0207 7215 6049

22.5 Total inland energy consumption
United Kingdom

Heat supplied basis

Million tonnes of oil equivalent

		1997	1998	1999	2000	2001	2002	2003	2004	2005	2006	2007
Inland energy consumption of primary fuels and equivalents[1]	KLWA	226.8	230.8	230.7	233.7	236.3	229.9	232.0	233.5	234.7	232.3	226.0
Coal[2]	KLWB	40.8	40.9	36.7	38.6	41.0	37.7	40.5	39.0	39.8	43.4	40.8
Petroleum[3]	KLWC	75.5	76.0	75.2	75.9	75.4	74.0	73.5	75.3	77.3	77.1	75.6
Primary electricity	KLWD	24.9	25.0	24.2	21.4	22.1	21.3	20.6	19.4	19.8	18.5	15.4
Natural gas	KLWE	83.5	86.9	92.5	95.6	95.4	94.2	94.5	96.6	93.9	89.1	90.0
Renewables and waste	GYUY	1.9	2.1	2.2	2.3	2.5	2.8	3.1	3.5	4.1	4.2	4.4
less Energy used by fuel producers and losses in conversion and distribution	KLWF	72.9	74.7	74.1	74.5	75.4	73.2	73.8	73.6	74.4	74.2	71.0
Total consumption by final users[1]	KLWG	153.9	155.9	156.5	159.2	160.9	156.5	158.0	159.8	160.2	157.9	154.9

Final energy consumption by type of fuel

		1997	1998	1999	2000	2001	2002	2003	2004	2005	2006	2007
Coal (direct use)	KLWH	4.3	3.7	3.5	2.7	2.7	2.2	2.1	2.0	1.7	1.6	1.7
Coke and breeze	KLWI	0.8	0.9	0.9	0.8	0.8	0.7	0.7	0.6	0.6	0.5	0.5
Other solid fuel[4]	KLWJ	0.7	0.7	0.6	0.4	0.5	0.5	0.3	0.3	0.4	0.4	0.4
Coke oven gas	KLWK	0.5	0.4	0.2	0.2	0.2	0.1	0.1	0.1	0.1	0.1	0.1
Natural gas (direct use)	KLWL	54.2	55.9	55.1	57.1	57.8	55.2	56.7	57.1	55.3	52.6	50.4
Electricity	KLWM	26.8	27.1	27.8	28.3	28.6	28.7	28.9	29.1	29.8	29.6	29.4
Petroleum (direct use)[5]	KLWN	65.4	66.1	65.1	66.3	67.1	66.1	66.8	68.6	70.4	71.0	70.3
Renewables	GYVA	0.9	0.9	0.7	0.7	0.7	0.7	0.7	0.7	0.7	0.8	0.9

Final energy consumption by class of consumer

		1997	1998	1999	2000	2001	2002	2003	2004	2005	2006	2007
Agriculture	KLWP	1.3	1.4	1.3	1.2	1.3	1.2	1.0	0.9	1.0	0.9	0.9
Iron and steel industry	KLWQ	4.2	4.0	3.8	2.2	2.3	2.0	1.9	1.9	1.8	1.9	1.7
Other industries	KLWR	30.4	30.5	30.5	33.1	33.2	32.0	32.4	31.3	31.9	30.9	30.0
Railways[6]	KLWS	1.2	1.3	1.4	1.4	1.4	1.4	1.4	1.4	1.5	1.4	1.4
Road transport	KLWT	41.3	41.0	41.4	41.1	41.1	41.9	41.8	42.2	42.4	42.5	42.8
Water transport	KLWU	1.3	1.2	1.1	1.0	0.8	0.7	1.2	1.2	1.4	1.8	1.6
Air transport	KLWV	9.3	10.2	11.0	12.0	11.8	11.7	11.9	12.9	13.9	14.0	14.0
Domestic	KLWW	44.8	46.1	46.1	46.9	48.2	47.0	47.7	48.6	47.2	45.7	44.0
Public administration	KLWX	8.4	8.1	8.2	8.1	8.0	7.0	6.7	7.2	7.2	7.1	6.7
Commercial and other services	KLWY	11.7	12.0	11.8	12.2	12.8	11.6	12.0	12.2	12.1	11.7	11.8

1 Includes heat sold from 1999.
2 Includes net trade and stock change in other solid fuels.
3 Refinery throughput of crude oil, *plus* net foreign trade and stock change in petroleum products. Petroleum products not used as fuels (chemical feedstock, industrial and white spirits, lubricants, bitumen and wax) are excluded.

4 Includes briquettes, ovoids, Phurnacite, Coalite, etc., and wood, waste etc., used for heat generation.
5 Includes manufactured liquid fuels from 1994.
6 Includes fuel used at transport premises.

Source: Department of Energy and Climate Change: 0207 7215 6049

22.6 Coal: supply and demand[1]
United Kingdom

Million tonnes

		1996	1997	1998	1999	2000	2001	2002	2003	2004	2005	2006	2007
Supply													
Production of deep-mined coal	KLXA	32.2	30.3	25.7	20.9	17.2	17.3	16.4	15.6	12.5	9.6	9.4	7.7
Production of opencast coal	KLXB	16.3	16.7	14.3	15.3	13.4	14.2	13.1	12.1	12.0	10.4	8.6	8.9
Total	KLXC	48.5	47.0	40.0	36.2	30.6	31.5	29.5	27.8	24.5	20.0	18.1	16.5
Recovered slurry, fines, etc	KLXD	1.7	1.5	1.1	0.9	0.6	0.4	0.4	0.5	0.6	0.5	0.4	0.5
Imports	KLXE	17.8	19.8	21.2	20.3	23.4	35.5	28.7	31.9	36.2	44.0	50.5	43.4
Total	KLXF	68.0	68.3	62.4	57.4	54.6	67.5	58.7	60.2	61.3	64.5	69.0	60.4
Change in stocks at collieries and opencast sites	KSOL	−3.0	0.7	−0.2	0.6	−3.5	−0.1	0.9	−0.9	−0.4	−0.1	−0.3	−0.1
Total supply	KLXI	70.9	67.6	62.7	56.8	58.2	67.5	57.8	61.0	61.7	64.6	69.4	60.5
Home consumption													
Total home consumption	KLXW	71.4	63.1	63.2	55.7	59.9	63.9	58.6	63.0	60.5	61.9	67.4	62.9
Overseas shipments and bunkers	KLXX	1.0	1.1	1.0	0.8	0.7	0.5	0.5	0.5	0.6	0.5	0.4	0.5
Total consumption and shipments	KLXY	72.4	64.2	64.1	56.5	60.6	64.4	59.1	63.6	61.1	62.4	67.8	63.4
Change in distributed stocks[2]	KLXZ	−0.9	3.0	−1.1	0.6	−2.3	3.5	−1.4	−2.4	0.5	1.9	1.2	−2.1
Balance[3]	KLYA	−0.6	0.3	−0.4	−0.3	−0.1	−0.3	0.1	−0.2	0.1	0.3	0.3	−0.8
Stocks at end of year													
Distributed[2]	KLYB	12.3	15.3	14.2	14.8	12.4	15.9	14.5	12.1	12.6	14.5	15.7	13.6
At collieries and opencast sites	KSOM	4.2	4.8	4.6	5.2	1.6	1.6	2.5	1.6	1.2	1.1	0.8	0.7
Total stocks	KLYE	16.4	20.1	18.8	19.9	14.1	17.5	17.0	13.7	13.8	15.6	16.5	14.3

1 See chapter text. Figures relate to periods of 52 weeks. For 1998, figures relate to 52 weeks estimate for period ended 26 December 1998.
2 Excludes distributed stocks held in merchant yards etc., mainly for the domestic market, and stocks held by the industrial sector.
3 This is the balance between supply and consumption, shipments and changes in known distributed stocks.

Source: Department of Energy and Climate Change: 020 7215 3839

22.7 Fuel input and gas output: gas consumption[1,2]
United Kingdom

Giga-watt hours

		1999	2000	2001	2002	2003	2004	2005	2006	2007
Analysis of gas consumption										
Transformation sector	I77I	341 678	349 454	336 525	351 856	344 410	362 668	351 448	332 412	373 961
Electricity generation	I77G	315 493	324 563	312 939	329 847	324 580	340 824	328 960	310 389	353 515
Heat generation[3]	I77H	26 185	24 891	23 586	22 009	19 830	21 844	22 488	22 023	20 446
Energy industry use total	I77N	76 973	77 941	91 451	91 260	88 907	88 468	86 273	80 184	74 504
Oil and gas extraction	I77J	64 634	65 555	78 457	79 364	76 837	77 753	74 187	70 130	65 305
Petroleum refineries	KIKN	4 155	3 641	4 189	3 350	2 773	3 076	4 274	3 225	3 381
Coal extraction and coke manufacture	I77K	265	241	220	196	188	150	114	112	91
Blast furnaces	I77L	643	712	375	222	539	728	941	611	719
Other	I77M	7 276	7 792	8 210	8 128	8 570	6 761	6 757	6 106	5 008
Final consumption total	I77F	654 312	678 142	683 753	653 151	669 457	673 860	652 570	623 557	597 068
Iron and steel industry	KIKR	21 622	8 953	8 502	8 791	10 327	9 715	8 469	8 406	7 337
Other industries	KIKS	155 193	174 488	171 341	156 375	155 890	144 238	142 923	135 411	129 475
Domestic	KIKT	358 066	369 909	379 426	376 372	386 486	396 411	384 009	364 850	349 943
Public administration	KIKU	43 253	44 552	46 232	42 998	44 362	51 934	50 319	48 816	44 589
Commercial	I77D	36 622	36 216	37 098	36 224	39 537	37 595	35 097	34 277	35 943
Agriculture	KIKV	1 155	1 522	2 329	2 346	2 324	2 355	2 261	2 013	1 999
Miscellaneous	KIKW	25 457	28 166	27 452	19 265	20 510	21 591	19 814	18 027	17 323
Non energy use	I77E	12 944	14 336	11 373	10 780	10 021	10 021	9 678	11 757	10 459
Total gas consumption	I77O	1 072 963	1 105 537	1 111 729	1 096 267	1 102 774	1 124 996	1 090 291	1 036 153	1 045 533

1 See chapter text. The breakdown of consumption by industrial users is made according to the 2003 Standard Industrial Classification.
2 Natural gas plus colliery methane.
3 Heat generation data are not available before 1999. For earlier years gas used to generate heat for sale is allocated to final consumption by the sector producing the heat.

Source: Department of Energy and Climate Change: 020 7215 2717

22.8 Electricity: generation, supply and consumption[1]
United Kingdom

Gigawatt-hours

		1997	1998	1999	2000	2001	2002	2003	2004	2005	2006	2007
Electricity generated												
Major power producers: total	KLUA	324 133	333 764	336 608	341 783	353 066	353 994	362 600	358 313	362 212	362 260	358 252
Conventional thermal and other[2]	AWLC	133 591	134 009	118 762	131 062	132 744	126 694	146 382	139 105	140 403	157 382	144 404
Combined cycle gas turbine stations	KJCS	86 974	93 832	114 620	117 935	123 846	132 016	121 076	131 182	130 689	118 495	139 826
Nuclear stations	KLUC	98 146	99 486	95 133	85 063	90 093	87 848	88 686	79 999	81 618	75 451	63 028
Hydro-electric stations:												
Natural flow	KLUE	3 337	4 237	4 431	4 331	3 215	3 927	2 568	3 908	3 826	3 693	4 144
Pumped storage	KLUF	1 486	1 624	2 902	2 694	2 422	2 652	2 734	2 649	2 930	3 853	3 859
Renewables other than hydro	KLUG	599	576	761	698	738	856	1 154	1 471	2 746	3 386	2 991
Other generators: total	KLUH	26 534	28 938	31 543	35 285	31 721	33 252	35 609	35 554	36 101	36 563	38 205
Conventional thermal and other[2]	AWLD	18 629	19 091	19 419	19 094	16 621	15 788	18 532	16 359	16 319	17 152	18 230
Combined cycle gas turbine stations	KJCT	4 412	5 428	7 141	10 859	8 979	10 577	10 879	11 852	11 792	11 561	11 516
Hydro-electric stations (natural flow)	KLUK	832	881	905	755	840	860	660	936	1 096	899	946
Renewables other than hydro	KILA	2 661	3 538	4 078	4 577	5 283	6 028	6 825	8 346	9 806	11 187	12 799
All generating companies: total	KLUL	350 667	362 702	368 151	377 068	384 787	387 246	398 209	393 867	398 313	398 823	396 457
Conventional thermal and other[2]	AWYH	152 220	153 100	138 181	150 156	149 365	142 482	164 914	155 464	156 722	174 534	162 634
Combined cycle gas turbine stations	KJCU	91 386	99 260	121 761	128 794	132 825	142 593	131 955	143 034	142 481	130 056	151 342
Nuclear stations	KLUN	98 146	99 486	95 133	85 063	90 093	87 848	88 686	79 999	81 618	75 451	63 028
Hydro-electric stations:												
Natural flow	KLUP	4 169	5 118	5 336	5 086	4 055	4 787	3 228	4 844	4 922	4 592	5 090
Pumped storage	KLUQ	1 486	1 624	2 902	2 694	2 422	2 652	2 734	2 649	2 930	3 853	3 859
Renewables other than hydro	KLUR	3 260	4 114	4 839	5 275	6 021	6 884	7 979	9 817	12 552	14 573	15 790
Electricity used on works: Total	KLUS	16 560	17 408	16 706	16 304	17 394	17 126	18 136	17 030	17 871	19 210	18 087
Major generating companies	KLUT	15 411	16 140	15 461	14 952	16 066	15 746	16 747	15 582	16 265	17 706	16 510
Other generators	KLUU	1 149	1 268	1 245	1 352	1 328	1 380	1 389	1 448	1 606	1 504	1 577
Electricity supplied (gross)												
Major power producers: total	KLUV	308 722	317 624	321 147	326 831	336 999	338 248	345 854	342 731	345 947	344 554	341 742
Conventional thermal and other[2]	AWYI	127 419	127 788	112 919	124 828	126 434	120 495	139 137	132 240	133 407	148 341	136 399
Combined cycle gas turbine stations	KJCV	86 682	93 005	112 768	116 110	121 344	129 384	118 546	128 983	128 179	116 398	137 561
Nuclear stations	KLUX	89 341	90 590	87 672	78 334	82 985	81 090	81 911	73 682	75 173	69 237	57 249
Hydro-electric stations:												
Natural flow	KLUZ	3 299	4 225	4 409	4 316	3 203	3 914	2 559	3 901	3 821	3 680	4 114
Pumped storage	KLVA	1 439	1 569	2 804	2 603	2 340	2 562	2 641	2 559	2 776	3 722	3 846
Renewables other than hydro	KLVB	542	447	574	640	692	802	1 059	1 367	2 592	3 175	2 574
Other generators: total	KLVC	25 385	27 670	30 298	33 933	30 393	31 873	34 220	34 106	34 495	35 059	36 628
Conventional thermal and other[2]	AWYJ	17 815	18 250	18 643	18 499	15 996	15 211	17 999	15 925	15 937	19 655	22 184
Combined cycle gas turbine stations	KJCW	4 192	5 157	6 785	10 318	8 531	10 049	10 336	11 260	11 204	10 984	10 941
Hydro-electric stations (natural flow)	KLVF	822	869	894	743	829	849	653	919	930	885	930
Renewables other than hydro	KIKZ	2 555	3 393	3 977	4 374	5 037	5 764	6 519	7 941	9 336	10 656	12 188
All generating companies: total	KLVG	334 107	345 294	351 445	360 764	367 392	370 121	380 074	376 837	380 442	379 613	378 370
Conventional thermal and other[2]	AWYK	145 234	146 038	131 562	143 327	142 430	135 706	157 136	148 165	149 344	167 996	158 583
Combined cycle gas turbine stations	KJCX	90 874	98 162	119 553	126 428	129 875	139 433	128 882	140 243	139 383	127 382	148 502
Nuclear stations	KLVI	89 341	90 590	87 672	78 334	82 985	81 090	81 911	73 682	75 173	69 237	57 249
Hydro-electric stations:												
Natural flow	KLVK	4 121	5 094	5 303	5 059	4 032	4 763	3 212	4 820	4 751	4 565	5 044
Pumped storage	KLVL	1 439	1 569	2 804	2 603	2 340	2 562	2 641	2 559	2 776	3 722	3 846
Renewables other than hydro	KLVM	3 097	3 840	4 551	5 014	5 729	6 566	7 578	9 308	11 928	13 831	14 762
Electricity used in pumping												
Major power producers	KLVN	2 477	2 594	3 774	3 499	3 210	3 463	3 546	3 497	3 707	4 918	5 071
Electricity supplied (net): Total	KLVO	331 630	342 700	347 671	357 266	364 182	366 657	376 528	373 340	376 735	374 695	373 299
Major power producers	KLVP	306 245	315 030	317 373	323 332	333 789	334 785	342 308	339 234	342 240	339 636	336 671
Other generators	KLVQ	25 385	27 670	30 298	33 933	30 393	31 873	34 220	34 106	34 495	35 059	36 628
Net imports	KGEZ	16 574	12 468	14 244	14 174	10 399	8 414	2 160	7 490	8 321	7 517	5 215
Electricity available	KGIZ	348 203	355 168	361 915	371 440	374 581	375 072	378 687	380 830	385 055	382 213	378 513
Losses in transmission etc	KGKW	27 138	29 818	29 862	31 146	32 077	30 963	32 070	33 115	30 056	28 974	27 912
Electricity consumption: Total	KGKX	321 065	325 350	332 053	340 294	342 504	344 109	346 617	347 715	354 999	353 239	350 601
Fuel industries	KGKY	8 624	8 406	8 037	9 703	8 625	10 060	9 752	8 142	7 850	7 913	8 048
Final users: total	KGKZ	312 441	316 944	324 016	330 593	333 879	334 049	336 865	339 573	347 150	345 327	342 552
Industrial sector	KGLZ	108 102	108 443	112 250	115 286	112 495	113 296	114 006	116 467	121 199	118 934	118 340
Domestic sector	KGMZ	104 455	109 410	110 308	111 842	115 337	114 534	115 761	116 526	116 811	116 449	115 050
Other sectors	KGNZ	99 884	99 091	101 457	103 465	106 047	106 219	107 098	107 580	109 140	109 944	109 162

1 See chapter text.
2 Includes electricity supplied by gas turbines and oil engines and plants producing electricity from renewable resources other than hydro.

Source: Department of Energy and Climate Change: 020 7215 5190

22.9 Electricity: plant capacity and demand
United Kingdom
At end of December

Megawatts

		1999	2000	2001	2002	2003	2004	2005	2006	2007
Major power producers:[1]										
Total declared net capability	GUFY	70 245	72 193	73 382	70 369	71 471	73 293	73 941	74 996	75 190
Conventional steam stations	GUFZ	35 647	34 835	34 835	30 687	31 867	31 982	32 292	33 608	33 776
Combined cycle gas turbine stations	GUGA	16 110	19 349	20 517	21 800	22 037	23 783	24 263	24 859	24 854
Nuclear stations[2]	GUGB	12 956	12 486	12 486	12 240	11 852	11 852	11 852	10 969	10 979
Gas turbines and oil engines	GUGC	1 301	1 291	1 291	1 433	1 537	1 495	1 356	1 444	1 404
Hydro-electric stations:										
Natural flow	GUGD	1 327	1 327	1 348	1 304	1 273	1 276	1 273	1 294	1 293
Pumped storage	GUGE	2 788	2 788	2 788	2 788	2 788	2 788	2 788	2 726	2 744
Renewables other than hydro	GUGF	117	117	117	117	117	117	117	96	140
Other generators:										
Total capacity of own generating plant[3]	GUGG	5 388	6 258	6 296	6 336	6 793	6 829	7 422	7 477	7 761
Conventional steam stations[4]	GUGH	3 315	3 544	3 464	3 325	3 480	3 275	3 269	3 106	3 047
Combined cycle gas turbine stations	GUGI	1 243	1 709	1 777	1 854	1 927	1 968	2 182	2 147	2 119
Hydro-electric stations (natural flow)	GUGJ	150	158	160	162	129	132	120	123	127
Renewables other than hydro	GUGK	680	847	895	995	1 257	1 454	1 852	2 100	2 467
All generating companies: Total capacity[3]	GUGL	75 633	78 451	79 678	76 705	78 264	80 122	81 363	82 473	82 951
Conventional steam stations[4]	GUGM	38 962	38 379	38 299	34 012	35 347	35 257	35 561	36 714	36 823
Combined cycle gas turbine stations	GUGN	17 353	21 058	22 294	23 654	23 964	25 751	26 445	27 006	26 973
Nuclear stations	GUGO	12 956	12 486	12 486	12 240	11 852	11 852	11 852	10 969	10 979
Gas turbines and oil engines	GUGP	1 301	1 291	1 291	1 433	1 537	1 495	1 356	1 444	1 404
Hydro-electric stations:										
Natural flow	GUGQ	1 477	1 485	1 508	1 466	1 402	1 408	1 393	1 417	1 420
Pumped storage	GUGR	2 788	2 788	2 788	2 788	2 788	2 788	2 788	2 726	2 744
Renewables other than hydro	GUGS	797	964	1 012	1 112	1 374	1 571	1 969	2 196	2 607
Major power producers:[1]										
Simultaneous maximum load met[5]	GUGT	57 849	58 452	58 589	61 717	60 501	61 013	61 697	59 071	61 527
System load factor[6] (percentages)	GUGU	67.0	67.0	69.0	65.0	67.0	67.0	66.0	69.0	66.0

1 See chapter text.
2 Nuclear generators are now included under "major power producers" only.
3 Capacity figures for other generators are as at end-December of the previous year.

4 For other generators, conventional steam stations cover all types of stations not separately listed.
5 Maximum load in year to end of March.
6 The average hourly quantity of electricity available during the year ending March expressed as a percentage of the maximum demand.

Source: Department of Energy and Climate Change : 020 7215 5190

22.10 Electricity: fuel used in generation
United Kingdom
At end of December[1]

Million tonnes of oil equivalent

		1997	1998	1999	2000	2001	2002	2003	2004	2005	2006	2007
Major power producers:[1] total all fuels	KGPS	71.50	74.90	73.60	74.40	77.38	75.79	77.53	76.82	78.19	78.75	75.65
Coal	FTAJ	27.71	28.72	24.51	27.77	30.57	28.62	31.57	30.37	31.65	35.00	31.93
Oil[2]	FTAK	1.38	0.85	0.82	0.77	0.82	0.69	24.48	26.18	25.42	23.92	27.59
Gas	KGPT	19.3	20.3	24.2	24.4	23.8	25.0	24.5	26.2	25.4	23.9	27.5
Nuclear[3]	FTAL	22.99	23.44	22.22	19.64	20.77	20.10	20.04	18.16	18.37	17.13	14.04
Hydro (natural flow)	FTAM	0.28	0.36	0.38	0.37	0.28	0.34	0.22	0.34	0.33	0.32	0.36
Other fuels used by UK companies	KGPU	0.2	0.2	0.2	0.2	0.3	0.3	0.4	0.5	0.8	0.7	0.6
Net imports	KGPV	1.4	1.1	1.2	1.2	0.9	0.7	0.2	0.6	0.7	0.6	0.4
Other generators: total all fuels	KGPW	6.7	7.1	7.3	8.0	7.6	8.0	8.7	8.4	8.9	8.9	9.1
Transport undertakings												
Gas	KGPX	0.200	0.200	0.200	0.200	0.200	0.200	0.008	–	–	–	0.002
Undertakings in industrial sector												
Coal	KGPY	1.2	1.2	1.0	0.9	1.0	1.0	1.0	0.9	0.9	0.9	1.0
Oil	KGPZ	0.8	0.7	0.7	0.8	0.6	0.6	0.5	0.5	0.5	0.5	0.5
Gas	KGQM	2.2	2.5	2.7	3.3	2.9	3.2	3.4	3.1	2.8	2.7	2.8
Hydro (natural flow)	KGQO	0.1	0.1	0.1	0.1	0.1	0.1	0.1	0.1	0.1	0.1	0.1
Other fuels	KGQP	2.186	2.420	2.640	2.770	2.740	2.968	3.660	3.781	4.619	4.661	4.708
All generating companies: total fuels	KGQQ	78.20	82.00	80.90	82.40	84.90	83.80	86.20	85.20	87.10	87.60	84.70
Coal	KGQR	28.3	29.9	25.5	28.7	31.6	29.6	32.5	31.3	32.6	35.9	32.9
Oil	KGQS	2.0	1.5	1.5	1.5	1.4	1.3	1.2	1.1	1.4	1.5	1.2
Gas	KGQT	21.7	23.0	27.1	27.9	26.9	28.4	27.9	29.3	28.2	26.6	30.3
Nuclear[3]	KGQU	22.0	23.4	22.2	19.6	20.8	20.1	20.0	18.2	18.4	17.1	14.0
Hydro (natural flow)	KGQV	0.4	0.4	0.5	0.4	0.3	0.4	0.3	0.4	0.4	0.4	0.4
Other fuels used by UK companies[4]	KGQW	2.351	2.597	2.863	3.007	2.993	3.242	4.041	4.321	5.437	5.392	5.333
Net imports	KGQX	1.4	1.1	1.2	1.2	0.9	0.7	0.2	0.6	0.7	0.6	0.4

1 See chapter text.
2 Includes oil used in gas turbine and diesel plant for lighting up coal fired boilers and Orimulsion.

3 Nuclear generators are now included under "major power producers" only.
4 Main fuels included are coke oven gas, blast furnace gas, waste products from chemical processes and sludge gas.

Source: Department of Energy and Climate Change: 020 7215 5190

Production

22.11 Indigenous petroleum production, refinery receipts, imports and exports of oil[1]

Thousand tonnes

		2000	2001	2002	2003	2004	2005	2006	2007	2008	2009	2010
Total indigenous petroleum production[2]	KMBA	126 245	116 678	115 944	106 073	95 374	84 721	76 578	76 832	..	..	..
Crude petroleum:[3]												
Refinery receipts total	KMBB	88 014	83 343	84 784	84 585	89 821	86 135	83 213	81 177	..	..	..
Foreign trade[4]												
Imports	KMBF	54 387	53 551	56 968	54 177	62 516	58 886	59 443	57 100	..	..	..
Exports	AXRB	92 918	86 930	87 144	74 898	64 504	54 098	50 195	50 999	..	..	..
Net imports	AXRC	−38 531	−33 378	−30 176	−20 720	−1 988	4 787	9 249	6 101	..	..	..
Petroleum products												
Foreign trade												
Imports[4]	BHMI	14 212	17 234	14 900	16 472	18 545	22 512	26 828	23 846	23 536	2 373	2 065
Exports[4]	AXRD	20 677	19 088	23 444	23 323	30 495	29 722	29 009	29 490	..	..	..
Net imports[4]	AXRE	−6 464	−1 854	−8 544	−6 851	−11 950	−7 211	−2 181	−5 644	..	..	..
International marine bunkers	BHMK	2 079	2 274	1 913	1 764	2 085	2 055	2 348	2 371	2 502	172	173

1 See chapter text. The term 'indigenous' is used in this table to cover oil produced on the UK Continental Shelf. This includes small amounts produced onshore.
2 Crude oil *plus* condensates and petroleum gases derived at onshore treatment plants.
3 Includes process (partly refined) oils.
4 Foreign trade as recorded by the petroleum industry and may differ from figures published in *Overseas Trade Statistics*.

Source: Department of Energy and Climate Change : 020 7215 2718

22.12 Throughput of crude and process oils and output of refined products from refineries[1]

United Kingdom

Thousand tonnes

		1997	1998	1999	2000	2001	2002	2003	2004	2005	2006	2007
Throughput of crude and process oils	KMAU	97 024	93 797	88 285	88 014	83 343	84 784	84 585	89 821	86 135	83 213	81 117
less: Refinery fuel:	KMAA	6 572	6 177	5 538	5 252	5 059	5 677	5 456	5 417	5 602	4 728	4 307
Losses	KMAB	86	1 004	1 550	1 632	1 233	788	58	−5	132	133	93
Total output of refined products	KMAC	90 366	86 616	81 197	81 130	77 051	78 319	79 071	84 409	80 402	78 352	76 903
Gases:												
Butane and propane	KMAE	1 950	1 961	1 975	1 917	1 764	2 139	2 281	2 150	2 184	2 105	2 259
Other petroleum	KMAF	139	394	361	288	272	537	715	520	427	661	517
Naphtha and other feedstock	KMAG	2 854	2 316	2 430	3 082	3 428	3 153	3 503	3 168	3 019	2 734	2 561
Aviation spirit	KMAH	–	–	16	30	101	28	26	31	32	25	–
Motor spirit	KMAJ	28 260	27 166	25 230	23 445	21 455	22 944	22 627	24 589	22 620	21 443	21 231
Industrial and white spirit	KMAK	128	135	129	122	121	121	104	100	136	107	70
Kerosene:												
Aviation turbine fuel	KMAL	8 342	7 876	7 249	6 484	5 910	5 365	5 277	5 615	5 167	6 261	6 176
Burning oil	KMAM	3 336	3 442	3 553	3 078	3 088	3 506	3 521	3 613	3 325	3 374	2 968
Gas/diesel oil	KMAN	28 778	27 542	25 755	28 229	26 748	28 343	27 380	28 647	28 486	26 038	26 391
Fuel oil	KMAO	11 747	11 125	10 446	10 296	10 179	8 507	9 495	11 308	10 155	11 280	10 690
Lubricating oil	KMAP	1 231	1 125	907	702	656	509	576	1 136	936	617	547
Bitumen	KMAQ	2 258	2 172	1 644	1 438	1 707	1 918	1 925	2 196	1 912	1 749	1 628
Petroleum wax	KMAR	65	59	261	437	416	430	460	94	98	16	12
Petroleum coke	KMAS	598	678	648	657	513	441	612	633	660	606	676
Other products	KMAT	680	625	593	927	692	378	569	607	1 005	1 186	1 177

1 See chapter text. Crude and process oils comprise all feedstocks, other than distillation benzines, for treatment at refinery plants. Refinery production does not cover further treatment of finished products for special grades such as in distillation plant for the preparation of industrial spirits.

Source: Department of Energy and Climate Change: 020 7215 2718

22.13 Deliveries of petroleum products for inland consumption[1]
United Kingdom

Thousand tonnes

		1998	1999	2000	2001	2002	2003	2004	2005	2006	2007	2008
Total (including refinery fuel)	KMCA	78 438	77 974	77 196	76 413	76 233	77 154	79 053	81 035	79 990	77 203	..
Total (excluding refinery fuel)	KMCB	72 261	72 436	71 944	71 354	70 556	71 697	73 642	75 133	75 110	72 896	..
Butane and propane	ECAQ	2 368	2 249	2 070	2 097	2 553	3 019	3 114	3 314	3 127	3 019	..
Other Petroleum Gases (includes Ethane)	ECAR	1 752	2 041	1 886	2 077	2 181	2 114	1 918	2 021	1 920	1 815	..
Naphtha	ECAS	2 882	3 100	2 344	1 592	1 592	2 332	2 029	1 916	2 279	1 006	..
Aviation spirit	KMCI	36	45	52	59	50	46	49	52	46	33	..
Motor spirit:												
Retail deliveries:												
Leaded Premium / Lead Replacement Petrol[2]	KMCK	4 595	2 629	1 462	838	401	183	74	25	19	..	..
Super Premium Unleaded[2]	KMCL	409	480	403	420	706	861	810	924	719	814	..
Premium Unleaded	KMCM	16 432	19 480	19 008	19 100	19 167	18 291	17 795	16 954	16 704	15 989	..
Total Retail Deliveries	ECAT	21 436	21 409	20 873	20 358	20 274	19 335	18 679	17 903	17 442	16 803	..
Commercial consumers:												
Leaded Premium / Lead Replacement Petrol[2]	KMCO	91	61	44	34	19	19	14	1	2	..	..
Super Premium Unleaded[2]	KMCP	4	6	6	9	17	22	26	16	63	22	..
Premium Unleaded	KMCQ	318	311	480	538	499	542	765	811	637	766	..
Total Commercial Consumers	ECAU	413	378	530	581	535	583	805	828	702	789	..
Total Motor spirit	BHOD	21 848	21 787	21 403	20 940	20 808	19 919	19 484	18 732	18 144	17 591	16 737
Industrial and white spirits	KMCS	179	174	170	151	157	147	281	284	156	167	..
Kerosene:												
Aviation turbine fuel	BHOE	9 241	9 939	10 806	10 614	10 519	10 764	11 637	12 497	12 641	12 633	12 147
Burning oil	KMCT	3 575	3 633	3 839	4 236	3 578	3 569	3 950	3 869	4 016	3 631	..
Gas/diesel oil:												
Derv fuel:												
Retail Deliveries	ECAV	6 602	7 137	7 181	7 846	8 153	9 057	9 517	10 679	11 453	12 285	..
Commercial Consumers	ECAW	8 541	8 371	8 451	8 213	8 774	8 655	8 997	8 757	8 693	8 754	..
Total Derv fuel	BHOI	15 143	15 508	15 632	16 059	16 926	17 712	18 514	19 436	20 146	21 039	20 613
Other gas/diesel oil (includes Mdf)	ECAX	7 908	7 454	7 576	6 960	6 099	6 326	6 017	6 797	6 565	6 110	..
Fuel oil	BHOK	2 935	2 414	2 120	2 579	1 723	1 540	2 064	1 965	2 151	2 209	2 372
Lubricating oils	BHOL	1 967	1 928	1 975	1 935	2 002	1 959	1 991	1 906	1 610	1 572	1 773
Bitumen	BHOM	813	790	801	846	829	868	914	750	713	672	510
Petroleum wax	KMCU	18	37	32	33	51	57	50	72	48	39	..
Petroleum coke	KMCV	887	660	776	702	893	880	1 145	1 042	925	1 678	..
Miscellaneous products	KMCW	537	388	463	475	596	449	476	484	628	551	..

1 See chapter text.
2 With effect from 2007, deliveries of Lead Replacement Petrol are now included with Super Premium Unleaded.

Source: Department of Energy and Climate Change: 020 7215 2718

Production

22.14 Iron and steel:[1] summary of steel supplies, deliveries and stocks
United Kingdom

		1996	1997	1998	1999	2000	2001	2002	2003	2004	2005	2006
Supply, disposal and consumption - (Finished product weight - Thousand tonnes)												
UK producers' home deliveries	KLTA	8 383	8 626	8 260	7 652	7 255	6 762	6 506	6 227	7 083	6 279	6 757
Imports excluding steelworks receipts	KLTB	5 147	5 894	6 466	6 014	6 387	6 978	6 793	6 893	7 272	6 297	7 403
Total deliveries to home market (a)	KLTC	13 530	14 520	14 726	13 666	13 642	13 740	13 299	13 120	14 355	12 576	14 160
Total exports (producers, consumers, merchants)	KLTD	8 917	9 060	8 008	7 623	7 446	6 512	6 320	7 007	7 455	8 408	7 862
Exports by UK producers	KLTE	8 305	8 534	7 876	7 416	7 163	6 182	5 594	6 202	6 275	6 594	6 852
Derived consumers' and merchants' exports (b)	KLTF	612	526	132	207	283	330	708	806	1 179	1 814	1 010
Net home disposals (a)-(b)	KLTG	12 918	13 994	14 594	13 460	13 359	13 410	12 591	12 314	13 176	10 762	13 150
Estimated home consumption	KLTI	12 918	13 994	14 594	13 460	13 359	13 410	12 591	12 114	13 176	10 762	13 150
Stocks - (Finished product weight - Thousand tonnes)												
Producers												
- ingots & semis	KLTJ	767	946	717	747	727	705	690	706	765	869	790
- finished steel	KLTK	1 515	1 358	1 495	1 318	1 039	981	932	917	901	947	876
Estimated home consumption - (Crude steel equivalent - Million tonnes)												
Crude steel production[2]	KLTN	17.99	18.50	17.32	16.28	15.15	13.54	11.53	13.13	13.77	13.23	13.90
Producers' stock change	KLTO	..	0.03	..	..	..	..	..	..	..	0.18	–
Re-usable material	KLTP	0.07	0.06	0.02	..	..	..	..	..	..	..	–
Total supply from home sources	KLTQ	18.13	18.53	17.45	16.47	15.48	13.68	11.61	13.13	13.77	13.20	13.90
Total imports[3]	KLTR	7.01	7.49	8.38	7.81	8.43	9.11	9.86	9.32	10.31	9.82	10.30
Total exports[3]	KLTS	10.26	10.43	9.25	8.70	8.61	7.53	7.39	8.65	9.15	8.93	10.40
Net home disposals	KLTT	14.88	15.59	16.58	15.58	15.30	15.26	14.08	14.20	14.99	13.09	14.70
Estimated home consumption	KLTV	14.88	15.59	16.58	15.58	15.30	15.26	14.08	14.20	14.99	13.09	14.70

1 See chapter text. The figures relate to periods of 52 weeks.
2 Includes liquid steel for castings only up to 2003.

3 Based on HM Customs Statistics, reflecting total trade rather than producers' trade.

Source: Iron and Steel Statistics Bureau: 020 8686 9050 ext 126

22.15 Iron and steel:[1] iron ore, manganese ore, pig iron and iron and steel scrap
United Kingdom

Thousand tonnes

		1996	1997	1998	1999	2000	2001	2002	2003	2004	2005	2006
Iron ore[2]	KLOF	19 720	20 820	19 532	18 754	16 991	15 113	13 185	15 766	16 013	15 991	16 539
Manganese ore[2]	KLOG	48	37	22	14	36	4	4	..	6	3	6
Pig iron (and blast furnace ferro-alloys)												
Average number of furnaces in blast during period	KLOH	9	9	9	9	8	7	5	6	6	6	7
Production Steelmaking iron	KLOI	12 830	13 054	12 746	12 139	10 890	9 870	8 561	10 228	10 180	10 189	10 696
In blast furnaces: total	KLOL	12 830	13 054	12 746	12 139	10 890	9 870	8 561	10 228	10 180	10 189	10 696
In steel works	KLOM	12 753	13 044	12 746	12 139	10 890	9 870	8 561	10 228	10 180	10 189	10 696
Consumption of pig iron: total	KLOO	12 753	13 044	12 746	12 139	10 890	9 870	8 561	10 228	10 180	10 189	10 696
Iron and steel scrap												
Steelworks and steel foundries Circulating scrap	KLOQ	2 639	2 459	2 380	2 488	2 287	2 019	1 882	1 926	1 787	1 737	1 669
Purchased receipts	KLOR	4 130	5 418	4 045	3 433	3 327	3 001	2 271	2 617	3 371	2 779	3 171
Consumption	KLOS	6 828	7 207	6 408	5 884	5 675	5 006	4 216	4 469	5 123	4 531	4 811
Stocks (end of period)	KLOT	260	236	253	290	229	224	161	234	242	228	257

1 See chapter text. The figures relate to periods of 52 weeks.
2 Consumption.

Source: Iron and Steel Statistics Bureau: 020 8686 9050 ext 126

Production

22.16 Iron and steel:[1] furnaces and production of steel
United Kingdom

		1996	1997	1998	1999	2000	2001	2002	2003	2004	2005	2006
Steel furnaces (numbers[2])	KLPA	192	192	190	181	181	181	173	..	..	..	..
Oxygen converters	KLPC	11	11	11	11	11	11	8	..	..	..	..
Electric	KLPD	181	181	179	170	170	170	165	..	..	..	..
Production of crude steel	KLPF	17 992	18 499	17 315	16 284	15 155	13 543	11 667	13 268	13 766	13 239	13 905
by process												
Oxygen converters	KLPH	13 758	13 986	13 426	12 634	11 551	10 271	8 956	10 630	10 667	10 550	11 203
Electric	KLPI	4 234	4 513	3 889	3 650	3 604	3 272	2 711	2 639	3 099	2 685	2 702
by cast method												
Cast to ingot	KLPK	1 892	1 660	784	534	539	369	339	354	383	281	206
Continuously cast	KLPL	15 912	16 653	16 346	15 637	14 470	13 024	11 182	12 766	13 383	12 958	13 698
Steel for castings	KLPM	188	186	185	127	146	150	146	148	..	..	..
by quality												
Non alloy steel	KLPN	16 708	17 193	16 145	15 263	14 004	12 482	10 657	12 294	12 809	12 376	..
Stainless and other alloy steel	KLPO	1 284	1 306	1 170	1 035	1 151	1 061	1 010	974	957	863	760

Production of finished steel products
(full quantities)[3]

		1996	1997	1998	1999	2000	2001	2002	2003	2004	2005	2006
Rods and bars for reinforcement (in coil and lengths)	KLPP	1 182	1 118	1 133	893	812	755	487	294	769	730	902
Wire rods and other rods and bars in coil	KLPQ	1 536	1 565	1 492	1 407	1 408	1 389	1 394	1 316	1 392	1 035	962
Hot rolled bars in lengths	KLPR	1 499	1 716	1 791	1 542	1 545	1 449	1 267	1 107	1 179	1 142	1 249
Bright steel bars[4]	KLPS	357	385	336	311	337	296	271	273	277	233	226
Light sections other than rails	KLPT	298	302	318	264	183	201	188	116	136	130	149
Heavy sections	KGQZ	2 557	2 397	2 346	2 303	1 915	1 931	1 873	1 774	1 694	1 414	1 527
Hot rolled plates, sheets and strip in coil and lengths	KLPW	8 512	8 956	8 454	7 893	7 293	5 841	5 756	6 145	6 437	5 823	6 010
Cold rolled plates and sheets in coil and lengths	KLPX	4 221	4 437	4 288	3 914	3 612	2 944	2 951	2 958	3 001	2 769	2 726
Cold rolled strip[4]	KLPZ	246	255	259	233	218	201	179	186	156	131	98
Tinplate	KLQW	739	754	772	736	753	602	562	493	507	471	421
Other coated sheet	KLQX	2 366	2 534	2 610	2 475	2 471	1 773	1 786	1 811	1 713	1 644	1 773
Tubes and pipes[4]	KLQY	1 317	1 310	1 276	1 100	1 061	1 096	940	1 066	1 076	932	993
Forged bars[4]	KLQZ	3	3	3	2	1	1	1	..	..	..	..

1 See chapter text. The figures relate to periods of 52 weeks.
2 Includes steel furnaces at steel foundries, only up to 2003.

3 Includes material for conversion into other products listed in the table.
4 Based on producers' deliveries.

Source: Iron and Steel Statistics Bureau: 020 8686 9050 ext 126

22.17 Non-ferrous metals
United Kingdom

Thousand tonnes

		1996	1997	1998	1999	2000	2001	2002	2003	2004	2005	2006
Copper												
Production of refined copper:												
Primary	KLAA	13.0	9.1	6.4	1.7	–	–	–	–	–	–	–
Secondary	KLAB	43.6	51.3	47.4	48.6	–	–	–	–	–	–	–
Home consumption:												
Refined	KLAC	396.0	408.3	374.1	305.3	322.7	285.9	260.8	242.2	243.4	165.4	172.1
Scrap (metal content)	KLAD	81.0	69.0	64.6	112.5	132.4	127.0	120.0	120.0	120.0	120.0	120.0
Stocks (end of period)[1,2]	KLAE	6.6	12.8	7.5	7.3	10.4	7.3	..	..	..	..	..
Analysis of home consumption (refined and scrap):[3,4] total	KLAF	477.3	477.4	438.7	417.8	455.5	212.7	..	..	..	..	..
Wire[5]	KLAG	309.4	312.5	287.2	276.1	310.2	151.8	..	..	..	..	..
Rods, bars and sections	KLAH	58.3	58.3	53.6	46.9	43.6	21.6	..	..	..	..	..
Sheet, strip and plate	KLAI	34.0	36.5	30.5	27.7	32.3	16.9	..	..	..	..	..
Tubes	KLAJ	75.6	70.1	67.4	67.1	69.4	22.4	..	..	..	..	..
Zinc												
Slab zinc:												
Production	KLAL	96.9	107.7	99.6	132.8	99.6	99.6	99.6	16.6	–	–	–
Home consumption	KLAM	195.7	194.8	187.9	198.9	206.5	197.1	202.4	176.2	150.1	161.7	161.7
Stocks (end of period)	KLAN	10.5	10.1	10.6	10.9	10.9	9.5	9.2	8.9	8.9	8.9	8.9
Other zinc (metal content):												
Consumption	KLAO	41.3	41.5	37.3	41.6	46.3	48.2	51.8	52.3	55.4	–	–
Analysis of home consumption (slab and scrap): total	KLAP	237.1	236.5	221.6	232.1	237.9	226.6	230.4	226.8	232.0		
Brass	KLAQ	39.1	41.6	36.6	33.6	34.4	32.2	30.0	30.0	31.2	..	..
Galvanized products	KLAR	110.3	108.4	103.8	116.6	120.9	111.8	117.3	113.3	116.2	..	..
Zinc sheet and strip	KLAS	3.0	3.3	3.3	3.3	3.3	3.3	3.4	3.3	3.3	..	..
Zinc alloy die castings	KLAT	46.5	46.5	46.5	46.5	46.5	46.5	46.5	46.5	46.5	..	..
Zinc oxide	KLAU	20.7	20.6	20.4	21.1	21.8	21.8	22.2	22.7	23.8	..	..
Other products	KLAV	17.5	16.1	11.0	11.0	11.0	11.0	11.0	11.0	11.0	..	..
Refined lead												
Production[6,7]	KLAW	351.4	384.1	349.7	351.0	328.0	366.3	366.3	364.6	245.9	304.3	306.7
Home consumption[7,8]												
Refined lead	KLAX	272.8	270.4	275.5	283.3	294.0	298.3	298.3	314.7	330.3	281.6	300.0
Scrap and remelted lead[7]	KLAY	43.4	39.1	38.4	32.2	39.5	40.6	40.7	34.1	40.8	..	..
Stocks (end of period)[9]												
Lead bullion	KLAZ	32.9	15.5	20.9	17.1	10.0	17.2	17.2	24.0	23.0	23.0	23.0
Refined soft lead at consumers	KLBA	28.8	29.1	27.4	25.7	25.8	26.1	26.1	25.3	25.9	25.9	25.9
In LME Warehouses (UK)	KLBB	3.0	2.4	0.1	0.1	0.1	0.1	0.1	0.1	0.1	0.1	..
Analysis of home consumption (refined and scrap): total	KLBC	316.2	309.5	313.9	315.5	333.5	338.9	339.0	348.8	371.1	281.6	300.0
Cables	KLBD	9.8	9.7	9.7	9.7	9.6	9.6	9.7	9.7	9.7	..	..
Batteries (excluding oxides)	KLBE	52.3	54.7	51.6	47.4	50.5	48.2	48.2	51.9	54.1	..	..
Oxides and compounds:												
Batteries	KLBF	54.9	56.1	54.4	53.1	55.9	54.7	54.7	55.9	59.0	..	..
Other uses	KLBG	56.1	54.5	56.4	57.0	56.8	53.8	53.8	60.6	64.5	..	..
Sheets and pipes	KLBH	94.1	91.1	96.1	94.9	102.3	102.3	102.3	109.8	111.4	..	..
Solder	KLBJ	7.4	7.4	7.4	7.4	7.4	7.4	7.4	7.2	7.4	..	..
Alloys	KLBK	12.1	9.4	9.4	11.9	15.2	24.3	24.3	25.7	33.3	..	..
Other uses	KLBL	29.5	26.6	28.9	34.1	35.8	38.6	38.6	28.0	31.7	..	..

Production

22.17 Non-ferrous metals
United Kingdom
continued

		1996	1997	1998	1999	2000	2001	2002	2003	2004	2005	2006
Tin												
Tin ore (metal content):												
Production	KLBM	2.1	2.3	0.4	0.4	..	..	1.9	1.9	–	–	–
Tin metal:[10]												
Production[11]	KLBO	–	..	..	..	..	..	1.9	1.9	–	–	–
Home consumption[11]	VQIX	10.5	10.4	10.6	9.6	10.0	10.3	6.9	7.1	5.3	3.2	4.1
Exports and re-exports[12]	KLBQ	0.6	0.3	3.4	0.1	0.1	0.4	1.9	0.3	0.6	1.7	11.8
Stocks (end of period):												
Consumers	KLBR	1.0	1.0	1.0	1.0	1.0	1.0	1.0	1.0	1.0	1.0	1.0
Analysis of home consumption												
(excluding scrap): total	KLBT	10.5	10.4	17.5	16.5	17.0	18.8	18.8	1.9	18.4	..	..
Tinplate	KLBU	3.6	2.8	2.6	3.0	3.0	3.0	1.9	1.9	3.0	..	..
Alloys	KLBV	3.5	3.4	12.1	11.2	11.6	2.6	1.9	1.9	2.6	..	..
Solder	KLBW	1.1	1.1	1.1	0.6	0.8	1.5	1.9	1.9	1.5	..	..
Other uses	KLBX	0.4	0.4	0.4	0.4	0.4	0.4	1.9	1.9	0.4	..	..
Aluminium												
Ingot production												
Primary	KLBY	240.0	247.7	258.4	269.7	305.1	340.8	344.3	342.7	359.6	368.5	360.3
Secondary[13]	KLCA	260.0	242.7	274.8	285.3	237.7	248.6	205.4	205.4	205.4	205.3	197.9
Wrought remelt production[14]	C6EW	500.0	490.4	533.2	555.0	542.8	589.4	549.7	548.1	565.0	573.8	558.2
Wrought and cast despatches												
Bar, section and tube[15]	C6EX	149.6	160.8	168.0	181.7	184.7	177.1	168.3	158.7	157.0	–	–
Plate, sheet, strip and circles	C6EY	327.9	350.4	352.5	349.7	419.1	384.8	312.2	274.3	267.3	–	–
Castings	KLCH	156.0	152.4	148.0	137.3	134.9	138.2	159.4	127.5	139.7	–	–
Exports												
Primary ingot	C6EZ	53.1	219.6	68.7	233.6	347.7	203.4	214.7	244.3	305.1	–	–
Secondary ingot	KLCC	152.2	153.3	156.6	143.1	84.2	59.9	35.7	26.9	30.8	–	–
Extruded products	C6F2	45.8	56.8	59.7	47.5	25.5	20.7	15.3	14.2	15.8	–	–
Rolled products	C6F3	155.5	157.7	160.1	166.6	222.9	198.3	208.8	193.9	192.2	–	–
Refined nickel												
Production (including ferro-nickel)	KLCM	38.6	36.1	39.1	39.5	38.0	33.8	33.8	26.8	38.6	37.6	36.8

1 Unwrought copper (electrolytic, fire refined and blister).
2 Reported stocks of refined copper held by consumers and those held in London Metal Exchange (LME) warehouses in the United Kingdom.
3 2001 figures only cover the period January to June.
4 Copper content.
5 Consumption for high-conductivity copper and cadmium copper wire represented by consumption of wire rods, production of which for export is also included.
6 Lead reclaimed from secondary and scrap material and lead refined from bullion and domestic ores.

7 Figures for production and consumption of refined lead include antimonial lead, and for scrap and remelted lead, exclude secondary antimonial lead.
8 Including toll transactions involving fabrication.
9 Excluding goverment stocks.
10 Including production from imported scrap and residues refined on toll.
11 Primary and secondary metal.
12 Including re-exports on toll transactions.
13 Predominantly from old scrap.
14 Predominantly using recycled scrap from fabrication.
15 Excluding forging bars.

Sources: World Bureau of Metal Statistics: 01920 461274;
Aluminium Federation: 0121 456 1103

22.18 Fertilisers
Years ending 30 June

Thousand tonnes

		1997	1998	1999	2000	2001	2002	2003	2004	2005	2006	2007
Nutrient Content												
Nitrogen (N):												
Straight	KGRM	957	912	819	819	714	751	664	662	691	631	656
Compounds	KGRN	483	463	465	449	448	446	467	463	370	372	352
Phosphate (P_2O_5)	KGRO	412	383	347	317	279	283	282	278	259	235	224
Potash (K_2O)	KGRP	501	487	451	409	369	391	375	375	352	325	317
Compounds - total product	KGRQ	3 238	3 037	3 013	2 851	2 471	2 511	2 558	2 550	2 221	2 134	2 039

Source: Agricultural Industries Confederation: 01733 385230

22.19 Minerals: production[1]
United Kingdom

Thousand tonnes

		1997	1998	1999	2000	2001	2002	2003	2004	2005	2006	2007
Great Britain												
Limestone	KLEA	84 252	85 382	82 714	80 810	83 492	88 013	84 445	86 846	81 830	82 598	83 482
Sandstone	KLEB	12 457	13 545	11 870	12 056	11 897	11 788	11 665	11 929	11 609	11 827	11 978
Igneous rock	KLEC	42 370	39 838	45 294	44 633	45 053	44 544	45 305	46 193	45 992	47 867	50 684
Clay/shale	KLED	11 322	12 230	11 355	10 838	10 426	10 306	10 680	11 164	10 898	10 432	10 104
Industrial sand	KLEE	4 704	4 662	4 092	4 095	3 848	3 833	4 073	5 011	4 146	5 174	4 909
Chalk	KLEF	9 550	9 934	9 667	9 213	8 205	8 587	8 066	7 997	7 105	7 376	7 565
Fireclay	KLEG	338	577	545	595	459	491	528	402	395	228	338
Barium sulphate	KLEH	57	64	59	54	70	56	..	..	62	44	54
Calcium fluoride	KLEI	58	52	46	21	46	22	..	..	44	133	..
Copper	KLEJ	–	–	–	–	–	–	–	..	–	–	..
Lead	KLEK	..	1	1	..	1	..	..	..	1	4	..
Tin	KLEL	2.0	–	–	–	–	–	..	..	–	–	..
Zinc	KLEM	–	–	–	–	–	–	–	..	–	–	..
Iron ore: crude	KLEN	2	2	1	1	1	1	–	..	–	–	..
Iron ore: iron content	KLEO	1	1	1	1	..	..	–	..	–	–	..
Calcspar	KLEP	13	15	..	..	12	..	–	..	–	..	..
China clay	KILC	2 798	2 866	2 841	2 779	2 804	2 467	2 378	2 148	1 908	..	1 821
Ball clay	KIMS	..	..	..	..	..	..	..	..	..	..	..
Chert and flint	KLER	..	..	6	..	2	2	..	2	2	..	1
Fuller's earth	KLES	162	111	83	103	..	33	19	11	–	–	..
Lignite	KLET	–	–	–	–	–	–	–	..	–	–	..
Salt[2]	I8AV	..	..	..	..	..	..	..	..	5 770	5 224	5 320
Anhydrite	KLEX	..	–	–	–	–	–	..	..	..	..	..
Dolomite	KLEY	17 282	15 632	13 698	13 069	14 314	12 946	..	..	11 514	12 100	7 622
Gypsum	KLEZ	..	..	..	..	..	..	..	1 686	..	..	..
Slate[3]	KLFA	347	425	361	479	551	742	832	901	928	865	1 428
Soapstone and talc	KLFB	5	5	6	5	5	6	6	4	6	4	3
Sand and gravel (land-won)	KLFC	74 362	73 016	74 785	74 877	74 599	69 889	68 090	73 061	69 368	66 268	66 724
Sand and gravel (marine dredged)	KLFD	12 004	12 952	13 424	14 356	13 611	12 832	12 131	12 996	13 024	13 974	13 777
Northern Ireland												
Sand and gravel	KLFG	5 138	5 300	5 517	5 073	6 194	5 512	4 894	5 084	5 803	5 150	8 086
Basalt and igneous rock (other than granite)	KLFH	6 286	6 107	7 861	9 480	6 448	6 681	6 051	6 844	7 112	6 087	8 225
Limestone	KLFI	3 500	3 892	4 219	3 538	4 746	4 514	4 887	5 634	5 588	6 385	5 904
Sandstone[4]	KLFJ	6 042	6 584	3 615	2 844	8 070	6 574	6 594	6 915	7 076	6 211	4 828
Granite	KLFL	–	–	–	–	–	–	–	..	..	..	..
Others[5]	KLFN	625	473	1 579	3 098	753	242	1 055	1 266	2 090	1 698	2 468

1 See chapter text.
2 Includes rock salt, salt from brine and salt in brine.
3 Roofing and vertically hanging slates, includes 'true' slate and stone slates produced from thinly bedded sandstones and limestones. Also includes 'true' and stone slates sold as sawn slabs for decorative cladding.
4 Prior to 1993 the 'Sandstone' heading was called 'Grit and conglomerate'. The new heading is all encompassing and was confirmed as correct with the Geological Survey in Northern Ireland.
5 Rock salt, Chalk, Diatomite and Fireclay.

Source: Office for National Statistics: 01633 812082

Production

22.20 Building materials and components[1]
Great Britain

	Building bricks (millions)		Concrete blocks (000 sq m)		Concrete roofing tiles (000 sq m of roof covered)		Slate[2] (tonnes)		Cement[3] (000 tonnes)		RMX[4] (000 cu m)	Sand and gravel (000 tonnes)
	Production	Deliveries	Production	Deliveries	Production	Deliveries	Production	Deliveries	Production	Deliveries	Deliveries	Deliveries
	BLDA	QXIH	BLDM	QXII	BLDN	QXIJ	BLDQ	QXIK	QXIM	QXIL	BLDP	BLDS
1999	245	252	7 314	7 154	2 164	2 114	8 239	8 330	1 058	978	1 963	6 819
2000	239	241	7 518	7 377	2 230	2 087	7 155	7 495	1 038	988	1 920	7 322
2001	230	235	7 327	7 376	2 069	2 036	7 760	7 852	924	888	1 917	8 121
2002	229	235	7 623	7 612	2 085	2 033	7 913	7 972	924	897	1 883	7 126
2003	231	245	7 973	8 032	1 786	1 783	6 591	6 543	935	923	1 857	6 896
2004	239	236	8 021	7 905	1 728	1 617	..	..	950	923	1 905	6 779
2005	229	214	7 500	7 463	2 143	2 041	..	..	935	917	1 869	6 708
2006	209	200	7 292	7 251	1 978	2 010	..	..	956	935	1 919	6 491
2007	206	201	7 496	7 395	1 963	1 984	..	..	991	970	1 962	6 293
2008	161	150	5 645	5 595	1 674	1 660	..	..	..	..	1 671	6 221
2006 Q4	199	182	7 102	6 674	1 830	1 929	..	..	950	891	1 847	5 952
2007 Q1	207	191	7 338	7 019	2 206	1 876	..	..	893	926	1 851	5 863
Q2	214	220	7 511	8 011	1 925	1 909	..	..	1 063	1 020	2 034	6 627
Q3	208	213	7 749	7 728	1 710	2 180	..	..	1 043	1 004	2 068	6 628
Q4	195	179	7 386	6 824	2 009	1 971	..	..	964	929	1 895	6 054
2008 Q1	193	167	7 044	6 285	1 903	1 807	..	..	870	850	1 731	6 051
Q2	195	180	6 744	6 571	1 938	1 893	..	..	934	939	1 924	6 758
Q3	158	141	4 965	5 436	1 552	1 659	..	..	840	832	1 634	6 447
Q4	97	112	3 829	4 086	1 301	1 283	..	..	..	..	1 394	5 628
2009 Q1	97	..	4 060	..	1 221	..	..	..	..	..	1 194	4 724
2007 Apr	200	202	6 645	7 427	..	..	..	..	1 004	939	..	..
May	209	219	7 759	8 299	..	..	..	..	1 113	1 082	..	..
Jun	232	240	8 129	8 307	..	..	..	..	1 071	1 040	..	..
Jul	193	208	8 099	7 882	..	..	..	..	1 089	1 011	..	..
Aug	188	204	7 021	7 739	..	..	..	..	1 017	1 014	..	..
Sep	242	228	8 128	7 564	..	..	..	..	1 024	986	..	..
Oct	203	211	8 202	8 013	..	..	..	..	1 065	1 116	..	..
Nov	219	188	8 287	7 531	..	..	..	..	1 054	1 046	..	..
Dec	162	138	5 668	4 928	..	..	..	..	772	625	..	..
2008 Jan	159	144	7 212	5 593	..	..	..	..	746	776	..	..
Feb	196	171	6 955	6 665	..	..	..	..	916	941	..	..
Mar	225	185	6 965	6 597	..	..	..	..	947	834	..	..
Apr	198	192	7 213	7 000	..	..	..	..	939	1 001	..	..
May	187	173	6 385	6 396	..	..	..	..	928	914	..	..
Jun	200	173	6 633	6 318	..	..	..	..	936	901	..	..
Jul	167	144	5 687	6 016	..	..	..	..	921	924	..	..
Aug	134	133	4 410	5 014	..	..	..	..	810	744	..	..
Sep	174	146	4 796	5 279	..	..	..	..	789	828	..	..
Oct	136	125	4 616	5 178	..	..	..	..	835	854	..	..
Nov	100	109	4 035	4 057	..	..	..	..	757	702	..	..
Dec	55	103	2 836	3 024	..	..	..	..	..	..	..	..
2009 Jan	63	..	3 776	..	..	..	..	..	..	..	..	..
Feb	96	..	3 828	..	..	..	..	..	..	..	..	..
Mar	132	..	4 576	..	..	..	..	..	..	..	..	..

1 See chapter text.
2 Excluding slate residue used as fill.
3 United Kingdom; Great Britain from January 2002.
4 United Kingdom; RMX stands for ready mixed concrete.

Sources: Department for Business, Enterprise and Regulatory Reform; (formerly the DTI) : 020 7215 1555

22.21 Volume of construction output by all agencies[1] by type of work at constant 2000 prices (seasonally adjusted)

Standard Industrial Classification 2003. Great Britain.

£ millions

	New work							Repair and maintenance						All work (seasonally adjusted volume index numbers)
	New housing for			Other new work for				Housing		Other work for				
					Private sector									
	Public sector	Private sector	Infrastr-ucture	Public sector	Industri-al	Commerci-al	Total new work	Public	Private	Public sector	Private sector	Total repair and main-tenance	Total all work	
	BLAC	BLAD	BAXF	BLAE	BLAF	BLAG	BLAB	BLBK	BLBL	BLAJ	BLAK	BLAH	FGAY	SFZX
2006	2 238	11 433	4 930	6 969	3 981	14 616	44 167	6 527	11 674	6 483	11 576	36 260	80 426	115.4
2007	2 576	11 273	5 069	6 629	3 996	16 458	46 001	6 256	11 847	5 804	12 567	36 474	82 474	118.4
2008[2]	2 394	9 132	5 843	7 686	3 224	16 719	44 998	6 408	12 206	6 362	12 153	37 130	82 129	117.9
2006 Q1	563	2 755	1 301	1 807	976	3 398	10 801	1 707	2 961	1 730	2 775	9 174	19 975	114.7
Q2	596	2 834	1 223	1 741	961	3 540	10 895	1 589	3 019	1 647	2 848	9 103	19 998	114.8
Q3	562	2 937	1 235	1 711	978	3 778	11 201	1 653	2 804	1 636	2 844	8 935	20 136	115.6
Q4	517	2 907	1 170	1 710	1 066	3 900	11 270	1 578	2 890	1 471	3 109	9 047	20 317	116.6
2007 Q1	675	2 823	1 140	1 650	1 038	3 868	11 194	1 712	2 886	1 501	3 095	9 194	20 388	117.0
Q2	690	2 862	1 254	1 625	1 025	4 045	11 501	1 542	3 031	1 431	3 064	9 069	20 570	118.1
Q3	636	2 875	1 355	1 664	970	4 236	11 736	1 482	2 820	1 446	3 168	8 917	20 653	118.6
Q4	575	2 713	1 319	1 689	964	4 309	11 569	1 519	3 111	1 425	3 240	9 295	20 864	119.8
2008 Q1	644	2 558	1 420	1 798	938	4 372	11 730	1 617	2 971	1 640	3 171	9 399	21 128	121.3
Q2	633	2 375	1 515	1 858	797	4 184	11 362	1 666	3 165	1 586	3 198	9 616	20 977	120.4
Q3	601	2 241	1 575	1 991	770	4 325	11 503	1 611	2 902	1 676	2 996	9 186	20 689	118.8
Q4[2]	516	1 958	1 333	2 039	720	3 838	10 404	1 514	3 168	1 460	2 788	8 930	19 334	111.0

1 Estimates of unrecorded output by small firms and self-employed workers, and output by the public sector's direct labour department are included.
2 Provisional.

Note: Responsibility for these statistics transferred from BERR (formerly DTI) to the ONS on 1st March 2008.

Source: Office for National Statistics;
Tel : 020 7215 1953

22.22 Value of new orders obtained by contractors for new work[1] at current prices

Great Britain

£ millions

| | New housing[2] | | | Other new work | | | | | | New work total |
	Public and housing association	Private	Total	Infrastructure	Other public	Private industrial	Private commercial	Total		
	BLBC	BLBD	FGAU	BAWT	BAWU	BAWV	BAWW	BLBE		FHAA
2006	2 653	13 468	16 121	4 319	6 162	3 634	17 528	31 643		47 764
2007	2 964	13 109	16 073	5 633	7 324	3 306	18 288	34 551		50 624
2008[3]	2 511	7 645	10 156	6 330	9 419	2 429	13 211	31 388		41 544
2006 Q1	833	3 333	4 166	1 025	1 625	961	4 410	8 021		12 187
Q2	586	3 704	4 290	1 279	1 375	804	5 133	8 590		12 880
Q3	696	3 317	4 014	1 089	1 672	955	4 386	8 102		12 116
Q4	537	3 114	3 651	926	1 491	914	3 599	6 929		10 581
2007 Q1	1 056	3 473	4 529	1 677	1 651	876	4 189	8 393		12 922
Q2	707	3 547	4 254	1 533	1 912	851	5 386	9 680		13 934
Q3	568	3 150	3 718	1 225	1 992	756	4 588	8 562		12 279
Q4	634	2 939	3 572	1 198	1 770	824	4 125	7 916		11 489
2008 Q1	797	2 658	3 455	1 780	2 283	711	3 982	8 756		12 211
Q2	669	2 268	2 937	1 895	2 211	526	3 510	8 141		11 078
Q3	582	1 502	2 084	1 389	2 681	669	3 360	8 099		10 183
Q4	462	1 218	1 680	1 266	2 244	523	2 359	6 392		8 072
2008 Jun	214	688	902	553	624	171	1 027	2 375		3 277
Jul	254	577	830	444	1 196	181	1 157	2 977		3 807
Aug	174	416	590	685	748	360	957	2 750		3 341
Sep	154	509	663	260	737	129	1 246	2 372		3 035
Oct	234	436	670	311	707	223	990	2 231		2 901
Nov[3]	128	432	559	197	913	148	739	1 998		2 557
Dec[3]	100	350	450	758	624	152	629	2 164		2 614

1 Including the value of speculative building when work starts on site.
2 Excluding orders for home improvement work.
3 Provisional.

Sources: Office for National Statistics;
Tel : 020 7215 1953

Note: Responsibility for these statistics transferred from BERR (formerly DTI) to the ONS on 1st March 2008.

Production

22.23 Total engineering: total turnover of UK based manufacturers[1]
Standard Industrial Classification 2003

£ millions

	Total			Home			Export		
	Orders on Hand	New Orders	Turnover	Orders on Hand	New Orders	Turnover	Orders on Hand	New Orders	Turnover
	HP62	HP65	HP5X	HP64	HP67	HP5Z	HP63	HP66	HP5Y
2004	27 256.9	79 680.2	79 961.2	19 980.7	48 174.6	48 555.3	7 276.2	31 505.3	31 405.7
2005	28 502.9	79 077.7	77 831.5	20 436.9	48 276.8	47 820.8	8 066.0	30 801.0	30 011.0
2006	29 131.0	81 089.5	80 461.3	19 729.9	47 417.5	48 124.5	9 401.1	33 672.2	32 336.9
2007	32 770.9	87 991.6	84 351.6	22 981.2	53 546.9	50 295.7	9 789.7	34 444.5	34 055.8
2008	33 034.6	87 076.7	86 813.2	22 459.4	50 672.1	51 193.8	10 575.2	36 404.8	35 619.3
2007 Q1	29 552.3	21 281.2	20 859.8	20 198.6	13 057.9	12 589.2	9 353.7	8 223.1	8 270.5
Q2	30 056.3	21 282.2	20 778.2	20 391.8	12 326.6	12 133.3	9 664.5	8 955.6	8 644.9
Q3	32 497.1	23 464.0	21 023.3	22 199.4	14 414.8	12 607.4	10 297.7	9 049.2	8 415.9
Q4	32 770.9	21 964.2	21 690.3	22 981.2	13 747.6	12 965.8	9 789.7	8 216.6	8 724.5
2008 Q1	34 144.2	22 824.4	21 451.1	23 108.1	13 134.8	13 007.7	11 036.1	9 689.7	8 443.3
Q2	34 828.9	22 764.8	22 080.2	23 143.9	12 958.2	12 922.6	11 685.0	9 806.6	9 157.6
Q3	35 094.1	21 639.5	21 374.3	23 890.3	13 351.0	12 604.5	11 203.8	8 288.5	8 769.8
Q4	33 034.6	19 848.0	21 907.6	22 459.4	11 228.1	12 659.0	10 575.2	8 620.0	9 248.6
2009 Q1	31 354.1	16 843.9	18 524.3	21 191.6	9 496.2	10 764.0	10 162.5	7 347.6	7 760.3
2007 Jul	32 002.4	8 883.4	6 937.3	21 918.3	5 691.5	4 165.1	10 084.1	3 191.9	2 772.2
Aug	32 195.1	6 994.3	6 801.6	22 292.0	4 487.0	4 113.3	9 903.1	2 507.3	2 688.3
Sep	32 497.1	7 586.3	7 284.4	22 199.4	4 236.3	4 329.0	10 297.7	3 350.0	2 955.4
Oct	32 164.5	7 043.1	7 375.7	22 017.1	4 191.2	4 373.5	10 147.3	2 851.9	3 002.2
Nov	32 385.9	7 686.0	7 464.5	22 318.6	4 754.0	4 452.5	10 067.4	2 932.0	3 012.0
Dec	32 770.9	7 235.1	6 850.1	22 981.2	4 802.4	4 139.8	9 789.7	2 432.7	2 710.3
2008 Jan	33 864.0	7 838.0	6 744.9	23 521.3	4 616.8	4 076.6	10 342.7	3 221.2	2 668.2
Feb	34 028.3	7 333.4	7 169.1	23 503.1	4 328.2	4 346.4	10 525.2	3 005.2	2 822.7
Mar	34 144.2	7 653.0	7 537.1	23 108.1	4 189.8	4 584.7	11 036.1	3 463.3	2 952.4
Apr	34 348.7	7 557.7	7 353.2	22 897.2	4 126.6	4 337.5	11 451.5	3 431.1	3 015.7
May	34 713.4	7 488.5	7 123.9	23 191.3	4 511.1	4 217.1	11 522.0	2 977.4	2 906.8
Jun	34 828.9	7 718.6	7 603.1	23 143.9	4 320.5	4 368.0	11 685.0	3 398.1	3 235.1
Jul	34 472.4	6 913.7	7 270.2	23 232.5	4 393.9	4 305.2	11 239.9	2 519.8	2 965.0
Aug	34 098.6	6 148.7	6 522.5	22 785.2	3 445.6	3 892.9	11 313.4	2 703.1	2 629.5
Sep	35 094.1	8 577.1	7 581.6	23 890.3	5 511.5	4 406.4	11 203.8	3 065.6	3 175.3
Oct	33 830.9	6 423.8	7 687.0	22 784.1	3 319.5	4 425.7	11 046.8	3 104.3	3 261.3
Nov	32 820.7	6 081.3	7 091.5	22 232.1	3 577.1	4 129.1	10 588.7	2 504.3	2 962.4
Dec	33 034.6	7 342.9	7 129.1	22 459.4	4 331.5	4 104.2	10 575.2	3 011.4	3 024.9
2009 Jan	31 961.7	4 662.9	5 735.8	21 556.6	2 444.2	3 346.9	10 405.0	2 218.7	2 388.9
Feb	31 664.5	5 637.9	5 935.1	21 365.9	3 210.8	3 401.6	10 298.6	2 427.1	2 533.5
Mar	31 354.1	6 543.1	6 853.4	21 191.6	3 841.2	4 015.5	10 162.5	2 701.8	2 837.9

1 New methodology was introduced from January 2008 affecting all historic estimates. See details in February ELMR in-brief page 3 found at: http://nswebcopy/elmr/02_08/downloads/ELMR_Feb08.pdf published on 11 February.

Source: Office for National Statistics

22.24 Manufacture of machinery and equipment not elsewhere classified[1]
Values at current prices

£ million

	Total			Home			Export		
	Orders on Hand	New Orders	Turnover	Orders on Hand	New Orders	Turnover	Orders on Hand	New Orders	Turnover
	HP6B	HP6E	HP68	HP6D	HP6G	HP6A	HP6C	HP6F	HP69
2004	13 669.4	33 228.0	33 524.0	10 192.8	20 242.2	20 652.8	3 476.6	12 985.8	12 871.3
2005	13 484.9	35 353.8	35 538.4	9 515.9	20 975.7	21 652.4	3 969.0	14 378.6	13 885.9
2006	14 095.2	38 110.7	37 500.3	9 260.9	22 047.4	22 302.1	4 834.3	16 063.6	15 198.2
2007	14 937.5	42 063.0	41 220.9	10 060.3	25 493.3	24 694.2	4 877.2	16 569.8	16 526.8
2008	16 281.7	45 897.8	44 553.7	11 165.9	26 653.3	25 547.8	5 115.7	19 244.7	19 006.2
2004 Q1	14 596.6	8 563.2	7 932.0	10 709.1	5 030.8	4 925.1	3 887.5	3 532.3	3 006.8
Q2	15 099.6	8 749.2	8 246.2	10 931.1	5 179.2	4 957.2	4 168.5	3 570.0	3 288.9
Q3	14 652.4	7 827.9	8 275.1	10 745.3	4 878.9	5 064.8	3 907.1	2 949.0	3 210.5
Q4	13 669.4	8 087.7	9 070.7	10 192.8	5 153.3	5 705.7	3 476.6	2 934.5	3 365.1
2005 Q1	14 361.2	9 200.2	8 508.3	10 349.8	5 455.7	5 298.6	4 011.4	3 744.6	3 209.7
Q2	14 482.6	8 972.7	8 851.2	10 367.1	5 404.6	5 387.3	4 115.5	3 568.1	3 463.9
Q3	13 961.1	8 343.8	8 865.5	9 998.9	5 030.8	5 398.9	3 962.1	3 313.3	3 466.6
Q4	13 484.9	8 837.1	9 313.4	9 515.9	5 084.6	5 567.6	3 969.0	3 752.6	3 745.7
2006 Q1	13 854.0	9 176.5	8 807.3	9 374.6	5 032.7	5 173.9	4 479.5	4 143.9	3 633.4
Q2	14 196.0	9 558.4	9 216.5	9 607.2	5 698.3	5 465.7	4 588.8	3 860.3	3 750.9
Q3	14 239.9	9 555.5	9 511.5	9 571.9	5 727.1	5 762.2	4 668.0	3 828.4	3 749.3
Q4	14 095.2	9 820.3	9 965.0	9 260.9	5 589.3	5 900.3	4 834.3	4 231.0	4 064.6
2007 Q1	13 794.4	9 494.2	9 795.0	9 239.4	5 960.9	5 982.6	4 555.1	3 533.3	3 812.4
Q2	14 234.4	10 482.7	10 042.7	9 465.3	6 179.3	5 953.3	4 769.1	4 303.5	4 089.5
Q3	15 237.0	11 484.1	10 481.6	10 127.8	6 959.2	6 296.8	5 100.1	4 524.9	4 184.8
Q4	14 937.5	10 000.0	10 901.0	10 060.3	6 393.9	6 461.5	4 877.2	4 208.1	4 440.1
2008 Q1	16 077.7	12 198.5	11 058.3	10 328.5	6 717.1	6 448.8	5 749.2	5 481.6	4 609.5
Q2	16 557.9	11 944.9	11 464.7	10 760.9	6 840.3	6 408.0	5 797.1	5 104.6	5 056.8
Q3	17 872.9	12 325.3	11 010.5	12 485.1	8 068.9	6 344.8	5 387.7	4 256.4	4 665.7
Q4	16 281.7	9 429.1	11 020.2	11 165.9	5 027.0	6 346.2	5 115.7	4 402.1	4 674.2
2009 Q1	15 396.6	8 094.6	8 979.7	10 629.6	4 795.2	5 331.5	4 767.0	3 299.5	3 648.2
2007 Mar	13 794.4	3 842.2	3 716.8	9 239.4	2 227.1	2 263.5	4 555.1	1 615.1	1 453.3
Apr	13 929.5	3 265.4	3 130.3	9 387.6	2 047.7	1 899.4	4 541.9	1 217.7	1 230.9
May	13 917.7	3 343.3	3 355.1	9 387.5	2 011.7	2 011.8	4 530.2	1 331.7	1 343.4
Jun	14 234.4	3 874.0	3 557.3	9 465.3	2 119.9	2 042.1	4 769.1	1 754.1	1 515.2
Jul	15 069.7	4 275.6	3 440.3	10 228.0	2 812.3	2 049.6	4 841.7	1 463.3	1 390.6
Aug	15 042.5	3 339.9	3 367.1	10 170.1	1 986.7	2 044.7	4 872.4	1 353.2	1 322.5
Sep	15 237.0	3 868.6	3 674.2	10 127.8	2 160.2	2 202.5	5 109.1	1 708.4	1 471.7
Oct	15 193.8	3 664.4	3 707.6	10 220.2	2 257.0	2 164.6	4 973.6	1 407.4	1 543.0
Nov	15 212.6	3 835.0	3 816.2	10 100.2	2 122.5	2 242.5	5 112.4	1 712.5	1 573.7
Dec	14 937.5	3 102.6	3 377.8	10 060.3	2 014.4	2 054.4	4 877.2	1 088.2	1 323.4
2008 Jan	16 003.0	4 523.4	3 457.9	10 598.5	2 563.4	2 025.2	5 404.6	1 960.1	1 432.7
Feb	15 910.0	3 638.3	3 731.3	10 428.4	2 030.8	2 200.8	5 481.6	1 607.6	1 530.5
Mar	16 077.7	4 036.8	3 869.1	10 328.5	2 122.9	2 222.8	5 749.2	1 913.9	1 646.3
Apr	16 143.9	3 913.6	3 847.5	10 253.8	2 108.0	2 182.7	5 890.0	1 805.6	1 664.8
May	16 533.5	4 077.9	3 688.2	10 681.0	2 513.0	2 085.8	5 852.5	1 564.9	1 602.4
Jun	16 557.9	3 953.4	3 929.0	10 760.9	2 219.3	2 139.5	5 797.1	1 734.1	1 789.6
Jul	16 552.5	3 825.7	3 831.2	10 958.0	2 371.6	2 174.5	5 594.4	1 454.1	1 656.7
Aug	16 789.0	3 497.5	3 261.0	11 147.8	2 091.8	1 902.1	5 641.2	1 405.7	1 358.9
Sep	17 872.9	5 002.1	3 918.3	12 485.1	3 605.5	2 268.2	5 387.7	1 396.6	1 650.1
Oct	17 017.3	3 117.2	3 972.7	11 679.2	1 479.1	2 285.0	5 338.1	1 638.1	1 687.8
Nov	16 271.7	2 802.1	3 547.7	11 277.5	1 648.5	2 050.2	4 994.1	1 153.6	1 497.6
Dec	16 281.7	3 509.8	3 499.8	11 165.9	1 899.4	2 011.0	5 115.7	1 610.4	1 488.8
2009 Jan	15 713.1	2 205.4	2 774.0	10 854.8	1 365.8	1 676.9	4 858.3	839.7	1 097.1
Feb	15 529.6	2 736.0	2 919.6	10 612.4	1 454.3	1 696.7	4 917.2	1 281.7	1 222.9
Mar	15 396.6	3 153.2	3 286.1	10 629.6	1 975.1	1 957.9	4 767.0	1 178.1	1 328.2

1 Note: New methodology was introduced from January 2008 affecting all historic estimates. See details in February ELMR in-brief page 3 found at: http://nswebcopy/elmr/02_08/downloads/ELMR_Feb08.pdf published on 11 February.

Source: Office for National Statistics

Production

22.25 Passenger cars
United Kingdom

	Total production					Production for export				
	1000cc and under	Over 1000cc and not over 1600cc	Over 1600cc and not over 2500cc	Over 2500cc	Total	1000cc and under	Over 1000cc and not over 1600cc	Over 1600cc and not over 2500cc	Over 2500cc	Total
	GKAB	GKAD	GKAF	GKAH	JCYM	GKAC	GKAE	GKAG	GKAI	JCYL
2000	96 043	676 438	723 294	145 677	1 641 452	56 556	375 528	509 591	121 315	1 062 990
2001	93 695	632 747	634 573	131 350	1 492 365	56 426	329 944	400 648	107 236	894 254
2002	79 545	711 553	720 067	118 579	1 629 744	35 866	442 975	470 285	98 158	1 047 284
2003	23 985	750 840	740 486	142 247	1 657 558	12 380	503 950	509 050	118 379	1 143 759
2004	15 471	796 174	690 759	144 346	1 646 750	10 316	560 505	492 564	116 371	1 179 756
2005	6 111	854 687	546 744	188 155	1 595 697	4 925	625 929	405 204	148 445	1 184 503
2006	–	792 187	446 143	203 755	1 442 085	–	622 205	324 880	159 008	1 106 093
2006 Feb	–	74 048	38 871	18 274	131 193	–	53 830	27 236	14 145	95 211
Mar	–	88 834	46 000	24 154	158 988	–	67 774	32 449	19 499	119 722
Apr	–	65 103	37 156	16 313	118 572	–	52 814	28 855	13 504	95 173
May	–	74 864	39 886	17 566	132 316	–	60 704	30 835	13 901	105 440
Jun	–	78 055	42 280	18 991	139 326	–	61 508	30 749	14 566	106 823
Jul	–	66 528	37 241	14 060	117 829	–	51 223	26 995	10 692	88 910
Aug	–	35 223	23 067	14 669	72 959	–	25 963	15 333	10 810	52 106
Sep	–	67 981	37 354	16 977	122 312	–	56 000	25 995	10 000	92 097
Oct	–	66 536	35 526	14 081	116 143	–	56 995	27 157	11 620	95 772
Nov	–	68 181	38 726	21 656	128 563	–	56 623	28 557	17 085	102 265
Dec	–	44 381	29 740	10 641	84 762	–	35 789	22 513	7 615	65 917
2007 Jan	–	58 476	44 747	20 974	124 197	–	45 690	32 511	16 683	94 884
Feb	–	50 765	45 021	19 863	115 649	–	35 745	34 582	14 634	84 961
Mar	–	60 556	57 299	20 154	138 009	–	43 991	39 465	16 697	100 153
Apr	–	51 685	52 171	16 584	120 440	–	39 791	41 062	13 694	94 547
May	–	52 566	55 754	19 063	127 383	–	42 253	44 341	15 687	102 281
Jun	–	58 890	58 327	20 312	137 529	–	46 020	45 812	16 984	108 816
Jul	–	61 021	52 489	16 178	129 688	–	47 046	38 221	12 964	98 231

*Note: The survey and publication of motor vehicle production ceased at
July reference period.

Source: Office for National Statistics

22.26 Alcoholic drink[1]
United Kingdom

			1998	1999	2000	2001	2002	2003	2004	2005	2006	2007	2008
Spirits[2]		Thousand hectolitres of alcohol											
Production	KMEA	"	5 145	4 705	4 210	4 368	4 508	4 553	4 081	4 365	4 485	5 673	6 949
Released for home consumption													
Home produced whisky	KMEE	"	289	323	314	321	321	318	319	301	283	286	289
Spirit-based Ready-to-drink[3]	SNET	"	..	..	..	..	105	124	114	84	65	52	42
Imported and other	KMEG	"	505	596	615	647	689	744	792	822	767	832	816
Total	KMEH	"	794	919	929	968	1 115	1 187	1 226	1 206	1 114	1 170	1 147
Beer		Thousand hectolitres											
Production	BFNK	"	56 652	57 854	55 279	56 802	56 672	58 014	57 459	56 255	53 763	51 341	49 469
Released for home consumption	BAYL	"	58 835	58 917	57 007	58 234	59 384	60 301	59 195	57 572	55 748	53 465	51 311
Production	JYXJ	Thousand hectolitres of pure alcohol	2 333	2 364	2 299	2 358	2 352	2 414	2 433	2 338	2 249	2 160	2 056
Released for home consumption	JYXK		2 439	2 428	2 382	2 429	2 473	2 515	2 499	2 398	2 335	2 247	2 138
Wine of fresh grapes													
Released for home consumption		Thousand hectolitres											
Fortified	KMEM		370	316	289	287	325	296	298	306	302	305	324
Still table	KMEN	"	7 979	8 391	8 864	9 534	10 319	10 647	11 768	12 117	11 655	12 559	12 402
Sparkling	KMEO	"	416	576	543	515	578	640	676	721	715	838	757
Total	KMEP	"	8 765	9 284	9 696	10 336	11 222	11 504	12 742	13 143	12 072	13 702	13 483
Made-wine													
Released for home consumption													
Other than coolers	KMEQ	"	406	416	431	364	367	339	351	334	317	348	382
Coolers[3]	KJDD	"	1 244	1 802	2 800	3 712	1 606	423	508	597	528	720	611
Cider and perry													
Released for home consumption	KMER	"	5 548	6 022	6 006	5 911	5 939	5 876	6 139	6 377	7 523	8 046	8 412

1 See chapter text.
2 Potable spirits distilled.
3 Made wine with alcoholic strength 1.2% to 5.5%. Includes alcoholic lemonade of appropriate strength and similar products. From 28 April 2002, duty on spirit-based "coolers" is charged at the same rate as spirits per litre of alcohol. Coolers for calendar year 2002 includes only wine based "coolers".

Sources: HM Revenue & Customs UK Trade Information website:;
http://www.uktradeinfo.com/index.cfm?task=bulletins

22.27 Tobacco products: released for home consumption[1]
United Kingdom

	Million			Thousand kilogrammes			
	Cigarettes			Other tobacco products			Total tobacco products other than cigarettes
	Home-produced	Imported	Total	Cigars	Hand-rolling	Other[2]	
	LUQN	LUQO	LUQP	LUQQ	LUQR	LUQS	LUQT
2004	48 166	4 454	52 620	826	3 052	549	4 428
2005	45 922	4 322	50 244	758	3 189	499	4 445
2006	44 392	4 570	48 962	689	3 454	439	4 581
2007	41 955	3 794	45 749	602	3 644	398	4 643
2008	42 053	3 680	45 733	546	4 154	381	5 081
2008 Jun	3 467	308	3 775	49	342	33	424
Jul	3 675	328	4 003	45	364	33	442
Aug	3 488	305	3 793	44	345	31	420
Sep	3 898	305	4 202	45	379	34	457
Oct	3 604	308	3 912	47	338	33	417
Nov	3 085	328	3 413	43	320	27	390
Dec	3 430	341	3 771	60	389	34	483
2009 Jan	4 224	281	4 505	38	336	28	402
Feb	2 846	237	3 084	39	393	31	462

1 See chapter text.
2 Excluding snuff.

Sources: HM Revenue and Customs Statistical Bulletins at;
http://www.uktradeinfo.com/index.cfm?task=bulletins

Banking, insurance

Chapter 23

Banking, insurance

Other banks balance sheet

(Table 23.3)

The table includes the business of all monthly and quarterly reporting banks in the UK.

The Channel Islands and Isle of Man are not treated as part of the UK for statistical purposes. Banking institutions in the Channel Islands and Isle of Man no longer have the option of being within the UK banking sector and their business, along with the business of offshore island branches of UK mainland banks, is excluded from the figures within this table. Additionally, the business of the UK banking sector with offshore island residents and entities are classified as 'non-residents'.

The table also contains details of business with building societies.

The aggregate balance sheet of the banking sector is reported on an accrual basis (accrued amounts that are payable and receivable are shown under liabilities and assets respectively). Additionally, acceptances are shown under both liabilities and assets.

The balance sheet of the Banking Department of the Bank of England is excluded from this table, and other banks business with the Issue Department is classified as 'UK banks'.

Data for 1999 reflect the acquisition of Birmingham Midshires Building Society by Halifax during that year.

Data for the end of 2000 reflect the entry of Bradford and Bingley plc to the banking sector during the year. Data for the end of 2000 also reflect the new reporting during the year of agency business as a result of collateral management via repurchase agreements (repos) and reverse repos.

Bank lending to, and bank deposits from, UK residents

(Tables 23.4 and 23.5)

These are series statistics based on the Standard Industrial Classification (SIC) 1992 (which was revised slightly in 2003).

Table 23.4. Until the third quarter of 2007, the analysis of lending covered loans, advances (including under reverse repos), finance leasing, acceptances and facilities (all in Sterling and other currencies) provided by reporting banks to their UK resident non-bank non-building society customers, as well as bank holdings of sterling and euro commercial paper issued by these resident customers. Following a review of statistical data collected, acceptances and holdings of sterling and euro commercial paper are no longer collected at the industry level detail with effect from fourth quarter 2007 data. Total lending therefore reflects loans and advances (including under reverse repos) only, from fourth quarter 2007 data.

Table 23.5 includes borrowing under sale and repo. Adjustments for transit items are not included.

Figures for both tables are supplied by monthly reporting banks and grossed to cover quarterly reporters. Following the transition of building societies' statistical reporting from the Financial Services Authority to the Bank of England on 1st January 2008, both tables will include data reported by building societies from the first quarter of 2008 onwards. They exclude lending to building societies and to residents of the Channel Islands and Isle of Man.

Building societies

(Table 23.13)

Building society figures are sourced from societies' annual returns and for each year relate to accounting years ending on dates between 1 February and 31 January of the following year. Figures are society-only as opposed to group consolidated.

Consumer credit

(Table 23.14)

Figures for net lending refer to changes in amounts outstanding adjusted to remove distortions caused by

revaluations of debt outstanding, such as write-offs. Class 3 loans are advanced under the terms of the Building Societies Act 1986.

A high proportion of credit advanced in certain types of agreement, notably on credit cards, is repaid within a month. This reflects use of such agreements as a method of payment rather than a way of obtaining credit. As from December 2006 the Bank of England has ceased to update the separate data on consumer credit provided by other specialist lenders, retailers and insurance companies previously contained in these tables. These categories have been merged into 'other consumer credit lenders'.

23.1 Bank of England Balance Sheet
Liabilities and assets outstanding at end of period

£ million

Consolidated statement

	Liabilities							Assets								
	Notes in circu- lation	Reserve balanc- es	Standi- ng facili- ty deposi- ts	Short term open market operat- ions	Foreign curren- cy public securi- ties issued	Cash ratio deposi- ts	Other liabil- ities	Standi- ng facili- ty assets	Short term open market operat- ions	Of which 1 week sterli- ng reverse repo	of which fine-t- uning sterli- ng reverse repo	of which other maturi- ty within mainte- nance period reverse repos	Longer term sterli- ng reverse repo	Ways and Means advanc- es to HMG	Bonds and other securi- ties acqured via market transa- ctions	Other assets	Total assets /liabil
	B55A	B56A	B57A	B58A	B59A	B62A	B63A	B65A	B66A	B67A	B68A	BL59	B69A	B72A	B73A	B74A	B75A
2008	45 923	–	–	–	5 534	–	56 200	–	7 257	–	7 257	–	9 796	370	7 257	60 120	89 346
2008 Jan	41 327	21 447	–	–	4 872	2 936	26 005	–	8 039	8 039	–	–	14 419	13 370	7 356	43 402	86 586
Feb	40 933	23 824	–	–	3 327	2 936	26 595	–	6 609	6 609	–	–	12 000	7 370	7 219	44 020	77 617
Mar	42 255	27 196	–	–	4 422	2 936	25 369	–	12 769	7 769	4 999	–	12 000	7 370	8 413	40 835	82 179
Apr	41 452	28 241	–	–	4 477	2 936	22 382	–	11 009	11 009	–	–	12 000	7 370	8 462	34 574	74 488
May	41 902	26 300	–	–	4 469	2 936	18 758	–	13 779	13 779	–	–	11 999	370	8 049	33 696	69 367
Jun	42 029	23 216	–	–	4 419	2 275	15 009	–	16 149	16 149	–	–	11 999	370	7 931	28 687	66 951
Jul	42 403	27 943	–	–	4 413	2 280	13 853	–	31 878	21 879	10 000	–	12 048	370	7 714	26 669	80 892
Aug	42 530	29 126	–	–	4 576	2 280	14 916	–	33 919	33 919	–	–	12 047	370	7 871	26 609	83 429
Sep	42 618	50 847	–	–	4 669	2 280	17 617	–	62 519	37 521	24 999	–	12 046	370	7 907	22 063	108 031
Oct	43 304	52 568	860	3 700	4 702	2 280	149 482	–	–	–	–	–	12 046	370	6 712	161 859	184 508
Nov	44 103	–	–	–	5 274	–	121 486	–	7 082	–	7 082	–	10 446	370	7 082	105 936	134 877
Dec	45 923	–	–	–	5 534	–	56 200	–	7 257	–	7 257	–	9 796	370	7 257	60 120	89 346

Issue Department

	Liabilities		Assets								
	Notes in circu- lation	Notes in Banking Departemnt	Short term open market operations	Of which 1 week sterling reverse repo	of which fine-tuning sterling reverse repo	Longer term sterling reverse repo	Ways and Means advances to HMG	Bonds and other securities acqured via market transactions	Other assets	Total assets/liabi- lities
	AEFA	AEFB	BL29	BL32	BL33	BL34	B54A	BL35	BL36	BL37
2008	45 923	–	–	–	15 436	9 796	370	4 547	31 210	45 923
2008 Jan	41 327	–	8 039	8 039	–	14 419	13 370	–	5 499	41 327
Feb	40 933	–	6 609	6 609	–	12 000	7 370	399	14 555	40 933
Mar	42 255	–	12 769	7 769	4 999	12 000	7 370	793	9 324	42 255
Apr	41 452	–	11 009	11 009	–	12 000	7 370	1 074	9 999	41 452
May	41 902	–	13 779	13 779	–	11 999	370	1 473	14 280	41 902
Jun	42 029	–	16 149	16 149	–	11 999	370	1 815	11 696	42 029
Jul	42 403	–	27 732	21 879	5 854	12 048	370	2 213	40	42 403
Aug	42 530	–	27 442	27 442	–	12 047	370	2 613	58	42 530
Sep	42 618	–	27 048	22 465	4 583	12 046	370	3 125	28	42 618
Oct	43 304	–	–	–	–	12 046	370	3 521	27 367	43 304
Nov	44 103	–	–	–	–	10 446	370	3 961	29 326	44 103
Dec	45 923	–	–	–	–	9 796	370	4 547	31 210	45 923

Banking Department

	Liabilities						Assets								
	Reserve balances	Standing facility deposits	Short term open market operatio- ns	Foreign currency public securiti- es issued	Cash ratio deposits	Other liabil- ities	Standing facility assets	Short term open market operatio- ns	Of which 1 week sterling reverse repo	of which fine-tun- ing sterling reverse repo	Longer term sterling reverse repo	Bonds and other securiti- es acqured via market transact- ions	Bank of England notes	Other assets	Total assets/l- iabilitie
	BL38	BL39	BL42	BL43	BL44	BL45	BL47	BL48	BL49	BL52	B3J2	BL53	BL54	BL55	BL56
2008	–	–	–	5 534	–	87 410	–	7 257	–	7 257	143 273	7 257	–	60 120	74 634
2008 Jan	21 447	–	–	4 872	2 936	31 504	–	–	–	–	10 000	7 356	–	43 402	50 758
Feb	23 824	–	–	3 327	2 936	41 151	–	–	–	–	19 999	7 219	–	44 020	51 239
Mar	27 196	–	–	4 422	2 936	34 694	–	–	–	–	19 999	8 413	–	40 835	49 248
Apr	28 241	–	–	4 477	2 936	32 381	–	–	–	–	24 999	8 462	–	34 574	43 036
May	26 300	–	–	4 469	2 936	33 039	–	–	–	–	24 999	8 049	–	33 696	41 745
Jun	23 216	–	–	4 419	2 275	26 705	–	–	–	–	19 998	7 931	–	28 687	36 617
Jul	27 943	–	–	4 413	2 280	13 892	–	4 146	–	4 146	9 999	7 714	–	26 669	38 529
Aug	29 126	–	–	4 576	2 280	14 914	–	6 477	6 477	–	9 999	7 871	–	26 609	40 957
Sep	50 847	–	–	4 669	2 280	17 646	–	35 472	15 056	20 416	10 000	7 907	–	22 063	65 442
Oct	52 568	860	3 700	4 702	2 280	176 849	–	–	–	–	92 239	6 712	–	161 859	168 571
Nov	–	–	–	5 274	–	150 812	–	7 082	–	7 082	134 768	7 082	–	105 936	120 100
Dec	–	–	–	5 534	–	87 410	–	7 257	–	7 257	143 273	7 257	–	60 120	74 634

Source: Bank of England

23.2 Value of inter-bank clearings
United Kingdom

£ billion

		1998	1999	2000	2001	2002	2003	2004	2005	2006	2007	2008
Bulk paper clearings[1]												
Cheque (formerly general)	KCYY	1 214	1 226	1 214	1 210	1 178	1 141	1 111	1 062	1 076	1 157	1 076
Credit	KCYZ	93	88	82	80	75	69	63	57	56	58	52
High-value clearings												
Town	KCZA	–	–	–	–	–	–	–	–	..	..	..
CHAPS Sterling only	KCZB	41 501	44 704	49 146	52 913	51 896	51 613	52 348	52 672	59 437	69 352	73 626
Electronic clearing (BACS)	KCZC	1 602	1 761	1 922	2 166	2 382	2 574	2 883	3 150	3 429	3 696	3 946

1 Excludes inter-branch clearings and clearings in Scotland and Northern Ireland.

Source: APACS - The UK payments association: 020 7711 6223

Banking, insurance

23.3 Other banks' balance sheet[1]

£ million

		1999[2]	2000[3,4]	2001	2002	2003	2004	2005	2006	2007	2008
Sterling liabilities											
Notes outstanding & cash loaded cards	TBFA	3 311	3 359	3 866	3 957	4 207	4 338	4 534	4 987	5 265	5 461
Sight deposits[5]											
UK banks[6]	TBFB	33 463	40 054	59 573	101 905	99 208	109 866	148 202	165 479	91 480	98 228
UK building societies	TBFC	841	1 168	1 466	2 403	1 736	1 697	2 314	2 277	2 653	5 745
UK public sector[7]	TBFD	3 450	3 403	4 283	3 997	5 679	6 635	7 341	9 046	8 190	12 829
Other UK residents	TBFE	325 392	372 725	415 180	457 077	502 359	566 524	638 684	701 743	765 627	748 155
Non-residents	TBFF	44 581	55 489	55 837	57 218	65 157	72 452	83 608	94 822	106 855	115 763
Time deposits											
UK banks[6]	TBFG	112 530	110 955	125 261	141 401	164 433	230 749	289 656	455 672	116 062	76 789
UK building societies	TBFH	4 253	4 688	4 856	4 487	3 643	4 045	4 098	3 573	4 182	3 247
UK public sector[7]	TBFI	8 064	8 241	8 306	8 936	8 934	10 872	11 378	16 504	16 820	53 319
Other UK residents	TBFJ	282 789	301 007	302 715	306 453	313 244	322 603	353 481	433 436	496 675	682 866
of which TESSAs	TBFK	22 868	24 265	9 752	5 235	1 832	–	–	–	..	..
of which SAYE	TBFL	2 840	2 726	2 439	2 367	2 226	2 301	2 164	1 900	1 049	698
of which cash ISAs	TFDG	5 210	13 684	31 298	42 269	52 118	61 033	68 584	76 323	83 827	..
Non-residents	TBFM	116 967	134 844	150 964	151 304	166 449	177 381	203 777	234 754	420 623	388 343
Acceptances granted	TBFN	12 854	10 012	10 627	9 954	2 856	1 446	928	1 105	1 860	1 280
Liabilities under sale and repurchase agreements											
of which British govt. securities[8]	TBFU	56 145	83 819	83 330	78 155	114 468	109 692	180 087	234 606	..	..
UK banks[7]	TBFP	48 213	56 408	60 551	52 079	95 922	86 876	133 938	190 384	167 057	193 086
UK building societies	TBFQ	200	36	–	107	170	62	345	–	175	50
UK public sector[7]	TBFR	–	14 351	5 127	1 402	1 521	113	155	35	3 792	3 850
Other UK residents	TBFS	17 165	22 974	25 732	19 759	19 906	35 038	55 378	58 312	71 150	108 505
Non-residents	TBFT	5 542	9 849	8 643	19 072	18 475	26 669	40 012	54 240	68 660	33 328
CDs and other short-term paper issued	TBFV	158 826	151 153	153 768	157 354	148 606	160 173	165 923	179 554	199 834	249 985
Total sterling deposits	TBFW	1 175 130	1 297 356	1 392 890	1 494 908	1 618 298	1 813 197	2 139 217	2 600 935	2 541 695	2 775 368
Sterling items in suspense and transmission	TBFX	17 307	15 261	16 702	13 318	18 371	17 923	27 479	34 047	29 469	30 830
Net derivatives	TBFY	8 324	10 992	4 029	2 491	−10 672	−15 457	9 894	−33 397	−25 459	51 752
Accrued amounts payable	TBFZ	22 122	23 726	22 836	21 541	22 624	26 262	27 108	35 267	44 909	38 695
Sterling capital and other internal funds	TBGA	100 575	133 436	148 294	173 320	204 295	265 344	243 392	299 359	275 685	302 045
Total sterling liabilities	TBGB	1 326 769	1 484 130	1 588 618	1 709 535	1 857 123	2 111 607	2 451 625	2 941 199	2 871 564	3 204 151
Foreign currency liabilities											
Sight and time deposits											
UK banks[9]	TBGC	77 684	99 447	106 368	111 536	139 018	151 946	153 024	184 880	179 964	331 139
UK building societies	TBGD	681	233	279	373	550	310	615	658	726	521
UK public sector[7]	TBGE	126	1 808	926	833	865	898	1 098	2 279	616	1 485
Other UK residents	TBGF	65 203	79 627	95 666	81 590	89 034	111 035	137 651	162 328	207 907	298 037
Non-residents	TBGG	736 792	914 888	1 001 321	997 398	1 055 183	1 185 037	1 427 857	1 551 892	1 994 229	2 584 477
Acceptances granted	TBGH	619	689	638	754	751	890	846	1 270	1 394	1 883
Sale and repurchase agreements											
UK banks	TBGJ	25 170	38 901	54 499	90 407	224 743	243 933	265 239	259 088	251 972	148 811
UK building societies	TBGK	–	–	–	–	–	–	–	–	–	19
UK public sector	TBGL	–	468	1	71	844	858	391	1	972	1 712
Other UK residents	TBGM	21 997	35 145	52 438	54 463	73 477	67 544	79 689	83 379	108 075	99 179
Non-residents	TBGN	115 357	139 656	154 976	211 276	289 674	379 695	433 712	419 744	526 493	436 143
CDs and other short-term paper issued	TBGO	151 009	199 510	224 225	234 731	255 590	278 440	341 866	406 487	530 751	648 555
Total foreign currency deposits	TBGP	1 194 637	1 510 373	1 691 336	1 783 432	2 129 730	2 420 587	2 841 988	3 072 007	3 803 098	4 551 961
Items in suspense and transmission	TBGQ	30 548	46 678	47 363	38 355	60 465	92 173	108 217	95 421	123 779	101 318
Net derivatives	TBGR	3 704	−4 472	−3 854	5 816	14 774	22 765	3 347	66 215	29 391	−205 224
Accrued amounts payable	TBGS	18 080	18 568	17 756	16 312	15 708	18 214	23 015	36 279	42 646	51 171
Capital and other internal funds	TBGT	69 798	89 359	85 489	87 047	81 778	45 835	93 991	50 759	93 285	219 455
Total foreign currency liabilities	TBGU	1 316 767	1 660 506	1 838 090	1 930 961	2 302 455	2 599 575	3 070 557	3 320 680	4 092 199	4 718 681
Total liabilities	TBGV	2 643 536	3 144 636	3 426 708	3 640 497	4 159 579	4 711 182	5 522 182	6 261 879	6 963 763	7 922 832

23.3 Other banks' balance sheet[1]
continued

£ million

		1999[2]	2000[3,4]	2001	2002	2003	2004	2005	2006	2007	2008
Sterling assets											
Notes and coins	TBGW	9 047	8 007	6 566	6 621	7 464	10 559	9 500	9 279	7 798	7 183
With UK central bank											
Cash ratio deposits	TBGX	1 141	1 275	1 386	1 495	1 609	1 759	1 953	2 271	2 599	2 144
Other	TBGY	676	117	143	249	54	100	1 388	17 645	21 268	51 017
Market loans											
UK banks[5,6]	TBGZ	144 537	149 174	181 350	237 771	263 004	342 699	438 572	618 742	185 890	176 075
UK bank CDs	TBHB	75 071	65 156	68 868	68 728	55 053	59 505	58 780	63 236	50 856	48 696
UK bank commercial paper	TBHC	208	8	52	62	5	54	75	410	399	783
UK building societies CDs etc and deposits	TBHD	5 093	4 748	3 933	4 293	7 200	7 222	5 655	7 481	7 827	3 673
Non-residents	TBHE	74 403	94 381	102 404	89 848	109 665	102 286	128 343	166 599	268 221	241 265
Acceptances granted											
UK building societies	TBHF	–	–	–	–	–	–	–	–	–	–
UK public sector[7]	TBHG	–	–	–	–	–	–	–	–	–	–
Other UK residents	TBHH	11 933	9 496	9 992	9 111	2 777	1 348	817	956	1 032	664
Non-residents	TBHI	920	516	635	842	79	99	111	148	828	615
Bills											
Treasury bills	TBHJ	2 749	1 612	8 474	18 752	18 265	14 507	15 707	11 984	4 837	2 762
UK bank bills	TBHA	11 426	7 011	8 098	8 491	1 265	646	24	103	51	56 586
UK building societies	TBHK	–	–	–	–	–	–	–	375	–	–
Other UK	TBHL	818	1 202	1 601	485	1 013	955	779	1 636	320	421
Non-residents	TBHM	206	287	744	979	733	702	1 063	1 831	4 099	2 622
Claims under sale and repurchase agreements											
of which British govt. securities[8]	TBHT	64 943	86 362	84 068	77 460	114 091	116 652	187 606	237 177	..	..
UK banks	TBHO	39 667	46 088	46 585	37 197	77 691	64 353	113 540	160 380	140 814	78 228
UK building societies	TBHP	91	116	327	86	114	263	1 048	76	4 650	4 607
UK public sector	TBHQ	–	9 067	4 692	5 159	5 231	10 801	11 695	9 168	8 026	1 506
Other UK residents	TBHR	30 338	35 058	36 222	31 363	35 885	50 371	61 311	65 569	102 677	125 017
Non-residents	TBHS	6 310	7 266	7 010	14 271	12 981	20 456	36 261	52 300	68 570	41 216
Advances											
UK public sector	TBHU	2 567	2 746	2 442	3 783	4 414	6 078	6 838	8 092	9 443	10 224
Other UK residents[10]	TBHV	732 649	823 787	891 790	986 835	1 062 650	1 159 833	1 252 836	1 376 190	1 555 938	1 665 414
Non-residents	TBHW	23 364	24 494	29 483	31 380	34 603	38 447	49 223	62 314	81 118	86 143
Banking dept. lending to central govt. (net)	TBNU	–	–	–	–	–	–	–	..	..	..
Investments											
British government stocks	TBHX	9 243	2 867	499	–3 545	–8 525	–4 210	–6 203	–11 173	–12 950	10 792
Other public sector	TBHY	124	88	116	158	385	328	459	569	767	416
UK banks[11]	TBHZ	13 584	22 935	23 965	23 542	34 971	34 664	36 365	36 655	37 633	61 700
UK building societies	TBIA	2 506	2 251	2 099	1 835	1 702	1 889	2 068	1 891	1 009	605
Other UK residents[12]	TBIB	57 391	77 647	82 013	76 773	84 813	100 892	112 593	165 898	165 949	265 092
Non-residents	TBIC	13 775	20 572	23 462	22 821	22 505	26 029	30 487	39 000	46 197	44 218
Items in suspense and collection	TBID	23 441	21 982	24 024	19 577	22 434	22 066	29 714	34 629	40 301	48 176
Accrued amounts receivable	TBIE	15 173	15 919	13 528	15 486	17 204	19 987	19 510	24 909	30 814	34 711
Other assets	TBIF	13 036	12 654	12 876	12 685	11 955	12 875	15 522	14 430	14 749	15 808
Total sterling assets[13]	TBIG	1 321 486	1 468 527	1 595 380	1 727 136	1 889 200	2 107 562	2 436 032	2 943 591	2 851 729	3 088 382

23.3 Other banks' balance sheet[1]
continued

£ million

		1999[2]	2000[3,4]	2001	2002	2003	2004	2005	2006	2007	2008
Foreign currency assets											
Market loans and advances											
UK banks[9]	TBIH	74 250	93 269	104 107	114 809	137 417	149 119	146 316	173 211	177 957	334 360
UK banks' CDs etc	TBII	14 364	13 171	13 298	10 128	13 162	11 026	18 412	13 023	12 851	8 635
UK building societies CDs etc. and deposits	TBIJ	451	173	354	357	591	448	411	422	608	304
UK public sector[7]	TBIK	20	30	13	83	91	50	153	105	153	52
Other UK residents	TBIL	88 847	107 707	118 106	117 669	134 894	153 574	161 488	199 147	279 617	389 404
Non-residents	TBIM	599 146	743 781	783 057	783 168	779 983	839 535	1 013 764	1 104 494	1 492 052	2 267 868
Claims under sale and repurchase agreement											
UK banks	TBIO	28 008	41 801	61 188	91 488	225 027	250 209	272 361	257 856	248 960	144 105
UK building societies	TBIP	–	–	–	–	–	–	100	67	2 152	4 434
UK public sector[7]	TBIQ	–	737	23	486	1 420	1 590	1 125	1	1 118	413
Other UK residents	TBIR	33 027	57 876	73 237	86 866	100 817	106 973	135 018	131 709	171 482	160 563
Non-residents	TBIS	146 756	199 990	219 449	256 663	382 672	506 157	612 065	595 615	751 407	539 082
Acceptances granted	TBIT	619	689	638	754	751	890	846	1 270	1 394	1 883
Bills	TBIU	19 508	21 878	25 399	20 803	31 429	24 250	24 230	25 917	35 841	40 709
Investments											
British government stocks	TBIV	4 473	3 518	890	226	19	−20	−30	104	9	2 702
Other public sector	TBIW	–	–	4	18	7	–	–	1	–	1
UK banks	TBIX	8 607	11 706	10 633	10 298	11 688	13 187	13 176	12 384	13 811	28 094
UK building societies	TBIY	631	939	850	1 170	1 570	2 400	2 974	2 683	2 590	3 399
Other UK residents	TBIZ	5 679	12 298	18 129	20 130	21 846	32 882	45 283	57 858	69 107	102 209
Non-residents	TBJA	243 147	297 404	324 073	326 035	334 371	398 040	484 874	566 025	662 689	599 092
Items in suspense and collection	TBJB	29 706	44 885	55 026	44 037	60 804	81 937	112 089	117 498	122 409	118 942
Accrued amounts receivable	TBJC	20 163	21 279	18 969	19 434	18 129	19 561	22 397	32 639	42 078	60 164
Other assets	TBJD	4 648	2 978	3 880	8 735	13 683	11 802	19 089	26 251	23 691	27 957
Total foreign currency assets[14]	TBJE	1 322 050	1 676 109	1 831 322	1 913 355	2 270 372	2 603 610	3 086 141	3 318 281	4 112 034	4 834 450
Total assets	TBJF	2 643 536	3 144 636	3 426 702	3 640 491	4 159 572	4 711 173	5 522 173	6 261 872	6 963 763	7 922 832
Holdings of own sterling acceptances	TBJG	1 725	1 231	916	1 220	411	265	24	19	20	14
Holdings of own FC acceptances	TBJH	150	135	118	58	104	170	222	247	526	888
Eligible banks' total sterling acceptances	TBJI	14 523	10 597	11 320	10 805	3 035	1 217	152	..	..	..
Eligible liabilities	TBJJ	849 289	952 062	1 012 194	1 087 877	1 163 917	1 266 726	1 420 348	1 636 053	1 873 503	2 086 706

1 See chapter text.

2 Data for 1999 reflect the acquisition of Birmingham Midshires Building Society by Halifax during that year.

3 Data for 2000 reflect the entry of Bradford & Bingley plc to the banking sector during the year.

4 Data for 2000 reflect the new reporting during the year of agency business as a result of collateral management via repos and reverse repos.

5 Sterling sight deposits from UK banks and sterling market loans to UK banks in 2003 were depressed by £19 bn following the consolidation of two banks balance sheets.

6 Sterling deposits (sight plus time) from, and lending to banks in 2007 were reduced by £386bn following changes in the reporting population.

7 From 2000 the UK public sector series reflects assumption by the Debt Management Office (an executive agency of HM Treasury) of responsibility for government cash management.

8 Due to changes to the forms completed by reporting institutions, the breakdown of sale and repurchase agreements into gilt and non-gilt collateral is not available after 2006.

9 Foreign currency sight and time deposits from UK banks and foreign currency market loans and advances to UK banks in 2001, 2003 and 2004 were each depressed by £14.5 bn, £0.5 bn and £4.7 bn respectively as a result of positions being consolidated out on the merger of two banks.

10 During 2000, 2001, 2002, 2003, 2004 and 2005 sterling advances to other UK residents were reduced by £10.3 bn, £12.9 bn, £16.2 bn, £29.1bn, £30.4bn and £33.6 bn respectively as a result of securitisations and other loan transfers to non-banks or non-residents.

11 Sterling investments in UK banks in 2000 were boosted by Barclay's £5.8 bn investment in Woolwich.

12 Sterling investments in other UK residents in 2000 were boosted by Lloyds TSB's £5.8 bn investment in Scottish Widows Group.

13 Changes in the reporting populations in 1998, 1999, 2000, 2001, 2003 and 2004 account for a net decrease of £7.3 bn, £11.3 bn £0.8 bn, £0.7bn, £0.2 bn and £4.5 bn respectively in sterling assets outstanding.

14 Changes in the reporting populations in 1998, 1999, 2000, 2001, 2003 and 2004 account for a net decrease of £4.6 bn, £6.6 bn, £0.2 bn, £0.2 bn £0.2 bn and £5.2 bn of foreign currency assets outstanding.

Source: Bank of England: 020 7601 3236

23.4 Industrial analysis of bank lending to UK residents[1]

Not seasonally adjusted

£ million

	UK residents		Agriculture, hunting and forestry	Fishing	Mining & quarrying	Manufacturing	Food, beverages & tobacco	Textiles & leather	Pulp, paper, publishing & printing
	Total	of which sterling				Total			

Amounts outstanding (sterling & other currencies)

Loans & advances (including under repo & sterling commercial paper)

	TBOA	TBOB	TBOC	TBOD	TBOE	TBOF	TBOG	TBOH	TBOI
2006	1 793 840	1 460 380	9 620	413	4 205	47 476	11 434	1 512	6 405
2007	..	..	..	..	..	–	..	..	..

Acceptances

	TBQA	TBQB	TBQC	TBQD	TBQE	TBQF	TBQG	TBQH	TBQI
2006	1 190	956	–	–	1	104	5	28	1
2007	..	..	..	..	..	–	..	..	..

Total

	TBSA		TBSC	TBSD	TBSE	TBSF	TBSG	TBSH	TBSI
2007	2 128 450		9 940	401	13 234	51 344	13 515	1 407	7 022
2008	2 629 622		10 711	356	16 895	64 273	18 676	1 588	7 735

of which in sterling

	TBUA		TBUC	TBUD	TBUE	TBUF	TBUG	TBUH	TBUI
2007	1 676 084		9 592	394	1 827	31 687	8 564	926	4 574
2008	2 077 692		10 137	347	2 204	32 622	9 310	953	4 354

Facilities granted

	TCAA		TCAC	TCAD	TCAE	TCAF	TCAG	TCAH	TCAI
2007	2 594 187		12 980	493	30 332	102 120	26 151	2 325	12 164
2008	3 098 001		13 925	453	28 384	110 472	29 016	2 380	12 988

of which in sterling

	TCCA		TCCC	TCCD	TCCE	TCCF	TCCG	TCCH	TCCI
2007	1 977 125		12 573	483	2 956	51 975	13 157	1 492	7 001
2008	2 368 451		13 317	444	3 243	50 061	13 010	1 429	6 693

	Manufacturing					Electricity, gas and water supply		
	Chemicals, man-made fibres, rubber & plastics	Non-metallic mineral products & metals	Machinery, equipment & transport equipment	Electrical, medical & optical equipment	Other manufacturing	Electricity, gas & heated water	Cold water purification & supply	Construction

Amounts outstanding (sterling & other currencies)

Loans & advances (including under repo & sterling commercial paper)

	TBOJ	TBOK	TBOL	TBOM	TBON	TBOO	TBOP	TBOQ
2006	5 681	6 122	6 678	3 741	5 903	7 075	4 235	20 671
2007	..	..	..	..	..	–	..	..

Acceptances

	TBQJ	TBQK	TBQL	TBQM	TBQN	TBQO	TBQP	TBQQ
2006	4	10	8	14	33	–	–	15
2007	..	..	..	..	..	–	..	..

Total

	TBSJ	TBSK	TBSL	TBSM	TBSN	TBSO	TBSP	TBSQ
2007	..	6 594	7 461	..	6 482	6 485	2 449	27 187
2008	..	8 036	10 605	..	6 148	9 765	3 728	31 165

of which in sterling

	TBUJ	TBUK	TBUL	TBUM	TBUN	TBUO	TBUP	TBUQ
2007	2 864	3 842	3 820	1 994	5 103	5 559	2 435	26 062
2008	3 191	3 703	4 968	2 127	4 017	7 605	3 697	30 087

Facilities granted

	TCAJ	TCAK	TCAL	TCAM	TCAN	TCAO	TCAP	TCAQ
2007	..	10 961	14 375	8 025	10 236	13 130	6 537	40 749
2008	..	12 928	18 231	9 003	11 498	18 712	8 042	42 884

of which in sterling

	TCCJ	TCCK	TCCL	TCCM	TCCN	TCCO	TCCP	TCCQ
2007	5 160	6 640	7 527	3 380	7 618	9 064	5 628	37 118
2008	4 760	6 113	8 847	3 464	5 746	11 825	7 184	40 030

Banking, insurance

23.4 Industrial analysis of bank lending to UK residents[1]
Not seasonally adjusted
continued

£ million

| | Wholesale and retail trade | | | | Hotels and restaurants | Transport, storage & communication | Real estate, renting, computer and other business activities | | |
	Total	Sale & repair of motor vehicles & fuel	Other wholesale trade	Other retail trade & repair			Total	Development, buying, selling, renting of real estate	Renting of machinery & equipment

Amounts outstanding (sterling & other currencies)

Loans & advances (including under repo & sterling commercial paper)

	TBOR	TBOS	TBOT	TBOU	TBOV	TBOW	TBOX	TBOY	TBPA
2005	40 548	9 293	13 312	17 943	25 064	20 836	177 152	137 281	6 661
2006	42 368	10 167	14 401	17 800	25 707	26 361	209 942	162 332	6 881

Acceptances

	TBQR	TBQS	TBQT	TBQU	TBQV	TBQW	TBQX	TBQY	TBRA
2005	151	7	120	25	–	–	721	714	–
2006	160	4	99	58	1	1	812	800	–

Total

	TBSR	TBSS	TBST	TBSU	TBSV	TBSW	TBSX	TBSY	TBTA
2007	53 512	9 429	20 104	23 979	28 559	26 881	252 901	196 183	9 125
2008	56 760	9 928	23 726	23 106	32 260	32 453	312 311	250 872	9 931

of which in sterling

	TBUR	TBUS	TBUT	TBUU	TBUV	TBUW	TBUX	TBUY	TBVA
2007	42 436	8 926	12 256	21 254	27 762	20 088	241 030	193 064	7 629
2008	42 840	9 291	12 903	20 646	31 060	23 253	291 173	242 639	8 093

Facilities granted

	TCAR	TCAS	TCAT	TCAU	TCAV	TCAW	TCAX	TCAY	TCBA
2007	78 796	12 932	28 659	37 205	34 485	43 951	318 035	239 785	10 682
2008	85 661	12 886	33 746	39 029	38 454	52 930	376 615	294 631	11 837

of which in sterling

	TCCR	TCCS	TCCT	TCCU	TCCV	TCCW	TCCX	TCCY	TCDA
2007	59 398	11 485	17 479	30 434	32 112	28 167	295 544	232 906	8 683
2008	62 388	11 573	18 434	32 380	35 431	33 534	343 391	281 546	9 338

| | Real estate, renting, computer and other business activities | | | | | Recreational, personal & community service activities | | Financial intermediation (excl. insurance & pension funds) | |
	Computer & related activities	Legal, accountancy, consultancy & other business activities	Public administration & defence	Education	Health & social work	Recreational, cultural & sporting activities	Personal & community services activities	Total	Financial leasing corporations

Amounts outstanding (sterling & other currencies)

Loans & advances (including under repo & sterling commercial paper)

	TBPB	TBPC	TBPD	TBPE	TBPF	TBPH	TBPG	TBPI	TBPJ
2006	4 431	36 299	17 227	7 498	15 854	12 255	5 594	491 121	41 068
2007	..	..	..	..	..	..	..	–	..

Acceptances

	TBRB	TBRC	TBRD	TBRE	TBRF	TBRH	TBRG	TBRI	TBRJ
2006	–	12	–	–	–	–	5	90	–
2007	..	..	..	..	..	..	..	–	..

Total

	TBTB	TBTC	TBTD	TBTE	TBTF	TBTH	TBTG	TBTI	TBTJ
2007	4 590	43 004	18 539	8 720	19 233	14 308	7 038	662 127	42 290
2008	5 405	46 103	31 792	10 533	21 434	14 245	7 023	832 718	46 518

of which in sterling

	TBVB	TBVC	TBVD	TBVE	TBVF	TBVH	TBVG	TBVI	TBVJ
2007	2 829	37 508	17 336	8 626	18 808	13 273	6 420	353 327	35 470
2008	2 813	37 629	31 282	10 347	20 945	12 722	6 232	489 589	35 862

Facilities granted

	TCBB	TCBC	TCBD	TCBE	TCBF	TCBH	TCBG	TCBI	TCBJ
2007	7 411	60 156	21 493	11 789	22 910	19 589	9 403	750 335	44 850
2008	7 703	62 443	35 094	13 871	24 582	19 977	9 293	920 092	50 169

of which in sterling

	TCDB	TCDC	TCDD	TCDE	TCDF	TCDH	TCDG	TCDI	TCDJ
2007	4 431	49 524	20 263	11 540	22 099	17 088	8 395	383 376	37 676
2008	3 892	48 614	33 737	13 431	23 710	16 416	8 012	515 630	39 211

23.4 Industrial analysis of bank lending to UK residents[1]
Not seasonally adjusted
continued

£ million

	Financial intermediation (excl. insurance & pension funds)								
	Non-bank credit grantors, excl. credit unions	Credit unions	Factoring corporations	Mortgage & housing credit corporations	Investment & unit trusts excl. money market mutual funds	Money market mutual funds	Bank holding companies	Securities dealers (f)	Other financial intermediaries

Amounts outstanding (sterling & other currencies)

Loans & advances (including under repo & sterling commercial paper)

	TBPK	TBPL	TBPM	TBPN	TBPO	TBPP	TBPQ	TBPR	TBPS
2005	17 833	28	4 633	62 869	20 394	1 377	19 707	165 421	93 916
2006	21 496	60	5 593	84 959	20 131	674	17 969	183 551	115 620

Acceptances

	TBRK	TBRL	TBRM	TBRN	TBRO	TBRP	TBRQ	TBRR	TBRS
2005	15	5	–	–	–	–	–	–	27
2006	15	5	–	–	–	–	–	–	69

Total

	TBTK	TBTL	TBTM	TBTN	TBTO	TBTP	TBTQ	TBTR	TBTS
2007	23 682	80	6 524	99 231	20 980	327	44 392	218 224	206 398
2008	25 167	83	7 072	176 722	11 583	394	53 453	200 244	311 483

of which in sterling

	TBVK	TBVL	TBVM	TBVN	TBVO	TBVP	TBVQ	TBVR	TBVS
2007	21 443	80	5 520	82 577	6 133	77	32 363	36 975	132 688
2008	21 919	82	5 742	147 755	6 700	29	38 476	33 451	199 573

Facilities granted

	TCBK	TCBL	TCDM	TCBN	TCBO	TCBP	TCBQ	TCBR	TCBS
2007	25 847	93	6 857	105 225	48 565	400	45 288	232 192	241 017
2008	27 248	95	7 367	179 845	44 006	481	56 075	206 462	348 344

of which in sterling

	TCDK	TCDL	TCDM	TCDN	TCDO	TCDP	TCDQ	TCDR	TCDS
2007	23 119	90	5 786	88 024	12 915	89	32 504	37 961	145 212
2008	23 378	94	5 965	150 263	12 972	29	39 367	33 994	210 358

	Activities auxiliary to financial intermediation			Individuals & individual trusts		
	Insurance companies & pension funds	Fund management activities	Other	Total	Lending secured on dwellings inc. bridging finance	Other loans & advances

Amounts outstanding (sterling & other currencies)

Loans & advances (including under repo & sterling commercial paper)

	TBPT	TBPU	TBPV	TBPW	TBPX	TBPY
2007	..	..	..	749 174	605 198	144 014
2008	..	..	..	896 809	755 982	140 827

Acceptances

	TBRT	TBRU	TBRV			
2006	1	–	–			
2007	..	–	..			

Total

	TBTT	TBTU	TBTV	TBTW	TBTX	TBTY
2007	30 306	52 748	93 324	749 174	605 198	144 014
2008	30 681	34 604	179 106	896 809	755 982	140 827

of which in sterling

	TBVT	TBVU	TBVV	TBVW	TBVX	TBVY
2007	27 965	15 774	58 154	747 490	..	142 853
2008	25 678	14 089	97 578	894 205	..	139 269

Facilities granted

	TCBT	TCBU	TCBV	TCBW	TCBX	TCBY
2007	58 775	56 988	96 108	865 188	667 425	197 762
2008	57 474	44 484	182 701	1 013 900	812 818	201 082

of which in sterling

	TCDT	TCDU	TCDV	TCDW	TCDX	TCDY
2007	38 374	17 865	59 923	863 182	666 897	142 853
2008	30 977	15 207	99 601	1 010 884	811 743	199 141

1 See chapter text.

Source: Bank of England: 020 7601 3236

Banking, insurance

23.5 Industrial analysis of bank deposits from UK residents[1]

£ million

	Total from UK residents	Agriculture, hunting and forestry	Fishing	Mining & quarrying	Manufacturing			
					Total	Food, beverages & tobacco	Textiles & leather	Pulp, paper, publishing & printing
Amounts outstanding (sterling & other currencies)								
Deposit liabilities (including under repos)								
	TDAA	TDAB	TDAC	TDAD	TDAE	TDAF	TDAG	TDAH
2007	1 679 824	5 096	208	6 336	40 578	3 632	1 393	4 760
2008	2 293 013	5 265	175	10 582	38 880	3 594	1 121	3 737
of which in sterling								
	TDCA	TDCB	TDCC	TDCD	TDCE	TDCF	TDCG	TDCH
2007	1 362 254	4 969	176	3 149	30 692	2 738	1 042	4 246
2008	1 889 330	5 024	162	2 868	28 101	2 370	850	3 030

	Manufacturing				Electricity, gas and water supply		
	Chemicals, man-made fibres, rubber & plastics	Non-metallic mineral products & metals	Machinery, equipment & transport equipment	Electrical, medical & optical equipment	Other manufacturing	Electricity, gas & heated water	Cold water purification & supply	Construction
Amounts outstanding (sterling & other currencies)								
Deposit liabilities (including under repos)								
	TDAI	TDAJ	TDAK	TDAL	TDAM	TDAN	TDAO	TDAP
2007	4 531	4 851	10 428	6 103	4 880	5 292	2 840	19 639
2008	6 313	4 559	9 348	6 130	4 077	5 446	3 030	18 236
of which in sterling								
	TDCI	TDCJ	TDCK	TDCL	TDCM	TDCN	TDCO	TDCP
2007	3 012	4 152	7 731	3 752	4 020	4 713	2 141	18 604
2008	4 188	3 782	6 542	3 830	3 511	4 380	2 999	17 726

	Wholesale and retail trade					Transport, storage & communication	Real estate, renting, computer and other business activities		
	Total	Sale & repair of motor vehicles & fuel	Other wholesale trade	Other retail trade & repair	Hotels and restaurants		Total	Development, buying, selling, renting of real estate	Renting of machinery & equipment
Amounts outstanding (sterling & other currencies)									
Deposit liabilities (including under repos)									
	TDAQ	TDAR	TDAS	TDAT	TDAU	TDAV	TDAW	TDAX	TDAY
2007	32 478	4 008	14 592	13 878	5 339	20 753	123 626	36 580	1 623
2008	30 492	4 063	13 461	12 968	4 380	19 345	121 518	33 599	1 750
of which in sterling									
	TDCQ	TDCR	TDCS	TDCT	TDCU	TDCV	TDCW	TDCX	TDCY
2007	27 713	3 558	11 110	13 045	5 042	16 350	113 982	35 531	1 419
2008	25 856	3 561	10 288	12 007	4 198	15 075	109 550	32 623	1 564

23.5 Industrial analysis of bank deposits from UK residents[1]

continued

£ million

	Real estate, renting, computer and other business activities					Recreational, personal & community service activities		Financial intermediation (excl. insurance & pension funds)	
	Computer & related activities	Legal, accountancy, consultancy & other business activities	Public administration & defence	Education	Health & social work	Recreational, cultural & sporting activities	Personal & community services activities	Total	Financial leasing corporations

Amounts outstanding (sterling & other currencies)

Deposit liabilities (including under repos)

	TDAZ	TDBA	TDBB	TDBC	TDBD	TDBF	TDBE	TDBG	TDBH
2007	9 163	76 260	25 895	9 163	13 653	16 203	15 627	439 552	4 164
2008	9 546	76 623	58 326	10 285	14 524	16 352	15 917	686 659	4 800

of which in sterling

	TDCZ	TDDA	TDDB	TDDC	TDDD	TDDF	TDDE	TDDG	TDDH
2007	7 600	69 432	24 641	8 907	13 254	15 217	15 094	246 642	3 252
2008	7 856	67 507	53 278	9 914	13 154	15 234	15 358	460 866	3 744

Financial intermediation (excl. insurance & pension funds)

	Non-bank credit grantors, excl. credit unions	Credit unions	Factoring corporations	Mortgage & housing credit corporations	Investment & unit trusts excl. money market mutual funds	Money market mutual funds	Bank holding companies	Securities dealers	Other financial intermediaries

Amounts outstanding (sterling & other currencies)

Deposit liabilities (including under repos)

	TDBI	TDBJ	TDBK	TDBL	TDBM	TDBN	TDBO	TDBP	TDBQ
2007	9 557	438	768	12 887	36 033	489	39 870	154 352	180 996
2008	8 818	443	829	110 840	41 004	377	64 918	143 430	311 200

of which in sterling

	TDDI	TDDJ	TDDK	TDDL	TDDM	TDDN	TDDO	TDDP	TDDQ
2007	7 753	438	631	12 601	19 093	358	27 013	41 855	133 648
2008	6 455	443	678	108 814	23 247	233	45 040	35 604	236 610

	Insurance companies & pension funds	Activities auxiliary to financial intermediation		Individuals & individual trusts
		Placed by fund managers	Other	

Amounts outstanding (sterling & other currencies)

Deposit liabilities (including under repos)

	TDBR	TDBS	TDBT	TDBU
2007	68 820	88 179	94 639	645 906
2008	65 941	112 317	154 182	901 159

of which in sterling

	TDDR	TDDS	TDDT	TDDU
2007	60 241	49 295	59 367	642 064
2008	55 564	52 637	100 657	896 732

1 See chapter text.

Source: Bank of England: 020 7601 3236

23.6 Public sector net cash requirement and other counterparts to changes in money stock during the year

Not seasonally adjusted

£ million

		1998	1999	2000	2001	2002	2003	2004	2005	2006	2007	2008
Public sector net cash requirement (surplus)	ABEN	−6 296	−3 205	−36 864	−2 019	18 010	37 160	41 915	41 278	33 916	32 362	79 456
Sales of public sector debt to M4 private sector	IDH8	1 698	−1 448	13 639	7 716	−9 258	−32 438	−32 007	−11 257	−20 082	−16 293	..
M4 lending[1]	AVBS	63 926	78 029	111 202	82 574	107 553	127 820	156 084	158 087	218 445	238 495	269 792
External and foreign currency finance of the public sector	VQDC	−4 717	6 199	3 616	3 875	2 486	−13 441	−2 395	−30 708	−33 554	−37 950	−52 360
Other external and foreign currency flows[2]	AVBW	14 033	−44 902	7 178	−21 631	−25 132	−27 124	4 288	33 643	−890	−43 674	163 177
Net non-deposit liabilities (increase)	AVBX	−8 222	−2 943	−31 050	−10 791	−25 130	−20 377	−67 401	−39 903	−29 964	−5 006	−149 662
Money stock (M4)	AUZI	60 097	33 329	67 198	58 994	68 834	73 271	100 014	150 869	167 008	181 535	270 845

1 Bank and building society lending, plus holdings of commercial bills by the Issue Department of the Bank of England.
2 Including sterling lending to non-residents sector.

Source: Bank of England: 020 7601 5468

23.7 Money stock and liquidity

£ million

		1998	1999	2000	2001	2002	2003	2004	2005	2006	2007	2008
Amounts outstanding at end-year												
Notes and coin in circulation with the M4 private sector[1]	VQKT	23 705	26 269	28 174	30 450	31 889	34 010	36 410	38 508	40 523	43 567	44 868
UK private sector sterling non-interest bearing sight deposits[2]	AUYA	36 765	42 130	45 867	50 548	45 594	51 274	50 845	55 208	54 800	62 051	70 114
Money stock (M2)[3]	VQXV	514 508	558 334	597 523	649 980	703 920	777 347	845 654	922 687	996 629	1 071 982	1 122 740
Money stock M4	AUYM	783 354	816 601	884 873	942 594	1 008 750	1 081 299	1 179 192	1 328 321	1 498 920	1 674 855	1 949 837
Changes during the year[4]												
Notes and coin in circulation with the M4 private sector[1]	VQLU	1 501	2 582	1 957	2 284	1 493	2 189	2 461	2 156	2 037	3 116	1 265
UK private sector sterling non-interest bearing sight deposits[2]	AUZA	−753	5 354	3 534	4 913	−6 760	5 322	−227	5 701	−408	9 292	−1 964
Money stock (M2)[3]	AUZE	30 781	41 992	39 123	52 813	53 698	72 255	68 901	78 428	72 764	65 042	48 558
Money stock M4	AUZI	60 097	33 329	67 198	58 994	68 834	73 271	100 014	150 869	167 008	181 535	270 845

1 The estimates of levels of coin in circulation include allowance for wastage, hoarding, etc.
2 Non-interest bearing deposits are confined to those with institutions included in the United Kingdom banks sector (See Table 23.3).
3 M2 comprises the UK non-monetary financial institutions and non-public sector, i.e. M4 private sector's holdings of notes and coin together with its sterling denominated retail deposits with UK monetary financial institutions.
4 As far as possible the changes exclude the effect of changes in the number of contributors to the series, and also of the introduction of new statistical returns. Changes are not seasonally adjusted.

Source: Bank of England: 020 7601 5468

23.8 Selected retail banks' base rate[1]
Operative between dates shown

Percentage rates

Date of change	New rate	Date of change	New rate	Date of change	New rate
1986 Jan 9	12.50	Oct 5	15.00		
Mar 19	11.50			1999 Jan 7	6.00
Apr 8	11.00-11.50	1990 Oct 8	14.00	Feb 4	5.50
Apr 9	11.00			Apr 8	5.25
Apr 21	10.50	1991 Feb 13	13.50	Jun 10	5.00
May 23	10.00-10.50	Feb 27	13.00	Sep 8	5.00-5.25
May 27	10.00	Mar 22	12.50	Sep 10	5.25
Oct 14	10.00-11.00	Apr 12	12.00	Nov 4	5.50
Oct 15	11.00	May 24	11.50		
		Jul 12	11.00	2000 Jan 13	5.75
1987 Mar 10	10.50	Sep 4	10.50	Feb 10	6.00
Mar 18	10.00-10.50				
Mar 19	10.00	1992 May 5	10.00	2001 Feb 8	5.75
Apr 28	9.50-10.00	Sep 16[2]	12.00	Apr 5	5.50
Apr 29	9.50	Sep 17[2]	10.00-12.00	May 10	5.25
May 11	9.00	Sep 18	10.00	Aug 2	5.00
Aug 6	9.00-10.00	Sep 22	9.00	Sep 18	4.75
Aug 7	10.00	Oct 16	8.00-9.00	Oct 4	4.50
Oct 23	9.50-10.00	Oct 19	8.00	Nov 8	4.00
Oct 29	9.50	Nov 13	7.00		
Nov 4	9.00-9.50			2003 Feb 6	3.75
Nov 5	9.00	1993 Jan 26	6.00	Jul 10	3.50
Dec 4	8.50	Nov 23	5.50	Nov 6	3.75
1988 Feb 2	9.00	1994 Feb 8	5.25	2004 Feb 5	4.00
Mar 17	8.50-9.00	Sep 12	5.75	May 6	4.25
Mar 18	8.50	Dec 7	6.25	Jun 10	4.50
Apr 11	8.00			Aug 5	4.75
May 17	7.50-8.00	1995 Feb 2[2]	6.25-6.75		
May 18	7.50	Feb 3	6.75	2005 Aug 4	4.50
Jun 2	7.50-8.00	Dec 13	6.50		
Jun 3	8.00			2006 Aug 3	4.75
Jun 6	8.00-8.50	1996 Jan 18	6.25	Nov 9	5.00
Jun 7	8.50	Mar 8	6.00		
Jun 22	8.50-9.00	Jun 6	5.75	2007 Jan 11	5.25
Jun 23	9.00	Oct 30	5.75-6.00	May 10	5.50
Jun 28	9.00-9.50	Oct 31	6.00	Jul 5	5.75
Jun 29	9.50			Dec 6	5.50
Jul 4	9.50-10.00	1997 May 6	6.25		
Jul 5	10.00	Jun 6	6.25-6.50	2008 Feb 7	5.25
Jul 18	10.00-10.50	Jun 9	6.50	Apr 10	5.00
Jul 19	10.50	Jul 10	6.75	Oct 8	4.50
Aug 8	10.50-11.00	Aug 7	7.00	Nov 6	3.00
Aug 9	11.00	Nov 6	7.25	Dec 4	2.00
Aug 25	11.00-12.00				
Aug 26	12.00	1998 Jun 4	7.50	2009 Jan 8	1.50
Nov 25	13.00	Oct 8	7.25	Feb 5	1.00
		Nov 5	6.75	Mar 5	0.50
1989 May 24	14.00	Dec 10	6.25		

1 Data obtained from Barclays Bank, Lloyds/TSB Bank, HSBC Bank and
  National Westminster Bank whose rates are used to compile this series.
2 Where all the rates did not change on the same day a spread is shown.

Source: Bank of England: 020 7601 3644

Banking, insurance

23.9 Average three month sterling money market rates[1]

Percentage rates

	1998	1999	2000	2001	2002	2003	2004	2005	2006	2007	2008
Treasury bills:[2] KDMM											
January	6.80	5.28	5.72	5.49	3.83	3.80	3.92	4.66	4.39	5.30	5.12
February	6.88	5.04	5.83	5.46	3.87	3.50	4.01	4.69	4.38	5.34	5.02
March	6.95	4.92	5.86	5.23	3.97	3.47	4.13	4.77	4.40	5.33	4.88
April	7.00	4.90	5.92	5.12	3.97	3.45	4.20	4.70	4.42	5.43	4.83
May	7.01	4.93	5.95	4.98	3.95	3.44	4.40	4.66	4.50	5.55	4.95
June	7.29	4.76	5.85	4.99	3.98	3.47	4.61	4.62	4.54	5.67	5.11
July	7.22	4.76	5.83	5.01	3.84	3.31	4.67	4.46	4.53	5.77	5.08
August	7.19	4.85	5.81	4.72	3.77	3.40	4.71	4.41	4.75	5.79	4.95
September	6.94	5.12	5.78	4.43	3.79	3.52	4.69	4.40	4.84	5.69	4.74
October	6.54	5.23	5.75	4.16	3.75	3.65	4.68	4.40	4.94	5.61	3.68
November	6.31	5.20	5.68	3.78	3.80	3.81	4.66	4.42	5.01	5.50	1.99
December	5.72	5.46	5.62	3.83	3.84	3.83	4.68	4.43	5.08	5.30	1.29
Eligible bill: KDMY[3]											
January	7.28	5.63	5.90	5.64	3.91	3.87	3.94	4.75	..	..	..
February	7.24	5.28	6.01	5.56	3.92	3.65	4.06	4.78	..	..	..
March	7.25	5.11	5.98	5.37	3.99	3.54	4.19	4.88	..	..	..
April	7.24	5.02	6.05	5.21	4.04	3.52	4.28	4.84	..	..	..
May	7.20	5.08	6.09	5.06	4.01	3.52	4.42	4.80	..	..	..
June	7.42	4.94	6.03	5.08	4.04	3.45	4.68	4.76	..	..	..
July	7.49	4.89	5.97	5.07	3.94	3.39	4.75	4.57	..	..	..
August	7.40	4.94	5.97	4.82	3.86	3.42	4.85	4.51	..	..	..
September	7.20	5.16	5.95	4.57	3.86	3.59	4.83	..	..	..	..
October	6.91	5.42	5.92	4.26	3.82	3.69	4.79	..	..	..	..
November	6.52	5.43	5.88	3.85	3.84	3.88	4.78	..	..	..	..
December	6.05	5.59	5.78	3.88	3.71	3.90	4.77	..	..	..	..
Interbank rate: AMIJ											
January	7.48	5.80	6.06	5.76	3.98	3.91	3.99	4.80	4.54	5.45	5.61
February	7.46	5.43	6.15	5.69	3.98	3.69	4.10	4.82	4.52	5.52	5.61
March	7.48	5.30	6.15	5.47	4.06	3.58	4.23	4.92	4.53	5.50	5.86
April	7.44	5.23	6.21	5.33	4.11	3.58	4.33	4.88	4.57	5.61	5.90
May	7.41	5.25	6.23	5.17	4.08	3.57	4.46	4.83	4.65	5.72	5.79
June	7.63	5.12	6.14	5.19	4.11	3.57	4.73	4.78	4.69	5.83	5.90
July	7.71	5.07	6.11	5.19	3.99	3.42	4.79	4.59	4.68	5.98	5.80
August	7.66	5.18	6.14	4.93	3.92	3.45	4.89	4.53	4.90	6.34	5.76
September	7.38	5.32	6.12	4.65	3.93	3.63	4.87	4.54	4.98	6.58	5.87
October	7.14	5.94	6.08	4.36	3.90	3.73	4.83	4.53	5.09	6.21	6.18
November	6.89	5.78	6.00	3.93	3.91	3.91	4.82	4.56	5.18	6.36	4.40
December	6.38	5.97	5.89	3.99	3.95	3.95	4.81	4.59	5.25	6.35	3.21
Certificate of deposits: KOSA											
January	7.44	5.74	6.02	5.73	3.96	3.90	3.98	4.80	4.54	5.45	5.61
February	7.42	5.38	6.10	5.66	3.96	3.68	4.09	4.82	4.52	5.51	5.60
March	7.43	5.26	6.09	5.44	4.04	3.57	4.22	4.91	4.53	5.52	5.85
April	7.40	5.19	6.17	5.30	4.08	3.57	4.32	4.86	4.57	5.69	5.89
May	7.37	5.22	6.19	5.15	4.06	3.56	4.45	4.82	4.65	5.84	5.79
June	7.59	5.09	6.10	5.16	4.09	3.56	4.72	4.78	4.69	5.94	5.89
July	7.66	5.03	6.08	5.17	3.97	3.41	4.79	4.60	4.68	6.11	5.80
August	7.61	5.14	6.09	4.90	3.90	3.44	4.89	4.53	4.89	6.35	5.75
September	7.34	5.28	6.08	4.62	3.91	3.62	4.87	4.54	4.98	6.54	5.86
October	7.09	5.86	6.05	4.33	3.88	3.72	4.83	4.52	5.09	6.21	6.16
November	6.82	5.72	5.98	3.91	3.89	3.90	4.81	4.56	5.18	6.34	4.40
December	6.32	5.89	5.85	3.96	3.93	3.94	4.80	4.58	5.24	6.35	3.21
Local authority deposits: KDPX[4]											
January	7.43	5.76	6.03	5.73	3.85	3.87	3.91	..	..	..	..
February	7.40	5.38	6.09	5.62	3.88	3.61	4.08	..	..	..	..
March	7.40	5.27	6.08	5.39	4.01	3.55	4.12	..	..	..	..
April	7.38	5.17	6.12	5.26	4.05	3.54	4.31	..	..	..	..
May	7.34	5.19	6.14	5.13	4.06	3.54	4.45	..	..	..	..
June	7.56	5.07	6.09	5.10	4.05	3.57	4.75	..	..	..	..
July	7.64	5.01	6.04	5.12	3.95	3.39	4.82	..	..	..	..
August	7.55	5.11	6.06	4.86	3.87	3.43	4.92	..	..	..	..
September	7.35	5.19	6.05	4.58	3.88	3.61	4.90	..	..	..	..
October	7.08	5.83	6.03	4.29	3.86	3.71	4.85	..	..	..	..
November	6.85	5.64	5.96	3.82	3.87	3.90	4.84	..	..	..	..
December	6.35	5.88	5.80	3.87	3.93	3.92	4.82	..	..	..	..

1 A full definition of these series is given in Section 7 of the ONS Financial
Statistics Explanatory Handbook.
2 Average rate of discount at weekly (Friday) tender.

3 This series discontinued at end of August 2005.
4 This series discontinued at end of December 2004.

Source: Bank of England: 020 7601 3644

23.10 Average foreign exchange rates[1]

	1998	1999	2000	2001	2002	2003	2004	2005	2006	2007	2008
Sterling exchange rate index (1990 = 100)[2] AGBG											
January	104.7	99.6	108.5	104.4	106.9	104.0	102.4	102.1	102.7	..	..
February	104.7	100.8	108.4	104.1	107.4	102.4	104.8	103.3	102.8	..	..
March	106.8	102.8	108.4	105.0	106.5	100.6	105.0	103.2	102.1	..	..
April	107.1	103.4	110.1	105.8	107.1	99.8	105.2	104.4	101.9	..	..
May	103.4	104.2	108.5	106.6	105.3	97.9	104.6	103.6	104.1	..	..
June	105.4	104.7	104.6	106.8	103.6	99.6	105.8	104.9	..	..	..
July	105.3	103.5	105.6	107.2	105.3	99.4	105.9	102.1	..	..	..
August	104.6	103.3	107.4	105.1	105.4	99.0	105.2	102.8	..	..	..
September	103.3	104.7	106.2	106.1	106.5	99.2	103.3	103.9	..	..	..
October	100.7	105.4	109.2	105.8	106.7	99.8	102.2	103.1	..	..	..
November	100.6	105.7	107.3	106.1	105.9	100.4	101.7	103.2	..	..	..
December	100.4	106.7	106.4	106.5	105.5	100.3	103.2	103.3	..	..	..
Effective Sterling exchange rate index (Jan 2005 = 100) BK67											
January	100.4	96.4	102.9	98.4	100.5	99.9	100.1	100.0	99.1	105.4	96.4
February	100.2	97.2	102.5	98.0	100.7	98.4	102.5	101.0	98.9	104.9	95.9
March	101.9	98.8	102.3	98.7	100.0	96.7	102.2	101.1	98.4	103.4	94.6
April	102.1	98.9	103.6	99.3	100.7	96.0	102.1	102.0	98.3	104.1	92.8
May	99.0	99.6	101.7	99.6	99.3	94.8	101.8	101.0	101.3	103.7	92.8
June	101.0	99.6	98.6	99.5	98.2	96.6	103.0	101.8	100.8	104.3	93.0
July	100.9	98.4	99.4	100.0	100.3	96.0	103.1	98.8	100.8	105.0	93.2
August	100.3	98.7	100.6	98.7	100.3	95.4	102.4	99.7	102.8	104.4	91.6
September	99.8	99.9	99.1	99.8	101.4	95.7	100.7	100.7	102.9	100.1	80.0
October	97.6	100.7	101.7	99.6	101.6	96.8	99.8	99.7	103.0	102.6	89.3
November	97.3	100.6	100.0	99.7	101.0	97.3	99.7	99.4	103.3	101.7	83.4
December	97.3	101.2	99.8	100.2	100.8	97.8	101.3	99.6	104.3	99.8	78.1
Sterling/US Dollar AUSS											
January	1.6	1.7	1.6	1.5	1.4	1.6	1.8	1.9	1.8	2.0	2.0
February	1.6	1.6	1.6	1.5	1.4	1.6	1.9	1.9	1.7	2.0	2.0
March	1.7	1.6	1.6	1.4	1.4	1.6	1.8	1.9	1.7	1.9	2.0
April	1.7	1.6	1.6	1.4	1.4	1.6	1.8	1.9	1.8	2.0	2.0
May	1.6	1.6	1.5	1.4	1.5	1.6	1.8	1.9	1.9	2.0	2.0
June	1.7	1.6	1.5	1.4	1.5	1.7	1.8	1.8	1.8	2.0	2.0
July	1.6	1.6	1.5	1.4	1.6	1.6	1.8	1.8	1.8	2.0	2.0
August	1.6	1.6	1.5	1.4	1.5	1.6	1.8	1.8	1.9	2.0	1.9
September	1.7	1.6	1.4	1.5	1.6	1.6	1.8	1.8	1.9	2.0	1.8
October	1.7	1.7	1.5	1.5	1.6	1.7	1.8	1.8	1.9	2.0	1.7
November	1.7	1.6	1.4	1.4	1.6	1.7	1.9	1.7	1.9	2.1	1.5
December	1.7	1.6	1.5	1.4	1.6	1.8	1.9	1.7	2.0	2.0	1.5
Sterling/Euro THAP											
January	1.5	1.4	1.6	1.6	1.6	1.5	1.4	1.4	1.5	1.5	1.3
February	1.5	1.5	1.6	1.6	1.6	1.5	1.5	1.4	1.5	1.5	1.3
March	1.6	1.5	1.6	1.6	1.6	1.5	1.5	1.4	1.5	1.5	1.3
April	1.5	1.5	1.7	1.6	1.6	1.5	1.5	1.5	1.4	1.5	1.3
May	1.5	1.5	1.7	1.6	1.6	1.4	1.5	1.5	1.5	1.5	1.3
June	1.5	1.5	1.6	1.6	1.6	1.4	1.5	1.5	1.5	1.5	1.3
July	1.5	1.5	1.6	1.6	1.6	1.4	1.5	1.5	1.5	1.5	1.3
August	1.5	1.5	1.6	1.6	1.6	1.4	1.5	1.5	1.5	1.5	1.3
September	1.5	1.5	1.6	1.6	1.6	1.4	1.5	1.5	1.5	1.5	1.3
October	1.4	1.5	1.7	1.6	1.6	1.4	1.4	1.5	1.5	1.4	1.3
November	1.4	1.6	1.7	1.6	1.6	1.4	1.4	1.5	1.5	1.4	1.2
December	1.4	1.6	1.6	1.6	1.6	1.4	1.4	1.5	1.5	1.4	1.1

1 Working day average. A full definition of these series is given in Section 7 of the ONS Explanatory Handbook.
2 Series discontinued from 31 May 2006.

Source: Bank of England: 020 7601 3644

23.11 Average zero coupon yields[1]

Percentage rates

	1997	1998	1999	2000	2001	2002	2003	2004	2005	2006	2007
Nominal Five Year Yield ZBRG											
January	7.15	6.18	4.30	6.28	5.07	4.90	4.15	4.61	4.43	4.11	5.06
February	6.82	6.10	4.46	6.13	5.04	4.94	3.85	4.63	4.53	4.17	5.08
March	7.07	6.09	4.69	5.89	4.86	5.22	3.93	4.56	4.73	4.33	5.00
April	7.28	5.93	4.66	5.80	4.96	5.21	4.09	4.80	4.54	4.48	5.20
May	6.94	5.95	4.95	5.82	5.14	5.22	3.85	5.01	4.31	4.67	5.32
June	6.96	6.04	5.28	5.61	5.25	5.05	3.72	5.15	4.17	4.69	5.59
July	7.01	6.12	5.49	5.58	5.26	4.88	3.98	5.07	4.16	4.69	5.55
August	6.97	5.80	5.75	5.65	5.03	4.54	4.36	4.96	4.23	4.74	5.25
September	6.72	5.32	6.00	5.65	4.90	4.31	4.46	4.83	4.12	4.67	5.02
October	6.51	4.94	6.25	5.46	4.74	4.36	4.73	4.65	4.26	4.76	4.95
November	6.69	4.92	5.86	5.33	4.55	4.38	4.91	4.58	4.29	4.73	4.64
December	6.46	4.51	5.90	5.14	4.88	4.34	4.71	4.43	4.21	4.80	4.57
Nominal Ten Year Yield ZBRH											
January	7.52	5.96	4.24	5.62	4.75	4.85	4.39	4.76	4.50	4.02	4.76
February	7.15	5.91	4.39	5.44	4.90	4.90	4.22	4.78	4.54	4.10	4.79
March	7.41	5.85	4.60	5.18	4.64	5.18	4.34	4.67	4.74	4.26	4.72
April	7.58	5.69	4.53	5.14	4.90	5.19	4.48	4.92	4.58	4.46	4.94
May	7.08	5.73	4.83	5.23	5.05	5.22	4.23	5.06	4.38	4.58	5.03
June	7.04	5.60	5.07	5.05	5.11	5.05	4.13	5.13	4.25	4.60	5.31
July	6.92	5.65	5.24	5.09	5.10	4.95	4.43	5.04	4.28	4.59	5.29
August	6.97	5.41	5.25	5.18	4.88	4.68	4.59	4.95	4.29	4.58	5.05
September	6.70	5.03	5.51	5.25	4.91	4.47	4.68	4.86	4.17	4.47	4.91
October	6.37	4.93	5.68	5.09	4.77	4.60	4.88	4.72	4.31	4.53	4.88
November	6.46	4.83	5.11	4.98	4.58	4.62	5.03	4.65	4.26	4.45	4.67
December	6.22	4.44	5.19	4.80	4.83	4.55	4.87	4.49	4.17	4.53	4.65
Nominal Twenty Year Yield ZBRI											
January	7.74	5.94	4.36	4.45	4.33	4.69	4.46	4.69	4.45	4.05	4.87
February	7.39	5.88	4.44	4.38	4.42	4.72	4.40	4.72	4.45	4.13	4.90
March	7.59	5.78	4.60	4.25	4.45	4.99	4.56	4.61	4.65	4.29	4.82
April	7.73	5.61	4.53	4.35	4.76	5.02	4.69	4.79	4.53	4.48	5.04
May	7.16	5.67	4.75	4.40	4.87	5.08	4.49	4.89	4.36	4.62	5.14
June	7.08	5.42	4.77	4.37	4.98	4.93	4.44	4.87	4.23	4.64	5.42
July	6.80	5.45	4.67	4.38	4.90	4.82	4.70	4.80	4.24	4.63	5.40
August	6.86	5.30	4.53	4.49	4.69	4.57	4.68	4.69	4.27	4.64	5.13
September	6.64	4.91	4.62	4.63	4.88	4.40	4.74	4.65	4.16	4.54	4.96
October	6.36	4.87	4.56	4.61	4.92	4.54	4.81	4.59	4.30	4.61	4.92
November	6.37	4.73	4.07	4.39	4.53	4.60	4.87	4.50	4.28	4.55	4.68
December	6.17	4.47	4.20	4.30	4.65	4.59	4.76	4.42	4.19	4.62	4.64
Real Ten Year Yield ZBRJ											
January	3.45	3.10	2.00	2.10	2.22	2.52	2.00	1.94	1.75	1.29	1.78
February	3.27	3.06	1.91	2.17	2.27	2.50	1.74	1.96	1.77	1.32	1.80
March	3.43	3.00	1.85	2.05	2.33	2.53	1.79	1.81	1.87	1.41	1.70
April	3.56	2.91	1.70	2.08	2.56	2.43	1.96	1.93	1.76	1.54	1.91
May	3.57	2.92	1.91	2.14	2.58	2.43	1.81	2.05	1.70	1.63	2.05
June	3.66	2.85	1.89	2.12	2.54	2.33	1.67	2.10	1.65	1.68	2.21
July	3.62	2.77	1.90	2.14	2.56	2.42	1.85	2.07	1.65	1.65	2.19
August	3.60	2.65	2.19	2.25	2.42	2.33	1.95	2.03	1.61	1.55	1.97
September	3.52	2.59	2.31	2.28	2.51	2.20	2.05	1.97	1.51	1.49	1.79
October	3.23	2.67	2.26	2.33	2.53	2.36	2.15	1.89	1.57	1.57	1.75
November	3.25	2.40	2.05	2.34	2.39	2.33	2.21	1.88	1.54	1.47	1.48
December	3.11	2.11	1.98	2.23	2.58	2.24	2.03	1.76	1.47	1.56	1.50
Real Twenty Year Yield ZBRK											
January	3.67	3.06	2.07	2.01	1.88	2.26	2.07	1.96	1.59	0.97	1.23
February	3.49	3.05	1.99	1.95	1.88	2.30	1.98	1.90	1.59	0.99	1.25
March	3.59	2.98	1.93	1.78	1.99	2.32	2.07	1.77	1.72	1.10	1.19
April	3.68	2.85	1.81	1.84	2.25	2.25	2.12	1.85	1.64	1.28	1.36
May	3.66	2.83	1.99	1.91	2.32	2.25	2.03	1.88	1.57	1.33	1.46
June	3.69	2.63	1.97	1.87	2.27	2.17	1.97	1.88	1.53	1.39	1.54
July	3.57	2.58	2.00	1.90	2.24	2.24	2.16	1.87	1.54	1.31	1.52
August	3.57	2.53	2.14	1.96	2.16	2.15	2.14	1.82	1.49	1.21	1.31
September	3.48	2.49	2.26	1.96	2.31	2.06	2.18	1.80	1.40	1.12	1.24
October	3.22	2.59	2.22	1.99	2.32	2.22	2.22	1.76	1.40	1.13	1.25
November	3.18	2.36	1.92	1.94	2.12	2.25	2.21	1.71	1.29	1.03	1.09
December	3.06	2.14	1.87	1.87	2.24	2.21	2.08	1.60	1.20	1.11	1.08

1 Working day average. Calculated using the Variable Roughness Penalty (VRP) model.

Source: Bank of England: 020 7601 3644

23.12 Average rates on representative British Government Stocks[1]

Percentage rates

	1998	1999	2000	2001	2002	2003	2004	2005	2006	2007	2008
5 Year Conventional Rate[2] KORP											
January	6.33	4.25	6.36	5.17	4.94	4.15	4.59	4.43	4.27	..	..
February	6.24	4.41	6.23	5.13	4.96	3.88	4.46	4.61	4.31	..	..
March	6.26	4.65	6.01	4.94	5.23	3.93	4.44	4.77	4.41	..	..
April	6.11	4.66	5.95	4.97	5.26	4.08	4.66	4.58	4.44	..	..
May	6.14	4.93	5.97	5.15	5.48	3.83	4.89	4.36	4.44	..	..
June	6.31	5.27	5.78	5.32	5.10	3.68	5.08	4.24	4.66	..	..
July	6.14	5.49	5.75	5.34	4.92	3.72	4.98	4.11	4.62	..	..
August	5.84	5.80	5.81	5.09	4.57	4.30	4.88	4.22	4.84	..	..
September	5.34	6.04	5.81	4.94	4.25	4.42	4.76	4.18	4.91	..	..
October	4.88	6.24	5.66	4.78	4.38	4.70	4.57	4.23	5.00	..	..
November	4.86	5.89	5.50	4.59	4.40	4.88	4.52	4.31	4.39	..	..
December	4.45	5.91	5.27	4.88	4.34	4.68	4.42	4.27	–	..	..
10 year Conventional Rate KORQ											
January	6.07	4.16	5.75	4.86	4.84	4.37	4.78	4.51	4.19	5.21	4.33
February	6.02	4.32	5.56	4.88	4.91	4.25	4.75	4.60	4.25	5.25	4.28
March	5.97	4.54	5.29	4.75	5.15	4.51	4.65	4.79	4.39	5.15	4.00
April	5.81	4.48	5.25	4.95	5.23	4.64	4.91	4.60	4.47	5.34	4.28
May	5.85	4.77	5.35	5.13	5.51	4.26	5.07	4.38	4.39	5.39	4.75
June	5.77	5.02	5.15	5.09	5.06	4.38	5.19	4.23	4.74	5.74	5.15
July	5.67	5.20	5.18	5.16	4.94	4.23	5.10	4.20	4.73	5.70	5.00
August	5.56	5.24	5.27	4.92	4.66	4.59	4.99	4.25	4.78	5.39	4.63
September	5.10	5.52	5.32	4.92	4.46	4.69	4.89	4.16	4.74	5.13	4.23
October	4.93	5.70	5.15	4.76	4.57	4.09	4.73	4.31	4.85	5.07	3.76
November	4.87	5.16	5.06	4.58	4.59	5.04	4.66	4.33	4.04	4.70	2.96
December	4.49	5.24	4.88	4.88	4.52	4.94	4.50	4.27	4.93	4.60	2.26
20 Year Conventional Rate KORR											
January	6.04	4.36	4.91	4.52	4.81	4.46	4.73	4.55	4.05	4.77	4.54
February	5.98	4.47	4.80	4.58	4.83	4.37	4.80	4.58	4.13	4.80	4.68
March	5.90	4.64	4.64	4.56	5.12	4.51	4.69	4.79	4.28	4.73	4.54
April	5.73	4.58	4.71	4.84	5.14	4.64	4.91	4.63	4.38	4.95	4.77
May	5.79	4.83	4.77	4.98	5.45	4.44	5.03	4.43	4.59	5.08	4.95
June	5.59	4.92	4.68	5.10	5.03	4.38	5.07	4.30	4.60	5.32	5.22
July	5.63	4.88	4.70	5.05	4.92	4.59	4.99	4.33	4.60	5.28	5.09
August	5.43	4.82	4.79	4.83	4.65	4.67	4.88	4.34	4.58	5.04	4.62
September	5.02	4.97	4.90	4.94	4.46	4.74	4.83	4.24	4.49	4.89	4.67
October	4.92	4.97	4.84	4.80	4.59	4.85	4.73	4.37	4.53	4.92	4.65
November	4.79	4.46	4.64	4.55	4.65	4.93	4.64	4.31	4.48	4.73	4.33
December	4.49	4.56	4.51	4.75	4.61	4.80	4.53	4.22	4.41	4.71	3.70
10 Year Index-Linked Rate KORS											
January	3.01	2.00	2.11	2.21	2.61	2.07	1.88	1.73	1.48	2.24	1.60
February	2.94	1.94	2.16	2.30	2.53	1.81	1.90	1.81	1.54	2.27	1.29
March	2.89	1.90	2.06	2.34	2.55	1.88	1.76	1.99	1.65	2.18	0.76
April	2.80	1.74	2.08	2.55	2.45	1.90	1.94	1.83	1.65	2.61	1.12
May	2.83	1.96	2.15	2.61	2.58	1.74	2.10	1.71	1.96	2.59	1.48
June	2.81	1.93	2.13	2.56	2.35	1.59	2.17	1.67	1.94	2.73	1.77
July	2.67	1.93	2.14	2.57	2.46	1.67	2.12	1.66	1.92	2.68	1.61
August	2.55	2.20	2.25	2.45	2.37	1.89	2.04	1.63	1.80	2.37	1.64
September	2.59	2.32	2.29	2.56	2.24	1.99	1.95	1.49	1.76	2.01	1.69
October	2.66	2.26	2.33	2.55	2.42	2.08	1.83	1.89	1.89	1.99	2.38
November	2.39	2.03	2.32	2.42	2.39	2.16	1.85	1.64	1.87	1.70	3.44
December	2.11	1.99	2.20	2.65	2.30	1.97	1.74	1.27	1.96	1.80	3.59
20 Year Index-Linked rate KORT											
January	3.01	2.06	2.01	1.96	2.35	2.10	1.95	1.68	1.17	1.63	1.25
February	3.01	1.97	1.98	1.99	2.36	1.99	1.94	1.72	1.22	1.65	1.30
March	2.92	1.93	1.83	2.09	2.39	2.07	1.80	1.89	1.34	1.57	1.04
April	2.80	1.81	1.90	2.35	2.32	2.10	1.91	1.77	1.38	1.77	1.24
May	2.79	1.99	1.97	2.41	2.43	2.00	1.99	1.67	1.56	1.91	1.38
June	2.61	1.97	1.94	2.38	2.23	1.93	2.01	1.63	1.61	2.07	1.34
July	2.56	1.97	1.96	2.36	2.30	2.05	1.99	1.63	1.55	2.07	1.27
August	2.51	2.12	2.03	2.25	2.21	2.09	1.93	1.58	1.45	1.83	1.14
September	2.51	2.23	2.04	2.39	2.12	2.13	1.89	1.48	1.37	1.67	1.26
October	2.58	2.18	2.08	2.38	2.29	2.17	1.84	1.51	1.44	1.65	1.99
November	2.35	1.91	2.02	2.19	2.31	2.16	1.80	1.45	1.34	1.41	2.47
December	2.12	1.88	1.94	2.33	2.26	2.04	1.69	1.38	1.43	1.41	2.14

1 Working day average.
2 Discontinued from 6 December 2006.

Source: Bank of England: 020 7601 3644

Banking, insurance

23.13 Building societies[1,2]
United Kingdom

		1998[3]	1999[3]	2000[4]	2001	2002	2003	2004	2005	2006	2007
Number and balance sheets											
Societies on register (numbers)	KRNA	71	69	67	65	65	63	63	63	60	59
Share investors (thousands)	KRNB	21 195	21 774	22 237	20 311	20 724	20 897	20 734	22 090	22 396	23 038
Depositors (thousands)	KRNC	909	722	740	568	511	520	525	449	472	460
Borrowers (thousands)	KRND	3 136	3 044	3 107	2 750	2 688	2 679	2 749	2 822	2 857	2 941
Assets and liabilities (£ million)											
Liabilities:											
Shares	KRNE	103 289.8	109 137.6	119 298.5	119 815.2	132 373.0	142 456.9	153 844.0	171 935.0	188 943.0	206 782.5
Deposits and wholesale	KRNF	33 432.5	34 579.2	43 578.5	37 985.2	37 650.8	49 204.4	63 797.5	71 703.7	82 759.8	98 364.5
Taxation and other	KRNG	2 105.0	2 259.8	2 033.6	1 532.0	1 401.1	1 498.8	1 761.5	2 983.6	4 655.4	5 417.8
General reserves	KRNH	8 305.6	8 733.0	9 577.0	9 152.2	9 932.8	10 592.8	11 385.6	12 151.1	12 532.7	13 607.5
Other Capital	KRNI	1 551.4	1 529.9	1 861.7	1 391.7	1 684.8	2 510.3	3 574.8	4 534.9	5 528.3	6 099.8
Assets:											
Mortgages	KRNK	116 284.5	120 409.5	134 100.1	128 321.6	138 884.0	156 396.1	180 172.4	203 259.7	228 095.9	257 810.2
Investments and cash	KHVZ	28 343.0	31 207.9	37 900.8	37 158.1	39 201.8	44 500.4	47 810.8	51 475.6	55 102.9	60 694.6
Other	KRNN	11 386.7	5 523.1	5 746.2	5 895.3	6 367.0	6 838.4	8 163.1	10 490.3	11 220.4	11 767.3
Total	KRNJ	156 014.2	157 140.5	177 747.1	171 375.0	184 452.8	207 734.9	236 146.3	265 225.6	294 419.2	330 272.1
Current transactions (£ million)											
Mortgage advances	KRNU	21 988.3	23 997.9	28 233.6	29 320.0	33 077.0	43 392.4	51 089.0	50 059.4	52 327.5	..
Management expenses	KRNX	1 501.7	1 573.8	1 640.7	1 528.0	1 623.6	1 746.4	1 844.2	1 939.9	2 116.2	..

1 See chapter text.
2 The figures for each year relate to accounting years ending on dates between 1 February of that year and 31 January of the following year.
3 The societies which have converted to the banking sector, namely Cheltenham & Gloucester (August 1995), National & Provincial (August 1996), Alliance & Leicester (April 1997), Halifax (June 1997), Woolwich (July 1997), Bristol & West (July 1997), Northern Rock (October 1997), and Birmingham Midshires (April 1999) have been included in flow figures (using flows up to the date of conversion), but have been excluded from the end of year balances.

4 Bradford & Bingley, which converted to the banking sector in December 2000, is included within flow figures and the end of year balances.

Source: Financial Services Authority: 020 7066 1000

23.14 Consumer credit
United Kingdom

£ million

		1998	1999	2000	2001	2002	2003	2004	2005	2006	2007
Total amount outstanding	VZRD	106 341	121 547	135 168	150 802	169 209	180 649	198 856	211 038	212 835	221 687
Total net lending	VZQC	15 503	16 133	15 969	19 673	23 443	22 401	25 337	19 666	13 054	13 471
of which											
Credit cards	VZQS	4 858	5 676	6 686	6 229	7 579	8 710	9 998	6 166	1 951	2 251
Other	VZQT	10 647	10 457	9 284	13 445	15 867	13 692	15 340	13 499	11 102	11 221
Banks	AIKN	11 738	11 057	13 217	16 055	17 452	15 269	19 370	11 317	9 346	6 075
Building societies' class 3 loans	ALPY	–	12	112	63	180	177	172	238	217	260
Other consumer credit lenders	BM59	3 764	5 065	2 640	3 554	5 811	6 954	5 796	8 112	3 489	7 135
Total gross lending	VZQG	134 847	148 623	160 744	177 452	196 451	207 255	221 318	217 467	207 460	204 631

As from Dec 2006 the Bank of England has ceased to update the separate data on consumer credit provided by other specialist lenders, retailers and insurance companies previously contained in these tables. These categories have been merged into 'other consumer credit lenders'.

Source: Office for National Statistics: 01633 456635

23.15 End-year assets and liabilities of investment trust companies, unit trusts[1] and property unit trusts[2]

United Kingdom

£ million

		1997	1998	1999	2000	2001	2002	2003	2004	2005	2006	2007
Investment trust companies												
Short-term assets and liabilities (net):	CBPL	1 157	2 263	71	423	161	–	73	866	921	..	1 194
Cash and UK bank deposits	AHAG	1 577	2 647	1 227	2 202	2 513	1 821	1 346	1 756	1 483	1 785	1 731
Other short-term assets	CBPN	1 445	1 734	1 097	1 082	656	805	1 189	1 344	1 549	353	1 572
Short-term liabilities	-CBPS	-1 865	-2 118	-2 253	-2 861	-3 008	-2 626	-2 462	-2 234	-2 111	..	-2 109
Medium and long-term liabilities and capital:	-CBPO	-54 117	-49 985	-57 616	-60 412	-54 630	-38 054	-48 076	-48 627	-55 076	..	..
Issued share and loan capital	-CBPQ	-8 625	-8 837	-8 565	-8 934	-8 796	-8 711	-9 873	-8 210	-7 155	-5 492	-5 659
Foreign currency borrowing	-CBPR	-658	-607	-880	-994	-933	-780	-682	-607	-839	-1 043	-1 118
Other borrowing	-CBQA	-1 296	-1 723	-1 716	-2 503	-3 251	-2 246	-2 181	-1 728	-1 420	..	..
Reserves and provisions, etc	-AHBC	-43 538	-38 818	-46 455	-47 981	-41 650	-26 317	-35 340	-38 082	-38 082	-43 444	-49 354
Investments:	CBPM	53 076	46 313	56 491	59 948	54 822	37 748	48 035	47 212	53 265	50 052	55 608
British government securities	AHBF	1 052	815	1 217	821	645	471	303	466	769	533	715
UK company securities:												
Loan capital and preference shares	CBGZ	1 320	1 351	1 425	1 654	1 516	946	1 079	1 270	673	1 071	1 259
Ordinary and deferred shares	CBGY	29 082	24 729	28 010	33 456	30 338	19 475	23 292	23 941	25 037	22 870	23 034
Overseas company securities:												
Loan capital and preference shares	CBHA	1 165	768	979	963	1 143	458	603	682	937	741	1 038
Ordinary and deferred shares	AHCC	17 747	17 741	23 330	21 355	19 476	14 453	20 294	18 967	23 065	21 659	25 795
Other investments	CBPT	2 868	1 051	1 530	1 699	1 704	1 945	2 464	1 886	2 784	3 178	3 767
Unit trusts												
Short-term assets and liabilities:	CBPU	5 048	6 883	5 894	8 340	7 979	8 041	10 256	10 229	13 944	..	..
Cash and UK bank deposits	AGYE	4 731	6 020	4 797	6 969	5 748	5 321	5 243	6 302	7 740	12 336	16 443
Other short term assets	CBPW	869	1 343	1 545	2 319	2 763	3 072	5 990	4 390	7 420	6 990	9 036
Short-term liabilities	-CBPX	-552	-480	-448	-948	-532	-352	-977	-403	-1 210	..	3 232
Foreign currency borrowing	-AGYK	–	–	–	–	–	–	–	–	–	–	–
Investments:	CBPZ	144 038	162 929	213 553	222 844	204 899	210 002	245 516	269 064	351 645	420 153	457 729
British government securities	CBHT	3 087	3 771	3 627	4 693	4 690	7 077	9 125	9 768	25 181	31 603	32 120
UK company securities:												
Loan capital and preference shares	CBHU	6 494	9 290	13 322	14 654	16 318	21 152	23 972	22 467	29 293	29 876	30 626
Ordinary and deferred shares	RLIB	85 742	93 291	119 496	116 808	103 704	82 851	116 407	130 230	157 149	185 637	195 009
Overseas company securities:												
Loan capital and preference shares	CBHV	1 834	1 801	3 032	3 212	4 113	5 916	9 840	13 142	16 057	25 617	30 029
Ordinary and deferred shares	RLIC	42 898	51 119	70 256	79 601	71 329	63 152	75 074	81 034	105 443	127 409	142 211
Other assets	CBQE	2 518	3 657	3 820	3 876	4 800	9 997	11 098	12 801	18 522	20 011	27 734
Property unit trusts												
Short-term assets and liabilities (net)	AGVC	328	176	205	285	247	242	459	466	686	1 258	785
Property	CBQG	3 895	2 740	2 722	3 488	2 078	4 026	5 125	5 909	9 623	12 781	12 480
Other assets	AGVL	168	202	436	380	151	677	373	1 366	1 864	2 713	1 648
Long-term borrowing	-AGVM	-247	-106	-75	-391	-90	-75	-76	-63	-250	-90	-158

Note: Assets are shown as positive: liabilities as negative.
1 Including open ended investment companies (OEICs).
2 Investments are at market value.

Source: Office for National Statistics: 01633 812789

23.16 Self-administered pension funds: market value of assets

United Kingdom

End year

£ million

		1995	1996	1997	1998	1999	2000	2001	2002	2003	2004	2005	2006	2007
Total pension funds[1]														
Total net assets	AHVA	508 581	543 879	656 874	699 191	812 228	765 199	711 572	610 441	692 694	761 066	914 955	1 010 794	1 023 979
Short-term assets	RYIQ	26 114	31 521	35 368	39 005	32 703	36 638	31 337	30 700	46 091	57 476	73 649	98 691	99 681
British government securities	AHVK	52 659	57 783	80 533	91 084	98 882	92 458	83 754	84 461	88 803	87 579	94 325	104 910	113 617
UK local authority long-term debt	AHVO	83	89	156	183	133	177	125	42	8	4	4	2	5
Overseas government securities	AHVT	11 721	11 800	13 079	15 493	16 684	19 206	20 383	16 031	16 340	15 075	19 037	21 776	22 434
UK company securities														
Ordinary shares	AHVP	256 625	276 001	339 687	334 648	357 230	299 318	260 696	186 437	186 426	180 561	199 199	208 473	152 048
Other	AHVQ	7 064	6 180	5 618	8 168	9 258	16 978	22 301	30 450	37 082	43 027	48 065	54 902	57 541
Overseas company securities														
Ordinary shares	AHVR	82 164	84 163	104 187	108 884	148 335	135 514	127 893	104 392	125 740	140 282	183 060	192 978	169 598
Other	AHVS	1 184	4 909	3 851	3 842	5 099	12 736	11 781	11 386	12 475	15 996	20 502	31 536	45 470
UK loans and mortgages	RLDQ	34	83	160	22	14	7	3	–	35	44	6	6	12
UK land, property and ground rent	AHWA	21 317	21 637	24 176	24 355	31 107	32 945	30 617	31 658	30 619	30 552	31 613	34 394	30 304
Authorised unit trust units	AHVU	15 212	21 767	21 979	30 596	33 731	34 587	38 083	36 530	62 029	67 482	86 660	94 638	134 176
Property unit trusts	AHVW	2 485	2 666	3 219	3 211	5 498	4 835	5 280	5 869	6 761	10 444	16 687	20 689	16 757
Other assets	RKPL	36 352	30 628	32 978	47 136	82 273	90 841	90 139	82 490	107 229	152 170	..	..	..
Total liabilities	GQFX	4 412	5 347	8 118	7 436	8 719	11 041	10 819	10 005	26 944	39 626	..	..	..

1 These figures cover funded schemes only and therefore exclude the main superannuation arrangements in the central government sector.

Source: Office for National Statistics: 01633 812726

23.17 Insurance companies: balance sheet market values
United Kingdom

End year

£ million

		1998	1999	2000	2001	2002	2003	2004	2005	2006	2007
Long-term insurance companies											
Assets											
Total current assets (gross)	RYEW	46 165	56 360	62 937	63 855	58 122	58 518	63 407	72 754	77 748	101 780
Agents' and reinsurance balances (net)	AHNY	1 383	508	384	620	6 373	4 720	3 755	3 933	5 100	984
Other debtors[1]	RKPN	18 210	18 613	21 045	27 285	34 391	35 414	30 504	27 591	52 253	60 063
British government securities	AHNJ	127 903	126 223	116 734	119 513	131 305	142 920	157 019	161 906	161 641	158 694
UK local authority securities etc	AHNN	1 722	1 456	1 170	1 407	1 427	1 547	2 044	1 840	1 614	998
UK company securities[2]	RKPO	438 666	539 834	557 293	505 691	443 535	468 910	487 034	601 681	643 433	664 717
Overseas company securities	RKPP	82 122	120 665	107 439	127 259	110 738	110 193	130 098	165 452	194 997	234 388
Overseas government securities	AHNS	17 515	18 494	18 004	21 285	19 762	20 561	20 161	16 065	21 078	25 787
Loans and mortgages	RKPQ	11 027	10 914	9 687	10 048	10 994	12 107	12 917	13 502	15 330	13 655
UK land, property and ground rent	AHNX	45 903	50 387	49 705	53 726	52 658	57 174	60 502	61 037	58 918	66 169
Overseas land, property and ground rent	RGCP	252	206	1 975	498	158	184	94	27	61	–
Other investments	RKPR	5 654	8 334	8 385	7 420	9 513	17 985	26 480	18 146	27 783	31 401
Total	RFXN	796 522	951 994	954 760	938 609	878 979	930 233	994 015	1 143 934	1 259 956	1 358 636
Net value of direct investment in:											
Non-insurance subsidiaries and associate companies in the United Kingdom	RYET	3 035	3 045	6 133	4 486	4 577	4 191	3 971	8 390	13 016	9 186
UK associate and subsidiary insurance companies and insurance holding companies	RYEU	148	2 245	3 586	4 206	4 569	5 054	3 473	2 528	6 114	7 578
Overseas subsidiaries and associates	RYEV	1 087	3 638	4 002	5 581	5 463	6 330	2 181	4 455	3 341	3 832
Total assets	RKBI	800 792	960 922	968 481	952 882	893 588	945 808	1 003 640	1 159 307	1 282 427	1 379 232
Liabilities											
Borrowing:											
Borrowing from UK banks	RGDF	3 252	6 064	8 272	8 790	4 958	4 164	5 358	5 037	2 862	3 795
Other UK borrowing	RGDE	1 040	3 070	2 823	5 350	7 406	10 923	8 385	9 036	9 542	6 705
Borrowing from overseas	RGDD	148	159	38	81	800	530	793	1 151	1 965	1 926
Long-term business:											
Funds	RKDC	669 301	800 184	838 485	831 051	794 177	824 766	873 071	1 037 658	1 125 221	1 205 183
Claims admitted but not paid	RKBM	1 712	2 032	2 249	2 547	3 234	3 699	3 579	3 481	3 513	3 848
Provision for taxation net of amounts receivable:											
UK authorities	RYPI	5 443	6 344	5 381	3 951	2 803	4 055	4 881	8 225	7 908	7 457
Overseas authorities	RYPJ	67	314	67	45	–20	2	–13	–2	199	5
Provision for recommended dividends	RYPK	359	201	183	87	32	27	93	22	13	27
Other creditors and liabilities	RYPL	12 509	17 042	19 031	18 468	23 261	15 870	16 738	16 907	33 192	39 527
Excess of assets over above liabilities:											
Excess of value of assets over liabilities in respect of long-term funds	RKBR	96 456	116 951	79 173	63 337	36 517	62 546	65 641	59 132	71 017	75 066
Minority interests in UK subsidiary companies	RKTI	..	25	..	..	..	1	267	..	..	192
Shareholders' capital and reserves in respect of general business	RKBS	6 299	6 139	10 287	17 044	18 629	15 698	20 719	18 717	27 315	35 855
Other reserves including profit and loss account balances	RKBT	4 206	2 396	2 492	2 130	1 791	3 527	4 129	–57	–320	–354
Total liabilities	RKBI	800 792	960 922	968 481	952 882	893 588	945 808	1 003 640	1 159 307	1 282 427	1 379 232

23.17
continued

Insurance companies: balance sheet market values
United Kingdom
End year

£ million

		1998	1999	2000	2001	2002	2003	2004	2005	2006	2007
Other than long-term insurance companies											
Assets											
Total current assets (gross)	RYME	8 524	10 468	8 772	12 264	17 671	20 036	29 258	26 561	24 942	25 810
Agents' and reinsurance balances (net)	AHMX	10 528	12 177	8 362	7 941	9 492	9 890	9 858	7 996	10 782	9 932
Other debtors[1]	RKPS	6 277	7 059	7 179	9 056	14 437	13 255	12 618	13 310	16 881	20 351
British government securities	AHMJ	16 409	15 938	14 561	15 064	18 390	19 645	19 662	19 818	19 296	16 026
UK local authority securities etc	AHMN	14	10	8	6	10	10	49	44	..	3
UK company securities[2]	RKPT	18 440	18 800	18 585	17 101	15 362	15 153	20 561	21 879	22 983	23 812
Overseas company securities	RKPU	8 676	6 284	8 190	6 402	7 394	7 124	11 520	12 645	18 636	14 773
Overseas government securities	AHMS	10 459	7 980	6 849	7 134	7 156	5 720	6 662	7 341	8 035	4 869
Loans and mortgages	RKPV	1 335	1 070	1 429	1 348	1 063	1 400	2 412	3 040	3 319	3 684
UK land, property and ground rent	AHMW	1 146	1 085	1 069	860	805	859	893	1 470	1 569	1 870
Overseas land, property and ground rent	RYNK	107	83	45	4	1	4	5	13	137	116
Other investments	RKPW	2 366	2 638	2 294	1 608	2 182	1 408	1 858	2 083	2 010	1 882
Total	RKAL	84 281	84 027	77 343	78 789	93 965	94 504	115 356	116 200	128 590	123 128
Net value of direct investment in:											
Non-insurance subsidiaries and associate companies in the United Kingdom	RYNR	5 553	7 074	7 038	10 456	11 706	13 408	19 028	20 530	20 111	21 954
UK associate and subsidiary insurance companies and insurance holding companies	RYNS	6 424	5 617	5 400	8 837	7 190	2 918	2 280	6 071	4 745	6 936
Overseas subsidiaries and associates	RYNT	14 239	17 775	15 993	14 260	9 014	5 718	5 507	6 446	9 657	9 445
Total assets	RKBY	110 497	114 493	105 774	112 342	121 875	116 548	142 171	149 247	163 103	161 463
Liabilities											
Borrowing:											
Borrowing from UK banks	RYMB	1 825	1 392	783	481	1 384	2 046	4 519	893	3 148	675
Other UK borrowing	RYMC	1 551	3 186	4 239	10 621	10 472	9 342	10 261	11 080	10 445	10 885
Borrowing from overseas	RYMD	1 600	3 045	1 867	1 964	2 916	2 918	2 476	2 817	5 459	7 037
General business technical reserves	RKCT	60 775	59 455	60 236	60 995	62 776	63 463	67 241	71 710	77 221	71 146
Long-term business:											
Funds	RKTF	–	–	–	–	–	–	–	–	–	–
Claims admitted but not paid	RKTK	–	–	–	–	–	–	–	–	–	–
Provision for taxation net of amounts receivable:											
UK authorities	RYPO	1 197	939	874	594	941	834	1 094	1 796	2 376	2 259
Overseas authorities	RYPP	11	11	11	7	5	84	24	5	10	5
Provision for recommended dividends	RYPQ	1 318	1 817	2 682	1 957	958	1 082	1 311	5	270	222
Other creditors and liabilities	RYPR	3 793	4 981	6 293	6 410	8 025	9 567	10 817	10 718	16 226	22 069
Excess of assets over above liabilities:											
Excess of value of assets over liabilities in respect of long-term funds	RKCG	–	–	–	–	–	–	–			–
Minority interests in UK subsidiary companies	RKCH	68	29	33	276	4	6	6	..	..	599
Shareholders' capital and reserves in respect of general business	RKCI	34 397	35 372	24 699	26 190	31 982	25 153	39 695	43 264	42 186	38 145
Other reserves including profit and loss account balances	RKCJ	4 215	4 265	4 056	2 847	2 411	2 053	4 727	6 959	5 762	8 421
Total liabilities	RKBY	110 497	114 493	105 774	112 342	121 875	116 548	142 171	149 247	163 103	161 463

1 Including outstanding interest, dividends and rents (net).
2 Including authorised unit trust units.

Source: Office for National Statistics: 01633 812726

Banking, insurance

23.18 Individual insolvencies
United Kingdom

		1998	1999	2000	2001	2002	2003	2004	2005	2006	2007	2008
England and Wales												
Bankruptcies[1]	AIHW	19 647	21 611	21 550	23 477	24 292	28 021	35 898	47 291	62 956	64 480	67 428
Individual voluntary arrangements[2,3]	AIHI	4 902	7 195	7 978	6 298	6 295	7 583	10 752	20 293	44 332	42 165	39 116
Total	AIHK	24 549	28 806	29 528	29 775	30 587	35 604	46 650	67 584	107 288	106 645	106 544
Scotland												
Sequestrations[4]	KRHA	3 016	3 195	2 965	3 048	3 215	3 328	3 297	4 965	5 430	6 219	12 322
Protected Trust Deeds	GJ2I	1 449	2 144	2 801	3 779	5 174	5 452	6 024	6 881	8 208	7 595	7 542
Total	GJ2J	4 465	5 339	5 766	6 827	8 389	8 780	9 321	11 846	13 638	13 814	19 864
Northern Ireland												
Bankruptcies[5]	KRHB	394	401	349	292	334	517	666	821	1 035	898	1 079
Individual voluntary arrangements[3,6]	KJRK	123	172	267	176	207	318	449	633	774	440	559
Total	KRHD	517	573	616	468	541	835	1 115	1 454	1 809	1 338	1 638

1 Comprises receiving and administration orders under the Bankruptcy Act 1914 and bankruptcy orders under the Insolvency Act 1986. Orders later consolidated or rescinded are included in these figures.
2 Introduced under the Insolvency Act 1986.
3 For statistical purposes deeds of arrangement are now included with individual voluntary arrangements.
4 Sequestrations awarded but not brought into operation are included in these figures.

5 Comprises bankruptcy adjudication orders, arrangement protection orders and orders for the administration of estates of deceased insolvents. Orders later set aside or dismissed are included in these figures.
6 Introduced under the Insolvency Northern Ireland order 1989.

Source: Insolvency Service: 020 7637 6504/6443

23.19 Company insolvencies
United Kingdom

		1998	1999	2000	2001	2002	2003	2004	2005	2006	2007	2008
England and Wales												
Compulsory liquidations	AIHR	5 216	5 209	4 925	4 675	6 231	5 234	4 584	5 233	5 418	5 165	5 494
Creditors' voluntary liquidations	AIHS	7 987	9 071	9 392	10 297	10 075	8 950	7 608	7 660	7 719	7 342	10 041
Total	AIHQ	13 203	14 280	14 317	14 972	16 306	14 184	12 192	12 893	13 137	12 507	15 535
Scotland												
Compulsory liquidations	KRGA	338	364	344	378	556	436	431	420	416	439	437
Creditors' voluntary liquidations	KRGB	228	208	239	224	232	195	190	149	133	100	87
Total	KRGC	566	572	583	602	788	631	621	569	549	539	524
Northern Ireland[1]												
Compulsory liquidations	KRGD	..	..	..	..	49	95	76	85	78	122	158
Creditors' voluntary liquidations	KRGE	..	..	..	..	53	47	45	53	50	42	51
Total	KRGF	..	..	..	..	102	142	121	138	128	164	209

1 Prior to 2002, the quality of the statistics on company liquidations in Northern Ireland are not robust enough and have been removed from this table.

Source: Insolvency Service: 020 7637 6504/6443

23.20 Selected financial statistics[1]

£ million

	Building societies Advances[2]		Unit trusts[3]	Net equity of households in life assurance and pension funds' reserves
	Not seasonally adjusted	Seasonally adjusted		
Amount outstanding as at 31 Dec	AHIF		AGXB	
2007	266 897		468 063	
Transactions	AAMN	AHHU	AGXE	NBYD
2004	22 078	21 886	5 718	44 942
2005	20 419	20 439	12 030	53 672
2006	27 057	27 147	20 678	55 989
2007	24 975	24 861	3 873	65 070
2007 Q4	5 611	6 059	-1 620	3 004
2008 Q1	..	..	410	5 682
Q2	..	..	1 919	12 655
Q3	..	..	-4 816	7 837
2007 Dec	1 323	1 625	-858	..
2008 Jan	..	..	-745	..
Feb	..	..	778	..
Mar	..	..	377	..
Apr	..	..	2 230	..
May	..	..	75	..
Jun	..	..	-386	..
Jul	..	..	-2 460	..
Aug	..	..	-716	..
Sep	..	..	-1 640	..
Oct	..	..	-1 585	..
Nov	..	..	-269	..

	Banks[4]				Consumer credit[5]		of which Credit cards[5]	
	UK private sector deposits		Lending to the private sector					
	Sterling (Not seasonally adjusted)	Other currencies	Sterling (Not seasonally adjusted)	Other currencies	Not seasonally adjusted	Seasonally adjusted	Not seasonally adjusted	Seasonally adjusted
Amount outstanding as at 31 Dec	AEAS	AGAK	AECE	AECK	VZRD	VZRI	VZRE	VZRJ
2008	1 670 430	483 258	2 077 656	657 846	233 565	..	..	..
Transactions					Net lending	Net lending	Net lending	Net lending
	AEAT	AEAZ	AECF		VZQC	RLMH	VZQS	VZQX
2005	137 241	39 735	137 555		19 666	19 801	6 166	6 109
2006	150 052	58 434	191 019		13 054	13 276	1 951	2 063
2007	155 314	71 345	213 352		13 471	13 206	2 251	2 060
2008	231 886	-39 476	233 509		11 267	..	4 029	..
2008 Q2	55 465	-24 499	93 831		3 855	3 190	1 577	1 185
Q3	45 570	-28 570	57 306		2 324	2 201	1 524	1 154
Q4	98 695	-25 468	31 958		1 788	..	1 583	..
2009 Q1	..	..	..		-838	..	-804	..
2008 May	10 284	-3 956	4 208		1 536	1 182	673	603
Jun	41 898	-29 848	58 380		888	1 055	588	429
Jul	-2 398	-2 463	9 085		671	853	195	248
Aug	27 653	-4 452	25 523		406	1 017	735	627
Sep	20 315	-21 655	22 698		1 246	330	594	279
Oct	54 688	8 645	50 731		497	754	-23	405
Nov	23 838	15 180	-4 902		531	751	677	396
Dec	20 169	-49 293	-13 871		760	..	929	..
2009 Jan	..	..	..		-142	..	-529	..
Feb	..	..	..		-755	..	-219	..
Mar	..	..	..		59	..	-55	..
Apr	..	..	..		762	..	520	..

1 For further details see *Financial Statistics,* Tables 1.2E, 3.2B, 4.2A, 4.3A, 4.3B, 5.2D, 6.2A, 10.5D.
2 Total administered by the Department for National Savings.
3 Including open ended investment companies (OEICs).
4 Monthly figures relate to calendar months.

5 Data have been revised back to February 2003 due to the inclusion of some additional other specialist lenders and the removal of some non-resident based securitisation vehicles.

Sources: Office for National Statistics;
Department for National Savings;
Building Societies Commission;
Association of Unit Trusts and Investment Funds;
Bank of England;
Department for Business, Enterprise and Regulatory Reform

23.21 Selected interest rates, exchange rates and security prices

	Selected retail banks' base rate	Average discount rate for 91 day Treasury bills	Inter bank 3 months bid rate	Inter bank 3 months offer rate	British government securities 20 years yield[1]	Exchange rate US spot
	ZCMG	AJNB	HSAJ	HSAK	AJLX	LUSS
2004 Dec	4.75	4.69	4.81	4.84	4.44	1.9199
2005 Jan	4.75	4.65	4.79	4.81	4.44	1.8859
Feb	4.75	4.73	4.87	4.90	4.53	1.9257
Mar	4.75	4.76	4.90	4.93	4.74	1.8904
Apr	4.75	4.69	4.86	4.88	4.60	1.9100
May	4.75	4.65	4.79	4.81	4.41	1.8225
Jun	4.75	4.52	4.69	4.73	4.29	1.7925
Jul	4.75	4.43	4.54	4.56	4.33	1.7607
Aug	4.50	4.38	4.52	4.54	4.34	1.7990
Sep	4.50	4.40	4.52	4.55	4.26	1.7688
Oct	4.50	4.42	4.54	4.56	4.36	1.7700
Nov	4.50	4.40	4.55	4.58	4.25	1.7304
Dec	4.50	4.43	4.57	4.59	4.14	1.7166
2006 Jan	4.50	4.40	4.52	4.54	3.81	1.7775
Feb	4.50	4.39	4.51	4.53	3.96	1.7511
Mar	4.50	4.41	4.54	4.56	4.15	1.7345
Apr	4.50	4.45	4.60	4.63	4.32	1.8179
May	4.50	4.51	4.66	4.68	4.43	1.8712
Jun	4.50	4.54	4.71	4.73	4.46	1.8494
Jul	4.50	4.58	4.73	4.74	4.45	1.8671
Aug	4.75	4.77	4.94	4.95	4.42	1.9018
Sep	4.75	4.87	5.02	5.05	4.29	1.8682
Oct	4.75	4.98	5.14	5.16	4.35	1.9073
Nov	5.00	5.04	5.20	5.22	4.27	1.9670
Dec	5.00	5.11	5.26	5.29	4.33	1.9570
2007 Jan	5.25	5.37	5.54	5.55	4.51	1.9574
Feb	5.25	5.31	5.48	5.50	4.59	1.9600
Mar	5.25	5.38	5.56	5.58	4.52	1.9613
Apr	5.25	5.47	5.66	5.70	4.72	1.9997
May	5.50	5.59	5.76	5.78	..	1.9782
Jun	5.50	5.77	5.93	5.98	..	2.0064
Jul	5.75	5.75	6.00	6.02	..	2.0322
Aug	5.75	5.77	6.55	6.65	4.80	2.0171
Sep	5.75	5.61	6.18	6.28	4.74	2.0374
Oct	5.75	5.57	6.17	6.25	4.74	2.0774
Nov	5.75	5.44	6.53	6.58	4.59	2.0561
Dec	5.50	5.24	5.95	5.95	4.59	1.9909
2008 Jan	5.50	5.01	5.50	5.58	4.46	1.9882
Feb	5.25	4.98	5.68	5.72	4.62	1.9892
Mar	5.25	4.77	5.95	6.02	4.54	1.9875
Apr	5.00	..	5.76	5.84	4.73	1.9803
May	5.00	..	5.80	5.87	4.85	1.9762
Jun	5.00	5.10	5.88	5.94	5.03	1.9901
Jul	5.00	5.09	5.75	5.79	4.94	1.9810
Aug	5.00	4.51	5.70	5.75	4.74	1.8237
Sep	5.00	4.74	6.15	6.30	4.66	1.7821
Oct	4.50	3.68	5.85	6.00	4.76	1.6158
Nov	3.00	1.99	3.85	4.10	4.69	1.5345
Dec	2.00	1.29	2.75	2.90	4.15	1.4376
2009 Jan	1.50	0.91	2.00	2.25	4.28	1.4416

1 Average of working days.

Source: Bank of England

23.22 Mergers and acquisitions in the UK by UK companies: category of expenditure

£ million

	Number of companies acquired	Total[1]	Cash Independent companies	Subsidiaries	Issues of ordinary shares[2]	Issues of fixed interest securities[2]
	AIHA	DUCM	DWVW	DWVX	AIHD	AIHE
1998	635	29 525	10 471	5 298	13 160	595
1999	493	26 163	12 605	3 615	9 592	351
2000	587	106 916	33 906	6 168	65 570	1 272
2001	492	28 994	8 489	6 704	12 356	1 445
2002	430	25 236	9 574	7 991	6 780	891
2003	558	18 679	8 956	7 183	1 667	873
2004	741	31 408	12 080	7 822	10 338	1 168
2005	769	25 134	13 425	8 510	2 768	431
2006	779	28 511	..	8 131	..	335
2007	869	26 778	13 671	6 507	4 909	1 691
1998 Q4	162	6 586	2 090	1 181	3 255	59
1999 Q1	117	8 735	2 299	625	5 735	76
Q2	127	7 212	4 893	728	1 509	82
Q3	145	6 479	2 618	1 682	2 098	81
Q4	104	3 737	2 795	580	250	112
2000 Q1	139	33 739	17 483	1 136	14 960	160
Q2	133	21 469	4 224	1 881	15 045	319
Q3	163	16 852	6 934	2 237	7 367	314
Q4	152	34 856	5 265	914	28 198	479
2001 Q1	131	6 181	2 606	2 255	982	300
Q2	108	4 890	1 679	2 214	555	442
Q3	129	16 079	3 457	1 526	10 649	447
Q4	124	1 844	747	709	170	218
2002 Q1	83	3 853	2 201	1 298	104	250
Q2	120	4 228	801	3 179	78	170
Q3	88	6 333	4 695	1 426	184	28
Q4	139	10 822	1 877	2 088	6 414	443
2003 Q1	107	3 857	1 003	1 892	609	353
Q2	122	3 753	1 437	1 713	258	345
Q3	153	4 700	2 495	1 919	153	133
Q4	176	6 369	4 021	1 659	647	42
2004 Q1	151	12 639	2 819	655	8 807	358
Q2	169	5 359	2 555	1 682	822	300
Q3	211	8 109	3 469	4 026	240	374
Q4	210	5 301	3 237	1 459	469	136
2005 Q1	166	3 516	1 334	1 918	166	98
Q2	215	8 983	4 869	2 715	1 285	114
Q3	211	7 287	4 106	1 878	1 207	96
Q4	177	5 348	3 116	1 999	110	123
2006 Q1	207	6 969	4 069	2 427	431	42
Q2	208	4 222	3 298	527	384	13
Q3	163	11 376	..	4 580	..	216
Q4	201	5 944	4 690	597	593	64
2007 Q1	191	5 649	2 824	276	2 407	142
Q2	212	10 122	3 605	4 361	1 874	282
Q3	258	7 846	5 545	833	358	1 110
Q4	208	3 161	1 697	1 037	270	157
2008 Q1	167	4 512	2 566	906	772	268
Q2	174	9 270	8 697	383	150	40
Q3	79	3 902	3 260	304	285	53

Missing data for any series have been suppressed to avoid the disclosure of information relating to individual enterprises.
1 Includes deferred payments.
2 Issued to the vendor as payment.

Source: Office for National Statistics

Service industry

Chapter 24

Service industry

Annual Business Inquiry

(Tables 24.1, 24.3 and 24.4)

For details of the Annual Business Inquiry, see the text accompanying Table **22.1.**

Retail trade: index numbers of value and volume

(Table 24.2)

The main purpose of the Retail Sales Inquiry (RSI) is to provide up-to-date information on short period movements in the level of retail sales. In principle, the RSI covers the retail activity of every business classified in the retail sector (Division 52 of the 2003 Standard Industrial Classification) in Great Britain. A business will be classified to the retail sector if its main activity is one of the individual 4 digit SIC categories within Division 52. The retail activity of a business is then defined by its retail turnover, that is, the sale of all retail goods (note that petrol, for example, is not a retail good).

The Retail Sales Index is compiled from the information returned to the statutory inquiries into the distribution and services sector. The inquiry is addressed to a stratified sample of 5,000 businesses classified to the retail sector, the stratification being by 'type of store' (the individual 4 digit SIC categories within Division 52) and by size. The sample structure is designed to ensure that the inquiry estimates are as accurate as possible. In terms of the selection, this means that:

- each of the individual 4 digit SIC categories are represented, their coverage depending upon the relative size of the category and the variability of the data

- within each 4 digit SIC category, the larger retailers tend to be fully enumerated with decreasing proportions of medium and smaller retailers

The structure of the inquiry is updated periodically, by reference to the more comprehensive results of the Annual Business Inquiry (ABI). The monthly inquiry also incorporates a rotation element for the smallest retailers. This helps to spread the burden more fairly, as well as improving the representativeness between successive benchmarks.

During 2003, the Retail Sales Index was rebased using detailed information from the 2000 Annual Business Inquiry. The reference year is currently set at 2000=100. A review of

the retail Sales Inquiry was published in October 2008. The findings are available at: www.statistics.gov.uk/StatBase/Product.asp?vlnk=13527

The latest summary statistics are published each month by First Release. More disaggregated indices (not seasonally adjusted) are published each month in the Business Monitor SDM28. See: www.statistics.gov.uk/rsi

24.1 Retail businesses[1]
United Kingdom

		2002	2003	2004	2005	2006
Number of businesses	ZABE	207 513	202 604	200 606	201 419	200 004
Total turnover[2]	ZABL	265 577	278 373	288 716	295 952	310 150
Value Added Tax in total turnover	ZABM	26 907	28 505	29 420	29 923	31 255
Retail turnover[2]	ZABN	238 456	250 849	258 903	264 427	277 298
Non-retail turnover[2]	ZABO	27 121	27 524	29 812	31 525	32 852
Other income						
Value of commercial insurance claims received	ZABP	105	65	40	76	81
Subsidies received from UK government sources and the EC	ZAEN	4	5	10	16	10
Employment costs[3]	ZABQ	29 779	31 367	32 806	34 729	36 035
Gross wages and salaries	ZABR	26 933	28 294	29 481	30 938	32 197
Redundancy and severance payments	ZABS	130	134	158	251	164
Employers' National Insurance contributions	ZABT	1 805	1 991	2 142	2 282	2 393
Contributions to pension funds	ZABU	911	948	1 026	1 258	1 280
Stocks						
Increase during year	ZABV	1 284	978	957	726	887
Value at end of year	ZABW	22 400	23 024	23 527	24 211	25 120
Total turnover[3] divided by end-year stocks (Quotient)	ZABX	10.7	10.9	11.0	11.0	11.1
Purchases of goods, materials and services[3]	ZABY	185 875	194 169	199 773	205 399	214 312
Goods bought for resale without processing	ZABZ	155 608	161 304	165 667	169 676	175 971
Energy and water products for own consumption	ZACA	1 918	2 048	2 191	2 522	3 048
Goods and materials	ZACB	3 845	3 917	4 166	4 271	4 587
Hiring, leasing or renting of plant, machinery and vehicles	ZACC	924	946	727	576	602
Commercial insurance premiums	ZACD	827	1 001	1 061	1 034	937
Road transport services	ZACE	2 137	2 545	2 557	2 737	2 499
Telecommunication services	ZACF	561	624	626	607	571
Computer and related services	ZACG	756	765	915	816	829
Advertising and marketing services	ZACH	3 047	3 378	3 298	3 540	3 601
Other services	ZACI	16 252	17 642	18 565	19 620	21 667
Taxes, duties and levies	ZACJ	4 576	4 715	4 896	5 990	6 361
National non-domestic (business) rates	ZACK	3 726	3 859	3 937	4 336	4 703
Other amounts paid for taxes, duties and levies	ZACL	850	855	958	1 654	1 658
Capital expenditure						
Cost of acquisitions	ZACM	9 355	8 776	9 936	10 138	10 065
Proceeds from disposals	ZACN	1 240	1 328	1 590	1 516	1 761
Net capital expenditure	ZACO	8 115	7 448	8 346	8 622	8 304
Amount included in acquisitions for assets under finance leasing arrangements	ZACP	587	304	332	303	443
Work of a capital nature carried out by own staff (included in acquisitions)	ZACQ	128	142	149	176	189
Gross margin						
Amount	ZACR	83 708	88 904	93 830	95 667	102 417
As a percentage of adjusted turnover[4]	ZACS	*34.9*	*35.6*	*36.2*	*36.0*	*36.7*
Approximate gross value added at basic prices	ZACT	53 545	56 104	59 764	60 020	64 157

Service industry

24.1 Retail businesses[1]
United Kingdom

£ million

		2002	2003	2004	2005	2006
Total turnover	ZABL	265 577	278 373	288 716	295 952	310 150
Retail turnover	ZABN	238 456	250 849	258 903	264 427	277 298
1 Fruit (including fresh, chilled, dried, frozen, canned and processed)	DSSX	3 997	4 507	4 499	4 657	5 279
2 Vegetables (including fresh, chilled, dried, frozen, canned and processed)	DSSY	6 871	8 354	8 470	9 205	9 077
3 Meat (including fresh, chilled, smoked, frozen, canned and processed)	DSSZ	11 671	13 505	13 727	13 520	14 876
4 Fish, crustaceans and molluscs (including fresh, chilled, frozen, canned and processed)	DSTA	2 299	2 549	2 671	2 866	2 858
5 Bakery products and cereals (including rice and pasta products)	DSTC	9 661	12 314	11 880	12 967	14 151
6 Sugar, jam, honey, chocolate and confectionery (including ice-cream)	DSTD	6 469	6 446	6 534	6 406	7 528
7 Alcoholic drink	DSTE	11 301	12 297	12 931	13 099	14 035
8 Non-alcoholic beverages (including tea, coffee, fruit drinks and vegetable drinks)	DSTF	6 476	6 713	7 386	7 514	7 379
9 Tobacco (excluding smokers requisites, eg pipes, lighters, etc)	DSTG	9 016	9 204	9 020	8 960	9 139
10 Milk, cheese and eggs (including yoghurts and cream)	DSTH	7 233	7 390	7 995	8 356	8 957
11 Oils and fats (including butter and margarine)	DSTI	1 222	1 162	1 287	1 329	1 295
12 Food products not elsewhere classified (including sauces, herbs, spices and soups)	DSTJ	9 185	4 112	4 399	4 327	4 572
13 Pharmaceutical products	DSTK	2 911	2 963	2 987	3 090	3 370
14 National Health Receipts	DSTL	7 740	8 647	9 006	9 673	9 966
15 Other medical products and therapeutic appliances and equipment	DSTN	2 753	3 122	3 388	3 387	3 758
16 Other appliances, articles and products for personal care	DSTO	9 611	10 698	11 111	11 405	12 314
17 Other articles of clothing, accessories for making clothing	DSTP	1 293	1 933	2 089	2 452	2 834
18 Garments	DSTQ	28 331	29 691	30 375	31 294	31 654
19 Footwear (excluding sports shoes)	DSTR	5 270	5 622	5 904	6 037	6 559
20 Travel goods and other personal effects not elsewhere classified	DSTT	1 007	1 175	1 120	1 124	1 332
21 Household textiles (including furnishing fabrics, curtains, etc)	DSTV	3 656	3 799	3 890	3 700	3 848
22 Household and personal appliances whether electric or not	DSUA	6 580	6 776	6 798	6 957	6 956
23 Glassware, tableware and household utensils (including non-electric)	DSUB	2 823	2 843	2 743	3 124	3 024
24 Furniture and furnishings	DSUC	12 094	13 285	13 493	13 620	13 998
25 Audio and visual equipment (including radios, televisions and video recorders)	DSUE	4 781	4 818	5 130	5 646	6 211
26 Recording material for pictures and sound (including audio and video tapes, blank and pre-recorded records, etc)	DSUG	3 591	3 788	4 488	4 366	4 000
27 Information processing equipment (including printers, software, calculators and typewriters)	DSUL	3 056	3 077	3 743	3 600	3 704
28 Decorating and DIY supplies	DSUM	6 548	6 631	7 427	6 928	5 652
29 Tools and equipment for house and garden	DSUN	3 007	3 452	2 838	2 983	3 187
30 Books	DSUP	2 752	2 748	3 004	2 646	3 017
31 Newspapers and periodicals	DSUQ	3 709	4 067	4 053	4 048	4 244
32 Stationery and drawing materials and miscellaneous printed matter	DSUW	3 864	3 824	3 989	4 201	4 583
33 Carpets and other floor coverings (excluding bathroom mats, rush and door mats)	DSUX	3 411	3 757	3 386	3 526	3 458
34 Photographic and cinematographic equipment and optical instruments	DSUZ	1 402	1 670	1 842	2 052	2 078
35 Telephone and telefax equipment (including mobile phones)	DSVA	2 238	2 293	3 272	3 476	3 480
36 Jewellery, silverware and plate; watches and clocks	DSVB	4 387	4 312	4 681	4 697	5 347
37 Works of art and antiques (including furniture, floor coverings and jewellery)	DSVF	1 509	1 493	1 619	1 720	1 568
38 Equipment and accessories for sport, camping, recreation and musical instruments	DSVH	3 624	3 803	3 732	3 612	4 431
39 Spare part and accessories for all types of vehicle and sales of bicycles	DSVI	1 082	572	610	556	768
40 Games, toys, hobbies (including video game software, video game computers that plug into the tv, video-games cassettes and CD-ROMs)	DSVM	5 468	5 962	5 920	5 745	5 933
41 Other goods not elsewhere classified (including sale of new postage stamps and sales of liquid and solid fuels)	DSVN	3 359	3 134	2 884	2 623	3 861
42 Non-durable household goods (including household cleaning, maintenance products) and paper products and other non-durable household goods	DSVO	4 405	5 017	5 429	5 291	4 809
43 Natural or artificial plants and flowers	DSVQ	3 266	3 745	3 117	3 253	3 810
44 Pets and related products (including pet food)	DSVR	2 497	2 681	3 012	3 228	3 314
45 Repair of household and personal items	DSVS	1 031	875	1 021	1 161	1 081

1 See chapter text.
2 Inclusive of VAT.
3 Exclusive of VAT.
4 Turnover is adjusted to take out VAT.

Source: Office for National Statistics: 01633 456592

24.2 Retail trade: index numbers of value and volume of sales[1]
Great Britain
Not seasonally adjusted

Weekly average (2000=100)

		Sales in 2000 £ million	1998	1999	2000	2001	2002	2003	2004	2005	2006	2007	2008
Value													
All retailing	EAFY	207 149	93.4	96.5	100.0	105.9	110.6	113.7	118.8	119.9	123.3	127.8	131.7
Large	EAFZ	153 022	91.7	95.8	100.0	106.5	112.2	118.2	123.9	126.0	130.7	136.1	140.0
Small	EAGA	54 128	98.6	98.5	100.0	104.1	105.8	101.1	104.1	102.8	102.2	104.5	108.4
Predominantly food stores	EAFS	89 041	93.4	96.6	100.0	106.0	110.4	114.8	119.6	123.6	128.3	132.7	140.1
Predominantly non-food stores	EAFT	106 359	93.2	96.3	100.0	106.8	111.8	114.8	119.9	119.1	121.6	125.8	126.5
Non specialised predominantly non-food stores	EAGE	18 781	92.6	95.2	100.0	105.0	107.4	109.2	111.2	110.8	114.0	117.9	116.0
Textiles, clothing, footwear and leather	EAFU	27 880	93.8	96.0	100.0	108.4	114.9	118.9	124.7	126.5	131.8	136.4	136.4
Household goods stores	EAFV	27 699	91.6	95.7	100.0	107.6	113.1	113.4	117.2	112.9	114.2	118.0	114.7
Other specialised non-food stores	EAFW	31 999	93.1	96.8	100.0	105.7	110.5	115.6	123.0	123.0	123.5	128.0	134.2
Other retail sale (non-store) and repair	EAFX	11 749	97.1	98.8	100.0	97.0	100.5	96.2	102.7	99.1	100.6	108.6	116.2
Volume													
All retailing	EAHC	207 149	92.5	95.7	100.0	106.1	112.2	116.3	123.3	125.8	129.8	135.3	139.7
Predominantly food stores	EAGW	89 041	95.5	97.2	100.0	104.1	108.2	111.9	116.5	119.7	122.7	124.2	125.7
Predominantly non-food stores	EAGX	106 359	89.9	94.3	100.0	108.5	116.2	121.3	129.6	131.8	136.4	144.0	149.1
Non specialised predominantly non-food stores	EAHI	18 781	91.5	94.0	100.0	106.0	110.5	113.8	118.0	119.3	124.1	129.7	130.3
Textiles, clothing, footwear and leather	EAGY	27 880	88.8	92.9	100.0	112.1	123.7	129.6	139.3	143.9	150.9	156.9	161.6
Household goods stores	EAGZ	27 699	85.8	92.6	100.0	109.6	117.8	122.3	130.8	131.2	137.7	148.5	151.3
Other specialised non-food stores	EAHA	31 999	93.6	97.1	100.0	105.9	111.6	117.5	127.0	129.1	130.0	137.2	147.3
Other retail sale (non-store) and repair	EAHB	11 749	93.2	96.2	100.0	99.6	106.5	105.4	117.1	118.0	123.6	141.1	161.4

1 See chapter text.

Source: Office for National Statistics

421

Service industry

24.3 Motor trades[1]
United Kingdom

		Sale, maintenance and repair of,motor vehicles and motorcycles; retail sale of automotive fuel (SIC 2003 50.00)					Sale of motor vehicles (SIC 2003 50.10)			
		2003	2004	2005	2006		2003	2004	2005	2006
Number of businesses	MKEQ	70 080	70 265	70 994	71 201	MKER	24 895	24 199	23 924	23 614
Total turnover	CMRH	150 629	153 447	158 018	156 349	EWRI	102 242	103 594	107 586	105 943
Motor trades turnover	CMRI	145 739	147 850	152 554	151 390	FDFZ	101 377	102 579	105 909	104 063
Retail sales of:										
New cars	CMRJ	31 050	30 645	30 699	29 501	FDGA	28 597	28 427	28 744	27 654
Other new motor vehicles and motorcycles	CMRK	4 070	5 223	5 099	4 597	FDGB	3 592	4 358	4 152	3 579
Sales to other dealers of:										
New cars	CMRL	22 855	23 209	23 770	24 085	FDGC	22 336	22 790	23 451	23 695
Other new motor vehicles and motorcycles	CMRM	3 949	3 692	3 520	3 579	FDGD	3 486	3 074	2 913	2 770
Gross sales of used motor vehicles and motorcycles	CMRN	32 050	32 951	34 968	34 735	FDGE	30 106	30 560	32 890	31 859
Turnover from sales of petrol, diesel, oil and other petroleum products	CMRO	17 738	17 998	18 014	17 260	FDGF	1 184	806	702	694
Other motor trades sales and receipts (including parts and accessories, workshop receipts)	CMRP	34 027	34 131	36 483	37 633	FDGG	12 076	12 564	13 058	13 813
Non-motor trades turnover	CMRQ	4 890	5 598	5 464	4 959	FDHJ	865	1 015	1 677	1 880
Purchases of goods, materials and services										
Total purchases	CMNR	127 823	131 600	135 467	132 450	FDGH	89 198	91 714	94 598	92 541
Energy, water and materials	CMRS	1 631	1 696	2 017	2 300	FDGI	666	704	835	806
Used motor vehicles and motorcycles	COBU	27 910	29 352	30 698	31 343	FDGJ	26 239	27 397	28 946	28 847
Parts used solely in repair and servicing activities	CMRT	6 481	7 079	7 544	7 702	FDGK	2 521	2 682	2 975	3 505
Other goods for resale	CMRU	83 396	84 679	86 139	82 314	FDGL	55 108	55 864	56 738	54 341
Hiring, leasing and renting of plant, machinery and vehicles	CMRV	349	369	307	290	FDGM	72	84	84	69
Commercial insurance premiums	CMRW	572	561	609	566	FDGN	224	215	245	246
Road transport services	CMRX	778	753	715	634	FDGO	368	415	317	260
Telecommunication services	CMRY	335	295	307	289	FDGP	150	128	145	130
Computer and related services	CMRZ	329	388	352	424	FDGQ	170	187	201	245
Advertising and marketing services	CMSA	2 076	2 267	2 405	2 544	FDGR	1 742	1 897	1 964	2 110
Other services	CMSB	3 967	4 161	4 374	4 044	FDGS	1 939	2 140	2 147	1 981
Taxes, duties and levies										
Total taxes and levies	CMSC	1 048	972	1 077	1 079	FDGT	520	516	625	624
National (non-domestic business) rates	CMSD	611	613	660	677	FDGU	278	280	343	339
Other amounts paid for taxes, duties and levies	CMSE	437	359	417	402	FDGV	243	236	281	285
Capital expenditure										
Cost of acquisitions	CMSF	2 290	2 346	2 499	2 616	FDGW	1 380	1 425	1 610	1 795
Cost of disposals	CMSG	778	987	1 015	1 450	FDGX	566	671	736	1 166
Net capital expenditure	CMSH	1 512	1 359	1 484	1 165	FDGY	813	755	874	628
Work of a capital nature carried out by own staff (included in acquisitions)	CMSI	31	5	10	52	FDGZ	1	5	10	41
Stocks										
Increase during year	CMSJ	1 363	1 344	550	290	FDHA	1 191	1 138	403	287
Value at end of year	CMSK	14 437	14 923	15 621	15 855	FDHB	10 632	11 104	11 469	11 413
Total turnover divided by end-year stocks (Quotient)	CMSL	10.4	10.3	10.1	9.9	FDHC	9.6	9.3	9.4	9.3
Employment costs										
Total employment costs	CMSM	9 726	10 238	10 716	11 098	FDHD	5 056	5 327	5 608	5 520
Gross wages and salaries paid	COBP	8 669	9 062	9 382	9 714	FDHE	4 487	4 701	4 851	4 789
National insurance and pension contributions	COBQ	1 056	1 175	1 334	1 384	FDHF	569	625	757	730
Gross margin										
Amount	COBR	34 080	33 580	34 042	35 171	FDHG	19 556	18 770	19 283	19 490
As a percentage of adjusted turnover	COBS	*22.6*	*21.9*	*21.5*	*22.5*	FDHH	*19.1*	*18.1*	*17.9*	*18.4*
Approximate gross value added at basic prices	COBT	24 072	23 125	22 979	24 116	FDHI	14 242	13 011	13 363	13 671

24.3 Motor trades[1]
United Kingdom
continued

		Maintenance and repair of motor vehicles (SIC 2003 50.20)					Sale of motor vehicle parts and accessories (SIC 2003 50.30)			
		2003	2004	2005	2006		2003	2004	2005	2006
Number of businesses	MKES	29 188	30 050	30 973	31 666	MKET	7 799	7 952	8 067	8 096
Total turnover	FDHK	12 542	13 337	14 445	14 261	FDIW	13 801	13 694	13 659	14 428
Motor trades turnover	FDHL	12 147	13 023	14 082	13 992	FDIX	13 304	12 702	12 722	13 426
Retail sales of:										
New cars	FDHM	1 081	939	1 000	768	FDIY	1 168	1 241	880	904
Other new motor vehicles and motorcycles	FDHN	153	213	164	283	FDIZ	..	172	233	206
Sales to other dealers of:										
New cars	FDHO	8	..	23	40	FDJA	509	..	294	322
Other new motor vehicles and motorcycles	FDHP	3	..	..	48	FDJB	..	..	75	51
Gross sales of used motor vehicles and motorcycles	FDHQ	1 109	1 380	1 276	1 316	FDJC	..	374	251	493
Turnover from sales of petrol, diesel, oil and other petroleum products	FDHR	117	100	119	240	FDJD	70	86	1	4
Other motor trades sales and receipts (including parts and accessories, workshop receipts)	FDHS	9 674	10 386	11 500	11 298	FDJE	11 085	10 362	10 987	11 447
Non-motor trades turnover	FDHT	396	314	363	269	FDJF	497	992	936	1 002
Purchases of goods, materials and services										
Total purchases	FDHU	8 100	8 795	9 406	9 045	FDJG	11 062	10 958	11 223	11 736
Energy, water and materials	FDHV	572	652	735	897	FDJH	220	227	329	439
Used motor vehicles and motorcycles	FDHW	897	1 041	1 046	1 134	FDJI	..	371	272	387
Parts used solely in repair and servicing activities	FDHX	3 374	3 980	4 184	3 909	FDJJ	410	183	208	158
Other goods for resale	FDHY	1 774	1 453	1 739	1 591	FDJK	..	9 000	8 976	9 268
Hiring, leasing and renting of plant, machinery and vehicles	FDHZ	77	111	120	140	FDJL	151	136	62	53
Commercial insurance premiums	FDIA	204	227	242	198	FDJM	89	78	84	82
Road transport services	FDIB	49	104	79	39	FDJN	267	126	207	237
Telecommunication services	FDIC	97	103	97	88	FDJO	60	45	45	44
Computer and related services	FDID	61	72	39	55	FDJP	75	107	96	104
Advertising and marketing services	FDIE	127	125	111	86	FDJQ	165	208	290	274
Other services	FDIF	868	926	1 015	908	FDJR	643	478	655	691
Taxes, duties and levies										
Total taxes and levies	FDIG	197	215	218	219	FDJS	102	116	128	135
National (non-domestic business) rates	FDIH	162	152	146	167	FDJT	84	89	96	106
Other amounts paid for taxes, duties and levies	FDII	35	63	72	52	FDJU	19	27	32	29
Capital expenditure										
Cost of acquisitions	FDIJ	433	442	441	348	FDJV	221	199	194	210
Cost of disposals	FDIK	87	98	109	93	FDJW	47	54	76	97
Net capital expenditure	FDIL	346	345	332	255	FDJX	173	144	118	113
Work of a capital nature carried out by own staff (included in acquisitions)	FDIM	1	–	–	–	FDJY	29	–	–	6
Stocks										
Increase during year	FDIN	102	36	−13	7	FDJZ	76	81	134	70
Value at end of year	FDIO	881	835	958	1 085	FDKA	1 750	1 807	1 818	2 047
Total turnover divided by end-year stocks (Quotient)	FDIP	14.2	16.0	15.1	13.1	FDKB	7.9	7.6	7.5	7.0
Employment costs										
Total employment costs	FDIQ	2 480	2 581	2 697	2 927	FDKC	1 427	1 565	1 618	1 773
Gross wages and salaries paid	FDIR	2 233	2 315	2 429	2 635	FDKD	1 268	1 391	1 423	1 556
National insurance and pension contributions	FDIS	247	266	268	292	FDKE	159	174	195	217
Gross margin										
Amount	FDIT	6 597	6 857	7 415	7 609	FDKF	4 501	4 199	4 313	4 671
As a percentage of adjusted turnover	FDIU	*52.6*	*51.4*	*51.3*	*53.4*	FDKG	*32.6*	*30.7*	*31.6*	*32.4*
Approximate gross value added at basic prices	FDIV	4 552	4 548	4 980	5 200	FDKH	2 831	2 796	2 547	2 753

24.3 Motor trades[1]
United Kingdom
continued

£ million and percentages

		Sale, maintenance and repair of motorcycles and related parts and accessories (SIC 2003 50.40)					Retail sale of automotive fuel (SIC 2003 50.50)			
		2003	2004	2005	2006		2003	2004	2005	2006
Number of businesses	MKEU	2 710	2 948	3 157	3 161	MKEV	5 488	5 116	4 873	4 664
Total turnover	FDKI	1 955	2 116	2 211	2 182	FDLV	20 089	20 708	20 118	19 536
Motor trades turnover	FDKJ	1 887	2 102	2 200	2 172	FDLW	17 024	17 444	17 641	17 736
Retail sales of:										
New cars	FDKK	49	–	35	54	FDLX	154	38	39	121
Other new motor vehicles and motorcycles	FDKL	215	479	550	465	FDLY	19	–	–	63
Sales to other dealers of:										
New cars	FDKM	–	–	–	–	FDLZ	1	1	2	29
Other new motor vehicles and motorcycles	FDKN	419	564	532	711	FDMA	2	–	–	–
Gross sales of used motor vehicles and motorcycles	FDKO	333	499	472	378	FDMB	160	138	80	689
Turnover from sales of petrol, diesel, oil and other petroleum products	FDKP	–	–	–	–	FDMC	16 367	17 006	17 192	16 323
Other motor trades sales and receipts (including parts and accessories, workshop receipts)	FDKQ	872	558	611	564	FDMD	319	261	328	512
Non-motor trades turnover	FDKR	68	14	11	10	FDME	3 065	3 263	2 476	1 799
Purchases of goods, materials and services										
Total purchases	FDKT	1 512	1 705	1 890	1 744	FDMF	17 951	18 428	18 350	17 384
Energy, water and materials	FDKU	59	13	21	24	FDMG	115	100	96	135
Used motor vehicles and motorcycles	FDKV	252	409	383	335	FDMH	140	134	51	641
Parts used solely in repair and servicing activities	FDKW	87	163	69	61	FDMI	90	71	108	69
Other goods for resale	FDKX	967	1 016	1 291	1 162	FDMJ	16 946	17 346	17 395	15 952
Hiring, leasing and renting of plant, machinery and vehicles	FDKY	7	1	2	1	FDMK	41	37	38	26
Commercial insurance premiums	FDKZ	23	8	13	9	FDML	32	32	25	31
Road transport services	FDLA	15	21	18	31	COBV	79	86	95	68
Telecommunication services	FDLB	9	5	6	6	COBW	20	14	14	20
Computer and related services	FDLC	4	3	5	5	COBX	18	19	11	15
Advertising and marketing services	FDLD	21	22	29	47	COBY	22	14	11	27
Other services	FDLE	67	42	52	64	COBZ	449	574	506	400
Taxes, duties and levies										
Total taxes and levies	FDLF	29	32	33	30	COCA	200	92	74	72
National (non-domestic business) rates	FDLG	..	..	..	11	COCB	..	..	..	55
Other amounts paid for taxes, duties and levies	FDLH	..	..	..	19	COCC	..	..	..	17
Capital expenditure										
Cost of acquisitions	FDLI	46	65	28	54	COCD	211	215	225	209
Cost of disposals	FDLJ	7	20	9	10	COCE	71	144	84	85
Net capital expenditure	FDLK	39	45	19	44	COCF	140	71	141	124
Work of a capital nature carried out by own staff (included in acquisitions)	FDLL	–	–	–	–	COCG	–	–	–	4
Stocks										
Increase during year	FDLM	–8	–1	–29	–65	COCH	2	90	55	–9
Value at end of year	FDLN	432	391	434	390	COCI	741	786	942	921
Total turnover divided by end-year stocks (Quotient)	FDLO	4.5	5.4	5.1	5.6	COCJ	27.1	26.3	21.3	21.2
Employment costs										
Total employment costs	FDLP	151	155	165	191	COCK	611	610	628	687
Gross wages and salaries paid	FDLQ	136	136	148	170	COCL	545	519	530	563
National insurance and pension contributions	FDLR	15	19	17	21	COCM	66	91	97	124
Gross margin										
Amount	FDLS	630	517	427	545	COCN	2 796	3 238	2 604	2 856
As a percentage of adjusted turnover	FDLT	*32.2*	*24.4*	*19.3*	*25.0*	CMQN	*13.9*	*15.6*	*12.9*	*14.6*
Approximate gross value added at basic prices	FDLU	424	400	281	359	CMQO	2 022	2 370	1 808	2 134

1 See chapter text. Figures are exclusive of VAT.

Source: Office for National Statistics: 01633 456592

24.4 Catering and allied trades[1]
United Kingdom

		Total catering and allied trades (SIC 2003 55.00)					Hotels and motels (SIC 2003 55.11 and 55.12)			
		2003	2004	2005	2006		2003	2004	2005	2006
Number of businesses	MKEK	123 491	126 706	130 180	132 563	MKEL	10 535	10 417	10 253	10 139
Total turnover[2]	CMKX	63 412	70 199	71 836	74 283	CMLW	12 172	13 009	13 438	14 734
Taxes and levies[3]										
Total taxes and levies	CMLM	1 622	1 848	1 949	1 995	CMML	395	427	461	501
National (non-domestic business) rates	CMLJ	1 495	1 673	1 749	1 847	CMMI	380	400	442	486
Other amounts paid for taxes, duties and levies	CMLL	126	175	200	147	CMMK	15	27	20	15
Capital expenditure[3]										
Capital acquisitions	CMLP	4 068	4 122	4 530	4 677	CMMO	960	934	1 110	1 325
Capital disposals	CMLQ	850	612	1 151	1 231	CMMP	144	150	336	176
Net capital expenditure	CMLK	3 217	3 510	3 379	3 446	CMMJ	815	783	773	1 149
Work of a capital nature carried out by your own staff (included in acquisitions)	CMLR	31	12	31	42	CMMQ	12	4	5	19
Stocks[3]										
Increase during year	CMLN	42	75	54	102	CMMM	2	2	2	2
Value at end of year	CMLO	1 106	1 253	1 267	1 311	CMMN	169	168	154	176
Purchases of goods and services[3]										
Total purchases	CMLI	29 230	31 813	33 358	34 052	CMMH	4 521	4 838	5 140	5 434
Energy, water and materials	CMKZ	12 130	13 374	12 839	12 755	CMLY	2 015	2 043	2 075	2 106
Goods for resale	CMLA	8 851	9 555	11 475	11 941	CMLZ	489	583	733	807
Hiring, leasing of plant, machinery etc	CMLB	275	303	262	256	CMMA	54	66	49	46
Commercial insurance premiums	CMLC	494	545	525	522	CMMB	124	105	102	109
Road transport services	CMLD	96	103	146	139	CMMC	22	8	10	16
Telecommunication services	CMLE	260	265	253	230	CMMD	71	68	60	62
Computer and related services	CMLF	149	169	197	164	CMME	50	45	72	69
Advertising and marketing services	CMLG	686	713	727	775	CMMF	183	203	202	241
Other services	CMLH	6 289	6 786	6 934	7 256	CMMG	1 513	1 687	1 806	1 949
Employment costs[3]										
Total employment costs	CMKY	14 116	15 287	16 541	16 652	CMLX	3 159	3 270	3 660	3 821
Gross wages and salaries paid	CMKV	12 998	14 075	15 134	15 336	CMLU	2 865	2 993	3 295	3 471
National insurance and pension contributions	CMKW	1 118	1 212	1 406	1 315	CMLV	294	277	364	350
Gross margin[4]										
Amount	CMQP	45 747	51 047	50 616	52 384	CMQS	9 889	10 525	10 726	11 858
As a percentage of turnover	CMQQ	*83.7*	*84.1*	*81.4*	*81.5*	CMQT	*95.3*	*94.6*	*93.5*	*93.7*
Value added at basic prices[4]	CMQR	25 435	28 833	28 757	30 311	CMQU	5 864	6 272	6 327	7 232
Accommodation										
Number of establishments	CMLS	28 209	28 332	83 134	..	CMMR	13 974	14 190	24 367	..
Letting bedplaces	CMLT	2 214 366	2 676 991	2 441 159	..	CMMS	1 198 410	964 733	1 589 498	..

24.4 Catering and allied trades[1]
United Kingdom

continued

£ million and percentages

		Camping sites and other provision of short-stay accommodation (SIC 2003 55.21 to 55.23)					Restaurants or cafes, take-away food shops (SIC 2003 55.30)			
		2003	2004	2005	2006		2003	2004	2005	2006
Number of businesses	MKEM	4 370	4 703	5 027	5 225	MKEN	55 475	57 674	60 539	62 062
Total turnover[2]	CMMV	3 032	3 620	3 699	4 212	CMNU	20 145	21 731	22 601	23 027
Taxes and levies[3]										
Total taxes and levies	CMNK	79	90	91	96	CMOJ	515	556	627	647
National (non-domestic business) rates	CMNH	75	81	83	93	CMOG	469	483	544	582
Other amounts paid for taxes, duties and levies	CMNJ	4	8	7	2	CMOI	46	73	83	65
Capital expenditure[3]										
Capital acquisitions	CMNN	345	336	345	461	CMOM	1 117	1 153	1 339	1 455
Capital disposals	CMNO	192	55	47	154	CMON	187	130	253	420
Net capital expenditure	CMNI	153	281	298	309	CMOH	930	1 023	1 086	1 035
Work of a capital nature carried out by your own staff (included in acquisitions)	CMNP	2	–	17	4	CMOO	3	4	8	9
Stocks[3]										
Increase during year	CMNL	2	10	19	40	CMOK	5	12	13	38
Value at end of year	CMNM	102	137	194	222	CMOL	313	328	338	374
Purchases of goods and services[3]										
Total purchases	CMNG	1 461	1 747	1 763	1 974	CMOF	9 546	10 056	10 614	10 738
Energy, water and materials	CMMX	360	449	444	418	CMNW	4 775	5 080	4 810	4 826
Goods for resale	CMMY	411	594	592	787	CMNX	2 345	2 399	3 125	3 270
Hiring, leasing of plant, machinery etc.	CMMZ	8	14	10	9	CMNY	54	47	38	30
Commercial insurance premiums	CMNA	59	59	48	51	CMNZ	117	140	138	118
Road transport services	CMNB	7	11	17	20	CMOA	30	51	55	45
Telecommunication services	CMNC	19	17	18	19	CMOB	71	72	71	60
Computer and related services	CMND	8	13	15	14	CMOC	34	41	46	25
Advertising and marketing services	CMNE	112	111	101	124	CMOD	231	251	268	257
Other services	CMNF	476	480	517	531	CMOE	1 888	1 975	2 063	2 108
Employment costs[3]										
Total employment costs	CMMW	554	578	683	737	CMNV	4 276	4 642	5 131	5 068
Gross wages and salaries paid	CMMT	507	523	618	671	CMNS	3 971	4 305	4 725	4 702
National insurance and pension contributions	CMMU	47	55	65	66	CMNT	305	337	406	366
Gross margin[4]										
Amount	CMQV	2 260	2 586	2 734	2 980	CMQY	14 936	16 289	16 343	16 665
As a percentage of turnover	CMQW	*84.7*	*81.4*	*82.9*	*80.0*	CMQZ	*86.3*	*86.9*	*83.7*	*83.6*
Value added at basic prices[4]	CMQX	1 212	1 435	1 565	1 796	CMRA	7 744	8 660	8 863	9 204
Accommodation										
Number of establishments	CMNQ	6 962	6 255	43 033	..	CMOP	1 965	1 604	4 195	..
Letting bedplaces	CMRR	857 489	1 533 656	674 684	..	CMOQ	51 974	42 383	65 339	..

24.4 Catering and allied trades[1]
United Kingdom
continued

£ million and percentages

		Licensed clubs with entertainment, independent, tenanted, managed public houses or wine bars (SIC 2003 55.40)[5]					Canteen operator, catering contractor (SIC 2003 55.51 and 55.52)			
		2003	2004	2005	2006		2003	2004	2005	2006
Number of businesses	MKEO	47 475	48 147	48 400	49 002	MKEP	5 636	5 765	5 961	6 135
Total turnover[2]	CMOT	21 392	24 455	23 830	24 784	CMPS	6 670	7 383	8 268	7 527
Taxes and levies[3]										
Total taxes and levies	CMPI	602	748	725	721	CMQH	31	28	46	30
National (non-domestic business) rates	CMPF	548	688	652	663	CMQE	23	21	28	23
Other amounts paid for taxes, duties and levies	CMPH	53	59	73	58	CMQG	8	8	17	7
Capital expenditure[3]										
Capital acquisitions	CMPL	1 482	1 489	1 588	1 349	CMQK	164	211	148	86
Capital disposals	CMPM	317	260	490	448	CMQL	11	17	25	34
Net capital expenditure	CMPG	1 166	1 229	1 098	902	CMQF	153	194	123	52
Work of a capital nature carried out by your own staff (included in acquisitions)	CMPN	13	4	1	10	CMQM	–	–	–	–
Stocks[3]										
Increase during year	CMPJ	28	41	5	19	CMQI	6	9	15	3
Value at end of year	CMPK	409	512	443	415	CMQJ	112	109	138	124
Purchases of goods and services[3]										
Total purchases	CMPE	10 675	11 844	12 002	12 427	CMQD	3 028	3 328	3 839	3 479
Energy, water and materials	CMOV	2 959	3 450	3 007	3 177	CMPU	2 022	2 344	2 503	2 228
Goods for resale	CMOW	5 151	5 522	6 434	6 560	CMPV	455	457	590	510
Hiring, leasing of plant, machinery etc.	CMOX	116	138	120	109	CMPW	44	38	45	62
Commercial insurance premiums	CMOY	150	182	170	176	CMPX	44	30	36	38
Road transport services	CMOZ	25	17	44	43	CMPY	13	15	20	16
Telecommunication services	CMPA	79	86	77	66	CMPZ	20	23	28	24
Computer and related services	CMPB	33	48	38	38	CMQA	24	22	26	19
Advertising and marketing services	CMPC	127	129	121	131	CMQB	32	19	35	23
Other services	CMPD	2 036	2 264	1 992	2 115	CMQC	374	380	557	553
Employment costs[3]										
Total employment costs	CMOU	3 834	4 294	4 376	4 375	CMPT	2 293	2 503	2 691	2 651
Gross wages and salaries paid	CMOR	3 566	3 974	4 037	4 068	CMPQ	2 090	2 281	2 459	2 424
National insurance and pension contributions	CMOS	268	320	339	307	CMPR	204	222	232	227
Gross margin[4]										
Amount	CMRB	13 182	15 408	13 931	14 689	CMRE	5 480	6 238	6 882	6 192
As a percentage of turnover	CMRC	*71.9*	*73.6*	*68.2*	*69.1*	CMRF	*92.3*	*93.2*	*92.3*	*92.3*
Value added at basic prices[4]	CMRD	7 708	9 098	8 368	8 849	CMRG	2 907	3 368	3 633	3 231
Accommodation										
Number of establishments	CMPO	5 018	6 046	11 288	..					
Letting bedplaces	CMPP	77 371	110 130	84 174	..					

1 See chapter text.
2 Inclusive of VAT.
3 Exclusive of VAT.

4 The total turnover figure used to calculate these data excludes VAT.
5 Includes figures for managed public houses owned by breweries.

Source: Office for National Statistics: 01633 456592

Sources

This index of sources gives the titles of official publications or other sources containing statistics allied to those in the tables of this *Annual Abstract*. These publications provide more detailed analyses than are shown in the *Annual Abstract*. This index includes publications to which reference should be made for short-term (monthly or quarterly) series. Further advice on published statistical sources is available from the National Statistics Public Enquiry Service on the numbers provided on page ii.

Table number in Abstract	Government department or other organisation	Official publication or other source
Chapter 1: Area		
1.1	Ordnance Survey	
	Ordnance Survey of Northern Ireland	
	Office for National Statistics	Regional Trends (annual, Palgrave Macmillan)
Chapter 2: Parliamentary elections		
Elections		
2.1	University of Plymouth for the Electoral Commission	British Electoral Facts 1832-2006 (Ashgate) Dod's Parliamentary Companion (annual)
By-elections		
2.2	University of Plymouth for the Electoral Commission	Vachers Parliamentary Companion (quarterly) Social Trends (annual, Palgrave Macmillan)
Devolved Assembly elections		
2.2 to 2.4	University of Plymouth for the Electoral Commission	British Electoral Facts 1832-2006 (Ashgate) Social Trends (annual, Palgrave Macmillan)
Chapter 3: International development		
3.1 to 3.2	Department for International Development	Statistics on International Development 2002/03-2007/08, Tables 1, 2, 3, 14 and 18
Chapter 4: Defence		
4.1 to 4.11	Ministry of Defence/DASA	UK Defence Statistics 2008 (The Stationery Office (TSO))
Chapter 5: Population		
Population		**Census**
5.1 to 5.3, 5.5	Office for National Statistics	*England and Wales*: Census reports 1911, 1921, 1931, 1951, 1961, 1971, 1981, 1991 and 2001 Key Population and Vital Statistics; Great Britain, Digest of Welsh Statistics (annual, National Assembly for Wales)
	General Register Office Scotland	*Scotland*: Census reports 1951, 1961, 1971, 1981, 1991 and 2001

Table number in Abstract	Government department or other organisation	Official publication or other source
	Northern Ireland Statistics and Research Agency	*Northern Ireland*: Census of population 1951, 1961, 1966, 1971, 1981, 1991 and 2001
		Resident population: mid-year estimates
5.1 to 5.3 and 5.5	Office for National Statistics	*England and Wales*: Series FM (Family statistics), DH (Death), MB (Morbidity), PP (Population estimates and projections), MN (Migration) and VS (Key population and vital statistics) Series PP1, Population estimates: The Registrar General's estimates of the population of regions and local government areas of England and Wales Population Trends (quarterly Palgrave Macmillan)
		Health Statistics Quarterly (Palgrave Macmillan)
	General Register Office Scotland	*Scotland*: Annual report of the Registrar General for Scotland Annual estimate of the population of Scotland
	Northern Ireland Statistics and Research Agency	*Northern Ireland*: Annual report of the Registrar General
5.6	Office for National Statistics	
Projections		
5.1 to 5.3	Office for National Statistics Government Actuary's Department	Series PP2, Population projections – national figures
Migration		
5.7 to 5.9	Office for National Statistics	International Migration - statistical bulletin of 2007 estimates Series MN (International migration) Population Trends (quarterly, Palgrave Macmillan)
5.10	Home Office	Control of immigration statistics United Kingdom (annual) Asylum Statistics United Kingdom (annual)
Vital statistics		
5.4 and 5.12 to 5.21	Office for National Statistics	*England and Wales*: Series FM (Births, marriages and divorce statistics) DH (Deaths), MB (Morbidity), PP (Population estimates and projections), MN (International migration) and VS (Key population and vital statistics)
	General Register Office Scotland	*Scotland*: Annual report of the Registrar General for Scotland Quarterly return of births, deaths and marriages
	Northern Ireland Statistics and Research Agency	*Northern Ireland*: Annual report of the Registrar General Quarterly return of births, deaths and marriages
5.14	Northern Ireland Court Service	Northern Ireland Judicial Statistics (annual)
5.18	Scottish Government Department of Health	

Sources

Table number in Abstract	Government department or other organisation	Official publication or other source
5.22	Office for National Statistics	*England and Wales*: Interim Life Table *Scotland*: Interim Life Table *Northern Ireland*: Annual Report of the Registrar General
5.23	Office for National Statistics General Register Office (Scotland) Northern Ireland Statistics and Research Agency	

Chapter 6: Education

6.1 to 6.11	Department for Children, Schools and Families (DCSF)	Education and Training Statistics for United Kingdom (Internet only) (annual, DCSF)
	Department For Innovation, Universities And Skills (DIUS)	United Kingdom higher education statistics (annual and ad-hoc, DIUS/Higher Education Statistics Agency (HESA))
	Welsh Assembly Government (WAG)	*Wales*: Statistics of education and training in Wales (annual and ad-hoc, WAG)
	Scottish Government (SG)	*Scotland*: Scottish educational statistics (annual and ad-hoc, SG)
	Northern Ireland Department of Education (DENI) Northern Ireland Department for Employment and Learning (DELNI)	*Northern Ireland*: Northern Ireland education statistics (annual and ad-hoc, DENI) Northern Ireland further and higher education statistics (annual and ad-hoc, DELNI)

Chapter 7: Labour market

Labour force survey

7.1 to 7.3, 7.6, 7.9, 7.10, 7.11, 7.13, 7.16 to 7.18	Office for National Statistics	Economic and Labour Market review (monthly, Palgrave Macmillan)
7.4, 7.5	Office for National Statistics	
7.7	Office for National Statistics	Labour Market Statistics
7.8	Office for National Statistics	Civil Service Statistics Monthly Digest of Statistics (Palgrave Macmillan)
7.9	Office for National Statistics	Economic and Labour Market review (monthly, Palgrave Macmillan)
	Scottish Executive	

Claimant count

7.12, 7.14, 7.15 and 7.25	Office for National Statistics	Economic and Labour Market review (monthly, Palgrave Macmillan)

Table number in Abstract	Government department or other organisation	Official publication or other source
7.19	Office for National Statistics	Economic and Labour Market review (monthly, Palgrave Macmillan) Monthly Digest of Statistics (Palgrave Macmillan)

Annual Survey of Hours and Earnings

7.20, 7.21, 7.24 and 7.25	Office for National Statistics	Annual Survey of Hours and Earnings (annual, ONS)

Average Earnings Index

7.22 and 7.23	Office for National Statistics	Economic and Labour Market review (monthly, Palgrave Macmillan) Monthly Digest of Statistics (Palgrave Macmillan)
7.26	Certification Office	Certification Officers Annual Report

Chapter 8: Personal income, expenditure and wealth

8.1	Board of HMRC	HMRC National Statistics http://www.hmrc.gov.uk/stats/income_distribution/menu.htm http://www.statistics.gov.uk/cci/article.asp?ID=2022
8.2	Office for National Statistics	National Statistics (http://www.statistics.gov.uk/cci/article.asp?ID=2022)
8.3 to 8.5	Office for National Statistics	Expenditure and Food Survey, (annual) (1990 onwards edition-Family Spending) (annual, Palgrave Macmillan)

Chapter 9: Health

National Health Service

9.1	The NHS Information Centre for health and social care Welsh Assembly Government The Scottish Government, ISD Scotland part of NHS National Services Scotland Department of Health, Social Services and Public Safety (Northern Ireland)	Summary of Health and Personal Social Services (Northern Ireland) Accounts (annual) Hospital Statistics (annual)
9.2	The Scottish Government, ISD Scotland part of NHS National Services Scotland	
9.3	Department of Health, Social Services and Public Safety (Northern Ireland)	Summary of Health and Personal Social Services (Northern Ireland) Accounts (annual) Hospital Statistics (annual)
9.4	NHS Information Centre for health and social care	*England*: Health and Personal Social Services Statistics for England (annual) NHS Hospital and Community Health Services (HCHS):

Table number in Abstract	Government department or other organisation	Official publication or other source
9.5	Welsh Assembly Government	*Wales*: Health Statistics Wales (annual)

Public Health

9.6	Office for National Statistics	*England and Wales*: Mortality statistics cause series DH2
	General Register Office Scotland	*Scotland*: Annual Report of the Registrar General for Scotland
	Northern Ireland Statistics and Research Agency	*Northern Ireland*: Annual Report of the Registrar General for Northern Ireland
9.7	HPA Centre for Infections	*England and Wales*: Communicable Disease Statistics Series MB2 (annual) Annual Review of Communicable Diseases
	NHS in Scotland NHS National Services Scotland	*Scotland*: Scottish Health Statistics (annual)
	Communicable Disease Surveillance Centre (NI)	*Northern Ireland*: Annual report of the Registrar General Northern Ireland
9.8 to 9.10	Health and Safety Executive	Health and Safety Statistics (annual)

Chapter 10: Social protection

Social security pensions, benefits and allowances

10.1	Department for Work and Pensions HM Revenue and Customs Department of Health, Social Services and Public Safety (Northern Ireland)	National Insurance Fund Account (annual)
10.2	Department for Work and Pensions	
10.3	HM Revenue and Customs	
10.4 and 10.5	Department for Work and Pensions (Information and Analysis Directorate) Ministry of Defence/DASA (Pay and Pensions)	Work and Pensions Longitudinal Study (WPLS, 100% sample)
	HM Revenue and Customs	
10.6 to 10.8, 10.12 to 10.19	Department for Work and Pensions (Information and Analysis Directorate)	Work and Pensions Longitudinal Study (WPLS, 100% sample)
10.9 and 10.11	HM Revenue and Customs	
10.15	Ministry of Defence/DASA (Health Information)	

Table number in Abstract	Government department or other organisation	Official publication or other source
Working Family Tax Credit		
10.10	Working Family Tax Credit Department for Work and Pensions (Information and Analysis Directorate)	Quarterly Enquiry United Kingdom (quarterly)
Social services		
10.20 to 10.24	Office for National Statistics Department for Education and Skills	Appropriation (annual) Northern Ireland Annual Abstract of Statistics
10.20	HM Treasury	HM Treasury Expenditure Statistical Analyses
Housing and community amenities		
10.25	Office for National Statistics	

Chapter 11: Crime and justice

11.1	Home Office	*England and Wales*: Police Service Strength England and Wales 2008 Home Office Statistical Bulletin 03/09
	Scottish Government Justice Analytical Services	
	The Police Service of Northern Ireland	*Northern Ireland*: The Chief Constable's Annual Report
11.3	Home Office	Crime in England and Wales 2007/08 (Home Office Statistical Bulletin 07/08)
11.4 to 11.9	Office for Criminal Justice Reform	Criminal Statistics, England and Wales (annual) (TSO) Offender Management Caseload Statistics 2008 (annual) Digest of Welsh Statistics (annual, Welsh Office)
11.2, 11.10 and 11.11	Ministry of Justice	Sentencing Statistics 2007 England & Wales Offender Management Caseload Statistics 2007
11.12	Ministry of Justice	HM Prison Service Annual Report and Accounts April 2007 – March 2008
11.13	Scottish Government Justice Analytical Services	Recorded Crime in Scotland, 2007/08
11.14 to 11.17	Scottish Government Justice Analytical Services	Criminal Proceedings in Scottish Courts, 2007/08
11.18 and 11.19	Scottish Government Justice Department	Prison Statistics Scotland, 2007/08 Scottish Prison Service Annual Report and Accounts

Table number in Abstract	Government department or other organisation	Official publication or other source
11.20	The Police Service of Northern Ireland	
11.21 to 11.24	Northern Ireland Office	A Commentary on Northern Ireland Crime Statistics 2004 'Court Prosecutions and Sentencing 2006' NIO Research and Statistical Bulletin 11/2008 Court Prosecutions and Sentencing for 10 to 17 year olds 2006' NIO Research and Statistical Bulletin 12/2008 The Northern Ireland Prison Population in 2007

Chapter 12. Lifestyles

12.1	Department for Culture, Media and Sports	
12.2	Department for Culture, Media and Sports	
12.3	Department for Culture, Media and Sports	
12.4	CAA Nielsen EDI	
12.5 and 12.6	UK Film Council, Nielsen EDI	08 Statistical Yearbook http://www.ukfilmcouncil.org.uk
12.7 and 12.10	Visit Britain	United Kingdom Tourism Survey
12.8 and 12.9	Office for National Statistics	International Passenger Survey Overseas Travel & Tourism MQ6 Overseas Travel & Tourism Statistical bulletin Travel Trends
12.11	Target Group Index, BMRB International	
12.12	Department for Culture, Media and Sports Gaming Commission National Lottery Commission	http://www.gamblingcommission.gov.uk/ http://www.natlotcomm.gov.uk/

Chapter 13: Environment

13.1, 13.2, 13.4, 13.8, 13.18 and 13.22	Office for National Statistics	Environmental Accounts Autumn 2008 http://www.statistics.gov.uk/downloads/theme_environment/EADec2008.pdf
13.3, 13.6, 13.7, and 13.16	Department for Environment Food and Rural Affairs	e-Digest of Environmental Statistics (annual) www.defra.gov.uk/environment/statistics/index.htm The Environment in your Pocket (annual)

Table number in Abstract	Government department or other organisation	Official publication or other source
13.9 and 13.13	Centre for Ecology and Hydrology, Wallingford	www.ceh-nerc.ac.uk/data/NWA.htm
13.10	The Met Office	www.met-office.gov.uk
13.11 and 13.17	Environment Agency	www.environment-agency.gov.uk
13.12	Scottish Environment Protection agency	http://www.sepa.org.uk/water/monitoring_and _classification/scottish_monitoring_strategy.aspx
13.14	Water Services Regulation Authority (OFWAT)	Financial performance and expenditure of the water companies 2007-08 (annual) http://www.ofwat.gov. uk/regulating/reporting/rpt_fpr_2007-08.pdf
13.15	Environment Agency	*England and Wales*: www.environment-agency.gov.uk
	Scottish Environment Protection agency	*Scotland*: www.sepa.org.uk
	Environment & Heritage Services Northern Ireland	*Northern Ireland*: www.ehsni.gov.uk
13.19 and 13.20	Department for Environment Food and Rural Affairs	*England*: www.defra.gov.uk/environment/statistics/index.htm
	Welsh Assembly Government	*Wales*: www.wales.gov.uk/statistics
	Scottish Environment Protection agency	*Scotland*: www.sepa.org.uk
	Environment & Heritage Services Northern Ireland	*Northern Ireland*: www.ehsni.gov.uk
13.21	The Chartered Institute of Environmental Health	
	The Royal Environmental Health Institute of Scotland	

Chapter 14: Housing

14.1	Communities and Local Government	
	Welsh Assembly Government	
	Scottish Government	
	Department for Social Development, Northern Ireland	
14.2	Office for National Statistics	General Household Survey

Sources

Table number in Abstract	Government department or other organisation	Official publication or other source
14.3	Communities and Local Government	
	Welsh Assembly Government	*Wales*: Welsh Housing Statistics (annual)
	Scottish Government	*Scotland*: Statistical Bulletins on Housing (SG)
	Department for Social Development, Northern Ireland	*Northern Ireland*: Northern Ireland Housing Statistics (annual)
14.4	Communities and Local Government	
14.5	Communities and Local Government	
	Welsh Assembly Government	
14.6	HM Court Service Northern Ireland Court Service	
14.7	Council of Mortgage Lenders	
14.8	Communities and Local Government	
	Welsh Assembly Government	
	Scottish Government	
14.9	Communities and Local Government	Statutory Homelessness Statistical Release (quarterly) http://www.communities.gov.uk/index.asp?id=1156302

Chapter 15: Transport and communications

General

15.1, 15.2 and 15.4	Department for Transport	
15.3	Office for National Statistics	

Road Transport

15.5 to 15.12	Department for Transport	Vehicle Licensing Statistics (annual, TSO) Road Casualties Great Britain (annual, TSO) Road accidents Wales (annual, Welsh Assembly Government) Office for National Statistics: Department for Transport
15.11		Driving Standards Agency
15.13 and 15.14	Department for Regional Development, Northern Ireland	Publication: Transport Statistics NISource: Driver and Vehicle Agency

Rail Transport

15.20 and 15.21	Department for Transport	Office for National Statistics Health and Safety Executive: Industry and Services (annual) Bulletin of Rail Statistics (quarterly)
15.22 and 15.23	Department for Regional Development, Northern Ireland	Translink

Table number in Abstract	Government department or other organisation	Official publication or other source
Air Transport		
15.24 to 15.27	Civil Aviation Authority	Civil Aviation Authority; Annual Statements of Movements, Passengers and Cargo Civil Aviation Authority; Monthly Statements of Movements, Passengers and Cargo
Communications		
15.28 and 15.29	Ofcom	
	Office for National Statistics	
15.30	Royal Mail Parcel Force Capita Business Services Ltd Post Office Counters Ltd.	Monthly Digest of Statistics (Palgrave Macmillan) Post Office report and accounts (annual)

Chapter 16: National accounts

16.1 to 16.22	Office for National Statistics	United Kingdom National Accounts (annual, Palgrave Macmillan) Monthly Digest of Statistics (Palgrave Macmillan)

Chapter 17: Prices

Producer Prices		
17.1 and 17.2	Office for National Statistics	Producer Price Index Press Notice (monthly) Business Monitor MM22, Producer Price Indices Monthly Digest of Statistics (Palgrave Macmillan)
Consumer Prices		
17.3 to 17.6	Office for National Statistics	Economic and Labour Market review (monthly, Palgrave Macmillan) Focus on Consumer Price Indices (monthly, National Statistics website)
17.7, 17.8	Department for Environment, Food and Rural Affairs	Agriculture in the UK (annual) Agricultural Price Indices, Statistical notice (monthly)
17.9	Eurostat Office for National Statistics	Economic and Labour Market Review (monthly)

Chapter 18: Government finance

Central Government		
18.1 to 18.3	Office for National Statistics	Financial Statistics (monthly, Palgrave Macmillan)
18.4 to 18.5 and 18.7	HM Treasury Office for National Statistics	Consolidated Fund and National Loans Fund Accounts Financial Statistics (monthly, Palgrave Macmillan)
18.5	HM Treasury Office for National Statistics	United Kingdom National Accounts (annual, Palgrave Macmillan)

Sources

Table number in Abstract	Government department or other organisation	Official publication or other source
18.6	Office for National Statistics	United Kingdom National Accounts (annual, Palgrave Macmillan)
18.8 and 18.9	HM Revenue & Customs	www.hmrc.gov.uk
18.10	Office for National Statistics	
Tax rates		
18.11 and 18.12	HM Revenue & Customs	www.hmrc.gov.uk
Rateable values		
18.13	HM Revenue & Customs	www.hmrc.gov.uk
Local Authorities		
18.14	Communities and Local Government Welsh Assembly Government Public Works Loan Board Scottish Executive Statistical Support for Local Government Department of Finance and Personnel for Northern Ireland Department of the Environment for Northern Ireland Chartered Institute of Public Finance and Accountancy	Local government financial statistics (England) (annual) Welsh local government financial statistics (annual) Annual report of the Public Works Loan Board Local Financial Returns (Scotland) (annual)
18.15 to 18.19	Communities and Local Government Welsh Assembly Government	Local government financial statistics (England) (annual) Welsh local government financial statistics (annual)
18.20 to 18.22	Scottish Government Statistical Support for Local Government	Local financial returns (Scotland) (annual) Capital Returns (Scotland) (annual)
18.23	Department of the Environment for Northern Ireland	District Council - Summary of Statement of Accounts (annual)

Chapter 19: External trade and investment

19.1 to 19.8	HM Revenue & Customs	OTS1 – Overseas Trade Statistics – Extra EC, (formerly MM20) (monthly) OTS2 – Overseas Trade Statistics – Intra EC and World (formerly MM20A) (monthly) OTSQ – Overseas Trade Statistics – Intra EC, (formerly MQ20) (quarterly) OTSA – Overseas Trade Statistics – Extra and Intra EC (formerly MA20) (annual)
	Office for National Statistics	Business Monitor MM24, Monthly Review of External Trade Statistics (monthly, Palgrave Macmillan) Overseas Trade Analysed in Terms of Industries MQ10 (quarterly, Palgrave Macmillan) Monthly Digest of Statistics (monthly, Palgrave Macmillan)

Table number in Abstract	Government department or other organisation	Official publication or other source
19.9 to 19.18	Office for National Statistics Bank of England	United Kingdom Balance of Payments (annual, Palgrave Macmillan) (quarterly, Palgrave Macmillan) figures: UK Economic Accounts Financial Statistics (monthly, Palgrave Macmillan) Foreign Direct Investment MA4 (annual, National Statistics website)

Chapter 20: Research and development

20.1 to 20.5	Office for National Statistics	Business Monitor MA14, Research and Development in UK Business (annual, ONS)

Chapter 21: Agriculture, fisheries and food

Agriculture

21.1 to 21.3	Department for Environment Food and Rural Affairs	Agriculture in the United Kingdom 2007 (annual)
21.6	Forestry Commission Department of agriculture and Rural Development (Northern Ireland)	Forestry Statistics (annual) Northern Ireland Annual Abstract of statistics

Fisheries

21.14 and 21.15	Department for Environment Food and Rural Affairs Scottish Government Agricultural Departments	

Family food

21.16	Department for Environment Food and Rural Affairs	Expenditure and Food Survey (annual) (1990 onwards edition-Family Spending) (annual, Palgrave Macmillan)

Chapter 22: Production

Production and construction

22.1	Office for National Statistics	Annual Business Inquiry (www.statistics.gov.uk/abi)

Manufacturers sales

22.2	Office for National Statistics	ProdCom: Product Sales and Trade Annual Reports - PRA series (annual, ONS) Product Sales and Trade Quarterly Reports - PRQ series (quarterly, ONS)
22.3	Office for National Statistics	UK Business: Activity, Size and Location (www.statistics.gov.uk/ukbusiness)

Sources

Table number in Abstract	Government department or other organisation	Official publication or other source
Energy		
22.4 to 22.13	Department of Energy and Climate Change	Digest of United Kingdom Energy Statistics (annual) Energy Trends (monthly and quarterly) Annual Business Inquiry (www.statistics.gov.uk/abi)
Iron and steel		
22.14 to 22.16	Iron and Steel Statistics Bureau	Iron and steel industry: annual statistics published by the Iron and Steel Statistics Bureau Corporation Regional Trends (annual, Palgrave Macmillan)
Industrial materials		
22.17	World Bureau of Metal Statistics Aluminium Federation	World Metal Statistics (monthly) Annual Business Inquiry (www.statistics.gov.uk/abi)
22.18	Agricultural Industries Confederation	Annual Business Inquiry (www.statistics.gov.uk/abi)
Minerals		
22.19	Communities and Local Government	Minerals (Business Monitor PA 1007) (annual, ONS)
	Department for Business, Enterprise and Regulatory Reform	Natural Environment Research Council: United Kingdom
	Department of Economic Development (Northern Ireland)	Minerals Yearbook Northern Ireland Annual Abstract of Statistics
Building materials		
22.20	Department for Business, Enterprise and Regulatory Reform	Monthly Statistics of Building Materials and Components (BERR) Monthly Digest of Statistics (Palgrave Macmillan)
Construction		
22.21 and 22.22	Office for National Statistics	Monthly Digest of Statistics (Palgrave Macmillan)
Engineering		
22.23 and 22.24	Office for National Statistics	Annual Business Inquiry (www.statistics.gov.uk/abi) UK Business: Activity, Size and Location (www.statistics.gov.uk/Ukbusiness)
Motor vehicle production		
22.25	Office for National Statistics	Monthly Digest of Statistics (Palgrave Macmillan)
Drink and tobacco		
22.26 and 22.27	HM Revenue & Customs	Annual report of the Commissioners of HM Revenue and Customs (www.hmrc.gov.uk/stats/tax_receipts/menu.htm) and HMRC Statistical Bulletins on UK Trade Information website (www.uktradeinfo.com/index.cfm?task=bulletins) Monthly Digest of Statistics (Palgrave Macmillan)

Table number in Abstract	Government department or other organisation	Official publication or other source

Chapter 23: Banking, insurance etc

Banking

23.1	Bank of England	Bank of England Annual Report and Accounts
23.2	Association for Payment Clearing Services	Yearbook of Payment Statistics 2008
23.3 to 23.7	Bank of England	Bank of England, Statistical Interactive Database
23.8	Bank of England	Bank of England Quarterly Bulletin
23.9 to 23.12	Bank of England	Financial Statistics (monthly, Palgrave Macmillan)

Other financial institutions

23.13	Financial Services Authority	Building Societies: Statistical Tables http://www.fsa.gov.uk/pages/Library/Other_publications/Miscellaneous/2007/bs_stats.shtml
23.14	Office for National Statistics	Business Monitor SDQ7, Assets and Liabilities of Finance Houses and Other Credit Companies (quarterly, ONS)
23.15	Office for National Statistics	Financial Statistics (monthly, Palgrave Macmillan) Monthly Digest of Statistics (Palgrave Macmillan) Business Monitor MQ5, Insurance Companies; Pension Funds and Trusts Investments (quarterly, ONS) Statistical bulletin
23.16 and 23.17	Office for National Statistics	Financial Statistics (monthly, Palgrave Macmillan) Business Monitor MQ5, Insurance Companies; Pension Funds and InsolvencyTrusts Investments (quarterly, ONS)
23.18 and 23.19	Insolvency service	
23.20	Association of Unit Trusts and Investment Funds	
	Bank of England	
	Building Societies Commission	
	Department for Business, Enterprise and Regulatory reform	
	Department for National Savings	
	Office for National Statistics	
23.21	Bank of England	
23.22	Office for National Statistics	

Sources

Table number in Abstract	Government department or other organisation	Official publication or other source
Chapter 24: Service industry		
Retail trades		
24.1	Office for National Statistics	Annual Business Inquiry (www.statistics.gov.uk/abi)
24.2	Office for National Statistics	Business Monitor SDM 28, www.statistics.gov.uk/rsi
Motor trades		
24.3	Office for National Statistics	Annual Business Inquiry (www.statistics.gov.uk/abi)
Catering		
24.4	Office for National Statistics	Annual Business Inquiry (www.statistics.gov.uk/abi)

Index

Figures indicate table numbers

Index

Index

Index

Index

Index